D1683622

Lingemann/von Steinau-Steinrück/Mengel

Employment & Labor Law in Germany

Employment & Labor Law in Germany

Stefan Lingemann
Robert von Steinau-Steinrück
Anja Mengel

Verlag C. H. Beck München 2012

The Authors

Dr. Stefan Lingemann, Prof. Dr. Robert von Steinau-Steinrück and Dr. Anja Mengel, LL.M. are attorneys in the Berlin offices of leading commercial law firms and a leading specialist law firm, respectively, in Germany – GLEISS LUTZ (Lingemann), LUTHER (von Steinau-Steinrück) and ALTENBURG (Mengel). They have extensive practical experience in advising international clients on employment and labor law. Their activities are primarily concentrated in the areas of collective labor law, employment and labor aspects of corporate restructuring and acquisition, remuneration plans and stock options, and company pension plans. Their numerous publications attest to their expertise of German employment and labor law.

www.beck.de

ISBN 978-3-406-60551-2
© 2012 Verlag C. H. Beck München

Druck und Bindung: Beltz Bad Langensalza GmbH
Neustädter Straße 1–4, 99947 Bad Langensalza

Satz: Druckerei C. H. Beck, Nördlingen

Umschlag: Siegfried Bütefisch, Schlaitdorf

Gedruckt auf säurefreiem, alterungsbeständigem Papier
(hergestellt aus chlorfrei gebleichtem Zellstoff)

Preface

Four years have passed since the second edition. It was, like the first edition, very well received in the market and has been sold out for over a year now. New laws relating to labor and employment law have been promulgated such as the EC Regulation on the law applicable to contractual obligations (Rome I) governing the international conflict of laws in employment relationships. On a national basis, new regulations were enacted with regard to employee data protection and minimum wages. The Federal Labor Court has been busy, not only giving quite a number of guidelines referring to the General Equal Treatment Act (*AGG*), but also extending the right to strike to new forms like „flash mobs". Employers and employees as well as the authorities are more than ever focussed on compliance issues. All of this urgently requires a third edition of this book, which, of course, covers these and other (new) matters, while our overall concept remains unaltered: This book explains the essential provisions of German employment and labor law and their interpretation by the Federal Labor Court.

Globalization calls upon international companies to increase their understanding of specific aspects of various national legal systems and economic cultures so as to be able to successfully establish production facilities and conduct business transactions abroad. Conversely, management personnel and human resources directors are increasingly finding themselves called upon to act as "interpreters" of German law and legal business standards for their companies, as are consultants for foreign clients. German employment and labor law, with its extensively developed system of individual and collective protection, is also strongly characterized by a reliance on case law and linkage with the social security laws, thus creating a special challenge for both German and non-German executives and advisors. Accordingly, this book explains the essential provisions of German employment and labor law, including the impact of social security and tax law, concisely and comprehensibly, while assuming no prior knowledge of the subject on the reader's part. Its purpose is to give executives and consultants a brief and succinct overview of the German system of employment and labor law. It is intended to help them recognize the issues which, in our opinion, present the most important problems and risks in establishing and managing German subsidiaries, as well as those arising from takeovers of German companies. The book focuses on those issues which, based on our extensive experience in the field, require the most legal advice and assistance. Academic questions of little practical relevance have been omitted.

We would appreciate any suggestions concerning (any) problems that are not addressed in the book. We would like to express our appreciation to the partners in our law firms for their suggestions and comments. We would also like to thank Ms. Bedene Greenspan for her translation of the legal texts, our valued colleague Dr. Rut Groneberg for her support as well as Ms. Susanne Bendrath and Ms. Virginie Dutrannoy for their work on the manuscript.

Berlin, August 2011

Dr. Stefan Lingemann   Prof. Dr. Robert   Dr. Anja Mengel, LL.M.
                             von Steinau-Steinrück

Abbreviations

AEU-Vertrag	Vertrag über die Arbeitsweise der Europäischen Union
AGG	Allgemeines Gleichbehandlungsgesetz
AktG	Aktiengesetz
ArbGG	Arbeitsgerichtsgesetz
AÜG	Arbeitnehmerüberlassungsgesetz
a.m.	ante meridiem (vormittags)
ArbZG	Arbeitszeitgesetz
Art.	article (Artikel)
BEEG	Bundeselterngeld- und Elternzeitgesetz
BErzGG	Bundeserziehungsgeldgesetz
BetrAVG	Gesetz zur Verbesserung der betrieblichen Altersvorsorge
BetrVG	Betriebsverfassungsgesetz
BUrlG	Bundesurlaubsgesetz
BGB	Bürgerliches Gesetzbuch
DrittelbG	Drittelbeteiligungsgesetz
e.g.	exempli gratia/for example (zum Beispiel)
EntgeltfortzG	Entgeltfortzahlungsgesetz
et seq.	et sequentes/and the following (und Folgende)
etc.	et cetera/and so forth (und so weiter)
ff.	and the following pages (und die folgenden Seiten)
GmbHG	GmbH-Gesetz
HGB	Handelsgesetzbuch
i.e.	id est/that is (das heißt)
KSchG	Kündigungsschutzgesetz
MitbestG	Mitbestimmungsgesetz
MuSchG	Mutterschutzgesetz
no.	number (pl. nos.) (Nummer(n))
NachwG	Nachweisgesetz
p.	page (pl. pp.) (Seite(n))
p.m.	post meridiem (nachmittags)
SGB III	3. Sozialgesetzbuch
SGB IV	4. Sozialgesetzbuch
SGB IX	9. Sozialgesetzbuch
TVG	Tarifvertragsgesetz
TzBfG	Gesetz über Teilzeitarbeit und befristete Arbeitsverträge

Table of Contents

Part I: Overview

A. Fundamentals	1
I. History and Introduction	1
II. Players	1
1. Employees and Employers	2
2. Works Councils	2
3. Trade Unions	3
4. Employers' Associations	3
III. Employment Agreement, Works Agreements, Collective Bargaining Agreements and other Legal Sources	4
1. Legal Sources	4
a) Employment Agreement	4
b) Works Agreements	4
c) Collective Bargaining Agreements	4
d) Statutes	5
e) Company Practice	5
f) Directives by the Employer	5
g) Equal Treatment	5
h) Constitution	6
i) European Law	6
j) International Law	7
k) Case Law	7
2. Order of Precedence	7
a) Hierarchy	7
b) Specificity	7
c) Replacement	7
d) Favorability	7
V. Social Security	8
V. Tax Law	8
VI. Conflict of laws	8
B. Employment Law	9
I. The General Equal Treatment Act	9
1. Scope of Application	9
2. Prohibition of Adverse Treatment	10
3. Organizational Duties of the Employer	11
4. Rights of the Employees	11
5. Legal Consequences	11
6. Consequences for Practice in the Workplace	12
II. Conclusion of Employment Agreements	13
1. Application	13
a) Prohibition of Discrimination	13
b) CV and References	13
c) Interview – What Questions Can Be Asked	14

d) Employment Questionnaire	15
e) Medical Examination	15
f) Interview Costs	15
g) Participation of the Works Council	15
2. Content of Employment Agreements	15
a) Conclusion of the Agreement	15
b) Limitation of Term	15
c) Part-Time Contract	16
d) Leasing of Employees	17
e) Foreign Employees	18
f) Prohibition of Discrimination	19
3. Control of General Terms and Conditions	19
a) Review of Subject Matter	20
b) Specific Clauses	20
4. Form	21
5. Invalid Employment Agreements	22
a) Minors	22
b) Fraudulent Misrepresentation	23
c) Error	23
d) Lack of Residence or Work Permit	23
III. Rights and Duties	23
1. Duty to Work/Right to Work	23
2. Remuneration	23
a) Minimum Remuneration	23
b) Bonus	24
c) Stock Options	24
d) Company Pension Plans	25
e) Capital Formation Benefits	26
3. Sick Pay	27
4. Working Time	27
5. Vacation	28
6. Maternity Protection – Parental Leave and Parental Benefits	29
a) Maternity Protection	29
b) Parental Leave and Parental Benefits	29
7. Confidentiality	31
8. Covenant Not to compete	31
9. Data Protection	31
a) Data Storage with the Consent of the Employee	31
b) Data Storage without the Consent of the Employee	31
10. Liability	32
11. Inventions	32
IV. Compliance	33
V. Termination of Employment Relationships	34
1. General Points	34
a) Declaration of Dismissal	34
b) Form	34
c) Delivery	35
d) Dismissal by Authorized Representatives	35
e) Dismissal Notice Periods	36
f) Calculating the Notice Periods	36
2. Consultation of the Works Council	36

Table of Contents

3. General Protection Against Dismissal	37
a) Conduct-Related Dismissals	38
b) Dismissals on Persononal Grounds	39
c) Dismissal for Operational Reasons	41
d) Dismissal for Variation of Contract	43
4. Ordinary Dismissal or Dismissal for Cause	43
a) Cause for Dismissal	43
b) Two-Week Period	43
c) Resignation for Good Cause	44
d) Employees Protected Due to Age	44
e) Tactical Advice	44
5. Special protection Against Dismissal	45
a) Maternity Protection	45
b) Parental Leave	45
c) Protection of Persons with Severe Disabilities	45
d) Works Council Members and Other Officers under the Works Constitution Act	45
e) Mass Layoffs	46
6. Termination Agreement	46
VI. Transfer of Business and Transformation	47
1. Transfer of Business	47
a) Introduction	47
b) Prerequisites	48
c) Passing of the Employment Relationships as a Legal Consequence	48
d) Information Requirements and Right of the Employees to Object	49
e) Distribution of Liability	50
f) Impact on the Employee Representative Bodies	50
g) Continued Application of Collective Norms	50
2. Transformations	51
VII. Assignment to Foreign Countries	52
1. Employment Law Issues	52
2. Social Insurance Issues	53
3. Tax Law Issues	54
C. Labor Law	**55**
I. Laws Governing Works Councils	55
1. Works Councils	55
a) Workplaces That Can Have Works Councils	55
b) Election of the Works Council	55
c) Election Committee	55
d) Election and Costs	56
e) Works Council Members	56
f) Joint Works Council	57
g) Group Works Council	58
h) European Works Council	58
i) Economic Committee	58
j) Youth and Trainee Representation	58
k) Spokespersons Committee for Managerial Employees	59
l) Severly Disabled Employees' Representation	59
m) Other Representative Bodies	59

2. Rights of Participation and Codetermination	59
a) Information and Consultation Rights	60
b) Codetermination Rights	60
c) Exercising Codetermination Rights	63
3. Works Agreements	64
a) Typical Content	64
b) Conclusion	64
c) Effectiveness	64
d) Termination	65
4. Disputes between Employer and Works Council	66
a) Suits before a Labor Court	66
b) Cease and Desist Claims	66
c) Temporary Hirings and Transfers	67
d) Conciliation Board	67
e) Other Remedies	67
5. Transfer of Business, Transformation and Restructuring	67
II. Collective Bargaining Agreements Law	68
1. Collective Bargaining Agreements	68
a) Typical Content	68
b) Conclusion	69
c) Effect	69
d) Termination	70
2. Labor Disputes/Industrial Action	70
a) Strike	70
b) Conduct of the Strike	70
c) Reaction of the Employer	70
d) Flash Mobs	71
III. Corporate Codetermination	71
D. Employee Protection Laws	**72**
I. Laws Governing Working Hours	73
II. Shop Closing Hours Act	73
III. Maternity Protection Act	74
IV. Federal Parental Allowance And Parental Leave Act	75
V. Young Persons' Protection in Employment Act	75
VI. Laws Regarding Employees with Disabilities	75
E. Social Insurance Laws	**76**
I. Statutory Social Insurance	76
1. Pension Insurance	77
2. Unemployment Insurance	78
3. Health Insurance	78
4. Home and Institutional Care Insurance	79
5. Employee Accident Insurance	80
II. Social Insurance Obligations	81
1. Total Social Insurance Contribution	81
2. Freelance Workers and Self-Employed Personnel	82
3. Pseudo-Independence	83
III. Termination of Employment Relationships	84
1. Disqualification Periods and Suspension Periods for the Employee	84
2. Severance Pay	85

F. Tax Laws 85
I. Withholding Tax on Wages 85
II. Special Issues 86
1. Company Car 86
2. Stock Options 87
3. Severance Payment 87

G. Labor Court Proceedings 88
I. Courts 88
II. Protection Against Dismissal Proceedings 88
1. Out-of-Court Negotiations 88
2. Three-Week Period for Filing Complaints 88
3. Course of Dismissal Proceedings and Tactical Considerations 88
4. Judicial Dissolution of Employment Relationships and Severance Pay 89
5. Remuneration Claims and Default in Acceptance 90
6. Right to Employment 90

H. Managing Directors, Management Board Members 91
I. Managing Directors of Limited Liability Companies 91
1. Appointment of Managing Directors 91
2. Removal of Managing Directors 91
3. Service Contract 92
4. Duties and Responsibilities of the Managing Directors 92
   a) Managing the Business of the Company 92
   b) Diligence 93
   c) Organisation Duties 93
   d) Duty to inform Shareholders 94
   e) Accounting 94
   f) Insolvency 94
   g) Raising and Maintenance of Capital 94
   h) Fiscal Obligations 95
   i) Social Security Obligations 95
II. Management Board Members of Stock Corporations 95
1. Appointment of Management Board Members 95
2. Removal of Management Board Members 95
3. Service Contract 95
4. Duties and Responsibilities of the Management Board Member 96
   a) Not bound by Directives 96
   b) Diligence 96
   c) Organisation Duties 96
   d) Information Duties 97
   e) Accounting 97
   f) Insolvency 97
   g) Raising and Maintenance of Share Capital 97
   h) Fiscal Obligations 97
   i) Social Security 97

Part II: Statutory Material
I. Civil Code (BGB) 99
II. General Equal Treatment Act (AGG) 128

III.	Part-Time and Limited Term Employment Act (TzBfG)	152
IV.	Continuation of Remuneration Act (EFZG)	166
V.	Protection Against Unfair Dismissal Act (KSchG)	178
VI.	Federal Vacation Act (BUrlG)	199
VII.	Act for the Improvement of Company Pension Plans (BetrAVG)	207
VIII.	Comercial Code (HGB)	253
IX.	Treaty on the Functioning of the European Union (AEU-Vertrag)	259
X.	Works Constitution Act (BetrVG)	261
XI.	Collective Bargaining Agreements Act (TVG)	371
XII.	Act on the Co-Determination of the Employees (MitbestG)	380
XIII.	One-Third Participation Act (DrittelbG)	409
XIV.	Hours of Employment Act (ArbZG)	418
XV.	Maternity Protection Act (MuSchG)	443
XVI.	Federal Parental Benefit and Parental Leave Act (BEEG)	461
XVII.	Social Security Code III (SGB III)	470
XVIII.	Social Security Code IV (SGB IV)	480
XIX.	Social Security Code IX (SGB IX)	506
XX.	Law Pertaining to Companies with Limited Liability (GmbH-Gesetz)	529
XXI.	Stock Corporation Act (AktG)	538
XXII.	Labor Court Act (ArbGG)	580
XXIII.	Act Regulating the Commercial Leasing of Employees (AÜG)	595
XXIV.	Law on Documenting Essential Applicable Conditions for an Employment Relationship (NachwG)	605

Glossary of Key Words English/German 608
Glossary of Key Words German/English 612

Part I: Overview

A. Fundamentals

I. History and Introduction

Modern German labor and employment law has its **origin** in the era of mass industrialization and the founding of the modern German state in the late 19th century. These developments were accompanied by the politicization of the labor force, leading to the formation of trade unions and, soon after the founding of the German Reich in 1871, to the passage of the first labor protection and social security laws under the "Iron Chancellor" **Otto von Bismarck.** The first two significant collective labor laws were promulgated during the Weimar Republic after World War I: the Collective Bargaining Agreements Act (*Tarifvertragsordnung*) of 1918 and the Works Councils Act (*Betriebsrätegesetz*) of 1920. During the "Third Reich" period between 1933 and 1945, employment and labor law was distorted to suit the National Socialist ideology as well as the war efforts for World War II (1939–1945). In particular, collective labor law was replaced by public law establishing the "Führer Principle" for companies. After World War II, the Federal Republic of Germany (West Germany) drew on the traditions of the Weimar Republic to establish a democratic, social market economy. Shortly after its founding, the West German government passed such laws as the Collective Bargaining Agreements Act of 1949 (*Tarifvertragsgesetz*), which remains essentially unchanged to this day, the first Works Constitution Act 1952 (*Betriebsverfassungsgesetz 1952 – BetrVG 1952*), and numerous other statutes regulating the relationships between individual employees and their employer. The German Democratic Republic (GDR), however, developed its employment and labor law to reflect its communist and socialist ideology. Since the unification of the two German states in 1990, West German law has applied throughout Germany, apart from a few exceptions, which applied only temporarily during the transition period.

Today, German labor and employment law is structurally divided into four areas that are very closely interlinked and in practice are virtually inseparable: a) **employment law,** which regulates the contractual relationship between the employer and an individual employee; b) **labor law,** which regulates the relationships between the employer and the employers' associations on the one hand and works councils and trade unions on the other, as well as the effect of collective agreements on individual employment agreements; c) public **labor protection law**, including accident prevention law; and d) **social security law**.

In addition to these four areas, labor and employment law in its broadest sense also covers the laws governing employment agreements for managing directors (*Geschäftsführer*) and members of a company's management board (*Vorstand*).

II. Players

Under German labor and employment law, a distinction is generally made between the relationships among individual parties – employees and employers – and those between representatives of collective interests – works councils, trade unions and employers. These are the major players:

1. Employees and Employers

An employer is a person, i.e., a natural person or a legal entity, who employs at least one employee.

An employee is a person who performs **"dependent" work** for the benefit of another person on the basis of a civil law contract. For example, civil servants and persons performing military service are not considered employees, as they are working on the basis of a public law relationship. The fact that an employee works dependently (*persönlich abhängig*) distinguishes the work of an employee from services performed by a freelancer or independent contractor (*freier Mitarbeiter oder Selbständiger*) as defined in section 84 German Commercial Code (*HGB*). An employee is personally dependent on the employer because the employer has the right to issue directives (*Weisungen*) on the place and time as well as details of the work of the employee. Typically, employees are also **integrated** into the works organization of another person, generally the employer, e.g. by being assigned a certain workplace and being integrated into workplace hierarchies.

Persons similar to employees (*arbeitnehmerähnliche Personen*) are not employees because they are not personally dependant on an employer. However, they are economically dependent on another person and enjoy protection similar to that of employees to a certain extent, e.g. they may also file suit over work-related issues with the labor courts pursuant to section 5 (3) German Labor Courts Act (*Arbeitsgerichtsgesetz – ArbGG*).

In addition, German law has traditionally distinguished between **blue-collar workers** (*Arbeiter*) and **white-collar workers** (*Angestellte*). Today, however, this distinction no longer has any legal relevance in practice, as German constitutional law requires both groups of employees to be treated equally unless objective grounds exist for unequal treatment. Differences remain with respect to employee representation and collective bargaining agreements.

Managerial employees (*leitende Angestellte*) are also employees, but often act as an employer vis-à-vis the other employees. For this reason, certain exceptions to the general labor and employment law rules are provided for managerial employees, notably with respect to protection against termination, pursuant to section 14 (2) of the Protection Against Unfair Dismissals Act 1969 (*Kündigungsschutzgesetz – KSchG*), and the applicability of the Works Constitution Act of 1972 (*Betriebsverfassungsgesetz – BetrVG*), pursuant to section 5 (3) BetrVG. In place of the Works Constitution Act, the Spokespersons Committee Act (*Sprecherausschußgesetz*) of 1989 provides for the codetermination of the managerial employees on the establishment level. It is important to note that the definition of a managerial employee can vary slightly depending on the particular statute involved.

2. Works Council

The works council (*Betriebsrat*) is the main employee **representative body** vis-à-vis the employer. It is elected by all of the establishment's employees every four years and has its own rights vis-à-vis the employer, i.e. the company's management. The election of a works council is not mandatory, but is relatively easy for employees or unions to initiate. An employer may not prevent the formation of a works council. The basic principle is one works council per establishment, but companies frequently consist of more than one establishment, in which case a company can have two or more works councils. Where a company has more than one works council, it must form a joint works council, whose competence generally covers all establishments of the company. Where a corporate group has more than one (joint) works council, the (joint) works councils may form a group works council, whose competence generally covers all of the companies in the group.

The rights and obligations of works councils, joint works councils and group works councils are laid down in the Works Constitution Act of 1972. In particular, works councils do not have the right to organize strikes. They are obligated to work together with the employer on the basis of mutual trust and cooperation (*vertrauensvolle Zusammenarbeit*).

3. Trade Unions

Trade unions are associations of individual employees organized to represent the interests of the employees vis-à-vis the employers and employers' associations, and in particular to conclude **collective bargaining agreements**. Trade unions must be a separate legal entity, formed freely and voluntarily, with the purpose of improving working conditions, including engaging in labor disputes. They must be independent and organized on a supra-company level and may not have members from the opposing side, i.e. employers (*Gegnerfreiheit*). German case law requires that the trade unions also be powerful enough to force an employer or employers' association to negotiate collective bargaining agreements with them (*Mächtigkeit*). Accordingly, it is rare that new trade unions are formed or at least recognized as such. However, recently the Federal Labor Court conferred union status on a new union of metal workers which is part of the group of Christian unions. Moreover, in the last few years, Germany has witnessed a wave of mergers of established trade unions. Most of the German trade unions belong to an umbrella organization known as the German Trade Union Association (*Deutscher Gewerkschaftsbund – DGB*). The DGB is organized according to the principle of "industrial sectors" (*Industriebranchenprinzip*), i.e. each DGB trade union is formed for one or more closely related industrial sector(s) and is responsible for negotiating collective bargaining agreements for employees of that particular sector. The DGB trade unions are also organized by region, with state and national boards coordinating the work of the various regions. Thus, collective bargaining agreements are often concluded for one particular region in Germany only, with that one region traditionally having a pilot function for the subsequent agreements in other regions, such as the Nord-Württemberg/Nord-Baden region, which plays this role for the entire metal industry. In addition to the DGB unions, there are unions that cover several sectors, such as **ver.di** (*Vereinte Dienstleistungsgewerkschaft*) with approximately two million members, that is mainly for white-collar employees. Approximately one quarter of all German employees belong to a union, but the degree of organization is much higher in some traditional sectors, such as the metal industry, and virtually non-existent in others, such as the information and technology sectors.

The formation and function of trade unions, as well as their internal democratic structures, are protected by constitutional law. An employee's freedom to choose whether or not to join a union is an individual constitutional right pursuant to Art. 9 (3) German Basic Law (*Grundgesetz – GG*).

4. Employers' Associations

Employers' associations are the **counterparts** of trade unions for the purpose of negotiating and concluding collective bargaining agreements. Like the trade unions, they have a matrix organization and are organized by industrial sectors as well as by region, with boards at both the state and national level. The associations, their formation, their work, as well as their internal democratic structures, enjoy constitutional protections. An employer's freedom to choose whether or not to join an association is an individual constitutional right pursuant to Art. 9 (3) GG.

III. Employment Agreement, Works Agreements, Collective Bargaining Agreements and Other Legal Sources

German labor and employment law draws on a great variety of legal sources to determine the rights and obligations of employees and employers in their employment relationship.

1. Legal Bases

The following legal bases, listed in descending order of importance, determine whether an employee has a claim:

a) Employment Agreement

The primary legal basis with respect to the employment relationship is the individual employment agreement concluded between the employer and an individual employee (for details, see pages 13 et seq.). In general, the employer and the employee are free to determine the provisions of their employment agreement. However, in practice, to a great extent the individual employment agreement merely supplements binding statutory law, collective bargaining agreements and works agreements. Furthermore, the German labor courts have the right to **review** the content of an individual employment agreement with respect to its fairness, pursuant to section 315 German Civil Code (*Bürgerliches Gesetzbuch – BGB*). For this reason, and for the purpose of efficiency, employers often use **standard employment contracts** for all employees and only amend them as necessary, particularly for higher-level employees. If standard contracts are used, the general laws regarding the review of standard conditions and terms pursuant to sections 305 et seq. BGB apply.

b) Works Agreements

Works agreements are special contracts concluded between an employer and a works council which contain general regulations pertaining to working conditions. They have direct and binding effect on the individual employment relationships of all employees in the establishment (for details, see pages 64 et seq.).

c) Collective Bargaining Agreements

Collective bargaining agreements are contracts concluded between a single employer or an employers' association on the one hand and a trade union on the other. Collective bargaining agreements generally regulate a large number of **key working conditions**, such as working time, remuneration, notice periods for termination, number of vacation days, overtime bonuses, etc. They also have direct and binding effect on individual employment relationships, pursuant to section 4 (1) German Collective Bargaining Agreements Act (*Tarifvertragsgesetz – TVG*), if the employer is bound by the collective bargaining agreement and the employee is a member of the union which concluded the contract (for details, see pages 68 et seq.). In addition, the individual employment agreements of non-union members often make reference to collective bargaining agreements, which thereby serve as baseline minimum labor standards for the respective industrial sector.

d) Statutes

There is no unified code of German labor and employment law. On the contrary, a great number of **fragmented** statutes exist, some of which go back as far as the 19th century and have been amended from time to time. Article 30 of the German Unification Treaty (*Einigungsvertrag*) obligates the German legislature to enact a code on employment law. However, despite several draft proposals, as of this writing, no employment code has yet been adopted.

In accordance with the protective nature of German labor and employment law in general, the statutory rules are largely binding in the sense that neither the parties to the individual employment agreement nor those to a works agreement or a collective bargaining agreement may deviate from the statutory rules to the employee's detriment, i.e., they set minimum standards. Deviations to an employee's benefit are possible under the **favorability principle** (see pages 7 et seq.). On an international scale of comparison, the level of protection provided by the German employment/labor statutes is relatively high.

e) Company Practice

Another source of law is what is known as "company practice" (*betriebliche Übung*). The principle of company practice also offers employees a basis for asserting claims which are not explicitly set forth in the employment agreement. If the employer **repeats** a certain action on a regular basis (at least three times), an employee can conclude that the employer intends to continue such actions in the future; as a result, the employee will have the right to demand the repetition of such actions in the future. In practice, this primarily creates employees' claims for special benefits, such as Christmas bonuses or other staff bonuses, if the employer has provided such benefits three times without explicitly stating that such benefits were being made on a voluntary basis; this is termed reservation of voluntariness (*Freiwilligkeitsvorbehalt*). For this reason, cautious employers always accompany special benefits with an explicit and written reservation of voluntariness, unless they are contractually stipulated in any case. They will then not be forced to eliminate a company practice with what is termed a "negative company practice", which requires that the employees accept the suspension of the usual benefit or the granting of such benefits with a reservation of voluntariness three times without objecting.

f) Directives by the Employer

Pursuant to section 106 German Industrial Code (GewO) and section 315 BGB, the employer has a comprehensive right to issue directives to employees regarding the working time, workplace and the work itself unless such matters are regulated elsewhere, e.g. in the employment agreement or collective bargaining agreements.

g) Equal Treatment

The principle of equal treatment is one of the most important principles in German employment and labor law. In practice it often forms a **basis for employees' (remuneration) claims** above and beyond those set forth in the employment agreement. Under the principle of equal treatment, an employer may not treat comparable employees in its establishment disparately without an objective reason for doing so and must issue generally uniform regulations unless it enters into a separate agreement with each individual employee. This also covers remuneration benefits under certain conditions, for example if the employer grants general benefits on a voluntary basis or does not negotiate different individual raises, but commits itself to a general pay raise. If individual employees or groups of employees are treated *unequally* in comparison to other employees without objective grounds, they will have a claim to the withheld benefit under the equal treatment principle. While it is true that the employer is not prevented from privileging individual employees, in practice it is often difficult to differentiate between permissible privileging and impermissible disadvantaging. Statutory provisions which regulate aspects of the equal treatment principle with respect to certain banned criteria, such as gender, ethnic origin, sexual orientation, religious or secular belief, disability and age, can be found in the General Equal Treatment Act of 2006 (*Allgemeines Gleichbehandlungsgesetz – AGG* see pages 9 et seq.) and in section 4 Part-Time and Limited Term Employment Act (*Teilzeit- und Befristungsgesetz – TzBfG*), which prohibits discrimination against part-time employees and employees hired for a limited term in comparison with permanent, fulltime employees (for details, see pages 15 et seq.).

h) Constitution

The German constitution, the Basic Law (*Grundgesetz – GG*), plays a relatively important role for the employment relationships despite the fact that the individual rights it confers do not apply directly between citizens. However, on the basis of general constitutional or case law, the **objective order of ethical values** derived from the Basic Law's list of human and civil rights (*objektive Wertordnung*) also affects the relationship between employer and employees. For example, the employer is compelled to respect an employee's rights of personal freedom (Art. 2 (1) GG), right to equal protection and equal treatment (Art. 3 GG), religious freedom (Art. 4 GG) and freedom of speech (Art. 5 GG) as well as protection of marriage and the family (Art. 6 GG) and freedom of choice of employment (Art. 12 GG) within the employment relationship.

Furthermore, the Basic Law guarantees freedom of association in Art. 9 (3) GG, which applies to the formation, organization and work of trade unions and employers' associations. This freedom of association also ensures the right not to join an association. Moreover, Art. 9 (3) GG guarantees the right to engage in labor disputes, particularly employees' and trade unions' right to strike.

Hence, the labor courts often turn to the constitution when the fragmented legislation does not provide a solution, particularly where legal labor dispute issues are involved.

i) European Law

European law is playing an **increasingly important role** in German employment and labor law. The primary European law, the European Treaties, only include a few articles with a direct effect on German national law, notably Art. 157 of the Treaty on the Functioning of the European Union (TFEU) on the equal remuneration of men and women and Art. 45 TFEU regarding the free movement of workers in the Common Market. In contrast, secondary European law, regulations and directives, has a very significant impact on German law. Over the years, the European Union (as well as the former European Community) has adopted a great number of directives in order to harmonize national legislation with respect to employment law, and, to a lesser extent, labor law. Two of the most important and best known directives are EC Directive 2001/23 (previously EC Directive 77/187) regarding the transfer of undertakings and EC Directive 98/59 regarding mass dismissals. European directives are not part of national law, but must be implemented by the national legislatures. However, as the European Court of Justice in Luxembourg is responsible for interpreting the directives, if it finds a certain provision of the national law or national case law to be inconsistent with its interpretation of a European Union directive, this will have a direct impact on the legal situation of that country.

j) International Law

Germany is a member of the most important international (labor law) organizations, such as the International Labor Organization and the Council of Europe, as well as the United Nations, and thus is subject to the relevant international labor law. International charters and conventions usually become binding national law through a national legal process of ratification.

k) Case Law

Case law and legal precedence are of importance in German employment and labor law to a much greater extent than is generally the case in the German national legal system, which is based on the concept of codification. However, since the German legislature has **not codified** German employment and labor law – for example, there is not even a statute covering labor disputes, strikes and lockouts –, the German labor courts are often responsible for filling gaps in the statutory law. Moreover, the courts are frequently compelled to interpret statutory provisions, particularly in recent years, as the legislation has become very complex and is ambiguously worded, and even new statutes often contain gaps or misleading provisions.

2. Order of Precedence

The various legal bases of German employment and labor law relate to each other in a matrix structure.

a) Hierarchy

On the one level there is a hierarchical order. A legal basis with a higher position in the hierarchy takes precedence over legal bases with a lower position. The hierarchy runs as follows in descending order: European law, constitutional law, statutes, collective bargaining agreements, works agreements, employment agreement, company practice, directives by the employer.

b) Specificity

The principle of specificity determines which legal basis will take precedence on the same hierarchical level. For example, a **special clause** stipulating that a company car arrangement in an employment agreement constitutes an entitlement of the employee takes precedence over a general clause regarding the voluntary nature of benefits.

c) Replacement

On the same hierarchical level of legal bases, the "replacement principle" (*Ablösungsprinzip*) plays an important role. A **newer provision** will always take precedence over an older provision (*lex posterior derogat legi priori*, also referred to as the *Ordnungsprinzip*).

d) Favorability

An important principle of German employment law is the favorability principle (*Günstigkeitsprinzip*), under which the legal regulation which is **more beneficial** to the employee will apply, irrespective of its hierarchical level or the date of its adoption, as long as it is still in force. The favorability principle is a legal exception to the other principles of precedence. However, there are also some important exceptions to the favorability principle itself, e.g. due to the relationship between works agreements and collective bargaining agreements pursuant to section 77 (3) and section 87 (1) sentence 1 BetrVG (see also page 65).

IV. Social Security

Germany has a national social security system, to which employees belong by **force of law**. Thus, it is very important to distinguish between a dependent employee and an independent contractor or freelancer with respect to the social security laws as well. The social security system comprises the following components: unemployment insurance, health insurance, nursing care insurance, statutory pension insurance and employee accident insurance. With the exception of the latter component, which the employers finance themselves, the employees and employers basically share the costs of the contributions to the social security system. The amount of the contribution is dependent on the gross income of the individual employee, and the payments are made by the employer, deducting the employees' share from their salary (for details on social security, see pages 76 et seq.).

This statutory social security system is regulated in the **Social Security Code** (*Sozialgesetzbuch – SGB*), which consists of twelve Books (SGB I–XII) that cover not only the social security system itself, but also such general social welfare matters as educational grants, child and youth welfare, welfare for persons with disabilities, welfare for unemployed persons (*Arbeitslosengeld I* and *Arbeitslosengeld II*) and social assistance as a subsidiary component of the general assistance rendered by the state (*Sozialhilfe*), etc. Separate statutes also contain provisions on social benefits, e.g. pensions for war victims and victims of crimes, and other social welfare matters, such as child and housing benefits.

V. Tax Law

Employees must pay income tax on the income they earn through employment. Depending on the amount of the gross income, the tax rates are graduated from the current rate (2010) of 14% to 45%, plus solidarity surcharge and church tax, if applicable. The employer is responsible for withholding the income tax accruing to the gross remuneration and forwarding it to the competent tax authority (*Finanzamt*). The employees may report deductible expenses or tax exemptions in their income tax declarations at the end of the calendar year (for details on employee-related tax law, see pages 85 et seq.).

VI. Conflict of Laws

Since 2009, the Rome I Regulation has governed conflict of laws in employment relationships in Germany (Regulation (EC) No 593/2008 of 17 June 2008 on the law applicable to contractual obligations). As a regulation of the European Union, Rome I applies directly in the EU Member States. Pursuant to Art. 8 (1) Rome I, the parties to the employment contract can generally stipulate the applicable (national) law freely (free choice of law). However, in order to protect employees, a number of regulations require that the rules of the national law chosen by the parties be superseded by the national law applicable without a choice of law or, specifically, by German employment law. In particular, the applicable national law/German law supersedes the chosen law insofar as the chosen law deviates from more favorable mandatory rules of the applicable national law/German law to the disadvantage of the employee. Further, there are *ordre public* exceptions. In practice, therefore, the choice of law is effectively quite limited since a large part of German employment law is mandatory under the conflict of laws regulations.

In the absence of a contractual choice of law, pursuant to Art. 8 (2) to (4) Rome I, German employment law is applicable if (i) an employee regularly works in Germany, even if he or she is temporarily seconded to a foreign country, or (ii), the branch which employs the employee is located in Germany, unless notwithstanding the aforementioned rules, the employment relationship is more closely tied to a country other than Germany, in which case the laws of that other country will apply. The same rules apply for determining whether the national laws of another country apply.

Art. 8 Rome I does not apply to the conflict of law rules regarding collective labor law or public labor law, including social security and tax law. Generally, conflict of law rules regarding these areas are governed by the territoriality principle (*Territorialitätsprinzip*). Accordingly, German law on works councils generally applies if the establishment is based in Germany, while German social security and tax law applies if the residence of the employee or his/her regular place of work is in Germany. In practice, however, many special rules have to be considered in each individual case.

B. Employment Law

I. The General Equal Treatment Act

The General Equal Treatment Act (*Allgemeines Gleichbehandlungsgesetz – AGG*) entered into force on 18 August 2006. With this Act, the German legislature fulfilled its duty to implement four European directives into national law. The aim of the AGG is to create comprehensive protection against discrimination. This can be expected to have sweeping consequences for labor and employment law practice.

1. Scope of Application

The purpose of the law is to **"prevent or eliminate adverse treatment on the grounds of race or ethnic origin, gender, religion or secular belief, a disability, age or sexual identity"** (section 1 AGG). The personal scope of application covers all employees, including apprentices and persons who, due to their economic dependency, are to be seen as "persons similar to employees" (*arbeitnehmerähnliche Personen*), persons working at home and those in an equivalent position, applicants for an employment relationship, and those whose employment relationship has been ended (section 6 (1) AGG). In the case of leased employees, the lessor and the client must comply with the AGG (section 6 (2) AGG).

Materially, the Act's scope of application extends in particular to the hiring of employees, their employment and working conditions, professional advancement, remuneration and dismissal (section 2 (1) AGG). The Federal Labor Court (*Bundesarbeitsgericht*) has ruled that notwithstanding the provision in section 2 (2) sentence 2 AGG, the AGG is also applicable to company pensions. However, the BetrAVG, as a special statute, has priority over the regulations in the AGG where any of the grounds set forth in section 1 AGG are involved, for example with respect to provisions on statutory vesting that are linked to the factor of "age". Pursuant to section

2 (4) AGG, the general and specific protection against unfair dismissal are also excluded from the AGG. But since prohibitions of discrimination apply within the scope of the German Protection Against Unfair Dismissal Act (KSchG), a dismissal that violates a prohibition of discrimination could be antisocial, and thus invalid. However, the creation of age groups pursuant to section 1 (3) sentence 2 KSchG is consistent with the AGG.

2. Prohibition of Adverse Treatment

Employees may not be subjected to adverse treatment due to any of the eight grounds specified in section 1 AGG (section 7 (1) AGG). In practice, apart from the issue of gender discrimination, the greatest problems arise from the issue of **age discrimination.**

The prohibition covers both direct and indirect adverse treatment (section 3 AGG). Pursuant to section 3 (1) AGG, **direct adverse treatment** exists if, due to one of the grounds set forth in section 1 AGG, one person is treated less favorably than another person is being, has been or would be treated in a comparable situation. Indirect adverse treatment exists if, due to one of the grounds set forth in section 1 AGG, an apparently neutral provision, criterion or practice would put certain persons at a particular disadvantage compared with other persons (section 3 (2) AGG). A classical example of **indirect adverse treatment** is the adverse treatment of part-time employees, who generally tend to be women. What is permissible, on the other hand, is a remuneration based on seniority or the deduction of parental leave from the seniority benefit. The requirement of at least ten years of professional experience represents an indirect age discrimination, but is justified if a certain amount of professional experience is necessary in order to do the job. The duty to wear certain items of clothing, e.g. certain headgear, is an indirect discrimination on grounds of religion, but can be justified on the grounds of industrial safety or demonstrably serious (including economic) disadvantages. **Harassment**, particularly sexual harassment, also constitutes adverse treatment within the meaning of the AGG (section 3 (3) and (4) AGG).

However, not every case of unequal treatment due to a feature specified in section 1 AGG represents impermissible adverse treatment. No indirect adverse treatment exists if the treatment in question is **justified** by a legitimate aim and the means of achieving that aim are appropriate and necessary (section 3 (2) AGG). Section 8 AGG permits as a general exception differences in treatment due to one of the specified grounds for discrimination if such grounds constitute a material and decisive occupational requirement. Hence, disabled persons may be treated unequally if the lack of such a disability is an absolute prerequisite for the performance of the work. Pursuant to section 9 AGG, the prohibition of differences in treatment due to religion will not apply if a particular religion or other secular belief constitutes a legitimate occupational requirement. On the basis of this provision, religious communities and the institutions associated with them will most likely be able to select their employees according to the criterion of religion. Finally, pursuant to section 10 AGG, differences in treatment due to age are permissible if they are objectively and reasonably justified by a legitimate aim. The means of achieving that aim must be appropriate and necessary. Legitimate aims can be not only those of the company or the sector, but also aims that are of general interest to the public. The Act presents in section 10 sentence 2 nos. 1 to 6 examples of situations in which a difference in treatment could be permissible. For example, while a sliding remuneration scale or promotions that are based purely on age would not be appropriate, the European Court of Justice (ECJ) has recognized years of service

I. The General Equal Treatment Act

(not years of age) as factors that can be used to determine remuneration for professional experience. Thus, company social security systems, typically company pension plans, or low age limits in high-risk professions, such as cockpit personnel, would also be permissible. Generally declining physical and mental capacity can also justify age limits for publicly appointed experts.

3. Organizational Duties of the Employer

The AGG is directed at employers, as is the prohibition of discrimination. Sections 11 and 12 AGG stipulate a number of actions the employer is obligated to take.

Pursuant to section 12 AGG, the employer must take the necessary measures to protect employees against adverse treatment due to one of the grounds set forth in section 1 AGG. This should also include **preventative measures**. Specifically, an employer can fulfill this duty by training its employees ("training defense"). The requirements placed on the nature, scope and frequency of the training vary according to the size of the workplace, and more extensive measures might be required of large enterprises than of small ones.

In the event that employees violate the prohibition of adverse treatment, the employer must take measures that are necessary, appropriate and suitable for the individual case (such as a warning, transfer, relocation or dismissal) to stop the adverse treatment (section 12 (3) AGG). It must additionally ensure that the employees are protected against adverse treatment by third parties (e.g. customers or suppliers) when performing their work (section 12 (4) AGG).

The employer should document its personnel decisions thoroughly, as section 22 AGG reverses the burden of proof, placing it on the employer once an employee proves the existence of circumstances that could give rise to a presumption of adverse treatment due to one of the grounds enumerated in section 1 AGG. In order to be able to present proof that the difference in treatment was not due to a violation of the prohibition of adverse treatment, the employer should be able to present extensive documentation.

4. Rights of the Employees

The employees have the right to make complaints to the competent persons (*Beschwerdestelle*) in the workplace, the company or the civil service workplace if they feel they have been subjected to adverse treatment by their employer, their superiors, other employees or third parties in connection with their employment relationship (section 13 AGG).

In the specific case of harassment at the workplace, section 14 AGG stipulates that if the employer takes no measures at all, or takes measures which are obviously unsuitable for stopping sexual or other harassment at the workplace, the employee will be entitled to stop working without losing his or her remuneration.

5. Legal Consequences

Provisions in agreements which are in violation of the prohibition of adverse treatment are **invalid** (section 7 (2) AGG). Since the AGG has no transitional provisions, it has been applicable to the existing individual and collective contractual provisions ever since 18 August 2006. For this reason, all employment agreements and collective agreements that were entered into **prior to 18 August 2006** should be examined to ascertain if they contain clauses that constitute impermissible adverse treatment.

A violation of the prohibition of adverse treatment does not create a claim to the formation of an employment relationship, a trainee relationship, or a promotion (section 15 (6) AGG). Thus, the employer is under no compulsion to conclude a contract due to this provision.

The employer is, however, obligated to **compensate** employees for any damage incurred due to a violation of the prohibition of adverse treatment. Pursuant to section 15 (1) AGG, the employer has to compensate for material damage if it was responsible for the violation of the prohibition of adverse treatment. In this respect, the employer generally bears liability in accordance with the general provisions for own fault and, pursuant to section 278 BGB, for its vicarious agents as well. Vicarious agents would presumably comprise all managerial employees to whom the employer has at least partially transferred the right to give directives.

Section 15 (2) AGG regulates compensation for **non-pecuniary damage**. A failure to hire a disadvantaged employee can entitle him or her to demand "appropriate monetary compensation", the amount of which, however, is limited to three months' salary if the employee would not have been hired had the selection been free of adverse treatment. The time period within which such claims must be asserted is two months, unless the parties to the collective bargaining agreements have agreed otherwise (section 15 (4) sentence 1 AGG). However, such ability to vary this time period by collective bargaining agreement may be in violation of European law.

Even if a violation has been committed not by vicarious agents of the employer but by other employees, the employer may be liable if it did not perform its organizational duties (see page 11 above).

6. Consequences for Practice in the Workplace

In order to avoid possible damages claims on the part of the employees, employers should **inform and educate** the employees who are entitled to issue directives, as well as members of the human resources departments, regarding the AGG. After that, all of the other employees should be trained and their participation in the sessions should be documented.

The entire **recruitment proceedings** have to avoid any possible adverse treatment, whereby it must particularly be ensured that the requirements contained in job advertisements are free of adverse treatment und the selection of applicants is carefully documented in order to prove that no violations against the prohibition of adverse treatment were committed. Job advertisements must be formulated such that they pertain exclusively to the job activity itself and only list criteria which are necessary for the position advertised.

When drafting **employment agreements**, age may not be cited as a criterion. Although it has been common for remuneration clauses to contain age levels, this is no longer permissible. Caution should also be used when agreeing upon severance pay clauses which stipulate minimum age limits and make the amount of the severance pay contingent solely on age. There is a risk that such provisions are now invalid, which would mean that employees have a full claim to severance pay regardless of their age.

It is most likely still permissible to agree upon age limits in the employment agreement, since section 10 no. 5 AGG clarifies that an agreement which provides for the termination of the employment relationship without a dismissal at the time at which the employee may apply for a pension due to his or her age does not represent impermissible adverse treatment.

Apart from age discrimination, the issues of sexual orientation and religion must be taken into account when drawing up employment agreements. For example, additional remuneration or severance payments for married employees should no longer be agreed upon in the future, since such provisions could indirectly represent discrimination due to sexual orientation. There is a risk that such provisions could be invalid, which would mean that all of the employees would have a claim to the additional remuneration components.

II. Conclusion of Employment Agreements

1. Application

a) Prohibition of Discrimination

The prohibition of discrimination applies to the advertising of a vacancy, as well as decisions made on the applications and the fulfillment of the employment agreement. In this context, the employer has to avoid discrimination on the grounds of race or ethnic origin, gender, religion or secular belief, a disability, age or sexual identity (sections 11, 7 (1) AGG). For details, see pages 12 et seq.

b) CV and References

Applications in Germany follow **fairly international standards,** including the CV and references from all former employers pursuant to section 630 BGB.

Employees are entitled to a written letter of reference with respect to the service relationship and its duration. An employee may demand a "simple" reference or a "qualified" reference. A simple reference merely indicates the nature and duration of the employment relationship, while a qualified reference also covers the employee's conduct during the employment relationship. Most important in practice is the qualified reference. If a legitimate interest (*berechtigtes Interesse*) exists, the employee may demand an interim reference (*Zwischenzeugnis*), particularly if the area of work changes within the operational unit, the company or the group, the employee's superior changes, a transfer of business is expected or, in particular, the employment agreement has been terminated but the termination notice period has not yet expired.

The reference must give the employee's full name. It must be written in German, even for foreign employees in Germany. However, upon request, the employer may also write a reference in a foreign language. The date of the reference must be that of the expiration of the employment agreement, even if the reference is written much later as a consequence of a legal dispute over its content. It must be signed by the employer (or its representative) by his own hand. A signature by a representative of the signatory, a facsimile signature or a photocopied signature will not be sufficient.

The reference must conform to the facts, but the language must be favorable to the employee (*wohlwollend*) and may not hinder the employee's further advancement without good cause. References therefore have a language of their own. There are certain codes related to specific "ratings". These ratings are, in descending order: "very good", "good", "satisfactory", "non-satisfactory".

For **conduct,** the **standard clause** for "good" is:

„Sein/ihr Verhalten gegenüber Vorgesetzten, Kollegen und nachgeordneten Mitarbeitern war stets vorbildlich." (His/her conduct toward his/her superiors, fellow employees and subordinates was always exemplary.)

For **performance,** the **standard clause** for "good" is:

„Er/sie hat die ihm/ihr übertragenen Aufgaben stets zu unserer vollen Zufriedenheit erledigt" (He/she always carried out the tasks assigned to him/her to our complete satisfaction.)

For **average performance** and conduct, the employer must use the code for "satisfactory".
For conduct, the standard clause for „satisfactory" is:

„Sein/ihr Verhalten gegenüber Vorgesetzten, Kollegen und nachgeordneten Mitarbeitern war einwandfrei." (His/her conduct toward his/her superiors, fellow employees and subordinates was beyond reproach.)

For performance, the standard clause for „satisfactory" is:

„Er/sie hat die ihm/ihr übertragenen Aufgaben zu unserer vollen Zufriedenheit erledigt" (He/she carried out the tasks assigned to him/her to our complete satisfaction.)

Below-average conduct would be expressed as follows:

„Sein/ihr Verhalten gegenüber Vorgesetzten, Kollegen und nachgeordneten Mitarbeitern war zufriedendstellend." (His/her conduct toward his/her superiors, fellow employees and subordinates was satisfactory.)

And for **below-average performance:**

„Er/sie hat die ihm/ihr übertragenen Aufgaben zu unserer Zufriedenheit erledigt." (He/she carried out the tasks assigned to him/her to our satisfaction.)

An employee is not entitled to a concluding passage, such as „*Er/sie verlässt uns auf eigenen Wunsch. Wir bedauern dies und wünschen ihm/ihr für die Zukunft alles Gute*" (He/she is leaving us of his/her own accord. We regret this and wish him/her all the best in the future). However, the lack of such a conclusion indicates particular disagreements between the employer and the employee.

If the reference is too unfavorable, the employer may be liable to pay damages to the employee, while if it is too favorable to the employee, the employer may be liable toward a subsequent employer, e.g. if the employer indicates that a bookkeeper was honest, when in fact he or she had defrauded the employer.

c) Interview – What Questions Can Be Asked

Essentially, the employer may ask any question **in connection with the possible employment relationship**, with only a few exceptions. If an applicant lies in response to permissible questions, the employer may contest the subsequent employment agreement on the grounds of fraudulent deception. As a rule, a female applicant cannot be asked whether she is pregnant. However, applicants may be asked whether they have a **criminal record** where this could be of relevance to the intended employment relationship, e.g. as a bookkeeper. Applicants may only be asked about their previous salary where this may be of relevance to the new employment relationship. The employer should refrain from asking questions related to race, ethnic origin, gender, religion or secular belief, disability, age or sexual identity, as such questions could be used as evidence for a difference in treatment due to one of the grounds set forth in section 1 AGG, unless such grounds constitute a material and decisive occupational requirement (sections 8, 9, 10 AGG). For details, see pages 9 et seq.

II. Conclusion of Employment Agreements

d) Employment Questionnaire
Employers usually use questionnaires, but they are subject to the prior approval of the works council. Without such approval, an employment relationship cannot be contested due to false answers given to permitted questions.

e) Medical Examination
A medical examination may be required by the employer; however, this is subject to the **employee's consent**. The employer may not ask employees to undergo genetic investigation or analysis or to present existing results, nor may the employer discriminate on grounds of genetic characteristics, sections 19, 21 Genetic Diagnostics Act (*Gendiagnostikgesetz – GenDG*).

f) Interview Costs
Interview costs are **borne by the employer,** including travel, meals, and perhaps even accommodation costs, but not including the time spent or compensation for income lost from the applicant's current employment relationship. The employer may preclude reimbursement of any out-of-pocket expenses in the invitation letter. However, this preclusion must be explicit and unambiguous.

g) Participation of the Works Council
Under section 99 (1) sentence 1 Works Constitution Act (*Betriebsverfassungsgesetz – BetrVG*), in companies with over 20 employees entitled to vote for the works council, the works council must be informed, and its **consent must be obtained**, before any new employee begins to work for the company. The employer must provide the works council with all personal data of all applicants. The works council may withhold its consent in the cases set forth in section 99 (2) BetrVG. In that case, the employer may obtain such consent from the Labor Court pursuant to section 99 (4) BetrVG. Even if the employer hires an employee without the works council's consent, the contract will still be valid, but the employer will not be allowed to assign the employee to perform his/her duties and will therefore terminate the contract within the first six months.

2. Content of Employment Agreements

a) Conclusion of the Agreement
All employment agreements require an offer and an acceptance.

b) Limitation of Term

aa) Formal Requirements. In order to be effective, a fixed term to an employment agreement must be in written form (section 14 (4) Part-Time and Limited Term Employment Act (*Teilzeit- und Befristungsgesetz – TzBfG*)). However, if a term is invalid only because it was not fixed in written form, the employment agreement may be ordinarily terminated before the end of the agreed upon term (section 16 TzBfG).

bb) Expiration/Termination. There are two types of fixed term employment relationships: according to the calendar and limited by purpose. An employment agreement with a fixed term according to the calendar **ends** at the **expiration of the agreed period** (section 15 (1) TzBfG). A fixed term limited by purpose ends upon **achieving the purpose**, but no earlier than two weeks after delivery of the employer's written notification to the employee on the time the purpose was achieved (section 15 (2) TzBfG). The employer should take note of the expiration date because if the employment relationship is continued beyond this date with the knowledge of the employer, it will be deemed to have been extended for an indefinite period if the employer does not object or convey the achievement of the purpose without delay (section 15 (5) TzBfG). As a rule, a fixed term agreement cannot be **ordinarily terminated** prior to the expiration of the agreed term or achievement of the purpose unless otherwise stipulated in the employment agreement or the applicable collective bargaining agreement. If the employment relationship has been concluded for a person's lifetime or for a period exceeding five years, it may be terminated by the employee once five years have elapsed with a notice period of six months (section 15 (4) TzBfG).

cc) Validity on Objective Grounds or Due to Legal Provision. Fixed-term agreements are only valid if the term is justified on objective grounds or a statutory law specifically allows for a fixed term agreement. The most **important examples of such objective grounds** are set forth in section 14 (1) sentence 2 TzBfG:

1. the operational need for the work involved is only temporary,
2. the term is fixed following training or study in order to facilitate the employee's transition to a subsequent job,
3. the employee is hired to fill in for another employee,
4. the type of work involved justifies a fixed term,
5. the fixed term is merely a probative period,
6. there are personal reasons residing with the employee which justify the fixed term,
7. the employee is remunerated from state budgetary funds which are earmarked for fixed term employment and he has been hired on that basis, or
8. the fixed term is based on a court settlement.

If no objective grounds exist, a term fixed according to the calendar may be extended no more than three times up to a total term of two years, unless the end of a previous fixed or unlimited term employment relationship had ended less than three jears before the new fixed ferm begins with the same employee (section 14 (2) sentences 1 and 2 TzBfG). As a consequence, an employer cannot validly conclude a fixed term agreement on the basis of section 14 (2) TzBfG with an employee who has already worked for this employer at any time in the past. Such an agreement would have no fixed term and run for an unlimited period.

If an employee is hired as a **temporary replacement for an employee on parental leave**, the employment agreement may be restricted to the period of such parental leave under section 21 Federal Parental Benefit and Parental Leave Act (*Bundeselterngeld- und Elternzeitgesetz – BEEG*).

c) Part-Time Contract

An employee is employed on a part-time basis if his or her regular weekly working time is less than that of a comparable fulltime employee (section 2 TzBfG).

aa) Claim for Part-Time Work. Under section 8 (1) TzBfG, employees who have been employed with the company for over six months may request a reduction in their contractual working time, unless the employer has **no more than 15 employees as a rule**, not counting trainees (section 8 (7) TzBfG).

Such employees must assert their right to a reduction in their working time and the extent of such reduction no later than three months before its onset (section 8 (2) TzBfG). It is of the utmost importance that the employer inform the employee of its decision on the reduction of the working time and its allocation **in writing at least one month before the desired onset of the reduction** (section 8 (5) sentence 1 TzBfG). If the employer misses this deadline, the working time will be reduced to the extent desired by the employee (section 8 (5) sentence 2 TzBfG).

II. Conclusion of Employment Agreements

The employer may deny the reduction in working time **on operational grounds** (*aus betrieblichen Gründen*). Pursuant to section 8 (4) sentence 2 TzBfG, such operational grounds exist if the reduction of the working time would severely encroach upon the establishment's organization, working process or safety or incur unreasonable costs. The assessment of whether such grounds entitle the employer to deny the employee's request for a change in working hours must be carried out in a three-stage examination. (1) It must be ascertained whether the working hours regulation the employer deems to be necessary is based on an organizational concept in the establishment, and if so what this concept is. (2) It must be ascertained to what degree the working hours regulation is actually opposed to the employee's request for a change in working hours. (3) Should it emerge that the employee's request for a change in working hours cannot be reconciled with the organizational concept and the resultant working hours regulation, then in a third stage the opposing operational grounds must be weighed against each other.

The employee may not request another reduction in his or her working time until at least **two years** have elapsed since the employer agreed to the reduction or rejected it on justifiable grounds (section 8 (6) TzBfG).

bb) Restrictions on Termination. The employer **may not terminate** the employment relationship **due to** an **employee's refusal** to switch from fulltime to parttime employment or vice versa. However, the right to terminate the employment relationship **on other grounds** remains **unaffected** (section 11 TzBfG). This means that if for operational reasons the company can no longer employ part-time employees, a termination on these grounds may be valid.

cc) Non-Discrimination. It is of particular importance that part-time employees **not be treated less favorably than** comparable fulltime employees on account of their part-time status unless objective grounds exist justifying unequal treatment (section 4 TzBfG).

dd) Further Legal Rules. There are additional rules concerning the extension of working time (section 9 TzBfG), job training and further qualification (section 10 TzBfG), on-call work (section 12 TzBfG) and job sharing (section 13 TzBfG), which are, however, of limited importance in practical employment law.

ee) Insignificant Employment. The insignificant employment (*geringfügige Beschäftigung*) is a special type of part-time work. It is subject to specific exemptions with respect to social security contributions if the employee regularly earns no more than **EUR 400 per month**, or his or her employment is restricted to a maximum of two months or 50 working days per year, is not performed as a profession (*berufsmäßig ausgeübt*) and the income for this period does not exceed EUR 400 per month (section 8 (1) Social Security Code IV (*SGB IV*).

d) Leasing of Employees (*Arbeitnehmerüberlassung*)

Employers who, as lessors, wish to **commercially lease out employees** (leased employees) to third parties (clients/lessees) for work **require** a **permit** pursuant to section 1 (1) sentence 1 Act Regulating the Commercial Leasing of Employees (*Arbeitnehmerüberlassungsgesetz – AÜG*). A distinction must be made between the employment agreement between the lessor and the leased employee and the lease agreement between the lessor and the lessee. Employees are "leased" if they are completely integrated into the lessee's establishment and do not continue to work for their employer alone.

In the **absence** of such a permit, it is extremely difficult to **distinguish** between permissible **service or work agreements** and impermissible **employee leasing**. If the employer determines the content, location and time of the employee's work, this would indicate employee leasing. To avoid this, the employer may only issue directives that pertain exclusively to the actual work.

Employee leasing is **"commercial"** and therefore requires a permit if it is not merely on an occasional basis, but is designed to last for a particular period of time and aims to achieve direct or indirect economic benefits. The case law construes the term "commercial" very broadly. Even more restrictions apply to the construction industry (section 1b AÜG).

A leased employee will, after six weeks of work, have the right to demand that the lessor pay the same remuneration as the client pays its regular employees in comparable positions (section 9 no. 2 in connection with section 10 (4) AÜG).

Foreign lessors who lease employees in Germany may be subject to the provisions of the Posted Workers Law (*Arbeitnehmer-Entsendegesetz – AEntG*). The leasing of employees between companies in a group pursuant to section 1 (3) no. 2 AÜG and in order to avoid short-time work or dismissal in accordance with section 1 (3) no. 1 and section 1a AÜG is less restricted.

If the **lessor does not have the permit required** pursuant to section 1 AÜG, an employment relationship between the client and the leased employee will be formed pursuant to section 10 (1) AÜG at the time the work is to commence under the contract between the client and the lessor. However, the employee may **object to the employment relationship with the client**, in which case periods of three weeks to four months after the lease comes to an end are accepted by the courts.

Before a leased employee is taken on, the client's works council must be consulted pursuant to section 99 of the Works Constitution Act (*Betriebsverfassungsgesetz – BetrVG*) and section 14 (3) AÜG. The works council can also exercise codetermination rights for the leased employee pursuant to section 87 (1) no. 2 BetrVG. However, if an (actual) service agreement or work agreement (*Werkvertrag*) is involved, then as a rule the works council will have no codetermination rights because the employee is not integrated into the client's establishment.

e) Foreign Employees

In order to take up residence and work in Germany, a foreigner who is not a citizen of an EEA member state must have a residence title (*Aufenthaltstitel*) pursuant to section 4 (1) sentence 1 Residence Act (*Aufenthaltsgesetz – AufenthG*). He or she must apply for this residence title at the Foreigners' Registration Office **before entering the country**. There are four types of residence titles: a visa (*Visum*, section 6 AufenthG), a (temporary) residence permit (*Aufenthaltserlaubnis*, section 7 AufenthG), a (permanent) settlement permit (*Niederlassungserlaubnis*, section 9 AufenthG) and a permanent EC residence permit (*Erlaubnis zum Daueraufenthalt-EG*, section 9a AufenthG).

The residence title specifies whether and to what extent a foreign national is entitled to take up work (section 4 (2) AufenthG). Foreigners may only take up employment if the residence permit so allows. A prerequisite for a **work permit** is a specific job offer to the employee (section 18 (5) AufenthG).

There are restrictions on the issuance of a residence title with work permit which are comparable to those of other countries: It may only be issued if the employment of foreign nationals will not negatively affect the employment market and no German or EEA national is available for the job. Foreign nationals may not be employed on terms less favorable than those applicable to comparable national employees, section 39 (2) AufenthG. There are **bilateral agreements** with several countries, particularly the USA, Canada and Australia, which allow their nationals

II. Conclusion of Employment Agreements

to travel to Germany without a visa and to apply for a residence title with a work permit **after entering the country**. The employment of foreign nationals without a work permit may be an administrative offense which could lead to the imposition of heavy fines upon the employer and of lesser fines upon the employee (section 404 (2) no. 3 and 4 SGB III).

The situation is much easier for EEA nationals, who do not require a residence title (sections 2 (4), 12 Act on the General Freedom of Movement for EU Citizens (*Freizügigkeitsgesetz – FreizügG*)). Unlike citizens of the Member States that joined the EU on 1 May 2004, citizens of Bulgaria and Romania still need to obtain a work permit from the Federal Employment Agency (*Bundesagentur für Arbeit*) until 2014 (section 284 (1) Social Security Code III (*SGB III*)).

f) Prohibition of Discrimination

Discrimination by **gender** is prohibited under the AGG. For details see pages 9 et seq. above.

3. Control of General Terms and Conditions

As a result of the reform of the law of obligations, the German legislation governing General Terms and Conditions now also applies to employment contracts; due consideration must, however, also be given to the special aspects of labor law. The control of employment contracts in line with the principles applicable to General Terms and Conditions is supposed to mitigate power imbalances between employer and employee, thereby preventing undue prejudice to the employee that can occur if employment contract terms are dictated unilaterally by the employer. This reform does not affect collective agreements or works agreements, which are still not subject to control.

General Terms and Conditions are all contractual terms that have been pre-formulated for a multitude of contracts by one party to the contract (the "user"). In practice, the user will normally be the employer. The employer presents the employee with a pre-formulated contract to sign. It is not relevant whether the employer is using such pre-formulated contractual terms for the first time or repeatedly. It suffices that the employer intends to use them on multiple occasions. In practical terms, almost every employment contract will therefore be subject to the control of General Terms and Conditions.

However, the control of the content in accordance with sections 305 et seq. BGB only applies where employment contract terms have been set by one of the parties upon conclusion of the contract. Contractual terms that have been negotiated individually are not subject to control, in accordance with sections 305 et seq. BGB. Negotiation means that the employer makes the core of the clause available for renegotiation by the employee and gives the employee an opportunity to co-determine the content of that clause. The requirements for this are very stringent.

"Surprising clauses" cannot become part of a contract (section 305c (1) BGB). The employer must ensure that the contractual terms are clear and comprehensible. Any doubts as to the interpretation of specific contract clauses will be construed to the detriment of the employer (section 305c (2) BGB). An employment contract must therefore be set out clearly. It is important to divide the contract into a number of paragraphs and subheadings and not to "conceal" any provisions. The employment contract should be as reader-friendly as possible. It must be designed for a legal layperson who should be able to understand it without consulting a lawyer.

a) Review of Subject Matter

The review of subject matter, as set forth in sections 307 et seq. BGB, lies at the heart of German law on General Terms and Conditions. A control of content is only performed if and where contractual stipulations deviate from the wording of the law. Clauses which merely replicate the law are not subject to a control of content. Clauses setting forth the terms of the performance or the consideration to be paid are not covered by the control of content for General Terms and Conditions, either, as this would be contrary to the basic concept of the provisions on General Terms and Conditions which specifically seek to avoid the court control of service proposals and prices. Thus, a below-standard wage can be agreed upon with an employee who is not bound by a collective agreement as long as it is not against *ordre public* (section 138 BGB).

Sections 308 and 309 BGB define special types of invalid clauses for which a contract must be examined prior to the general control of content pursuant to section 307 BGB. Only if a clause is not deemed to be invalid under the provisions of sections 308, 309 BGB will the general control of content pursuant to section 307 BGB be carried out. Under this provision, a stipulation in a pre-formulated employment contract is invalid if, contrary to the principles of good faith, it unreasonably disadvantages the employee. Unreasonable disadvantage may also result from a stipulation which is not clear and comprehensible. In case of doubt, unreasonable disadvantage to an employee will be presumed if a stipulation in the employment contract cannot be reconciled with the basic rationale of the legal provision from which it deviates or if essential rights or duties inherent to the nature of the contract are restricted in such a manner as to jeopardize the achievement of the contractual purpose.

If a clause in the contract proves to be invalid as a result of the control of content, the validity of the remainder of the contract will remain unaffected (section 306 (1) BGB). Individual clauses cannot be reduced to the extent in which they would be permissible in order to retain their validity (*geltungserhaltende Reduktion*). A clause that contravenes the law on General Terms and Conditions will always be invalid as a result. If a clause is only partly unlawful, the lawful portion can remain valid. Using the "blue pencil test", it should be examined whether the invalid portion of a clause can be readily severed from the contract without rendering the remainder of the clause incomprehensible. If a clause is divisible in this sense, the lawful portion of the clause will remain effective.

b) Specific Clauses

In labor law practice, the control of General Terms and Conditions is particularly relevant for contractual penalties, rights of revocation, cut-off periods and reference clauses.

aa) Contractual penalties. Contrary to section 309 no. 6 BGB, which prohibits such arrangements in General Terms and Conditions, contractual penalties may be agreed upon in standard form employment agreements, as such penalties are specific features of labor law. However, contractual penalties may constitute an unreasonable disadvantage if they are disproportionately high. In that case, the clause as a whole will be ineffective.

A penalty can be unreasonable if there is a discrepancy between a breach of duty and the amount of the contractual penalty demanded. For example, a contractual penalty for failure to commence work in the amount of a gross monthly salary would be too high if the notice period is only two weeks. As a consequence, the contractual penalty clause would be ineffective – a reduction would not be possi-

II. Conclusion of Employment Agreements

ble. The employee would also be unreasonably disadvantaged if the employment contract provides for contractual penalties ranging in amount from one to three months' salary for each violation of competition rules. The employer can, however, stipulate the exact amount of penalty depending on the gravity of the violation.

bb) Exclusion clauses. Cut-off periods have always been common in labor law and also are permissible in standard form employment agreements as long as certain minimum terms are adhered to. According to case law, there is a minimum cut-off period of three months for asserting claims. In the case of two-stage cut-off periods, i.e. those which require that the claim be asserted in court within a certain period after the claim has been asserted against the employer, the Federal Labor Court has adjudged a period of three months to be appropriate for the second term as well.

cc) Revocation clauses. Revocation clauses allowing the employer to revoke benefits for the future must conform to section 308 no. 4 BGB, which renders any standard form stipulation of the employer's right to modify or deviate from the promised compensation invalid, unless the agreement to the modification or deviation can reasonably be expected of the employee when the interests of the employer are taken into account. The Federal Labor Court has ruled that the employee may be reasonably expected to agree to a right of revocation – which would therefore be valid – if the employee is granted no less than the standard wage or the customary compensation, and protection against dismissal with the option of altered conditions of reemployment is not circumvented. Subject to these prerequisites, no more than 25 to 30% of the overall compensation can be revoked. Furthermore, a revocation may only be effected for good cause. This must be derived from the contractual clause, which must state at least the nature of the grounds for the revocation (e.g. financial reasons, reasons relating to the employee's conduct).

dd) Reference clauses. Individual employment contracts often incorporate entire collective agreements or parts thereof by reference. As collective agreements are on an equal footing with legal provisions, they are not subject to a control of contents in accordance with sections 307 et seq. BGB. However, reference to a collective agreement relating to an entirely different industry may be invalid due to the protection against surprising clauses (section 305c (1) BGB). "Dynamic" reference clauses, which incorporate future amendments into collective agreements in an employment contract, can also pose a problem as they hinder the required transparency and clarity. For reference clauses concluded after December 31, 2001, the Federal Labor Court has abandoned the rule of interpretation wherein a contractual reference to collective agreements is merely designed to place unorganized employees on an equal footing with organized employees. This means that even once the employer has left an employers' association, employees will still participate in collective wage increases through the reference clause. Accordingly, the employer's intent to treat employees equally should now be included explicitly in such clauses in order to ensure that if an employer leaves the employers' association, the employees will cease to participate in future collective wage increases.

4. Form

Basically, there are no formal requirements for employment agreements. But according to section 2 Documentation Act (*Nachweisgesetz*), no later than one month after the agreed upon commencement of the employment relationship the employer must **record** the essential contractual terms in writing, sign the record and

hand it over to the employee. This record must contain at least the following information:
1. the name and address of the parties to the agreement,
2. the date of commencement of the employment relationship,
3. the anticipated duration of the employment relationship (in the case of fixed term employment relationships),
4. the location of the workplace or, if the employee will not only be working at one site, an acknowledgement to the fact that the employee can be assigned to work at various locations,
5. a brief characterization or description of the activity to be performed by the employee,
6. the composition and amount of the remuneration, including the extra pay, incentive payments and special payments, as well as other components of the remuneration and their payability,
7. the agreed upon working hours,
8. the length of the annual vacation,
9. the notice periods for terminating the employment relationship,
10. a general reference to the collective bargaining agreements, works or service agreements applicable to the employment relationship.

In the case of employees engaged in insignificant employment (see page 17) pursuant to section 8 (1) Social Security Code IV (*SGB IV*), the record must further contain a reference to the fact that the employee can attain the position of a regular employee, subject to contributions to the statutory pension insurance fund, if he or she waives the exemption from compulsory insurance pursuant to section 5 (2) sentence 2 SGB VI by declaration to the employer.

Section 2 (2) Documentation Act lists the facts that, at a minimum, must be provided in the document. However, if the employer does not comply with this Act, this will not affect the validity of the employment relationship; but this could create procedural disadvantages for the employer in the event of a legal dispute on the conditions of employment. The employer may then need to bear the burden of proof with respect to its allegations regarding employment conditions in the legal proceeding.

In practice, employment agreements are usually concluded in writing. **Certain special laws require written documentation** such as
– the conclusion of a fixed term agreement (section 14 (4) TzBfG)
– agreements with apprentices (*Auszubildende*) (section 11 Vocational Training Act (*Berufsbildungsgesetz – BBiG*)).

5. Invalid Employment Agreements

Employment agreements are declared invalid only in very rare cases. Usually, even if the employment agreement itself is not valid, the employment relationship is deemed to be legitimate until it is challenged by the employer or employee.

a) Minors

Minors may only be employed in accordance with the Young Persons' Protection in Employment Act (*Jugendarbeitsschutzgesetz – JArbSchG*). Adolescents (between the age of 15 and 18 years) are allowed to work up to eight hours per day and 40 hours per week. Children between 13 and 15 years may enter into an employment agreement with the consent of their guardian, provided that such work is suitable for a child and does not jeopardize the child's health, safety, development or education.

The working times are restricted to two hours per day between 8:00 a.m. and 6:00 p.m.

If the parents do not agree, the contract will presumptively be invalid and unenforceable unless such consent is declared in response to the employer's request within an adequate period of time.

b) Fraudulent Misrepresentation

An employment agreement may be challenged if it was concluded on the basis of fraudulent deception on the part of one of the parties (section 123 (I) BGB). The most frequent case is an inaccurate answer to a legitimate question raised by the employer during the employment interview.

c) Error

According to section 119 (2) BGB, an **error about the characteristics of the employee** concerning the specific skills required for the job may, in very narrowly defined cases, give the employer the right to rescind the employment agreement.

d) Lack of Residence or Work Permit

In addition to the general restrictions, an employment agreement **may** also **be invalid** due to lack of a residence title permitting a foreign national to take up employment. If the residence title or work permit is revoked or invalidated or an extension is denied, the employer may terminate the contract for person-related reasons with an ordinary termination notice period.

III. Rights and Duties

1. Duty to Work/Right to Work

Under the employment contract, the employee has both the right and duty to work. Accordingly, the employer **may not suspend** the employee unless otherwise validly provided in the employment agreement.

2. Remuneration

a) Minimum Remuneration

There is no **statutory wage law** in Germany. Only in certain branches of industries is a minimum wage set in accordance with the Law on the Posting of Workers (*Arbeitnehmer-Entsendegesetz – AEntG*): construction work, industrial cleaning, nursing care, laundry services, waste management, including street cleaning and snow clearing, security services, electric installation, painting and varnishing. However, the actual amount is not specified in this law, but rather in collective bargaining agreements concluded in relationship to it. A minimum wage for an economic sector is binding on all employers domiciled in Germany or abroad if their employees fall under the scope of application of the collective bargaining agreement. It is further binding for all lessor employers if the client assigns the leased employees to perform work that falls within the scope of application of the collective bargaining agreement. A minimum wage is also legally possible, but at present not in force, in the sectors of mail services, leasing of employees, scrapping services and training services pursuant to Social Security Code II and III. A general minimum wage that was envisioned for the mail services sector was found to be invalid on formal grounds by the Federal Administrative Court (*Bundesverwaltungsgericht*) at the beginning of 2010. There is controversy over the question of whether the Posted

Workers Directive was implemented into national law to the necessary extent with the AEntG, since its scope of application is limited to just a few sectors.

Moreover, an agreed wage may be grossly unfair if it does not exceed two-thirds of the relevant trade union agreement or if wages for fulltime work amount to less than the protected social welfare minimum. Finally, collective bargaining agreements may be generally binding and fix the minimum wages of a specific sector.

b) Bonus

There are a great number of different **types of bonuses** in Germany, such as supplemental pay, profit sharing, commission, piecework remuneration, incentives (*Prämien*) and staff bonuses such as Christmas bonuses (*Gratifikationen*):

Supplemental pay (*Zulagen/Zuschläge*) is offered in addition to the basic remuneration. It may be granted for a particular reason, e.g. to compensate for particular difficulties on the job or for work at inconvenient hours (night work, Sundays, holidays), or it may be granted for no particular reason, but merely in order to increase the income so that it is above the level of the wage scale which is deemed to be too low.

Profit sharing (*Tantieme*) is often granted on or above the level of managerial employees (*leitende Angestellte*) in addition to the fixed remuneration. It enables the employee to participate in the company's results, regardless of whether they were the result of his or her activities.

Commission, on the other hand, is linked to the employee's own activities and success. As a rule, it is paid as remuneration for the brokering or conclusion of contracts on behalf of the company and is the standard compensation for commercial agents pursuant to sections 87 to 87c of the German Commercial Code (*Handelsgesetzbuch – HGB*).

Piecework rates (*Akkordlöhne*) are strictly tied to performance. In contrast to incentive payments, the reference point is solely the quantity of work done.

Attendance bonuses (*Anwesenheitsprämien*) may be paid if the employee is absent less than a given number of days per year and a **loyalty bonus** awarded for a given number of years with the company.

The employer can **pay staff** bonuses at certain points in time above and beyond the remuneration for work done. In addition to the Christmas bonus (often one monthly salary) and/or vacation bonus, an employee can also receive anniversary bonuses. Staff bonuses and supplementary payments may also be agreed upon as a voluntary benefit or be made subject to a right of revocation on grounds to be specified in the contract, such as economic reasons or the employee's performance or conduct. The revocable part of the total remuneration must be limited to 25% to 30%. Independent of that, wage scale increases may be set off against extra payments made above scale, even if this is not explicitly provided for in the contract.

c) Stock Options

Employees may be granted stock options on the basis of a binding agreement as an enforceable component of their remuneration or as a voluntary benefit. Generally, such an individual agreement is not contained in the employment agreement, but rather in a separate granting agreement. With the stock options, the employees receive direct or indirect subscription rights to the employing company's stocks. In many cases the agreement to grant stock options is limited to a certain class of employees, generally management personnel. The principle of stock options is that the exercise price of the shares an employee can acquire is set in the **granting agreement**. If the market price rises above the exercise price, this will be to the benefit of the employee. Typically, an option agreement provides for a **waiting**

period before the option can be exercised, which may not be less than four years for board members; this period also serves as a basis for calculating the waiting period with regard to employees. The exercise of the option can also be restricted to certain times or excluded for a certain period of time. This is designed to prevent insider trading and is therefore deemed permissible under the labor and employment laws. Moreover, the (contractual) **transfer** of the stock options may be excluded for a number of years.

The stock option plans generally provide for the option rights to be forfeited if an employee leaves the company. Such **forfeiture clauses** are generally allowed and are not viewed as impermissible impediments to resignation, because the granting of future advantages may be made contingent upon the continuation of the employment relationship. In particular, this does not present a problem if the stock options were granted free of charge. It has not yet been determined whether stock option rights for which an employee had to pay a consideration can be forfeited without compensation, but better arguments can be made for the permissibility of a forfeiture without compensation even where stock option rights were granted for a consideration.

In granting stock options, the **principle of equal treatment** must be observed, if they are granted based on a particular concept, which is almost always the case. This applies even if the employer is providing voluntary benefits. However, the equal treatment principle only applies within the company, not within the corporate group. Accordingly, if the stock options are granted by the parent company of the group – which may be domiciled in a different country – this principle cannot be enforced.

The options are not **taxed** at the time they are granted, but after they have been exercised. The monetary value of the options is calculated as the difference between the exercise price and the current market price. The further taxation of the shares acquired in this way follows the general tax rules.

If the company has a works council – and the employees entitled to receive options are not exclusively members of governing bodies or managerial personnel within the meaning of section 5 BetrVG – then a **codetermination right** pursuant to section 87 (1) no. 10 BetrVG may exist. Although no such right exists with respect to the question of whether stock options should be granted at all and, if so within what scope they should be granted, but they would have a say in the details of the distribution, in particular the allocation to individual groups of employees or even individual employees. However, the instructions issued by the shareholders' meeting would most likely not be subject to codetermination, since it cannot negotiate with the works council, but only with the management board as the employer. Thus, the scope of decisions not subject to codetermination is expanded to include instructions issued by the shareholders' meeting by sections 192, 193 (2) Stock Corporation Act (*Aktiengesetz – AktG*), as the management board is bound by these instructions. This would presumably also apply – within the limits of a proper exercise of legal rights – to those instructions which are not mandatory under the Stock Corporation Act, but are set forth in shareholder resolutions. The codetermination rights with regard to the implementation of these instructions would likely be limited to a requirement of the works council's consent.

d) Company Pension Plans

The law provides for five types of company pension plans:
– direct pension (*Direktzusage*)
– direct insurance policies (*Direktversicherung*)
– staff pension funds (*Pensionskasse*)

- pension funds (*Pensionsfonds*)
- benevolent funds (*Unterstützungskasse*).

Direct pensions are based on an agreement between employer and employee that the employer will pay a certain pension after the employee's retirement pursuant to section 1b (1) Act for the Improvement of Company Pension Plans (*Gesetz zur Verbesserung der betrieblichen Altersvorsorge – BetrAVG*). The employer is directly obligated to make the future pension payments. It may create accruals in the annual balance sheet, which would lead to substantial tax benefits.

Direct insurance policies (section 1b (2) BetrAVG) are based on life insurance policies the employer takes out on the employee. The employee is the insured person and the insurance policy's beneficiary. He or she can therefore, upon retirement, claim the pension benefits directly from the insurance company. The employer, however, remains liable within the scope of the pension commitment (section 1 (1) sentence 3 BetrAVG).

Pension funds are separate legal entities which execute a company pension plan. If the employee has a direct claim against the fund, this is a "staff pension fund" (section 1b (3) BetrAVG) or "pension fund" (section 1b (3) BetrAVG), otherwise such funds are "benevolent funds" (section 1b (4) BetrAVG). Payments from a benevolent fund are made entirely at the discretion of the fund, but the courts have held that if the benevolent fund does not pay, the employee will have a claim against the employer.

If an employee is at least 30 years of age and the pension commitment to him or her has been in effect for at least five years, then the pension expectancy is vested (section 1b (1) sentence 1 BetrAVG). If a pension expectancy is vested and an employee leaves the company before reaching retirement age, he or she will retain the right to future benefits which will then be calculated according to section 2 BetrAVG *pro rata temporis*.

An employee may **not waive pension expectancies** either with or without compensation if such an agreement is concluded in connection with the termination of the employment relationship or thereafter until the commencement of his retirement. Only in extremely rare cases of very low pension expectancies would such an agreement be valid against compensation (section 3 BetrAVG).

Furthermore, vested pension expectancies may only be **transferred** if (1) the employment relationship is terminated, (2) the expectancies are transferred to the new employer, (3) the three parties (employee, former employer and new employer) conclude a trilateral agreement on the transfer and (4) the new employer takes over either the existing pension commitment or the transfer value of the vested pension expectancies and grants an equivalent pension commitment (section 4 (2) BetrAVG). If no such trilateral agreement is concluded, the employee will, in principle, be entitled to have the transfer value of the pension expectancies transferred to him or her if the company pension scheme was operated by a pension fund, staff pension fund or direct insurance (section 4 (3) BetrAVG). The new employer will then be obligated to provide an equivalent pension commitment and implement this commitment via a pension fund, staff pension fund or direct insurance.

If pension expectancies are vested, the employee is insured against the **employer's insolvency** by the pension guarantee fund (*Pensionssicherungsverein*) up to a certain limit (section 7 (3) BetrAVG). Finally, there are certain obligations under section 16 BetrAVG to adjust pension payments on a regular basis.

e) Capital Formation Benefits

The employer may make certain payments (not exceeding EUR 470 per year) to its employees which gives them the right to an additional state payment, depending

III. Rights and Duties

on the kind of contribution involved ("capital formation benefits" – *vermögenswirksame Leistungen*).

3. Sick Pay

The Continuation of Remuneration Act (*Entgeltfortzahlungsgesetz – EFZG*) gives every employee the right to receive sick pay up to the amount of 100% of his or her wages. The duration of such benefits is limited to the **first six weeks of the illness**. However, this six-week period will **commence anew** with the onset of each illness if it is not due to the same underlying ailment. On the basis of the same basic underlying ailment, it will recommence after six months have elapsed since the end of the last sick leave, and one year has elapsed since the beginning of the first sick leave.

If the sickness exceeds this six-week period, employees are entitled to receive a sickness allowance (*Krankengeld*) paid by their statutory health insurance scheme. The sickness allowance amounts to 70% of an employee's normal pay. The maximum period for payment of this allowance is 78 weeks.

4. Working Time

The **working hours** during working days (*Werktage*) may not exceed **eight hours** pursuant to section 3 sentence 1 Working Hours Act (*Arbeitszeitgesetz – ArbZG*), and thus **48 hours per week** for a six-day workweek (Monday to Saturday). This can be extended to **ten hours** if the average shift within six months or 24 weeks does not exceed eight hours a working day (section 3 sentence 2 ArbZG). After completion of their work shift, the employees must have **an uninterrupted rest period of at least eleven hours** (section 5 (1) ArbZG). **Night work** is only permissible for eight hours per working day; if the shift is extended to ten hours, it must be ensured that, within a compensatory period of one month or four weeks, the average shift per working day does not exceed eight hours (section 6 (2) ArbZG). **On-call work** (*Bereitschaftsdienst*) also counts as working time and, where applicable, as overtime, where such work is rendered in the form of the employee's physical presence at the workplace; on-call work in the form of constant availability, i.e. stand-by work (*Rufbereitschaft*), on the other hand, does not count as working time. However, it makes no difference whether the employee is active or idle during this period.

Pursuant to section 7 ArbZG extensions of working hours are possible on the basis of a **collective bargaining agreement or a works agreement:** if stand-by work is assigned regularly or to a great extent, the working day shift can be extended even beyond ten hours (section 7 (1) no. 1 lit. a and no. 4 lit. a ArbZG), if the working time does not exceed an average of 48 hours a week in 12 calendar months (section 7 (8) ArbZG). The compensatory period can also be extended (section 7 (1) no. 1 lit. a and no. 4 lit. b ArbZG). With rotating shifts and public transport enterprises, short breaks of less than 15 minutes can be permitted (section 7 (1) no. 2 ArbZG). The breaks can also be reduced by up to two hours if the nature of the work requires this and the reduction is compensated for within a period to be established (section 7 (1) nos. 3 ArbZG). Thus, where corresponding collective bargaining agreements exist, their working-time provisions can be incorporated. If the employer is not bound by a collective bargaining agreement, but its establishment falls within the territorial, operational and objective purview of a collective bargaining agreement, it may also incorporate that agreement's working time provisions into a works agreement or – if there is no works council – into individual employment agreements. Such an agreement with the employee must be in written form. If the collective bargaining agreement contains a clause allowing for variations, an employer who is not bound by a collective bargaining agreement may take advantage of this in its establishment by way of a works agreement (section 7 (3) ArbZG).

The general rule prohibiting **Sunday and holiday work** (section 9 (1) ArbZG) is modified by numerous exceptions (section 10 ArbZG). Even if only one of the exceptions applies, 15 Sundays per year must be work-free and Sunday work must be compensated for by an additional day off (section 11 ArbZG). Here too, statutory compensation periods can be altered in a collective bargaining agreement or a works agreement based on a collective bargaining agreement (section 12 ArbZG). The above statements on the incorporation of collective bargaining provisions into works agreements apply (section 12 sentence 2, section 7 (3) ArbZG).

5. Vacation

Pursuant to the German Federal Vacation Act (*Bundesurlaubsgesetz – BUrlG*), the minimum vacation entitlement is 24 working days. With each week consisting of six working days (excluding Sundays), this comes to four weeks in all (section 3 BUrlG). The German system distinguishes between working days (*Werktage*) and office days (*Arbeitstage*). Since office days are only from Monday to Friday, the four-week minimum vacation amounts to 20 office days.

The **purpose** of a vacation is to give employees an opportunity to relax and restore their energy – they therefore may not enter into any other employment arrangements during this time which might be at odds with this purpose. The vacation entitlement **commences** once the employment relationship has existed for **six months** (section 4 BUrlG). If the employment relationship is terminated before these six months have elapsed or within the first half of a calendar year, an employee will only be entitled to 1/12 of the annual vacation entitlement for each month of the employment relationship. In the event of termination after the first six months of the employment relationship and within the second half of the calendar year, an employee will be entitled to the full annual vacation (section 5 BUrlG). The vacation entitlement **expires** at the end of the calendar year, but it can be retained until 31 March of the following year if an employee was not able to take his or her vacation for operational or personal reasons (section 7 (2) sentence 2 BUrlG). Even employees who are sick during the entire year will be entitled to a vacation which will not extinguish, but must be granted to them once they regain their health. An ECJ Advocate General has argued that these vacation claims should be allowed to expire after 18 months, but this has not yet been ruled on by the ECJ.

Employees must **apply** for vacation and the employer must approve the written request unless prevented from doing so due to urgent operational reasons or vacation applications of other employees who, due to "social factors", have a higher priority (section 7 (1) sentence 1 BUrlG). If the employment agreement has been terminated, an employee must apply for vacation in such a way that it can be taken before the termination notice period has elapsed.

There is no vacation entitlement where an employee has already taken vacation leave in a **previous employment relationship** during the same calendar year (section 6 (1) BUrlG). Hence, the previous employer must certify the vacation the employee took while under its employ (section 6 (2) BUrlG).

During the vacation period, employees are entitled to **full remuneration**, calculated in accordance with the average employment earnings they received during the last 13 weeks prior to the commencement of their vacation (section 11 (1) BUrlG). Frequently, the employer also grants a special vacation bonus as a voluntary staff bonus (*Gratifikation*), see page 24.

III. Rights and Duties

If the vacation cannot be granted due to a **termination of the employment agreement**, the employee will be entitled to **compensation** for vacation not taken in an amount equivalent to the vacation pay. In order to assert such a claim the employee must have applied for vacation prior to 31 March of the following year and prior to the expiration of the employment agreement. However, this does not apply to employees who were prevented from applying for vacation due to an inability to work.

6. Maternity Protection – Parental Leave and Parental Benefits

a) Maternity Protection.

Pursuant to sections 3 and 4 Maternity Protection Act (*Mutterschutzgesetz – MuSchG*), women are **not permitted to perform certain tasks during pregnancy** and for a certain period after giving birth which are considered hazardous to the health or safety of the mother or child. Pregnant women are **not obligated to work** at all in the last six weeks leading up to the expected date of birth, unless they explicitly declare their willingness to do so. Such a declaration can be revoked at any time pursuant to section 3 (2) MuSchG. The same applies to a period of **eight weeks** following the birth (or twelve weeks in cases of multiple or premature births), during which the mother is absolutely forbidden to work. During the period in which the mother is nursing her child, there are specific tasks she may not perform (section 6 (3) MuSchG), and the employer is obligated to give her sufficient time to nurse her baby (section 7 MuSchG).

During these periods (six weeks prior to delivery date to 8/12 weeks following delivery) women are entitled to **maternity pay** equivalent to their monthly remuneration during the last three months before the commencement of their maternity leave. A part of this remuneration, amounting to a maximum of EUR 13 per day, is contributed by the health insurer.

In order to benefit from these regulations, a pregnant woman must **inform her employer** of her pregnancy and the expected delivery date as soon as they have been ascertained. The employer must notify the competent authorities (*Aufsichtsbehörde*) in good time but is not entitled to inform third parties.

The employer **may not dismiss** pregnant women until four months after they have given birth, unless it was not given notice of the pregnancy or had not received such information within **two weeks** after the dismissal was served. Only in very specific cases, such as the shutdown of the entire operation, may the employer give notice of dismissal upon the prior consent of the competent authority. It is very important that such a declaration of termination not only be in written form, but also that the employee **be informed of the grounds for the dismissal in writing**, otherwise it would be invalid. A woman's right to terminate her employment agreement during this period remains unrestricted.

b) Parental Leave and Parental Benefits.

Both the father and the mother of the newborn child are entitled to parental leave for a period of up to three years, until the child has reached the age of three, pursuant to section 15 Act on Parental Benefits and Parental Leave (*Bundeselterngeld- und Elternzeitgesetz – BEEG*; see also page 75).

Parental leave can be taken **by the father or mother separately or together**. However, it is restricted to **three years for each child**. The 8 (or 12) week period of maternity leave pursuant to section 6 (2) MuSchG is included in this period (section 15 (2) sentence 2 BEEG). Up to **12 months** of the three-year period can be transferred to a later time until the child reaches the **age of 8** (section 15 (2) sentence 4 BEEG). However, such a transfer requires the consent of the employer.

An employee on parental leave may be employed **part-time** for a maximum of **30 hours per week**. Any employment relationship with another employer or on a self-employed basis requires the consent of the regular employer, which may only be withheld within a four-week period for urgent operational reasons (section 15 (4) BEEG).

During their parental leave, employees may **apply twice for a reduction of their working time** (section 15 (6) BEEG), provided that, among other conditions, the working time is reduced to 15 to 30 working hours per week for a period of at least three months (section 15 (7) BEEG). The employer may only deny such a request within **four weeks**, stating the **grounds for the denial in writing** (section 15 (7) sentence 4 BEEG).

In order to provide a clear situation for both parties, an employee must **request parental leave** in writing **seven weeks** before its onset, stating the precise time he or she wishes to take parental leave within **two years** (section 16 (1) BEEG). Because parental leave can be taken for up to three years, the employee may submit another application eight weeks before the expiration of the first two years for the final year of parental leave. The leave may only be terminated prior to the agreed date **or extended** beyond that date with the **employer's consent** (section 16 (3) sentence 1 BEEG). An employee who has requested parental leave **cannot be dismissed** as of the moment of the request, but at most eight weeks prior to the commencement of the parental leave or during the leave itself, except for extreme cases with the consent of the competent authority (section 18 (1) BEEG).

As outlined above, **fixed-term agreements** are only valid if the term is justified on objective grounds or a statute specifically authorizes fixed-term agreements. Pursuant to section 21 (1) BEEG, material grounds justifying the limitation of the term of an employment relationship exist if an **employee is hired to take the place** of another employee for the duration of the period in which employment is prohibited pursuant to the Maternity Protection Act, of parental leave, of release from work responsibilities in order to care for a child under the provisions of a collective bargaining agreement, a works agreement or an individual agreement, or the duration of these periods cumulatively or parts thereof. Under section 21 (3) BEEG, it is sufficient if the duration of the fixed term agreement is set according to the calendar or can be fixed or derived from the purpose of the replacement for parental leave. Such a replacement agreement may be **terminated** with a notice period of three weeks, but no earlier than as of the end of the parental leave (section 21 (4) BEEG).

During parental leave, employees may be entitled to **parental benefits** which are provided by the state. Under the BEEG, which has meanwhile replaced the Federal Education Allowance Act (*Bundeserziehungsgeldgesetz*), the parental benefits (*Elterngeld*) amount to 67% of the employee's average income in the 12 months prior to the child's birth (section 2 (1) BEEG). There is no income limit, but the maximum amount of parental benefits is EUR 1,800 (section 2 (1) BEEG) and the minimum amount is EUR 300 (section 2 (5) BEEG). Parents are entitled to parental benefits for 14 months starting from the date of the child's birth (section 4 (1) BEEG). One parent may only receive the parental benefits for 12 months. Thus, the other parent has to take parental leave for at least two months in order to claim the full 14 months' benefit; exceptions apply especially for single parents (section 4 (3) BEEG).

III. Rights and Duties   31

7. Confidentiality

Employees are obligated not to disclose any confidential information. This obligation applies during and after termination of the employment agreement. A provision to this effect is also standard in any employment contract.

8. Covenant Not to Compete

After the termination of the employment, a **confidentiality clause** will be enforceable without obligation to pay compensation, whereas a post-contractual **covenant not to compete** will be enforceable only if
- it does not exceed a period of two years
- it is concluded in writing
- it is necessary to safeguard a justified commercial interest of the employer
- it does not unfairly jeopardize the employee's further career
- the employer undertakes to pay compensation for the duration of the covenant in the amount of at least one-half of all contractual benefits the employee last received.

Other eqarnings are only deducted if, together with the compensation, they exceed 110% of the employee's previous remuneration. If he or she must change his or her residence due to the covenant not to compete, the limit is 125% (section 74c HGB). If one party has provided grounds for terminating the employment relationship for cause, the other party may declare within one month that it is **no longer bound** by the restrictive covenant (section 75 HGB). The same applies in favor of the employee if the employer terminates the employment agreement without justification. The employer may **waive** the covenant at any time **before** the employment agreement expires. However, in that case it must pay the **compensation an additional year**. Consequently, if it waives the covenant one year or more before the employment agreement comes to an end, no compensation will need to be paid since it will be set off against the paid remuneration.

9. Data Protection

The collection, processing and use of personal data within an employment relationship are subject to the restrictions set forth in the **Federal Data Protection Act** (*Bundesdatenschutzgesetz – BDSG*). Personal data means any information concerning the personal or material circumstances of a given natural person, in this case an employee, section 3 (1) BDSG.

a) Data Storage with the Consent of the Employee

For the protection of their personal rights, employees are entitled to decide themselves when and to what purpose their personal circumstances may be disclosed. Thus, the collection, processing and use of the data is generally only permissible with the employee's consent or is permitted by statute (section 4 (1) BDSG). Such consent must be obtained in advance and be in written form (section 4a (1) sentence 3 BDSG). It must be declared voluntarily and unequivocally. The employer must inform the employee of the purpose of the data collection, processing or use (section 4a (1) sent, 2 BDSG).

b) Data Storage Without the Consent of the Employee

Personal data of an employee may be collected, processed or used for employment-related purposes where necessary for **hiring** decisions or, after hiring, for **carrying out** or **terminating** the employment relationship (section 32 (1) sentence 1 BDSG).

The storage of all data from the personnel questionnaire is not necessary in this sense, since the information the employer can legitimately ask about does not always correspond to the knowledge necessary to fulfill the contract. Under these principles, only the following information may be stored from the data contained in the personnel questionnaire:
- gender and marital status for tax purposes
- data on education and languages spoken
- absentee and sick days.

Recording the employee's religion or military history, on the other hand, is not allowed, although it would be permissible with the employee's consent.

Additionally, employees' personal data may be collected, processed or used to investigate crimes only if (i) there is a documented reason to believe the data subject (i.e. the employee) has committed a crime while employed, (ii) the collection, processing or use of such data is necessary to investigate the crime, and (iii) the employee does not have an overriding legitimate interest in ruling out the possibility of collection, processing or use, and in particular the type and extent are not disproportionate to the reason (section 32 (1) sentence 2 BDSG). The reasons underlying such suspicion must be documented.

10. Liability

Principles have been established in the realm of compensation for damage within a company which will **mitigate the employee's liability** for activities performed in the course of the employment. Thus, employees are
- not liable at all for extremely slight negligence
- liable pro rata for medium negligence
- **fully liable** for **gross negligence and intentional acts**.

Even in the case of gross negligence, however, the possibility of reducing the extent of liability is not completely excluded. It could come into consideration especially if a claim for full damages would threaten the employee's ability to make a living. Therefore, such liability is often reduced to the deductible (*Selbstbehalt*) under any insurance policy for the damages incurred.

Provisions on liability that deviate from the above principles and are to an employee's detriment will only be valid if an increase in exposure is accompanied by financial compensation for the risk. For this reason, employers prefer to invest such additional compensation in adequate **insurance coverage.**

11. Inventions

Generally, the employer is entitled to all fruits of the employees' labor without needing to pay additional compensation. The **Employee Inventions Act** (*Arbeitnehmererfindungsgesetz – ArbNErfG*) basically sets forth the formal requirements for determining exploitation rights when the employer declares that it wishes to use the invention either without limitation, with limitation, or not at all. In the latter case, the employee will be free to use the invention himself or herself (section 8 (1) no. 3 ArbNErfG).

If an employee notifies the employer of an invention which, in his or her view, was developed outside the course of employment, the employer must formally declare within three months that it was in fact created in the course of employment, thereby preserving its rights. If the employer fails to act within this period, the employee will again be free to use the invention himself or herself.

As a rule, employment contracts simply make reference to the provisions of the Employee Inventions Act.

IV. Compliance

Compliance has become an issue of ever-growing importance for companies in Germany in recent years. Some compliance matters have, in fact, attracted considerable international attention, such as corruption prevention methods, the implementation of codes of business ethics and conduct, and whistleblowing systems. International companies, in particular US-led groups, started introducing ethics codes in the last decade, especially in response to the enactment of the Sarbanes-Oxley Act in 2002. German companies, notably those listed on the New York Stock Exchange, have begun to follow these examples. Accordingly, the content of ethics codes adopted by German employers often mirrors that of typical US or international standards, and includes general ethical principles, rules on legal and financial compliance, as well as the prohibition of various acts, such as insider trading, corruption, discrimination and harassment.

With respect to implementing compliance rules under German employment and labor law, in addition to the multitude of universally known general issues that need to be addressed when establishing a functioning compliance system for companies, certain particular aspects have to be considered as well. Contrary to internationally applied standards, employers in Germany are often well-advised not to implement ethic codes or compliance rules in a general fashion by way of contractual agreement with the employees, in particular an amendment or supplement to the employment contract. In order to retain the broadest level of flexibility, companies should instead analyze carefully what matters are better dealt with in employer's instructions to the employees (*Weisungen/Arbeitsanweisungen*) than in (standard) employment contracts. For instance, setting out rules for employees' compliance with mandatory statutory rules, such as competition laws, accounting standards, the German Criminal Code, etc., may often merely require declaratory directions and explanations that can be issued in the form of written instructions to all employees or to the selected group of employees concerned. As the employer remains free to amend such instructions at any time, full flexibility regarding the wording will be maintained. If, however, a company establishes rules for employees that go beyond the statutory (minimum) standard, instructions may no longer suffice, and it may be necessary to obtain employees' consent in order for the additional obligations to become binding. Furthermore, a significant number of matters that lie at the core of modern compliance rules, such as guidelines on the acceptance of gifts as well as professional conduct, will require co-determination by the works council, and are therefore best implemented by way of a works agreement that supplements the consent of each individual employee; in such cases, an employee's consent alone would not suffice.

Similarly, the implementation of a whistleblowing system typically also triggers a multitude of legal issues under German law, not only because the consent of the works council is required and a detailed works agreement is usually called for, but also in light of mandatory European/German data protection laws. While at present these laws are widely deemed to permit US-style whistleblowing systems, including the option of anonymous whistleblowing, a lengthy controversial debate on this issue that was sparked a number of years ago has led to the imposition of a relatively strict test of proportionality with respect to the scope of the whistleblowing system and the data collected and stored, etc. Special issues come into play where a whistleblowing system is operated internationally and encompasses the US, since European/German data protection laws require that special precautions be taken for the transfer of personal data (of employees) from within the European Union to the US (see also pages 31 et seq.).

A functioning compliance system will also require the monitoring and investigation of (potential) violations of the rules. In this respect, it is important to note that German employee data protection and employment laws also impose strict standards. In particular, employers are generally restricted in their ability to conduct ongoing (automatic) or special (targeted) reviews of (private) e-mails of employees on the company's IT system, and are well-advised to carefully plan and implement internal rules governing the (private) use of IT facilities when implementing a compliance system. Furthermore, the works council enjoys extremely far-reaching co-determination rights with respect to IT matters, and works agreements are therefore often required to deal with these matters, including the company's rights in the event of an internal investigation. Finally, under German law, an employee's violation of compliance rules will not necessarily entitle the employer to dismiss him or her, as most employees are granted protection against dismissal (see pages 37 et seq.). As a result, a careful case-by-case analysis is required to determine whether or not the threshold for justifying a dismissal on grounds of the employee's wrongful behavior has been reached, or any other disciplinary action by the employer is permitted.

V. Termination of Employment Relationships

1. General Points

a) Declaration of Dismissal

Due to their serious consequences, dismissals must be declared **clearly** and **unambiguously**. The case law is very stringent on this point. The will to end an employment relationship, and the point in time at which it should end, must therefore be stated with absolute clarity in the dismissal notice.

b) Form

Since 1 May 2000, the termination of employment relationships by dismissal or termination agreement, as well as limitations of term are required to be in **written form** to be valid (section 623 BGB). The statutory written form requirement cannot be waived by employment agreement, collective bargaining agreement or works agreement.

A dismissal that has formal defects is **void** and cannot be remedied subsequently (section 125 (1) BGB). The statutory written form requirement means that the dismissal must be declared in a written document and signed by its issuer. The signature must cover the content of the dismissal notice, i.e. immediately follow and close the text. The signature must be rendered by the issuer in his or her own hand and contain his or her name in full. If the employer is a legal entity, such as a limited liability company (GmbH), the dismissal needs to be signed by the legal representative. A merchant (*Kaufmann*) may sign with his company name, and legal representatives with their own name, if their position as a representative is clearly indicated in the document. However, a representative may also sign with the name of the person represented.

It is important to note that in light of this new statutory written form requirement, transmission by telefax or telegram is no longer sufficient, even if it is signed by hand. A mere duplication of the signature is legally insufficient.

The grounds for the dismissal need not be stated in the notice, unless this has been expressly provided, e.g. in a vocational training relationship. Generally, in the

V. Termination of Employment Relationships

case of dismissals, a premature statement of grounds could be detrimental to the employer if, in later court proceedings pertaining to the dismissal, the grounds are subsequently inserted on the advice of an attorney.

The dismissal notice also need not identify the date on which the notice period will expire. The declaration "as of the next possible date" is sufficient. If a notice period is identified but is too brief, or otherwise incorrect, this will not affect the validity of the dismissal; rather, it would be constructed to be a dismissal as of the next permissible date.

c) Delivery

Dismissals only become effective once they are delivered to the recipient. Delivery to an **absent person** is effected when the dismissal comes into the receiver's domain in such a way that under normal circumstances he or she would have the ability to learn of the content of the notice. Thus, dropping the notice into a mailbox will bring about delivery at the time of the next collection under ordinary circumstances. The safest way is to hand the dismissal notice directly to the employee in question and have him or her sign a confirmation of receipt.

If the dismissal is handed over to a **representative** of the recipient, the relevant issue is whether he or she is authorized to receive service. If not, then that person will become a messenger whose actions are to be attributed to the sender. The sender would then bear the risk of any delay.

Registered letters are not considered to be delivered until they are handed over to the recipient by the post office, since the notification slip merely puts the recipient in a position to bring the registered letter into his or her sphere of control. The recipient can therefore delay the delivery of a registered letter by simply not picking it up from the post office. Dismissals should therefore not be sent by registered mail.

If a recipient **refuses** to accept the dismissal notice without legal grounds, then as a rule delivery, will be deemed to be effective as of the moment of refusal.

The party that invokes the timeliness of the delivery bears the **burden of proof**. Thus, in the case of a dismissal, the employer must substantiate the burden of proving that the employee received the notice in a timely manner and in proper form. Evidentiary problems can arise, particularly when the employer itself, or a managing director, has signed the dismissal notice, because they would then be barred from testifying on the matter under German rules of evidence. It is therefore advisable to have coworkers present when a dismissal is handed over who can later testify in court as witnesses.

d) Dismissal by Authorized Representatives

When a dismissal is declared by authorized representatives, caution should be exercised. If the dismissal is declared by an authorized representative of the employer without presenting a **power of attorney,** an employee will have legal grounds for immediately rejecting the dismissal. Authorized representatives must present the **original** power of attorney document together with the dismissal notice.

However, a rejection due to a failure to present a power of attorney is **precluded** if the recipient of the declaration is aware of the representative's empowerment. For example, if the head of the human resources department declares the dismissal, the employee cannot reject it, because it is generally known that the head of a human resources department is authorized to render such declarations. The same would apply to a dismissal declared by a procuration officer (*Prokurist*), at if his or her authorization is recorded in the Commercial Register and has been announced.

e) Dismissal Notice Periods

The basic dismissal notice period is four weeks (i.e. 28 days) counting back from the 15th or the last day of a calendar month (section 622 BGB). This notice period increases depending upon the **seniority** of the employee. If the employee has 2 years of seniority with the company, the notice period increases to one month; and to 2 months for 5 years' seniority; 3 months for 8 years' seniority; 4 months for 10 years' seniority, 5 months for 12 years' seniority, 6 months for 15 years' seniority and 7 months for 20 years' seniority; each time to the end of the month. The level of seniority that determines the notice periods is that already attained at the time the dismissal notice was delivered. Previous employment with the same employer without a legal connection, or in another company in the same corporate group will generally not be counted.

If the parties agree to a **probationary period**, then for the duration of the probation, but no longer than six months, the dismissal notice period will be two weeks (section 622 (3) BGB). This notice period need not be agreed upon; it is statutorily mandated if a probationary period is stipulated. The date on which the dismissal is to go into effect need not be specified.

All statutory dismissal notice periods (during probation, basic notice period, and extended notice period) may be changed in **collective bargaining agreements** pursuant to section 622 (4) BGB. The parties to the collective bargaining agreements may depart from the statutory notice periods in the employees' favor as well as to their disadvantage. under the amended BGB, not only the notice periods, but also the effective dates and conditions under which notice periods can be extended (seniority, calculation of seniority as of a certain age) can now be regulated in collective bargaining agreements.

An extension of the statutory dismissal notice periods in individual employment agreements is permissible for both parties. However, the notice period for resignation by an employee cannot be longer than that for dismissal by the employer (section 622 (6) BGB); since otherwise, the contractual provision would constitute impermissible discrimination and thereby be void.

An employment relationship with a fixed term (i.e., without the possibility of ordinary termination) for a period of over five years may in any case be terminated by an employee after five years with a six-month notice period (section 624 BGB).

f) Calculating the Notice Periods

The day on which the dismissal or resignation notice is delivered is not counted as part of the notice period. Rather, the notice period commences on the next day. The notice must therefore be delivered one day before the commencement of the notice period if it is to enter into effect at the soonest possible date. Accordingly, if a dismissal or resignation can be declared each month up to the end of the month, it must be delivered by the last day of the previous month at the latest.

2. Consultation of the Works Council

If a works council exists, it must be **heard before every dismissal** (section 102 BetrVG). However, the hearing of the works council does not toll the dismissal notice period. This must particularly be borne in mind when declaring a dismissal for cause (*aus wichtigem Grund*), for which a two-week notice period must be observed. The hearing must be scheduled to leave sufficient time for declaring the dismissal before this two-week period has elapsed.

There are no formal requirements for the hearing. However, it is advisable to record it in **writing**, so that it can serve as evidence at a later point if necessary. The notification must be made to the chairperson of the works council (section 26 (2) sentence 2 BetrVG).

The notification made to the works council must **contain** the affected worker's personal data, the type of dismissal, notice period and the grounds for the dismissal. As a rule, vague, generalized catchphrases will not suffice. This also applies to dismissals within the first six months of employment.

The relevant circumstances must be described in such a way as to put the works council in a position to **assess** the validity of the dismissal grounds, take a position on them and raise substantive objections without needing to conduct additional research on its own. However, in presenting the grounds for dismissal, the employer need only impart those circumstances which, from its **subjective point of view**, are relevant to the dismissal. The **employer cannot introduce in subsequent court proceedings grounds which it did not offer to the works council** regarding the dismissal, assuming that such grounds already existed and were known to the employer at the time of the hearing.

This means that the employer is generally not obligated to inform the works council of of the grounds for dismissal, but must merely inform the it of the grounds on which it actually intends to base the dismissal. A dismissal will therefore only be in violation of section 102 BetrVG if multiple grounds for dismissal exist and the employer is actually basing the dismissal on all of them, but fails to inform the works council of all of the grounds involved. The employer must also inform the works council of mitigating circumstances favorable to the employee.

The works council must state its objections in writing within **one week** in the case of an **ordinary dismissal**, or within **three days** in the case of a **dismissal for cause** (*aus wichtigem Grund*). The one-week period can be extended by agreement, but it cannot be reduced. However, the works council can issue a final statement before the time period elapses.

The works council may consent to the dismissal, raise doubts about it or object to it. If the works council **does not respond** at all, it will be deemed to have rendered its consent once the time period for responding has elapsed. If the works council validly objects to a dismissal, pursuant to section 102 (3) BetrVG, the employee involved will have a right to retain his or her employment after the expiration of the dismissal notice period until the legal proceeding on the dismissal has been resolved. This means that the employer must pay the employee's remuneration for the duration of these proceedings, even if the employee ultimately loses the case.

A dismissal may nonetheless be validly declared despite the objection of the works council, as its consent is not a prerequisite for validity. However, the employer may conclude a valid agreement with the works council stipulating that a dismissal is only possible with the consent of the works council.

If in a works council hearing pursuant to section 102 BetrVG was conducted in an erroneous manner, it must always be ascertained who is responsible for this error. If it falls within the employer's sphere of responsibility, the dismissal will be invalid. This legal defect cannot be remedied at a later date. Experienced counsel for an employee may wait to file a complaint against a faulty works council hearing until the judicial proceeding is well underway. However, errors that fall within the works council's sphere of responsibility (e.g. failure to properly convene a works council meeting) will have no impact on the validity of the dismissal.

3. General Protection Against Dismissal

An employer's ability to (unilaterally) terminate an employment relationship is very severely restricted by the Protection Against Unfair Dismissal Act (*Kündi-*

gungsschutzgesetz – KSchG). This statute is applicable in all establishments with **more than five employees**. In establishments regularly employing ten employees or less, excluding those employed for vocational training, these provisions do not apply for employees whose employment relationship commenced after 31 December 2003.

Where the statute applies, the employees fall within its protection after a **six-month waiting period** (which is not to be confused with the contractual probationary period). This means that an ordinary dismissal (i.e. with notice) will only be effective on one of the three grounds for termination explicitly permitted pursuant to section 1 (2) KSchG. These grounds are: conduct-related dismissal (i.e. due to the employee's misconduct at the workplace), dismissal for reasons connected with the individual employee (i.e. the employee's inability to do the work) and for operational reasons. On the other hand, where the Protection Against Dismissal Act does not apply, the employer is free to dismiss any employees it chooses at any time, as long as the dismissal is not arbitrary. However, this freedom of discretion is restricted by the principles governing abuse of legal rights and ethical considerations.

a) Conduct-Related Dismissals

The employer can respond to an employee's breach of contractual duties with a conduct-related dismissal. Generally speaking, this requires a breach of duty on the part of the employee. After all, terminating the employment relationship has to appear to be a reasonable measure after taking the interests of employer and employee duly into consideration.

aa) Warning. As a rule, the case law requires that an employee receive at **least one prior warning**. Nevertheless, such warning(s) will not be required if it is evident that the employee does not wish to behave in compliance with his or her contract or is aware that his or her conduct is in violation of the contract, but nonetheless stubbornly and unrepentantly continues to act in breach of duty. Under the most recent case law, the warning requirement pertains to the area of both performance and trust; in any case, it applies whenever controllable behavior on the employee's part is involved and the employer can expect that the trust will not be restored.

A conduct-related dismissal undertaken without the previous issuance of a warning notice is **invalid**. Such an oversight could ruin the employer's chances of being able to carry out a conduct-related dismissal. It is therefore advisable to take the necessary precautionary measures of having the individual employee's violations documented and to discuss with the human resources department or management whether a warning notice should be issued in each particular case.
A valid warning notice must contain the following components:
- reprimand, citing the specific conduct in violation of the contract
- **demand** that the employee **cease** such conduct
- statement that in the event of a repeated violation the employee faces **termination** of his or her employment.

Warning notices should be issued in writing for evidentiary purposes, but they are not subject to any form requirements. Moreover, the employer should not wait too long to issue a warning notice. There are no fixed rule on the amount of time that can elapse between the issuance of the warning and the declaration of dismissal, but a warning notice can become "stale" and lose its relevance with the passage of time. In the case of slight violations, this would probably occur after six months, and in the case of serious violations, after two years. Depending upon the seriousness of the violation, two or three warnings may be necessary before an or-

V. Termination of Employment Relationships

dinary dismissal can be performed. As warning notices are not subject to codetermination requirements, the works council does not have the right to participate in such matters.

In practice, the main grounds for conduct-related dismissals are breaches of ancillary contractual duties, failure to adequately perform assigned tasks, failure to perform their duty to work, as well as misconduct outside of work and breach of fiduciary duties toward the employer.

bb) Dismissal on Suspicion. A special case of conduct-related dismissals is what is termed a "dismissal on suspicion". This occurs if the employer states that the very suspicion of unproven misconduct has destroyed the trust necessary for the continuation of the employment relationship and is thus grounds for dismissal. However, if the employer is convinced that the employee has actually committed a certain punishable offense or a very serious breach of duty, then only a dismissal based on fact can be pursued.

In order for a dismissal on suspicion to be valid, the **employee must first be heard**; he or she must be given an opportunity to respond to the allegations raised against him or her. Such a hearing may take place orally or in writing at the employer's discretion. However, a written hearing is definitely advisable, as it can serve as evidence later.

The works council must be informed of the grounds for the suspicion as well as of the employee's response thereto.

b) Dismissals on Personal Grounds (personenbedingte Kündigungen)

Dismissals on personal grounds must take into account the principle that an employment relationship has the character of an **exchange**. The primary duties of performance (work performance by the employee on the one hand and remuneration by the employer on the other hand) must be in a balanced relationship to each other. Above all, absence due to illness can seriously damage this exchange relationship.

Astonishingly, the **inability** to perform the work owed under the employment contract does not constitute legitimate grounds for dismissal, unless the employee's performance falls well below the average performance of the other employees.

The primary area of application of such dismissals is an **inability to work due to illness**. The most common cases in practice tend to involve frequent absences due to illness.

Pursuant to case law, there are **three prerequisites** for dismissal due to illness in cases of frequent brief illnesses:

aa) Negative Prognosis. A dismissal due to illness is only justified as a "dismissal on personal grounds" if at the time the dismissal is served, it can be presumed that the employee will continue to be absent due to illness in the future. Within the framework of what is termed a "negative prognosis", the case law requires proof of **frequent absences due to short-term illness in the past**. This is a reasonable indication that, due to illness, the employee will also be unable to work in the same capacity in the future. However, it is typically the case that the employer does not know what kind of illness is involved. As far as the duty to provide evidence is concerned, it is sufficient if reference is made to the absentee periods in the past and it is asserted that the employee will continue to be absent in the future with the same frequency.

However, a decisive factor in accepting such circumstantial evidence is the type of illness involved. Chronic conditions, such as gastritis or bronchitis, provide a rational basis for assuming future **repeated absenteeism**. On the other hand, illnesses that by their nature are not chronic, such as injuries from accidents, appendectomies, etc., are "individual events" which **cannot** be invoked for the "negative prognosis".

The **minimum duration** of absenteeism pursuant to the case law (due to illnesses with a danger of recurrence) varies from at least 14 to approximately 25% of the total working time per year over a reference period of at least three years, or four if possible. However, these figures must be taken with a **grain of salt**, since the legal commentaries and the case law repeatedly state that no fixed reference values exist. The rate of absenteeism is expressed as the proportion of working days per year (around230 for a five-day week and 30 vacation days) to the number of the employee's sick days (not counting vacation days and maternity/parental leave).

For example, an absenteeism rate of 25% would mean that the employee missed 58 working days per year, calculated over a three year period, a total of around 173 sick days.

If there was frequent absenteeism due to illness in the past, it can be presumed that the employee will miss just as many days in the future. However, the employee can refute such circumstantial evidence by making a plausible case that the past illnesses were of a **one-time nature** or that a **complete recovery** can be expected in the near future. To this end, he or she can release the treating physician from the responsibility to maintain professional confidentiality. As a rule, the question of the danger of recurrence can only be resolved by an independent expert opinion. Thus, the employer bears the risk involved in the prognosis. This risk is impossible to assess, because in most cases the employer would not know what illness the employee was suffering from in the first place.

bb) Serious Detriment to Business Interests. Absenteeism may only serve as the basis for a dismissal if it is seriously detrimental to the employer's business interests. Such detriment can take the form of **disruptions to the business operations, or serious economic burden** on the employer.

Disruptions of business operations include:
– loss of production, machinery breakdowns
– loss of customers
– excessive strain on the remaining personnel
– removal of necessary employees from other areas
– impossibility of finding substitute personnel
– adverse effect on the other employees' willingness to work
– increased difficulty assigning shifts.

Serious economic burdens will be presumed where **salary continues to be paid during the employee's illness for more than six weeks per year** over a period of several years. This applies particularly to short-term illnesses where no chronic disease or medical condition exists.

cc) Weighing of Interests. In weighing the interests involved, from the **employer's point of view,** anticipated future adverse effects on the business (extent of the disruption of business, financial condition of the company, security risks, etc.) must all be taken into account.

From the employee's point of view, the factors to be considered are: the duration of the employment relationship; the employee's seniority with the company without periods of illness, age, number of dependents, and other factors entitling him or her to special protection, as well as the question of whether the illness(es) is (are) work-related.

V. Termination of Employment Relationships

A dismissal due to **lengthy illness** is subject to the following prerequisites:
- The employee must still be ill at the time the dismissal is delivered.
- The time of recovery must not yet be objectively foreseeable, according to a prognosis made at the time the dismissal is delivered.
- The uncertainty about the time of recovery must inevitably lead to an unreasonable impairment of company interests.

An employee's permanent inability to work would also constitute grounds for a dismissal on personal grounds.

In the case of **alcohol or drug dependency,** the same principles apply as for dismissal due to illness. The decisive factor is whether the employee is willing to undergo **therapy.** Before declaring a dismissal, the employer is obligated to urge the employee to check into a drug/alcohol treatment center; refusal to do so is grounds for dismissal. The employer may only dismiss a cooperative employee if the therapy fails.

c) Dismissal for Operational Reasons

aa) Entrepreneurial decision (*unternehmerische Entscheidung*). A dismissal for operational reasons plays a central role in the termination of employment relationships. Unlike conduct-related dismissals or dismissals on personal grounds, the grounds for the dismissal do not lie within the **control** of the employee, but are based on a **structural entrepreneurial decision** on the employer's part. With a dismissal for operational reasons, the employer may adjust the number of personnel to the company's needs in the interest of profitability. The following prerequisites must be met:

The specific job must have been eliminated. This could be due to circumstances lying outside of the company's control ("external causes"), such as a drop in orders or sales, scarcity of raw materials, etc.. The employer bears the burden of proof with regard to both the causes and the direct impact on the specific jobs. In practice, experience shows that it is virtually impossible to meet this burden.

As a result, an **"entrepreneurial decision"** is a much more important basis for cutting jobs. The main feature of an entrepreneurial decision is that its implementation will result in a reduction of the volume of work or personnel needs. Such decisions are primarily made in the course of performing efficiency measures, introducing new work or production methods, or carrying out plant closures, outsourcing, relocation of operations, etc. The dismissal itself cannot be the sole subject of the entrepreneurial decision; otherwise, the statutory protection of employees against unfair dismissal would be meaningless. However, the Federal Labor Court has recognized a decision to implement a permanent reduction in personnel as a permissible entrepreneurial decision. Nonetheless, the closer the entrepreneurial decision comes to an actual decision to dismiss, the more extensively must the employer examine the feasibility of the decision , in order to avoid the appearance of subjectivity or arbitrariness. To this end, the employer must present a **plausible conception** demonstrating that it will be possible to permanently operate the work area in question in the future with a reduced number of personnel and how this will be done.

The labor courts may only review an entrepreneurial decision to ascertain whether it **prima facie unlucky objectivity,** is unreasonable or arbitrary. This does not alter the fact that the employer must describe in detail how the implementation of its decision will impact the workplace in the long run and what the underlying operational concept is.

bb) Possibility of Reassignment. A dismissal for operational reasons is not an option if the employee can be assigned to another **vacant position** within the company. In practice, it is frequently the case that dismissals are carried out while at the same time, vacancies are being advertised on the Internet, in the newspaper, on the bulletin board, etc. If the dismissed employee can be reassigned to a vacant position, a dismissal for operational reasons is prohibited. If there are fewer vacant positions than employees to be dismissed, the vacant positions will have to be offered to those employees who most merit protection on the basis of various social criteria. A vacant position will then have to be offered by way of dismissal for variation of contract (*Änderungskündigung*), even if the conditions of employment (hours of work, salary) are different or less favorable. The employer's obligation to retain the employee means that it must be prepared to offer reasonable possibilities for further education or retraining and to give the employee time to learn the new job, typically up to three months.

cc) "Social Selection" *(Sozialauswahl)*. If a job has been eliminated and there is no way the employee can be reassigned, the employer must carry out a "social selection" in order to determine who merits protection against dismissal according to various criteria. This must be carried out in **three stages**:

1. **Determination of the employees to be included in the "social selection".**
   The "social selection" must be carried out among all comparable employees within the entire **establishment.** Employees who have not completed the six-month waiting period until the Protection Against Unfair Dismissal Act becomes applicable cannot participate in the social selection; they must be the first to be dismissed, since they do not yet enjoy statutory protection against dismissal. The decisive factor in ascertaining the comparability of the employees is whether they are **interchangeable**. Employees are interchangeable if they can exchange jobs immediately or after a reasonable training period. This is based on objective, as well as subjective considerations. The objective considerations include the job category, the skilled work, the classification of the work and the pay scale. Subjective considerations include the individual's ability and skills, willingness to work, etc.

2. **Determination of eligibility for "social" protection based on social factors (section 1 (3) sentence 1 KSchG).**
   – From the group of comparable employees, those with the **least** eligibility for "social" protection must be the **first** to be dismissed. The need for social protection is based on the following four criteria:
   – seniority with the company
   – age
   – number of dependents
   – severe disability of the employee.

   Pursuant to section 2 (4) AGG, the criteria of the AGG do not apply to dismissals. The protection against dismissal is regulated in the laws governing general and special dismissal protection. According to the Federal Labor Court (*Bundesarbeitsgericht*), section 2 (4) AGG should be interpreted to mean that the AGG needs to be taken into account when interpreting the KSchG. In evaluating the individual social criteria, the employer may exercise a certain amount of **discretion.** In practice, when a large number of employees are to be laid off, a point system is often used to make the evaluation. In companies with works councils, it is advisable to set guidelines for selection, in which the weighing of the social factors is agreed to by the works council, to be implemented for future dismissals on operational grounds.

V. Termination of Employment Relationships

3. Determination of whether the retention of one or more employees is justified by legitimate operational requirements (section 1 (3) sentence 2 KSchG).
If individual employees have special qualifications, knowledge or skills, and if their retention is of particular importance to the company, such employees may be excluded from the social selection procedure. Moreover, ensuring a balanced range of ages is one of the operational interests that would justify deviating from the social selection rules.

d) Dismissal for Variation of Contract

If the employer would like to unilaterally change the working conditions, a "dismissal for variation of contract" (*Änderungskündigung*) could be considered. This is a **termination** of the employment agreement **connected** with an **offer** to continue the employment relationship under different conditions. Such a dismissal is a suitable vehicle for such measures as reassigning employees to other areas of operations, or perhaps transferring them to another location. On the other hand, it is not suitable for bringing about a reduction in salary. Pursuant to the case law, dismissals for variation of contract are permissible only if the company otherwise would have to reduce the workforce or even shut down the works.

4. Ordinary Dismissal or Dismissal for Cause

a) Cause for Dismissal (*wichtiger Grund*)

An ordinary dismissal ends the employment relationship after the expiration of the dismissal notice period. A dismissal for cause (extraordinary dismissal) ends the employment relationship either immediately without observing a dismissal notice period (= dismissal without notice) or with what is termed an "phase-out period" (*Auslauffrist*).

Cause for dismissal within the meaning of section 626 BGB exists if circumstances are present which, taking the entire situation of the individual case into account and weighing the interests of both parties, render it **unreasonable** to expect the terminating party to continue the employment relationship until the termination period has elapsed or until the agreed upon conclusion of the employment relationship.

In case of dispute, the competent court will examine whether cause for dismissal is present in two stages. First, it will ask whether certain circumstances generally create **reasonable grounds for dismissal,** without taking into account the specific situation involved in the individual case. Only if this question is answered in the affirmative will a **comprehensive weighing of the interests** on both sides in the individual case be undertaken. This weighing of interests must take such factors as seniority, age, consequences of a dismissal, etc. into account even if the dismissal is due to a criminal offense that was committed to the detriment of the employer.

Section 626 BGB is mandatory law. Accordingly, the right to dismiss for cause cannot be abrogated or restricted and any contractual provisions to that effect would be invalid. The same applies to an employment agreement stipulating that certain grounds beyond the standard set forth in section 626 BGB will be deemed to constitute cause for dismissal.

b) Two-Week Period

Under section 626 (2) BGB, the right to dismiss for cause is **forfeited** if it is not exercised within **two weeks after obtaining knowledge** of the facts giving rise to the dismissal. In practice, this provision can create serious difficulties, as it cannot always be definitively ascertained at what precise point in time the employer obtained certain knowledge of such facts.

The two-week time period can be controlled to a minimal extent by giving the employee a hearing. However, in order to avoid delaying the commencement of this period more than absolutely necessary, the first hearing should be held as soon as possible, generally within one week.

While it is up to the employer's discretion to decide whether or not to grant the employee a hearing before it declares a dismissal for cause due to demonstrable breaches of duty, a hearing is mandatory prior to a declaration of dismissal on suspicion of unlawful conduct, i.e. a serious breach of contract (*Verdachtskündigung*) (for details, see page 39).

Finally, it is important to note that the works council also has to be heard within the two-week period (for details, see page 36).

c) Resignation for Cause

An employee has the right to resign for cause. This is subject to the same requirements as a dismissal for cause by the employer.

The Federal Labor Court has held that an employer's violation of its employment obligations may entitle an employee to resign for good cause, for instance if no salary is paid. It is therefore necessary that the employment agreement explicitly reserve the employer's right to release the employee from his/her duties or at least to transfer the employee to another location.

d) Employees Protected Due to Age

Dismissal can be even more problematic if an ordinary dismissal is prohibited. Often, collective bargaining agreements provide that employees cannot be ordinarily dismissed after they have reached a certain age or worked for the company for a certain length of time. Such clauses may, in some cases, violate the AGG. However, as there are no precedents on this issue to date, we assume that these provisions are still valid. In that case, if an establishment (or part of one) is to be closed down, the question arises whether and how the employment relationships with these employees enjoying special protection can be dissolved.

The Federal Labor Court has found that it is unreasonable to expect an employer to continue to pay an employee the agreed remuneration for years and years without being able to avail itself of his or her services. On the other hand, the employees may not incur disadvantages due to the special legal protection against dismissal they enjoy.

The Federal Labor Court will therefore presume that in such cases, the employment relationship can be extraordinarily terminated, but the employer must observe the dismissal notice period pursuant to the statutes, collective bargaining agreement or individual employment agreements that would apply if the right of ordinary dismissal existed This is termed an "extraordinary dismissal with ordinary notice periods" (*entfristete außerordentliche Kündigung*).

In the hearing of the works council, the employer must ensure that it nonetheless declares an extraordinary dismissal. The hearing of the work council pursuant to section 102 BetrVG will therefore only be properly conducted if the employer has informed the works council in advance that it intends to declare an extraordinary dismissal with ordinary notice periods.

e) Tactical Advice

If there is any doubt as to the validity of a dismissal for cause, then, purely as a precaution, an ordinary dismissal should also be declared (but note that this is also contingent upon a hearing of the works council).

5. Special Protection Against Dismissal

a) Maternity Protection

In general, it is impermissible to dismiss a woman during a pregnancy and in the first four months after delivery if the employer was **aware of the pregnancy** or delivery when issuing the dismissal, or learned of it within **two weeks** of delivery of the dismissal notice (section 9 Maternity Protection Act (*Mutterschutzgesetz – MuSchG*)). This two-week period is a preclusive period under substantive law, i.e. if knowledge was obtained only subsequently, the dismissal is permissible; however, a failure to observe this time period will only lead to a loss of protection against dismissal if the employee culpably failed to inform the employer in due time. Thus, the employee will not forfeit this protection against dismissal if she was unaware of her pregnancy through no fault of her own and informs her employer immediately upon learning of it.

In special cases (e.g. establishment shutdowns), however, it is possible to dismiss such employees. The state authority responsible for the protection of employees may declare the dismissals to be permissible upon application by the employer.

b) Parental Leave

Employees (male and female) have a claim to parental leave under the conditions set forth in section 15 et seq. of the Federal Parental Allowance and Parental Leave Act (*Bundeselterngeld- und Elternzeitgesetz – BEEG*) of 2007 (previously: Federal Educational Allowance Act (*Bundeserziehungsgeldgesetz – BErzGG*)) until a child's third birthday. Pursuant to section 18 (1) sentence 1 BEEG, the employer may not dismiss an employee during this parental leave. As provided in section 9 (3) sentence 1 MuSchG, the state authority responsible for the protection of employees may nevertheless declare dismissals to be permissible in exceptional cases.

c) Protection of Persons with Severe Disabilities

With respect to persons with disabilities or in an equivalent position, both ordinary dismissals and dismissals for cause require the **prior consent** of the competent authority for the integration of severely disabled persons (*Integrationsamt*) pursuant to section 85 SGB IX. A dismissal issued without such consent is invalid.

Persons with severe disabilities are generally protected against dismissals of any kind (section 85 SGB IX). Accordingly, before issuing a dismissal on operational grounds, the employer will need the prior consent of the competent authority. Pursuant to section 90 (1) no. 1 SGB IX, however, a prerequisite for such protection against dismissal is that the employment relationship already have been in existence for six consecutive months at the time the dismissal notice is delivered.

In the case of a dismissal for cause, the employer must submit an application for consent to the competent authority within **two weeks** of learning of the facts providing the grounds for the dismissal. This authority must then render a decision within two weeks of receipt of the application; otherwise, its consent will be deemed to have been granted pursuant to section 91 (3) SGB IX.

d) Works Council Members and Other Officers under the Works Constitution Act

Members of the works council and certain other employee representational bodies enjoy special protection against dismissal under section 15 KSchG. These people can only be dismissed for cause within the meaning of section 626 BGB if the **consent** of the works council required under section 103 BetrVG has been granted or replaced by a court decision. An ordinary dismissal of such employees in observance of the notice periods is not valid.

Such special protection against dismissal continues for one year after the expiration of the term of office. This prolongation of the protection period also applies to substitute members, regardless of whether they actually succeed to the works council or only acted as deputies on a temporary basis. During this prolongation phase, however, the protection against dismissal is weakened somewhat in that the consent of the works council is no longer required. There remains (only) the general obligation to hear the works council as set forth in sections 102 and 626 BetrVG.

When issuing a dismissal for cause, a differentiation must be made between a works council member's breach of official duties and a breach of duties under the employment agreement. Even a substantial breach of official duties will not automatically justify a dismissal for cause. Such breaches can be punished by removal from the works council pursuant to section 23 BetrVG. A summary dismissal is only permissible if the breach of official duties simultaneously constitutes a gross breach of the employment agreement which justifies dismissal for cause.

It is possible to terminate employment agreements by mutual consent at any time; this does not require the consent or hearing of the works council.

e) Mass Layoffs

Under section 17 (1) nos. 1 to 3 KSchG, the employer must **notify the Agency for Employment** (*Agentur für Arbeit*) of layoffs that reach a certain threshold, depending on the size of the establishment concerned. If the employer fails to submit such a mass layoff notification pursuant to section 17 KSchG, then all dismissals carried out on the basis of the layoff will be invalid.

According to the European Court of Justice, the mass layoff notification has to be submitted before the dismissals are delivered to the employees. It is of no consequence whether the dismissals are carried out on operational grounds. The language of the statute strongly implies that even ordinary dismissals based on an employee's conduct and/or on personal grounds must be included in the headcount of employees to be laid off. On the other hand, dismissals for cause are not to be included in the headcount. However, employees who resign on the basis of termination agreements must also be included in the count.

Once the mass layoff notification has been submitted to the Agency for Employment, a **waiting period** of one month goes into effect. In individual cases, this period can be extended to up to two months. During this waiting period, dismissal is permissible only with the consent of the Agency for Employment. The dismissals (as opposed to the issuance of the dismissal notices) therefore cannot be carried out until the waiting period has expired, but then must be carried out within the 90-day **"free period"** stipulated in section 18 (4) KSchG. If this is not possible, a new notification will need to be filed for dismissals pursuant to section 17 (1) KSchG,.

6. Termination Agreement (*Aufhebungsvertrag*)

As a rule, the termination of an employment relationship by way of a termination agreement makes the most **economic sense.** In many cases, following the declaration of an ordinary dismissal or a dismissal for cause, a mutual agreement to end the employment relationship with a termination agreement or court settlement is reached in or out of court. By statute, termination agreements must be in **written form** (section 623 BGB). This means that both parties must sign the agreement in their own hand. A telefax will not suffice. In order to avoid errors that can often be very costly, an attorney should be engaged before a termination agreement is concluded.

Essentially, a termination agreement can contain the following information:
- Date and type of termination
- Severance pay
- Continued payment of remuneration up to the end of the employment relationship
- Release from work duties
- Company pension plan
- Post-contractual covenant not to compete
- Duty to maintain confidentiality
- Inventions
- Return of company car
- General duty to return company property
- Reference
- Discharge of obligations.

VI. Transfer of Business and Transformation

1. Transfer of Business (*Betriebsübergang*)

a) Introduction

Protective legislation for employees plays a major role in the acquisition of companies and participations in Germany. Accordingly, when planning a transaction, the impact of these laws should always be taken into account. **Section 613a BGB is the key legal provision** with regard to the acquisition of a company. Its purpose is to protect employees by retaining their employment relationships unchanged. It also provides for the continued existence of the works council and employee representative bodies. Further, it establishes the allocation of responsibility between the selling and the acquiring company for employment and labor law obligations. This provision is largely based on EU directives.

Corporate acquisitions differ according to the type and form of the acquisition. The purchaser can either acquire the shares in a company **(share deal)** or some or all of its assets and liabilities **(asset deal).** The acquisition can take the form of either a singular succession or a universal succession. In a singular succession, each individual asset is transferred by a separate contract, while in a universal succession, the acquirer steps into all the seller's rights and duties by force of law or by means of a contract. One example of a universal succession is the vesting of an heir in an estate. Of particular significance for corporate acquisitions is the German Transformation Act (*Umwandlungsgesetz – UmwG*), which provides **for four types of company transformations** (merger, split-up, transfer of assets and change of corporate form). What these four types of transformation have in common is that rights are acquired within the framework of a universal succession. In a pure share deal, the company's identity is preserved and the acquirer takes over the target company, with all of its rights and obligations. No special protective legislation for employees is necessary in this case, because the employment relationships remain unchanged. In the case of an asset deal, on the other hand, section 613a BGB applies if the sale of a business or part of a business is involved. Under this provision, the employment relationships automatically pass from the seller to the acquirer. For example, if a company sells the entire assets of a certain production site to an acquirer who wishes to continue with the production at that site, the consequence would be that all employees working there will automatically pass to the acquirer, who must continue to employ them. Any dismissals made in connection with the transfer of the business are invalid. Section 613a BGB applies not only to asset deals, but also to transformations of companies under the Transformation Act.

A flood of court decisions have been occasioned by section 613a BGB, due to the fact that the provision is not comprehensible in and of itself. A business or part of a business is not an item that is normally transferred as such through a legal transaction. For every corporate acquisition, it is therefore necessary to examine whether the transferred items constitute a business within the meaning of section 613a BGB. If so, the employment relationships will pass from the seller to the acquirer.

b) Prerequisites

In order for employment relationships to be transferred from the seller to the acquirer in a transfer of a business as defined by section 613a BGB, **a business or part of a business** must pass over to a new proprietor by virtue of a legal transaction.

The case law of the Federal Labor Court, in accordance with the European case law, defines a business or part of a business as a **"long-term economic unit"**. The term "unit" is defined by the European Court of Justice as an organized totality of persons and things for the purpose of carrying out economic activity with its own objectives. The determining factor will be whether the acquirer has taken over the organization of work underlying the business. This is the case, in the Federal Labor Court's opinion, if the essential elements of the functional relationship which are required to create value are preserved.

A determination of whether an economic unit within the meaning of the case law has been transferred is based on the following seven criteria:
- Type of business or company involved
- Transfer of tangible assets
- Transfer of intangible assets (customer lists, know-how, etc.)
- Assumption of the personnel or part of the personnel (key employees) by the acquirer
- Transfer of the customers
- Similarity between activities before and after the transfer
- Duration of any interruption of activity.

These criteria determine in an overall evaluation whether a transfer of business has taken place within the meaning of section 613a BGB. It is also sufficient if only a part of a business is transferred. A part of a business is an organizational subdivision of a business.

In addition to a transfer of business, section 613a BGB also requires a change in the proprietor of the business. The decisive factor here is a **change in the proprietor's legal personality.** A change in the proprietor is not necessarily contingent upon a change in ownership of the business assets; it is sufficient if merely the right of use is transferred. Thus, a leaseholder is deemed to be the proprietor of the business if it runs the business in its own name.

Finally, section 613a BGB requires that a business or part of a business pass over to a new proprietor by virtue of a legal transaction and not by law. A transfer by legal transaction can be effected by sale, lease or gift.

c) Passing of the Employment Relationships as a Legal Consequence

If these criteria are met, then as a legal consequence of section 613a BGB, the employment relationships will pass over to the acquirer. The transfer of business will comprise the employment relationships that are attributable to the transferred business or part of business. Section 613a BGB does not cover managing directors of a GmbH (*Geschäftsführer*, see pages 91 et seq.) or members of the management

VI. Transfer of Business and Transformation

board of stock corporations (*Vorstandsmitglieder*, see pages 95 et seq.). Additionally, former employees and retirees who still have claims under the company pension plan are not included in the transfer of the employment relationships; section 613a BGB applies only with respect to the active employees.

Under section 613a (1) sentence 1 BGB, the **acquirer succeeds to the rights and duties** arising from the existing employment relationships. The contractual relationship as a whole passes over to the acquirer; in other words, there is a substitution of the contractual party on the employer's side. This means that the acquirer must fulfill all obligations arising from the transferred employment relationships as if it were the original contracting party.

d) Information Requirements and Right of the Employees to Object

The acquirer or the seller (as co-debtors) are obligated to inform each individual employee prior to the transfer of the business in a form similar to written form (section 126b BGB) containing the following information: the acquirer; the date or planned date of the transfer of business; the grounds for the transfer of business for the employees; the legal, economic and social consequences of the transfer of business for the employees; the intended measures to be taken with respect to employees (section 613a (5) BGB); and the employees' right of objection. The employees are entitled to object to the transfer of their employment relationships from the seller to the acquirer within one month after being informed as described above (section 613a (6) BGB), even if the employment relationship has been terminated. The one-month time period only begins to run after the employees have been provided with complete information. Otherwise the employees have an unlimited right to object to the transfer of their employment relationships. However, employees can forfeit their right to object. This occurred in a case before the Federal Labor Court, for example, in which an employee did not object to the transfer of the undertaking until 15 ½ months after the transfer. However, the circumstances involved have to be taken into account in each particular case Essentially, this right has been developed by case law on the premise that forcing a new employer upon the employees against their will would be in violation of their basic rights. If any employees exercises their right to object, their **employment relationships** will remain with the seller. If it is not possible for the seller itself to retain the employees, perhaps because the entire business has been sold, it can **dismiss the objecting employees** on operational grounds. The exercise of an employee's right to object can lead to serious problems if the seller has retained part of the business. In that case, objecting employees cannot simply be dismissed. Since these employees fall within the purview of the Protection Against Unfair Dismissals Act, a "social selection" must be carried out to determine the degree to which employees enjoy protection against dismissal under that Act due to social factors. If the seller cannot retain the objecting employees, it may be necessary to carry out a social selection between the objecting employees (from the transferred part of the business) and those employees who are not affected by the transfer of business at all. In such cases, according to the Federal Labor Court, the motives for an employee's objection are not to be taken into account. If it becomes evident that an objecting employee is, due to social factors, more in need of protection, that employee may supplant employees in another part of the seller's business.

Pursuant to section 613a (4) BGB, dismissals are invalid if they are "**due to**" the transfer of part of a business. According to the case law, a dismissal is deemed to be "due to" a transfer of business if this was the motive for the dismissal. The intent of this prohibition of dismissals is to prevent the circumvention of provisions that safeguard labor and employment standards.

On the other hand, dismissals **on other grounds,** e.g. relating to the employee's conduct or for operational reasons, are permissible. Thus, a seller can carry out efficiency measures to make the business more saleable. Such dismissals would not be "due to" the transfer of business. However, drawing such a distinction can be difficult in individual cases.

e) Distribution of Liability

Section 613a BGB also provides for an allocation of liability between the seller and the acquirer. The acquirer is liable for all obligations arising from the assumed employment relationships. This liability extends, without restriction, to **all outstanding claims,** regardless of when they arose. In particular, the acquirer is additionally liable for all claims arising from the company pension plan.

The seller is liable solely for claims arising from employment relationships that have already ended at the time of the transfer of business; these employment relationships are not included in the transfer of business. On the other hand, the seller and acquirer are jointly and severally liable under section 613a 1 sentence 1 BGB for obligations that arose prior to the transfer date and are payable within one year of that date.

Where the seller and acquirer are jointly and severally liable, they are liable as co-debtors. This means that a creditor can assert its claim against either of the two co-debtors at its discretion. Thus, for example, employees who retired shortly before the transfer of business could assert their pension claims against the acquirer without limitation. Such eventualities should be covered by an explicit clause in the company acquisition agreement on the internal allocation of risk between the seller and the acquirer.

f) Impact on the Employee Representative Bodies

In the case of a pure **transfer of the whole business,** the works council has no codetermination rights. A transfer of business in and of itself is not an operational change within the meaning of section 111 BetrVG, and thus is not subject to codetermination. However, if the transfer of business is accompanied by an operational change (split-up, merger of businesses), codetermination rights may exist. The sale of **part of a business,** on the other hand, is generally a split-up of the business and thus would constitute an operational change which is subject to codetermination (section 111 sentence 2 no. 3 BetrVG), and thus the its codetermination rights (right to negotiate a conciliation of interest and a social plan) would have to be respected.

A transfer of business per se generally has no effect on the works council as a governing body or on its members, as they will remain in their positions in the acquirer's business as well.

g) Continued Application of Collective Norms

Finally, section 613a (1) sentences 2 to 4 BGB also covers the effects of a transfer of business on the provisions of collective agreements that are applicable to the seller's business (works agreements and collective bargaining agreements). If the business as a whole passes over and retains its identity, the works agreements previously concluded will remain in force. On the other hand, if only part of the business is sold, with the consequence that this part does not retain its identity, the **works agreements** concluded previously for the personnel as a whole may be transformed into individual contractual provisions for each employee (section 613a (1) sentence 2 BGB). But this will not be the case if the acquirer operates the transferred part of the business as a separate undertaking, as they will then have the same legal character as provisions in an employment agreement. However, if the

VI. Transfer of Business and Transformation

acquirer's business has works agreements with identical parameters, they will replace the works agreement that had been in force in the seller's business (section 613a (1) sentence 3 BGB). As an exception, the works agreements will not be transformed into individual contractual provisions as described above if the acquirer continues the part of the business as a separate entity.

If a **collective bargaining agreement** exists, it will essentially continue in force with the acquirer on a collective basis if the business falls within its purview even after the transfer of business and a bilateral commitment to the agreement has been made by the employees and the employer. This means that in the case of regional collective bargaining agreements, the acquirer must belong to the competent employers' association. The seller's membership in the employers' association is a strictly personal matter and will not automatically pass over in the course of a transfer of business. If a company-union agreement is in force, as a rule it will not continue to apply on a collective basis after the transfer of the business, since the acquirer will ordinarily not have been a party to that agreement. In this case as well, the provisions in the collective bargaining agreement which apply collectively will be transformed into provisions of the individual employment agreement and continue to have effect on that basis (section 613a (1) sentence 2 BGB). Consequently, it will not be possible to modify them to the employee's detriment until one year has elapsed. On the other hand, if a collective bargaining agreement with similar provisions is already in force with the acquirer, it can, under certain conditions, replace the collective bargaining agreement with the seller that had been in force up to the moment of transfer. In that case, the acquirer's collective bargaining agreement would continue in force for the transferred business with collective applicability.

2. Transformations

The German Transformation Act provides for four types of corporate transformations: merger, division, asset transfer and form change (sections 1 (1), 2, 123, 174, 190 UmwG). It contains a number of provisions designed to protect employees, which complement section 613a BGB, and relate primarily to the **duty to inform the works council.** Above and beyond its other rights and powers in the workplace, the works council must be kept apprised of all relevant transformation measures by presentation of the transformation agreements or resolutions (sections 5 (3), 126 (3), 176 (1), 194 (2) UmwG). The transformation notification must describe the specifies of the transformation and its consequences for the employees and their representative bodies, as well as the planned measures for providing compensation in this area. It is mandatory that the information necessary for this purpose be contained in the transformation agreement. The transformation agreement, or a draft thereof, must be submitted to the works council at least one month before the date of the shareholders' meeting which is to adopt a resolution consenting to the transformation.

If, in the course of the transformation, a business unit is divided, **the works council will have a transitional mandate** (section 21a BetrVG). The works council of the divided business unit will generally remain in office and continue to manage the affairs for the parts of the business unit newly created by the division on a transitional basis for up to, but no longer than six months. The mandate ends as soon as a new works council has been elected in the divided parts of the business unit and the results of the election have been announced (section 21a (1) sentence 3 BetrVG). Where business units or parts of business units are combined as a result of divisions and mergers, the works council representing the most employees will also assume the transitional mandate (section 21a (2) BetrVG). If the legal prerequisites for the works council's participation rights are no longer met due to the division of the business unit, the continued applicability of these rights may be agreed upon by a works agreement or collective bargaining agreement (section 325 (2) UmwG).

In the case of certain transformations, the Act provides for the **retention of codetermination rights** in the supervisory board (see pages 71 et seq.) for a five-year period (section 325 (1) sentence 1 UmwG). If the legal prerequisites for the works council's participation in the supervisory board are no longer met due to a spin-off or drop-down, the codetermination will continue in the form that it had up to that point. However, this will not apply if the number of employees in the business unit falls to less than one quarter of the minimum number required for codetermination (section 325 (1) sentence 2 UmwG). If codetermination is retained when the company changes form, a new election of the employee representatives will not be necessary. The supervisory board members will remain in office for the balance of their term as members of the legal entity in its new legal form (section 203 (1) sentence 1 UmwG). In all other respects, the general rules will apply (procedure to determine its composition pursuant to sections 97 et seq. AktG).

Apart from section 613a (4) BGB, special provisions apply to protection against dismissal. If the division of a company also engenders a division of a business unit, then even after the division, the parts of the business unit belonging to different companies will be deemed to constitute a single business unit within the meaning of such protective provisions (section 322 UmwG). Moreover, the former position of the employee under such provisions will be protected in the event of a division or partial transfer for a period of two years.

In the event of a merger, divestiture or asset transfer, by conducting a **reconciliation of interests** (*Interessenausgleich*, see page 63), it will be possible to allocate employees to certain business units or parts of business units following the transformation (section 323 (2) UmwG). The labor court can only review the allocation according to the reconciliation of interests for "gross error". The power of the works council and the employer to perform an allocation, however, is limited by the fact that they must comply with the prerequisites set forth in section 613a BGB. An allocation performed in a reconciliation of interests will most likely only be found to contain such "gross errors" if they lack any factual or objective basis whatsoever.

In addition to the allocation of liability pursuant to section 613a (2) BGB, which is of great significance in transformations, section 134 (1) sentence 1 UmwG contains a special liability provision for cases of a typical **"business unit division"** (*Betriebsaufspaltung*). If a company is split up into a company that holds the fixed assets (*Besitzgesellschaft*) and an operating company (*Betriebsgesellschaft*), the former will also be liable for any claims of employees of the latter that arise within five years of the transformation.

VII. Assignment to Foreign Countries

1. Employment Law Issues

If a German company wishes to assign its employees to work abroad, there are two possible ways to do so:

Firstly, the employment agreement can be terminated or suspended due to the transfer. In its place, the employee will receive both a "parent company binding agreement" (*Stammhausbindungsvertrag*) with the German main office and a local employment agreement with the respective foreign subsidiary. Such a **division into two contracts** is advisable if a local employment agreement is required in order for the employee to be granted a residence permit. On the other hand, social security issues or provisions regarding moving expenses would have no place in the contract with the foreign subsidiary. These must also be worked out vis-à-vis the German main office.

The other model is **"secondment"**, in which case the original employment agreement would remain intact and an additional secondment agreement would cover the particularities of the foreign assignment. This model is advisable if there is no active employment relationship with the foreign company. As a rule, a parent company binding agreement is governed by German law, while in practice large corporate groups also tend to reserve the right to issue directives. However, the Federal Labor Court recently ruled that a parent company binding agreement is to be categorized as an employment agreement, thus falling under the purview of the German Protection Against Unfair Dismissals Act. This means that the employee of the German subsidiary can be dismissed only if a notice of termination of both the local employment agreement with the foreign subsidiary and the parent company binding agreement with the German main office has been validly rendered.

2. Social Insurance Issues

When German employees are assigned to work abroad, it is usually important that their social insurance coverage in Germany be maintained even during their foreign assignment, as they would not wish to lose any claims due to their stays abroad. In Although the regulations governing the statutory retirement, health, accident, nursing care and unemployment insurance in fact apply only if an employee is employed in Germany (**"territoriality principle"**), there are some exceptions that would permit the social insurance regulations to be extended to cover employment abroad.

Employees assigned to work in an **EU country** or one belonging to the European Economic Area (Iceland, Liechtenstein and Norway) will be subject solely to the statutory social insurance provisions of the state in which they are actually working. Thus, they will remain in the German social insurance system only if the employing company has its place of business (*Sitz*) in Germany and they are assigned to the territory of another EU Member State on its account. Moreover, the anticipated duration of the assignment may not exceed twelve months, whereby an employee may not take over a position from another employee whose assignment term has expired, for example. However, the assignment can be extended by another twelve months.

In the case of assignments to countries outside of Europe, the decisive question is whether the Federal Republic of Germany has concluded a **bilateral social insurance agreement** with the country in question. Such agreements have been concluded with the US, Japan, China, Australia, Canada, India, Poland, the Czech Republic, Croatia, Israel, Chile, Switzerland, Morocco, Turkey, Tunisia and Romania, among other countries. Some of these agreements provide for the continued application of German social insurance law, but this tends to apply only to certain areas of the social insurance.

If no such agreement exists, then the rules on what is termed **"extended application"** (*Ausstrahlung*) will apply. This means that employees working abroad can remain in the German social insurance system only if their foreign assignment constitutes a "secondment" within the scope of an employment relationship with a

German company. As a rule, they must, at the instruction of an employer domiciled in Germany have traveled directly from Germany to the foreign country in order to work there. Moreover, they must remain organizationally integrated in the German employer's operation, and the essential employer functions (right to give directives, right to dismiss) must remain with the German company. In addition, the term of the foreign assignment must be set in advance. While there is no fixed maximum term, the secondment should not last more than two or three years to be on the safe side. **If the membership in the German social insurance is then extended**, its rules will apply with one exception: the employee will remain obligated to contribute to the health insurance fund, but will not be entitled to any direct claim against the insurance fund for medical services.

However, if the German social insurance laws do not apply either on the basis of a bilateral/multilateral agreement or by way of extension, an employee will be free to take out private retirement, health and nursing care insurance and, to some extent, accident insurance.

3. Tax Law Issues

The rules of international employee taxation are virtually incomprehensible. Under German law, employees in the Federal Republic of Germany are subject to unlimited tax liability, i.e. on their income worldwide, if they are either resident in Germany or normally live there. This applies even if they earn income from their work in another country.

Where **double taxation treaties** exist, pursuant to the OECD Model Treaty, in most cases the country in which labor is performed has jurisdiction to impose taxes on the employee remuneration received there (territoriality principle). However, under the Model Treaty, this taxation right then reverts to the country of legal residence if the length of stay of employee assigned to the foreign country does not exceed 183 days, along with other prerequisites, i.e. that the employee was not present in the country of performance for over 183 days within a 12-month period (commencing or ending during the tax year involved); that the remuneration was paid by or for an employer which is not domiciled in the other country; and finally that the remuneration was not borne by an establishment or fixed installation which the employer has in the other country.

This **183-day period** includes both days of physical presence and days of mere partial presence. That is to say, even if the employee is present for merely part of the day, it will still be calculated as a full day. The day of arrival the day of departure and all other days of the stay in the country of performance (weekends, etc.) will all be counted as days of presence. However, full days spent out of the country of performance, including days of transit within that country on a trip between two other countries will not be counted.

In order to avoid double taxation, the German double taxation treaties allow the foreign income to be exempted from the German income tax, albeit with a proviso. While this income will not be subject to German income tax, it will increase the tax rate of the German income. If no double taxation treaty exists, then pursuant to the "decree on foreign work" (*Auslandstätigkeitserlass*), certain privileged activities abroad may be exempted from German income tax, provided that the work was carried out in the other country for at least three consecutive months.

Finally, if there is no treaty and the prerequisites for a foreign work exemption are not met, double taxation can be eliminated by setting the foreign taxes off against the German income tax. In this case, the income received in Germany and abroad will be subject to German tax, but the foreign taxes will be set off against the German taxes.

C. Labor Law

I. Laws Governing Works Councils

With respect to codetermination, German law distinguishes between an "establishment" (*Betrieb*) and a "company". An establishment is the "organizational labor unit", while the company is the economic unit. Generally, a company has several establishments. However, it is possible for a (smaller) company to consist of just one establishment. A works council (*Betriebsrat*) exercises employee codetermination at the establishment level, as opposed to codetermination at the supervisory board level (see pages 71 et seq.). For the most part, employee codetermination within an establishment is regulated in the Works Constitution Act of 1972 (*Betriebsverfassungsgesetz – BetrVG*).

1. Works Councils

The **most important codetermining body** under the BetrVG is the works council, an elected employee representative body which has rights of its own vis-à-vis the employer. It exercises most of the codetermination rights.

a) Workplaces That Can Have Works Councils

The formation of a works council is **not mandatory** for employees. The initiative for creating one must come from the employees or the unions. The only requirement is that an establishment has at least five regularly employed workers. If a company has more than one establishment, it is generally possible to create a works council for each establishment, provided that it has five or more employees.

b) Election of the Works Council

The works council is elected by the employees **every four years** by direct and secret ballot. Up to 2001, blue collar workers (*Arbeiter*) and white collar employees (*Angestellte*) had voted separately, but an extensive reform has since eliminated this distinction. Now, all of the employees vote for the works council in a common election.

c) Election Committee

An election committee (*Wahlvorstand*) must be formed to organize the election of the works council (sections 16, 17 BetrVG). If a works council already exists, the **works council currently in office** appoints the election committee for the next election (section 16 (1) BetrVG). If there is no election committee eight weeks before the term of office expires, a joint works council (*Gesamtbetriebsrat*) or a group works council (*Konzernbetriebsrat*) may also appoint the election committee pursuant to section 16 (3) BetrVG. If necessary, this can be done by the labor court upon application by three employees or a trade union.

If no works council exists, the **joint works council or group works council** will appoint the election committee pursuant to section 17 BetrVG. If there is no joint works council, or group works council, or if they do not appoint an election committee, the election committee will be elected in a **works meeting** (*Betriebsversammlung*) pursuant to section 17 BetrVG. This works meeting may be initiated by three employees of the establishment or a trade union. A representative of the relevant trade union may enter the establishment for the purpose of convening an election meeting. If the employees do not attend the works meeting, and as a result no election committee is elected, or if they do attend, but no election committee is elected, the labor court may, upon application by three employees or a trade union, appoint the members of the election committee pursuant to section 17 (4) BetrVG.

Special rules apply to small establishments with up to 50 employees pursuant to sections 17a and 14a BetrVG.

d) Election and Costs

The employees must hold a works meeting to elect the works council members who have been nominated. Any employee of the establishment who has been nominated may be elected. Nominations may also be made by the trade unions. The rules for the actual holding of the election are set forth in a separate statute, the Election Code (*Wahlordnung*). The costs of the election are borne by the employer. As a rule, elections are held during working hours.

e) Works Council Members

The size of the works council depends on the number of employees in the establishment. Pursuant to section 9 BetrVG:

1   works council member is to be elected for 5 to 20 employees,
3   works council members are to be elected for 21 to 50 employees,
5   works council members are to be elected for 51 to 100 employees,
7   works council members are to be elected for 101 to 200 employees,
9   works council members are to be elected for 201 to 400 employees,
11   works council members are to be elected for 401 to 700 employees,
13   works council members are to be elected for 701 to 1,000 employees,
     etc.

Nominees who are not elected can become alternate members. Alternate members will become full members if the works council loses a member (section 25 BetrVG).

Members of the works council and election committee, as well as nominated candidates, enjoy **special protection against dismissals.** Pursuant to section 15 of the KSchG, an employer may only dismiss a works council member, an election committee member, or a nominated candidate for cause (*aus wichtigem Grund*). In practice, this criterion is virtually impossible to meet. Indeed, even where cause does exist, a works council member can only be dismissed with the consent of the remaining works council members (section 103 BetrVG). If the works council withholds its consent, the labor court may, at the request of the employer, overrule the lack of consent, whereupon the employer may dismiss the relevant work council member for cause.

Furthermore, pursuant to section 103 (3) BetrVG, the **employer may not transfer a works council member** to another establishment without the consent of the remaining works council members, unless the member in question agrees to the transfer. Here too, the employer may request that the labor court order the transfer, superceding the consent of the works council.

aa) Management, Meetings and Works Meetings of the Works Council.

Pursuant to section 2 BetrVG, the employer must work together with the works council on a basis of mutual trust (*vertrauensvolle Zusammenarbeit*). The works council may not call upon the employees to go on strike or engage in any other labor dispute measures (section 74 BetrVG). Section 74 (1) BetrVG also states that the employer and the works council should meet once a month.

The works council has one **chairman** pursuant to section 26 BetrVG. If the establishment has more than 100 employees, the works council may form committees

I. Laws Governing Works Councils

and assign tasks to them (section 28 BetrVG). The works council holds its meetings during working hours. It must hold a meeting at the employer's request, which the employer may attend. The employer may not attend meetings the works council schedules itself unless invited to do so. Pursuant to section 43 BetrVG, the works council must hold a works meeting (*Betriebsversammlung*) every quarter, to be attended by all of the employees of the establishment, in which the works council informs the employees of its activities. The employer may also attend. He must inform the employees at least once a year during a works meeting about personnel and social matters, as well as the economic situation and development of the establishment, among other things, provided that no trade secrets are jeopardized thereby (section 43 (2) BetrVG).

If the works council is of a particular size, the employer must generally **release individual works council members from their work duties** pursuant to section 38 BetrVG. These works council members will only carry out works council tasks and continue to receive their remuneration from the employer. The number of works council members the employer must release is contingent upon the number of employees in the establishment. The number of employees to be relieved of duties is to be calculated as follows:

200–500 employees	1 works council member to be released from duties,
501–900 employees	2 works council members to be released from duties,
901–1,500 employees	3 works council members to be released from duties,
1,501–2,000 employees	4 works council members to be released from duties,
2,001–3,000 employees	5 works council members to be released from duties,
3,001–4,000 employees	6 works council members to be released from duties, etc.

The works council, in consultation with the employer, selects the works council members that are to be released.

The employer must also release the other works council members from their work duties to the extent necessary for them to perform the duties of their office (section 37 BetrVG). A works council member who performs works council duties outside of working hours, must be provided by the employer with an equivalent amount of free time. In addition, the employer must release works council members for any training sessions necessary for them to perform their works council duties; in practice, it is frequently disputed whether a given session is in fact necessary for the works council's activities. Moreover, a works council member must be excused for a total of three weeks per year for such training sessions that are recognized by the government as suitable (section 37 (7) BetrVG).

bb) Costs. Pursuant to section 40 BetrVG, the **employer must bear all costs** of the works council; this includes providing the works council with offices, equipment and staff as necessary for the performance of the its duties. However, since the works council has a certain amount of discretion in determining the equipment it deems necessary, in practice, disputes over this point are very common. Section 40 BetrVG explicitly stipulates that the employer must provide the works council with information and communication technology.

f) Joint Works Council

Pursuant to sections 47 et seq. BetrVG, if a company has two or more works councils, a joint works council (*Gesamtbetriebsrat*) must be formed, to which each works council delegates members. The joint works council is responsible for matters concerning the **entire company, or multiple establishments.** As a rule, it might be difficult to ascertain whether a given matter is to be handled by the works council or the joint works council. The individual works councils can also pass certain matters on to the joint works council. Pursuant to section 50 BetrVG, the joint works council is also responsible for establishments in the company that do not have a works council.

g) Group Works Council

If two or more companies are part of a group (*Konzern*) then pursuant to section 18 (1) Stock Corporation Act (*Aktiengesetz – AktG*), the joint works councils may elect a group works council (*Konzernbetriebsrat*) pursuant to sections 54 et seq. BetrVG. The creation of a group works council is voluntary. The group works council is responsible for matters concerning **a group or multiple companies.** A joint works council may pass individual matters on to the group works council. Under section 58 BetrVG, the group works council is also responsible for companies or establishments that have no joint works council and establishments without a works council. Thus, a works agreement concluded by the group works council will also apply to companies that do not even have a works council at all.

h) European Works Council

A European works council can be formed in a company domiciled in Germany that has at least 1,000 employees in Member States of the **European Union,** of which at least 150 employees are employed in least two Member States, by concluding an agreement. If the employer refuses to conclude such an agreement, the employees may initiate a European works council by way of the national works council in Germany. A European works council only has the right to be informed about various aspects of the economic situation of the company and the staff and does not play a major role in practice. However, the company must provide the works council upon request with information that will enable it to ascertain whether or not a European works council can be formed.

i) Economic Committee

If a company has more than 100 employees and a works council exists, an economic committee (*Wirtschaftsausschuss*) to the works council must be formed pursuant to section 106 BetrVG. The economic committee has no actual codetermination rights, but serves merely in an **advisory capacity.** It should meet once a month (section 108 (1) BetrVG). The employer must attend these sessions pursuant to section 108 (2) BetrVG. Pursuant to section 106 (2) and (3) BetrVG, the employer must inform the economic committee about various economic matters relating to the company (provided that no trade or business secrets are jeopardized thereby), in particular with respect to the economic and financial condition of the company, the production and sales situation, the production and investment programs, rationalization projects, manufacturing and working methods, cutbacks or shut-downs of establishments or of parts of establishments, the relocation of establishments or parts of establishments, the amalgamation or split-up of establishments, changes in the establishment's organization or purpose and other events and projects which could materially affect the interests of the employees of the company, as well as questions of environmental protection in the establishment.

The economics committee then passes this information on to the works council. However, the works council members are obligated to treat this information confidentially pursuant to section 79 BetrVG.

j) Youth and Trainee Representation

If an establishment has at least five employees who are under the age of 18 or are employed as trainees, a youth and trainee representative body (*Jugend- und Auszu-*

I. Laws Governing Works Councils

bildendenvertretung) must be formed pursuant to sections 60 et seq. BetrVG. It has no rights vis-à-vis the employer, rather it represents the interests of the trainees vis-à-vis the works council. It is not of any great importance in practice, but pursuant to section 78a (2) BetrVG, the youth and trainee representatives have a claim to be hired permanently upon completion of their training.

k) Spokespersons Committee for Managerial Employees

The BetrVG does not apply to managerial employees (*leitende Angestellte*). However, the employer must inform the works council on the hiring of **managerial employees** and keep it apprised regarding special personnel measures involving them (section 105 BetrVG). The managerial employees may elect a spokespersons committee (*Sprecherausschuss*) pursuant to the Spokespersons Committee Act (*Sprecherausschussgesetz – SprAuG*). This committee primarily has a right to be heard with respect to the dismissal of managerial employees, as otherwise, the dismissal will be invalid. In all other respects, the spokespersons committee is of but slight importance.

l) Severely Disabled Employees' Representation

Pursuant to sections 93 to 100 SGB IX, a special representative and a deputy representative for employees with severe disabilities must be elected in establishments with at least five regularly employed workers with severe disabilities within the meaning of sections 2 and 68 SGB IX. If a joint works council or a group works council exists on the company or group level, the representatives of the establishment must elect a joint representative and a group representative pursuant to section 97 SGB IX. These representatives have the right to participate in all meetings of the works councils and the joint and group works councils in a non-voting capacity, pursuant to sections 32, 52 and 59a BetrVG. Furthermore, the representatives have their own participation rights, particularly information and consultation rights, regarding all matters involving an individual employee with severe disabilities or the severely disabled employees as a group (section 95 SGB IX). A measure may not be carried out if the representative has not been informed or consulted. The information and consultation must then take place within seven days, whereupon the employer must come to a new decision. Pursuant to section 96 SGB IX, the representatives enjoy protection similar to that of works council members regarding their personal status and work, particularly with respect to termination (see page 45). The employer must also appoint a representative, or more if necessary, to represent it in matters concerning employees with severe disabilities (section 98 SGB IX).

m) Other Representative Bodies

Since 2001, it has been possible for collective bargaining agreements to create other governing or representational bodies, such as a works council which would be responsible for the entire company or for an individual division (section 3 BetrVG). Accordingly, employers and trade unions occasionally form other bodies in collective bargaining agreements for an individual company or group of companies (see pages 68 for company collective bargaining agreements).

2. Rights of Participation and Codetermination

The individual codetermination rights of the works council are important in practice. Apart from codetermination rights, it also has a number of participation rights, including information and consultation rights.

a) Information and Consultation Rights

Information and consultation rights are not actual codetermination rights, in that the employer may carry out a measure even without the works council's consent, despite its obligation to inform and consult. However, under certain circumstances, the works council can enforce its right to be informed through the labor courts (see pages 66 et seq.).

Generally, the stronger forms of participation rights, namely consultation rights and codetermination rights, include the works council's right to receive adequate information. But the works council is entitled to receive additional information beyond that. The most important of these informational rights relate to the **general duties** of the works council, of which is has a great variety pursuant to section 80 BetrVG. Since the employer must provide the works council with all information it needs to carry out these tasks, this right is very far-reaching. The works council is entitled to request documents or other data that will affect its duties, including in particular payroll documents. The employer can be compelled to fulfill this duty by the labor courts. The works council may also obtain information by visiting the workplace of an employee. Its right to receive information is directed against the employer, who is the owner of the establishment. Whether and to what extent employers within corporate groups must obtain information from parent companies and pass it on to the works council has not yet been determined by the labor courts. As a rule, however, the employer need only provide the works council with the information in its possession. The works council may discuss the topics set forth in section 80 BetrVG in its meetings, bringing in experts as necessary, at the employer's expense, to assist it in carrying out its tasks (section 80 (3) BetrVG). To this end, it must conclude an agreement with the employer.

Moreover, pursuant to section 89 BetrVG, the employer must inform the works council about occupational safety measures undertaken in the establishment. The works council members are obligated to maintain secrecy if the employer classifies an item of information as confidential and informs the works council thereof (section 79 BetrVG).

The works council also has **informational and consultation rights in personnel matters** which apply to all employees. These rights cover, *inter alia*, personnel planning pursuant to sections 92 and 93 BetrVG, personnel questionnaires pursuant to section 94 BetrVG, selection guidelines, training measures and proposals to the employer to secure jobs pursuant to section 92a BetrVG, as well as the introduction of new work routines and technical facilities pursuant to section 97 BetrVG.

b) Codetermination Rights

The works council has codetermination rights under special circumstances as provided for in the BetrVG. The codetermination rights make up the **strongest form of works council participation** and generally include informational and consultation rights.

aa) Structuring of Jobs. Under section 90 BetrVG, the employer must inform the works council of, and consult with it on, the planning of renovation and expansion of production areas, technical installations, work procedures and routines, or work places. Pursuant to section 91 BetrVG, if a change in the workplace, work routine or working environment would place significant burdens on the employees, the works council may demand compensatory measures for the employees. In the event that the works council and the employer cannot reach agreement, they may appeal to the conciliation board, which would then rule on the matter (see page 67).

I. Laws Governing Works Councils

bb) Social Matters. Pursuant to section 87 (1) BetrVG, the works council participates in the determination of a variety of social matters, to the extent that they are not already regulated by statute or collective bargaining agreements.

In practice, some of the most important of these matters are set forth in section 87 (1) nos. 1 and 3 BetrVG, including overtime work. Section 87 (1) no. 6 BetrVG also cites as an important social matter the introduction and use of information technology within the establishment. This means, for example, that the employer must involve the works council in the introduction of a computer system with which the employees' conduct can be monitored. In order to fall within the scope of section 87 BetrVG it is sufficient if the employer can see what e-mails the employees receive.

Under section 87 BetrVG, the works council has a **genuine codetermination right,** meaning that the employer cannot implement certain planned measures without the consent of the works council. In the event that the works council and the employer cannot come to an agreement, either may appeal to the conciliation board, which would then rule on the matter (see page 67).

cc) Hiring and Transfers. The works council has **very important codetermination rights** in personnel matters, particularly in regard to the hiring and transfer of employees.

Pursuant to section 99 BetrVG, if a company has more than 20 employees, it is generally necessary to obtain the works council's consent to every single hiring and transfer. Accordingly, if a company has a total of more than 20 employees, the consent of an existing works council must be obtained, even if the establishment involved only has five employees. To this end, the employer must provide the works council with all necessary documents, such as the application documents, which the works council members are obligated to keep confidential.

However, pursuant to section 99 (2) nos. 1 to 6 BetrVG, the works council may withhold its consent on certain grounds, but not arbitrarily. If an employee is to be transferred from one establishment to another within a company and both establishments have a works council, the employer must generally involve both of the works councils in the decision. The employer is only released from its obligation to involve the works council of the establishment from which the employee is to be transferred if the employee is in agreement with the transfer. If the employer wishes to hire or transfer an applicant or employee against the will of the works council, the employer must petition the labor court for a ruling with respect to such transfer or hire. In certain urgent cases, the employer may also temporarily employ or transfer the employee. However, in that case it would also need to petition the labor court for a ruling on the transfer or hire within three days, section 100 BetrVG (see also page 67).

If the employer fails to consult the works council, the latter can demand the suspension of the hire or transfer. If this demand is upheld by the labor court, the employer must then dismiss the applicant involved. Under certain circumstances, the applicant may then claim damages.

dd) Dismissals. In practice, codetermination pursuant to section 102 BetrVG plays a major role in dismissals, even though the works council generally only has a right to be informed and consulted and essentially cannot prevent a dismissal. If the employer does not grant the works council a proper consultation, the **dismissal will be invalid.** Indeed, dismissals are frequently invalidated for that very reason. If the employer wishes to dismiss an employee without cause – ordinary termination with prior notice (*ordentliche Kündigung*) – the employer must inform the works council of the grounds for its decision pursuant to section 102 (1) and (2), sentences 1 and 2 BetrVG.

Under the Protection Against Unfair Dismissals Act (KSchG), employees who have worked for a company with more than five employees (for employees hired after 31 December 2003, the threshold is ten employees) for over six months may only be dismissed on certain grounds, in particular if their position ceases to exist and it is impossible for the employer to reassign them to another vacant position (see page 42). In practice, works council consultations are very often invalid because the employer failed to state the basis for the termination in sufficient detail. Where the KSchG is not applicable, the employer may terminate the employment agreement at its sole discretion and without particular cause, but the grounds may not be discriminatory and the employer must still inform the works council of its reason for the dismissal.

The works council has **one week to raise objections** to a dismissal. The employer must then wait until the expiration of this period before it effects the dismissal. If it terminates the employment agreement before this period has elapsed, the dismissal will be invalid unless the works council has agreed in writing to a reduction of the information period. Even if the works council objects to a dismissal, the employer can still terminate the employment agreement despite the objection. If the employee then files a suit for wrongful dismissal, however, the employer will, under certain circumstances, have to continue to employ the employee due to the works council's objection until the legal dispute has been resolved.

If the employer wishes to dismiss an employee without notice for cause, e.g. due to a criminal offence, it must inform the in advance works council of the grounds for the dismissal (section 102 (1) and (2), sentence 3 BetrVG). The works council will then have **three days** in which to state its position on the dismissal. The employer may not terminate the employment agreement for cause until these three days have elapsed, otherwise, the dismissal will be invalid.

Pursuant to section 103 BetrVG and section 15 KSchG, an employer may only dismiss a works council member or any of the three employees who initiated the works council election for cause, except in the case of a (partial) closure of the establishment, and then only with the consent of the remaining works council members. If the works council withholds its consent, the employer may petition the labor court to overrule the works council's decision on the dismissal. In practice, the requirement that an employee be dismissed for cause sets a very high standard, since a dismissal for cause can have very severe consequences for the employee. If an employer wishes to dismiss a large number of employees at once (mass dismissal), under section 17 KSchG, it must inform the works council of the grounds for the planned dismissals, the number and occupational classifications of the employees to be dismissed, the number of people employed in the establishment, the timeframe in which it plans to carry out the dismissals, the intended criteria for the selection as well as the names of those to be dismissed. The employer must also consult with the works council on these dismissals. Additionally, the employer must inform the works council how it is calculating the severance pay for the dismissals, if it wishes to make any severance payments at all. If the employer fails to inform the works council, under certain circumstances it will not be allowed to carry out the dismissals.

ee) Economic Matters. The works council has codetermination rights if the employer wishes to restructure or shut down the establishment, including the preparation of mass dismissals. This can lead to problems in certain transactions. Section 111 BetrVG provides that in companies with more than 20 employees, the employer must inform the works council of plans to implement any **operational changes** in the establishment (*Betriebsänderung*) that would be of material disadvantage to the employees. Accordingly, it could be the case that the employer will need to negotiate with the works council on a spin-off or the closure of an establishment that has fewer than five employees. If the company has more than 300 employees, the works council may call in an external consultant at the employer's expense to assist in the negotiations. The employer must also consult with the works council on the planned change. Pursuant to section 111 sentence 2 nos. 1 to 5 BetrVG, an operational change is always initially deemed to exist in any case of a cutback, shutdown or relocation of the establishment (or significant parts thereof), a split-up and an amalgamation with other establishments.

If the employer plans an operational change, it must attempt to agree on a **reconciliation of interests** (*Interessenausgleich*) with the works council before implementing the change (section 112 BetrVG). This reconciliation of interests describes the organizational execution of the operational change. The works council may not force the employer to agree to a reconciliation of interests, but if the employer does not negotiate, works councils will generally attempt to prevent the planned operational change by obtaining a temporary injunction. Some regional labor courts (*Landesarbeitsgericht*) do issue such injunctions, which can significantly delay a transaction.

If the employer deviates from the reconciliation of interests and dismisses an employee in violation thereof, that employee can sue the employer for compensation pursuant to section 113 BetrVG. However, the works council may not assert any damages claims against an employer.

In order to compensate the employees for the disadvantages the operational change will bring upon them, the employer has to agree with the works council on a **social plan** (*Sozialplan*) pursuant to section 112 BetrVG. This social plan regulates matters such as compensation payments for disadvantages incurred by the employees as a result of operational change. The employees may file claims on the basis of this social plan. If no agreement is reached on a social plan, the works council or the employer may appeal to the conciliation board (see page 67), which would then be authorized to draw up the social plan itself. Further, pursuant to recent case law, the unions (see page 68) may also call a strike for a trade union social plan independent of the conciliation board proceedings. This generally places the employer under considerable pressure in the negotiations.

c) Exercising Codetermination Rights

How a works council exercises its codetermination rights is generally dependent upon the particular right involved. If the works council has a codetermination right, it may consent or object to individual measures by the employer, e.g. the planned hiring or firing of an employee.

It is primarily in the area of social codetermination rights, which apply to all employees, that the works council concludes a **written works agreement** (*Betriebsvereinbarung*) with the employer (for details, see below and pages 64 et seq.). Where the consent of the works council must be obtained to a planned measure that is to apply to all employees, it may demand that the employer conclude a works agreement. However, it is also possible for the employer to voluntarily conclude a works agreement with the works council on a matter on which the works council has no codetermination rights, i.e. a **"voluntary works agreement"** (*freiwillige Betriebsvereinbarung*). The employer normally concludes works agreements with the works council for a fixed term. If no fixed term is stipulated, the works agreement will remain in force until terminated by the employer or the works council.

The works council may also conclude a **"regulatory arrangement"** (*Regelungsabrede*). This is an informal contract between the employer and the works council which does not have a direct or binding effect on the individual employment relationships.

3. Works Agreements

A works agreement is a special type of contract concluded between the employer and the works council containing general provisions regarding the working conditions of the individual employees. Pursuant to section 77 (4) sentence 1 BetrVG, works agreements have the same **a direct and binding effect** on the individual employment relationships as statutory law. Works councils, joint works councils and group works councils may conclude works agreements for the establishment, the company and the group, respectively.

a) Typical Content

The content of works agreements is not regulated by statutory law. Usually a distinction is made between works agreements involving enforceable codetermination and voluntary works agreements. In practice, a large number of works agreements cover issues of enforceable codetermination and social matters pursuant to section 87 BetrVG. Particularly common are works agreements regarding workplace rules and regulations and employee conduct, including, increasingly, ethics codes and codes of conduct (see also page 33), the daily work schedule, including breaks and overtime, the introduction and use of technical equipment that is specially designed to monitor the conduct or performance of the employees, the wage structure of the establishment, including company pensions and the establishment of piecework and bonus rates, and comparable pay based on performance.

The content of voluntary works agreements is described in section 88 BetrVG. However, in practice, voluntary works agreements can cover any matters the employer and the works council deem necessary to regulate in a general way.

b) Conclusion

Section 77 (2) BetrVG requires that a works agreement be concluded by the employer and the works council and set down **in writing**. It must be signed by both parties unless it resulted from a ruling by a conciliation board. The written form requirement mandates that if the works agreement consists of two or more pages, all of the pages must be physically affixed to each other, i.e. bound together. The employer is obligated to display a copy of the works agreements in the establishment in an adequate manner, i.e. on an accessible bulletin board.

c) Effectiveness

Works agreements generally contain clauses binding both the employer and the works council. They also contain normative clauses regulating the working conditions for the establishment's employees which have a direct and binding effect pursuant to section 77 (1) sentence 1 BetrVG. Accordingly, the content of the works agreement regulates the individual employee's employment relationship in the same way as **mandatory statutory law**. A works agreement need not be formally incorporated into the individual employment agreements. The employer and the individual employee may not deviate from the works agreements to the employee's disadvantage except with the consent of the works council (section 77 (4) sentence 2 BetrVG). However, employees may still demand better treatment than

I. Laws Governing Works Councils

that provided for in the works agreement, on the basis of their individual employment contract or other sources of law, pursuant to the **favorability principle** (*"Günstigkeitsprinzip"*, see pages 7 et seq.). Pursuant to case law, exceptions are made if the works agreement supersedes the more favorable contractual claim or rule. This is the case if (i) the contractual claim is based on either company practice (see page 5) or a general (collective) commitment by the employer and (ii) the works agreement compares favorably to the contractual claim from the point of view of the employees concerned as a whole (*kollektiver Günstigkeitsvergleich*), or if the general commitment was made subject to an explicit reservation of the right to make a subsequent change in a works agreement.

While the parties to works agreements are generally free to determine its content, they may not violate binding statutory law or regulate issues that are typically covered by collective bargaining agreements pursuant to section 77 (3) BetrVG, or with regard to social matters, those items that are actually covered in the applicable collective bargaining agreement (section 87 (1) sentence 1 BetrVG). In addition, the labor courts may review works agreements for fairness, particularly in light of the principles of equal treatment and equal protection pursuant to section 75 BetrVG.

The works council has the right to demand that the employer **perform the works agreements.** If the employer fails to do so, it may be sued for specific performance or prevented from violating the works agreement by a temporary injunction issued by the labor court. However, the works council may not demand the specific performance of an individual employee's claims against the employer.

Works agreements may only cover issues that fall within the statutory scope of a works council's responsibility. If the written form requirement is breached, a works agreement will be invalid. However, it could nevertheless be interpreted as a "regulatory arrangement" and thus still have effect between the employer and works council without having a direct effect on the individual employment relationships.

d) Termination

Works agreements terminate without notice if they are explicitly concluded for a limited term. They may also be terminated with notice pursuant to section 77 (5) BetrVG. The statutory notice period is **three months.** However, the parties are free to stipulate a shorter or longer termination notice period. Generally, neither the employer nor the works council require grounds to terminate a works agreement with prior notice, but the employer's right to do so is limited where works agreements on company pensions are concerned. Moreover, works agreements may also be terminated without prior notice for cause, but this is very rare in practice since the standard for cause for termination is relatively difficult to meet.

A works agreement also terminates when **replaced by a new works agreement** covering the same issues. Old works agreements may generally also be replaced with new works agreements containing new working conditions that are disadvantageous for the employees. However, pursuant to the case law, the new works agreement may not be more disadvantageous to the employees if certain matters are concerned and the employees have already acquired a certain right or expectation from the previous works agreement, particularly regarding remuneration or company pensions. However, the new works agreement will replace the previous agreement if the principles of proportionality (*Verhältnismäßigkeit*) and protection of trust (*Vertrauensschutz*) are complied with in each individual case.

If a works agreement terminates without being replaced by a new works agreement, it will continue to have direct and binding effect on the individual employment relationships, pursuant to section 77 (6) BetrVG, as far as provisions on matters of enforceable codetermination are concerned (*Nachwirkung* – *"after-effect"*). An "after-effect" may be excluded in the works agreement itself or expressly stipulated with respect to voluntary works agreements or voluntary codetermination issues in works agreements covering matters of both enforceable and non-enforceable codetermination. If works agreements have an "after-effect", they may be replaced by another agreement which need not be a new works agreement, but can also be an agreement between the employer and the individual employee.

4. Disputes between Employer and Works Council

Disputes between the employer and the works council are often finally resolved by suits before a labor court. However, alternative dispute resolution options exist, such as submission to a conciliation board and other remedies.

a) Suits before a Labor Court

If an employer violates a participation or codetermination right, the works council may file suit with the labor court. For example, if the works council has the right to receive information, it may sue for disclosure of the item of information involved. If the employer is only allowed to carry out a given measure with the consent of the works council and fails to consult it, the works council may file for injunctive relief at the labor court. If the employer and works council do not agree on whether the works council has a codetermination right at all, the works council may petition the labor court to issue a declaration that such a codetermination right exists.

Some courts have found that in urgent cases, it may be possible for the works council to obtain a **temporary injunction in order to enforce its rights** subject to the general procedural provisions. Moreover, under section 23 (3) BetrVG, the works council may obtain injunctive relief, including a restraining order, if an employer is guilty of serious breaches of its duties under the BetrVG, such as intentionally failing to consult the works council in a social measure pursuant to section 87 BetrVG. The works council or a trade union may petition the labor court to order the employer to cease and desist (see section below). If the employer fails to comply with the labor court's order (e.g. continues to exclude the works council from participation in such matters), the labor court may impose a fine of up to EUR 10,000 to compel the employer to comply with the court order.

Should any works council members severely breach their duties under the BetrVG, the employer may petition the labor court to exclude them from the works council, pursuant to section 23 (1) BetrVG.

There are special procedures for resolving disputes between the employer and the works council (*Beschlussverfahren*). Regardless of whether the employer wins or loses in a judicial proceeding against the works council, as a rule it must bear the entire cost of the proceeding, including attorney's fees.

b) Cease and Desist Claims

If an employer violates a codetermination right of the works council, for example by attempting to carry out a social measure pursuant to section 87 BetrVG without the participation of the works council, the works council may demand that the employer cease and desist, not only if the employer has severely violated its duties within the meaning of section 23 (3) BetrVG (see section above) but also pursuant to the **general procedural provisions**, according to which the works council can assert this claim before the labor court and, in urgent cases, petition it for an injunction. Of particular importance in practice is the fact that a great many labor courts also grant temporary injunctions to prevent an employer from carrying out an alteration or restructuring of its works within the meaning of section 111 BetrVG if the works council has not been properly consulted on the plans for such measures and involved in negotiations on a reconciliation of interests (see pages 63 et seq.).

c) Temporary Hirings and Transfers

Pursuant to sections 100 et seq. BetrVG, the employer has the right to temporarily hire or transfer an employee in urgent cases even if the works council has not (yet) consented to this measure as provided in section 99 BetrVG. The employer must then inform the works council of the **temporary measure** without delay. If the works council disputes the urgency of the measure, the employer may only uphold the temporary measure if it petitions the labor court within three days to rule that the temporary measure was necessary and issue an order in lieu of the works council's consent.

d) Conciliation Board

The BetrVG provides that in some cases the works council must consent to a planned measure of the employer and in such cases should arrive at an agreement with the employer. If attempts to reach such an agreement fail, the employer or the works council may appeal unilaterally to the conciliation board (*Einigungsstelle*) if the BetrVG provides that a conciliation board ruling replaces an agreement between the parties (section 76 (5) BetrVG). A conciliation board may also be appealed to by both parties in other matters pursuant to section 76 (6) BetrVG. The conciliation board is a kind of **arbitration tribunal for the establishment.** It has a chairperson on whom the employer and the works council must agree and who will otherwise be appointed by the labor court. The employer and the works council then each appoint one to three additional members (section 76 (2) BetrVG).

The conciliation board must hold oral discussions and reach a decision by majority vote, which will be binding on the employer and the works council if it is empowered to issue an order in lieu of agreement between the parties (section 76 (5) and (6) BetrVG). The works council and the employer may seek a review of the conciliation board's decision by the labor court. However, such a judicial review would be restricted to determining whether the conciliation board was actually competent to rule on the issue involved, and if so, whether its decision was reasonable.

e) Other Remedies

Members of the works council or the economic committee who breach their duty of confidentiality may be criminally liable (section 120 BetrVG). An employer obstructing an election of a works council would be guilty of a criminal offense and could be sentenced to up to one year in prison pursuant to section 119 BetrVG. If the employer conveys information to the works council that is false, incomplete or delayed, it may be guilty of an administrative offense and subject to a fine of up to EUR 10,000 (section 121 BetrVG). However, this does not apply to the right to receive general information pursuant to section 80 BetrVG.

5. Transfer of Business, Transformation and Restructuring

Generally, transfers of an entire company by way of an asset deal, or a transformation pursuant to the Transformation Act have no effect on the establishment level. Therefore, **works agreements remain in force** and the works council remains in office when the entire company is sold. However, the existence of a joint works council or a group works council, as well as joint and group works agreements, are often affected.

The structure and organization of an individual establishment may also be affected if only parts of a company are transferred and the split of the company also affects the establishment. If the structure and organization of the establishment are fundamentally altered by a partial transfer of the company, works agreements will generally terminate and the works council will be dissolved. However, there are special rules for the continued application of works agreements in the event of a transfer of business pursuant to section 613a BGB or a transformation pursuant to section 324 UmwG (for details, see pages 47 et seq.). But these special rules do not apply if the transferor and the transferee continue to run the establishment unchanged after the acquisition as a joint establishment of two companies. Further, works agreements will generally terminate if the structure and organization of the establishment are altered not by a partial transfer, but merely by internal restructurings or internal restructuring before or after mergers and acquisitions. The works council has a transitional mandate pursuant to section 21a BetrVG if the organization of the establishment is fundamentally altered. The works council then is charged with organizing new works council elections in the remaining (split) parts if they themselves are considered to be establishments within the meaning of section 1 BetrVG.

II. Collective Bargaining Agreements Law

Collective bargaining can refer to two kinds of agreements: either agreements **between the employer and the works council** (works agreements), or agreements with **trade unions** (trade union agreements). Works agreements are described above (see pages 64 et seq.). This chapter only covers collective bargaining agreements in the sense of trade union agreements.

1. Collective Bargaining Agreements

There are also two kinds of collective bargaining agreements with trade unions: those concluded between the employers' association and the trade union (hereinafter: "association agreement" – *Verbandstarifvertrag*) and those concluded between the employer and the trade union (hereinafter: "company agreement" – *Firmentarifvertrag*).

a) Typical Content

Both forms of collective bargaining agreements typically regulate **working conditions, particularly remuneration and working hours,** but also bonuses, holidays and notice periods. Generally, collective bargaining agreements are divided into two distinct agreements. The first is the collective framework agreement on general working and employment conditions (*Manteltarifvertrag*) and the other is the collective bargaining agreement on payment, or "pay agreement" (*Gehaltstarifvertrag*). Pay agreements cover those conditions which are altered from time to time due to collective bargaining, basically remuneration, whereas framework agreements cover those conditions which remain unchanged for longer periods of time, such as classification of employees, notice periods, working hours, including percentage to be paid for differentials for overtime, Sunday and holiday work and regulations on the length of vacations. If the working hours are changed without an equivalent change in pay, both kinds of collective bargaining agreements have to be renegotiated at the same time.

An increasing number of collective bargaining agreements are being concluded between the employers and the trade unions in cases of larger restructurings and

II. Collective Bargaining Agreements Law

layoffs; these agreements are termed "trade union social plans" (*Tarifsozialpläne*). For a long time there was a great deal of dispute over the permissibility of such agreements since pursuant to sections 111, 112 BetrVG, the procedure and severance payments must also be subjected to a reconciliation of interests and a social plan, which the employer was supposed to negotiate not with the trade unions, but with the works council. Even though this could mean that in the case of larger restructurings and layoffs, the employer might have to fight on two fronts, i.e. with the trade union with respect to the trade union social plan and with the works council with respect to the reconciliation of interests and the social plan, the Federal Labor Court has found that such trade union social plans, and even the trade unions' right to call a strike to demand such plans, are in fact permissible.

b) Conclusion

As mentioned above, collective bargaining agreements are concluded between trade unions on the one hand and either the respective employers' association or the employer itself on the other. According to section 1 (2) of the Collective Bargaining Agreements Act (*Tarifvertragsgesetz – TVG*), collective bargaining agreements must be made in writing.

c) Effect

Members of the parties to a collective bargaining agreement, or the employer if it is itself a party thereto, are bound by the collective bargaining agreement subject to the following conditions:

- **Company agreements**
  - the employee is a member of the trade union that is a party to it
- **Association agreements**
  - the employer is a member of the employers' association that is a party to it and the employee is a member of the respective trade union

  or

  - the Federal Minister of Labor and Social Affairs or the supreme state labor authority has declared the trade union agreement to be generally binding (section 5 (1) and (6) TVG). Such association agreements are registered in the Collective Bargaining Agreements Register (*Tarifregister*) at the Federal Ministry of Labor and Social Affairs (section 6 TVG).

If the collective bargaining agreement is binding, the employees covered by it have a **direct claim against the employer** on all issues concerning their relationship with the employer as stipulated in the agreement. Moreover, arrangements which depart from the collective bargaining agreement shall be permissible only if they are allowed under the collective bargaining agreement or authorized by the parties to such agreement or the departure is to the employee's advantage (*Günstigkeitsprinzip*) pursuant to section 4 (3) TVG.

Until recently, the legal principle of uniform collective bargaining agreements (*Tarifeinheit*) had applied, under which only the most specific and relevant collective bargaining agreement was to be applied to employees in a given establishment. The Federal Labor Court overturned this concept in 2010, with the result that multiple collective bargaining agreements and multiple trade unions can now coexist in a single establishment (*Tarifpluralität*). If collective bargaining agreements have different terms, they must also be renegotiated at different times, whereby strikes are possible in each case.

d) Termination

All collective bargaining agreements are **concluded for a fixed term** and will often contain a notice period for the termination of the agreement itself.

During the fixed term of a collective bargaining agreement, it cannot validly be terminated without cause. **Industrial action** (i.e. strikes) during this time **is not permitted**. Upon expiration of the collective bargaining agreement, the legal norms set forth therein will continue to apply until they are superseded by a subsequent arrangement, i.e. an "after effect" will occur (section 4 (5) TVG). Such arrangements include the conclusion of individual employment contracts.

2. Labor Disputes/Industrial Action

The typical industrial action taken by employees and trade unions is the strike, while employers engage in lockouts or payment of strike-breaking premiums.

a) Strike

To be legal, a strike must meet certain formal requirements and pursue a legitimate purpose.

Formally, a strike must (i) be organized by a trade union and (ii) be called following a strike vote conducted according to democratic principles. Accordingly, "wildcat" strikes, which are not organized by a trade union, are illegal.

The strike must further pursue a **legitimate purpose**, which can only be a change in working conditions. Therefore, a strike is illegal if:
- the underlying collective bargaining agreements are still fully in force, i.e. have not yet expired (and not merely due to "after effects"),
- it is intended as a political action and not to change working conditions,
- the actions taken in the strike are in violation of general applicable law,
- it is unreasonable and out of proportion. This would particularly be the case if a strike commences before negotiations have proven to be unsuccessful; however, there is a wide discretion of the unions in this respect. There is a narrow exception for "warning strikes", which may already begin before the negotiations have failed in order to exert pressure on the employers. However, such warning strikes may legally only last a few hours.

For clarification: an employee's right to withhold his or her labor until the employer meets its obligations is not a strike, but rather the exercising of rights on a purely individual basis.

b) Conduct of the Strike

A strike must also be conducted in a **reasonable and lawful manner**. Therefore, the union may not occupy the premises, call on customers of the employer to boycott its products or prevent employees willing to work from entering the premises and working. However, **picketing** for the sole purpose of monitoring who enters the premises is permissible.

c) Reaction of the Employer

The employer is not obligated to remunerate workers during a strike. The union usually pays strike benefits to its members.

During and after a legal strike, the employer may not sanction the employees for their participation in the action. In the case of an **illegal strike**, the employer may seek a **preliminary injunction** to prevent the employees from violating the law by participating in the strike. If the trade union is involved in the illegal strike, the injunction may also be directed against it. Finally, the employers' side may impose a **lockout**. However, lockouts may not be used offensively, but only as a defensive reaction to a strike. Moreover, it must be proportionate. If less than 25% of the employees are on strike, the employers may only lock out up to an additional 25% of the employees. If over 25% are on strike, the employers may only lock out up to 50% of the workforce. The employer may **close the entire operation down** for a period of time, but it must explicitly announce this to all of the employees, specifying the dates involved. The duties of both parties under the employment agreement are then suspended for the announced lockout period, which may not substantially exceed the duration of the strike.

Strike-breaker premiums are, in principle, legal if paid out during the strike, rather than after it. In practice, such premiums are rare as the collective bargaining agreements concluded in the course of a strike often provide for the reversal of any unequal treatment of strikers and strike-breakers in connection with the strike. Lockouts, shutdowns of the operation and strike-breaker premiums may only be introduced in reaction to a strike, and in no event may they be employed as pre-emptory tactics.

d) Flash Mobs

A "flash mob" occurs when a group of people, who generally do not know each other personally, assemble briefly and apparently spontaneously in public or semi-public places and do unusual things. Flash mobs are organized via online communities, viral e-mails or mobile phone messages.

The trade union ver.di has used flash mobs as a new strike action to support industrial action in the retail business. It called upon people to buy low-priced goods in a retail store and/or fill up shopping carts and leave them standing in the store, in order to disrupt the course of business. In the view of the Federal Labor Court, such an action accompanying a strike in order to exert pressure on the employers to achieve collective bargaining goals is not generally impermissible. The intrusion involved can be justified under the laws governing industrial actions if the employers have effective means at their disposal to defend against them.

III. Corporate Codetermination

Corporate codetermination is codetermination **on the supervisory board** (*Aufsichtsrat*). It is part of the corporate governance and must be distinguished from the codetermination of the works council in relationship to the employer (pages 59 et seq.). The supervisory board oversees officers (legal representatives) and in particular is responsible for appointing and dismissing the managing directors, concluding and terminating their service contracts with the company. With regard to codetermination in the supervisory board, the German system distinguishes between companies with up to 500 employees, those with 501 to 2,000 employees, and those with more than 2,000 employees.

In companies with **up to 500 employees**, there is no mandatory employee codetermination in the supervisory board.

In stock corporations (*Aktiengesellschaften – AG*) or partnerships limited by shares (*Kommanditgesellschaften auf Aktien – KGaA*) with more than 500 employees, one third of the members of the supervisory board must consist of employee representatives who are directly elected by the employees. The same applies to a limited liability company (*Gesellschaft mit beschränkter Haftung – GmbH*) of this size, which must form a supervisory board, section 1 (1) no. 3 One-Third Participation Act (*Drittelbeteiligungsgesetz – DrittelbG*).

If a stock corporation, a partnership limited by shares or a limited liability company regularly employs **more than 2,000 employees**, the Codetermination Act (*Mitbestimmungsgesetz – MitbestG*) will apply. With very rare exceptions, these companies must form a supervisory board, section 6 (1) MitbestG, consisting of an equal number of representatives of employees and of the shareholders. As a result of the system for electing the chairperson of the supervisory board (section 27 (1) and (2) MitbestG), the chairperson is a representative of the shareholders, while the deputy chairperson is a representative of the employees. This is very significant, because under section 29 (2) MitbestG, in the event of a tie, the chairperson will have two votes (section 29 (2) sentence 1 in connection with sentence 3 MitbestG). The same applies analogously to the supervisory board's decision on the appointment of the officers (legal representatives) of the company, i.e. the management board or managing director (section 31 (3) sentence 2 in connection with (4) MitbestG).

An explicit exception is made for codetermination in the **coal and steel industries**, which is regulated by the Act Concerning the Codetermination of Employees in the Supervisory Boards and Management Boards in the Mining and the Iron and Steel Manufacturing Industry (*Montan-Mitbestimmungsgesetz – Montan-MitbestG*). For these companies, the codetermination threshold is more than 1,000 employees (section 1 (2) Montan-MitbestG). The supervisory board consists of eleven members, one of whom must be neutral (section 4 (1) and (2) in connection with section 8 Montan-MitbestG). If the nominal capital exceeds EUR 10 million, the supervisory board can be increased to 15 members, and to 21 members if it exceeds EUR 25 million. In each case, there is one neutral member who is elected by a special committee out of those nominated by the other supervisory board members, sometimes following a rather complicated proceeding involving the higher regional court (*Oberlandesgericht*) in case of a dispute (section 8 Montan-MitbestG). However, in practice, it is unusual for the court to get involved.

D. Employee Protection Laws

In addition to the private individual and collective employment and labor laws, public employee protection laws constitute the **third pillar of German employment and labor law**. The public law protective provisions are, almost without exception, mandatory law, which can only be derogated from by agreement to the benefit of the employees. Only in exceptional cases can they be derogated from to the employees' detriment in collective bargaining agreements or through other private law agreements on the basis of an empowerment to do so in a collective bargaining agreement. Important employee protection laws are the Law on Safety and Health at Work (*Arbeitsschutzgesetz*) of 1996 which regulates the fundamental duties of the employer and employees regarding health protection, the Act on Industrial Physicians, Safety Engineers and Other Occupational Safety Specialists (*Gesetz über Betriebsärzte, Sicherheitsingenieure und andere Fachkräfte für Arbeitssicherheit*) of 1973, the Federal Immission Control Act (*Bundesimmissionsschutzgesetz*) of 1974, the Federal Data Protection Act (*Bundesdatenschutzgesetz*) of 1978 to protect general rights of personal freedom and regulate the use of personal data in employment relationships, including the international transfer of personal data of employees, the General Equal Treatment Act (*AGG*) of 2006, the Home Workers Act (*Heimarbeitsgesetz*) of 1951 and the Act Regulating the Commercial Leasing of Employees (*Arbeitnehmerüberlassungsgesetz*) of 1972. Provisions on employee protection in the narrower sense of the term can also be found in the accident prevention provisions and SGB VII on statutory employee accident insurance, which is overseen by the professional associations (see pages 80 et seq.).

Compliance with the public law employment protection statutes is monitored and enforced by various public authorities as designated in the individual statutes. As a rule, these authorities are also authorized to impose fines for infractions of employee protection provisions. Serious violations of such provisions may also be subject to criminal prosecution.

The following are the most important employee protection statutes in practice:

I. Laws Governing Working Hours

The Hours of Employment Act (*Arbeitszeitgesetz* – *ArbZG*) of 1994 regulates the **maximum length of an employee's working day**. Pursuant to section 3 ArbZG, it generally may not exceed eight hours. In exceptional cases it can be extended to **ten hours**, provided the working day does not exceed an average of eight hours over a period of six calendar months or 24 calendar weeks. A working day is every day except Sundays and public holidays. Section 4 ArbZG regulates the **minimum length of breaks**. They must be at least **30 minutes** long for a working day of six to nine hours, and at least 45 minutes long for a working day of over nine hours. Pursuant to section 5 ArbZG, at the end of the working day the employee must have an uninterrupted **rest period** of **at least 11 hours** before beginning the next working day. Exceptions to this rule are only permissible under special circumstances in certain industry sectors. **Night work and rotating shift** work are strictly regulated in section 6 ArbZG. A night shift may generally not exceed eight hours. In exceptional cases it can be extended to ten hours, as long as the average daily shift does not exceed eight hours over a period of one calendar month or four calendar weeks. Pursuant to section 7 ArbZG, **collective bargaining agreements, or works agreements** based on a collective bargaining agreement, may provide for deviations from this rule, even to the employee's detriment, particularly with respect to the maximum working hours per day and the compensation period. Section 9 ArbZG generally prohibits employers from assigning employees to Sunday or holiday work between midnight to midnight. True, sections 10 to 12 ArbZG provide for numerous exceptions to this general rule, but manufacturing operations in Germany which are to be run on a two or three shift system should generally be set up in close consultation with the authorities competent to monitor compliance with the employee protection laws. In some cases, official waivers pursuant to section 13 ArbZG can also be obtained for shifts which are normally not allowed. It should be noted that, *inter alia*, managerial employees, as defined under section 18 ArbZG, are exempted from the statutory regulations on working hours.

II. Shop Closing Hours Act

The former federal Shop Closing Hours Act (*Ladenschlussgesetz* – *LadenschlussG*) of 1956 was originally conceived as protective legislation for employees. The provisions concerning the business hours of retail outlets of all kinds on weekdays, as well as Sundays and holidays, were intended to protect the employees of such establishments against adverse working hours. This Act has since been repealed due to amendments to the federal constitution (Basic Law) in 2006, and the shop closing hours are now governed by state law in each of the 16 Federal States of Germany. So far, the States have largely passed state legislation providing for much less restrictive shop opening hours than before. For instance in the state of Berlin, opening hours are generally 24 hours on Monday through Saturday with an extensive list of exceptions for shops which may be open on Sundays and holidays as well. However, the laws on shop opening hours govern the relationship between a business and its customers or the public at large, and not the employment relationships. The maximum working hours of the employees are regulated exclusively in the ArbZG.

III. Maternity Protection Act

The purpose of the Maternity Protection Act (*Mutterschutzgesetz – MuSchG*) is to provide special legal protections for women during pregnancy and after giving birth. Pregnant women should **inform their employers** of their pregnancy and the anticipated delivery date as soon as they learn of their condition. The Act **prohibits assigning them from performing certain jobs** in order to protect them from excessive physical strain. Under section 3 MuSchG, mothers-to-be may not be assigned to work that, according to a doctor's certificate, would jeopardize the life or health of mother or fetus. Likewise, pregnant women may not be assigned to work during the six weeks leading up to the expected delivery date unless they expressly declare their willingness to do so. Such a declaration can be revoked at any time. Section 4 MuSchG contains special prohibitions of work assignments in order to prevent pregnant women from performing heavy physical labor or work that would expose them to the harmful effects of hazardous substances, heat, cold or dampness, as well as vibrations or noise. Furthermore, pursuant to section 8 MuSchG, pregnant women may not be assigned to nightshifts between 8:00 p.m. and 6:00 a.m. or Sunday and holiday work. Moreover, mothers may not be assigned work for eight weeks after delivery, pursuant to section 6 MuSchG. Section 7 MuSchG contains additional protective provisions for nursing mothers.

The MuSchG also provides **financial protection** for pregnant women and mothers after delivery. Under section 11 MuSchG, a claim for remuneration largely remains intact even when the women cannot be assigned work. Under section 13 MuSchG, mothers receive maternity benefits from their health insurance scheme or from the federal government for the period in which they generally may not be assigned to work, i.e. six weeks before the expected delivery date and eight weeks after delivery. Under section 14 MuSchG, the employer must make a contribution toward the maternity benefit in the amount of the difference between the maternity benefit and the net pay per calendar day. However, the employer has a claim to be fully reimbursed by the woman's health insurance scheme pursuant to the Act on the Compensation for Employer's Expenditures for the Continuation of Payment (*Gesetz über den Ausgleich von Arbeitgeberaufwendungen für Entgeltfortzahlung – AAG*).

During pregnancy and for the first four months after delivery, a mother enjoys a comprehensive protection against dismissal pursuant to section 9 MuSchG, which prohibits dismissals with notice or for cause if the employer was aware of the pregnancy or the delivery when issuing the dismissal or was informed thereof within two weeks of receipt of the dismissal notice. Only in exceptional cases can the competent federal authority declare a dismissal permissible if it is unrelated to the pregnancy or the delivery. It is important for the employer to note that, despite the legal and financial burdens associated with the pregnancy of a female employee, it may not ask an applicant if she is pregnant before hiring her (see page 14).

IV. Federal Parental Allowance And Parental Leave Act

Under section 15 of the Federal Parental Allowance and Parental Leave Act (*Bundeselterngeld- und Elternzeitgesetz – BEEG*) of 2007 (previously: Federal Educational Allowance Act (*Bundeserziehungsgeldgesetz – BErzGG*)), both the mother and the father have a claim to parental leave up to the **child's third birthday**. With the employer's consent, up to twelve months of this leave time can be subsequently applied up to the child's eighth birthday. Parental leave can be taken by the mother, the father or both parents together, but may not exceed three years per child. Pursuant to sections 3 et seq. BEEG, subject to certain prerequisites, the parents are entitled to a parental allowance, which is for a maximum of 12 or, if both parents take parental leave, 14 months.

Under section 15 (7) BEEG, parents have a general right to demand that the employer organize **part-time work** with a minimum of 15 and a maximum of 30 weekly working hours for the duration of the parental leave; the employer may refuse to grant permission for such part-time work only in the event of urgent operational reasons. Further, pursuant to section 15 (4) BEEG, parents generally have the right to work part-time for another employer or as a free lancer for up to 30 hours per week during parental leave; the employer may refuse to grant permission for such secondary employment only on urgent operational grounds.

Under section 18 BEEG, the employer may generally not terminate the employment relationship after the point at which parental leave is applied for or during the parental leave. Only in special cases can the competent authorities, as an exception, declare a termination to be permissible. Accordingly, employees generally have a right to return to their old job after the parental leave has ended. If they were working part-time during the parental leave, they also have the right to work their old shift upon their return.

V. Young Persons' Protection in Employment Act

The Young Persons' Protection in Employment Act (*Jugendarbeitsschutzgesetz – JArbSchG*) regulates the special protection of young employees. A young employee is anyone **between 15 and 18 years of age**. Under section 5 JArbSchG the employment of children is generally prohibited, a child being anyone younger than 15 years of age. Section 5 (2) and sections 6 and 7 JArbSchG provide for exceptions to this prohibition. These exemptions are supplemented in detail in the Child Labor Protection Ordinance (*Verordnung über den Kinderarbeitsschutz*) of 1998.

Pursuant to section 8 JArbSchG, young employees may generally not be assigned to work more than eight hours per day and 40 hours per week. There are only a few narrowly defined exceptions to this rule. Sections 11 to 21 JArbSchG contain additional special working time provisions for young employees regarding such matters as breaks, Saturday work, Sunday and holiday work, and vacation days. Sections 22 to 31 JArbSchG list a number of restrictions and prohibitions regarding the assignment of young employees to certain tasks. Sections 32 to 46 JArbSchG contain special regulations on monitoring the health of young employees and providing them with medical care.

VI. Laws Regarding Employees with Disabilities

In July 2001, the **Persons with Disabilities Act** (*Schwerbehindertengesetz – SchwbG*) of 1986 was incorporated into the Social Security Code (*Sozialgesetzbuch*) in its entirety in Book IX. The provisions regarding employees with severe disabilities in Part 2 of SGB IX are designed to facilitate the integration of severely disabled persons into the workplace and afford special protection to such employees. A severely disabled person within the meaning of the law is anyone with an impaired function due to an abnormal physical, mental or psychological condition resulting in a 50% reduction in such person's ability to participate in social life and to work (sections 2, 68 SGB IX). Persons with a 30% incapacitation are equivalent to severely disabled persons if their impairment would otherwise prevent them from obtaining or holding a suitable job.

Employers with over 20 positions must employ persons with severe disabilities to fill at least 5% of these jobs pursuant to sections 71 et seq. SGB IX. An employer failing to hire the prescribed **quota** will need to make a monthly compensation payment for each unfilled post reserved for persons with severe disabilities (section 77 SGB IX). This compensation payment currently amounts to between EUR 105 and EUR 260 per unfilled post. Pursuant to sections 85 to 92 SGB IX, severely disabled employees enjoy special protection against dismissal which, however, only commences after six months of employment. Under these provisions, any dismissal of a severely disabled employee must have the prior consent of a special authority, the "Integration Authority" (*Integrationsamt*), regardless of whether or not the dismissal is due to the disability. Both the employee and the employer can contest this authority's decision on the dismissal before the administrative courts. Pursuant to section 125 SGB IX, severely disabled employees also have a claim to additional vacation time, generally amounting to five working days per year.

The SGB IX further provides in sections 93 to 100 for the establishment of a representation for severely disabled persons in the establishment. Section 81 SGB IX contains special rules regarding the hiring of severely disabled persons and special support during employment. Further, the AGG contains general rules on the prohibition of discrimination, including discrimination against employees with disabilities, particularly with regard to the commencement of an employment relationship, directives and promotion within the employment relationship and the termination of an employment relationship (for details, see pages 9 et seq.).

E. Social Insurance Laws

The social insurance laws are tightly bound up with employment and labor law, because the **statutory social insurance is mandatory for most employees.** Accordingly, the criteria for differentiating between employees and the self-employed under the employment laws are largely identical to those set forth under the social insurance laws (see pages 81 et seq.). One important inconsistency pertains to external managing directors (*Fremdgeschäftsführer*) who, as a governing body, are not employees under employment and labor law, but are categorized as employees for social insurance purposes.

I. Statutory Social Insurance

In Germany, social insurance is divided into the following categories: pension insurance, unemployment insurance, health insurance, nursing care insurance and employee accident insurance. Other important social services provided by the state are child benefits, housing benefits, educational benefits, care of war victims and

I. Statutory Social Insurance

soldiers, compensation for victims of crime, and social welfare, which, however, do not fall within the scope of social insurance, because they are financed solely by direct taxation. The statutory social insurance is largely a **compulsory insurance system for the collective allocation of risk**.

1. Pension Insurance

In the last few years, the statutory pension scheme has been the subject of numerous reform statutes and proposals. More than the other branches of social insurance, it is based on the concept of a **"contract between the generations"**, in which the current contributors finance the pensions of the current pensioners on a pay-as-you-go basis (*Umlageverfahren*). The statutory pension insurance does not operate on the principle of a fully funded basis, but merely creates certain fluctuation reserves (section 216 SGB VI). As a result, the system is very vulnerable to the current negative demographic developments in Germany, which are expected to grow worse in the future. Ever fewer employees will be forced to finance the pensions of the growing number of baby boomer retirees. So far, the legislature has addressed this problem primarily through increases in the contributions, but also increasingly by reducing pension payments and raising the statutory retirement age. The long-term structure of the statutory pension insurance is still under discussion. At present, 75% of the ongoing pension payments are financed by contributions, and 25% by state subsidy out of tax revenues.

Up to now, the statutory pension insurance pursuant to SGB VI has primarily served to provide financial security in old age with **retirement pensions,** but also serves to provide security against reduction of earning capacity and for survivors of diseased employees/retirees. The primary carrier of the statutory pension insurance is the German Pension Insurance Institution (*Deutsche Rentenversicherung*) which, for historical reasons, is internally divided into a federal division (*Deutsche Rentenversicherung Bund*) and a regional one, as well as a special division for certain industries. Persons subject to the mandatory insurance system are primarily dependent employees. This generally applies regardless of the amount of income, so even highly paid employees are subject to compulsory pension insurance, unlike the statutory health insurance system (see pages 78 et seq.). The contributions to pension insurance are divided equally between the employer and the employee as a joint social insurance contribution (see pages 81 et seq.). Like the joint social insurance contributions, they are assessed by income. However, there is a contribution assessment ceiling for pensions (*Beitragsbemessungsgrenze*), which in 2010 amounted to EUR 5,500 gross per month (in the former West Germany), and EUR 4,650 gross per month (in the former East Germany). Special rules apply to those engaged in insignificant employment, short-term employment and students. The primary service rendered by the pension insurance is the retirement pension, which insured persons may avail themselves of upon reaching the statutory age threshold, provided that they have complied with a general five-year waiting period in which the contributions were paid. The statutory pension age is currently 65 years of age in most cases (section 35 SGB VI), but it will be increased gradually over a 20-year period to the age of 67 starting in 2012. However, the age thresholds are lower for persons who have been insured for a long time, for the handicapped, those who are unable to work or engage in a profession, etc., and those who have a claim to a partial-retirement pension. The retirement pensions will depend on the period of time in which contributions have been paid in and the total amount of contributions, up to a certain ceiling, as well as on such social factors as time spent on education and child rearing. Moreover, it is dynamically linked to wages and adjusted to reflect the wage and salary developments nationally. Aside from retirement pensions, the pension insurance also provides survivors' pensions for widows, widowers and orphans, pensions for reduced ability to work or engage in a profession and services and measures for medical rehabilitation in order to preserve the ability to work.

Apart from the statutory pension insurance, the two other pillars of old-age security in Germany are the company pension plans, including deferred compensation and, increasingly, private pension plans, some of which are tax-subsidized.

2. Unemployment Insurance

Unemployment insurance under SGB III provides protection against unemployment and unemployment assistance. The carriers of the unemployment insurance are the German Federal Agency for Employment (*Bundesagentur für Arbeit*) as well as state and local employment agencies (*Agentur für Arbeit*). Above all, dependent employees are subject to the compulsory insurance scheme. Unlike statutory health insurance, unemployment insurance has no compulsory insurance limits, but, like pension insurance, it does have a contribution assessment ceiling. The contributions to unemployment insurance are shared equally by the employer and the employees as a joint social insurance contribution (see pages 81 et seq.). Special rules apply to persons engaged in insignificant employment or short-term employment and students. The most important function of unemployment insurance is the **payment of benefits to unemployed people.** An unemployed person has a claim to unemployment benefits if he or she has worked for at least 12 months in the past two years in an employment relationship subject to compulsory insurance, is available for placement in another job and has applied for unemployment benefits. However, the claim to unemployment benefits will be suspended or blocked under certain circumstances (see pages 84 et seq.). In 2010, unemployment benefits generally amounted to 60% of the average net remuneration for work in the last 52 weeks, which is calculated as a lump sum. Unemployed persons with at least one child eligible for child benefits receive a benefit rate of 67%. The duration of the payment of unemployment benefits depends on the length of the previous employment relationship, as well as the age of the unemployed person. Payment will be made for at least six months and at most 24 months, for an unemployed person over the age of 58 whose last job lasted at least 48 months. The unemployment insurance also pays unemployment benefits to needy unemployed persons who do not have a claim to unemployment benefits. Other compensatory payments made by the unemployment insurance are support money for further education, transition funding for the integration of the handicapped, benefits for short-time work, winter benefits in the construction sector, and insolvency benefits. The unemployment insurance also finances various measures such as professional training, continuing education and ability to move to a different location to accept work.

3. Health Insurance

The goal of the statutory health insurance pursuant to SGB V is to maintain, restore or improve the health of the insured party. The carriers of the statutory health insurance are the statutory health insurance schemes (*Krankenkassen*), which include the local health care funds (*Allgemeinen Ortskrankenkassen – AOK*) having regional jurisdiction, works health insurance schemes established by the employer for one or more large establishments, the guild health insurance schemes established for members of the handicraft guilds, and the substitutional social health insurance funds (*Ersatzkassen*). With certain restrictions, the **insured persons are free to choose** among the statutory health insurance schemes. Persons subject to compulsory insurance are primarily dependent employees, but may also be unemployed persons and retirees, et al. However, employees with an income exceeding one of the annual remuneration thresholds are exempted. Various thresholds apply: in 2010 the general threshold was EUR 4,162.50 gross per month, but there is also a special threshold for employees who were exempt until January 1, 2003 and continue to be exempt with up to a gross monthly salary of EUR 3,712.50. Exempt employees are free to become members of private health insurance schemes (*Privatkassen*), but they can also voluntarily remain with the statutory health insurance scheme. This is more advantageous than a private health insurance scheme for single-income families, for example, since the spouse and children of an insured party are included in the statutory health insurance scheme free of charge in the form of "family insurance" (*Familienversicherung*) pursuant to section 10 SGB V. Since 2009, the health insurance contributions have been consistent in all of the statutory health insurance schemes. They are shared equally by the employer and the employees, but the employee has to pay an additional contribution for dentures. Moreover, if health insurance schemes cannot finance their expenses with the regular contributions, they are allowed to impose additional contributions on the employees. Special rules apply to persons engaged in insignificant employment or short-term employment and students.

The benefits provided by the statutory health insurance scheme in case of illness consist primarily of the necessary medical and other services, which are rendered to the insured party by physicians, hospitals and pharmacies without (advance) payment by the employee on the basis of contracts with the statutory health insurance scheme. The health insurance fund pays the parties to its contracts for expenses subsequent to the provision of services pursuant to fee regulations. However, the insured parties must make co-payments for certain services, in particular pharmaceuticals, hospital care, and dental treatments. The benefits rendered in case of illness include medical treatment, including psychotherapy, dental treatment, including provision of dentures and orthodontic treatment of children (and adults in a few exceptional cases), provision of pharmaceuticals, bandages, remedies and aids, hospital care, rehabilitation services, as well as stress tests and occupational therapy, and pregnancy and maternity care. The statutory health insurance schemes also provide benefits for the prevention of illness and early detection, in particular dental and cancer preventive care, as well as spa therapy. The health insurance schemes further provide benefits in case of illness to replace remuneration to persons whose insurance is based on drawing remuneration and other benefits. Employees receive sickness benefits at a rate of 70% of their normal remuneration, which is oriented to the remuneration regularly paid in line with certain legal provisions. The payment of sickness benefits is suspended until the end of the employer's continued payment of remuneration (see page 27). As a rule, the payment of sickness benefits is limited to a maximum of 78 weeks within three years, even in the case of separate illnesses.

4. Home and Institutional Care Insurance

The purposes of the statutory nursing care insurance pursuant to SGB XI are rehabilitation, the provision of legal and financial security and the expansion of domestic, out-patient and, where necessary, in-patient care of those in need of nursing care. The carriers of nursing care insurance are the nursing care funds established in every statutory health insurance fund. The nursing care insurance is also **closely bound up with the statutory health insurance** (see pages 78 et seq.). In general, those subject to compulsory statutory health insurance are also subject to compulsory nursing care insurance. As in the case of statutory health insurance, the entire family is insured. Members of a private health insurance fund must, however, take out private nursing care insurance.

The contributions to nursing care insurance are shared equally by the employer and the employees as a joint social insurance contribution (see pages 81 et seq.). Special rules apply to persons engaged in insignificant employment or short-term employment and students. Insured parties in need of care have claims under the nursing care insurance, i.e. anyone one who – regardless of age – due to a physical, mental or psychological illness or impairment requires a significant amount of assistance to carry out for his or her normal daily routine on a long-term basis, but presumably for at least six months. The need for nursing care is divided into three categories of severity and reviewed by the medical service of the health insurance scheme. Depending upon the category, the persons in need of care will receive upon application nursing services, money for nursing assistance to be obtained on their own, home care, nursing aids, partial in-patient day and night care, short-time care, complete in-patient care, subsidy of care in institutions for the handicapped, payments to procure nursing staff, and nursing courses for family members and voluntary care providers.

5. Employee Accident Insurance

Statutory employee accident insurance pursuant to SGB VII essentially performs the following functions: preventing accidents at the workplace and occupational diseases, improving protection against hazards at the workplace, rehabilitating the insured parties who have had accidents at the workplace or have contracted occupational diseases, and providing compensation to them or their survivors. The insured parties are primarily dependent employees. The insurance covers **accidents at the workplace,** including accidents on the way to or from work, and occupational diseases. The carriers of the accident insurance are the professional associations (*Berufsgenossenschaften*) to which all companies are allocated by trade. Unlike the other statutory social insurance branches, the **contributions are made by the employer alone** on a pay-as-you-go basis for the previous calendar year by the member companies of the individual professional associations. The amount of the contributions is based on the risk of accidents at the respective company and the expenses for damage based on hazard classification. The essential services of the statutory employee accident insurance are accident prevention, medical and occupational rehabilitation measures, payment of benefits to injured parties or transition benefits and, above all, benefits to injured parties suffering permanent damage to their health.

To compensate for the fact that the statutory employee accident insurance is financed by the employers alone, sections 104 et seq. SGB VII provide for **far-reaching exclusions of liability** in favor of the employers and their other employees in the event of an accident that is brought about through the negligence of a third party, for instance a contractor of the employer or colleagues of the injured employee. However, this exclusion of liability does not extend to intentional acts. In cases of grossly negligent and intentional conduct, the tortfeasors are also obligated to pay compensation to the social insurance fund pursuant to section 110 SGB VII.

Often, companies in Germany take out additional private accident insurance policies for higher-level employees and managerial personnel, which generally provide lump sum payments for accidents.

II. Social Insurance Obligations

The general social insurance regulations can be found in SGB I and SGB IV. The essential duty of an employer under social insurance law is **to register an employee for social insurance** with the competent health insurance fund, pursuant to sections 28 a to 28 i SGB IV. This registration duty also covers persons who are engaged in insignificant employment or are only working for a short term. The beginning and end of, or changes to, the duty to make contributions are notifiable, and annual reports must be made. The insured person must give the employer and the social insurance carrier the information necessary for the reports and provide the necessary documents pursuant to section 28o SGB IV. The employer must further pay the joint social insurance contribution pursuant to sections 28 d to 28 i SGB IV, to the health insurance fund as the collecting agency (see section below) and maintain and preserve proof of payment of the contributions. Accordingly, pursuant to section 28o SGB IV, the employees must assist in the payment of contributions by providing information and documents. An employee's essential duty is to present his or her social insurance ID card at the onset of the employment, pursuant to section 18 h SGB IV. If the employee fails to do so upon request, the employer will, under certain circumstances, have the right to render a notice of dismissal. The ID card is issued by the competent pension insurance carrier for each employee. It serves to combat abuse of services and illegal employment. Thus, in certain sectors particularly liable to engage in illegal employment, such as the construction industry, employees should actually keep their ID card on their person at all times when they are at work.

1. Total Social Insurance Contribution

The employees and the employer each pay half of the contributions to social insurance pursuant to sections 346 et seq. SGB III, sections 249 et seq. SGB V and sections 157 et seq. SGB VI. The amount of these joint contributions depends upon the gross income of the individual employee, unlike accident insurance, which is financed by the employer alone. Presently, the joint social insurance contribution amounts to around 40% of the gross salary, i. e. about 20% for the employee and the employer, respectively.

Pursuant to sections 28 e and 28h SGB IV, the employer is responsible for paying the contributions into the **competent health insurance fund as the collecting agency.** The contributions to the individual social insurance branches are consolidated into a single contribution. The employer is also responsible for ascertaining whether an employment relationship is subject to compulsory social insurance and correctly calculating the required contributions. In case of doubt, it must obtain a binding confirmation from the collecting agency, pursuant to section 28h (2) SGB IV.

The employer is the sole debtor to the social insurance for the contributions to be made pursuant to sections 28d, 28e SGB IV, section 253 SGB V and section 174 (1) SGB VI. It may only claim half of these contributions from the employees by deducting it from their remuneration, pursuant to section 28g SGB IV. This is generally done in the month of payment with the monthly salary remittance. As a rule, if the employer fails to perform these deductions, it can only make up for it in the next three salary payment periods. The amount which may be deducted in one month is limited. After that, the employer can only do so if it was not at fault in failing to deduct the contributions. However, because even slight negligence constitutes fault, in most cases such failure is the employer's fault. The only exception would be if the employer has obtained a binding confirmation from the collection agency and in fact relied upon it. Accordingly, if the contributions the employer pays in are too low over a long period of time, it will be obligated to pay the difference in full, and thereby also the outstanding employee's share beyond the amount which may be deducted over the course of the next three salary payment periods. If the employee has already left the company, the employer can generally, with a very few narrowly defined exceptions, no longer claim the employee's share of the contributions, even for the last three months, as it is no longer possible to deduct it from his or her remuneration. Deduction from remuneration is the only legal way the employer can obtain the employee's share of the social insurance contributions. On the other hand, the employer's duty to offset shortfalls in the contributions lasts at least four years, because under section 25 SGB IV, the statute of limitations for claims for contributions is four years after the end of the calendar year in which they fell due. If the contributions were intentionally not paid in, the statute of limitations is 30 years.

These provisions represent a serious financial risk for the employer, especially in the case of pseudo-independence (see pages 83 et seq.). Any agreements made in derogation of these provisions to the detriment of the employee are null and void, pursuant to section 32 SGB I.

If the employer is a corporation, claims may be asserted not only against the company itself, but also against the members of its governing bodies personally, including, for example, the managing director of a GmbH. Under section 266a (1) of the German Criminal Code (*Strafgesetzbuch – StGB*), the intentional withholding of social insurance contributions is a criminal offense. If the managing director is responsible for the violation, he or she will also be liable for compensatory damages claims under general tort law, section 823 (2) BGB.

2. Freelance Workers and Self-Employed Personnel

In contrast to employees, self-employed service providers or contractors or freelance employees are not personally dependent in their activity. Thus, they do not enjoy the protection of employment and labor law and are not subject to compulsory social insurance regulations. They can conclude agreements to provide services on the basis of freedom of contract and the general rules of civil law. Whether an employment relationship or freelance work is involved, however, is dependent upon the circumstances of the individual case. The decisive factor is the content of the contract and its practical execution. If they conflict with each other, the decisive factor is how the contract is put into practice. Under the general rules of employment and labor law and pursuant to the special standard in social insurance law as set forth in section 7 (1) sentence 2 SGB IV, the points of reference for a dependent employment relationship are both "work according to directives" and "integration into the work organization of the issuer of the directives".

The main criterion is the employee's **dependence on directives** regarding the place, time and specifics of the work performed. One indication of personal dependency, and thus employee status, is therefore detailed instructions as to where the work is to be done, the manner in which it is to be performed, when work is to begin each day, when breaks can be taken and the end of the working day. Freelancers are free to choose whether, where, when and how they will carry out the work they were hired to do. The object of a freelancer's contract must therefore be described so precisely that directives are dispensable to the greatest possible extent. Detailed instructions on the manner in which the duties are to be discharged can trigger subjection to compulsory insurance. The principal cannot dictate every single step of the execution of the order. However, the principal can convey its own quality requirements, or those of the end-customer, and set technical standards that must be observed. Instructions on working time are an indication of personal dependency, and thus employee status. A contractor must have the ability to influence the timing of the performance of the work, for example by informing the principal each week which days of the following week or week after that he or she would be available to work. It is also possible to set commencement or completion dates for the performance of the work in contracts with self-employed persons.

Contractors are **not integrated into the operation** of the principal if they performs their services separately from the principal's organization. While an employee performs his or her work on the employer's premises with its materials and equipment, a self-employed person generally works in his or her own facilities. If this is impossible due to the nature of the service to be provided, a self-employed person will not be integrated into the principal's organization of work if he or she is not given a specific workplace of his or her own, such as an office. Generally, self-employed persons are not entered into the company's internal telephone or mailing lists. If this is unavoidable, it should be indicated that such persons are self-employed, for example by highlighting their names and set them apart from those of the employees, i.e. by designating them as "external consultants". Freelancers generally work with their own materials and equipment. Contractors are not obligated to document their working time in a system internal to the company, at most they might record their working time according to their own system for the purpose of billing by the hour. Employees must generally perform their own work personally and are often restricted in their ability to enter into secondary employment. Thus, other indications of self-employment are if a contractor can assign third parties to perform the contract and take on any other employment without restriction. A further characteristic of self-employment is that a contractor is free to choose whether or not to accept individual orders.

It has recently become possible under section 7a SGB IV for the parties involved to file an application with the German Pension Insurance Federal Institution (*Deutsche Rentenversichtung Bund*) for an official declaration of the status of the person engaged.

3. Pseudo-Independence

Pseudo-independence (*Scheinselbständigkeit*) occurs if, according to the criteria established by employment and labor and/or social security law, a contractual relationship is not a true freelance relationship, but actually an employment relationship. In order to prevent a circumvention of employees' protections against termination and claims to social insurance, **a pseudo-independent person will be legally deemed to be an employee** under the employment and labor and social security laws as of the date on which the pseudo-independence was ascertained. If the remuneration was at a higher level when the employee was treated as a freelancer, it may be reduced to the normal rate for employees. However, the employee may also need to be added to the company pension plan. In particular, if certain criteria are met, as an employee he or she will enjoy protection against unfair dismissal, vacation claims, claims to continuation of remuneration in case of illness, etc. Pseudo-independence can also lead to **serious financial burdens for the company** retroactively. The employer will then need to pay the social insurance contributions for the current year as well as the past four years pursuant to section 25

SGB IV. This retroactive payment comprises both the employer's and the employee's contributions if a deduction from the employee's remuneration cannot be performed pursuant to section 28g SGB IV out of the next three remuneration payments (see pages 81 et seq.). Moreover, the tax authority may compel the employer to make up for unpaid withholding taxes and wrongfully deducted value added taxes (input tax) incurred within the typical four-year statute of limitations. The employee may also need to pay a higher amount of value added tax retroactively.

III. Termination of Employment Relationships

The termination of employment relationships can also have consequences under the social insurance laws, which must be taken into account before carrying out a dismissal or concluding a termination agreement.

1. Disqualification Periods and Suspension Periods for the Employee

Particularly when concluding a termination agreement, whether or not the employer has previously given notice, employees must bear in mind that their claim to unemployment benefits may be suspended or disqualified under certain circumstances.

Pursuant to section 143 SGB III, a claim to unemployment benefits is suspended during the period in which the unemployed person is still receiving, or has a claim for, remuneration. The same applies to the period for which the unemployed person receives, or has a claim to, payments discharging outstanding vacation claims resulting from the termination of the employment relationship. In practice, the suspension of the claim for benefits is particularly important in cases of hidden remuneration for work performed and subsequent remuneration payments as severance pay.

Further, under section 143a SGB III, a claim to unemployment benefits will also be suspended if the unemployed person is receiving, or has a claim to, severance pay due to the termination of the employment relationship and the employment relationship is terminated without adherence to the proper notice period. It will be assumed that at least part of the severance payment consists of remuneration for the period between the actual termination date and that stipulated by law. The claim for unemployment benefits will generally be suspended in accordance with the reduction of the notice period. Generally, if a suspension of the claim for unemployment benefits is prescribed by statute, the right to benefits must be postponed for the duration of the suspension period.

There are also circumstances leading to a disqualification of the claim for unemployment benefits, which reduces such claims. The most important circumstance leading to a disqualification of a claim is set forth in section 144 SGB III, under which the claim is generally disqualified for a maximum of 12 weeks if an employee **voluntarily gives up his or her job by resigning or concluding a termination agreement.** Generally no disqualification will occur if the termination agreement was preceded by a notice of a (valid) dismissal by the employer and the agreement merely serves to execute the termination of the employment relationship by mutual agreement, in particular to provide for severance pay. However, the employer must not give notice in the termination agreement with the employee, as, pursuant to current case law, this would generally also trigger a disqualification period.

2. Severance Pay

Severance pay which is paid after the termination of the employment relationship for the **loss of the vested rights in social status** (*sozialer Besitzstand*) resulting from a dismissal by the employer or a termination agreement, does not constitute remuneration subject to social insurance contributions, but is exempt from such contributions, or at most contributions are reduced to the wage withholding tax incurred (see section below). This does not apply if some or all of the severance pay is rendered for work performed in the past, vacation days not taken, etc., in a terminated employment relationship (pseudo-severance). In that case, the unemployment benefits could be subjected to suspension periods under the social insurance laws (see section above).

F. Tax Laws

Experts agree that the German tax code is extremely complex and difficult to navigate. From the point of view of employment and labor law, the relevant regulations are those governing income tax, in particular withholding tax, i.e. the tax laws for earned income from a employment relationship.

I. Withholding Tax on Wages

In general, employees must pay taxes on work remuneration paid by a German employer save in exceptional cases where the employer enjoys tax-exempt status. Employees must pay withholding tax, a special "solidarity surcharge" to finance the unification of the two German states, and church tax if they belong to an authorized church. Although the employee is the taxpayer pursuant to sections 38 et seq. of the German Income Tax Act (*Einkommenssteuergesetz – EStG*), the employer **must calculate the employees' taxes, deduct them from their gross remuneration and send them to the competent tax authority** (withholding tax deduction procedure – *Lohnsteuerabzugsverfahren*). To this extent, the employer is liable toward the tax authority, pursuant to section 42 d EStG for the employees' payment of their tax debt if it fails to properly withhold and forward the withholding tax. The employer must document the remuneration and payment of the withholding tax, as well as payment of the social security contributions (certificate of withholding tax deduction). To this end, employees subject to the income tax without modifications (the overwhelming majority of employees), must submit to the employer a wage tax deduction card at the commencement of the employment relationship. This card, which will be replaced by an electronic procedure as of the year 2012, is a public document that is issued by the municipality or the competent tax authority at the employees' place of residence; the employer must use its entries to calculate and pay out the withholding tax, even if they are obviously incorrect. At the end of the calendar year or the employment relationship, the card will be returned to the employees, who can then assert a claim against the tax authority by way of an annual wage tax adjustment (*Lohnsteuerjahresausgleich*), i.e., assert a claim for a tax refund by filling out their employee income tax returns and declaring various deductions, such as employment-related expenses. The employer may also be obligated to execute an annual wage tax adjustment if, due to fluctuations in wages or alterations to the entries on the wage tax card, an employee has paid an excessive amount of withholding tax given his or her annual income. Here too, the tax authority can hold the employer for an inaccurate income tax return under section 42 d EStG.

To oversimplify somewhat, the key factor in calculating the withholding tax is the amount of earned income, because the withholding tax in Germany increases on a progressive scale with the income (see page 8). However, it also depends on other important factors such as marital status, number of dependent children and religious affiliation. The calculation is then made by assigning the employee to a certain withholding tax class (Classes I–VI), which is also entered on the wage tax deduction card.

At the end of each period in which the employer is to file a self-assessment wage tax return (*Lohnsteueranmeldung*), generally every calendar month, it must file such a return for each establishment with the respective tax authority pursuant to the withholding tax laws declaring the withholding tax to be retained and to be assumed during the period involved. This return must be made by electronic data transmission. In order to monitor the collection of the wage withholding tax, the tax authority competent for the establishment may perform a field audit of the employer at its own discretion.

If the tax authority asserts a claim against an employer based on the employer's liability for an employee's tax debt, the employer is generally entitled to recourse against the employee. However, this right may be abrogated in individual cases by exclusionary periods set forth in the collective bargaining agreements, or by the employer's incorrect calculation of the withholding tax in breach of its duties. Since the employer is obligated to calculate the withholding tax correctly due to its duty of general care toward the employee under the employment and labor laws, a wrongful calculation in breach of duty can also result in damages claims for the employee against the employer.

Special regulations pertain to part-time and temporary employees, which in particular allow for a lump sum payment of the withholding tax. Where a lump sum is declared, the employer is the taxpayer if it takes over the withholding tax.

II. Special Issues

The following special forms of remuneration or extraordinary payments and the special tax treatment thereof are important in practice:

1. Company Car

If an employer provides an employee with a company car that can be used privately (i.e. not only for company purposes), this permission to use the car for private purposes constitutes a **benefit of monetary value,** which the employee must declare as income. This applies even if the permission to use the car is not granted on the basis of an explicit agreement, but rather on a de facto basis, but in any case with the employer's consent. There are two ways to calculate the taxable amount of such benefits: by itemization in a logbook or by making a lump sum payment on the use. In practice, the latter method is primarily employed, in which the use benefit is posted each month as 1% of the gross list price rounded down to the nearest hundred, plus 0.03% of the list price per kilometer for travel between the residence and the workplace. Where the employee bears part of the private-use costs him or herself on the basis of an agreement with the employer, i.e. makes additional payments, the lump sum use benefit will be reduced accordingly. Since the provision of a company car is an ongoing benefit of monetary value, it is subject to the withholding tax procedure (see page 85 et seq.).

II. Special Issues

2. Stock Options

Stock options (see pages 24 et seq.) that employees receive in the employment relationship as compensation for their work and, perhaps, as a reward for their loyalty to the company, are deemed to constitute earned income under the tax laws and are therefore taxable.

Taxation of remuneration is based on the "stream of income" principle (*Lohnzuflussprinzip*) pursuant to section 11 (1) sentence 1 EStG. That is, the remuneration is generally taxed at the time at which it actually flows to an employee. Accordingly, it does not matter when the employee's claim to the wages arose; it is assessed to him or her only when the payment is actually received.

Thus, in Germany, unlike in many other countries, the resulting financial benefit arising from the granting of **stock options will not be taxed until the employee actually exercises the option.** As a rule, the difference between the current market value of the shares and the strike price is deemed to constitute profit, i.e. a benefit of monetary value, and thus taxable wages. On the other hand, the benefit from stock options is often not subject to withholding tax. This particularly applies to the granting of stock options by a third party, as is often the practice, often by a company affiliated with the employer in the same group.

The taxable benefit of equivalent monetary value that generally flows to the employee upon exercise of the stock options is subject to a withholding tax procedure (see page 85), both if the employer had granted the options itself and if a third party granted the employee the stock options and the employer knows about this or must know about it (section 38 (1) and (4) EStG), as often happens in corporate groups. As this issue has not yet been conclusively resolved in every aspect, it is recommended that the employer withhold the tax if the options are granted by an affiliated company.

From the point of view of the social security laws, the granting of stock options also constitutes remuneration for work upon which contributions must be paid. Typically, they are provided as one-time payments and not regularly recurring remuneration for work. In contrast to tax law, under the laws governing social security contributions, the actual receipt of the money is of no consequence for assessment purposes. Accordingly, stock options must be appraised at the time they are granted and the corresponding contributions must be paid by the employer, including the employee's share. Hence, neither a subsequent gain in the share's market price before the option is exercised nor even the exercising of the option itself are relevant. However, at present the umbrella organizations of the social security carriers hold the dissident view that stock option benefits should generally only be taken into account when they are exercised. If the employment relationship has already ended by the time of the exercise, the benefit should be allocated to the last accounting period in the then-current calendar year. If the employment relationship ended in the previous year, the benefit will only be subject to contributions after being exercised if the option was exercised by 31 March of the then-current year.

3. Severance Payment

Up to 2006, severance payments made by the employer to an employee as a result of a dissolution of the employment relationship at the employer's instigation or by order of a court had been **tax-exempt** up to the amount of EUR 8,181 pursuant to section 3 no. 9 EStG. However, this tax exemption has since been repealed, and currently severance payments may merely be tax-privileged pursuant to section 24 no. 1a, section 34 EStG.

G. Labor Court Proceedings

I. Courts

The courts for labor matters are organized into three levels. The court of first instance is the labor court (*Arbeitsgericht*), which has exclusive subject matter jurisdiction over all disputes arising from an employment relationship, regardless of the value of the matter in dispute. Appeals are heard in the regional labor courts (*Landesarbeitsgerichte*). In order for an appeal to be admitted, the value of the matter in dispute must generally exceed EUR 600. In the third instance, the Federal Labor Court (*Bundesarbeitsgericht*) can, upon special petition, rule on appeals of the final decisions of the regional labor courts. The Federal Labor Court serves as the final court of appeal.

The labor courts are composed of both **professional and lay judges**. The tribunals of the labor court and the regional labor courts each comprise one professional judge and two lay judges. The lay judges are nominated by the trade unions and employers' associations in the respective judicial district. The lay judges have the same rights and powers as the professional judges, but as a rule, the latter play the leading role in the proceedings.

II. Protection Against Dismissal Proceedings

1. Out-of-Court Negotiations

Once a dismissal notice has been issued, out-of-court negotiations tend not to be successful. For one thing, there is considerable time pressure, because the employee must file a complaint against the dismissal within three weeks of notification. Frequently, any attempt by the employer to settle out of court will be perceived as a sign of having a weak case. With a few exceptions, such as in the case of senior employees, it is therefore advisable to wait for the conciliation hearings (*Güteverhandlung*) to seek an amicable settlement.

2. Three-Week Period for Filing Complaints

Once a dismissal has been issued, an employee who wishes to invoke protection against dismissal must **file a complaint with the labor court within three weeks** of receiving the dismissal notice. According to the language of the statute, the employee must petition the labor court to find that the employment relationship has not been dissolved legally by the termination.

If the three-week period set forth in section 4 KSchG is not observed, the complaint can only be admitted retroactively upon petition if, despite exercising all reasonable efforts under the circumstances, an employee was hindered from filing a complaint within this period (section 5 KSchG).

3. Course of Dismissal Proceedings and Tactical Considerations

Dismissal proceedings are initiated with the **conciliation hearing**. This is mandated by law. This hearing is not held before the full panel of judges in the chamber, but only before the presiding judge.

The parties are not obligated to prepare for the conciliation hearing with written briefs. However, even if the statutes do not compel it, one should examine in each individual case whether and to what extent preparations for the conciliation hearing should be made. The more substantial the basis for the dismissal, the more sense it makes to present these grounds in writing so that the presiding judge can familiarize him or herself with the arguments before the hearing even starts. It may be necessary for tactical reasons to submit the brief relatively late, even moments before the hearing, so the other side will not have a chance to respond in writing.

The court can order one or both of the **parties to appear personally** pursuant to section 51 (1) in connection with section 141 (2) and (3) of the German Code of Civil Procedure (*Zivilprozessordnung – ZPO*). If the summoned party fails to appear, an administrative fine may be imposed. Moreover, the presiding judge can refuse an appearance by legal counsel if the client has failed to appear without just cause, despite a court order, and thus the purpose of the order was frustrated. There is then a danger that the refusal will mean that the party is deemed to be in default, and a default judgment will be entered.

The primary goal of the conciliation hearing is to come to an **amicable settlement**. Both parties should make careful preparations for the conclusion of a settlement in a conciliation hearing in order to prevent a situation in which false declarations are rendered at the termination of the employment relationship, thereby disadvantaging one of the parties. This can particularly occur if existing claims are overlooked and then excluded by the adoption of a general discharge clause.

If the conciliation hearing is unsuccessful, it will be followed by another hearing. In practice, this generally means that a new court date will be scheduled and legal briefs will have to be submitted in preparation of the hearing.

4. Judicial Dissolution of Employment Relationships and Severance Pay

If the parties are unable to come to a mutual agreement in the conciliation hearings, they should not overlook the possibility that **the court will dissolve the employment relationship under certain circumstances**. This can occur in cases where, although the dismissal was socially unacceptable and is therefore invalid, neither party can reasonably be expected to continue to work together with the other (sections 9 and 10 KSchG).

A judicial dissolution of the employment relationship in exchange for a severance payment can only be considered in the case of a socially unwarranted dismissal and requires that one of the parties to the dismissal protection procedure file a petition before the oral hearings in the appellate court come to an end. The Federal Labor Court has ruled that a petition pursuant to section 9 KSchG can be filed only if the employee bases his or her claim that the dismissal is invalid on the lack of social justification.

If the court grants the petition for dissolution, it must set the date of the dissolution of the employment relationship. Pursuant to section 9 (2) KSchG, the employment relationship must be dissolved as of the date on which it would have ended had the dismissal been socially justified.

The court will only dissolve the employment relationship pursuant to section 9 KSchG if, at the same time, it orders the employer to offer reasonable severance pay. The court is bound to the limitations set forth in section 10 KSchG. The maximum limits provided in section 10 KSchG are linked to the concept of monthly earnings, which, pursuant to the prevailing opinion, are defined as the gross monthly remuneration. Remuneration that is paid for work over a longer period of time, such as one year (13th or 14th monthly salary) must be evenly spread over the individual months. On the other hand, sums that are only paid on special occasions, (anniversary bonuses) are not to be counted. The maximum limit set is the sum of up to 12 months' earnings. If the employee has reached the age of 50 and the employment relationship has lasted 15 years, the maximum limit is 15 months' earnings. If the employee has reached the age of 55 and the employment relationship has lasted 20 years, the maximum limit is 18 months' earnings.

Factors to be taken into account in calculating the amount of the severance pay include the length of the employment relationship, the employee's age, marital status, number of dependents, etc.

5. Remuneration Claims and Default in Acceptance

Employees are obligated to **work up to the expiration of the notice period**. Accordingly, they generally also have a claim to wages for this period. If the employer no longer assigns an employee to work after giving notice, i.e. grants paid leave of absence (*Freistellung*), the employer will generally find itself in default of acceptance pursuant to section 615 BGB. This means that it will still need to pay the remuneration up to the expiration of the notice period.

If the employee has meanwhile earned income elsewhere, he or she must allow these earnings to be set off against the remuneration claims (section 615 sentence 2 BGB).

After the notice period has expired, if the dismissal was invalid, the employer will be in default of acceptance if it did not call upon the employee to resume his or her work. Filing a complaint for protection against the dismissal constitutes an offer to work on the employee's part.

6. Right to Employment

During the course of the notice period, the employee not only has a claim to continuation of remuneration, but also to actually be assigned to work. The employer is only entitled to release employees from their duties if and to the extent that it can demonstrate a legitimate compelling interest in doing so. Once the notice period has expired, the employees will have a claim to continued employment pursuant to section 102 BetrVG if:
– an ordinary dismissal has been issued,
– the works council has objected in due time and in the proper manner
– and the employee has filed a claim for protection against the dismissal.

This duty to employ the employee will survive until the complaint has been finally dismissed. It is left to the **employee's discretion whether or not to assert his or her claim** to continued employment pursuant to section 102 (5) BetrVG. Even if the employee does not assert the claim, the employer will still be in **default of acceptance**.

The employer can petition to be released from the duty to continue to employ the employee with the help of a temporary injunction in the judicial proceedings pursuant to section 102 (5) BetrVG. The statute contains a conclusive list of the circumstances under which a claim for such a release exists.

Finally, once the notice period has expired, an employee also has what is termed a "general social claim to continued employment" if he or she obtains a finding from the lower court that the dismissal was invalid. If he or she is unsuccessful in the first instance, but then successful on the appellate level, the claim for continued employment will only commence with the entering of appellate judgment. If he or she is successful in the first instance, but not on the appellate level, on the other hand, the claim for continued employment will end with the entering of the appellate judgment.

H. Managing Directors, Management Board Members

I. Managing Directors of Limited Liability Companies

A limited liability company (*Gesellschaft mit beschränkter Haftung – GmbH*) must have one or more managing directors (*Geschäftsführer*) who are responsible for managing the affairs of the company and representing it vis-à-vis third parties.

The most important aspects are the appointment and removal of managing directors, their service contracts (*Dienstverträge*) and their powers, duties and responsibilities under the Limited Liability Companies Act (*GmbH-Gesetz – GmbHG*). One must bear in mind, however, that the GmbHG gives the shareholders extensive powers to diverge from the provisions of this Act (section 45 GmbHG), so the managing directors' position can be tailored to meet the needs of each individual case. This freedom is restricted in the case of companies falling within one of the Codetermination Acts, such as those having more than 500 employees (one-third employees' representation on the supervisory board under section 1 (1) no. 3 One-Third Participation Act (*DrittelbG*)), or more than 2,000 employees (one-half employees' representation on the supervisory board under the Codetermination Act (*MitbestG*)). Such companies will not be discussed in this section (see pages 71 et seq.).

1. Appointment of Managing Directors

The managing directors constitute the executive body of a GmbH. Managing directors are vested with executive powers as of their appointment. Their appointment to the position is distinct from their employment under their service contracts, which regulate their personal relations with the company.

The GmbHG provides that the managing directors are to be appointed by the shareholders' meeting by a simple majority of the votes cast (sections 46 (5) and 47 (1) GmbHG). The articles of association may specify a different majority or delegate the appointment of managing directors to one particular shareholder, a group of shareholders, or a specific body within the company (e.g. the supervisory board).

Only natural persons not subject to any restriction on their capacity to transact business may be appointed managing directors (section 6 (2) sentence 1 GmbHG). They do not need to have German citizenship or be resident in Germany. But there are specific restrictions relating to previous convictions for criminal offenses.

The articles of association can lay down further requirements in connection with the appointment of managing directors; they may provide, for example, that only shareholders of the GmbH may become managing directors.

The names of the managing directors and their powers of representation must be entered in the Commercial Register (*Handelsregister*) pursuant to section 10 GmbHG.

2. Removal of Managing Directors

The shareholders' meeting can remove managing directors from office at any time by a simple majority of votes cast, whereby no compelling reason for their removal is necessary (sections 38, 46 no. 5 and 47 (1) GmbHG). As a rule, the service contract remains unaffected by the removal from office. The articles of association can make the removal of managing directors dependent on other criteria (removal only for cause, stricter majority requirements), or allocate this function to another body (in particular a supervisory board), but may not exclude the right to remove a managing director for cause.

A managing director can resign from his or her office at any time. A resignation without notice is only invalid if it constitutes an abuse of rights. Again, it should be noted that a managing director's service contract does not automatically end upon his or her resignation. If a managing director resigns from office without notice and without cause for doing so, he or she may be liable for damages to the company under the service contract. A managing director may not remain in office if he or she can no longer fulfill the requirements for his or her appointment under the law or the articles of association.

The expiration date of the managing directors' terms must be entered in the Commercial Register (section 39 GmbHG). Although registration is not a prerequisite for validity, uninformed third parties may rely on the persons registered still being managing directors until such time as the expiration of their appointment is entered in the Commercial Register.

3. Service Contract

The relationship between a managing director and the GmbH is determined by the service contract between them, usually – but not necessarily – in writing. For the purpose of negotiating and concluding the managing director's contract, the company is normally represented by the body entrusted with the appointment of the managing directors. The managing director's contract covers matters such as salary, vacation entitlement, continued payment of salary in case of illness, old-age pension and surviving dependents' pension, as well as other matters which concern the managing director as a person performing services for the company. Employee protection rules in German labor law only apply to a limited extent to GmbH managing directors. In particular, the Protection Against Unfair Dismissal Act (see pages 37 et seq.), the Federal Vacation Act (see pages 28 et seq.) and the Employee Inventions Act (see page 32) do not apply. However, the ECJ recently ruled that board members bound by instructions are 'workers' under the Pregnant Workers Directive (92/85/EEC) which argues for the fact that the regulations governing maternity protection (see pages 29 et seq.) will also apply to female managing directors, restricting the GmbH's right of termination. This does not, however, result in the application of other employee protection laws to managing directors.

4. Duties and Responsibilities of the Managing Directors

a) Managing the Business of the Company

The managing directors are responsible for managing the business of the company, which includes taking the decisions necessary for the pursuit of the company's purpose, in particular with regard to the organization of the company, business plans and objectives, the control and supervision of all the affairs of the company, the day-to-day business and the legal conduct of the company vis-à-vis third parties. The management of the company also includes its representation in and out of court (section 35 GmbHG). As a rule, transactions entered into by managing directors in the name of the company empower and obligate the company itself and only the company (section 36 GmbHG).

Unless the articles of association provide otherwise, declarations in the name of the GmbH can only be made by all the managing directors jointly (collective representation). However, frequently one or more of the managing directors is granted

I. Managing Directors of Limited Liability Companies

power of sole representation, or, if a GmbH has several managing directors, the articles of association can provide that the company may be represented by two of them jointly or by one managing director jointly with a procuration officer (*Prokurist*), who holds full commercial powers of attorney). The managing directors have an obligation to the company to observe restrictions on the scope of their powers of representation that are imposed by law, the articles of association or individual shareholder resolutions (section 37 GmbHG). The articles of association, or the internal rules of procedure for the management, if any have been drawn up, frequently contain a list of measures (usually important ones) that require the prior consent of the shareholders.

Unlike the board of directors of a stock corporation (*Aktiengesellschaft*), GmbH managing directors are bound by shareholders' resolutions, in which they can be instructed to take or refrain from taking certain measures. The managing directors' powers of representation cannot, however, be restricted. If restrictions are imposed upon their power of management in the articles of association or by a shareholders' resolution, these restrictions will have no effect vis-à-vis third parties; if they act ultra vires, their conduct can, at worst, only result in claims for damages by the company against the managing directors and justify their removal for cause.

b) Diligence

The managing directors must exercise the diligence of a prudent businessman in the conduct of the company's affairs. They have a paramount duty of loyalty to the company. For example, each managing director must cooperate in a spirit of good faith with the other managing directors, the shareholders and the other bodies of the GmbH, keep themselves informed about all material affairs of the company, maintain silence on all confidential information and secrets of the company, conscientiously supervise and direct subordinate bodies and employees, and be led by the common good of the company and not their own benefit in all matters which affect the company's interests. A managing director who violates his or her obligations towards the company may be liable for damages (section 43 GmbHG). Likewise, the business judgment rule set forth in section 93 (1) sentence 2 AktG also applies to GmbH managing directors, even though there is no corresponding provision in the laws governing GmbHs. According to this rule, no breach of duty occurs if a managing director had good reason to assume that in taking an entrepreneurial decision he or she was acting on the basis of adequate information for the benefit of the company.

c) Organizational Duties

The managing directors are responsible for the convening of the shareholders' meetings (section 49 GmbHG). The ordinary shareholders' meeting is particularly responsible for resolving on the approval of the annual financial statement and the appropriation of results (section 46 (1) GmbHG). Since the shareholders have to adopt such resolutions by the end of the first eight months of the fiscal year at the latest or, in the case of small companies as defined in section 267 (1) of the German Commercial Code (*Handelsgesetzbuch – HGB*), within the first eleven months of the financial year (section 42a (2) GmbHG), the shareholders meeting has to be convened within this period each year. If the financial statement has to be audited, the auditor must be chosen by the shareholders' meeting. The shareholders' meeting also adopts resolutions on the discharge of the managing directors from liability (*Entlastung*) and, where applicable, their re-appointment, as well as on the appointment of procuration officers and agents empowered to bind the company in all aspects of its business (*Handlungsbevollmächtigte*). In discharging the managing directors from liability the shareholders are formally approving the former's management of the company. Thus, once a GmbH has discharged its managing directors, it cannot assert any claims which were already discernible on the basis of the information made available for the purpose of the discharge.

d) Duty to inform Shareholders

The managing directors must provide each shareholder, upon request, with information about the company's affairs and grant access to the accounts and records unless there is a risk that the shareholder would use the information for purposes unrelated to the company, and thereby cause considerable damage to the company (section 51 a GmbHG).

e) Accounting

The managing directors are obligated to ensure that the company keeps proper accounts and to prepare the annual financial statement (*Jahresabschluß*) pursuant to section 41 (1) GmbHG and section 264 (1) HGB. The managing directors have to convene a shareholders' meeting if the annual financial statement or a balance sheet drawn up in the course of the financial year shows that half of the share capital has been lost (section 49 (3) GmbHG). If they fail to do so, they will be liable for damages (section 43 (2) GmbHG) and render themselves liable to prosecution (section 84 (1) no. 1 GmbHG).

f) Insolvency

If the company becomes illiquid, the managing directors must, without undue delay, but no later than three weeks after the illiquidity occurs, petition for the opening of insolvency proceedings or court composition proceedings. This applies analogously if the company is overindebted (section 15 a (1) German Insolvency Statute (*Insolvenzordnung – InsO*)). The managing directors are liable towards the company for compensation for any payments made after the company became insolvent or was found to be overindebted unless these were consistent with the diligence of a prudent businessman (section 64 sentences 1 and 2 GmbHG). The same obligation is imposed on the managing directors for payments to shareholders that were bound to lead to the company's insolvency (section 64 sentence 3 GmbHG).

g) Raising and Maintenance of Capital

The managing directors are also responsible for the due and proper raising and maintenance of capital:

The application for entry of the company into the Commercial Register, which is the responsibility of the managing directors, may not be submitted until one quarter of each original **capital contribution** has been paid in – except in the case of contributions in kind, which have to be made in full prior to registration. The amount of share capital paid in must be at least enough to ensure that the total of all paid in cash contributions, plus the full amount of contributions in kind equals at least EUR 12,500 (section 7 GmbHG). If false statements are made for the purpose of setting up the company, not only the shareholders, but also the managing directors will be liable for payment of any outstanding contributions and obligated to reimburse the company for any payment not provided for as part of the formation costs and to indemnify the company for any other damages sustained if they were, or should have been, aware of the facts which triggered the obligation for compensation (section 9 a GmbHG). The same applies in the case of capital increases.

The assets of the company required in order to maintain the share capital may not be distributed to the shareholders (section 30 GmbHG). If, contrary to the capital maintenance provisions, payments are made from the assets required to maintain the capital, the managing directors will be liable for damages (section 43 (3) GmbHG).

As of November 2008, it is also possible to form an "entrepreneur limited liability company" (*Unternehmergesellschaft*), known colloquially as a "**mini-GmbH**", in which – in contrast to a GmbH – share capital of one euro is sufficient. The share capital must be paid in immediately and in full as a cash contribution (section 5a (2) GmbHG). Both GmbHs and entrepreneur limited liability companies can be formed more quickly and at a lower cost if the model protocol provided in the Annex to the GmbHG is used. In this case, the company may not have more than three shareholders and one managing director. Otherwise, an individual shareholders agreement will have to be concluded.

h) Fiscal Obligations

The managing directors must fulfill the GmbH's fiscal obligations pursuant to section 34 of the General Tax Code (*Abgabenordnung – AO*). If they fail to do so, they will be liable; if their failure to fulfill the obligations is due to intent or gross negligence, they will be directly liable toward the tax authorities (section 69 AO). This may also constitute a criminal offense (sections 380, 370 AO).

i) Social Security Obligations

The managing directors are responsible for ensuring that the social security contributions payable by the GmbH are paid punctually and in full to the respective collecting agency. If they fail to do so, they may be liable for damages under section 823 (2) BGB and may render themselves liable to prosecution under section 266a (1) to (3) German Criminal Code (*Strafgesetzbuch – StGB*).

II. Management Board Members of Stock Corporations

The rules for the GmbH's managing director also apply to a great extent to AG management board members (*Vorstände*). However, there are some significant differences:

1. Appointment of Management Board Members

The AG management board members are appointed by the supervisory board by a simple majority of votes cast pursuant to section 84 (1) sentence 1 of the Stock Corporation Act (*Aktiengesetz – AktG*). The restrictions regarding personal prerequisites for being a managing director of a GmbH (see page 91) also apply to management board members of an AG (section 76 (3) AktG).

2. Removal of Management Board Members

Unlike GmbH managing directors, an AG management board member can only be removed from office for cause. Such cause includes in particular a gross breach of duty, inability to manage the company properly, or a vote of no-confidence by the shareholders' meeting, unless such vote of no-confidence was passed for manifestly arbitrary reasons (section 84 (3) sentence 2 AktG).

3. Service Contract

Like the relationship between the managing director and the GmbH, that between the management board member and the AG is governed by a service contract (section 84 (3) sentence 5 AktG). The remuneration must bear a reasonable relationship to the duties of the management board members and the condition of the company and may not exceed the customary remuneration without special grounds for doing so (section 87 (1) sentence 1 AktG). At listed companies, the remuneration must be geared towards sustainable company development (section 87 (1) sentence 2 AktG). Variable remuneration components should therefore be based on a multi-year assessment; in the event of extraordinary developments, the supervisory board should agree on a compensation cap (section 87 (1) sentence 3 AktG). Employee protection regulations in German employment law do not apply to a member of an AG management board

4. Duties and Responsibilities of the Management Board Members

The following differences from and similarities to the duties and responsibilities of a GmbH managing director (see pages 92 et seq.) are worthy of note:

a) Not bound by Directives

The AG management board manages the company under its own responsibility. It is not bound by directives issued by the supervisory board. However, if there is a dependency/control agreement between the AG and a controlling enterprise, the controlling enterprise is entitled to issue instructions to the management board of the AG regarding the management of the company (section 308 (1) AktG). Unless the contract stipulates otherwise, the controlling enterprise may also issue instructions to the detriment of the controlled AG if they are to the benefit of the controlling enterprise or other affiliates (section 308 (1) sentence 2 AktG). In that case, the management board members will be obligated to comply with such instructions pursuant to section 308 (2) sentence 1 AktG. However, the managements of the controlling enterprise and the controlling enterprise themselves may be liable if they do not act with the diligence of prudent businessmen. In any case, the shareholders' meeting can decide on matters concerning the management of the company only if requested to do so by the management board (section 119 (2) AktG).

b) Diligence

The management board must exercise the same diligence as a GmbH managing director or be liable for damages (section 93 AktG); in particular the business judgment rule set forth in section 93 (1) sentence 2 AktG applies. However, unlike a GmbH, an AG may not waive liability claims against its management board members until three years have elapsed since the claim has arisen, provided that the shareholders' meeting consents thereto and no minority whose aggregate holding amounts to at least one-tenth of the share capital records an objection in the minutes. This time restriction will not apply if a management board member is insolvent or is threatened with insolvency.

c) Organization Duties

Like a GmbH managing director, an AG management board member must convene shareholders' meetings pursuant to section 121 AktG. However, it is not the shareholders' meeting, but the supervisory board, which is responsible for the approval of the annual financial statement (section 172 AktG), unless the management board and supervisory board decide to leave this to the shareholders' meeting.

However, the shareholders' meeting does decide on the use of the distributable profits (section 119 (1) no. 2 AktG), but in doing so it is bound by the approved annual financial statement (section 174 (1) AktG). The shareholders' meeting also appoints the members of the supervisory board representing the owners (sec-

II. Management Board Members of Stock Corporations

tion 119 (1) no. 1 AktG), while the members representing the employees are elected by the employees. Pursuant to section 119 (1) nos. 4 to 8 AktG, the shareholders' meeting further decides on
- the appointment of auditors
- amendments to the articles of association
- measures to increase or reduce the share capital
- the appointment of auditors for the examination of matters in connection with the formation or the management of the company
- the dissolution of the company.

d) Information Duties

Shareholders are provided with information on the company's affairs by the management board in the shareholders' meeting (section 131 AktG).

e) Accounting

Like GmbH managing directors, AG management board members are responsible for proper accounts and the preparation of the annual financial statement (section 170 AktG). The management board members also have to convene a shareholders' meeting if the annual financial statement or the balance sheet drawn up in the course of the financial year shows that half of the share capital has been lost (section 92 (1) AktG), see page 94.

f) Insolvency

In case of insolvency, management board members have the same duties as GmbH managing directors (section 92 (2) AktG, see page 94).

g) Raising and Maintenance of Share Capital

Management board members are also responsible for the proper raising and maintenance of the share capital. The minimum share capital is EUR 50,000 (section 7 AktG). Before the company can be entered into the Commercial Register (*Handelsregister*), at least one quarter of this amount of share capital must be paid in in the case of cash contributions, and the full amount in the case of contributions in kind (section 36 a AktG). If false statements are made, the management board members will be liable (section 41 AktG). They also may not distribute share capital to the shareholders pursuant to section 57 AktG.

h) Fiscal Obligations

The management board members must fulfill the AG's fiscal obligations (section 34 AO).

i) Social Security

They are also responsible for ensuring that the social security contributions payable by the AG are paid in punctually and in full to the respective collecting agency. With regard to violations, the same liability applies as for the managing director of a GmbH (see page 95).

Part II: Statutory Material

I. Civil Code
(Bürgerliches Gesetzbuch – BGB)

of 18 August 1896 in the version of the Publication of 2 January 2002
(Federal Law Gazette I p. 42)

in the amended version of 24 July 2010

(excerpts)

§ 119
Anfechtbarkeit wegen Irrtums

(1) Wer bei der Abgabe einer Willenserklärung über deren Inhalt im Irrtum war oder eine Erklärung dieses Inhalts überhaupt nicht abgeben wollte, kann die Erklärung anfechten, wenn anzunehmen ist, dass er sie bei Kenntnis der Sachlage und bei verständiger Würdigung des Falles nicht abgegeben haben würde.

(2) Als Irrtum über den Inhalt der Erklärung gilt auch der Irrtum über solche Eigenschaften der Person oder der Sache, die im Verkehr als wesentlich angesehen werden.

Section 119
Rescission Due to Error

(1) Any person who, upon making a declaration of intention, was in error as to its content or did not intend to make a declaration with such content at all, may rescind the declaration if it may be assumed that he would not have made it had he been aware of the facts and had a reasonable appreciation of the situation.

(2) An error regarding those characteristics of a person or thing which are regarded in business as essential is also deemed to be an error as to the content of the declaration.

§ 121
Anfechtungsfrist

(1) [1] Die Anfechtung muss in den Fällen der §§ 119, 120 ohne schuldhaftes Zögern (unverzüglich) erfolgen, nachdem der Anfechtungsberechtigte von dem Anfechtungsgrund Kenntnis erlangt hat. [2] Die einem Abwesenden gegenüber erfolgte Anfechtung gilt als rechtzeitig erfolgt, wenn die Anfechtungserklärung unverzüglich abgesendet worden ist.

(2) Die Anfechtung ist ausgeschlossen, wenn seit der Abgabe der Willenserklärung zehn Jahre verstrichen sind.

Section 121
Rescission Period

(1) [1] Rescission must be effected, in the cases set out in sections 119 and 120, without culpable delay (without undue delay) after the person entitled to rescind gains knowledge of the grounds for the rescission. [2] A rescission effected against an absent person shall be deemed to be effected in due time if the declaration of rescission is dispatched without undue delay.

(2) Rescission shall be excluded if ten years have elapsed since the declaration of intent was made.

§ 123
Anfechtbarkeit wegen Täuschung oder Drohung

(1) Wer zur Abgabe einer Willenserklärung durch arglistige Täuschung oder widerrechtlich durch Drohung bestimmt worden ist, kann die Erklärung anfechten.

(2) ¹Hat ein Dritter die Täuschung verübt, so ist eine Erklärung, die einem anderen gegenüber abzugeben war, nur dann anfechtbar, wenn dieser die Täuschung kannte oder kennen musste. ²Soweit ein anderer als derjenige, welchem gegenüber die Erklärung abzugeben war, aus der Erklärung unmittelbar ein Recht erworben hat, ist die Erklärung ihm gegenüber anfechtbar, wenn er die Täuschung kannte oder kennen musste.

§ 124
Anfechtungsfrist

(1) Die Anfechtung einer nach § 123 anfechtbaren Willenserklärung kann nur binnen Jahresfrist erfolgen.

(2) ¹Die Frist beginnt im Falle der arglistigen Täuschung mit dem Zeitpunkt, in welchem der Anfechtungsberechtigte die Täuschung entdeckt, im Falle der Drohung mit dem Zeitpunkt, in welchem die Zwangslage aufhört. ²Auf den Lauf der Frist finden die für die Verjährung geltenden Vorschriften der §§ 206, 210 und 211 entsprechende Anwendung.

(3) Die Anfechtung ist ausgeschlossen, wenn seit der Abgabe der Willenserklärung zehn Jahre verstrichen sind.

§ 138
Sittenwidriges Rechtsgeschäft; Wucher

(1) Ein Rechtsgeschäft, das gegen die guten Sitten verstößt, ist nichtig.

Section 123
Rescission on Grounds of Fraud or Threats

(1) Any person who has been induced to make a declaration of intent by deception or unlawfully by threats may rescind such declaration.

(2) ¹If a third party committed the deception, a declaration which was to be made to another person may only be rescinded if the recipient of the declaration knew or should have known of the deception. ²If a person other than the recipient of the declaration to be made has acquired a right directly through the declaration, the declaration may be rescinded vis-à-vis such person if he knew or should have known of the fraud.

Section 124
Rescission Period

(1) The rescission of a declaration of intent which may be rescinded under section 123 may be effected only within a period of one year.

(2) ¹In a case of fraudulent deception, the period shall begin to run from the moment the person entitled to rescind the deception, and in case of duress, from the time the duress ceases. ²The provisions set forth in sections 206, 210 and 211 applicable to limitation periods apply *mutatis mutandis* to the running of this period.

(3) Rescission is barred if ten years have elapsed since the declaration of intent was made.

Section 138
Legal Transaction Against Public Policy; Usury

(1) A legal transaction which is against public policy is invalid.

(2) Nichtig ist insbesondere ein Rechtsgeschäft, durch das jemand unter Ausbeutung der Zwangslage, der Unerfahrenheit, des Mangels an Urteilsvermögen oder der erheblichen Willensschwäche eines anderen sich oder einem Dritten für eine Leistung Vermögensvorteile versprechen oder gewähren lässt, die in einem auffälligen Missverhältnis zu der Leistung stehen.

(2) In particular, a legal transaction by which a person exploiting another person's predicament, inexperience, lack of sound judgment or substantial lack of will power causes to be promised or granted to himself or to a third party pecuniary advantages in exchange for a performance which are in obvious disproportion to the performance is also invalid.

§ 142
Wirkung der Anfechtung

(1) Wird ein anfechtbares Rechtsgeschäft angefochten, so ist es als von Anfang an nichtig anzusehen.

(2) Wer die Anfechtbarkeit kannte oder kennen musste, wird, wenn die Anfechtung erfolgt, so behandelt, wie wenn er die Nichtigkeit des Rechtsgeschäfts gekannt hätte oder hätte kennen müssen.

Section 142
Effect of Rescission

(1) If a legal transaction which is subject to rescission, is rescinded it shall be deemed to have been void from the outset.

(2) If a person knew or should have known of the possibility of rescission, if a transaction is rescinded he shall treated as if he had known or should have known of the nullity of the legal transaction.

§ 242
Leistung nach Treu und Glauben

Der Schuldner ist verpflichtet, die Leistung so zu bewirken, wie Treu und Glauben mit Rücksicht auf die Verkehrssitte es erfordern.

Section 242
Performance in Good Faith

The debtor shall be obligated to perform in a manner consistent with the principles of good faith taking into account accepted practice.

§ 249
Art und Umfang des Schadensersatzes

(1) Wer zum Schadensersatz verpflichtet ist, hat den Zustand herzustellen, der bestehen würde, wenn der zum Ersatz verpflichtende Umstand nicht eingetreten wäre.

(2) ¹Ist wegen Verletzung einer Person oder wegen Beschädigung einer Sache Schadensersatz zu leisten, so kann der Gläubiger statt der Herstellung den dazu erforderlichen Geldbetrag verlangen. ²Bei der Beschädigung einer Sache schließt der nach Satz 1 erforderliche Geldbetrag die Umsatzsteuer nur mit ein, wenn und soweit sie tatsächlich angefallen ist.

Section 249
Type and Scope of Compensation

(1) A person who is obligated to pay compensation shall restore the situation which would have existed had the circumstance leading to the compensation not occurred.

(2) ¹If compensation is to be paid due to personal injury or property damage, the creditor may, in lieu of restoration, demand the sum of money necessary for that purpose. ²In the case or property damage, the monetary sum necessary pursuant to sentence 1 shall only include turnover tax if and to the extent it was actually incurred.

§ 252
Entgangener Gewinn

¹Der zu ersetzende Schaden umfasst auch den entgangenen Gewinn. ²Als entgangen gilt der Gewinn, welcher nach dem gewöhnlichen Lauf der Dinge oder nach den besonderen Umständen, insbesondere nach den getroffenen Anstalten und Vorkehrungen, mit Wahrscheinlichkeit erwartet werden konnte.

§ 253
Immaterieller Schaden

(1) Wegen eines Schadens, der nicht Vermögensschaden ist, kann Entschädigung in Geld nur in den durch das Gesetz bestimmten Fällen gefordert werden.

(2) Ist wegen einer Verletzung des Körpers, der Gesundheit, der Freiheit oder der sexuellen Selbstbestimmung Schadensersatz zu leisten, kann auch wegen des Schadens, der nicht Vermögensschaden ist, eine billige Entschädigung in Geld gefordert werden.

§ 254
Mitverschulden

(1) Hat bei der Entstehung des Schadens ein Verschulden des Beschädigten mitgewirkt, so hängt die Verpflichtung zum Ersatz sowie der Umfang des zu leistenden Ersatzes von den Umständen, insbesondere davon ab, inwieweit der Schaden vorwiegend von dem einen oder dem anderen Teil verursacht worden ist.

(2) ¹Dies gilt auch dann, wenn sich das Verschulden des Beschädigten darauf beschränkt, dass er unterlassen hat, den Schuldner auf die Gefahr eines ungewöhnlich hohen Schadens aufmerksam zu machen, die der Schuldner weder kannte noch kennen musste, oder dass er unterlassen hat, den Schaden abzuwenden oder zu mindern. ²Die Vorschrift des § 278 findet entsprechende Anwendung.

Section 252
Lost Profit

¹The compensation shall also include lost profit. ²Profit is deemed to be lost that could probably have been expected in the ordinary course of events or under the particular circumstances involved, in particular in view of the preparations and arrangements made.

Section 253
Intangible Damages

(1) For damage which is not a financial loss, compensation in money can only be demanded in the cases determined by law.

(2) If compensation is to be made due to bodily injury, damage to health, loss of liberty or sexual self-determination, a reasonable compensation in money can also be claimed for damage which is not a financial loss.

Section 254
Contributory Negligence

(1) If the damaged party was also at fault for the occurrence of damage, the obligation to provide compensation, as well as the amount of compensation to be rendered, shall particularly depend upon the extent to which the damage was primarily caused by the one party or the other.

(2) ¹This shall also apply if the damaged party's culpability is limited to the fact that he failed to call the debtor's attention to the danger of an unusually high degree of damage of which the debtor was unaware and was not obligated to be aware, or that he failed to avert or mitigate the damage. ²The provision set forth in section 278 applies *mutatis mutandis*.

§ 305
Einbeziehung Allgemeiner Geschäftsbedingungen in den Vertrag

Section 305
Incorporation of General Terms and Conditions Into the Contract

(1) ¹Allgemeine Geschäftsbedingungen sind alle für eine Vielzahl von Verträgen vorformulierten Vertragsbedingungen, die eine Vertragspartei (Verwender) der anderen Vertragspartei bei Abschluss eines Vertrags stellt. ²Gleichgültig ist, ob die Bestimmungen einen äußerlich gesonderten Bestandteil des Vertrags bilden oder in die Vertragsurkunde selbst aufgenommen werden, welchen Umfang sie haben, in welcher Schriftart sie verfasst sind und welche Form der Vertrag hat. ³Allgemeine Geschäftsbedingungen liegen nicht vor, soweit die Vertragsbedingungen zwischen den Vertragsparteien im Einzelnen ausgehandelt sind.

(1) ¹General Terms and Conditions are all contractual terms which have been pre-formulated for a multitude of contracts which one party to the contract (the user) presents to the other party upon conclusion of the contract. ²It is irrelevant whether the provisions appear as a separate part of a contract or are included in the contractual document itself, how extensive they are, what typeface is used for them, or what form the contract takes. ³Contractual terms do not constitute General Terms and Conditions where they have been individually negotiated between the parties.

(2) Allgemeine Geschäftsbedingungen werden nur dann Bestandteil eines Vertrags, wenn der Verwender bei Vertragsschluss

(2) General Terms and Conditions only become a part of a contract, if the user upon concluding the contract

1. die andere Vertragspartei ausdrücklich oder, wenn ein ausdrücklicher Hinweis wegen der Art des Vertragsschlusses nur unter unverhältnismäßigen Schwierigkeiten möglich ist, durch deutlich sichtbaren Aushang am Ort des Vertragsschlusses auf sie hinweist und
2. der anderen Vertragspartei die Möglichkeit verschafft, in zumutbarer Weise, die auch eine für den Verwender erkennbare körperliche Behinderung der anderen Vertragspartei angemessen berücksichtigt, von ihrem Inhalt Kenntnis zu nehmen,

und wenn die andere Vertragspartei mit ihrer Geltung einverstanden ist.

1. refers the other contracting party to them explicitly or, where explicit reference due to the nature of the conclusion of the contract is only possible with considerable difficulties, by posting a clearly visible notice at the place of the conclusion of the contract, and
2. provides the other contracting party with the opportunity, in an acceptable manner, that also appropriately takes into account a physical handicap of the other contracting party discernible by the user, of taking notice of their contents,

and if the other contracting party is in agreement with their application.

(3) Die Vertragsparteien können für eine bestimmte Art von Rechtsgeschäften die Geltung bestimmter Allgemeiner Geschäftsbedingungen unter Beachtung der in Absatz 2 bezeichneten Erfordernisse im Voraus vereinbaren.

(3) Subject to observance of the requirements set out in subsection (2) above, the parties may agree in advance that particular General Terms and Conditions will apply to a particular type of legal transaction.

§ 305 a
Einbeziehung in besonderen Fällen

Auch ohne Einhaltung der in § 305 Abs. 2 Nr. 1 und 2 bezeichneten Erfordernisse werden einbezogen, wenn die andere Vertragspartei mit ihrer Geltung einverstanden ist,

1. die mit Genehmigung der zuständigen Verkehrsbehörde oder auf Grund von internationalen Übereinkommen erlassenen Tarife und Ausführungsbestimmungen der Eisenbahnen und die nach Maßgabe des Personenbeförderungsgesetzes genehmigten Beförderungsbedingungen der Straßenbahnen, Obusse und Kraftfahrzeuge im Linienverkehr in den Beförderungsvertrag,
2. die im Amtsblatt der Bundesnetzagentur für Elektrizität, Gas, Telekommunikation, Post und Eisenbahnen veröffentlichten und in den Geschäftsstellen des Verwenders bereitgehaltenen Allgemeinen Geschäftsbedingungen
   a) in Beförderungsverträge, die außerhalb von Geschäftsräumen durch den Einwurf von Postsendungen in Briefkästen abgeschlossen werden,
   b) in Verträge über Telekommunikations-, Informations- und andere Dienstleistungen, die unmittelbar durch Einsatz von Fernkommunikationsmitteln und während der Erbringung einer Telekommunikationsdienstleistung in einem Mal erbracht werden, wenn die Allgemeinen Geschäftsbedingungen der anderen Vertragspartei nur unter unverhältnismäßigen Schwierigkeiten vor dem Vertragsschluss zugänglich gemacht werden können.

§ 305 b
Vorrang der Individualabrede

Individuelle Vertragsabreden haben Vorrang vor Allgemeinen Geschäftsbedingungen.

Section 305 a
Incorporation in Special Cases

Even without compliance with the requirements cited in section 305 (2) nos. 1 and 2, if the other contracting party is in agreement with their application,

1. tariffs and regulations adopted with the approval of the competent transport authority or on the basis of international conventions and terms of transport, authorized in accordance with the Passenger Transport Act, of trams, buses and motor vehicles in scheduled services are incorporated into the transport contract,
2. general and conditions published in the official journal of the Federal Network Agency for Electricity, Gas, Telecommunications, Post and Railway and kept available in the user's business premises are incorporated,
   a) into contracts of carriage concluded away from business premises by the posting of items in post boxes,
   b) into contracts for telecommunications, information and other services that are provided directly and in one go by means of remote communication and during the provision of a telecommunications service, if it is unreasonably difficult to make the General Terms and Conditions available to the other party before conclusion of the contract.

Section 305 b
Precedence of Individually Negotiated Terms

Individually negotiated terms take precedence over General Terms and Conditions.

§ 305 c
Überraschende und mehrdeutige Klauseln

(1) Bestimmungen in Allgemeinen Geschäftsbedingungen, die nach den Umständen, insbesondere nach dem äußeren Erscheinungsbild des Vertrags, so ungewöhnlich sind, dass der Vertragspartner des Verwenders mit ihnen nicht zu rechnen braucht, werden nicht Vertragsbestandteil.

(2) Zweifel bei der Auslegung Allgemeiner Geschäftsbedingungen gehen zu Lasten des Verwenders.

§ 306
Rechtsfolgen bei Nichteinbeziehung und Unwirksamkeit

(1) Sind Allgemeine Geschäftsbedingungen ganz oder teilweise nicht Vertragsbestandteil geworden oder unwirksam, so bleibt der Vertrag im Übrigen wirksam.

(2) Soweit die Bestimmungen nicht Vertragsbestandteil geworden oder unwirksam sind, richtet sich der Inhalt des Vertrags nach den gesetzlichen Vorschriften.

(3) Der Vertrag ist unwirksam, wenn das Festhalten an ihm auch unter Berücksichtigung der nach Absatz 2 vorgesehenen Änderung eine unzumutbare Härte für eine Vertragspartei darstellen würde.

§ 306 a
Umgehungsverbot

Die Vorschriften dieses Abschnitts finden auch Anwendung, wenn sie durch anderweitige Gestaltungen umgangen werden.

§ 307
Inhaltskontrolle

(1) [1]Bestimmungen in Allgemeinen Geschäftsbedingungen sind unwirk-

Section 305 c
Surprising and Ambiguous Clauses

(1) Provisions in General Terms and Conditions which in the circumstances, in particular in view of the outward appearance of the contract, are so unusual that the contractual partner of the user could not reasonably have expected them, do not form part of the contract.

(2) In case of doubt, General Terms and Conditions shall be interpreted against the user.

Section 306
Legal Consequences of Non-incorporation and Ineffectiveness

(1) If some or all General Terms and Conditions have not become part of the contract or are ineffective, the remainder of the contract continues to be effective.

(2) Where provisions have not become part of the contract or are ineffective, the content of the contract shall be determined by the statutory regulations.

(3) The contract is invalid if one party would suffer unreasonable hardship, if it were bound by the contract even after the amendment provided for in subsection (2) above.

Section 306 a
Prohibition of Circumvention

The rules in this chapter apply even if they are circumvented by other arrangements.

Section 307
Review of Subject Matter

(1) [1]Provisions in General Terms and Conditions are invalid if, contrary to

sam, wenn sie den Vertragspartner des Verwenders entgegen den Geboten von Treu und Glauben unangemessen benachteiligen. ²Eine unangemessene Benachteiligung kann sich auch daraus ergeben, dass die Bestimmung nicht klar und verständlich ist.

(2) Eine unangemessene Benachteiligung ist im Zweifel anzunehmen, wenn eine Bestimmung
1. mit wesentlichen Grundgedanken der gesetzlichen Regelung, von der abgewichen wird, nicht zu vereinbaren ist oder
2. wesentliche Rechte oder Pflichten, die sich aus der Natur des Vertrags ergeben, so einschränkt, dass die Erreichung des Vertragszwecks gefährdet ist.

(3) ¹Die Absätze 1 und 2 sowie die §§ 308 und 309 gelten nur für Bestimmungen in Allgemeinen Geschäftsbedingungen, durch die von Rechtsvorschriften abweichende oder diese ergänzende Regelungen vereinbart werden. ²Andere Bestimmungen können nach Absatz 1 Satz 2 in Verbindung mit Absatz 1 Satz 1 unwirksam sein.

§ 308
Klauselverbote mit Wertungsmöglichkeit

In Allgemeinen Geschäftsbedingungen ist insbesondere unwirksam
1. (Annahme- und Leistungsfrist)
eine Bestimmung, durch die sich der Verwender unangemessen lange oder nicht hinreichend bestimmte Fristen für die Annahme oder Ablehnung eines Angebots oder die Erbringung einer Leistung vorbehält; ausgenommen hiervon ist der Vorbehalt, erst nach Ablauf der Widerrufs- oder Rückgabefrist nach § 355 Abs. 1 bis 3 und § 356 zu leisten;
2. (Nachfrist)
eine Bestimmung, durch die sich der Verwender für die von ihm zu be-

the requirements of good faith, they place the contractual partner of the user at an unreasonable disadvantage.² An unreasonable disadvantage may also result from the fact that the provision is not clear and comprehensible.

(2) In case of doubt, an unreasonable disadvantage must be assumed if a provision
1. is not compatible with the essential principles of the statutory regulation from which it deviates, or
2. limits material rights or duties inherent in the nature of the contract to such an extent that attainment of the contractual objective is jeopardized.

(3) ¹Subsections (1) and (2) above, and sections 308 and 309 apply only to provisions in General Terms and Conditions with which provisions derogating from or supplementing legal rules are agreed. ²Other provisions may be invalid under subsection (1) sentence 2 in conjunction with subsection (1) sentence 1 above.

Section 308
Prohibited Clauses with the Option of Appraisal

In General Terms and Conditions, the following are in particular invalid
1. (Period of time for acceptance and performance)
a provision whereby the user makes reservation for unreasonably protracted or inadequately determined periods of time for acceptance or rejection of an offer or for the rendering of a performance; an exception is the reservation to perform only after the end of the period of time for revocation or return under sections 355 (1) to (3) and section 356;
2. (Additional period)
a provision whereby the user makes reservation for an unreasonably pro-

wirkende Leistung abweichend von Rechtsvorschriften eine unangemessen lange oder nicht hinreichend bestimmte Nachfrist vorbehält;

3. (Rücktrittsvorbehalt)
die Vereinbarung eines Rechts des Verwenders, sich ohne sachlich gerechtfertigten und im Vertrag angegebenen Grund von seiner Leistungspflicht zu lösen; dies gilt nicht für Dauerschuldverhältnisse;

4. (Änderungsvorbehalt)
die Vereinbarung eines Rechts des Verwenders, die versprochene Leistung zu ändern oder von ihr abzuweichen, wenn nicht die Vereinbarung der Änderung oder Abweichung unter Berücksichtigung der Interessen des Verwenders für den anderen Vertragsteil zumutbar ist;

5. (Fingierte Erklärungen)
eine Bestimmung, wonach eine Erklärung des Vertragspartners des Verwenders bei Vornahme oder Unterlassung einer bestimmten Handlung als von ihm abgegeben oder nicht abgegeben gilt, es sei denn, dass
a) dem Vertragspartner eine angemessene Frist zur Abgabe einer ausdrücklichen Erklärung eingeräumt ist und
b) der Verwender sich verpflichtet, den Vertragspartner bei Beginn der Frist auf die vorgesehene Bedeutung seines Verhaltens besonders hinzuweisen;

6. (Fiktion des Zugangs)
eine Bestimmung, die vorsieht, dass eine Erklärung des Verwenders von besonderer Bedeutung dem anderen Vertragsteil als zugegangen gilt;

7. (Abwicklung von Verträgen)
eine Bestimmung, nach der der Verwender für den Fall, dass eine Vertragspartei vom Vertrag zurücktritt oder den Vertrag kündigt,
a) eine unangemessen hohe Vergütung für die Nutzung oder den Gebrauch einer Sache oder eines Rechts oder für erbrachte Leistungen oder

tracted or inadequately determined additional period of time contrary to legal provisions for the performance he is to render;

3. (Reservation of rescission)
agreement of a right of the user to free himself from his obligation to perform without any objectively justified reason indicated in the contract; this does not apply to recurring obligations;

4. (Reservation of modification)
the agreement of a right by the user to modify the performance promised or deviate from it, unless the agreement of the modification or deviation can reasonably be expected of the other contracting party taking the users interests into account;

5. (Constructive declarations)
a provision according to which a declaration by the party to the contract with the user is deemed to have been made or not made when undertaking or omitting a specific action, unless

a) the contracting party is granted a reasonable period of time for making an explicit declaration, and

b) the user undertakes to draw the other party's attention to the intended significance of his behavior at the beginning of the period of time;

6. (Constructive receipt)
a provision providing that a declaration by the user of special importance to the other contracting party is deemed to have been received;

7. (Winding up of contracts)
a provision according to which the user, in the event that a contracting party rescinds the contract or gives notice of termination, may demand,
a) unreasonably high remuneration for enjoyment or use of a thing or a right or for performances rendered, or

b) einen unangemessen hohen Ersatz von Aufwendungen verlangen kann;
8. (Nichtverfügbarkeit der Leistung) die nach Nummer 3 zulässige Vereinbarung eines Vorbehalts des Verwenders, sich von der Verpflichtung zur Erfüllung des Vertrags bei Nichtverfügbarkeit der Leistung zu lösen, wenn sich der Verwender nicht verpflichtet,
a) den Vertragspartner unverzüglich über die Nichtverfügbarkeit zu informieren und
b) Gegenleistungen des Vertragspartners unverzüglich zu erstatten.

§ 309
Klauselverbote ohne Wertungsmöglichkeit

Auch soweit eine Abweichung von den gesetzlichen Vorschriften zulässig ist, ist in Allgemeinen Geschäftsbedingungen unwirksam:
1. (Kurzfristige Preiserhöhungen) Eine Bestimmung, welche die Erhöhung des Entgelts für Waren oder Leistungen vorsieht, die innerhalb von vier Monaten nach Vertragsschluss geliefert oder erbracht werden sollen; dies gilt nicht bei Waren oder Leistungen, die im Rahmen von Dauerschuldverhältnissen geliefert oder erbracht werden;
2. (Leistungsverweigerungsrechte) eine Bestimmung, durch die
a) das Leistungsverweigerungsrecht, das dem Vertragspartner des Verwenders nach § 320 zusteht, ausgeschlossen oder eingeschränkt wird oder
b) ein dem Vertragspartner des Verwenders zustehendes Zurückbehaltungsrecht, soweit es auf demselben Vertragsverhältnis beruht, ausgeschlossen oder eingeschränkt, insbesondere von der Anerkennung von Mängeln

b) unreasonably high compensation for expenses;
8. (Unavailability of performance) an agreement, permissible under no. 3, of a reservation by the user to free himself from the duty to fulfill the contract in the absence of availability of performance, if the user does not oblige himself to,
a) inform the contracting party of the unavailability without undue delay, and
b) reimburse the contracting party for counter performances without undue delay.

Section 309
Prohibited Clauses without the Option of Appraisal

Even where derogation from the statutory provisions is permissible, the following are invalid in General Terms and Conditions:
1. (Price increases on short notice) a provision providing for an increase in remuneration for goods or services that are to be delivered or rendered within four months of conclusion of the contract; this does not apply to goods or services delivered or rendered in the framework of recurring obligations;
2. (Rights to refuse service) a provision whereby
a) the right to refuse performance which the party to the contract with the user is entitled to exercise under section 320, or is excluded from or restricted in exercising, or
b) a right of retention which the party to the contract with the user is entitled to exercise to the extent that it is based on the same contractual relationship, or is excluded from or restricted in exercising, is particularly made

durch den Verwender abhängig gemacht wird;
3. (Aufrechnungsverbot)
Eine Bestimmung, durch die dem Vertragspartner des Verwenders die Befugnis genommen wird, mit einer unbestrittenen oder rechtskräftig festgestellten Forderung aufzurechnen;
4. (Mahnung, Fristsetzung)
eine Bestimmung, durch die der Verwender von der gesetzlichen Obliegenheit freigestellt wird, den anderen Vertragsteil zu mahnen oder ihm eine Frist für die Leistung oder Nacherfüllung zu setzen;

5. (Pauschalierung von Schadensersatzansprüchen)
die Vereinbarung eines pauschalierten Anspruchs des Verwenders auf Schadensersatz oder Ersatz einer Wertminderung, wenn
a) die Pauschale den in den geregelten Fällen nach dem gewöhnlichen Lauf der Dinge zu erwartenden Schaden oder die gewöhnlich eintretende Wertminderung übersteigt oder
b) dem anderen Vertragsteil nicht ausdrücklich der Nachweis gestattet wird, ein Schaden oder eine Wertminderung sei überhaupt nicht entstanden oder wesentlich niedriger als die Pauschale;
6. (Vertragsstrafe)
eine Bestimmung, durch die dem Verwender für den Fall der Nichtabnahme oder verspäteten Abnahme der Leistung, des Zahlungsverzugs oder für den Fall, dass der andere Vertragsteil sich vom Vertrag löst, Zahlung einer Vertragsstrafe versprochen wird;
7. (Haftungsausschluss bei Verletzung von Leben, Körper, Gesundheit und bei grobem Verschulden)
a) (Verletzung von Leben, Körper, Gesundheit)
ein Ausschluss oder eine Begrenzung der Haftung für Schäden

dependent upon an acknowledgement of defects by the user;
3. (Prohibition of set-off)
a provision whereby the party to the contract with the user is deprived of the right to set off a claim that is uncontested or has been established with final and binding effect
4. (Demand for Payment, setting of a time period)
a provision whereby the user is exempted from the statutory requirement of giving the other contracting party a demand for payment or setting a period of time for the latter's performance or subsequent performance;

5. (Lump-sum claims for compensation)
the agreement of a lump-sum claim by the user for damages or for compensation for a reduction in value if

a) the lump-sum exceeds the damage expected in the cases included under normal circumstances or the normally occurring reduction in value, or

b) the other contracting party is not explicitly permitted to show that absolutely no damage or reduction in value has occurred or that it is considerably less than the lump-sum
6. (Contractual penalty)
a provision whereby the user is promised the payment of a contractual penalty in the event of non-acceptance or late acceptance of the performance, default in payment or in the event that the other contracting party frees itself from the contract;
7. (Exclusion of liability for death, personal injury, impairment to health and in case of gross culpability)
a) (Death, personal injury, impairment to health)
any exclusion or limitation of liability for damage due to death,

aus der Verletzung des Lebens, des Körpers oder der Gesundheit, die auf einer fahrlässigen Pflichtverletzung des Verwenders oder einer vorsätzlichen oder fahrlässigen Pflichtverletzung eines gesetzlichen Vertreters oder Erfüllungsgehilfen des Verwenders beruhen;

b) (Grobes Verschulden)
ein Ausschluss oder eine Begrenzung der Haftung für sonstige Schäden, die auf einer grob fahrlässigen Pflichtverletzung des Verwenders oder auf einer vorsätzlichen oder grob fahrlässigen Pflichtverletzung eines gesetzlichen Vertreters oder Erfüllungsgehilfen des Verwenders beruhen; die Buchstaben a und b gelten nicht für Haftungsbeschränkungen in den nach Maßgabe des Personenbeförderungsgesetzes genehmigten Beförderungsbedingungen und Tarifvorschriften der Straßenbahnen, Obusse und Kraftfahrzeuge im Linienverkehr, soweit sie nicht zum Nachteil des Fahrgastes von der Verordnung über die Allgemeinen Beförderungsbedingungen für den Straßenbahn- und Obusverkehr sowie den Linienverkehr mit Kraftfahrzeugen vom 27. Februar 1970 abweichen; Buchstabe b gilt nicht für Haftungsbeschränkungen für staatlich genehmigte Lotterie- oder Ausspielverträge

8. (Sonstige Haftungsausschlüsse bei Pflichtverletzung)
a) (Ausschluss des Rechts, sich vom Vertrag zu lösen)
eine Bestimmung, die bei einer vom Verwender zu vertretenden, nicht in einem Mangel der Kaufsache oder des Werkes bestehenden Pflichtverletzung das Recht des anderen Vertragsteils, sich vom Vertrag zu lösen, ausschließt oder einschränkt; dies gilt nicht für die in der Nummer 7 bezeichneten Beförderungsbedingungen und Tarifvorschriften unter den

personal injury, or an impairment to health caused by a negligent breach of duty by the user or intentional or negligent breach of duty by a legal representative or a person employed to perform an obligation of the user;

b) (Gross fault)
any exclusion or limitation of liability for other reasons due to negligent breach of duty by the user or intentional or negligent breach of duty by a legal representative or vicarious agent of the user;

the letters (a) and (b) do not apply to limitations on liability in terms of transport and tariff rules, authorized in accordance with the Passenger Transport Act, of trams, buses and motor vehicles in scheduled services, to the extent that they do not deviate to the disadvantage of the passenger from the Ordinance on Standard Transport Terms for Tram and Bus Traffic as well as Scheduled Traffic with Motor Vehicles of 27 February 1970; letter (b) does not apply to limitations on liability for government-approved lottery or raffle contracts;

8. Other exclusions of liability for breaches of duty)
a) (Exclusion of the right to free oneself from the contract)
a provision which, in the case of a breach of duty for which the user is responsible and which does not consist of a defect in the thing sold or the work, excludes or restricts the other party's right to free itself from the contract; this does not apply to the terms of contract and tariff rules referred to in no. 7 under the conditions set out therein;

dort genannten Voraussetzungen;
b) (Mängel)
eine Bestimmung, durch die bei Verträgen über Lieferungen neu hergestellter Sachen und über Werkleistungen
   aa) (Ausschluss und Verweisung auf Dritte)
   die Ansprüche gegen den Verwender wegen eines Mangels insgesamt oder bezüglich einzelner Teile ausgeschlossen, auf die Einräumung von Ansprüchen gegen Dritte beschränkt oder von der vorherigen gerichtlichen Inanspruchnahme Dritter abhängig gemacht werden;
   bb) (Beschränkung auf Nacherfüllung)
   die Ansprüche gegen den Verwender insgesamt oder bezüglich einzelner Teile auf ein Recht auf Nacherfüllung beschränkt werden, sofern dem anderen Vertragsteil nicht ausdrücklich das Recht vorbehalten wird, bei Fehlschlagen der Nacherfüllung zu mindern oder, wenn nicht eine Bauleistung Gegenstand der Mängelhaftung ist, nach seiner Wahl vom Vertrag zurückzutreten;
   cc) (Aufwendungen bei Nacherfüllung)
   die Verpflichtung des Verwenders ausgeschlossen oder beschränkt wird, die zum Zwecke der Nacherfüllung erforderlichen Aufwendungen, insbesondere Transport-, Wege-, Arbeits- und Materialkosten, zu tragen;
   dd) (Vorenthalten der Nacherfüllung)
   der Verwender die Nacherfüllung von der vorherigen

b) (Defects)
a provision whereby in contracts relating to newly produced things and the performance of work
   aa) (Exclusion and Referral to Third Parties)
   the claims against the user due to defects in their entirety or with regard to individual parts are excluded, limited to the granting of claims against third parties or made contingent upon prior court action taken against third parties;

   bb) (Limitation to subsequent performance)
   the claims against the user are limited in their entirety or with regard to individual parts to the right to subsequent performance to the extent the other contracting party has not explicitly reserved the right to reduce the purchase price if the subsequent performance should fail or, unless a construction performance is the object of the liability for defects, to withdraw from the contract at its option;

   cc) (Expenses for subsequent performance)
   the user's duty to bear expenses for the purpose of subsequent performance, in particular to bear transport, road, work and materials costs, is excluded or limited;

   dd) (Withholding subsequent performance)
   the user makes subsequent performance dependent

Zahlung des vollständigen Entgelts oder eines unter Berücksichtigung des Mangels unverhältnismäßig hohen Teils des Entgelts abhängig macht;

ee) (Ausschlussfrist für Mängelanzeige)
der Verwender dem anderen Vertragsteil für die Anzeige nicht offensichtlicher Mängel eine Ausschlussfrist setzt, die kürzer ist als die nach dem Doppelbuchstaben ff zulässige Frist;

ff) (Erleichterung der Verjährung)
die Verjährung von Ansprüchen gegen den Verwender wegen eines Mangels in den Fällen des § 438 Abs. 1 Nr. 2 und des § 634a Abs. 1 Nr. 2 erleichtert oder in den sonstigen Fällen eine weniger als ein Jahr betragende Verjährungsfrist ab dem gesetzlichen Verjährungsbeginn erreicht wird;

9. (Laufzeit bei Dauerschuldverhältnissen)
bei einem Vertragsverhältnis, das die regelmäßige Lieferung von Waren oder die regelmäßige Erbringung von Dienst- oder Werkleistungen durch den Verwender zum Gegenstand hat,
a) eine den anderen Vertragsteil länger als zwei Jahre bindende Laufzeit des Vertrags,
b) eine den anderen Vertragsteil bindende stillschweigende Verlängerung des Vertragsverhältnisses um jeweils mehr als ein Jahr oder
c) zu Lasten des anderen Vertragsteils eine längere Kündigungsfrist als drei Monate vor Ablauf der zunächst vorgesehenen oder stillschweigend verlängerten Vertragsdauer;
dies gilt nicht für Verträge über die Lieferung als zusammengehörig

upon prior payment of the entire fee or a portion of the fee that is disproportionate in view of the defect;

ee) (Exclusion period for notification of defects)
the user imposes an exclusionary period of time for the other contracting party to notify non-evident defects which is shorter than the period of time permissible under double letter (ff);

ff) (Facilitation of limitation)
the statute-barring of claims against the user due to a defect in the cases cited in section 438 (1) no. 2 and section 634a (1) no. 2 is facilitated, or in other cases a limitation period of less than one year reckoned as of the onset of the statutory limitation period is attained;

9. (Term in the case of recurring obligations)
in a contractual relationship the subject matter of which is the regular delivery of goods or the regular performance of services or work by the user,
a) a contractual term binding the other contracting party for more than two years,
b) a tacit extension of the contractual relationship by more than one year at a time which is binding on the other contracting party, or
c) a termination notice period which is longer than three months prior to expiry of the next planned or tacitly extended contractual term at the expense of the other contracting party;
this does not apply to contracts relating to delivery of things which

verkaufter Sachen, für Versicherungsverträge sowie für Verträge zwischen den Inhabern urheberrechtlicher Rechte und Ansprüche und Verwertungsgesellschaften im Sinne des Gesetzes über die Wahrnehmung von Urheberrechten und verwandten Schutzrechten;

10. (Wechsel des Vertragspartners) eine Bestimmung, wonach bei Kauf-, Darlehens-, Dienst- oder Werkverträgen ein Dritter anstelle des Verwenders in die sich aus dem Vertrag ergebenden Rechte und Pflichten eintritt oder eintreten kann, es sei denn, in der Bestimmung wird
    a) der Dritte namentlich bezeichnet oder
    b) dem anderen Vertragsteil das Recht eingeräumt, sich vom Vertrag zu lösen;

11. (Haftung des Abschlussvertreters) eine Bestimmung, durch die der Verwender einem Vertreter, der den Vertrag für den anderen Vertragsteil abschließt,
    a) ohne hierauf gerichtete ausdrückliche und gesonderte Erklärung eine eigene Haftung oder Einstandspflicht oder
    b) im Falle vollmachtsloser Vertretung eine über § 179 hinausgehende Haftung auferlegt;

12. (Beweislast) eine Bestimmung, durch die der Verwender die Beweislast zum Nachteil des anderen Vertragsteils ändert, insbesondere indem er
    a) diesem die Beweislast für Umstände auferlegt, die im Verantwortungsbereich des Verwenders liegen, oder
    b) den anderen Vertragsteil bestimmte Tatsachen bestätigen lässt;
    Buchstabe b gilt nicht für Empfangsbekenntnisse, die gesondert unterschrieben oder mit einer gesonderten qualifizierten elektronischen Signatur versehen sind;

belong together, to insurance contracts as well as to contracts between the holders of intellectual property rights and claims and royalty collecting societies within the meaning of the Act on the Administration of Copyright and related Trade Rights;

10. (Change in contracting parties) a provision under which in case of purchase, loan, service or work agreements a third party accedes, or may accede, to the rights and duties under the contract in lieu of the user unless in that provision
    a) the third party is identified by name, or
    b) the other contracting party is granted the right to free itself from the contract;

11. (Liability of the contract agent) a provision whereby the user imposes on the agent entering into a contract for the other contracting party
    a) the latter's own liability or duty of responsibility without any explicit and separate declaration addressing the same, or
    b) liability going beyond that under section 179 in the case of representation without authority

12. (Burden of Proof) a provision whereby the user modifies the burden of proof to the disadvantage of the other contracting party, in particular by
    a) imposing on the latter the burden of proof for circumstances lying in the sphere of the user's responsibility, or
    b) having the other contracting party confirm certain facts;
    Letter (b) does not apply to acknowledgements of receipt that are signed separately or provided with a separate qualified electronic signature;

13. (Form von Anzeigen und Erklärungen)
eine Bestimmung, durch die Anzeigen oder Erklärungen, die dem Verwender oder einem Dritten gegenüber abzugeben sind, an eine strengere Form als die Schriftform oder an besondere Zugangserfordernisse gebunden werden.

§ 310
Anwendungsbereich

(1) [1]§ 305 Abs. 2 und 3 und die §§ 308 und 309 finden keine Anwendung auf Allgemeine Geschäftsbedingungen, die gegenüber einem Unternehmer, einer juristischen Person des öffentlichen Rechts oder einem öffentlich-rechtlichen Sondervermögen verwendet werden. [2]§ 307 Abs. 1 und 2 findet in den Fällen des Satzes 1 auch insoweit Anwendung, als dies zur Unwirksamkeit von in den §§ 308 und 309 genannten Vertragsbestimmungen führt; auf die im Handelsverkehr geltenden Gewohnheiten und Gebräuche ist angemessen Rücksicht zu nehmen. In den Fällen des Satzes 1 findet § 307 Abs. 1 und 2 auf Verträge, in die die Vergabe- und Vertragsordnung für Bauleistungen Teil B (VOB/B) in der jeweils zum Zeitpunkt des Vertragsschlusses geltenden Fassung ohne inhaltliche Abweichungen insgesamt einbezogen ist, in Bezug auf eine Inhaltskontrolle einzelner Bestimmungen keine Anwendung.

(2) [1]Die §§ 308 und 309 finden keine Anwendung auf Verträge der Elektrizitäts-, Gas-, Fernwärme- und Wasserversorgungsunternehmen über die Versorgung von Sonderabnehmern mit elektrischer Energie, Gas, Fernwärme und Wasser aus dem Versorgungsnetz, soweit die Versorgungsbedingungen nicht zum Nachteil der Abnehmer von Verordnungen über Allgemeine Bedingungen für die Versorgung von Tarifkunden mit elektrischer Energie, Gas, Fernwärme und Wasser abweichen. [2]Satz 1 gilt entsprechend für

13. (Form of notices and declarations)

a provision whereby notices or declarations that are to be made to the user or a third party are subject to a more stringent form than the written form or special receipt requirements.

Section 310
Scope of Application

(1) [1]Section 305 (2) and (3) and sections 308 and 309 do not apply to General Terms and Conditions which are used vis-à-vis an entrepreneur, a legal entity governed by public law or a special fund governed by public law. [2]In such cases, section 307 (1) and (2) shall nevertheless apply to the extent that this results in the invalidity of the contractual provisions referred to in sections 308 and 309; the customs and practices applicable to business transactions shall be duly taken into account. In the cases of sentence 1, section 307 (1) and (2) shall not apply to contracts which incorporate the Standard Official Contracting Terms for Construction Work, Part B *(Vergabe- und Vertragsordnung für Bauleistungen Teil B – VOB/B)*, in the version applicable at the time of the conclusion of the contract as a whole, without changes to their content, with respect to an examination of the content of individual provisions.

(2) [1]Sections 308 and 309 do not apply to contracts of electricity, gas, district heating or water supply companies for the supply to special customers of electricity, gas, district heating or water from the supply grid unless the conditions for the supply derogate, to the detriment of the customers, from regulations on general conditions for the supply of tariff customers with electricity, gas, district heating or water. [2]Sentence 1 applies *mutatis mutandis* to contracts for the disposal of sewage.

Verträge über die Entsorgung von Abwasser.

(3) Bei Verträgen zwischen einem Unternehmer und einem Verbraucher (Verbraucherverträge) finden die Vorschriften dieses Abschnitts mit folgenden Maßgaben Anwendung:
1. Allgemeine Geschäftsbedingungen gelten als vom Unternehmer gestellt, es sei denn, dass sie durch den Verbraucher in den Vertrag eingeführt wurden;
2. § 305c Abs. 2 und die §§ 306 und 307 bis 309 dieses Gesetzes sowie Artikel 29a des Einführungsgesetzes zum Bürgerlichen Gesetzbuche finden auf vorformulierte Vertragsbedingungen auch dann Anwendung, wenn diese nur zur einmaligen Verwendung bestimmt sind und soweit der Verbraucher auf Grund der Vorformulierung auf ihren Inhalt keinen Einfluss nehmen konnte;
3. bei der Beurteilung der unangemessenen Benachteiligung nach § 307 Abs. 1 und 2 sind auch die den Vertragsschluss begleitenden Umstände zu berücksichtigen.

(4) [1] Dieser Abschnitt findet keine Anwendung bei Verträgen auf dem Gebiet des Erb-, Familien- und Gesellschaftsrechts sowie auf Tarifverträge, Betriebs- und Dienstvereinbarungen. [2] Bei der Anwendung auf Arbeitsverträge sind die im Arbeitsrecht geltenden Besonderheiten angemessen zu berücksichtigen; § 305 Abs. 2 und 3 ist nicht anzuwenden. Tarifverträge, Betriebs- und Dienstvereinbarungen stehen Rechtsvorschriften im Sinne von § 307 Abs. 3 gleich.

§ 312
Widerrufsrecht bei Haustürgeschäften

(1) [1] Bei einem Vertrag zwischen einem Unternehmer und einem Verbraucher, der eine entgeltliche Leistung zum Ge-

(3) In the case of contracts between an entrepreneur and a consumer (consumer contracts), the rules in this chapter shall apply, subject to the following provisions:
1. General Terms and Conditions are deemed to have been imposed by the entrepreneur, unless the consumer has introduced them into the contract;
2. section 305c (2) and sections 306 and 307 to 309 of this Act as well as Article 29a of the Introductory Act to the Civil Code shall also apply to pre-formulated contractual terms and conditions, if they are only intended for use a single time, and to the extent that, due to the pre-formulation, the consumer was not able to exert an influence over their content;
3. in judging unreasonable discrimination pursuant to section 307 (1) and (2), the other circumstances involved in the conclusion of the contract must be taken into account.

(4) [1] This chapter does not apply to contracts in the field of the law of succession, family law and company law or to collective bargaining agreements, or works agreements. [2] When applied to employment contracts the particularities applicable in employment and labor law must be appropriately taken into account; section 305 (2) and (3) shall be applied. [3] Collective bargaining agreements and works agreements shall be equivalent to legal provisions within the meaning of section 307 (3).

Section 312
Right of Revocation in the Case of Doorstep Transactions

(1) [1] In the case of a contract between a businessperson and a consumer concerning performance for remuneration

genstand hat und zu dessen Abschluss der Verbraucher

1. durch mündliche Verhandlungen an seinem Arbeitsplatz oder im Bereich einer Privatwohnung,
2. anlässlich einer vom Unternehmer oder von einem Dritten zumindest auch im Interesse des Unternehmers durchgeführten Freizeitveranstaltung oder
3. im Anschluss an ein überraschendes Ansprechen in Verkehrsmitteln oder im Bereich öffentlich zugänglicher Verkehrsflächen

bestimmt worden ist (Haustürgeschäft), steht dem Verbraucher ein Widerrufsrecht gemäß § 355 zu. ²Dem Verbraucher kann anstelle des Widerrufsrechts ein Rückgaberecht nach § 356 eingeräumt werden, wenn zwischen dem Verbraucher und dem Unternehmer im Zusammenhang mit diesem oder einem späteren Geschäft auch eine ständige Verbindung aufrechterhalten werden soll.

(2) Der Unternehmer ist verpflichtet, den Verbraucher gemäß § 360 über sein Widerrufs- oder Rückgaberecht zu belehren. Die Belehrung muss auf die Rechtsfolgen des § 357 Abs. 1 und 3 hinweisen. Der Hinweis ist nicht erforderlich, soweit diese Rechtsfolgen tatsächlich nicht eintreten können.

(3) Das Widerrufs- oder Rückgaberecht besteht unbeschadet anderer Vorschriften nicht bei Versicherungsverträgen oder wenn

1. im Falle von Absatz 1 Nr. 1 die mündlichen Verhandlungen, auf denen der Abschluss des Vertrags beruht, auf vorhergehende Bestellung des Verbrauchers geführt worden sind oder
2. die Leistung bei Abschluss der Verhandlungen sofort erbracht und bezahlt wird und das Entgelt 40 Euro nicht übersteigt oder
3. die Willenserklärung des Verbrauchers von einem Notar beurkundet worden ist.

which the consumer has been induced to conclude

1. as a result of oral negotiations at his place of work or in a private residence,
2. on the occasion of a leisure event organized by the businessperson or a third party, which was at least also in the interest of the businessperson, or
3. subsequent to a surprise approach in a means of transport or a publicly accessible area,

(doorstep transactions), the consumer is entitled to a right of revocation in accordance with section 355. ²In lieu of the right of revocation the consumer may be given a right of return under section 356 if a permanent connection is also to be maintained between the businessperson and the consumer in connection with this or a subsequent transaction.

(2) The entrepreneur shall be obliged to instruct consumers pursuant to section 360 on their right of revocation or return. Such information must refer to the legal consequences of section 357 (1) and (3). This reference shall not be required where such legal consequences cannot, in fact, occur.

(3) Without prejudice to other provisions, there shall be no right of revocation or return in the case of insurance contracts or if

1. in the case of subsection (1) no. 1, the oral negotiations on which the conclusion of the contract was based were conducted pursuant to a previous order placed by the consumer, or
2. the performance is paid for and rendered immediately upon conclusion of the contract and such payment does not exceed 40 euro, or
3. the consumer's declaration of intention has been certified by a notary.

Part II – Statutory Material 117

§ 312a
Verhältnis zu anderen Vorschriften

Steht dem Verbraucher zugleich nach Maßgabe anderer Vorschriften ein Widerrufs- oder Rückgaberecht nach § 355 oder § 356 dieses Gesetzes, nach § 126 des Investmentgesetzes zu, ist das Widerrufs- oder Rückgaberecht nach § 312 ausgeschlossen.

Section 312a
Relationship to Other Provisions

If the consumer is simultaneously entitled to a right of revocation or return pursuant to section 355 or section 356 of this statute, pursuant to section 126 of the Investment Act (*Investmentgesetz*), then the right of revocation or return pursuant to section 312 shall be excluded.

§ 611
Vertragstypische Pflichten beim Dienstvertrag

(1) Durch den Dienstvertrag wird derjenige, welcher Dienste zusagt, zur Leistung der versprochenen Dienste, der andere Teil zur Gewährung der vereinbarten Vergütung verpflichtet.

(2) Gegenstand des Dienstvertrags können Dienste jeder Art sein.

Section 611
Nature of the Service Agreement

(1) With the service agreement, the party promising service is obligated to perform the service promised, and the other party is bound to pay the remuneration agreed upon.

(2) Services of any kind may be the subject of the service agreement.

§§ 611a und 611b
(weggefallen)

Sections 611a and 611b
(repealed)

§ 612
Vergütung

(1) Eine Vergütung gilt als stillschweigend vereinbart, wenn die Dienstleistung den Umständen nach nur gegen eine Vergütung zu erwarten ist.

(2) Ist die Höhe der Vergütung nicht bestimmt, so ist bei dem Bestehen einer Taxe die taxmäßige Vergütung, in Ermangelung einer Taxe die übliche Vergütung als vereinbart anzusehen.

(3) *(weggefallen)*

Section 612
Remuneration

(1) Remuneration shall be deemed to have been tacitly agreed upon if, under the circumstances, it is to be expected that service will be only performed against remuneration.

(2) If the amount of the remuneration is not specified, where an official rate has been fixed, this rate of remuneration shall be deemed to have been agreed; where no official rate has been fixed, the usual remuneration shall be deemed to have been agreed.

(3) *(repealed)*

§ 612a
Maßregelungsverbot

Der Arbeitgeber darf einen Arbeitnehmer bei einer Vereinbarung oder einer Maßnahme nicht benachteiligen, weil

Section 612a
Prohibition of Disciplinary Actions

The employer may not discriminate against the employee in any agreement or measure because the employee has

der Arbeitnehmer in zulässiger Weise seine Rechte ausübt.

§ 613
Unübertragbarkeit

¹Der zur Dienstleistung Verpflichtete hat die Dienste im Zweifel in Person zu leisten. ²Der Anspruch auf die Dienste ist im Zweifel nicht übertragbar.

§ 613a
Rechte und Pflichten bei Betriebsübergang

(1) ¹Geht ein Betrieb oder Betriebsteil durch Rechtsgeschäft auf einen anderen Inhaber über, so tritt dieser in die Rechte und Pflichten aus den im Zeitpunkt des Übergangs bestehenden Arbeitsverhältnissen ein. ²Sind diese Rechte und Pflichten durch Rechtsnormen eines Tarifvertrags oder durch eine Betriebsvereinbarung geregelt, so werden sie Inhalt des Arbeitsverhältnisses zwischen dem neuen Inhaber und dem Arbeitnehmer und dürfen nicht vor Ablauf eines Jahres nach dem Zeitpunkt des Übergangs zum Nachteil des Arbeitnehmers geändert werden. ³Satz 2 gilt nicht, wenn die Rechte und Pflichten bei dem neuen Inhaber durch Rechtsnormen eines anderen Tarifvertrags oder durch eine andere Betriebsvereinbarung geregelt werden. ⁴Vor Ablauf der Frist nach Satz 2 können die Rechte und Pflichten geändert werden, wenn der Tarifvertrag oder die Betriebsvereinbarung nicht mehr gilt oder bei fehlender beiderseitiger Tarifgebundenheit im Geltungsbereich eines anderen Tarifvertrags dessen Anwendung zwischen dem neuen Inhaber und dem Arbeitnehmer vereinbart wird.

(2) ¹Der bisherige Arbeitgeber haftet neben dem neuen Inhaber für Ver-

exercised his or her rights in a legitimate manner.

Section 613
Strictly Personal Obligation and Entitlement

¹In case of doubt, the person obligated to perform the service shall perform it in person. ²In case of doubt the claim to the services is not transferable.

Section 613a
Rights and Obligations Upon the Transfer of a Business

(1) ¹Where a business or part of a business is transferred to another owner by means of a legal transaction, the new owner enters into the rights and obligations arising from the employment relationships in existence at the time of transfer. ²Where these rights and obligations are regulated by means of the legal standards set in a collective bargaining agreement or by a works agreement, they shall become an integral part of the employment contract between the new owner and the employee and may not be altered to the detriment of the employee until one year has elapsed following the date of transfer. ³Sentence 2 shall not apply if the rights and obligations in the relationship with the new owner are regulated by means of the legal standards set in another collective bargaining agreement or another works agreement. ⁴The rights and obligations may be altered prior to the expiration of the period pursuant to sentence 2 if the collective bargaining agreement or the works agreement has ceased to exist or, if neither party is bound to a collective bargaining agreement, within the scope of application of another collective bargaining agreement, the application of which is agreed upon between the new owner and the employee.

(2) ¹The former owner shall be jointly and severally liable together with the

pflichtungen nach Absatz 1, soweit sie vor dem Zeitpunkt des Übergangs entstanden sind und vor Ablauf von einem Jahr nach diesem Zeitpunkt fällig werden, als Gesamtschuldner. [2]Werden solche Verpflichtungen nach dem Zeitpunkt des Übergangs fällig, so haftet der bisherige Arbeitgeber für sie jedoch nur in dem Umfang, der dem im Zeitpunkt des Übergangs abgelaufenen Teil ihres Bemessungszeitraums entspricht.

(3) Absatz 2 gilt nicht, wenn eine juristische Person oder eine Personenhandelsgesellschaft durch Umwandlung erlischt.

(4) [1]Die Kündigung des Arbeitsverhältnisses eines Arbeitnehmers durch den bisherigen Arbeitgeber oder durch den neuen Inhaber wegen des Übergangs eines Betriebs oder eines Betriebsteils ist unwirksam. [2]Das Recht zur Kündigung des Arbeitsverhältnisses aus anderen Gründen bleibt unberührt.

(5) Der bisherige Arbeitgeber oder der neue Inhaber hat die von einem Übergang betroffenen Arbeitnehmer vor dem Übergang in Textform zu unterrichten über:
1. den Zeitpunkt oder den geplanten Zeitpunkt des Übergangs,
2. den Grund für den Übergang,
3. die rechtlichen, wirtschaftlichen und sozialen Folgen des Übergangs für die Arbeitnehmer und
4. die hinsichtlich der Arbeitnehmer in Aussicht genommenen Maßnahmen.

(6) [1]Der Arbeitnehmer kann dem Übergang des Arbeitsverhältnisses innerhalb eines Monats nach Zugang der Unterrichtung nach Absatz 5 schriftlich widersprechen. [2]Der Widerspruch kann gegenüber dem bisherigen Arbeitgeber oder dem neuen Inhaber erklärt werden.

new owner for those obligations pursuant to subsection (1) which arise prior to the date of transfer and become due before the expiration of one year after that date. [2]Where such obligations become due after the date of transfer, the previous owner shall be liable for them, however only for the fraction of the total assessment period reflecting the time elapsed before the transfer date.

(3) Subsection (2) shall not apply if a legal entity or a commercial partnership ceases to exist by virtue of transformation.

(4) [1]Any termination of an employee's employment relationship by the former employer or the new owner on account of the transfer of a business or part of a business shall be invalid. [2]The right to terminate the employment relationship for other reasons remains unaffected.

(5) The former employer or new owner shall inform the employees affected by a transfer in writing prior to the transfer with respect to:
1. the date or planned date of the transfer,
2. the reason for the transfer,
3. the legal, economic and social ramifications of the transfer for the employers, and
4. the prospective measures to be taken with respect to the employees.

(6) [1]The employee may object to the transfer of the employment relationship in writing within one month after receiving the notification pursuant to subsection (5). [2]The objection may be declared to the former employer or the new owner.

§ 614
Fälligkeit der Vergütung

[1]Die Vergütung ist nach der Leistung der Dienste zu entrichten. [2]Ist die Ver-

Section 614
Payability of the Remuneration

[1]The remuneration shall be payable after performance of the service. [2]If the

gütung nach Zeitabschnitten bemessen, so ist sie nach dem Ablauf der einzelnen Zeitabschnitte zu entrichten.

remuneration is calculated by periods of time, it shall be payable at the end of each individual time period.

§ 615
Vergütung bei Annahmeverzug und bei Betriebsrisiko

Section 615
Remuneration in Case of Default in Acceptance and Operational Risk

[1] Kommt der Dienstberechtigte mit der Annahme der Dienste in Verzug, so kann der Verpflichtete für die infolge des Verzugs nicht geleisteten Dienste die vereinbarte Vergütung verlangen, ohne zur Nachleistung verpflichtet zu sein. [2] Er muss sich jedoch den Wert desjenigen anrechnen lassen, was er infolge des Unterbleibens der Dienstleistung erspart oder durch anderweitige Verwendung seiner Dienste erwirbt oder zu erwerben böswillig unterlässt. [3] Die Sätze 1 und 2 gelten entsprechend in den Fällen, in denen der Arbeitgeber das Risiko des Arbeitsausfalls trägt.

[1] If the party entitled to the service is in default of acceptance of the service, the party obligated to render the service may demand the agreed upon remuneration for the service not performed as a result of the default, without being obligated to make up for services not performed. [2] The obligated party must, however, deduct what he has saved as a result of not performing such service or has acquired or maliciously failed to acquire. [3] Sentences 1 and 2 apply *mutatis mutandis* in cases in which the employer bears the risk of the loss of work hours.

§ 616
Vorübergehende Verhinderung

Section 616
Temporary Hindrance

[1] Der zur Dienstleistung Verpflichtete wird des Anspruchs auf die Vergütung nicht dadurch verlustig, dass er für eine verhältnismäßig nicht erhebliche Zeit durch einen in seiner Person liegenden Grund ohne sein Verschulden an der Dienstleistung verhindert wird. [2] Er muss sich jedoch den Betrag anrechnen lassen, welcher ihm für die Zeit der Verhinderung aus einer auf Grund gesetzlicher Verpflichtung bestehenden Kranken- oder Unfallversicherung zukommt.

[1] The obligated party shall not lose his claim to remuneration due to being hindered, through no fault of his own, from performing the service for a comparatively insignificant period of time due to personal reasons. [2] He must, however, deduct the amount accruing to him for the period of his incapacity of the health and accident insurance he has taken out due to a statutory obligation.

§ 618
Pflicht zu Schutzmaßnahmen

Section 618
Duty to Take Precautions

(1) Der Dienstberechtigte hat Räume, Vorrichtungen oder Gerätschaften, die er zur Verrichtung der Dienste zu beschaffen hat, so einzurichten und zu unterhalten und Dienstleistungen, die unter seiner Anordnung oder seiner

(1) The entitled party shall furnish and maintain the rooms, equipment and tools he needs to supply for the performance of the services in such a way that the obligated party is protected against danger to his health and safety,

Leitung vorzunehmen sind, so zu regeln, dass der Verpflichtete gegen Gefahr für Leben und Gesundheit soweit geschützt ist, als die Natur der Dienstleistung es gestattet.

(2) Ist der Verpflichtete in die häusliche Gemeinschaft aufgenommen, so hat der Dienstberechtigte in Ansehung des Wohn- und Schlafraums, der Verpflegung sowie der Arbeits- und Erholungszeit diejenigen Einrichtungen und Anordnungen zu treffen, welche mit Rücksicht auf die Gesundheit, die Sittlichkeit und die Religion des Verpflichteten erforderlich sind.

(3) Erfüllt der Dienstberechtigte die ihm in Ansehung des Lebens und der Gesundheit des Verpflichteten obliegenden Verpflichtungen nicht, so finden auf seine Verpflichtung zum Schadensersatz die für unerlaubte Handlungen geltenden Vorschriften der §§ 842 bis 846 entsprechende Anwendung.

§ 619
Unabdingbarkeit der Fürsorgepflichten

Die dem Dienstberechtigten nach den §§ 617, 618 obliegenden Verpflichtungen können nicht im Voraus durch Vertrag aufgehoben oder beschränkt werden.

§ 619 a
Beweislast bei Haftung des Arbeitnehmers

Abweichend von § 280 Abs. 1 hat der Arbeitnehmer dem Arbeitgeber Ersatz für den aus der Verletzung einer Pflicht aus dem Arbeitsverhältnis entstehenden Schaden nur zu leisten, wenn er die Pflichtverletzung zu vertreten hat.

§ 620
Beendigung des Dienstverhältnisses

(1) Das Dienstverhältnis endigt mit dem Ablauf der Zeit, für die es eingegangen ist.

to the extent permitted by the nature of the services to be performed.

(2) Where the obligated party is taken into the household, the entitled party shall make such arrangements and measures with respect to his living and sleeping quarters, his board, as well as time for work and recreation as are necessary in light of the health, morals and religion of the obligated party.

(3) If the entitled party does not fulfill the obligations imposed upon him with respect to the obligated party's health and safety, the provisions of sections 842 to 846 applicable to tort shall apply *mutatis mutandis* to his obligation to pay damages.

Section 619
Mandatory Nature of Duties of Care

The obligations imposed upon the entitled party pursuant to sections 617 and 618 cannot be avoided or limited by contractual provisions in advance.

Section 619 a
Burden of Proof Where Employee is Liable

Notwithstanding section 280 (1), the employee shall only compensate the employer for damage arising from the breach of a duty under the employment relationship if he is responsible for the breach of duty.

Section 620
Termination of the Service Relationship

(1) The service relationship shall end with the expiration of the agreed term.

(2) Ist die Dauer des Dienstverhältnisses weder bestimmt noch aus der Beschaffenheit oder dem Zwecke der Dienste zu entnehmen, so kann jeder Teil das Dienstverhältnis nach Maßgabe der §§ 621 bis 623 kündigen.

(3) Für Arbeitsverträge, die auf bestimmte Zeit abgeschlossen werden, gilt das Teilzeit- und Befristungsgesetz.

§ 621
Kündigungsfristen bei Dienstverhältnissen

Bei einem Dienstverhältnis, das kein Arbeitsverhältnis im Sinne des § 622 ist, ist die Kündigung zulässig,

1. wenn die Vergütung nach Tagen bemessen ist, an jedem Tag für den Ablauf des folgenden Tages;
2. wenn die Vergütung nach Wochen bemessen ist, spätestens am ersten Werktag einer Woche für den Ablauf des folgenden Sonnabends;
3. wenn die Vergütung nach Monaten bemessen ist, spätestens am fünfzehnten eines Monats für den Schluss des Kalendermonats;
4. wenn die Vergütung nach Vierteljahren oder längeren Zeitabschnitten bemessen ist, unter Einhaltung einer Kündigungsfrist von sechs Wochen für den Schluss eines Kalendervierteljahrs;
5. wenn die Vergütung nicht nach Zeitabschnitten bemessen ist, jederzeit; bei einem die Erwerbstätigkeit des Verpflichteten vollständig oder hauptsächlich in Anspruch nehmenden Dienstverhältnis ist jedoch eine Kündigungsfrist von zwei Wochen einzuhalten.

§ 622
Kündigungsfristen bei Arbeitsverhältnissen

(1) Das Arbeitsverhältnis eines Arbeiters oder eines Angestellten (Arbeit-

(2) Where the term of the service relationship is not fixed or cannot be inferred from the nature or purpose of the service to be rendered, either party may give notice to terminate the service relationship as provided for in sections 621 to 623.

(3) For employment agreements concluded for a fixed period of time, the Part-Time and Limited Term Employment Act *(Teilzeit- und Befristungsgesetz)* shall apply.

Section 621
Termination Notice Periods in Service Relationships

In a service relationship which is not an employment relationship within the meaning of section 622, notice of termination is permissible

1. on any day, for the end of the following day, if the remuneration is calculated by the day;
2. no later than on the first working day of a week for the end of the following Saturday, if the remuneration is calculated by the week;
3. no later than on the fifteenth day of any month for the end of the calendar month, if the remuneration is calculated by the month;
4. with the observance of a six-week notice period for the end of a calendar quarter, if the remuneration is calculated by the quarter or a longer period;
5. at any time if the remuneration is not calculated by a time period; however, where a service relationship completely or predominantly engages the working activities of the obligated party, a two-week notice period shall be observed.

Section 622
Termination Notice Period for an Employment Relationship

(1) The employment relationship of a wage worker or salaried employee (em-

nehmers) kann mit einer Frist von vier Wochen zum Fünfzehnten oder zum Ende eines Kalendermonats gekündigt werden.

(2) Für eine Kündigung durch den Arbeitgeber beträgt die Kündigungsfrist, wenn das Arbeitsverhältnis in dem Betrieb oder Unternehmen
1. zwei Jahre bestanden hat, einen Monat zum Ende eines Kalendermonats,
2. fünf Jahre bestanden hat, zwei Monate zum Ende eines Kalendermonats,
3. acht Jahre bestanden hat, drei Monate zum Ende eines Kalendermonats,
4. zehn Jahre bestanden hat, vier Monate zum Ende eines Kalendermonats,
5. zwölf Jahre bestanden hat, fünf Monate zum Ende eines Kalendermonats,
6. 15 Jahre bestanden hat, sechs Monate zum Ende eines Kalendermonats,
7. 20 Jahre bestanden hat, sieben Monate zum Ende eines Kalendermonats.

Bei der Berechnung der Beschäftigungsdauer werden Zeiten, die vor der Vollendung des 25. Lebensjahrs des Arbeitnehmers liegen, nicht berücksichtigt.

(3) Während einer vereinbarten Probezeit, längstens für die Dauer von sechs Monaten, kann das Arbeitsverhältnis mit einer Frist von zwei Wochen gekündigt werden.

(4) [1] Von den Absätzen 1 bis 3 abweichende Regelungen können durch Tarifvertrag vereinbart werden. [2] Im Geltungsbereich eines solchen Tarifvertrags gelten die abweichenden tarifvertraglichen Bestimmungen zwischen nicht tarifgebundenen Arbeitgebern und Arbeitnehmern, wenn ihre Anwendung zwischen ihnen vereinbart ist.

(5) [1] Einzelvertraglich kann eine kürzere als die in Absatz 1 genannte Kündigungsfrist nur vereinbart werden,

ployee) may be terminated by observing a four-week termination notice period, to be effective on the fifteenth or the last day of a calendar month.

(2) [1] The notice period for a termination by the employer shall have the following length: if the employment relationship has lasted
1. two years, one month up to the end of a calendar month,
2. five years, two months up to the end of a calendar month,
3. eight years, three months up to the end of a calendar month,
4. ten years, four months up to the end of a calendar month,
5. twelve years, five months up to the end of a calendar month,
6. fifteen years, six months up to the end of a calendar month,
7. twenty years, seven months up to the end of a calendar month.

[2] The period preceding the employee's 25th birthday shall not be taken into account when determining the duration of employment.

(3) During an agreed probation period, to last no longer than six months, the employment relationship may be terminated with a notice period of two weeks.

(4) [1] Termination notice periods differing from those set forth in subsections (1) through (3) may be agreed upon in a collective bargaining agreement. [2] In the area of applicability of such a collective bargaining agreement, the divergent collective bargaining agreement provisions between employers and employees not bound by a collective bargaining agreement shall apply if their applicability is agreed upon between them.

(5) [1] Termination notice periods shorter than those set forth in subsection (1) may only be agreed upon on an individual contractual basis

1. wenn ein Arbeitnehmer zur vorübergehenden Aushilfe eingestellt ist; dies gilt nicht, wenn das Arbeitsverhältnis über die Zeit von drei Monaten hinaus fortgesetzt wird;
2. wenn der Arbeitgeber in der Regel nicht mehr als 20 Arbeitnehmer ausschließlich der zu ihrer Berufsbildung Beschäftigten beschäftigt und die Kündigungsfrist vier Wochen nicht unterschreitet.

²Bei der Feststellung der Zahl der beschäftigten Arbeitnehmer sind teilzeitbeschäftigte Arbeitnehmer mit einer regelmäßigen wöchentlichen Arbeitszeit von nicht mehr als 20 Stunden mit 0,5 und nicht mehr als 30 Stunden mit 0,75 zu berücksichtigen. ³Die einzelvertragliche Vereinbarung längerer als der in den Absätzen 1 bis 3 genannten Kündigungsfristen bleibt hiervon unberührt.

(6) Für die Kündigung des Arbeitsverhältnisses durch den Arbeitnehmer darf keine längere Frist vereinbart werden als für die Kündigung durch den Arbeitgeber.

1. if an employee is hired on a temporary basis to provide help; this shall not apply, if the employment relationship exceeds three months.
2. if the employer, as a rule, employs no more than twenty employees, not including apprentices and the termination notice period is not less than four weeks.

²In establishing the number of employees, those part-time employees whose regular hours of work do not exceed 20 hours weekly shall be counted as 0.5 of an employee and those whose regular hours of work do not exceed 30 hours monthly shall be counted as 0.75 of an employee. ³Individual agreements providing for longer termination notice periods than those set forth in subsections (1) through (3) shall not be affected.

(6) It may not be stipulated that the notice period for termination by the employee will be longer than for termination by the employer.

§ 623
Schriftform der Kündigung

Die Beendigung von Arbeitsverhältnissen durch Kündigung oder Auflösungsvertrag bedürfen zu ihrer Wirksamkeit der Schriftform; die elektronische Form ist ausgeschlossen.

Section 623
Written Form of Termination

The termination of an employment relationship by dismissal, resignation or a termination agreement must be in written form to be effective; electronic form is excluded.

§ 624
Kündigungsfrist bei Verträgen über mehr als 5 Jahre

¹Ist das Dienstverhältnis für die Lebenszeit einer Person oder für längere Zeit als fünf Jahre eingegangen, so kann es von dem Verpflichteten nach dem Ablauf von fünf Jahren gekündigt werden. ²Die Kündigungsfrist beträgt sechs Monate.

Section 624
Termination Notice Period for Contracts Exceeding Five Years

¹Where the service relationship is entered into for the lifetime of a person or for longer than five years, it may be terminated by the obligated party after the expiration of five years. ²The termination notice period shall be six months.

§ 625
Stillschweigende Verlängerung

Wird das Dienstverhältnis nach dem Ablauf der Dienstzeit von dem Verpflichteten mit Wissen des anderen Teiles fortgesetzt, so gilt es als auf unbestimmte Zeit verlängert, sofern nicht der andere Teil unverzüglich widerspricht.

§ 626
Fristlose Kündigung aus wichtigem Grund

(1) Das Dienstverhältnis kann von jedem Vertragsteil aus wichtigem Grund ohne Einhaltung einer Kündigungsfrist gekündigt werden, wenn Tatsachen vorliegen, auf Grund derer dem Kündigenden unter Berücksichtigung aller Umstände des Einzelfalles und unter Abwägung der Interessen beider Vertragsteile die Fortsetzung des Dienstverhältnisses bis zum Ablauf der Kündigungsfrist oder bis zu der vereinbarten Beendigung des Dienstverhältnisses nicht zugemutet werden kann.

(2) [1]Die Kündigung kann nur innerhalb von zwei Wochen erfolgen. [2]Die Frist beginnt mit dem Zeitpunkt, in dem der Kündigungsberechtigte von den für die Kündigung maßgebenden Tatsachen Kenntnis erlangt. [3]Der Kündigende muss dem anderen Teil auf Verlangen den Kündigungsgrund unverzüglich schriftlich mitteilen.

§ 627
Fristlose Kündigung bei Vertrauensstellung

(1) Bei einem Dienstverhältnis, das kein Arbeitsverhältnis im Sinne des § 622 ist, ist die Kündigung auch ohne die in § 626 bezeichnete Voraussetzung zulässig, wenn der zur Dienstleistung Verpflichtete, ohne in einem dauernden Dienstverhältnis mit festen Bezügen zu stehen, Dienste höherer Art zu leisten

Section 625
Tacit Extension

Where the obligated party continues the service relationship beyond the expiration of the service period, with the knowledge of the other party, it shall be extended for an indefinite period unless the other party immediately objects.

Section 626
Termination Without Notice

(1) The employment relationship may be terminated without notice by either contractual party for good cause *(aus wichtigem Grund)* if circumstances are present which, taking the entire situation of the individual case into account and weighing the interests of both parties, render it unreasonable to expect the terminating party to continue the employment relationship until the termination period has elapsed or until the agreed upon conclusion of the employment relationship.

(2) [1]The termination must take place within two weeks. [2]The two-week period commences when the party entitled to terminate learns of the circumstances justifying the termination. [3]On request, the terminating party must immediately inform the other party in writing of the reasons for the termination.

Section 627
Termination Without Notice in Case of a Position of Confidence

(1) In the case of a service relationship which is not an employment relationship within the meaning of section 622, termination is possible even without the prerequisites set forth in section 626 if the obligated party must, without being in a continuous service relationship with fixed remuneration, perform

hat, die auf Grund besonderen Vertrauens übertragen zu werden pflegen.

(2) ¹Der Verpflichtete darf nur in der Art kündigen, dass sich der Dienstberechtigte die Dienste anderweit beschaffen kann, es sei denn, dass ein wichtiger Grund für die unzeitige Kündigung vorliegt. ²Kündigt er ohne solchen Grund zur Unzeit, so hat er dem Dienstberechtigten den daraus entstehenden Schaden zu ersetzen.

higher level services which are regularly entrusted on the basis of special confidence.

(2) ¹The obligated party may only give notice of termination in such a way that the entitled party can obtain the services elsewhere, unless good cause for the untimely notice exists. ²If he gives untimely notice without such good cause, he must compensate the entitled party for any damages resulting therefrom.

§ 628
Teilvergütung und Schadensersatz bei fristloser Kündigung

Section 628
Partial Remuneration and Damages in Case of Termination Without Notice

(1) ¹Wird nach dem Beginn der Dienstleistung das Dienstverhältnis auf Grund des § 626 oder des § 627 gekündigt, so kann der Verpflichtete einen seinen bisherigen Leistungen entsprechenden Teil der Vergütung verlangen. ²Kündigt er, ohne durch vertragswidriges Verhalten des anderen Teiles dazu veranlasst zu sein, oder veranlasst er durch sein vertragswidriges Verhalten die Kündigung des anderen Teiles, so steht ihm ein Anspruch auf die Vergütung insoweit nicht zu, als seine bisherigen Leistungen infolge der Kündigung für den anderen Teil kein Interesse haben. ³Ist die Vergütung für eine spätere Zeit im Voraus entrichtet, so hat der Verpflichtete sie nach Maßgabe des § 346 oder, wenn die Kündigung wegen eines Umstands erfolgt, den er nicht zu vertreten hat, nach den Vorschriften über die Herausgabe einer ungerechtfertigten Bereicherung zurückzuerstatten.

(1) ¹Where, upon commencement of the provision of service, notice of termination of the service relationship is given on the basis of section 626 or section 627, the obligated party may demand a part of the remuneration in proportion to the services already rendered. ²If he gives notice without being caused to do so by the other party's conduct in breach of the contract, or if he causes the other party to give notice by his conduct in breach of the contract, he shall have no claim to remuneration to the extent that the services he has already performed are of no interest to the other party as a result of the notice of termination. ³If the remuneration has been paid in advance for a later time, the obligated party must reimburse it pursuant to section 347 or, if the notice of termination results from circumstances beyond his control, in accordance with the provisions regarding the restitution of unjust enrichment.

(2) Wird die Kündigung durch vertragswidriges Verhalten des anderen Teiles veranlasst, so ist dieser zum Ersatz des durch die Aufhebung des Dienstverhältnisses entstehenden Schadens verpflichtet.

(2) If the notice was caused by the other part's conduct in breach of contract, the latter shall be liable for the damages resulting from the termination of the service relationship.

§ 629
Freizeit zur Stellungssuche

Nach der Kündigung eines dauernden Dienstverhältnisses hat der Dienstberechtigte dem Verpflichteten auf Verlangen angemessene Zeit zum Aufsuchen eines anderen Dienstverhältnisses zu gewähren.

§ 630
Pflicht zur Zeugniserteilung

¹Bei der Beendigung eines dauernden Dienstverhältnisses kann der Verpflichtete von dem anderen Teil ein schriftliches Zeugnis über das Dienstverhältnis und dessen Dauer fordern. ²Das Zeugnis ist auf Verlangen auf die Leistungen und die Führung im Dienst zu erstrecken. ³Die Erteilung des Zeugnisses in elektronischer Form ist ausgeschlossen. ⁴Wenn der Verpflichtete ein Arbeitnehmer ist, findet § 109 der Gewerbeordnung Anwendung.

Section 629
Time Off to Seek Employment

Following notice of termination of an ongoing service relationship, the party entitled to the services shall, upon request, grant the party obligated to render the services adequate time to seek other employment.

Section 630
Duty to Provide a Reference

¹At the end of an ongoing continuous service relationship, the obligated party may demand from the other party a written reference with respect to the service relationship and its duration. ²Such reference shall, upon request, also cover the obligated party's performance and conduct while rendering the service. ³The reference may not be provided in electronic form ⁴If the obligated party is an employee, section 109 of the Trade Code *(Gewerbeordnung)* shall apply.

II. General Equal Treatment Act
(Allgemeines Gleichbehandlungsgesetz – AGG)

14 August 2006, Federal Law Gazette I 2006, p. 1897

in the amended version of 5 February 2009

Abschnitt 1
Allgemeiner Teil

Chapter 1
General Provisions

§ 1
Ziel des Gesetzes

Section 1
Aim of the Act

Ziel des Gesetzes ist, Benachteiligungen aus Gründen der Rasse oder wegen der ethnischen Herkunft, des Geschlechts, der Religion oder Weltanschauung, einer Behinderung, des Alters oder der sexuellen Identität zu verhindern oder zu beseitigen.

The purpose of this Act is to prevent or eliminate adverse treatment on the grounds of race or ethnic origin, gender, religion or secular belief, a disability, age or sexual identity.

§ 2
Anwendungsbereich

Section 2
Scope of Application

(1) Benachteiligungen aus einem in § 1 genannten Grund sind nach Maßgabe dieses Gesetzes unzulässig in Bezug auf:

(1) Adverse treatment on one of the grounds set forth in section 1 shall be impermissible under this Act with respect to:

1. die Bedingungen, einschließlich Auswahlkriterien und Einstellungsbedingungen, für den Zugang zu unselbstständiger und selbstständiger Erwerbstätigkeit, unabhängig von Tätigkeitsfeld und beruflicher Position, sowie für den beruflichen Aufstieg,
2. die Beschäftigungs- und Arbeitsbedingungen einschließlich Arbeitsentgelt und Entlassungsbedingungen, insbesondere in individual- und kollektivrechtlichen Vereinbarungen und Maßnahmen bei der Durchführung und Beendigung eines Beschäftigungsverhältnisses sowie beim beruflichen Aufstieg,
3. den Zugang zu allen Formen und allen Ebenen der Berufsberatung, der Berufsbildung einschließlich der Be-

1. conditions for access to employment or self-employment, including selection criteria and recruitment conditions, whatever the branch of activity and at all levels of the professional hierarchy, including promotion,
2. employment and working conditions, including pay and dismissals, in particular in individual and collective bargaining agreements and measures for the execution and termination of an employment relationship as well as with respect to promotions,
3. access to all forms and all levels of vocational guidance, vocational training, including vocational education,

rufsausbildung, der beruflichen Weiterbildung und der Umschulung sowie der praktischen Berufserfahrung,
4. die Mitgliedschaft und Mitwirkung in einer Beschäftigten- oder Arbeitgebervereinigung oder einer Vereinigung, deren Mitglieder einer bestimmten Berufsgruppe angehören, einschließlich der Inanspruchnahme der Leistungen solcher Vereinigungen,
5. den Sozialschutz, einschließlich der sozialen Sicherheit und der Gesundheitsdienste,
6. die sozialen Vergünstigungen,
7. die Bildung,
8. den Zugang zu und die Versorgung mit Gütern und Dienstleistungen, die der Öffentlichkeit zur Verfügung stehen, einschließlich von Wohnraum.

(2) ¹Für Leistungen nach dem Sozialgesetzbuch gelten § 33c des Ersten Buches Sozialgesetzbuch und § 19a des Vierten Buches Sozialgesetzbuch. ¹Für die betriebliche Altersvorsorge gilt das Betriebsrentengesetz.

(3) ¹Die Geltung sonstiger Benachteiligungsverbote oder Gebote der Gleichbehandlung wird durch dieses Gesetz nicht berührt. ²Dies gilt auch für öffentlich-rechtliche Vorschriften, die dem Schutz bestimmter Personengruppen dienen.

(4) Für Kündigungen gelten ausschließlich die Bestimmungen zum allgemeinen und besonderen Kündigungsschutz.

§ 3
Begriffsbestimmungen

(1) ¹Eine unmittelbare Benachteiligung liegt vor, wenn eine Person wegen eines in § 1 genannten Grundes eine weniger günstige Behandlung erfährt, als eine andere Person in einer vergleichbaren

advanced vocational training and retraining, including practical work experience,
4. membership of and involvement in an organization of employees or employers, or any organization whose members carry on a particular profession, including the benefits provided by such organizations,
5. social protection, including social security and health services,
6. social advantages,
7. education,
8. access to and supply of goods and services which are available to the public, including housing.

(2) ¹Benefits pursuant to the Social Security Code (*Sozialgesetzbuch*) shall be governed by section 33c of the First Book of the Social Security Code and section 19a of the Fourth Book of the Social Security Code. ²The company pension schemes shall be governed by the Act for the Improvement of Company Pension Plans (*Betriebsrentengesetz*).

(3) ¹The validity of any other prohibitions of adverse treatment or requirements of equal treatment shall not be affected by this Act. ²This shall also apply with respect to public law regulations which serve to protect certain groups of persons.

(4) Dismissals shall be governed exclusively by the provisions on general and specific protection against unfair dismissal.

Section 3
Definition of Terms

(1) ¹Direct adverse treatment exists if, based on one of the grounds set forth in section 1, a person is treated less favorably than another is, has been or would be treated in a comparable situa-

Situation erfährt, erfahren hat oder erfahren würde. ²Eine unmittelbare Benachteiligung wegen des Geschlechts liegt in Bezug auf § 2 Abs. 1 Nr. 1 bis 4 auch im Falle einer ungünstigeren Behandlung einer Frau wegen Schwangerschaft oder Mutterschaft vor.

(2) Eine mittelbare Benachteiligung liegt vor, wenn dem Anschein nach neutrale Vorschriften, Kriterien oder Verfahren Personen wegen eines in § 1 genannten Grundes gegenüber anderen Personen in besonderer Weise benachteiligen können, es sei denn, die betreffenden Vorschriften, Kriterien oder Verfahren sind durch ein rechtmäßiges Ziel sachlich gerechtfertigt und die Mittel sind zur Erreichung dieses Ziels angemessen und erforderlich.

(3) Eine Belästigung ist eine Benachteiligung, wenn unerwünschte Verhaltensweisen, die mit einem in § 1 genannten Grund in Zusammenhang stehen, bezwecken oder bewirken, dass die Würde der betreffenden Person verletzt und ein von Einschüchterungen, Anfeindungen, Erniedrigungen, Entwürdigungen oder Beleidigungen gekennzeichnetes Umfeld geschaffen wird.

(4) Eine sexuelle Belästigung ist eine Benachteiligung in Bezug auf § 2 Abs. 1 Nr. 1 bis 4, wenn ein unerwünschtes, sexuell bestimmtes Verhalten, wozu auch unerwünschte sexuelle Handlungen und Aufforderungen zu diesen, sexuell bestimmte körperliche Berührungen, Bemerkungen sexuellen Inhalts sowie unerwünschtes Zeigen und sichtbares Anbringen von pornographischen Darstellungen gehören, bezweckt oder bewirkt, dass die Würde der betreffenden Person verletzt wird, insbesondere wenn ein von Einschüchterungen, Anfeindungen, Erniedrigungen, Entwürdigungen oder Beleidigungen gekennzeichnetes Umfeld geschaffen wird.

(5) ¹Die Anweisung zur Benachteiligung einer Person aus einem in § 1 genannten Grund gilt als Benachteiligung.

tion. ²Direct adverse treatment on grounds of gender also exists with respect to section 2 (1) nos. 1 to 4 where a woman is treated less favorably due to her pregnancy or maternity.

(2) Indirect adverse treatment exists if, on the basis of one of the grounds set forth in section 1, an apparently neutral provision, criterion or practice would put certain persons at a particular disadvantage compared with other persons, unless such provision, criterion or practice is objectively justified by a legitimate aim and the means of achieving that aim are appropriate and necessary.

(3) Harassment constitutes adverse treatment where unwanted conduct related to one of the grounds set forth in section 1 occurs with the purpose or effect of violating the dignity of the affected person and of creating an intimidating, hostile, degrading, humiliating or offensive environment.

(4) Sexual harassment constitutes adverse treatment with respect to section 2 (1) nos. 1 to 4 where any unwanted, sexually motivated conduct, which also includes unwanted sexual acts and demands to perform such acts, sexually motivated physical contact, remarks of a sexual content as well as the unwanted display and visible posting of pornographic images, occurs with the purpose or effect of violating the dignity of the affected person, in particular by creating an intimidating, hostile, degrading, humiliating or offensive environment.

(5) ¹Instructions to treat a person adversely on the basis of one of the grounds set forth in section 1 shall be

² Eine solche Anweisung liegt in Bezug auf § 2 Abs. 1 Nr. 1 bis 4 insbesondere vor, wenn jemand eine Person zu einem Verhalten bestimmt, das einen Beschäftigten oder eine Beschäftigte wegen eines in § 1 genannten Grundes benachteiligt oder benachteiligen kann.

deemed to constitute adverse treatment. ²Such instructions are in particular rendered with respect to section 2 (1) nos. 1 to 4 if someone orders a person to behave in a way which treats or could treat an employee adversely on the basis of one of the grounds set forth in section 1.

§ 4
Unterschiedliche Behandlung wegen mehrerer Gründe

Erfolgt eine unterschiedliche Behandlung wegen mehrerer der in § 1 genannten Gründe, so kann diese unterschiedliche Behandlung nach den §§ 8 bis 10 und 20 nur gerechtfertigt werden, wenn sich die Rechtfertigung auf alle diese Gründe erstreckt, derentwegen die unterschiedliche Behandlung erfolgt.

Section 4
Differences in Treatment on Multiple Grounds

If a difference in treatment occurs on the basis of two or more of the grounds set forth in section 1, then such difference in treatment may only be justified pursuant to sections 8 to 10 and 20 if the justification extends to all of the grounds for the difference in treatment.

§ 5
Positive Maßnahmen

Ungeachtet der in den §§ 8 bis 10 sowie in § 20 benannten Gründe ist eine unterschiedliche Behandlung auch zulässig, wenn durch geeignete und angemessene Maßnahmen bestehende Nachteile wegen eines in § 1 genannten Grundes verhindert oder ausgeglichen werden sollen.

Section 5
Positive Action

Apart from the grounds set forth in sections 8 to 10 as well as section 20, a difference in treatment shall also be permissible if suitable and appropriate measures are taken to prevent or compensate for existing disadvantages resulting from one of the grounds set forth in section 1.

Abschnitt 2
Schutz der Beschäftigten vor Benachteiligung

Unterabschnitt 1
Verbot der Benachteiligung

Chapter 2
Protection of Employees Against Adverse Treatment

Subchapter 1
Prohibition of Adverse Treatment

§ 6
Persönlicher Anwendungsbereich

(1) ¹Beschäftigte im Sinne dieses Gesetzes sind
1. Arbeitnehmerinnen und Arbeitnehmer,

Section 6
Personal Scope of Application

(1) ¹Employees within the meaning of this Act are
1. employees,

2. die zu ihrer Berufsbildung Beschäftigten,
3. Personen, die wegen ihrer wirtschaftlichen Unselbstständigkeit als arbeitnehmerähnliche Personen anzusehen sind; zu diesen gehören auch die in Heimarbeit Beschäftigten und die ihnen Gleichgestellten.
²Als Beschäftigte gelten auch die Bewerberinnen und Bewerber für ein Beschäftigungsverhältnis sowie die Personen, deren Beschäftigungsverhältnis beendet ist.

(2) ¹Arbeitgeber (Arbeitgeber und Arbeitgeberinnen) im Sinne dieses Abschnitts sind natürliche und juristische Personen sowie rechtsfähige Personengesellschaften, die Personen nach Absatz 1 beschäftigen. ²Werden Beschäftigte einem Dritten zur Arbeitsleistung überlassen, so gilt auch dieser als Arbeitgeber im Sinne dieses Abschnitts. ³Für die in Heimarbeit Beschäftigten und die ihnen Gleichgestellten tritt an die Stelle des Arbeitgebers der Auftraggeber oder Zwischenmeister.

(3) Soweit es die Bedingungen für den Zugang zur Erwerbstätigkeit sowie den beruflichen Aufstieg betrifft, gelten die Vorschriften dieses Abschnitts für Selbstständige und Organmitglieder, insbesondere Geschäftsführer oder Geschäftsführerinnen und Vorstände, entsprechend.

§ 7
Benachteiligungsverbot

(1) Beschäftigte dürfen nicht wegen eines in § 1 genannten Grundes benachteiligt werden; dies gilt auch, wenn die Person, die die Benachteiligung begeht, das Vorliegen eines in § 1 genannten Grundes bei der Benachteiligung nur annimmt.

(2) Bestimmungen in Vereinbarungen, die gegen das Benachteiligungsverbot des Absatzes 1 verstoßen, sind unwirksam.

2. apprentices,
3. persons who, due to their economic dependency, are to be seen as "persons similar to employees" (*arbeitnehmerähnliche Personen*); they also include persons working at home and those in an equivalent position.
²Applicants for an employment relationship are likewise deemed to be employees, as are those whose employment relationship has been ended.

(2) ¹Employers within the meaning of this Chapter are natural persons and legal entities, as well as partnerships having legal capacity, who employ persons as defined in subsection (1). ²If employees are being leased to a third party for the performance of work, such third party shall also be deemed to be an employer within the meaning of this Chapter. ³For those working at home and persons in an equivalent position, the principal or intermediary shall take the place of the employer.

(3) As far as the conditions for access to employment and promotion are concerned, the provisions in this chapter shall also apply to self-employed persons and members of governing bodies, in particular managing directors and members of the management board mutatis mutandis.

Section 7
Prohibition of Adverse Treatment

(1) Employees may not be treated adversely on the basis of one of the grounds set forth in section 1, this also applies if the person performing the adverse treatment merely assumed that one of the grounds set forth in section 1 was the case when carrying out the adverse treatment.

(2) Provisions in agreements which violate the prohibition of adverse treatment set forth in subsection (1) shall be invalid.

(3) Eine Benachteiligung nach Absatz 1 durch Arbeitgeber oder Beschäftigte ist eine Verletzung vertraglicher Pflichten.

(3) Adverse treatment pursuant to subsection (1) by the employer or employees shall constitute a breach of contractual duties.

§ 8
Zulässige unterschiedliche Behandlung wegen beruflicher Anforderungen

(1) Eine unterschiedliche Behandlung wegen eines in § 1 genannten Grundes ist zulässig, wenn dieser Grund wegen der Art der auszuübenden Tätigkeit oder der Bedingungen ihrer Ausübung eine wesentliche und entscheidende berufliche Anforderung darstellt, sofern der Zweck rechtmäßig und die Anforderung angemessen ist.

(2) Die Vereinbarung einer geringeren Vergütung für gleiche oder gleichwertige Arbeit wegen eines in § 1 genannten Grundes wird nicht dadurch gerechtfertigt, dass wegen eines in § 1 genannten Grundes besondere Schutzvorschriften gelten.

Section 8
Permissible Difference in Treatment Due to Occupational Requirements

(1) A difference of treatment which is based on one of the grounds set forth in section 1 shall be permissible if, due to the nature of the activity to be performed or the conditions of the performance, such grounds constitute a material and determining occupational requirement, when the objective is legitimate and the requirement is proportionate.

(2) Agreement on lower remuneration for equal or equivalent work on the basis of one of the grounds set forth in section 1 shall not be justified by the fact that special protective provisions apply on the basis of one of the grounds set forth in section 1.

§ 9
Zulässige unterschiedliche Behandlung wegen der Religion oder Weltanschauung

(1) Ungeachtet des § 8 ist eine unterschiedliche Behandlung wegen der Religion oder der Weltanschauung bei der Beschäftigung durch Religionsgemeinschaften, die ihnen zugeordneten Einrichtungen ohne Rücksicht auf ihre Rechtsform oder durch Vereinigungen, die sich die gemeinschaftliche Pflege einer Religion oder Weltanschauung zur Aufgabe machen, auch zulässig, wenn eine bestimmte Religion oder Weltanschauung unter Beachtung des Selbstverständnisses der jeweiligen Religionsgemeinschaft oder Vereinigung im Hinblick auf ihr Selbstbestimmungsrecht oder nach der Art der Tätigkeit eine gerechtfertigte berufliche Anforderung darstellt.

Section 9
Permissible Difference in Treatment Due to Religion or Secular Belief

(1) Apart from the cases set forth in section 8, a difference in treatment due to religion or secular belief shall be also permissible with regard to employment by religious communities and institutions associated with them, regardless of their legal form, or by associations which have set themselves the task of collectively cultivating a religion or secular belief if, taking into account the self-conception of the respective religious community or association in view of its right of self-determination or the nature of the activity to be performed, a certain religion or secular belief constitutes a justified occupational requirement.

(2) Das Verbot unterschiedlicher Behandlung wegen der Religion oder der Weltanschauung berührt nicht das Recht der in Absatz 1 genannten Religionsgemeinschaften, der ihnen zugeordneten Einrichtungen ohne Rücksicht auf ihre Rechtsform oder der Vereinigungen, die sich die gemeinschaftliche Pflege einer Religion oder Weltanschauung zur Aufgabe machen, von ihren Beschäftigten ein loyales und aufrichtiges Verhalten im Sinne ihres jeweiligen Selbstverständnisses verlangen zu können.

(2) The prohibition of differences in treatment due to religion or secular belief shall not affect the right of the religious communities mentioned in subsection (1), the institutions allocated to them, regardless of their legal form, or the associations which have set themselves the task of collectively cultivating a religion or secular belief, from being able to require their employees to act in good faith and with loyalty to their respective self-concept.

§ 10
Zulässige unterschiedliche Behandlung wegen des Alters

Section 10
Permissible Differences in Treatment Due to Age

¹Ungeachtet des § 8 ist eine unterschiedliche Behandlung wegen des Alters auch zulässig, wenn sie objektiv und angemessen und durch ein legitimes Ziel gerechtfertigt ist. ²Die Mittel zur Erreichung dieses Ziels müssen angemessen und erforderlich sein. ³Derartige unterschiedliche Behandlungen können insbesondere Folgendes einschließen:

¹Apart from the cases set forth in section 8, differences in treatment on grounds of age shall also be permissible if they are objectively and reasonably justified by a legitimate aim. ²The means of achieving that aim must be proportionate and necessary. ³Such differences in treatment may specifically include, among others:

1. die Festlegung besonderer Bedingungen für den Zugang zur Beschäftigung und zur beruflichen Bildung sowie besonderer Beschäftigungs- und Arbeitsbedingungen, einschließlich der Bedingungen für Entlohnung und Beendigung des Beschäftigungsverhältnisses, um die berufliche Eingliederung von Jugendlichen, älteren Beschäftigten und Personen mit Fürsorgepflichten zu fördern oder ihren Schutz sicherzustellen,
2. die Festlegung von Mindestanforderungen an das Alter, die Berufserfahrung oder das Dienstalter für den Zugang zur Beschäftigung oder für bestimmte mit der Beschäftigung verbundene Vorteile,
3. die Festsetzung eines Höchstalters für die Einstellung auf Grund der spezifischen Ausbildungsanforderungen eines bestimmten Arbeitsplatzes oder auf Grund der Notwen-

1. setting special conditions on access to employment and vocational training, employment and occupation, including conditions regarding remuneration and the termination of the employment relationship, in order to promote the vocational integration or ensure the protection of young people, older employees and persons with caring responsibilities,
2. fixing minimum requirements of age, professional experience or seniority in service for access to employment or to certain advantages linked to employment,
3. fixing a maximum age for recruitment which is based on the training requirements of the post in question or the need for a proportionate period of employment before retire-

digkeit einer angemessenen Beschäftigungszeit vor dem Eintritt in den Ruhestand,

4. die Festsetzung von Altersgrenzen bei den betrieblichen Systemen der sozialen Sicherheit als Voraussetzung für die Mitgliedschaft oder den Bezug von Altersrente oder von Leistungen bei Invalidität einschließlich der Festsetzung unterschiedlicher Altersgrenzen im Rahmen dieser Systeme für bestimmte Beschäftigte oder Gruppen von Beschäftigten und die Verwendung von Alterskriterien im Rahmen dieser Systeme für versicherungsmathematische Berechnungen,

5. eine Vereinbarung, die die Beendigung des Beschäftigungsverhältnisses ohne Kündigung zu einem Zeitpunkt vorsieht, zu dem der oder die Beschäftigte eine Rente wegen Alters beantragen kann; § 41 des Sechsten Buches Sozialgesetzbuch bleibt unberührt,

6. Differenzierungen von Leistungen in Sozialplänen im Sinne des Betriebsverfassungsgesetzes, wenn die Parteien eine nach Alter oder Betriebszugehörigkeit gestaffelte Abfindungsregelung geschaffen haben, in der die wesentlich vom Alter abhängenden Chancen auf dem Arbeitsmarkt durch eine verhältnismäßig starke Betonung des Lebensalters erkennbar berücksichtigt worden sind, oder Beschäftigte von den Leistungen des Sozialplans ausgeschlossen haben, die wirtschaftlich abgesichert sind, weil sie, gegebenenfalls nach Bezug von Arbeitslosengeld, rentenberechtigt sind.

ment,

4. fixing age limits in the company social security systems as a prerequisite for membership or the receipt of old-age pensions or of benefits in case of disability, including the fixing of different age limits within the framework of these systems for certain employees or groups of employees and the application of age criteria within the framework of these systems for actuarial calculations,

5. an agreement providing for the termination of the employment relationship without a dismissal at the time at which the employee may apply for a pension due to his or her age; section 41 of the Sixth Book of the Social Security Code remains unaffected,

6. making differentiations in the benefits provided under "social plans" (Sozialpläne) within the meaning of the Works Constitution Act (Betriebsverfassungsgesetz) if the parties have provided for a severance payment provision staggered according to age or seniority in which the chances on the labor market, which are materially dependent upon age, are discernibly taken into account by a relatively strong emphasis on age, or employees are excluded from the benefits of the social plan who are economically secured because they are entitled to pensions, after receiving unemployment benefits if applicable.

Unterabschnitt 2
Organisationspflichten des Arbeitgebers

§ 11
Ausschreibung

Ein Arbeitsplatz darf nicht unter Verstoß gegen § 7 Abs. 1 ausgeschrieben werden.

Subchapter 2
Organizational Duties of the Employer

Section 11
Advertising

A job position may not be advertised in violation of section 7 (1).

§ 12
Maßnahmen und Pflichten des Arbeitgebers

(1) ¹Der Arbeitgeber ist verpflichtet, die erforderlichen Maßnahmen zum Schutz vor Benachteiligungen wegen eines in § 1 genannten Grundes zu treffen. ²Dieser Schutz umfasst auch vorbeugende Maßnahmen.

(2) ¹Der Arbeitgeber soll in geeigneter Art und Weise, insbesondere im Rahmen der beruflichen Aus- und Fortbildung, auf die Unzulässigkeit solcher Benachteiligungen hinweisen und darauf hinwirken, dass diese unterbleiben. ²Hat der Arbeitgeber seine Beschäftigten in geeigneter Weise zum Zwecke der Verhinderung von Benachteiligung geschult, gilt dies als Erfüllung seiner Pflichten nach Absatz 1.

(3) Verstoßen Beschäftigte gegen das Benachteiligungsverbot des § 7 Abs. 1, so hat der Arbeitgeber die im Einzelfall geeigneten, erforderlichen und angemessenen Maßnahmen zur Unterbindung der Benachteiligung wie Abmahnung, Umsetzung, Versetzung oder Kündigung zu ergreifen.

(4) Werden Beschäftigte bei der Ausübung ihrer Tätigkeit durch Dritte nach § 7 Abs. 1 benachteiligt, so hat der Arbeitgeber die im Einzelfall geeigneten, erforderlichen und angemessenen Maßnahmen zum Schutz der Beschäftigten zu ergreifen.

(5) ¹Dieses Gesetz und § 61b des Arbeitsgerichtsgesetzes sowie Informationen über die für die Behandlung von Beschwerden nach § 13 zuständigen Stellen sind im Betrieb oder in der Dienststelle bekannt zu machen. ²Die Bekanntmachung kann durch Aushang oder Auslegung an geeigneter Stelle oder den Einsatz der im Betrieb oder der Dienststelle üblichen Informations- und Kommunikationstechnik erfolgen.

Section 12
Measures and Duties of the Employer

(1) ¹The employer shall be obliged to take the necessary measures to protect employees against adverse treatment based on one of the grounds set forth in section 1. ²Such protection also includes preventative measures.

(2) ¹The employer shall, in an appropriate manner, particularly in the course of the professional training and advanced vocational training, call attention to the impermissibility of such adverse treatment and act to ensure that it does not occur. ²If the employer has trained its employees in an appropriate manner for the purpose of preventing adverse treatment, it shall be deemed to have met its duty pursuant to subsection (1).

(3) If employees violate the prohibition of adverse treatment pursuant to section 7 (1), the employer shall take the measures that are necessary, appropriate and suitable for the individual case to stop the adverse treatment, such as a warning, transfer, relocation or dismissal.

(4) If employees are treated adversely by third parties pursuant to section 7 (1) while they are performing their work, the employer shall take the measures that are necessary, appropriate and suitable for the individual case to protect the employees.

(5) ¹This Act and section 61b of the Labor Court Act *(Arbeitsgerichtsgesetz)*, as well as information on the persons responsible for handling complaints pursuant to section 13 shall be made known in the workplace or the civil service workplace. ²Such announcement may be made by posting a notice or displaying it in an appropriate place or by means of the information and communication technology customarily used in the workplace or the civil service workplace.

Unterabschnitt 3 **Rechte des Beschäftigten**	**Subchapter 3** **Employee's Rights**
§ 13 **Beschwerderecht**	**Section 13** **Right to Make Complaints**
(1) ¹Die Beschäftigten haben das Recht, sich bei den zuständigen Stellen des Betriebs, des Unternehmens oder der Dienststelle zu beschweren, wenn sie sich im Zusammenhang mit ihrem Beschäftigungsverhältnis vom Arbeitgeber, von Vorgesetzten, anderen Beschäftigten oder Dritten wegen eines in § 1 genannten Grundes benachteiligt fühlen. ²Die Beschwerde ist zu prüfen und das Ergebnis der oder dem beschwerdeführenden Beschäftigten mitzuteilen.	(1) ¹Employees shall have the right to make a complaint to the competent person in the workplace, the company or the civil service workplace if they feel they have been subjected to adverse treatment by their employer, superior, other employees or third parties in connection with their employment on the basis of one of the grounds set forth in section 1. ²The complaint must be reviewed and the result communicated to the complaining employee.
(2) Die Rechte der Arbeitnehmervertretungen bleiben unberührt.	(2) The rights of the employees' representative bodies remain unaffected.
§ 14 **Leistungsverweigerungsrecht**	**Section 14** **Right to Refuse Performance**
¹Ergreift der Arbeitgeber keine oder offensichtlich ungeeignete Maßnahmen zur Unterbindung einer Belästigung oder sexuellen Belästigung am Arbeitsplatz, sind die betroffenen Beschäftigten berechtigt, ihre Tätigkeit ohne Verlust des Arbeitsentgelts einzustellen, soweit dies zu ihrem Schutz erforderlich ist. ²§ 273 des Bürgerlichen Gesetzbuchs bleibt unberührt.	¹If the employer takes no measures or obviously unsuitable measures to stop harassment or sexual harassment in the workplace, the affected employees shall be entitled to stop working without losing their remuneration to the extent this is necessary for their protection. ²Section 273 of the German Civil Code remains unaffected.
§ 15 **Entschädigung und Schadensersatz**	**Section 15** **Compensation and Damages**
(1) ¹Bei einem Verstoß gegen das Benachteiligungsverbot ist der Arbeitgeber verpflichtet, den hierdurch entstandenen Schaden zu ersetzen. ²Dies gilt nicht, wenn der Arbeitgeber die Pflichtverletzung nicht zu vertreten hat.	(1) ¹In the case of a violation of the prohibition of adverse treatment, the employer shall be obligated to pay compensation for the damage resulting therefrom. ²This shall not apply if the employer is not responsible for the breach of duty.
(2) ¹Wegen eines Schadens, der nicht Vermögensschaden ist, kann der oder die Beschäftigte eine angemessene Entschädigung in Geld verlangen. ²Die Entschädigung darf bei einer Nichtein-	(2) ¹Where the damage does not involve a financial loss, the employee or employees may demand an appropriate monetary compensation. ²In the event of a failure to hire a person, the com-

stellung drei Monatsgehälter nicht übersteigen, wenn der oder die Beschäftigte auch bei benachteiligungsfreier Auswahl nicht eingestellt worden wäre.

(3) Der Arbeitgeber ist bei der Anwendung kollektivrechtlicher Vereinbarungen nur dann zur Entschädigung verpflichtet, wenn er vorsätzlich oder grob fahrlässig handelt.

(4) [1] Ein Anspruch nach Absatz 1 oder 2 muss innerhalb einer Frist von zwei Monaten schriftlich geltend gemacht werden, es sei denn, die Tarifvertragsparteien haben etwas anderes vereinbart. [2] Die Frist beginnt im Falle einer Bewerbung oder eines beruflichen Aufstiegs mit dem Zugang der Ablehnung und in den sonstigen Fällen einer Benachteiligung zu dem Zeitpunkt, in dem der oder die Beschäftigte von der Benachteiligung Kenntnis erlangt.

(5) Im Übrigen bleiben Ansprüche gegen den Arbeitgeber, die sich aus anderen Rechtsvorschriften ergeben, unberührt.

(6) Ein Verstoß des Arbeitgebers gegen das Benachteiligungsverbot des § 7 Abs. 1 begründet keinen Anspruch auf Begründung eines Beschäftigungsverhältnisses, Berufsausbildungsverhältnisses oder einen beruflichen Aufstieg, es sei denn, ein solcher ergibt sich aus einem anderen Rechtsgrund.

pensation may not exceed three months' salary if the employee would not have been hired had the selection been free of adverse treatment.

(3) In the course of implementing collective agreements, the employer shall only be obliged to pay compensation if it has acted with intent or gross negligence.

(4) [1] A claim pursuant to subsections (1) or (2) must be asserted in writing within a period of two months unless the parties to the collective bargaining agreements have agreed otherwise. [2] This period shall begin to run in the case of a job application or a promotion upon receipt of the rejection and in the other cases of adverse treatment at the time at which the employee obtains knowledge of the adverse treatment.

(5) Otherwise, claims against the employer arising from other legal provisions shall remain unaffected.

(6) A violation of the prohibition of adverse treatment pursuant to section 7 (1) by the employer shall not create a claim to the formation of an employment relationship, a trainee relationship, or a promotion, unless such a claim arises on other grounds.

§ 16
Maßregelungsverbot

(1) [1] Der Arbeitgeber darf Beschäftigte nicht wegen der Inanspruchnahme von Rechten nach diesem Abschnitt oder wegen der Weigerung, eine gegen diesen Abschnitt verstoßende Anweisung auszuführen, benachteiligen. [2] Gleiches gilt für Personen, die den Beschäftigten hierbei unterstützen oder als Zeuginnen oder Zeugen aussagen.

(2) [1] Die Zurückweisung oder Duldung benachteiligender Verhaltensweisen durch betroffene Beschäftigte darf nicht

Section 16
Prohibition of Disciplinary Action

(1) [1] The employer may not subject employees to adverse treatment due to their exercising of rights under this Chapter or refusal to carry out instructions which are in violation of this Chapter. [2] The same shall apply to persons who support the employees against such treatment or testify as witnesses.

(2) [1] The rejection or toleration of conduct involving adverse treatment by the affected employees may not be in-

als Grundlage für eine Entscheidung herangezogen werden, die diese Beschäftigten berührt. ²Absatz 1 Satz 2 gilt entsprechend.

(3) § 22 gilt entsprechend.

Unterabschnitt 4
Ergänzende Vorschriften

§ 17
Soziale Verantwortung der Beteiligten

(1) Tarifvertragsparteien, Arbeitgeber, Beschäftigte und deren Vertretungen sind aufgefordert, im Rahmen ihrer Aufgaben und Handlungsmöglichkeiten an der Verwirklichung des in § 1 genannten Ziels mitzuwirken.

(2) ¹In Betrieben, in denen die Voraussetzungen des § 1 Abs. 1 Satz 1 des Betriebsverfassungsgesetzes vorliegen, können bei einem groben Verstoß des Arbeitgebers gegen Vorschriften aus diesem Abschnitt der Betriebsrat oder eine im Betrieb vertretene Gewerkschaft unter der Voraussetzung des § 23 Abs. 3 Satz 1 des Betriebsverfassungsgesetzes die dort genannten Rechte gerichtlich geltend machen; § 23 Abs. 3 Satz 2 bis 5 des Betriebsverfassungsgesetzes gilt entsprechend. ²Mit dem Antrag dürfen nicht Ansprüche des Benachteiligten geltend gemacht werden.

§ 18
Mitgliedschaft in Vereinigungen

(1) Die Vorschriften dieses Abschnitts gelten entsprechend für die Mitgliedschaft oder die Mitwirkung in einer

1. Tarifvertragspartei,

2. Vereinigung, deren Mitglieder einer bestimmten Berufsgruppe angehören oder die eine überragende Machtstellung im wirtschaftlichen oder sozialen Bereich innehat, wenn ein grundlegendes Interesse am Erwerb der

voked as a basis for a decision involving these employees. ²Para. (1) sentence 2 applies *mutatis mutandis*.

(3) Section 22 applies *mutatis mutandis*.

Subchapter 4
Supplementary Provisions

Section 17
Social Responsibility of the Parties

(1) Parties to collective bargaining agreements, employers, employees and their representative bodies are called upon to contribute to the realization of the purpose defined in section 1 to the extent they are able in the course of carrying out their tasks.

(2) ¹In workplaces in which the prerequisites set forth in section 1 (1) sentence 1 of the Works Constitution Act are met, and where the employer is grossly in violation of provisions in this Chapter, the works council or a trade union represented in the workplace may, if the prerequisites set forth in section 23 (3) sentence 1 Works Constitution Act are met, assert the rights mentioned therein before a court; section 23 (3) sentences 2 to 5 Works Constitution Act apply *mutatis mutandis*. ²Claims of victims of adverse treatment may not be asserted by such bodies.

Section 18
Membership in Associations

(1) The provisions of this Chapter shall apply *mutatis mutandis* for membership or participation in

1. a party to a collective bargaining agreement,

2. an association whose members belong to a certain professional group or which holds a dominant position of power in the economic or social realm, if a fundamental interest in the acquisition of membership exists,

Mitgliedschaft besteht, sowie deren jeweiligen Zusammenschlüssen.

(2) Wenn die Ablehnung einen Verstoß gegen das Benachteiligungsverbot des § 7 Abs. 1 darstellt, besteht ein Anspruch auf Mitgliedschaft oder Mitwirkung in den in Absatz 1 genannten Vereinigungen.

as well as their respective combinations.

(2) If a rejection constitutes a violation of the prohibition of adverse treatment pursuant to section 7 (1), a claim for membership or participation in the associations set forth in subsection (1) shall exist.

Abschnitt 3
Schutz vor Benachteiligung im Zivilrechtsverkehr

Chapter 3
Protection Against Adverse Treatment Under Civil Law

§ 19
Zivilrechtliches Benachteiligungsverbot

Section 19
Prohibition of Adverse Treatment Under Civil Law

(1) Eine Benachteiligung aus Gründen der Rasse oder wegen der ethnischen Herkunft, wegen des Geschlechts, der Religion, einer Behinderung, des Alters oder der sexuellen Identität bei der Begründung, Durchführung und Beendigung zivilrechtlicher Schuldverhältnisse, die

(1) Adverse treatment on the grounds of race or ethnic origin, gender, religion, a disability, age or sexual identity is impermissible in the formation, performance and termination of civil law contractual relationships which

1. typischerweise ohne Ansehen der Person zu vergleichbaren Bedingungen in einer Vielzahl von Fällen zustande kommen (Massengeschäfte) oder bei denen das Ansehen der Person nach der Art des Schuldverhältnisses eine nachrangige Bedeutung hat und die zu vergleichbaren Bedingungen in einer Vielzahl von Fällen zustande kommen oder

1. would typically come about under comparable conditions without distinction as to person in a great number of cases (bulk transactions) or where, given the type of contractual relationship involved, a distinction as to person would only be of secondary importance, and such contractual relationships come about under comparable conditions in a great number of cases or

2. eine privatrechtliche Versicherung zum Gegenstand haben, ist unzulässig.

2. involve private law insurance.

(2) Eine Benachteiligung aus Gründen der Rasse oder wegen der ethnischen Herkunft ist darüber hinaus auch bei der Begründung, Durchführung und Beendigung sonstiger zivilrechtlicher Schuldverhältnisse im Sinne des § 2 Abs. 1 Nr. 5 bis 8 unzulässig.

(2) Moreover, adverse treatment on the grounds of race or ethnic origin is also impermissible in the formation, performance and termination of all other civil law contractual relationships within the meaning of section 2 (1) nos. 5 to 8.

(3) Bei der Vermietung von Wohnraum ist eine unterschiedliche Behandlung im Hinblick auf die Schaffung und Er-

(3) In connection with the letting of housing, a difference in treatment with a view to the creation and maintenance

haltung sozial stabiler Bewohnerstrukturen und ausgewogener Siedlungsstrukturen sowie ausgeglichener wirtschaftlicher, sozialer und kultureller Verhältnisse zulässig.

(4) Die Vorschriften dieses Abschnitts finden keine Anwendung auf familien- und erbrechtliche Schuldverhältnisse.

(5) ¹Die Vorschriften dieses Abschnitts finden keine Anwendung auf zivilrechtliche Schuldverhältnisse, bei denen ein besonderes Nähe- oder Vertrauensverhältnis der Parteien oder ihrer Angehörigen begründet wird. ²Bei Mietverhältnissen kann dies insbesondere der Fall sein, wenn die Parteien oder ihre Angehörigen Wohnraum auf demselben Grundstück nutzen. ³Die Vermietung von Wohnraum zum nicht nur vorübergehenden Gebrauch ist in der Regel kein Geschäft im Sinne des Absatzes 1 Nr. 1, wenn der Vermieter insgesamt nicht mehr als 50 Wohnungen vermietet.

of socially stable residential structures and well-balanced settlements, as well as well-balanced economic, social and cultural conditions shall be permissible.

(4) The provisions of this Chapter shall have no application to contractual relationships governed by family law or dealing with inheritances.

(5) ¹The provisions of this Chapter shall have no application to civil law contractual relationships which create a special relationship of trust between the parties or their relatives. ²This can particularly be the case with leases if the parties or their relatives use housing space on the same property. ³The letting of housing space for not merely temporary use is, as a rule, not a transaction within the meaning of subsection (1) no. 1 if the does not rent out more than 50 residences in all.

§ 20
Zulässige unterschiedliche Behandlung

(1) ¹Eine Verletzung des Benachteiligungsverbots ist nicht gegeben, wenn für eine unterschiedliche Behandlung wegen der Religion, einer Behinderung, des Alters, der sexuellen Identität oder des Geschlechts ein sachlicher Grund vorliegt. ²Das kann insbesondere der Fall sein, wenn die unterschiedliche Behandlung

1. der Vermeidung von Gefahren, der Verhütung von Schäden oder anderen Zwecken vergleichbarer Art dient,
2. dem Bedürfnis nach Schutz der Intimsphäre oder der persönlichen Sicherheit Rechnung trägt,
3. besondere Vorteile gewährt und ein Interesse an der Durchsetzung der Gleichbehandlung fehlt,
4. an die Religion eines Menschen anknüpft und im Hinblick auf die Aus-

Section 20
Permissible Differences in Treatment

(1) ¹A difference in treatment due to religion, a disability, age, sexual identity or gender shall not constitute a violation of the prohibition of adverse treatment if there are objective grounds for such treatment. ²This can in particular be the case if the difference in treatment

1. serves to avoid danger, to prevent damage or serves other purposes of a comparable nature,
2. takes the need for protection of privacy or personal security into account,
3. grants special benefits and there is no interest in enforcing equal treatment,
4. is linked to the religion of a person and is justified in view of the exercise

übung der Religionsfreiheit oder auf das Selbstbestimmungsrecht der Religionsgemeinschaften, der ihnen zugeordneten Einrichtungen ohne Rücksicht auf ihre Rechtsform sowie der Vereinigungen, die sich die gemeinschaftliche Pflege einer Religion zur Aufgabe machen, unter Beachtung des jeweiligen Selbstverständnisses gerechtfertigt ist.

(2) [1] Eine unterschiedliche Behandlung wegen des Geschlechts ist im Falle des § 19 Abs. 1 Nr. 2 bei den Prämien oder Leistungen nur zulässig, wenn dessen Berücksichtigung bei einer auf relevanten und genauen versicherungsmathematischen und statistischen Daten beruhenden Risikobewertung ein bestimmender Faktor ist. [2] Kosten im Zusammenhang mit Schwangerschaft und Mutterschaft dürfen auf keinen Fall zu unterschiedlichen Prämien oder Leistungen führen. [3] Eine unterschiedliche Behandlung wegen der Religion, einer Behinderung, des Alters oder der sexuellen Identität ist im Falle des § 19 Abs. 1 Nr. 2 nur zulässig, wenn diese auf anerkannten Prinzipien risikoadäquater Kalkulation beruht, insbesondere auf einer versicherungsmathematisch ermittelten Risikobewertung unter Heranziehung statistischer Erhebungen.

of religious freedom or the right to self-determination of a religious community or the institutions attributed to it, regardless of their legal form, as well as associations which have set themselves the task of collectively cultivating a religion taking into account their self-conception.

(2) [1] In the cases set forth in section 19 (1) no. 2, a difference in treatment due to gender shall only be permissible in relation to premiums and to benefits where gender is a determining factor in the assessment of risk based on relevant and accurate actuarial and statistical data. [2] Costs related to pregnancy or maternity shall under no circumstances lead to differences in premiums and benefits. [3] A difference in treatment due to religion, a disability, age or sexual identity shall only be permissible in the cases set forth in section 19 (1) no. 2 if this is based on recognized principles of risk-adjusted calculations, in particular an assessment of risk based on an actuarial calculation, taking statistical data into account.

§ 21
Ansprüche

(1) [1] Der Benachteiligte kann bei einem Verstoß gegen das Benachteiligungsverbot unbeschadet weiterer Ansprüche die Beseitigung der Beeinträchtigung verlangen. [2] Sind weitere Beeinträchtigungen zu besorgen, so kann er auf Unterlassung klagen.

(2) [1] Bei einer Verletzung des Benachteiligungsverbots ist der Benachteiligende verpflichtet, den hierdurch entstandenen Schaden zu ersetzen. [2] Dies gilt nicht, wenn der Benachteiligende die Pflichtverletzung nicht zu vertreten hat. [2] Wegen eines Schadens, der nicht Ver-

Section 21
Claims

(1) [1] In the event of a violation of the prohibition of adverse treatment, the disadvantaged party may, irrespective of further claims, demand the removal of the impairment. [2] If further impairments are to be feared, he or she may file a cease and desist action.

(2) [1] In the event of a violation of the prohibition of adverse treatment, the offender shall be obligated to compensate the victim for the damage resulting from his actions. [2] This shall not apply if the offender is not responsible for the breach of duty. [3] Where the damage

mögensschaden ist, kann der Benachteiligte eine angemessene Entschädigung in Geld verlangen.

(3) Ansprüche aus unerlaubter Handlung bleiben unberührt.

(4) Auf eine Vereinbarung, die von dem Benachteiligungsverbot abweicht, kann sich der Benachteiligende nicht berufen.

(5) [1] Ein Anspruch nach den Absätzen 1 und 2 muss innerhalb einer Frist von zwei Monaten geltend gemacht werden. [2] Nach Ablauf der Frist kann der Anspruch nur geltend gemacht werden, wenn der Benachteiligte ohne Verschulden an der Einhaltung der Frist verhindert war.

does not involve a financial loss, the disadvantaged person may demand appropriate monetary compensation.

(3) Tort claims remain unaffected.

(4) The offender may not invoke an agreement which derogates from the prohibition of adverse treatment.

(5) [1] A claim pursuant to paragraphs 1 and 2 must be asserted within a period of two months. [2] After this period, a claim may only be asserted if the disadvantaged person was prevented from adhering to this time period due to circumstances beyond his or her control.

Abschnitt 4
Rechtsschutz

Chapter 4
Legal Protection

§ 22
Beweislast

Section 22
Burden of Proof

Wenn im Streitfall die eine Partei Indizien beweist, die eine Benachteiligung wegen eines in § 1 genannten Grundes vermuten lassen, trägt die andere Partei die Beweislast dafür, dass kein Verstoß gegen die Bestimmungen zum Schutz vor Benachteiligung vorgelegen hat.

If one party to a dispute proves the existence of indications that would give rise to an assumption of adverse treatment based on one of the grounds set forth in section 1, it shall be for the other party to prove that no violation of the provisions for the protection against adverse treatment occurred.

§ 23
Unterstützung durch Antidiskriminierungsverbände

Section 23
Support from Anti-Discrimination Organizations

(1) [1] Antidiskriminierungsverbände sind Personenzusammenschlüsse, die nicht gewerbsmäßig und nicht nur vorübergehend entsprechend ihrer Satzung die besonderen Interessen von benachteiligten Personen oder Personengruppen nach Maßgabe von § 1 wahrnehmen. [2] Die Befugnisse nach den Absätzen 2 bis 4 stehen ihnen zu, wenn sie mindestens 75 Mitglieder haben oder einen Zusammenschluss aus mindestens sieben Verbänden bilden.

(1) [1] Anti-discrimination organizations are associations of persons which represent the special interests of victims of adverse treatment or groups of such persons as defined in section 1 on a non-commercial and ongoing basis in accordance with their bylaws. [2] They are entitled to the powers set forth in subsections (2) to (4) if they have at least 75 members or form a combination of at least seven organizations.

(2) ¹Antidiskriminierungsverbände sind befugt, im Rahmen ihres Satzungszwecks in gerichtlichen Verfahren als Beistände Benachteiligter in der Verhandlung aufzutreten. ²Im Übrigen bleiben die Vorschriften der Verfahrensordnungen, insbesondere diejenigen, nach denen Beiständen weiterer Vortrag untersagt werden kann, unberührt.

(3) Antidiskriminierungsverbänden ist im Rahmen ihres Satzungszwecks die Besorgung von Rechtsangelegenheiten Benachteiligter gestattet.

(4) Besondere Klagerechte und Vertretungsbefugnisse von Verbänden zu Gunsten von behinderten Menschen bleiben unberührt.

(2) ¹ Anti-discrimination organizations are authorized, within the scope of their purpose as set forth in their bylaws, to appear in court proceedings as a legal advisor *(Beistand)* to victims of adverse treatment. ²In all other respects, the provisions of the procedural statutes remain unaffected, in particular those pursuant to which legal advisors can be prohibited from continuing with their arguments.

(3) Anti-discrimination organizations shall be permitted to handle the legal affairs of victims of adverse treatment as permitted within the scope of their purpose as set forth in their by-laws.

(4) The special rights of organizations supporting disabled persons to file suit and their powers of representation remain unaffected.

Abschnitt 5
Sonderregelungen für öffentlich-rechtliche Dienstverhältnisse

Chapter 5
Special Regulations for Civil Service Positions

§ 24
Sonderregelung für öffentlich-rechtliche Dienstverhältnisse

Section 24
Special Regulations for Civil Service Positions

Die Vorschriften dieses Gesetzes gelten unter Berücksichtigung ihrer besonderen Rechtsstellung entsprechend für

1. Beamtinnen und Beamte des Bundes, der Länder, der Gemeinden, der Gemeindeverbände sowie der sonstigen der Aufsicht des Bundes oder eines Landes unterstehenden Körperschaften, Anstalten und Stiftungen des öffentlichen Rechts,
2. Richterinnen und Richter des Bundes und der Länder,
3. Zivildienstleistende sowie anerkannte Kriegsdienstverweigerer, soweit ihre Heranziehung zum Zivildienst betroffen ist.

Taking their special legal position into account, the provisions of this Act shall apply *mutatis mutandis* for

1. civil servants working for the federal government or the federal states, the municipalities, the municipal associations and the other public law bodies, institutions and foundations that are subject to the supervision of the federal government or a federal state,
2. federal and state judges,
3. conscientious objectors, to the extent that their assignment to perform civilian alternative service is affected.

Abschnitt 6
Antidiskriminierungsstelle

§ 25
Antidiskriminierungsstelle des Bundes

(1) Beim Bundesministerium für Familie, Senioren, Frauen und Jugend wird unbeschadet der Zuständigkeit der Beauftragten des Deutschen Bundestages oder der Bundesregierung die Stelle des Bundes zum Schutz vor Benachteiligungen wegen eines in § 1 genannten Grundes (Antidiskriminierungsstelle des Bundes) errichtet.

(2) ¹Der Antidiskriminierungsstelle des Bundes ist die für die Erfüllung ihrer Aufgaben notwendige Personal- und Sachausstattung zur Verfügung zu stellen. ²Sie ist im Einzelplan des Bundesministeriums für Familie, Senioren, Frauen und Jugend in einem eigenen Kapitel auszuweisen.

§ 26
Rechtsstellung der Leitung der Antidiskriminierungsstelle des Bundes

(1) ¹Die Bundesministerin oder der Bundesminister für Familie, Senioren, Frauen und Jugend ernennt auf Vorschlag der Bundesregierung eine Person zur Leitung der Antidiskriminierungsstelle des Bundes. ²Sie steht nach Maßgabe dieses Gesetzes in einem öffentlich-rechtlichen Amtsverhältnis zum Bund. ³Sie ist in Ausübung ihres Amtes unabhängig und nur dem Gesetz unterworfen.

(2) Das Amtsverhältnis beginnt mit der Aushändigung der Urkunde über die Ernennung durch die Bundesministerin oder den Bundesminister für Familie, Senioren, Frauen und Jugend.

Chapter 6
Anti-Discrimination Office

Section 25
Federal Anti-Discrimination Office

(1) Notwithstanding the competence of the commissioners of the Lower House of the German Parliament *(Bundestag)* or the Federal Government, a federal authority for protection against adverse treatment based on one of the grounds set forth in section 1 (Federal Anti-Discrimination Office) shall be established within the Federal Ministry for Family Affairs, Senior Citizens, Women and Youth *(Bundesministerium für Familie, Senioren, Frauen und Jugend)*.

(2) ¹The Federal Anti-Discrimination Office shall be provided with the personnel and equipment necessary for it to perform its tasks. ²It shall be posted as its own item in the section of the budget for the Federal Ministry for Family Affairs, Senior Citizens, Women and Youth.

Section 26
Legal Position of the Directorate of the Federal Anti-Discrimination Office

(1) ¹The Federal Minister for Family Affairs, Senior Citizens, Women and Youth shall appoint a person nominated by the Federal Government as director of the Federal Anti-Discrimination Office. ²This person shall then be in a public law official relationship *(Amtsverhältnis)* with the federal government pursuant to this Act. ³The director shall be independent in the performance of his or her office and only subject to the law.

(2) The official relationship commences with the handover of the appointment certificate by the Federal Minister for Family Affairs, Senior Citizens, Women and Youth.

(3) ¹Das Amtsverhältnis endet außer durch Tod

1. mit dem Zusammentreten eines neuen Bundestages,
2. durch Ablauf der Amtszeit mit Erreichen der Altersgrenze nach § 51 Abs. 1 und 2 des Bundesbeamtengesetzes,
3. mit der Entlassung.

²Die Bundesministerin oder der Bundesminister für Familie, Senioren, Frauen und Jugend entlässt die Leiterin oder den Leiter der Antidiskriminierungsstelle des Bundes auf deren Verlangen oder wenn Gründe vorliegen, die bei einer Richterin oder einem Richter auf Lebenszeit die Entlassung aus dem Dienst rechtfertigen. ³Im Falle der Beendigung des Amtsverhältnisses erhält die Leiterin oder der Leiter der Antidiskriminierungsstelle des Bundes eine von der Bundesministerin oder dem Bundesminister für Familie, Senioren, Frauen und Jugend vollzogene Urkunde. ⁴Die Entlassung wird mit der Aushändigung der Urkunde wirksam.

(4)¹Das Rechtsverhältnis der Leitung der Antidiskriminierungsstelle des Bundes gegenüber dem Bund wird durch Vertrag mit dem Bundesministerium für Familie, Senioren, Frauen und Jugend geregelt. ²Der Vertrag bedarf der Zustimmung der Bundesregierung.

(5) ¹Wird eine Bundesbeamtin oder ein Bundesbeamter zur Leitung der Antidiskriminierungsstelle des Bundes bestellt, scheidet er oder sie mit Beginn des Amtsverhältnisses aus dem bisherigen Amt aus. ²Für die Dauer des Amtsverhältnisses ruhen die aus dem Beamtenverhältnis begründeten Rechte und Pflichten mit Ausnahme der Pflicht zur Amtsverschwiegenheit und des Verbots der Annahme von Belohnungen oder Geschenken. ³Bei unfallverletzten Beamtinnen oder Beamten bleiben die gesetzlichen Ansprüche auf das Heil-

(3) ¹The official relationship shall end either with the death of the director or

1. with the convening of a new Bundestag,
2. with the expiration of the official term upon reaching the age limit set forth in section 51 (1) and (2) of the German Federal Civil Service Act (Bundesbeamtengesetz),
3. with his or her dismissal.

²The Federal Minister for Family Affairs, Senior Citizens, Women and Youth shall dismiss the director of the Federal Anti-Discrimination Office at his or her request or if grounds exist which would justify the dismissal of a judge from his or her post for life. ³Should the official relationship come to an end, the director of the Federal Anti-Discrimination Office shall receive a certificate signed by the Federal Minister for Family Affairs, Senior Citizens, Women and Youth. ⁴The dismissal shall enter into effect once the certificate is handed over.

(4) ¹The legal relationship between the directorate of the Federal Anti-Discrimination Office and the Federal Government shall be regulated in a contract with the Federal Ministry for Family Affairs, Senior Citizens, Women and Youth. ²This contract shall require the consent of the Federal Government.

(5) ¹If a federal civil servant is appointed as director of the Federal Anti-Discrimination Office, he or she ceases to hold his or her current position upon commencing the official relationship. ²For the duration of the official relationship, the rights and duties arising from the federal civil servant's position shall be suspended with the exception of the duty to maintain official secrecy and the prohibition of accepting rewards or gifts. ³If a federal civil servant is injured in an accident, the statutory claims for medical treatment and com-

verfahren und einen Unfallausgleich unberührt.

§ 27
Aufgaben

(1) Wer der Ansicht ist, wegen eines in § 1 genannten Grundes benachteiligt worden zu sein, kann sich an die Antidiskriminierungsstelle des Bundes wenden.

(2) ¹Die Antidiskriminierungsstelle des Bundes unterstützt auf unabhängige Weise Personen, die sich nach Absatz 1 an sie wenden, bei der Durchsetzung ihrer Rechte zum Schutz vor Benachteiligungen. ²Hierbei kann sie insbesondere

1. über Ansprüche und die Möglichkeiten des rechtlichen Vorgehens im Rahmen gesetzlicher Regelungen zum Schutz vor Benachteiligungen informieren,
2. Beratung durch andere Stellen vermitteln,
3. eine gütliche Beilegung zwischen den Beteiligten anstreben

³Soweit Beauftragte des Deutschen Bundestages oder der Bundesregierung zuständig sind, leitet die Antidiskriminierungsstelle des Bundes die Anliegen der in Absatz 1 genannten Personen mit deren Einverständnis unverzüglich an diese weiter.

(3) Die Antidiskriminierungsstelle des Bundes nimmt auf unabhängige Weise folgende Aufgaben wahr, soweit nicht die Zuständigkeit der Beauftragten der Bundesregierung oder des Deutschen Bundestages berührt ist:
1. Öffentlichkeitsarbeit,
2. Maßnahmen zur Verhinderung von Benachteiligungen aus den in § 1 genannten Gründen,
3. Durchführung wissenschaftlicher Untersuchungen zu diesen Benachteiligungen.

pensation for the accident shall remain unaffected.

Section 27
Tasks

(1) Anyone who is of the opinion that he or she has been subjected to adverse treatment based on one of the grounds set forth in section 1 may turn to the Federal Anti-Discrimination Office for assistance.

(2) ¹The Federal Anti-Discrimination Office shall support in an independent manner the persons who turn to it for assistance pursuant to subsection (1) in enforcing their right to protection against adverse treatment. ²In particular, it may

1. inform them of claims and the possibility of legal action within the scope of statutory regulations on the protection against adverse treatment,
2. refer them to other agencies for counseling,
3. strive to achieve a mutually agreeable settlement between the parties.

³In cases in which German Bundestag or Federal Government commissioners have competency, the Federal Anti-Discrimination Office shall pass the concerns of the persons mentioned in subsection (1) on to these commissioners without delay, provided that the persons involved give their consent.

(3) The Federal Anti-Discrimination Office shall carry out the following tasks in an independent manner, to the extent that the competence of the Federal Government or German Bundestag commissioners is not affected:
1. public relations work,
2. measures to prevent adverse treatment based on one of the grounds set forth in section 1,
3. performance of scientific investigations into such adverse treatment.

(4) ¹Die Antidiskriminierungsstelle des Bundes und die in ihrem Zuständigkeitsbereich betroffenen Beauftragten der Bundesregierung und des Deutschen Bundestages legen gemeinsam dem Deutschen Bundestag alle vier Jahre Berichte über Benachteiligungen aus den in § 1 genannten Gründen vor und geben Empfehlungen zur Beseitigung und Vermeidung dieser Benachteiligungen. ²Sie können gemeinsam wissenschaftliche Untersuchungen zu Benachteiligungen durchführen.

(5) Die Antidiskriminierungsstelle des Bundes und die in ihrem Zuständigkeitsbereich betroffenen Beauftragten der Bundesregierung und des Deutschen Bundestages sollen bei Benachteiligungen aus mehreren der in § 1 genannten Gründe zusammenarbeiten.

(4) ¹Every four years the Federal Anti-Discrimination Office and the Federal Government and German Bundestag commissioners whose area of responsibility is involved shall jointly present to the German Bundestag reports on adverse treatment based on the grounds set forth in section 1 and give recommendations for the elimination and prevention of such adverse treatment. ²They may jointly carry out scientific investigations into adverse treatment.

(5) In the event of adverse treatment on the basis of two or more of the grounds set forth in section 1, the Federal Anti-Discrimination Office should work together with the Federal Government and German Bundestag commissioners whose area of responsibility is involved.

§ 28
Befugnisse

(1) Die Antidiskriminierungsstelle des Bundes kann in Fällen des § 27 Abs. 2 Satz 2 Nr. 3 Beteiligte um Stellungnahmen ersuchen, soweit die Person, die sich nach § 27 Abs. 1 an sie gewandt hat, hierzu ihr Einverständnis erklärt.

(2) ¹Alle Bundesbehörden und sonstigen öffentlichen Stellen im Bereich des Bundes sind verpflichtet, die Antidiskriminierungsstelle des Bundes bei der Erfüllung ihrer Aufgaben zu unterstützen, insbesondere die erforderlichen Auskünfte zu erteilen. ²Die Bestimmungen zum Schutz personenbezogener Daten bleiben unberührt.

Section 28
Powers

(1) In the cases set forth in section 27 (2) sentence 2 no. 3, the Federal Anti-Discrimination Office may ask the persons involved to comment on the complaint, but only with the consent of the persons who had sought assistance from it pursuant to section 27 (1).

(2) ¹All federal agencies and other federal official offices are obligated to support the Federal Anti-Discrimination Office in the performance of its tasks and in particular to provide it with all necessary information. ²The legal provisions on the protection of personal data remain unaffected.

§ 29
Zusammenarbeit mit Nichtregierungsorganisationen und anderen Einrichtungen

Die Antidiskriminierungsstelle des Bundes soll bei ihrer Tätigkeit Nichtregierungsorganisationen sowie Einrichtungen, die auf europäischer, Bundes-,

Section 29
Cooperation with Non-Governmental Organizations and other Institutions

The Federal Anti-Discrimination Office should involve in its activities (in an appropriate form) non-governmental organizations and institutions that are

Landes- oder regionaler Ebene zum Schutz vor Benachteiligungen wegen eines in § 1 genannten Grundes tätig sind, in geeigneter Form einbeziehen.

§ 30
Beirat

(1) [1] Zur Förderung des Dialogs mit gesellschaftlichen Gruppen und Organisationen, die sich den Schutz vor Benachteiligungen wegen eines in § 1 genannten Grundes zum Ziel gesetzt haben, wird der Antidiskriminierungsstelle des Bundes ein Beirat beigeordnet. [2] Der Beirat berät die Antidiskriminierungsstelle des Bundes bei der Vorlage von Berichten und Empfehlungen an den Deutschen Bundestag nach § 27 Abs. 4 und kann hierzu sowie zu wissenschaftlichen Untersuchungen nach § 27 Abs. 3 Nr. 3 eigene Vorschläge unterbreiten.

(2) [1] Das Bundesministerium für Familie, Senioren, Frauen und Jugend beruft im Einvernehmen mit der Leitung der Antidiskriminierungsstelle des Bundes sowie den entsprechend zuständigen Beauftragten der Bundesregierung oder des Deutschen Bundestages die Mitglieder dieses Beirats und für jedes Mitglied eine Stellvertretung. [2] In den Beirat sollen Vertreterinnen und Vertreter gesellschaftlicher Gruppen und Organisationen sowie Expertinnen und Experten in Benachteiligungsfragen berufen werden. [3] Die Gesamtzahl der Mitglieder des Beirats soll 16 Personen nicht überschreiten. [4] Der Beirat soll zu gleichen Teilen mit Frauen und Männern besetzt sein.

(3) Der Beirat gibt sich eine Geschäftsordnung, die der Zustimmung des Bundesministeriums für Familie, Senioren, Frauen und Jugend bedarf.

(4) [1] Die Mitglieder des Beirats üben die Tätigkeit nach diesem Gesetz ehrenamtlich aus. [2] Sie haben Anspruch auf Auf-

active on a European, national, state or regional level for protection against adverse treatment based on one of the grounds set forth in section 1.

Section 30
Advisory board

(1) [1] In order to promote dialogue with social groups and organizations which have set themselves the goal of protecting people against adverse treatment based on one of the grounds set forth in section 1, an advisory board shall be assigned to the Federal Anti-Discrimination Office. [2] This advisory board shall advise the Federal Anti-Discrimination Office in connection with the presentation of reports and recommendations to the German Bundestag pursuant to section 27 (4) and can make its own proposals on these as well as on scientific investigations pursuant to section 27 (3) no. 3.

(2) [1] The Federal Ministry for Family Affairs, Senior Citizens, Women and Youth shall appoint the members of this advisory board, and a substitute for each member, in consultation with the directorate of the Federal Anti-Discrimination Office and the respective competent Federal Government or German Bundestag commissioners. [2] Representatives of social groups and organizations, as well as experts on discrimination issues, should be appointed to the advisory board. [3] The total number of members of the advisory board should not exceed 16 persons. [4] The advisory board should have an equal number of male and female members.

(3) The advisory board shall draft its own rules of procedure which shall require the consent of the Federal Ministry for Family Affairs, Senior Citizens, Women and Youth.

(4) [1] The members of the advisory board shall perform their activities under this Act on a pro bono basis. [2] They are enti-

wandsentschädigung sowie Reisekostenvergütung, Tagegelder und Übernachtungsgelder. ³Näheres regelt die Geschäftsordnung.

tled to the reimbursement of travel and other expenses, as well as to per diem and accommodation expenses. ³Details shall be regulated in the rules of procedure.

Abschnitt 7
Schlussvorschriften

Chapter 7
Final provisions

§ 31
Unabdingbarkeit

Section 31
Mandatory character

Von den Vorschriften dieses Gesetzes kann nicht zu Ungunsten der geschützten Personen abgewichen werden.

No derogations from the provisions of this Act to the detriment of the protected persons shall be permissible.

§ 32
Schlussbestimmungen

Section 32
Final provision

Soweit in diesem Gesetz nicht Abweichendes bestimmt ist, gelten die allgemeinen Bestimmungen.

Unless otherwise provided in this Act, the general provisions shall apply.

§ 33
Übergangsbestimmungen

Section 33
Transitional provisions

(1) Bei Benachteiligungen nach den §§ 611a, 611b und 612 Abs. 3 des Bürgerlichen Gesetzbuchs oder sexuellen Belästigungen nach dem Beschäftigtenschutzgesetz ist das vor dem 18. August 2006 maßgebliche Recht anzuwenden.

(1) In cases of adverse treatment in violation of sections 611a, 611b and 612 (3) of the German Civil Code (*Bürgerliches Gesetzbuch*) or sexual harassment in violation of the Employee Protection Act (*Beschäftigtenschutzgesetz*), the law that prevailed before 18 August 2006 shall be applied.

(2) ¹Bei Benachteiligungen aus Gründen der Rasse oder wegen der ethnischen Herkunft sind die §§ 19 bis 21 nicht auf Schuldverhältnisse anzuwenden, die vor dem 18. August 2006 begründet worden sind. ²Satz 1 gilt nicht für spätere Änderungen von Dauerschuldverhältnissen.

(2) ¹In cases of adverse treatment due to race or ethnic origin, sections 19 to 21 shall not be applied to contractual relationships which were formed prior to 18 August 2006. ²Sentence 1 shall not apply to subsequent amendments to ongoing contractual relationships.

(3) ¹Bei Benachteiligungen wegen des Geschlechts, der Religion, einer Behinderung, des Alters oder der sexuellen Identität sind die §§ 19 bis 21 nicht auf Schuldverhältnisse anzuwenden, die vor dem 1. Dezember 2006 begründet worden sind. ²Satz 1 gilt nicht für spätere Änderungen von Dauerschuldverhältnissen.

(3) ¹In cases of adverse treatment due to gender, religion, a disability, age or sexual identity, sections 19 to 21 shall not be applied to contractual relationships which were formed prior to 1 December 2006. ²Sentence 1 shall not apply to subsequent amendments to ongoing contractual relationships.

(4) ¹Auf Schuldverhältnisse, die eine privatrechtliche Versicherung zum Gegenstand haben, ist § 19 Abs. 1 nicht anzuwenden, wenn diese vor dem 22. Dezember 2007 begründet worden sind. ²Satz 1 gilt nicht für spätere Änderungen solcher Schuldverhältnisse.

(4) ¹Section 19 (1) shall not be applied to contractual relationships for private law insurance if they were formed prior to 22 December 2007. ²Sentence 1 shall not apply to subsequent amendments to such contractual relationships.

III. Part-Time and Limited Term Employment Act (Gesetz über Teilzeitarbeit und befristete Arbeitsverträge – TzBfG)

of 21 December 2000 (Federal Law Gazette I p. 1966)

in the amended version of 19 April 2007

Erster Abschnitt Allgemeine Vorschriften	Chapter 1 General Provisions

§ 1
Zielsetzung

Section 1
Purpose

Ziel des Gesetzes ist, Teilzeitarbeit zu fördern, die Voraussetzungen für die Zulässigkeit befristeter Arbeitsverträge festzulegen und die Diskriminierung von teilzeitbeschäftigten und befristet beschäftigten Arbeitnehmern zu verhindern.

The purpose of this Act is to promote part-time work, to define the prerequisites for the permissibility of employment agreements for limited terms and to prevent discrimination against part-time and limited term employees.

§ 2
Begriff des teilzeitbeschäftigten Arbeitnehmers

Section 2
Definition of the Term "Part-Time Employee"

(1) [1] Teilzeitbeschäftigt ist ein Arbeitnehmer, dessen regelmäßige Wochenarbeitszeit kürzer ist als die eines vergleichbaren vollzeitbeschäftigten Arbeitnehmers [2] Ist eine regelmäßige Wochenarbeitszeit nicht vereinbart, so ist ein Arbeitnehmer teilzeitbeschäftigt, wenn seine regelmäßige Arbeitszeit im Durchschnitt eines bis zu einem Jahr reichenden Beschäftigungszeitraums unter der eines vergleichbaren vollzeitbeschäftigten Arbeitnehmers liegt. [3] Vergleichbar ist ein vollzeitbeschäftigter Arbeitnehmer des Betriebes mit derselben Art des Arbeitsverhältnisses und der gleichen oder einer ähnlichen Tätigkeit. [4] Gibt es im Betrieb keinen vergleichbaren vollzeitbeschäftigten Arbeitnehmer, so ist der vergleichbare vollzeitbeschäftigte Arbeitnehmer auf Grund des anwendbaren Tarifvertrages zu bestimmen; in allen anderen Fällen ist darauf abzustellen, wer im jeweiligen Wirt-

(1) [1] An employee is employed on a part-time basis if his regular weekly working time is less than that of a comparable fulltime employee. [2] If no regular weekly working time has been agreed, an employee shall be deemed to be working part time if his average regular working time over a period of up to one year of employment falls below that of a comparable fulltime employee. [3] A comparable fulltime employee of the establishment is one who has the same type of employment relationship and performs the same or similar work. [4] If there are no comparable fulltime employees in the establishment then a comparable fulltime employee shall be determined on the basis of the applicable collective bargaining agreement; in all other cases such determination shall be based on those in the respective industry sector who are normally deemed to be comparable fulltime employees.

schaftszweig üblicherweise als vergleichbarer vollzeitbeschäftigter Arbeitnehmer anzusehen ist.

(2) Teilzeitbeschäftigt ist auch ein Arbeitnehmer, der eine geringfügige Beschäftigung nach § 8 Abs. 1 Nr. 1 des Vierten Buches Sozialgesetzbuch ausübt.

(2) An employee engaged in insignificant employment within the meaning of section 8 (1) no. 1 of the Fourth Book of the Social Security Code is also a part-time employee.

§ 3
Begriff des befristet beschäftigten Arbeitnehmers

(1) [1] Befristet beschäftigt ist ein Arbeitnehmer mit einem auf bestimmte Zeit geschlossenen Arbeitsvertrag. [2] Ein auf bestimmte Zeit geschlossener Arbeitsvertrag (befristeter Arbeitsvertrag) liegt vor, wenn seine Dauer kalendermäßig bestimmt ist (kalendermäßig befristeter Arbeitsvertrag) oder sich aus Art, Zweck oder Beschaffenheit der Arbeitsleistung ergibt (zweckbefristeter Arbeitsvertrag).

(2) [1] Vergleichbar ist ein unbefristet beschäftigter Arbeitnehmer des Betriebes mit der gleichen oder einer ähnlichen Tätigkeit. [2] Gibt es im Betrieb keinen vergleichbaren unbefristet beschäftigten Arbeitnehmer, so ist der vergleichbare unbefristet beschäftigte Arbeitnehmer auf Grund des anwendbaren Tarifvertrages zu bestimmen; in allen anderen Fällen ist darauf abzustellen, wer im jeweiligen Wirtschaftszweig üblicherweise als vergleichbarer unbefristet beschäftigter Arbeitnehmer anzusehen ist.

Section 3
Definition of Employees for a Limited Term

(1) [1] An employee employed for a limited term has an employment agreement concluded for a fixed period of time. [2] An employment agreement is concluded for a fixed period of time (limited term employment agreement) if its duration has been fixed according to the calendar (limited calendar term employment agreement) or results from the nature, purpose or quality of the work to be rendered (employment agreement with a term limited by purpose).

(2) [1] Such an employee shall be compared to an employee in the establishment who has been employed for an unlimited term to perform the same or similar work. [2] If there is no comparable employee in the establishment employed for an unlimited term, then the comparable employee employed for an unlimited term shall be determined on the basis of the applicable collective bargaining agreement; in all other cases, such determination shall be based on those in the respective industry sector who are normally deemed to be comparable employees employed for an unlimited term.

§ 4
Verbot der Diskriminierung

(1) [1] Ein teilzeitbeschäftigter Arbeitnehmer darf wegen der Teilzeitarbeit nicht schlechter behandelt werden als ein vergleichbarer vollzeitbeschäftigter Arbeitnehmer, es sei denn, dass sachliche Gründe eine unterschiedliche

Section 4
Prohibition of Discrimination

(1) [1] A part-time employee may not be treated worse due to his part-time work than a comparable fulltime employee unless there are objective grounds justifying different treatment. [2] A part-time employee shall be paid remuneration

Behandlung rechtfertigen. ²Einem teilzeitbeschäftigten Arbeitnehmer ist Arbeitsentgelt oder eine andere teilbare geldwerte Leistung mindestens in dem Umfang zu gewähren, der dem Anteil seiner Arbeitszeit an der Arbeitszeit eines vergleichbaren vollzeitbeschäftigten Arbeitnehmers entspricht.

(2) ¹Ein befristet beschäftigter Arbeitnehmer darf wegen der Befristung des Arbeitsvertrages nicht schlechter behandelt werden, als ein vergleichbarer unbefristet beschäftigter Arbeitnehmer, es sei denn, dass sachliche Gründe eine unterschiedliche Behandlung rechtfertigen. ²Einem befristet beschäftigten Arbeitnehmer ist Arbeitsentgelt oder eine andere teilbare geldwerte Leistung, die für einen bestimmten Bemessungszeitraum gewährt wird, mindestens in dem Umfang zu gewähren, der dem Anteil seiner Beschäftigungsdauer am Bemessungszeitraum entspricht. ³Sind bestimmte Beschäftigungsbedingungen von der Dauer des Bestehens des Arbeitsverhältnisses in demselben Betrieb oder Unternehmen abhängig, so sind für befristet beschäftigte Arbeitnehmer dieselben Zeiten zu berücksichtigen wie für unbefristet beschäftigte Arbeitnehmer, es sei denn, dass eine unterschiedliche Berücksichtigung aus sachlichen Gründen gerechtfertigt ist.

for work or another divisible non-monetary benefit at least to a degree corresponding to the proportion of his working time to the working time of a comparable fulltime employee.

(2) ¹An employee employed for a limited term may not be treated worse due to his limited term work than a comparable employee employed for an unlimited term unless there are objective grounds justifying different treatment. ²A limited term employee shall be paid remuneration for work or another divisible non-monetary benefit for a certain calculation period at least to a degree corresponding to the proportion of his employment term to the calculation period. ³If certain employment conditions are dependent upon the seniority of the employee in the same establishment or company, then for employees employed for a limited term the same time periods shall be taken into consideration as for employees employed for an unlimited term, unless there are objective reasons justifying different consideration.

§ 5
Benachteiligungsverbot

Der Arbeitgeber darf einen Arbeitnehmer nicht wegen der Inanspruchnahme von Rechten nach diesem Gesetz benachteiligen.

Section 5
Prohibition of Unfavorable Treatment

The employer may not treat an employee unfavorably because the employee enforces his rights set forth under this Act.

Zweiter Abschnitt
Teilzeitarbeit

Chapter 2
Part-Time Work

§ 6
Förderung von Teilzeitarbeit

Der Arbeitgeber hat den Arbeitnehmern, auch in leitenden Positionen,

Section 6
Promotion of Part-Time Work

The employer shall enable the employees, including those in managerial

Teilzeitarbeit nach Maßgabe dieses Gesetzes zu ermöglichen.

§ 7
Ausschreibung; Information über freie Arbeitsplätze

(1) Der Arbeitgeber hat einen Arbeitsplatz, den er öffentlich oder innerhalb des Betriebes ausschreibt, auch als Teilzeitarbeitsplatz auszuschreiben, wenn sich der Arbeitsplatz hierfür eignet.

(2) Der Arbeitgeber hat einen Arbeitnehmer, der ihm den Wunsch nach einer Veränderung von Dauer und Lage seiner vertraglich vereinbarten Arbeitszeit angezeigt hat, über entsprechende Arbeitsplätze zu informieren, die im Betrieb oder Unternehmen besetzt werden sollen.

(3) [1] Der Arbeitgeber hat die Arbeitnehmervertretung über Teilzeitarbeit im Betrieb und Unternehmen zu informieren, insbesondere über vorhandene oder geplante Teilzeitarbeitsplätze und über die Umwandlung von Teilzeitarbeitsplätzen in Vollzeitarbeitsplätze oder umgekehrt [2] Der Arbeitnehmervertretung sind auf Verlangen die erforderlichen Unterlagen zur Verfügung zu stellen; § 92 des Betriebsverfassungsgesetzes bleibt unberührt.

§ 8
Verringerung der Arbeitzeit

(1) Ein Arbeitnehmer, dessen Arbeitsverhältnis länger als sechs Monate bestanden hat, kann verlangen, dass seine vertraglich vereinbarte Arbeitszeit verringert wird.

(2) [1] Der Arbeitnehmer muss die Verringerung seiner Arbeitszeit und den Umfang der Verringerung spätestens drei Monate vor deren Beginn geltend machen. [2] Er soll dabei die gewünschte Verteilung der Arbeitszeit angeben.

(3) [1] Der Arbeitgeber hat mit dem Arbeitnehmer die gewünschte Verringerung der Arbeitszeit mit dem Ziel zu erörtern, zu einer Vereinbarung zu gelangen. [2] Er hat mit dem Arbeitnehmer Einverneh-

positions, to work part-time in accordance with this Act.

Section 7
Announcements; Information of Vacancies

(1) Any vacancy the employer announces publicly or within the establishment shall also be announced as a part-time job if the position is deemed suitable.

(2) The employer shall inform an employee who has already declared his interest in changing the length or timing of his contractual working time about relevant vacancies to be filled in the establishment or the company.

(3) [1] The employer shall inform the employee representative body of part-time work in the establishment and the company, in particular of current or planned vacancies for part-time employment and of the transformation of part-time jobs into fulltime jobs and vice versa. [2] The employee representative body shall be provided with the requisite documents upon request; section 92 of the Works Constitution Act remains unaffected.

Section 8
Reduction of Working Time

(1) An employee who has been employed with the company for over six months may request a reduction in his contractual working time.

(2) [1] The employee must assert his right to a reduction in his working time and the scope of such reduction no later than three months before its onset. [2] He shall state his preference for a division of the working time.

(3) [1] The employer shall discuss with the employee the desired reduction of the working time with the goal of coming to an agreement. [2] He shall achieve agreement with the em-

men über die von ihm festzulegende Verteilung der Arbeitszeit zu erzielen.

(4) ¹Der Arbeitgeber hat der Verringerung der Arbeitszeit zuzustimmen und ihre Verteilung entsprechend den Wünschen des Arbeitnehmers festzulegen, soweit betriebliche Gründe nicht entgegenstehen. ²Ein betrieblicher Grund liegt insbesondere vor, wenn die Verringerung der Arbeitszeit die Organisation, den Arbeitsablauf oder die Sicherheit im Betrieb wesentlich beeinträchtigt oder unverhältnismäßige Kosten verursacht. ³Die Ablehnungsgründe können durch Tarifvertrag festgelegt werden. ⁴Im Geltungsbereich eines solchen Tarifvertrages können nicht tarifgebundene Arbeitgeber und Arbeitnehmer die Anwendung der tariflichen Regelungen über die Ablehnungsgründe vereinbaren.

(5) ¹Die Entscheidung über die Verringerung der Arbeitszeit und ihre Verteilung hat der Arbeitgeber dem Arbeitnehmer spätestens einen Monat vor dem gewünschten Beginn der Verringerung schriftlich mitzuteilen. ²Haben sich Arbeitgeber und Arbeitnehmer nicht nach Absatz 3 Satz 1 über die Verringerung der Arbeitszeit geeinigt und hat der Arbeitgeber die Arbeitszeitverringerung nicht spätestens einen Monat vor deren gewünschtem Beginn schriftlich abgelehnt, verringert sich die Arbeitszeit in dem vom Arbeitnehmer gewünschten Umfang. ³Haben Arbeitgeber und Arbeitnehmer über die Verteilung der Arbeitszeit kein Einvernehmen nach Absatz 3 Satz 2 erzielt und hat der Arbeitgeber nicht spätestens einen Monat vor dem gewünschten Beginn der Arbeitszeitverringerung die gewünschte Verteilung der Arbeitszeit schriftlich abgelehnt, gilt die Verteilung der Arbeitszeit entsprechend den Wünschen des Arbeitnehmers als festgelegt. ⁴Der Arbeitgeber kann die nach Satz 3 oder Absatz 3 Satz 2 festgelegte Verteilung der Arbeitszeit wieder ändern, wenn das betriebliche Interesse daran das Interesse des Arbeitnehmers

ployee on the division of the working time.

(4) ¹The employer shall consent to the reduction in the working time and its division in accordance with the employee's wishes, unless there are operational reasons standing in the way of such reduction. ²Such operational reasons exist in particular if the reduction of the working time would fundamentally impair the establishment's organization, working process or safety or incur unreasonable costs. ³The reasons for rejecting a request for reduced working time may be set forth in a collective bargaining agreement. ⁴Within the scope of such a collective bargaining agreement, employers and employees not bound to such agreements may agree that the contractual provisions with respect to the reasons for rejection will apply.

(5) ¹The employer shall inform the employee of his decision on the reduction and division of the working time and in writing at least one month before the desired onset of the reduction. ²If the employer and employee cannot agree on the reduction pursuant to subsection (3) sentence 1, and if the employer has not rejected the reduction of working time in writing at least one month before the desired onset of the reduction, the working time shall be reduced to the extent desired by the employee. ³If the employer and the employee have not reached agreement on the division of the working time pursuant to subsection (3) sentence 2, and if the employer has not rejected the desired division of working time in writing at least one month before the desired onset of the reduction, the division of the working time desired by the employee shall be deemed to be set. ⁴The employer may change the division of the working time pursuant to sentence 3 or subsection (3) sentence 2 again if the interests of the establishment in doing so substantially outweighs the employee's interest in maintaining the status quo and the employer has an-

an der Beibehaltung erheblich überwiegt und der Arbeitgeber die Änderung spätestens einen Monat vorher angekündigt hat.

(6) Der Arbeitnehmer kann eine erneute Verringerung der Arbeitszeit frühestens nach Ablauf von zwei Jahren verlangen, nachdem der Arbeitgeber einer Verringerung zugestimmt oder sie berechtigt abgelehnt hat.

(7) Für den Anspruch auf Verringerung der Arbeitszeit gilt die Voraussetzung, dass der Arbeitgeber, unabhängig von der Anzahl der Personen in Berufsbildung, in der Regel mehr als 15 Arbeitnehmer beschäftigt.

§ 9
Verlängerung der Arbeitszeit

Der Arbeitgeber hat einen teilzeitbeschäftigten Arbeitnehmer, der ihm den Wunsch nach einer Verlängerung seiner vertraglich vereinbarten Arbeitszeit angezeigt hat, bei der Besetzung eines entsprechenden freien Arbeitsplatzes bei gleicher Eignung bevorzugt zu berücksichtigen, es sei denn, dass dringende betriebliche Gründe oder Arbeitszeitwünsche anderer teilzeitbeschäftigter Arbeitnehmer entgegenstehen.

§ 10
Aus- und Weiterbildung

Der Arbeitgeber hat Sorge zu tragen, dass auch teilzeitbeschäftigte Arbeitnehmer an Aus- und Weiterbildungsmaßnahmen zur Förderung der beruflichen Entwicklung und Mobilität teilnehmen können, es sei denn, dass dringende betriebliche Gründe oder Aus- und Weiterbildungswünsche anderer teilzeit- oder vollzeitbeschäftigter Arbeitnehmer entgegenstehen.

§ 11
Kündigungsverbot

[1]Die Kündigung eines Arbeitsverhältnisses wegen der Weigerung eines Ar-

nounced the change at least one month in advance.

(6) The employee may not request another reduction in his working time until at last two years have elapsed since the employer agreed to the reduction or rejected it for justifiable reasons.

(7) The claim to reduction of working time is subject to the prerequisite that as a rule the employer has more than 15 employees, not counting trainees.

Section 9
Extension of Working Time

If a part-time employee has informed the employer of his interest in extending his contractual working time, such employee shall be given preference in filling a suitable vacancy, assuming equivalent qualification, unless urgent operational grounds or the desires of other part-time employees to change their working times stand in the way.

Section 10
Job Training and Further Qualification

The employer shall ensure that part-time employees are also able to participate in training and further qualification measures to promote their professional development and mobility, unless urgent operational grounds or the desire of other part-time employees to receive such training stand in the way.

Section 11
Prohibition of Dismissal

[1]Any termination of an employment relationship due to an employee's re-

beitnehmers, von einem Vollzeit- in ein Teilzeitarbeitsverhältnis oder umgekehrt zu wechseln, ist unwirksam. [2]Das Recht zur Kündigung des Arbeitsverhältnisses aus anderen Gründen bleibt unberührt.

fusal to switch from fulltime to parttime employment or vice versa shall be invalid. [2]The right to terminate the employment relationship for other reasons remains unaffected.

§ 12
Arbeit auf Abruf

(1) [1]Arbeitgeber und Arbeitnehmer können vereinbaren, dass der Arbeitnehmer seine Arbeitsleistung entsprechend dem Arbeitsanfall zu erbringen hat (Arbeit auf Abruf). [2]Die Vereinbarung muss eine bestimmte Dauer der wöchentlichen und täglichen Arbeitszeit festlegen. [3]Wenn die Dauer der wöchentlichen Arbeitszeit nicht festgelegt ist, gilt eine Arbeitszeit von zehn Stunden als vereinbart. [4]Wenn die Dauer der täglichen Arbeitszeit nicht festgelegt ist, hat der Arbeitgeber die Arbeitsleistung des Arbeitnehmers jeweils für mindestens drei aufeinander folgende Stunden in Anspruch zu nehmen.

(2) Der Arbeitnehmer ist nur zur Arbeitsleistung verpflichtet, wenn der Arbeitgeber ihm die Lage seiner Arbeitszeit jeweils mindestens vier Tage im Voraus mitteilt.

(3) [1]Durch Tarifvertrag kann von den Absätzen 1 und 2 auch zuungunsten des Arbeitnehmers abgewichen werden, wenn der Tarifvertrag Regelungen über die tägliche und wöchentliche Arbeitszeit und die Vorankündigungsfrist vorsieht. [2]Im Geltungsbereich eines solchen Tarifvertrages können nicht tarifgebundene Arbeitgeber und Arbeitnehmer die Anwendung der tariflichen Regelungen über die Arbeit auf Abruf vereinbaren.

Section 12
On-Call Work

(1) [1]The employer and the employee may agree that the employee must perform his services in accordance with the workload (on-call work). [2]The agreement must lay down a set period of time to be worked weekly and daily. [3]If the number of working hours per week has not been set, then a working time of ten hours per week shall be deemed to have been agreed. [4]If the number of working hours per day has not been set, then the employer shall call upon the employee's services for at least three consecutive hours.

(2) The employee shall only be obligated to render his services if the employer informs him at least four days in advance of what hours the employee will be working.

(3) [1]It is possible to diverge from subsections (1) and (2) in a collective bargaining agreement, even to the detriment of the employee, if the collective bargaining agreement contains provisions governing the daily and weekly working time and the advance notice required. [2]Within the scope of such a collective bargaining agreement, employers and employees not bound to such agreements may agree on the application of the contractual provisions regarding on-call work.

§ 13
Arbeitsplatzteilung

(1) [1]Arbeitgeber und Arbeitnehmer können vereinbaren, dass mehrere Arbeitnehmer sich die Arbeitszeit an ei-

Section 13
Job Sharing

(1) [1]The employer and employee may agree that several employees can share the working time at one workplace (job

nem Arbeitsplatz teilen (Arbeitsplatzteilung) ²Ist einer dieser Arbeitnehmer an der Arbeitsleistung verhindert, sind die anderen Arbeitnehmer zur Vertretung verpflichtet, wenn sie der Vertretung im Einzelfall zugestimmt haben. ³Eine Pflicht zur Vertretung besteht auch, wenn der Arbeitsvertrag bei Vorliegen dringender betrieblicher Gründe eine Vertretung vorsieht und diese im Einzelfall zumutbar ist.

(2) ¹Scheidet ein Arbeitnehmer aus der Arbeitsplatzteilung aus, so ist die darauf gestützte Kündigung des Arbeitsverhältnisses eines anderen in die Arbeitsplatzteilung einbezogenen Arbeitnehmers durch den Arbeitgeber unwirksam. ²Das Recht zur Änderungskündigung aus diesem Anlass und zur Kündigung des Arbeitsverhältnisses aus anderen Gründen bleibt unberührt.

(3) Die Absätze 1 und 2 sind entsprechend anzuwenden, wenn sich Gruppen von Arbeitnehmern auf bestimmten Arbeitsplätzen in festgelegten Zeitabschnitten abwechseln, ohne dass eine Arbeitsplatzteilung im Sinne des Absatzes 1 vorliegt.

(4) ¹Durch Tarifvertrag kann von den Absätzen 1 und 3 auch zuungunsten des Arbeitnehmers abgewichen werden, wenn der Tarifvertrag Regelungen über die Vertretung der Arbeitnehmer enthält. ²Im Geltungsbereich eines solchen Tarifvertrages können nicht tarifgebundene Arbeitgeber und Arbeitnehmer die Anwendung der tariflichen Regelungen über die Arbeitsplatzteilung vereinbaren.

sharing). ²If one of these employees is unable to work, the other employees shall fill in for him, provided that they have consented to do so in the individual case. ³A duty to fill in shall also exist if the employment agreement provides for such on urgent operational grounds and it can by reasonably demanded in the individual case.

(2) ¹If an employee withdraws from the job sharing relationship, the employer's dismissal of another employee involved in the job sharing shall be invalid. ²The right to terminate the employment relationship for this reason in order to modify it, or on other grounds, remains unaffected.

(3) Subsections (1) and (2) shall be applied *mutatis mutandis* if groups of employees relieve each other at certain jobs at fixed intervals, but a job sharing within the meaning of subsection (1) does not exist.

(4) ¹It is possible to diverge from subsections (1) and (3) in a collective bargaining agreement, even to the detriment of the employee, if the collective bargaining agreement contains provisions governing the way in which employees fill in for each other. ²Within the scope of such a collective bargaining agreement, employers and employees not bound to such agreements may agree on the application of the contractual provisions regarding job sharing.

Dritter Abschnitt
Befristete Arbeitsverträge

Chapter 3
Fixed Term Employment Agreements

§ 14
Zulässigkeit der Befristung

Section 14
Permissibility of Fixing Terms

(1) ¹Die Befristung eines Arbeitsvertrages ist zulässig, wenn sie durch einen

(1) ¹The term of an employment agreement may be fixed if this is justified on

sachlichen Grund gerechtfertigt ist. ²Ein sachlicher Grund liegt insbesondere vor, wenn

1. der betriebliche Bedarf an der Arbeitsleistung nur vorübergehend besteht,
2. die Befristung im Anschluss an eine Ausbildung oder ein Studium erfolgt, um den Übergang des Arbeitnehmers in eine Anschlussbeschäftigung zu erleichtern,
3. der Arbeitnehmer zur Vertretung eines anderen Arbeitnehmers beschäftigt wird,
4. die Eigenart der Arbeitsleistung die Befristung rechtfertigt,
5. die Befristung zur Erprobung erfolgt,
6. in der Person des Arbeitnehmers liegende Gründe die Befristung rechtfertigen,
7. der Arbeitnehmer aus Haushaltsmitteln vergütet wird, die haushaltsrechtlich für eine befristete Beschäftigung bestimmt sind, und er entsprechend beschäftigt wird oder
8. die Befristung auf einem gerichtlichen Vergleich beruht.

(2) ¹Die kalendermäßige Befristung eines Arbeitsvertrages ohne Vorliegen eines sachlichen Grundes ist bis zur Dauer von zwei Jahren zulässig; bis zu dieser Gesamtdauer von zwei Jahren ist auch die höchstens dreimalige Verlängerung eines kalendermäßig befristeten Arbeitsvertrages zulässig. ²Eine Befristung nach Satz 1 ist nicht zulässig, wenn mit demselben Arbeitgeber bereits zuvor ein befristetes oder unbefristetes Arbeitsverhältnis bestanden hat. ³Durch Tarifvertrag kann die Anzahl der Verlängerungen oder die Höchstdauer der Befristung abweichend von Satz 1 festgelegt werden. ⁴Im Geltungsbereich eines solchen Tarifvertrages können nicht tarifgebundene Arbeitgeber und Arbeitnehmer die Anwendung der tariflichen Regelungen vereinbaren.

(2a) ¹In den ersten vier Jahren nach der Gründung eines Unternehmens ist die

objective grounds. ²Such objective grounds exist in particular if

1. the operational need for the work involved is only temporary,
2. the term is fixed following training or study in order to facilitate the employee's transition to a subsequent job,
3. the employee is hired to fill in for another employee,
4. the type of work involved justifies a fixed term,
5. the fixed term is intended to try the employee out,
6. there are personal reasons residing with the employee which justify the fixed term,
7. the employee is remunerated from public funds which are earmarked for fixed term employment and he has been hired on that basis, or
8. the fixed term is based on a court settlement.

(2) ¹The limitation of the term of an employment agreement according to the calendar to up to two years where no objective grounds exist is permissible; moreover, a term fixed according to the calendar may be extended no more than three times up to a total term of two years. ²A fixed term pursuant to sentence 1 is not permissible if a fixed or unlimited term employment relationship had previously existed with the same employer. ³It is possible to stipulate the number of extensions or the maximum duration of the fixed term in deviation from sentence 1 in a collective bargaining agreement. ⁴Within the scope of such a collective bargaining agreement, employers and employees not bound to such agreements may agree on the application of the contractual provisions.

(2a) ¹In the first four years after the formation of a company, the limitation

kalendermäßige Befristung eines Arbeitsvertrages ohne Vorliegen eines sachlichen Grundes bis zur Dauer von vier Jahren zulässig; bis zu dieser Gesamtdauer von vier Jahren ist auch die mehrfache Verlängerung eines kalendermäßig befristeten Arbeitsvertrages zulässig. ²Dies gilt nicht für Neugründungen im Zusammenhang mit der rechtlichen Umstrukturierung von Unternehmen und Konzernen. ³Maßgebend für den Zeitpunkt der Gründung des Unternehmens ist die Aufnahme einer Erwerbstätigkeit, die nach § 138 der Abgabenordnung der Gemeinde oder dem Finanzamt mitzuteilen ist. ⁴Auf die Befristung eines Arbeitsvertrages nach Satz 1 findet Absatz 2 Satz 2 bis 4 entsprechende Anwendung.

(3) ¹Die kalendermäßige Befristung eines Arbeitsvertrages ohne Vorliegen eines sachlichen Grundes ist bis zu einer Dauer von fünf Jahren zulässig, wenn der Arbeitnehmer bei Beginn des befristeten Arbeitsverhältnisses das 52. Lebensjahr vollendet hat und unmittelbar vor Beginn des befristeten Arbeitsverhältnisses mindestens vier Monate beschäftigungslos im Sinne des § 119 Abs. 1 Nr. 1 des Dritten Buches Sozialgesetzbuch gewesen ist, Transferkurzarbeitergeld, bezogen oder an einer öffentlich geförderten Beschäftigungsmaßnahme nach dem Zweiten oder Dritten Buch Sozialgesetzbuch teilgenommen hat. ²Bis zu der Gesamtdauer von fünf Jahren ist auch die mehrfache Verlängerung des Arbeitsvertrages zulässig.

(4) Die Befristung eines Arbeitsvertrages bedarf zu ihrer Wirksamkeit der Schriftform.

§ 15
Ende des befristeten Arbeitsvertrages

(1) Ein kalendermäßig befristeter Arbeitsvertrag endet mit Ablauf der vereinbarten Zeit.

of the term of an employment agreement according to the calendar where no objective grounds exist is permissible; moreover, a term fixed according to the calendar may be extended several times up to the expiration of this four-year period. ²This shall not apply to new formations in connection with the legal restructuring of companies and corporate groups. ³Decisive for the time of formation of a company shall be the assumption of a business activity which must be reported to the municipality or the tax authority pursuant to section 138 of the Tax Code (*Abgabenordnung*). ⁴With respect to the limitation of the term of an employment agreement pursuant to sentence 1, subsection (2) sentences 2 to 4 shall apply *mutatis mutandis*.

(3) ¹The limitation of the term of an employment agreement according to the calendar to up to five years where no objective grounds exist is permissible if the employee is 52 years of age and was unemployed within the meaning of section 119 (1) no. 1 of the Third Book of the Social Security Code for at least four months immediately prior to the commencement of the fixed term employment agreement, received transfer short-time allowances or took part in a publicly subsidized employment measure pursuant to the Second or Third Book of the Social Security Code. ²The employment agreement may also be extended two or more times for up to a total period of five years.

(4) In order to be effective, a fixed term to an employment agreement must be in written form.

Section 15
End of the Fixed Term Employment Agreement

(1) An employment agreement with a fixed term according to the calendar shall end at the expiration of the agreed period.

(2) Ein zweckbefristeter Arbeitsvertrag endet mit Erreichen des Zwecks, frühestens jedoch zwei Wochen nach Zugang der schriftlichen Unterrichtung des Arbeitnehmers durch den Arbeitgeber über den Zeitpunkt der Zweckerreichung.

(3) Ein befristetes Arbeitsverhältnis unterliegt nur dann der ordentlichen Kündigung, wenn dies einzelvertraglich oder im anwendbaren Tarifvertrag vereinbart ist.

(4) ¹Ist das Arbeitsverhältnis für die Lebenszeit einer Person oder für längere Zeit als fünf Jahre eingegangen, so kann es von dem Arbeitnehmer nach Ablauf von fünf Jahren gekündigt werden. ²Die Kündigungsfrist beträgt sechs Monate.

(5) Wird das Arbeitsverhältnis nach Ablauf der Zeit, für die es eingegangen ist, oder nach Zweckerreichung mit Wissen des Arbeitgebers fortgesetzt, so gilt es als auf unbestimmte Zeit verlängert, wenn der Arbeitgeber nicht unverzüglich widerspricht oder dem Arbeitnehmer die Zweckerreichung nicht unverzüglich mitteilt.

(2) An employment agreement with a fixed term limited by purpose shall end upon achieving the purpose, but no earlier than two weeks after delivery of the employer's written notification to the employee on the time the purpose was achieved.

(3) A fixed term employment relationship shall only be subject to ordinary termination if this has been agreed in the individual agreement or the applicable collective bargaining agreement.

(4) ¹If the employment relationship has been concluded for a person's lifetime or for a period exceeding five years, it may be terminated by the employee once five years have elapsed. ²The termination notice period shall be six months.

(5) If, upon expiration of the term for which it was entered into, or after the purpose has been achieved, the employment relationship is continued with the knowledge of the employer, then it shall be deemed to have been extended for an indefinite period if the employer does not object without delay or the employer does not convey achievement of the purpose to the employee without delay.

§ 16
Folgen unwirksamer Befristung

¹Ist die Befristung rechtsunwirksam, so gilt der befristete Arbeitsvertrag als auf unbestimmte Zeit geschlossen; er kann vom Arbeitgeber frühestens zum vereinbarten Ende ordentlich gekündigt werden, sofern nicht nach § 15 Abs. 3 die ordentliche Kündigung zu einem früheren Zeitpunkt möglich ist. ²Ist die Befristung nur wegen des Mangels der Schriftform unwirksam, kann der Arbeitsvertrag auch vor dem vereinbarten Ende ordentlich gekündigt werden.

Section 16
Consequences of Invalid Setting of Term

¹If the fixing of the term is not legally valid, then the employment agreement with the limited term shall be deemed to have been concluded for an indefinite period of time; it may be ordinarily terminated by the employer at the earliest upon expiration of the agreed upon term, unless an ordinary termination is possible pursuant to section 15 (3). ²If the term is invalid only because it was not fixed in written form, the employment agreement may also be ordinarily terminated before the end of the agreed upon term.

§ 17
Anrufung des Arbeitsgerichts

[1]Will der Arbeitnehmer geltend machen, dass die Befristung eines Arbeitsvertrages rechtsunwirksam ist, so muss er innerhalb von drei Wochen nach dem vereinbarten Ende des befristeten Arbeitsvertrages Klage beim Arbeitsgericht auf Feststellung erheben, dass das Arbeitsverhältnis auf Grund der Befristung nicht beendet ist. [2]Die §§ 5 bis 7 des Kündigungsschutzgesetzes gelten entsprechend. [3]Wird das Arbeitsverhältnis nach dem vereinbarten Ende fortgesetzt, so beginnt die Frist nach Satz 1 mit dem Zugang der schriftlichen Erklärung des Arbeitgebers, dass das Arbeitsverhältnis auf Grund der Befristung beendet sei.

Section 17
Appealing to the Labor Courts

[1]If the employee wishes to assert that the term of an employment agreement is invalid, he must, within three weeks of the agreed upon expiration of the employment agreement, bring an action before the labor court for declaratory judgment that the employment relationship has not come to an end due to expiration of the term. [2]Sections 5 to 7 of the Protection Against Dismissals Act *(Kündigungsschutzgesetz)* shall apply *mutatis mutandis*. [3]If the employment relationship is continued after the expiration of the agreed term, the time period pursuant to sentence 1 shall commence upon receipt of the employer's written declaration that the employment relationship has ended due to expiration of the term.

§ 18
Information über unbefristete Arbeitsplätze

[1]Der Arbeitgeber hat die befristet beschäftigten Arbeitnehmer über entsprechende unbefristete Arbeitsplätze zu informieren, die besetzt werden sollen. [2]Die Information kann durch allgemeine Bekanntgabe an geeigneter, den Arbeitnehmern zugänglicher Stelle im Betrieb und Unternehmen erfolgen.

Section 18
Information on Jobs for Unlimited Terms

[1]The employer shall inform employees working under a contract with a limited term of corresponding vacancies for unlimited terms. [2]This information may be rendered by a general announcement posted at a suitable location in the establishment and company which is accessible to the employees.

§ 19
Aus- und Weiterbildung

Der Arbeitgeber hat Sorge zu tragen, dass auch befristet beschäftigte Arbeitnehmer an angemessenen Aus- und Weiterbildungsmaßnahmen zur Förderung der beruflichen Entwicklung und Mobilität teilnehmen können, es sei denn, dass dringende betriebliche Gründe oder Aus- und Weiterbildungswünsche anderer Arbeitnehmer entgegenstehen.

Section 19
Training and Further Qualification

The employer shall ensure that employees working for fixed terms can also participate in appropriate training and further qualification measures to further their professional development and mobility, unless urgent operational grounds or the desire of other part-time employees to receive such training stand in the way.

§ 20
Information der Arbeitnehmervertretung

Der Arbeitgeber hat die Arbeitnehmervertretung über die Anzahl der befristet beschäftigten Arbeitnehmer und ihren Anteil an der Gesamtbelegschaft des Betriebes und des Unternehmens zu informieren.

Section 20
Informing the Employee Representatives

The employer shall inform the employee representative body of the number of employees working for fixed terms and their percentage of the total employees of the establishment and the company.

§ 21
Auflösend bedingte Arbeitsverträge

Wird der Arbeitsvertrag unter einer auflösenden Bedingung geschlossen, gelten § 4 Abs. 2, § 5, § 14 Abs. 1 und 4, § 15 Abs. 2, 3 und 5 sowie die §§ 16 bis 20 entsprechend.

Section 21
Employment Agreements with Conditions Subsequent

If the employment agreement was concluded subject to a resolutory condition subsequent, section 4 (2), sections 5, 14 (1) and (4), section 15 (2), (3) and (5) as well as sections 16 to 20 shall apply *mutatis mutandis*.

Vierter Abschnitt. Gemeinsame Vorschriften

Chapter 4. Common Provisions

§ 22
Abweichende Vereinbarungen

(1) Außer in den Fällen des § 12 Abs. 3, § 13 Abs. 4 und § 14 Abs. 2 Satz 3 und 4 kann von den Vorschriften dieses Gesetzes nicht zuungunsten des Arbeitnehmers abgewichen werden.

(2) Enthält ein Tarifvertrag für den öffentlichen Dienst Bestimmungen im Sinne des § 8 Abs. 4 Satz 3 und 4, § 12 Abs. 3, § 13 Abs. 4, § 14 Abs. 2 Satz 3 und 4 oder § 15 Abs. 3, so gelten diese Bestimmungen auch zwischen nicht tarifgebundenen Arbeitgebern und Arbeitnehmern außerhalb des öffentlichen Dienstes, wenn die Anwendung der für den öffentlichen Dienst geltenden tarifvertraglichen Bestimmungen zwischen ihnen vereinbart ist und die Arbeitgeber die Kosten des Betriebes überwiegend mit Zuwendungen im Sinne des Haushaltsrechts decken.

Section 22
Diverging Agreements

(1) Except in the cases set forth in section 12 (3), section 13 (4) and section 14 (2) sentences 3 and 4, employment agreements may not diverge from this statute to the detriment of the employee.

(2) Should a collective bargaining agreement for civil service contain provisions within the meaning of section 8 (4) sentences 3 and 4, section 12 (3), section 13 (4), section 14 (2) sentences 3 and 4 or section 15 (3), then such provisions shall be deemed to have also been concluded between non-civil service employers and employees who are not bound by such agreements if they have agreed to the application of the provisions in such agreements for civil service and the employer covers the costs of the establishment primarily with payments granted as part of a governmental budget.

§ 23
Besondere gesetzliche Regelungen

Besondere Regelungen über Teilzeitarbeit und über die Befristung von Arbeitsverträgen nach anderen gesetzlichen Vorschriften bleiben unberührt.

Section 23
Special Statutory Regulations

Special regulations governing part-time work and limited terms for employment agreements in other statutes remain unaffected.

IV. Act on the Payment of Wages and Salaries on Statutory Holidays and in Case of Illness (Continuation of Remuneration Act) (Entgeltfortzahlungsgesetz – EntgeltfortzG)

of 26 May 1994 (Federal Law Gazette I p. 1014)

in the amended version of 23 December 2003

§ 1
Anwendungsbereich

(1) Dieses Gesetz regelt die Zahlung des Arbeitsentgelts an gesetzlichen Feiertagen und die Fortzahlung des Arbeitsentgelts im Krankheitsfall an Arbeitnehmer sowie die wirtschaftliche Sicherung im Bereich der Heimarbeit für gesetzliche Feiertage und im Krankheitsfall.

(2) Arbeitnehmer in Sinne dieses Gesetzes sind Arbeiter und Angestellte sowie die zu ihrer Berufsbildung Beschäftigten.

§ 2
Entgeltzahlung an Feiertagen

(1) Für Arbeitszeit, die infolge eines gesetzlichen Feiertages ausfällt, hat der Arbeitgeber dem Arbeitnehmer das Arbeitsentgelt zu zahlen, das er ohne den Arbeitsausfall erhalten hätte.

(2) Die Arbeitszeit, die an einem gesetzlichen Feiertag gleichzeitig infolge von Kurzarbeit ausfällt und für die an anderen Tagen als an gesetzlichen Feiertagen Kurzarbeitergeld geleistet wird, gilt als infolge eines gesetzlichen Feiertages nach Absatz 1 ausgefallen.

(3) Arbeitnehmer, die am letzten Arbeitstag vor oder am ersten Arbeitstag nach Feiertagen unentschuldigt der

Section 1
Area of Applicability

(1) This Act governs the payment of wages and salaries to employees on statutory holidays and the continuation of payment of remuneration in case of illness, as well as the provision of economic security for statutory holidays and in case of illness in the area of work conducted in the home.

(2) Employees in the meaning of this Act are wage earners and salaried employees as well as trainees and apprentices.

Section 2
Payment of Remuneration on Holidays

(1) For hours not worked due to a statutory holiday, the employer must pay the employee the remuneration which he would have received had he worked.

(2) The working time on a statutory holiday which is not worked due to short-time work and for which on days other than statutory holidays short-time work remuneration is paid, shall be deemed to be working time not worked due to a statutory holiday pursuant to subsection (1).

(3) Employees who are absent without an excuse on the working day immediately preceding or following statutory

Arbeit fernbleiben, haben keinen Anspruch auf Bezahlung für diese Feiertage.

§ 3
Anspruch auf Entgeltfortzahlung im Krankheitsfall

(1) [1]Wird ein Arbeitnehmer durch Arbeitsunfähigkeit infolge Krankheit an seiner Arbeitsleistung verhindert, ohne dass ihn ein Verschulden trifft, so hat er Anspruch auf Entgeltfortzahlung im Krankheitsfall durch den Arbeitgeber für die Zeit der Arbeitsunfähigkeit bis zur Dauer von sechs Wochen. [2]Wird der Arbeitnehmer infolge derselben Krankheit erneut arbeitsunfähig, so verliert er wegen der erneuten Arbeitsunfähigkeit den Anspruch nach Satz 1 für einen weiteren Zeitraum von höchstens sechs Wochen nicht, wenn

1. er vor der erneuten Arbeitsunfähigkeit mindestens sechs Monate nicht infolge derselben Krankheit arbeitsunfähig war oder
2. seit Beginn der ersten Arbeitsunfähigkeit infolge derselben Krankheit eine Frist von zwölf Monaten abgelaufen ist.

(2) [1]Als unverschuldete Arbeitsunfähigkeit im Sinne des Absatzes 1 gilt auch eine Arbeitsverhinderung, die infolge einer nicht rechtswidrigen Sterilisation oder eines nicht rechtswidrigen Abbruchs der Schwangerschaft eintritt. [2]Dasselbe gilt für einen Abbruch der Schwangerschaft, wenn die Schwangerschaft innerhalb von zwölf Wochen nach der Empfängnis durch einen Arzt abgebrochen wird, die schwangere Frau den Abbruch verlangt und dem Arzt durch eine Bescheinigung nachgewiesen hat, dass sie sich mindestens drei Tage vor dem Eingriff von einer anerkannten Beratungsstelle hat beraten lassen.

(3) Der Anspruch nach Absatz 1 entsteht nach vierwöchiger ununterbrochener Dauer des Arbeitsverhältnisses.

Section 3
Claim to Continued Remuneration in Case of Illness

(1) [1]Should an employee be prevented from working due to an incapacitation caused by illness for which he is not at fault, he shall not lose his claim to remuneration for the time of his incapacitation for a period of up to six weeks. [2]Should the employee then become incapacitated again due to the same illness, he shall retain his claim to remuneration for the time of his incapacitation pursuant to sentence 1 for a further period of up to six weeks, provided that

1. for a period of at least six months up to the renewed incapacitation, he had not been unable to work due to the same illness, or
2. twelve months have elapsed since the onset of the first incidence of incapacitation due to the same illness.

(2) [1]Other cases deemed to constitute a non-culpable incapacitation within the meaning of subsection (1) shall be an incapacitation due to a not illegal sterilization or a not illegal termination of pregnancy. [2]The same shall hold for a termination of pregnancy if the pregnancy is terminated within twelve weeks of conception by a doctor, the pregnant woman has requested the abortion and has presented the doctor with proof that she had obtained counseling from a recognized counseling center at least three days prior to the procedure.

(3) The claim pursuant to subsection (1) shall take effect once the employee has been employed with the employer for four consecutive weeks.

§ 4
Höhe des fortzuzahlenden Arbeitsentgelts

(1) Für den in § 3 Abs. 1 bezeichneten Zeitraum ist dem Arbeitnehmer das ihm bei der für ihn maßgebenden regelmäßigen Arbeitszeit zustehende Arbeitsentgelt fortzuzahlen.

(1a) [1] Zum Arbeitsentgelt nach Absatz 1 gehören nicht das zusätzlich für Überstunden gezahlte Arbeitsentgelt und Leistungen für Aufwendungen des Arbeitnehmers, soweit der Anspruch auf sie im Falle der Arbeitsfähigkeit davon abhängig ist, dass dem Arbeitnehmer entsprechende Aufwendungen tatsächlich entstanden sind, und dem Arbeitnehmer solche Aufwendungen während der Arbeitsunfähigkeit nicht entstehen. [2] Erhält der Arbeitnehmer eine auf das Ergebnis der Arbeit abgestellte Vergütung, so ist der von dem Arbeitnehmer in der für ihn maßgebenden regelmäßigen Arbeitszeit erzielbare Durchschnittsverdienst der Berechnung zugrunde zu legen.

(2) Ist der Arbeitgeber für Arbeitszeit, die gleichzeitig infolge eines gesetzlichen Feiertages ausgefallen ist, zur Fortzahlung des Arbeitsentgelts nach § 3 verpflichtet, bemisst sich die Höhe des fortzuzahlenden Arbeitsentgelts für diesen Feiertag nach § 2.

(3) [1] Wird in dem Betrieb verkürzt gearbeitet und würde deshalb das Arbeitsentgelt des Arbeitnehmers im Falle seiner Arbeitsfähigkeit gemindert, so ist die verkürzte Arbeitszeit für ihre Dauer als die für den Arbeitnehmer maßgebende regelmäßige Arbeitszeit im Sinne des Absatzes 1 anzusehen. [2] Dies gilt nicht im Falle des § 2 Abs. 2.

(4) [1] Durch Tarifvertrag kann eine von den Absätzen 1, 1a und 3 abweichende Bemessungsgrundlage des fortzuzahlenden Arbeitsentgelts festgelegt werden. [2] Im Geltungsbereich eines solchen Tarifvertrages kann zwischen

Section 4
Amount of Remuneration to be Continuously Paid

(1) For the period of time set forth in section 3 (1), the employee shall continue to be paid the amount of remuneration he would receive for the working time normally worked.

(1a) [1] Remuneration pursuant to subsection (1) shall not include additional remuneration for overtime and reimbursements for expenses of the employee where the employee's claim to them while able to work is dependent upon the employee's actually incurring such expenses and the employee does not incur such expenses during his period of incapacitation. [2] Should the employee receive remuneration based upon the results of his work, his remuneration shall be based on in the amount of his average earnings during the working time he normally works.

(2) Should the employer be obligated to continue to pay remuneration for time not worked due to a statutory holiday pursuant to section 3, the amount of the payment for this holiday shall be calculated pursuant to section 2.

(3) [1] Should the establishment be reduced to short-time work, causing the wages of the employee to be reduced as a result of the lowering of his work capacity, then, for the duration of the incapacitation, the reduced shift shall be deemed to constitute the normal working time in the meaning of subsection (1). [2] This does not apply in the case of section 2 (2).

(4) [1] A basis for calculating the amount of continued remuneration payments in deviation from that set forth in subsections (1), (1a) and (3) may be established by virtue of a collective bargaining agreement. [2] In the area of applicability

nichttarifgebundenen Arbeitgebern und Arbeitnehmern die Anwendung der tarifvertraglichen Regelung über die Fortzahlung des Arbeitsentgelts im Krankheitsfalle vereinbart werden.

of such a collective bargaining agreement, employers and employees not bound by a collective bargaining agreement may agree to apply the provisions therein with regard to continued remuneration in case of illness.

§ 4a
Kürzung von Sondervergütungen

[1]Eine Vereinbarung über die Kürzung von Leistungen, die der Arbeitgeber zusätzlich zum laufenden Arbeitsentgelt erbringt (Sondervergütungen), ist auch für Zeiten der Arbeitsunfähigkeit infolge Krankheit zulässig. [2]Die Kürzung darf für jeden Tag der Arbeitsunfähigkeit infolge Krankheit ein Viertel des Arbeitsentgelts, das im Jahresdurchschnitt auf einen Arbeitstag entfällt, nicht überschreiten.

Section 4a
Reduction of Special Bonuses

[1]An agreement to reduce the payments the employer renders in addition to the regular wage or salary (special bonuses) shall also be permitted for periods of incapacitation resulting from illness. [2]The reduction for each day of incapacity resulting from illness may not exceed one quarter of the wage or salary payable for each working day on an annual average.

§ 5
Anzeige- und Nachweispflichten

(1) [1]Der Arbeitnehmer ist verpflichtet, dem Arbeitgeber die Arbeitsunfähigkeit und deren voraussichtliche Dauer unverzüglich mitzuteilen. [2]Dauert die Arbeitsunfähigkeit länger als drei Kalendertage, hat der Arbeitnehmer eine ärztliche Bescheinigung über das Bestehen der Arbeitsunfähigkeit sowie deren voraussichtliche Dauer spätestens an dem darauffolgenden Arbeitstag vorzulegen. [3]Der Arbeitgeber ist berechtigt, die Vorlage der ärztlichen Bescheinigung früher zu verlangen. [4]Dauert die Arbeitsunfähigkeit länger als in der Bescheinigung angegeben, ist der Arbeitnehmer verpflichtet, eine neue ärztliche Bescheinigung vorzulegen. [5]Ist der Arbeitnehmer Mitglied einer gesetzlichen Krankenkasse, muss die ärztliche Bescheinigung einen Vermerk des behandelnden Arztes darüber enthalten, dass der Krankenkasse unverzüglich eine Bescheinigung über die Arbeitsunfähigkeit mit Angaben über den Befund und die voraussichtliche

Section 5
Duty of Notification and Provision of Proof

(1) [1]The employee shall notify the employer without delay of his incapacity and its presumed duration. [2]Should the incapacity last longer than three calendar days, the employee must, at the latest by the next working day, present a medical certificate from a doctor confirming the incapacity and its presumed duration. [3]The employer is entitled to demand that the certificate be presented earlier. [4]Should the incapacity last longer than is stated in the certificate, the employee shall be obligated to present a new medical certificate. [5]Should the employee be insured by a statutory health insurance fund, the medical certificate must contain a note from his doctor stating that a certificate verifying the incapacity and including information on the findings and presumed duration of the incapacity will be sent to the insurance fund without delay.

Dauer der Arbeitsunfähigkeit übersandt wird.

(2) ¹Hält sich der Arbeitnehmer bei Beginn der Arbeitsunfähigkeit im Ausland auf, so ist er verpflichtet, dem Arbeitgeber die Arbeitsunfähigkeit, deren voraussichtliche Dauer und die Adresse am Aufenthaltsort in der schnellstmöglichen Art der Übermittlung mitzuteilen ²Die durch die Mitteilung entstehenden Kosten hat der Arbeitgeber zu tragen. ³Darüber hinaus ist der Arbeitnehmer, wenn er Mitglied einer gesetzlichen Krankenkasse ist, verpflichtet, auch dieser die Arbeitsunfähigkeit und deren voraussichtliche Dauer unverzüglich anzuzeigen. ⁴Dauert die Arbeitsunfähigkeit länger als angezeigt, so ist der Arbeitnehmer verpflichtet, der gesetzlichen Krankenkasse die voraussichtliche Fortdauer der Arbeitsunfähigkeit mitzuteilen. ⁵Die gesetzlichen Krankenkassen können festlegen, dass der Arbeitnehmer Anzeige- und Mitteilungspflichten nach den Sätzen 3 und 4 auch gegenüber einem ausländischen Sozialversicherungsträger erfüllen kann. ⁶Absatz 1 Satz 5 gilt nicht. ⁷Kehrt ein arbeitsunfähig erkrankter Arbeitnehmer in das Inland zurück, so ist er verpflichtet, dem Arbeitgeber und der Krankenkasse seine Rückkehr unverzüglich anzuzeigen.

(2) ¹Should the employee be out of the country during the onset of his incapacity, he shall notify his employer by the quickest means possible of his incapacity, its presumed duration and the address at which he can be reached. ²Costs incurred by relaying this notification shall be borne by the employer. ³Further, if the employee is insured by a statutory health insurance fund, he shall inform this fund as well of his incapacity and its presumed duration without delay. ⁴Should the incapacity last longer than was originally stated, the employee shall inform the insurance fund of the presumed continued duration of the incapacity. ⁵The insurance fund may determine that the employee can also fulfill his notification and information duties pursuant to sentences 3 and 4 through a foreign social insurance fund. ⁶Subsection (1) sentence 5 does not apply. ⁷Should an employee who is incapacitated due to illness return to this country, he shall notify his employer and insurance fund of his return without delay.

§ 6
Forderungsübergang bei Dritthaftung

(1) Kann der Arbeitnehmer auf Grund gesetzlicher Vorschriften von einem Dritten Schadensersatz wegen des Verdienstausfalls beanspruchen, der ihm durch die Arbeitsunfähigkeit entstanden ist, so geht dieser Anspruch insoweit auf den Arbeitgeber über, als dieser dem Arbeitnehmer nach diesem Gesetz Arbeitsentgelt fortgezahlt und darauf entfallende vom Arbeitgeber zu tragende Beiträge zur Bundesagentur für Arbeit, Arbeitgeberanteile an Beiträgen zur Sozialversicherung und zur

Section 6
Assignment of Rights in Third Party Liability

(1) Should the employee, by force of statutory provisions, have a statutory claim to damages from a third party due to the loss of earnings arising from his incapacitation, this claim shall be assigned to the employer insofar as the latter continues to pay remuneration to the employee pursuant to this Act, plus any contributions the employer is obligated to make to the Federal Employment Office, social security and nursing care insurance, as well as to additional old age and survivors insurance plans.

Pflegeversicherung sowie zu Einrichtungen der zusätzlichen Alters- und Hinterbliebenenversorgung abgeführt hat.

(2) Der Arbeitnehmer hat dem Arbeitgeber unverzüglich die zur Geltendmachung des Schadensersatzanspruchs erforderlichen Angaben zu machen.

(3) Der Forderungsübergang nach Absatz 1 kann nicht zum Nachteil des Arbeitnehmers geltend gemacht werden.

(2) The employee shall give the employer all information necessary for the assertion of the damage claim without delay.

(3) The assignment of the claim pursuant to subsection (1) may not be asserted to the detriment of the employee.

§ 7
Leistungsverweigerungsrecht des Arbeitgebers

(1) Der Arbeitgeber ist berechtigt, die Fortzahlung des Arbeitsentgelts zu verweigern,

1. solange der Arbeitnehmer die von ihm nach § 5 Abs. 1 vorzulegende ärztliche Bescheinigung nicht vorlegt oder den ihm nach § 5 Abs. 2 obliegenden Verpflichtungen nicht nachkommt;
2. wenn der Arbeitnehmer den Übergang eines Schadensersatzanspruchs gegen einen Dritten auf den Arbeitgeber (§ 6) verhindert.

(2) Absatz 1 gilt nicht, wenn der Arbeitnehmer die Verletzung dieser ihm obliegenden Verpflichtungen nicht zu vertreten hat.

Section 7
Right of Employer to Refuse Performance

(1) The employer has the right to refuse the continuation of remuneration

1. as long as the employee does not present the medical certificate pursuant to section 5 (1) or fulfill his obligations pursuant to section 5 (2)

2. if the employee prevents assignment of damage claims against a third party to the employer (section 6).

(2) Subsection (1) shall not apply if the employee has been in breach of his obligations due to reasons beyond his control.

§ 8
Beendigung des Arbeitsverhältnisses

(1) ¹Der Anspruch auf Fortzahlung des Arbeitsentgelts wird nicht dadurch berührt, dass der Arbeitgeber das Arbeitsverhältnis aus Anlass der Arbeitsunfähigkeit kündigt. ²Das gleiche gilt, wenn der Arbeitnehmer das Arbeitsverhältnis aus einem vom Arbeitgeber zu vertretenden Grunde kündigt, der den Arbeitnehmer zur Kündigung aus wichtigem Grund ohne Einhaltung einer Kündigungsfrist berechtigt.

Section 8
Termination of the Employment Relationship

(1) ¹Should the employer terminate the employment relationship on grounds of incapacity, this shall not affect the claim to continuation of remuneration. ²The same shall hold for cases in which the employee terminates the employment relationship due to culpable behavior on the part of the employer, which entitles the employee to terminate for good cause *(aus wichtigem Grund)* without observing a notice period.

(2) Endet das Arbeitsverhältnis vor Ablauf der in § 3 Abs. 1 bezeichneten Zeit nach dem Beginn der Arbeitsunfähigkeit, ohne dass es einer Kündigung bedarf, oder infolge einer Kündigung aus anderen als den in Absatz 1 bezeichneten Gründen, so endet der Anspruch mit dem Ende des Arbeitsverhältnisses.

(2) Should the employment relationship end before the period set forth in section 3 (1) following the onset of the incapacity has elapsed, without need of a termination or as a consequence of a termination for reasons other than those set forth in subsection (1), the claim shall end with the conclusion of the employment relationship.

§ 9
Maßnahmen der medizinischen Vorsorge und Rehabilitation

Section 9
Preventative Medicine and Rehabilitation Measures

(1) ¹Die Vorschriften der §§ 3 bis 4a und 6 bis 8 gelten entsprechend für die Arbeitsverhinderung infolge einer Maßnahme der medizinischen Vorsorge oder Rehabilitation, die ein Träger der gesetzlichen Renten-, Kranken- oder Unfallversicherung, eine Verwaltungsbehörde der Kriegsopferversorgung oder ein sonstiger Sozialleistungsträger bewilligt hat und die in einer Einrichtung der medizinischen Vorsorge oder Rehabilitation durchgeführt wird. ²Ist der Arbeitnehmer nicht Mitglied einer gesetzlichen Krankenkasse oder nicht in der gesetzlichen Rentenversicherung versichert, gelten die §§ 3 bis 4a und 6 bis 8 entsprechend, wenn eine Maßnahme der medizinischen Vorsorge oder Rehabilitation ärztlich verordnet worden ist und in einer Einrichtung der medizinischen Vorsorge oder Rehabilitation oder einer vergleichbaren Einrichtung durchgeführt wird.

(1) ¹In cases where the employee is prevented from working due to a preventative or rehabilitative medical procedure which has been approved by a statutory insurance fund for retirement insurance, health insurance or accident insurance, an administrative agency responsible for pensions and benefits for war victims or another social welfare agency, and for which the employee requires stationary treatment in an institution for medical prevention or rehabilitation, the provisions of sections 3 to 4a and 6 to 8 shall apply *mutatis mutandis*. ²If the employee is not a member of a statutory insurance fund or eligible for retirement benefits, sections 3 to 4a and 6 to 8 shall apply *mutatis mutandis*, provided that a preventative or rehabilitative medical procedure has been prescribed by a doctor and will require inpatient treatment in an institution for medical prevention or rehabilitation or a comparable institution.

(2) Der Arbeitnehmer ist verpflichtet, dem Arbeitgeber den Zeitpunkt des Antritts der Maßnahme, die voraussichtliche Dauer und die Verlängerung der Maßnahme im Sinne des Absatzes 1 unverzüglich mitzuteilen und ihm

(2) The employee shall notify the employer without delay of the time at which this procedure is to be performed, its presumed duration and the extension of the procedure in the meaning of subsection (1) and submit without delay

a) eine Bescheinigung über die Bewilligung der Maßnahme durch einen Sozialleistungsträger nach Absatz 1 Satz 1 oder

a) a certificate by a social benefits provider pursuant to subsection (1) sentence 1 verifying approval of the procedure or

b) eine ärztliche Bescheinigung über die Erforderlichkeit der Maßnahme im Sinne des Absatzes 1 Satz 2

unverzüglich vorzulegen.

§ 10
Wirtschaftliche Sicherung für den Krankheitsfall im Bereich der Heimarbeit

(1) ¹In Heimarbeit Beschäftigte (§ 1 Abs. 1 des Heimarbeitsgesetzes) und ihnen nach § 1 Abs. 2 Buchstabe a bis c des Heimarbeitsgesetzes Gleichgestellte haben gegen ihren Auftraggeber oder, falls sie von einem Zwischenmeister beschäftigt werden, gegen diesen Anspruch auf Zahlung eines Zuschlags zum Arbeitsentgelt. ²Der Zuschlag beträgt

1. für Heimarbeiter, für Hausgewerbetreibende ohne fremde Hilfskräfte und die nach § 1 Abs. 2 Buchstabe a des Heimarbeitsgesetzes Gleichgestellten 3,4 vom Hundert,

2. für Hausgewerbetreibende mit nicht mehr als zwei fremden Hilfskräften und die nach § 1 Abs. 2 Buchstabe b und c des Heimarbeitsgesetzes Gleichgestellten 6,4 vom Hundert

des Arbeitsentgelts vor Abzug der Steuern, des Beitrags zur Bundesagentur für Arbeit und der Sozialversicherungsbeiträge ohne Unkostenzuschlag und ohne die für den Lohnausfall an gesetzlichen Feiertagen, den Urlaub und den Arbeitsausfall infolge Krankheit zu leistenden Zahlungen. ³Der Zuschlag für die unter Nummer 2 aufgeführten Personen dient zugleich zur Sicherung der Ansprüche der von ihnen Beschäftigten.

(2) Zwischenmeister, die den in Heimarbeit Beschäftigten nach § 1 Abs. 2 Buchstabe d des Heimarbeitsgesetzes gleichgestellt sind, haben gegen ihren Auftraggeber Anspruch auf Vergütung

b) a medical certificate verifying the necessity of the procedure within the meaning of subsection (1) sentence 2.

Section 10
Economic Protection for Cases of Illness in the Area of Work Conducted in the Home

(1) ¹Those involved in work conducted in the home (section 1 (1) of the Home Work Act) and those with equal status pursuant to section 1 (2) a to c of the Home Work Act have a claim to payment of a premium to their remuneration on the part of their contractor, or, if they are employed by an intermediary, from him. ²This premium shall be calculated as follows:

1. for work conducted in the home, self-employed work conducted in the home with no employees outside their family and those with equal status pursuant to section 1 (2) a of the Home Work Act, 3.4%,

2. for self-employed work conducted in the home with no more than two employees outside their family and those with equal status pursuant to section 1 (2) b and c of the Home Work Act, 6.4%

of the remuneration before taxes and contributions to the Federal Employment Office and social security, excluding compensation for expenses or payments for the loss of wages on legal holidays, vacation and incapacitation due to illness. ³The premium for the persons set forth in no. 2. above shall also serve as a security for the claims of those employed by them.

(2) Intermediaries who have an equal status with those engaged in work conducted in the home pursuant to section 1 (2) d of the Home Work Act have a claim against their contractor for re-

der von ihnen nach Absatz 1 nachweislich zu zahlenden Zuschläge.

(3) Die nach den Absätzen 1 und 2 in Betracht kommenden Zuschläge sind gesondert in den Entgeltbeleg einzutragen.

(4) ¹Für Heimarbeiter (§ 1 Abs. 1 Buchstabe a des Heimarbeitsgesetzes) kann durch Tarifvertrag bestimmt werden, dass sie statt der in Absatz 1 Satz 2 Nr. 1 bezeichneten Leistungen die den Arbeitnehmern im Falle ihrer Arbeitsunfähigkeit nach diesem Gesetz zustehenden Leistungen erhalten. ²Bei der Bemessung des Anspruchs auf Arbeitsentgelt bleibt der Unkostenzuschlag außer Betracht.

(5) ¹Auf die in den Absätzen 1 und 2 vorgesehenen Zuschläge sind die §§ 23 bis 25, 27 und 28 des Heimarbeitsgesetzes, auf die in Absatz 1 dem Zwischenmeister gegenüber vorgesehenen Zuschläge außerdem § 21 Abs. 2 des Heimarbeitsgesetzes entsprechend anzuwenden. ²Auf die Ansprüche der fremden Hilfskräfte der in Absatz 1 unter Nummer 2 genannten Personen auf Entgeltfortzahlung im Krankheitsfall ist § 26 des Heimarbeitsgesetzes entsprechend anzuwenden.

§ 11
Feiertagsbezahlung der in Heimarbeit Beschäftigten

(1) ¹Die in Heimarbeit Beschäftigen (§ 1 Abs. 1 des Heimarbeitsgesetzes) haben gegen den Auftraggeber oder Zwischenmeister Anspruch auf Feiertagsbezahlung nach Maßgabe der Absätze 2 bis 5. ²Den gleichen Anspruch haben die in § 1 Abs. 2 Buchstabe a bis d des Heimarbeitsgesetzes bezeichneten Personen, wenn sie hinsichtlich der Feiertagsbezahlung gleichgestellt werden; die Vorschriften des § 1 Abs. 3 Satz 3 und Abs. 4 und 5 des Heimarbeitsgesetzes finden Anwendung. ³Eine Gleichstellung, die sich auf die Entgelt-

muneration of the premiums pursuant to subsection (1) for which they can furnish proof.

(3) The premiums which come under consideration pursuant to subsections (1) and (2) must be separately entered in the remuneration statement.

(4) ¹Home workers (section 1 (1) a of the Home Work Act) may agree in a collective bargaining agreement that, in case of incapacity, they may receive from the employers the performances set forth in the Act in lieu of the premium set forth in subsection (1) sentence 2 no. 1. ²In gauging the claim to remuneration, the compensation for expenses shall not be taken into account.

(5) ¹For the premiums set forth in subsections (1) and (2), sections 23 to 25, 27 and 28 of the Home Work Act shall apply *mutatis mutandis*; for the premium to the intermediary set forth in subsection (1), section 21 (2) of the Home Work Act shall also apply *mutatis mutandis*. ²For the claims of the non-family employees of the persons named in subsection (2) no. 1 to continuation of remuneration in case of illness, section 26 of the Home Work Act shall apply *mutatis mutandis*.

Section 11
Holiday Pay for Those Engaged in Home Work

(1) ¹Those engaged in home work (section 1 (1) of the Home Work Act) have a claim to payment for statutory holidays from their contractor or intermediary pursuant to subsections (2) to (5). ²Those persons described in section 1 (2) a to d of the Home Work Act have the same claim if they have the same status with regard to payment for statutory holidays; the provisions of section 1 (3) sentence 3 and subsections (4) and (5) of the Home Work Act shall apply. ³An equal status which extends to the remuneration provision shall also

regelung erstreckt, gilt auch für die Feiertagsbezahlung, wenn diese nicht ausdrücklich von der Gleichstellung ausgenommen ist.

(2) ¹Das Feiertagsgeld beträgt für jeden Feiertag im Sinne des § 2 Abs. 1 0,72 vom Hundert des in einem Zeitraum von sechs Monaten ausgezahlten reinen Arbeitsentgelts ohne Unkostenzuschläge. ²Bei der Berechnung des Feiertagsgeldes ist für die Feiertage, die in den Zeitraum vom 1. Mai bis 31. Oktober fallen, der vorhergehende Zeitraum vom 1. November bis 30. April und für die Feiertage, die in den Zeitraum vom 1. November bis 30. April fallen, der vorhergehende Zeitraum vom 1. Mai bis 31. Oktober zugrunde zu legen. ³Der Anspruch auf Feiertagsgeld ist unabhängig davon, ob im laufenden Halbjahreszeitraum noch eine Beschäftigung in Heimarbeit für den Auftraggeber stattfindet.

(3) ¹Das Feiertagsgeld ist jeweils bei der Entgeltzahlung vor dem Feiertag zu zahlen. ²Ist die Beschäftigung vor dem Feiertag unterbrochen worden, so ist das Feiertagsgeld spätestens drei Tage vor dem Feiertag auszuzahlen. ³Besteht bei der Einstellung der Ausgabe von Heimarbeit zwischen den Beteiligten Einvernehmen, das Heimarbeitsverhältnis nicht wieder fortzusetzen, so ist dem Berechtigten bei der letzten Entgeltzahlung das Feiertagsgeld für die noch übrigen Feiertage des laufenden sowie die Feiertage des folgenden Halbjahreszeitraumes zu zahlen. ⁴Das Feiertagsgeld ist jeweils bei der Auszahlung in die Entgeltbelege (§ 9 des Heimarbeitsgesetzes) einzutragen.

(4) ¹Übersteigt das Feiertagsgeld, das der nach Absatz 1 anspruchsberechtigte Hausgewerbetreibende oder im Lohnauftrag arbeitende Gewerbetreibende (Anspruchsberechtigte) für einen Feiertag auf Grund des § 2 seinen fremden

hold for payment for statutory holidays, unless such is explicitly excluded from the equalization of status.

(2) ¹For each statutory holiday within the meaning of section 2 (1), the payment shall amount to 0.72% of the net remuneration paid in a six-month period excluding compensation for expenses. ²In calculating the payment for the statutory holiday, those statutory holidays falling between May 1 and October 31 shall be based upon the previous period between November 1 and April 30, and those falling between November 1 and April 30 shall be based upon the previous period between May 1 and October 31. ³The claim to payment for statutory holiday holds regardless of whether the employee is still engaged in work conducted in the home for the contractor in the current six month period.

(3) ¹Payment for statutory holidays shall be remitted together with the remuneration immediately preceding the holiday. ²Should the employment be interrupted before the statutory holiday, the payment shall be remitted no later than three days before the statutory holiday. ³Should the parties involved agree upon terminating the engagement for work conducted in the home that they shall not resume the work conducted in the home relationship at a later date, the entitled party shall receive with his final remuneration payment for statutory holidays for those statutory holidays yet remaining in the current and the following six months. ⁴The payment for statutory holidays must be entered into the remuneration statement (section 9 of the Home Work Act).

(4) ¹Should the amount of the payment for statutory holidays which the person engaged in work conducted in the home who is entitled to holiday pay pursuant to subsection (1) or a tradesman working for wages (entitled claim-

Hilfskräften (§ 2 Abs. 6 des Heimarbeitsgesetzes) gezahlt hat, den Betrag, den er auf Grund der Absätze 2 und 3 für diesen Feiertag erhalten hat, so haben ihm auf Verlangen seine Auftraggeber oder Zwischenmeister den Mehrbetrag anteilig zu erstatten. ²Ist der Anspruchsberechtigte gleichzeitig Zwischenmeister, so bleibt hierbei das für die Heimarbeiter oder Hausgewerbetreibenden empfangene und weiter gezahlte Feiertagsgeld außer Ansatz. ³Nimmt ein Anspruchsberechtigter eine Erstattung nach Satz 1 in Anspruch, so können ihm bei Einstellung der Ausgabe von Heimarbeit die erstatteten Beträge auf das Feiertagsgeld angerechnet werden, das ihm auf Grund des Absatzes 2 und des Absatzes 3 Satz 3 für die dann noch übrigen Feiertage des laufenden sowie für die Feiertage des folgenden Halbjahreszeitraumes zu zahlen ist.

ant) for a statutory holiday pursuant to section 2 remits to his non-family employees (section 2 (6) of the Home Work Act) exceed the amount which he has received pursuant to subsections (2) and (3) for this holiday, his contractor or intermediary shall recompense the difference on a pro rata basis. ²Should the entitled claimant also be the intermediary, the payment for statutory holidays received hereby for the work conducted in the home or self-employed work conducted in the home, which they in turn have paid to others, shall not be taken into account. ³Should an entitled claimant receive a reimbursement pursuant to sentence 1, then, in the event that the contracting of work conducted in the home is terminated, the reimbursed amount be set off against the payment for statutory holidays which he is to receive on the basis of subsections (2) and (3) sentence 3 for the holidays remaining from the current and the following six month periods.

(5) Das Feiertagsgeld gilt als Entgelt im Sinne der Vorschriften des Heimarbeitsgesetzes über Mithaftung des Auftraggebers (§ 21 Abs. 2), über Entgeltschutz (§§ 23 bis 27) und über Auskunftspflicht über Entgelte (§ 28); hierbei finden die §§ 24 bis 26 des Heimarbeitsgesetzes Anwendung, wenn ein Feiertagsgeld gezahlt ist, das niedriger ist als das in diesem Gesetz festgesetzte.

(5) Payment for statutory holidays is deemed remuneration in the meaning of the provisions of the Home Work Act on the joint liability of the contractor (section 21 (2)), on remuneration protection (sections 23 to 27) and on the duty of providing information on remunerations (section 28); here, sections 24 to 26 of the Home Work Act shall apply if payment is remitted which is less than that set forth in this Act.

§ 12
Unabdingbarkeit

§ 10 berechtigten Personen abgewichen Abgesehen von § 4 Abs. 4 kann von den Vorschriften dieses Gesetzes nicht zuungunsten des Arbeitnehmers oder der nach werden.

Section 12
Mandatory Nature

With the exception of section 4 (4), there shall be no deviation from the provisions in these Acts to the detriment of the employee or those persons entitled thereto pursuant to section 10.

§ 13
Übergangsvorschrift

Ist der Arbeitnehmer von einem Tag nach dem 9. Dezember 1998 bis zum

Section 13
Transitional Provision

If the employee is prevented from working between one day after 9 December

1. Januar 1999 oder darüber hinaus durch Arbeitsunfähigkeit infolge Krankheit oder infolge einer Maßnahme der medizinischen Vorsorge oder Rehabilitation an seiner Arbeitsleistung verhindert, sind für diesen Zeitraum die seit dem 1. Januar 1999 geltenden Vorschriften maßgebend, es sei denn, dass diese für den Arbeitnehmer ungünstiger sind.

1998 and 1 January 1999 or beyond that as a result of illness or a medicinal procedure or rehabilitation, then the provisions that have been in force since 1 January 1999 shall prevail, unless this would be less favorable for the employee.

V. Protection Against Unfair Dismissal Act (Kündigungsschutzgesetz – KSchG)

of 25 August 1969 (Federal Law Gazette I p. 1317)

in the amended version of 26 March 2008

Erster Abschnitt
Allgemeiner Kündigungsschutz

Chapter 1
General Dismissal Protection

§ 1
Sozial ungerechtfertigte Kündigungen

Section 1
Socially Unjustified Dismissals

(1) Die Kündigung des Arbeitsverhältnisses gegenüber einem Arbeitnehmer, dessen Arbeitsverhältnis in demselben Betrieb oder Unternehmen ohne Unterbrechung länger als sechs Monate bestanden hat, ist rechtsunwirksam, wenn sie sozial ungerechtfertigt ist.

(2) ¹Sozial ungerechtfertigt ist die Kündigung, wenn sie nicht durch Gründe, die in der Person oder in dem Verhalten des Arbeitnehmers liegen, oder durch dringende betriebliche Erfordernisse, die einer Weiterbeschäftigung des Arbeitnehmers in diesem Betrieb entgegenstehen, bedingt ist. ²Die Kündigung ist auch sozial ungerechtfertigt, wenn

1. in Betrieben des privaten Rechts
   a) die Kündigung gegen eine Richtlinie nach § 95 des Betriebsverfassungsgesetzes verstößt,

   b) der Arbeitnehmer an einem anderen Arbeitsplatz in demselben Betrieb oder in einem anderen Betrieb des Unternehmens weiterbeschäftigt werden kann

und der Betriebsrat oder eine andere nach dem Betriebsverfassungsgesetz insoweit zuständige Vertretung der Arbeitnehmer aus einem dieser Gründe der Kündigung innerhalb der Frist des § 102 Abs. 2 Satz 1 des Betriebsverfassungsgesetzes schriftlich widersprochen hat,

(1) The termination of the employment relationship of an employee who has been employed in the same establishment or the same company without interruption for more than six months is legally invalid if it is socially unjustified.

(2) ¹A dismissal is socially unjustified if it is not due to reasons related to the person, the conduct of the employee, or to compelling operational requirements which preclude the continued employment of the employee in the establishment. ²The termination is also socially unjustified if:

1. in private law establishments
   a) the termination violates a guideline pursuant to section 95 of the Works Constitution Act *(Betriebsverfassungsgesetz)*,

   b) the employee can continue to be employed in another position in the same establishment or in another establishment of the company

and the works council or another competent representative body of the employees, pursuant to the Works Constitution Act, has objected to the dismissal in writing for one of these reasons within the period set forth in section 102 (2) sentence 1 of the Works Constitution Act,

2. in Betrieben und Verwaltungen des öffentlichen Rechts
   a) die Kündigung gegen eine Richtlinie über die personelle Auswahl bei Kündigungen verstößt,
   b) der Arbeitnehmer an einem anderen Arbeitsplatz in derselben Dienststelle oder in einer anderen Dienststelle desselben Verwaltungszweigs an demselben Dienstort einschließlich seines Einzugsgebiets weiterbeschäftigt werden kann

und die zuständige Personalvertretung aus einem dieser Gründe fristgerecht gegen die Kündigung Einwendungen erhoben hat, es sei denn, dass die Stufenvertretung in der Verhandlung mit der übergeordneten Dienststelle die Einwendungen nicht aufrechterhalten hat.

³Satz 2 gilt entsprechend, wenn die Weiterbeschäftigung des Arbeitnehmers nach zumutbaren Umschulungs- oder Fortbildungsmaßnahmen oder eine Weiterbeschäftigung des Arbeitnehmers unter geänderten Arbeitsbedingungen möglich ist und der Arbeitnehmer sein Einverständnis hiermit erklärt hat. ⁴Der Arbeitgeber hat die Tatsachen zu beweisen, die die Kündigung bedingen.

(3) ¹Ist einem Arbeitnehmer aus dringenden betrieblichen Erfordernissen im Sinne des Absatzes 2 gekündigt worden, so ist die Kündigung trotzdem sozial ungerechtfertigt, wenn der Arbeitgeber bei der Auswahl des Arbeitnehmers die Dauer der Betriebszugehörigkeit, das Lebensalter, die Unterhaltspflichten und die Schwerbehinderung des Arbeitnehmers nicht oder nicht ausreichend berücksichtigt hat; auf Verlangen des Arbeitnehmers hat der Arbeitgeber dem Arbeitnehmer die Gründe anzugeben, die zu der getroffenen sozialen Auswahl geführt haben. ²In die soziale Auswahl nach Satz 1 sind Arbeitnehmer nicht einzubeziehen, deren Weiterbeschäftigung, insbesondere wegen ihrer Kenntnisse, Fähigkei-

2. in public sector establishments and public administrations
   a) the termination violates a guideline regarding the selection of personnel for dismissal,
   b) the employee can continue to be employed in another position in the same office or in another office of the same administrative branch in the same locality or its commuting area,

and the competent employee representative body has raised objections to the dismissal in a timely manner for one of these reasons, unless a superior representative body in negotiations with a superior office has not upheld these objections.

³Sentence 2 applies *mutatis mutandis* if the continued employment of the employee is possible after a reasonable amount of re-training or additional training or under modified working conditions and the employee has given his consent. ⁴The employer has the burden of proving the facts which caused the dismissal.

(3) ¹Where an employee is dismissed due to compelling operational requirements within the meaning of subsection (2), the dismissal is nevertheless held to be socially unjustified if, in selecting the employee, the employer has not, or has not sufficiently, considered the employee's seniority, age, duties to support dependents and severe disability; at the employee's request, the employer must state to the employee the reasons on which the selection in question was made. ²Employees shall not be included in the social selection pursuant to sentence 1 if their continued employment is in the justified operational interest of the employer, in particular due to their knowledge, skills and performance or in order to ensure a bal-

ten und Leistungen oder zur Sicherung einer ausgewogenen Personalstruktur des Betriebes, im berechtigten betrieblichen Interesse liegt. ³Der Arbeitnehmer hat die Tatsachen zu beweisen, die die Kündigung als sozial ungerechtfertigt im Sinne des Satzes 1 erscheinen lassen.

(4) Ist in einem Tarifvertrag, in einer Betriebsvereinbarung nach § 95 des Betriebsverfassungsgesetzes oder in einer entsprechenden Richtlinie nach den Personalvertretungsgesetzen festgelegt, wie die sozialen Gesichtspunkte nach Absatz 3 Satz 1 im Verhältnis zueinander zu bewerten sind, so kann die Bewertung nur auf grobe Fehlerhaftigkeit überprüft werden.

(5) ¹Sind bei einer Kündigung auf Grund einer Betriebsänderung nach § 111 des Betriebsverfassungsgesetzes die Arbeitnehmer, denen gekündigt werden soll, in einem Interessenausgleich zwischen Arbeitgeber und Betriebsrat namentlich bezeichnet, so wird vermutet, dass die Kündigung durch dringende betriebliche Erfordernisse im Sinne des Absatzes 2 bedingt ist. ²Die soziale Auswahl der Arbeitnehmer kann nur auf grobe Fehlerhaftigkeit überprüft werden. ³Die Sätze 1 und 2 gelten nicht, soweit sich die Sachlage nach Zustandekommen des Interessenausgleichs wesentlich geändert hat. ⁴Der Interessenausgleich nach Satz 1 ersetzt die Stellungnahme des Betriebsrates nach § 17 Abs. 3 Satz 2.

anced personnel structure in the establishment. ³The employee has the burden of proving the facts which make the dismissal appear to be socially unjustified within the meaning of sentence 1.

(4) Where a collective bargaining agreement, a works agreement pursuant to section 95 of the Works Constitution Act or a corresponding guideline under the laws governing personnel representation stipulate how the social factors pursuant to subsection (3) sentence 1 are to be evaluated in relationship to each other, such evaluation may only be reviewed for gross errors.

(5) ¹If, in the event of a termination on the basis of a change in business pursuant to section 111 of the Works Constitution Act, the employees who are to be dismissed are designated by name in a reconciliation of interests between the employer and the works council, then it shall be presumed that the dismissal is due to compelling operational requirements within the meaning of subsection (2). ²The social selection of the employees may only be reviewed for gross errors. ³Sentences 1 and 2 shall not apply to the extent that the situation has materially changed after the reconciliation of interests came about. ⁴The reconciliation of interests pursuant to sentence 1 shall replace the works council's comments pursuant to section 17 (3) sentence 2.

§ 1 a
Abfindungsanspruch bei betriebsbedingter Kündigung

Section 1 a
Claim for Severance Payment in the Case of a Dismissal on Operational Grounds

(1) ¹Kündigt der Arbeitgeber wegen dringender betrieblicher Erfordernisse nach § 1 Abs. 2 Satz 1 und erhebt der Arbeitnehmer bis zum Ablauf der Frist des § 4 Satz 1 keine Klage auf Feststellung, dass das Arbeitsverhältnis durch die Kündigung nicht aufgelöst ist, hat

(1) ¹If the employee dismisses an employee due to compelling operational requirements pursuant to section 1 (2) sentence 1 and the employee does not petition the Labor Court to find that the employment relationship has not been dissolved due to the termination by the

der Arbeitnehmer mit dem Ablauf der Kündigungsfrist Anspruch auf eine Abfindung. ²Der Anspruch setzt den Hinweis des Arbeitgebers in der Kündigungserklärung voraus, dass die Kündigung auf dringende betriebliche Erfordernisse gestützt ist und der Arbeitnehmer bei Verstreichenlassen der Klagefrist die Abfindung beanspruchen kann.

(2) ¹Die Höhe der Abfindung beträgt 0,5 Monatsverdienste für jedes Jahr des Bestehens des Arbeitsverhältnisses. ²§ 10 Abs. 3 gilt entsprechend. ³Bei der Ermittlung der Dauer des Arbeitsverhältnisses ist ein Zeitraum von mehr als sechs Monaten auf ein volles Jahr aufzurunden.

§ 2
Änderungskündigung

¹Kündigt der Arbeitgeber das Arbeitsverhältnis und bietet er dem Arbeitnehmer im Zusammenhang mit der Kündigung die Fortsetzung des Arbeitsverhältnisses zu geänderten Arbeitsbedingungen an, so kann der Arbeitnehmer dieses Angebot unter dem Vorbehalt annehmen, dass die Änderung der Arbeitsbedingungen nicht sozial ungerechtfertigt ist (§ 1 Abs. 2 Satz 1 bis 3, Abs. 3 Satz 1 und 2). ²Diesen Vorbehalt muss der Arbeitnehmer dem Arbeitgeber innerhalb der Kündigungsfrist, spätestens jedoch innerhalb von drei Wochen nach Zugang der Kündigung erklären.

§ 3
Kündigungseinspruch

¹Hält der Arbeitnehmer eine Kündigung für sozial ungerechtfertigt, so kann er binnen einer Woche nach der Kündigung Einspruch beim Betriebsrat einlegen. ²Erachtet der Betriebsrat den Einspruch für begründet, so hat er zu versuchen, eine Verständigung mit dem

expiration of the period set forth in section 4 sentence 1, the employee shall have a claim to a severance payment upon expiration of the notice period for dismissal. ²This claim is subject to the condition that the employer has stated in its declaration of dismissal that the dismissal is based on compelling operational requirements and the employee may claim the severance pay once he has allowed the period in which it may petition the court to elapse.

(2) ¹The severance pay shall amount to 0.5 monthly remuneration for each year the employment relationship existed. ²Section 10 (3) applies *mutatis mutandis*. ³In calculating the duration of the employment relationship, a period of more than six months shall be rounded up to a full year.

Section 2
Dismissal for Variation of Contract

¹Where the employer terminates the employment relationship and, in connection with the dismissal, offers the employee continued employment under modified working conditions, the employee may accept this offer subject to the proviso that the modified working conditions are not socially unjustified (section 1 (2) sentences 1 to 3, (3) sentences 1 and 2). ²The employee must declare this proviso to the employer within the dismissal notice period, at the latest, however, within three weeks after having been given notice of dismissal.

Section 3
Objection to Dismissal

¹Where an employee believes his dismissal to be socially unjustified, he may submit an objection to the works council within one week after the notice of dismissal. ²Where the works council believes the objection to be justified it shall attempt to reach an understanding

Arbeitgeber herbeizuführen. ³Er hat seine Stellungnahme zu dem Einspruch dem Arbeitnehmer und dem Arbeitgeber auf Verlangen schriftlich mitzuteilen.

with the employer. ³Upon request, it shall inform the employee and the employer in writing of its position regarding the objection.

§ 4
Anrufung des Arbeitsgerichts

¹Will ein Arbeitnehmer geltend machen, dass eine Kündigung sozial ungerechtfertigt oder aus anderen Gründen rechtsunwirksam ist, so muss er innerhalb von drei Wochen nach Zugang der schriftlichen Kündigung Klage beim Arbeitsgericht auf Feststellung erheben, dass das Arbeitsverhältnis durch die Kündigung nicht aufgelöst ist. ²Im Falle des § 2 ist die Klage auf Feststellung zu erheben, dass die Änderung der Arbeitsbedingungen sozial ungerechtfertigt oder aus anderen Gründen rechtsunwirksam ist. ³Hat der Arbeitnehmer Einspruch beim Betriebsrat eingelegt (§ 3), so soll er der Klage die Stellungnahme des Betriebsrats beifügen. ⁴Soweit die Kündigung der Zustimmung einer Behörde bedarf, läuft die Frist zur Anrufung des Arbeitsgerichts erst von der Bekanntgabe der Entscheidung der Behörde an den Arbeitnehmer ab.

Section 4
Seeking Redress in the Labor Court

¹Where an employee wishes to assert a claim that his dismissal is socially unjustified or legally invalid on other grounds, he must petition the Labor Court within three weeks after receiving the written termination notice to find that the employment relationship has not been dissolved due to the termination. ²If section 2 is the case, the petition shall seek a finding that the modified working conditions are socially unjustified or legally invalid on other grounds. ³Where an employee has submitted an objection to the works council (section 3), he should include the position of the works council with the complaint. ⁴To the extent the dismissal requires the approval of an authority, the time period for seeking redress in the Labor Court shall commence only once the employee has been notified of the decision of such authority.

§ 5
Zulassung verspäteter Klagen

(1) ¹War ein Arbeitnehmer nach erfolgter Kündigung trotz Anwendung aller ihm nach Lage der Umstände zuzumutenden Sorgfalt verhindert, die Klage innerhalb von drei Wochen nach Zugang der schriftlichen Kündigung zu erheben, so ist auf seinen Antrag die Klage nachträglich zuzulassen. ²Gleiches gilt, wenn eine Frau von ihrer Schwangerschaft aus einem von ihr nicht zu vertretenden Grund erst nach Ablauf der Frist des § 4 Satz 1 Kenntnis erlangt hat.

(2) ¹Mit dem Antrag ist die Klageerhebung zu verbinden; ist die Klage bereits

Section 5
Admissibility of Late Complaints

(1) ¹Where despite exercising all reasonable efforts under the circumstances, an employee was hindered from filing a complaint within three weeks of receiving a written notice of dismissal, the complaint shall be accepted retroactively for filing upon request. ²The same shall apply if, due to circumstances beyond her control, a woman did not learn of her pregnancy until the time period set forth in section 4 sentence 1 has elapsed.

(2) ¹The filed complaint shall be submitted together with the petition; whe-

eingereicht, so ist auf sie im Antrag Bezug zu nehmen. ²Der Antrag muß ferner die Angabe der die nachträgliche Zulassung begründenden Tatsachen und der Mittel für deren Glaubhaftmachung enthalten.

(3) ¹Der Antrag ist nur innerhalb von zwei Wochen nach Behebung des Hindernisses zulässig. ²Nach Ablauf von sechs Monaten, vom Ende der versäumten Frist an gerechnet, kann der Antrag nicht mehr gestellt werden.

(4) ¹Das Verfahren über den Antrag auf nachträgliche Zulassung ist mit dem Verfahren über die Klage zu verbinden. ²Das Arbeitsgericht kann das Verfahren zunächst auf die Verhandlung und Entscheidung über den Antrag beschränken. ³In diesem Fall ergeht die Entscheidung durch Zwischenurteil, das wie ein Endurteil angefochten werden kann.

(5) Hat das Arbeitsgericht über einen Antrag auf nachträgliche Klagezulassung nicht entschieden oder wird ein solcher Antrag erstmals vor dem Landesarbeitsgericht gestellt, entscheidet hierüber die Kammer des Landesarbeitsgerichts. Absatz 4 gilt entsprechend.

re the complaint has already been submitted it shall be referenced in the petition. ²The petition must also describe the circumstances justifying the delayed submission, providing *prima facie* substantiation.

(3) ¹The petition shall be permitted only within two weeks after the hindrance has been removed. ²Once six months have elapsed following the missed deadline, the petition may no longer be filed.

(4) ¹The proceeding on the petition for a delayed submission shall be bound to the proceeding on the complaint. ²The Labor Court may initially limit the proceeding to the hearing and the decision regarding the petition. ³In that case, the decision shall be rendered by way of an interim judgment, which can be contested as if it were a final judgment.

(5) If the Labor Court has not decided on a petition for delayed submission of complaint or if such a petition is initially filed with the Regional Labor Court, the division of the Labor Court shall decide on it. Subsection (4) shall apply *mutatis mutandis*.

§ 6
Verlängerte Anrufungsfrist

¹Hat ein Arbeitnehmer innerhalb von drei Wochen nach Zugang der schriftlichen Kündigung im Klagewege geltend gemacht, dass eine rechtswirksame Kündigung nicht vorliege, so kann er sich in diesem Verfahren bis zum Schluss der mündlichen Verhandlung erster Instanz zur Begründung der Unwirksamkeit der Kündigung auch auf innerhalb der Klagefrist nicht geltend gemachte Gründe berufen. ²Das Arbeitsgericht soll ihn hierauf hinweisen.

Section 6
Extended Petition Period

¹Where an employee asserts in a complaint within three weeks after receiving the written dismissal notice that the dismissal was invalid, he may invoke grounds that had not been asserted within the petition period to substantiate the invalidity of the dismissal in this proceeding up to the conclusion of the oral hearing in the first instance. ²The Labor Court shall inform him of this fact.

§ 7
Wirksamwerden der Kündigung

Wird die Rechtsunwirksamkeit einer Kündigung nicht rechtzeitig geltend

Section 7
Effectiveness of Dismissal

Where the invalidity of a dismissal is not asserted in a timely manner (sec-

gemacht (§ 4 Satz 1, §§ 5 und 6), so gilt die Kündigung als von Anfang an rechtswirksam; ein vom Arbeitnehmer nach § 2 erklärter Vorbehalt erlischt.

tion 4 sentence 1, sections 5 and 6), the dismissal is held to be legally effective from the outset; any proviso declared by the employee pursuant to section 2 shall lapse.

§ 8
Wiederherstellung der früheren Arbeitsbedingungen

Stellt das Gericht im Falle des § 2 fest, dass die Änderung der Arbeitsbedingungen sozial ungerechtfertigt ist, so gilt die Änderungskündigung als von Anfang an rechtsunwirksam.

Section 8
Restoration of Previous Working Conditions

If, according to section 2 the Court finds that the modification of the working conditions is socially unjustified, the dismissal for variation of contract shall be deemed to have been invalid from the outset.

§ 9
Auflösung des Arbeitsverhältnisses durch Urteil des Gerichts; Abfindung des Arbeitnehmers

(1) ¹Stellt das Gericht fest, dass das Arbeitsverhältnis durch die Kündigung nicht aufgelöst ist, ist jedoch dem Arbeitnehmer die Fortsetzung des Arbeitsverhältnisses nicht zuzumuten, so hat das Gericht auf Antrag des Arbeitnehmers das Arbeitsverhältnis aufzulösen und den Arbeitgeber zur Zahlung einer angemessenen Abfindung zu verurteilen. ²Die gleiche Entscheidung hat das Gericht auf Antrag des Arbeitgebers zu treffen, wenn Gründe vorliegen, die eine den Betriebszwecken dienliche weitere Zusammenarbeit zwischen Arbeitgeber und Arbeitnehmer nicht erwarten lassen. ³Arbeitnehmer und Arbeitgeber können den Antrag auf Auflösung des Arbeitsverhältnisses bis zum Schluss der letzten mündlichen Verhandlung in der Berufungsinstanz stellen.

(2) Das Gericht hat für die Auflösung des Arbeitsverhältnisses den Zeitpunkt festzusetzen, an dem es bei sozial gerechtfertigter Kündigung geendet hätte.

Section 9
Dissolution of the Employment Relationship through a Court Decision; Severance Payment for the Employee

(1) ¹Where the Court finds that an employment relationship was not dissolved by the dismissal, but the employee cannot reasonably be expected to continue with the employment relationship, the Court shall, upon the employee's petition, dissolve the employment relationship and order the employer to make an appropriate severance payment. ²The Court shall make the same decision upon petition of the employer if there are factors rendering it unlikely that a continued working relationship between the employer and the employee would be beneficial to the company's business interests. ³The employee and the employer may petition for dissolution of the employment contract up to the conclusion of the final oral hearing at the appellate level.

(2) If the employment relationship is to be dissolved, the Court must determine at what time it would have ended had a socially justified dismissal taken place.

§ 10
Höhe der Abfindung

(1) Als Abfindung ist ein Betrag bis zu zwölf Monatsverdiensten festzusetzen.

(2) ¹Hat der Arbeitnehmer das fünfzigste Lebensjahr vollendet und hat das Arbeitsverhältnis mindestens fünfzehn Jahre bestanden, so ist ein Betrag bis zu fünfzehn Monatsverdiensten, hat der Arbeitnehmer das fünfundfünfzigste Lebensjahr vollendet und hat das Arbeitsverhältnis mindestens zwanzig Jahre bestanden, so ist ein Betrag bis zu achtzehn Monatsverdiensten festzusetzen. ²Dies gilt nicht, wenn der Arbeitnehmer in dem Zeitpunkt, den das Gericht nach § 9 Abs. 2 für die Auflösung des Arbeitsverhältnisses festsetzt, das in der Vorschrift des Sechsten Buches Sozialgesetzbuch über die Regelaltersrente bezeichnete Lebensalter erreicht hat.

(3) Als Monatsverdienst gilt, was dem Arbeitnehmer bei der für ihn maßgebenden regelmäßigen Arbeitszeit in dem Monat, in dem das Arbeitsverhältnis endet (§ 9 Abs. 2), an Geld und Sachbezügen zusteht.

Section 10
Amount of the Severance Payment

(1) A severance payment in the amount of up to twelve months' pay shall be set.

(2) ¹Where the employee has reached the age of 50 and the employment relationship has lasted a minimum of 15 years, the amount shall be up to 15 months' salary; where the employee has reached the age of 55 and the employment relationship has lasted a minimum of 20 years, an amount of up to 18 months' salary shall be established. ²This shall not apply if, at the time when the Court has found the employment relationship to have been dissolved pursuant to section 9 (2), the employee has reached the age for regular retirement benefits, pursuant to the Sixth Book of the Social Security Code.

(3) A monthly salary shall be deemed to constitute the monetary and non-monetary remuneration the employee receives for his regular monthly working time at the time the employment relationship comes to an end (section 9 (2)).

§ 11
Anrechnung auf entgangenen Zwischenverdienst

¹Besteht nach der Entscheidung des Gerichts das Arbeitsverhältnis fort, so muss sich der Arbeitnehmer auf das Arbeitsentgelt, das ihm der Arbeitgeber für die Zeit nach der Entlassung schuldet, anrechnen lassen,
1. was er durch anderweitige Arbeit verdient hat,
2. was er hätte verdienen können, wenn er es nicht böswillig unterlassen hätte, eine ihm zumutbare Arbeit anzunehmen,
3. was ihm an öffentlich-rechtlichen Leistungen infolge Arbeitslosigkeit aus der Sozialversicherung, der Ar-

Section 11
Set-Off for Lost Interim Earnings

¹If the Court determines that the employment relationship continues to exist, the employee must allow the following to be deducted from the remuneration the employer owes him for the period following the dismissal
1. what he has earned through other work,
2. what he could have earned, had he not maliciously declined a reasonable offer of work,
3. what he has received on an interim basis as public aid due to his unemployment status, including social in-

beitslosenversicherung, der Sicherung des Lebensunterhalts nach dem Zweiten Buch Sozialgesetzbuch oder der Sozialhilfe für die Zwischenzeit gezahlt worden ist. ²Diese Beträge hat der Arbeitgeber der Stelle zu erstatten, die sie geleistet hat.

§ 12
Neues Arbeitsverhältnis des Arbeitnehmers; Auflösung des alten Arbeitsverhältnisses

¹Besteht nach der Entscheidung des Gerichts das Arbeitsverhältnis fort, ist jedoch der Arbeitnehmer inzwischen ein neues Arbeitsverhältnis eingegangen, so kann er binnen einer Woche nach der Rechtskraft des Urteils durch Erklärung gegenüber dem alten Arbeitgeber die Fortsetzung des Arbeitsverhältnisses bei diesem verweigern. ²Die Frist wird auch durch eine vor ihrem Ablauf zur Post gegebene schriftliche Erklärung gewahrt. ³Mit dem Zugang der Erklärung erlischt das Arbeitsverhältnis. ⁴Macht der Arbeitnehmer von seinem Verweigerungsrecht Gebrauch, so ist ihm entgangener Verdienst nur für die Zeit zwischen der Entlassung und dem Tag des Eintritts in das neue Arbeitsverhältnis zu gewähren. ⁵§ 11 findet entsprechende Anwendung.

§ 13
Außerordentliche, sittenwidrige und sonstige Kündigungen

(1) ¹Die Vorschriften über das Recht zur außerordentlichen Kündigung eines Arbeitsverhältnisses werden durch das vorliegende Gesetz nicht berührt. ²Die Rechtsunwirksamkeit einer außerordentlichen Kündigung kann jedoch nur nach Maßgabe des § 4 Satz 1 und der §§ 5 bis 7 geltend gemacht werden. ³Stellt das Gericht fest, dass die außerordentliche Kündigung unbegründet ist, ist jedoch dem Arbeitnehmer die Fortsetzung des Arbeitsverhältnisses nicht zuzumuten, so hat auf seinen An-

surance, unemployment insurance, securing of his livelihood pursuant to the Second Book of the Social Security Code, or social assistance. ²The employer shall reimburse this amount to the agency which made these payments.

Section 12
New Employment Relationship of the Employee, Dissolution of the Former Employment Relationship

¹Where an employment relationship continues to exist due to the Court's decision, but the employee has meanwhile accepted other employment, he may decline to continue the employment relationship by declaration to the former employer within one week after the judgment becomes final and non-appealable. ²A declaration in written form mailed prior to the expiration of this period shall be in compliance with this requirement. ³The employment relationship ceases to exist upon receipt of the declaration. ⁴Where the employee exercises his legal right to decline continued employment, back-pay shall only be due to him for the period between the dismissal and the date on which he entered into the new employment relationship. ⁵Section 11 applies *mutatis mutandis*.

Section 13
Extraordinary, Unethical and Other Dismissals

(1) ¹The provisions regarding the right to an extraordinary dismissal of an employment relationship are not affected by this Act. ²However, the validity of an extraordinary dismissal may only be challenged on the basis of section 4 sentence 1 and sections 5 to 7. ³Where the Court finds that an extraordinary dismissal is unfounded, but the employee cannot reasonably be expected to continue the employment relationship, he may dissolve the employment relationship upon petition to the Court and the

trag das Gericht das Arbeitsverhältnis aufzulösen und den Arbeitgeber zur Zahlung einer angemessenen Abfindung zu verurteilen. ⁴Das Gericht hat für die Auflösung des Arbeitsverhältnisses den Zeitpunkt festzulegen, zu dem die außerordentliche Kündigung ausgesprochen wurde. ⁵Die Vorschriften der §§ 10 bis 12 gelten entsprechend.

(2) Verstößt eine Kündigung gegen die guten Sitten, so finden die Vorschriften des § 9 Abs. 1 Satz 1 und Abs. 2 und der §§ 10 bis 12 entsprechende Anwendung.

(3) Im Übrigen finden die Vorschriften dieses Abschnitts mit Ausnahme der §§ 4 bis 7 auf eine Kündigung, die bereits aus anderen als den in § 1 Abs. 2 und 3 bezeichneten Gründen rechtsunwirksam ist, keine Anwendung.

employer shall be ordered to make an appropriate severance payment. ⁴The Court shall determine for the dissolution of the employment relationship the date on which the extraordinary dismissal was declared. ⁵The provisions of 10 to 12 apply *mutatis mutandis.*

(2) Where a dismissal is contrary to public policy, the provisions of section 9 (1) sentences 1 and (2) and sections 10 to 12 shall apply *mutatis mutandis* .

(3) Otherwise, the provisions of this Chapter, with the exception of sections 4 to 7, are not applicable to a dismissal which is invalid for reasons other than those provided in section 1 (2) and (3).

§ 14
Angestellte in leitender Stellung

(1) Die Vorschriften dieses Abschnitts gelten nicht
1. in Betrieben einer juristischen Person für die Mitglieder des Organs, das zur gesetzlichen Vertretung der juristischen Person berufen ist,
2. in Betrieben einer Personengesamtheit für die durch Gesetz, Satzung oder Gesellschaftsvertrag zur Vertretung der Personengesamtheit berufenen Personen.

(2) ¹Auf Geschäftsführer, Betriebsleiter und ähnliche leitende Angestellte, soweit diese zur selbständigen Einstellung oder Entlassung von Arbeitnehmern berechtigt sind, finden die Vorschriften dieses Abschnitts mit Ausnahme des § 3 Anwendung. ²§ 9 Abs. 1 Satz 2 findet mit der Maßgabe Anwendung, dass der Antrag des Arbeitgebers auf Auflösung des Arbeitsverhältnisses keiner Begründung bedarf.

Section 14
Salaried Employees and Managerial Positions

(1) The provisions of this Chapter do not apply
1. in establishments of a legal entity, members of the body appointed to legally represent the legal entity,
2. in establishments of a partnership, the persons appointed by law, the articles of association or the bylaws to represent the partnership.

(2) ¹The provisions of this Chapter, with the exception of section 3, are not applicable to managing directors, directors of establishments and similar managerial employees who have the authority to independently hire or dismiss employees. ²Section 9 (1) sentence 2 shall apply, with the proviso that the employer's petition for dissolution of the employment relationship shall not require substantiation.

Chapter 2
Protection against Dismissal Within the Scope of the Provisions Governing the Works Constitution and of Public Employees Representatives

Section 15
Inadmissibility of Dismissal

(1) [1] The dismissal of a member of a works council, a youth and trainee representative body, for a ship's crew or a marine works council, shall be unlawful unless circumstances exist which entitle the employer to dismiss for good cause without notice, and the required consent, pursuant to section 103 of the Works Constitution Act, has been obtained or a court ruling has been obtained in lieu of such consent. [2] Members of a works council, a youth and trainee representative body, or a marine works council, may not be dismissed within one year, and members of a representative body of a ship's crew may not be dismissed within six months of expiration of such member's term of office, calculated from the date on which such member's term of office expires, unless circumstances exist which entitle the employer to dismiss for good cause without notice; the foregoing shall not apply if membership has been terminated by virtue of a court ruling.

(2) [1] The dismissal of a member of a body representing public employees or employees who are minors or apprentices is unlawful unless circumstances exist which entitle the employer to dismiss for good cause without notice and the required consent, pursuant to public employees representation law, has been obtained or a court ruling has been made in lieu of such consent. [2] After the expiration of the term of office of the persons mentioned in

Amtszeit der in Satz 1 genannten Personen ist ihre Kündigung innerhalb eines Jahres, vom Zeitpunkt der Beendigung der Amtszeit an gerechnet, unzulässig, es sei denn, dass Tatsachen vorliegen, die den Arbeitgeber zur Kündigung aus wichtigem Grund ohne Einhaltung einer Kündigungsfrist berechtigen; dies gilt nicht, wenn die Beendigung der Mitgliedschaft auf einer gerichtlichen Entscheidung beruht.

(3) ¹Die Kündigung eines Mitglieds eines Wahlvorstands ist vom Zeitpunkt seiner Bestellung an, die Kündigung eines Wahlbewerbers vom Zeitpunkt der Aufstellung des Wahlvorschlags an, jeweils bis zur Bekanntgabe des Wahlergebnisses unzulässig, es sei denn, dass Tatsachen vorliegen, die den Arbeitgeber zur Kündigung aus wichtigem Grund ohne Einhaltung einer Kündigungsfrist berechtigen, und dass die nach § 103 des Betriebsverfassungsgesetzes oder nach dem Personalvertretungsrecht erforderliche Zustimmung vorliegt oder durch eine gerichtliche Entscheidung ersetzt ist. ²Innerhalb von sechs Monaten nach Bekanntgabe des Wahlergebnisses ist die Kündigung unzulässig, es sei denn, dass Tatsachen vorliegen, die den Arbeitgeber zur Kündigung aus wichtigem Grund ohne Einhaltung einer Kündigungsfrist berechtigen; dies gilt nicht für Mitglieder des Wahlvorstands, wenn dieser durch gerichtliche Entscheidung durch einen anderen Wahlvorstand ersetzt worden ist.

(3a) ¹Die Kündigung eines Arbeitnehmers, der zu einer Betriebs-, Wahl- oder Bordversammlung nach § 17 Abs. 3, § 17a Nr. 3 Satz 2, § 115 Abs. 2 Nr. 8 Satz 1 des Betriebsverfassungsgesetzes einlädt oder die Bestellung eines Wahlvorstands nach § 16 Abs. 2 Satz 1, § 17 Abs. 4, § 17a Nr. 4, § 63 Abs. 3, § 115 Abs. 2 Nr. 8 Satz 2 oder § 116 Abs. 2 Nr. 7 Satz 5 des Betriebsverfassungsgesetzes beantragt, ist vom Zeitpunkt der Einladung oder Antragstellung an bis zur Bekanntgabe des Wahlergebnisses

sentence 1, they may not be dismissed within one year, counting from the date of expiration of the term of office, unless circumstances exist which entitle the employer to terminate for good cause without notice; the foregoing shall not apply if membership has been terminated by virtue of a court ruling.

(3) ¹A member of an election committee shall not be dismissed from the time of his appointment, and an election candidate shall not be dismissed from the time of his nomination until the election results have been announced, unless circumstances exist which entitle the employer to dismiss the member or candidate for good cause without notice and the required consent, pursuant to section 103 of the Works Constitution Act or the laws governing personnel representation, has been obtained or a court ruling has been obtained in lieu of such consent. ²No dismissal may be made within six months of the announcement of the election results unless circumstances exist which entitle the employer to dismiss the member or candidate for good cause without notice; the foregoing shall not apply to members of the election committee if the committee has been replaced, pursuant to a court ruling, by another election committee.

(3a) ¹An employee who, pursuant to section 17 (1), section 17a no. 3 sentence 2, section 115 (2) no. 8 sentence 1 of the Works Constitution Act invites an establishment meeting, electoral rally, or crew meeting or who, pursuant to 316 (2) sentence 1, section 17 (4), section 17a no. 4, section 63 (3), section 115 (2) no. 8 sentence 2 or section 116 (2) no. 7 sentence 5 of the Works Constitution Act, petitions for the appointment of an electoral committee may not be dismissed from the time of the invitation

unzulässig, es sei denn, dass Tatsachen vorliegen, die den Arbeitgeber zur Kündigung aus wichtigem Grund ohne Einhaltung einer Kündigungsfrist berechtigen; der Kündigungsschutz gilt für die ersten drei in der Einladung oder Antragstellung aufgeführten Arbeitnehmer. ²Wird ein Betriebsrat, eine Jugend- und Auszubildendenvertretung, eine Bordvertretung oder ein Seebetriebsrat nicht gewählt, besteht der Kündigungsschutz nach Satz 1 vom Zeitpunkt der Einladung oder Antragstellung an drei Monate.

(4) Wird der Betrieb stillgelegt, so ist die Kündigung der in den Absätzen 1 bis 3 genannten Personen frühestens zum Zeitpunkt der Stilllegung zulässig, es sei denn, dass ihre Kündigung zu einem früheren Zeitpunkt durch zwingende betriebliche Erfordernisse bedingt ist.

(5) ¹Wird eine der in den Absätzen 1 bis 3 genannten Personen in einer Betriebsabteilung beschäftigt, die stillgelegt wird, so ist sie in eine andere Betriebsabteilung zu übernehmen. ²Ist dies aus betrieblichen Gründen nicht möglich, so findet auf ihre Kündigung die Vorschrift des Absatzes 4 über die Kündigung bei Stilllegung des Betriebs sinngemäß Anwendung.

§ 16
Neues Arbeitsverhältnis, Auflösung des alten Arbeitsverhältnisses

¹Stellt das Gericht die Unwirksamkeit der Kündigung einer der in § 15 Abs. 1 bis 3a genannten Personen fest, so kann diese Person, falls sie inzwischen ein neues Arbeitsverhältnis eingegangen ist, binnen einer Woche nach Rechtskraft des Urteils durch Erklärung gegenüber dem alten Arbeitgeber die Wiederbeschäftigung bei diesem verweigern. ²Im übrigen finden die Vorschriften des § 11 und des § 12

or the petition until the election results have been announced, unless circumstances exist which entitle the employer to dismiss the employee for good cause without notice; the dismissal protection applies for the first three employees listed in the invitation or petition. ²Should a works council, a representative body for young employees and apprentices, ship's committee, or a works council of the merchant fleet not be elected the dismissal protection set forth in sentence 1 shall apply for three months beginning at the time of the invitation or petition.

(4) If the establishment is closed down, the dismissal of the persons mentioned in subsections (1) to (3) above shall be permissible no earlier than the date of closure, unless their earlier dismissal is necessary for compelling operational reasons.

(5) ¹Where one of the persons mentioned in subsections (1) to (3) above is employed in a section of the establishment which has been closed down, he shall be transferred to another section of the establishment. ²Where this is not possible for operational reasons, the provision set forth in subsection (4) regarding dismissal upon closure of the establishment shall apply accordingly.

Section 16
New Employment Relationship, Dissolution of the Old Employment Relationship

¹Where the Court establishes the invalidity of the dismissal of one of the persons mentioned in section 15 (1) to (3a) and such person has entered into a new employment relationship, he may decline continued employment with the former employer by making a declaration to the latter to this effect within one week after the judgment has become final and non-appealable. ²Otherwise, the provisions contained in section 11

Satz 2 bis 4 entsprechende Anwendung.

Dritter Abschnitt
Anzeigepflichtige Entlassungen

§ 17
Anzeigepflicht

(1) ¹Der Arbeitgeber ist verpflichtet, der Agentur für Arbeit Anzeige zu erstatten, bevor er

1. in Betrieben mit in der Regel mehr als 20 und weniger als 60 Arbeitnehmern mehr als 5 Arbeitnehmer,
2. in Betrieben mit in der Regel mindestens 60 und weniger als 500 Arbeitnehmern 10 vom Hundert der im Betrieb regelmäßig beschäftigten Arbeitnehmer oder aber mehr als 25 Arbeitnehmer,
3. in Betrieben mit in der Regel mindestens 500 Arbeitnehmern mindestens 30 Arbeitnehmer

innerhalb von 30 Kalendertagen entlässt. ²Den Entlassungen stehen andere Beendigungen des Arbeitsverhältnisses gleich, die vom Arbeitgeber veranlasst werden.

(2) ¹Beabsichtigt der Arbeitgeber, nach Absatz 1 anzeigepflichtige Entlassungen vorzunehmen, hat er dem Betriebsrat rechtzeitig die zweckdienlichen Auskünfte zu erteilen und ihn schriftlich insbesondere zu unterrichten über

1. die Gründe für die geplanten Entlassungen,
2. die Zahl und die Berufsgruppen der zu entlassenden Arbeitnehmer,
3. die Zahl und die Berufsgruppen der in der Regel beschäftigten Arbeitnehmer,
4. den Zeitraum, in dem die Entlassungen vorgenommen werden sollen,
5. die vorgesehenen Kriterien für die Auswahl der zu entlassenden Arbeitnehmer,
6. die für die Berechnung etwaiger Abfindungen vorgesehenen Kriterien.

and section 12 sentence 2 to 4 shall apply *mutatis mutandis*.

Chapter 3
Dismissals Requiring Notification

Section 17
Duty of Notification

(1) ¹The employer shall notify the Agency for Employment within 30 calendar days prior to dismissing

1. more than 5 employees in establishments with regularly more than 20 and fewer than 60 employees,
2. 10 per cent of the regularly employed employees or more than 25 employees in establishments with at least 60 and fewer than 500 employees,
3. at least 30 employees in establishments with regularly at least 500 employees.

²These dismissals shall be equivalent to other terminations of the employment relationship which are brought about by the employer.

(2) ¹Where an employer intends to make dismissals which are notifiable pursuant to subsection (1), he must inform the works council in writing and in a timely manner of, in particular,

1. the reasons for the planned dismissals,
2. the number and occupational group of the employees to be dismissed,
3. the number and occupational group of the employees regularly employed,
4. the period of time over which these dismissals are to take place,
5. the intended criteria for the selection of the employees to be dismissed,
6. the criteria for calculating any severance payments.

²Arbeitgeber und Betriebsrat haben insbesondere die Möglichkeiten zu beraten, Entlassungen zu vermeiden oder einzuschränken und ihre Folgen zu mildern.

(3) ¹Der Arbeitgeber hat gleichzeitig der Agentur für Arbeit eine Abschrift der Mitteilung an den Betriebsrat zuzuleiten; sie muss zumindest die in Absatz 2 Satz 1 Nr. 1 bis 5 vorgeschriebenen Angaben enthalten. ²Die Anzeige nach Absatz 1 ist schriftlich unter Beifügung der Stellungnahme des Betriebsrats zu den Entlassungen zu erstatten. ³Liegt eine Stellungnahme des Betriebsrats nicht vor, so ist die Anzeige wirksam, wenn der Arbeitgeber glaubhaft macht, dass er den Betriebsrat mindestens zwei Wochen vor Erstattung der Anzeige nach Absatz 2 Satz 1 unterrichtet hat, und er den Stand der Beratungen darlegt. ⁴Die Anzeige muss Angaben über den Namen des Arbeitgebers, den Sitz und die Art des Betriebes enthalten, ferner die Gründe für die geplanten Entlassungen, die Zahl und die Berufsgruppen der zu entlassenden und der in der Regel beschäftigten Arbeitnehmer, den Zeitraum, in dem die Entlassungen vorgenommen werden sollen und die vorgesehenen Kriterien für die Auswahl der zu entlassenden Arbeitnehmer. ⁵In der Anzeige sollen ferner im Einvernehmen mit dem Betriebsrat für die Arbeitsvermittlung Angaben über Geschlecht, Alter, Beruf und Staatsangehörigkeit der zu entlassenden Arbeitnehmer gemacht werden. ⁶Der Arbeitgeber hat dem Betriebsrat eine Abschrift der Anzeige zuzuleiten. ⁷Der Betriebsrat kann gegenüber der Agentur für Arbeit weitere Stellungnahmen abgeben. ⁸Er hat dem Arbeitgeber eine Abschrift der Stellungnahme zuzuleiten.

(3a) ¹Die Auskunfts-, Beratungs- und Anzeigepflichten nach den Absätzen 1 bis 3 gelten auch dann, wenn die Entscheidung über die Entlassungen von einem den Arbeitgeber beherrschenden Unternehmen getroffen wurde. ²Der

²Employer and works council shall, in particular, have the opportunity to discuss ways in which the dismissals can be prevented or limited and their consequences can be mitigated.

(3) ¹The employer must, at the same time, send the Agency for Employment a copy of the notification to the works council; this notification must at least contain the information set forth in subsection 2 sentence 1 nos. 1 to 5 above. ²The notification pursuant to subsection (1) must be in writing and include the works council's comments regarding the dismissals. ³Where the works council has not given its comments, the notification shall be effective if the employer can demonstrate that he informed the works council at least two weeks prior to submitting the notification pursuant to subsection (2) sentence 1 and describes the status of the discussions. ⁴The notification shall give the employer's name, the seat and nature of the establishment, the reasons for the planned dismissals, the number and occupational group of employees to be dismissed and of those regularly employed, the period of time over which the dismissals are to take place and the intended criteria for the selection of the employees to be dismissed. ⁵Further, in agreement with the works council, for the use of the Agency for Employment, the notification should give the sex, age, occupation and nationality of the employees to be dismissed. ⁶The employer shall send a copy of the notification to the works council. ⁷The works council may submit further comments to the Agency for Employment. ⁸It shall send the employer a copy of such comments.

(3a) ¹The duty to provide information, to consult with the works council and to notify the Agency for Employment pursuant to subsections (1) to (3) shall apply even if the decision on the dismissals was made by a company con-

Arbeitgeber kann sich nicht darauf berufen, dass das für die Entlassungen verantwortliche Unternehmen die notwendigen Auskünfte nicht übermittelt hat.

(4) ¹Das Recht zur fristlosen Entlassung bleibt unberührt. ²Fristlose Entlassungen werden bei Berechnung der Mindestzahl der Entlassungen nach Absatz 1 nicht mitgerechnet.

(5) Als Arbeitnehmer im Sinne dieser Vorschrift gelten nicht

1. in Betrieben einer juristischen Person die Mitglieder des Organs, das zur gesetzlichen Vertretung der juristischen Person berufen ist,
2. in Betrieben einer Personengesamtheit die durch Gesetz, Satzung oder Gesellschaftsvertrag zur Vertretung der Personengesamtheit berufenen Personen,
3. Geschäftsführer, Betriebsleiter und ähnliche leitende Personen, soweit diese zur selbständigen Einstellung oder Entlassung von Arbeitnehmern berechtigt sind.

§ 18
Entlassungssperre

(1) Entlassungen, die nach § 17 anzuzeigen sind, werden vor Ablauf eines Monats nach Eingang der Anzeige bei der Agentur für Arbeit nur mit deren Zustimmung wirksam; die Zustimmung kann auch rückwirkend bis zum Tage der Antragstellung erteilt werden.

(2) Die Agentur für Arbeit kann im Einzelfall bestimmen, dass die Entlassungen nicht vor Ablauf von längstens zwei Monaten nach Eingang der Anzeige wirksam werden.

(3) *(weggefallen)*

trolling the employer. ²The employer cannot invoke the fact that the company responsible for the dismissals did not convey the necessary information.

(4) ¹The right of dismissal without notice shall remain unaffected. ²Dismissals without notice shall not be counted in the calculation of the minimum number of dismissals pursuant to subsection (1).

(5) The following shall not be deemed to be employees within the meaning of this provision:

1. in establishments of a legal entity, members of the body appointed to legally represent that legal entity,
2. in establishments of a partnership, the persons appointed by law or in the articles of association or by-laws to represent the partnership,
3. managers, directors of establishments and similar persons exercising management functions insofar as they have the authority to independently hire or dismiss employees.

Section 18
Period Before Dismissal Takes Effect

(1) Dismissals which are notifiable pursuant to section 17 shall not become effective sooner than one month of the date of the Agency for Employment's receipt of the notification without its consent; such consent may also be granted with retroactive effect as of the date of application.

(2) The Agency for Employment may, in individual cases, determine that dismissals shall not become effective before at most two months have elapsed following the date of the Agency for Employment's receipt of the notification.

(3) *(repealed)*

(4) Soweit die Entlassungen nicht innerhalb von 90 Tagen nach dem Zeitpunkt, zu dem sie nach den Absätzen 1 und 2 zulässig sind, durchgeführt werden, bedarf es unter den Voraussetzungen des § 17 Abs. 1 einer erneuten Anzeige.

(4) If the dismissals are not carried out within 90 days following the date as from which they are permissible pursuant to subsections (1) and (2), a new notification must be filed for dismissals pursuant to section 17 (1).

§ 19
Zulässigkeit von Kurzarbeit

(1) Ist der Arbeitgeber nicht in der Lage, die Arbeitnehmer bis zu dem in § 18 Abs. 1 und 2 bezeichneten Zeitpunkt voll zu beschäftigen, so kann die Bundesagentur für Arbeit zulassen, dass der Arbeitgeber für die Zwischenzeit Kurzarbeit einführt.

(2) Der Arbeitgeber ist im Falle der Kurzarbeit berechtigt, Lohn oder Gehalt der mit verkürzter Arbeitszeit beschäftigten Arbeitnehmer entsprechend zu kürzen; die Kürzung des Arbeitsentgelts wird jedoch erst von dem Zeitpunkt an wirksam, an dem das Arbeitsverhältnis nach den allgemeinen gesetzlichen oder den vereinbarten Bestimmungen enden würde.

(3) Tarifvertragliche Bestimmungen über die Einführung, das Ausmaß und die Bezahlung von Kurzarbeit werden durch die Absätze 1 und 2 nicht berührt.

Section 19
Permissibility of Short-Time Work

(1) Where the employer is not able to occupy the employees fully up to the time described in section 18 (1) and (2), the Federal Agency for Employment may permit the employer to introduce short time work for the interim period.

(2) In the case of short-time work, the employer shall be entitled to reduce proportionately the wages or salaries of employees occupied on a short-time work basis; this reduction shall, however, only be effective as from the time when the employment relationship would have ended under general statutory or contractual provisions.

(3) Provisions of collective bargaining agreements relating to the introduction, duration and remuneration of short-time work shall not be affected by subsections (1) and (2).

§ 20
Entscheidungen der Agentur für Arbeit

(1) [1]Die Entscheidungen der Agentur für Arbeit nach § 18 Abs. 1 und 2 trifft deren Geschäftsführung oder ein Ausschuss (Entscheidungsträger). [2]Die Geschäftsführung darf nur dann entscheiden, wenn die Zahl der Entlassungen weniger als 50 beträgt.

(2) [1]Der Ausschuss setzt sich aus dem Geschäftsführer, der Geschäftsführerin oder dem oder der Vorsitzenden der Geschäftsführung der Agentur für Arbeit oder einem von ihm oder ihr beauftragten Angehörigen der Agentur für Arbeit als Vorsitzenden und je zwei

Section 20
Decisions of the Agency for Employment

[1]Decisions of the Agency for Employment pursuant to section 18 (1) and (2) shall be reached by its management or a committee (decision-maker). [2]The management may only decide if less than 50 dismissals are involved.

(2) [1]The committee shall consist of the managing director or the chairperson of the management of the Agency for Employment, or an employee of the Agency for Employment appointed by him or her, as chairperson and two representatives each for the employees, the

Vertretern der Arbeitnehmer, der Arbeitgeber und der öffentlichen Körperschaften zusammen, die von dem Verwaltungsausschuss der Agentur für Arbeit benannt werden. ²Er trifft seine Entscheidungen mit Stimmenmehrheit.

(3) ¹Der Entscheidungsträger hat vor seiner Entscheidung von Arbeitgeber und den Betriebsrat anzuhören. ²Dem Entscheidungsträger sind, insbesondere vom Arbeitgeber und Betriebsrat, die von ihm für die Beurteilung des Falles erforderlich gehaltenen Auskünfte zu erteilen.

(4) Der Entscheidungsträger hat sowohl das Interesse des Arbeitgebers als auch das der zu entlassenden Arbeitnehmer, das öffentliche Interesse und die Lage des gesamten Arbeitsmarktes unter besonderer Beachtung des Wirtschaftszweiges, dem der Betrieb angehört, zu berücksichtigen.

§ 21
Entscheidungen der Zentrale der Bundesagentur für Arbeit

¹Für Betriebe, die zum Geschäftsbereich des Bundesministers für Verkehr oder des Bundesministers für Post und Telekommunikation gehören, trifft, wenn mehr als 500 Arbeitnehmer entlassen werden sollen, ein gemäß § 20 Abs. 1 bei der Zentrale der Bundesagentur für Arbeit zu bildender Ausschuss die Entscheidungen nach § 18 Abs. 1 und 2 ²Der zuständige Bundesminister kann zwei Vertreter mit beratender Stimme in den Ausschuss entsenden. ³Die Anzeigen nach § 17 sind in diesem Falle an die Zentrale der Bundesagentur für Arbeit zu erstatten. ⁴Im übrigen gilt § 20 Abs. 1 bis 3 entsprechend.

§ 22
Ausnahmebetriebe

(1) Auf Saisonbetriebe und Kampagne-Betriebe finden die Vorschriften dieses

employer and public bodies, to be nominated by the administrative committee of the Agency for Employment. ²The committee shall arrive at its decisions by a simple majority of votes.

(3) ¹The decision-maker shall hear the employer and the works council before reaching its decision. ²The committee shall receive, in particular from the employer and the works council, all information it considers necessary for evaluating the case.

(4) The decision-maker shall take into account the interests of the employer as well as those of the employees to be dismissed, the public interest, and the entire employment market situation, particularly taking into consideration the branch of industry to which the establishment belongs.

Section 21
Decisions of the Headquarters of the Federal Agency for Employment

¹For establishments belonging to the area of business for which the Federal Minister of Transport or the Federal Minister of Post and Telecommunications is responsible, if more than 500 employees are to be dismissed, a committee to be formed pursuant to section 20(1) by the Headquarters of the Federal Agency for Employment shall make the decisions pursuant to section 18(1) and (2). ²The competent Federal Minister may appoint two representatives in an advisory capacity to the committee. ³Notifications pursuant to section 17 shall, in this case, be submitted to the Headquarters of the Federal Agency for Employment. ⁴Otherwise section 20(1) to (3) apply *mutatis mutandis*.

Section 22
Exempted Establishments

(1) The provisions of this chapter shall not apply to seasonal and project-

Abschnitts bei Entlassungen, die durch diese Eigenart der Betriebe bedingt sind, keine Anwendung.

(2) ¹Keine Saisonbetriebe oder Kampagne-Betriebe sind Betriebe des Baugewerbes, in denen die ganzjährige Beschäftigung nach dem Dritten Buch Sozialgesetzbuch gefördert wird. ²Das Bundesministerium für Arbeit und Soziales wird ermächtigt, durch Rechtsverordnung Vorschriften zu erlassen, welche Betriebe als Saisonbetriebe oder Kampagne-Betriebe im Sinne des Absatzes 1 gelten.

orientated establishments in the case of dismissals made necessary by the special nature of such establishments.

(2) ¹Establishments in the construction industry, in which year-round occupation pursuant to the Third Book of the Social Security Code is promoted, shall not be deemed to be seasonal or project-orientated establishments. ²The Federal Minister Labor and Social Affairs shall be empowered to issue provisions by decree defining which establishments are deemed to be seasonal or project-orientated enterprises within the meaning of subsection (1).

Vierter Abschnitt
Schlussbestimmungen

Chapter 4
Final Provisions

§ 23
Geltungsbereich

Section 23
Scope of Application

(1) ¹Die Vorschriften des Ersten und Zweiten Abschnitts gelten für Betriebe und Verwaltungen des privaten und des öffentlichen Rechts, vorbehaltlich der Vorschriften des § 24 für die Seeschifffahrts-, Binnenschifffahrts- und Luftverkehrsbetriebe. ²Die Vorschriften des Ersten Abschnitts gelten mit Ausnahme der §§ 4 bis 7 und des § 13 Abs. 1 Satz 1 und 2 nicht für Betriebe und Verwaltungen, in denen in der Regel fünf oder weniger Arbeitnehmer ausschließlich der zu ihrer Berufsbildung Beschäftigten beschäftigt werden. ³In Betrieben und Verwaltungen, in denen in der Regel zehn oder weniger Arbeitnehmer ausschließlich der zu ihrer Berufsbildung Beschäftigten beschäftigt werden, gelten die Vorschriften des Ersten Abschnitts mit Ausnahme der §§ 4 bis 7 und des § 13 Abs. 1 Satz 1 und 2 nicht für Arbeitnehmer, deren Arbeitsverhältnis nach dem 31. Dezember 2003 begonnen hat; diese Arbeitnehmer sind bei der Feststellung der Zahl der beschäftigten Arbeitnehmer nach Satz 2 bis zur Beschäftigung von in der Regel zehn Arbeitnehmern

(1) ¹The provisions of the Chapters 1 and 2 apply to establishments and administrations constituted under private and public law, subject to the provisions of section 24 with regard to establishments involved in shipping on the high seas or on inland waterways and in air transport. ²With the exception of sections 4 to 7 and section 13 (1) sentences 1 and 2, the provisions of Chapter 1 do not apply to establishments and administrations regularly employing five or fewer employees, excluding persons employed for vocational training. ³In establishments and administrations regularly employing ten or fewer employees, excluding persons employed for vocational training, the provisions of Chapter 1 with the exception of sections 4 to 7 and section 13 (1) sentences 1 and 2 shall not apply for employees whose employment relationship commenced after 31 December 2003; in determining the number of employees pursuant to sentence 2, these employees shall not be taken into account until ten employees are regularly employed. ⁴In determining the

nicht zu berücksichtigen. ⁴Bei der Feststellung der Zahl der beschäftigten Arbeitnehmer nach den Sätzen 2 und 3 sind teilzeitbeschäftigte Arbeitnehmer mit einer regelmäßigen wöchentlichen Arbeitszeit von nicht mehr als 20 Stunden mit 0,5 und nicht mehr als 30 Stunden mit 0,75 zu berücksichtigen.

(2) ¹Die Vorschriften des Dritten Abschnitts gelten für Betriebe und Verwaltungen des privaten Rechts sowie für Betriebe, die von einer öffentlichen Verwaltung geführt werden, soweit sie wirtschaftliche Zwecke verfolgen. ²Sie gelten nicht für Seeschiffe und ihre Besatzung.

§ 24
Anwendung des Gesetzes auf Betriebe der Schifffahrt und des Luftverkehrs

(1)¹Die Vorschriften des Ersten und Zweiten Abschnitts finden nach Maßgabe der Absätze 2 bis 5 auf Arbeitsverhältnisse der Besatzung von Seeschiffen, Binnenschiffen und Luftfahrzeugen Anwendung. ²Als Betrieb im Sinne dieses Gesetzes gilt jeweils die Gesamtheit der Seeschiffe oder der Binnenschiffe eines Schifffahrtsbetriebs oder der Luftfahrzeuge eines Luftverkehrsbetriebs.

(2) Dauert die erste Reise eines Besatzungsmitglieds im Dienst einer Reederei oder eines Luftverkehrsbetriebs länger als sechs Monate, so verlängert sich die Sechsmonatsfrist des § 1 Abs. 1 bis drei Tage nach Beendigung dieser Reise.

(3) ¹Die Klage nach § 4 ist binnen drei Wochen, nachdem das Besatzungsmitglied zum Sitz des Betriebs zurückgekehrt ist, zu erheben, spätestens jedoch binnen sechs Wochen nach Zugang der Kündigung. ²Wird die Kündigung während der Fahrt des Schiffes oder des Luftfahrzeugs ausgesprochen, so beginnt die sechswöchige Frist nicht vor dem Tage, an dem das Schiff oder das Luftfahrzeug einen deutschen Hafen

number of employees pursuant to sentences 2 and 3, those part-time employees whose regular working time does not exceed 20 hours weekly shall be counted as 0.5 of an employee and those whose working time does not exceed 30 hours weekly shall be counted as 0.75 of an employee.

(2) ¹The provisions of the Chapter 3 apply to establishments and administrations constituted under private law and to establishments operated by a public administration insofar as they pursue commercial objectives. ²They do not apply to seagoing vessels and their crews.

Section 24
Application of the Act to Establishments Concerned with Shipping and Air Transport

(1) ¹The provisions of Chapters 1 and 2 apply subject to subsections (2) to (5) to employment relationships of crews of seagoing vessels, inland waterway vessels and aircraft. ²All the seagoing vessels or the inland waterway vessels of a shipping concern or the aircraft of an air transport concern shall be deemed to be an establishment within the meaning of this Act.

(2) Where the first journey of a crew member in the service of a shipping establishment or of an air transport establishment lasts longer than six months, the six-month period pursuant to section 1 (1) shall be extended to three days after the end of this journey.

(3) ¹Complaints pursuant to section 4 shall be filed within three weeks following the return of the crew member to the legal domicile of the establishment, but no later than six weeks following receipt of the notice of dismissal. ²If the notice of dismissal is given during the voyage of the ship or flight of the aircraft, the six-week period shall not begin until the day on which the ship or the aircraft reaches a

oder Liegeplatz erreicht. ³An die Stelle der Dreiwochenfrist in § 6 treten die hier in den Sätzen 1 und 2 bestimmten Fristen.

(4) ¹Für Klagen der Kapitäne und der Besatzungsmitglieder im Sinne der §§ 2 und 3 des Seemannsgesetzes nach § 4 dieses Gesetzes tritt an die Stelle des Arbeitsgerichts das Gericht, das für Streitigkeiten aus dem Arbeitsverhältnis dieser Personen zuständig ist. ²Soweit in Vorschriften des Seemannsgesetzes für die Streitigkeiten aus dem Arbeitsverhältnis Zuständigkeiten des Seemannsamts begründet sind, finden die Vorschriften auf Streitigkeiten über Ansprüche aus diesem Gesetz keine Anwendung.

(5) Der Kündigungsschutz des Ersten Abschnitts gilt, abweichend von § 14, auch für den Kapitän und die übrigen als leitende Angestellte im Sinne des § 14 anzusehenden Angehörigen der Besatzung.

German seaport or airport. ³The periods specified here in sentences 1 and 2 shall replace the three-week period set forth in section 6.

(4) ¹For complaints pursuant to section 4 of this Act by captains and crew members within the meaning of sections 2 and 3 of the Seafarers Act, the court which is competent for disputes arising out of the employment relationships of such persons shall replace the Labor Court. ²Insofar as the competency of the Seaman's Authority is established by provisions of the Seafarers Act for disputes arising out of the employment relationship, such provisions shall not apply to disputes concerning claims arising from this Act.

(5) Notwithstanding section 14, the protection against dismissals contained in Chapter 1 shall apply to the captain and the other crew members who are to be regarded as managerial employees within the meaning of section 14.

§ 25
Kündigung in Arbeitskämpfen

Die Vorschriften dieses Gesetzes finden keine Anwendung auf Kündigungen und Entlassungen, die lediglich als Maßnahmen in wirtschaftlichen Kämpfen zwischen Arbeitgebern und Arbeitnehmern vorgenommen werden.

Section 25
Dismissal during Labor Disputes

The provisions of this Act do not apply to dismissals which are effected simply as measures in economic disputes between employers and employees.

§ 25a
Berlin-Klausel

¹Dieses Gesetz gilt nach Maßgabe des § 13 Abs. 1 des Dritten Überleitungsgesetzes auch im Land Berlin. ²Rechtsverordnungen, die auf Grund dieses Gesetzes erlassen werden, gelten im Land Berlin nach § 14 des Dritten Überleitungsgesetzes.

Section 25a
Berlin Clause

¹This Act also applies in the Federal State of Berlin on the basis of section 13 (1) of the Third Transitional Act. ²Statutory orders which are enacted on the basis of this Act shall apply in the State of Berlin pursuant to section 14 of the Third Transitional Act.

§ 26
Inkrafttreten

Dieses Gesetz tritt am Tag nach seiner Verkündung in Kraft.

Section 26
Date of Coming into Force

This Act shall enter into force on the day following its promulgation.

VI. Minimum Vacation Act for Employees (Federal Vacation Act) (Bundesurlaubsgesetz – BUrlG)

of 8 January 1963 (Federal Law Gazette I p. 2)

in the amended version of 7 May 2002

§ 1
Urlaubsanspruch

Jeder Arbeitnehmer hat in jedem Kalenderjahr Anspruch auf bezahlten Erholungsurlaub.

Section 1
Claim to Vacation

Each employee has a claim to paid recreational vacation in every calendar year.

§ 2
Geltungsbereich

[1] Arbeitnehmer im Sinne des Gesetzes sind Arbeiter und Angestellte sowie die zu ihrer Berufsausbildung Beschäftigten. [2] Als Arbeitnehmer gelten auch Personen, die wegen ihrer wirtschaftlichen Unselbständigkeit als arbeitnehmerähnliche Personen anzusehen sind; für den Bereich der Heimarbeit gilt § 12.

Section 2
Scope of Application

[1] Employees within the meaning of the Act are workers and salaried employees as well as the employees in vocational training. [2] Those persons are also deemed employees who are to be regarded as similar to employees due their economic dependence; with respect to work to be conducted in the home, section 12 applies.

§ 3
Dauer des Urlaubs

(1) Der Urlaub beträgt jährlich mindestens 24 Werktage.

(2) Als Werktage gelten alle Kalendertage, die nicht Sonn- oder gesetzliche Feiertage sind.

Section 3
Length of Vacation

(1) The vacation amounts to at least 24 working days annually.

(2) All calendar days which are neither Sundays nor statutory holidays are considered to be working days.

§ 4
Wartezeit

Der volle Urlaubsanspruch wird erstmalig nach sechsmonatigem Bestehen des Arbeitsverhältnisses erworben.

Section 4
Waiting Period

A full vacation claim is acquired only when the employment relationship has existed for six months.

§ 5
Teilurlaub

(1) Anspruch auf ein Zwölftel des Jahresurlaubs für jeden vollen Monat des

The employee has a claim to one-twelfth of the annual vacation for each

Bestehens des Arbeitsverhältnisses hat der Arbeitnehmer

a) für Zeiten eines Kalenderjahrs, für die er wegen Nichterfüllung der Wartezeit in diesem Kalenderjahr keinen vollen Urlaubsanspruch erwirbt;
b) wenn er vor erfüllter Wartezeit aus dem Arbeitsverhältnis ausscheidet;
c) wenn er nach erfüllter Wartezeit in der ersten Hälfte eines Kalenderjahrs aus dem Arbeitsverhältnis ausscheidet.

(2) Bruchteile von Urlaubstagen, die mindestens einen halben Tag ergeben, sind auf volle Urlaubstage aufzurunden.

(3) Hat der Arbeitnehmer im Falle des Absatzes 1 Buchstabe c bereits Urlaub über den ihm zustehenden Umfang hinaus erhalten, so kann das dafür gezahlte Urlaubsentgelt nicht zurückgefordert werden.

§ 6
Ausschluss von Doppelansprüchen

(1) Der Anspruch auf Urlaub besteht nicht, soweit dem Arbeitnehmer für das laufende Kalenderjahr bereits von einem früheren Arbeitgeber Urlaub gewährt worden ist.

(2) Der Arbeitgeber ist verpflichtet, bei Beendigung des Arbeitsverhältnisses dem Arbeitnehmer eine Bescheinigung über den im laufenden Kalenderjahr gewährten oder abgegoltenen Urlaub auszuhändigen.

§ 7
Zeitpunkt, Übertragbarkeit und Abgeltung des Urlaubs

(1) [1]Bei der zeitlichen Festlegung des Urlaubs sind die Urlaubswünsche des Arbeitnehmers zu berücksichtigen, es sei denn, dass ihrer Berücksichtigung dringende betriebliche Belange oder Urlaubswünsche anderer Arbeitnehmer, die unter sozialen Gesichtspunkten den

full month the employment relationship has existed

a) with respect to periods of a calendar year for which he has not acquired a full vacation claim because the waiting period had not elapsed in that calendar year;
b) if he leaves the employment relationship before the waiting period has elapsed;
c) if, after the waiting period has elapsed, he leaves the employment relationship in the first half of a calendar year.

(2) Fractions of vacation days in the amount of at least one half-day shall be rounded up to full vacation days.

(3) Where the employee, in the case of subsection (1) c, has already taken vacation exceeding the amount due to him, the vacation pay rendered for this purpose may not be reclaimed.

Section 6
Exclusion of Duplicate Claims

(1) The claim to vacation does not exist to the extent that the employee has already been granted vacation by a previous employer for the current calendar year.

(2) Upon termination of the employment relationship the employer is obligated to provide the employee with a certification of the vacation granted or compensated during the current calendar year.

Section 7
Time, Carryover and Compensation in Lieu of Vacation

(1) [1]In determining the time at which vacation is taken, the employee's vacation requests shall be taken into consideration, unless urgent business interests or other employees' vacation requests deserving priority from a social point of view stand in the way. [2]Vacation shall

Vorrang verdienen, entgegenstehen. ²Der Urlaub ist zu gewähren, wenn der Arbeitnehmer dies im Anschluss an eine Maßnahme der medizinischen Vorsorge oder Rehabilitation verlangt.

(2) ¹Der Urlaub ist zusammenhängend zu gewähren, es sei denn, dass dringende betriebliche oder in der Person des Arbeitnehmers liegende Gründe eine Teilung des Urlaubs erforderlich machen. ²Kann der Urlaub aus diesen Gründen nicht zusammenhängend gewährt werden, und hat der Arbeitnehmer Anspruch auf Urlaub von mehr als zwölf Werktagen, so muss einer der Urlaubsteile mindestens zwölf aufeinanderfolgende Werktage umfassen.

(3) ¹Der Urlaub muss im laufenden Kalenderjahr gewährt und genommen werden. ²Eine Übertragung des Urlaubs auf das nächste Kalenderjahr ist nur statthaft, wenn dringende betriebliche oder in der Person des Arbeitnehmers liegende Gründe dies rechtfertigen. ³Im Fall der Übertragung muss der Urlaub in den ersten drei Monaten des folgenden Kalenderjahrs gewährt und genommen werden.⁴ Auf Verlangen des Arbeitnehmers ist ein nach § 5 Abs. 1 Buchstabe a entstehender Teilurlaub jedoch auf das nächste Kalenderjahr zu übertragen.

(4) Kann der Urlaub wegen Beendigung des Arbeitsverhältnisses ganz oder teilweise nicht mehr gewährt werden, so ist er abzugelten.

be granted upon the employee's request following a preventative course of medical treatment or rehabilitation.

(2) ¹The vacation days shall be granted consecutively, unless compelling operational reasons or reasons personal to the employee necessitate apportionment of the vacation. ²Where the vacation days cannot be granted consecutively for these reasons and the employee has a claim to vacation of more than 12 working days, one portion of the vacation shall comprise at least 12 consecutive working days.

(3) ¹The vacation shall be granted and taken in the current calendar year. ²Carryover of vacation to the next calendar year is only permissible if compelling operational reasons or reasons personal to the employee justify it. ³In the case of a carryover, the vacation must be granted and taken within the first three months of the succeeding calendar year. ⁴At the employee's request, however, partial vacation arising pursuant to section 5 (1) a shall be carried over to the next calendar year.

(4) Where the vacation can no longer be granted either in full or in part due to the termination of the employment relationship, compensation shall be paid instead.

§ 8
Erwerbstätigkeit während des Urlaubs

Während des Urlaubs darf der Arbeitnehmer keine dem Urlaubszweck widersprechende Erwerbstätigkeit leisten.

Section 8
Business Activity during acation

During vacation, the employee shall not pursue any business activity conflicting with the purpose of the vacation.

§ 9
Erkrankung während des Urlaubs

Erkrankt ein Arbeitnehmer während des Urlaubs, so werden die durch ärzt-

Section 9
Illness during Vacation

If an employee becomes ill during his vacation, the days of inability to work

liches Zeugnis nachgewiesenen Tage der Arbeitsunfähigkeit auf den Jahresurlaub nicht angerechnet.

as evidenced by a physician's certificate shall not be applied toward annual vacation.

§ 10
Maßnahmen der mdizinischen Vorsorge oder Rhabilitation

Maßnahmen der medizinischen Vorsorge oder Rehabilitation dürfen nicht auf den Urlaub angerechnet werden, soweit ein Anspruch auf Fortzahlung des Arbeitsentgelts nach den gesetzlichen Vorschriften über die Entgeltfortzahlung im Krankheitsfall besteht.

Section 10
Preventative medicine and Rehabilitation Treatments

Periods where an employee is receiving preventative or rehabilitative medicine shall not be applied toward vacation insofar as a right to continued payment of employment remuneration exists pursuant to the statutory provisions concerning continued payment of remuneration in case of illness.

§ 11
Urlaubsentgelt

(1) [1]Das Urlaubsentgelt bemisst sich nach dem durchschnittlichen Arbeitsverdienst, das der Arbeitnehmer in den letzten dreizehn Wochen vor dem Beginn des Urlaubs erhalten hat, mit Ausnahme des zusätzlich für Überstunden gezahlten Arbeitsverdienstes. [2]Bei Verdiensterhöhungen nicht nur vorübergehender Natur, die während des Berechnungszeitraums oder des Urlaubs eintreten, ist von dem erhöhten Verdienst auszugehen. [3]Verdienstkürzungen, die im Berechnungszeitraum infolge von Kurzarbeit, Arbeitsausfällen oder unverschuldeter Arbeitsversäumnis eintreten, bleiben für die Berechnung des Urlaubsentgelts außer Betracht. [4]Zum Arbeitsentgelt gehörende Sachbezüge, die während des Urlaubs nicht weitergewährt werden, sind für die Dauer des Urlaubs angemessen in bar abzugelten.

(2) Das Urlaubsentgelt ist vor Antritt des Urlaubs auszuzahlen.

Section 11
Vacation Pay

(1) [1]Vacation pay shall be calculated in accordance with the average employment earnings received by the employee during the last 13 weeks prior to the commencement of vacation additional payments for overtime will not be included. [2]In the case of nontemporary increases in earnings which occur during the calculation period or the vacation, the higher earnings shall be applied to the computation. [3]Reductions in earnings occurring in the calculation period due to short-time work, loss of working hours or absence from work, due to reasons beyond the employee's control, shall not be considered in computing vacation pay. [4]Payments in kind being part of the employment remuneration, which are no longer granted during the vacation, shall instead be compensated appropriately in cash for the period of the vacation.

(2) Vacation pay shall be paid prior to commencement of vacation.

§ 12
Urlaub im Bereich der Heimarbeit

Für die in Heimarbeit Beschäftigten und die ihnen nach § 1 Abs. 2 Buchsta-

Section 12
Vacation for Work conducted in the Home

For persons working at home and those in an equivalent position pursuant to

ben a bis c des Heimarbeitsgesetzes Gleichgestellten, für die die Urlaubsregelung nicht ausdrücklich von der Gleichstellung ausgenommen ist, gelten die vorstehenden Bestimmungen mit Ausnahme der §§ 4 bis 6, 7 Abs. 3 und 4 und § 11 nach Maßgabe der folgenden Bestimmungen:

1. Heimarbeiter (§ 1 Abs. 1 Buchstabe a des Heimarbeitsgesetzes) und nach § 1 Abs. 2 Buchstabe a des Heimarbeitsgesetzes Gleichgestellte erhalten von ihrem Auftraggeber oder, falls sie von einem Zwischenmeister beschäftigt werden, von diesem bei einem Anspruch auf 24 Werktage ein Urlaubsentgelt von 9,1 vom Hundert des in der Zeit vom 1. Mai bis zum 30. April des folgenden Jahres oder bis zur Beendigung des Beschäftigungsverhältnisses verdienten Arbeitsentgelts vor Abzug der Steuern und Sozialversicherungsbeiträge ohne Unkostenzuschlag und ohne die für den Lohnausfall an Feiertagen, den Arbeitsausfall infolge Krankheit und den Urlaub zu leistenden Zahlungen.
2. War der Anspruchsberechtigte im Berechnungszeitraum nicht ständig beschäftigt, so brauchen unbeschadet des Anspruches auf Urlaubsentgelt nach Nummer 1 nur so viele Urlaubstage gegeben zu werden, wie durchschnittliche Tagesverdienste, die er in der Regel erzielt hat, in dem Urlaubsentgelt nach Nummer 1 enthalten sind.
3. Das Urlaubsentgelt für die in Nummer 1 bezeichneten Personen soll erst bei der letzten Entgeltzahlung vor Antritt des Urlaubs ausgezahlt werden.
4. Hausgewerbetreibende (§ 1 Abs. 1 Buchstabe b des Heimarbeitsgesetzes) und nach § 1 Abs. 2 Buchstaben b und c des Heimarbeitsgesetzes Gleichgestellte erhalten von ihrem Auftraggeber oder, falls sie von einem Zwischenmeister beschäftigt werden, von diesem als eigenes Urlaubsentgelt und zur Sicherung der

section 1 (2) a to c of the Home Work Act *(Heimarbeitsgesetz)*, for whom the provisions governing vacations are not explicitly excluded from the equivalent status, the above provisions shall apply with the exception of sections 4 to 6, 7 (3) and (4) and section 11 on the basis of the following provisions:

1. Home Workers (section 1 (1) a of the Home Work Act) and those in an equivalent position pursuant to section 1 (2) a of the Home Work Act shall receive from their employer, or, if they are employed by an intermediary, from the intermediary – with a claim for 24 working days – vacation pay of 9.1% of the remuneration for work performed between 1 May and 30 April of the following year or up to the end of the employment relationship before deduction of taxes and social security contributions, not including the allowance for expenses or payments to be made for loss of wages on holidays, inability to work due to illness or vacation.
2. If the claimant was not consistently employed during the entire calculation period, then, notwithstanding the claim for vacation pay pursuant to no. 1 above, only that amount of vacation days need be granted as the number average daily earnings he attained as a rule which are contained in the vacation pay pursuant to no. 1.
3. The vacation pay for the persons designated in no. 1 shall only be paid together with the last remuneration prior to the commencement of the vacation.
4. Home workers (section 1 (1) b of the Home Work Act) and those in an equivalent position pursuant to section 1 (2) b and c of the Home Work Act shall receive from their employer or, if they are employed by an intermediary, then from him, as their employees' own vacation pay and to secure their vacation claims a sum in

Urlaubsansprüche der von ihnen Beschäftigten einen Betrag von 9,1 vom Hundert des an sie ausgezahlten Arbeitsentgelts vor Abzug der Steuern und Sozialversicherungsbeiträge ohne Unkostenzuschlag und ohne die für den Lohnausfall an Feiertagen, den Arbeitsausfall infolge Krankheit und den Urlaub zu leistenden Zahlungen.

5. Zwischenmeister, die den in Heimarbeit Beschäftigten nach § 1 Abs. 2 Buchstabe d des Heimarbeitsgesetzes gleichgestellt sind, haben gegen ihren Auftraggeber Anspruch auf die von ihnen nach den Nummern 1 und 4 nachweislich zu zahlenden Beträge.

6. Die Beträge nach den Nummern 1, 4 und 5 sind gesondert im Entgeltbeleg auszuweisen.

7. Durch Tarifvertrag kann bestimmt werden, dass Heimarbeiter (§ 1 Abs. 1 Buchstabe a des Heimarbeitsgesetzes), die nur für einen Auftraggeber tätig sind und tariflich allgemein wie Betriebsarbeiter behandelt werden, Urlaub nach den allgemeinen Urlaubsbestimmungen erhalten.

8. Auf die in den Nummern 1, 4 und 5 vorgesehenen Beträge finden die §§ 23 bis 25, 27 und 28 und auf die in den Nummern 1 und 4 vorgesehenen Beträge außerdem § 21 Abs. 2 des Heimarbeitsgesetzes entsprechende Anwendung. Für die Urlaubsansprüche der fremden Hilfskräfte der in Nummer 4 genannten Personen gilt § 26 des Heimarbeitsgesetzes entsprechend.

§ 13
Unabdingbarkeit

(1) ¹Von den vorstehenden Vorschriften mit Ausnahme der §§ 1, 2 und 3 Abs. 1 kann in Tarifverträgen abgewichen werden. ²Die abweichenden Bestimmungen haben zwischen nichttarifgebundenen Arbeitgebern und Arbeitnehmern Geltung, wenn zwischen diesen die Anwendung der einschlägi-

the amount of 9.1% of the remuneration for work paid to them before deduction of taxes and social security contributions, not counting the allowance for expenses or payments to be made for loss of wages on statutory holidays, inability to work due to illness or vacation.

5. Intermediaries who are in an equivalent position to those working in the home pursuant to section 1 (2) d of the Home Work Act shall have a claim against their employer for the sums they are demonstrably owed pursuant to nos. 1 and 4 above.

6. The sums pursuant to nos. 1, 4 and 5 above shall be posted separately in the remuneration statement.

7. It may be provided in a collective bargaining agreement that home workers (section 1 (1) a of the Home Work Act) who are only employed by one employer and, with respect to the collective bargaining agreement, are treated as works employees, receive vacation pursuant to the general vacation provisions.

8. Sections 23 to 25, 27 and 28 of the Home Work Act shall be applicable to the sums set forth in nos. 1, 4 and 5 and section 21 (2) of the Home Work Act shall also be applicable to the sums set forth in nos. 1 and 4 *mutatis mutandis*. For the vacation claims of the outside temporary workers designated in no. 4, section 26 of the Home Work Act shall apply *mutatis mutandis*.

Section 13
Mandatory Nature of Provisions

(1) ¹Collective bargaining agreements may contain provisions differing from the above provisions, except for sections 1, 2 and 3 (1). ²The deviating provisions shall apply between employers and employees not bound by a collective bargaining agreement if the application of the relevant collective bargain-

gen tariflichen Urlaubsregelung vereinbart ist. ³Im übrigen kann, abgesehen von § 7 Abs. 2 Satz 2, von den Bestimmungen dieses Gesetzes nicht zuungunsten des Arbeitnehmers abgewichen werden.

(2) ¹Für das Baugewerbe oder sonstige Wirtschaftszweige, in denen als Folge häufigen Ortswechsels der von den Betrieben zu leistenden Arbeit Arbeitsverhältnisse von kürzerer Dauer als einem Jahr in erheblichem Umfange üblich sind, kann durch Tarifvertrag von den vorstehenden Vorschriften über die in Absatz 1 Satz 1 vorgesehene Grenze hinaus abgewichen werden, soweit dies zur Sicherung eines zusammenhängenden Jahresurlaubs für alle Arbeitnehmer erforderlich ist. ²Absatz 1 Satz 2 findet entsprechende Anwendung.

(3) Für den Bereich der Deutsche Bahn Aktiengesellschaft sowie einer gemäß § 2 Abs. 1 und § 3 Abs. 3 des Deutsche Bahn Gründungsgesetzes vom 27. Dezember 1993 (BGBl. I S. 2378, 2386) ausgegliederten Gesellschaft und für den Bereich der Nachfolgeunternehmen der Deutschen Bundespost kann von der Vorschrift über das Kalenderjahr als Urlaubsjahr (§ 1) in Tarifverträgen abgewichen werden.

ing agreement rules concerning vacation have been agreed upon. ³Otherwise, except for section 7 (2) sentence 2, no deviation from the provisions of this Act detrimental to the employee shall be made.

(2) ¹In the construction business or other branches of business, in which as a result of a frequent relocation of the services to be performed by the works, employment relationships with a term of less than one year are significantly common collective bargaining agreements may depart from the above provisions in excess of the limit set forth in subsection (1) sentence 1, where this is necessary for securing an uninterrupted annual vacation for all employees. ²Subsection (1) sentence 2 shall apply mutatis *mutandis*.

(3) For the sphere of Deutsche Bahn Aktiengesellschaft, as well as a spin off companies pursuant to section 2 (1) and section 3 (3) of the Deutsche Bahn Formation Act of 27 December 1993 (Federal Law Gazette I pp. 2378, 2386) and for the sphere of the successor of Deutsche Bundespost, the provision on the calendar year as a vacation year (section 1) may be varied in the collective bargaining agreements.

§ 14
Berlin-Klausel

Dieses Gesetz gilt nach Maßgabe des § 13 Abs. 1 des Dritten Überleitungsgesetzes vom 4. Januar 1952 (Bundesgesetzbl. I S. 1) auch im Land Berlin.

Section 14
Berlin-Clause

This Act shall also apply in the Federal State of Berlin subject to section 13 (1) of the Third Transitional Act of 4 January 1952 (Federal Law Gazette I p. 1)

§ 15
Änderung und Aufhebung von Gesetzen

(1) Unberührt bleiben die urlaubsrechtlichen Bestimmungen des Arbeitsplatzschutzgesetzes vom 30. März 1957 (Bundesgesetzbl. I S. 293), geändert durch Gesetz vom 22. März 1962 (Bundesgesetzbl. I S. 169), des Neunten Bu-

Section 15
Amendment and Annulment of Acts

(1) The provisions governing vacation in the Job Protection Act (*Arbeitsplatzschutzgesetz*) of 30 March 1957 (Federal Law Gazette I p. 293), as amended by the Act of 22 March 1962 (Federal Law Gazette I p. 169), the Ninth Book

ches Sozialgesetzbuch des Jugendarbeitsschutzgesetzes vom 9. August 1960 (Bundesgesetzbl. I S. 665), geändert durch Gesetz vom 20. Juli 1962 (Bundesgesetzbl. I S. 449), und des Seemannsgesetzes vom 26. Juli 1957 (Bundesgesetzbl. II S. 713), geändert durch Gesetz vom 25. August 1961 (Bundesgesetzbl. II S. 1391), jedoch wird

a) und b) *(Änderungsvorschriften hier nicht abgedruckt)*

(2) [1] Mit dem Inkrafttreten dieses Gesetzes treten die landesrechtlichen Vorschriften über den Erholungsurlaub außer Kraft. [2] In Kraft bleiben jedoch die landesrechtlichen Bestimmungen über den Urlaub für Opfer des Nationalsozialismus und für solche Arbeitnehmer, die geistig oder körperlich in ihrer Erwerbsfähigkeit behindert sind.

§ 15 a
Übergangsvorschrift

Befindet sich der Arbeitnehmer von einem Tag nach dem 9. Dezember 1998 bis zum 1. Januar 1999 oder darüber hinaus in einer Maßnahme der medizinischen Vorsorge oder Rehabilitation, sind für diesen Zeitraum die seit dem 1. Januar 1999 geltenden Vorschriften maßgebend, es sei denn, dass diese für den Arbeitnehmer ungünstiger sind.

§ 16
Inkrafttreten

Dieses Gesetz tritt mit Wirkung vom 1. Januar 1963 in Kraft.

of the Social Security Code, the Youth Labor Protection Act *(Jugendarbeitsschutzgesetz)* of 9 August 1960 (Federal Law Gazette I p. 665), amended by the Act of 20 July 1962 (Federal Law Gazette I p. 449) and the Seaman's Act of 26 July 1957 (Federal Law Gazette II p. 713), amended by the Act of 25 August 1961 (Federal Law Gazette I p. 1391) shall remain unaffected; however,

a) and b) *(amendment provisions not printed here)*

(2) [1] Once this Act enters into effect, the Federal State statutory provisions on vacation shall lose their effect. [2] However, the Federal State provisions on vacation for victims of National Socialism [i.e. the Nazi regime] and for employees whose mental or physical ability to work has been impaired shall remain in force.

Section 15 a
Transition Provision

If the employee was receiving preventative medicine or rehabilitation treatment from one day after 9 December 1998 to 1 January 1999 or beyond, then the provisions applicable as of 1 January 1999 shall apply to that period unless they are less favourable to the employee.

Section 16
Entering into Effect

This Act shall enter into effect on 1 January 1963.

VII. Act for the Improvement of Company Pension Plans (Gesetz zur Verbesserung der betrieblichen Altersversorgung – BetrAVG)

of 19 December 1974 (Federal Law Gazette I p. 3610)

in the amended version of 21 December 2008

Erster Teil Arbeitsrechtliche Vorschriften	Part 1 Employment Law Provisions
Erster Abschnitt **Durchführung der betrieblichen Altersversorgung**	**Chapter 1** **Execution of Company Pension Plans**
§ 1 **Zusage des Arbeitgebers auf betriebliche Altersvorsorge**	**Section 1** **Employer's Company Pension Plan Commitment**
(1) ¹Werden einem Arbeitnehmer Leistungen der Alters-, Invaliditäts- oder Hinterbliebenenversorgung aus Anlass seines Arbeitsverhältnisses vom Arbeitgeber zugesagt (betriebliche Altersversorgung), gelten die Vorschriften dieses Gesetzes. ²Die Durchführung der betrieblichen Altersversorgung kann unmittelbar über den Arbeitgeber oder über einen der in § 1b Abs. 2 bis 4 genannten Versorgungsträger erfolgen. ³Der Arbeitgeber steht für die Erfüllung der von ihm zugesagten Leistungen auch dann ein, wenn die Durchführung nicht unmittelbar über ihn erfolgt.	(1) ¹If an employer has promised an employee payment of old-age, invalidity or survivor's pension in connection with his employment (company pension plan), the provisions of this Act shall apply. ²The company pension plan may be executed directly though the employer or through one of the pension carrier designated in section 1b (2) to (4). ³The employer shall be responsible for the fulfillment of its pension commitments even if they are not directly executed through the employer.
(2) Betriebliche Altersversorgung liegt auch vor, wenn	(2) A company pension plan also exists if
1. der Arbeitgeber sich verpflichtet, bestimmte Beiträge in einer Anwartschaft auf Alters-, Invaliditäts- oder Hinterbliebenenversorgung umzuwandeln (beitragsorientierte Leistungszusage),	1. the employer makes a commitment to convert certain contributions into an expectancy for old-age, invalidity or survivor's pension (contribution-based payment commitment),
2. der Arbeitgeber sich verpflichtet, Beiträge zur Finanzierung von Leistungen der betrieblichen Altersversorgung an einen Pensionsfonds, eine Pensionskasse oder eine Direktversi-	2. the employer makes a commitment to contribute to the financing of company pension plan benefits by making payments to a retirement fund *(Pensionsfonds)*, staff pension fund

cherung zu zahlen und für Leistungen zur Altersversorgung das planmäßig zuzurechnende Versorgungskapital auf der Grundlage der gezahlten Beiträge (Beiträge und die daraus erzielten Erträge), mindestens die Summe der zugesagten Beiträge, soweit sie nicht rechnungsmäßig für einen biometrischen Risikoausgleich verbraucht wurden, hierfür zur Verfügung zu stellen (Beitragszusage mit Mindestleistung),

3. künftige Entgeltansprüche in eine wertgleiche Anwartschaft auf Versorgungsleistungen umgewandelt werden (Entgeltumwandlung) oder

4. der Arbeitnehmer Beiträge aus seinem Arbeitsentgelt zur Finanzierung von Leistungen der betrieblichen Altersversorgung an einen Pensionsfonds, eine Pensionskasse oder eine Direktversicherung leistet und die Zusage des Arbeitgebers auch die Leistungen aus diesen Beiträgen umfasst; die Regelungen für Entgeltumwandlung sind hierbei entsprechend anzuwenden, soweit die zugesagten Leistungen aus diesen Beiträgen im Wege der Kapitaldeckung finanziert werden.

(Pensionskasse) or a direct insurance and to provide the pension capital to be allocated for old-age pension benefits according to the plan on the basis of the contributions paid (contributions plus the return therefrom), in the amount of at least the sum of the committed contributions, where they were not used mathematically for a biometric balancing portfolio (contribution commitment with minimum payment,

3. future remuneration claims are converted into an expectancy for pension benefits of equal value (remuneration conversion = *deferred compensation*), or

4. the employee contributes to the financing of company pension plan benefits by making payments from his remuneration to a retirement fund, staff pension fund or a direct insurance and the employer's commitment also covers the benefits deriving from these contributions; in this respect the provision for remuneration conversion shall apply *mutatis mutandis* to the extent that the committed benefits are financed by these contributions by way of the formation of coverage capital.

§ 1a
Anspruch auf betriebliche Altersversorgung durch Entgeltumwandlung

(1) ¹Der Arbeitnehmer kann vom Arbeitgeber verlangen, dass von seinen künftigen Entgeltansprüchen bis zu 4 vom Hundert der jeweiligen Beitragsbemessungsgrenze in der allgemeinen Rentenversicherung durch Entgeltumwandlung für seine betriebliche Altersversorgung verwendet werden. ²Die Durchführung des Anspruchs des Arbeitnehmers wird durch Vereinbarung geregelt. ³Ist der Arbeitgeber zu einer Durchführung über einen Pensionsfonds oder eine Pensionskasse (§ 1b Abs. 3) bereit, ist die betriebliche Altersversorgung dort durchzuführen;

Section 1a
Claim to Company Pension Plan Through Remuneration Conversion

(1) ¹The employee may demand of the employer that up to four percent of the respective contribution assessment limits in the general statutory pension insurance be taken from his future remuneration claims and used for his company pension plan by way of remuneration conversion. ²The execution of the employee's claim shall be regulated through an agreement. ³If the employer is willing to have the execution performed through a retirement fund or a staff pension fund (section 1b (3)), the company pension plan shall be executed there; otherwise, the

andernfalls kann der Arbeitnehmer verlangen, dass der Arbeitgeber für ihn eine Direktversicherung (§ 1 b Abs. 2) abschließt. ⁴Soweit der Anspruch geltend gemacht wird, muss der Arbeitnehmer jährlich einen Betrag in Höhe von mindestens einem Hundertsechzigstel der Bezugsgröße nach § 18 Abs. 1 des Vierten Buches Sozialgesetzbuch für seine betriebliche Altersversorgung verwenden. ⁵Soweit der Arbeitnehmer Teile seines regelmäßigen Entgelts für betriebliche Altersversorgung verwendet, kann der Arbeitgeber verlangen, dass während eines laufenden Kalenderjahres gleich bleibende monatliche Beträge verwendet werden.

(2) Soweit eine durch Entgeltumwandlung finanzierte betriebliche Altersversorgung besteht, ist der Anspruch des Arbeitnehmers auf Entgeltumwandlung ausgeschlossen.

(3) Soweit der Arbeitnehmer einen Anspruch auf Entgeltumwandlung für betriebliche Altersversorgung nach Abs. 1 hat, kann er verlangen, dass die Voraussetzungen für eine Förderung nach den §§ 10 a, 82 Abs. 2 des Einkommensteuergesetzes erfüllt werden, wenn die betriebliche Altersversorgung über einen Pensionsfonds, eine Pensionskasse oder eine Direktversicherung durchgeführt wird.

(4) ¹Falls der Arbeitnehmer bei fortbestehendem Arbeitsverhältnis kein Entgelt erhält, hat er das Recht, die Versicherung oder Versorgung mit eigenen Beiträgen fortzusetzen. ²Der Arbeitgeber steht auch für die Leistungen aus diesen Beiträgen ein. ³Die Regelungen über Entgeltumwandlung gelten entsprechend.

employee may demand that the employer take out direct insurance for him (section 1 b (2)). ⁴Where the claim is asserted, the employee must defer a contribution in the amount of at least $1/160$ of the reference value set forth in section 18 (1) of the Fourth Book of the Social Security Code *(Sozialgesetzbuch)* to his company pension plan. ⁵Where the employee defers portions of his regular remuneration to his company pension plan, the employer may demand that equivalent monthly contributions be deferred during a calendar year.

(2) Where a company pension plan financed by remuneration conversion is in place, the employee's claim to conversion of remuneration shall be excluded.

(3) Where the employee has a claim to conversion of remuneration claims for a company pension plan pursuant to subsection (1), he may demand that the prerequisites for a claim pursuant to sections 10a, 82 (2) of the Income Tax Act will be met if the company pension plan is executed through a retirement fund, a staff pension fund or direct insurance.

(4) ¹If the employee in an ongoing employment relationship has not received remuneration, he has the right to continue the insurance or pension with his own contributions. ²The employer shall also be responsible for the payments out of these contributions. ³The provisions on conversion of remuneration apply *mutatis mutandis*.

§ 1 b
Unverfallbarkeit und Durchführung der betrieblichen Altersversorgung

(1) ¹Einem Arbeitnehmer, dem Leistungen aus der betrieblichen Altersversorgung zugesagt worden sind, bleibt die

Section 1 b
Vesting and Execution of the Company Pension Plan

(1) ¹An employee who has been promised payments from the company pension plan shall retain his right to future

Anwartschaft erhalten, wenn das Arbeitsverhältnis vor Eintritt des Versorgungsfalls, jedoch nach Vollendung des 25. Lebensjahres endet und die Versorgungszusage zu diesem Zeitpunkt mindestens fünf Jahre bestanden hat (unverfallbare Anwartschaft). ²Ein Arbeitnehmer behält seine Anwartschaft auch dann, wenn er aufgrund einer Vorruhestandsregelung ausscheidet und ohne das vorherige Ausscheiden die Wartezeit und die sonstigen Voraussetzungen für den Bezug von Leistungen der betrieblichen Altersversorgung hätte erfüllen können. ³Eine Änderung der Versorgungszusage oder ihre Übernahme durch eine andere Person unterbricht nicht den Ablauf der Fristen nach Satz 1. ⁴Der Verpflichtung aus einer Versorgungszusage stehen Versorgungsverpflichtungen gleich, die auf betrieblicher Übung oder dem Grundsatz der Gleichbehandlung beruhen. ⁵Der Ablauf einer vorgesehenen Wartezeit wird durch die Beendigung des Arbeitsverhältnisses nach Erfüllung der Voraussetzungen der Sätze 1 und 2 nicht berührt. ⁶Wechselt ein Arbeitnehmer vom Geltungsbereich dieses Gesetzes in einen anderen Mitgliedstaat der Europäischen Union, bleibt die Anwartschaft in gleichem Umfange wie für Personen erhalten, die auch nach Beendigung eines Arbeitsverhältnisses innerhalb des Geltungsbereichs dieses Gesetzes verbleiben.

(2) ¹Wird für die betriebliche Altersversorgung eine Lebensversicherung auf das Leben des Arbeitnehmers durch den Arbeitgeber abgeschlossen und sind der Arbeitnehmer oder seine Hinterbliebenen hinsichtlich der Leistungen des Versicherers ganz oder teilweise bezugsberechtigt (Direktversicherung), so ist der Arbeitgeber verpflichtet, wegen Beendigung des Arbeitsverhältnisses nach Erfüllung der in Absatz 1 Satz 1 und 2 genannten Voraussetzungen das Bezugsrecht nicht mehr zu widerrufen. ²Eine Vereinbarung, nach der das Bezugsrecht durch die Beendigung des

benefits if his employment relationship ends before the pension goes into effect, but after the employer reaches the age of 25 years and the pension commitment to him has been in effect for at least five years at that point (vested expectancy). ²An employer shall retain his right to future payments even if he leaves the company due to an early retirement agreement and could have fulfilled the waiting period and other requirements for receiving company pension benefits had he not left the company earlier. ³A change in the pension commitment or its assumption by another person shall not interrupt the running of the time periods set forth in sentence 1. ⁴The obligation arising from a pension commitment is equivalent to pension obligations based on company practice or the principle of equal treatment. ⁵The course of a waiting period shall not be affected by the termination of an employment relationship once the prerequisites set forth in sentences 1 and 2 have been met. ⁶An employee who moves from the jurisdiction of this Act to another member state in the European Union, shall retain his right to future benefits to the same extent as for those remaining within the jurisdiction of this Act even after their employment relationship comes to an end.

(2) ¹If the employer has taken out a life insurance policy on the employee for the company pension plan and the employee or his survivors are entitled to receive all or part of the insurance benefits (direct insurance), then if the employment comes to an end and the prerequisites set forth in subsection (1) sentences 1 and 2 have been met, the employer is no longer obligated to revoke the employee's right to the life insurance benefits. ²Any agreement which stipulates that the right to the life insurance benefits to the condition subsequent that the employment relation-

Arbeitsverhältnisses nach Erfüllung der in Absatz 1 Satz 1 und 2 genannten Voraussetzungen auflösend bedingt ist, ist unwirksam. ³Hat der Arbeitgeber die Ansprüche aus dem Versicherungsvertrag abgetreten oder beliehen, so ist er verpflichtet, den Arbeitnehmer, dessen Arbeitsverhältnis nach Erfüllung der in Absatz 1 Satz 1 und 2 genannten Voraussetzungen geendet hat, bei Eintritt des Versicherungsfalles so zu stellen, als ob die Abtretung oder Beleihung nicht erfolgt wäre. ⁴Als Zeitpunkt der Erteilung der Versorgungszusage im Sinne des Absatzes 1 gilt der Versicherungsbeginn, frühestens jedoch der Beginn der Betriebszugehörigkeit.

(3) ¹Wird die betriebliche Altersversorgung von einer rechtsfähigen Versorgungseinrichtung durchgeführt, die dem Arbeitnehmer oder seinen Hinterbliebenen auf ihre Leistungen einen Rechtsanspruch gewährt (Pensionskasse und Pensionsfonds), so gilt Absatz 1 entsprechend. ²Als Zeitpunkt der Erteilung der Versorgungszusage im Sinne des Absatzes 1 gilt der Versicherungsbeginn, frühestens jedoch der Beginn der Betriebszugehörigkeit.

(4) ¹Wird die betriebliche Altersversorgung von einer rechtsfähigen Versorgungseinrichtung durchgeführt, die auf ihre Leistungen keinen Rechtsanspruch gewährt (Unterstützungskasse), so sind die nach Erfüllung der in Absatz 1 Satz 1 und 2 genannten Voraussetzungen und vor Eintritt des Versorgungsfalles aus dem Unternehmen ausgeschiedenen Arbeitnehmer und ihre Hinterbliebenen den bis zum Eintritt des Versorgungsfalles dem Unternehmen angehörenden Arbeitnehmern und deren Hinterbliebenen gleichgestellt. ²Die Versorgungszusage gilt in dem Zeitpunkt als erteilt im Sinne des Absatzes 1, von dem an der Arbeitnehmer zum Kreis der Begünstigten der Unterstützungskasse gehört.

ship comes to an end after the prerequisites set forth in subsection (1) sentences 1 and 2 have been met shall be invalid. ³If the employer has assigned claims under the insurance policy or borrowed against it, once pensionable status has been reached, the employer shall be obligated to put the employee whose employment relationship comes to an end after the prerequisites set forth in subsection (1) sentences 1 and 2 have been met in the same position he would have been in had such assignment or loan never taken place. ⁴The date of the granting of the pension commitment within the meaning of subsection (1) shall be that of the commencement of the insurance policy, but not before the date on which the employment begins.

(3) ¹If the company pension plan is executed by a pension organization of legal capacity which grants the employee or his survivors a legal claim to its benefits (staff pension fund and retirement fund), then subsection (1) shall apply *mutatis mutandis*. ²The date of the granting of the pension commitment within the meaning of subsection (1) shall be that of the commencement of the insurance policy, but not before the date on which the employment begins.

(4) ¹If the company pension plan is executed by a pension organization of legal capacity which does not grant a legal claim to its benefits (support fund), then, upon fulfilment of the prerequisites set forth in subsection (1) sentences 1 and 2 and prior to the pensionable status being reached within the meaning of subsection (1), employees who have left the company and their survivors shall be equivalent to employees working for the company up to the point when pensionable status is reached and their survivors. ²The pension commitment shall be deemed to have been rendered within the meaning of subsection (1) as of from the time at which the employee becomes a beneficiary of the support fund.

(5) Soweit betriebliche Altersversorgung durch Entgeltumwandlung erfolgt, behält der Arbeitnehmer seine Anwartschaft, wenn sein Arbeitsverhältnis vor Eintritt des Versorgungsfalles endet; in den Fällen der Absätze 2 und 3

1. dürfen die Überschussanteile nur zur Verbesserung der Leistung verwendet,
2. muss dem ausgeschiedenen Arbeitnehmer das Recht zur Fortsetzung der Versicherung oder Versorgung mit eigenen Beiträgen eingeräumt und
3. muss das Recht zur Verpfändung, Abtretung oder Beleihung durch den Arbeitgeber ausgeschlossen werden.

Im Fall einer Direktversicherung ist dem Arbeitnehmer darüber hinaus mit Beginn der Entgeltumwandlung ein unwiderrufliches Bezugsrecht einzuräumen.

§ 2
Höhe der unverfallbaren Anwartschaft

(1) ¹Bei Eintritt des Versorgungsfalles wegen Erreichens der Altersgrenze, wegen Invalidität oder Tod haben ein vorher ausgeschiedener Arbeitnehmer, dessen Anwartschaft nach § 1b fortbesteht, und seine Hinterbliebenen einen Anspruch mindestens in Höhe des Teiles der ohne das vorherige Ausscheiden zustehenden Leistung, der dem Verhältnis der Dauer der Betriebszugehörigkeit zu der Zeit vom Beginn der Betriebszugehörigkeit zum Erreichen der Regelaltersgrenze in der gesetzlichen Rentenversicherung entspricht; an die Stelle des Erreichens der Regelaltersgrenze tritt ein früherer Zeitpunkt, wenn dieser in der Versorgungsregelung als feste Altersgrenze vorgesehen ist, spätestens der Zeitpunkt, in dem der Arbeitnehmer ausscheidet und gleichzeitig eine Altersrente aus der gesetzlichen Rentenversicherung für besonders langjährig Versicherte in An-

(5) Where company pension plans are executed through conversion of remuneration claims, the employee shall retain his right to future payments if the employment relationship ends before the benefits become payable; in the cases set forth in subsections (2) and (3)

1. surpluses may only be used to improve the benefits,
2. an employee who leaves the company must be granted the right to continue the insurance or pension plan with his own contributions, and
3. the employee's right to pledge, assign or borrow against his claims must be excluded.

In the case of a direct insurance, the employer shall further be granted an irrevocable right to receive payments upon commencement of the conversion of remuneration claims.

Section 2
Amount of the Vested Pension Right

(1) ¹Upon the employee reaching pensionable status, due to a certain age having been reached or invalidity or death, an employee who had previously left the company but whose expectancy pursuant to section 1b continues to be in force, and his survivors, shall have a claim to at least that part of the benefits which would have been due had the premature retirement not taken place which corresponds to the ratio of the length of his employment with the company to the time between the onset of his employment and his normal retirement age in the statutory pension insurance; the normal retirement age shall be replaced by an earlier point in time if so provided by a fixed age limit in the pension provisions, at the latest the point in time at which the employee retires and at the same time makes use of old-age benefits from the statutory pension insurance for persons

spruch nimmt. ²Der Mindestanspruch auf Leistungen wegen Invalidität oder Tod vor Erreichen der Altersgrenze ist jedoch nicht höher als der Betrag, den der Arbeitnehmer oder seine Hinterbliebenen erhalten hätten, wenn im Zeitpunkt des Ausscheidens der Versorgungsfall eingetreten wäre und die sonstigen Leistungsvoraussetzungen erfüllt gewesen wären.

(2) ¹Ist bei einer Direktversicherung der Arbeitnehmer nach Erfüllung der Voraussetzungen des § 1b Abs. 1 und 5 vor Eintritt des Versorgungsfalls ausgeschieden, so gilt Absatz 1 mit der Maßgabe, dass sich der vom Arbeitgeber zu finanzierende Teilanspruch nach Absatz 1, soweit er über die von dem Versicherer nach dem Versicherungsvertrag auf Grund der Beiträge des Arbeitgebers zu erbringende Versicherungsleistung hinausgeht, gegen den Arbeitgeber richtet. ²An die Stelle der Ansprüche nach Satz 1 tritt auf Verlangen des Arbeitgebers die von dem Versicherer auf Grund des Versicherungsvertrags zu erbringende Versicherungsleistung, wenn

1. spätestens nach 3 Monaten seit dem Ausscheiden des Arbeitnehmers das Bezugsrecht unwiderruflich ist und eine Abtretung oder Beleihung des Rechts aus dem Versicherungsvertrag durch den Arbeitgeber und Beitragsrückstände nicht vorhanden sind,
2. vom Beginn der Versicherung, frühestens jedoch vom Beginn der Betriebszugehörigkeit an, nach dem Versicherungsvertrag die Überschussanteile nur zur Verbesserung der Versicherungsleistung zu verwenden sind und
3. der ausgeschiedene Arbeitnehmer nach dem Versicherungsvertrag das Recht zur Fortsetzung der Versicherung mit eigenen Beiträgen hat.

³Der Arbeitgeber kann sein Verlangen nach Satz 2 nur innerhalb von 3 Monaten seit dem Ausscheiden des Arbeitnehmers diesem und dem Versicherer

who have been insured for a particularly long period of time. ²The minimum claim to benefits due to invalidity or death before the age limit is reached, however, shall not exceed the amount the employee or his survivors would have received had the employee reached pensionable status at the time he left the company and the other prerequisites had been met.

(2) ¹If, in the case of a direct insurance, the employee leaves the company after fulfilling the prerequisites set forth in section 1b (1) and (5) prior to the employee reaching pensionable status, subsection (1) shall apply with the proviso that to the extent that the partial claim to be financed by the employer pursuant to subsection (1) exceeds the insurance benefit to be paid by the insurer under the insurance policy on the basis of the employer's contributions, such claim shall be directed against the employer. ²At the employer's request, the claims pursuant to sentence 1 shall be replaced by the insurance benefits to be paid by the insurer on the basis of the insurance policy if

1. no later than three months after the employee leaves the company the right to receive benefits is irrevocable and the employer has not assigned or borrowed against the right under the insurance policy and no outstanding premiums are due,
2. under the insurance policy, as of the commencement of the insurance, but at the earliest as of the commencement of employment, the surpluses are only to be used to improve the insurance benefits, and
3. under the insurance policy the former employee has the right to continue the insurance by paying his own premiums.

³The employer may only convey his request pursuant to sentence 2 to the former employee and the insurer within three months after the employee

mitteilen. ⁴Der ausgeschiedene Arbeitnehmer darf die Ansprüche aus dem Versicherungsvertrag in Höhe des durch Beitragszahlungen des Arbeitgebers gebildeten geschäftsplanmäßigen Deckungskapitals oder, soweit die Berechnung des Deckungskapitals nicht zum Geschäftsplan gehört, das nach § 169 Abs. 3 und 4 des Versicherungsvertragsgesetzes berechneten Wertes weder abtreten noch beleihen. ⁵In dieser Höhe darf der Rückkaufswert auf Grund einer Kündigung des Versicherungsvertrags nicht in Anspruch genommen werden; im Falle einer Kündigung wird die Versicherung in eine prämienfreie Versicherung umgewandelt. ⁶§ 169 Abs. 1 des Versicherungsvertrags-gesetzes findet insoweit keine Anwendung. ⁷Eine Abfindung des Anspruchs nach § 3 ist weiterhin möglich.

(3) ¹Für Pensionskassen gilt Absatz 1 mit der Maßgabe, dass sich der vom Arbeitgeber zu finanzierende Teilanspruch nach Absatz 1, soweit er über die von der Pensionskasse nach dem aufsichtsbehördlich genehmigten Geschäftsplan oder, soweit eine aufsichtsbehördliche Genehmigung nicht vorgeschrieben ist, nach den allgemeinen Versicherungsbedingungen und den fachlichen Geschäftsunterlagen im Sinne des § 5 Abs. 3 Nr. 2 Halbsatz 2 des Versicherungsaufsichtsgesetzes (Geschäftsunterlagen) auf Grund der Beiträge des Arbeitgebers zu erbringende Leistung hinausgeht, gegen den Arbeitgeber richtet. ²An die Stelle der Ansprüche nach Satz 1 tritt auf Verlangen des Arbeitgebers die von der Pensionskasse auf Grund des Geschäftsplans oder der Geschäftsunterlagen zu erbringende Leistung, wenn nach dem aufsichtsbehördlich genehmigten Geschäftsplan oder den Geschäftsunterlagen
1. vom Beginn der Versicherung, frühestens jedoch vom Beginn der Betriebszugehörigkeit an, Überschussanteile, die auf Grund des Finanzie-

leaves the company. ⁴The former employee may neither assign nor borrow against the claims arising from the insurance policy in the amount of the premium reserve created by the employer's contributions as per the business plan or, where the calculation of the premium reserve is not part of the business plan, the value as calculated pursuant to section 169 (3) and (4) of the Insurance Policies Act (*Versicherungsvertragsgesetz*). ⁵The repurchase value in this amount may not be utilized due to a termination of the insurance premium; in the event of such termination, the insurance shall be converted into a premium-free insurance policy. ⁶Section 169 (1) of the Insurance Policies Act shall not apply in this regard. ⁷It shall still be possible to pay compensation for a claim pursuant to section 3.

(3) ¹Subsection (1) shall apply to staff pension funds with the proviso that the partial claim to be financed by the employer pursuant to subsection (1) shall be directed against the employer where it exceeds the benefits to be rendered by the staff pension fund pursuant to a business plan approved by the regulatory authorities or, where no approval by the regulatory authorities is required, pursuant to the general insurance terms and conditions and the professional business documents within the meaning of section 5 (3) no. 2, 2nd half-sentence of the Insurance Supervision Act (business documents) on the basis of the employer's contributions. ²At the employer's request, the claims pursuant to sentence 1 shall be replaced by the benefits to be rendered by the staff pension fund on the basis of the business plan or the business documents, if, according to the business plan or the business documents approved by the regulatory authority,
1. as of the commencement of the insurance, but at the earliest as of the commencement of employment, surpluses shares which regularly arise in

rungsverfahrens regelmäßig entstehen, nur zur Verbesserung der Versicherungsleistung zu verwenden sind oder die Steigerung der Versorgungsanwartschaften des Arbeitnehmers der Entwicklung seines Arbeitsentgelts, soweit es unter den jeweiligen Beitragsbemessungsgrenzen der gesetzlichen Rentenversicherungen liegt, entspricht und

2. der ausgeschiedene Arbeitnehmer das Recht zur Fortsetzung der Versicherung mit eigenen Beiträgen hat.

³ Absatz 2 Satz 3 bis 7 gilt entsprechend.

(3a) Für Pensionsfonds gilt Absatz 1 mit der Maßgabe, dass sich der vom Arbeitgeber zu finanzierende Teilanspruch, soweit er über die vom Pensionsfonds auf der Grundlage der nach dem geltenden Pensionsplan im Sinne des § 112 Abs. 1 Satz 2 in Verbindung mit § 113 Abs. 2 Nr. 5 des Versicherungsaufsichtsgesetzes berechnete Deckungsrückstellung hinausgeht, gegen den Arbeitgeber richtet.

(4) Eine Unterstützungskasse hat bei Eintritt des Versorgungsfalls einem vorzeitig ausgeschiedenen Arbeitnehmer, der nach § 1b Abs. 4 gleichgestellt ist, und seinen Hinterbliebenen mindestens den nach Absatz 1 berechneten Teil der Versorgung zu gewähren.

(5) ¹ Bei der Berechnung des Teilanspruchs nach Absatz 1 bleiben Veränderungen der Versorgungsregelung und der Bemessungsgrundlagen für die Leistung der betrieblichen Altersversorgung, soweit sie nach dem Ausscheiden des Arbeitnehmers eintreten, außer Betracht; dies gilt auch für die Bemessungsgrundlagen anderer Versorgungsbezüge, die bei der Berechnung der Leistung der betrieblichen Altersversorgung zu berücksichtigen sind. ² Ist eine Rente der gesetzlichen Rentenversicherung zu berücksichtigen, so kann das bei der Berechnung von Pensionsrückstellungen allgemein zulässige Verfahren zugrunde gelegt werden,

the course of the financing procedures are only to be used to improve the insurance benefits, or the increase in the employee's pension expectancies corresponds to the development of his remuneration, if it falls below the respective contribution assessment limits of the statutory pension insurance and

2. the former employee has a right to continue the insurance policy with his own contributions.

³ Subsection (2) sentences 3 to 7 applies *mutatis mutandis*.

(3a) Subsection (1) shall apply to retirement funds with the proviso that to the extent that the partial claim to be financed by the employee exceeds the pro rata unearned premium reserve calculated on the basis of the current pension plan within the meaning of section 112 (1) sentence 2 in connection with section 113 (2) no. 5 of the Insurance Supervisory Act shall be directed against the employer.

(4) Once benefits become payable, a support fund shall grant an employee who retired prematurely but is in an equivalent position pursuant to section 1b (4) and shall grant his survivors at least the portion of the pension calculated pursuant to subsection (1).

(5) ¹ In calculating partial claims pursuant to subsection (1), if changes in the pension regulations and the basis for assessment of the claims of the company pension plans occur after the employee has left the company, they shall not be taken into account; this also applies with respect to the basis for assessment of other pension benefits which must be taken into account in calculating the benefits of the company pension plan. ² If a retirement benefit under the statutory pension insurance is to be taken into account, the calculation of the pension reserves can be based on the generally permissible proceedings unless the former employee

wenn nicht der ausgeschiedene Arbeitnehmer die Anzahl der im Zeitpunkt des Ausscheidens erreichten Entgeltpunkte nachweist; bei Pensionskassen sind der aufsichtsbehördlich genehmigte Geschäftsplan oder die Geschäftsunterlagen maßgebend. ³Bei Pensionsfonds sind der Pensionsplan und die sonstigen Geschäftsunterlagen maßgebend. ⁴Versorgungsanwartschaften, die der Arbeitnehmer nach seinem Ausscheiden erwirbt, dürfen zu keiner Kürzung des Teilanspruchs nach Absatz 1 führen.	demonstrates the number of remuneration points achieved at the time he left the company; in the case of staff pension funds, the business plan approved by the regulatory authorities or the business documents will be decisive. ³In the case of retirement funds, the pension plan and the other business documents shall be decisive. ⁴Pension expectancies the employee acquires after leaving the company may not lead to a reduction of the partial claim pursuant to subsection (1).
(5a) Bei einer unverfallbaren Anwartschaft aus Entgeltumwandlung tritt an die Stelle der Ansprüche nach Absatz 1, 3a oder 4 die vom Zeitpunkt der Zusage auf betriebliche Altersversorgung bis zum Ausscheiden des Arbeitnehmers erreichte Anwartschaft auf Leistungen aus den bis dahin umgewandelten Entgeltbestandteilen; dies gilt entsprechend für eine unverfallbare Anwartschaft aus Beiträgen im Rahmen einer beitragsorientierten Leistungszusage.	(5a) In the case of a vested expectancy arising from conversion of remuneration claims, the claims pursuant to subsections (1), (3a) or (4) shall be replaced by the right to payments out of those parts of the remuneration that have already been converted which the employee has attained from the time of the commitment to the company pension plan until he leaves the company; this shall apply *mutatis mutandis* for a vested expectancy arising from contributions made within the scope of a contribution based pension commitment.
(5b) An die Stelle der Ansprüche nach den Absätzen 2, 3, 3a und 5a tritt bei einer Beitragszusage mit Mindestleistung das dem Arbeitnehmer planmäßig zuzurechnende Versorgungskapital auf der Grundlage der bis zu seinem Ausscheiden geleisteten Beiträge (Beiträge und die bis zum Eintritt des Versorgungsfalls erzielten Erträge), mindestens die Summe der bis dahin zugesagten Beiträge, soweit sie nicht rechnungsmäßig für einen biometrischen Risikoausgleich verbraucht wurden.	(5b) In the case of a contribution commitment with minimum payment, the claims pursuant to subsections (2), (3), (3a) and (5a) shall be replaced by a claim for pension capital to be allocated to the employee according to plan on the basis of the contributions made up until the date of retirement (contributions plus the income earned on it until benefits become payable), at least the to sum of the committed contributions to date, where they were not used mathematically for a biometric balancing portfolio.
(6) *(weggefallen)*	(6) *(repealed)*

§ 3	Section 3
Abfindung	**Compensation**
(1) Unverfallbare Anwartschaften im Falle der Beendigung des Arbeitsverhältnisses und laufende Leistungen	(1) Vested expectancies in the event that the employment relationship comes to an end and ongoing pension benefits

dürfen nur unter den Voraussetzungen der folgenden Absätze abgefunden werden.

(2) ¹Der Arbeitgeber kann eine Anwartschaft ohne Zustimmung des Arbeitnehmers abfinden, wenn der Monatsbetrag der aus der Anwartschaft resultierenden laufenden Leistung bei Erreichen der vorgesehenen Altersgrenze 1 vom Hundert, bei Kapitalleistungen zwölf Zehntel der monatlichen Bezugsgröße nach § 18 des Vierten Buches Sozialgesetzbuch nicht übersteigen würde. ²Dies gilt entsprechend für die Abfindung einer laufenden Leistung. ³Die Abfindung ist unzulässig, wenn der Arbeitnehmer von seinem Recht auf Übertragung der Anwartschaft Gebrauch macht.

(3) Die Anwartschaft ist auf Verlangen des Arbeitnehmers abzufinden, wenn die Beiträge zur gesetzlichen Rentenversicherung erstattet worden sind.

(4) Der Teil der Anwartschaft, der während eines Insolvenzverfahrens erdient worden ist, kann ohne Zustimmung des Arbeitnehmers abgefunden werden, wenn die Betriebstätigkeit vollständig eingestellt und das Unternehmen liquidiert wird.

(5) Für die Berechnung des Abfindungsbetrages gilt § 4 Abs. 5 entsprechend.

(6) Die Abfindung ist gesondert auszuweisen und einmalig zu zahlen.

§ 4
Übertragung

(1) Unverfallbare Anwartschaften und laufende Leistungen dürfen nur unter den Voraussetzungen der folgenden Absätze übertragen werden.

(2) Nach Beendigung des Arbeitsverhältnisses kann im Einvernehmen des

may only be compensated subject to the prerequisites set forth in the following subsections.

(2) ¹The employer may compensate a pension expectancy without the employee's consent if the employee has reached the stipulated age limit, the monthly amount of the ongoing pension benefit resulting from the expectancy does not exceed one percent of the monthly reference figure and in the case of payments of capital, twelve tenths of the monthly reference figure set forth in section 18 of the Fourth Book of the Social Security Code. ²This applies for compensation for ongoing benefits *mutatis mutandis*. ³The compensation shall not be permissible if the employee avails itself of his right to transfer the expectancy.

(3) The expectancy shall be compensated at the employee's request if the contributions to the statutory pension insurance have been refunded.

(4) The portion of the expectancy that accrues in the course of an insolvency proceeding may be compensated without the employee's consent if the business operations have been completely closed down and the company is being liquidated.

(5) For the calculation of the amount of the compensation, section 4 (5) shall apply *mutatis mutandis*.

(6) The compensation shall be posted separately and paid on a one-off basis.

Section 4
Transfer

(1) Vested expectancies and ongoing benefits may only be transferred subject to the prerequisites set forth in the following subsections.

(2) Once the employment relationship comes to an end, by mutual agreement

ehemaligen mit dem neuen Arbeitgeber sowie dem Arbeitnehmer
1. die Zusage vom neuen Arbeitgeber übernommen werden oder
2. der Wert der vom Arbeitnehmer erworbenen unverfallbaren Anwartschaft auf betriebliche Altersversorgung (Übertragungswert) auf den neuen Arbeitgeber übertragen werden, wenn dieser eine wertgleiche Zusage erteilt; für die neue Anwartschaft gelten die Regelungen über Entgeltumwandlung entsprechend.

(3) ¹Der Arbeitnehmer kann innerhalb eines Jahres nach Beendigung des Arbeitsverhältnisses von seinem ehemaligen Arbeitgeber verlangen, dass der Übertragungswert auf den neuen Arbeitgeber übertragen wird, wenn
1. die betriebliche Altersversorgung über einen Pensionsfonds, eine Pensionskasse oder eine Direktversicherung durchgeführt worden ist und
2. der Übertragungswert die Beitragsbemessungsgrenze in der allgemeinen Rentenversicherung nicht übersteigt.
²Der Anspruch richtet sich gegen den Versorgungsträger, wenn der ehemalige Arbeitgeber die versicherungsförmige Lösung nach § 2 Abs. 2 oder 3 gewählt hat oder soweit der Arbeitnehmer die Versicherung oder Versorgung mit eigenen Beiträgen fortgeführt hat. ³Der neue Arbeitgeber ist verpflichtet, eine dem Übertragungswert wertgleiche Zusage zu erteilen und über einen Pensionsfonds, eine Pensionskasse oder eine Direktversicherung durchzuführen. ⁴Für die neue Anwartschaft gelten die Regelungen über Entgeltumwandlung entsprechend.

(4) ¹Wird die Betriebstätigkeit eingestellt und das Unternehmen liquidiert, kann eine Zusage von einer Pensionskasse oder einem Unternehmen der Lebensversicherung ohne Zustimmung des Arbeitnehmers oder Versorgungsempfängers übernommen werden, wenn sichergestellt ist, dass die Über-

between the former and new employer, as well as the employee
1. the commitment may be assumed by the new employer or
2. the value of the vested pension expectancy acquired by the employee (transfer value) may be transferred to the new employer if it renders a commitment of equivalent value; the rules on conversion of remuneration shall apply to the new expectancy *mutatis mutandis*.

(3) ¹Within one year after his employment relationship comes to an end, the employee may demand that his former employer transfer the transfer value to the new employer if
1. the company pension plan is executed through a retirement fund, a staff pension fund or a direct insurance and
2. the transfer value does not exceed the contribution assessment limits in the general statutory pension insurance.
²The claim shall be directed against the pension carrier if the former employer has selected the insurance solution set forth in section 2 (2) or (3) or to the extent the employee has continued the insurance or pension with his own contributions. ³The new employer shall be obligated to render a commitment equivalent in value to the transfer value and execute it through a retirement fund, a staff pension fund or a direct insurance. ⁴The rules on conversion of remuneration shall apply to the new expectancy *mutatis mutandis*.

(4) ¹If the company ceases operations and is liquidated, a commitment by a staff pension fund or a life insurance company may be assumed without the consent of the beneficiary or employee if it has been ensured that the surplus shares will be used as of the onset of retirement in accordance with sec-

schussanteile ab Rentenbeginn entsprechend § 16 Abs. 3 Nr. 2 verwendet werden. ²§ 2 Abs. 2 Satz 4 bis 6 gilt entsprechend.

(5) ¹Der Übertragungswert entspricht bei einer unmittelbar über den Arbeitgeber oder über eine Unterstützungskasse durchgeführten betrieblichen Altersversorgung dem Barwert der nach § 2 bemessenen künftigen Versorgungsleistung im Zeitpunkt der Übertragung; bei der Berechnung des Barwerts sind die Rechnungsgrundlagen sowie die anerkannten Regeln der Versicherungsmathematik maßgebend. ²Soweit die betriebliche Altersversorgung über einen Pensionsfonds, eine Pensionskasse oder eine Direktversicherung durchgeführt worden ist, entspricht der Übertragungswert dem gebildeten Kapital im Zeitpunkt der Übertragung.

(6) Mit der vollständigen Übertragung des Übertragungswerts erlischt die Zusage des ehemaligen Arbeitgebers.

§ 4 a
Auskunftsanspruch

(1) Der Arbeitgeber oder der Versorgungsträger hat dem Arbeitnehmer bei einem berechtigten Interesse auf dessen Verlangen schriftlich mitzuteilen,
1. in welcher Höhe aus der bisher erworbenen unverfallbaren Anwartschaft bei Erreichen der in der Versorgungsregelung vorgesehenen Altersgrenze ein Anspruch auf Altersversorgung besteht und
2. wie hoch bei einer Übertragung der Anwartschaft nach § 4 Abs. 3 der Übertragungswert ist.

(2) Der neue Arbeitgeber oder der Versorgungsträger hat dem Arbeitnehmer auf dessen Verlangen schriftlich mitzuteilen, in welcher Höhe aus dem Übertragungswert ein Anspruch auf Altersversorgung und ob eine Invaliditäts- oder Hinterbliebenenversorgung bestehen würde.

tion 16 (3) no. 2. ²Section 2 (2) sentences 4 to 6 shall apply *mutatis mutandis*.

(5) ¹In the case of a company pension plan executed directly through the employer or a support fund, the transfer value corresponds to the cash value of the future pension benefit calculated pursuant to section 2 at the time of the transfer; in calculating the cash value, the basis of calculation, as well as the recognized rules of actuarial mathematics shall prevail. ²Where the company pension plan is executed through a retirement fund, a staff pension fund or a direct insurance, the transfer value shall correspond to the capital formed at the time of the transfer.

(6) The former employer's commitment shall extinguish with the complete transfer of the transfer value.

Section 4 a
Claim for Disclosure

(1) The employer or the pension carrier must inform the employee in writing at his request, provided he has a justified interest in receiving such information,
1. of the amount of the vested expectancy achieved thus far to which he would have a claim to old-age pension benefits upon reaching the age provided for in the pension provisions and
2. the amount of the transfer value upon a transfer of the expectancy pursuant to section 4 (3).

(2) The new employer or the pension carrier must inform the employee in writing at his request of the amount of the transfer value to which he has a claim to old-age pension benefits and whether an invalidity or survivor's pension would exist.

Zweiter Abschnitt
Auszehrungsverbot

§ 5
Auszehrung und Anrechnung

(1) Die bei Eintritt des Versorgungsfalls festgesetzten Leistungen der betrieblichen Altersversorgung dürfen nicht mehr dadurch gemindert oder entzogen werden, dass Beträge, um die sich andere Versorgungsbezüge nach diesem Zeitpunkt durch Anpassung an die wirtschaftliche Entwicklung erhöhen, angerechnet oder bei der Begrenzung der Gesamtversorgung auf einen Höchstbetrag berücksichtigt werden.

(2) [1] Leistungen der betrieblichen Altersversorgung dürfen durch Anrechnung oder Berücksichtigung anderer Versorgungsbezüge, soweit sie auf eigenen Beiträgen des Versorgungsempfängers beruhen, nicht gekürzt werden. [2] Dies gilt nicht für Renten aus den gesetzlichen Rentenversicherungen, soweit sie auf Pflichtbeiträgen beruhen, sowie für sonstige Versorgungsbezüge, die mindestens zur Hälfte auf Beiträgen oder Zuschüssen des Arbeitgebers beruhen.

Dritter Abschnitt
Altersgrenze

§ 6
Vorzeitige Altersleistung

[1] Einem Arbeitnehmer, der die Altersrente aus der gesetzlichen Rentenversicherung als Vollrente in Anspruch nimmt, sind auf sein Verlangen nach Erfüllung der Wartezeit und sonstiger Leistungsvoraussetzungen Leistungen der betrieblichen Altersversorgung zu gewähren. [2] Fällt die Altersrente aus der gesetzlichen Rentenversicherung wieder weg oder wird sie auf einen Teilbetrag beschränkt, so können auch die Leistungen der betrieblichen Altersversorgung eingestellt werden. [3] Der aus-

Chapter 2
Prohibition of Erosion of Benefits

Section 5
Erosion and Set-Off

(1) The amount of company pension plan benefits set at the point when pensionable status is reached may not be reduced or withdrawn by setting off sums by which other pension benefits increase after this time due to adjustments to the economic developments, or by taking such sums into account in limiting the overall pension to a maximum sum.

(2) [1] Company pension plan benefits may not be reduced by setoff or taking other pension benefits into account that are based on the beneficiary's own contributions. [2] This shall not apply to statutory pension insurance benefits where they are based on mandatory contributions or for other pension benefits which are based on at least fifty percent of the employer's contributions or subsidies.

Chapter 3
Age Limit

Section 6
Premature Old-Age Benefits

[1] An employee who makes use of old-age benefits from the statutory pension insurance as full retirement benefits shall, at his request, upon compliance with a waiting period and other prerequisites, be granted company pension plan benefits. [2] If the old-age benefits from the statutory pension fund should be withdrawn or limited to a partial amount, the company pension plan benefits may also be discontinued. [3] The former employee shall be obligated to notify the employer or other pension

geschiedene Arbeitnehmer ist verpflichtet, die Aufnahme oder Ausübung einer Beschäftigung oder Erwerbstätigkeit, die zu einem Wegfall oder zu einer Beschränkung der Altersrente aus der gesetzlichen Rentenversicherung führt, dem Arbeitgeber oder sonstigen Versorgungsträger unverzüglich anzuzeigen.

payer of the assumption of employment or professional activities leading to the cessation or limitation of the old-age benefits from the state pension fund without delay.

Vierter Abschnitt
Insolvenzsicherung

Chapter 4
Insolvency Insurance

§ 7
Umfang des Versicherungsschutzes

Section 7
Scope of the Insurance Coverage

(1) ¹Versorgungsempfänger, deren Ansprüche aus einer unmittelbaren Versorgungszusage des Arbeitgebers nicht erfüllt werden, weil über das Vermögen des Arbeitgebers oder über seinen Nachlass das Insolvenzverfahren eröffnet worden ist, und ihre Hinterbliebenen haben gegen den Träger der Insolvenzsicherung einen Anspruch in Höhe der Leistung, die der Arbeitgeber aufgrund der Versorgungszusage zu erbringen hätte, wenn das Insolvenzverfahren nicht eröffnet worden wäre. ²Satz 1 gilt entsprechend,

(1) ¹Pension beneficiaries whose claims arising from a direct pension commitment by the employer are not fulfilled because insolvency proceedings have been initiated against the employer's assets or its estate, and their survivors shall have a claim against the insolvency insurance carrier in the amount of the benefits the employer would have been obligated to render had the insolvency proceeding not been initiated. ²Sentence 1 applies *mutatis mutandis*

1. wenn Leistungen aus einer Direktversicherung aufgrund der in § 1b Abs. 2 Satz 3 genannten Tatbestände nicht gezahlt werden und der Arbeitgeber seiner Verpflichtung nach § 1b Abs. 2 Satz 3 wegen der Eröffnung des Insolvenzverfahrens nicht nachkommt,

1. if benefits from a direct insurance are not paid due to the circumstances described in section 1b (2) sentence 3 and the employer does not fulfil his obligation pursuant to section 1b (2) sentence 3 due to the initiation of insolvency proceedings,

2. wenn eine Unterstützungskasse oder ein Pensionsfonds die nach ihrer Versorgungsregelung vorgesehene Versorgung nicht erbringt, weil über das Vermögen oder den Nachlass eines Arbeitgebers, der der Unterstützungskasse oder dem Pensionsfonds Zuwendungen leistet (Trägerunternehmen), das Insolvenzverfahren eröffnet worden ist.

2. a support fund or retirement fund does not render the benefits as required by its own rules and regulations because insolvency proceedings have been initiated against the assets or estate of an employer which is subsidizing the support fund or the retirement fund (carrier company).

³§ 14 des Versicherungsvertragsgesetzes findet entsprechende Anwendung.

³Section 14 of the Insurance Policy Act applies *mutatis mutandis*. ⁴In the appli-

⁴Der Eröffnung des Insolvenzverfahrens stehen bei der Anwendung der Sätze 1 bis 3 gleich

1. die Abweisung des Antrags auf Eröffnung des Insolvenzverfahrens mangels Masse,
2. der außergerichtliche Vergleich (Stundungs-, Quoten- oder Liquidationsvergleich) des Arbeitgebers mit seinen Gläubigern zur Abwendung eines Insolvenzverfahrens, wenn ihm der Träger der Insolvenzsicherung zustimmt,
3. die vollständige Beendigung der Betriebstätigkeit im Geltungsbereich dieses Gesetzes, wenn ein Antrag auf Eröffnung des Insolvenzverfahrens nicht gestellt worden ist und ein Insolvenzverfahren offensichtlich mangels Masse nicht in Betracht kommt.

(1 a) ¹Der Anspruch gegen den Träger der Insolvenzsicherung entsteht mit dem Beginn des Kalendermonats, der auf den Eintritt des Sicherungsfalles folgt. ²Der Anspruch endet mit Ablauf des Sterbemonats des Begünstigten, soweit in der Versorgungszusage des Arbeitgebers nicht etwas anderen bestimmt ist. ³In den Fällen des Absatzes 1 Satz 1 und 4 Nr. 1 und 3 umfasst der Anspruch auch rückständige Versorgungsleistungen, soweit diese bis zu zwölf Monaten vor Entstehen der Leitungspflicht des Trägers der Insolvenzsicherung entstanden sind.

(2) ¹Personen, die bei Eröffnung des Insolvenzverfahrens oder bei Eintritt der nach Absatz 1 Satz 4 gleichstehenden Voraussetzungen (Sicherungsfall) eine nach § 1b unverfallbare Versorgungsanwartschaft haben, und ihre Hinterbliebenen haben bei Eintritt des Versorgungsfalls einen Anspruch gegen den Träger der Insolvenzsicherung, wenn die Anwartschaft beruht

1. auf einer unmittelbaren Versorgungszusage des Arbeitgebers oder
2. auf einer Direktversicherung und der Arbeitnehmer hinsichtlich der Leis-

cation of sentences 1 to 3, the initiation of insolvency proceedings shall be equivalent to

1. the denial of the application for initiation of insolvency proceedings for lack of assets,
2. out-of-court composition proceedings (respite on debt, quota share or liquidation settlement) between the employer and his creditors to avert insolvency proceedings, with the consent of the carrier of the insolvency insurance,
3. the complete cessation of operations within the scope of this Act if no application for initiation of insolvency proceedings has been filed and such proceedings are obviously out of the question due to lack of assets.

(1 a) ¹The claim against the carrier of the insolvency insurance shall come into being at the beginning of the calendar month following the occurrence of the insured event. ²The claim shall end at the end of the month in which the beneficiary dies unless otherwise provided in the employer's pension commitment. ³In the cases described in subsections (1) sentence 1 and (4) nos. 1 and 3, the claim shall also comprise outstanding pension benefits provided that they have arisen up to twelve months before the insolvency insurance carrier's duty to pay benefits comes into being.

(2) ¹Persons who have a vested pension expectancy upon the initiation of insolvency proceedings or on the occurrence of the conditions equivalent to those set forth in subsection (1 b) sentence 4 (insured event), and their survivors shall have a claim against the carrier of the insolvency insurance once pensionable status has been reached if the expectancy is based on

1. a direct pension commitment by the employer or
2. a direct insurance policy and the employee is irrevocably entitled to draw

tungen des Versicherers widerruflich bezugsberechtigt ist oder die Leistungen aufgrund der in § 1b Abs. 2 Satz 3 genannten Tatbestände nicht gezahlt werden und der Arbeitgeber seiner Verpflichtung aus § 1b Abs. 2 Satz 3 wegen der Eröffnung des Insolvenzverfahrens nicht nachkommt. ²Satz 1 gilt entsprechend für Personen, die zum Kreis der Begünstigten einer Unterstützungskasse oder eines Pensionsfonds gehören, wenn der Sicherungsfall bei einem Trägerunternehmen eingetreten ist. ³Die Höhe des Anspruchs richtet sich nach der Höhe der Leistungen gemäß § 2 Abs. 1, 2 Satz 2 und Abs. 5, bei Unterstützungskassen nach dem Teil der nach der Versorgungsregelung vorgesehenen Versorgung, der dem Verhältnis der Dauer der Betriebszugehörigkeit zu der Zeit vom Beginn der Betriebszugehörigkeit bis zum Erreichen der in der Versorgungsregelung vorgesehenen festen Altersgrenze entspricht, es sei denn, § 2 Abs. 5a ist anwendbar. ⁴Für die Berechnung der Höhe des Anspruchs nach Satz 3 wird die Betriebszugehörigkeit bis zum Eintritt des Sicherungsfalles berücksichtigt. ⁵Bei Pensionsfonds mit Leistungszusagen gelten für die Höhe des Anspruchs die Bestimmungen für unmittelbare Versorgungszusagen entsprechend, bei Beitragszusagen mit Mindestleistung gilt für die Höhe des Anspruchs § 2 Abs. 5b.

benefits from the insurance company or the benefits are not paid due to the circumstances set forth in section 1b (2) sentence 3 and the employer does not fulfill his obligation under section 1b (2) sentence 3 due to the initiation of insolvency proceedings. ²Sentence 1 applies *mutatis mutandis* for persons who are among the beneficiaries of a support fund or a pension fund if the event insured against occurs to a company supporting such support fund or retirement fund. ³The amount of the claim is based upon the amount of the benefits pursuant to section 2 (1) and (2) sentence 2 and (5); in the case of support funds the amount of the claim is based on the portion of the pension which, under the pension rules and regulations, corresponds to the ratio between the length of employment with the company and the time elapsed from the commencement of employment to the fixed age set forth in the pension rules and regulations, unless section 2 (5a) applies. ⁴In calculating the amount of the claim pursuant to sentence 3, employment with the company up to the point when pensionable status is reached will be taken into account. ⁵In the case of retirement funds with payment commitments, the provisions on direct pension claims shall apply *mutatis mutandis* to the amount of the claim; in the case of contribution commitments with minimum payments, section 2 (5b) shall apply with respect to the amount of the claim.

(3) ¹Ein Anspruch auf laufende Leistungen gegen den Träger der Insolvenzsicherung beträgt jedoch im Monat höchstens das Dreifache der im Zeitpunkt der ersten Fälligkeit maßgebenden monatlichen Bezugsgröße gemäß § 18 des Vierten Buches Sozialgesetzbuch. ²Satz 1 gilt entsprechend bei einem Anspruch auf Kapitalleistungen mit der Maßgabe, dass zehn vom Hundert der Leistung als Jahresbetrag einer laufenden Leistung anzusetzen sind.

(3) ¹However, a claim to ongoing benefits against the insolvency insurance carrier shall each month amount to at most triple the monthly reference figure pursuant to section 18 of the Fourth Book of the Social Security Code that is relevant when the claims first become due. ²Sentence 1 applies *mutatis mutandis* for a claim to capital benefits with the proviso that ten percent of the benefits must be posted as the annual sum of an ongoing benefit.

(4) ¹Ein Anspruch auf Leistungen gegen den Träger der Insolvenzsicherung vermindert sich in dem Umfang, in dem der Arbeitgeber oder sonstige Träger der Versorgung die Leistungen der betrieblichen Altersversorgung erbringt. ²Wird im Insolvenzverfahren ein Insolvenzplan bestätigt, vermindert sich der Anspruch auf Leistungen gegen den Träger der Insolvenzsicherung insoweit, als nach dem Insolvenzplan der Arbeitgeber oder sonstige Träger der Versorgung einen Teil der Leistungen selbst zu erbringen hat. ³Sieht der Insolvenzplan vor, dass der Arbeitgeber oder sonstige Träger der Versorgung die Leistungen der betrieblichen Altersversorgung von einem bestimmten Zeitpunkt an selbst zu erbringen hat, so entfällt der Anspruch auf Leistungen gegen den Träger der Insolvenzsicherung von diesem Zeitpunkt an. ⁴Die Sätze 2 und 3 sind für den außergerichtlichen Vergleich nach Absatz 1 Satz 4 Nr. 2 entsprechend anzuwenden. ⁵Im Insolvenzplan soll vorgesehen werden, dass bei einer nachhaltigen Besserung der wirtschaftlichen Lage des Arbeitgebers die vom Träger der Insolvenzsicherung zu erbringenden Leistungen ganz oder zum Teil vom Arbeitgeber oder sonstigen Träger der Versorgung wieder übernommen werden.

(4) ¹A claim to benefits against the insolvency insurance carrier shall be reduced to the degree that the employer or other carrier of the pension renders the benefits of the company pension plan. ²If an insolvency plan is confirmed in insolvency proceedings, the claim for benefits against the insolvency insurance carrier shall be reduced to the extent that under the insolvency plan the employer or other pension carrier must render a portion of the benefits itself. ³If the insolvency plan provides that the employer or other pension carrier must render the benefits under the company pension plan itself from a certain point in time on, the claim for benefits against the insolvency insurance carrier shall lapse from this time on. ⁴Sentences 2 and 3 shall apply *mutatis mutandis* to out-of-court settlements pursuant to subsection (1) sentence 4 no. 2. ⁵The insolvency plan shall provide that in the event of a sustained improvement in the employer's economic position, the benefits to be paid by the insolvency insurance carrier shall be reassumed by the employer or other pension carrier in whole or in part.

(5) ¹Ein Anspruch gegen den Träger der Insolvenzsicherung besteht nicht, soweit nach den Umständen des Falles die Annahme gerechtfertigt ist, dass es der alleinige oder überwiegende Zweck der Versorgungszusage oder ihre Verbesserung oder der für die Direktversicherung in § 1b Abs. 2 Satz 3 genannten Tatbestände gewesen ist, den Träger der Insolvenzsicherung in Anspruch zu nehmen. ²Diese Annahme ist insbesondere dann gerechtfertigt, wenn bei Erteilung oder Verbesserung der Versorgungszusage wegen der wirtschaftlichen Lage des Arbeitgebers zu erwarten war, dass die Zusage nicht erfüllt werde. ³Ein Anspruch auf Leistungen gegen den Träger der Insolvenzsiche-

(5) ¹No claim shall exist against the insolvency insurance carrier where the circumstances of the case justify an assumption that the sole or predominant purpose of the pension commitment or its improvement or the prerequisite for direct insurance set forth in section 1b (2) sentence 3 was to assert a claim against the insolvency insurance carrier. ²Such assumption shall in particular be justified if upon granting or improving the pension commitment it was to be anticipated that, in light of the employer's economic situation, such commitment would not be fulfilled. ³A claim for benefits against the insolvency insurance carrier shall only exist in the case of commitments and

rung besteht bei Zusagen und Verbesserungen von Zusagen, die in den beiden letzten Jahren vor dem Eintritt des Sicherungsfalls erfolgt sind, nur

1. für ab dem 1. Januar 2002 gegebene Zusagen, soweit bei Entgeltumwandlung Beträge von bis zu 4 vom Hundert der Beitragsbemessungsgrenze in der allgemeinen Rentenversicherung für eine betriebliche Altersversorgung verwendet werden oder
2. für im Rahmen von Übertragungen gegebene Zusagen, soweit der Übertragungswert die Beitragsbemessungsgrenze in der allgemeinen Rentenversicherung nicht übersteigt.

(6) Ist der Sicherungsfall durch kriegerische Ereignisse, innere Unruhen, Naturkatastrophen oder Kernenergie verursacht worden, kann der Träger der Insolvenzsicherung mit Zustimmung der Bundesanstalt für Finanzdienstleistungsaufsicht die Leistungen nach billigem Ermessen abweichend von den Absätzen 1 bis 5 festsetzen.

improvements of commitments which were made in the two years preceding the onset of the insolvency

1. for commitments rendered as of 1 January 2002, where in the course of the remuneration conversion, sums of up to four percent of the contribution assessment limit in the general statutory pension insurance are used for a company pension plan or
2. for commitments rendered in the course of transferring commitments that had been rendered where the transfer value does not exceed the contribution assessment limits in the general statutory pension insurance.

(6) If the insured event is caused by armed conflicts, internal unrest, natural catastrophes or atomic energy, the insolvency insurance carrier may, with the consent of the Federal Financial Supervisory Authority *(Bundesanstalt für Finanzdienstleistungsaufsicht)*, set the amount of the benefits according to its fair discretion, in deviation of subsections (1) to (5).

§ 8
Übertragung der Leistungspflicht und Abfindung

Section 8
Transfer of the Duty to Pay Benefits and Compensation

(1) Ein Anspruch gegen den Träger der Insolvenzsicherung auf Leistungen nach § 7 besteht nicht, wenn eine Pensionskasse oder ein Unternehmen der Lebensversicherung sich dem Träger der Insolvenzsicherung gegenüber verpflichtet, diese Leistungen zu erbringen, und die nach § 7 Berechtigten ein unmittelbares Recht erwerben, die Leistungen zu fordern.

(1a) [1]Der Träger der Insolvenzsicherung hat die gegen ihn gerichteten Ansprüche auf den Pensionsfonds, dessen Trägerunternehmen die Eintrittspflicht nach § 7 ausgelöst hat, im Sinne von Absatz 1 zu übertragen, wenn die Bundesanstalt für Finanzdienstleistungsaufsicht hierzu die Genehmigung er-

(1) No claim against the insolvency insurance carrier for benefits pursuant to section 7 shall exist if a staff pension fund or a life insurance company commits itself to the insolvency insurance carrier to render such benefits and the beneficiaries pursuant to section 7 acquire a direct right to demand such benefits.

(1a) [1]The insolvency insurance carrier shall transfer, within the meaning of subsection (1), the claims directed at it to the retirement fund whose carrier company has triggered the duties engendered by the onset of the occurrence pursuant to section 7 if the Federal Financial Supervisory Authority grants

teilt. ²Die Genehmigung kann nur erteilt werden, wenn durch Auflagen der Bundesanstalt für Finanzdienstleistungsaufsicht die dauernde Erfüllbarkeit der Leistungen aus dem Pensionsplan sichergestellt werden kann. ³Die Genehmigung der Bundesanstalt für Finanzdienstleistungsaufsicht kann der Pensionsfonds nur innerhalb von drei Monaten nach Eintritt des Sicherungsfalles beantragen.

permission to do so. ²Such permission may only be granted if the ongoing ability to make the payments under the pension plan can be ensured by orders issued by the Federal Financial Supervisory Authority. ³The retirement fund may only apply for permission by the Federal Financial Supervisory Authority within a period of three months after the point when pensionable status is reached.

(2) ¹Der Träger der Insolvenzsicherung kann eine Anwartschaft ohne Zustimmung des Arbeitnehmers abfinden, wenn der Monatsbetrag der aus der Anwartschaft resultierenden laufenden Leistung bei Erreichen der vorgesehenen Altersgrenze 1 vom Hundert, bei Kapitalleistungen zwölf Zehntel der monatlichen Bezugsgröße nach § 18 des Vierten Buches Sozialgesetzbuch nicht übersteigen würde oder wenn dem Arbeitnehmer die Beiträge zur gesetzlichen Rentenversicherung erstattet worden sind. ²Dies gilt entsprechend für die Abfindung einer laufenden Leistung. ³Die Abfindung ist darüber hinaus möglich, wenn sie an ein Unternehmen der Lebensversicherung gezahlt wird, bei dem der Versorgungsberechtigte im Rahmen einer Direktversicherung versichert ist. ⁴§ 2 Abs. 2 Satz 4 bis 6 und § 3 Abs. 5 gelten entsprechend.

(2) ¹The insolvency insurance carrier may provide compensation for an expectancy without the employee's consent if the monthly amount of the ongoing pension benefit resulting from the expectancy would not exceed one percent of the monthly reference figure and in the case of payments of capital, twelve tenths of the monthly reference figure set forth in section 18 Fourth Book of the Social Security Code or if the employee has been reimbursed for his contributions to the statutory pension insurance. ²This applies for compensation for an ongoing benefit *mutatis mutandis*. ³Compensation is further possible if it is paid to a life insurance company with which the pension beneficiary is insured within the scope of a direct insurance. ⁴Section 2 (2) sentences 4 to 6 and section 3 (2) apply *mutatis mutandis*.

§ 9
Mitteilungspflicht, Forderungs- und Vermögensübergang

Section 9
Notification Duty, Transfer of Claims and Assets

(1) ¹Der Träger der Insolvenzsicherung teilt dem Berechtigten die ihm nach § 7 oder § 8 zustehenden Ansprüche oder Anwartschaften schriftlich mit. ²Unterbleibt die Mitteilung, so ist der Anspruch oder die Anwartschaft spätestens ein Jahr nach dem Sicherungsfall bei dem Träger der Insolvenzsicherung anzumelden; erfolgt die Anmeldung später, so beginnen die Leistungen frühestens mit dem Ersten des Monats der Anmeldung, es sei denn, dass der Be-

(1) ¹The insolvency insurance carrier shall notify the beneficiary in writing of the claims or expectancies accruing to him pursuant to section 7 or 8. ²If no such notification is made, then the claim or expectancy shall be registered with the insolvency insurance carrier no later than one year after the onset of insolvency; if such registration is made later, then the benefits shall commence no earlier than at the first of the month of the registration, unless the benefici-

rechtigte an der rechtzeitigen Anmeldung ohne sein Verschulden verhindert war.

(2) ¹Ansprüche oder Anwartschaften des Berechtigten gegen den Arbeitgeber auf Leistungen der betrieblichen Altersversorgung, die den Anspruch gegen den Träger der Insolvenzsicherung begründen, gehen im Falle eines Insolvenzverfahrens mit dessen Eröffnung, in den übrigen Sicherungsfällen dann auf den Träger der Insolvenzsicherung über, wenn dieser nach Absatz 1 Satz 1 dem Berechtigten die ihm zustehenden Ansprüche oder Anwartschaften mitteilt. ²Der Übergang kann nicht zum Nachteil des Berechtigten geltend gemacht werden. ³Die mit der Eröffnung des Insolvenzverfahrens übergegangenen Anwartschaften werden im Insolvenzverfahren als unbedingte Forderungen nach § 45 der Insolvenzordnung geltend gemacht.

(3) ¹Ist der Träger der Insolvenzsicherung zu Leistungen verpflichtet, die ohne den Eintritt des Sicherungsfalls eine Unterstützungskasse erbringen würde, geht deren Vermögen einschließlich der Verbindlichkeiten auf ihn über; die Haftung für die Verbindlichkeiten beschränkt sich auf das übergegangene Vermögen. ²Wenn die übergegangenen Vermögenswerte den Barwert der Ansprüche und Anwartschaften gegen den Träger der Insolvenzsicherung übersteigen, hat dieser den übersteigenden Teil entsprechend der Satzung der Unterstützungskasse zu verwenden. ³Bei einer Unterstützungskasse mit mehreren Trägerunternehmen hat der Träger der Insolvenzsicherung einen Anspruch gegen die Unterstützungskasse auf einen Betrag, der dem Teil des Vermögens der Kasse entspricht, der auf das Unternehmen entfällt, bei dem der Sicherungsfall eingetreten ist. ⁴Die Sätze 1 bis 3 gelten nicht, wenn der Sicherungsfall auf den in § 7 Abs. 1 Satz 4 Nr. 2 genannten Gründen beruht, es sei denn, dass das Trägerunternehmen seine Betriebstätig-

ary was prevented from registering on time by reasons beyond his control.

(2) ¹Claims or expectancies of the beneficiary against the employer for company pension plan benefits which intern create claims against the insolvency insurance carrier shall pass over to the insolvency insurance carrier, upon the initiation of insolvency proceedings or, in other cases insured against, once the insolvency insurance carrier informs the beneficiary of his accrued claims or expectancies pursuant to subsection (1) sentence 1. ²The transfer may not be effected to the detriment of the beneficiary. ³The expectancies passing over upon the initiation of insolvency proceedings shall be asserted in the insolvency proceedings as unconditional claims pursuant to section 45 of the Insolvency Code (*Insolvenzordnung*).

(3) ¹If the insolvency insurance carrier is obliged to pay benefits which a support fund would have rendered if the case insured against had not transpired, the support fund's assets, including liabilities, shall pass to the insolvency insurance carrier; liability for the liabilities shall be limited to the assets transferred. ²If the value of the transferred assets exceeds the cash value of the claims and expectancies against the insolvency insurance carrier, it shall use this excess value in accordance with the support funds statutes. ³If a support fund has two or more carrier companies, the insolvency insurance carrier shall have a claim against the support fund for a sum corresponding to the portion of the fund's assets accruing to the company which has suffered the event insured against. ⁴Sentences 1 to 3 shall not apply if the event insured against is due to the grounds set forth in section 7 (1) sentence 4 no. 2, unless the carrier company does not continue operations upon occurrence of such event and is dissolved (liquidation settlement).

keit nach Eintritt des Sicherungsfall nicht fortsetzt und aufgelöst wird (Liquidationsvergleich).

(3a) Absatz 3 findet entsprechende Anwendung auf einen Pensionsfonds, wenn die Bundesanstalt für Finanzdienstleistungsaufsicht die Genehmigung für die Übertragung der Leistungspflicht durch den Träger der Insolvenzsicherung nach § 8 Abs. 1a nicht erteilt.

(4) ¹In einem Insolvenzplan, der die Fortführung des Unternehmens oder eines Betriebes vorsieht, kann für den Träger der Insolvenzsicherung eine besondere Gruppe gebildet werden. ²Sofern im Insolvenzplan nichts anderes vorgesehen ist, kann der Träger der Insolvenzsicherung, wenn innerhalb von drei Jahren nach der Aufhebung des Insolvenzverfahrens ein Antrag auf Eröffnung eines neuen Insolvenzverfahrens über das Vermögen des Arbeitgebers gestellt wird, in diesem Verfahren als Insolvenzgläubiger Erstattung der von ihm erbrachten Leistungen verlangen.

(5) Dem Träger der Insolvenzsicherung steht gegen den Beschluss, durch den das Insolvenzverfahren eröffnet wird, die sofortige Beschwerde zu.

§ 10
Beitragspflicht und Beitragsbemessung

(1) Die Mittel für die Durchführung der Insolvenzsicherung werden auf Grund öffentlich-rechtlicher Verpflichtung durch Beiträge aller Arbeitgeber aufgebracht, die Leistungen der betrieblichen Altersversorgung unmittelbar zugesagt haben oder eine betriebliche Altersversorgung über eine Unterstützungskasse, eine Direktversicherung der in § 7 Abs. 1 Satz 2 und Absatz 2 Satz 1 Nr. 2 bezeichneten Art oder einen Pensionsfonds durchführen.

(2) ¹Die Beiträge müssen den Barwert der im laufenden Kalenderjahr entste-

(3a) Subsection 3 shall apply to a retirement fund *mutatis mutandis* if the Federal Financial Supervisory Authority does not issue permission for the transfer of the duty to make payments by the carrier of the insolvency insurance pursuant to section 8 (1a).

(4) ¹In an insolvency plan which provides for the continuation of the company or an establishment, a special group may be created for the insolvency insurance carrier. ²Unless otherwise provided in the insolvency plan, if within three years of the termination of the insolvency proceeding a petition for initiation of new insolvency proceedings is filed, the insolvency insurance carrier may during the course of the proceedings demand as an insolvency creditor reimbursement of the benefits it has rendered.

(5) The insolvency insurance carrier has the right to object immediately to a resolution initiating insolvency proceedings.

Section 10
Duty to Pay and Assessment of Premiums

(1) The funds for executing the insolvency insurance shall be raised by premiums made pursuant to public law obligations by every employer which has directly committed itself to pay company pension plan benefits or carry out a company pension plan by way of a support fund, a direct insurance of the type described in section 7 (1) sentence 2 and (2) sentence 1 no. 2 or a retirement fund.

(2) ¹The premiums must cover the cash value of claims for insolvency insur-

henden Ansprüche auf Leistungen der Insolvenzsicherung decken zuzüglich eines Betrages für die aufgrund eingetretener Insolvenzen zu sichernden Anwartschaften, der sich aus dem Unterschied der Barwerte dieser Anwartschaften am Ende des Kalenderjahres und am Ende des Vorjahres bemisst. ²Der Rechnungszinsfuss bei der Berechnung des Barwertes der Ansprüche auf Leistungen der Insolvenzsicherung bestimmt sich nach § 65 des Versicherungsaufsichtsgesetzes; soweit keine Übertragung nach § 8 Abs. 1 stattfindet, ist der Rechnungszinsfuss bei der Berechnung des Barwerts der Anwartschaften um ein Drittel höher. ³Darüber hinaus müssen die Beiträge die im gleichen Zeitraum entstehenden Verwaltungskosten und sonstigen Kosten, die mit der Gewährung der Leistungen zusammenhängen, und die Zuführung zu einem von der Bundesanstalt für Finanzdienstleistungsaufsicht festgesetzten Ausgleichsfonds decken; § 37 des Versicherungsaufsichtsgesetzes bleibt unberührt. ⁴Auf die am Ende des Kalenderjahres fälligen Beiträge können Vorschüsse erhoben werden. ⁵Sind die nach den Sätzen 1 bis 3 erforderlichen Beiträge höher als im vorangegangenen Kalenderjahr, so kann der Unterschiedsbetrag auf das laufende und die folgenden vier Kalenderjahre verteilt werden. ⁶In Jahren, in denen sich außergewöhnlich hohe Beiträge ergeben würden, kann zu deren Ermäßigung der Ausgleichsfonds in einem von der Bundesanstalt für Finanzdienstleistungsaufsicht zu genehmigenden Umfang herangezogen werden.

(3) Die nach Absatz 2 erforderlichen Beiträge werden auf die Arbeitgeber nach Maßgabe der nachfolgenden Beträge umgelegt, soweit sie sich auf die laufenden Versorgungsleistungen und die nach § 1b unverfallbaren Versorgungsanwartschaften beziehen (Beitragsbemessungsgrundlage); diese Beträge sind festzustellen auf den Schluss des Wirtschaftsjahrs des Arbeitgebers,

ance benefits arising in the current calendar year plus a sum for the expectancies to be secured due to insolvency events which equals the difference between the cash value of these expectancies at the end of the calendar year and that at the end of the previous year. ²The discount to be used in calculating the cash value shall be determined pursuant to section 65 of the Insurance Supervisory Act; where no transfer pursuant to section 8 (1) take place, the discount to be used in calculating the cash value of the expectancies shall be one-third hither. ³Moreover, the sums must cover the administrative and other costs incurred in the same period in connection with the payment of these benefits and the allocation for an equalization fund as determined by the Financial Supervisory Authority; section 37 of the Insurance Supervisory Act (*Versicherungsaufsichtsgesetz*) remains unaffected. ⁴Advance payments on the premiums due at the end of the calendar year may be demanded. ⁵If the sums required pursuant to sentences 1 to 3 are greater than in the previous calendar year, then the amount of the difference may be divided over the current and four subsequent calendar years. ⁶In years in which these sums are extraordinarily high, the equalization fund may be drawn upon to reduce the premiums to an extent to be approved by the Federal Financial Supervisory Authority.

(3) The premiums required pursuant to subsection (2) shall be apportioned to the employer on the basis of the following sums, where they pertain to the current payment of benefits and the vested expectancies pursuant to section 1b (basis for assessing premiums); these sums shall be determined at the end of the employer's business year which ended in the preceding calendar

das im abgelaufenen Kalenderjahr geendet hat:

1. Bei Arbeitgebern, die Leistungen der betrieblichen Altersversorgung unmittelbar zugesagt haben, ist Beitragsbemessungsgrundlage der Teilwert der Pensionsverpflichtung (§ 6a Abs. 3 des Einkommensteuergesetzes).

2. Bei Arbeitgebern, die eine betriebliche Altersversorgung über eine Direktversicherung mit widerruflichem Bezugsrecht durchführen, ist Beitragsbemessungsgrundlage das geschäftsplanmäßige Deckungskapital oder, soweit die Berechnung des Deckungskapitals nicht zum Geschäftsplan gehört, die Deckungsrückstellung. Für Versicherungen, bei denen der Versicherungsfall bereits eingetreten ist, und für Versicherungsanwartschaften, für die ein unwiderrufliches Bezugsrecht eingeräumt ist, ist das Deckungskapital oder die Deckungsrückstellung nur insoweit zu berücksichtigen, als die Versicherungen abgetreten oder beliehen sind.

3. Bei Arbeitgebern, die eine betriebliche Altersversorgung über eine Unterstützungskasse durchführen, ist Beitragsbemessungsgrundlage das Deckungskapital für die laufenden Leistungen (§ 4d Abs. 1 Nr. 1 Buchstabe a des Einkommensteuergesetzes) zuzüglich des Zwanzigfachen der nach § 4d Abs. 1 Nr. 1 Buchstabe b Satz 1 des Einkommensteuergesetzes errechneten jährlichen Zuwendungen für Leistungsanwärter im Sinne von § 4d Abs. 1 Nr. 1 Buchstabe b Satz 2 des Einkommensteuergesetzes.

4. Bei Arbeitgebern, soweit sie betriebliche Altersversorgung über einen Pensionsfonds durchführen, ist Beitragsbemessungsgrundlage 20 vom Hundert des entsprechend Nummer 1 ermittelten Betrages.

(4) ¹Aus den Beitragsbescheiden des Trägers der Insolvenzsicherung findet

year:

1. In the case of employers who have made a direct company pension plan commitment, the basis for assessing the premiums shall be the going concern value of the pension obligation (section 6a (3) of the Income Tax Act).

2. In the case of employers who carry out a company pension plan by way of a direct insurance with revocable rights to benefits, the basis for assessing the premiums shall be the premium reserve as per the business plan or, where the calculation of the premium reserve is not part of the business plan, the pro rata unearned premium reserve. For insurance policies where the event insured against has already occurred and for insurance expectancies for which a vested right to benefits has been granted, the premium reserve or the pro rata unearned premium reserve shall only be taken into account where the insurance policies have been assigned or were used as collateral for a loan.

3. In the case of employers which carry out a company pension plan by way of a support fund, the basis for assessing the premiums shall be the premium reserve for the current benefits (section 4d (1) no. 1a of the Income Tax Act) plus 20 times the annual sum allocated for potential beneficiaries within the meaning of section 4d (1) no. 1b sentence 1 of the Income Tax Act as calculated pursuant to section 4d (1) no. 1b sentence 2 of the Income Tax Act.

4. In the case of employers who execute company pension plans through a pension fund, 20 percent of the sum calculated pursuant to no. 1 shall be applied as the basis for assessing the premiums.

(4) ¹The insolvency insurance carrier's premium notices shall be enforced in

die Zwangsvollstreckung in entsprechender Anwendung der Vorschriften der Zivilprozessordnung statt. [2]Die vollstreckbare Ausfertigung erteilt der Träger der Insolvenzsicherung.

analogous application of the provisions of the Code of Civil Procedure (Zivilprozessordnung). [2]The enforceable execution shall be issued by the insolvency insurance carrier.

§ 10 a
Säumniszuschläge, Zinsen, Verjährung

(1) Für Beiträge, die wegen Verstoßes des Arbeitgebers gegen die Meldepflicht erst nach Fälligkeit erhoben werden, kann der Träger der Insolvenzsicherung für jeden angefangenen Monat vom Zeitpunkt der Fälligkeit an einen Säumniszuschlag in Höhe von bis zu eins vom Hundert der nacherhobenen Beiträge erheben.

(2) [1]Für festgesetzte Beiträge und Vorschüsse, die der Arbeitgeber nach Fälligkeit zahlt, erhebt der Träger der Insolvenzsicherung für jeden Monat Verzugszinsen in Höhe von 0,5 vom Hundert der rückständigen Beiträge. [2]Angefangene Monate bleiben außer Ansatz.

(3) [1]Vom Träger der Insolvenzsicherung zu erstattende Beiträge werden vom Tage der Fälligkeit oder bei Feststellung des Erstattungsanspruchs durch gerichtliche Entscheidung vom Tage der Rechtshängigkeit an für jeden Monate mit 0,5 vom Hundert verzinst. [2]Angefangene Monate bleiben außer Ansatz.

(4) [1]Ansprüche auf Zahlung der Beiträge zur Insolvenzsicherung gemäß § 10 sowie Erstattungsansprüche nach Zahlung nicht geschuldeter Beiträge zur Insolvenzsicherung verjähren in sechs Jahren. [2]Die Verjährungsfrist beginnt mit Ablauf des Kalenderjahres, in dem die Beitragspflicht entstanden oder der Erstattungsanspruch fällig geworden ist. [3]Auf die Verjährung sind die Vorschriften des Bürgerlichen Gesetzbuchs anzuwenden.

Section 10 a
Extra Charge for Late Payments, Interest, Statute of Limitations

(1) For premiums that are only levied after their due date because the employer was in breach of his notification duty, the insolvency insurance carrier may levy a late charge for each month or part thereof as of the due date in the amount of up to one percent of the premiums levied at that time.

(2) [1]In the case of fixed premiums and advance payments which the employer pays after their due date, the insolvency insurance carrier shall levy default interest at a rate of 0.5 percent of the outstanding premiums for each month. [2]No default interest shall be charged for partial months.

(3) [1]The premiums to be refunded by the insolvency insurance carrier shall be charged interest from the due date or, where a reimbursement claim has been determined by judicial decision, from the date on which the determination became legally binding, for each month at a rate of 0.5 percent. [2]No interest shall be charged for partial months.

(4) [1]Claims for payment of the insolvency insurance premiums pursuant to section 10 as well as reimbursement claims following payment of insolvency insurance premiums that were not owed shall become statute barred in six years. [2]The statute of limitations shall commence at the end of the calendar year in which the duty to pay premiums arose or the reimbursement claim became payable. [3]The provisions of the German Civil Code (Bürgerliches Gesetzbuch) shall be applied to the statute of limitations.

§ 11
Melde-, Auskunfts- und Mitteilungspflichten

(1) ¹Der Arbeitgeber hat dem Träger der Insolvenzsicherung eine betriebliche Altersversorgung nach § 1b Abs. 1 bis 4 für seine Arbeitnehmer innerhalb von 3 Monaten nach Erteilung der unmittelbaren Versorgungszusage, dem Abschluss einer Direktversicherung oder der Errichtung einer Unterstützungskasse oder eines Pensionsfonds mitzuteilen. ²Der Arbeitgeber, der sonstige Träger der Versorgung, der Insolvenzverwalter und die nach § 7 Berechtigten sind verpflichtet, dem Träger der Insolvenzsicherung alle Auskünfte zu erteilen, die zur Durchführung der Vorschriften dieses Abschnitts erforderlich sind, sowie Unterlagen vorzulegen, aus denen die erforderlichen Angaben ersichtlich sind.

(2) ¹Ein beitragspflichtiger Arbeitgeber hat dem Träger der Insolvenzsicherung spätestens bis zum 30. September eines jeden Kalenderjahrs die Höhe des nach § 10 Abs. 3 für die Bemessung des Beitrages maßgebenden Betrages bei unmittelbaren Versorgungszusagen und Pensionsfonds auf Grund eines versicherungsmathematischen Gutachtens, bei Direktversicherungen auf Grund einer Bescheinigung des Versicherers und bei Unterstützungskassen auf Grund einer nachprüfbaren Berechnung mitzuteilen. ²Der Arbeitgeber hat die in Satz 1 bezeichneten Unterlagen mindestens 6 Jahre aufzubewahren.

(3) ¹Der Insolvenzverwalter hat dem Träger der Insolvenzsicherung die Eröffnung des Insolvenzverfahrens, Namen und Anschriften der Versorgungsempfänger und die Höhe ihrer Versorgung nach § 7 unverzüglich mitzuteilen. ²Er hat zugleich Namen und Anschriften der Personen, die bei Eröffnung des Insolvenzverfahrens eine nach § 1 unverfallbare Versorgungsan-

Section 11
Duty to Notify, Disclose Information and Communicate

(1) ¹The employer shall inform the insolvency insurance carrier about a company pension plan pursuant to section 1b (1) to (4) for its employees within three months of issuing the direct pension commitment, the conclusion of a direct insurance contract or the establishment of a support fund or a retirement fund. ²The employer, the other pension carriers, the insolvency receiver and the beneficiaries pursuant to section 7 shall be obligated to provide the insolvency insurance carrier with all information necessary to carry out the provisions in this Chapter, as well as to provide documents from which the necessary information can be derived.

(2) ¹An employer obligated to pay premiums shall inform the insolvency insurance carrier by no later than 30 September of each calendar year of the amount of the sum decisive for calculating the premium pursuant to section 10 (3), in the case of direct pension commitments and retirement funds on the basis of an actuarial report, in the case of direct insurance on the basis of a certificate issued by the insurance company and in the case of support funds and premium commitments with a minimum payment on the basis of a verifiable calculation. ²The employer shall preserve the documents set forth in sentence 1 for at least six years.

(3) ¹The insolvency receiver shall inform the insolvency insurance carrier without delay of the initiation of insolvency proceedings and provide it with the names and addresses of the pension recipients and the amount of their benefits pursuant to section 7. ²At the same time it shall convey the names and addresses of the persons having vested pension rights pursuant to section 1 as

wartschaft haben, sowie die Höhe ihrer Anwartschaft nach § 7 mitzuteilen.

(4) Der Arbeitgeber, der sonstige Träger der Versorgung und die nach § 7 Berechtigten sind verpflichtet, dem Insolvenzverwalter Auskünfte über alle Tatsachen zu erteilen, auf die sich die Mitteilungspflicht nach Absatz 3 bezieht.

(5) In den Fällen, in denen ein Insolvenzverfahren nicht eröffnet wird (§ 7 Abs. 1 Satz 4) oder nach § 207 der Insolvenzordnung eingestellt worden ist, sind die Pflichten des Insolvenzverwalters nach Absatz 3 vom Arbeitgeber oder dem sonstigen Träger der Versorgung zu erfüllen.

(6) Kammern und andere Zusammenschlüsse von Unternehmern oder anderen selbständigen Berufstätigen, die als Körperschaften des öffentlichen Rechts errichtet sind, ferner Verbände und andere Zusammenschlüsse, denen Unternehmer oder andere selbständige Berufstätige kraft Gesetzes angehören oder anzugehören haben, haben den Träger der Insolvenzsicherung bei der Ermittlung der nach § 10 beitragspflichtigen Arbeitgeber zu unterstützen.

(7) Die nach den Absätzen 1 bis 3 und 5 zu Mitteilungen und Auskünften und die nach Absatz 6 zur Unterstützung Verpflichteten haben die vom Träger der Insolvenzsicherung vorgesehenen Vordrucke zu verwenden.

(8) ¹Zur Sicherung der vollständigen Erfassung der nach § 10 beitragspflichtigen Arbeitgeber können die Finanzämter dem Träger der Insolvenzsicherung mitteilen, welche Arbeitgeber für die Beitragspflicht in Betracht kommen. ²Die Bundesregierung wird ermächtigt, durch Rechtsverordnung mit Zustimmung des Bundesrates das Nähere zu bestimmen und Einzelheiten des Verfahrens zu regeln.

well as the amount of their expectancies pursuant to section 7.

(4) The employer, the other pension carriers and the beneficiaries pursuant to section 7 are obligated to provide the insolvency receiver with information on any and all circumstances pertaining to the notification duty pursuant to subsection 3.

(5) In the cases where no insolvency proceeding is initiated (section 7 (1) sentence 4) or one is suspended pursuant to section 207 of the Insolvency Code *(Insolvenzordnung)*, the duties of the insolvency receiver pursuant to subsection 3 shall be fulfilled by the employer or the other pension carrier.

(6) Chambers and other combinations of enterprises or other self-employed professionals who are established as corporations under public law, as well as associations and other combinations to which entrepreneurs or other self-employed professionals belong or have belonged by force of law, shall support the insolvency insurance carrier in identifying the employers who are obligated to pay premiums pursuant to section 10.

(7) Those obligated to convey notifications and information pursuant to subsections 1 to 3 and 5 and to render assistance pursuant to subsection 6 shall use the forms provided by the insolvency insurance carrier.

(8) ¹In order to ensure that the information compiled regarding the employers obligation to pay premiums pursuant to section 10 is complete, the tax authorities may inform the insolvency insurance carrier which employers come under consideration for such a duty. ²The Federal Government shall be empowered to enact regulations, ratified by the upper house of the German Parliament, setting forth the details of such a procedure.

§ 12
Ordnungswidrigkeiten

(1) Ordnungswidrig handelt, wer vorsätzlich oder fahrlässig

1. entgegen § 11 Abs. 1 Satz 1, Abs. 2, Satz 1, Abs. 3 oder Abs. 5 eine Mitteilung nicht, nicht richtig, nicht vollständig oder nicht rechtzeitig vornimmt,

2. entgegen § 11 Abs. 1 Satz 2 oder Abs. 4 eine Auskunft nicht, nicht richtig, nicht vollständig oder nicht rechtzeitig erteilt oder

3. entgegen § 11 Abs. 1 Satz 2 Unterlagen nicht, nicht richtig, nicht vollständig oder nicht rechtzeitig vorlegt oder entgegen § 11 Abs. 2 Satz 2 Unterlagen nicht aufbewahrt.

(2) Die Ordnungswidrigkeit kann mit einer Geldbusse bis zu zweitausendfünfhundert Euro geahndet werden.

(3) Verwaltungsbehörde im Sinne des § 36 Abs. 1 Nr. 1 des Gesetzes über Ordnungswidrigkeiten ist die Bundesanstalt für Finanzdienstleistungsaufsicht.

Section 12
Breach of Regulations

(1) Anyone who intentionally or negligently

1. fails to make a notification or such notification is not correct, not complete or was not made in a timely manner in contravention of section 11 (1) sentence 1, (2) sentence 1, (3) or (5),

2. fails to provide information or such information is not correct, not complete or was not made in a timely manner in contravention of section 11 (1) sentence 2, or (4),

3. fails to provide documentation or such documentation is not correct, not complete or was not made in a timely manner in contravention of section 11 (1) sentence 2, or fails to preserve such documentation in contravention of section 11 (2) sentence 2 is acting in breach of regulations.

(2) The breach of regulations may be subject to a fine or up to two thousand five hundred euro.

(3) The administrative authority within the meaning of section 36 (1) no. 1 of the Act of Breaches of Regulations (*Gesetz über Ordnungswidrigkeiten*) shall be the Federal Financial Supervisory Authority.

§ 13
(weggefallen)

Section 13
(repealed)

§ 14
Träger der Insolvenzsicherung

(1) ¹Träger der Insolvenzsicherung ist der Pensions-Sicherungs-Verein Versicherungsverein auf Gegenseitigkeit. ²Er ist zugleich Träger der Insolvenzsicherung von Versorgungszusagen Luxemburger Unternehmen nach Maßgabe des Abkommens vom 22. September 2000 zwischen der Bundesrepublik Deutschland und dem Großherzogtum Luxemburg über Zusammenarbeit im

Section 14
Insolvency Insurance Carrier

(1) ¹The carrier of the insolvency insurance is the Pensions-Sicherungs-Verein Versicherungsverein auf Gegenseitigkeit. ²At the same time it is the carrier of the insolvency insurance of pension commitments of Luxembourg companies in accordance with the Agreement of 22 September 2000 between the Federal Republic of Germany and the Grand Duchy of Luxembourg on coop-

Bereich der Insolvenzsicherung betrieblicher Altersversorgung. [3]Er unterliegt der Aufsicht durch die Bundesanstalt für Finanzdienstleistungsaufsicht. [4]Die Vorschriften des Versicherungsaufsichtsgesetzes gelten, soweit dieses Gesetz nichts anderes bestimmt.

(2) Der Bundesminister für Arbeit und Sozialordnung weist durch Rechtsverordnung mit Zustimmung des Bundesrates die Stellung des Trägers der Insolvenzsicherung der Kreditanstalt für Wiederaufbau zu, bei der ein Fonds zur Insolvenzsicherung der betrieblichen Altersversorgung gebildet wird, wenn

1. bis zum 31. Dezember 1974 nicht nachgewiesen worden ist, dass der in Absatz 1 genannte Träger die Erlaubnis der Aufsichtsbehörde zum Geschäftsbetrieb erhalten hat,
2. der in Absatz 1 genannte Träger aufgelöst worden ist oder
3. die Aufsichtsbehörde den Geschäftsbetrieb des in Absatz 1 genannten Trägers untersagt oder die Erlaubnis zum Geschäftsbetrieb widerruft.

[2]In den Fällen der Nummern 2 und 3 geht das Vermögen des in Absatz 1 genannten Trägers einschließlich der Verbindlichkeiten auf die Kreditanstalt für Wiederaufbau über, die es dem Fonds zur Insolvenzsicherung der betrieblichen Altersversorgung zuweist.

(3) [1]Wird die Insolvenzsicherung von der Kreditanstalt für Wiederaufbau durchgeführt, gelten die Vorschriften dieses Abschnittes mit folgenden Abweichungen:
1. In § 7 Abs. 6 entfällt die Zustimmung der Bundesanstalt für Finanzdienstleistungsaufsicht.
2. [2]§ 10 Abs. 2 findet keine Anwendung. Die von der Kreditanstalt für Wiederaufbau zu erhebenden Beiträge müssen den Bedarf für die laufenden Leistungen der Insolvenzsicherung im laufenden Kalenderjahr und die im gleichen Zeitraum entstehenden Verwaltungskosten und

eration in the area of the insolvency insurance of company pension plans. [3]It is supervised by the Federal Financial Supervisory Authority. [4]The provisions of the Insurance Supervisory Act shall apply unless otherwise provided in this Act.

(2) [1]The Federal Minister for Labor and Social Order shall enact a statute, to be ratified by the upper house of German Parliament, assigning the position of insolvency insurance carrier to the Kreditanstalt für Wiederaufbau, at which a fund to provide insolvency insurance for company pension plans shall be created if

1. it has not been proven by 31 December 1974 that the carrier set forth in subsection 1 has received the permission of the Supervisory Office to operate its business,
2. the carrier set forth in subsection 1 has been dissolved or
3. the Supervisory Office prohibits the carrier set forth in subsection 1 from operating its business or revokes its permission to do so.

[2]In the cases set forth in numbers 2 and 3 the assets of the carrier set forth in subsection 1, including its liabilities, shall pass to Kreditanstalt für Wiederaufbau, which shall allocate such assets to the fund for insolvency insurance for company pension plans.

(3) [1]If the insolvency insurance is carried out by Kreditanstalt für Wiederaufbau, the provisions of this Chapter shall apply with the following variations:
1. In section 7 (6), the consent of the Federal Financial Supervisory Authority shall no longer be required.
2. [2]Section 10 (2) shall not apply. [2]The premiums to be levied by Kreditanstalt für Wiederaufbau must cover the needs for the current insolvency insurance benefits and the administrative costs arising during the same period and other costs associated with the granting of the benefits. [3]In

sonstigen Kosten, die mit der Gewährung der Leistungen zusammenhängen, decken. ³Bei einer Zuweisung nach Absatz 2 Nr. 1 beträgt der Beitrag für die ersten 3 Jahre mindestens 0,1 vom Hundert der Beitragsbemessungsgrundlage gemäß § 10 Abs. 3; der nicht benötigte Teil dieses Beitragsaufkommens wird einer Betriebsmittelreserve zugeführt. ⁴Bei einer Zuweisung nach Absatz 2 Nr. 2 oder 3 wird in den ersten 3 Jahren zu dem Beitrag nach Nummer 2 Satz 2 ein Zuschlag von 0,08 vom Hundert der Beitragsbemessungsgrundlage gemäß § 10 Abs. 3 zur Bildung einer Betriebsmittelreserve erhoben. ⁵Auf die Beiträge können Vorschüsse erhoben werden.

3. ⁶In § 12 Abs. 3 tritt an die Stelle der Bundesanstalt für Finanzdienstleistungsaufsicht die Kreditanstalt für Wiederaufbau.

⁷Die Kreditanstalt für Wiederaufbau verwaltet den Fonds im eigenen Namen. ⁸Für Verbindlichkeiten des Fonds haftet sie nur mit dem Vermögen des Fonds. ⁹Dieser haftet nicht für die sonstigen Verbindlichkeiten der Bank. ¹⁰§ 11 Abs. 1 Satz 1 des Gesetzes über die Kreditanstalt für Wiederaufbau in der Fassung der Bekanntmachung vom 23. Juni 1969 (BGBl. I S. 573), das zuletzt durch Artikel 14 des Gesetzes vom 21. Juni 2002 (BGBl. I S. 2010) geändert worden ist, ist in der jeweils geltenden Fassung auch für den Fonds anzuwenden.

the case of an assignment pursuant to subsection (2) no. 1, the premium for the first three years shall amount to at least 0.1 percent of the premium assessment basis pursuant to section 10 (3); the portion of the premium revenues that is not needed shall be allocated to an operating funds reserve. ⁴In the case of an assignment pursuant to subsection (2) no. 2 or 3, in the first three years a surcharge of 0.08 percent of the premium assessment basis pursuant to section 10 (3) shall be added to the premium pursuant to no. 2 sentence 2 for the creation of an operating funds reserve. ⁵Advance payments of the premiums may be levied.

3. ⁶In Section 12 (3), the Federal Financial Supervisory Authority shall be replaced by Kreditanstalt für Wiederaufbau.

⁷Kreditanstalt für Wiederaufbau shall administer the fund in its own name. ⁸It shall only be liable to pay the fund's liabilities with the fund's assets. ⁹The fund shall not be liable for any other liabilities the Bank incurs. ¹⁰Section 11 (1) sentence 1 of the Act on Kreditanstalt für Wiederaufbau in the version of the promulgation of 23 July 1969 (Federal Law Gazette I p. 573), as most recently amended by Article 14 of the Act of 21 June 2002 (Federal Law Gazette I p. 2010) shall be applied in the version applicable at the time.

§ 15
Verschwiegenheitspflicht

¹Personen, die bei dem Träger der Insolvenzsicherung beschäftigt oder für ihn tätig sind, dürfen fremde Geheimnisse, insbesondere Betriebs- oder Geschäftsgeheimnisse, nicht unbefugt offenbaren oder verwerten. ²Sie sind nach dem Gesetz über die förmliche Verpflichtung nichtbeamteter Personen vom 2. März 1974 (Bundesgesetzbl. I

Section 15
Duty of Confidentiality

¹Persons who are employed by or work for the insolvency insurance carrier may not disclose or exploit outside secrets, in particular trade or business secrets, without authorization. ²Pursuant to the Act on the Formal Obligation of Non-Permanent Status Civil Servants of 2 March 1974 (Federal Law Gazette I p. 469, 547), the duty to con-

S. 469, 547) von der Bundesanstalt für Finanzdienstleistungsaufsicht auf die gewissenhafte Erfüllung ihrer Obliegenheiten zu verpflichten.

scientiously fulfill their obligations shall be imposed upon them by the Federal Financial Supervisory Authority.

<h3 style="text-align:center">Fünfter Abschnitt
Anpassung</h3>

<h3 style="text-align:center">Chapter 5
Adjustment</h3>

<h3 style="text-align:center">§ 16
Anpassungsprüfungspflicht</h3>

<h3 style="text-align:center">Section 16
Adjustment Examination Duty</h3>

(1) Der Arbeitgeber hat alle drei Jahre eine Anpassung der laufenden Leistungen der betrieblichen Altersversorgung zu prüfen und hierüber nach billigem Ermessen zu entscheiden; dabei sind insbesondere die Belange des Versorgungsempfängers und die wirtschaftliche Lage des Arbeitgebers zu berücksichtigen.

(1) Every three years the employer shall examine whether an adjustment of the ongoing company pension plan benefits is necessary and reach a conclusion according to its own fair assessment; particular factors to be considered are the interests of the beneficiaries and the financial position of the employer.

(2) Die Verpflichtung nach Absatz 1 gilt als erfüllt, wenn die Anpassung nicht geringer ist als der Anstieg

(2) The obligation set forth in subsection (1) shall be deemed to have been fulfilled if the adjustment is no lower than the increase

1. des Verbraucherpreisindexes für Deutschland oder
2. der Nettolöhne vergleichbarer Arbeitnehmergruppen des Unternehmens

im Prüfungszeitraum.

1. of the consumer price index for Germany or
2. the net wages of comparable employee groups of the company

during the period of the examination.

(3) Die Verpflichtung nach Absatz 1 entfällt wenn
1. der Arbeitgeber sich verpflichtet, die laufenden Leistungen jährlich um wenigstens eins vom Hundert anzupassen,
2. die betriebliche Altersversorgung über eine Direktversicherung im Sinne des § 1b Abs. 2 oder über eine Pensionskasse im Sinne des § 1b Abs. 3 durchgeführt wird, ab Rentenbeginn sämtliche auf den Rentenbestand entfallende Überschussanteile zur Erhöhung der laufenden Leistungen verwendet werden und zur Berechnung der garantierten Leistung der nach § 65 Abs. 1 Nr. 1 Buchstabe a des Versicherungsaufsichtsgesetzes festgesetzte Höchstzinssatz zur Berechnung der De-

(3) The obligation pursuant to subsection (1) shall not apply if
1. the employer obligates itself to adjust the ongoing benefits by at least one percent per year or
2. the company pension plan is carried out through a direct insurance within the meaning of section 1b (2) or a state pension fund within the meaning of section 1b (3), as of the onset of benefits all surpluses accruing to the bond holdings are used to increase the ongoing benefits, and in calculating the guaranteed benefit, the maximum interest rate set pursuant to section 65 (1) no. 1a of the Supervision of Private Insurance Companies Act to calculate the premium reserve is not exceeded or

ckungsrückstellung nicht überschritten wird oder

3. eine Beitragszusage mit Mindestleistung erteilt wurde; Absatz 5 findet insoweit keine Anwendung.

3. a pension commitment with a minimum payment has been issued; subsection (5) does not apply in this respect.

(4) ¹Sind laufende Leistungen nach Absatz 1 nicht oder nicht in vollem Umfang anzupassen (zu Recht unterbliebene Anpassung), ist der Arbeitgeber nicht verpflichtet, die Anpassung zu einem späteren Zeitpunkt nachzuholen. ²Eine Anpassung gilt als zu Recht unterblieben, wenn der Arbeitgeber dem Versorgungsempfänger die wirtschaftliche Lage des Unternehmens schriftlich dargelegt, der Versorgungsempfänger nicht binnen drei Kalendermonaten nach Zugang der Mitteilung schriftlich widersprochen hat und er auf die Rechtsfolgen eines nicht fristgemäßen Widerspruchs hingewiesen wurde.

(4) ¹If ongoing benefits pursuant to subsection subsection1 are not or not completely to be adjusted (an adjustment has been correctly foregone) the employer shall not be obligated to make up for it at a later date. ²An adjustment is deemed to have been correctly foregone if the employer represents the company's financial position to the beneficiary in writing, the beneficiary has not objected in writing within three calendar months of receiving the notification and he was informed on the legal consequences of failing to object in time.

(5) Soweit betriebliche Altersversorgung durch Entgeltumwandlung finanziert wird, ist der Arbeitgeber verpflichtet, die Leistungen mindestens entsprechend Absatz 3 Nr. 1 anzupassen oder im Falle der Durchführung über eine Direktversicherung oder eine Pensionskasse sämtliche Überschussanteile entsprechend Absatz 3 Nr. 2 zu verwenden.

(5) To the extent that the company pension plan is financed by conversion of remuneration, the employer shall be obligated to adjust the payments at least in accordance with subsection (3) no. 1 or, if it is executed through a direct insurance or a retirement fund, to use all surpluses pursuant to subsection 3 no. 2.

(6) Eine Verpflichtung zur Anpassung besteht nicht für monatliche Raten im Rahmen eines Auszahlungsplans sowie für Renten ab Vollendung des 85. Lebensjahres im Anschluss an einen Auszahlungsplan.

(6) There will be no obligation to adjust monthly installments within the scope of a payment plan or for pensions as of the age of 85 immediately following a payment plan.

Sechster Abschnitt
Geltungsbereich

Chapter 6
Scope of Application

§ 17
Persönlicher Geltungsbereich und Tariföffnungsklausel

Section 17
Applicable Personnel and Opening Clause in Collective Agreements

(1) ¹Arbeitnehmer im Sinne der §§ 1 bis 16 sind Arbeiter und Angestellte einschließlich der zu ihrer Berufsausbil-

(1) ¹Employees within the meaning of sections 1 to 16 are workers and white collar employees, including trainees; a

dung Beschäftigten; ein Berufsausbildungsverhältnis steht einem Arbeitsverhältnis gleich. ²Die §§ 1 bis 16 gelten entsprechend für Personen, die nicht Arbeitnehmer sind, wenn ihnen Leistungen der Alters-, Invaliditäts- oder Hinterbliebenenversorgung aus Anlass ihrer Tätigkeit für ein Unternehmen zugesagt worden sind. ³Arbeitnehmer im Sinne von § 1a Abs. 1 sind nur Personen nach den Sätzen 1 und 2, soweit sie aufgrund der Beschäftigung oder Tätigkeit bei dem Arbeitgeber, gegen den sich der Anspruch nach § 1a richten würde, in der gesetzlichen Rentenversicherung pflichtversichert sind.

(2) Die §§ 7 bis 15 gelten nicht für den Bund, die Länder, die Gemeinden sowie die Körperschaften, Stiftungen und Anstalten des öffentlichen Rechts, bei denen das Insolvenzverfahren nicht zulässig ist, und solche juristische Personen des öffentlichen Rechts, bei denen der Bund, ein Land oder eine Gemeinde kraft Gesetzes die Zahlungsfähigkeit sichert.

(3) ¹Von den §§ 1a, 2 bis 5, 16, 18a Satz 1, §§ 27 und 28 kann in Tarifverträgen abgewichen werden. ²Die abweichenden Bestimmungen haben zwischen nichttarifgebundenen Arbeitgebern und Arbeitnehmern Geltung, wenn zwischen diesen die Anwendung der einschlägigen tariflichen Regelung vereinbart ist. ³Im übrigen kann von den Bestimmungen dieses Gesetzes nicht zuungunsten des Arbeitnehmers abgewichen werden.

(4) Gesetzliche Regelungen über Leistungen der betrieblichen Altersversorgung werden unbeschadet des § 18 durch die §§ 1 bis 16 und 26 bis 30 nicht berührt.

(5) Soweit Entgeltansprüche auf einem Tarifvertrag beruhen, kann für diese eine Entgeltumwandlung nur vorgenommen werden, soweit dies durch Tarifvertrag vorgesehen oder durch Tarifvertrag zugelassen ist.

trainee position is equivalent to an employment relationship. ²Sections 1 to 16 apply *mutatis mutandis* to persons who are not employees if they were promised old age, invalidity or survivor's pension due to their activity for a company. ³Employees within the meaning of section 1a (1) are only those persons pursuant to sentences 1 and 2, to the extent that due to their work or activity for the employer against whom the claim pursuant to section 1a would be directed, they are covered by mandatory insurance in the statutory pension insurance.

(2) Sections 7 to 15 shall not apply with respect to the Federal Government, the Federal State Governments, the municipalities, as well as public law corporations, foundations and institutions for which insolvency proceedings are not permitted, and in addition those public law entities for which the Federal Government, a federal state or a municipality guaranties solvency by force of law.

(3) ¹Collective bargaining agreements may contain provisions differing from sections 1a, 2 to 5, 16, 18a sentence 1, sections 27 and 28. ²The provisions differing from these sections shall be valid between employers and employees who are not bound by such agreements if they agree that the relevant passages will apply. ³Otherwise, no variations may be made to the provisions in this Act which are to the employee's detriment.

(4) Notwithstanding section 18, statutory provisions on company pension plan benefits shall not be affected by sections 1 to 16 and 26 to 30.

(5) Where remuneration claims are based on a collective bargaining agreement, a conversion of remuneration may only be performed for them if so provided or permitted in the collective bargaining agreement.

§ 18
Sonderregelungen für den öffentlichen Dienst

(1) Für Personen, die

1. bei der Versorgungsanstalt des Bundes und der Länder (VBL) oder einer kommunalen oder kirchlichen Zusatzversorgungseinrichtung pflichtversichert sind, oder

2. bei einer anderen Zusatzversorgungseinrichtung pflichtversichert sind, die mit einer der Zusatzversorgungseinrichtungen nach Nummer 1 ein Überleitungsabkommen abgeschlossen hat oder aufgrund satzungsrechtlicher Vorschriften von Zusatzversorgungseinrichtungen nach Nummer 1 ein solches Abkommen abschließen kann, oder

3. unter das Gesetz über die zusätzliche Alters- und Hinterbliebenenversorgung für Angestellte und Arbeiter der Freien und Hansestadt Hamburg (Erstes Ruhegeldgesetz – 1. RGG), das Gesetz zur Neuregelung der zusätzlichen Alters- und Hinterbliebenenversorgung für Angestellte und Arbeiter der Freien und Hansestadt Hamburg (Zweites Ruhegeldgesetz – 2. RGG) oder unter das Bremische Ruhelohngesetz in ihren jeweiligen Fassungen fallen oder auf die diese Gesetze sonst Anwendung finden,

gelten die §§ 2, 5, 16, 27 und 28 nicht, soweit sich aus den nachfolgenden Regelungen nichts Abweichendes ergibt; § 4 gilt nicht, wenn die Anwartschaft oder die laufende Leistung ganz oder teilweise umlage- oder haushaltsfinanziert ist.

(2) Bei Eintritt des Versorgungsfalles erhalten die in Absatz 1 Nr. 1 und 2 bezeichneten Personen, deren Anwartschaft nach § 1b fortbesteht und deren Arbeitsverhältnis vor Eintritt des Versorgungsfalles geendet hat, von der Zusatzversorgungseinrichtung eine Zusatzrente nach folgenden Maßgaben:

Section 18
Special Rules for Public Service

(1) For persons who

1. are covered by mandatory insurance with the Federal and State Pension Office *(Versorgungsanstalt des Bundes und der Länder)* or a supplementary pension fund institution of a municipality or church, or

2. are covered by mandatory insurance with a supplementary pension fund institution which has concluded a transitional agreement with one of the supplementary pension fund institution pursuant to no. 1 or, under provisions in the bylaws of supplementary pension fund institutions pursuant to no. 1, may conclude such an agreement, or

3. fall under the Act on Supplemental Old-Age and Survivor's Pensions for Employees of the Free and Hanseatic City of Hamburg (First Pension Act *[Erstes Ruhegeldgesetz]* – 1. RGG), the Act to Newly Regulate the Supplemental Old-Age and Survivor's Pensions for Employees of the Free and Hanseatic City of Hamburg (Second Pension Act *[Zweites Ruhegeldgesetz]* – 2. RGG), or under the Bremen Retirement Pay Act in its current versions or for whom these acts are otherwise applicable,

sections 2, 5, 16, 27 and 28 shall not apply in as far as no derivation can be ensured from the following provisions; section 4 shall not apply if the expectancy or the ongoing benefit has been wholly or partly financed by unfunded pension plans or from a budget.

(2) Upon reaching pensionable age, the persons designated in subsection (1) nos. 1 and 2, whose expectancy pursuant to section 1b continues to exist and whose employment relationship ends before eligibility commences shall receive a supplementary pension from the supplemental pension fund subject to the following conditions:

1. Der monatliche Betrag der Zusatzrente beträgt für jedes Jahr der aufgrund des Arbeitsverhältnisses bestehenden Pflichtversicherung bei einer Zusatzversorgungseinrichtung 2,25 vom Hundert, höchstens jedoch 100 vom Hundert der Leistung, die bei dem höchstmöglichen Versorgungssatz zugestanden hätte (Voll-Leistung). Für die Berechnung der Voll-Leistung
   a) ist der Versicherungsfall der Regelaltersrente maßgebend,
   b) ist das Arbeitsentgelt maßgebend, das nach der Versorgungsregelung für die Leistungsbemessung maßgebend wäre, wenn im Zeitpunkt des Ausscheidens der Versicherungsfall im Sinne der Versorgungsregelung eingetreten wäre,
   c) finden § 2 Abs. 5 Satz 1 und § 2 Abs. 6 entsprechend Anwendung,
   d) ist im Rahmen einer Gesamtversorgung der im Falle einer Teilzeitbeschäftigung oder Beurlaubung nach der Versorgungsregelung für die gesamte Dauer des Arbeitsverhältnisses maßgebliche Beschäftigungsquotient nach der Versorgungsregelung als Beschäftigungsquotient auch für die übrige Zeit maßgebend,
   e) finden die Vorschriften der Versorgungsregelung über eine Mindestleistung keine Anwendung und
   f) ist eine anzurechnende Grundversorgung nach dem bei der Berechnung von Pensionsrückstellungen für die Berücksichtigung von Renten aus der gesetzlichen Rentenversicherung allgemein zulässigen Verfahren zu ermitteln. Hierbei ist das Arbeitsentgelt nach Buchstabe b zugrunde zu legen und – soweit während der Pflichtversicherung Teilzeitbeschäftigung bestand – diese nach Maßgabe der Versorgungsregelung zu berücksichtigen.

1. The sum of the monthly supplementary pension benefit shall, for each year of mandatory insurance with a supplemental pension fund due to the employment relationship amount to at least 2.25 percent, but nor more than 100 percent of the benefits that would have been payable at the highest possible benefit rate (full payment). In order to calculate the full payment
   a) the date of occurrence of the standard old-age pension shall be decisive,
   b) the remuneration for work that would have been decisive under the pension regulations for assessing benefits if at the time of ceasing to work the eligibility within the meaning of the pension regulations had commenced shall be decisive,
   c) section 2 (5) sentence 1 and section 2 (6) shall apply *mutatis mutandis*,
   d) within the scope of an overall pension, in the event of part-time work or leave of absence under the pension regulations the decisive employment quotient under the pension regulations for the entire duration of the employment relation is also decisive as the employment quotient for the remaining time,
   e) the provisions of the pension regulations shall not apply above a minimum benefit payment,
   f) a creditable basic pension shall be calculated in accordance with the generally permissible procedure for taking pensions from the statutory pension insurance into account when calculating pension reserves. Such calculation shall be based on the remuneration for work pursuant to b) above and – where part-time work was performed during the mandatory insurance period – this shall be taken into account pursuant to the pension regulations.

2. Die Zusatzrente vermindert sich um 0,3 vom Hundert für jeden vollen Kalendermonat, den der Versorgungsfall vor Vollendung des 65. Lebensjahres eintritt, höchstens jedoch um den in der Versorgungsregelung für die Voll-Leistung vorgesehenen Vomhundertsatz.
3. Übersteigt die Summe der Vomhundertsätze nach Nummer 1 aus unterschiedlichen Arbeitsverhältnissen 100, sind die einzelnen Leistungen im gleichen Verhältnis zu kürzen.
4. Die Zusatzrente muss monatlich mindestens den Betrag erreichen, der sich aufgrund des Arbeitsverhältnisses nach der Versorgungsregelung als Versicherungsrente aus den jeweils maßgeblichen Vomhundertsätzen der zusatzversorgungspflichtigen Entgelte oder der gezahlten Beiträge und Erhöhungsbeträge ergibt.
5. Die Vorschriften der Versorgungsregelung über das Erlöschen, das Ruhen und die Nichtleistung der Versorgungsrente gelten entsprechend. Soweit die Versorgungsregelung eine Mindestleistung in Ruhensfällen vorsieht, gilt dies nur, wenn die Mindestleistung der Leistung im Sinne der Nummer 4 entspricht.
6. Verstirbt die in Absatz 1 genannte Person, erhält eine Witwe oder ein Witwer 60 vom Hundert, eine Witwe oder ein Witwer im Sinne des § 46 Abs. 1 des Sechsten Buches Sozialgesetzbuch 42 vom Hundert, eine Halbwaise 12 vom Hundert und eine Vollwaise 20 vom Hundert der unter Berücksichtigung der in diesem Absatz genannten Maßgaben zu berechnenden Zusatzrente; die §§ 46, 48, 103 bis 105 des Sechsten Buches Sozialgesetzbuch sind entsprechend anzuwenden. ²Die Leistungen an mehrere Hinterbliebene dürfen den Betrag der Zusatzrente nicht übersteigen; gegebenenfalls sind die Leistungen im gleichen Verhältnis zu kürzen.

2. The supplemental pension shall be reduced by 0.3 percent for each full calendar month in which the beneficiary becomes eligible before reaching the age of 65, but at most by the percentage stipulated in the pension regulations for full payments.
3. If the sum of the percentages pursuant to number 1 from various employment relationships exceeds 100, the individual payments shall be reduced in the same proportion.
4. The supplemental pension payment each month shall amount to at least the sum calculated on the basis of the employment relationship under the provision regulations as pension insurance from the respective decisive percentages of the remuneration which is mandatory for supplemental pension fund or the paid sums and amounts of increases.
5. The provisions of the pension regulations on the cancellation, suspension and non-payment of the pension benefits shall apply *mutatis mutandis*. Where the pension regulations provide for a minimum payment in case of suspension, this shall only apply if such minimum payment corresponds to payment within the meaning of number 4.
6. Should the person designated in subsection (1) die, his widow or her widower shall receive 60 percent, a widow or widower within the meaning of section 46 (1) of the Sixth Book of the Social Security Code shall receive 42 percent, a child who has lost one parent shall receive 12 percent and an orphan shall receive 20 percent of the supplemental pension to be calculated taking the provisions in this subsection into account; sections 46, 48, 103 to 105 of the Sixth Book of the Social Security Code shall be applied *mutatis mutandis*. The payments to two or more surviving dependents may not exceed the amount of the supplemental pension; if appropriate, the payments shall be reduced in the same proportion.

7. Versorgungsfall ist der Versicherungsfall im Sinne der Versorgungsregelung.	7. Pensionable status is the insured event within the meaning of the pension provisions.
(3) Personen, auf die bis zur Beendigung ihre Arbeitsverhältnisses die Regelungen des Ersten Ruhegeldgesetzes, des Zweiten Ruhegeldgesetzes oder des Bremischen Ruhelohngesetzes in ihren jeweiligen Fassungen Anwendung gefunden haben, haben Anspruch gegenüber ihrem ehemaligen Arbeitgeber auf Leistungen in sinngemäßer Anwendung des Absatzes 2 mit Ausnahme von Absatz 2 Nr. 3 und 4 sowie Nr. 5 Satz 2; bei Anwendung des Zweiten Ruhegeldgesetzes bestimmt sich der monatliche Betrag der Zusatzrente abweichend von Absatz 2 nach der nach dem Zweiten Ruhegeldgesetz maßgebenden Berechnungsweise.	(3) Persons to whom the provisions in the First Pension Act, the Second Pension Act or the Bremen Retirement Pay Act in their respective valid versions apply shall have a claim against their former employer for payments corresponding to subsection (2) with the exception of subsection (2) nos. 3 and 4 as well as no. 5 sentence 2; where the Second Pension Act applies, the monthly amount of the supplementary pension shall, notwithstanding subsection (2), be calculated pursuant to the Second Pension Act.
(4) Die Leistungen nach den Absätzen 2 und 3 werden, mit Ausnahme der Leistungen nach Absatz 2 Nr. 4, jährlich zum 1. Juli um 1 vom Hundert erhöht, soweit in diesem Jahr eine allgemeine Erhöhung der Versorgungsrenten erfolgt.	(4) The payments pursuant to subsections (2) and (3) shall, with the exception of payments pursuant to subsection (2) no. 4, be increased on 1 July of each year by one percent, where in that year a general increase of pension payments occurs.
(5) Besteht der Eintritt des Versorgungsfalles neben dem Anspruch auf Zusatzrente oder auf die in Absatz 3 oder Absatz 7 bezeichneten Leistungen auch Anspruch auf eine Versorgungsrente oder Versicherungsrente der in Absatz 1 Satz 1 Nr. 1 und 2 bezeichneten Zusatzversorgungseinrichtungen oder Anspruch auf entsprechende Versorgungsleistungen der Versorgungsanstalt der deutschen Kulturorchester oder der Versorgungsanstalt der deutschen Bühnen oder nach den Regelungen des Ersten Ruhegeldgesetzes, des Zweiten Ruhegeldgesetzes oder des Bremischen Ruhelohngesetzes, in deren Berechnung auch die der Zusatzrente zugrunde liegenden Zeiten berücksichtigt sind, ist nur die im Zahlbetrag höhere Rente zu leisten.	(5) If, the pensionable status is achieved along with the claim to supplemental pension or the benefits set forth in subsection (3) or (7), there is also a claim to pension payments from the supplementary pension funds designated in subsection (1) sentence 1 nos. 1 and 2 or claim to corresponding payments from the pension fund of the German *Kulturorchester* or the pension fund of the German Theater or pursuant to the provisions of First Pension Act, the Second Pension Act or the Bremen Retirement Pay Act, the calculation of which shall also take into account the time periods on which the supplemental pension is based, only the pension with the highest amount shall be paid out.
(6) Eine Anwartschaft auf Zusatzrente nach Absatz 2 oder auf Leistungen nach Absatz 3 kann bei Übertritt der anwart-	(6) If a person holding expectancies to future supplemental pension pursuant to subsection (2) or to payments pursu-

schaftsberechtigten Person in ein Versorgungssystem einer überstaatlichen Einrichtung in das Versorgungssystem dieser Einrichtung übertragen werden, wenn ein entsprechendes Abkommen zwischen der Zusatzversorgungseinrichtung oder der Freien und Hansestadt Hamburg oder der Freien Hansestadt Bremen und der überstaatlichen Einrichtung besteht.

(7) [1] Für Personen, die bei der Versorgungsanstalt der deutschen Kulturorchester oder der Versorgungsanstalt der deutschen Bühnen pflichtversichert sind, gelten die §§ 2 bis 5, 16, 27 und 28 nicht. [2] Bei Eintritt des Versorgungsfalles treten an die Stelle der Zusatzrente und der Leistungen an Hinterbliebene nach Absatz 2 und an die Stelle der Regelung in Absatz 4 die satzungsgemäß vorgesehenen Leistungen; Absatz 2 Nr. 5 findet entsprechend Anwendung. [3] Die Höhe der Leistungen kann nach dem Ausscheiden aus dem Beschäftigungsverhältnis nicht mehr geändert werden. [4] Als pflichtversichert gelten auch die freiwillig Versicherten der Versorgungsanstalt der deutschen Kulturorchester und der Versorgungsanstalt der deutschen Bühnen.

(8) Gegen Entscheidungen der Zusatzversorgungseinrichtungen über Ansprüche nach diesem Gesetz ist der Rechtsweg gegeben, der für Versicherte der Einrichtung gilt.

(9) Bei Personen, die aus einem Arbeitsverhältnis ausscheiden, in dem sie nach § 5 Abs. 1 Satz 1 Nr. 2 des Sechsten Buches Sozialgesetzbuch versicherungsfrei waren, dürfen die Ansprüche nach § 2 Abs. 1 Satz 1 und 2 nicht hinter dem Rentenanspruch zurückbleiben, der sich ergeben hätte, wenn der Arbeitnehmer für die Zeit der versicherungsfreien Beschäftigung in der gesetzlichen Rentenversicherung nachversichert worden wäre; die Vergleichsberechnung ist im Versorgungsfall aufgrund einer Auskunft der Deutschen Rentenversicherung Bund vorzunehmen.

ant to subsection (3) transfers to the pension system of a supranational agency, such expectancies may be transferred to the pension system of such agency if a corresponding agreement has been reached between the supplemental pension fund or the Free and Hanseatic City of Hamburg or the Free and Hanseatic City of Bremen and such supranational agency.

(7) [1] For persons covered by the mandatory insurance of the pension fund of the German *Kulturorchester* or the pension fund of the German Theater, sections 2 to 5, 16, 27 and 28 shall not apply. [2] Upon reaching pensionable status the benefits provided in the bylaws shall replace the supplemental pension and the survivors' benefits pursuant to subsection (2) and the provision in subsection (4); subsection (2) no. 5 shall apply *mutatis mutandis*. [3] The amount of the payments may not be changed once the beneficiary's employment relationship comes to an end. [4] The holders of voluntary insurance in the pension fund of the German *Kulturorchester* or the pension fund of the German Theater shall also be deemed to be covered by mandatory insurance.

(8) Appeals against decisions made by the supplemental pension funds on claims under this Act may be judicially pursued in the manner applicable for persons insured by the fund.

(9) For persons who leave an employment relationship in which they were exempt from the compulsory insurance pursuant to section 5 (1) sentence 1 no. 2 of the Sixth Book of the Social Security Code, the claims pursuant to section 2 (1) sentences 1 and 2 may not amount to less than the pension claim they would have had if the employee had been insured with the statutory pension insurance for the time of the employment in which he had been exempted from insurance; the comparative calculation shall be performed in the event of the pensionable status be-

ing reached on the basis of information provided by the German Pension Insurance Federal Institution *(Deutschen Rentenversicherung Bund)*.

§ 18 a
Verjährung

¹Der Anspruch auf Leistungen aus der betrieblichen Altersversorgung verjährt in 30 Jahren. ²Ansprüche auf regelmäßig wiederkehrende Leistungen unterliegen der regelmäßigen Verjährungsfrist nach den Vorschriften des Bürgerlichen Gesetzbuchs.

Section 18 a
Statute of Limitations

¹The statute of limitations for claims to benefits from company pension plans shall be 30 years. ²Claims for regularly recurring benefits are subject to the regular statute of limitations pursuant to the provisions of the German Civil Code *(Bürgerliches Gesetzbuch)*.

Zweiter Teil
Steuerrechtliche Vorschriften

§§ 19–24
(Änderungsvorschriften – hier nicht enthalten)

§ 25
(Aufhebungsvorschrift – hier nicht enthalten)

Part 2
Tax Provisions

Sections 19–24
(Amending provisions – not contained herein)

Section 24
(Repealing provision – not contained hierin)

Dritter Teil
Übergangs- und Schlussvorschriften

§ 26
Ausschluss der Rückwirkung

Die §§ 1 bis 4 und 18 gelten nicht, wenn das Arbeitsverhältnis oder Dienstverhältnis vor dem Inkrafttreten des Gesetzes beendet worden ist.

Part 3
Transitional and Final Provisions

Section 26
Exclusion of retroactive effect

Sections 1 to 4 and 18 shall not apply if the employment or service relationship ends before this Act comes into effect.

§ 27
Direktversicherungen und Pensionskassen

§ 2 Abs. 2 Satz 2 Nr. 2 und 3 und Abs. 3 Satz 2 Nr. 1 und 2 gelten in Fällen, in denen vor dem Inkrafttreten des Gesetzes die Direktversicherung abgeschlossen worden ist oder die Versicherung des Ar-

Section 27
Direct Insurances and Pension Funds

Section 2 (2) sentence 2 nos. 2 and 3 and (3) sentence 2 nos. 1 and 2 shall apply in cases in which a direct insurance was entered into or the employee's insurance with a pension fund began before

beitnehmers bei einer Pensionskasse begonnen hat, mit der Maßgabe, dass die in diesen Vorschriften genannten Voraussetzungen spätestens für die Zeit nach Ablauf eines Jahres seit dem Inkrafttreten des Gesetzes erfüllt sein müssen.

this Act went into effect, subject to the proviso that the prerequisites set forth in these provisions must be fulfilled at the latest for the period following the expiration of one year after this Act enters into force.

§ 28
Auszehrungs- und Anrechnungsverbot

§ 5 gilt für Fälle, in denen der Versorgungsfall vor dem Inkrafttreten des Gesetzes eingetreten ist, mit der Maßgabe, dass diese Vorschrift bei der Berechnung der nach dem Inkrafttreten des Gesetzes fällig werdenden Versorgungsleistungen anzuwenden ist.

Section 28
Prohibition of Depletion and Set-off

Section 5 shall apply to cases in which the pensionable status is reached prior to the coming into force of this Act, subject to the proviso that this clause is applied when calculating the pension benefits that become payable after this Act enters into force.

§ 29
Vorzeitige Altersleistungen

§ 6 gilt für die Fälle, in denen das Altersruhegeld der gesetzlichen Rentenversicherung bereits vor dem Inkrafttreten des Gesetzes in Anspruch genommen worden ist, mit der Maßgabe, dass die Leistungen der betrieblichen Altersversorgung vom Inkrafttreten des Gesetzes an zu gewähren sind.

Section 29
Premature old Age Benefits

Section 6 shall apply to cases in which the old age pension benefits paid from the statutory pension insurance have been claimed before this Act enters into force, subject to the proviso that the company pension plan benefits must be granted from the time this Act comes into force on.

§ 30
Erstmalige Beitrags- und Leistungspflicht bei Insolvenzversicherung

[1]Ein Anspruch gegen den Träger der Insolvenzsicherung nach § 7 besteht nur, wenn der Sicherungsfall nach dem Inkrafttreten der §§ 7 bis 15 eingetreten ist; er kann erstmals nach dem Ablauf von sechs Monaten nach diesem Zeitpunkt geltend gemacht werden. [2]Die Beitragspflicht des Arbeitgebers beginnt mit dem Inkrafttreten der §§ 7 bis 15.

Section 30
First-Time Contribution and Payment Obligation for Insolvency Insurance

[1]A claim against the insolvency insurance carrier pursuant to section 7 shall only exist if the insolvency occurred after sections 7 to 15 entered into force; such a claim may be asserted for the first time six months after this time. [2]The employer's duty to pay premiums commences with the coming into force of sections 7 to 15.

§ 30 a
Leistungen der betrieblichen Altersversorgung

(1) [1]Männlichen Arbeitnehmern,
1. die vor dem 1. Januar 1952 geboren sind,

Section 30 a
Benefits from the Company Pension Plan

(1) [1]Male employees
1. who were born before 1 January 1952,

2. die das 60. Lebensjahr vollendet haben,
3. die nach Vollendung des 40. Lebensjahres mehr als 10 Jahre Pflichtbeiträge für eine in der gesetzlichen Rentenversicherung versicherte Beschäftigung oder Tätigkeit nach den Vorschriften des Sechsten Buches Sozialgesetzbuch haben,
4. die die Wartezeit von 15 Jahren in der gesetzlichen Rentenversicherung erfüllt haben und
5. deren Arbeitsentgelt oder Arbeitseinkommen die Hinzuverdienstgrenze nach § 34 Abs. 3 Nr. 1 des Sechsten Buches Sozialgesetzbuch nicht überschreitet,

sind auf deren Verlangen nach Erfüllung der Wartezeit und sonstiger Leistungsvoraussetzungen der Versorgungsregelung für nach dem 17. Mai 1990 zurückgelegte Beschäftigungszeiten Leistungen der betrieblichen Altersversorgung zu gewähren. ²§ 6 Satz 3 gilt entsprechend.

(2) Haben der Arbeitnehmer oder seine anspruchsberechtigten Angehörigen vor dem 17. Mai 1990 gegen die Versagung der Leistungen der betrieblichen Altersversorgung Rechtsmittel eingelegt, ist Absatz 1 für Beschäftigungszeiten nach dem 8. April 1976 anzuwenden.

(3) Die Vorschriften des Bürgerlichen Gesetzbuchs über die Verjährung von Ansprüchen aus dem Arbeitsverhältnis bleiben unberührt.

2. who have reached the age of 60,
3. who, upon reaching the age of 40 have more than ten years of mandatory premiums for an employment insured by the statutory pension insurance or activities pursuant to the provisions of the Sixth Book of the Social Security Code,
4. who have fulfilled the waiting period of 15 years in the statutory pension insurance
5. whose remuneration or income for their work does not exceed the supplementary earnings ceiling set forth in section 43 (3) no. 1 of the Sixth Book of the Social Security Code

shall, at their request, upon fulfilling the waiting period and other prerequisites for benefits set forth in the pension regulations for employment periods after 17 May 1990 shall be granted company pension plan benefits. ²Section 6 sentence 3 applies *mutatis mutandis*.

(2) If the employee or his entitled dependents have appealed a denial of company pension plan benefits prior to 17 May 1990, subsection (1) shall be applied to employment periods after 8 April 1976.

(3) The provisions of the German Civil Code on the statute of limitations of claims arising from employment relationships shall remain unchanged.

§ 30 b
Anwendbarkeit § 4 Abs. 3

§ 4 Abs. 3 gilt nur für Zusagen, die nach dem 31. Dezember 2004 erteilt wurden.

Section 30 b
Applicability of Section 4 (3)

Section 4 (3) shall only apply to commitments rendered after 31 December 2004.

§ 30 c
Anwendbarkeit des § 16 Abs. 3 Nr. 1

(1) § 16 Abs. 3 Nr. 1 gilt nur für laufende Leistungen, die auf Zusagen beru-

Section 30 c
Applicability of Section 16 (3) no. 1

(1) Section 16 (3) no. 1 applies only to ongoing benefits based on commit-

hen, die nach dem 31. Dezember 1998 erteilt werden.

(2) § 16 Abs. 4 gilt nicht für vor dem 1. Januar 1999 zu Recht unterbliebene Anpassungen.

(3) § 16 Abs. 5 gilt nur für laufende Leistungen, die auf Zusagen beruhen, die nach dem 31. Dezember 2000 erteilt werden.

(4) Für die Erfüllung der Anpassungsprüfungspflicht für Zeiträume vor dem 1. Januar 2003 gilt § 16 Abs. 2 Nr. 1 mit der Maßgabe, dass an die Stelle des Verbraucherpreisindexes für Deutschland der Preisindex für die Lebenshaltung von 4-Personen-Haushalten von Arbeitern und Angestellten mit mittlerem Einkommen tritt.

§ 30 d
Übergangsregelung zu § 18

(1) ¹Ist der Versorgungsfall vor dem 1. Januar 2001 eingetreten oder ist der Arbeitnehmer vor dem 1. Januar 2001 aus dem Beschäftigungsverhältnis bei einem öffentlichen Arbeitgeber ausgeschieden und der Versorgungsfall nach dem 31. Dezember 2000 eingetreten, sind für die Berechnung der Voll-Leistung die Regelungen der Zusatzversorgungseinrichtungen nach § 18 Abs. 1 Satz 1 Nr. 1 und 2 oder die Gesetze im Sinne des § 18 Abs. 1 Satz 1 Nr. 3 sowie die weiteren Berechnungsfaktoren jeweils in der am 31. Dezember 2000 geltenden Fassung maßgebend; § 18 Abs. 2 Nr. 1 Buchstabe b bleibt unberührt. ²Die Steuerklasse III/O ist zugrunde zu legen. ³Ist der Versorgungsfall vor dem 1. Januar 2001 eingetreten, besteht der Anspruch auf Zusatzrente mindestens in der Höhe, wie er sich aus § 18 in der Fassung vom 16. Dezember 1997 (BGBl. I S. 2998) ergibt.

(2) Die Anwendung des § 18 ist in den Fällen des Absatzes 1 ausgeschlossen, soweit eine Versorgungsrente der in § 18 Abs. 1 Satz 1 Nr. 1 und 2 bezeichneten Zusatzversorgungseinrichtungen

ments made after 31 December 1998.

(2) Section 16 (4) does not apply to adjustments which were correctly foregone prior to 1 January 1999.

(3) Section 16 (5) applies only to ongoing benefits based on commitments made after 31 December 2000.

(4) With respect to the fulfilment of the adjustment examination duty for periods prior to 1 January 2003, section 16 (2) no. 1 shall apply subject to the proviso that the consumer price index for Germany shall be replaced by the price index for four-person households of mid-income workers and white collar employees.

Section 30 d
Transitional Provision on section 18

(1) ¹If pensionable status is reached before 1 January 2001 or if the employee left his employment with a public employer before 1 January 2001 and eligibility occurred after 31 December 2000, the provisions of the supplementary pension fund pursuant to section 18 (1) sentence 1 nos. 1 and 2 or the statutes set forth in section 18 (1) sentence 1 no. 3, as well as the other calculation factors respectively, shall be decisive for the calculation of the full payment in the version applicable on 31 December 2000; section 18 (2) no. 1b remains unaffected. ²The tax classification III/O shall be used as a basis. ³If pensionable status is reached before 1 January 2001, a claim for supplemental pension shall exist at least in the amount resulting from section 18 in the version of 16 December 1997 (Federal Law Gazette I p. 2998).

(2) The application of section 18 shall be excluded in the cases set forth in subsection (1), where a pension from one of the supplementary pension funds designated in section 18 (1) sentence 1

oder eine entsprechende Leistung aufgrund der Regelungen des Ersten Ruhegeldgesetzes, des Zweiten Ruhegeldgesetzes oder des Bremischen Ruhelohngesetzes bezogen wird, oder eine Versicherungsrente abgefunden wurde.

(3) ¹Für Arbeitnehmer im Sinne des § 18 Abs. 1 Satz 1 Nr. 4, 5 und 6 in der bis zum 31. Dezember 1998 geltenden Fassung, für die bis zum 31. Dezember 1998 ein Anspruch auf Nachversicherung nach § 18 Abs. 6 entstanden ist, gilt Absatz 1 Satz 1 für die aufgrund der Nachversicherung zu ermittelnde Voll-Leistung entsprechend mit der Maßgabe, dass sich der nach § 2 zu ermittelnde Anspruch gegen den ehemaligen Arbeitgeber richtet. ²Für den nach § 2 zu ermittelnden Anspruch gilt § 18 Abs. 2 Nr. 1 Buchstabe b entsprechend; für die übrigen Bemessungsfaktoren ist auf die Rechtslage am 31. Dezember 2000 abzustellen. ³Leistungen der gesetzlichen Rentenversicherung, die auf einer Nachversicherung wegen Ausscheidens aus einem Dienstordnungsverhältnis beruhen, und Leistungen, die die zuständige Versorgungseinrichtung aufgrund von Nachversicherungen im Sinne des § 18 Abs. 6 in der am 31. Dezember 1998 geltenden Fassung gewährt, werden auf den Anspruch nach § 2 angerechnet. ⁴Hat das Arbeitsverhältnis im Sinne des § 18 Abs. 9 bereits am 31. Dezember 1998 bestanden, ist in die Vergleichsberechnung nach § 18 Abs. 9 auch die Zusatzrente nach § 18 in der bis zum 31. Dezember 1998 geltenden Fassung einzubeziehen.

nos. 1 and 2 or a corresponding benefit on the basis of the First Pension Act, the Second Pension Act or the Bremen Retirement Pay Act is received or an insurance pension has been compensated.

(3) ¹For employees within the meaning of section 18 (1) sentence 1 nos. 4, 5 and 6 in the version valid up to 31 December 1998, for whom a claim for collateral insurance pursuant to section 18 (6) has been created, subsection (1) sentence 1 shall apply *mutatis mutandis* for the full payment to be calculated on the basis of the collateral insurance, subject to the proviso that the claim to be calculated pursuant to section 2 is directed against the former employer. ²For the claim to be calculated pursuant to section 2, section 18 (2) no. 1b applies *mutatis mutandis*; for the remaining calculation factors, the position of the law on 31 December 2000 shall be used as a basis. ³Benefits from the statutory pension insurance which are based on a collateral insurance due to the employee's retirement from a public employment and benefits which the competent pension funds render on the basis of a collateral reinsurance within the meaning of section 18 (6) in the version valid on 31 December 1998 shall be set off against the claim pursuant to section 2. ⁴If the employment relationship within the meaning of section 18 (9) had already commenced on 31 December 1998, the supplementary pension pursuant to section 18 of the version valid until 31 December 1998 shall be included in the settlement calculation pursuant to section 18 (9).

§ 30 e
Anwendungsbereich des § 1 Abs. 2 Nr. 4

(1) § 1 Abs. 2 Nr. 4 zweiter Halbsatz gilt für Zusagen, die nach dem 31. Dezember 2002 erteilt werden.

(2) ¹§ 1 Abs. 2 Nr. 4 zweiter Halbsatz findet auf Pensionskassen, deren Leis-

Section 30 e
Scope of Application of section 12 no. 4

(1) Section 1 (2) no. 4 second half-sentence shall apply for commitments rendered after 31 December 2002.

(2) ¹Section 1 (2) no. 4 second half-sentence shall apply to staff pension

tungen der betrieblichen Altersversorgung durch Beiträge der Arbeitnehmer und Arbeitgeber gemeinsam finanziert und die als beitragsorientierte Leistungszusage oder als Leistungszusage durchgeführt werden, mit der Maßgabe Anwendung, dass dem ausgeschiedenen Arbeitnehmer das Recht zur Fortführung mit eigenen Beiträgen nicht eingeräumt werden und eine Überschussverwendung gemäß § 1b Abs. 5 Nr. 1 nicht erfolgen muss. ²Wird dem ausgeschiedenen Arbeitnehmer ein Recht zur Fortführung nicht eingeräumt, gilt für die Höhe der unverfallbaren Anwartschaft § 2 Abs. 5a entsprechend. ³Für die Anpassung laufender Leistungen gelten die Regelungen nach § 16 Abs. 1 bis 4. Die Regelung in Absatz 1 bleibt unberührt.

funds whose company pension plan benefits are jointly financed by contributions of the employees and the employer and are administered as contribution-based payment commitments or as payment commitments, subject to the proviso that the former employee shall not be granted the right to continue them with his own contributions and the surplus need not be used pursuant to section 1b (5) no. 1. ²If the former employee is not granted a right to continue them, section 2 (5a) shall apply for the amount of the vested expectancy *mutatis mutandis*. ³For the adjustment of ongoing benefits, the provisions set forth in Section 16 (1) to (4) shall apply. The provision in subsection (1) remains unaffected.

§ 30f
Unverfallbare Anwartschaft

(1) ¹Wenn Leistungen der betrieblichen Altersversorgung vor dem 1. Januar 2001 zugesagt worden sind, ist § 1b Abs. 1 mit der Maßgabe anzuwenden, dass die Anwartschaft erhalten bleibt, wenn das Arbeitsverhältnis vor Eintritt des Versorgungsfalles, jedoch nach Vollendung des 35. Lebensjahres endet und die Versorgungszusage zu diesem Zeitpunkt

1. mindestens zehn Jahre oder
2. bei mindestens zwölfjähriger Betriebszugehörigkeit mindestens drei Jahre

bestanden hat; in diesen Fällen bleibt die Anwartschaft auch erhalten, wenn die Zusage ab dem 1. Januar 2001 fünf Jahre bestanden hat und bei Beendigung des Arbeitsverhältnisses das 30. Lebensjahr vollendet ist. ²§ 1b Abs. 5 findet für Anwartschaften aus diesen Zusagen keine Anwendung.

(2) Wenn Leistungen der betrieblichen Altersversorgung vor dem 1. Januar 2009 und nach dem 31. Dezember 2000 zugesagt worden sind, ist § 1b Abs. 1 Satz 1 mit der Maßgabe anzuwenden,

Section 30f
Vested Expectancy

(1) ¹If company pension plan benefits were promised before 1 January 2001, section 1b (1) shall apply with the proviso that the expectancy will be retained if the employment relationship ends before the employee reaches pensionable status, but after the employee reaches the age of 35 and the pension plan commitment had at that time existed for

1. at least ten years or
2. where length of service is not less than twelve years, at least three years;

in these cases the expectancy shall also be retained if the commitment has existed for five years as of 1 January 2001 and the employee has reached the age of 30 by the time the employment relationship comes to an end. ²Section 1b (5) shall not apply to expectancies based on such commitments.

(2) ¹If company pension plan benefits were promised before 1 January 2009 and after 31 December 2000, section 1b (1) sentence 1 shall apply with the proviso that the expectancy will be re-

dass die Anwartschaft erhalten bleibt, wenn das Arbeitsverhältnis vor Eintritt des Versorgungsfalls, jedoch nach Vollendung des 30. Lebensjahres endet und die Versorgungszusage zu diesem Zeitpunkt fünf Jahre bestanden hat; in diesen Fällen bleibt die Anwartschaft auch erhalten, wenn die Zusage ab dem 1. Januar 2009 fünf Jahre bestanden hat und bei Beendigung des Arbeitsverhältnisses das 25. Lebensjahr vollendet ist.

tained if the employment relationship ends before the employee reaches pensionable status, but after the employee reaches the age of 30 and the pension plan commitment had at that time existed for five years; in such cases the expectancy shall also be retained if the commitment has existed for five years as of 1 January 2009 and the employee has reached the age of 25 by the time the employment relationship comes to an end.

§ 30 g
Anwendbarkeit des § 2 Abs. 5 a

(1) [1]§ 2 Abs. 5a gilt nur für Anwartschaften, die auf Zusagen beruhen, die nach dem 31. Dezember 2000 erteilt worden sind. [2]Im Einvernehmen zwischen Arbeitgeber und Arbeitnehmer kann § 2 Abs. 5a auch auf Anwartschaften angewendet werden, die auf Zusagen beruhen, die vor dem 1. Januar 2001 erteilt worden sind.

(2) § 3 findet keine Anwendung auf laufende Leistungen, die vor dem 1. Januar 2005 erstmals gezahlt worden sind.

Section 30 g
Applicability of section 2 (5 a)

(1) [1]Section 2 (5a) applies only to expectancies based on commitments granted after 31 December 2000. [2]By mutual agreement of the employer and the employee, section 2 (5a) may also be applied to expectancies based on commitments granted before 1 January 2001.

(2) Section 3 shall not apply to ongoing benefits which were paid for the first time before 1 January 2005.

§ 30 h
Entgeltumwandlungen nach dem 19. 6. 2001

§ 17 Abs. 5 gilt für Entgeltumwandlungen, die auf Zusagen beruhen, die nach dem 29. Juni 2001 erteilt werden.

Section 30 h
Remuneration Conversions after 19 June 2001

Section 17 (5) shall apply to remuneration conversions based on commitments granted after 29 June 2001.

§ 30 i
Insolvenzsicherung

(1) [1]Der Barwert der bis zum 31. Dezember 2005 aufgrund eingetretener Insolvenzen zu sichernden Anwartschaften wird einmalig auf die beitragspflichtigen Arbeitgeber entsprechend § 10 Abs. 3 umgelegt und vom Träger der Insolvenzsicherung nach Maßgabe der Beträge zum Schluss des Wirtschaftsjahres, das im Jahr 2004 geendet hat, erhoben. [2]Der Rechnungs-

Section 30 i
Insolvency insurance

(1) [1]The cash value of the expectancies to be secured due to insolvencies up to 31 December 2005 shall be apportioned one time to the employer obligated to pay premiums pursuant to section 10 (3) and imposed by the carrier of the insolvency insurance in accordance with the sums at the end of the economic year that ended in the year 2004. [2]The discount to be used in

zinsfuss bei der Berechnung des Barwerts beträgt 3,67 vom Hundert.

(2) [1]Der Betrag ist in 15 gleichen Raten fällig. [2]Die erste Rate wird am 31. März 2007 fällig, die weiteren zum 31. März der folgenden Kalenderjahre. [3]Bei vorfälliger Zahlung erfolgt eine Diskontierung der einzelnen Jahresraten mit dem zum Zeitpunkt der Zahlung um ein Drittel erhöhten Rechnungszinsfuss nach § 65 des Versicherungsaufsichtsgesetzes, wobei nur volle Monate berücksichtigt werden.

(3) Der abgezinste Gesamtbetrag ist gemäß Absatz 2 am 31. März 2007 fällig, wenn die sich ergebende Jahresrate nicht höher als 50 Euro ist.

(4) Insolvenzbedingte Zahlungsausfälle von ausstehenden Raten werden im Jahr der Insolvenz in die erforderlichen jährlichen Beiträge gemäß § 10 Abs. 2 eingerechnet.

§ 31
Sicherungsfälle vor dem 1. 1. 1999

Auf Sicherungsfälle, die vor dem 1. Januar 1999 eingetreten sind, ist dieses Gesetz in der bis zu diesem Zeitpunkt geltenden Fassung anzuwenden.

§ 32
Inkrafttreten

[1]Dieses Gesetz tritt vorbehaltlich des Satzes 2 am Tag nach seiner Verkündung in Kraft. [2]Die §§ 7 bis 15 treten am 1. Januar 1975 in Kraft.

calculating the cash value shall be 3.67 percent.

(2) [1]The sum shall be payable in 15 equal instalments. [2]The first installment shall fall due on 31 March 2007, the others on 31 March of the following calendar years. [3]In case of a premature payment, the individual annual rates shall be discounted by the discount rate pursuant to the Insurance Supervisory Act *(Versicherungsaufsichtsgesetz)* at the time of the payment increased by one-third, whereby only full months shall be taken into account.

(3) The reduced total sum shall be payable pursuant to subsection (2) on 31 March 2007 if the annual instalment so calculated is no more than 50 euro.

(4) Cessations of payment of outstanding installments due to insolvency shall be calculated into the required annual sums pursuant to section 10 (2) in the year of the insolvency.

Section 31
Insolvency Prior to 1 January 1999

If an insolvency arises prior to 1 January 1999, this Act shall be applied in the version valid up to that point.

Section 31
Entry into Force

[1]This Act shall, subject to sentence 2, enter into force on the day following its promulgation. [2]Sections 7 to 15 shall enter into effect on 1 January 1975.

VIII. Commercial Code (Handelsgesetzbuch – HGB)

of 10 May 1897 (Federal Law Gazette I, p. 219)

in the amended version of 31 July 2009

(excerpts)

§ 74
Vertragliches Wettbewerbverbot

(1) Eine Vereinbarung zwischen dem Prinzipal und dem Handlungsgehilfen, die den Gehilfen für die Zeit nach Beendigung des Dienstverhältnisses in seiner gewerblichen Tätigkeit beschränkt (Wettbewerbsverbot), bedarf der Schriftform und der Aushändigung einer vom Prinzipal unterzeichneten, die vereinbarten Bestimmungen enthaltenden Urkunde an den Gehilfen.

(2) Das Wettbewerbsverbot ist nur verbindlich, wenn sich der Prinzipal verpflichtet, für die Dauer des Verbots eine Entschädigung zu zahlen, die für jedes Jahr des Verbots mindestens die Hälfte der von dem Handlungsgehilfen zuletzt bezogenen vertragsmäßigen Leistungen erreicht.

§ 74 a
Unverbindliches Verbot

(1) [1] Das Wettbewerbsverbot ist insoweit unverbindlich, als es nicht zum Schutz eines berechtigten geschäftlichen Interesses des Prinzipals dient. [2] Es ist ferner unverbindlich, soweit es unter Berücksichtigung der gewährten Entschädigung nach Ort, Zeit oder Gegenstand eine unbillige Erschwerung des Fortkommens des Gehilfen enthält. [3] Das Verbot kann nicht auf einen Zeitraum von mehr als zwei Jahren von der

Section 74
Contractual Prohibition of Competition

(1) An agreement between the principal and the dependent commercial employee which restricts the commercial employee in his business activity during the period following termination of the employment relationship (prohibition of competition) must be made in writing, and a copy of the document signed by the principal and containing the agreed conditions must be provided to the commercial employee.

(2) The prohibition of competition shall only be binding if the principal is obligated, for the term of the prohibition, to pay compensation equal to at least one-half of the most recent contractual remuneration received by the commercial employee for each year of the prohibition.

Section 74 a
Non-Binding or Void Prohibition of Competition

(1) [1] The prohibition of competition is non-binding insofar as it does not serve to protect a legitimate business interest of the principal. [2] Furthermore, it is non-binding insofar as, taking the compensation granted into account, it constitutes unreasonable interference with the commercial employee's career, with respect to the place, time or subject matter. [3] The prohibition cannot be extended beyond a period of two years

Beendigung des Dienstverhältnisses an erstreckt werden.

(2) ¹Das Verbot ist nichtig, wenn der Gehilfe zur Zeit des Abschlusses minderjährig ist oder wenn sich der Prinzipal die Erfüllung auf Ehrenwort oder unter ähnlichen Versicherungen versprechen lässt. ²Nichtig ist auch die Vereinbarung, durch die ein Dritter an Stelle des Gehilfen die Verpflichtung übernimmt, dass sich der Gehilfe nach der Beendigung des Dienstverhältnisses in seiner gewerblichen Tätigkeit beschränken werde.

(3) Unberührt bleiben die Vorschriften des § 138 des Bürgerlichen Gesetzbuchs über die Nichtigkeit von Rechtsgeschäften, die gegen die guten Sitten verstoßen.

§ 74 b
Zahlung der Entschädigung

(1) Die nach § 74 Abs. 2 dem Handlungsgehilfen zu gewährende Entschädigung ist am Schluss jedes Monats zu zahlen.

(2) ¹Soweit die dem Gehilfen zustehenden vertragsmäßigen Leistungen in einer Provision oder in anderen wechselnden Bezügen bestehen, sind sie bei der Berechnung der Entschädigung nach dem Durchschnitt der letzten drei Jahre in Ansatz zu bringen. ²Hat die für die Bezüge bei der Beendigung des Dienstverhältnisses maßgebende Vertragsbestimmung noch nicht drei Jahre bestanden, so erfolgt der Ansatz nach dem Durchschnitt des Zeitraums, für den die Bestimmung in Kraft war.

(3) Soweit Bezüge zum Ersatz besonderer Auslagen dienen sollen, die infolge der Dienstleistung entstehen, bleiben sie außer Ansatz.

following the end of the employment relationship.

(2) ¹The prohibition is void if the commercial employee is a minor at the time the contract was concluded or the principal causes the commercial employee to give his word of honor or a similar assurance. ²An agreement under which a third party, in lieu of the commercial employee, assumes the obligation to ensure that the commercial employee will restrict his professional activity following the end of the employment relationship, is also void.

(3) The provisions of section 138 of the Civil Code with regard to the nullity of legal acts contrary to public policy remain unaffected.

Section 74 b
Payment and Calculation of Compensation

(1) The compensation guaranteed to the commercial employee pursuant to section 74 (2) shall be paid at the end of each month.

(2) ¹Where the contractual remuneration due to the commercial employee consists of a commission or other variable payments, the average of such remuneration received over the last three years shall be used to calculate the compensation due the employee. ²If the contractual provision applicable to such payments has not been in force for three years by the end of the employment relationship, the amount of compensation due shall be calculated by averaging the contractual remuneration paid during the period in which the provision was in force.

(3) Where certain payments were intended to reimburse for specific expenditures arising as a result of the performance of services, they shall not be included in the assessment of compensation due.

§ 74 c
Anrechnung anderweitigen Erwerbs

(1) ¹Der Handlungsgehilfe muss sich auf die fällige Entschädigung anrechnen lassen, was er während des Zeitraums, für den die Entschädigung gezahlt wird, durch anderweite Verwertung seiner Arbeitskraft erwirbt oder zu erwerben böswillig unterlässt, soweit die Entschädigung unter Hinzurechnung dieses Betrags den Betrag der zuletzt von ihm bezogenen vertragsmäßigen Leistungen um mehr als ein Zehntel übersteigen würde. ²Ist der Gehilfe durch das Wettbewerbsverbot gezwungen worden, seinen Wohnsitz zu verlegen, so tritt an die Stelle des Betrags von einem Zehntel der Betrag von einem Viertel. ³Für die Dauer der Verbüßung einer Freiheitsstrafe kann der Gehilfe eine Entschädigung nicht verlangen.

(2) Der Gehilfe ist verpflichtet, dem Prinzipal auf Erfordern über die Höhe seines Erwerbs Auskunft zu erteilen.

§ 75
Unwirksamwerden des Verbots

(1) Löst der Gehilfe das Dienstverhältnis gemäß den Vorschriften der §§ 70 und 71 wegen vertragswidrigen Verhaltens des Prinzipals auf, so wird das Wettbewerbsverbot unwirksam, wenn der Gehilfe vor Ablauf eines Monats nach der Kündigung schriftlich erklärt, dass er sich an die Vereinbarung nicht gebunden erachte.

(2) ¹In gleicher Weise wird das Wettbewerbsverbot unwirksam, wenn der Prinzipal das Dienstverhältnis kündigt, es sei denn, dass für die Kündigung ein erheblicher Anlass in der Person des

Section 74 c
Deduction of Other Earnings

(1) ¹The commercial employee must allow any sums he earns through utilization of his work capacity elsewhere, or maliciously fails to earn, during the period for which compensation is to be paid, to be deducted from the compensation due, if the compensation plus these sums would exceed the most recent contractual remuneration by more than ten percent. ²If the commercial employee has been compelled by the prohibition of competition to change his residence, this ten percent figure shall be replaced by twenty-five percent. ³The commercial employee may not claim compensation while serving a prison sentence.

(2) The commercial employee shall be obligated to inform the principal on demand of the amount he has earned.

Section 75
Invalidity of the Prohibition of Competition

(1) Where the commercial employee dissolves the employment relationship pursuant to the provisions of *sections 70 and 71*[1] due to breach of contract by the principal, the prohibition of competition shall be invalid if the commercial employee declares in writing within one month after giving notice of termination that he does not consider himself bound by the agreement.

(2)[1] Likewise, the prohibition of competition becomes invalid if the principal terminates the employment relationship, unless there are significant grounds for the termination relating to

---

[1] Repealed by the First Labor Law Simplification Act *(Erstes Arbeitsrechtsbereinigungsgesetz)* of August 14, 1969 (BGBl. I p. 1106), cf. § 626 of the German Civil Code.

Gehilfen vorliegt oder dass sich der Prinzipal bei der Kündigung bereit erklärt, während der Dauer der Beschränkung dem Gehilfen die vollen zuletzt von ihm bezogenen vertragsmäßigen Leistungen zu gewähren. ²Im letzteren Falle finden die Vorschriften des § 74b entsprechende Anwendung.

(3) Löst der Prinzipal das Dienstverhältnis gemäß den Vorschriften der §§ 70 und 72 wegen vertragswidrigen Verhaltens des Gehilfen auf, so hat der Gehilfe keinen Anspruch auf die Entschädigung.

the person of the commercial employee or the principal declares, upon giving notice, that he will pay the commercial employee the full contractual remuneration last earned by him for the duration of the prohibition of competition. ²In the latter case the provisions of section 74b shall apply mutatis mutandis.

(3) Where the principal dissolves the employment relationship pursuant to the provisions of *sections 70 and 72* due to breach of contract by the commercial employee, the commercial employee shall have no claim to compensation.[2]

§ 75 a
Verzicht des Prinzipals

Der Prinzipal kann vor der Beendigung des Dienstverhältnisses durch schriftliche Erklärung auf das Wettbewerbsverbot mit der Wirkung verzichten, dass er mit dem Ablauf eines Jahres seit der Erklärung von der Verpflichtung zur Zahlung der Entschädigung frei wird.

Section 75 a
The Principal's Waiver

Prior to expiration of the employment relationship, the principal may waive the prohibition of competition by means of a written statement, with the effect that, beginning one year after the date of the declaration, he will be free of the obligation to pay compensation.

§ 75 b
(weggefallen)

Section 75 b
(repealed)

§ 75 c
Vertragsstrafe

(1) ¹Hat der Handlungsgehilfe für den Fall, dass er die in der Vereinbarung übernommene Verpflichtung nicht erfüllt, eine Strafe versprochen, so kann der Prinzipal Ansprüche nur nach Maßgabe der Vorschriften des § 340 des Bürgerlichen Gesetzbuchs geltend machen. ²Die Vorschriften des Bürgerlichen Gesetzbuchs über die Herabsetzung einer unverhältnismäßig hohen Vertragsstrafe bleiben unberührt.

(2) Ist die Verbindlichkeit der Vereinbarung nicht davon abhängig, dass sich

Section 75 c
Contractual Penalty

(1) ¹Where the commercial employee has promised to pay a penalty in the event of non-fulfillment of his contractual obligation, the principal may assert claims only pursuant to the provisions of section 340 of the German Civil Code. ²The provisions of the German Civil Code regarding the reduction of a disproportionately high contractual penalty remain unaffected.

(2) If the binding force of the agreement is not contingent upon the principal's

---

[2] Pursuant to the decision rendered by the Federal Labor Court *(Bundesarbeitsgericht)* on 23 February 1977, 3 AZR 620/75, (AP No. 6 to § 75 Commercial Code – NJW 1977, p. 1357), § 75 (3) of the Commercial Code violates Article 3 of the Basic Law *(Grundgesetz)* and is, therefore, null and void.

der Prinzipal zur Zahlung einer Entschädigung an den Gehilfen verpflichtet, so kann der Prinzipal, wenn sich der Gehilfe einer Vertragsstrafe der in Absatz 1 bezeichneten Art unterworfen hat, nur die verwirkte Strafe verlangen; der Anspruch auf Erfüllung oder auf Ersatz eines weiteren Schadens ist ausgeschlossen.

obligation to pay compensation to the commercial employee, the principal may only demand the forfeited penalty if the commercial employee is subject to a contractual penalty of the kind outlined in subsection (1); the right to specific performance or compensation for additional damages is excluded.

§ 75d
Unabdingbarkeit

Section 75d
Mandatory Nature

[1] Auf eine Vereinbarung, durch die von den Vorschriften der §§ 74 bis 75c zum Nachteil des Handlungsgehilfen abgewichen wird, kann sich der Prinzipal nicht berufen. [2] Das gilt auch von Vereinbarungen, die bezwecken, die gesetzlichen Vorschriften über das Mindestmass der Entschädigung durch Verrechnungen oder auf sonstige Weise zu umgehen.

[1] The principal may not enforce an agreement which deviates from the provisions of sections 74 to 75c, to the disadvantage of the commercial employee. [2] This also applies to agreements which seek to circumvent legal provisions concerning the minimum compensation by means of set-off or other methods.

§ 75e
(aufgehoben)

Section 75e
(repealed)

§ 75f
Geheimes Wettbewerbverbot

Section 75f
Secret Prohibition of Competition

[1] Im Falle einer Vereinbarung, durch die sich ein Prinzipal einem anderen Prinzipal gegenüber verpflichtet, einen Handlungsgehilfen, der bei diesem im Dienst ist oder gewesen ist, nicht oder nur unter bestimmten Voraussetzungen anzustellen, steht beiden Teilen der Rücktritt frei. [2] Aus der Vereinbarung findet weder Klage noch Einrede statt.

[1] In the event of an agreement by which a principal obligates himself to another principal not to employ a commercial employee who has been employed by the latter, or to employ him only under specific conditions, both parties are free to rescind the agreement. [2] Neither a cause of action nor a defense is created by the agreement.

§ 75g
Vermittlungsgehilfe

Section 75g
Clerical Employee Capable of Soliciting for the Principal

[1] § 55 Abs. 4 gilt auch für einen Handlungsgehilfen, der damit betraut ist, außerhalb des Betriebs des Prinzipals für diesen Geschäfte zu vermitteln. [2] Eine Beschränkung dieser Rechte braucht ein Dritter gegen sich nur gelten zu lassen, wenn er sie kannte oder kennen musste.

[1] Section 55 (4) also applies to a commercial employee entrusted to solicit business for the principal as an agent outside of the principal's establishment. [2] A third party must accept a limitation of these rights only if he knew or should have known of them.

§ 75 h
Unkenntnis des Mangels der Vertretungsmacht

(1) Hat ein Handlungsgehilfe, der nur mit der Vermittlung von Geschäften außerhalb des Betriebs des Prinzipals betraut ist, ein Geschäft im Namen des Prinzipals abgeschlossen, und war dem Dritten der Mangel der Vertretungsmacht nicht bekannt, so gilt das Geschäft als von dem Prinzipal genehmigt, wenn dieser dem Dritten gegenüber nicht unverzüglich das Geschäft ablehnt, nachdem er von dem Handlungsgehilfen oder dem Dritten über Abschluss und wesentlichen Inhalt benachrichtigt worden ist.

(2) Das gleiche gilt, wenn ein Handlungsgehilfe, der mit dem Abschluss von Geschäften betraut ist, ein Geschäft im Namen des Prinzipals abgeschlossen hat, zu dessen Abschluss er nicht bevollmächtigt ist.

Section 75 h
Ignorance as to the Absence of Agency Relationship

(1) Where a commercial employee who is only authorized to solicit business outside of the principal's establishment has concluded a transaction in the principal's name, and the third party did not know of this lack of authority, the transaction will be regarded as approved by the principal if he fails to repudiate it without undue delay after he has been informed by the commercial employee or the third party of the conclusion of the agreement and its material terms.

(2) The same applies where a commercial employee authorized to enter into business transactions has concluded a transaction in the principal's name which he was not authorized to conclude.

IX. Treaty on the Functioning of the European Union (Vertrag über die Arbeitsweise der Europäischen Union – AEU-Vertrag)

of 9 May 2008 (Official Journal C 115)

(prior to the Treaty of Lisbon known as Treaty Establishing the European Community)

(excerpts)

Art. 157 (ex-Artikel 141 EGV) [Gleiches Entgelt für Männer und Frauen]

(1) Jeder Mitgliedstaat stellt die Anwendung des Grundsatzes des gleichen Entgelts für Männer und Frauen bei gleicher oder gleichwertiger Arbeit sicher.

(2) ¹Unter „Entgelt" im Sinne dieses Artikels sind die üblichen Grund- oder Mindestlöhne und -gehälter sowie alle sonstigen Vergütungen zu verstehen, die der Arbeitgeber aufgrund des Dienstverhältnisses dem Arbeitnehmer unmittelbar oder mittelbar in bar oder in Sachleistungen zahlt.
²Gleichheit des Arbeitsentgelts ohne Diskriminierung aufgrund des Geschlechts bedeutet,

a) dass das Entgelt für eine gleiche nach Akkord bezahlte Arbeit aufgrund der gleichen Maßeinheit festgesetzt wird,
b) dass für eine nach Zeit bezahlte Arbeit das Entgelt bei gleichem Arbeitsplatz gleich ist.

(3) Das Europäische Parlament und der Rat beschließen gemäß dem ordentlichen Gesetzgebungsverfahren und nach Anhörung des Wirtschafts- und Sozialausschusses Maßnahmen zur Gewährleistung der Anwendung des Grundsatzes der Chancengleichheit und der Gleichbehandlung von Männern und Frauen in Arbeits- und Be-

Article 157 (ex Article 141) [Equal Pay for Men and Women]

(1) Each Member State shall ensure that principle of equal pay for male and female workers for equal work or work of equal value is applied.

(2) ¹For the purpose of this Article, "pay" means the ordinary basic or minimum wage or salary and any other consideration, whether in cash or in kind, which the worker receives directly or indirectly, in respect of his employment, from his employer.

²Equal pay without discrimination based on sex means:

a) that pay for the same work at piece rates shall be calculated on the basis of the same unit of measurement;

b) that pay for work at time rates shall be the same for the same job.

(3) The European Parliament and the Council, acting in accordance with the ordinary legislative procedure, and after consulting the Economic and Social Committee, shall adopt measures to ensure the application of the principle of equal opportunities and equal treatment of men and women in matters of employment and occupation, including

schäftigungsfragen, einschließlich des Grundsatzes des gleichen Entgelts bei gleicher oder gleichwertiger Arbeit.

(4) Im Hinblick auf die effektive Gewährleistung der vollen Gleichstellung von Männern und Frauen im Arbeitsleben hindert der Grundsatz der Gleichbehandlung die Mitgliedstaaten nicht daran, zur Erleichterung der Berufstätigkeit des unterrepräsentierten Geschlechts oder zur Verhinderung bzw. zum Ausgleich von Benachteiligungen in der beruflichen Laufbahn spezifische Vergünstigungen beizubehalten oder zu beschließen.

the principle of equal pay for equal work or work of equal value.

(4) With a view to ensuring full equality in practice between men and women in working life, the principle of equal treatment shall not prevent any Member State from maintaining or adopting measures providing for specific advantages in order to make it easier for the under-represented sex to pursue a vocational activity or to prevent or compensate for disadvantages in professional careers.

X. Works Constitution Act (Betriebsverfassungsgesetz – BetrVG)

of 15 January 1972 (Federal Law Gazette I p. 13)

in the amended version of 29 July 2009

Erster Teil
Allgemeine Vorschriften

§ 1
Errichtung von Betriebsräten

(1) ¹In Betrieben mit in der Regel mindestens fünf ständigen wahlberechtigten Arbeitnehmern, von denen drei wählbar sind, werden Betriebsräte gewählt. ²Dies gilt auch für gemeinsame Betriebe mehrerer Unternehmen.

(2) Ein gemeinsamer Betrieb mehrerer Unternehmen wird vermutet, wenn

1. zur Verfolgung arbeitstechnischer Zwecke die Betriebsmittel sowie die Arbeitnehmer von den Unternehmen gemeinsam eingesetzt werden oder
2. die Spaltung eines Unternehmens zur Folge hat, dass von einem Betrieb ein oder mehrere Betriebsteile einem an der Spaltung beteiligten anderen Unternehmen zugeordnet werden, ohne dass sich dabei die Organisation des betroffenen Betriebs wesentlich ändert.

§ 2
Stellung der Gewerkschaften und Vereinigungen der Arbeitgeber

(1) Arbeitgeber und Betriebsrat arbeiten unter Beachtung der geltenden Tarifverträge vertrauensvoll und im Zusammenwirken mit den im Betrieb vertretenen Gewerkschaften und Arbeitgebervereinigungen zum Wohl der Arbeitnehmer und des Betriebs zusammen.

Part 1
General Provisions

Section 1
Establishment of Works Councils

(1) ¹Works councils are elected in establishments which regularly have at least five permanent employees eligible to vote, of whom three are eligible for election. ²This shall also apply to joint establishments of two or more companies.

(2) A joint establishment of two or more companies shall be presumed to exist if

1. the working capital and the employees are jointly deployed by the company for the pursuit of the same technical labor purposes or
2. as a result of the divestiture of a company, one establishment or two or more sections of an establishment *(Betriebsteile)* are allocated to another company participating in the divestiture with no essential change having occurred in the organization of the affected establishment.

Section 2
Position of Trade Unions and Employer Associations

(1) The employer and works council shall work together in accordance with the valid collective bargaining agreement in a spirit of mutual trust and in cooperation with the trade unions and employers' associations represented in the establishment for the benefit of both the employees and the establishment.

(2) Zur Wahrnehmung der in diesem Gesetz genannten Aufgaben und Befugnisse der im Betrieb vertretenen Gewerkschaften ist deren Beauftragten nach Unterrichtung des Arbeitgebers oder seines Vertreters Zugang zum Betrieb zu gewähren, soweit dem nicht unumgängliche Notwendigkeiten des Betriebsablaufs, zwingende Sicherheitsvorschriften oder der Schutz von Betriebsgeheimnissen entgegenstehen.

(3) Die Aufgaben der Gewerkschaften und der Vereinigungen der Arbeitgeber, insbesondere die Wahrnehmung der Interessen ihrer Mitglieder, werden durch dieses Gesetz nicht berührt.

§ 3
Abweichende Regelungen

(1) Durch Tarifvertrag können bestimmt werden:

1. für Unternehmen mit mehreren Betrieben
    a) die Bildung eines unternehmenseinheitlichen Betriebsrats oder
    b) die Zusammenfassung von Betrieben,
    wenn dies die Bildung von Betriebsräten erleichtert oder einer sachgerechten Wahrnehmung der Interessen der Arbeitnehmer dient;
2. für Unternehmen und Konzerne, soweit sie nach produkt- oder projektbezogenen Geschäftsbereichen (Sparten) organisiert sind und die Leitung der Sparte auch Entscheidungen in beteiligungspflichtigen Angelegenheiten trifft, die Bildung von Betriebsräten in den Sparten (Spartenbetriebsräte), wenn dies der sachgerechten Wahrnehmung der Aufgaben des Betriebsrats dient;
3. andere Arbeitnehmervertretungsstrukturen, soweit dies insbesondere aufgrund der Betriebs-, Unternehmens- oder Konzernorganisation oder aufgrund anderer Formen der Zusammenarbeit von Unternehmen

(2) In order to exercise the powers and duties set forth in this Act, the trade unions represented in the establishment shall, through their representatives and after informing the employer or his representative, be granted access to the establishment, unless unavoidable operational requirements, mandatory safety regulations, or the protection of the establishment's secrets stand in the way.

(3) The duties of the trade unions and the employers' associations, in particular the safeguarding of the interests of its members, shall not be affected by this Act.

Section 3
Variable Regulations

(1) The following may be determined by means of a collective bargaining agreement:

1. for companies with two or more establishments
    a) the formation of a unified works council for the entire company or
    b) the amalgamation of establishments
    if this will facilitate the formation of works councils or the proper safeguarding of the employees' interests;
2. for companies and groups that are organized along product or project-oriented lines (divisions) where the management of the division also makes decisions in matters requiring the participation of the works council, the formation of works councils in the divisions (division works councils) if this will facilitate the proper fulfillment of the works council's duties;
3. other employee representational structures where, particularly in light of the governing organization of the establishment, company or group or in light of other forms of cooperation between companies, this will facili-

einer wirksamen und zweckmäßigen Interessenvertretung der Arbeitnehmer dient;
4. zusätzliche betriebsverfassungsrechtliche Gremien (Arbeitsgemeinschaften), die der unternehmensübergreifenden Zusammenarbeit von Arbeitnehmervertretungen dienen;
5. zusätzliche betriebsverfassungsrechtliche Vertretungen der Arbeitnehmer, die die Zusammenarbeit zwischen Betriebsrat und Arbeitnehmern erleichtern.

(2) Besteht in den Fällen des Absatzes 1 Nr. 1, 2, 4 oder 5 keine tarifliche Regelung und gilt auch kein anderer Tarifvertrag, kann die Regelung durch Betriebsvereinbarung getroffen werden.

(3) ¹Besteht im Fall des Absatzes 1 Nr. 1 Buchstabe a keine tarifliche Regelung und besteht in dem Unternehmen kein Betriebsrat, können die Arbeitnehmer mit Stimmenmehrheit die Wahl eines unternehmenseinheitlichen Betriebsrats beschließen. ²Die Abstimmung kann von mindestens drei wahlberechtigten Arbeitnehmern des Unternehmens oder einer im Unternehmen vertretenen Gewerkschaft veranlasst werden.

(4) ¹Sofern der Tarifvertrag oder die Betriebsvereinbarung nichts anderes bestimmt, sind Regelungen nach Absatz 1 Nr. 1 bis 3 erstmals bei der nächsten regelmäßigen Betriebsratswahl anzuwenden, es sei denn, es besteht kein Betriebsrat oder es ist aus anderen Gründen eine Neuwahl des Betriebsrats erforderlich. ²Sieht der Tarifvertrag oder die Betriebsvereinbarung einen anderen Wahlzeitpunkt vor, endet die Amtszeit bestehender Betriebsräte, die durch die Regelungen nach Absatz 1 Nr. 1 bis 3 entfallen, mit Bekanntgabe des Wahlergebnisses.

(5) ¹Die aufgrund eines Tarifvertrages oder einer Betriebsvereinbarung nach Absatz 1 Nr. 1 bis 3 gebildeten betriebs-

tate an effective and expedient representation of the employees' interests;
4. additional bodies (workgroups) within the meaning of this act to facilitate the cooperation of employee representative bodies of different companies;
5. additional representative bodies of employees to facilitate the cooperation between the works council and the employees.

(2) If, in the cases set forth in subsection (1) nos. 1, 2, 4 or 5 there is no provision in the collective bargaining agreements and if no other collective agreement applies, such a provision may be concluded by way of a works agreement.

(3) ¹If, in the case set forth in subsection (1) no. 1a, there is no provision in the collective bargaining agreements and there is no works council in the company, the employees may resolve with a majority of votes cast to elect a unified works council for the entire company. ²The voting may be initiated by at least three employees of the company who are eligible to vote or a trade union represented in the company.

(4) ¹Unless otherwise provided in the collective bargaining agreement or the works agreement, provisions pursuant to subsection (1) nos. 1 to 3 shall first be applied during the next regular works council election, unless no works council exists or a new election of the works council is necessary for other reasons. ²If the collective bargaining agreement or the works agreement provides for another time for the election, the period of office of the existing works council which cease to exist due to the provisions in subsection (1) nos. 1 to 3, shall end upon the announcement of the results of the election.

(5) ¹The governing organizational units within the meaning of this act, formed on the basis of a collective bargaining

verfassungsrechtlichen Organisationseinheiten gelten als Betriebe im Sinne dieses Gesetzes. ²Auf die in ihnen gebildeten Arbeitnehmervertretungen finden die Vorschriften über die Rechte und Pflichten des Betriebsrats und die Rechtsstellung seiner Mitglieder Anwendung.

agreement or a works agreement pursuant to subsection (1) nos. 1 to 3 shall be deemed to be establishments within the meaning of this Act. ²The provisions on the rights and duties of the works council and the legal position of its members shall be applicable to the employee representative bodies formed in such establishments.

§ 4
Betriebsteile, Kleinstbetriebe

Section 4
Sections of Establishments and Small Businesses

(1) ¹Betriebsteile gelten als selbständige Betriebe, wenn sie die Voraussetzungen des § 1 Abs. 1 Satz 1 erfüllen und

1. räumlich weit vom Hauptbetrieb entfernt oder
2. durch Aufgabenbereich und Organisation eigenständig sind.

²Die Arbeitnehmer eines Betriebsteils, in dem kein eigener Betriebsrat besteht, können mit Stimmenmehrheit formlos beschließen, an der Wahl des Betriebsrats im Hauptbetrieb teilzunehmen; § 3 Abs. 3 Satz 2 gilt entsprechend. ³Die Abstimmung kann auch vom Betriebsrat des Hauptbetriebs veranlasst werden. ⁴Der Beschluss ist dem Betriebsrat des Hauptbetriebs spätestens zehn Wochen vor Ablauf seiner Amtszeit mitzuteilen. ⁵Für den Widerruf des Beschlusses gelten die Sätze 2 bis 4 entsprechend.

(1) ¹Sections of establishments shall qualify as independent establishments if they fulfill the prerequisites of section 1 (1) and

1. are a great distance away from the primary establishment or
2. are autonomous in terms of scope of duties and governing organization.

²The employees of a section in which no works council exists may resolve with a majority of votes cast to participate in the election of the works council in the primary establishment; section 3 (3) sentence 2 applies *mutatis mutandis*. ³The vote may also be initiated by the works council of the primary establishment. ⁴The resolution shall be communicated to the works council of the primary establishment no later than ten weeks before its term of office comes to an end. ⁵For the revocation of the resolution, sentences 2 to 4 apply *mutatis mutandis*.

(2) Betriebe, die die Voraussetzungen des § 1 Abs. 1 Satz 1 nicht erfüllen, sind dem Hauptbetrieb zuzuordnen.

(2) Establishments which do not fulfill the prerequisites set forth in section 1 (1) sentence 1 shall be allocated to the primary establishment.

§ 5
Arbeitnehmer

Section 5
Employees

(1) ¹Arbeitnehmer (Arbeitnehmerinnen und Arbeitnehmer) im Sinne dieses Gesetzes sind Arbeiter und Angestellte einschließlich der zu ihrer Berufsausbildung Beschäftigten, unabhängig da-

(1) ¹Employees within the meaning of this Act are workers and salaried employees including those that are engaged in vocational training, regardless of whether they are working in the es-

von, ob sie im Betrieb, im Außendienst oder mit Telearbeit beschäftigt werden ²Als Arbeitnehmer gelten auch die in Heimarbeit Beschäftigten, die in der Hauptsache für den Betrieb arbeiten. ³Als Arbeitnehmer gelten ferner Beamte (Beamtinnen und Beamte), Soldaten (Soldatinnen und Soldaten) sowie Arbeitnehmer des öffentlichen Dienstes einschließlich der zu ihrer Berufsausbildung Beschäftigten, die in Betrieben privatrechtlich organisierter Unternehmen tätig sind.	tablishment, in the field or by teleworking. ²Those working at home who mainly work for the establishment shall also be deemed to be employees. ³Moreover, civil servants, soldiers, as well as public employees, including those that are engaged in vocational training who are working in establishments of organized companies under private law, are considered to be employees.
(2) Als Arbeitnehmer im Sinne dieses Gesetzes gelten nicht	(2) Those engaged in the following activities are not employees within the meaning of this Act:
1. in Betrieben einer juristischen Person die Mitglieder des Organs, das zur gesetzlichen Vertretung der juristischen Person berufen ist;	1. in establishments of a legal entity, the members of the governing body which has the legal authority to represent such legal entity;
2. die Gesellschafter einer offenen Handelsgesellschaft oder die Mitglieder einer anderen Personengesamtheit, soweit sie durch Gesetz, Satzung oder Gesellschaftsvertrag zur Vertretung der Personengesamtheit oder zur Geschäftsführung berufen sind, in deren Betrieben;	2. the partners in a commercial partnership or the members of another unincorporated association, to the extent they have the authority by law, bylaws, or articles of association to represent or manage the unincorporated association in such establishments;
3. Personen, deren Beschäftigung nicht in erster Linie ihrem Erwerb dient, sondern vorwiegend durch Beweggründe karitativer oder religiöser Art bestimmt ist;	3. persons whose employment is not primarily to earn a salary and is principally inspired by charitable or religious motives;
4. Personen, deren Beschäftigung nicht in erster Linie ihrem Erwerb dient und die vorwiegend zu ihrer Heilung, Wiedereingewöhnung, sittlichen Besserung oder Erziehung beschäftigt werden;	4. persons whose employment is not primarily to earn a salary but are employed mainly for as therapy, rehabilitation, or for their moral improvement or education;
5. der Ehegatte, der Lebenspartner, Verwandte und Verschwägerte ersten Grades, die in häuslicher Gemeinschaft mit dem Arbeitgeber leben.	5. the spouse, life partner and relatives by blood or marriage of the first degree who live in the same household as the employer.
(3) ¹Dieses Gesetz findet, soweit in ihm nicht ausdrücklich etwas anderes bestimmt ist, keine Anwendung auf leitende Angestellte. ²Leitender Angestellter ist, wer nach Arbeitsvertrag und Stellung im Unternehmen oder im Betrieb	(3) ¹This Act shall not apply to managerial employees, unless otherwise expressly stipulated in this Act. ²Managerial employees are those who, by their employment contract and status in the company or establishment,
1. zur selbständigen Einstellung und Entlassung von im Betrieb oder in	1. have the independent authority to hire and dismiss employees in the es-

der Betriebsabteilung beschäftigten Arbeitnehmern berechtigt ist oder
2. Generalvollmacht oder Prokura hat und die Prokura auch im Verhältnis zum Arbeitgeber nicht unbedeutend ist oder

3. regelmäßig sonstige Aufgaben wahrnimmt, die für den Bestand und die Entwicklung des Unternehmens oder eines Betriebs von Bedeutung sind und deren Erfüllung besondere Erfahrungen und Kenntnisse voraussetzt, wenn er dabei entweder die Entscheidungen im Wesentlichen frei von Weisungen trifft oder sie maßgeblich beeinflusst; dies kann auch bei Vorgaben insbesondere aufgrund von Rechtsvorschriften, Plänen oder Richtlinien sowie bei Zusammenarbeit mit anderen leitenden Angestellten gegeben sein.

Für die in Absatz 1 Satz 3 genannten Beamten und Soldaten gelten die Sätze 1 und 2 entsprechend.

(4) Leitender Angestellter nach Absatz 3 Nr. 3 ist im Zweifel, wer

1. aus Anlass der letzten Wahl des Betriebsrats, des Sprecherausschusses oder von Aufsichtsratsmitgliedern der Arbeitnehmer oder durch rechtskräftige gerichtliche Entscheidung den leitenden Angestellten zugeordnet worden ist oder
2. einer Leitungsebene angehört, auf der in dem Unternehmen überwiegend leitende Angestellte vertreten sind, oder
3. ein regelmäßiges Jahresarbeitsentgelt erhält, das für leitende Angestellte in dem Unternehmen üblich ist, oder,
4. falls auch bei der Anwendung der Nummer 3 noch Zweifel bleiben, ein regelmäßiges Jahresarbeitsentgelt erhält, das das Dreifache der Bezugsgröße nach § 18 des Vierten Buches Sozialgesetzbuch überschreitet.

tablishment or in one of its departments or
2. have a general power of attorney or a full power of representation (*Prokura*) and the extent of such full power of representation is not significantly limited by internal restrictions or

3. regularly assume other duties that are significant for the existence and development of the company or an establishment, where the performance of such duties requires special experience and knowledge, if, in so doing, he makes decisions essentially free of directives or exerts a major influence on such decisions; this may also be the case if there are certain fixed standards based in particular on statutory provisions, plans, or guidelines, as well as cooperation with other managerial employees.

For the civil servants and soldiers mentioned in subsection (1) sentence 3, sentences 1 and 2 apply *mutatis mutandis*.

(4) In case of doubt, a managerial employee pursuant to subsection (3) no. 3 is someone who

1. has been designated a managerial employee at the most recent election of the works council, the spokesperson's committee (*Sprecherausschuss*), or the employees' representatives in the supervisory board or through non-appealable judicial decisions; or
2. belongs to a level of management which in that company consists primarily of managerial employees; or
3. earns a regular annual income customary for managerial employees or
4. in case there is still doubt in the application of no. 3., regularly earns an annual income which is more than triple the income pursuant to section 18 of the Fourth Book of the Social Security Code (*Viertes Buch Sozialgesetzbuch*).

§ 6
(weggefallen)

Section 6
(repealed)

Zweiter Teil
Betriebsrat, Betriebsversammlung, Gesamt- und Konzernbetriebsrat

Part 2
Works Council, Works Assembly, General and Group Works Councils

Erster Abschnitt
Zusammensetzung und Wahl des Betriebsrats

Chapter 1
Composition and Election of the Works Council

§ 7
Wahlberechtigung

Section 7
Right to Vote

¹Wahlberechtigt sind alle Arbeitnehmer des Betriebs, die das 18. Lebensjahr vollendet haben. ²Werden Arbeitnehmer eines anderen Arbeitgebers zur Arbeitsleistung überlassen, so sind diese wahlberechtigt, wenn sie länger als drei Monate im Betrieb eingesetzt werden.

¹All employees of the establishment who have reached the age of 18 shall be eligible to vote. ²If employees of another employer are delegated to work in the establishment, they shall be eligible to vote if they have been assigned to the establishment for longer than three months.

§ 8
Wählbarkeit

Section 8
Eligibility for Election

(1) ¹Wählbar sind alle Wahlberechtigten, die sechs Monate dem Betrieb angehören oder als in Heimarbeit Beschäftigte in der Hauptsache für den Betrieb gearbeitet haben. ²Auf diese sechsmonatige Betriebszugehörigkeit werden Zeiten angerechnet, in denen der Arbeitnehmer unmittelbar vorher einem anderen Betrieb desselben Unternehmens oder Konzerns (§ 18 Abs. 1 des Aktiengesetzes) angehört hat. ³Nicht wählbar ist, wer infolge strafgerichtlicher Verurteilung die Fähigkeit, Rechte aus öffentlichen Wahlen zu erlangen, nicht besitzt.

(1) ¹All those employed that have been with an establishment or employed at home principally for the establishment for six months are eligible for election. ²Included in this six month work period are periods in which the employee was employed with another establishment in the same company or group (section 18 (1) of the Stock Corporation Act) immediately prior to his employment with the present employer. ³Those who, due to a criminal conviction do not have the right to run for public office, shall not be eligible for election.

(2) Besteht der Betrieb weniger als sechs Monate, so sind abweichend von der Vorschrift in Absatz 1 über die sechsmonatige Betriebszugehörigkeit diejenigen Arbeitnehmer wählbar, die bei der Einleitung der Betriebsratswahl im Betrieb beschäftigt sind und die übrigen

(2) Where the establishment has been in existence for less than six months, employees shall be eligible for election notwithstanding the six-month employment requirement set forth in subsection (1), employees employed at the establishment when the election of the

Voraussetzungen für die Wählbarkeit erfüllen.

works council is initiated and fulfil all other requirements for eligibility shall be eligible for election.

§ 9
Zahl der Betriebsratsmitglieder

Section 9
Number of Works Councils Members

[1] Der Betriebsrat besteht in Betrieben mit in der Regel

    5 bis 20 wahlberechtigten Arbeitnehmern aus einer Person,
    21 bis 50 wahlberechtigten Arbeitnehmern aus 3 Mitgliedern,
    51 wahlberechtigten Arbeitnehmern bis 100 Arbeitnehmern aus 5 Mitgliedern,
    101 bis 200 Arbeitnehmern aus 7 Mitgliedern,
    201 bis 400 Arbeitnehmern aus 9 Mitgliedern,
    401 bis 700 Arbeitnehmern aus 11 Mitgliedern,
    701 bis 1.000 Arbeitnehmern aus 13 Mitgliedern,
    1.001 bis 1.500 Arbeitnehmern aus 15 Mitgliedern,
    1.501 bis 2.000 Arbeitnehmern aus 17 Mitgliedern,
    2.001 bis 2.500 Arbeitnehmern aus 19 Mitgliedern,
    2.501 bis 3.000 Arbeitnehmern aus 21 Mitgliedern,
    3.001 bis 3.500 Arbeitnehmern aus 23 Mitgliedern,
    3.501 bis 4.000 Arbeitnehmern aus 25 Mitgliedern,
    4.001 bis 4.500 Arbeitnehmern aus 27 Mitgliedern,
    4.501 bis 5.000 Arbeitnehmern aus 29 Mitgliedern,
    5.001 bis 6.000 Arbeitnehmern aus 31 Mitgliedern,
    6.001 bis 7.000 Arbeitnehmern aus 33 Mitgliedern,
    7.001 bis 9.000 Arbeitnehmern aus 35 Mitgliedern.

[2] In Betrieben mit mehr als 9.000 Arbeitnehmern erhöht sich die Zahl der Mitglieder des Betriebsrats für je angefan-

[1] The number of works council members per number of employees eligible to vote who are regularly employed in the establishment shall be as follows:

    5–20 employees – 1 person
    21–50 employees – 3 members
    51–100 employees – 5 members
    101–200 employees – 7 members
    201–400 employees – 9 members
    401–700 employees – 11 members
    701-1,000 employees – 13 members
    1,001-1,500 employees – 15 members
    1,501-2,000 employees – 17 members
    2,001–2,500 employees – 19 members
    2,501-3,000 employees – 21 members
    3,001–3,500 employees – 23 members
    3,501-4,000 employees – 25 members
    4,001–4,500 employees – 27 members
    4,501-5,000 employees – 29 members
    5,001–6,000 employees – 31 members
    6,001–7,000 employees – 33 members
    7,001–9,000 employees – 35 members.

[2] In establishments with more than 9,000 employees the number of members of the works council shall increase

gene weitere 3.000 Arbeitnehmer um 2 Mitglieder.

by two members for each additional fraction of 3,000 employees.

§ 10
(weggefallen)

Section 10
(repealed)

§ 11
Ermäßigte Zahl der Betriebsratsmitglieder

Hat ein Betrieb nicht die ausreichende Zahl von wählbaren Arbeitnehmern, so ist die Zahl der Betriebsratsmitglieder der nächstniedrigeren Betriebsgröße zugrunde zu legen.

Section 11
Reduction in Number of Works Council Members

Where an establishment does not have the sufficient number of employees eligible to vote, the number of works council members shall be reduced to that for a works council for the next smaller sized establishment.

§ 12
(weggefallen)

Section 12
(repealed)

§ 13
Zeitpunkt der Betriebsratswahlen

(1) [1]Die regelmäßigen Betriebsratswahlen finden alle vier Jahre in der Zeit vom 1. März bis 31. Mai statt. [2]Sie sind zeitgleich mit den regelmäßigen Wahlen nach § 5 Abs. 1 des Sprecherausschussgesetzes einzuleiten.

(2) Außerhalb dieser Zeit ist der Betriebsrat zu wählen, wenn

1. mit Ablauf von 24 Monaten, vom Tage der Wahl an gerechnet, die Zahl der regelmäßig beschäftigten Arbeitnehmer um die Hälfte, mindestens aber um fünfzig, gestiegen oder gesunken ist,
2. die Gesamtzahl der Betriebsratsmitglieder nach Eintreten sämtlicher Ersatzmitglieder unter die vorgeschriebene Zahl der Betriebsratsmitglieder gesunken ist,
3. der Betriebsrat mit der Mehrheit seiner Mitglieder seinen Rücktritt beschlossen hat,
4. die Betriebsratswahl mit Erfolg angefochten worden ist,

Section 13
Time Period for Works Councils Elections

(1) [1]Regular elections for works councils shall take place every four years between 1 March and 31 May. [2]They shall coincide with the regular election pursuant to section 5 (1) of the Spokesperson's Committee Act *(Sprecherausschussgesetz)*.

(2) Works council elections shall be held outside of this time period if

1. within 24 months from the day of the election, the number of regular employees increased or decreased by one-half, but at least by 50 employees,
2. the total number of works council members, after all alternative members have taken office, has fallen below the required number of works council members,
3. the works council has decided to resign by the vote of a majority of its members,
4. the works council election has been successfully challenged,

5. der Betriebsrat durch eine gerichtliche Entscheidung aufgelöst ist oder
6. im Betrieb ein Betriebsrat nicht besteht.

(3) ¹Hat außerhalb des für die regelmäßigen Betriebsratswahlen festgelegten Zeitraums eine Betriebsratswahl stattgefunden, so ist der Betriebsrat in dem auf die Wahl folgenden nächsten Zeitraum der regelmäßigen Betriebsratswahlen neu zu wählen. ²Hat die Amtszeit des Betriebsrats zu Beginn des für die regelmäßigen Betriebsratswahlen festgelegten Zeitraums noch nicht ein Jahr betragen, so ist der Betriebsrat in dem übernächsten Zeitraum der regelmäßigen Betriebsratswahlen neu zu wählen.

§ 14
Wahlvorschriften

(1) Der Betriebsrat wird in geheimer und unmittelbarer Wahl gewählt.

(2) ¹Die Wahl erfolgt nach den Grundsätzen der Verhältniswahl. ²Sie erfolgt nach den Grundsätzen der Mehrheitswahl, wenn nur ein Wahlvorschlag eingereicht wird oder wenn der Betriebsrat im vereinfachten Wahlverfahren nach § 14a zu wählen ist.

(3) Zur Wahl des Betriebsrats können die wahlberechtigten Arbeitnehmer und die im Betrieb vertretenen Gewerkschaften Wahlvorschläge machen.

(4) ¹Jeder Wahlvorschlag der Arbeitnehmer muss von mindestens einem Zwanzigstel der wahlberechtigten Arbeitnehmer, mindestens jedoch von drei Wahlberechtigten unterzeichnet sein; in Betrieben mit in der Regel bis zu zwanzig wahlberechtigten Arbeitnehmern genügt die Unterzeichnung durch zwei Wahlberechtigte. ²In jedem Fall genügt die Unterzeichnung durch fünfzig wahlberechtigte Arbeitnehmer.

(5) Jeder Wahlvorschlag einer Gewerkschaft muss von zwei Beauftragten unterzeichnet sein.

5. the works council is dissolved by a court order, or
6. no works council exists in the establishment.

(3) ¹If the works council election is held at a time other than that regularly set for works council elections, a new election shall be held during the next period designated for regular works council elections. ²If, at the beginning of the period for the regular works council elections, the works council has not yet been in office for one year, the election shall be held during the second regular works council election period following that period.

Section 14
Election Regulations

(1) The works council shall be elected in a direct election by secret ballot.

(2) ¹The election shall be held pursuant to the principles of proportional representation. ²Where only one nomination is made or the works council is to be elected according to the simplified procedure set forth in section 14a, the election shall be held pursuant to the principles of majority voting.

(3) The employees eligible to vote and the trade unions represented in the establishment may make nominations for the works council election.

(4) ¹Each nomination by the employees must be signed by at least 1/20 of the employees eligible to vote, but no fewer than three employees eligible to vote; in establishments which regularly employ up to 20 employees, the signature of two employees eligible to vote shall suffice. ²In any case, the signatures of 50 employees eligible to vote shall suffice.

(5) Each nomination by a trade union must be signed by two authorized representatives.

§ 14a
Vereinfachtes Wahlverfahren für Kleinbetriebe

(1) ¹In Betrieben mit in der Regel fünf bis fünfzig wahlberechtigten Arbeitnehmern wird der Betriebsrat in einem zweistufigen Verfahren gewählt. ²Auf einer ersten Wahlversammlung wird der Wahlvorstand nach § 17a Nr. 3 gewählt. ³Auf einer zweiten Wahlversammlung wird der Betriebsrat in geheimer und unmittelbarer Wahl gewählt. ⁴Diese Wahlversammlung findet eine Woche nach der Wahlversammlung zur Wahl des Wahlvorstands statt.

(2) Wahlvorschläge können bis zum Ende der Wahlversammlung zur Wahl des Wahlvorstands nach § 17a Nr. 3 gemacht werden; für Wahlvorschläge der Arbeitnehmer gilt § 14 Abs. 4 mit der Maßgabe, dass für Wahlvorschläge, die erst auf dieser Wahlversammlung gemacht werden, keine Schriftform erforderlich ist.

(3) ¹Ist der Wahlvorstand in Betrieben mit in der Regel fünf bis fünfzig wahlberechtigten Arbeitnehmern nach § 17a Nr. 1 in Verbindung mit § 16 vom Betriebsrat, Gesamtbetriebsrat oder Konzernbetriebsrat oder nach § 17a Nr. 4 vom Arbeitsgericht bestellt, wird der Betriebsrat abweichend von Absatz 1 Satz 1 und 2 auf nur einer Wahlversammlung in geheimer und unmittelbarer Wahl gewählt. ²Wahlvorschläge können bis eine Woche vor der Wahlversammlung zur Wahl des Betriebsrats gemacht werden; § 14 Abs. 4 gilt unverändert.

(4) Wahlberechtigten Arbeitnehmern, die an der Wahlversammlung zur Wahl des Betriebsrats nicht teilnehmen können, ist Gelegenheit zur schriftlichen Stimmabgabe zu geben.

(5) In Betrieben mit in der Regel 51 bis 100 wahlberechtigten Arbeitnehmern können der Wahlvorstand und der Ar-

Section 14a
Simplified Election Procedure for Small Businesses

(1) ¹In establishments which regularly employ five to fifty employees eligible to vote, the works council shall be elected in a two-stage procedure. ²In a first election assembly the election committee shall be elected pursuant to section 17a no. 3. ³In a second election assembly, the works council shall be elected in a direct election by secret ballot. ⁴This election assembly shall be held one week after the election of the election committee.

(2) Nominations may be made up to the end of the assembly for the election of the election committee pursuant to section 17a no. 3; for nominations by the employees, section 14 (4) shall apply subject to the proviso that nominations made for the first time at this assembly need not be in writing.

(3) ¹If the election committee in establishments regularly employing five to fifty employees eligible to vote has been appointed by the works council, joint works council or group works council pursuant to section 17a no. 1 in connection with section 16, or by the Labor Court pursuant to section 17a no. 4, the works council shall, notwithstanding subsection (1) sentences 1 and 2, be elected in a single election assembly in a direct election by secret ballot. ²Nominations may be made up to one week before the election assembly to elect the works council; section 14 (4) applies unchanged.

(4) Employees eligible to vote who cannot participate in the election assembly to elect the works council shall be given an opportunity to vote in writing.

(5) In establishments which regularly employ 51 to 100 employees eligible to vote, the election committee and the

beitgeber die Anwendung des vereinfachten Wahlverfahrens vereinbaren.

§ 15
Zusammensetzung nach Beschäftigungsarten und Geschlechter

(1) Der Betriebsrat soll sich möglichst aus Arbeitnehmern der einzelnen Organisationsbereiche und der verschiedenen Beschäftigungsarten der im Betrieb tätigen Arbeitnehmer zusammensetzen.

(2) Das Geschlecht, das in der Belegschaft in der Minderheit ist, muss mindestens entsprechend seinem zahlenmäßigen Verhältnis im Betriebsrat vertreten sein, wenn dieser aus mindestens drei Mitgliedern besteht.

§ 16
Bestellung des Wahlvorstands

(1) [1] Spätestens zehn Wochen vor Ablauf seiner Amtszeit bestellt der Betriebsrat einen aus drei Wahlberechtigten bestehenden Wahlvorstand und einen von ihnen als Vorsitzenden. [2] Der Betriebsrat kann die Zahl der Wahlvorstandsmitglieder erhöhen, wenn dies zur ordnungsgemäßen Durchführung der Wahl erforderlich ist. [3] Der Wahlvorstand muss in jedem Fall aus einer ungeraden Zahl von Mitgliedern bestehen. [4] Für jedes Mitglied des Wahlvorstands kann für den Fall seiner Verhinderung ein Ersatzmitglied bestellt werden. [5] In Betrieben mit weiblichen und männlichen Arbeitnehmern sollen dem Wahlvorstand Frauen und Männer angehören. [6] Jede im Betrieb vertretene Gewerkschaft kann zusätzlich einen dem Betrieb angehörenden Beauftragten als nicht stimmberechtigtes Mitglied in den Wahlvorstand entsenden, sofern ihr nicht ein stimmberechtigtes Wahlvorstandsmitglied angehört.

(2) [1] Besteht acht Wochen vor Ablauf der Amtszeit des Betriebsrats kein Wahlvorstand, so bestellt ihn das Ar-

employer may agree to apply the simplified election procedure.

Section 15
Composition According to Type of Employment and Gender

(1) If possible, the works council should be composed of employees of the individual organizational areas and the various types of employment of the employees in the establishment.

(2) Where the works council has at least three members, the gender in the minority shall be represented in it in proportion to its numerical strength.

Section 16
Appointment of the election committee

(1) [1] No later than ten weeks before the expiration of its term the works council shall appoint an election committee consisting of three employees eligible to vote, one of whom shall be chairperson. [2] The works council may increase the number of election committee members if this is necessary to ensure the proper conduct of the election. [3] The election committee must in each case have an odd number of members. [4] An alternate member may be assigned for each election committee member should the regular member be unable to perform his duties. [5] In establishments with male and female employees, both men and women shall be in the election committee. [6] Each union represented in the establishment may also appoint a representative employed in the establishment to the election committee as a non-voting member provided that no member of this union is already a voting member of the election committee.

(2) [1] If there is no election committee eight weeks before the expiration of the term of the works council, one shall be

beitsgericht auf Antrag von mindestens drei Wahlberechtigten oder einer im Betrieb vertretenen Gewerkschaft; Absatz 1 gilt entsprechend. ²In dem Antrag können Vorschläge für die Zusammensetzung des Wahlvorstands gemacht werden. ³Das Arbeitsgericht kann für Betriebe mit in der Regel mehr als zwanzig wahlberechtigten Arbeitnehmern auch Mitglieder einer im Betrieb vertretenen Gewerkschaft, die nicht Arbeitnehmer des Betriebs sind, zu Mitgliedern des Wahlvorstands bestellen, wenn dies zur ordnungsgemäßen Durchführung der Wahl erforderlich ist.

(3) ¹Besteht acht Wochen vor Ablauf der Amtszeit des Betriebsrats kein Wahlvorstand, kann auch der Gesamtbetriebsrat oder, falls ein solcher nicht besteht, der Konzernbetriebsrat den Wahlvorstand bestellen. ²Absatz 1 gilt entsprechend.

§ 17
Bestellung des Wahlvorstands in Betrieben ohne Betriebsrat

(1) ¹Besteht in einem Betrieb, der die Voraussetzungen des § 1 Abs. 1 Satz 1 erfüllt, kein Betriebsrat, so bestellt der Gesamtbetriebsrat oder, falls ein solcher nicht besteht, der Konzernbetriebsrat einen Wahlvorstand. ²§ 16 Abs. 1 gilt entsprechend.

(2) ¹Besteht weder ein Gesamtbetriebsrat noch ein Konzernbetriebsrat, so wird in einer Betriebsversammlung von der Mehrheit der anwesenden Arbeitnehmer ein Wahlvorstand gewählt; § 16 Abs. 1 gilt entsprechend. ²Gleiches gilt, wenn der Gesamtbetriebsrat oder Konzernbetriebsrat die Bestellung des Wahlvorstands nach Absatz 1 unterlässt.

(3) Zu dieser Betriebsversammlung können drei wahlberechtigte Arbeitnehmer des Betriebs oder eine im Betrieb vertretene Gewerkschaft einladen

appointed by the Labor Court upon application of at least three people eligible to vote or a union represented in the establishment; subsection (1) applies *mutatis mutandis*. ²The application may contain nominations for election committee members. ³For establishments regularly employing more than 20 employees eligible to vote, the Labor Court may also appoint members of a union represented in the establishment who are not employees of the establishment as election committee members if this is necessary for the proper conduct of the election.

(3) ¹If there is no election committee eight weeks before the expiration of the term of the works council, the joint works council or, if none exists, the group works council may appoint the election committee. ²Subsection (1) applies *mutatis mutandis*.

Section 17
Appointment of the Election Committee in Establishments Without Works Councils

(1) ¹Where no works council exists in an establishment meeting the prerequisites set forth in section 1 (1) sentence 1, the joint works council or, if none exists, the group works council shall appoint the election committee. ²Section 16 (1) applies *mutatis mutandis*.

(2) ¹If neither a joint works council or a group works council exists, an election committee shall be elected by a majority of the employees present in a works assembly; section 16 (1) applies *mutatis mutandis*. ²The same shall apply if the joint works council or the group works council fails to appoint the election committee pursuant to subsection (1).

(3) Three employees of the establishment eligible to vote or a union represented in the establishment may convene a works assembly and nomi-

und Vorschläge für die Zusammensetzung des Wahlvorstands machen.

(4) ¹Findet trotz Einladung keine Betriebsversammlung statt oder wählt die Betriebsversammlung keinen Wahlvorstand, so bestellt ihn das Arbeitsgericht auf Antrag von mindestens drei wahlberechtigten Arbeitnehmern oder einer im Betrieb vertretenen Gewerkschaft. ²§ 16 Abs. 2 gilt entsprechend.

§ 17a
Bestellung des Wahlvorstands im vereinfachten Wahlverfahren

Im Fall des § 14a finden die §§ 16 und 17 mit folgender Maßgabe Anwendung:
1. Die Frist des § 16 Abs. 1 Satz 1 wird auf vier Wochen und die des § 16 Abs. 2 Satz 1, Abs. 3 Satz 1 auf drei Wochen verkürzt.
2. § 16 Abs. 1 Satz 2 und 3 findet keine Anwendung.
3. ¹In den Fällen des § 17 Abs. 2 wird der Wahlvorstand in einer Wahlversammlung von der Mehrheit der anwesenden Arbeitnehmer gewählt. ²Für die Einladung zu der Wahlversammlung gilt § 17 Abs. 3 entsprechend.
4. § 17 Abs. 4 gilt entsprechend, wenn trotz Einladung keine Wahlversammlung stattfindet oder auf der Wahlversammlung kein Wahlvorstand gewählt wird.

§ 18
Vorbereitung und Durchführung der Wahl

(1) ¹Der Wahlvorstand hat die Wahl unverzüglich einzuleiten, sie durchzuführen und das Wahlergebnis festzustellen. ²Kommt der Wahlvorstand dieser Verpflichtung nicht nach, so ersetzt ihn das Arbeitsgericht auf Antrag des Betriebsrats, von mindestens drei wahlberechtigten Arbeitnehmern oder einer

nate candidates for the election committee.

(4) ¹If a works assembly is not held despite being convened, or the works assembly does not elect an election committee, the Labor Court shall appoint it upon application by at least three persons eligible to vote or a union represented in the establishment. ²Section 16 (2) applies *mutatis mutandis*.

Section 17a
Appointment of the Election Committee in a Simplified Election Procedure

In the case set forth in section 14a, sections 16 and 17 shall apply with the following exceptions:
1. The time period set forth in section 16(1) sentence 1 shall be reduced to four weeks and that set forth in section 16(2) sentence 1 and (3) sentence 1 shall be reduced to three weeks.
2. Section 16 (1) sentences 2 and 3 shall not apply.
3. ¹In the cases set forth in section 17 (2) the election committee shall be elected in an election assembly by the majority of employees present. ²For the convening of the election assembly, section 17 (3) applies *mutatis mutandis*.
4. Section 17 (4) applies *mutatis mutandis* where no election assembly takes place despite being convened or no election committee is elected at the election assembly.

Section 18
Preparation and Conduct of the Election

(1) ¹The election committee shall promptly initiate, and execute the election and determine its result. ²Where the election committee does not comply with this obligation, it shall be replaced by the Labor Court upon application by the works council, at least three employees eligible to vote or a

²Werden Angelegenheiten behandelt, die besonders die in § 60 Abs. 1 genannten Arbeitnehmer betreffen, so hat zu diesen Tagesordnungspunkten die gesamte Jugend- und Auszubildendenvertretung ein Teilnahmerecht.

(2) Die Jugend- und Auszubildendenvertreter haben Stimmrecht, soweit die zu fassenden Beschlüsse des Betriebsrats überwiegend die in § 60 Abs. 1 genannten Arbeitnehmer betreffen.

(3) ¹Die Jugend- und Auszubildendenvertretung kann beim Betriebsrat beantragen, Angelegenheiten, die besonders die in § 60 Abs. 1 genannten Arbeitnehmer betreffen und über die sie beraten hat, auf die nächste Tagesordnung zu setzen. ²Der Betriebsrat soll Angelegenheiten, die besonders die in § 60 Abs. 1 genannten Arbeitnehmer betreffen, der Jugend- und Auszubildendenvertretung zur Beratung zuleiten.

§ 68
Teilnahme an gemeinsamen Besprechungen

Der Betriebsrat hat die Jugend- und Auszubildendenvertretung zu Besprechungen zwischen Arbeitgeber und Betriebsrat beizuziehen, wenn Angelegenheiten behandelt werden, die besonders die in § 60 Abs. 1 genannten Arbeitnehmer betreffen.

§ 69
Sprechstunden

¹In Betrieben, die in der Regel mehr als fünfzig der in § 60 Abs. 1 genannten Arbeitnehmer beschäftigen, kann die Jugend- und Auszubildendenvertretung Sprechstunden während der Arbeitszeit einrichten. ²Zeit und Ort sind durch Betriebsrat und Arbeitgeber zu vereinbaren. ³§ 39 Abs. 1 Satz 3 und 4 und Abs. 3 gilt entsprechend. ⁴An den Sprechstunden der Jugend- und Auszubildendenvertretung kann der Betriebsratsvorsitzende oder ein beauf-

youth and trainee representative body has a right to participate in those matters discussed which particularly concern the employees referred to in section 60 (1).

(2) The youth and trainee representative body has the right to vote on resolutions which predominantly apply to the employees referred to in section 60 (1).

(3) ¹The youth and trainee representative body may petition the works council to place on the agenda matters which apply particularly to the employees referred to in section 60 (1) and have already been discussed. ²The works council shall pass matters which particularly affect the employees referred to in section 60 (1) on to the youth and trainee representative body for its consideration.

Section 68
Participation in Joint Consultations

The works council shall consult with the youth and trainee representative body regarding matters between the employer and works council which particularly affect the employees referred to in section 60 (1).

Section 69
Consultation Periods

¹The youth and trainee representative body may hold consultation sessions during normal working hours in establishments which regularly employ more than fifty of the employees referred to in section 60 (1). ²The time and place shall be agreed upon with the works council and the employer. ³Section 39 (1) sentences 3 and 4 and (3) apply *mutatis mutandis*. ⁴The works council chairman or a designated works council member may participate in the youth and

tragtes Betriebsratsmitglied beratend teilnehmen.

§ 70
Allgemeine Aufgaben

(1) Die Jugend- und Auszubildendenvertretung hat folgende allgemeine Aufgaben:

1. Maßnahmen, die den in § 60 Abs. 1 genannten Arbeitnehmern dienen, insbesondere in Fragen der Berufsbildung und der Übernahme der zu ihrer Berufsausbildung Beschäftigten in ein Arbeitsverhältnis, beim Betriebsrat zu beantragen;

1a. Maßnahmen zur Durchsetzung der tatsächlichen Gleichstellung der in § 60 Abs. 1 genannten Arbeitnehmer entsprechend § 80 Abs. 1 Nr. 2a und 2b beim Betriebsrat zu beantragen;

2. darüber zu wachen, dass die zugunsten der in § 60 Abs. 1 genannten Arbeitnehmer geltenden Gesetze, Verordnungen, Unfallverhütungsvorschriften, Tarifverträge und Betriebsvereinbarungen durchgeführt werden;

3. Anregungen von in § 60 Abs. 1 genannten Arbeitnehmern, insbesondere in Fragen der Berufsbildung, entgegenzunehmen und, falls sie berechtigt erscheinen, beim Betriebsrat auf eine Erledigung hinzuwirken. Die Jugend- und Auszubildendenvertretung hat die betroffenen in § 60 Abs. 1 genannten Arbeitnehmer über den Stand und das Ergebnis der Verhandlungen zu informieren;

4. die Integration ausländischer, in § 60 Abs. 1 genannter Arbeitnehmer im Betrieb zu fördern und entsprechende Maßnahmen beim Betriebsrat zu beantragen.

(2) ¹Zur Durchführung ihrer Aufgaben ist die Jugend- und Auszubildendenvertretung durch den Betriebsrat rechtzeitig und umfassend zu unterrichten. ²Die Jugend- und Auszubildendenvertretung kann verlangen, dass ihr der

trainee representative body's sessions as a consultant.

Section 70
General Duties

(1) The youth and trainee representative body has the following general duties:

1. to request that the works council take measures to benefit those employees referred to in section 60 (1), in particular with respect vocational training and the assumption of trainees as employees;

1a. to request that the works council take measures to enforce actual equal treatment of the employees referred to in section 60 (1) in accordance with section 80 (1) nos. 2a and 2b;

2. to monitor compliance with the applicable laws, rules, safety regulations, collective bargaining agreements and works agreements for the benefit of the employees referred to in section 60 (1);

3. to receive suggestions from the employees referred to in section 60 (1), especially with regard to issues involving vocational training, and if they appear to be justified, to seek to have them implemented by the works council. The youth and trainee representative body shall inform the employees referred to in section 60 (1) of the status and results of the negotiations;

4. to request that the works council promote and take the corresponding measures to integrate foreign employees referred to in section 60 (1) in the establishment.

(2) ¹The youth and trainee representative body shall be promptly and completely informed by the works council so that it can perform its duties. ²The youth and trainee representative body may demand the works council provide

Betriebsrat die zur Durchführung ihrer Aufgaben erforderlichen Unterlagen zur Verfügung stellt.

it with all documents necessary to perform its duties.

§ 71
Jugend- und Auszubildendenversammlung

[1] Die Jugend- und Auszubildendenvertretung kann vor oder nach jeder Betriebsversammlung im Einvernehmen mit dem Betriebsrat eine betriebliche Jugend- und Auszubildendenversammlung einberufen. [2] Im Einvernehmen mit Betriebsrat und Arbeitgeber kann die betriebliche Jugend- und Auszubildendenversammlung auch zu einem anderen Zeitpunkt einberufen werden. [3] § 43 Abs. 2 Satz 1 und 2, die §§ 44 bis 46 und § 65 Abs. 2 Satz 2 gelten entsprechend.

Section 71
Youth and Trainee Representative Body Meetings

[1] The youth and trainee representatives may, in agreement with the works council, call a works meeting for the youth and trainees before or after each works meeting. [2] The youth and trainees works meeting may also, in agreement with the works council and the employer, be convened at a different time. [3] Section 43 (2) sentences 1 and 2, sections 44 through 46 and section 65 (2) sentence 2 apply *mutatis mutandis*.

Zweiter Abschnitt
Gesamt-Jugend- und Auszubildendenvertretung

Chapter 2
Joint Youth and Trainee Representative Body

§ 72
Voraussetzungen der Errichtung, Mitgliederzahl, Stimmengewicht

(1) Bestehen in einem Unternehmen mehrere Jugend- und Auszubildendenvertretungen, so ist eine Gesamt-Jugend- und Auszubildendenvertretung zu errichten.

(2) In die Gesamt-Jugend- und Auszubildendenvertretung entsendet jede Jugend- und Auszubildendenvertretung ein Mitglied.

(3) Die Jugend- und Auszubildendenvertretung hat für das Mitglied der Gesamt-Jugend- und Auszubildendenvertretung mindestens ein Ersatzmitglied zu bestellen und die Reihenfolge des Nachrückens festzulegen.

(4) Durch Tarifvertrag oder Betriebsvereinbarung kann die Mitgliederzahl der Gesamt-Jugend- und Auszubildenden-

Section 72
Prerequisites for the Formation, Number of Members, Weight of Votes

(1) Where several youth and trainee representative bodies exist in an company, a joint youth representative may be formed.

(2) Each youth and trainee representative body shall designate one member to the joint youth and trainee representative body.

(3) The youth and trainee representative bodies shall appoint at least one alternate member to the joint youth and trainee representative body and establish the order of succession.

(4) A collective bargaining agreement or a works agreement may provide for a different number of joint youth and

vertretung abweichend von Absatz 2 geregelt werden.

(5) Gehören nach Absatz 2 der Gesamt-Jugend- und Auszubildendenvertretung mehr als zwanzig Mitglieder an und besteht keine tarifliche Regelung nach Absatz 4, so ist zwischen Gesamtbetriebsrat und Arbeitgeber eine Betriebsvereinbarung über die Mitgliederzahl der Gesamt-Jugend- und Auszubildendenvertretung abzuschließen, in der bestimmt wird, dass Jugend- und Auszubildendenvertretungen mehrerer Betriebe eines Unternehmens, die regional oder durch gleichartige Interessen miteinander verbunden sind, gemeinsam Mitglieder in die Gesamt-Jugend- und Auszubildendenvertretung entsenden.

(6) [1] Kommt im Fall des Absatzes 5 eine Einigung nicht zustande, so entscheidet eine für das Gesamtunternehmen zu bildende Einigungsstelle. [2] Der Spruch der Einigungsstelle ersetzt die Einigung zwischen Arbeitgeber und Gesamtbetriebsrat.

(7) [1] Jedes Mitglied der Gesamt-Jugend- und Auszubildendenvertretung hat so viele Stimmen, wie in dem Betrieb, in dem es gewählt wurde, in § 60 Abs. 1 genannte Arbeitnehmer in der Wählerliste eingetragen sind. [2] Ist ein Mitglied der Gesamt-Jugend- und Auszubildendenvertretung für mehrere Betriebe entsandt worden, so hat es so viele Stimmen, wie in den Betrieben, für die es entsandt ist, in § 60 Abs. 1 genannte Arbeitnehmer in den Wählerlisten eingetragen sind. [3] Sind mehrere Mitglieder der Jugend- und Auszubildendenvertretung entsandt worden, so stehen diesen die Stimmen nach Satz 1 anteilig zu.

(8) Für Mitglieder der Gesamt-Jugend- und Auszubildendenvertretung, die aus einem gemeinsamen Betrieb mehrerer Unternehmen entsandt worden sind, können durch Tarifvertrag oder Be-

trainee representatives from that set forth in subsection (2).

(5) Where, pursuant to subsection (2), more than 20 members belong to the joint youth and trainee representative body and there is no collective bargaining provision pursuant to subsection (4), a works agreement shall be concluded between the joint works council and the employer with regard to the number of members of the joint youth and trainee representative body, which shall provide that the youth and trainee representative bodies of the several establishments within one company which are bound together geographically or through the same interests will jointly delegate members to the joint youth and trainee representative body.

(6) [1] If an agreement cannot be reached pursuant to subsection (5), a conciliation board formed for the entire company shall render the decision. [2] The decision of the conciliation board shall replace a decision between the employer and the joint works council.

(7) [1] The number of votes held by each member of the joint youth and trainee representatives shall be equivalent to the number of employees referred to in section 60 (1) registered on the voting lists of the establishment in which it was elected. [2] If one member of the joint youth and trainee representative body has been delegated by several establishments, he shall have as many votes as there are employees referred to in section 60 (1) registered on the voting list in the establishment which delegated him. [3] If two or more members of the youth and trainee representative body have been delegated, they shall have proportional votes pursuant to sentence 1.

(8) For members of the joint youth and trainee representative body who were delegated by a joint works of several companies, a collective bargaining agreement or works agreement may

triebsvereinbarung von Absatz 7 abweichende Regelungen getroffen werden.

agree upon a provision varying from subsection (7).

§ 73
Geschäftsführung und Geltung sonstiger Vorschriften

Section 73
Management and Application of Other Regulations

(1) ¹Die Gesamt-Jugend- und Auszubildendenvertretung kann nach Verständigung des Gesamtbetriebsrats Sitzungen abhalten. ²An den Sitzungen kann der Vorsitzende des Gesamtbetriebsrats oder ein beauftragtes Mitglied des Gesamtbetriebsrats teilnehmen.

(1) ¹The joint youth and trainee representative body may, upon agreement with the joint works council, hold meetings. ²The chairman or a delegated member of the joint works council may participate in this meeting.

(2) Für die Gesamt-Jugend- und Auszubildendenvertretung gelten § 25 Abs. 1, die §§ 26, 28 Abs. 1 Satz 1, die §§ 30, 31, 34, 36, 37 Abs. 1 bis 3, die §§ 40, 41, 48, 49, 50, 51 Abs. 2 bis 5 sowie die §§ 66 bis 68 entsprechend.

(2) For the joint youth and trainee body, section 25 (1), sections 26, 28 (1) sentence 1, sections 30, 31, 34, 36, 37 (1) to (3), sections 40, 41, 48, 49, 50, 51 (2) to (5), as well as sections 66 through 68 apply *mutatis mutandis*.

Dritter Abschnitt
Konzern-Jugend- und Auszubildendenvertretung

Chapter 3
Group Youth and Trainee Representative Body

§ 73 a
Voraussetzung der Errichtung, Mitgliederzahl, Stimmengewicht

Section 73 a
Prerequisites for the Formation, Number of Members, Weight of Votes

(1) ¹Bestehen in einem Konzern (§ 18 Abs. 1 des Aktiengesetzes) mehrere Gesamt-Jugend- und Auszubildendenvertretungen, kann durch Beschlüsse der einzelnen Gesamt-Jugend- und Auszubildendenvertretungen eine Konzern-Jugend- und Auszubildendenvertretung errichtet werden. ²Die Errichtung erfordert die Zustimmung der Gesamt-Jugend- und Auszubildendenvertretungen der Konzernunternehmen, in denen insgesamt mindestens 75 vom Hundert der in § 60 Abs. 1 genannten Arbeitnehmer beschäftigt sind. ³Besteht in einem Konzernunternehmen nur eine Jugend- und Auszubildendenvertretung, so nimmt diese die Aufgaben einer Gesamt-Jugend- und Auszubildendenvertretung nach den Vorschriften dieses Abschnitts wahr.

(1) ¹Where several joint youth and trainee representative bodies exist within an group (section 18 (1) of the Stock Corporation Act), the individual joint youth and trainee representative bodies may adopt a resolution to form a group youth and trainee representative body. ²The formation shall require the consent of the joint youth and trainee representative bodies of the group companies in which at least 75% of the employees referred to in section 60 (1) are employed. ³If a group company only has one youth and trainee representative body, it shall assume the duties of a joint youth and trainee representative body pursuant to the provisions of this Chapter.

(2) ¹In die Konzern-Jugend- und Auszubildendenvertretung entsendet jede Gesamt-Jugend- und Auszubildendenvertretung eines ihrer Mitglieder. ²Sie hat für jedes Mitglied mindestens ein Ersatzmitglied zu bestellen und die Reihenfolge des Nachrückens festzulegen.

(3) Jedes Mitglied der Konzern-Jugend- und Auszubildendenvertretung hat so viele Stimmen, wie die Mitglieder der entsendenden Gesamt-Jugend- und Auszubildendenvertretung insgesamt Stimmen haben.

(4) § 72 Abs. 4 bis 8 gilt entsprechend.

(2) ¹Each joint youth and trainee representative body shall designate one of its members to the group youth and trainee representative body. ²They shall appoint at least one alternate for each member and establish the order of succession.

(3) The number of votes held by each member of the group youth and trainee representatives shall be equivalent to the total number of members of the delegating joint youth and trainee representative body.

(4) Section 72 (4) to (8) applies *mutatis mutandis*.

§ 73 b
Geschäftsführung und Geltung sonstiger Vorschriften

(1) ¹Die Konzern-Jugend- und Auszubildendenvertretung kann nach Verständigung des Konzernbetriebsrats Sitzungen abhalten. ²An den Sitzungen kann der Vorsitzende oder ein beauftragtes Mitglied des Konzernbetriebsrats teilnehmen.

(2) Für die Konzern-Jugend- und Auszubildendenvertretung gelten § 25 Abs. 1, die §§ 26, 28 Abs. 1 Satz 1, die §§ 30, 31, 34, 36, 37 Abs. 1 bis 3, die §§ 40, 41, 51 Abs. 3 bis 5, die §§ 56, 57, 58, 59 Abs. 2 und die §§ 66 bis 68 entsprechend.

Section 73 b
Management and Application of Other Regulations

(1) ¹The group youth and trainee representative body may, upon agreement with the group works council, hold meetings. ²The chairman or a delegated member of the group works council may participate in this meeting.

(2) For the group youth and trainee body, sections 25 (1), 26, 28 (1) sentence 1, sections 30, 31, 34, 36, 37 (1) to (3), sections 40, 41, 51 (3) to (5), sections 56, 57, 58, 59 (2) as well as sections 66 through 68 apply *mutatis mutandis*.

Vierter Teil
Mitwirkung und Mitbestimmung der Arbeitnehmer

Part 4
Participation and Codetermination of the Employee

Erster Abschnitt
Allgemeines

Chapter 1
General Information

§ 74
Grundsätze für die Zusammenarbeit

Section 74
Principles of Cooperation

(1) ¹Arbeitgeber und Betriebsrat sollen mindestens einmal im Monat zu einer

(1) ¹The employer and the joint works council shall arrange to meet at least

Besprechung zusammentreten. ²Sie haben über strittige Fragen mit dem ernsten Willen zur Einigung zu verhandeln und Vorschläge für die Beilegung von Meinungsverschiedenheiten zu machen.

(2) ¹Maßnahmen des Arbeitskampfes zwischen Arbeitgeber und Betriebsrat sind unzulässig; Arbeitskämpfe tariffähiger Parteien werden hierdurch nicht berührt. ²Arbeitgeber und Betriebsrat haben Betätigungen zu unterlassen, durch die der Arbeitsablauf oder der Frieden des Betriebs beeinträchtigt werden. ³Sie haben jede parteipolitische Betätigung im Betrieb zu unterlassen; die Behandlung von Angelegenheiten tarifpolitischer, sozialpolitischer, umweltpolitischer und wirtschaftlicher Art, die den Betrieb oder seine Arbeitnehmer unmittelbar betreffen, wird hierdurch nicht berührt.

(3) Arbeitnehmer, die im Rahmen dieses Gesetzes Aufgaben übernehmen, werden hierdurch in der Betätigung für ihre Gewerkschaft auch im Betrieb nicht beschränkt.

§ 75
Grundsätze für die Behandlung der Betriebsangehörigen

(1) Arbeitgeber und Betriebsrat haben darüber zu wachen, dass alle im Betrieb tätigen Personen nach den Grundsätzen von Recht und Billigkeit behandelt werden, insbesondere, dass jede Benachteiligung von Personen aus Gründen ihrer Rasse oder wegen ihrer ethnischen Herkunft, ihrer Abstammung oder sonstigen Herkunft, ihrer Nationalität, ihrer Religion oder Weltanschauung, ihrer Behinderung, ihres Alters, ihrer politischen oder gewerkschaftlichen Betätigung oder Einstellung oder wegen ihres Geschlechts oder ihrer sexuellen Identität unterbleibt.

(2) ¹Arbeitgeber und Betriebsrat haben die freie Entfaltung der Persönlichkeit

once a month. ²They shall discuss disputed issues with a sincere desire to come to an agreement and make suggestions for resolving differences of opinion.

(2) ¹Labor dispute measures between the employer and the works council shall not be permitted; this shall not apply to labor disputes between parties competent to conclude collective bargaining agreements. ²Employers and works councils shall refrain from any activities which could impair the flow of the establishment or the order in the establishment. ³They shall refrain from all party politics in the establishment; this shall not apply to the treatment of matters involving collective bargaining policies, social policies, environmental policies and economic policies which directly affect the establishment or its employees.

(3) Employees who undertake duties pursuant to this Act shall not be restricted by the foregoing with regard to their trade union activities in the establishment.

Section 75
Principles Regarding the Treatment of the Staff of the Establishment

(1) The employer and the works council shall ensure that all persons working in the establishment are treated in accordance with the principles of justice and fairness, in particular, that no persons are disadvantaged due to their race or their ethic origin, descent or other origin, nationality, religion or secular belief, their disability, age, political or trade union activities or views or due to their gender or sexual identity.

(2) ¹The employer and the works council shall safeguard and promote the free

der im Betrieb beschäftigten Arbeitnehmer zu schützen und zu fördern. ²Sie haben die Selbständigkeit und Eigeninitiative der Arbeitnehmer und Arbeitsgruppen zu fördern.

§ 76
Einigungsstelle

(1) ¹Zur Beilegung von Meinungsverschiedenheiten zwischen Arbeitgeber und Betriebsrat, Gesamtbetriebsrat oder Konzernbetriebsrat ist bei Bedarf eine Einigungsstelle zu bilden. ²Durch Betriebsvereinbarung kann eine ständige Einigungsstelle errichtet werden.

(2) ¹Die Einigungsstelle besteht aus einer gleichen Anzahl von Beisitzern, die vom Arbeitgeber und Betriebsrat bestellt werden, und einem unparteiischen Vorsitzenden, auf dessen Person sich beide Seiten einigen müssen. ²Kommt eine Einigung über die Person des Vorsitzenden nicht zustande, so bestellt ihn das Arbeitsgericht. ³Dieses entscheidet auch, wenn kein Einverständnis über die Zahl der Beisitzer erzielt wird.

(3) ¹Die Einigungsstelle hat unverzüglich tätig zu werden. ²Sie fasst ihre Beschlüsse nach mündlicher Beratung mit Stimmenmehrheit. ³Bei der Beschlussfassung hat sich der Vorsitzende zunächst der Stimme zu enthalten; kommt eine Stimmenmehrheit nicht zustande, so nimmt der Vorsitzende nach weiterer Beratung an der erneuten Beschlussfassung teil. ⁴Die Beschlüsse der Einigungsstelle sind schriftlich niederzulegen, vom Vorsitzenden zu unterschreiben und Arbeitgeber und Betriebsrat zuzuleiten.

(4) Durch Betriebsvereinbarung können weitere Einzelheiten des Verfahrens vor der Einigungsstelle geregelt werden.

(5) ¹In den Fällen, in denen der Spruch der Einigungsstelle die Einigung zwischen Arbeitgeber und Betriebsrat ersetzt, wird die Einigungsstelle auf Antrag einer Seite tätig. ²Benennt eine

development of the personality of the employees of the establishment. ²They shall promote the independence and initiative of the employees and work groups.

Section 76
Conciliation Board

(1) ¹A conciliation board shall be formed, where necessary, to resolve any differences of opinion between the employer and works council, joint works council or group works council. ²A permanent conciliation board may be formed pursuant to a works agreement.

(2) ¹The employer and the works council shall appoint an equal number of members to the conciliation board and an impartial chairman agreed upon by both sides. ²The Labor Court shall appoint a chairman if no agreement can be reached. ³It shall also decide if an agreement cannot be reached regarding the number of board members.

(3) ¹The conciliation board shall begin working without delay. ²The conciliation board shall discuss the matter and decide by majority vote. ³The chairman shall initially abstain from voting on the resolution; in case of a tie, he shall participate in the next round of voting after further discussion. ⁴The resolutions of the conciliation board shall be recorded in writing, signed by the chairman, and then forwarded to the employer and works council.

(4) Additional details regarding the conciliation board proceedings may be regulated by a works agreement.

(5) ¹In cases where the decision of the conciliation board replaces an agreement between the employer and the works council, the conciliation board act at the request of either party.

Seite keine Mitglieder oder bleiben die von einer Seite genannten Mitglieder trotz rechtzeitiger Einladung der Sitzung fern, so entscheiden der Vorsitzende und die erschienenen Mitglieder nach Maßgabe des Absatzes 3 allein. ³Die Einigungsstelle fasst ihre Beschlüsse unter angemessener Berücksichtigung der Belange des Betriebs und der betroffenen Arbeitnehmer nach billigem Ermessen. ⁴Die Überschreitung der Grenzen des Ermessens kann durch den Arbeitgeber oder den Betriebsrat nur binnen einer Frist von zwei Wochen, vom Tage der Zuleitung des Beschlusses an gerechnet, beim Arbeitsgericht geltend gemacht werden.

(6) ¹Im Übrigen wird die Einigungsstelle nur tätig, wenn beide Seiten es beantragen oder mit ihrem Tätigwerden einverstanden sind. ²In diesen Fällen ersetzt ihr Spruch die Einigung zwischen Arbeitgeber und Betriebsrat nur, wenn beide Seiten sich dem Spruch im Voraus unterworfen oder ihn nachträglich angenommen haben.

(7) Soweit nach anderen Vorschriften der Rechtsweg gegeben ist, wird er durch den Spruch der Einigungsstelle nicht ausgeschlossen.

(8) Durch Tarifvertrag kann bestimmt werden, dass an die Stelle der in Absatz 1 bezeichneten Einigungsstelle eine tarifliche Schlichtungsstelle tritt.

²Where one side fails to appoint any members or despite timely notice, the members of one side are absent, the chairman and the members present shall decide the matter alone in accordance with subsection (3). ³The conciliation board shall adopt its resolutions according to its best judgment, taking the concerns of the establishment and of the employees involved duly into account. ⁴The employer or the works council may only file a petition with the Labor Court charging the conciliation board with exceeding the limits of its discretion within two weeks after receiving the decision.

(6) ¹Otherwise, the conciliation board shall only act if both sides so request or agree that it should act. ²In such cases its decision shall only replace an agreement between the employer and the works council if both sides have agreed in advance to be bound by this decision or if they ratify it subsequently.

(7) If other provisions provide for legal recourse, it shall not be excluded by a decision of the conciliation board.

(8) A collective bargaining agreement may provide that an arbitration tribunal set up pursuant to the collective bargaining agreement will take the place of a conciliation board as referred to in subsection (1).

§ 76a
Kosten der Einigungsstelle

(1) Die Kosten der Einigungsstelle trägt der Arbeitgeber.

(2) ¹Die Beisitzer der Einigungsstelle, die dem Betrieb angehören, erhalten für ihre Tätigkeit keine Vergütung; § 37 Abs. 2 und 3 gilt entsprechend. ²Ist die Einigungsstelle zur Beilegung von Meinungsverschiedenheiten zwischen Arbeitgeber und Gesamtbetriebsrat oder Konzernbetriebsrat zu bilden, so gilt

Section 76a
Cost of the Conciliation Board

(1) The costs of the conciliation board shall be borne by the employer.

(2) ¹Members of the conciliation board who belong to the establishment shall not be compensated for their activities; Section 37 (2) and (3) apply *mutatis mutandis*. ²Where the conciliation board is formed to resolve differences of opinion between the employer and the joint works council or group works council,

Satz 1 für die einem Betrieb des Unternehmens oder eines Konzernunternehmens angehörenden Beisitzer entsprechend.

(3) ¹Der Vorsitzende und die Beisitzer der Einigungsstelle, die nicht zu den in Absatz 2 genannten Personen zählen, haben gegenüber dem Arbeitgeber Anspruch auf Vergütung ihrer Tätigkeit. ²Die Höhe der Vergütung richtet sich nach den Grundsätzen des Absatzes 4 Satz 3 bis 5.

(4) ¹Das Bundesministerium für Arbeit und Soziales kann durch Rechtsverordnung die Vergütung nach Absatz 3 regeln. ²In der Vergütungsordnung sind Höchstsätze festzusetzen. ³Dabei sind insbesondere der erforderliche Zeitaufwand, die Schwierigkeit der Streitigkeit sowie ein Verdienstausfall zu berücksichtigen. ⁴Die Vergütung der Beisitzer ist niedriger zu bemessen als die des Vorsitzenden. ⁵Bei der Festsetzung der Höchstsätze ist den berechtigten Interessen der Mitglieder der Einigungsstelle und des Arbeitgebers Rechnung zu tragen.

(5) Von Absatz 3 und einer Vergütungsordnung nach Absatz 4 kann durch Tarifvertrag oder in einer Betriebsvereinbarung, wenn ein Tarifvertrag dies zulässt oder eine tarifliche Regelung nicht besteht, abgewichen werden.

§ 77
Durchführung gemeinsamer Beschlüsse, Betriebsvereinbarungen

(1) ¹Vereinbarungen zwischen Betriebsrat und Arbeitgeber, auch soweit sie auf einem Spruch der Einigungsstelle beruhen, führt der Arbeitgeber durch, es sei denn, dass im Einzelfall etwas anderes vereinbart ist. ²Der Betriebsrat darf nicht durch einseitige Handlungen in die Leitung des Betriebs eingreifen.

sentence 1 shall apply with respect to the conciliation board members belonging to the company or a group company.

(3) ¹The chairman and members of the conciliation board who are not among those persons referred to in subsection (2) above, shall be entitled to compensation from the employer for their activity. ²The amount of the compensation shall be determined in accordance with the principles set forth in subsection (4) sentences 3 through 5.

(4) ¹The Federal Ministry of Labor and Social Affairs may enact an order regulating the compensation pursuant to subsection (3). ²This order shall stipulate the maximum rates for such compensation. ³Particular consideration shall be given to the amount of time spent, the complexity of the dispute and lost earnings. ⁴The members shall receive less compensation than the chairman. ⁵In determining the maximum rates, the legitimate interests of the conciliation board members and the employer shall be taken into account.

(5) A collective bargaining agreement or a works agreement may provide for a variation from subsection (3) and the compensation order pursuant to subsection (4) if so permitted by a collective bargaining agreement or if no collective bargaining provision exists.

Section 77
Implementation of Joint Resolutions, Works Agreements

(1) ¹Agreements between the works council and the employer, including those based on a decision of the conciliation board, shall be implemented by the employer unless otherwise specifically agreed in an individual case. ²The works council may not unilaterally intervene in the management of the establishment.

(2) ¹Betriebsvereinbarungen sind von Betriebsrat und Arbeitgeber gemeinsam zu beschließen und schriftlich niederzulegen. ²Sie sind von beiden Seiten zu unterzeichnen; dies gilt nicht, soweit Betriebsvereinbarungen auf einem Spruch der Einigungsstelle beruhen. ³Der Arbeitgeber hat die Betriebsvereinbarungen an geeigneter Stelle im Betrieb auszulegen.

(3) ¹Arbeitsentgelte und sonstige Arbeitsbedingungen, die durch Tarifvertrag geregelt sind oder üblicherweise geregelt werden, können nicht Gegenstand einer Betriebsvereinbarung sein. ²Dies gilt nicht, wenn ein Tarifvertrag den Abschluss ergänzender Betriebsvereinbarungen ausdrücklich zulässt.

(4) ¹Betriebsvereinbarungen gelten unmittelbar und zwingend. ²Werden Arbeitnehmern durch die Betriebsvereinbarung Rechte eingeräumt, so ist ein Verzicht auf sie nur mit Zustimmung des Betriebsrats zulässig. ³Die Verwirkung dieser Rechte ist ausgeschlossen. ⁴Ausschlussfristen für ihre Geltendmachung sind nur insoweit zulässig, als sie in einem Tarifvertrag oder einer Betriebsvereinbarung vereinbart werden; dasselbe gilt für die Abkürzung der Verjährungsfristen.

(5) Betriebsvereinbarungen können, soweit nichts anderes vereinbart ist, mit einer Frist von drei Monaten gekündigt werden.

(6) Nach Ablauf einer Betriebsvereinbarung gelten ihre Regelungen in Angelegenheiten, in denen ein Spruch der Einigungsstelle die Einigung zwischen Arbeitgeber und Betriebsrat ersetzen kann, weiter, bis sie durch eine andere Abmachung ersetzt werden.

§ 78
Schutzbestimmungen

¹Die Mitglieder des Betriebsrats, des Gesamtbetriebsrats, des Konzernbetriebsrats, der Jugend- und Auszubildendenvertretung, der Gesamt-Jugend-

(2) ¹Works agreements shall be concluded jointly by the works council and the employer and recorded in writing. ²They shall be signed by both parties; this does not apply if the works agreement is based on a decision of the conciliation board. ³The employer shall display the works agreements in a suitable place in the establishment.

(3) ¹Remuneration and other working conditions which are regulated or normally regulated by collective bargaining agreements may not be the subject of a works agreement. ²This does not apply if a collective bargaining agreement expressly permits the conclusion of supplementary works agreements.

(4) ¹Works agreements have direct and mandatory application. ²If a works agreement grants employees rights, they may only be waived with the consent of the works council. ³These rights may not be forfeited. ⁴Preclusive periods for the exercise of such rights shall only be permitted if they are agreed upon in a collective bargaining agreement or a works agreement; the same shall apply for the reduction of the period within which such rights must be exercised.

(5) Unless otherwise agreed, works agreements may be terminated with three months' notice.

(6) Upon expiration of a works agreement, its provisions shall continue to apply with respect to matters in which a decision of the conciliation board may replace an agreement between the employer and the works council until it is replaced by another agreement.

Section 78
Protective Provisions

¹The members of the works council, the joint works council, the group works council, the youth and trainee representative body, the joint youth and trainee

und Auszubildendenvertretung, der Konzern-Jugend- und Auszubildendenvertretung, des Wirtschaftsausschusses, der Bordvertretung, des Seebetriebsrats, der in § 3 Abs. 1 genannten Vertretungen der Arbeitnehmer, der Einigungsstelle, einer tariflichen Schlichtungsstelle (§ 76 Abs. 8) und einer betrieblichen Beschwerdestelle (§ 86) sowie Auskunftspersonen (§ 80 Abs. 2 Satz 3) dürfen in der Ausübung ihrer Tätigkeit nicht gestört oder behindert werden. ²Sie dürfen wegen ihrer Tätigkeit nicht benachteiligt oder begünstigt werden; dies gilt auch für ihre berufliche Entwicklung.

representative body, the economic committee, the ship's committee, the works council of the merchant fleet, the representatives of the employees referred to in section 3 (1), the conciliation board, an arbitration board pursuant to collective bargaining agreement (section 76 (8)) and a complaints board of the establishment (section 86), as well as persons providing information (section 80 (2) sentence 3) may not be disturbed or hindered from performing their activities. ²They may not be disadvantaged or advantaged due to their activities; the same applies to their occupational advancement.

§ 78a
Schutz Auszubildender in besonderen Fällen

Section 78a
Protection of Trainees in Special Cases

(1) Beabsichtigt der Arbeitgeber, einen Auszubildenden, der Mitglied der Jugend- und Auszubildendenvertretung, des Betriebsrats, der Bordvertretung oder des Seebetriebsrats ist, nach Beendigung des Berufsausbildungsverhältnisses nicht in ein Arbeitsverhältnis auf unbestimmte Zeit zu übernehmen, so hat er dies drei Monate vor Beendigung des Berufsausbildungsverhältnisses dem Auszubildenden schriftlich mitzuteilen.

(1) If an employer does not intend to enter into an employment relationship for an indefinite term after the end of the training period of a trainee who is a member of the youth and trainee representative body, the works council, the ship's committee or the works council of the merchant fleet, the employer must inform such trainee in writing thereof three months before the end of the training period.

(2) ¹Verlangt ein in Absatz 1 genannter Auszubildender innerhalb der letzten drei Monate vor Beendigung des Berufsausbildungsverhältnisses schriftlich vom Arbeitgeber die Weiterbeschäftigung, so gilt zwischen Auszubildendem und Arbeitgeber im Anschluss an das Berufsausbildungsverhältnis ein Arbeitsverhältnis auf unbestimmte Zeit als begründet. ²Auf dieses Arbeitsverhältnis ist insbesondere § 37 Abs. 4 und 5 entsprechend anzuwenden.

(2) ¹If a trainee referred to in subsection (1) makes a written request for continued employment by the employer within the three months prior the end of the vocational training period, the trainee and the employer shall be deemed to have entered into an employment relationship for an indefinite term following the training period. ²Section 37 (4) and (5) in particular apply *mutatis mutandis* to this employment relationship.

(3) Die Absätze 1 und 2 gelten auch, wenn das Berufsausbildungsverhältnis vor Ablauf eines Jahres nach Beendigung der Amtszeit der Jugend- und Auszubildendenvertretung, des Betriebsrats,

(3) Subsections (1) and (2) shall also apply if the trainee period ends within one year after the end of the trainee's term of office as a youth and trainee representative, a works council mem-

der Bordvertretung oder des Seebetriebsrats endet.

(4) ¹Der Arbeitgeber kann spätestens bis zum Ablauf von zwei Wochen nach Beendigung des Berufsausbildungsverhältnisses beim Arbeitsgericht beantragen,
1. festzustellen, dass ein Arbeitsverhältnis nach Absatz 2 oder 3 nicht begründet wird, oder
2. das bereits nach Absatz 2 oder 3 begründete Arbeitsverhältnis aufzulösen,

wenn Tatsachen vorliegen, aufgrund derer dem Arbeitgeber unter Berücksichtigung aller Umstände die Weiterbeschäftigung nicht zugemutet werden kann. ²In dem Verfahren vor dem Arbeitsgericht sind der Betriebsrat, die Bordvertretung, der Seebetriebsrat, bei Mitgliedern der Jugend- und Auszubildendenvertretung auch diese Beteiligte.

(5) Die Absätze 2 bis 4 finden unabhängig davon Anwendung, ob der Arbeitgeber seiner Mitteilungspflicht nach Absatz 1 nachgekommen ist.

§ 79
Geheimhaltungspflicht

(1) ¹Die Mitglieder und Ersatzmitglieder des Betriebsrats sind verpflichtet, Betriebs- oder Geschäftsgeheimnisse, die ihnen wegen ihrer Zugehörigkeit zum Betriebsrat bekannt geworden und vom Arbeitgeber ausdrücklich als geheimhaltungsbedürftig bezeichnet worden sind, nicht zu offenbaren und nicht zu verwerten. ²Dies gilt auch nach dem Ausscheiden aus dem Betriebsrat. ³Die Verpflichtung gilt nicht gegenüber Mitgliedern des Betriebsrats. ⁴Sie gilt ferner nicht gegenüber dem Gesamtbetriebsrat, dem Konzernbetriebsrat, der Bordvertretung, dem Seebetriebsrat und den Arbeitnehmervertretern im Aufsichtsrat sowie im Verfahren vor der Einigungsstelle, der tariflichen Schlichtungsstelle

ber, a ship's committee member, or a works council member for the merchant fleet.

(4) ¹The employer may, within two weeks after the end of the vocational trainee period at the latest, petition the Labor Court to:
1. determine that no employment relationship was established pursuant to subsection (2) or (3), or
2. dissolve an employment relationship established pursuant to subsection (2) or (3)

if, taking all circumstances duly into account, the employer cannot reasonably be expected to employee the trainee. ²The works council, the ship's committee, the works council for the merchant fleet, members of the youth and trainee representative body shall also be parties to the proceedings before the Labor Court.

(5) Subsections (2) through (4) shall apply regardless of whether or not the employer fulfilled his obligation to notify the trainee pursuant to subsection (1).

Section 79
Duty of Confidentiality

(1) ¹The members and alternate members of the works council shall refrain from disclose or utilizing trade or business secrets which have become known to them due to their membership in the works council and which the employer has expressly designated as confidential. ²This shall continue to apply after the membership on the works council comes to an end. ³This obligation does not apply vis-à-vis other members of the works council. ⁴It does also not apply vis-à-vis the joint works council, the group works council, the ship's committee, the works council of the merchant fleet, and the representatives of the employee on the supervisory board as well as in proceedings before the

(§ 76 Abs. 8) oder einer betrieblichen Beschwerdestelle (§ 86).

(2) Absatz 1 gilt sinngemäß für die Mitglieder und Ersatzmitglieder des Gesamtbetriebsrats, des Konzernbetriebsrats, der Jugend- und Auszubildendenvertretung, der Gesamt-Jugend- und Auszubildendenvertretung, der Konzern-Jugend- und Auszubildendenvertretung, des Wirtschaftsausschusses, der Bordvertretung, des Seebetriebsrats, der gemäß § 3 Abs. 1 gebildeten Vertretungen der Arbeitnehmer, der Einigungsstelle, der tariflichen Schlichtungsstelle (§ 76 Abs. 8) und einer betrieblichen Beschwerdestelle (§ 86) sowie für die Vertreter von Gewerkschaften oder von Arbeitgebervereinigungen.

§ 80
Allgemeine Aufgaben

(1) Der Betriebsrat hat folgende allgemeine Aufgaben:
1. darüber zu wachen, dass die zugunsten der Arbeitnehmer geltenden Gesetze, Verordnungen, Unfallverhütungsvorschriften, Tarifverträge und Betriebsvereinbarungen durchgeführt werden;
2. Maßnahmen, die dem Betrieb und der Belegschaft dienen, beim Arbeitgeber zu beantragen;
2a. die Durchsetzung der tatsächlichen Gleichstellung von Frauen und Männern, insbesondere bei der Einstellung, Beschäftigung, Aus-, Fort- und Weiterbildung und dem beruflichen Aufstieg, zu fördern;
2b. die Vereinbarkeit von Familie und Erwerbstätigkeit zu fördern;
3. Anregungen von Arbeitnehmern und der Jugend- und Auszubildendenvertretung entgegenzunehmen und, falls sie berechtigt erscheinen, durch Verhandlungen mit dem Arbeitgeber auf eine Erledigung hinzuwirken; er

conciliation board, the arbitration board formed under the collective bargaining agreement (section 76 (8)) or a complaints committee of the establishment (section 86).

(2) Subsection (1) applies *mutatis mutandis* for the members and alternate members of the joint works council, the group works council, the youth and trainee representative body, the joint youth and trainee representative body, the economics committee, the ship's committee, the works council of the merchant fleet, the designated representatives of the employees pursuant to section 3 (1), the conciliation board, the arbitration board formed under the collective bargaining agreement (section 76 (8)) and a complaints committee of the establishment (section 86), as well as representatives of the union or employers' associations.

Section 80
General Duties

(1) The works council shall have the following general duties:
1. to ensure implementation of the laws, regulations, safety regulations, collective bargaining agreements and works agreements concluded for the benefit of the employees;
2. to request that the employer implement measures that serve the interest of the establishment and the staff;
2a. to promote the genuine equality of women and men, especially with respect to hiring, employment, training, continuing and further education and promotion;
2b. to promote the compatibility of family with employment;
3. to accept suggestions by employees and the youth and trainee representative body and where they appear to be justified, to negotiate with the employer for their implementation; it shall inform the affected employees

hat die betreffenden Arbeitnehmer über den Stand und das Ergebnis der Verhandlungen zu unterrichten;
4. die Eingliederung Schwerbehinderter und sonstiger besonders schutzbedürftiger Personen zu fördern;
5. die Wahl einer Jugend- und Auszubildendenvertretung vorzubereiten und durchzuführen und mit dieser zur Förderung der Belange der in § 60 Abs. 1 genannten Arbeitnehmer eng zusammenzuarbeiten; er kann von der Jugend- und Auszubildendenvertretung Vorschläge und Stellungnahmen anfordern;
6. die Beschäftigung älterer Arbeitnehmer im Betrieb zu fördern;
7. die Integration ausländischer Arbeitnehmer im Betrieb und das Verständnis zwischen ihnen und den deutschen Arbeitnehmern zu fördern, sowie Maßnahmen zur Bekämpfung von Rassismus und Fremdenfeindlichkeit im Betrieb zu beantragen;
8. die Beschäftigung im Betrieb zu fördern und zu sichern;
9. Maßnahmen des Arbeitsschutzes und des betrieblichen Umweltschutzes zu fördern.

(2) ¹Zur Durchführung seiner Aufgaben nach diesem Gesetz ist der Betriebsrat rechtzeitig und umfassend vom Arbeitgeber zu unterrichten; die Unterrichtung erstreckt sich auch auf die Beschäftigung von Personen, die nicht in einem Arbeitsverhältnis zum Arbeitgeber stehen. ²Dem Betriebsrat sind auf Verlangen jederzeit die zur Durchführung seiner Aufgaben erforderlichen Unterlagen zur Verfügung zu stellen; in diesem Rahmen ist der Betriebsausschuss oder ein nach § 28 gebildeter Ausschuss berechtigt, in die Listen über die Bruttolöhne und -gehälter Einblick zu nehmen. ³Soweit es zur ordnungsgemäßen Erfüllung der Aufgaben des Betriebsrats erforderlich ist, hat der Arbeitgeber ihm sachkundige Arbeitnehmer als Auskunftspersonen zur Verfügung zu stellen; er hat hierbei die Vorschläge des Betriebsrats zu berück-

of the status and results of such negotiations;
4. to promote the integration of the severely disabled and other persons requiring special protection;
5. to prepare and hold the election of the youth and trainee representative body and to work closely with it to further the interests of the employees referred to in section 60 (1); it may request suggestions and comments from the youth and trainee representative body;
6. to promote the employment of older employees in the establishment;
7. to promote the integration of foreign employees in the establishment and understanding between them and the German employees, as well as to petition measures to combat racism and xenophobia in the establishment;
8. to promote and secure employment in the establishment;
9. to promote industrial safety and operational environmental measures.

(2) ¹The employer shall promptly and completely inform the works council so it may execute its duties pursuant to this Act; such information shall extend to the employment of persons who are not in an employment relationship with the employer. ²Upon request the works council shall have necessary documents made available to it so it may execute its duties; in this connection the works committee, or a committee formed pursuant to section 28, shall be entitled to inspect the lists of gross wages and salaries. ³To the extent necessary for the proper fulfillment of the works council's duties, the employer shall provide it with knowledgeable employees to furnish information; in so doing the employer shall take the works council's suggestions into account, unless prevented from doing so by operational requirements.

sichtigen, soweit betriebliche Notwendigkeiten nicht entgegenstehen.

(3) Der Betriebsrat kann bei der Durchführung seiner Aufgaben nach näherer Vereinbarung mit dem Arbeitgeber Sachverständige hinzuziehen, soweit dies zur ordnungsgemäßen Erfüllung seiner Aufgaben erforderlich ist.

(4) Für die Geheimhaltungspflicht der Auskunftspersonen und der Sachverständigen gilt § 79 entsprechend.

(3) The works council may call for experts to assist it in its execution of its duties, with an additional agreement from the employer, to the extent this is necessary for the orderly execution of its duties.

(4) The duty of confidentiality of section 79 applies *mutatis mutandis* for the suppliers of information and the experts.

Zweiter Abschnitt
Mitwirkungs- und Beschwerderecht des Arbeitnehmers

Chapter 2
Employees' Rights of Participation and Complaint

§ 81
Unterrichtungs- und Erörterungspflicht des Arbeitgebers

Section 81
Employer's Duty to Inform and Discuss

(1) ¹Der Arbeitgeber hat den Arbeitnehmer über dessen Aufgabe und Verantwortung sowie über die Art seiner Tätigkeit und ihre Einordnung in den Arbeitsablauf des Betriebs zu unterrichten. ¹Er hat den Arbeitnehmer vor Beginn der Beschäftigung über die Unfall- und Gesundheitsgefahren, denen dieser bei der Beschäftigung ausgesetzt ist, sowie über die Maßnahmen und Einrichtungen zur Abwendung dieser Gefahren und die nach § 10 Abs. 2 des Arbeitsschutzgesetzes getroffenen Maßnahmen zu belehren.

(2) ¹Über Veränderungen in seinem Arbeitsbereich ist der Arbeitnehmer rechtzeitig zu unterrichten. ²Absatz 1 gilt entsprechend.

(3) In Betrieben, in denen kein Betriebsrat besteht, hat der Arbeitgeber die Arbeitnehmer zu allen Maßnahmen zu hören, die Auswirkungen auf Sicherheit und Gesundheit der Arbeitnehmer haben können.

(4) ¹Der Arbeitgeber hat den Arbeitnehmer über die aufgrund einer Pla-

(1) ¹The employer shall inform employees of their duties and responsibilities as well as the nature of their activities and classification in the operation of the establishment. ²Before commencing their employment, the employer shall instruct the employees with respect to the health and safety hazards to which they will be exposed at the workplace, as well about the measures to be taken and facilities to be used to avert such risks, as well as the measures taken pursuant to section 10 (2) of the Worker Protection Act (*Arbeitsschutzgesetz*).

(2) ¹Employees shall be informed in good time of any changes in their area of work. ²Subsection (1) applies *mutatis mutandis*.

(3) In establishments without a works council, the employer shall give the employees a right to be heard with respect to any measures that could affect their healthy and safety.

(4) ¹The employer shall provide the employees with information on the

nung von technischen Anlagen, von Arbeitsverfahren und Arbeitsabläufen oder der Arbeitsplätze vorgesehenen Maßnahmen und ihre Auswirkungen auf seinen Arbeitsplatz, die Arbeitsumgebung sowie auf Inhalt und Art seiner Tätigkeit zu unterrichten. ²Sobald feststeht, dass sich die Tätigkeit des Arbeitnehmers ändern wird und seine beruflichen Kenntnisse und Fähigkeiten zur Erfüllung seiner Aufgaben nicht ausreichen, hat der Arbeitgeber mit dem Arbeitnehmer zu erörtern, wie dessen berufliche Kenntnisse und Fähigkeiten im Rahmen der betrieblichen Möglichkeiten den künftigen Anforderungen angepasst werden können. ³Der Arbeitnehmer kann bei der Erörterung ein Mitglied des Betriebsrats hinzuziehen.

proposed introduction of measures to be taken on the basis of plans for the technical facilities, work procedures and the flow of work or the workplaces, as well as on effect such measures would have on his workplace, work environment and the content and type of work they do. ²As soon as it becomes evident that an employee's work will change and his professional knowledge and capabilities will not suffice to fulfill his duties, the employer must discuss with the employee how, within the capacity of the establishment, his professional knowledge and capabilities can be adapted to meet the future requirements. ³The employee may invite a member of the works council to participate in the discussion.

§ 82
Anhörungs- und Erörterungsrecht des Arbeitnehmers

Section 82
Employee's Right to be Heard and to Discuss

(1) ¹Der Arbeitnehmer hat das Recht, in betrieblichen Angelegenheiten, die seine Person betreffen, von den nach Maßgabe des organisatorischen Aufbaus des Betriebs hierfür zuständigen Personen gehört zu werden. ²Er ist berechtigt, zu Maßnahmen des Arbeitgebers, die ihn betreffen, Stellung zu nehmen sowie Vorschläge für die Gestaltung des Arbeitsplatzes und des Arbeitsablaufs zu machen.

(1) ¹Employees have the right to be heard with regard to matters in the establishment affecting them personally by the competent persons within the organizational structure of the establishment. ²The employees are entitled to state their position on the employer's measures which affect them as well as make suggestions for organizing the work and the workplace.

(2) ¹Der Arbeitnehmer kann verlangen, dass ihm die Berechnung und Zusammensetzung seines Arbeitsentgelts erläutert und dass mit ihm die Beurteilung seiner Leistungen sowie die Möglichkeiten seiner beruflichen Entwicklung im Betrieb erörtert werden. ²Er kann ein Mitglied des Betriebsrats hinzuziehen. ³Das Mitglied des Betriebsrats hat über den Inhalt dieser Verhandlungen Stillschweigen zu bewahren, soweit es vom Arbeitnehmer im Einzelfall nicht von dieser Verpflichtung entbunden wird.

(2) ¹Employees may demand an explanation of the calculation and breakdown of their remuneration and a discussion of their performance evaluations, as well as of the possibility of their advancement in the establishment. ²They may invite a member of the works council to participate in this discussion. ³The works council member shall maintain confidentiality with respect to the content of such discussions unless the employee involved releases him from this obligation in an individual case.

§ 83
Einsicht in die Personalakten

(1) [1]Der Arbeitnehmer hat das Recht, in die über ihn geführten Personalakten Einsicht zu nehmen. [2]Er kann hierzu ein Mitglied des Betriebsrats hinzuziehen. [3]Das Mitglied des Betriebsrats hat über den Inhalt der Personalakte Stillschweigen zu bewahren, soweit es vom Arbeitnehmer im Einzelfall nicht von dieser Verpflichtung entbunden wird.

(2) Erklärungen des Arbeitnehmers zum Inhalt der Personalakte sind dieser auf sein Verlangen beizufügen.

§ 84
Beschwerderecht

(1) [1]Jeder Arbeitnehmer hat das Recht, sich bei den zuständigen Stellen des Betriebs zu beschweren, wenn er sich vom Arbeitgeber oder von Arbeitnehmern des Betriebs benachteiligt oder ungerecht behandelt oder in sonstiger Weise beeinträchtigt fühlt. [2]Er kann ein Mitglied des Betriebsrats zur Unterstützung oder Vermittlung hinzuziehen.

(2) Der Arbeitgeber hat den Arbeitnehmer über die Behandlung der Beschwerde zu bescheiden und, soweit er die Beschwerde für berechtigt erachtet, ihr abzuhelfen.

(3) Wegen der Erhebung einer Beschwerde dürfen dem Arbeitnehmer keine Nachteile entstehen.

§ 85
Behandlung von Beschwerden durch den Betriebsrat

(1) Der Betriebsrat hat Beschwerden von Arbeitnehmern entgegenzunehmen und, falls er sie für berechtigt erachtet, beim Arbeitgeber auf Abhilfe hinzuwirken.

(2) [1]Bestehen zwischen Betriebsrat und Arbeitgeber Meinungsverschiedenheiten über die Berechtigung der Be-

Section 83
Inspection of the Personnel Files

(1) [1]The employee has the right to inspect the personnel files which are kept on him. [2]He may invite a member of the works council to accompany him. [3]The works council member shall maintain confidentiality with respect to the content of the personnel file unless the employee involved releases him from this obligation in an individual case.

(2) The employee's comments on the content of the personnel file shall be added to the file at his request.

Section 84
Right to Make Complaints

(1) [1]Each employee has the right to make a complaint to the competent authority of the establishment if he feels he has been discriminated against or unfairly treated or otherwise disadvantaged by the employer or employees of the establishment. [2]He may invite a member of the works council to assist or mediate.

(2) The employer shall inform the employee of how the complaint will be handled and, if he considers the complaint justified, rectify the situation.

(3) The employee may not be subjected to any disadvantage for filing a complaint.

Section 85
Handling of the Complaint by the Works Council

(1) The works council shall be authorized to accept complaints from the employee and, if it considers them to be justified, to influence the employer to rectify the situation.

(2) [1]Where differences of opinion exist between the works council and the employee regarding the justification of a

schwerde, so kann der Betriebsrat die Einigungsstelle anrufen. ²Der Spruch der Einigungsstelle ersetzt die Einigung zwischen Arbeitgeber und Betriebsrat. ³Dies gilt nicht, soweit Gegenstand der Beschwerde ein Rechtsanspruch ist.

(3) ¹Der Arbeitgeber hat den Betriebsrat über die Behandlung der Beschwerde zu unterrichten. ²§ 84 Abs. 2 bleibt unberührt.

§ 86
Ergänzende Vereinbarungen

¹Durch Tarifvertrag oder Betriebsvereinbarung können die Einzelheiten des Beschwerdeverfahrens geregelt werden. ²Hierbei kann bestimmt werden, dass in den Fällen des § 85 Abs. 2 an die Stelle der Einigungsstelle eine betriebliche Beschwerdestelle tritt.

§ 86 a
Vorschlagsrecht der Arbeitnehmer

¹Jeder Arbeitnehmer hat das Recht, dem Betriebsrat Themen zur Beratung vorzuschlagen. ²Wird ein Vorschlag von mindestens 5 vom Hundert der Arbeitnehmer des Betriebs unterstützt, hat der Betriebsrat diesen innerhalb von zwei Monaten auf die Tagesordnung einer Betriebsratssitzung zu setzen.

Dritter Abschnitt
Soziale Angelegenheiten

§ 87
Mitbestimmungsrechte

(1) Der Betriebsrat hat, soweit eine gesetzliche oder tarifliche Regelung nicht besteht, in folgenden Angelegenheiten mitzubestimmen:
1. Fragen der Ordnung des Betriebs und des Verhaltens der Arbeitnehmer im Betrieb;

complaint, the works council may appeal to the conciliation board. ²The decision of the conciliation board shall replace an agreement between the employer and the works council. ³This does not apply if the subject of the complaint is a legal claim.

(3) ¹The employer shall inform the works council regarding the handling of the complaint. ²Section 84 (2) remains unaffected.

Section 86
Supplementary Agreements

¹The specifics of the complaint procedure may be regulated by a collective bargaining agreement or a works agreement. ²Such agreements may provide that in situations falling under section 85 (2), a works grievance committee will replace the conciliation board.

Section 86 a
Employees' Right to Make Suggestions

¹Each employer shall have the right to suggest topics for the works council to discuss. ²If a suggestion is supported by at least five percent of the employees in the establishment, the works council shall add it to the agenda of a works council meeting within two months.

Chapter 3
Social Matters

Section 87
Codetermination Rights

(1) The works council has a right of codetermination on the following matters where no statutory or collective bargaining provision exists:
1. questions of order in the establishment and the conduct of the employees in the establishment;

2. Beginn und Ende der täglichen Arbeitszeit einschließlich der Pausen sowie Verteilung der Arbeitszeit auf die einzelnen Wochentage;

3. vorübergehende Verkürzung oder Verlängerung der betriebsüblichen Arbeitszeit;

4. Zeit, Ort und Art der Auszahlung der Arbeitsentgelte;

5. Aufstellung allgemeiner Urlaubsgrundsätze und des Urlaubsplans sowie die Festsetzung der zeitlichen Lage des Urlaubs für einzelne Arbeitnehmer, wenn zwischen dem Arbeitgeber und den beteiligten Arbeitnehmern kein Einverständnis erzielt wird;

6. Einführung und Anwendung von technischen Einrichtungen, die dazu bestimmt sind, das Verhalten oder die Leistung der Arbeitnehmer zu überwachen;

7. Regelungen über die Verhütung von Arbeitsunfällen und Berufskrankheiten sowie über den Gesundheitsschutz im Rahmen der gesetzlichen Vorschriften oder der Unfallverhütungsvorschriften;

8. Form, Ausgestaltung und Verwaltung von Sozialeinrichtungen, deren Wirkungsbereich auf den Betrieb, das Unternehmen oder den Konzern beschränkt ist;

9. Zuweisung und Kündigung von Wohnräumen, die den Arbeitnehmern mit Rücksicht auf das Bestehen eines Arbeitsverhältnisses vermietet werden, sowie die allgemeine Festlegung der Nutzungsbedingungen;

10. Fragen der betrieblichen Lohngestaltung, insbesondere die Aufstellung von Entlohnungsgrundsätzen und die Einführung und Anwendung von neuen Entlohnungsmethoden sowie deren Änderung;

11. Festsetzung der Akkord- und Prämiensätze und vergleichbarer leistungsbezogener Entgelte, einschließlich der Geldfaktoren;

2. beginning and end of the daily working hours, including breaks, as well as the distribution of the working hours over the individual days of the week;

3. temporary reduction or increase in the normal working hours;

4. time, place, and method of payment of the remuneration;

5. establishment of general principles on vacations and the vacation schedule, as well as the fixing of vacation periods for the individual employees, if no agreement can be reached between the employer and the employees involved;

6. introduction and use of technical equipment which is specifically designed to monitor the conduct or performance of the employee;

7. regulations regarding the prevention of accidents at work and work-related illnesses as well as health protection measures within the scope of the statutory provisions or the safety regulations;

8. the form, organization and administration of social services affecting the establishment, the company, or the group;

9. allocation and termination of housing rented to employees on the basis of the employment relationship, as well as the establishment of the general conditions for use;

10. questions pertaining to the wage structure of the establishment, in particular the establishment of remuneration principles and the introduction and implementation of new remuneration methods, as well as any changes made thereto;

11. establishment of piecework and bonus rates and comparable performance-based remuneration, including the unit rates;

12. Grundsätze über das betriebliche Vorschlagswesen;
13. Grundsätze über die Durchführung von Gruppenarbeit; Gruppenarbeit im Sinne dieser Vorschrift liegt vor, wenn im Rahmen des betrieblichen Arbeitsablaufs eine Gruppe von Arbeitnehmern eine ihr übertragene Gesamtaufgabe im Wesentlichen eigenverantwortlich erledigt.

(2) ¹Kommt eine Einigung über eine Angelegenheit nach Absatz 1 nicht zustande, so entscheidet die Einigungsstelle. ²Der Spruch der Einigungsstelle ersetzt die Einigung zwischen Arbeitgeber und Betriebsrat.

12. principles regarding the suggestion system in the establishment;
13. principles regarding the performance of group work; „group work" within the meaning of this provision exists if, in the course of the flow of work, a group of employees performs a task assigned to it essentially on its own authority.

(2) ¹Where no agreement can be reached regarding one of the matters set forth in subsection (1), the conciliation board shall render a decision. ²The conciliation board's decision shall replace an agreement between the employer and the works council.

§ 88
Freiwillige Betriebsvereinbarungen

Durch Betriebsvereinbarung können insbesondere geregelt werden

1. zusätzliche Maßnahmen zur Verhütung von Arbeitsunfällen und Gesundheitsschädigungen;
1a. Maßnahmen des betrieblichen Umweltschutzes;
2. die Errichtung von Sozialeinrichtungen, deren Wirkungsbereich auf den Betrieb, das Unternehmen oder den Konzern beschränkt ist;
3. Maßnahmen zur Förderung der Vermögensbildung;
4. Maßnahmen zur Integration ausländischer Arbeitnehmer sowie zur Bekämpfung von Rassismus und Fremdenfeindlichkeit im Betrieb.

Section 88
Voluntary Works Agreements

The following may be specifically regulated in a works agreement:

1. additional measures for protection against industrial accidents and health hazards;
1a. environmental measures in the establishment;
2. the establishment of social benefits whose scope is limited to the establishment, the company or the group;
3. measures for the promotion of capital formation;
4. measures for the integration of foreign employees as well as to combat racism and xenophobia in the establishment.

§ 89
Arbeits- und betrieblicher Umweltschutz

(1) ¹Der Betriebsrat hat sich dafür einzusetzen, dass die Vorschriften über den Arbeitsschutz und die Unfallverhütung im Betrieb sowie über den betrieblichen Umweltschutz durchgeführt werden. ²Er hat bei der Bekämpfung von Unfall- und Gesundheitsgefahren

Section 89
Industrial Safety and Environmental Protection in the Establishment

(1) ¹The works council shall endeavor to ensure that the provisions on industrial safety and accident prevention in the establishment, as well as on environmental protection in the establishment are implemented. ²The works council shall support the authorities

die für den Arbeitsschutz zuständigen Behörden, die Träger der gesetzlichen Unfallversicherung und die sonstigen in Betracht kommenden Stellen durch Anregung, Beratung und Auskunft zu unterstützen.

(2) ¹Der Arbeitgeber und die in Absatz 1 Satz 2 genannten Stellen sind verpflichtet, den Betriebsrat oder die von ihm bestimmten Mitglieder des Betriebsrats bei allen im Zusammenhang mit dem Arbeitsschutz oder der Unfallverhütung stehenden Besichtigungen und Fragen und bei Unfalluntersuchungen hinzuzuziehen. ²Der Arbeitgeber hat den Betriebsrat auch bei allen im Zusammenhang mit dem betrieblichen Umweltschutz stehenden Besichtigungen und Fragen hinzuzuziehen und ihm unverzüglich die den Arbeitsschutz, die Unfallverhütung und den betrieblichen Umweltschutz betreffenden Auflagen und Anordnungen der zuständigen Stellen mitzuteilen.

(3) Als betrieblicher Umweltschutz im Sinne dieses Gesetzes sind alle personellen und organisatorischen Maßnahmen sowie alle die betrieblichen Bauten, Räume, technische Anlagen, Arbeitsverfahren, Arbeitsabläufe und Arbeitsplätze betreffenden Maßnahmen zu verstehen, die dem Umweltschutz dienen.

(4) An Besprechungen des Arbeitgebers mit den Sicherheitsbeauftragten im Rahmen des § 22 Abs. 2 des Siebten Buches Sozialgesetzbuch nehmen vom Betriebsrat beauftragte Betriebsratsmitglieder teil.

(5) Der Betriebsrat erhält vom Arbeitgeber die Niederschriften über Untersuchungen, Besichtigungen und Besprechungen, zu denen er nach den Absätzen 2 und 4 hinzuzuziehen ist.

(6) Der Arbeitgeber hat dem Betriebsrat eine Durchschrift der nach § 193 Abs. 5

responsible for industrial safety, statutory accident insurers and other appropriate agencies in the prevention of accidents and the elimination of health risks by providing suggestions, advice and information.

(2) ¹The employer and the agencies mentioned in subsection (1) sentence 2 shall involve the works council or the members it delegates in all inspections and matters connected with industrial safety or the prevention of accidents and in the investigation of accidents. ²The employer shall involve the works council in all inspections and matters connected with environmental protection in the establishment and inform the works council without delay of any conditions and orders issued by the competent authorities concerning industrial safety, accident prevention and environmental protection in the establishment.

(3) Environmental protection in the establishment within the meaning of this Act is defined to encompass all personnel and organizational measures as well as all measures affecting the structures, rooms, technical facilities, working procedures, flow of work and workplaces in the establishment which serve to protect the environment.

(4) Members of the works council delegated by the works council shall participate in meetings between the employer and the safety officers or the safety committee pursuant to section 22 (2) of the Seventh Book of the Social Security Code (*Siebtes Buch Sozialgesetzbuch*).

(5) The employer shall provide the works council with written records of investigations, inspections and meetings to which it must be invited pursuant to subsections (2) and (4).

(6) The employer shall provide the works council with a copy of the acci-

des Siebten Buches Sozialgesetzbuch vom Betriebsrat zu unterschreibenden Unfallanzeige auszuhändigen.

dent report, which must be signed by the works council, pursuant to section 193 (5) of the Seventh Book of the Social Security Code.

**Vierter Abschnitt.
Gestaltung von Arbeitsplatz, Arbeitsablauf und Arbeitsumgebung**

**Chapter 4.
Organization of Workplace, Work Flow and Work Environment**

**§ 90
Unterrichtungs- und Beratungsrechte**

**Section 90
Right to Receive Information and Be Consulted**

Der Arbeitgeber hat den Betriebsrat über die Planung

(1) The employer shall inform the works council in good time, providing the necessary documents, regarding the planning of:

1. von Neu-, Um- und Erweiterungsbauten von Fabrikations-, Verwaltungs- und sonstigen betrieblichen Räumen,
2. von technischen Anlagen,
3. von Arbeitsverfahren und Arbeitsabläufen oder
4. der Arbeitsplätze

rechtzeitig unter Vorlage der erforderlichen Unterlagen zu unterrichten.

1. new construction, renovation and expansion of production, administration and other work areas;
2. technical installations;
3. work procedures and the flow of work; or
4. the workplace.

(2) ¹Der Arbeitgeber hat mit dem Betriebsrat die vorgesehenen Maßnahmen und ihre Auswirkungen auf die Arbeitnehmer, insbesondere auf die Art ihrer Arbeit sowie die sich daraus ergebenden Anforderungen an die Arbeitnehmer so rechtzeitig zu beraten, dass Vorschläge und Bedenken des Betriebsrats bei der Planung berücksichtigt werden können. ²Arbeitgeber und Betriebsrat sollen dabei auch die gesicherten arbeitswissenschaftlichen Erkenntnisse über die menschengerechte Gestaltung der Arbeit berücksichtigen.

(2) ¹The employer shall confer with the works council in good time regarding the proposed measures and their impact on the employees, in particular on the nature of the work as well as the resulting demands on the employees, so that the works council's suggestions and concerns can be taken into consideration with regard to the planning. ²The employer and the works council shall consider the accepted scientific principles regarding the creation of humane working conditions.

**§ 91
Mitbestimmungsrecht**

**Section 91
Right of Codetermination**

¹Werden die Arbeitnehmer durch Änderungen der Arbeitsplätze, des Arbeitsablaufs oder der Arbeitsumgebung, die den gesicherten arbeitswissenschaftli-

¹Where the employer obviously acts contrary to generally accepted scientific principles regarding the humaneness of the working process by making chan-

chen Erkenntnissen über die menschengerechte Gestaltung der Arbeit offensichtlich widersprechen, in besonderer Weise belastet, so kann der Betriebsrat angemessene Maßnahmen zur Abwendung, Milderung oder zum Ausgleich der Belastung verlangen. ²Kommt eine Einigung nicht zustande, so entscheidet die Einigungsstelle. ³Der Spruch der Einigungsstelle ersetzt die Einigung zwischen Arbeitgeber und Betriebsrat.

ges in the workplace, the flow of work or the working environment, the works council may demand measures to eliminate, mitigate or compensate for the burden. ²Where a decision cannot be reached the conciliation board shall render a decision. ³The decision of the conciliation board shall replace an agreement between the employer and the works council.

Fünfter Abschnitt
Personelle Angelegenheiten

Chapter 5
Personnel Matters

Erster Unterabschnitt
Allgemeine personelle Angelegenheiten

Subchapter 1
General Personnel Matters

§ 92
Personalplanung

Section 92
Personnel Planning

(1) ¹Der Arbeitgeber hat den Betriebsrat über die Personalplanung, insbesondere über den gegenwärtigen und künftigen Personalbedarf sowie über die sich daraus ergebenden personellen Maßnahmen und Maßnahmen der Berufsbildung anhand von Unterlagen rechtzeitig und umfassend zu unterrichten. ²Er hat mit dem Betriebsrat über Art und Umfang der erforderlichen Maßnahmen und über die Vermeidung von Härten zu beraten.

(1) ¹The employer shall inform the works council completely and in a timely manner, with the aid of documents, with respect to personnel planning, in particular the present and future personnel requirements as well as the resulting personnel and vocational training measures. ²It shall discuss with the works council the nature and scope of the necessary measures and the avoidance of hardship.

(2) Der Betriebsrat kann dem Arbeitgeber Vorschläge für die Einführung einer Personalplanung und ihre Durchführung machen.

(2) The works council may make suggestions to the employer for the introduction of a personnel plan and its implementation.

(3) Die Absätze 1 und 2 gelten entsprechend für Maßnahmen im Sinne des § 80 Abs. 1 Nr. 2a und 2b, insbesondere für die Aufstellung und Durchführung von Maßnahmen zur Förderung der Gleichstellung von Frauen und Männern.

(3) Subsections (1) and (2) shall apply *mutatis mutandis* with respect to measures within the meaning of Section 80 (1) no. 2a and 2b, in particular for the establishment and implementation of measures to promote the equal standing of women and men.

§ 92a
Beschäftigungssicherung

Section 92a
Job Security

(1) ¹Der Betriebsrat kann dem Arbeitgeber Vorschläge zur Sicherung und

(1) ¹The works council may make suggestions to the employer for securing

Förderung der Beschäftigung machen. ²Diese können insbesondere eine flexible Gestaltung der Arbeitszeit, die Förderung von Teilzeitarbeit und Altersteilzeit, neue Formen der Arbeitsorganisation, Änderungen der Arbeitsverfahren und Arbeitsabläufe, die Qualifizierung der Arbeitnehmer, Alternativen zur Ausgliederung von Arbeit oder ihrer Vergabe an andere Unternehmen sowie zum Produktions- und Investitionsprogramm zum Gegenstand haben.

(2) ¹Der Arbeitgeber hat die Vorschläge mit dem Betriebsrat zu beraten. ²Hält der Arbeitgeber die Vorschläge des Betriebsrats für ungeeignet, hat er dies zu begründen; in Betrieben mit mehr als 100 Arbeitnehmern erfolgt die Begründung schriftlich. ³Zu den Beratungen kann der Arbeitgeber oder der Betriebsrat einen Vertreter der Bundesagentur für Arbeit hinzuziehen.

and promoting employment. ²They may in particular cover such topics as a flexible scheduling of working hours, the promotion of part-time work and part-time work for older workers, new forms of organizing the work, changes in work procedures and the flow of work, the qualification of the employees, alternatives to outsourcing work or suggestions for a production and investment program.

(2) ¹The employer shall discuss such suggestions with the works council. ²If the employer considers the works council's suggestions to be unsuitable, it shall substantiate this assessment; in establishments with over 100 employees, such substantiation must be in writing. ³The employer or the works council may invite a representative of the Federal Employment Agency to participate in these discussions.

§ 93
Ausschreibung von Arbeitsplätzen

Der Betriebsrat kann verlangen, dass Arbeitsplätze, die besetzt werden sollen, allgemein oder für bestimmte Arten von Tätigkeiten vor ihrer Besetzung innerhalb des Betriebs ausgeschrieben werden.

Section 93
Announcement of Vacancies

The works council may require that vacancies for general or specific types of work be announced within the establishment before they are filled.

§ 94
Personalfragebogen, Beurteilungsgrundsätze

(1) ¹Personalfragebogen bedürfen der Zustimmung des Betriebsrats. ²Kommt eine Einigung über ihren Inhalt nicht zustande, so entscheidet die Einigungsstelle. ³Der Spruch der Einigungsstelle ersetzt die Einigung zwischen Arbeitgeber und Betriebsrat.

(2) Absatz 1 gilt entsprechend für persönliche Angaben in schriftlichen Arbeitsverträgen, die allgemein für den Betrieb verwendet werden sollen, sowie

Section 94
Personnel Questionnaire, Evaluation Principles

(1) ¹Personnel questionnaires require the approval of the works council. ²Where an agreement cannot be reached regarding their content, the conciliation board shall decide. ³The decision of the conciliation board shall replace an agreement between the employer and the works council.

(2) Subsection 1 applies *mutatis mutandis* with respect to personal information in written employment contracts which is to be used generally for the estab-

für die Aufstellung allgemeiner Beurteilungsgrundsätze.

§ 95
Auswahlrichtlinien

(1) ¹Richtlinien über die personelle Auswahl bei Einstellungen, Versetzungen, Umgruppierungen und Kündigungen bedürfen der Zustimmung des Betriebsrats. ²Kommt eine Einigung über die Richtlinien oder ihren Inhalt nicht zustande, so entscheidet auf Antrag des Arbeitgebers die Einigungsstelle. ³Der Spruch der Einigungsstelle ersetzt die Einigung zwischen Arbeitgeber und Betriebsrat.

(2) ¹In Betrieben mit mehr als 500 Arbeitnehmern kann der Betriebsrat die Aufstellung von Richtlinien über die bei Maßnahmen des Absatzes 1 Satz 1 zu beachtenden fachlichen und persönlichen Voraussetzungen und sozialen Gesichtspunkte verlangen. ²Kommt eine Einigung über die Richtlinien oder ihren Inhalt nicht zustande, so entscheidet die Einigungsstelle. ³Der Spruch der Einigungsstelle ersetzt die Einigung zwischen Arbeitgeber und Betriebsrat.

(3) ¹Versetzung im Sinne dieses Gesetzes ist die Zuweisung eines anderen Arbeitsbereichs, die voraussichtlich die Dauer von einem Monat überschreitet, oder die mit einer erheblichen Änderung der Umstände verbunden ist, unter denen die Arbeit zu leisten ist. ²Werden Arbeitnehmer nach der Eigenart ihres Arbeitsverhältnisses üblicherweise nicht ständig an einem bestimmten Arbeitsplatz beschäftigt, so gilt die Bestimmung des jeweiligen Arbeitsplatzes nicht als Versetzung.

Zweiter Unterabschnitt
Berufsbildung

§ 96
Förderung der Berufsbildung

(1) ¹Arbeitgeber und Betriebsrat haben im Rahmen der betrieblichen Personal-

lishment, as well as for the establishment of general evaluation principles.

Section 95
Selection Guidelines

(1) ¹Guidelines for the selection of personnel to be hired, transferred, assigned to a different group and dismissed shall require the approval of the works council. ²If no agreement regarding the guidelines or their content can be reached, the conciliation board shall render a decision at the employer's request. ³The decision of the conciliation board shall replace an agreement between the employer and the works council.

(2) ¹In establishments with more than 500 employees the works council may require that guidelines be established on the technical and personal requirements and social factors to be taken into account when the measures set forth in subsection (1) sentence 1 are taken. ²If no agreement regarding the guidelines or their content can be reached, the conciliation board shall render a decision. ³The decision of the conciliation board shall replace an agreement between the employer and the works council.

(3) ¹A transfer within the meaning of this act is an assignment to another area of work for a period which is likely to last more than one month or which involves a significant change in the circumstances under which the work is to be performed. ²Where due to the unique nature of their employment relationship, employees are not regularly employed at one workplace, assignment to each respective workplace shall not constitute a transfer.

Subchapter 2
Vocational Training

Section 96
Promotion of Vocational Training

(1) ¹The employer and the works council shall support vocational training

planung und in Zusammenarbeit mit den für die Berufsbildung und den für die Förderung der Berufsbildung zuständigen Stellen die Berufsbildung der Arbeitnehmer zu fördern. ²Der Arbeitgeber hat auf Verlangen des Betriebsrats den Berufsbildungsbedarf zu ermitteln und mit ihm Fragen der Berufsbildung der Arbeitnehmer des Betriebs zu beraten. ³Hierzu kann der Betriebsrat Vorschläge machen.

(2) ¹Arbeitgeber und Betriebsrat haben darauf zu achten, dass unter Berücksichtigung der betrieblichen Notwendigkeiten den Arbeitnehmern die Teilnahme an betrieblichen oder außerbetrieblichen Maßnahmen der Berufsbildung ermöglicht wird. ²Sie haben dabei auch die Belange älterer Arbeitnehmer, Teilzeitbeschäftigter und von Arbeitnehmern mit Familienpflichten zu berücksichtigen.

§ 97
Einrichtungen und Maßnahmen der Berufsbildung

(1) Der Arbeitgeber hat mit dem Betriebsrat über die Errichtung und Ausstattung betrieblicher Einrichtungen zur Berufsbildung, die Einführung betrieblicher Berufsbildungsmaßnahmen und die Teilnahme an außerbetrieblichen Berufsbildungsmaßnahmen zu beraten.

(2) ¹Hat der Arbeitgeber Maßnahmen geplant oder durchgeführt, die dazu führen, dass sich die Tätigkeit der betroffenen Arbeitnehmer ändert und ihre beruflichen Kenntnisse und Fähigkeiten zur Erfüllen ihrer Aufgaben nicht mehr ausreichen, so hat der Betriebsrat bei der Einführung von Maßnahmen der betrieblichen Berufsbildung mitzubestimmen. ²Kommt eine Einigung nicht zustande, so entscheidet die Einigungsstelle. ³Der Spruch der Einigungsstelle ersetzt die Einigung zwischen Arbeitgeber und Betriebsrat.

within the context of personnel planning within the establishment and in cooperation with the authorities competent for the employee's vocational training and the support thereof. ²Upon request of the works council, the employee shall consult with it to ascertain the vocational training requirements and discuss questions of vocational training of the establishment's employees. ³Suggestions may be made by the works council.

(2) ¹The employer and the works council shall ensure that, taking into account the requirements of the establishment, the employees are able to participate in vocational training within or outside the establishment. ²They shall also take the interests of older employees, part-time employees and employees with familial responsibilities into account.

Section 97
Vocational Training Facilities and Programs

(1) The employer shall confer with the works council regarding the establishment and equipment of vocational training facilities and the introduction of vocational training measures within the establishment, as well as the participation in vocational training programs outside the establishment.

(2) ¹If the employer has planned for the introduction of technical facilities, work methods or work procedures which would lead to a change in the activities of the affected employees and their professional knowledge and skills are no longer sufficient for the performance of their tasks, the works council shall have a right of codetermination with respect to the introduction of vocational training measures in the establishment. ²If no agreement can be reached, the conciliation board shall render a decision. ³The decision of the conciliation board

§ 98
Durchführung betrieblicher Bildungsmaßnahmen

(1) Der Betriebsrat hat bei der Durchführung von Maßnahmen der betrieblichen Berufsbildung mitzubestimmen.

(2) Der Betriebsrat kann der Bestellung einer mit der Durchführung der betrieblichen Berufsbildung beauftragten Person widersprechen oder ihre Abberufung verlangen, wenn diese die persönliche oder fachliche, insbesondere die berufs- und arbeitspädagogische Eignung im Sinne des Berufsbildungsgesetzes nicht besitzt oder ihre Aufgaben vernachlässigt.

(3) Führt der Arbeitgeber betriebliche Maßnahmen der Berufsbildung durch oder stellt er für außerbetriebliche Maßnahmen der Berufsbildung Arbeitnehmer frei oder trägt er die durch die Teilnahme von Arbeitnehmern an solchen Maßnahmen entstehenden Kosten ganz oder teilweise, so kann der Betriebsrat Vorschläge für die Teilnahme von Arbeitnehmern oder Gruppen von Arbeitnehmern des Betriebs an diesen Maßnahmen der beruflichen Bildung machen.

(4) [1] Kommt im Fall des Absatzes 1 oder über die nach Absatz 3 vom Betriebsrat vorgeschlagenen Teilnehmer eine Einigung nicht zustande, so entscheidet die Einigungsstelle. [2] Der Spruch der Einigungsstelle ersetzt die Einigung zwischen Arbeitgeber und Betriebsrat.

(5) [1] Kommt im Fall des Absatzes 2 eine Einigung nicht zustande, so kann der Betriebsrat beim Arbeitsgericht beantragen, dem Arbeitgeber aufzugeben, die Bestellung zu unterlassen oder die Abberufung durchzuführen. [2] Führt der

Section 98
Vocational Training Programs Within the Establishment

(1) The works council has the right of codetermination with respect to the implementation of vocational training programs within the establishment.

(2) The works council may object to the appointment of or demand the dismissal of a person appointed to execute the vocational training program within the establishment if such person does not have the personal or the technical qualifications, in particular the pedagogic skills required for vocational training within the meaning of the Vocational Training Act *(Berufsbildungsgesetz)* or if he neglects his duties.

(3) Where the employer conducts with vocational training within the establishment or releases employees for vocational training outside the establishment or assumes some or all of the costs for employees to participate in such programs, the works council may make suggestions for the participation of employees or groups of employees in the establishment in such vocational training programs.

shall replace an agreement between the employer and the works council.

(4) [1] If an agreement cannot be reached with respect to subsection (1) or regarding the participants suggested by the works council pursuant to subsection (3), the decision shall be rendered by the conciliation board. [2] The decision of the conciliation board shall replace an agreement between the employer and the works council.

(5) [1] If an agreement cannot be reached pursuant to subsection (2), the works council may petition the Labor Court to order the employer to refrain from making such appointments or to perform the dismissals. [2] If an employee makes

Arbeitgeber die Bestellung einer rechtskräftigen gerichtlichen Entscheidung zuwider durch, so ist er auf Antrag des Betriebsrats vom Arbeitsgericht wegen der Bestellung nach vorheriger Androhung zu einem Ordnungsgeld zu verurteilen; das Höchstmaß des Ordnungsgeldes beträgt 10.000 Euro. ³Führt der Arbeitgeber die Abberufung einer rechtskräftigen gerichtlichen Entscheidung zuwider nicht durch, so ist auf Antrag des Betriebsrats vom Arbeitsgericht zu erkennen, dass der Arbeitgeber zur Abberufung durch Zwangsgeld anzuhalten sei; das Höchstmaß des Zwangsgeldes beträgt für jeden Tag der Zuwiderhandlung 250 Euro. ⁴Die Vorschriften des Berufsbildungsgesetzes über die Ordnung der Berufsbildung bleiben unberührt.

(6) Die Absätze 1 bis 5 gelten entsprechend, wenn der Arbeitgeber sonstige Bildungsmaßnahmen im Betrieb durchführt.

an appointment despite a legally valid and final court order, then, upon request of the works council, the Labor Court shall impose an administrative fine upon the employer following a prior warning; the maximum amount of the fine shall be 10,000 euro. ³If an employer does not perform a dismissal in violation of a legally valid and final court order, the Labor Court shall, upon application of the works council, order the employer to perform such dismissal or face a coercive fine; the maximum amount of the coercive fine shall be 250 euro for each day of the violation. ⁴The provisions of the Vocational Training Act regarding the organization of vocational training remain unaffected.

(6) Subsections (1) to (5) apply *mutatis mutandis* if the employer carries out other vocational training programs within the establishment.

Dritter Unterabschnitt
Personelle Einzelmaßnahmen

Subchapter 3
Individual Personnel Measures

§ 99
Mitbestimmung bei personellen Einzelmaßnahmen

Section 99
Codetermination with Regard to Individual Personnel Measures

(1) ¹In Unternehmen mit in der Regel mehr als zwanzig wahlberechtigten Arbeitnehmern hat der Arbeitgeber den Betriebsrat vor jeder Einstellung, Eingruppierung, Umgruppierung und Versetzung zu unterrichten, ihm die erforderlichen Bewerbungsunterlagen vorzulegen und Auskunft über die Person der Beteiligten zu geben; er hat dem Betriebsrat unter Vorlage der erforderlichen Unterlagen Auskunft über die Auswirkungen der geplanten Maßnahme zu geben und die Zustimmung des Betriebsrats zu der geplanten Maßnahme einzuholen. ²Bei Einstellungen und Versetzungen hat der Arbeitgeber insbesondere den in Aussicht genommenen Arbeitsplatz und die vorgesehe-

(1) ¹In companies normally employing more than 20 employees eligible to vote, the employer shall inform the works council prior to every hiring, classification, re-classification and transfer and provide it with the requisite application documents and information on the person involved; the employee shall inform the works council, presenting the necessary documents, of the effects of the measures planned and obtain the consent of the works council with regard to the measures planned. ²With hirings and transfers, the employer must, in particular, provide information on the job involved and the proposed classification. ³The members of the works council are bound to se-

ne Eingruppierung mitzuteilen. ³Die Mitglieder des Betriebsrats sind verpflichtet, über die ihnen im Rahmen der personellen Maßnahmen nach den Sätzen 1 und 2 bekanntgewordenen persönlichen Verhältnisse und Angelegenheiten der Arbeitnehmer, die ihrer Bedeutung oder ihrem Inhalt nach einer vertraulichen Behandlung bedürfen, Stillschweigen zu bewahren; § 79 Abs. 1 Satz 2 bis 4 gilt entsprechend.

crecy with regard to personal relationships and matters of an employee which have become known to them due to the personnel measures pursuant to sentences 1 and 2 and which, due to their significance or subject matter, require confidential treatment; section 79 (1) sentences 2 through 4 apply *mutatis mutandis*.

(2) Der Betriebsrat kann die Zustimmung verweigern, wenn

1. die personelle Maßnahme gegen ein Gesetz, eine Verordnung, eine Unfallverhütungsvorschrift oder gegen eine Bestimmung in einem Tarifvertrag oder in einer Betriebsvereinbarung oder gegen eine gerichtliche Entscheidung oder eine behördliche Anordnung verstoßen würde,
2. die personelle Maßnahme gegen eine Richtlinie nach § 95 verstoßen würde,
3. die durch Tatsachen begründete Besorgnis besteht, dass infolge der personellen Maßnahme im Betrieb beschäftigte Arbeitnehmer gekündigt werden oder sonstige Nachteile erleiden, ohne dass dies aus betrieblichen oder persönlichen Gründen gerechtfertigt ist; als Nachteil gilt bei unbefristeter Einstellung auch die Nichtberücksichtigung eines gleich geeigneten befristet Beschäftigten,
4. der betroffene Arbeitnehmer durch die personelle Maßnahme benachteiligt wird, ohne dass dies aus betrieblichen oder in der Person des Arbeitnehmers liegenden Gründen gerechtfertigt ist,
5. eine nach § 93 erforderliche Ausschreibung im Betrieb unterblieben ist oder
6. die durch Tatsachen begründete Besorgnis besteht, dass der für die personelle Maßnahme in Aussicht genommene Bewerber oder Arbeitnehmer den Betriebsfrieden durch gesetzwidriges Verhalten oder durch grobe Verletzung der in § 75 Abs. 1

(2) The works council may refuse to render consent if

1. the personnel measure violates a statute, an ordinance, a safety regulation, a provision in a collective bargaining agreement or works agreement, a court order, or an administrative order,
2. the personnel measure would violate a guideline pursuant to section 95,
3. a well-founded concern exists that as a consequence of the personnel measure, employees in the establishment will be dismissed or incur other hardships, even though this would not be justified on operational or personal grounds; in the case of a permanent hiring, such hardship would also be deemed to be the failure to consider an equally suitable fixed term employee,
4. the employee involved would be disadvantaged by the personnel measure, even though this would not be justified on operational or personal grounds,
5. an announcement of the vacancy, as required by section 93, has not been posted in the establishment, or
6. a well-founded concern exists that the applicant or employee under consideration for the personnel measure would disturb the peace of the establishment through illegal conduct or a gross violation of the principles contained in section 75 (1),

enthaltenen Grundsätze, insbesondere durch rassistische oder fremdenfeindliche Betätigung, stören werde.

(3) ¹Verweigert der Betriebsrat seine Zustimmung, so hat er dies unter Angabe von Gründen innerhalb einer Woche nach Unterrichtung durch den Arbeitgeber diesem schriftlich mitzuteilen. ²Teilt der Betriebsrat dem Arbeitgeber die Verweigerung seiner Zustimmung nicht innerhalb der Frist schriftlich mit, so gilt die Zustimmung als erteilt.

(4) Verweigert der Betriebsrat seine Zustimmung, so kann der Arbeitgeber beim Arbeitsgericht beantragen, die Zustimmung zu ersetzen.

§ 100
Vorläufige personelle Maßnahmen

(1) ¹Der Arbeitgeber kann, wenn dies aus sachlichen Gründen dringend erforderlich ist, die personelle Maßnahme im Sinne des § 99 Abs. 1 Satz 1 vorläufig durchführen, bevor der Betriebsrat sich geäußert oder wenn er die Zustimmung verweigert hat. ²Der Arbeitgeber hat den Arbeitnehmer über die Sach- und Rechtslage aufzuklären.

(2) ¹Der Arbeitgeber hat den Betriebsrat unverzüglich von der vorläufigen personellen Maßnahme zu unterrichten. ²Bestreitet der Betriebsrat, dass die Maßnahme aus sachlichen Gründen dringend erforderlich ist, so hat er dies dem Arbeitgeber unverzüglich mitzuteilen. ³In diesem Fall darf der Arbeitgeber die vorläufige personelle Maßnahme nur aufrechterhalten, wenn er innerhalb von drei Tagen beim Arbeitsgericht die Ersetzung der Zustimmung des Betriebsrats und die Feststellung beantragt, dass die Maßnahme aus sachlichen Gründen dringend erforderlich war.

(3) ¹Lehnt das Gericht durch rechtskräftige Entscheidung die Ersetzung der Zustimmung des Betriebsrats ab oder stellt es rechtskräftig fest, dass offen-

in particular by engaging in racist or xenophobic behavior.

(3) ¹Should the works council refuse to render consent, it shall inform the employer of such in writing, stating its reasons, within one week of being informed by the employer. ²If the works council fails to inform the employer of its refusal to render consent in writing within this time period, such consent shall be deemed to have been rendered.

(4) Where the works council refuses to render consent, the employer may petition the Labor Court to rule in lieu of the works council's consent.

Section 100
Provisional Personnel Measures

(1) ¹The employer, if urgently necessary on objective grounds, carry out personnel measures within the meaning of section 99 (1) sentence 1 on a provisional basis before the works council has expressed its views or after it refuses its consent. ²The employer must explain the objective and legal situation to the employee.

(2) ¹The employer shall inform the works council without delay of such provisional personnel measures. ²Where the works council disputes that the measures are urgently necessary on objective grounds, it shall inform the employer without delay. ³In such a case the employer may only continue the provisional personnel measures if he petitions the Labor Court within three days for a ruling to replace the consent of the works council and determining that the measures are urgently necessary on objective grounds.

(3) ¹Where the court refuses to supersede the works council's consent by a legal ruling or determines that the measure was evidently not urgently neces-

sichtlich die Maßnahme aus sachlichen Gründen nicht dringend erforderlich war, so endet die vorläufige personelle Maßnahme mit Ablauf von zwei Wochen nach Rechtskraft der Entscheidung. ²Von diesem Zeitpunkt an darf die personelle Maßnahme nicht aufrechterhalten werden.

sary on objective grounds, the provisional personnel measures shall end upon the expiration of two weeks after the ruling becomes final. ²After that date, the personnel measure may not be continued.

§ 101
Zwangsgeld

¹Führt der Arbeitgeber eine personelle Maßnahme im Sinne des § 99 Abs. 1 Satz 1 ohne Zustimmung des Betriebsrats durch oder hält er eine vorläufige personelle Maßnahme entgegen § 100 Abs. 2 Satz 3 oder Abs. 3 aufrecht, so kann der Betriebsrat beim Arbeitsgericht beantragen, dem Arbeitgeber aufzugeben, die personelle Maßnahme aufzuheben. ²Hebt der Arbeitgeber entgegen einer rechtskräftigen gerichtlichen Entscheidung die personelle Maßnahme nicht auf, so ist auf Antrag des Betriebsrats vom Arbeitsgericht zu erkennen, dass der Arbeitgeber zur Aufhebung der Maßnahme durch Zwangsgeld anzuhalten sei. ³Das Höchstmaß des Zwangsgeldes beträgt für jeden Tag der Zuwiderhandlung 250 Euro.

Section 101
Coercive Fine

¹If an employer implements a personnel measure within the meaning of section 99 (1) sentence 1 without the works council's consent or continues a preliminary personnel measure in violation of section 100 (2) sentence 3 or (3), the works council may petition the Labor Court to order the employer to discontinue such personnel measure. ²Where the employer fails to do so in violation of a legally valid court decision, the Labor Court may, upon application of the works council, impose a coercive fine upon the employer if it fails to discontinue the measure. ³The maximum amount of the coercive fine shall be 250 euro for each day of violation.

§ 102
Mitbestimmung bei Kündigungen

(1) ¹Der Betriebsrat ist vor jeder Kündigung zu hören. ²Der Arbeitgeber hat ihm die Gründe für die Kündigung mitzuteilen. ³Eine ohne Anhörung des Betriebsrats ausgesprochene Kündigung ist unwirksam.

(2) ¹Hat der Betriebsrat gegen eine ordentliche Kündigung Bedenken, so hat er diese unter Angabe der Gründe dem Arbeitgeber spätestens innerhalb einer Woche schriftlich mitzuteilen. ²Äußert er sich innerhalb dieser Frist nicht, gilt seine Zustimmung zur Kündigung als erteilt. ³Hat der Betriebsrat gegen eine

Section 102
Codetermination in the Event of Dismissals

(1) ¹The works council shall be consulted prior to any dismissal. ²The employer shall inform it of the grounds for the dismissal. ³A dismissal without prior consultation of the works council is invalid.

(2) ¹If the works council objects to an ordinary dismissal, it shall communicate its objection within one week to the employer in writing, citing its grounds. ²If it does not do so within this period, it shall be deemed to have consented to the dismissal. ³If the works council objects to a dismissal for cause, it shall

außerordentliche Kündigung Bedenken, so hat er diese unter Angabe der Gründe dem Arbeitgeber unverzüglich, spätestens jedoch innerhalb von drei Tagen, schriftlich mitzuteilen. ⁴Der Betriebsrat soll, soweit dies erforderlich erscheint, vor seiner Stellungnahme den betroffenen Arbeitnehmer hören. ⁴§ 99 Abs. 1 Satz 3 gilt entsprechend.

(3) Der Betriebsrat kann innerhalb der Frist des Absatzes 2 Satz 1 der ordentlichen Kündigung widersprechen, wenn

1. der Arbeitgeber bei der Auswahl des zu kündigenden Arbeitnehmers soziale Gesichtspunkte nicht oder nicht ausreichend berücksichtigt hat,
2. die Kündigung gegen eine Richtlinie nach § 95 verstößt,
3. der zu kündigende Arbeitnehmer an einem anderen Arbeitsplatz im selben Betrieb oder in einem anderen Betrieb des Unternehmens weiterbeschäftigt werden kann,
4. die Weiterbeschäftigung des Arbeitnehmers nach zumutbaren Umschulungs- oder Fortbildungsmaßnahmen möglich ist oder
5. eine Weiterbeschäftigung des Arbeitnehmers unter geänderten Vertragsbedingungen möglich ist und der Arbeitnehmer sein Einverständnis hiermit erklärt hat.

(4) Kündigt der Arbeitgeber, obwohl der Betriebsrat nach Absatz 3 der Kündigung widersprochen hat, so hat er dem Arbeitnehmer mit der Kündigung eine Abschrift der Stellungnahme des Betriebsrats zuzuleiten.

(5) ¹Hat der Betriebsrat einer ordentlichen Kündigung frist- und ordnungsgemäß widersprochen und hat der Arbeitnehmer nach dem Kündigungsschutzgesetz Klage auf Feststellung erhoben, dass das Arbeitsverhältnis durch die Kündigung nicht aufgelöst ist, so muss der Arbeitgeber auf Verlangen des Arbeitnehmers diesen nach Ablauf der Kündigungsfrist bis zum rechts-

communicate its objection to the employer immediately, but at the latest within three days, giving its reasons in writing. ⁴The works council should, if it appears necessary to do so, consult with the employee in question before submitting its report. ⁴Section 99 (1) sentence 3 applies *mutatis mutandis.*

(3) The works council may, within the period stipulated in subsection (2) sentence 1, object to an ordinary dismissal if

1. the employer has not, or not sufficiently, taken social factors into account in selecting of the employee to be dismissed,
2. the dismissal is in contravention of a guideline pursuant to section 95,
3. the employee to be dismissed can continue to be employed in a different position within the same establishment or in another establishment belonging to the company,
4. the continued employment of the employee is possible after reasonable further training or retraining, or
5. the continued employment of the employee is possible under amended contractual terms to which the employee has consented.

(4) If the employer gives notice of dismissal, even though the works council has objected to the dismissal pursuant to subsection (3), the employer shall send the employee a copy of the works council's statement along with the notice of termination.

(5) ¹If the works council has objected to an ordinary dismissal promptly and properly and the employee has petitioned for a declaratory ruling pursuant to the Protection Against Unfair Dismissals Act *(Kündigungsschutzgesetz)* that the employment was been terminated by the notice of dismissal, the employer shall, at the employee's request and until the final judicial resolu-

kräftigen Abschluss des Rechtsstreits bei unveränderten Arbeitsbedingungen weiterbeschäftigen. ²Auf Antrag des Arbeitgebers kann das Gericht ihn durch einstweilige Verfügung von der Verpflichtung zur Weiterbeschäftigung nach Satz 1 entbinden, wenn

1. die Klage des Arbeitnehmers keine hinreichende Aussicht auf Erfolg bietet oder mutwillig erscheint oder
2. die Weiterbeschäftigung des Arbeitnehmers zu einer unzumutbaren wirtschaftlichen Belastung des Arbeitgebers führen würde oder
3. der Widerspruch des Betriebsrats offensichtlich unbegründet war.

(6) Arbeitgeber und Betriebsrat können vereinbaren, dass Kündigungen der Zustimmung des Betriebsrats bedürfen und dass bei Meinungsverschiedenheiten über die Berechtigung der Nichterteilung der Zustimmung die Einigungsstelle entscheidet.

(7) Die Vorschriften über die Beteiligung des Betriebsrats nach dem Kündigungsschutzgesetz bleiben unberührt.

§ 103
Außerordentliche Kündigung und Versetzung in besonderen Fällen

(1) Die außerordentliche Kündigung von Mitgliedern des Betriebsrats, der Jugend- und Auszubildendenvertretung, der Bordvertretung und des Seebetriebsrats, des Wahlvorstands sowie von Wahlbewerbern bedarf der Zustimmung des Betriebsrats.

(2) ¹Verweigert der Betriebsrat seine Zustimmung, so kann das Arbeitsgericht sie auf Antrag des Arbeitgebers ersetzen, wenn die außerordentliche Kündigung unter Berücksichtigung aller Umstände gerechtfertigt ist. ²In dem Verfahren vor dem Arbeitsgericht ist der betroffene Arbeitnehmer Beteiligter.

tion of the dispute, continue his employment under the same conditions even after the expiration of the dismissal notice period. ²At the employer's request, the Court may temporarily release him from the obligation to continue the employment pursuant to sentence 1 if:

1. the employee's action does not offer sufficient prospect of success or appears to be frivolous, or
2. the continued employment of the employee would create an unreasonable economic burden on the employer, or
3. the objection of the works council was obviously without foundation.

(6) Employer and works council may agree that dismissals shall require the consent of the works council and that, in the event of a difference of opinion over the justification of a refusal to grant consent, the conciliation board shall decide.

(7) The provisions of the Protection Against Unfair Dismissals Act concerning the participation of the works council shall not be affected.

Section 103
Dismissal for Cause and Transfer In Special Cases

(1) Dismissal for cause of members of the works council, the youth and trainee representative body, the ship's committee or the works council of the merchant fleet, of the election committee or candidates for election shall require the consent of the works council.

(2) ¹Should the works council withhold its consent, the Labor Court may upon petition by the employer supersede it if the termination for cause is justified once all the circumstances are taken into account. ²The employee concerned shall participate in the proceedings before the Labor Court.

(3) ¹Die Versetzung der in Absatz 1 genannten Personen, die zu einem Verlust des Amtes oder der Wählbarkeit führen würde, bedarf der Zustimmung des Betriebsrats; dies gilt nicht, wenn der betroffene Arbeitnehmer mit der Versetzung einverstanden ist. ²Absatz 2 gilt entsprechend mit der Maßgabe, dass das Arbeitsgericht die Zustimmung zu der Versetzung ersetzen kann, wenn diese auch unter Berücksichtigung der betriebsverfassungsrechtlichen Stellung des betroffenen Arbeitnehmers aus dringenden betrieblichen Gründen notwendig ist.

§ 104
Entfernung betriebsstörender Arbeitnehmer

¹Hat ein Arbeitnehmer durch gesetzwidriges Verhalten oder durch grobe Verletzung der in § 75 Abs. 1 enthaltenen Grundsätze, insbesondere durch rassistische oder fremdenfeindliche Betätigungen, den Betriebsfrieden wiederholt ernstlich gestört, so kann der Betriebsrat vom Arbeitgeber die Entlassung oder Versetzung verlangen. ²Gibt das Arbeitsgericht einem Antrag des Betriebsrats statt, dem Arbeitgeber aufzugeben, die Entlassung oder Versetzung durchzuführen, und führt der Arbeitgeber die Entlassung oder Versetzung einer rechtskräftigen gerichtlichen Entscheidung zuwider nicht durch, so ist auf Antrag des Betriebsrats vom Arbeitsgericht zu erkennen, dass er zur Vornahme der Entlassung oder Versetzung durch Zwangsgeld anzuhalten sei. ³Das Höchstmaß des Zwangsgeldes beträgt für jeden Tag der Zuwiderhandlung 250 Euro.

§ 105
Leitende Angestellte

Eine beabsichtigte Einstellung oder personelle Veränderung eines in § 5 Abs. 3 genannten leitenden Angestellten ist dem Betriebsrat rechtzeitig mitzuteilen.

(3) ¹A transfer of the persons set forth in subsection (1) which would lead to the loss of their office or eligibility to be elected shall require the consent of the works council; this shall not apply if the employee concerned is in agreement with the transfer. ²Para. (2) shall apply *mutatis mutandis* with the proviso that the Labor Court may supersede the works council's consent to the transfer if, even taking the employee's position in the establishment into account, such transfer is necessary on urgent operational grounds.

Section 104
Dismissal of Disruptive Employees Within the Establishment

¹If an employee repeatedly causes a serious disturbance of the peace in the establishment through unlawful conduct or gross violation of the principles contained in section 75 (1), particularly racist or xenophobic behaviour, the works council may demand that the employer dismiss or transfer him. ²If the Labor Court approves the works council's petition to order the employer to execute the dismissal or transfer and the employer fails to execute such dismissal or transfer in violation of a legally valid and final court decision, the Labor Court may, at the works council's request, compel the employer to carry out the dismissal or transfer or face a coercive fine. ³The maximum amount of such fine shall be 250 euro for each day of violation.

Section 105
Managerial Employees

The works council must be notified in good time of an intended appointment or change of a managerial employee as defined in section 5 (3).

Sechster Abschnitt
Wirtschaftliche Angelegenheiten

Erster Unterabschnitt
Unterrichtung in wirtschaftlichen Angelegenheiten

§ 106
Wirtschaftsausschuss

(1) ¹In allen Unternehmen mit in der Regel mehr als einhundert ständig beschäftigten Arbeitnehmern ist ein Wirtschaftsausschuss zu bilden. ²Der Wirtschaftsausschuss hat die Aufgabe, wirtschaftliche Angelegenheiten mit dem Unternehmer zu beraten und den Betriebsrat zu unterrichten.

(2) Der Unternehmer hat den Wirtschaftsausschuss rechtzeitig und umfassend über die wirtschaftlichen Angelegenheiten des Unternehmens unter Vorlage der erforderlichen Unterlagen zu unterrichten, soweit dadurch nicht die Betriebs- und Geschäftsgeheimnisse des Unternehmens gefährdet werden, sowie die sich daraus ergebenden Auswirkungen auf die Personalplanung darzustellen. Zu den erforderlichen Unterlagen gehört in den Fällen des Absatzes 3 Nr. 9 a insbesondere die Angabe über den potentiellen Erwerber und dessen Absichten im Hinblick auf die künftige Geschäftstätigkeit des Unternehmens sowie die sich daraus ergebenden Auswirkungen auf die Arbeitnehmer; Gleiches gilt, wenn im Vorfeld der Übernahme des Unternehmens ein Bieterverfahren durchgeführt wird.

(3) Zu den wirtschaftlichen Angelegenheiten im Sinne dieser Vorschrift gehören insbesondere

1. die wirtschaftliche und finanzielle Lage des Unternehmens;
2. die Produktions- und Absatzlage;
3. das Produktions- und Investitionsprogramm;
4. Rationalisierungsvorhaben;

Chapter 6
Economic Matters

Subchapter 1
Information on Economic Matters

Section 106
Economic Committee

(1) ¹An economic committee (*Wirtschaftsausschuss*) shall be formed in all companies with more than 100 regular employees. ²The economic committee has the duty to confer with the owner of the company about economic matters and to inform the works council.

(2) The company shall inform the economic committee promptly and comprehensively about the economic matters of the company, providing the necessary documents, to the extent this does not jeopardize the company's trade and business secrets, and describe the impact these matters will have on the personnel planning. In the cases set forth in subsection (3) no. 9 a, such necessary documents shall in particular include information on the potential acquirer and its intentions with respect to the future business activity of the company, as well as the resultant impact on the employees; the same shall apply if a bidding procedure is carried out in advance of the takeover of the company.

(3) Economic matters within the meaning of this provision include in particular:

1. the economic and financial situation of the company;
2. the production and sales situation;
3. the production and investment program;
4. rationalization projects;

5. Fabrikations- und Arbeitsmethoden, insbesondere die Einführung neuer Arbeitsmethoden;
5a. Fragen des betrieblichen Umweltschutzes;
6. die Einschränkung oder Stilllegung von Betrieben oder von Betriebsteilen;
7. die Verlegung von Betrieben oder Betriebsteilen;
8. der Zusammenschluss oder die Spaltung von Unternehmen oder Betrieben;
9. die Änderung der Betriebsorganisation oder des Betriebszwecks;
9a. die Übernahme des Unternehmens, wenn hiermit der Erwerb der Kontrolle verbunden ist, sowie
10. sonstige Vorgänge und Vorhaben, welche die Interessen der Arbeitnehmer des Unternehmens wesentlich berühren können.

5. manufacturing and working methods, in particular the introduction of new working methods;
5a. questions of environmental protection in the establishment;
6. cutbacks or shut-downs of establishments or of parts of establishments;
7. the relocation of establishments or parts of establishments;
8. the amalgamation or split-up of establishments;
9. changes in the organization or purpose of the establishment;
9a. the takeover of the company if this involves the acquisition of control, as well as
10. other events and projects which could materially affect the interests of the employees of the company.

§ 107
Bestellung und Zusammensetzung des Wirtschaftsausschusses

(1) [1] Der Wirtschaftsausschuss besteht aus mindestens drei und höchstens sieben Mitgliedern, die dem Unternehmen angehören müssen, darunter mindestens einem Betriebsratsmitglied. [2] Zu Mitgliedern des Wirtschaftsausschusses können auch die in § 5 Abs. 3 genannten Angestellten bestimmt werden. [3] Die Mitglieder sollen die zur Erfüllung ihrer Aufgaben erforderliche fachliche und persönliche Eignung besitzen.

(2) [1] Die Mitglieder des Wirtschaftsausschusses werden vom Betriebsrat für die Dauer seiner Amtszeit bestimmt. [2] Besteht ein Gesamtbetriebsrat, so bestimmt dieser die Mitglieder des Wirtschaftsausschusses; die Amtszeit der Mitglieder endet in diesem Fall in dem Zeitpunkt, in dem die Amtszeit der Mehrheit der Mitglieder des Gesamtbetriebsrats, die an der Bestimmung mitzuwirken berechtigt waren, abgelaufen ist. [3] Die Mitglieder des Wirtschaftsausschusses können jederzeit abberufen

Section 107
Appointment and Composition of the Economic Committee

(1) [1] The economic committee shall comprise 3 to 7 members belonging to the company, one of whom must be a works council member. [2] The managerial employees described in section 5 (3) may also be appointed as members of the economic committee. [3] The members should have the necessary professional and personal qualifications to fulfill their duties.

(2) [1] The economic committee members shall be appointed by the works council for the duration of their term of office. [2] If a joint works council exists, it shall appoint the members of the economic committee; in this case, the term of office of the members shall end at the same time as the expiration of the term of office of the majority of those joint works council members entitled participate in the appointment. [3] Members of the economic committee may be removed at any time; sentences 1 and 2

werden; auf die Abberufung sind die Sätze 1 und 2 entsprechend anzuwenden.

(3) ¹Der Betriebsrat kann mit der Mehrheit der Stimmen seiner Mitglieder beschließen, die Aufgaben des Wirtschaftsausschusses einem Ausschuss des Betriebsrats zu übertragen. ²Die Zahl der Mitglieder des Ausschusses darf die Zahl der Mitglieder des Betriebsausschusses nicht überschreiten. ³Der Betriebsrat kann jedoch weitere Arbeitnehmer einschließlich der in § 5 Abs. 3 genannten leitenden Angestellten bis zur selben Zahl, wie der Ausschuss Mitglieder hat, in den Ausschuss berufen; für die Beschlussfassung gilt Satz 1. ⁴Für die Verschwiegenheitspflicht der in Satz 3 bezeichneten weiteren Arbeitnehmer gilt § 79 entsprechend. ⁵Für die Abänderung und den Widerruf der Beschlüsse nach den Sätzen 1 bis 3 sind die gleichen Stimmenmehrheiten erforderlich wie für die Beschlüsse nach den Sätzen 1 bis 3. ⁶Ist in einem Unternehmen ein Gesamtbetriebsrat errichtet, so beschließt dieser über die anderweitige Wahrnehmung der Aufgaben des Wirtschaftsausschusses; die Sätze 1 bis 5 gelten entsprechend.

apply *mutatis mutandis* to such removal.

(3) ¹The works council may, with a majority vote of its members, decide to delegate the duties of the economic committee to a committee of the works council. ²Such committee cannot have more members than the works committee. ³The works council may, however, appoint additional employees to the committee, including those managerial employees described in section 5 (3), up to the number of members of the committee; sentence 1 applies to such resolutions. ⁴Section 79 applies *mutatis mutandis* to the duty of confidentiality regarding the additional employees pursuant to sentence 3. ⁵The same number of majority votes is necessary for the amendment and revocation of the provisions pursuant to sentences 1 to 3 as for the adoption of provisions pursuant to sentences 1 to 3. ⁶Where a joint works council is formed in an company, it shall determine who will assume the duties of the economic committees elsewhere; sentences 1 to 5 apply accordingly.

§ 108
Sitzungen

(1) Der Wirtschaftsausschuss soll monatlich einmal zusammentreten.

(2) ¹An den Sitzungen des Wirtschaftsausschusses hat der Unternehmer oder sein Vertreter teilzunehmen. ²Er kann sachkundige Arbeitnehmer des Unternehmens einschließlich der in § 5 Abs. 3 genannten Angestellten hinzuziehen. ³Für die Hinzuziehung und die Verschwiegenheitspflicht von Sachverständigen gilt § 80 Abs. 3 und 4 entsprechend.

(3) Die Mitglieder des Wirtschaftsausschusses sind berechtigt, in die nach § 106 Abs. 2 vorzulegenden Unterlagen Einsicht zu nehmen.

Section 108
Meetings

(1) The economic committee shall meet once per month.

(2) ¹The owner or his representatives shall participate in the meetings of the economic committee. ²He may invite competent employees of the company, including those referred to in section 5 (3). ³Section 80 (3) and (4) apply *mutatis mutandis* with respect to the invitation and the duty of confidentiality of such persons.

(3) The members of the economic committee are entitled to inspect the documents to be presented pursuant to section 106 (2).

(4) Der Wirtschaftsausschuss hat über jede Sitzung dem Betriebsrat unverzüglich und vollständig zu berichten.

(5) Der Jahresabschluss ist dem Wirtschaftsausschuss unter Beteiligung des Betriebsrats zu erläutern.

(6) Hat der Betriebsrat oder der Gesamtbetriebsrat eine anderweitige Wahrnehmung der Aufgaben des Wirtschaftsausschusses beschlossen, so gelten die Absätze 1 bis 5 entsprechend.

§ 109
Beilegung von Meinungsverschiedenheiten

[1] Wird eine Auskunft über wirtschaftliche Angelegenheiten des Unternehmens im Sinne des § 106 entgegen dem Verlangen des Wirtschaftsausschusses nicht, nicht rechtzeitig oder nur ungenügend erteilt und kommt hierüber zwischen Unternehmer und Betriebsrat eine Einigung nicht zustande, so entscheidet die Einigungsstelle. [2] Der Spruch der Einigungsstelle ersetzt die Einigung zwischen Arbeitgeber und Betriebsrat. [3] Die Einigungsstelle kann, wenn dies für ihre Entscheidung erforderlich ist, Sachverständige anhören; § 80 Abs. 4 gilt entsprechend. [4] Hat der Betriebsrat oder der Gesamtbetriebsrat eine anderweitige Wahrnehmung der Aufgaben des Wirtschaftsausschusses beschlossen, so gilt Satz 1 entsprechend.

§ 109 a
Unternehmensübernahme

In Unternehmen, in denen kein Wirtschaftsausschuss besteht, ist im Fall des § 106 Abs. 3 Nr. 9 a der Betriebsrat entsprechend § 106 Abs. 1 und 2 zu beteiligen; § 109 gilt entsprechend.

§ 110
Unterrichtung der Arbeitnehmer

(1) In Unternehmen mit in der Regel mehr als 1.000 ständig beschäftigten

(4) The economic committee shall inform the works council promptly and completely about every meeting.

(5) The annual statement of accounts shall be explained to the economic committee with the works council in attendance.

(6) If the works council or the joint works council decides to assign the duties of the economic committee to another body, subsections (1) to (5) shall apply *mutatis mutandis*.

Section 109
Settlement of Differences of Opinion

[1] If information regarding economic matters of the company within the meaning of section 106 is not given contrary to the request of the economic committee, is not given in a timely manner or is inadequate and an agreement cannot be reached between the owner and the works council, the conciliation board shall render the decision. [2] The decision of the conciliation board replaces an agreement between the employer and the works council. [3] The conciliation board may consult experts, if this is necessary for reaching a decision; section 80 (4) applies mutatis mutandis. [4] Where the works council or the joint works council has decided to assign the economic committee's duties to another body, sentence 1 shall apply *mutatis mutandis*.

Section 109 a
Company Takeovers

In companies in which no economic committee exists, in the event of section 106 (3) no. 9 a, the works council must be involved in accordance with section 106 (1) and (2); section 109 shall apply *mutatis mutandis*.

Section 110
Informing the Employees

(1) In companies with more than 1,000 regular employees, the owner shall,

Arbeitnehmern hat der Unternehmer mindestens einmal in jedem Kalendervierteljahr nach vorheriger Abstimmung mit dem Wirtschaftsausschuss oder den in § 107 Abs. 3 genannten Stellen und dem Betriebsrat die Arbeitnehmer schriftlich über die wirtschaftliche Lage und Entwicklung des Unternehmens zu unterrichten.

(2) ¹In Unternehmen, die die Voraussetzungen des Absatzes 1 nicht erfüllen, aber in der Regel mehr als zwanzig wahlberechtigte ständige Arbeitnehmer beschäftigen, gilt Absatz 1 mit der Maßgabe, dass die Unterrichtung der Arbeitnehmer mündlich erfolgen kann. ²Ist in diesen Unternehmen ein Wirtschaftsausschuss nicht zu errichten, so erfolgt die Unterrichtung nach vorheriger Abstimmung mit dem Betriebsrat.

upon prior consultation with the economic committee or the committees referred to in section 107 (3) and the works council, inform the employees in writing with regard to the economic situation and development of the company once every quarter.

(2) ¹In companies that do not meet the prerequisites of subsection (1) but regularly have more than 20 employees eligible to vote, subsection (1) shall apply with the proviso that the employees may be informed orally. ²If no economic committee has been formed in this company, the information shall be provided after prior consultation with the works council.

Zweiter Unterabschnitt
Betriebsänderungen

Subchapter 2
Operational Changes

§ 111
Betriebsänderungen

Section 111
Operational Changes

¹In Unternehmen mit in der Regel mehr als zwanzig wahlberechtigten Arbeitnehmern hat der Unternehmer den Betriebsrat über geplante Betriebsänderungen, die wesentliche Nachteile für die Belegschaft oder erhebliche Teile der Belegschaft zur Folge haben können, rechtzeitig und umfassend zu unterrichten und die geplanten Betriebsänderungen mit dem Betriebsrat zu beraten. ²Der Betriebsrat kann in Unternehmen mit mehr als 300 Arbeitnehmern zu seiner Unterstützung einen Berater hinzuziehen; § 80 Abs. 4 gilt entsprechend; im Übrigen bleibt § 80 Abs. 3 unberührt. ³Als Betriebsänderungen im Sinne des Satzes 1 gelten

1. Einschränkung und Stilllegung des ganzen Betriebs oder von wesentlichen Betriebsteilen,
2. Verlegung des ganzen Betriebs oder von wesentlichen Betriebsteilen,

¹In companies with more than 20 regular employees eligible to vote, the owner shall promptly and comprehensively inform the works council of planned operational changes which could result in significant disadvantages for the personnel or a considerable part of the personnel and confer with the works council with respect to the planned operational changes. ²In companies with over 300 employees the works council may engage a consultant to assist it; section 80 (4) applies *mutatis mutandis*; otherwise, section 80 (3) remains unaffected. ³Operational changes within the meaning of sentence 1 include:

1. cutback or closure of the entire establishment or significant parts of the establishment;
2. relocation of the establishment or considerable parts of the establishment;

3. Zusammenschluss mit anderen Betrieben oder die Spaltung von Betrieben,
4. grundlegende Änderungen der Betriebsorganisation, des Betriebszwecks oder der Betriebsanlagen,
5. Einführung grundlegend neuer Arbeitsmethoden und Fertigungsverfahren.

§ 112
Interessenausgleich über die Betriebsänderung, Sozialplan

(1) [1]Kommt zwischen Unternehmer und Betriebsrat ein Interessenausgleich über die geplante Betriebsänderung zustande, so ist dieser schriftlich niederzulegen und vom Unternehmer und Betriebsrat zu unterschreiben. [2]Das Gleiche gilt für eine Einigung über den Ausgleich oder die Milderung der wirtschaftlichen Nachteile, die den Arbeitnehmern infolge der geplanten Betriebsänderung entstehen (Sozialplan). [3]Der Sozialplan hat die Wirkung einer Betriebsvereinbarung. [4]§ 77 Abs. 3 ist auf den Sozialplan nicht anzuwenden.

(2) [1]Kommt ein Interessenausgleich über die geplante Betriebsänderung oder eine Einigung über den Sozialplan nicht zustande, so können der Unternehmer oder der Betriebsrat den Vorstand der Bundesagentur für Arbeit um Vermittlung ersuchen, der Vorstand kann die Aufgabe auf andere Bedienstete der Bundesagentur für Arbeit übertragen. [2]Erfolgt kein Vermittlungsersuchen oder bleibt der Vermittlungsversuch ergebnislos, so können der Unternehmer oder der Betriebsrat die Einigungsstelle anrufen. [3]Auf Ersuchen des Vorsitzenden der Einigungsstelle nimmt ein Mitglied des Vorstands der Bundesagentur für Arbeit oder ein vom Vorstand der Bundesagentur für Arbeit benannter Bediensteter der Bundesagentur für Arbeit an der Verhandlung teil.

3. amalgamation with other establishments or the divestiture of establishments;
4. fundamental changes in the organization, purpose or technical facilities of the establishment;
5. introduction of fundamentally new work methods and production processes.

Section 112
Reconciliation of Interests with Respect to Operational Change, Social Plan

(1) [1]If a reconciliation of interests is agreed upon between the owner and the works council with regard to the planned operational changes, this shall be recorded in writing and be signed by the owner and the works council. [2]The same applies for an agreement with regard to a settlement or the mitigation of financial disadvantages the employees will suffer due to the planned operational changes (social plan). [3]The social plan *(Sozialplan)* shall have the effect of a works agreement. [4]Section 77 (3) is not applicable to the social plan.

(2) [1]If a reconciliation of interests with regard to the planned operational changes or agreement on a social plan cannot be achieved, the owner or the works council may call upon the Governing Board of the Federal Employment Agency to mediate, which may pass this task on to other staff members of the Federal Employment Agency. [2]If this does not occur or the attempt to mediate fails, the owner or the works council may appeal to the conciliation board. [3]At the request of the conciliation board's chairman, a member of the Governing Board of the Federal Employment Agency or a staff member of the Federal Employment Agency appointed Governing Board shall participate in the negotiations.

(3) ¹Unternehmer und Betriebsrat sollen der Einigungsstelle Vorschläge zur Beilegung der Meinungsverschiedenheiten über den Interessenausgleich und den Sozialplan machen. ²Die Einigungsstelle hat eine Einigung der Parteien zu versuchen. ³Kommt eine Einigung zustande, so ist sie schriftlich niederzulegen und von den Parteien und vom Vorsitzenden zu unterschreiben.

(4) ¹Kommt eine Einigung über den Sozialplan nicht zustande, so entscheidet die Einigungsstelle über die Aufstellung eines Sozialplans. ²Der Spruch der Einigungsstelle ersetzt die Einigung zwischen Arbeitgeber und Betriebsrat.

(5) ¹Die Einigungsstelle hat bei ihrer Entscheidung nach Absatz 4 sowohl die sozialen Belange der betroffenen Arbeitnehmer zu berücksichtigen als auch auf die wirtschaftliche Vertretbarkeit ihrer Entscheidung für das Unternehmen zu achten. ²Dabei hat die Einigungsstelle sich im Rahmen billigen Ermessens insbesondere von folgenden Grundsätzen leiten zu lassen:

1. Sie soll beim Ausgleich oder bei der Milderung wirtschaftlicher Nachteile, insbesondere durch Einkommensminderung, Wegfall von Sonderleistungen oder Verlust von Anwartschaften auf betriebliche Altersversorgung, Umzugskosten oder erhöhte Fahrtkosten, Leistungen vorsehen, die in der Regel den Gegebenheiten des Einzelfalles Rechnung tragen.
2. ¹Sie hat die Aussichten der betroffenen Arbeitnehmer auf dem Arbeitsmarkt zu berücksichtigen. ²Sie soll Arbeitnehmer von Leistungen ausschließen, die in einem zumutbaren Arbeitsverhältnis im selben Betrieb oder in einem anderen Betrieb des Unternehmens oder eines zum Konzern gehörenden Unternehmens weiterbeschäftigt werden können

(3) ¹The owner and the works council shall make suggestions to the conciliation board to resolve the differences of opinion on the reconciliation of interests and the social plan. ²The conciliation board shall attempt to bring the parties to an agreement. ³If no agreement is reached, this shall be recorded in writing and signed by the parties and the chairman.

(4) ¹If no agreement on the social plan is reached, the conciliation board shall decide on the establishment of the social plan. ²The conciliation board's decision shall replace an agreement between the employer and the works council.

(5) ¹In making its decision pursuant to subsection (4), the conciliation board shall consider the social concerns of the affected employees as well as the economic feasibility of its decision for the company. ²The conciliation board shall, in its reasonable discretion, particularly be guided by the following principles:

1. When compensating for or mitigating financial disadvantages, in particular those resulting from loss of income, fringe benefits or expectancies in company pension plans, from moving costs or increased travel costs, it should provide for benefits which generally take the individual's circumstances into account.
2. ¹It must consider the affected employee's prospects on the labor market. ²It should exclude from any benefits employees who could be further employed and who reject continued and reasonable employment in the same establishment or in a different establishment of the company or of companies belonging to the group; continued employment in

und die Weiterbeschäftigung ablehnen; die mögliche Weiterbeschäftigung an einem anderen Ort begründet für sich allein nicht die Unzumutbarkeit.

2a. Sie soll insbesondere die im Dritten Buch des Sozialgesetzbuches vorgesehenen Förderungsmöglichkeiten zur Vermeidung von Arbeitslosigkeit berücksichtigen.

3. Sie hat bei der Bemessung des Gesamtbetrages der Sozialplanleistungen darauf zu achten, dass der Fortbestand des Unternehmens oder die nach Durchführung der Betriebsänderung verbleibenden Arbeitsplätze nicht gefährdet werden.

a different locality shall not be deemed to be unreasonable for that reason alone.

2a. In particular it should take into consideration the possibilities for advancement in order to prevent unemployment that are set forth in the Third Book of the Social Security Code.

3. When calculating the total amount of the social plan benefits, it shall ensure that the continuation of the company or the jobs remaining after the execution of the operational changes will not be endangered.

§ 112a
Erzwingbarer Sozialplan bei Personalabbau, Neugründungen

Section 112a
Compulsory Social Plan due to Reduction Personnel, New Formations

(1) ¹Besteht eine geplante Betriebsänderung im Sinne des § 111 Satz 3 Nr. 1 allein in der Entlassung von Arbeitnehmern, so findet § 112 Abs. 4 und 5 nur Anwendung, wenn

1. in Betrieben mit in der Regel weniger als 60 Arbeitnehmern 20 vom Hundert der regelmäßig beschäftigten Arbeitnehmer, aber mindestens 6 Arbeitnehmer,
2. in Betrieben mit in der Regel mindestens 60 und weniger als 250 Arbeitnehmern 20 vom Hundert der regelmäßig beschäftigten Arbeitnehmer oder mindestens 37 Arbeitnehmer,
3. in Betrieben mit in der Regel mindestens 250 und weniger als 500 Arbeitnehmern 15 vom Hundert der regelmäßig beschäftigten Arbeitnehmer oder mindestens 60 Arbeitnehmer,
4. in Betrieben mit in der Regel mindestens 500 Arbeitnehmern 10 vom Hundert der regelmäßig beschäftigten Arbeitnehmer, aber mindestens 60 Arbeitnehmer

(1) ¹If a planned operational change within the meaning of section 111 sentence 3 no. 1 consists solely of a layoff of employees, section 112 (4) and (5) shall only apply if in

1. establishments which regularly employ less than 60 employees, 20% of the regular employees, but at least 6 employees,
2. establishments which regularly employ at least 60 and less than 250 employees, 20% of the regular employees or at least 37 employees,
3. establishments which regularly employ at least 250 and less than 500 employees, 15% of the regular employees or at least 60 employees
4. establishments which regularly employ at least 500 employees, 10% of the regular employees, but at least 60 employees.

aus betriebsbedingten Gründen entlassen werden sollen. ²Als Entlassung gilt auch das vom Arbeitgeber aus Gründen der Betriebsänderung veranlasste Ausscheiden von Arbeitnehmern auf Grund von Aufhebungsverträgen.

(2) ¹§ 112 Abs. 4 und 5 findet keine Anwendung auf Betriebe eines Unternehmens in den ersten vier Jahren nach seiner Gründung. ²Dies gilt nicht für Neugründungen im Zusammenhang mit der rechtlichen Umstrukturierung von Unternehmen und Konzernen. ³Maßgebend für den Zeitpunkt der Gründung ist die Aufnahme einer Erwerbstätigkeit, die nach § 138 der Abgabenordnung dem Finanzamt mitzuteilen ist.

are to be laid off for operational reasons. ²If the employer instigates the departure of an employee on the basis of a termination agreement, this shall also be deemed to be a layoff due to operational changes.

(2) ¹Section 112 (4) and (5) shall not apply to the establishment of an company during the first four years following its formation. ²This shall not apply for new formations in connection with the legal restructuring of an company or a group. ³Decisive for determining the time of formation is the commencement of business operations which must be reported to the tax authority pursuant to section 138 of the Tax Code (*Abgabenordnung*).

§ 113
Nachteilsausgleich

(1) Weicht der Unternehmer von einem Interessenausgleich über die geplante Betriebsänderung ohne zwingenden Grund ab, so können Arbeitnehmer, die infolge dieser Abweichung entlassen werden, beim Arbeitsgericht Klage erheben mit dem Antrag, den Arbeitgeber zur Zahlung von Abfindungen zu verurteilen; § 10 des Kündigungsschutzgesetzes gilt entsprechend.

(2) Erleiden Arbeitnehmer infolge einer Abweichung nach Absatz 1 andere wirtschaftliche Nachteile, so hat der Unternehmer diese Nachteile bis zu einem Zeitraum von zwölf Monaten auszugleichen.

(3) Die Absätze 1 und 2 gelten entsprechend, wenn der Unternehmer eine geplante Betriebsänderung nach § 111 durchführt, ohne über sie einen Interessenausgleich mit dem Betriebsrat versucht zu haben, und infolge der Maßnahme Arbeitnehmer entlassen werden oder andere wirtschaftliche Nachteile erleiden.

Section 113
Compensation for Disadvantages

(1) Where the owner deviates from a reconciliation of interests with regard to the planned operational changes without a compelling reason, the employees who have been dismissed due to this deviation may file a complaint with the Labor Court, petitioning it to order the employer to make severance payments; section 10 of the Protection Against Unfair Dismissals Act shall apply *mutatis mutandis*.

(2) If employees incur other financial disadvantages as a result of a deviation pursuant to subsection (1), the owner shall compensate for these disadvantages within a period of twelve months.

(3) Subsections (1) and (2) apply *mutatis mutandis* if the company executes a planned operational change pursuant to section 111 without attempting to reach a reconciliation of interests with the works council and as a result of this change employees are laid off or incur other financial disadvantages.

Fünfter Teil
Besondere Vorschriften für einzelne Betriebsarten

Erster Abschnitt
Seeschifffahrt

§ 114
Grundsätze

(1) Auf Seeschifffahrtsunternehmen und ihre Betriebe ist dieses Gesetz anzuwenden, soweit sich aus den Vorschriften dieses Abschnitts nichts anderes ergibt.

(2) [1] Seeschifffahrtsunternehmen im Sinne dieses Gesetzes ist ein Unternehmen, das Handelsschifffahrt betreibt und seinen Sitz im Geltungsbereich dieses Gesetzes hat. [2] Ein Seeschifffahrtsunternehmen im Sinne dieses Abschnitts betreibt auch, wer als Korrespondenzreeder, Vertragsreeder, Ausrüster oder aufgrund eines ähnlichen Rechtsverhältnisses Schiffe zum Erwerb durch die Seeschifffahrt verwendet, wenn er Arbeitgeber des Kapitäns und der Besatzungsmitglieder ist oder überwiegend die Befugnisse des Arbeitgebers ausübt.

(3) Als Seebetrieb im Sinne dieses Gesetzes gilt die Gesamtheit der Schiffe eines Seeschifffahrtsunternehmens einschließlich der in Absatz 2 Satz 2 genannten Schiffe.

(4) [1] Schiffe im Sinne dieses Gesetzes sind Kauffahrteischiffe, die nach dem Flaggenrechtsgesetz die Bundesflagge führen. [2] Schiffe, die in der Regel binnen 24 Stunden nach dem Auslaufen an den Sitz eines Landbetriebs zurückkehren, gelten als Teil dieses Landbetriebs des Seeschifffahrtsunternehmens.

(5) Jugend- und Auszubildendenvertretungen werden nur für die Landbetriebe von Seeschifffahrtsunternehmen gebildet.

Part 5
Miscellaneous Provisions for Specific Types of Establishments

Chapter 1
Maritime Shipping

Section 114
Principles

(1) This Act is applicable to maritime enterprises and their establishments unless otherwise provided in the provisions of this Chapter.

(2) [1] A maritime enterprise within the meaning of this Act is an company which is engaged in merchant shipping and has its seat within the jurisdiction of this Act. [2] An owner of a maritime enterprise within the meaning of this Chapter is also someone who acts as the managing owner of a ship, a contractual ship owner, ship's chandler or on the basis of a similar legal relationship uses ships in sea transport for gain, if he is the employer of the captain and the crew members or generally exercises the authority of the employer.

(3) A fleet establishment within the meaning of this Act is the aggregate of the ships of a maritime enterprise, including the ships mentioned in subsection (2) sentence 2.

(4) [1] Ships within the meaning of this Act are trading vessels which fly the flag of the Federal Republic of Germany pursuant to the Law of the Flag Act *(Flaggenrechtsgesetz)*. [2] Ships which normally return to the seat of a land establishment within 24 hours after departure are considered as part of the land establishment of the maritime enterprise.

(5) Youth and trainee representatives are only formed for the land establishment of the maritime shipping companies.

(6) ¹Besatzungsmitglieder sind die in § 3 des Seemannsgesetzes genannten Personen. ²Leitende Angestellte im Sinne des § 5 Abs. 3 dieses Gesetzes sind nur die Kapitäne.

§ 115
Bordvertretung

(1) ¹Auf Schiffen, die mit in der Regel mindestens fünf wahlberechtigten Besatzungsmitgliedern besetzt sind, von denen drei wählbar sind, wird eine Bordvertretung gewählt. ²Auf die Bordvertretung finden, soweit sich aus diesem Gesetz oder aus anderen gesetzlichen Vorschriften nicht etwas anderes ergibt, die Vorschriften über die Rechte und Pflichten des Betriebsrats und die Rechtsstellung seiner Mitglieder Anwendung.

(2) Die Vorschriften über die Wahl und Zusammensetzung des Betriebsrats finden mit folgender Maßgabe Anwendung:
1. Wahlberechtigt sind alle Besatzungsmitglieder des Schiffes.
2. Wählbar sind die Besatzungsmitglieder des Schiffes, die am Wahltag das 18. Lebensjahr vollendet haben und ein Jahr Besatzungsmitglied eines Schiffes waren, das nach dem Flaggenrechtsgesetz die Bundesflagge führt. § 8 Abs. 1 Satz 3 bleibt unberührt.
3. Die Bordvertretung besteht auf Schiffen mit in der Regel
5 bis 20 wahlberechtigten Besatzungsmitgliedern aus einer Person,
21 bis 75 wahlberechtigten Besatzungsmitgliedern aus drei Mitgliedern,
über 75 wahlberechtigten Besatzungsmitgliedern aus fünf Mitgliedern.
4. *(weggefallen)*
5. § 13 Abs. 1 und 3 findet keine Anwendung. Die Bordvertretung ist vor Ablauf ihrer Amtszeit unter den in § 13 Abs. 2 Nr. 2 bis 5 genannten Voraussetzungen neu zu wählen.

(6) ¹Crew members are those persons referred to in section 3 of the Seaman's Act (*Seemannsgesetz*). ²Only captains are managerial employees within the meaning of section 5 (3) of this Act.

Section 115
Board Representation

(1) ¹A ship's committee shall be elected on ships on which five crew members are normally occupied, of which three are eligible for election. ²To the extent not otherwise provided by this Act or of another legal provision the ship's committee shall consist of the provisions with regard to the rights and duties of the works council and the legal status of its members apply.

(2) The provisions with regard to the election and co-operation of the works council applies with the following provisions:
1. All crew members of the ship are eligible to vote.
2. Crew members of the ship are eligible for election if they have reached the age of 18 on the day of the election and have been a crew member of the ship for one year on a ship under the flag of the Federal Republic of Germany pursuant to the Law of the Flag Act. Section 8 (1) sentence 3 remains unaffected.
3. The ship's committee shall consist on ships with as a rule
5 to 20 crew members eligible to vote, of one person,
21 through 75 crew members eligible to vote, of three members,
over 75 crew members eligible to vote, of five members.
4. *(repealed)*
5. Section 13 (1) and (3) shall not apply. The ship's committee shall be newly elected before the expiration of its office, subject to the provisions set forth in section 13 (2) nos. 2 to 5.

6. Die wahlberechtigten Besatzungsmitglieder können mit der Mehrheit aller Stimmen beschließen, die Wahl der Bordvertretung binnen 24 Stunden durchzuführen.

7. Die in § 16 Abs. 1 Satz 1 genannte Frist wird auf zwei Wochen, die in § 16 Abs. 2 Satz 1 genannte Frist wird auf eine Woche verkürzt.

8. Bestellt die im Amt befindliche Bordvertretung nicht rechtzeitig einen Wahlvorstand oder besteht keine Bordvertretung, wird der Wahlvorstand in einer Bordversammlung von der Mehrheit der anwesenden Besatzungsmitglieder gewählt; § 17 Abs. 3 gilt entsprechend. Kann aus Gründen der Aufrechterhaltung des ordnungsgemäßen Schiffsbetriebs eine Bordversammlung nicht stattfinden, so kann der Kapitän auf Antrag von drei Wahlberechtigten den Wahlvorstand bestellen. Bestellt der Kapitän den Wahlvorstand nicht, so ist der Seebetriebsrat berechtigt, den Wahlvorstand zu bestellen. Die Vorschriften über die Bestellung des Wahlvorstands durch das Arbeitsgericht bleiben unberührt.

9. Die Frist für die Wahlanfechtung beginnt für Besatzungsmitglieder an Bord, wenn das Schiff nach Bekanntgabe des Wahlergebnisses erstmalig einen Hafen im Geltungsbereich dieses Gesetzes oder einen Hafen, in dem ein Seemannsamt seinen Sitz hat, anläuft. Die Wahlanfechtung kann auch zu Protokoll des Seemannsamtes erklärt werden. Wird die Wahl zur Bordvertretung angefochten, zieht das Seemannsamt die an Bord befindlichen Wahlunterlagen ein. Die Anfechtungserklärung und die eingezogenen Wahlunterlagen sind vom Seemannsamt unverzüglich an das für die Anfechtung zuständige Arbeitsgericht weiterzuleiten.

6. The crew members eligible to vote may decide by majority of all votes cast to conduct the election of the ship's committee within 24 hours.

7. The time period referred to in section 16 (1) sentence 1 shall be reduced to two weeks and the time period referred to in section 16 (2) sentence 1 shall be reduced to one week.

8. Where the ship's committee in office does not appoint an election committee in a timely manner or no ship's committee has been formed, the election committee shall be elected in a crew meeting by the majority of the crew members present; section 17 (3) applies mutatis mutandis. If the proper running of the ship prevents a crew meeting from being held, the captain may, at the request of three persons eligible to vote, appoint an election committee. If the captain fails to appoint an election committee the ship's works council shall be entitled to do so. The provisions with regard to the appointment of an election committee through the Labor Court remain unaffected.

9. The time period for challenging an election commences for the crew members on board when the ship first reaches a port subject to the jurisdiction of this Act or a port in which a seamen's employment authority has its seat after the announcement of the election results. The declaration of the election challenge may also recorded by the seamen's employment authority. If the election of the ship's committees is challenged, the seamen's employment authority shall take possession the election documents which are on board. The declaration of the challenge and the confiscated election documents shall be submitted without delay to the Labor Court competent to rule on the challenge.

(3) Auf die Amtszeit der Bordvertretung finden die §§ 21, 22 bis 25 mit der Maßgabe Anwendung, dass

1. die Amtszeit ein Jahr beträgt,
2. die Mitgliedschaft in der Bordvertretung auch endet, wenn das Besatzungsmitglied den Dienst an Bord beendet, es sei denn, dass es den Dienst an Bord vor Ablauf der Amtszeit nach Nummer 1 wieder antritt.

(4) [1]Für die Geschäftsführung der Bordvertretung gelten die §§ 26 bis 36, § 37 Abs. 1 bis 3 sowie die §§ 39 bis 41 entsprechend. [2]§ 40 Abs. 2 ist mit der Maßgabe anzuwenden, dass die Bordvertretung in dem für ihre Tätigkeit erforderlichen Umfang auch die für die Verbindung des Schiffes zur Reederei eingerichteten Mittel zur beschleunigten Übermittlung von Nachrichten in Anspruch nehmen kann.

(5) [1]Die §§ 42 bis 46 über die Betriebsversammlung finden für die Versammlung der Besatzungsmitglieder eines Schiffes (Bordversammlung) entsprechende Anwendung. [2]Auf Verlangen der Bordvertretung hat der Kapitän der Bordversammlung einen Bericht über die Schiffsreise und die damit zusammenhängenden Angelegenheiten zu erstatten. [3]Er hat Fragen, die den Schiffsbetrieb, die Schiffsreise und die Schiffssicherheit betreffen, zu beantworten.

(6) Die §§ 47 bis 59 über den Gesamtbetriebsrat und den Konzernbetriebsrat finden für die Bordvertretung keine Anwendung.

(7) Die §§ 74 bis 105 über die Mitwirkung und Mitbestimmung der Arbeitnehmer finden auf die Bordvertretung mit folgender Maßgabe Anwendung:

1. Die Bordvertretung ist zuständig für die Behandlung derjenigen nach diesem Gesetz der Mitwirkung und Mitbestimmung des Betriebsrats unterliegenden Angelegenheiten, die den

(3) The term of office of the ship's committee shall be subject to sections 21, 22 to 25, provided, however, that

1. the term of office shall be one year;
2. the membership of the ship's committee shall also end when the crew member ends his service on board unless he resumes service on board prior to the expiration of his term of office pursuant to no. 1.

(4) [1]Sections 26 through 36, section 37 (1) through (3) as well as sections 39 through 41 shall apply *mutatis mutandis* for the management of the ship's committee. [2]Section 40 (2) shall apply except that, to the extent necessary for its activities, the ship's committee may also use the equipment installed for the rapid transmission of information between the ship and the shipping company.

(5) [1]Sections 42 through 46 regarding the works meeting apply *mutatis mutandis* for the meeting of the crew members of a ship (crew meeting). [2]At the request of the ship's committee the captain shall issue a report on the ship's voyage and any related matters to the crew meeting. [3]He shall answer questions concerning the ships establishment, the ship's voyage and the ship's safety.

(6) Sections 47 through 59 regarding the joint works council and the group works council are not applicable to the ship's committee.

(7) Sections 74 through 105 regarding the employees' participation and codetermination shall apply to the ship's committee subject to the following conditions:

1. The ship's committee is responsible for handling those matters which are subject to the participation and codetermination of the works council pursuant to this Act and which affect

Bordbetrieb oder die Besatzungsmitglieder des Schiffes betreffen und deren Regelung dem Kapitän auf Grund gesetzlicher Vorschriften oder der ihm von der Reederei übertragenen Befugnisse obliegt.
2. Kommt es zwischen Kapitän und Bordvertretung in einer der Mitwirkung oder Mitbestimmung der Bordvertretung unterliegenden Angelegenheit nicht zu einer Einigung, so kann die Angelegenheit von der Bordvertretung an den Seebetriebsrat abgegeben werden. Der Seebetriebsrat hat die Bordvertretung über die weitere Behandlung der Angelegenheit zu unterrichten. Bordvertretung und Kapitän dürfen die Einigungsstelle oder das Arbeitsgericht nur anrufen, wenn ein Seebetriebsrat nicht gewählt ist.
3. Bordvertretung und Kapitän können im Rahmen ihrer Zuständigkeiten Bordvereinbarungen abschließen. Die Vorschriften über Betriebsvereinbarungen gelten für Bordvereinbarungen entsprechend. Bordvereinbarungen sind unzulässig, soweit eine Angelegenheit durch eine Betriebsvereinbarung zwischen Seebetriebsrat und Arbeitgeber geregelt ist.
4. In Angelegenheiten, die der Mitbestimmung der Bordvertretung unterliegen, kann der Kapitän, auch wenn eine Einigung mit der Bordvertretung noch nicht erzielt ist, vorläufige Regelungen treffen, wenn dies zur Aufrechterhaltung des ordnungsgemäßen Schiffsbetriebs dringend erforderlich ist. Den von der Anordnung betroffenen Besatzungsmitgliedern ist die Vorläufigkeit der Regelung bekannt zu geben. Soweit die vorläufige Regelung der endgültigen Regelung nicht entspricht, hat das Schifffahrtsunternehmen Nachteile auszugleichen, die den Besatzungsmitgliedern durch die vorläufige Regelung entstanden sind.
5. Die Bordvertretung hat das Recht auf regelmäßige und umfassende Unter-

the ship's committee or the crew members of the ship and which are handled by the captain due to statutory provisions or the authority conferred upon to him by the shipping company.
2. If the captain and the ship's committee do not come to an agreement in a matter subject to the participation or codetermination of the ship's committee, the ship's committee may delegate the matter to the works council of the fleet works council. ²The fleet works council shall inform the ship's committee of the continued handling of the matter. The ship's committee and captain may only appeal to the conciliation board or the Labor Court if no fleet works council has been elected.
3. The ship's committee and the captain have the authority to conclude a board agreement within the scope of their competence. The provisions with regard to the works agreement apply mutatis mutandis for the board agreement. Board agreements are prohibited where a matter has been resolved by a works agreement between the fleet works council and the employer.
4. In matters which are subject to the codetermination of the ship's committee, even where no agreement with the ship's committee has yet been reached, the captain can implement provisional regulations if this is urgently necessary for the proper running of the ship. The crew members affected shall be informed that the regulation is provisional. To the extent the provisional regulation does not correspond to the final regulation, the shipping company shall compensate for any disadvantages the crew members incurred due to the provisional regulation.
5. The ship's committee has the right to be informed in a regular and thor-

richtung über den Schiffsbetrieb. Die erforderlichen Unterlagen sind der Bordvertretung vorzulegen. Zum Schiffsbetrieb gehören insbesondere die Schiffssicherheit, die Reiserouten, die voraussichtlichen Ankunfts- und Abfahrtszeiten sowie die zu befördernde Ladung.

6. Auf Verlangen der Bordvertretung hat der Kapitän ihr Einsicht in die an Bord befindlichen Schiffstagebücher zu gewähren. In den Fällen, in denen der Kapitän eine Eintragung über Angelegenheiten macht, die der Mitwirkung oder Mitbestimmung der Bordvertretung unterliegen, kann diese eine Abschrift der Eintragung verlangen und Erklärungen zum Schiffstagebuch abgeben. In den Fällen, in denen über eine der Mitwirkung oder Mitbestimmung der Bordvertretung unterliegenden Angelegenheit eine Einigung zwischen Kapitän und Bordvertretung nicht erzielt wird, kann die Bordvertretung dies zum Schiffstagebuch erklären und eine Abschrift dieser Eintragung verlangen.

7. Die Zuständigkeit der Bordvertretung im Rahmen des Arbeitsschutzes bezieht sich auch auf die Schiffssicherheit und die Zusammenarbeit mit den insoweit zuständigen Behörden und sonstigen in Betracht kommenden Stellen.

ough manner with regard to activities on the ship. The necessary documents shall be presented to the ship's committee. Such activities include in particular the ship's safety, the routes of the voyage, the estimate time of arrival and departure as well as the goods to be shipped.

6. At the request of the ship's committee the captain shall allow it to inspect the ship's log which is on board. Where the captain makes an entry with regard to matters which are subject to the participation or codetermination of the ship's committee, the ship's committee may demand a copy of such entry and make declarations in the ship's log. In those cases in which an agreement cannot be reached between the captain and the ship's committee with regard to matters which are subject to the participation or codetermination of the ship's committee, the ship's committee declare this in the ship's log and demand a copy of the entry.

7. The authority of the ship's committee with respect to industrial safety also applies to the safety of the ship and cooperation with the competent authorities and other agencies concerned.

§ 116
Seebetriebsrat

(1) ¹In Seebetrieben werden Seebetriebsräte gewählt. ²Auf die Seebetriebsräte finden, soweit sich aus diesem Gesetz oder aus anderen gesetzlichen Vorschriften nicht etwas anderes ergibt, die Vorschriften über die Rechte und Pflichten des Betriebsrats und die Rechtsstellung seiner Mitglieder Anwendung.

(2) Die Vorschriften über die Wahl, Zusammensetzung und Amtszeit des Be-

Section 116
Fleet Works Council

(1) ¹Fleet works councils shall be elected in maritime establishments. ²Unless otherwise provided in this Act or in other statutory provisions, the provisions on the rights and obligations of the works council and legal status of its members shall apply to the fleet works council.

(2) The provisions with regard to the election, composition and term of office

triebsrats finden mit folgender Maßgabe Anwendung:

1. Wahlberechtigt zum Seebetriebsrat sind alle zum Seeschifffahrtsunternehmen gehörenden Besatzungsmitglieder.
2. Für die Wählbarkeit zum Seebetriebsrat gilt § 8 mit der Maßgabe, dass

    a) in Seeschifffahrtsunternehmen, zu denen mehr als acht Schiffe gehören oder in denen in der Regel mehr als 250 Besatzungsmitglieder beschäftigt sind, nur nach § 115 Abs. 2 Nr. 2 wählbare Besatzungsmitglieder wählbar sind;
    b) in den Fällen, in denen die Voraussetzungen des Buchstabens a nicht vorliegen, nur Arbeitnehmer wählbar sind, die nach § 8 die Wählbarkeit im Landbetrieb des Seeschifffahrtsunternehmens besitzen, es sei denn, dass der Arbeitgeber mit der Wahl von Besatzungsmitgliedern einverstanden ist.
3. Der Seebetriebsrat besteht in Seebetrieben mit in der Regel
5 bis 400 wahlberechtigten Besatzungsmitgliedern aus einer Person,
401 bis 800 wahlberechtigten Besatzungsmitgliedern aus drei Mitgliedern,
über 800 wahlberechtigten Besatzungsmitgliedern aus fünf Mitgliedern.
4. Ein Wahlvorschlag ist gültig, wenn er im Fall des § 14 Abs. 4 Satz 1 erster Halbsatz und Satz 2 mindestens von drei wahlberechtigten Besatzungsmitgliedern unterschrieben ist.
5. § 14a findet keine Anwendung.
6. Die in § 16 Abs. 1 Satz 1 genannte Frist wird auf drei Monate, die in § 16 Abs. 2 Satz 1 genannte Frist auf zwei Monate verlängert.
7. Zu Mitgliedern des Wahlvorstands können auch im Landbetrieb des Seeschifffahrtsunternehmens beschäftig-

of the works council shall apply subject to the following conditions:

1. All crew members belonging to the maritime enterprise are eligible to vote for the fleet works council.
2. With respect to the eligibility for election to the fleet works council, section 8 shall apply subject to the condition that

    a) in maritime enterprises with more than eight ships or which normally employ more than 250 crew members, only those crew members eligible for pursuant to section 115 (2) no. 2 shall be eligible;
    b) in those cases in which the prerequisites set forth of a) are not met, only those employees are eligible who are eligible pursuant to section 8 in the land works of the maritime enterprise, unless the employer consents to the election of crew members.
3. The fleet works council consists in maritime enterprises with, as a rule,
5 to 400 crew members eligible to vote of one person
401 to 800 crew members eligible to vote of three members

over 800 crew members eligible to vote of five members.
4. A nomination for the election is valid if, in the case of section 14 (4) first half of sentence 1 and sentence 2, it is signed by at least three crew members eligible to vote.
5. Section 14a shall not apply.
6. The time period mentioned in section 16 (1) sentence 1 shall be extended to three months and the time period mentioned in Section 16 (2) sentence 1 shall be extended to two months.
7. The employees of the land establishment of the maritime enterprise may be appointed as members of the

te Arbeitnehmer bestellt werden. § 17 Abs. 2 bis 4 findet keine Anwendung. Besteht kein Seebetriebsrat, so bestellt der Gesamtbetriebsrat oder, falls ein solcher nicht besteht, der Konzernbetriebsrat den Wahlvorstand. Besteht weder ein Gesamtbetriebsrat noch ein Konzernbetriebsrat wird der Wahlvorstand gemeinsam vom Arbeitgeber und den im Seebetrieb vertretenen Gewerkschaften bestellt; Gleiches gilt, wenn der Gesamtbetriebsrat oder der Konzernbetriebsrat die Bestellung des Wahlvorstands nach Satz 3 unterlässt. Einigen sich Arbeitgeber und Gewerkschaften nicht, so bestellt ihn das Arbeitsgericht auf Antrag des Arbeitgebers, einer im Seebetrieb vertretenen Gewerkschaft oder von mindestens drei wahlberechtigten Besatzungsmitgliedern. § 16 Abs. 2 Satz 2 und 3 gilt entsprechend.

8. Die Frist für die Wahlanfechtung nach § 19 Abs. 2 beginnt für Besatzungsmitglieder an Bord, wenn das Schiff nach Bekanntgabe des Wahlergebnisses erstmalig einen Hafen im Geltungsbereich dieses Gesetzes oder einen Hafen, in dem ein Seemannsamt seinen Sitz hat, anläuft. Nach Ablauf von drei Monaten seit Bekanntgabe des Wahlergebnisses ist eine Wahlanfechtung unzulässig. Die Wahlanfechtung kann auch zu Protokoll des Seemannsamtes erklärt werden. Die Anfechtungserklärung ist vom Seemannsamt unverzüglich an das für die Anfechtung zuständige Arbeitsgericht weiterzuleiten.

9. Die Mitgliedschaft im Seebetriebsrat endet, wenn der Seebetriebsrat aus Besatzungsmitgliedern besteht, auch, wenn das Mitglied des Seebetriebsrats nicht mehr Besatzungsmitglied ist. Die Eigenschaft als Besatzungsmitglied wird durch die Tätigkeit im Seebetriebsrat oder durch eine Beschäftigung gemäß Absatz 3 Nr. 2 nicht berührt.

election committee. Section 17 (2) to (4) shall not apply. If no fleet works council exists, the joint works council or, if none exists, the group works council shall appoint the election committee. If neither a joint works council nor a group works council exists, the election committee shall be appointed jointly by the employer and the union represented in the maritime enterprise; the same shall apply if the joint works council or the group works council refrains from appointing the election committee pursuant to sentence 3. Where the employer and the union cannot come to an agreement it shall be appointed by the Labor Court upon application of the employer, a union representative in the ship's establishment or by at least three crew members eligible to vote. Section 16 (2) sentence 2 and (3) apply *mutatis mutandis*.

8. The time period for challenging an election pursuant to section 19 (2) commences for the crew members on board when the ship first reaches a harbor which is subject to jurisdiction of this Act or a harbor in which a seamen's employment authority has a seat after the announcement of the election results. An election may not be challenged after three months have elapsed since the election results were announced. The declaration of the election challenge may also recorded by the seamen's employment authority. The seamen's employment authority shall submit the declaration of the challenge to the Labor Court competent to rule on the challenge without delay.

9. If the fleet works council consists of crew members, membership in the fleet works council ends when the fleet works council member ceases to be a crew member. The status as crew member is not affected by the activities of the works council or work pursuant to subsection (3) no. 2.

(3) Die §§ 26 bis 41 über die Geschäftsführung des Betriebsrats finden auf den Seebetriebsrat mit folgender Maßgabe Anwendung:

1. In Angelegenheiten, in denen der Seebetriebsrat nach diesem Gesetz innerhalb einer bestimmten Frist Stellung zu nehmen hat, kann er, abweichend von § 33 Abs. 2, ohne Rücksicht auf die Zahl der zur Sitzung erschienenen Mitglieder einen Beschluss fassen, wenn die Mitglieder ordnungsgemäß geladen worden sind.
2. Soweit die Mitglieder des Seebetriebsrats nicht freizustellen sind, sind sie so zu beschäftigen, dass sie durch ihre Tätigkeit nicht gehindert sind, die Aufgaben des Seebetriebsrats wahrzunehmen. Der Arbeitsplatz soll den Fähigkeiten und Kenntnissen des Mitglieds des Seebetriebsrats und seiner bisherigen beruflichen Stellung entsprechen. Der Arbeitsplatz ist im Einvernehmen mit dem Seebetriebsrat zu bestimmen. Kommt eine Einigung über die Bestimmung des Arbeitsplatzes nicht zustande, so entscheidet die Einigungsstelle. Der Spruch der Einigungsstelle ersetzt die Einigung zwischen Arbeitgeber und Seebetriebsrat.
3. Den Mitgliedern des Seebetriebsrats, die Besatzungsmitglieder sind, ist die Heuer auch dann fortzuzahlen, wenn sie im Landbetrieb beschäftigt werden. Sachbezüge sind angemessen abzugelten. Ist der neue Arbeitsplatz höherwertig, so ist das diesem Arbeitsplatz entsprechende Arbeitsentgelt zu zahlen.
4. Unter Berücksichtigung der örtlichen Verhältnisse ist über die Unterkunft der in den Seebetriebsrat gewählten Besatzungsmitglieder eine Regelung zwischen dem Seebetriebsrat und dem Arbeitgeber zu treffen, wenn der Arbeitsplatz sich nicht am Wohnort befindet. Kommt eine Eini-

(3) Sections 26 through 41 with regard to the management of the works council applies to the fleet works council as follows:

1. In matters on which the fleet works council must take a position within a certain period pursuant to this Act it may, notwithstanding section 33 (2), validly adopt a resolution irregardless of the number of members present at a meeting, provided that the members had been given proper notice.
2. Where members of the fleet work council are not to be released from their duties, they shall be employed in such a manner that their tasks do not prevent them from carrying out the duties of the fleet works council. The fleet works council member's workplace should correspond to his abilities and skills and his previous employment position. His workplace shall be determined in agreement with the fleet works council. Where no agreement on the determination of the workplace is reached, the conciliation board shall render the decision. The decision of the conciliation board shall replace an agreement between the employer and the fleet works council.
3. Members of the fleet works council who are crew members shall continue to receive their wages as sailors if they are employed in a land establishment. Appropriate compensation shall be made for benefits in kind. If the new workplace calls for higher remuneration, the remuneration corresponding to this workplace shall be paid.
4. Taking local conditions into account, an agreement shall be reached between the fleet works council and the employer with regard to the accommodation of the crew members elected to the fleet works council if their workplace is not located in their place of residence. If no agreement is

gung nicht zustande, so entscheidet die Einigungsstelle. Der Spruch der Einigungsstelle ersetzt die Einigung zwischen Arbeitgeber und Seebetriebsrat.

5. Der Seebetriebsrat hat das Recht, jedes zum Seebetrieb gehörende Schiff zu betreten, dort im Rahmen seiner Aufgaben tätig zu werden sowie an den Sitzungen der Bordvertretung teilzunehmen. § 115 Abs. 7 Nr. 5 Satz 1 gilt entsprechend.
6. Liegt ein Schiff in einem Hafen innerhalb des Geltungsbereichs dieses Gesetzes, so kann der Seebetriebsrat nach Unterrichtung des Kapitäns Sprechstunden an Bord abhalten und Bordversammlungen der Besatzungsmitglieder durchführen.
7. Läuft ein Schiff innerhalb eines Kalenderjahres keinen Hafen im Geltungsbereich dieses Gesetzes an, so gelten die Nummern 5 und 6 für europäische Häfen. ²Die Schleusen des Nordostseekanals gelten nicht als Häfen.
8. Im Einvernehmen mit dem Arbeitgeber können Sprechstunden und Bordversammlungen, abweichend von den Nummern 6 und 7, auch in anderen Liegehäfen des Schiffes durchgeführt werden, wenn ein dringendes Bedürfnis hierfür besteht. Kommt eine Einigung nicht zustande, so entscheidet die Einigungsstelle. Der Spruch der Einigungsstelle ersetzt die Einigung zwischen Arbeitgeber und Seebetriebsrat.

(4) Die §§ 42 bis 46 über die Betriebsversammlung finden auf den Seebetrieb keine Anwendung.

(5) Für den Seebetrieb nimmt der Seebetriebsrat die in den §§ 47 bis 59 dem Betriebsrat übertragenen Aufgaben, Befugnisse und Pflichten wahr.

(6) Die §§ 74 bis 113 über die Mitwirkung und Mitbestimmung der Arbeit-

reached, the decision shall be rendered by the conciliation board. The decision of the conciliation board shall replace an agreement between the employer and the fleet works council.

5. The fleet works council shall have the right to board every ship belonging to the maritime establishment to act within the scope of its duties, as well as participate in the meetings of the ship's committee. Section 115 (7) no. 5 sentence 1 applies *mutatis mutandis*.
6. If a ship is docked in a port within the jurisdiction of this Act, the fleet works council may, after informing the captain, hold a consulting hours on board and conduct a meeting of the crew members.
7. If a ship does not enter a port within the jurisdiction of this Act within one quarter year, nos. 5 and 6 shall apply to European ports. The locks of the Kiel canal shall not qualify as ports.
8. Notwithstanding nos. 6 and 7, consulting hours and crew meetings may be held in other ports where the ship docks upon agreement with the owner in case of urgent necessity. If no agreement can be reached the conciliation board shall render the decision. The decision of the conciliation board shall replace an agreement between the employer and the fleet works council.

(4) Sections 42 through 46 regarding to works meetings shall not apply to the maritime establishment.

(5) The fleet works council shall assume the duties, authority and rights assumed by the works council pursuant to sections 47 through 59 for the maritime establishment.

(6) Sections 74 through 113 concerning employees' participation and codeter-

nehmer finden auf den Seebetriebsrat mit folgender Maßgabe Anwendung:

1. Der Seebetriebsrat ist zuständig für die Behandlung derjenigen nach diesem Gesetz der Mitwirkung oder Mitbestimmung des Betriebsrats unterliegenden Angelegenheiten,
   a) die alle oder mehrere Schiffe des Seebetriebs oder die Besatzungsmitglieder aller oder mehrerer Schiffe des Seebetriebs betreffen,
   b) die nach § 115 Abs. 7 Nr. 2 von der Bordvertretung abgegeben worden sind oder
   c) für die nicht die Zuständigkeit der Bordvertretung nach § 115 Abs. 7 Nr. 1 gegeben ist.
2. Der Seebetriebsrat ist regelmäßig und umfassend über den Schiffsbetrieb des Seeschifffahrtsunternehmens zu unterrichten. Die erforderlichen Unterlagen sind ihm vorzulegen.

mination shall be applicable to the fleet works councils as follows:

1. The fleet works council is competent to handle all matters subject to the participation and codetermination of the works council pursuant to this Act:
   a) affecting all or several ships of the maritime establishment or the crew members of all or several of the maritime establishments;
   b) which are delegated by the ship's committee pursuant to section 115 (7) no. 2; or
   c) where the ship's committee is not competent pursuant to section 115 (7) no.1.
2. The fleet works council shall be informed regularly and thoroughly with regard to the activities of the maritime establishment and the maritime enterprise. The necessary documents shall be provided to it.

**Zweiter Abschnitt
Luftfahrt**

**Chapter 2
Air Transportation**

**§ 117
Geltung für die Luftfahrt**

**Section 117
Applicability to Air Transportation**

(1) Auf Landbetriebe von Luftfahrtunternehmen ist dieses Gesetz anzuwenden.

(2) ¹Für im Flugbetrieb beschäftigte Arbeitnehmer von Luftfahrtunternehmen kann durch Tarifvertrag eine Vertretung errichtet werden. ²Über die Zusammenarbeit dieser Vertretung mit den nach diesem Gesetz zu errichtenden Vertretungen der Arbeitnehmer der Landbetriebe des Luftfahrtunternehmens kann der Tarifvertrag von diesem Gesetz abweichende Regelungen vorsehen.

(1) This Act is applicable to land establishments of air transportation companies.

(2) ¹Employees of air traffic and air transportation companies may form a representative body by collective bargaining agreement. ²The collective bargaining agreement may contain resolutions departing from the provisions of this Act with respect to the cooperation between such bodies and the bodies to be formed to represent the employees of the ground establishments of air transportation companies under this Act.

Dritter Abschnitt
Tendenzbetriebe und Religionsgemeinschaften

§ 118
Geltung für Tendenzbetriebe und Religionsgemeinschaften

(1) ¹Auf Unternehmen und Betriebe, die unmittelbar und überwiegend

1. politischen, koalitionspolitischen, konfessionellen, karitativen, erzieherischen, wissenschaftlichen oder künstlerischen Bestimmungen oder
2. Zwecken der Berichterstattung oder Meinungsäußerung, auf die Artikel 5 Abs. 1 Satz 2 des Grundgesetzes Anwendung findet,

dienen, finden die Vorschriften dieses Gesetzes keine Anwendung, soweit die Eigenart des Unternehmens oder des Betriebs dem entgegensteht. ²Die §§ 106 bis 110 sind nicht, die §§ 111 bis 113 nur insoweit anzuwenden, als sie den Ausgleich oder die Milderung wirtschaftlicher Nachteile für die Arbeitnehmer infolge von Betriebsänderungen regeln.

(2) Dieses Gesetz findet keine Anwendung auf Religionsgemeinschaften und ihre karitativen und erzieherischen Einrichtungen unbeschadet deren Rechtsform.

Sechster Teil
Straf- und Bußgeldvorschriften

§ 119
Straftaten gegen Betriebsverfassungsorgane und ihre Mitglieder

(1) Mit Freiheitsstrafe bis zu einem Jahr oder mit Geldstrafe wird bestraft, wer

1. eine Wahl des Betriebsrats, der Jugend- und Auszubildendenvertre-

Chapter 3
Ideological Establishments and Religious Communities

Section 118
Applicability for Ideological Establishments and Religious Communities

(1) ¹The provisions of this Act shall not be applicable to companies and establishments engaged directly and primarily in

1. political, coalition political, religious, charitable, educational, scientific or artistic activities; or
2. reporting of news or expression of opinion where Article 5 (1) sentence 2 of the Basic Law (*Grundgesetz*) would be applicable

where the nature of the company or the establishment would preclude their application. ²Sections 106 to 110 do not apply and sections 111 to 113 apply only to the extent that they provide for a compensation or mitigation of economic disadvantages for employees resulting from operational changes.

(2) This Act does not apply to religious communities and their charitable and educational institutions, regardless of their legal form.

Part 6
Penal Provisions and Provisions for Fines

Section 119
Offenses Against Bodies Formed Pursuant to this Act and their Members

(1) A maximum sentence of one year's imprisonment or a fine shall be imposed on anyone who:

1. obstructs an election of the works council, the youth and trainee repre-

tung, der Bordvertretung, des Seebetriebsrats oder der in § 3 Abs. 1 Nr. 1 bis 3 oder 5 bezeichneten Vertretungen der Arbeitnehmer behindert oder durch Zufügung oder Androhung von Nachteilen oder durch Gewährung oder Versprechen von Vorteilen beeinflusst,
2. die Tätigkeit des Betriebsrats, des Gesamtbetriebsrats, des Konzernbetriebsrats, der Jugend- und Auszubildendenvertretung, der Gesamt-Jugend- und Auszubildendenvertretung, der Konzern-Jugend- und Auszubildendenvertretung, der Bordvertretung, des Seebetriebsrats, der in § 3 Abs. 1 bezeichneten Vertretungen der Arbeitnehmer, der Einigungsstelle, der in § 76 Abs. 8 bezeichneten tariflichen Schlichtungsstelle, der in § 86 bezeichneten betrieblichen Beschwerdestelle oder des Wirtschaftsausschusses behindert oder stört, oder
3. ein Mitglied oder ein Ersatzmitglied des Betriebsrats, des Gesamtbetriebsrats, des Konzernbetriebsrats, der Jugend- und Auszubildendenvertretung, der Gesamt-Jugend- und Auszubildendenvertretung, der Konzern-Jugend- und Auszubildendenvertretung, der Bordvertretung, des Seebetriebsrats, der in § 3 Abs. 1 bezeichneten Vertretungen der Arbeitnehmer, der Einigungsstelle, der in § 76 Abs. 8 bezeichneten Schlichtungsstelle, der in § 86 bezeichneten betrieblichen Beschwerdestelle oder des Wirtschaftsausschusses um seiner Tätigkeit willen oder eine Auskunftsperson nach § 80 Abs. 2 Satz 3 um ihrer Tätigkeit willen benachteiligt oder begünstigt.

(2) Die Tat wird nur auf Antrag des Betriebsrats, des Gesamtbetriebsrats, des Konzernbetriebsrats, der Bordvertretung, des Seebetriebsrats, einer der in § 3 Abs. 1 bezeichneten Vertretungen der Arbeitnehmer, des Wahlvorstands, des Unternehmers oder einer im Betrieb vertretenen Gewerkschaft verfolgt.

sentative body, the ship's committee, the fleet works council or the employee representative bodies referred to in Section 3 (1) nos. 1 to 3 or 5, or influences such election by causing or threatening disadvantages or by granting or promising advantages;
2. obstructs or disturbs the activities of the works council, the joint works council, the group works council, the youth and the trainee representative body, the general youth and trainee representative body, the ship's committee, the fleet works council, the employee representative bodies referred to in section 3 (1), the conciliation board, the collective arbitration body referred to in section 76 (8), the grievance board referred to in section 86 or the economic affairs committee; or
3. discriminates against or favors a member or an alternative member of the works council, the joint works council, the group works council, the youth and trainee representative body, the general youth and trainee representative body, the ship's committee, the fleet works council, the employee representative bodies the referred to in section 3 (1), the conciliation board, the arbitration body referred to in Section 76 (8), the grievance board referred to in Section 86 or the economic affairs committee, due to its activities, or an employee called upon to furnish information pursuant to Section 80 (2) sentence 3 due to his or her activities.

(2) Offenders shall only be prosecuted at the request of the works council, the joint works council, the group works council, the ship's committee, the fleet works council, one of the employee representative bodies referred to in section 3 (1), the election board, the company, or a trade union represented in the establishment.

§ 120
Verletzung von Geheimnissen

(1) Wer unbefugt ein fremdes Betriebs- oder Geschäftsgeheimnis offenbart, das ihm in seiner Eigenschaft als

1. Mitglied oder Ersatzmitglied des Betriebsrats oder einer der in § 79 Abs. 2 bezeichneten Stellen,
2. Vertreter einer Gewerkschaft oder Arbeitgebervereinigung,
3. Sachverständiger, der vom Betriebsrat nach § 80 Abs. 3 hinzugezogen oder von der Einigungsstelle nach § 109 Satz 3 angehört worden ist,
3a. Berater, der vom Betriebsrat nach § 111 Satz 2 hinzugezogen worden ist,
3b. Auskunftsperson, die dem Betriebsrat nach § 80 Abs. 2 Satz 3 zur Verfügung gestellt worden ist, oder
4. Arbeitnehmer, der vom Betriebsrat nach § 107 Abs. 3 Satz 3 oder vom Wirtschaftsausschuss nach § 108 Abs. 2 Satz 2 hinzugezogen worden ist,

bekannt geworden und das vom Arbeitgeber ausdrücklich als geheimhaltungsbedürftig bezeichnet worden ist, wird mit Freiheitsstrafe bis zu einem Jahr oder mit Geldstrafe bestraft.

(2) Ebenso wird bestraft, wer unbefugt ein fremdes Geheimnis eines Arbeitnehmers, namentlich ein zu dessen persönlichen Lebensbereich gehörendes Geheimnis, offenbart, das ihm in seiner Eigenschaft als Mitglied oder Ersatzmitglied des Betriebsrats oder einer der in § 79 Abs. 2 bezeichneten Stellen bekannt geworden ist und über das nach den Vorschriften dieses Gesetzes Stillschweigen zu bewahren ist.

(3) [1] Handelt der Täter gegen Entgelt oder in der Absicht, sich oder einen anderen zu bereichern oder einen anderen zu schädigen, so ist die Strafe Freiheitsstrafe bis zu zwei Jahren oder Geldstrafe. [2] Ebenso wird bestraft, wer unbefugt ein fremdes Geheimnis, na-

Section 120
Violation of Confidentiality

(1) Anyone who divulges a trade or business secret without authorization to a third party that was made known to him in his capacity as

1. a member or alternate member of the works council or one of the positions referred to in section 79 (2),
2. a representative of a trade union or an employers' association,
3. an expert who was called in by a works council pursuant to section 80 (3) or consulted by the conciliation board pursuant to section 109 sentence 3,
3a. a consultant who was called in by the works council pursuant to section 111 sentence 2,
3b. an expert who was provided to the works council pursuant to section 80 (2) sentence 3,
4. an employee who was called upon by the works council pursuant to section 107 (3) sentence 3 or by the economic affairs committee pursuant to section 108 (2) sentence 2

and was clearly designated as confidential by the employer shall be punished with imprisonment for up to one year or a fine.

(2) The same penalty shall be imposed on anyone who divulges without authorization a secret of an employee, especially a secret relating to his personal life which became known to the offender in his capacity as a member or an alternate member of the works council or one of the positions referred to in section 79 (2) and which he is obligated to treat confidentially pursuant to this Act.

(3) [1] If the offender commits this offense in exchange for payment or with the intention of enriching himself or another person or in order to harm another person, the penalty shall be imprisonment for up to 2 years or a fine. [2] The same penalty shall be imposed on

mentlich ein Betriebs- oder Geschäftsgeheimnis, zu dessen Geheimhaltung er nach den Absätzen 1 oder 2 verpflichtet ist, verwertet.

(4) Die Absätze 1 bis 3 sind auch anzuwenden, wenn der Täter das fremde Geheimnis nach dem Tode des Betroffenen unbefugt offenbart oder verwertet.

(5) [1] Die Tat wird nur auf Antrag des Verletzten verfolgt. [2] Stirbt der Verletzte, so geht das Antragsrecht nach § 77 Abs. 2 des Strafgesetzbuches auf die Angehörigen über, wenn das Geheimnis zum persönlichen Lebensbereich des Verletzten gehört; in anderen Fällen geht es auf die Erben über. [3] Offenbart der Täter das Geheimnis nach dem Tode des Betroffenen, so gilt Satz 2 sinngemäß.

anyone who, without authority, exploits a secret belonging to a third party, particularly a trade or business secret which he is obligated to treat confidentially pursuant to subsections (1) or (2).

(4) Subsections (1) through (3) are also applicable if the offender divulges or exploits the secret of another person without authorization after the death of the person concerned.

(5) [1] The offense will only be prosecuted upon petition by the injured party. [2] If the injured party dies, the right to prosecute the offense pursuant to section 77 (2) of the German Criminal Code *(Strafgesetzbuch)* shall vest in his relatives if the secret concerned the personal life of the injured party; in all other cases it shall vest in his heirs. [3] Where the offender reveals the secret after the death of the party concerned, sentence 2 shall apply *mutatis mutandis*.

§ 121
Bußgeldvorschriften

(1) Ordnungswidrig handelt, wer eine der in § 90 Abs. 1, 2 Satz 1, § 92 Abs. 1 Satz 1 auch in Verbindung mit Absatz 3, § 99 Abs. 1, § 106 Abs. 2, § 108 Abs. 5, § 110 oder § 111 bezeichneten Aufklärungs- oder Auskunftspflichten nicht, wahrheitswidrig, unvollständig oder verspätet erfüllt.

(2) Die Ordnungswidrigkeit kann mit einer Geldbuße bis zu 10.000 Euro geahndet werden.

Section 121
Administrative Fine Provisions

(1) Failure to provide clarification or information as required in section 90 (1) and (2) sentence 1, section 92 (1) sentence 1, also in connection with (3), section 99 (1), section 106 (2), section 108 (5), section 110 or section 111 or to do so in a truthful, complete or timely manner shall constitute an administrative offense.

(2) An administrative offense may be punished with an administrative fine of up to 10,000 euro.

Siebenter Teil
Änderung von Gesetzen

Part 7
Amendments of Acts

§ 122
(Änderung des Bürgerlichen Gesetzbuchs)

(gegenstandslos)

Section 122
(Amendment of the Civil Code)

(obsolete)

§ 123
(Änderung des Kündigungsschutzgesetzes)

(gegenstandslos)

§ 124
(Änderung des Arbeitsgerichtsgesetzes)

(gegenstandslos)

Achter Teil
Übergangs- und Schlussvorschriften

§ 125
Erstmalige Wahlen nach diesem Gesetz

(1) Die erstmaligen Betriebsratswahlen nach § 13 Abs. 1 finden im Jahre 1972 statt.

(2) ¹Die erstmaligen Wahlen der Jugend- und Auszubildendenvertretung nach § 64 Abs. 1 Satz 1 finden im Jahre 1988 statt. ²Die Amtszeit der Jugendvertretung endet mit der Bekanntgabe des Wahlergebnisses der neu gewählten Jugend- und Auszubildendenvertretung, spätestens am 30. November 1988.

(3) Auf Wahlen des Betriebsrats, der Bordvertretung, des Seebetriebsrats und der Jugend- und Auszubildendenvertretung, die nach dem 28. Juli 2001 eingeleitet werden, finden die Erste Verordnung zur Durchführung des Betriebsverfassungsgesetzes vom 16. Januar 1972 (BGBl. I S. 49), zuletzt geändert durch die Verordnung vom 16. Januar 1995 (BGBl. I S. 43), die Zweite Verordnung zur Durchführung des Betriebsverfassungsgesetzes vom 24. Oktober 1972 (BGBl. I S. 2029), zuletzt geändert durch die Verordnung vom 28. September 1989 (BGBl. I S. 1795) und die Verordnung zur Durchführung der Betriebsratswahlen bei den Postunternehmen vom 26. Juni 1995 (BGBl. I

Section 123
(Amendment of the Protection Against Unfair Dismissal Act)

(obsolete)

Section 124
(Amendment of the Labor Court Act)

(obsolete)

Part 8
Transitional and Final Provisions

Section 125
The Initial Election Pursuant to this Act

(1) The initial works council's election pursuant to section 13 (1) shall be held in the year 1972.

(2) ¹The initial election for the youth and trainee representative body pursuant to section 64 (1) sentence 1 shall be held in the year 1988. ²The term of office for the youth representatives shall end with the announcement of the election results of the newly elected youth and trainee representatives, but no later than 30 November 1988.

(3) Elections of works councils, ship's committees fleet works councils and youth and trainee representative bodies, which are introduced after 28 July 2001, shall be governed by the First Ordinance on the Execution of the Works Constitution Act of 16 January 1972 (Federal Law Gazette I p. 49), most recently amended by the Ordinance of 16 January 1995 (Federal Law Gazette I. p. 43), the Second Ordinance on the Execution of the Works Constitution Act of 24 October 1972 (Federal Law Gazette I. p. 2029), most recently amended by the Ordinance of 28 September 1989 (Federal Law Gazette I. p. 1795) and the Ordinance on the Execution of the works council elections in post en-

S. 871) bis zu deren Änderung entsprechende Anwendung.

(4) Ergänzend findet für das vereinfachte Wahlverfahren nach § 14a die Erste Verordnung zur Durchführung des Betriebsverfassungsgesetzes bis zu deren Änderung mit folgenden Maßgaben entsprechende Anwendung:
1. Die Frist für die Einladung zur Wahlversammlung zur Wahl des Wahlvorstands nach § 14a Abs. 1 des Gesetzes beträgt mindestens sieben Tage. Die Einladung muss Ort, Tag und Zeit der Wahlversammlung sowie den Hinweis enthalten, dass bis zum Ende dieser Wahlversammlung Wahlvorschläge zur Wahl des Betriebsrats gemacht werden können (§ 14a Abs. 2 des Gesetzes).
2. § 3 findet wie folgt Anwendung:
a) Im Fall des § 14a Abs. 1 des Gesetzes erlässt der Wahlvorstand auf der Wahlversammlung das Wahlausschreiben. Die Einspruchsfrist nach § 3 Abs. 2 Nr. 3 verkürzt sich auf drei Tage. Die Angabe nach § 3 Abs. 2 Nr. 4 muss die Zahl der Mindestsitze des Geschlechts in der Minderheit (§ 15 Abs. 2 des Gesetzes) enthalten. Die Wahlvorschläge sind abweichend von § 3 Abs. 2 Nr. 7 bis zum Abschluss der Wahlversammlung zur Wahl des Wahlvorstands bei diesem einzureichen. Ergänzend zu § 3 Abs. 2 Nr. 10 gibt der Wahlvorstand den Ort, Tag und Zeit der nachträglichen Stimmabgabe an (§ 14a Abs. 4 des Gesetzes).

b) Im Fall des § 14a Abs. 3 des Gesetzes erlässt der Wahlvorstand unverzüglich das Wahlausschreiben mit den unter Buchstabe a genannten Maßgaben zu § 3 Abs. 2 Nr. 3, 4 und 10. Abweichend von § 3 Abs. 2 Nr. 7 sind die Wahlvorschläge spätestens eine Woche vor

terprises of 26 June 1995 (Federal Law Gazette I. p. 871) until they are amended.

(4) Additionally, the simplified election procedure pursuant to section 14a shall be governed by the First Ordinance on the Execution of the Works Constitution Act until it is amended, subject to the following provisos:
1. The time period for convening the assembly for the election of the election committee pursuant to section 14a (1) of this Act shall be at least seven days. The invitation shall state the location, date and time of the assembly and mention that nominations for the election of the works council can be made up to the end of this assembly (section 14a (2) of this Act).
2. Section 3 shall apply as follows:
a) In the case of section 14a (1) of this Act the election committee shall issue the declaration of the election at the election assembly. The time period for raising objections pursuant to section 3 (2) no. 3 shall be reduced to three days. The statement pursuant to section 3 (2) no. 4 shall state the minimum number of seats held by the minority gender (section 15 (2) of this Act). The nominations for election shall, notwithstanding section 3 (2) no. 7, be submitted to the election committee by the end of the assembly for the election of the election committee. Supplementing section 3 (2) no. 10, the election committee shall state the location, date and time of the subsequent casting of votes (section 14a (4) of this Act).

b) In the case of section 14a (3) of this Act, the election committee shall issue the declaration of the election without delay, subject to the provisos regarding section 3 (2) nos. 3, 4 and 10 set forth in a) above. Notwithstanding section 3 (2) no. 7, the nominations

der Wahlversammlung zur Wahl des Betriebsrats (§ 14 a Abs. 3 Satz 2 des Gesetzes) beim Wahlvorstand einzureichen.

3. Die Einspruchsfrist des § 4 Abs. 1 verkürzt sich auf drei Tage.
4. Die §§ 6 bis 8 und § 10 Abs. 2 finden entsprechende Anwendung mit der Maßgabe, dass die Wahl aufgrund von Wahlvorschlägen erfolgt. Im Fall des § 14 a Abs. 1 des Gesetzes sind die Wahlvorschläge bis zum Abschluss der Wahlversammlung zur Wahl des Wahlvorstands bei diesem einzureichen; im Fall des § 14 a Abs. 3 des Gesetzes sind die Wahlvorschläge spätestens eine Woche vor der Wahlversammlung zur Wahl des Betriebsrats (§ 14 a Abs. 3 Satz 2 des Gesetzes) beim Wahlvorstand einzureichen.
5. § 9 findet keine Anwendung.
6. Auf das Wahlverfahren finden die §§ 21 ff. entsprechende Anwendung. Auf den Stimmzetteln sind die Bewerber in alphabetischer Reihenfolge unter Angabe von Familienname, Vorname und Art der Beschäftigung im Betrieb aufzuführen.
7. § 25 Abs. 5 bis 8 findet keine Anwendung.
8. § 26 Abs. 1 findet mit der Maßgabe Anwendung, dass der Wahlberechtigte sein Verlangen auf schriftliche Stimmabgabe spätestens drei Tage vor dem Tag der Wahlversammlung zur Wahl des Betriebsrats dem Wahlvorstand mitgeteilt haben muss.
9. § 31 findet entsprechende Anwendung mit der Maßgabe, dass die Wahl der Jugend- und Auszubildendenvertretung aufgrund von Wahlvorschlägen erfolgt.

§ 126
Ermächtigung zum Erlass von Wahlordnungen

Das Bundesministerium für Arbeit und Soziales wird ermächtigt, mit Zustim-

shall be submitted to the election committee at least one week before the assembly to elect the works council (section 14 a (3) sentence 2 of this Act).

3. The time period for raising objections pursuant to section 4 (1) shall be reduced to three days.
4. Sections 6 to 8 and 10 (2) shall apply *mutatis mutandis* subject to the proviso that the election shall be conducted on the basis of nominations. In the case of section 14 a (1) of this Act, the nominations shall be submitted to the election committee by the end of the assembly for the election of such election committee; in the case of section 14 a (3) of this Act, the nominations shall be submitted to the election committee at least one week before the assembly to elect the works council (section 14 a (3) sentence 2 of this Act).
5. Section 9 shall not apply.
6. Sections 21 ff. shall apply to the election procedure *mutatis mutandis*. The ballots shall list the candidates in alphabetical order, stating their last name, first name and position in the establishment.
7. Section 25 (5) to (8) shall not apply.
8. Section 26 (1) shall apply subject to the proviso that the person entitled to vote shall must have submitted his request for a written ballot to the election committee at least three days before the day of the assembly to elect the works council.
9. Section 31 shall apply *mutatis mutandis* subject to the proviso that the election of the youth and trainee representative body shall be held on the basis of nominations.

Section 126
Authorization to Issue Election Regulations

The Federal Ministry of Labor and Social Affairs shall be authorized, with the

mung des Bundesrates Rechtsverordnungen zu erlassen zur Regelung der in den §§ 7 bis 20, 60 bis 63, 115 und 116 bezeichneten Wahlen über

1. die Vorbereitung der Wahl, insbesondere die Aufstellung der Wählerlisten und die Errechnung der Vertreterzahl;
2. die Frist für die Einsichtnahme in die Wählerlisten und die Erhebung von Einsprüchen gegen sie;
3. die Vorschlagslisten und die Frist für ihre Einreichung;
4. das Wahlausschreiben und die Fristen für seine Bekanntmachung;
5. die Stimmabgabe;
5a. die Verteilung der Sitze im Betriebsrat, in der Bordvertretung, im Seebetriebsrat sowie in der Jugend- und Auszubildendenvertretung auf die Geschlechter, auch soweit die Sitze nicht gemäß § 15 Abs. 2 und § 62 Abs. 3 besetzt werden können;
6. die Feststellung des Wahlergebnisses und die Fristen für seine Bekanntmachung;
7. die Aufbewahrung der Wahlakten.

approval of the Upper House of Parliament *(Bundesrat)*, to issue legal regulations for the elections referred to in sections 7 to 20, 60 to 63, 115 and 116 with regard to

1. the preparations for the elections, in particular the preparation of the voter lists and the calculation of the number of representatives;
2. the period for inspecting the voter lists and the filing of objections to them;
3. the lists of candidates and the period within which they must be submitted;
4. the declaration of the election and the time period for its announcement;
5. the casting of votes;
5a. the distribution by gender of the seats in the works council, the ship's committee, the fleet works council, as well as in the youth and trainee representative body, even where the seats cannot be apportioned pursuant to section 15 (2) and section 62 (3);
6. the determination of the election results and the time period for their announcement;
7. the preservation of election documents.

§ 127
Verweisungen

Soweit in anderen Vorschriften auf Vorschriften verwiesen wird oder Bezeichnungen verwendet werden, die durch dieses Gesetz aufgehoben oder geändert werden, treten an ihre Stelle die entsprechenden Vorschriften oder Bezeichnungen dieses Gesetzes.

Section 127
References

To the extent other provisions refer to provisions or descriptions which have been repealed or amended under this Act, such provisions shall be superseded by the corresponding provisions and designations in this Act.

§ 128
Bestehende abweichende Tarifverträge

Die im Zeitpunkt des Inkrafttretens dieses Gesetzes nach § 20 Abs. 3 des Betriebsverfassungsgesetzes vom

Section 128
Collective Bargaining Agreements Departing from this Act

Collective bargaining agreements that were concluded pursuant to section 20 (3) of the Works Constitution

11. Oktober 1952 geltenden Tarifverträge über die Errichtung einer anderen Vertretung der Arbeitnehmer für Betriebe, in denen wegen ihrer Eigenart der Errichtung von Betriebsräten besondere Schwierigkeiten entgegenstehen, werden durch dieses Gesetz nicht berührt.

Act of 11 October 1952 and are valid at this time this Act goes into effect and regulate the formation of other representational bodies for the employees of establishments in which, due to their special nature, the formation of works councils is particularly difficult, shall not be affected by this Act.

§ 129
Außerkrafttreten von Vorschriften

(aufgehoben)

Section 129
Repeal of Provisions

(repealed)

§ 130
Öffentlicher Dienst

Dieses Gesetz findet keine Anwendung auf Verwaltungen und Betriebe des Bundes, der Länder, der Gemeinden und sonstiger Körperschaften, Anstalten und Stiftungen des öffentlichen Rechts.

Section 130
Public Service

This Act shall apply to the organizations and establishments of the Federal Government, the States, the municipalities and other public corporations, institutions and foundations governed by public law.

§ 131
Berlin-Klausel

(gegenstandslos)

Section 131
Berlin Clause

(obsolete)

§ 132

(Inkrafttreten)

Section 132

(Coming Into Force)

XI. Collective Bargaining Agreements Act (Tarifvertragsgesetz – TVG)

of 25 August 1969 (Federal Law Gazette I p. 1323)

in the amended version of 31 October 2006

§ 1
Inhalt und Form des Tarifvertrags

(1) Der Tarifvertrag regelt die Rechte und Pflichten der Tarifvertragsparteien und enthält Rechtsnormen, die den Inhalt, den Abschluss und die Beendigung von Arbeitsverhältnissen sowie betriebliche und betriebsverfassungsrechtliche Fragen ordnen können.

(2) Tarifverträge bedürfen der Schriftform.

§ 2
Tarifvertragsparteien

(1) Tarifvertragsparteien sind Gewerkschaften, einzelne Arbeitgeber sowie Vereinigungen von Arbeitgebern.

(2) Zusammenschlüsse von Gewerkschaften und von Vereinigungen von Arbeitgebern (Spitzenorganisationen) können im Namen der ihnen angeschlossenen Verbände Tarifverträge abschließen, wenn sie eine entsprechende Vollmacht haben.

(3) Spitzenorganisationen können selbst Parteien eines Tarifvertrags sein, wenn der Abschluss von Tarifverträgen zu ihren satzungsgemäßen Aufgaben gehört.

(4) In den Fällen der Absätze 2 und 3 haften sowohl die Spitzenorganisationen wie die ihnen angeschlossenen Verbände für die Erfüllung der gegenseitigen Verpflichtungen der Tarifvertragsparteien.

Section 1
Content and Form of Collective Bargaining Agreements

(1) Collective bargaining agreements shall govern the rights and obligations of the parties thereto and contain legal norms which may regulate the content, commencement and termination of employment relationships and matters relating to the operation of the establishment and legal aspects of the works' constitution.

(2) Collective bargaining agreements shall be made in writing.

Section 2
Parties to a Collective Bargaining Agreement

(1) The parties to a collective bargaining agreement shall be trade unions, individual employers or associations of employers.

(2) Federations of trade unions and of employers' associations (central organizations may conclude collective bargaining agreements on behalf of their affiliates if empowered to do so.

(3) Central organizations may themselves be parties to a collective bargaining agreement if concluding of collective bargaining agreements is one of the tasks specified in their articles of association.

(4) Where subsections (2) and (3) apply, both the central organizations and their affiliates shall be bound to fulfill the mutual obligations of the parties under the collective bargaining agreements.

§ 3
Tarifgebundenheit

(1) Tarifgebunden sind die Mitglieder der Tarifvertragsparteien und der Arbeitgeber, der selbst Partei des Tarifvertrags ist.

(2) Rechtsnormen des Tarifvertrags über betriebliche und betriebsverfassungsrechtliche Fragen gelten für alle Betriebe, deren Arbeitgeber tarifgebunden ist.

(3) Die Tarifgebundenheit bleibt bestehen, bis der Tarifvertrag endet.

§ 4
Wirkung der Rechtsnormen

(1) [1] Die Rechtsnormen des Tarifvertrags, die den Inhalt, den Abschluss oder die Beendigung von Arbeitsverhältnissen ordnen, gelten unmittelbar und zwingend zwischen den beiderseits Tarifgebundenen, die unter den Geltungsbereich des Tarifvertrags fallen. § 80 para. [2] Diese Vorschrift gilt entsprechend für Rechtsnormen des Tarifvertrags über betriebliche und betriebsverfassungsrechtliche Fragen.

(2) Sind im Tarifvertrag gemeinsame Einrichtungen der Tarifvertragsparteien vorgesehen und geregelt (Lohnausgleichskassen, Urlaubskassen usw.), so gelten diese Regelungen auch unmittelbar und zwingend für die Satzung dieser Einrichtung und das Verhältnis der Einrichtung zu den tarifgebundenen Arbeitgebern und Arbeitnehmern.

(3) Abweichende Abmachungen sind nur zulässig, soweit sie durch den Ta-

Section 3
Binding Nature of Collective Bargaining Agreements

(1) Members of the parties to a collective bargaining agreement and the employer who is himself a party thereto shall be bound by the collective bargaining agreement.

(2) The legal norms set forth in a collective bargaining agreement which regulate matters relating to the operation of the establishment and legal aspects of the works' constitution shall apply to all establishments where the employers are bound by the collective bargaining agreement.

(3) A collective bargaining agreement shall continue to be binding until it expires or is terminated.

Section 4
Effect of the Legal Norms

(1) [1] The legal norms contained in a collective bargaining agreement which regulate the content, commencement or termination of employment relationships shall apply directly and with mandatory effect as between both parties bound by the agreement who fall within its scope of application. [2] This provision shall apply, *mutatis mutandis*, to legal norms contained in a collective bargaining agreement which govern matters relating to the operation of the establishment and legal aspects of the works' constitution.

(2) Where a collective bargaining agreement provides for and governs institutions jointly established by the parties thereto (wage equalization and vacation funds, etc.), the provisions shall also apply directly and unreservedly to the bylaws of these institutions and to the relationship between the institutions and the employers and employees bound by the agreement.

(3) Arrangements which depart from the foregoing shall be permissible only

rifvertrag gestattet sind oder eine Änderung der Regelungen zugunsten des Arbeitnehmers enthalten.

(4) ¹Ein Verzicht auf entstandene tarifliche Rechte ist nur in einem von den Tarifvertragsparteien gebilligten Vergleich zulässig. ²Die Verwirkung von tariflichen Rechten ist ausgeschlossen. ³Ausschlussfristen für die Geltendmachung tariflicher Rechte können nur im Tarifvertrag vereinbart werden.

(5) Nach Ablauf des Tarifvertrags gelten seine Rechtsnormen weiter, bis sie durch eine andere Abmachung ersetzt werden.

if they are authorized by the collective bargaining agreement or the departure is to the employees' advantage.

(4) ¹Rights acquired by virtue of a collective bargaining agreement may be waived only in a settlement approved by the parties to the agreement. ²Such rights shall not be forfeited. ³Preclusive periods for the assertion of rights under a collective bargaining agreement shall be permitted only if the collective bargaining agreement provides therefore.

(5) Upon the expiration of a collective bargaining agreement, the legal norms set forth therein shall continue to apply until they are replaced by another arrangement.

§ 5
Allgemeinverbindlichkeit

(1) Das Bundesministerium für Arbeit und Soziales kann einen Tarifvertrag im Einvernehmen mit einem aus je drei Vertretern der Spitzenorganisationen der Arbeitgeber und der Arbeitnehmer bestehenden Ausschuss auf Antrag einer Tarifvertragspartei für allgemeinverbindlich erklären, wenn

1. die tarifgebundenen Arbeitgeber nicht weniger als 50 vom Hundert der unter den Geltungsbereich des Tarifvertrags fallenden Arbeitnehmer beschäftigen und
2. die Allgemeinverbindlicherklärung im öffentlichen Interesse geboten erscheint.

Von den Voraussetzungen der Nummern 1 und 2 kann abgesehen werden, wenn die Allgemeinverbindlicherklärung zur Behebung eines sozialen Notstands erforderlich erscheint.

(2) Vor der Entscheidung über den Antrag ist Arbeitgebern und Arbeitnehmern, die von der Allgemein-

Section 5
Generally Binding Nature of Collective Bargaining Agreements

(1) ¹On request by a party to a collective bargaining agreement, the Federal Ministry of Labor and Social Affairs, acting in consultation with a committee consisting of three representatives of the central organizations of the employers and three representatives of the central organizations of the employees, may declare the agreement to be generally binding if

1. the employers bound by the agreement employ not less than fifty percent of the employees coming within its sphere of application and
2. the declaration that the agreement is generally binding appears necessary for the public interest.

²Departures from the requirements set forth in nos. 1 and 2 shall be permissible if the declaration that a collective bargaining agreement is generally binding appears necessary in order to overcome a social emergency.

(2) Before a decision is made on the request, the employers and employees who would be affected by the declara-

verbindlicherklärung betroffen werden würden, den am Ausgang des Verfahrens interessierten Gewerkschaften und Vereinigungen der Arbeitgeber sowie den obersten Arbeitsbehörden der Länder, auf deren Bereich sich der Tarifvertrag erstreckt, Gelegenheit zur schriftlichen Stellungnahme sowie zur Äußerung in einer mündlichen und öffentlichen Verhandlung zu geben.

(3) Erhebt die oberste Arbeitsbehörde eines beteiligten Landes Einspruch gegen die beantragte Allgemeinverbindlicherklärung, so kann das Bundesministerium für Arbeit und Soziales dem Antrag nur mit Zustimmung der Bundesregierung stattgeben.

(4) Mit der Allgemeinverbindlicherklärung erfassen die Rechtsnormen des Tarifvertrags in seinem Geltungsbereich auch die bisher nicht tarifgebundenen Arbeitgeber und Arbeitnehmer.

(5) [1] Das Bundesministerium für Arbeit und Soziales kann die Allgemeinverbindlicherklärung eines Tarifvertrags im Einvernehmen mit dem in Absatz 1 genannten Ausschuss aufheben, wenn die Aufhebung im öffentlichen Interesse geboten erscheint. [2] Die Absätze 2 und 3 gelten entsprechend. [3] Im übrigen endet die Allgemeinverbindlichkeit eines Tarifvertrags mit dessen Ablauf.

(6) Das Bundesministerium für Arbeit und Soziales kann der obersten Arbeitsbehörde eines Landes für einzelne Fälle das Recht zur Allgemeinverbindlicherklärung sowie zur Aufhebung der Allgemeinverbindlichkeit übertragen.

(7) Die Allgemeinverbindlicherklärung und die Aufhebung der Allgemeinverbindlichkeit bedürfen der öffentlichen Bekanntmachung.

tion, the trade unions and employers' associations interested in the outcome of the procedure and the supreme labor authorities of the Federal States in whose areas the collective bargaining agreement applies shall have an opportunity to express their opinion in writing and state their views in a public discussion.

(3) If the supreme labor authority of an interested Federal State opposes the request that the collective bargaining agreement be declared generally binding, the Federal Ministry of Labor and Social Affairs shall not accede to the request without the approval of the Federal Government.

(4) If a collective bargaining agreement is declared generally binding, the legal norms it contains shall also apply, within its sphere of application, to employers and employees not previously bound by the agreement.

(5) [1] The Federal Ministry of Labor and Social Affairs, acting in consultation with the committee referred to in subsection (1), may revoke its declaration that a collective bargaining agreement is generally binding if this appears to be in the public interest. [2] Subsections (2) and (3) apply *mutatis mutandis*. [3] An agreement shall otherwise cease to be generally binding upon its expiration.

(6) In specific cases the Federal Ministry of Labor and Social Affairs may delegate the right to declare a collective bargaining agreement generally binding and to revoke any such declaration to the supreme labor authority of a Federal State.

(7) Public notice shall be given of the declaration that a collective bargaining agreement is generally binding and of the withdrawal of such a declaration.

§ 6
Tarifregister

Bei dem Bundesministerium für Arbeit und Soziales wird ein Tarifregister geführt, in das der Abschluss, die Änderung und die Aufhebung der Tarifverträge sowie der Beginn und die Beendigung der Allgemeinverbindlichkeit eingetragen werden.

Section 6
Register of Collective bargaining agreements

The Federal Ministry of Labor and Social Affairs shall keep a register of collective bargaining agreements in which the conclusion, amendment and cancellation of collective bargaining agreements and the dates on which declarations that collective bargaining agreements are generally binding come into force and expire shall be recorded.

§ 7
Übersendungs- und Mitteilungspflicht

(1) ¹Die Tarifvertragsparteien sind verpflichtet, dem Bundesministerium für Arbeit und Soziales innerhalb eines Monats nach Abschluss kostenfrei die Urschrift oder eine beglaubigte Abschrift sowie zwei weitere Abschriften eines jeden Tarifvertrags und seiner Änderungen zu übersenden; sie haben ihm das Außerkrafttreten eines jeden Tarifvertrags innerhalb eines Monats mitzuteilen. ²Sie sind ferner verpflichtet, den obersten Arbeitsbehörden der Länder, auf deren Bereich sich der Tarifvertrag erstreckt, innerhalb eines Monats nach Abschluss kostenfrei je drei Abschriften des Tarifvertrags und seiner Änderungen zu übersenden und auch das Außerkrafttreten des Tarifvertrags innerhalb eines Monats mitzuteilen. ³Erfüllt eine Tarifvertragspartei die Verpflichtungen, so werden die übrigen Tarifvertragsparteien davon befreit.

(2) ¹Ordnungswidrig handelt, wer vorsätzlich oder fahrlässig entgegen Absatz 1 einer Übersendungs- oder Mitteilungspflicht nicht, unrichtig, nicht vollständig oder nicht rechtzeitig genügt. ²Die Ordnungswidrigkeit kann mit einer Geldbuße geahndet werden.

Section 7
Obligation to Submit Documents and Information

(1) ¹The parties to collective bargaining agreements shall submit to the Federal Ministry of Labor and Social Affairs free of charge the original or a certified copy and two further copies of any collective bargaining agreements and amendments thereto within one month of the conclusion of the agreement and adoption of amendments; they shall inform him of the expiration or termination of any collective bargaining agreement within one month. ²They shall also submit to the supreme labor authority of each Federal State in which a collective bargaining agreement is valid three copies of the collective bargaining agreement and amendments thereto free of charge within one month of the conclusion of the agreement and adoption of amendments and inform it of the expiration or termination of the collective bargaining agreement within one month. ³If one party to a collective bargaining agreement fulfills these obligations, the other parties shall be released therefrom.

(2) ¹It shall be an offense for any person to intentionally or negligently fail to fulfill his obligation under subsection (1) to submit documents or information or to do so accurately, fully or within the appointed period. ²A fine may be imposed for any such offense.

(3) Verwaltungsbehörde im Sinne des § 36 Abs. 1 Nr. 1 des Gesetzes über Ordnungswidrigkeiten ist die Behörde, der gegenüber die Pflicht nach Absatz 1 zu erfüllen ist.

(3) The administrative authority within the meaning of section 36 (1) no. 1 of the Administrative Offenses Act shall be the authority to which the obligation referred to in subsection (1) shall be fulfilled.

§ 8
Bekanntgabe des Tarifvertrags

Die Arbeitgeber sind verpflichtet, die für ihren Betrieb maßgebenden Tarifverträge an geeigneter Stelle im Betrieb auszulegen.

Section 8
Public Display of Collective Bargaining Agreements

Each employer shall display collective bargaining agreements relevant to his establishment at an appropriate place in the establishment.

§ 9
Feststellung der Rechtswirksamkeit

Rechtskräftige Entscheidungen der Gerichte für Arbeitssachen, die in Rechtsstreitigkeiten zwischen Tarifvertragsparteien aus dem Tarifvertrag oder über das Bestehen oder Nichtbestehen des Tarifvertrags ergangen sind, sind in Rechtsstreitigkeiten zwischen tarifgebundenen Parteien sowie zwischen diesen und Dritten für die Gerichte und Schiedsgerichte bindend.

Section 9
Determination of Validity

Final decisions taken by labor courts in litigation between the parties to a collective bargaining agreement over matters arising from the collective bargaining agreement or over the existence or non-existence of a collective bargaining agreement in litigation between parties bound by the agreement and between these and third parties shall be binding on the courts and arbitration tribunals.

§ 10
Tarifvertrag und Tarifordnungen

(1) Mit dem Inkrafttreten eines Tarifvertrags treten Tarifordnungen und Anordnungen auf Grund der Verordnung über die Lohngestaltung vom 25. Juni 1938 (Reichsgesetzbl. I S. 691) und ihrer Durchführungsverordnung vom 23. April 1941 (Reichsgesetzbl. I S. 222), die für den Geltungsbereich des Tarifvertrags oder Teile desselben erlassen worden sind, außer Kraft, mit Ausnahme solcher Bestimmungen, die durch den Tarifvertrag nicht geregelt worden sind.

(2) Das Bundesministerium für Arbeit und Soziales kann Tarifordnungen

Section 10
Collective Bargaining Agreements and Pay Schedules

(1) When a collective bargaining agreement comes into force, pay schedules and orders issued pursuant to the Ordinance of 25 June 1938 concerning wage structures (Reich Law Gazette I p. 692) and the Implementing Regulation of 23 April 1941 made there under (Reich Law Gazette I p. 222) for the sphere of application of the collective bargaining agreement or parts thereof shall cease to apply, except that provisions not governed by the collective bargaining agreement shall remain in force.

(2) The Federal Ministry of Labor and Social Affairs may cancel pay schedules

und die in Absatz 1 bezeichneten Anordnungen aufheben; die Aufhebung bedarf der öffentlichen Bekanntmachung.

and the orders referred to in subsection (1); public notice shall be given of cancellations.

§ 11
Durchführungsbestimmungen

Section 11
Implementing Regulations

Das Bundesministerium für Arbeit und Soziales kann unter Mitwirkung der Spitzenorganisationen der Arbeitgeber und der Arbeitnehmer die zur Durchführung des Gesetzes erforderlichen Verordnungen erlassen, insbesondere über

The Federal Ministry off Labor, acting in co-operation with the central organizations of the employers and employees, may issue the ordinances required for the implementation of this Act, concerning in particular

1. die Errichtung und die Führung des Tarifregisters und des Tarifarchivs;
2. das Verfahren bei der Allgemeinverbindlicherklärung von Tarifverträgen und der Aufhebung von Tarifordnungen und Anordnungen, die öffentlichen Bekanntmachungen bei der Antragstellung, der Erklärung und Beendigung der Allgemeinverbindlichkeit und der Aufhebung von Tarifordnungen und Anordnungen sowie die hierdurch entstehenden Kosten;
3. den im § 5 genannten Ausschuss.

1. the creation and maintenance of the register and archives of collective bargaining agreements;
2. the procedure to be followed when collective bargaining agreements are declared generally binding or pay schedules and orders are cancelled, the public notice to be given of applications for such declarations, the declarations themselves and their expiration or termination and of the cancellation of pay schedules and orders, and the expenses incurred in connection therewith;
3. the committee referred to in section 5.

§ 12
Spitzenorganisationen

Section 12
Central Organizations

¹Spitzenorganisationen im Sinne dieses Gesetzes sind – unbeschadet der Regelung in § 2 – diejenigen Zusammenschlüsse von Gewerkschaften oder von Arbeitgebervereinigungen, die für die Vertretung der Arbeitnehmer- oder der Arbeitgeberinteressen im Arbeitsleben des Bundesgebiets wesentliche Bedeutung haben. ²Ihnen stehen gleich Gewerkschaften und Arbeitgebervereinigungen, die keinem solchen Zusammenschluss angehören, wenn sie die Voraussetzungen des letzten Halbsatzes in Satz 1 erfüllen.

¹For the purposes of this Act and without prejudice to the provisions of section 2 the term "central organizations" shall mean such federations of trade unions or of employers' associations as are of major importance for the representation of employees' and employers' interests in gainful activities in the Federal Republic. ²Trade unions and employers' associations which do not belong to any such federation shall be deemed equivalent to such organizations if they satisfy the requirements of the second half of the first sentence.

§ 12a
Arbeitnehmerähnliche Personen

Section 12a
Persons Similar to Employees

(1) Die Vorschriften dieses Gesetzes gelten entsprechend

1. für Personen, die wirtschaftlich abhängig und vergleichbar einem Arbeitnehmer sozial schutzbedürftig sind (arbeitnehmerähnliche Personen), wenn sie auf Grund von Dienst- oder Werkverträgen für andere Personen tätig sind, die geschuldeten Leistungen persönlich und im wesentlichen ohne Mitarbeit von Arbeitnehmern erbringen und
    a) überwiegend für eine Person tätig sind oder
    b) ihnen von einer Person im Durchschnitt mehr als die Hälfte des Entgelts zusteht, das ihnen für ihre Erwerbstätigkeit insgesamt zusteht; ist dies nicht voraussehbar, so sind für die Berechnung, soweit im Tarifvertrag nichts anderes vereinbart ist, jeweils die letzten sechs Monate, bei kürzerer Dauer der Tätigkeit dieser Zeitraum, maßgebend,
2. für die in Nummer 1 genannten Personen, für die die arbeitnehmerähnlichen Personen tätig sind, sowie für die zwischen ihnen und den arbeitnehmerähnlichen Personen durch Dienst- oder Werkverträge begründeten Rechtsverhältnisse.

(2) Mehrere Personen, für die arbeitnehmerähnliche Personen tätig sind, gelten als eine Person, wenn diese mehreren Personen nach der Art eines Konzerns (§ 18 des Aktiengesetzes) zusammengefasst sind oder zu einer zwischen ihnen bestehenden Organisationsgemeinschaft oder nicht nur vorübergehenden Arbeitsgemeinschaft gehören.

(3) Die Absätze 1 und 2 finden auf Personen, die künstlerische, schriftstellerische oder journalistische Leistungen erbringen, sowie auf Personen, die an der Erbringung, insbesondere der technischen Gestaltung solcher Leistungen unmittelbar mitwirken, auch dann An-

(1) The provisions of this Act shall apply *mutatis mutandis*

1. to persons who are financially dependent and, like employees, in need of social protection (persons similar to employees) if they work for other persons under contracts of service or contracts for work, perform the work thus contracted personally and largely without the assistance of employees and
    a) work predominantly for one person or
    b) are entitled to receive from one person on average more than half of the remuneration to which they are entitled for their gainful activity; if this cannot be predicted, the calculation shall be based, unless a collective bargaining agreement provides otherwise, on the previous six months or, if the work has been performed for a shorter period, on this period,
2. to the persons referred to in subsection (1) for whom persons similar to employees work and to the legal relationship between them and the persons similar to employees established by contracts of service or contracts for work.

(2) Two or more persons for whom persons similar to employees work shall be deemed to be one person if they are combined in the nature of a group (section 18 of the Stock Corporations Act) or belong to a joint organization or more than temporary working association consisting of their number.

(3) Subsections (1) and (2) shall apply to persons engaged in artistic, literary or journalistic activities and to persons directly involved in the performance and particularly the technical aspects of such activities even if, notwithstanding subsection (1) no. 1b, first half-sen-

wendung, wenn ihnen abweichend von Absatz 1 Nr. 1 Buchstabe b erster Halbsatz von einer Person im Durchschnitt mindestens ein Drittel des Entgelts zusteht, das ihnen für ihre Erwerbstätigkeit insgesamt zusteht.

(4) Die Vorschrift findet keine Anwendung auf Handelsvertreter im Sinne des § 84 des Handelsgesetzbuchs.

tence, they are entitled to receive from one person on average at least one third of the total remuneration to which they are entitled for their gainful activity.

(4) These provisions shall not apply to commercial representatives within the meaning of section 84 of the Commercial Code.

§ 12 b
Berlin-Klausel

(gegenstandslos)

Section 12 b
Berlin Clause

(repealed)

§ 13
Inkrafttreten

(1) Dieses Gesetz tritt mit seiner Verkündung in Kraft.

(2) Tarifverträge, die vor dem Inkrafttreten dieses Gesetzes abgeschlossen sind, unterliegen diesem Gesetz.

Section 13
Entry into Force

(1) This Act shall come into force on the date of its promulgation.

(2) Collective bargaining agreements concluded before this Act comes into force shall be governed by this Act.

XII. Act on the Co-Determination of the Employees (Mitbestimmungsgesetz – MitbestG)

of 4 May 1976 (Federal Law Gazette I p. 1153)

in the amended version of 30 July 2009

Erster Teil
Geltungsbereich

Part 1
Scope Of Application

§ 1
Erfasste Unternehmen

Section 1
Enterprises Affected

(1) In Unternehmen, die

1. in der Rechtsform einer Aktiengesellschaft, einer Kommanditgesellschaft auf Aktien, einer Gesellschaft mit beschränkter Haftung oder einer Genossenschaft betrieben werden und

2. in der Regel mehr als 2.000 Arbeitnehmer beschäftigen,

haben die Arbeitnehmer ein Mitbestimmungsrecht nach Maßgabe dieses Gesetzes.

(2) Dieses Gesetz ist nicht anzuwenden auf die Mitbestimmung in Organen von Unternehmen, in denen die Arbeitnehmer nach

1. dem Gesetz über die Mitbestimmung der Arbeitnehmer in den Aufsichtsräten und Vorständen der Unternehmen des Bergbaus und der Eisen und Stahl erzeugenden Industrie vom 21. Mai 1951 (Bundesgesetzbl. I S. 347) – Montan-Mitbestimmungsgesetz –, oder

2. dem Gesetz zur Ergänzung des Gesetzes über die Mitbestimmung der Arbeitnehmer in den Aufsichtsräten und Vorständen der Unternehmen des Bergbaus und der Eisen und Stahl erzeugenden Industrie vom 7. August

(1) In enterprises which:

1. are operated in the legal form of a stock corporation *(Aktiengesellschaft)*, a commercial partnership limited by shares *(Kommanditgesellschaft auf Aktien)*, a limited liability company *(Gesellschaft mit beschränkter Haftung)*, or a cooperative society *(Genossenschaft)* and

2. as a rule employ over 2,000 persons,

the employees shall have a right of co-determination as provided in this Act.

(2) This Act shall not be applicable with regard to co-determination in governing bodies of enterprises in which the employees have the right to co-determination pursuant to

1. the Act Concerning Co-Determination of Employees in the Supervisory Boards and Management Boards of Enterprises of the Mining and the Iron and Steel Manufacturing Industries of 21 May 1951 (Federal Law Gazette I p. 347) – the Iron, Coal and Steel Co-determination Act *(Montan-Mitbestimmungsgesetz)* –, or

2. the Act to Amend the Act Concerning the Co-Determination of Employees in the Supervisory Boards and Management Boards of Enterprises of the Mining and the Iron and Steel Manufacturing Industries of 7 August 1956

1956 (Bundesgesetzbl. I S. 707) – Mitbestimmungsergänzungsgesetz – ein Mitbestimmungsrecht haben.

(3) Die Vertretung der Arbeitnehmer in den Aufsichtsräten von Unternehmen, in denen die Arbeitnehmer nicht nach Absatz 1 oder nach den in Absatz 2 bezeichneten Gesetzen ein Mitbestimmungsrecht haben, bestimmt sich nach den Vorschriften des Drittelbeteiligungsgesetzes (BGBl. 2004 I S. 974).

(4) Dieses Gesetz ist nicht anzuwenden auf Unternehmen, die unmittelbar und überwiegend

1. politischen, koalitionspolitischen, konfessionellen, karitativen, erzieherischen, wissenschaftlichen oder künstlerischen Bestimmungen oder
2. Zwecken der Berichterstattung oder Meinungsäußerung, auf die Artikel 5 Abs. 1 Satz 2 des Grundgesetzes anzuwenden ist,

dienen. Dieses Gesetz ist nicht anzuwenden auf Religionsgemeinschaften und ihre karitativen und erzieherischen Einrichtungen unbeschadet deren Rechtsform.

(Federal Law Gazette I p. 707) – the Co-determination Amendment Act *(Mitbestimmungsergänzungsgesetz)*.

(3) The representation of employees in the supervisory boards of enterprises in which the employees do not have a right of co-determination pursuant to subsection (1) or the statutes referred in subsection (2), shall be governed by the provisions of the One-Third Participation Act (Federal Law Gazette 2004 I p. 974).

(4) [1] This Act shall not be applicable to enterprises engaged directly and primarily in:

1. political, coalition political, religious, charitable, educational, scientific or artistic activities; or
2. news reporting or expressions of opinion where Article 5 (1) sentence 2 of the Basic Law *(Grundgesetz)* would be applicable.

[2] This Act shall not be applicable to religious communities or their charitable and educational institutions regardless of their legal form.

§ 2
Anteilseigner

Anteilseigner im Sinne dieses Gesetzes sind je nach der Rechtsform der in § 1 Abs. 1 Nr. 1 bezeichneten Unternehmen Aktionäre, Gesellschafter oder Mitglieder einer Genossenschaft.

Section 2
Shareholders

Shareholders within the meaning of this Act are, depending on the legal form of the enterprises designated in section 1 (1) no. 1, stockholders, partners, or members of a cooperative society.

§ 3
Arbeitnehmer und Betrieb

(1) [1] Arbeitnehmer im Sinne dieses Gesetzes sind

1. die in § 5 Abs. 1 des Betriebsverfassungsgesetzes bezeichneten Personen mit Ausnahme der in § 5

Section 3
Employees and Works

(1) [1] Employees within the meaning of this Act are;

1. those persons named in section 5 (1) of the Works Constitution Act with the exception of those executive em-

Abs. 3 des Betriebsverfassungsgesetzes bezeichneten leitenden Angestellten,

2. die in § 5 Abs. 3 des Betriebsverfassungsgesetzes bezeichneten leitenden Angestellten.

²Keine Arbeitnehmer im Sinne dieses Gesetzes sind die in § 5 Abs. 2 des Betriebsverfassungsgesetzes bezeichneten Personen.

(2) ¹Betriebe im Sinne dieses Gesetzes sind solche des Betriebsverfassungsgesetzes. ²§ 4 Abs. 2 des Betriebsverfassungsgesetzes ist anzuwenden.

ployees listed in section 5 (3) of the Works Constitution Act,

2. those executive employees named in section 5 (3) of the Works Constitution Act.

²Those persons named in section 5 (2) of the Works Constitution Act are not employees within the meaning of this Act.

(2) ¹Works within the meaning of this Act are the same as those of the Works Constitution Act. ²Section 4 (2) of the Works Constitution Act has effect.

§ 4
Kommanditgesellschaft

(1) ¹Ist ein in § 1 Abs. 1 Nr. 1 bezeichnetes Unternehmen persönlich haftender Gesellschafter einer Kommanditgesellschaft und hat die Mehrheit der Kommanditisten dieser Kommanditgesellschaft, berechnet nach der Mehrheit der Anteile oder der Stimmen, die Mehrheit der Anteile oder der Stimmen in dem Unternehmen des persönlich haftenden Gesellschafters inne, so gelten für die Anwendung dieses Gesetzes auf den persönlich haftenden Gesellschafter die Arbeitnehmer der Kommanditgesellschaft als Arbeitnehmer des persönlich haftenden Gesellschafters, sofern nicht der persönlich haftende Gesellschafter einen eigenen Geschäftsbetrieb mit in der Regel mehr als 500 Arbeitnehmern hat. ²Ist die Kommanditgesellschaft persönlich haftender Gesellschafter einer anderen Kommanditgesellschaft, so gelten auch deren Arbeitnehmer als Arbeitnehmer des in § 1 Abs. 1 Nr. 1 bezeichneten Unternehmens. ³Dies gilt entsprechend, wenn sich die Verbindung von Kommanditgesellschaften in dieser Weise fortsetzt.

(2) Das Unternehmen kann von der Führung der Geschäfte der Kommanditgesellschaft nicht ausgeschlossen werden.

Section 4
Limited Partnership

(1) ¹If an enterprise designated in section 1 (1) no. 1 is a general partner of a limited partnership and the majority of the limited partners of this limited partnership, computed on the basis of the majority of shares or votes, has the majority of the shares or the votes in the enterprise of the general partner, then, with regard to the applicability of this Act to the general partner, the employees of the limited partnership shall be deemed to be employees of the general partner as long as the general partner does not have a separate business which, as a rule, has more than 500 employees. ²Where the limited partner is a general partner of another limited partnership, those employees shall be deemed to be employees of the enterprise referred to in section 1 (1) no. 1. ³This applies accordingly if the relationship of the limited partnerships continues in this manner.

(2) The enterprise cannot be excluded from the business management of the limited partnership.

§ 5
Konzern

(1) ¹Ist ein in § 1 Abs. 1 Nr. 1 bezeichnetes Unternehmen herrschendes Unternehmen eines Konzerns (§ 18 Abs. 1 des Aktiengesetzes), so gelten für die Anwendung dieses Gesetzes auf das herrschende Unternehmen die Arbeitnehmer der Konzernunternehmen als Arbeitnehmer des herrschenden Unternehmens. ²Dies gilt auch für die Arbeitnehmer eines in § 1 Abs. 1 Nr. 1 bezeichneten Unternehmens, das persönlich haftender Gesellschafter eines abhängigen Unternehmens (§ 18 Abs. 1 des Aktiengesetzes) in der Rechtsform einer Kommanditgesellschaft ist.

(2) ¹Ist eine Kommanditgesellschaft, bei der für die Anwendung dieses Gesetzes auf den persönlich haftenden Gesellschafter die Arbeitnehmer der Kommanditgesellschaft nach § 4 Abs. 1 als Arbeitnehmer des persönlich haftenden Gesellschafters gelten, herrschendes Unternehmen eines Konzerns (§ 18 Abs. 1 des Aktiengesetzes), so gelten für die Anwendung dieses Gesetzes auf den persönlich haftenden Gesellschafter der Kommanditgesellschaft die Arbeitnehmer der Konzernunternehmen als Arbeitnehmer des persönlich haftenden Gesellschafters. ²Absatz 1 Satz 2 sowie § 4 Abs. 2 sind entsprechend anzuwenden.

(3) Stehen in einem Konzern die Konzernunternehmen unter der einheitlichen Leitung eines anderen als eines in Absatz 1 oder 2 bezeichneten Unternehmens, beherrscht aber die Konzernleitung über ein in Absatz 1 oder 2 bezeichnetes Unternehmen oder über mehrere solcher Unternehmen andere Konzernunternehmen, so gelten die in Absatz 1 oder 2 bezeichneten und der Konzernleitung am nächsten stehenden Unternehmen, über die die Konzernleitung andere Konzernunternehmen beherrscht, für die Anwendung dieses Gesetzes als herrschende Unternehmen.

Section 5
Corporate Groups

(1) ¹Where the enterprise referred to in section 1 (1) no. 1 is the controlling enterprise within a corporate group (section 18 (1) of the Stock Corporation Act), then for the purposes of applying this Act to the controlling enterprise, the employees of the enterprises in such groups shall be considered to be employees of the controlling enterprise. ²This applies also for the employees of an enterprise referred to in section 1 (1) no. 1 if it is a general partner of a dependent enterprise (section 18 (1) of the Stock Corporation Act) having the legal form of a limited partnership.

(2) ¹If a limited partnership, in which the employees are deemed to be employees of the general partner pursuant to section 4 (1) for the purposes of the application of this Act to the general partner, is the controlling enterprise of a group (section 18 (1) of the Stock Corporation Act), then, for the purposes of the application of this Act to the general partner of the limited partnership, the employees of the enterprise of the group shall be deemed to be employees of the general partner. ²Subsection (1) sentence 2 as well as section 4 (2) apply *mutatis mutandis*.

(3) Where the companies within a group are under the unified management of an enterprise other than those referred to in subsection (1) or (2), but the group management controls group companies other than those referred to in subsection (1) or (2), then the enterprises referred to in subsection (1) or (2) which are most closely connected to the group management, and through which the group management controls other enterprises within the group, shall be deemed to be the controlling enterprises for the purposes of this Act.

Zweiter Teil
Aufsichtsrat

Erster Abschnitt
Bildung und Zusammensetzung

§ 6
Grundsatz

(1) Bei den in § 1 Abs. 1 bezeichneten Unternehmen ist ein Aufsichtsrat zu bilden, soweit sich dies nicht schon aus anderen gesetzlichen Vorschriften ergibt.

(2) [1] Die Bildung und die Zusammensetzung des Aufsichtsrats sowie die Bestellung und die Abberufung seiner Mitglieder bestimmen sich nach den §§ 7 bis 24 dieses Gesetzes und, soweit sich dies nicht schon aus anderen gesetzlichen Vorschriften ergibt, nach § 96 Abs. 2, den §§ 97 bis 101 Abs. 1 und 3 und den §§ 102 bis 106 des Aktiengesetzes mit der Maßgabe, dass die Wählbarkeit eines Prokuristen als Aufsichtsratsmitglied der Arbeitnehmer nur ausgeschlossen ist, wenn dieser dem zur gesetzlichen Vertretung des Unternehmens befugten Organ unmittelbar unterstellt und zur Ausübung der Prokura für den gesamten Geschäftsbereich des Organs ermächtigt ist. [2] Andere gesetzliche Vorschriften und Bestimmungen der Satzung (des Gesellschaftsvertrags, des Status) über die Zusammensetzung des Aufsichtsrats sowie über die Bestellung und die Abberufung seiner Mitglieder bleiben unberührt, soweit Vorschriften dieses Gesetzes dem nicht entgegenstehen.

(3) [1] Auf Genossenschaften sind die §§ 100, 101 Abs. 1 und 3 und die §§ 103 und 106 des Aktiengesetzes nicht anzuwenden. [2] Auf die Aufsichtsratsmitglieder der Arbeitnehmer ist § 9 Abs. 2 des Genossenschaftsgesetzes nicht anzuwenden.

Part 2
Supervisory Board

Chapter 1
Formation and Composition

Section 6
Principles

(1) A supervisory board shall be formed in those enterprises referred to in section 1 (1) unless otherwise provided in other statutory provisions.

(2) [1] The formation and composition of the supervisory board, as well as the appointment and dismissal of its members, shall be determined pursuant to sections 7 through 24 of this Act, and, where not otherwise already provided in other statutory provisions, pursuant to section 96 (2), sections 97 through 101 (1) and (3) and sections 102 through 106 of the Stock Corporation Act; with the proviso that a procuration officer's eligibility to be elected supervisory board member as an employee representative shall only be excluded if he is directly subordinate to the body legally representing the company and he is empowered to exercise his authorization for this body's entire scope of business. [2] Other statutory provisions and provisions of the articles of association (the partnership agreement, the statutes) with regard to the composition of the supervisory board as well as with regard to the appointment and the dismissal of its members shall remain unaffected, to the extent they do not conflict with other provisions of this Act.

(3) [1] Sections 100, 101 (1) and (3) and sections 103 and 106 of the Stock Corporation Act shall not be applicable to cooperative societies. [2] Section 9 (2) of the Act on Cooperatives (*Genossenschaftsgesetz*) shall not be applicable to the employee supervisory board members.

§ 7
Zusammensetzung des Aufsichtsrats

Section 7
Composition of the Supervisory Board

(1) ¹Der Aufsichtsrat eines Unternehmens

1. mit in der Regel nicht mehr als 10.000 Arbeitnehmern setzt sich zusammen aus je sechs Aufsichtsratsmitgliedern der Anteilseigner und der Arbeitnehmer;
2. mit in der Regel mehr als 10.000, jedoch nicht mehr als 20.000 Arbeitnehmern setzt sich zusammen aus je acht Aufsichtsratsmitgliedern der Anteilseigner und der Arbeitnehmer;
3. mit in der Regel mehr als 20.000 Arbeitnehmern setzt sich zusammen aus je zehn Aufsichtsratsmitgliedern der Anteilseigner und der Arbeitnehmer.

²Bei den in Satz 1 Nr. 1 bezeichneten Unternehmen kann die Satzung (der Gesellschaftsvertrag) bestimmen, dass Satz 1 Nr. 2 oder 3 anzuwenden ist. ³Bei den in Satz 1 Nr. 2 bezeichneten Unternehmen kann die Satzung (der Gesellschaftsvertrag) bestimmen, dass Satz 1 Nr. 3 anzuwenden ist.

(2) Unter den Aufsichtsratsmitgliedern der Arbeitnehmer müssen sich befinden

1. in einem Aufsichtsrat, dem sechs Aufsichtsratsmitglieder der Arbeitnehmer angehören, vier Arbeitnehmer des Unternehmens und zwei Vertreter von Gewerkschaften;
2. in einem Aufsichtsrat, dem acht Aufsichtsratsmitglieder der Arbeitnehmer angehören, sechs Arbeitnehmer des Unternehmens und zwei Vertreter von Gewerkschaften;
3. in einem Aufsichtsrat, dem zehn Aufsichtsratsmitglieder der Arbeitnehmer angehören, sieben Arbeitnehmer des Unternehmens und drei Vertreter von Gewerkschaften.

(1) ¹The supervisory board of an enterprise which has

1. as a rule not more than 10,000 employees, shall consist of six supervisory board members each for shareholders and employees;
2. as a rule more than 10,000 employees but not fewer than 20,000 employees, shall consist of eight supervisory board members each for shareholders and employees;
3. as a rule more than 20,000 employees, shall consist of ten supervisory board members each for shareholders and employees.

²The articles of association (the partnership agreement) can provide with regard to the enterprises referred to in sentence 1 no. 1 that sentence 1 no. 2 or 3 is applicable. ³In the case of the enterprises referred to in sentence 1 no. 2, the articles of association (the partnership agreement) may provide that sentence 1 no. 3 will apply.

(2) The employee supervisory board members be allocated as follows:

1. In a supervisory board with six supervisory board members belonging to the employees, four shall be for employees of the enterprise and two shall be union representatives;
2. In a supervisory board with eight supervisory board members belonging to the employees, six shall be for employees of the enterprise and two shall be union representatives;
3. In a supervisory board with ten supervisory board members belonging to the employees, seven shall be for employees of the enterprise and three shall be union representatives.

(3) ¹Die in Absatz 2 bezeichneten Arbeitnehmer des Unternehmens müssen das 18. Lebensjahr vollendet haben und ein Jahr dem Unternehmen angehören. ²Auf die einjährige Unternehmensangehörigkeit werden Zeiten der Angehörigkeit zu einem anderen Unternehmen, dessen Arbeitnehmer nach diesem Gesetz an der Wahl von Aufsichtsratsmitgliedern des Unternehmens teilnehmen, angerechnet. ³Diese Zeiten müssen unmittelbar vor dem Zeitpunkt liegen, ab dem die Arbeitnehmer zur Wahl von Aufsichtsratsmitgliedern des Unternehmens berechtigt sind. ⁴Die weiteren Wählbarkeitsvoraussetzungen des § 8 Abs. 1 des Betriebsverfassungsgesetzes müssen erfüllt sein.

(4) Die in Absatz 2 bezeichneten Gewerkschaften müssen in dem Unternehmen selbst oder in einem anderen Unternehmen vertreten sein, dessen Arbeitnehmer nach diesem Gesetz an der Wahl von Aufsichtsratsmitgliedern des Unternehmens teilnehmen.

(3) [1]The employees of the enterprise referred to in subsection (2) must be at least 18 years of age and have been with the enterprise for one year. [2]After being with the enterprise for one year, time that the employee spent with another enterprise in which the employer participated in the electing of enterprise supervisory board members in accordance with this Act will be deducted. [3]This period must have been directly before the point in time from which the employee was entitled to vote in elections for enterprise supervisory board members. [4]The further eligibility prerequisites set forth in section 8 (1) of the Works Constitution Act must be fulfilled.

(4) The unions referred to in subsection (2) must be represented in the enterprise itself or in another enterprise whose employees participate in the election of the enterprise's supervisory board members pursuant to this Act.

Zweiter Abschnitt
Bestellung der Aufsichtsratsmitglieder

Chapter 2
Appointment of the Supervisory Board Members

Erster Unterabschnitt
Aufsichtsratsmitglieder der Anteilseigner

Subchapter 1
Supervisory Board Members of the Shareholders

§ 8
Aufsichtsratsmitglieder der Anteilseigner

Section 8
Supervisory board members of Shareholders

(1) Die Aufsichtsratsmitglieder der Anteilseigner werden durch das nach Gesetz, Satzung oder Gesellschaftsvertrag zur Wahl von Mitgliedern des Aufsichtsrats befugte Organ (Wahlorgan) und, soweit gesetzliche Vorschriften dem nicht entgegenstehen, nach Maßgabe der Satzung oder des Gesellschaftsvertrags bestellt.

(2) § 101 Abs. 2 des Aktiengesetzes bleibt unberührt.

(1) The supervisory board members of the shareholders shall be appointed by the body (elective body) authorized under the law, the articles of association or the partnership agreement to elect members to the supervisory board, and pursuant to the articles of association or the partnership agreement, unless contrary to legal provisions.

(2) Section 101 (2) of the Stock Corporation Act remains unaffected.

Zweiter Unterabschnitt
Aufsichtsratsmitglieder der Arbeitnehmer, Grundsatz

§ 9
Aufsichtsratsmitglieder der Arbeitnehmer, Grundsatz

(1) Die Aufsichtsratsmitglieder der Arbeitnehmer (§ 7 Abs. 2) eines Unternehmens mit in der Regel mehr als 8.000 Arbeitnehmern werden durch Delegierte gewählt, sofern nicht die wahlberechtigten Arbeitnehmer die unmittelbare Wahl beschließen.

(2) Die Aufsichtsratsmitglieder der Arbeitnehmer (§ 7 Abs. 2) eines Unternehmens mit in der Regel nicht mehr als 8.000 Arbeitnehmern werden in unmittelbarer Wahl gewählt, sofern nicht die wahlberechtigten Arbeitnehmer die Wahl durch Delegierte beschließen.

(3) [1] Zur Abstimmung darüber, ob die Wahl durch Delegierte oder unmittelbar erfolgen soll, bedarf es eines Antrags, der von einem Zwanzigstel der wahlberechtigten Arbeitnehmer des Unternehmens unterzeichnet sein muss. [2] Die Abstimmung ist geheim. [3] Ein Beschluss nach Absatz 1 oder 2 kann nur unter Beteiligung von mindestens der Hälfte der wahlberechtigten Arbeitnehmer und nur mit der Mehrheit der abgegebenen Stimmen gefasst werden.

Dritter Unterabschnitt
Wahl der Aufsichtsratsmitglieder der Arbeitnehmer durch Delegierte

§ 10
Wahl der Delegierten

(1) In jedem Betrieb des Unternehmens wählen die Arbeitnehmer in geheimer Wahl und nach den Grundsätzen der Verhältniswahl Delegierte.

Subchapter 2
Supervisory Board Members of the Employees, Principles

Section 9
Supervisory Board Members of the Employees, Principles

(1) The employee supervisory board members (section 7 (2)) of an enterprise normally employing more than 8,000 employees shall be elected through delegates as long as the employees eligible to vote do not resolve to hold a direct election.

(2) The employee supervisory board members (section 7 (2)) of an enterprise normally employing no more than 8,000 employees shall be elected in a direct election as long as the employees eligible to vote do not resolve to hold the election through delegates.

(3) [1] The vote on whether elections shall be held through delegates or by direct election requires a petition which must be signed by one twentieth of the employees of the enterprise who are eligible to vote. [2] The vote shall be by secret ballot. [3] A resolution pursuant to subsection (1) or (2) can only be passed with the participation of at least half of the employees eligible to vote and only with a majority of the votes cast.

Subchapter 3
Election of the Employee Supervisory Board Members Through Delegates

Section 10
Election of the Delegates

(1) In every establishment of the enterprise, the employees shall elect delegates by secret ballot and according to the principles of proportional representation.

(2) ¹Wahlberechtigt für die Wahl von Delegierten sind die Arbeitnehmer des Unternehmens, die das 18. Lebensjahr vollendet haben. ²§ 7 Satz 2 des Betriebsverfassungsgesetzes gilt entsprechend.

(3) Zu Delegierten wählbar sind die in Absatz 2 Satz 1 bezeichneten Arbeitnehmer, die die weiteren Wählbarkeitsvoraussetzungen des § 8 des Betriebsverfassungsgesetzes erfüllen.

(4) ¹Wird für einen Wahlgang nur ein Wahlvorschlag gemacht, so gelten die darin aufgeführten Arbeitnehmer in der angegebenen Reihenfolge als gewählt. ²§ 11 Abs. 2 ist anzuwenden.

§ 11
Errechnung der Zahl der Delegierten

(1) ¹In jedem Betrieb entfällt auf je 90 wahlberechtigte Arbeitnehmer ein Delegierter. ²Ergibt die Errechnung nach Satz 1 in einem Betrieb mehr als

1. 25 Delegierte, so vermindert sich die Zahl der zu wählenden Delegierten auf die Hälfte; diese Delegierten erhalten je zwei Stimmen;
2. 50 Delegierte, so vermindert sich die Zahl der zu wählenden Delegierten auf ein Drittel; diese Delegierten erhalten je drei Stimmen;
3. 75 Delegierte, so vermindert sich die Zahl der zu wählenden Delegierten auf ein Viertel; diese Delegierten erhalten je vier Stimmen;
4. 100 Delegierte, so vermindert sich die Zahl der zu wählenden Delegierten auf ein Fünftel; diese Delegierten erhalten je fünf Stimmen;
5. 125 Delegierte, so vermindert sich die Zahl der zu wählenden Delegierten auf ein Sechstel; diese Delegierten erhalten je sechs Stimmen;
6. 150 Delegierte, so vermindert sich die Zahl der zu wählenden Delegier-

(2) ¹Employees of the enterprise who have reached the age of 18 are eligible to vote for the election of the delegates. ²Section 7 sentence 2 of the Works Constitution Act applies *mutatis mutandis*.

(3) Those employees referred to in subsection (2) sentence 1 who fulfill the further prerequisites for candidacy referred to in section 8 of the Works Constitution Act may be elected as delegates.

(4) ¹Where only one nomination is made for a ballot, then the employees listed shall be deemed to be elected in the order indicated. ²Section 11 (2) shall apply.

Section 11
Calculation of Number of Delegates

(1) ¹There shall be one delegate for every 90 employees eligible to vote in each establishment. ²Where pursuant to the computation of sentence 1 there are for an establishment more than:

1. 25 delegates, then the number of elected delegates will be reduced by one half; each delegate shall have two votes;
2. 50 delegates, then the number of elected delegates will be reduced to one third; each delegate shall have three votes;
3. 75 delegates, then the number of elected delegates will be reduced to one quarter; each delegate shall have four votes;
4. 100 delegates, then the number of elected delegates will be reduced to one fifth; each delegate shall have five votes;
5. 125 delegates, then the number of elected delegates will be reduced to one sixth; each delegate shall have six votes;
6. 150 delegates, then the number of elected delegates will be reduced to

ten auf ein Siebtel; diese Delegierten erhalten je sieben Stimmen.

³Bei der Errechnung der Zahl der Delegierten werden Teilzahlen voll gezählt, wenn sie mindestens die Hälfte der vollen Zahl betragen.

(2) ¹Unter den Delegierten müssen in jedem Betrieb die in § 3 Abs. 1 Nr. 1 bezeichneten Arbeitnehmer und die leitenden Angestellten entsprechend ihrem zahlenmäßigen Verhältnis vertreten sein. ²Sind in einem Betrieb mindestens neun Delegierte zu wählen, so entfällt auf die in § 3 Abs. 1 Nr. 1 bezeichneten Arbeitnehmer und die leitenden Angestellten mindestens je ein Delegierter; dies gilt nicht, soweit in dem Betrieb nicht mehr als fünf in § 3 Abs. 1 Nr. 1 bezeichnete Arbeitnehmer oder leitende Angestellte wahlberechtigt sind. ³Soweit auf die in § 3 Abs. 1 Nr. 1 bezeichneten Arbeitnehmer und die leitenden Angestellten lediglich nach Satz 2 Delegierte entfallen, vermehrt sich die nach Absatz 1 errechnete Zahl der Delegierten des Betriebs entsprechend.

(3) ¹Soweit nach Absatz 2 auf die in § 3 Abs. 1 Nr. 1 bezeichneten Arbeitnehmer und die leitenden Angestellten eines Betriebs nicht mindestens je ein Delegierter entfällt, gelten diese für die Wahl der Delegierten als Arbeitnehmer des Betriebs der Hauptniederlassung des Unternehmens. ²Soweit nach Absatz 2 und nach Satz 1 auf die in § 3 Abs. 1 Nr. 1 bezeichneten Arbeitnehmer und die leitenden Angestellten des Betriebs der Hauptniederlassung nicht mindestens je ein Delegierter entfällt, gelten diese für die Wahl der Delegierten als Arbeitnehmer des nach der Zahl der wahlberechtigten Arbeitnehmer größten Betriebs des Unternehmens.

(4) Entfällt auf einen Betrieb oder auf ein Unternehmen, dessen Arbeitnehmer

one seventh; each delegate shall have seven votes.

³In computing the number of delegates, fractional amounts shall be counted in full if they amount to at least one half of the full number.

(2) ¹Among the salaried employee delegates, the salaried employees referred to in section 3 (1) no. 1 and the managerial employees must be represented in proportion to their numbers. ²Where at least nine delegates are to be delegated in one establishment, the workers, the salaried employees referred to in section 3 (1) no. 1 and the managerial employees shall each have at lest one delegate; this does not apply where no more than five workers, salaried employees referred to in section 3 (1) no. 1 or managerial employees are eligible to vote. ³To the extent that the workers, the salaried employees referred to in section 3 (1) no. 1 and the managerial employees are only allocated delegates pursuant to sentence 3, the computed number of delegates of the establishment pursuant to sentence 1 shall increase *mutatis mutandis*.

(3) ¹If pursuant to subsection (2) the workers, the salaried employees referred to in section 3 (3) no. 1 and the managerial employees of an establishment do not each have at least one delegate, they shall, for the purpose of electing the delegates, be deemed to be employees of the establishment of the headquarters of the enterprise. ²If pursuant to subsection (2) and sentence 1 the workers, the salaried employees referred to in section 3 (3) no. 1 and the managerial employees of a establishment of the headquarters do not each have at least one delegate, they shall, for purpose of electing the delegates, be deemed to be employees of that establishment of the enterprise with the greatest number of employees eligible to vote.

(4) If an establishment or enterprise in which the employer participates in elec-

nach diesem Gesetz an der Wahl von Aufsichtsratsmitgliedern des Unternehmens teilnehmen, kein Delegierter, so ist Absatz 3 entsprechend anzuwenden.

(5) Die Eigenschaft eines Delegierten als Delegierter der Arbeitnehmer nach § 3 Abs. 1 Nr. 1 oder § 3 Abs. 1 Nr. 2 bleibt bei einem Wechsel der Eigenschaft als Arbeitnehmer nach § 3 Abs. 1 Nr. 1 oder § 3 Abs. 1 Nr. 2 erhalten.

tions for enterprise supervisory board members in accordance with this Act, has no delegates allocated to it subsection (3) shall be applied accordingly.

(5) The status of a delegate as the delegate of the employees pursuant to section 3 (1) no. 1 or section 3 (1) no. 2 will continue even if his status changes from that of an employer pursuant to section 3 (1) no. 1 to that of one pursuant to section 3 (1) no. 2.

§ 12
Wahlvorschläge für Delegierte

(1) [1] Zur Wahl der Delegierten können die wahlberechtigten Arbeitnehmer des Betriebs Wahlvorschläge machen. [2] Jeder Wahlvorschlag muss von einem Zwanzigstel oder 50 der jeweils wahlberechtigten in § 3 Abs. 1 Nr. 1 bezeichneten Arbeitnehmer oder der leitenden Angestellten des Betriebs unterzeichnet sein.

(2) Jeder Wahlvorschlag soll mindestens doppelt so viele Bewerber enthalten, wie in dem Wahlgang Delegierte zu wählen sind.

Section 12
Nominations of Delegates

(1) [1] The employees of the establishment eligible to vote may make nominations for election of the delegates. [2] Every nomination must be signed by one twentieth or 50 of the respectively eligible employees named in section 3 (1) no. 1 or the managerial employees of the establishment.

(2) Each nomination should have twice as many candidates as there are delegates to be elected.

§ 13
Amtszeit der Delegierten

(1) [1] Die Delegierten werden für eine Zeit gewählt, die der Amtszeit der von ihnen zu wählenden Aufsichtsratsmitglieder entspricht. [2] Sie nehmen die ihnen nach den Vorschriften dieses Gesetzes zustehenden Aufgaben und Befugnisse bis zur Einleitung der Neuwahl der Aufsichtsratsmitglieder der Arbeitnehmer wahr.

(2) In den Fällen des § 9 Abs. 1 endet die Amtszeit der Delegierten, wenn

1. die wahlberechtigten Arbeitnehmer nach § 9 Abs. 1 die unmittelbare Wahl beschließen;
2. das Unternehmen nicht mehr die Voraussetzungen für die Anwendung des § 9 Abs. 1 erfüllt, es sei

Section 13
Terms of Office of Delegates

(1) [1] The delegates shall be elected for a period corresponding to the term of office for the supervisory board members to be elected by them. [2] They shall assume their rightful duties and powers pursuant to the provisions of this Act until commencement of the new election of the employee supervisory board members.

(2) Where a situation pursuant to section 9 (1) arises, the term of office of the delegate shall end if:

1. the employees eligible to vote pursuant to section 9 (1) resolve to hold a direct election;
2. the enterprise no longer fulfils the prerequisites for the application of section 9 (1), unless the employees

denn, die wahlberechtigten Arbeitnehmer beschließen, dass die Amtszeit bis zu dem in Absatz 1 genannten Zeitpunkt fortdauern soll; § 9 Abs. 3 ist entsprechend anzuwenden.

(3) In den Fällen des § 9 Abs. 2 endet die Amtszeit der Delegierten, wenn die wahlberechtigten Arbeitnehmer die unmittelbare Wahl beschließen; § 9 Abs. 3 ist anzuwenden.

(4) Abweichend von Absatz 1 endet die Amtszeit der Delegierten eines Betriebs, wenn nach Eintreten aller Ersatzdelegierten des Wahlvorschlags, dem die zu ersetzenden Delegierten angehören, die Gesamtzahl der Delegierten des Betriebs unter die im Zeitpunkt ihrer Wahl vorgeschriebene Zahl der auf den Betrieb entfallenden Delegierten gesunken ist.

§ 14
Vorzeitige Beendigung der Amtszeit oder Verhinderung von Delegierten

(1) Die Amtszeit eines Delegierten endet vor dem in § 13 bezeichneten Zeitpunkt
1. durch Niederlegung des Amtes,
2. durch Beendigung der Beschäftigung des Delegierten in dem Betrieb, dessen Delegierter er ist,
3. durch Verlust der Wählbarkeit.

(2) ¹Endet die Amtszeit eines Delegierten vorzeitig oder ist er verhindert, so tritt an seine Stelle ein Ersatzdelegierter. ²Die Ersatzdelegierten werden der Reihe nach aus den nicht gewählten Arbeitnehmern derjenigen Wahlvorschläge entnommen, denen die zu ersetzenden Delegierten angehören.

§ 15
Wahl der unternehmensangehörigen Aufsichtsratsmitglieder der Arbeitnehmer

(1) ¹Die Delegierten wählen die Aufsichtsratsmitglieder, die nach § 7 Abs. 2

eligible to vote resolve that the term of office shall continue up to the time period mentioned in subsection (1); section 9 (3) applies *mutatis mutandis*.

(3) In the cases described in section 9 (2), the term of office of the delegates shall end if the employees eligible to vote resolve to hold a direct election; section 9 (3) shall apply.

(4) Deviating from subsection (1), the term of office of a delegate of a establishment shall end if, after the assumption of office by all the alternate delegates on the nomination list to which the delegates to be replaced belong, the total number of delegates of the establishment has fallen below the number of delegates to which the establishment is entitled at the time of the election.

Section 14
Delegates' Premature Termination of Office or Inability to Serve

(1) The term of office of a delegate shall end prior to the time period mentioned in section 13
1. by resignation;
2. by termination of the delegate's employment in the establishment; he was delegated for
3. by loss of his eligibility for election.

(2) ¹Where the term of office of a delegate ends prematurely or he is prevented from serving, an alternate delegate shall assume the position. ²The alternate delegates shall be taken from the employees not elected in the order in which they appear on the nomination lists to which the replaced delegates belonged.

Section 15
Election of Supervisory Board Members of the Employees Belonging to the Enterprise

(1)¹The delegates elect the supervisory board members, who must be employees

Arbeitnehmer des Unternehmens sein müssen, geheim und nach den Grundsätzen der Verhältniswahl für die Zeit, die im Gesetz oder in der Satzung (im Gesellschaftsvertrag) für die durch das Wahlorgan der Anteilseigner zu wählenden Mitglieder des Aufsichtsrats bestimmt ist. ²Dem Aufsichtsrat muss ein leitender Angestellter angehören.

(2) ¹Die Wahl erfolgt auf Grund von Wahlvorschlägen. ²Jeder Wahlvorschlag für

1. Aufsichtsratsmitglieder der Arbeitnehmer nach § 3 Abs. 1 Nr. 1 muss von einem Fünftel oder 100 der wahlberechtigten Arbeitnehmer des Unternehmens unterzeichnet sein;
2. das Aufsichtsratsmitglied der leitenden Angestellten wird auf Grund von Abstimmungsvorschlägen durch Beschluss der wahlberechtigten leitenden Angestellten aufgestellt. Jeder Abstimmungsvorschlag muss von einem Zwanzigstel oder 50 der wahlberechtigten leitenden Angestellten unterzeichnet sein. Der Beschluss wird in geheimer Abstimmung gefasst. Jeder leitende Angestellte hat so viele Stimmen, wie für den Wahlvorschlag nach Absatz 3 Satz 2 Bewerber zu benennen sind. In den Wahlvorschlag ist die nach Absatz 3 Satz 2 vorgeschriebene Anzahl von Bewerbern in der Reihenfolge der auf sie entfallenden Stimmenzahlen aufzunehmen.

(3) ¹Abweichend von Absatz 1 findet Mehrheitswahl statt, soweit nur ein Wahlvorschlag gemacht wird. ²In diesem Fall muss der Wahlvorschlag doppelt so viele Bewerber enthalten, wie Aufsichtsratsmitglieder auf die Arbeitnehmer nach § 3 Abs. 1 Nr. 1 und auf die leitenden Angestellten entfallen.

§ 16
Wahl der Vertreter von Gewerkschaften in den Aufsichtsrat

(1) Die Delegierten wählen die Aufsichtsratsmitglieder, die nach § 7 Abs. 2

of the enterprise pursuant to section 7 (2), by secret ballot and pursuant to the principles of proportional representation for a term, the length of which is set by law or the articles of association (the partnership agreement) for those members of the supervisory board who are to be elected by the electoral body of the shareholders. ²The supervisory board must include one managerial employee.

(2) ¹The election shall follow the principles of nominations. ²Every nomination for:

1. supervisory board members of those employees defined in section 3 (1) no. 1 must be signed by one fifth or 100 of those employees of the company entitled to vote.
2. supervisory board members of the managerial employees shall proceed on the basis of nomination by resolution of the managerial employees eligible to vote. Each nomination must be signed by one twentieth or 50 managerial employees eligible to vote. The resolution shall be passed with the majority of votes cast in a secret ballot. Each managerial employee shall have as many votes as the number of candidates which are to be nominated pursuant to subsection (3) sentence 2. The nomination shall list the number of candidates prescribed by subsection (3) sentence 2 in the order of the number of votes cast for them.

(3) ¹Notwithstanding subsection (1) election by majority vote shall take place where only one nomination has been made. ²In this case the nomination shall include twice as many candidates as there are supervisory board members for the employees pursuant to section 3 (1) no. 1 and for the managerial employees.

Section 16
Election of the Union Representatives to the Supervisory Board

(1) The delegates shall elect the supervisory board members who are union

Vertreter von Gewerkschaften sind, in geheimer Wahl und nach den Grundsätzen der Verhältniswahl für die in § 15 Abs. 1 bestimmte Zeit.

(2) ¹Die Wahl erfolgt auf Grund von Wahlvorschlägen der Gewerkschaften, die in dem Unternehmen selbst oder in einem anderen Unternehmen vertreten sind, dessen Arbeitnehmer nach diesem Gesetz an der Wahl von Aufsichtsratsmitgliedern des Unternehmens teilnehmen. ²Wird nur ein Wahlvorschlag gemacht, so findet abweichend von Satz 1 Mehrheitswahl statt. ³In diesem Fall muss der Wahlvorschlag mindestens doppelt so viele Bewerber enthalten, wie Vertreter von Gewerkschaften in den Aufsichtsrat zu wählen sind.

§ 17
Ersatzmitglieder

(1) ¹In jedem Wahlvorschlag kann zusammen mit jedem Bewerber für diesen ein Ersatzmitglied des Aufsichtsrats vorgeschlagen werden. ²Für einen Bewerber, der Arbeitnehmer nach § 3 Abs. 1 Nr. 1 ist, kann nur ein Arbeitnehmer nach § 3 Abs. 1 Nr. 1 und für einen leitenden Angestellten nach § 3 Abs. 1 Nr. 2 nur ein leitender Angestellter als Ersatzmitglied vorgeschlagen werden. ³Ein Bewerber kann nicht zugleich als Ersatzmitglied vorgeschlagen werden.

(2) Wird ein Bewerber als Aufsichtsratsmitglied gewählt, so ist auch das zusammen mit ihm vorgeschlagene Ersatzmitglied gewählt.

Vierter Unterabschnitt
Unmittelbare Wahl der Aufsichtsratsmitglieder der Arbeitnehmer

§ 18
Unmittelbare Wahl

¹Sind nach § 9 die Aufsichtsratsmitglieder der Arbeitnehmer in unmittel-

representatives pursuant to section 7 (2) in a common election with a secret ballot and pursuant to the principles of proportional representation for the time period defined in section 15 (1).

(2) ¹The election shall be based on nominations by the unions which are represented within the enterprise itself or in another enterprise whose employees participate in the election of the supervisory board members of the enterprise pursuant to this Act. ²Where only one nomination is made, an election by majority vote shall take place notwithstanding sentence 1. ³In such a case, the nomination shall include at least twice as many candidates as union representatives to be elected to the supervisory board.

Section 17
Alternate members

(1) ¹Each nomination for each candidate may include an alternate member to the supervisory board. ²A worker may only be nominated as an alternate member for another worker who is a candidate, a salaried employee as defined in section 3 (1) no. 1 can only be named as an alternate for a like employee and a managerial employee may only be named as an alternate for another managerial employee. ³A candidate may not be nominated simultaneously as an alternate member.

(2) Where a candidate is elected as a supervisory board member, the alternate member nominated with him shall also be elected.

Subchapter 4
Direct Election of the Supervisory Board of the Employees

Section 18
Direct Election

¹Where the supervisory board of the employees are to be elected in a direct

barer Wahl zu wählen, so sind die Arbeitnehmer des Unternehmens, die das 18. Lebensjahr vollendet haben, wahlberechtigt. ²§ 7 Satz 2 des Betriebsverfassungsgesetzes gilt entsprechend. ³Für die Wahl sind die §§ 15 bis 17 mit der Maßgabe anzuwenden, dass an die Stelle der Delegierten die wahlberechtigten Arbeitnehmer des Unternehmens treten.

election pursuant to section 9, the employees of the enterprise who have reached the age of 18 are eligible to vote. ²Section 7 sentence 2 of the Works Constitution Act shall apply *mutatis mutandis*. ³Sections 15 to 17 shall apply to such an election with the proviso that the employees eligible to vote shall assume the role of the delegates.

Fünfter Unterabschnitt
Weitere Vorschriften über das Wahlverfahren sowie über die Bestellung und Abberufung von Aufsichtsratsmitgliedern

Subchapter 5
Further Provisions with Regard to the Election Procedures as well as the Appointment and Dismissal of Supervisory Board Members

§ 19
Bekanntmachung der Mitglieder des Aufsichtsrats

Section 19
Announcement of Supervisory Board Members

¹Das zur gesetzlichen Vertretung des Unternehmens befugte Organ hat die Namen der Mitglieder und der Ersatzmitglieder des Aufsichtsrats unverzüglich nach ihrer Bestellung in den Betrieben des Unternehmens bekanntzumachen und im elektronischen Bundesanzeiger zu veröffentlichen. ²Nehmen an der Wahl der Aufsichtsratsmitglieder des Unternehmens auch die Arbeitnehmer eines anderen Unternehmens teil, so ist daneben das zur gesetzlichen Vertretung des anderen Unternehmens befugte Organ zur Bekanntmachung in seinen Betrieben verpflichtet.

¹The body authorized to legally represent the enterprise shall publicize the names of the members and the alternate members of the supervisory board immediately upon their appointment in the establishment of the enterprise and in the electronic Federal Gazette *(Bundesanzeiger)*. ²Where the employees of an enterprise other than the enterprise having elections for their enterprise supervisory board member take part in those elections then the governing body authorized to legally represent the other enterprise is obligated to make a notification in its establishment.

§ 20
Wahlschutz und Wahlkosten

Section 20
Protection of the Election and Cost of Election

(1) ¹Niemand darf die Wahlen nach den §§ 10, 15, 16 und 18 behindern. ²Insbesondere darf niemand in der Ausübung des aktiven und passiven Wahlrechts beschränkt werden.

(1) ¹No one may obstruct the elections held in accordance with sections 10, 15, 16 and 18. ²In particular, no one may be limited in exercising their right to vote and the right to be a candidate.

(2) Niemand darf die Wahlen durch Zufügung oder Androhung von Nachteilen oder durch Gewährung oder Versprechen von Vorteilen beeinflussen.

(2) No one may influence the elections by inflicting or threatening to cause disadvantages or by granting or promising advantages.

(3) ¹Die Kosten der Wahlen trägt das Unternehmen. ²Versäumnis von Arbeitszeit, die zur Ausübung des Wahlrechts oder der Betätigung im Wahlvorstand erforderlich ist, berechtigt den Arbeitgeber nicht zur Minderung des Arbeitsentgelts.

§ 21
Anfechtung der Wahl von Delegierten

(1) Die Wahl der Delegierten eines Betriebs kann beim Arbeitsgericht angefochten werden, wenn gegen wesentliche Vorschriften über das Wahlrecht, die Wählbarkeit oder das Wahlverfahren verstoßen worden und eine Berichtigung nicht erfolgt ist, es sei denn, dass durch den Verstoß das Wahlergebnis nicht geändert oder beeinflusst werden konnte.

(2) ¹Zur Anfechtung berechtigt sind

1. mindestens drei wahlberechtigte Arbeitnehmer des Betriebs,
2. der Betriebsrat,
3. der Sprecherausschuss,
4. das zur gesetzlichen Vertretung des Unternehmens befugte Organ.

²Die Anfechtung ist nur binnen einer Frist von zwei Wochen, vom Tage der Bekanntgabe des Wahlergebnisses an gerechnet, zulässig.

§ 22
Anfechtung der Wahl von Aufsichtsratsmitgliedern der Arbeitnehmer

(1) Die Wahl eines Aufsichtsratsmitglieds oder eines Ersatzmitglieds der Arbeitnehmer kann beim Arbeitsgericht angefochten werden, wenn gegen wesentliche Vorschriften über das Wahlrecht, die Wählbarkeit oder das Wahlverfahren verstoßen worden und eine Berichtigung nicht erfolgt ist, es sei denn, dass durch den Verstoß das Wahlergebnis nicht geändert oder beeinflusst werden konnte.

(3) ¹The cost of the election shall be borne by the enterprise. ²Absence from work which is necessary to exercise the right to vote or to serve on the election committee does not entitle the employer to make a reduction in the remuneration.

Section 21
Challenging the Election of the Delegates

(1) An action to challenge the election of the delegates of an establishment may be brought before the Labor Court if there has been an infringement of material provisions of the voting rights, eligibility or the election procedure and this was not followed by a remedy, unless such infringement could not have changed or influenced the results of the election.

(2) ¹Those empowered to challenge the election are

1. at least three employees of the establishment who are eligible to vote,
2. the works council (Betriebsrat),
3. the spokesperson's committee,
4. the governing body authorized to legally represent the enterprise.

²A challenge to the election is only permissible within two weeks of the date on which the election results were announced.

Section 22
Challenge of the Election of the Supervisory Board Members of the Employees

(1) An action to challenge the election of an employee supervisory board member or alternate member may be brought before a labor court if material provisions with regard to the voting rights, eligibility or the election procedures have been infringed upon and this was not followed with a remedy, unless such infringement could not have changed or influenced the results of the election.

(2) ¹ Those entitled to challenge the election are

1. at least three employees of the enterprise who are eligible to vote,
2. the joint works council of the enterprise or, if only one works council exists in an enterprise, the works council, as well as, where the enterprise is the controlling enterprise of a group, the works council of the group if one exists;
3. the joint or enterprise spokesperson's committee of the enterprise, or, if there is only a spokesperson's committee in the enterprise, the spokesperson's committee as well as, if the company dominating the enterprise is a group, the group spokesperson's committee if one exists,
4. the joint works council of another enterprise, the employees of which participated in the election of the supervisory board members of the enterprise pursuant to this Act, or, if in another enterprise only a works council exists, the works council,
5. the joint or enterprise spokesperson's committee of another enterprise, the employees of which participated in the election of the supervisory board members of the enterprise pursuant to this Act, or, if in the other enterprise only a spokesperson's committee exists, the spokesperson's committee,
6. each union entitled to make nominations pursuant to section 16 (2);
7. the body authorized to legally represent the enterprise.

² A challenge to the election is only permissible within two weeks of the date of the publication in the electronic Federal Law Gazette.

Section 23
Dismissal of Supervisory Board Members of the Employees

(1) ¹ A supervisory board member of the employees may be dismissed by peti-

zeit auf Antrag abberufen werden. ²Antragsberechtigt sind für die Abberufung eines
1. Aufsichtsratsmitglieds der Arbeitnehmer nach § 3 Abs. 1 Nr. 1 drei Viertel der wahlberechtigten Arbeitnehmer nach § 3 Abs. 1 Nr. 1,

2. Aufsichtsratsmitglieds der leitenden Angestellten drei Viertel der wahlberechtigten leitenden Angestellten,

3. Aufsichtsratsmitglieds, das nach § 7 Abs. 2 Vertreter einer Gewerkschaft ist, die Gewerkschaft, die das Mitglied vorgeschlagen hat.

(2) ¹Ein durch Delegierte gewähltes Aufsichtsratsmitglied wird durch Beschluss der Delegierten abberufen. ²Dieser Beschluss wird in geheimer Abstimmung gefasst; er bedarf einer Mehrheit von drei Vierteln der abgegebenen Stimmen.

(3) ¹Ein von den Arbeitnehmern unmittelbar gewähltes Aufsichtsratsmitglied wird durch Beschluss der wahlberechtigten Arbeitnehmer abberufen. ²Dieser Beschluss wird in geheimer, unmittelbarer Abstimmung gefasst; er bedarf einer Mehrheit von drei Vierteln der abgegebenen Stimmen.

(4) Die Absätze 1 bis 3 sind für die Abberufung von Ersatzmitgliedern entsprechend anzuwenden.

tion prior to the expiration of his term of office. ²The persons entitled to make a motion to dismiss a member of;
1. a supervisory board member for the employees defined in section 3 (1) no. 1, will be three quarters of those employees defined in section 3 (1) no. 1 who are eligible to vote,

2. a supervisory board member for managerial employees, will be three quarters of those managerial employees who are eligible to vote,

3. a supervisory board member, where the member is a union representative as defined in section 7 (2), will be the union that nominated the member.

(2) ¹A supervisory board member elected by delegate shall be dismissed by a resolution of the delegates. ²This resolution shall be passed in a secret ballot; it requires a three quarters majority of the votes cast.

(3) ¹A supervisory board member elected by direct election of the employees shall be dismissed by resolution of those employees eligible to vote. ²This resolution shall be passed in a secret and direct ballot; it requires a majority of three quarters of the votes cast.

(4) Subsections (1) through (3) apply accordingly for the dismissal of alternate members.

§ 24
Verlust der Wählbarkeit und Änderung der Zuordnung unternehmensangehöriger Aufsichtsratsmitglieder

(1) Verliert ein Aufsichtsratsmitglied, das nach § 7 Abs. 2 Arbeitnehmer des Unternehmens sein muss, die Wählbarkeit, so erlischt sein Amt.

(2) Die Änderung der Zuordnung eines Aufsichtsratsmitglieds zu den in § 3 Abs. 1 Nr. 1 oder § 3 Abs. 1 Nr. 2 genannten Arbeitnehmern führt nicht zum Erlöschen seines Amtes.

Section 24
Loss of Eligibility for Election and Change of Group Membership of Supervisory Board Members of the Enterprise

(1) If a supervisory board member who is required to be an employee of the enterprise pursuant to section 7 (2) loses his eligibility for election, his term of office expires.

(2) A change in group membership of a supervisory board member of those employees named in section 3 (1) no. 1 or section 3 (1) no. 2 shall not result in the expiration of his term of office.

Dritter Abschnitt
Innere Ordnung, Rechte und Pflichten des Aufsichtsrats

§ 25
Grundsatz

(1) ¹Die innere Ordnung, die Beschlussfassung sowie die Rechte und Pflichten des Aufsichtsrats bestimmen sich nach den §§ 27 bis 29, den §§ 31 und 32 und, soweit diese Vorschriften dem nicht entgegenstehen,

1. für Aktiengesellschaften und Kommanditgesellschaften auf Aktien nach dem Aktiengesetz,
2. für Gesellschaften mit beschränkter Haftung nach § 90 Abs. 3, 4 und 5 Satz 1 und 2, den §§ 107 bis 116, 118 Abs. 3, § 125 Abs. 3 und 4 und den §§ 170, 171 und 268 Abs. 2 des Aktiengesetzes,
3. für Genossenschaften nach dem Genossenschaftsgesetz.

²§ 4 Abs. 2 des Gesetzes über die Überführung der Anteilsrechte an der Volkswagenwerk Gesellschaft mit beschränkter Haftung in private Hand vom 21. Juli 1960 (Bundesgesetzbl. I S. 585), zuletzt geändert durch das Zweite Gesetz zur Änderung des Gesetzes über die Überführung der Anteilsrechte an der Volkswagenwerk Gesellschaft mit beschränkter Haftung in private Hand vom 31. Juli 1970 (Bundesgesetzbl. I S. 1149), bleibt unberührt.

(2) Andere gesetzliche Vorschriften und Bestimmungen der Satzung (des Gesellschaftsvertrags) oder der Geschäftsordnung des Aufsichtsrats über die innere Ordnung, die Beschlussfassung sowie die Rechte und Pflichten des Aufsichtsrats bleiben unberührt, soweit Absatz 1 dem nicht entgegensteht.

Chapter 3
Internal Regulation, Rights and Obligations of the Supervisory Board

Section 25
Principles

(1) ¹The internal regulation and decision making, as well as the rights and obligations of the supervisory board are determined pursuant to sections 27 through 29, sections 31 and 32, and, to the extent that these provisions do not conflict with them,

1. for stock corporations and partnership limited by shares, pursuant to the Stock Corporation Act;
2. for limited liability companies, pursuant to section 90 (3), (4) and (5) sentences 1 and 2, sections 107 through 116, section 118 (3), section 125 (3) and (4) and sections 170, 171 and 268 (2) of the Stock Corporation Act;
3. for cooperative societies, pursuant to the Act on Cooperatives.

²Section 4 (2) of the Act Concerning the Transfer of Shares of the Volkswagenwerk Gesellschaft mit beschränkter Haftung into Private Ownership of 21 July 1960 (Federal Law Gazette I p. 585), last amended by the Second Act Amending the Act Concerning the Transfer of Shares of the Volkswagenwerk Gesellschaft mit beschränkter Haftung into Private Ownership of 31 July 1970 (Federal Law Gazette I p. 1149), remains unaffected.

(2) Other statutory provisions and conditions of the articles of association (the partnership agreement) or the rules of procedure of the supervisory board concerning the internal regulation and decision making, as well as the rights and obligations of the supervisory board, remain unaffected to the extent they do not conflict with subsection (1).

§ 26
Schutz von Aufsichtsratsmitgliedern vor Benachteiligung

[1]Aufsichtsratsmitglieder der Arbeitnehmer dürfen in der Ausübung ihrer Tätigkeit nicht gestört oder behindert werden. [2]Sie dürfen wegen ihrer Tätigkeit im Aufsichtsrat eines Unternehmens, dessen Arbeitnehmer sie sind oder als dessen Arbeitnehmer sie nach § 4 oder § 5 gelten, nicht benachteiligt werden. [3]Dies gilt auch für ihre berufliche Entwicklung.

Section 26
Protection of Supervisory Board Members Against Discrimination

[1]Supervisory board members of the employees may not be interfered with or hindered from carrying out their activities. [2]They may not be discriminated against due to their activities on the supervisory board of the enterprise which is their employer pursuant to section 4 or 5. [3]This also applies to their professional advancement.

§ 27
Vorsitz im Aufsichtsrat

(1) Der Aufsichtsrat wählt mit einer Mehrheit von zwei Dritteln der Mitglieder, aus denen er insgesamt zu bestehen hat, aus seiner Mitte einen Aufsichtsratsvorsitzenden und einen Stellvertreter.

(2) [1]Wird bei der Wahl des Aufsichtsratsvorsitzenden oder seines Stellvertreters die nach Absatz 1 erforderliche Mehrheit nicht erreicht, so findet für die Wahl des Aufsichtsratsvorsitzenden und seines Stellvertreters ein zweiter Wahlgang statt. [2]In diesem Wahlgang wählen die Aufsichtsratsmitglieder der Anteilseigner den Aufsichtsratsvorsitzenden und die Aufsichtsratsmitglieder der Arbeitnehmer den Stellvertreter jeweils mit der Mehrheit der abgegebenen Stimmen.

(3) Unmittelbar nach der Wahl des Aufsichtsratsvorsitzenden und seines Stellvertreters bildet der Aufsichtsrat zur Wahrnehmung der in § 31 Abs. 3 Satz 1 bezeichneten Aufgabe einen Ausschuss, dem der Aufsichtsratsvorsitzende, sein Stellvertreter sowie je ein von den Aufsichtsratsmitgliedern der Arbeitnehmer und von den Aufsichtsratsmitgliedern der Anteilseigner mit der Mehrheit der abgegebenen Stimmen gewähltes Mitglied angehören.

Section 27
Chairman of the Supervisory Board

(1) The supervisory board shall elect from within its ranks a chairman of the supervisory board and a deputy with a majority of two thirds of the total members of which it is to consist.

(2) [1]Where the majority stipulated in subsection (1) is not achieved for the election of the chairman of the supervisory board or his deputy, a second ballot shall be cast for the election of the chairman of the supervisory board and the deputy. [2]In this ballot, the supervisory board members of the shareholders shall elect the chairman of the supervisory board with a majority vote and the supervisory board members of the employees shall elect the deputy with the majority of votes.

(3) Immediately after the election of the supervisory board chairman and his deputy, the supervisory board shall form a committee to exercise those duties as designated in section 31 (3) sentence 1, which shall consist of the chairman of the supervisory board, his deputy, as well as one member to be elected by the supervisory board members of the employees and one member to be elected by the supervisory board members of the shareholders, with the majority of the votes cast.

§ 28
Beschlussfähigkeit

[1] Der Aufsichtsrat ist nur beschlussfähig, wenn mindestens die Hälfte der Mitglieder, aus denen er insgesamt zu bestehen hat, an der Beschlussfassung teilnimmt. [2] § 108 Abs. 2 Satz 4 des Aktiengesetzes ist anzuwenden.

§ 29
Abstimmungen

(1) Beschlüsse des Aufsichtsrats bedürfen der Mehrheit der abgegebenen Stimmen, soweit nicht in Absatz 2 und in den §§ 27, 31 und 32 etwas anderes bestimmt ist.

(2) [1] Ergibt eine Abstimmung im Aufsichtsrat Stimmengleichheit, so hat bei einer erneuten Abstimmung über denselben Gegenstand, wenn auch sie Stimmengleichheit ergibt, der Aufsichtsratsvorsitzende zwei Stimmen. [2] § 108 Abs. 3 des Aktiengesetzes ist auch auf die Abgabe der zweiten Stimme anzuwenden. [3] Dem Stellvertreter steht die zweite Stimme nicht zu.

Dritter Teil
Gesetzliches Vertretungsorgan

§ 30
Grundsatz

Die Zusammensetzung, die Rechte und Pflichten des zur gesetzlichen Vertretung des Unternehmens befugten Organs sowie die Bestellung seiner Mitglieder bestimmen sich nach den für die Rechtsform des Unternehmens geltenden Vorschriften, soweit sich aus den §§ 31 bis 33 nichts anderes ergibt.

§ 31
Bestellung und Widerruf

(1) [1] Die Bestellung der Mitglieder des zur gesetzlichen Vertretung des Unter-

Section 28
Quorum

[1] The supervisory board shall only have a quorum if at least one-half of the total number of members of which it is to consist participates in the adoption of a resolution. [2] Section 108 (2) sentence 4 of the Stock Corporation Act shall apply.

Section 29
Voting

(1) Resolutions of the supervisory board shall require the majority of votes cast unless otherwise provided in subsection (2) and in sections 27, 31 and 32.

(2) [1] Where the votes cast in the supervisory board result in a tie, a new ballot shall be cast on the same resolution. [2] If this again results in a tie, the chairman of the supervisory board shall have two votes. [3] Section 108 (3) of the Stock Corporation Act is also applicable to the casting of the second vote. [4] The deputy shall not have the right to such second vote.

Part 3
Body Authorized to Legally Represent the Enterprise

Section 30
Principles

The composition, rights and obligations of the body authorized to legally represent the enterprise, as well as the appointment of its members, are stipulated in the statutory provisions applicable to the enterprise's legal form, unless otherwise provided in sections 31 through 33.

Section 31
Appointment and Revocation of Appointment

(1) [1] The appointment and revocation of members of the body authorized to le-

nehmens befugten Organs und der Widerruf der Bestellung bestimmen sich nach den §§ 84 und 85 des Aktiengesetzes, soweit sich nicht aus den Absätzen 2 bis 5 etwas anderes ergibt. ²Dies gilt nicht für Kommanditgesellschaften auf Aktien.	gally represent the enterprise and the revocation of such appointment shall be conducted as set forth in sections 84 and 85 of the Stock Corporation Act unless otherwise provided in subsections (2) through (5). ²This does not apply for partnerships limited by shares (Kommanditgesellschaft auf Aktien – KGaA).
(2) Der Aufsichtsrat bestellt die Mitglieder des zur gesetzlichen Vertretung des Unternehmens befugten Organs mit einer Mehrheit, die mindestens zwei Drittel der Stimmen seiner Mitglieder umfasst.	(2) The supervisory board shall appoint the members of the body authorized to legally represent the enterprise with a majority comprising at least two thirds of its members' votes.
(3) ¹Kommt eine Bestellung nach Absatz 2 nicht zustande, so hat der in § 27 Abs. 3 bezeichnete Ausschuss des Aufsichtsrats innerhalb eines Monats nach der Abstimmung, in der die in Absatz 2 vorgeschriebene Mehrheit nicht erreicht worden ist, dem Aufsichtsrat einen Vorschlag für die Bestellung zu machen; dieser Vorschlag schließt andere Vorschläge nicht aus. ²Der Aufsichtsrat bestellt die Mitglieder des zur gesetzlichen Vertretung des Unternehmens befugten Organs mit der Mehrheit der Stimmen seiner Mitglieder.	(3) ¹If an appointment pursuant to subsection (2) is not made, the committee of the supervisory board referred to in section 27 (3) shall, within one month after the vote in which the number of votes required by subsection (2) was not reached, make a proposal to the supervisory board for such an appointment; this proposal shall not exclude other proposals. ²The supervisory board shall appoint the members of the body authorized to legally represent the enterprise with the majority of its members' votes.
(4) ¹Kommt eine Bestellung nach Absatz 3 nicht zustande, so hat bei einer erneuten Abstimmung der Aufsichtsratsvorsitzende zwei Stimmen; Absatz 3 Satz 2 ist anzuwenden. ²Auf die Abgabe der zweiten Stimme ist § 108 Abs. 3 des Aktiengesetzes anzuwenden. ³Dem Stellvertreter steht die zweite Stimme nicht zu.	(4) ¹If an appointment pursuant to subsection (3) is not made, the chairman of the supervisory board shall have two votes during the next balloting; subsection (3) sentence 2 shall apply. ²Section 108 (3) of the Stock Corporation Act shall apply with regard to the casting of the second vote. ³The deputy shall not have the right to a second vote.
(5) Die Absätze 2 bis 4 sind für den Widerruf der Bestellung eines Mitglieds des zur gesetzlichen Vertretung des Unternehmens befugten Organs entsprechend anzuwenden.	(5) Subsections (2) through (4) shall apply mutatis mutandis for the revocation of the appointment of a member of the body authorized to legally represent the enterprise.

<table><tr><td colspan="2" align="center">

§ 32
Ausübung von Beteiligungsrechten

</td><td colspan="2" align="center">

Section 32
Exercise of Participation Rights

</td></tr></table>

(1) ¹Die einem Unternehmen, in dem die Arbeitnehmer nach diesem Gesetz	(1) ¹The rights accruing to an enterprise in which the employees have a right of

ein Mitbestimmungsrecht haben, auf Grund von Beteiligungen an einem anderen Unternehmen, in dem die Arbeitnehmer nach diesem Gesetz ein Mitbestimmungsrecht haben, zustehenden Rechte bei der Bestellung, dem Widerruf der Bestellung oder der Entlastung von Verwaltungsträgern sowie bei der Beschlussfassung über die Auflösung oder Umwandlung des anderen Unternehmens, den Abschluss von Unternehmensverträgen (§§ 291, 292 des Aktiengesetzes) mit dem anderen Unternehmen, über dessen Fortsetzung nach seiner Auflösung oder über die Übertragung seines Vermögens können durch das zur gesetzlichen Vertretung des Unternehmens befugte Organ nur auf Grund von Beschlüssen des Aufsichtsrats ausgeübt werden. ²Diese Beschlüsse bedürfen nur der Mehrheit der Stimmen der Aufsichtsratsmitglieder der Anteilseigner; sie sind für das zur gesetzlichen Vertretung des Unternehmens befugte Organ verbindlich.

(2) Absatz 1 ist nicht anzuwenden, wenn die Beteiligung des Unternehmens an dem anderen Unternehmen weniger als ein Viertel beträgt.

co-determination pursuant to this Act, due to its participation in another enterprise in which employees have the right of co-determination pursuant to this Act, with respect to the appointment, revocation of the appointment or the discharge of administrators, as well as the adoption of resolutions concerning the dissolution, merger, or transformation of that other enterprise, the conclusion of enterprise agreements (sections 291, 292 of the Stock Corporation Act) with that other enterprise, its continuation upon dissolution or the transfer of its assets, can only be exercised by the body authorized to legally represent the enterprise through a resolution of the supervisory board. ²Such resolutions require only a majority of the votes of the shareholders' supervisory board members; they are binding on the body authorized to legally represent the enterprise.

(2) Subsection (1) shall not apply if the participation of the enterprise in the other enterprise consists of less than one fourth.

§ 33
Arbeitsdirektor

(1) ¹Als gleichberechtigtes Mitglied des zur gesetzlichen Vertretung des Unternehmens befugten Organs wird ein Arbeitsdirektor bestellt. ²Dies gilt nicht für Kommanditgesellschaften auf Aktien.

(2) ¹Der Arbeitsdirektor hat wie die übrigen Mitglieder des zur gesetzlichen Vertretung des Unternehmens befugten Organs seine Aufgaben im engsten Einvernehmen mit dem Gesamtorgan auszuüben. ²Das Nähere bestimmt die Geschäftsordnung.

Section 33
Director Representing the Employees

(1) ¹A director representing the employees shall be appointed as a member with equivalent rights to the body authorized to legally represent the enterprise. ²This does not apply to partnerships limited by shares (*Kommanditgesellschaft auf Aktien*).

(2) ¹The director representing the employees shall, like the other members of the body authorized to legally represent the enterprise, assume his duties in close cooperation with the entire body. ²Details shall be prescribed by the internal rules of procedure.

(3) Bei Genossenschaften ist auf den Arbeitsdirektor § 9 Abs. 2 des Genossenschaftsgesetzes nicht anzuwenden.

(3) Section 9 (2) of the Act on Co-Operatives shall not apply to the director representing the employees of cooperative societies.

Vierter Teil
Seeschifffahrt

Part 4
Maritime Shipping

§ 34
[Schiffe]

Section 34
[Ships]

(1) Die Gesamtheit der Schiffe eines Unternehmens gilt für die Anwendung dieses Gesetzes als ein Betrieb.

(1) The entire fleet of ships of one enterprise shall, for the purposes of the application of this Act, constitute a single establishment.

(2) [1] Schiffe im Sinne dieses Gesetzes sind Kauffahrteischiffe, die nach dem Flaggenrechtsgesetz die Bundesflagge führen. [2] Schiffe, die in der Regel binnen 48 Stunden nach dem Auslaufen an den Sitz eines Landbetriebs zurückkehren, gelten als Teil dieses Landbetriebs.

(2) [1] Vessels within the meaning of this Act are merchant vessels which fly the flag of the Federal Republic of Germany, pursuant to the Law of the Flag Act *(Flaggenrechtsgesetz)*. [2] Vessels which normally return to the seat of a land establishment within 48 hours after departure shall be considered as part of the land establishment.

(3) Leitende Angestellte im Sinne des § 3 Abs. 1 Nr. 2 dieses Gesetzes sind in einem in Absatz 1 bezeichneten Betrieb nur die Kapitäne.

(3) For an establishment mentioned in subsection (1), only masters shall qualify as managerial employees as defined in section 3 (3) no. 2 of this Act.

(4) Die Arbeitnehmer eines in Absatz 1 bezeichneten Betriebs nehmen an einer Abstimmung nach § 9 nicht teil und bleiben für die Errechnung der für die Antragstellung und für die Beschlussfassung erforderlichen Zahl von Arbeitnehmern außer Betracht.

(4) The employees of an establishment referred to in subsection (1) shall not participate in the voting pursuant to section 9 and shall not be taken into account in the computation of the requisite number of employees for petitions and for adopting resolutions.

(5) [1] Werden die Aufsichtsratsmitglieder der Arbeitnehmer durch Delegierte gewählt, so werden abweichend von § 10 in einem in Absatz 1 bezeichneten Betrieb keine Delegierten gewählt. [2] Abweichend von § 15 Abs. 1 nehmen die Arbeitnehmer dieses Betriebs unmittelbar an der Wahl der Aufsichtsratsmitglieder der Arbeitnehmer teil mit der Maßgabe, dass die Stimme eines dieser Arbeitnehmer als ein Neunzigstel der Stimme eines Delegierten zu zählen ist; § 11 Abs. 1 Satz 3 ist entsprechend anzuwenden.

(5) [1] If the employees' supervisory board members are elected by the delegates, then notwithstanding section 10, no delegates shall be elected in an establishment as defined in subsection (1). [2] Notwithstanding section 15 (1), the employees of the establishment shall participate directly in the election of the supervisory board members of the employees with the proviso that the vote of one of these employees shall constitute one ninetieth of the vote of one delegate; section 11 (1) sentence 3 shall apply accordingly.

Fünfter Teil
Übergangs- und Schlussvorschriften

Part 5
Transitional and Final Provisions

§ 35
(aufgehoben)

Section 35
(repealed)

§ 36
Verweisungen

Section 36
References

(1) Soweit in anderen Vorschriften auf Vorschriften des Betriebsverfassungsgesetzes 1952 über die Vertretung der Arbeitnehmer in den Aufsichtsräten von Unternehmen verwiesen wird, gelten diese Verweisungen für die in § 1 Abs. 1 dieses Gesetzes bezeichneten Unternehmen als Verweisungen auf dieses Gesetz.

(1) Where other provisions refer to provisions of the Works Constitution Act of 1952 with regard to the representation of employees in the supervisory boards of enterprises, such references apply to this Act for those enterprises referred to in section 1 (1) of this Act.

(2) Soweit in anderen Vorschriften für das Gesetz über die Mitbestimmung der Arbeitnehmer in den Aufsichtsräten und Vorständen der Unternehmen des Bergbaus und der Eisen und Stahl erzeugenden Industrie vom 21. Mai 1951 (Bundesgesetzbl. I S. 347) die Bezeichnung „Mitbestimmungsgesetz" verwendet wird, tritt an ihre Stelle die Bezeichnung „Montan-Mitbestimmungsgesetz".

(2) Where the term "Co-Determination Act" appears in other provisions with respect to the Act Concerning the Co-Determination of the Employees in the Supervisory Board and Management Boards of Mining and Iron and Steel Industries of 21 May 1951 (Federal Law Gazette I p. 347) this term shall be superseded by the term "Mining, Coal and steel Co-Determination Act".

§ 37
Erstmalige Anwendung des Gesetzes auf ein Unternehmen

Section 37
Initial Application of this Act to an Enterprise

(1) [1] Andere als die in § 97 Abs. 2 Satz 2 des Aktiengesetzes bezeichneten Bestimmungen der Satzung (des Gesellschaftsvertrags), die mit den Vorschriften dieses Gesetzes nicht vereinbar sind, treten mit dem in § 97 Abs. 2 Satz 2 des Aktiengesetzes bezeichneten Zeitpunkt oder, im Fall einer gerichtlichen Entscheidung, mit dem in § 98 Abs. 4 Satz 2 des Aktiengesetzes bezeichneten Zeitpunkt außer Kraft. [2] Eine Hauptversammlung (Gesellschafterversammlung, Generalversammlung), die bis zu diesem Zeitpunkt stattfindet,

(1) [1] Provisions other than those in the articles of association (the partnership agreement, the statutes) referred to in section 97 (2) sentence 2 of the Stock Corporation Act which conflict with the provisions of this Act shall cease to be valid as of the time designated in section 97 (2) sentence 2 of the Stock Corporation Act, or, in the case of a judicial decision, at the time designated in section 98 (4) sentence 2 of the Stock Corporation Act. [2] A shareholders' meeting (of a limited liability company, a mining company, a stock corporation) held

kann an Stelle der außer Kraft tretenden Satzungsbestimmungen mit einfacher Mehrheit neue Satzungsbestimmungen beschließen.

(2) Die §§ 25 bis 29, 31 bis 33 sind erstmalig anzuwenden, wenn der Aufsichtsrat nach den Vorschriften dieses Gesetzes zusammengesetzt ist.

(3) ¹Die Bestellung eines vor dem Inkrafttreten dieses Gesetzes bestellten Mitglieds des zur gesetzlichen Vertretung befugten Organs eines Unternehmens, auf das dieses Gesetz bereits bei seinem Inkrafttreten anzuwenden ist, kann, sofern die Amtszeit dieses Mitglieds nicht aus anderen Gründen früher endet, nach Ablauf von fünf Jahren seit dem Inkrafttreten dieses Gesetzes von dem nach diesem Gesetz gebildeten Aufsichtsrat jederzeit widerrufen werden. ²Für den Widerruf bedarf es der Mehrheit der abgegebenen Stimmen der Aufsichtsratsmitglieder, aller Stimmen der Aufsichtsratsmitglieder der Anteilseigner oder aller Stimmen der Aufsichtsratsmitglieder der Arbeitnehmer. ³Für die Ansprüche aus dem Anstellungsvertrag gelten die allgemeinen Vorschriften. ⁴Bis zum Widerruf bleiben für diese Mitglieder Satzungsbestimmungen über die Amtszeit abweichend von Absatz 1 Satz 1 in Kraft.⁵Diese Vorschriften sind entsprechend anzuwenden, wenn dieses Gesetzes auf ein Unternehmen erst nach dem Zeitpunkt des Inkrafttretens dieses Gesetzes erstmalig anzuwenden ist.

(4) Absatz 3 gilt nicht für persönlich haftende Gesellschafter einer Kommanditgesellschaft auf Aktien.

prior to this time may, by simple majority, adopt new clauses in its articles of association to supersede the clauses in the articles of association which are about to become invalid.

(2) Sections 25 through 29 and 31 through 33 shall apply for the first time once the supervisory board has been formed pursuant to the provisions of this Act.

(3) ¹The appointment of a member of a body authorized to legally represent the enterprise prior to the coming into effect of this Act, to which this Act shall be applicable once it comes into effect, may, to the extent his term of office does not end earlier for other reasons, be revoked at any time by the supervisory board formed pursuant to this Act once this Act has been in effect for five years. ²Such a revocation shall require either the majority of the votes cast by the supervisory board, a unanimous vote by the shareholders' supervisory board members, or a unanimous vote by the employees' supervisory board members. ³The general provisions shall apply for the claims arising from the employment agreement. ⁴Notwithstanding subsection (1) sentence 1, the provisions in the articles of association regarding the term of office shall remain in effect until the appointment of these members has been revoked. ⁵These provisions shall apply accordingly if this Act was not initially applied to an enterprise until after this Act went into effect.

(4) Subsection (3) does not apply to general partners of a partnership limited by shares.

§ 38
(aufgehoben)

Section 38
(repealed)

§ 39
Ermächtigung zum Erlass von Rechtsverordnungen

Die Bundesregierung wird ermächtigt, durch Rechtsverordnung Vorschriften

Section 39
Authorization to Issue Legal Regulations

The federal government shall be empowered to issue provisions concerning

über das Verfahren für die Wahl und die Abberufung von Aufsichtsratsmitgliedern der Arbeitnehmer zu erlassen, insbesondere über

1. die Vorbereitung der Wahl oder Abstimmung, die Bestellung der Wahlvorstände und Abstimmungsvorstände sowie die Aufstellung der Wählerlisten,
2. die Abstimmungen darüber, ob die Wahl der Aufsichtsratsmitglieder in unmittelbarer Wahl oder durch Delegierte erfolgen soll,
3. die Frist für die Einsichtnahme in die Wählerlisten und die Erhebung von Einsprüchen,
4. die Errechnung der Zahl der Aufsichtsratsmitglieder der Arbeitnehmer sowie ihre Verteilung auf die in § 3 Abs. 1 Nr. 1 bezeichneten Arbeitnehmer, die leitenden Angestellten und die Gewerkschaftsvertreter,
5. die Errechnung der Zahl der Delegierten,
6. die Wahlvorschläge und die Frist für ihre Einreichung,
7. die Ausschreibung der Wahl oder der Abstimmung und die Fristen für die Bekanntmachung des Ausschreibens,
8. die Teilnahme von Arbeitnehmern eines in § 34 Abs. 1 bezeichneten Betriebs an Wahlen und Abstimmungen,
9. die Stimmabgabe,
10. die Feststellung des Ergebnisses der Wahl oder der Abstimmung und die Fristen für seine Bekanntmachung,
11. die Aufbewahrung der Wahlakten und der Abstimmungsakten.

the election procedure and the recall of supervisory board members of the employees through legal regulations, particularly with regard to:

1. the preparation of the election or ballots, the appointment of election committees and ballot committees as well as the drawing up of election lists;
2. voting on whether the supervisory board members will be chosen by a direct election or through delegates and whether a common election is to be held;
3. the deadline for inspecting the election lists and raising objections to them;
4. the computation of the number of supervisory board members of the employees as well as their allocation to the workers, to the salaried employees as defined in section 3 (3) no. 1, the managerial employees and the representatives of the union;
5. the computation of the number of delegates;
6. the nominations and filing deadline;
7. the announcement of the election or ballots and the deadline for the announcing them;
8. the participation of employees for elections and voting in an establishment specified in section 34 (1);
9. the casting of votes;
10. the determination of the results of the election or the ballots and the deadline for announcing them;
11. the retention of election files and ballot files.

§ 40
Übergangsregelung

(1) Auf Wahlen oder Abberufungen von Aufsichtsratsmitgliedern der Arbeitnehmer, die nach dem 28. Juli 2001 bis zum 26. März 2002 eingeleitet wurden,

Section 40
Transitional Provision

(1) For elections or recalls of supervisory board members of the employees which were initiated between 28 July 2001 and 26 March 2002, by the Code-

ist das Mitbestimmungsgesetz vom 4. Mai 1976 (BGBl. I S. 1153) in der durch Artikel 12 des Betriebsverfassungs-Reformgesetzes vom 23. Juli 2001 (BGBl. I S. 1852) geänderten Fassung anzuwenden. Abweichend von Satz 1 findet § 11 des Mitbestimmungsgesetzes vom 4. Mai 1976 (BGBl. I S. 1153) in der durch Artikel 1 des Gesetzes zur Vereinfachung der Wahl der Arbeitnehmervertreter in den Aufsichtsrat vom 23. März 2002 (BGBl. I S. 1130) geänderten Fassung Anwendung, wenn feststeht, dass die Aufsichtsratsmitglieder der Arbeitnehmer durch Delegierte zu wählen sind und bis zum 26. März 2002 die Errechnung der Zahl der Delegierten noch nicht erfolgt ist.

(2) ¹Auf Wahlen oder Abberufungen von Aufsichtsratsmitgliedern der Arbeitnehmer, die nach dem 28. Juli 2001 eingeleitet wurden, finden die Erste Wahlordnung zum Mitbestimmungsgesetz vom 23. Juni 1977 (BGBl. I S. 861), geändert durch Artikel 1 der Verordnung vom 9. November 1990 (BGBl. I S. 2487), die Zweite Wahlordnung zum Mitbestimmungsgesetz vom 23. Juni 1977 (BGBl. I S. 893), geändert durch Artikel 2 der Verordnung vom 9. November 1990 (BGBl. I S. 2487) und die Dritte Wahlordnung zum Mitbestimmungsgesetz vom 23. Juni 1977 (BGBl. I S. 934), geändert durch Artikel 3 der Verordnung vom 9. November 1990 (BGBl. I S. 2487) bis zu deren Änderung entsprechende Anwendung. ²Für die entsprechende Anwendung ist für Wahlen oder Abberufungen von Aufsichtsratsmitgliedern der Arbeitnehmer, die in dem Zeitraum nach dem 28. Juli 2001 bis zum 26. März 2002 eingeleitet wurden, das Mitbestimmungsgesetz vom 4. Mai 1976 (BGBl. I S. 1153) in der nach Absatz 1 anzuwendenden Fassung maßgeblich; für Wahlen oder Abberufungen von Aufsichtsratsmitgliedern der Arbeitnehmer, die nach dem 26. März 2002 eingeleitet werden, ist das Mitbestimmungsgesetz vom 4. Mai

termination Act of 4 May 1976 (Federal Law Gazette I p. 1153) in the version as amended by Article 12 of the Act to Reform the Works Constitutional Act of 23 July 2001 (Federal Law Gazette I p. 1852) shall apply. Notwithstanding sentence 1, section 11 of the Codetermination Act of 4 May 1976 (Federal Law Gazette I p. 1153) in the version as amended by Article 1 of the Act to Simplify the Election of the Employees' Representatives in the Supervisory Board of 23 March 2002 (Federal Law Gazette I p. 1130) shall apply, if it has been established that the supervisory board members of the employees are to be elected by delegates and the number of delegates has not been calculated by 26 March 2002.

(2) ¹For elections or recalls of supervisory board members of the employees which were initiated after 28 July 2001 the First Electoral Regulations Regarding the Codetermination Act of 23 June 1977 (Federal Law Gazette I p. 861), as amended by Article 1 of the Ordinance of 9 November 1990 (Federal Law Gazette I p. 2487), the Second Electoral Regulations Regarding the Codetermination Act of 23 June 1977 (Federal Law Gazette I p. 893), as amended by Article 2 of the Ordinance of 9 November 1990 (Federal Law Gazette p. 2487) and the Third Electoral Regulations Regarding the Codetermination Act of 23 June 1977 (Federal Law Gazette I p. 934), as amended by Article 3 of the Ordinance of 9 November 1990 (Federal Law Gazette I p. 2487) shall apply mutatis mutandis until they are amended. ²The analogous application for elections or recalls of supervisory board members initiated between 28 July 2001 and 26 March 2002 shall be subject to the Codetermination Act of 4 May 1976 (Federal Law Gazette I p. 1153) in the version to be applied pursuant to subsection (1); for elections or recalls of supervisory board members initiated after 26 March 2002, the Codetermination Act of 4 May 1976 (Federal Law

1976 (BGBl. I S. 1153) in der durch Artikel 1 des Gesetzes zur Vereinfachung der Wahl der Arbeitnehmervertreter in den Aufsichtsrat vom 23. März 2002 (BGBl. I S. 1130) geänderten Fassung maßgeblich.

Gazette I p. 1153) in the version as amended by Article 1 of the Act to Simplify the Election of the Employees' Representatives in the Supervisory Board of 23 March 2002 (Federal Law Gazette I p. 1130) shall prevail.

§ 41
Inkrafttreten

Section 41
Entry into force

Dieses Gesetz tritt am 1. Juli 1976 in Kraft.

This Act shall enter into effect on 1 July 1976.

XIII. One-Third Participation Act (Drittelbeteiligungsgesetz – DrittelbG)

of 18 May 2004 (Federal Law Gazette I p. 974)

in the amended version of 30 July 2009

(excerpts)

Part 1
Scope of Application

Section 1
Enterprises Covered

(1) The employees have a right of codetermination in the supervisory board (*Aufsichtsrat*) in accordance with this Act in

1. a stock corporation (*Aktiengesellschaft*) with, as a rule, more than 500 employees. A right of codetermination in the supervisory board shall also exist in a stock corporation with, as a rule, less than 500 employees, if it was registered before 10 August 1994 and is not a family-owned company. Family-owned companies are deemed to be those stock corporations whose shareholder is an individual natural person or whose shareholders are related by blood or marriage within the meaning of Section 15 (1) nos. 2 to 8 and (2) of the Tax Code (*Abgabenordnung*);
2. a partnership limited by shares (*Kommanditgesellschaft auf Aktien*) with, as a rule, more than 500 employees. No. 1 sentence 2 and 3 apply *mutatis mutandis*;
3. a limited liability company (*Gesellschaft mit beschränkter Haftung*) with, as a rule, more than 500 employees. The company must form a supervisory board; its composition, as well as its rights and duties, are determined pursuant to section 90 (3), (4), (5) sentences 1 and 2, pursuant to

Abs. 2, § 125 Abs. 3 und 4 und nach den §§ 170, 171, 268 Abs. 2 des Aktiengesetzes;	sections 95 to 114, 116, 118 (2), section 125 (3) and (4) and pursuant to sections 170, 171, 268 (2) of the German Stock Corporation Act *(Aktiengesetz)*;
4. einem Versicherungsverein auf Gegenseitigkeit mit in der Regel mehr als 500 Arbeitnehmern, wenn dort ein Aufsichtsrat besteht;	4. a mutual insurance company *(Versicherungsverein auf Gegenseitigkeit)* with, as a rule, more than 500 employees if it has a supervisory board;
5. einer Genossenschaft mit in der Regel mehr als 500 Arbeitnehmern. § 96 Abs. 2 und die §§ 97 bis 99 des Aktiengesetzes sind entsprechend anzuwenden. Die Satzung kann nur eine durch drei teilbare Zahl von Aufsichtsratsmitgliedern festsetzen. Der Aufsichtsrat muss zwei Sitzungen im Kalenderhalbjahr abhalten.	5. a cooperative society *(Genossenschaft)* with, as a rule, more than 500 employees. Section 96 (2) and sections 97 to 99 of the Stock Corporation Act apply *mutatis mutandis*. The articles of association may only stipulate a number of supervisory board members which is divisible by three. The supervisory board must hold two meetings in a calendar half-year.
(2) Dieses Gesetz findet keine Anwendung auf	(2) This Act shall not apply to
1. die in § 1 Abs. 1 des Mitbestimmungsgesetzes, die in § 1 des Montan-Mitbestimmungsgesetzes und die in den §§ 1 und 3 Abs. 1 des Montan-Mitbestimmungsergänzungsgesetzes bezeichneten Unternehmen;	1. the enterprises designated in section 1 (1) of the Codetermination Act *(Mitbestimmungsgesetz)*, in section 1 of the Coal, Iron and Steel Codetermination Act *(Montan-Mitbestimmungsgesetz)* and in sections 1 and 3 (1) of the Amended Coal, Iron and Steel Codetermination Act *(Montan-Mitbestimmungsergänzungsgesetz)*;
2. Unternehmen, die unmittelbar und überwiegend a) politischen, koalitionspolitischen, konfessionellen, karitativen, erzieherischen, wissenschaftlichen oder künstlerischen Bestimmungen oder b) Zwecken der Berichterstattung oder Meinungsäußerung, auf die Artikel 5 Abs. 1 Satz 2 des Grundgesetzes anzuwenden ist, dienen.	2. enterprises that directly and predominantly serve a) political, trade union/employee association, denominational, charitable, educational, academic or artistic purposes or b) the purpose of reporting news or expressing opinions which are governed by Article 5 (1) sentence 2 of the Basic Law *(Grundgesetz)*.
Dieses Gesetz ist nicht anzuwenden auf Religionsgemeinschaften und ihre karitativen und erzieherischen Einrichtungen unbeschadet deren Rechtsform.	This Act shall not be applied to religious communities or their charitable and educational facilities, regardless of their legal form.
(3) Die Vorschriften des Genossenschaftsgesetzes über die Zusammensetzung des Aufsichtsrats sowie über die	(3) The provisions of the Cooperative Societies Act *(Genossenschaftsgesetz)* on the composition of the supervisory

Wahl und die Abberufung von Aufsichtsratsmitgliedern gelten insoweit nicht, als sie den Vorschriften dieses Gesetzes widersprechen.

§ 2
Konzern

(1) An der Wahl der Aufsichtsratsmitglieder der Arbeitnehmer des herrschenden Unternehmens eines Konzerns (§ 18 Abs. 1 des Aktiengesetzes) nehmen auch die Arbeitnehmer der übrigen Konzernunternehmen teil.

(2) Soweit nach § 1 die Beteiligung der Arbeitnehmer im Aufsichtsrat eines herrschenden Unternehmens von dem Vorhandensein oder der Zahl von Arbeitnehmern abhängt, gelten die Arbeitnehmer eines Konzernunternehmens als solche des herrschenden Unternehmens, wenn zwischen den Unternehmen ein Beherrschungsvertrag besteht oder das abhängige Unternehmen in das herrschende Unternehmen eingegliedert ist.

§ 3
Arbeitnehmer, Betrieb

(1) Arbeitnehmer im Sinne dieses Gesetzes sind die in § 5 Abs. 1 des Betriebsverfassungsgesetzes bezeichneten Personen mit Ausnahme der in § 5 Abs. 3 des Betriebsverfassungsgesetzes bezeichneten leitenden Angestellten.

(2) [1]Betriebe im Sinne dieses Gesetzes sind solche des Betriebsverfassungsgesetzes. [2]§ 4 Abs. 2 des Betriebsverfassungsgesetzes ist anzuwenden.

(3) [1]Die Gesamtheit der Schiffe eines Unternehmens gilt für die Anwendung dieses Gesetzes als ein Betrieb. [2]Schiffe im Sinne dieses Gesetzes sind Kauffahrteischiffe, die nach dem Flaggenrechtsgesetz die Bundesflagge führen. [3]Schiffe, die in der Regel binnen 48 Stunden

board as well as on the election and dismissal of supervisory board members shall not apply where they conflict with the provisions of this Act.

Section 2
Corporate Group

(1) Where supervisory board members are elected for the employees of the controlling enterprise of a group (section 18 (1) of the Stock Corporation Act), employees of the other group enterprises shall also participate in the election.

(2) Where the participation of the employees in the supervisory board of a controlling enterprise is dependent on the existence or number of employees pursuant to section 1, the employees of a group enterprise shall be deemed to be employees of the controlling enterprise if a control agreement exists between the enterprises or the controlled enterprise is integrated into the controlling enterprise.

Section 3
Employees, Establishments

(1) Employees within the meaning of this Act are those persons designated in section 5 (1) of the Works Constitution Act (*Betriebsverfassungsgesetz*), with the exception of the managerial employees designated in section 5 (3) of the Works Constitution Act.

(2) [1]Establishments within the meaning of this Act are those defined in the Works Constitution Act. [2]Section 4 (2) of the Works Constitution Act shall apply.

(3) [1]The total number of ships in an enterprise shall be deemed to constitute an establishment for the application of this Act. [2]Ships within the meaning of this Act are merchant ships who fly the flag of the Federal Republic of Germany pursuant to the Law of the Flag

nach dem Auslaufen an den Sitz eines Landbetriebs zurückkehren, gelten als Teil dieses Landbetriebs.

Act *(Flaggenrechtsgesetz)*. ³Ships which as a rule return to the seat of the land establishment within 48 hours of setting sail shall be deemed to be part of this land establishment.

Teil 2
Aufsichtsrat

Part 2
Supervisory Board

§ 4
Zusammensetzung

Section 4
Composition

(1) Der Aufsichtsrat eines in § 1 Abs. 1 bezeichneten Unternehmens muss zu einem Drittel aus Arbeitnehmervertretern bestehen.

(1) At least one third of the supervisory board of an enterprise designated in section 1 (1) must be employee representatives.

(2) ¹Ist ein Aufsichtsratsmitglied der Arbeitnehmer oder sind zwei Aufsichtsratsmitglieder der Arbeitnehmer zu wählen, so müssen diese als Arbeitnehmer im Unternehmen beschäftigt sein. ²Sind mehr als zwei Aufsichtsratsmitglieder der Arbeitnehmer zu wählen, so müssen mindestens zwei Aufsichtsratsmitglieder als Arbeitnehmer im Unternehmen beschäftigt sein.

(2) ¹If one or two employee supervisory board members are to be elected, they must be working for the enterprise as employees. ²If more than two employee supervisory board members are to be elected, at least two supervisory board members must be working for the enterprise as employees.

(3) ¹Die Aufsichtsratsmitglieder der Arbeitnehmer, die Arbeitnehmer des Unternehmens sind, müssen das 18. Lebensjahr vollendet haben und ein Jahr dem Unternehmen angehören. ²Auf die einjährige Unternehmensangehörigkeit werden Zeiten der Angehörigkeit zu einem anderen Unternehmen, dessen Arbeitnehmer nach diesem Gesetz an der Wahl von Aufsichtsratsmitgliedern des Unternehmens teilnehmen, angerechnet. ³Diese Zeiten müssen unmittelbar vor dem Zeitpunkt liegen, ab dem die Arbeitnehmer zur Wahl von Aufsichtsratsmitgliedern des Unternehmens berechtigt sind. ⁴Die weiteren Wählbarkeitsvoraussetzungen des § 8 Abs. 1 des Betriebsverfassungsgesetzes müssen erfüllt sein.

(3) ¹The employee supervisory board members who are employees of the enterprise must be at least 18 years of age and have worked for the enterprise for one year. ²Periods of employment with another enterprise whose employees participate in the election of members of the enterprise's supervisory board under this Act shall be counted toward this one-year seniority requirement. ³These periods must immediately precede the point in time from which the employees are entitled to vote for members of the enterprise's supervisory board. ⁴The further eligibility requirements set forth in section 8 (1) of the Works Constitution Act must be met.

(4) Unter den Aufsichtsratsmitgliedern der Arbeitnehmer sollen Frauen und Männer entsprechend ihrem zahlenmä-

(4) Men and women should be represented among the employee supervisory board members in accordance with

ßigen Verhältnis im Unternehmen vertreten sein.

their proportional numbers in the enterprise.

§ 5
Wahl der Aufsichtsratsmitglieder der Arbeitnehmer

(1) Die Aufsichtsratsmitglieder der Arbeitnehmer werden nach den Grundsätzen der Mehrheitswahl in allgemeiner, geheimer, gleicher und unmittelbarer Wahl für die Zeit gewählt, die im Gesetz oder in der Satzung für die von der Hauptversammlung zu wählenden Aufsichtsratsmitglieder bestimmt ist.

(2) ^{1}Wahlberechtigt sind die Arbeitnehmer des Unternehmens, die das 18. Lebensjahr vollendet haben. ^{2}§ 7 Satz 2 des Betriebsverfassungsgesetzes gilt entsprechend.

Section 5
Election of the Employee Supervisory Board Members

(1) The employee supervisory board members shall be elected according to the principles of majority vote in a general, secret, equitable and direct vote for the period set forth in the statute or the articles of association for the supervisory board members to be elected by the general shareholder meeting.

(2) ^{1}All employees of the enterprise who have reached the age of 18 shall be eligible to vote. ^{2}Section 7 sentence 2 of the Works Constitution Act applies *mutatis mutandis*.

§ 6
Wahlvorschläge

^{1}Die Wahl erfolgt auf Grund von Wahlvorschlägen der Betriebsräte und der Arbeitnehmer. ^{2}Die Wahlvorschläge der Arbeitnehmer müssen von mindestens einem Zehntel der Wahlberechtigten oder von mindestens 100 Wahlberechtigten unterzeichnet sein.

Section 6
Nominations

^{1}The election shall be held on the basis of nominations by the works councils and the employees. ^{2}The nominations by the employees must be signed by at least one tenth of the eligible voters or at least 100 eligible voters.

§ 7
Ersatzmitglieder

(1) ^{1}In jedem Wahlvorschlag kann zusammen mit jedem Bewerber für diesen ein Ersatzmitglied des Aufsichtsrats vorgeschlagen werden. ^{2}Ein Bewerber kann nicht zugleich als Ersatzmitglied vorgeschlagen werden.

(2) Wird ein Bewerber als Aufsichtsratsmitglied gewählt, so ist auch das zusammen mit ihm vorgeschlagene Ersatzmitglied gewählt.

Section 7
Deputy Members

(1) ^{1}In each nomination, a deputy member of the supervisory board may be proposed together with each candidate. ^{2}A candidate may not simultaneously be proposed as a deputy member.

(2) If a candidate is elected to the supervisory board, the deputy member proposed together with him shall also be elected.

§ 8
Bekanntmachung der Mitglieder des Aufsichtsrats

^{1}Das zur gesetzlichen Vertretung des Unternehmens befugte Organ hat die

Section 8
Announcement of the Members of the Supervisory Board

^{1}The governing body authorized to legally represent the enterprise shall

Namen der Mitglieder und der Ersatzmitglieder des Aufsichtsrats unverzüglich nach ihrer Bestellung in den Betrieben des Unternehmens bekannt zu machen und im elektronischen Bundesanzeiger zu veröffentlichen. ²Nehmen an der Wahl der Aufsichtsratsmitglieder des Unternehmens auch die Arbeitnehmer eines anderen Unternehmens teil, so ist daneben das zur gesetzlichen Vertretung des anderen Unternehmens befugte Organ zur Bekanntmachung in seinen Betrieben verpflichtet.

announce the names of the members and deputy members of the supervisory board immediately following their appointment in the establishments of the enterprise and in the electronic Federal Gazette *(Bundesanzeiger)*. ²Should the employees of another enterprise also participate in the election of the enterprise's supervisory board members, then the governing body authorized to legally represent the other enterprise shall also be obligated to make the same announcement in its establishments.

§ 9
Schutz von Aufsichtsratsmitgliedern vor Benachteiligung

Section 9
Protection of Supervisory Board Members Against Detrimental Treatment

¹Aufsichtsratsmitglieder der Arbeitnehmer dürfen in der Ausübung ihrer Tätigkeit nicht gestört oder behindert werden. ²Sie dürfen wegen ihrer Tätigkeit im Aufsichtsrat nicht benachteiligt oder begünstigt werden. ³Dies gilt auch für ihre berufliche Entwicklung.

¹Employee supervisory board members may not be interfered with or hindered in the performance of their activities. ²They may not be treated detrimentally or preferentially due to their activity in the supervisory board. ³This also applies to their professional development.

§ 10
Wahlschutz und Wahlkosten

Section 10
Protection of the Election and Cost of the Election

(1) ¹Niemand darf die Wahl der Aufsichtsratsmitglieder der Arbeitnehmer behindern. ²Insbesondere darf niemand in der Ausübung des aktiven und passiven Wahlrechts beschränkt werden.

(1) ¹No one may hinder the election of the employee supervisory board members. ²In particular, no one may be restricted in the exercise of their active and passive right to vote.

(2) Niemand darf die Wahlen durch Zufügung oder Androhung von Nachteilen oder durch Gewährung oder Versprechen von Vorteilen beeinflussen.

(2) No one may influence the elections by imposing or threatening disadvantages or by granting or promising advantages.

(3) ¹Die Kosten der Wahlen trägt das Unternehmen. ²Versäumnis von Arbeitszeit, die zur Ausübung des Wahlrechts oder der Betätigung im Wahlvorstand erforderlich ist, berechtigt nicht zur Minderung des Arbeitsentgelts.

(3) ¹The cost of the election shall be borne by the enterprise. ²Working time which is lost due to employees' exercise of their voting rights or activity in the election committee shall not justify a reduction of their remuneration.

§ 11
Anfechtung der Wahl von Aufsichtsratsmitgliedern der Arbeitnehmer

(1) Die Wahl eines Aufsichtsratsmitglieds oder eines Ersatzmitglieds der Arbeitnehmer kann beim Arbeitsgericht angefochten werden, wenn gegen wesentliche Vorschriften über das Wahlrecht, die Wählbarkeit oder das Wahlverfahren verstoßen worden und eine Berichtigung nicht erfolgt ist, es sei denn, dass durch den Verstoß das Wahlergebnis nicht geändert oder beeinflusst werden konnte.

(2) Zur Anfechtung berechtigt sind

1. mindestens drei Wahlberechtigte,
2. die Betriebsräte,
3. das zur gesetzlichen Vertretung des Unternehmens befugte Organ.

Die Anfechtung ist nur binnen einer Frist von zwei Wochen, vom Tag der Veröffentlichung im elektronischen Bundesanzeiger an gerechnet, zulässig.

§ 12
Abberufung von Aufsichtsratsmitgliedern der Arbeitnehmer

(1) Ein Aufsichtsratsmitglied der Arbeitnehmer kann vor Ablauf der Amtszeit auf Antrag eines Betriebsrats oder von mindestens einem Fünftel der Wahlberechtigten durch Beschluss abberufen werden. Der Beschluss der Wahlberechtigten wird in allgemeiner, geheimer, gleicher und unmittelbarer Abstimmung gefasst; er bedarf einer Mehrheit von drei Vierteln der abgegebenen Stimmen. Auf die Beschlussfassung findet § 2 Abs. 1 Anwendung.

(2) Absatz 1 ist für die Abberufung von Ersatzmitgliedern entsprechend anzuwenden.

Section 11
Action to Set Aside the Election of Employee Supervisory Board Members

(1) An action to set aside the election of a supervisory board member or deputy member of the employees may be filed with the Labor Court if material provisions on voting rights, eligibility of candidates or the election procedure were violated and this was not corrected, unless the result of the election could not be changed or influenced due to the violation.

(2) The following shall be entitled to file such an action:

1. at least three eligible voters,
2. the works councils,
3. the governing body authorized to represent the enterprise.

Such an action shall only be permissible within a period of two weeks, calculated as of the date of publication in the electronic Federal Gazette.

Section 12
Dismissal of Employee Supervisory Board Members

(1) A supervisory board member of the employees may be dismissed before his term has ended by means of a resolution upon application by a works council or at least one-fifth of the eligible voters. The resolution of the eligible voters shall be adopted by a general, secret, equitable and direct vote; it shall require a three-quarters majority of the votes cast. Section 2 (1) shall apply with respect to the adoption of the resolution.

(2) For the dismissal of deputy members, subsection (1) shall apply *mutatis mutandis*.

Teil 3
Übergangs- und Schlussvorschriften

§ 13
Ermächtigung zum Erlass von Rechtsverordnungen

Die Bundesregierung wird ermächtigt, durch Rechtsverordnung Vorschriften über das Verfahren für die Wahl und die Abberufung von Aufsichtsratsmitgliedern der Arbeitnehmer zu erlassen, insbesondere über

1. die Vorbereitung der Wahl, insbesondere die Aufstellung der Wählerlisten und die Errechnung der Zahl der Aufsichtsratsmitglieder der Arbeitnehmer;
2. die Frist für die Einsichtnahme in die Wählerlisten und die Erhebung von Einsprüchen gegen sie;
3. die Wahlvorschläge und die Frist für ihre Einreichung;
4. das Wahlausschreiben und die Frist für seine Bekanntmachung;
5. die Teilnahme von Arbeitnehmern eines in § 3 Abs. 3 bezeichneten Betriebs an der Wahl;
6. die Stimmabgabe;
7. die Feststellung des Wahlergebnisses und die Fristen für seine Bekanntmachung;
8. die Anfechtung der Wahl;
9. die Aufbewahrung der Wahlakten.

§ 14
Verweisungen

Soweit in anderen Gesetzen auf Vorschriften verwiesen wird, die durch Artikel 6 Abs. 2 des Zweiten Gesetzes zur Vereinfachung der Wahl der Arbeitnehmervertreter in den Aufsichtsrat aufgehoben werden, treten an ihre Stelle die entsprechenden Vorschriften dieses Gesetzes.

Part 3
Transitional and Final Provisions

Section 13
Empowerment to Issue Ordinances

The Federal Government shall be empowered to issue ordinances containing provisions on the procedure for the election and dismissal of employee supervisory board members, in particular regarding

1. the preparations for the election, in particular drawing up the list of voters and calculating the number of employee supervisory board members;
2. the time period for inspecting the voter lists and the raising of objections to them;
3. the nominations for election and the deadline for submitting them;
4. the calling of the election and the deadline for announcing it;
5. the participation in the election by employees of an establishment described in section 3 (3);
6. the casting of votes;
7. the determination of the results of the voting and deadline for announcing them;
8. the filing of an action to set aside the election;
9. the preservation of the election files.

Section 14
References

Where reference is made in other statutes to provisions which were repealed by Article 6 (2) of the Second Act for the Simplification of the Election of the Employee Representatives in the supervisory board (*Zweites Gesetz zur Vereinfachung der Wahl der Arbeitnehmervertreter in den Aufsichtsrat*), they shall be replaced by the respective provisions of this Act.

§ 15
Übergangsregelung

Auf Wahlen oder Abberufungen, die vor dem 1. Juli 2004 eingeleitet worden sind, ist das Betriebsverfassungsgesetz 1952 in der im Bundesgesetzblatt Teil III, Gliederungsnummer 801–1, veröffentlichten bereinigten Fassung, zuletzt geändert durch Artikel 9 des Gesetzes vom 23. Juli 2001 (BGBl. I S. 1852), auch nach seinem Außerkrafttreten anzuwenden.

Section 15
Transitional Provisions

Elections or dismissals which were initiated prior to 1 July 2004 shall be governed by the Works Constitution Act 1952 in the revised version published in the Federal Law Gazette Part III, Classification Number 801–1, most recently amended by Article 9 of the Act of 23 July 2001 (Federal Law Gazette I p. 1852), even once it has expired.

XIV. Hours of Employment Act (Arbeitszeitgesetz – ArbZG)

of 6 June 1994 (Federal Law Gazette I p. 1170)

in the amended version of 15 July 2009

Erster Abschnitt
Allgemeine Vorschriften

Chapter 1
General Provisions

§ 1
Zweck des Gesetzes

Section 1
Purpose of the Act

Zweck des Gesetzes ist es,

1. die Sicherheit und den Gesundheitsschutz der Arbeitnehmer bei der Arbeitszeitgestaltung zu gewährleisten und die Rahmenbedingungen für flexible Arbeitszeiten zu verbessern sowie
2. den Sonntag und die staatlich anerkannten Feiertage als Tage der Arbeitsruhe und der seelischen Erhebung der Arbeitnehmer zu schützen.

The purpose of the Act is:

1. to ensure the safety and protection of the health of the employees in the establishment of work shifts and to improve the general conditions for creating flexible work shifts, as well as
2. to preserve Sundays and legal holidays as days of rest and edification for the employees.

§ 2
Begriffsbestimmungen

Section 2
Definition of Terms

(1) [1]Arbeitszeit im Sinne dieses Gesetzes ist die Zeit vom Beginn bis zum Ende der Arbeit ohne die Ruhepausen; Arbeitszeiten bei mehreren Arbeitgebern sind zusammenzurechnen. [2]Im Bergbau unter Tage zählen die Ruhepausen zur Arbeitszeit.

(1) [1]Hours of employment (work shifts) within the meaning of this Act shall be defined as the time from the beginning to the end of the work shift minus breaks; work shifts for multiple employers are to be added together. [2]For underground mining, the breaks shall be included as part of the work shift.

(2) Arbeitnehmer im Sinne dieses Gesetzes sind Arbeiter und Angestellte sowie die zu ihrer Berufsbildung Beschäftigten.

(2) Employees within the meaning of this Act are wage earners and salaried employees as well as trainees and apprentices.

(3) Nachtzeit im Sinne dieses Gesetzes ist die Zeit von 23 bis 6 Uhr, in Bäckereien und Konditoreien die Zeit von 22 bis 5 Uhr.

(3) Nighttime, within the meaning of this Act, is the time between 11:00 p.m. and 6:00 a.m., and in bakeries and pastry shops, the time between 10:00 p.m. and 5:00 a.m.

(4) Nachtarbeit im Sinne dieses Gesetzes ist jede Arbeit, die mehr als zwei Stunden der Nachtzeit umfasst.

(5) Nachtarbeitnehmer im Sinne dieses Gesetzes sind Arbeitnehmer, die
1. auf Grund ihrer Arbeitszeitgestaltung normalerweise Nachtarbeit in Wechselschicht zu leisten haben oder
2. Nachtarbeit an mindestens 48 Tagen im Kalenderjahr leisten.

**Zweiter Abschnitt
Werktägliche Arbeitszeit
und arbeitsfreie Zeiten**

**§ 3
Arbeitszeit der Arbeitnehmer**

¹Die werktägliche Arbeitszeit der Arbeitnehmer darf acht Stunden nicht überschreiten. ²Sie kann auf bis zu zehn Stunden nur verlängert werden, wenn innerhalb von sechs Kalendermonaten oder innerhalb von 24 Wochen im Durchschnitt acht Stunden werktäglich nicht überschritten werden.

**§ 4
Ruhepausen**

¹Die Arbeit ist durch im voraus feststehende Ruhepausen von mindestens 30 Minuten bei einer Arbeitszeit von mehr als sechs bis zu neun Stunden und 45 Minuten bei einer Arbeitszeit von mehr als neun Stunden insgesamt zu unterbrechen. ²Die Ruhepausen nach Satz 1 können in Zeitabschnitte von jeweils mindestens 15 Minuten aufgeteilt werden. ³Länger als sechs Stunden hintereinander dürfen Arbeitnehmer nicht ohne Ruhepause beschäftigt werden.

**§ 5
Ruhezeit**

(1) Die Arbeitnehmer müssen nach Beendigung der täglichen Arbeitszeit eine ununterbrochene Ruhezeit von mindestens elf Stunden haben.

(4) Night shift, within the meaning of this Act, is all work which is conducted during more than two hours of nighttime.

(5) Night shift workers within the meaning of this Act are employees who
1. due to their work shifts must normally work nights in rotating shifts, or
2. work night shifts at least 48 days in the calendar year.

**Chapter 2
Work Shifts on Working Days
and Breaks**

**Section 3
Work Shifts of the Employees**

¹The work shifts of the employees on working days may not exceed eight hours. ²They may be extended to ten hours only if the average shift within six calendar months or twenty-four weeks does not exceed eight hours per working day.

**Section 4
Breaks**

¹The work shall be interrupted by previously set breaks of at least 30 minutes for a shift of more than six and up to nine hours, and 45 minutes for a shift of over nine hours in all. ²The breaks pursuant to sentence 1 may be split up into units of at least 15 minutes each. ³Employees may not work more than six hours at a stretch without a break.

**Section 5
Periods of Rest**

(1) After completion of their work shift, the employees must have an uninterrupted rest period of at least eleven hours.

(2) Die Dauer der Ruhezeit des Absatzes 1 kann in Krankenhäusern und anderen Einrichtungen zur Behandlung, Pflege und Betreuung von Personen, in Gaststätten und anderen Einrichtungen zur Bewirtung und Beherbergung, in Verkehrsbetrieben, beim Rundfunk sowie in der Landwirtschaft und in der Tierhaltung um bis zu eine Stunde verkürzt werden, wenn jede Verkürzung der Ruhezeit innerhalb eines Kalendermonats oder innerhalb von vier Wochen durch Verlängerung einer anderen Ruhezeit auf mindestens zwölf Stunden ausgeglichen wird.

(3) Abweichend von Absatz 1 können in Krankenhäusern und anderen Einrichtungen zur Behandlung, Pflege und Betreuung von Personen Kürzungen der Ruhezeit durch Inanspruchnahme während der Rufbereitschaft, die nicht mehr als die Hälfte der Ruhezeit betragen, zu anderen Zeiten ausgeglichen werden.

§ 6
Nacht- und Schichtarbeit

(1) Die Arbeitszeit der Nacht- und Schichtarbeitnehmer ist nach den gesicherten arbeitswissenschaftlichen Erkenntnissen über die menschengerechte Gestaltung der Arbeit festzulegen.

(2) [1] Die werktägliche Arbeitszeit der Nachtarbeitnehmer darf acht Stunden nicht überschreiten. [2] Sie kann auf bis zu zehn Stunden nur verlängert werden, wenn abweichend von § 3 innerhalb von einem Kalendermonat oder innerhalb von vier Wochen im Durchschnitt acht Stunden werktäglich nicht überschritten werden. [3] Für Zeiträume, in denen Nachtarbeitnehmer im Sinne des § 2 Abs. 5 Nr. 2 nicht zur Nachtarbeit herangezogen werden, findet § 3 Satz 2 Anwendung.

(3) [1] Nachtarbeitnehmer sind berechtigt, sich vor Beginn der Beschäftigung und danach in regelmäßigen Zeitabständen

(2) For employees of hospitals and other institutions devoted to the treatment, nursing and care of persons, restaurants and other establishments for the provision of food and lodging, in public transport enterprises, in radio or in the area of agriculture and livestock, the duration of the rest period set forth in subsection (1) may be decreased by up to one hour, provided that each decrease in the rest period is compensated for within one calendar month, or four weeks, by the extension of another period of rest to at least twelve hours.

(3) Notwithstanding subsection (1), in hospitals and other institutions devoted to the treatment, nursing and care of persons, a shortening of the rest period due to a call to duty during on-call service, which does not amount to more than half of the period of rest, may be compensated for at other times.

Section 6
Night Shifts and Rotating Shifts

(1) The work shifts of those working nights and on rotating shifts shall be established in compliance with confirmed ergonomic findings with regard to the humane scheduling of work shifts.

(2) [1] Night shifts on working days may not exceed eight hours. [2] They may only be extended to ten hours if, notwithstanding section 3, the average shift within one calendar month or four weeks does not exceed eight hours on working days. [3] For those periods of time in which night shift workers within the meaning of section 2 (5) no. 2 are not called upon to perform night shifts, section 3 sentence 2 shall apply.

(3) [1] Night shift workers shall be entitled to medical examinations prior to beginning their employment and thereaf-

von nicht weniger als drei Jahren arbeitsmedizinisch untersuchen zu lassen. ²Nach Vollendung des 50. Lebensjahres steht Nachtarbeitnehmern dieses Recht in Zeitabständen von einem Jahr zu. ³Die Kosten der Untersuchungen hat der Arbeitgeber zu tragen, sofern er die Untersuchungen den Nachtarbeitnehmern nicht kostenlos durch einen Betriebsarzt oder einen überbetrieblichen Dienst von Betriebsärzten anbietet.

(4) ¹Der Arbeitgeber hat den Nachtarbeitnehmer auf dessen Verlangen auf einen für ihn geeigneten Tagesarbeitsplatz umzusetzen, wenn

a) nach arbeitsmedizinischer Feststellung die weitere Verrichtung von Nachtarbeit den Arbeitnehmer in seiner Gesundheit gefährdet oder
b) im Haushalt des Arbeitnehmers ein Kind unter zwölf Jahren lebt, das nicht von einer anderen im Haushalt lebenden Person betreut werden kann, oder
c) der Arbeitnehmer einen schwerpflegebedürftigen Angehörigen zu versorgen hat, der nicht von einem anderen im Haushalt lebenden Angehörigen versorgt werden kann,

sofern dem nicht dringende betriebliche Erfordernisse entgegenstehen. ²Stehen der Umsetzung des Nachtarbeitnehmers auf einen für ihn geeigneten Tagesarbeitsplatz nach Auffassung des Arbeitgebers dringende betriebliche Erfordernisse entgegen, so ist der Betriebs- oder Personalrat zu hören. ³Der Betriebs- oder Personalrat kann dem Arbeitgeber Vorschläge für eine Umsetzung unterbreiten.

(5) Soweit keine tarifvertraglichen Ausgleichsregelungen bestehen, hat der Arbeitgeber dem Nachtarbeitnehmer für die während der Nachtzeit geleisteten Arbeitsstunden eine angemessene Zahl bezahlter freier Tage oder einen angemessenen Zuschlag auf das ihm hierfür zustehende Bruttoarbeitsentgelt zu gewähren.

ter in regular intervals of no less than three years. ²Upon turning 51 years of age, night shift workers shall be entitled to such examinations on an annual basis. ³The costs of the examinations shall be borne by the employer if he does not offer night shift workers such examinations through a company doctor or through a service of company doctor for several establishments.

(4) ¹The employer shall transfer a night shift worker to a suitable day shift position at his request if:

a) a medical examination has shown that further night work would endanger the health of the employee; or
b) the employee has a child in his home under twelve years of age who cannot be cared for by another member of his household; or
c) the employee must care for a person in need of constant nursing care who cannot be cared for by another member of his household,

as long as this does not conflict with urgent operating needs. ²If, in the opinion of the employer, such needs are in opposition to transferring the night shift worker to a day shift position suitable for him, the works council or staff council must hold a hearing. ³The works council or staff council may make suggestions to the employer for a transfer.

(5) Insofar as no compensatory provisions exist in a collective agreement, the employer must guarantee the night shift worker a reasonable number of paid days off for the hours worked on night shift or a reasonable bonus in addition to his wages.

(6) Es ist sicherzustellen, dass Nachtarbeitnehmer den gleichen Zugang zur betrieblichen Weiterbildung und zu aufstiegsfördernden Maßnahmen haben wie die übrigen Arbeitnehmer.

§ 7
Abweichende Regelungen

(1) In einem Tarifvertrag oder auf Grund eines Tarifvertrags in einer Betriebs- oder Dienstvereinbarung kann zugelassen werden,
1. abweichend von § 3
   a) die Arbeitszeit über zehn Stunden werktäglich zu verlängern, wenn in die Arbeitszeit regelmäßig und in erheblichem Umfang Arbeitsbereitschaft oder Bereitschaftsdienst fällt,
   b) einen anderen Ausgleichszeitraum festzulegen,
2. abweichend von § 4 Satz 2 die Gesamtdauer der Ruhepausen in Schichtbetrieben und Verkehrsbetrieben auf Kurzpausen von angemessener Dauer aufzuteilen,
3. abweichend von § 5 Abs. 1 die Ruhezeit um bis zu zwei Stunden zu kürzen, wenn die Art der Arbeit dies erfordert und die Kürzung der Ruhezeit innerhalb eines festzulegenden Ausgleichszeitraums ausgeglichen wird,
4. abweichend von § 6 Abs. 2
   a) die Arbeitszeit über zehn Stunden werktäglich hinaus zu verlängern, wenn in die Arbeitszeit regelmäßig und in erheblichem Umfang Arbeitsbereitschaft oder Bereitschaftsdienst fällt,
   b) einen anderen Ausgleichszeitraum festzulegen,
5. den Beginn des siebenstündigen Nachtzeitraums des § 2 Abs. 3 auf die Zeit zwischen 22 und 24 Uhr festzulegen.

(2) Sofern der Gesundheitsschutz der Arbeitnehmer durch einen entsprechenden Zeitausgleich gewährleistet wird, kann in einem Tarifvertrag oder

(6) It must be ensured that night shift workers have the same access as the other employees to further training in the establishment and to measures aiding their opportunities for advancement.

Section 7
Deviating Provisions

(1) In a collective agreement or a works or service agreement based upon a collective agreement, the following may be permitted:
1. in deviation from section 3
   a) to extend the work shift to over ten hours on working days if there is a substantial amount of stand-by or emergency service work on a regular basis,
   b) to alter the period for which the compensation is to be rendered;
2. in deviation from section 4 sentence 2, to divide the total duration of rest breaks in plants with rotating shifts and public transport enterprises into shorter breaks of a reasonable length;
3. in deviation from section 5 (1), to shorten the rest breaks by up to two hours, provided that this is required by the type of work performed and the reduction of the break time is compensated for within a deadline to be determined;
4. in deviation from section 6 (2)
   a) to extend the work shift to over ten hours on working days if a substantial amount of stand-by or emergency service work exists on a regular basis,
   b) to alter the period for which the compensation is to be rendered;
5. to set the commencement of the seven-hour night period set forth in section 2 (3) as the time between 10:00 p.m. and midnight.

(2) Insofar as the protection of the health of the employees is safeguarded by virtue of a corresponding compensation in time, a collective agreement or a

auf Grund eines Tarifvertrags in einer Betriebs- oder Dienstvereinbarung ferner zugelassen werden,

1. abweichend von § 5 Abs. 1 die Ruhezeiten bei Rufbereitschaft den Besonderheiten dieses Dienstes anzupassen, insbesondere Kürzungen der Ruhezeit infolge von Inanspruchnahmen während dieses Dienstes zu anderen Zeiten auszugleichen,

2. die Regelungen der §§ 3, 5 Abs. 1 und § 6 Abs. 2 in der Landwirtschaft der Bestellungs- und Erntezeit sowie den Witterungseinflüssen anzupassen,

3. die Regelungen der §§ 3, 4, 5 Abs. 1 und § 6 Abs. 2 bei der Behandlung, Pflege und Betreuung von Personen der Eigenart dieser Tätigkeit und dem Wohl dieser Personen entsprechend anzupassen,

4. die Regelungen der §§ 3, 4, 5 Abs. 1 und § 6 Abs. 2 bei Verwaltungen und Betrieben des Bundes, der Länder, der Gemeinden und sonstigen Körperschaften, Anstalten und Stiftungen des öffentlichen Rechts sowie bei anderen Arbeitgebern, die der Tarifbindung eines für den öffentlichen Dienst geltenden oder eines im wesentlichen inhaltsgleichen Tarifvertrags unterliegen, der Eigenart der Tätigkeit bei diesen Stellen anzupassen.

(2a) In einem Tarifvertrag oder auf Grund eines Tarifvertrags in einer Betriebs- oder Dienstvereinbarung kann abweichend von den §§ 3, 5 Abs. 1 und § 6 Abs. 2 zugelassen werden, die werktägliche Arbeitszeit auch ohne Ausgleich über acht Stunden zu verlängern, wenn in die Arbeitszeit regelmäßig und in erheblichem Umfang Arbeitsbereitschaft oder Bereitschaftsdienst fällt und durch besondere Regelungen sichergestellt wird, dass die Gesundheit der Arbeitnehmer nicht gefährdet wird.

works or service agreement on the basis of a collective agreement may further permit the following:

1. in deviation from section 5 (1), to adjust the break times of employees on on-call service to suit the particularities of such service, in particular to compensate for reductions of break times resulting from being called to duty at other times during this service;

2. in the case of agricultural workers, to adjust the provisions of sections 3, 5 (1) and section 6 (2) to take planting and harvesting times into account as well as weather conditions;

3. in the case of workers employed in the treatment, nursing and care of persons, to adjust the provisions of sections 3, 4, 5 (1) and section 6 (2) to take the particularities of these activities and the well-being of the persons being treated into account;

4. in the case of employees involved in the administration and management of the national, state, community governments or other governmental bodies, institutions and foundations as well as those employed by other employers who are subject to the obligations of a collective agreement valid for workers in public service or one which is essentially identical in content, to adjust the provisions of sections 3, 4, 5 (1) and section 6 (2) to take the particularities of the activities of these posts into account.

(2a) Notwithstanding sections 3, 4, 5 (1) and section 6 (2), a collective agreement or a works agreement or a service agreement in the public sector on the basis of a collective agreement, may permit the work shifts on working days to be extended over eight hours, even without compensation, if a substantial amount of stand-by or emergency service work time exists on a regular basis, and it is ensured through special regulations that the health of the employees is not jeopardized.

(3) ¹Im Geltungsbereich eines Tarifvertrags nach Absatz 1, 2 oder 2a können abweichende tarifvertragliche Regelungen im Betrieb eines nicht tarifgebundenen Arbeitgebers durch Betriebs- oder Dienstvereinbarung oder, wenn ein Betriebs- oder Personalrat nicht besteht, durch schriftliche Vereinbarung zwischen dem Arbeitgeber und dem Arbeitnehmer übernommen werden. ²Können auf Grund eines solchen Tarifvertrags abweichende Regelungen in einer Betriebs- oder Dienstvereinbarung getroffen werden, kann auch in Betrieben eines nicht tarifgebundenen Arbeitgebers davon Gebrauch gemacht werden. ³Eine nach Absatz 2 Nr. 4 getroffene abweichende tarifvertragliche Regelung hat zwischen nicht tarifgebundenen Arbeitgebern und Arbeitnehmern Geltung, wenn zwischen ihnen die Anwendung der für den öffentlichen Dienst geltenden tarifvertraglichen Bestimmungen vereinbart ist und die Arbeitgeber die Kosten des Betriebs überwiegend mit Zuwendungen im Sinne des Haushaltsrechts decken.

(3) ¹Where a collective agreement applies pursuant to subsection (1) or (2), deviating contractual provisions in the establishment of an employer not bound by the contract may be adopted by virtue of a works or service agreement, or, if there is no works or personnel council, by virtue of a written agreement between the employer and the employee. ²If, due to such a collective agreement, deviating provisions are made in a works or service agreement, these provisions may also be utilized in the establishment of an employer not bound by the contract. ³A deviating provision in the collective agreement made pursuant to subsection (2) no. 4 above is valid between employers and employees not bound by the collective bargaining agreement, providing that they have agreed to the application of those collective agreement provisions which apply to those engaged in public service, and the employers cover the costs of the establishment primarily with subsidies within the meaning of budgetary law.

(4) Die Kirchen und die öffentlich-rechtlichen Religionsgesellschaften können die in Absatz 1, 2 oder 2a genannten Abweichungen in ihren Regelungen vorsehen.

(4) Churches and public law religious societies may incorporate the deviations set forth in subsection (1) or (2) into their regulations.

(5) In einem Bereich, in dem Regelungen durch Tarifvertrag üblicherweise nicht getroffen werden, können Ausnahmen im Rahmen des Absatzes 1, 2 oder 2a durch die Aufsichtsbehörde bewilligt werden, wenn dies aus betrieblichen Gründen erforderlich ist und die Gesundheit der Arbeitnehmer nicht gefährdet wird.

(5) In an area where provisions are generally not contained by collective agreements, exceptions within the framework of subsection (1), (2) or (2a) may be approved by the supervisory authority if this is necessary for operational reasons and does not endanger the health of the employees.

(6) Die Bundesregierung kann durch Rechtsverordnung mit Zustimmung des Bundesrates Ausnahmen im Rahmen des Absatzes 1 oder 2 zulassen, sofern dies aus betrieblichen Gründen erforderlich ist und die Gesundheit der Arbeitnehmer nicht gefährdet wird.

(6) The Federal Government may pass a regulation with approval from the Upper House of Parliament *(Bundesrat)* permitting exceptions within the framework of subsection (1) or (2) insofar as this is necessary for operational reasons and it does not endanger the health of the employees.

(7) ¹Auf Grund einer Regelung nach Absatz 2a oder den Absätzen 3 bis 5 jeweils in Verbindung mit Absatz 2a darf die Arbeitszeit nur verlängert werden, wenn der Arbeitnehmer schriftlich eingewilligt hat. ²Der Arbeitnehmer kann die Einwilligung mit einer Frist von sechs Monaten schriftlich widerrufen. ³Der Arbeitgeber darf einen Arbeitnehmer nicht benachteiligen, weil dieser die Einwilligung zur Verlängerung der Arbeitszeit nicht erklärt oder die Einwilligung widerrufen hat.

(8) ¹Werden Regelungen nach Absatz 1 Nr. 1 und 4, Absatz 2 Nr. 2 bis 4 oder solche Regelungen auf Grund der Absätze 3 und 4 zugelassen, darf die Arbeitszeit 48 Stunden wöchentlich im Durchschnitt von zwölf Kalendermonaten nicht überschreiten. ²Erfolgt die Zulassung auf Grund des Absatzes 5, darf die Arbeitszeit 48 Stunden wöchentlich im Durchschnitt von sechs Kalendermonaten oder 24 Wochen nicht überschreiten.

(9) Wird die werktägliche Arbeitszeit über zwölf Stunden hinaus verlängert, muss im unmittelbaren Anschluss an die Beendigung der Arbeitszeit eine Ruhezeit von mindestens elf Stunden gewährt werden.

(7) ¹The work shifts may only be extended on the basis of a provision in subsection (2a) or subsections (3) to (5) each in connection with subsection (2a) with the written consent of the employee. ²The employee may revoke such consent in writing with six months' advance notice. ³The employer may not disadvantage an employee for refusing to declare or revoking his consent.

(8) ¹If regulations are permitted pursuant to subsection (1) nos. 1 and 4, subsection (2) nos. 2 to 4 or on the basis of subsections (3) and (4), the work shifts may not exceed an average of 48 hours per week in twelve calendar months. ²If the permission derives from subsection (5), the work shift may not exceed an average 48 hours within a six calendar months or 24 weeks.

(9) If the work shift on working days is extended beyond twelve hours, then immediately after the end of the shift, a rest period of at least eleven hours must be granted.

§ 8
Gefährliche Arbeiten

¹Die Bundesregierung kann durch Rechtsverordnung mit Zustimmung des Bundesrates für einzelne Beschäftigungsbereiche, für bestimmte Arbeiten oder für bestimmte Arbeitnehmergruppen, bei denen besondere Gefahren für die Gesundheit der Arbeitnehmer zu erwarten sind, die Arbeitszeit über § 3 hinaus beschränken, die Ruhepausen und Ruhezeiten über die §§ 4 und 5 hinaus ausdehnen, die Regelungen zum Schutz der Nacht- und Schichtarbeitnehmer in § 6 erweitern und die Abweichungsmöglichkeiten nach § 7 beschränken, soweit dies zum Schutz der Gesundheit der Arbeitneh-

Section 8
Dangerous Work

¹In the case of individual sectors, certain occupations or certain groups of employees where particular danger to the health of the employees is to be expected, the Federal Government may pass a regulation with the ratification of the Upper House of Parliament (*Bundesrat*) limiting the working time beyond section 3, extending the breaks and time off beyond sections 4 and 5, expanding the provisions governing the protection of night shift and shift workers beyond section 6 and limiting the possibilities for deviating from such rules pursuant to section 7, insofar as this is necessary for the safeguarding of

mer erforderlich ist. ²Satz 1 gilt nicht für Beschäftigungsbereiche und Arbeiten in Betrieben, die der Bergaufsicht unterliegen.

the health of the employees. ²Sentence 1 does not apply to sectors and jobs in establishments subject to the supervision of the mining authorities.

Dritter Abschnitt
Sonn- und Feiertagsruhe

Chapter 3
Sunday and Holiday Rest Periods

§ 9
Sonn- und Feiertagsruhe

Section 9
Sunday and Holiday Rest Periods

(1) Arbeitnehmer dürfen an Sonn- und gesetzlichen Feiertagen von 0 bis 24 Uhr nicht beschäftigt werden.

(1) Employees may not be scheduled to work on Sundays and holidays between midnight and midnight.

(2) In mehrschichtigen Betrieben mit regelmäßiger Tag- und Nachtschicht kann Beginn oder Ende der Sonn- und Feiertagsruhe um bis zu sechs Stunden vor- oder zurückverlegt werden, wenn für die auf den Beginn der Ruhezeit folgenden 24 Stunden der Betrieb ruht.

(2) In establishments with multiple shifts and regular day and night shifts, the beginning or the end of the Sunday and holiday days off may be put forward or back by up to six hours if the establishment will then be inactive for the 24 hours following the beginning of this period.

(3) Für Kraftfahrer und Beifahrer kann der Beginn der 24stündigen Sonn- und Feiertagsruhe um bis zu zwei Stunden vorverlegt werden.

(3) In the case of truck drivers and co-drivers, the beginning of the 24-hour Sunday and holiday days off may be put forward by up to two hours.

§ 10
Sonn- und Feiertagsbeschäftigung

Section 10
Sunday and Holiday Work

(1) Sofern die Arbeiten nicht an Werktagen vorgenommen werden können, dürfen Arbeitnehmer an Sonn- und Feiertagen abweichend von § 9 beschäftigt werden

(1) Where the work cannot be performed on working days, the employers may, notwithstanding section 9, assign employees shifts on Sundays and holidays under the following circumstances:

1. in Not- und Rettungsdiensten sowie bei der Feuerwehr,

2. zur Aufrechterhaltung der öffentlichen Sicherheit und Ordnung sowie der Funktionsfähigkeit von Gerichten und Behörden und für Zwecke der Verteidigung,

3. in Krankenhäusern und anderen Einrichtungen zur Behandlung, Pflege und Betreuung von Personen,

1. for workers in emergency and rescue services as well as the Fire Department;

2. to maintain public safety and order as well as for the function of courts and governmental agencies and for purposes of defense;

3. in hospitals and other institutions devoted to the treatment, nursing and care of persons;

4. in Gaststätten und anderen Einrichtungen zur Bewirtung und Beherbergung sowie im Haushalt,	4. in restaurants and other establishments for the provision of food and lodging as well as in households;
5. bei Musikaufführungen, Theatervorstellungen, Filmvorführungen, Schaustellungen, Darbietungen und anderen ähnlichen Veranstaltungen,	5. for musical and theatrical performances, film showings, exhibitions, performances and other similar programs;
6. bei nichtgewerblichen Aktionen und Veranstaltungen der Kirchen, Religionsgesellschaften, Verbände, Vereine, Parteien und anderer ähnlicher Vereinigungen,	6. for non-commercial events and programs held by churches, religious societies, associations, clubs, political parties and other similar organizations;
7. beim Sport und in Freizeit-, Erholungs- und Vergnügungseinrichtungen, beim Fremdenverkehr sowie in Museen und wissenschaftlichen Präsenzbibliotheken,	7. for sports events and in leisure, recreational and amusement establishments, tourist offices as well as museums and scientific reference libraries;
8. beim Rundfunk, bei der Tages- und Sportpresse, bei Nachrichtenagenturen sowie bei den der Tagesaktualität dienenden Tätigkeiten für andere Presseerzeugnisse einschließlich des Austragens, bei der Herstellung von Satz, Filmen und Druckformen für tagesaktuelle Nachrichten und Bilder, bei tagesaktuellen Aufnahmen auf Ton- und Bildträger sowie beim Transport und Kommissionieren von Presseerzeugnissen, deren Ersterscheinungstag am Montag oder am Tag nach einem Feiertag liegt,	8. for workers in radio, daily and sports newspapers, wire services as well as activities involved in the timely preparation of other press media including delivery, typesetting, producing film and printing forms for current news and pictures, for sound and image recording as well as the transport and commissioning of news products which are to appear on Monday or the day after a holiday;
9. bei Messen, Ausstellungen und Märkten im Sinne des Titels IV der Gewerbeordnung sowie bei Volksfesten,	9. for trade fairs, exhibits and markets within the meaning of Title IV of the Trade Code *(Gewerbeordnung)* as well as for public celebrations *(Volksfeste)*;
10. in Verkehrsbetrieben sowie beim Transport und Kommissionieren von leichtverderblichen Waren im Sinne des § 30 Abs. 3 Nr. 2 der Straßenverkehrsordnung,	10. in public transport works as well as for the transport and commissioning of perishable goods within the meaning of section 30 (3) no. 2 of the Traffic Code (Straßenverkehrsordnung);
11. in den Energie- und Wasserversorgungsbetrieben sowie in Abfall- und Abwasserentsorgungsbetrieben,	11. in the energy and water supply works as well as in waste and sewage disposal works;
12. in der Landwirtschaft und in der Tierhaltung sowie in Einrichtungen zur Behandlung und Pflege von Tieren,	12. in agriculture and livestock businesses as well as in establishments for the treatment and care of animals;

13. im Bewachungsgewerbe und bei der Bewachung von Betriebsanlagen,
14. bei der Reinigung und Instandhaltung von Betriebseinrichtungen, soweit hierdurch der regelmäßige Fortgang des eigenen oder eines fremden Betriebs bedingt ist, bei der Vorbereitung der Wiederaufnahme des vollen werktägigen Betriebs sowie bei der Aufrechterhaltung der Funktionsfähigkeit von Datennetzen und Rechnersystemen,
15. zur Verhütung des Verderbens von Naturerzeugnissen oder Rohstoffen oder des Misslingens von Arbeitsergebnissen sowie bei kontinuierlich durchzuführenden Forschungsarbeiten,
16. zur Vermeidung einer Zerstörung oder erheblichen Beschädigung der Produktionseinrichtungen.

(2) Abweichend von § 9 dürfen Arbeitnehmer an Sonn- und Feiertagen mit den Produktionsarbeiten beschäftigt werden, wenn die infolge der Unterbrechung der Produktion nach Absatz 1 Nr. 14 zulässigen Arbeiten den Einsatz von mehr Arbeitnehmern als bei durchgehender Produktion erfordern.

(3) Abweichend von § 9 dürfen Arbeitnehmer an Sonn- und Feiertagen in Bäckereien und Konditoreien für bis zu drei Stunden mit der Herstellung und dem Austragen oder Ausfahren von Konditorwaren und an diesem Tag zum Verkauf kommenden Bäckerwaren beschäftigt werden.

(4) Sofern die Arbeiten nicht an Werktagen vorgenommen werden können, dürfen Arbeitnehmer zur Durchführung des Eil- und Großbetragszahlungsverkehrs und des Geld-, Devisen-, Wertpapier- und Derivatehandels abweichend von § 9 Abs. 1 an den auf einen Werktag fallenden Feiertagen beschäftigt werden, die nicht in allen Mitgliedstaaten der Europäischen Union Feiertage sind.

13. in security services and while guarding industrial plants;
14. during the cleaning and maintaining of plant equipment insofar as the regular continuation of the employer's own operation or that of another is dependent upon this, during preparations for the resumption of the full workday operations as well as in maintaining the functionality of data networks and computer systems;
15. for the prevention of spoilage of natural products or raw materials or the prevention of factors which may seriously impede production, as well as during research which must be conducted on a continuous basis;
16. to avoid the destruction or severe damaging of manufacturing equipment.

(2) Notwithstanding section 9, employees may be put to work on production on Sundays and holidays provided that the work permitted due to the interruption of production pursuant to subsection (1) no. 14 requires a greater number of employees than would be needed for ongoing production.

(3) Notwithstanding section 9, employees may be put to work on the production and delivery of confectioneries and bakery products for sale on the day in bakeries and confectioneries on Sundays and on holidays for up to three hours.

(4) Notwithstanding section 9 (1), to the extent the work cannot be carried forward to working days, employees may be put to work on the transaction of urgent and large sum payments and of money, foreign currency, share and derivative dealings on holidays that fall on working days but which are not holidays in all member states of the European Union.

§ 11
Ausgleich für Sonn- und Feiertagsbeschäftigung

(1) Mindestens 15 Sonntage im Jahr müssen beschäftigungsfrei bleiben.

(2) Für die Beschäftigung an Sonn- und Feiertagen gelten die §§ 3 bis 8 entsprechend, jedoch dürfen durch die Arbeitszeit an Sonn- und Feiertagen die in den §§ 3, 6 Abs. 2, §§ 7 und 21a Abs. 4 bestimmten Höchstarbeitszeiten und Ausgleichszeiträume nicht überschritten werden.

(3) [1]Werden Arbeitnehmer an einem Sonntag beschäftigt, müssen sie einen Ersatzruhetag haben, der innerhalb eines den Beschäftigungstag einschließenden Zeitraums von zwei Wochen zu gewähren ist. [2]Werden Arbeitnehmer an einem auf einen Werktag fallenden Feiertag beschäftigt, müssen sie einen Ersatzruhetag haben, der innerhalb eines den Beschäftigungstag einschließenden Zeitraums von acht Wochen zu gewähren ist.

(4) Die Sonn- oder Feiertagsruhe des § 9 oder der Ersatzruhetag des Absatzes 3 ist den Arbeitnehmern unmittelbar in Verbindung mit einer Ruhezeit nach § 5 zu gewähren, soweit dem technische oder arbeitsorganisatorische Gründe nicht entgegenstehen.

§ 12
Abweichende Regelungen

[1]In einem Tarifvertrag oder auf Grund eines Tarifvertrags in einer Betriebs- oder Dienstvereinbarung kann zugelassen werden,

1. abweichend von § 11 Abs. 1 die Anzahl der beschäftigungsfreien Sonntage in den Einrichtungen des § 10 Abs. 1 Nr. 2, 3, 4 und 10 auf mindestens zehn Sonntage, im Rundfunk, in Theaterbetrieben, Orchestern sowie

Section 11
Compensation for Sunday and Holiday Work

(1) At least fifteen Sundays per year must be without work.

(2) For Sunday and holiday work, sections 3 to 8 apply accordingly, however the amount of time worked on Sundays and holidays may not exceed the maximum working times and deadlines for compensation set forth in sections 3, 6 (2), sections 7 and 21a (4).

(3) [1]Should employees be assigned Sunday work, they must be granted a substitute day off, which shall fall within a two week period encompassing the Sunday worked. [2]Should employees be assigned work on a holiday which falls on a working day, they shall be granted a substitute day off, which shall fall within an eight-week period encompassing the holiday worked.

(4) The Sunday and holiday day of rest pursuant to section 9, or the substitute day off pursuant to subsection (3), shall be granted to the employee in direct connection to a time of rest pursuant to section 5, insofar as there are no technical or organizational reasons opposing this.

Section 12
Deviating Provisions

[1]The following may be permitted in a collective bargaining agreement or a works or service agreement in the public sector based upon a collective bargaining agreement:

1. in deviation from section 11 (1), to reduce the number of Sundays on which may not be worked in those establishments, as set forth in section 10 (1) nos. 2, 3, 4 and 10, to at least ten Sundays; in radio, theatre

bei Schaustellungen auf mindestens acht Sonntage, in Filmtheatern und in der Tierhaltung auf mindestens sechs Sonntage im Jahr zu verringern,
2. abweichend von § 11 Abs. 3 den Wegfall von Ersatzruhetagen für auf Werktage fallende Feiertage zu vereinbaren oder Arbeitnehmer innerhalb eines festzulegenden Ausgleichszeitraums beschäftigungsfrei zu stellen,
3. abweichend von § 11 Abs. 1 bis 3 in der Seeschiffahrt die den Arbeitnehmern nach diesen Vorschriften zustehenden freien Tage zusammenhängend zu geben,
4. abweichend von § 11 Abs. 2 die Arbeitszeit in vollkontinuierlichen Schichtbetrieben an Sonn- und Feiertagen auf bis zu zwölf Stunden zu verlängern, wenn dadurch zusätzliche freie Schichten an Sonn- und Feiertagen erreicht werden.

[2]§ 7 Abs. 3 bis 6 findet Anwendung.

companies and orchestras as well as performances to at least eight Sundays, in cinemas and livestock facilities to at least six Sundays per year;
2. in deviation from section 11 (3), to agree not to provide a substitute day off for holidays falling on working days or to give employees time off within a period of time to be determined;
3. in deviation from section 11 (1) to (3), in the case of maritime shipping, to schedule consecutive days off to which the employees are entitled pursuant to this provision;
4. in deviation from section 11 (2), to extend the working time on Sundays and holidays to up to twelve hours in establishments with continuous shifts, provided that this will result in additional free shifts on Sundays and holidays.

[2]Section 7 (3) to (6) shall apply.

§ 13
Ermächtigung, Anordnung, Bewilligung

(1) Die Bundesregierung kann durch Rechtsverordnung mit Zustimmung des Bundesrates zur Vermeidung erheblicher Schäden unter Berücksichtigung des Schutzes der Arbeitnehmer und der Sonn- und Feiertagsruhe

1. die Bereiche mit Sonn- und Feiertagsbeschäftigung nach § 10 sowie die dort zugelassenen Arbeiten näher bestimmen,
2. über die Ausnahmen nach § 10 hinaus weitere Ausnahmen abweichend von § 9
   a) für Betriebe, in denen die Beschäftigung von Arbeitnehmern an Sonn- oder Feiertagen zur Befriedigung täglicher oder an diesen Tagen besonders hervortretender Bedürfnisse der Bevölkerung erforderlich ist,

Section 13
Empowerment, Decree, Permits

(1) In order to avoid substantial damage, and with due regard to the safeguarding of the employees and their days of rest on Sundays and holidays, the Federal Government may issue an ordinance, to be ratified by the Upper House of Parliament,

1. more specifically defining the areas in which Sunday and holiday work is permitted pursuant to section 10;
2. in deviation from section 9, permitting exceptions over and above those set forth in section 10
   a) for enterprises in which the scheduling of employees to work Sundays or holidays is necessary in order to meet needs of the population which arise on a daily basis or particularly on such days,

b) für Betriebe, in denen Arbeiten vorkommen, deren Unterbrechung oder Aufschub	b) for enterprises in which tasks arise, the interruption or deferment of which would
aa) nach dem Stand der Technik ihrer Art nach nicht oder nur mit erheblichen Schwierigkeiten möglich ist,	aa) in light of the current state of technology, be impossible or present grave difficulties,
bb) besondere Gefahren für Leben oder Gesundheit der Arbeitnehmer zur Folge hätte,	bb) result in particular danger to the life or health of the employees,
cc) zu erheblichen Belastungen der Umwelt oder der Energie- oder Wasserversorgung führen würde,	cc) lead to significant pollution of the environment or burden on the energy or water supply,
c) aus Gründen des Gemeinwohls, insbesondere auch zur Sicherung der Beschäftigung,	c) in the interests of common welfare, in particular for securing the employment,
zulassen und die zum Schutz der Arbeitnehmer und der Sonn- und Feiertagsruhe notwendigen Bedingungen bestimmen.	and determine the conditions necessary for the protection of the employees and of the days of rest on Sundays and holidays.
(2) ¹Soweit die Bundesregierung von der Ermächtigung des Absatzes 1 Nr. 2 Buchstabe a keinen Gebrauch gemacht hat, können die Landesregierungen durch Rechtsverordnung entsprechende Bestimmungen erlassen. ²Die Landesregierungen können diese Ermächtigung durch Rechtsverordnung auf oberste Landesbehörden übertragen.	(2) ¹Insofar as the Federal Republic has not made use of the empowerment pursuant to subsection (1) no. 2a, the state *(Land)* governments may issue corresponding ordinances. ²The state governments may transfer this empowerment to the highest governmental agencies of the state by virtue of an ordinance.
(3) Die Aufsichtsbehörde kann	(3) The regulatory authority may
1. feststellen, ob eine Beschäftigung nach § 10 zulässig ist,	1. determine whether work pursuant to section 10 is permissible,
2. abweichend von § 9 bewilligen, Arbeitnehmer zu beschäftigen	2. notwithstanding section 9, permit employees to be scheduled to work
a) im Handelsgewerbe an bis zu zehn Sonn- und Feiertagen im Jahr, an denen besondere Verhältnisse einen erweiterten Geschäftsverkehr erforderlich machen,	a) in trading enterprises, up to ten Sundays and holidays per year if special circumstances necessitate expanded business operations,
b) an bis zu fünf Sonn- und Feiertagen im Jahr, wenn besondere Verhältnisse zur Verhütung eines unverhältnismäßigen Schadens dies erfordern,	b) up to five Sundays and holidays per year, if special circumstances necessitate it in order to prevent a disproportionate degree of damage
c) an einem Sonntag im Jahr zur Durchführung einer gesetzlich vorgeschriebenen Inventur,	c) one Sunday per year in order to carry out a legally mandatory inventory,
und Anordnungen über die Beschäftigungszeit unter Berücksichtigung der	and issue directives on work times, giving due consideration to the time

für den öffentlichen Gottesdienst bestimmten Zeit treffen.

(4) Die Aufsichtsbehörde soll abweichend von § 9 bewilligen, dass Arbeitnehmer an Sonn- und Feiertagen mit Arbeiten beschäftigt werden, die aus chemischen, biologischen, technischen oder physikalischen Gründen einen ununterbrochenen Fortgang auch an Sonn- und Feiertagen erfordern.

(5) Die Aufsichtsbehörde hat abweichend von § 9 die Beschäftigung von Arbeitnehmern an Sonn- und Feiertagen zu bewilligen, wenn bei einer weitgehenden Ausnutzung der gesetzlich zulässigen wöchentlichen Betriebszeiten und bei längeren Betriebszeiten im Ausland die Konkurrenzfähigkeit unzumutbar beeinträchtigt ist und durch die Genehmigung von Sonn- und Feiertagsarbeit die Beschäftigung gesichert werden kann.

Vierter Abschnitt
Ausnahmen in besonderen Fällen

§ 14
Außergewöhnliche Fälle

(1) Von den §§ 3 bis 5, 6 Abs. 2, §§ 7, 9 bis 11 darf abgewichen werden bei vorübergehenden Arbeiten in Notfällen und in außergewöhnlichen Fällen, die unabhängig vom Willen der Betroffenen eintreten und deren Folgen nicht auf andere Weise zu beseitigen sind, besonders wenn Rohstoffe oder Lebensmittel zu verderben oder Arbeitsergebnisse zu misslingen drohen.

(2) Von den §§ 3 bis 5, 6 Abs. 2, §§ 7, 11 Abs. 1 bis 3 und § 12 darf ferner abgewichen werden,

1. wenn eine verhältnismäßig geringe Zahl von Arbeitnehmern vorüberge-

scheduled for public church services.

(4) Notwithstanding section 9, the regulatory authority shall permit workers to be scheduled on Sundays and holidays to perform tasks which, for chemical, biological, technical or physical reasons, must be performed continuously, even on Sundays and holidays.

(5) Notwithstanding section 9, the regulatory authority must approve the assignment of workers to shifts on Sundays and holidays, providing that, although the company is extensively utilizing the legally permissible amount of operating hours per week, the fact that foreign companies are permitted longer working weeks impairs the competitiveness of the company to an unreasonable extent, and that this could be counteracted by approving Sunday and holiday work.

Chapter 4
Exceptions in Special Cases

Section 14
Extraordinary Cases

(1) Deviations from sections 3 to 5, 6 (2), sections 7 and 9 to 11 may be made for work performed on a temporary basis in the event of emergencies and extraordinary cases which arise independent of the will of those affected, when the consequences thereof cannot be eliminated in any other way, particularly if the threat of spoilage of raw materials or foodstuffs or of impediment to production exists.

(2) Furthermore, provided that the employer cannot reasonably be expected to make other arrangements, deviations from sections 3 to 5, 6 (2), sections 7 and 11 (1) to (3) and section 12 may be made in the following cases:

1. if a relatively low number of employees are assigned work on a tem-

hend mit Arbeiten beschäftigt wird, deren Nichterledigung das Ergebnis der Arbeiten gefährden oder einen unverhältnismäßigen Schaden zur Folge haben würden,

2. bei Forschung und Lehre, bei unaufschiebbaren Vor- und Abschlussarbeiten sowie bei unaufschiebbaren Arbeiten zur Behandlung, Pflege und Betreuung von Personen oder zur Behandlung und Pflege von Tieren an einzelnen Tagen,

wenn dem Arbeitgeber andere Vorkehrungen nicht zugemutet werden können.

(3) Wird von den Befugnissen nach Absatz 1 oder 2 Gebrauch gemacht, darf die Arbeitszeit 48 Stunden wöchentlich im Durchschnitt von sechs Kalendermonaten oder 24 Wochen nicht überschreiten.

§ 15
Bewilligung, Ermächtigung

(1) Die Aufsichtsbehörde kann

1. eine von den §§ 3, 6 Abs. 2 und § 11 Abs. 2 abweichende längere tägliche Arbeitszeit bewilligen
   a) für kontinuierliche Schichtbetriebe zur Erreichung zusätzlicher Freischichten,
   b) für Bau- und Montagestellen,

2. eine von den §§ 3, 6 Abs. 2 und § 11 Abs. 2 abweichende längere tägliche Arbeitszeit für Saison- und Kampagnebetriebe für die Zeit der Saison oder Kampagne bewilligen, wenn die Verlängerung der Arbeitszeit über acht Stunden werktäglich durch eine entsprechende Verkürzung der Arbeitszeit zu anderen Zeiten ausgeglichen wird,

3. eine von den §§ 5 und 11 Abs. 2 abweichende Dauer und Lage der Ruhezeit bei Arbeitsbereitschaft, Bereitschaftsdienst und Rufbereitschaft den Besonderheiten dieser Inanspruch-

porary basis, the non-performance of which would endanger the results of the work or result in a disproportionate degree of damage;

2. in the case of research and teaching, during preparatory and finishing work which cannot be re-scheduled, as well as tasks which cannot be re-scheduled with regard to the treatment, nursing and care of persons, or treatment and care of animals on individual days.

(3) If the powers granted under subsection (1) or (2) are utilized, the work shift may not exceed an average of 48 hours per week within six calendar months or 24 weeks.

Section 15
Permits, Empowerment

(1) The regulatory authority may issue permits in the following cases:

1. for a longer daily work shift notwithstanding sections 3, 6 (2) and 11 (2)
   a) for continuous shift work to attain extra free shifts,
   b) for construction and assembly positions;

2. for a longer daily work shift notwithstanding sections 3, 6 (2) and 11 (2) for seasonal businesses and campaign activities during the time of the season or the campaign, provided that the extension of the shift to over eight hours per workday is compensated by a corresponding reduction of the shift during other times;

3. for a deviation from sections 5 and 11 (2) with regard to the duration and scheduling of the rest time in case of stand-by duty, emergency service and on-call service, in accor-

nahmen im öffentlichen Dienst entsprechend bewilligen,

4. eine von den §§ 5 und 11 Abs. 2 abweichende Ruhezeit zur Herbeiführung eines regelmäßigen wöchentlichen Schichtwechsels zweimal innerhalb eines Zeitraums von drei Wochen bewilligen.

(2) Die Aufsichtsbehörde kann über die in diesem Gesetz vorgesehenen Ausnahmen hinaus weitergehende Ausnahmen zulassen, soweit sie im öffentlichen Interesse dringend nötig werden.

(3) Das Bundesministerium der Verteidigung kann in seinem Geschäftsbereich durch Rechtsverordnung mit Zustimmung des Bundesministeriums für Arbeit und Soziales aus zwingenden Gründen der Verteidigung Arbeitnehmer verpflichten, über die in diesem Gesetz und in den auf Grund dieses Gesetzes erlassenen Rechtsverordnungen und Tarifverträgen festgelegten Arbeitszeitgrenzen und -beschränkungen hinaus Arbeit zu leisten.

(4) Werden Ausnahmen nach Absatz 1 oder 2 zugelassen, darf die Arbeitszeit 48 Stunden wöchentlich im Durchschnitt von sechs Kalendermonaten oder 24 Wochen nicht überschreiten.

dance with the particularities of the use of these services in public service occupations;

4. for a deviation from sections 5 and 11 (2) with regard to the rest time in order to effect a regular weekly shift change twice in every three-week period.

(2) The regulatory authority may permit exceptions above and beyond those set forth in this Act, insofar as they are of urgent necessity to the public interest.

(3) In cases of urgent necessity, the Federal Defense Ministry may conscript employees for defense purposes by virtue of the issuance of an ordinance, ratified by the Federal Ministry of Labor and Social Affairs, to work shifts which go beyond the work shift limitations and restrictions set forth in this Act and in ordinances and collective agreements based upon this Act.

(4) If exceptions are permitted pursuant to subsection (1) or (2), the work shift may not exceed an average of 48 hours per week within six calendar months or 24 weeks.

Fünfter Abschnitt
Durchführung des Gesetzes

Chapter 5
Implementation of the Act

§ 16
Aushang und Arbeitszeitnachweise

Section 16
Display of Notice and of Working Hours

(1) Der Arbeitgeber ist verpflichtet, einen Abdruck dieses Gesetzes, der auf Grund dieses Gesetzes erlassenen, für den Betrieb geltenden Rechtsverordnungen und der für den Betrieb geltenden Tarifverträge und Betriebs- oder Dienstvereinbarungen im Sinne des § 7 Abs. 1 bis 3, §§ 12 und 21a Abs. 6 an geeigneter Stelle im Betrieb zur Einsichtnahme auszulegen oder auszuhängen.

(1) The employer shall display or post a copy of this Act for inspection in an appropriate place in the establishment, as well as any ordinances issued on the basis of this Act, and the collective bargaining agreements and works or service agreements within the meaning of section 7 (1) to (3), section 12 and 21a (6) which are applicable to the establishment.

(2) ¹Der Arbeitgeber ist verpflichtet, die über die werktägliche Arbeitszeit des § 3 Satz 1 hinausgehende Arbeitszeit der Arbeitnehmer aufzuzeichnen und ein Verzeichnis der Arbeitnehmer zu führen, die in eine Verlängerung der Arbeitszeit gemäß § 7 Abs. 7 eingewilligt haben. ²Die Nachweise sind mindestens zwei Jahre aufzubewahren.

§ 17
Aufsichtsbehörde

(1) Die Einhaltung dieses Gesetzes und der auf Grund dieses Gesetzes erlassenen Rechtsverordnungen wird von den nach Landesrecht zuständigen Behörden (Aufsichtsbehörden) überwacht.

(2) Die Aufsichtsbehörde kann die erforderlichen Maßnahmen anordnen, die der Arbeitgeber zur Erfüllung der sich aus diesem Gesetz und den auf Grund dieses Gesetzes erlassenen Rechtsverordnungen ergebenden Pflichten zu treffen hat.

(3) Für den öffentlichen Dienst des Bundes sowie für die bundesunmittelbaren Körperschaften, Anstalten und Stiftungen des öffentlichen Rechts werden die Aufgaben und Befugnisse der Aufsichtsbehörde vom zuständigen Bundesministerium oder den von ihm bestimmten Stellen wahrgenommen; das gleiche gilt für die Befugnisse nach § 15 Abs. 1 und 2.

(4) ¹Die Aufsichtsbehörde kann vom Arbeitgeber die für die Durchführung dieses Gesetzes und der auf Grund dieses Gesetzes erlassenen Rechtsverordnungen erforderlichen Auskünfte verlangen. ²Sie kann ferner vom Arbeitgeber verlangen, die Arbeitszeitnachweise und Tarifverträge oder Betriebs- oder Dienstvereinbarungen im Sinne des § 7 Abs. 1 bis 3, §§ 12 und 21a Abs. 6 vorzulegen oder zur Einsicht einzusenden.

(5) ¹Die Beauftragten der Aufsichtsbehörde sind berechtigt, die Arbeitsstätten während der Betriebs- und Arbeits-

(2) ¹The employer shall make a record of the times worked by employees on working days in excess of the times set forth in section 3 sentence 1 and a list of the employees who have consented to an extension of the work shift pursuant to section 7 (7). ²Such proof shall be kept for at least two years.

Section 17
Regulatory Authority

(1) Compliance with this Act and any ordinances enacted on the basis of this Act shall be supervised by the competent agency (regulatory authority) pursuant to the laws of the state.

(2) The regulatory authority may decree the necessary measures which the employer must take in order to fulfill the duties arising from this Act and the ordinances enacted on the basis of this Act.

(3) In the case of federal public service as well as for bodies, institutions and public foundations immediately linked with the Federal Government, the tasks and powers of the regulatory authority shall be assumed by the competent Federal Ministry or those appointed by it; the same holds for the powers pursuant to section 15 (1) and (2).

(4) ¹The regulatory authority may demand that the employer submit information necessary for the execution of this Act and the ordinances enacted on the basis of this Act. ²Moreover, it may demand that the employer present proof of work shifts and collective bargaining agreements or works or service agreements within the meaning of section 7 (1) to (3), sections 12 and 21a (6) or to submit them for inspection.

(5) ¹The authorized representatives of the regulatory authority are entitled to enter and inspect the workplaces dur-

zeit zu betreten und zu besichtigen; außerhalb dieser Zeit oder wenn sich die Arbeitsstätten in einer Wohnung befinden, dürfen sie ohne Einverständnis des Inhabers nur zur Verhütung von dringenden Gefahren für die öffentliche Sicherheit und Ordnung betreten und besichtigt werden. [2]Der Arbeitgeber hat das Betreten und Besichtigen der Arbeitsstätten zu gestatten. [3]Das Grundrecht der Unverletzlichkeit der Wohnung (Artikel 13 des Grundgesetzes) wird insoweit eingeschränkt.

(6) Der zur Auskunft Verpflichtete kann die Auskunft auf solche Fragen verweigern, deren Beantwortung ihn selbst oder einen der in § 383 Abs. 1 Nr. 1 bis 3 der Zivilprozessordnung bezeichneten Angehörigen der Gefahr strafgerichtlicher Verfolgung oder eines Verfahrens nach dem Gesetz über Ordnungswidrigkeiten aussetzen würde.

ing operating and working hours; outside of this time or in cases in which the workplace is in a private home, they may enter and inspect the premises without the owner's consent solely for the purpose of preventing imperative danger to public safety and order. [2]The employer must permit entry and inspection of the workplace. [3]The basic right of the inviolability of the home (Article 13 of the Basic Law – *Grundgesetz*) is restricted to this extent.

(6) The person obligated to give information may refuse to answer those questions to which a response could subject him or one of his relatives as defined in section 383 (1) nos. 1 to 3 of the Code of Civil Procedure (*Zivilprozeßordnung*) to the risk of prosecution by a criminal court or proceedings for an administrative offense.

Sechster Abschnitt
Sonderregelungen

§ 18
Nichtanwendung des Gesetzes

(1) Dieses Gesetz ist nicht anzuwenden auf
1. leitende Angestellte im Sinne des § 5 Abs. 3 des Betriebsverfassungsgesetzes sowie Chefärzte,
2. Leiter von öffentlichen Dienststellen und deren Vertreter sowie Arbeitnehmer im öffentlichen Dienst, die zu selbständigen Entscheidungen in Personalangelegenheiten befugt sind,
3. Arbeitnehmer, die in häuslicher Gemeinschaft mit den ihnen anvertrauten Personen zusammenleben und sie eigenverantwortlich erziehen, pflegen oder betreuen,
4. den liturgischen Bereich der Kirchen und der Religionsgemeinschaften.

Chapter 6
Special Provisions

Section 18
Inapplicability of the Act

(1) This Act is not applicable to:
1. managerial employees within the meaning of section 5 (3) of the Works Constitution Act (*Betriebsverfassungsgesetz*) as well as the chief of medical staff of a hospital;
2. heads of governmental service agencies and their representatives as well as public servants who are authorized to make independent decisions in personnel matters;
3. employees who share a household with the persons entrusted to them and raise, nurse or care for them on their own responsibility;
4. the liturgical realm of the churches and the religious societies.

(2) Für die Beschäftigung von Personen unter 18 Jahren gilt anstelle dieses Gesetzes das Jugendarbeitsschutzgesetz.

(3) Für die Beschäftigung von Arbeitnehmern auf Kauffahrteischiffen als Besatzungsmitglieder im Sinne des § 3 des Seemannsgesetzes gilt anstelle dieses Gesetzes das Seemannsgesetz.

§ 19
Beschäftigung im öffentlichen Dienst

Bei der Wahrnehmung hoheitlicher Aufgaben im öffentlichen Dienst können, soweit keine tarifvertragliche Regelung besteht, durch die zuständige Dienstbehörde die für Beamte geltenden Bestimmungen über die Arbeitszeit auf die Arbeitnehmer übertragen werden; insoweit finden die §§ 3 bis 13 keine Anwendung.

§ 20
Beschäftigung in der Luftfahrt

Für die Beschäftigung von Arbeitnehmern als Besatzungsmitglieder von Luftfahrzeugen gelten anstelle der Vorschriften dieses Gesetzes über Arbeits- und Ruhezeiten die Vorschriften über Flug-, Flugdienst- und Ruhezeiten der Zweiten Durchführungsverordnung zur Betriebsordnung für Luftfahrtgerät in der jeweils geltenden Fassung.

§ 21
Beschäftigung in der Binnenschifffahrt

¹Die Vorschriften dieses Gesetzes gelten für die Beschäftigung von Fahrpersonal in der Binnenschifffahrt, soweit die Vorschriften über Ruhezeiten der Binnenschiffsuntersuchungsordnung in der jeweils geltenden Fassung dem nicht entgegenstehen. ²Sie können durch Ta-

(2) With regard to the employment of persons under 18 years of age, the Act to Protect Minors at Work *(Jugendarbeitsschutzgesetz)* shall apply in lieu of this Act.

(3) With regard to the employment of members of the merchant marines as crew within the meaning of section 3 of the Seaman's Law *(Seemannsgesetz)*, that Law shall apply in lieu of this Act.

Section 19
Employment in Public Service

Where there are no collective bargaining agreement provisions with regard to the assumption of sovereign assignments in public service, the competent service agency may apply the provisions governing the working time of civil servants to the employees as well; to this extent, sections 3 to 13 shall not apply.

Section 20
Employment in Aviation

With regard to the employment of crew members of aircraft, the provisions governing flying time, aviation staff time and rest time as set forth in the valid version of the Second Regulation for the Implementation of Working Regulations in Aircraft *(Zweite Durchführungsverordnung zur Betriebsordnung für Luftfahrtgerät)* shall apply in lieu of the provisions of this Act on working and rest time.

Section 21
Employment in Inland Navigation

¹The provisions of this Act apply to the employment of crew members in inland navigation, insofar as they do not contradict the regulations governing rest times as set forth in the valid versions of the Inland Navigation Inspection Ordinance *(Binnenschiffsuntersu-*

rifvertrag der Eigenart der Binnenschifffahrt angepasst werden.

chungsverordnung) respectively. ²These provisions may be adjusted in a collective bargaining agreement to suit the particular character of the inland navigation.

§ 21 a
Beschäftigung im Straßentransport

Section 21 a
Employment in Road Transport

¹Für die Beschäftigung von Arbeitnehmern als Fahrer oder Beifahrer bei Straßenverkehrstätigkeiten im Sinne der Verordnung (EG) Nr. 561/2006 des Europäischen Parlaments und des Rates vom 15. März 2006 zur Harmonisierung bestimmter Sozialvorschriften im Straßenverkehr und zur Änderung der Verordnungen (EWG) Nr. 3821/85 und (EG) Nr. 2135/98 des Rates sowie zur Aufhebung der Verordnung (EWG) Nr. 3820/85 des Rates (ABl. EG Nr. L 102 S. 1) oder des Europäischen Übereinkommens über die Arbeit des im internationalen Straßenverkehr beschäftigten Fahrpersonals (AETR) vom 1. Juli 1970 (BGBl. II 1974 S. 1473) in ihren jeweiligen Fassungen gelten die Vorschriften dieses Gesetzes, soweit nicht die folgenden Absätze abweichende Regelungen enthalten. ²Die Vorschriften der Verordnung (EG) Nr. 561/2006 und des AETR bleiben unberührt.

¹For employee's service as drivers or co-drivers in road transport activities within the meaning of Council Regulation (EC) No. 561/2006 of the European Parliament and the Council of 15 March 2006 on the harmonization of certain social legislation relating to road transport and amending Council Regulations (EEC) No. 3821/85 and (EC) No. 2135/98 and repealing Council Regulation (EEC) No. 3820/85 (OJ L 102 P. 1) or the European Agreement concerning the Work of Crews of Vehicles Engaged in International Road Transport (AETR) of 1 July 1970 (Federal Law Gazette II 1974 p. 1473) in their current versions, the provisions of this Act shall apply unless otherwise provided in the following paragraphs. ²The provisions of the Council Regulation (EC) No. 561/2006 and the AETR remain unaffected.

(2) Eine Woche im Sinne dieser Vorschriften ist der Zeitraum von Montag 0 Uhr bis Sonntag 24 Uhr.

(2) A week within the meaning of these provisions shall be the period from Monday 0:00 to Sunday 24:00.

(3) ¹Abweichend von § 2 Abs. 1 ist keine Arbeitszeit:

(3) ¹Notwithstanding section 2 (1) a work shift is not:

1. die Zeit, während derer sich ein Arbeitnehmer am Arbeitsplatz bereithalten muss, um seine Tätigkeit aufzunehmen,

1. the time an employee needs be available at the work place in order to begin his work,

2. die Zeit, während derer sich ein Arbeitnehmer bereithalten muss, um seine Tätigkeit auf Anweisung aufnehmen zu können, ohne sich an seinem Arbeitsplatz aufhalten zu müssen;

2. the time an employee needs be available in order, to be able to begin his work upon direction without needing to be present at the work place;

3. für Arbeitnehmer, die sich beim Fahren abwechseln, die während der

3. for employees who take turns driving, the time in which they sit next to

Fahrt neben dem Fahrer oder in einer Schlafkabine verbrachte Zeit. ²Für die Zeiten nach Satz 1 Nr. 1 und 2 gilt dies nur, wenn der Zeitraum und dessen voraussichtliche Dauer im Voraus, spätestens unmittelbar vor Beginn des betreffenden Zeitraums bekannt ist. ³Die in Satz 1 genannten Zeiten sind keine Ruhezeiten. ⁴Die in Satz 1 Nr. 1 und 2 genannten Zeiten sind keine Ruhepausen.	the driver during the trip or in a sleeping compartment. ²This shall only apply for the time spent pursuant to sentence 1 nos. 1 and 2 if the period of time and its anticipated duration is known at the latest right before the onset of such time period. ³The times mentioned in sentence 1 are not rest periods. ⁴The times mentioned in sentence 1 nos. 1 and 2 are not breaks.
(4) ¹Die Arbeitszeit darf 48 Stunden wöchentlich nicht überschreiten. ²Sie kann auf bis zu 60 Stunden verlängert werden, wenn innerhalb von vier Kalendermonaten oder 16 Wochen im Durchschnitt 48 Stunden wöchentlich nicht überschritten werden.	(4) ¹The work shift may not exceed 48 hours per week. ²It may be extended to up to 60 hours if an average of 48 hours is not exceeded within four calendar months or 16 weeks.
(5) ¹Die Ruhezeiten bestimmen sich nach den Vorschriften der Europäischen Gemeinschaften für Kraftfahrer und Beifahrer sowie nach dem AETR. ²Dies gilt auch für Auszubildende und Praktikanten.	(5) ¹The rest periods shall be determined according to the provisions of the European Community for truck drivers and co-drivers as well as the AETR. ²This also applies to apprentices and trainees.
(6) In einem Tarifvertrag oder auf Grund eines Tarifvertrags in einer Betriebs- oder Dienstvereinbarung kann zugelassen werden,	(6) It may be permitted under a collective agreement or a works or service agreement based upon a collective agreement
1. nähere Einzelheiten zu den in Absatz 3 Satz 1 Nr. 1, 2 und Satz 2 genannten Voraussetzungen zu regeln,	1. to regulate specific details regarding the prerequisites set forth in subsection (3) sentence 1 nos. 1, 2 and sentence 2,
2. abweichend von Absatz 4 sowie den §§ 3 und 6 Abs. 2 die Arbeitszeit festzulegen, wenn objektive, technische oder arbeitszeitorganisatorische Gründe vorliegen. Dabei darf die Arbeitszeit 48 Stunden wöchentlich im Durchschnitt von sechs Kalendermonaten nicht überschreiten. § 7 Abs. 1 Nr. 2 und Abs. 2a gilt nicht. § 7 Abs. 3 gilt entsprechend.	2. notwithstanding subsection (4) as well as sections 3 und 6 (2), to define the work shift if there are objective, technical or organizational grounds for doing so. However, the work shift may not exceed an average of 48 hours per week within six calendar months. Section 7 (1) nos. 2 and (2a) shall not apply. Section 7 (3) applies *mutatis mutandis*.
(7) ¹Der Arbeitgeber ist verpflichtet, die Arbeitszeit der Arbeitnehmer aufzuzeichnen. ²Die Aufzeichnungen sind mindestens zwei Jahre aufzubewahren. ³Der Arbeitgeber hat dem Arbeitnehmer auf Verlangen eine Kopie der Auf-	(7) ¹The employer shall be obligated to record the employees' work shifts. ²These records shall be preserved for at least two years. ³The employer shall provide the employee with a copy of the records of his work shift upon request.

zeichnungen seiner Arbeitszeit auszuhändigen.

(8) ¹Zur Berechnung der Arbeitszeit fordert der Arbeitgeber den Arbeitnehmer schriftlich auf, ihm eine Aufstellung der bei einem anderen Arbeitgeber geleisteten Arbeitszeit vorzulegen. ²Der Arbeitnehmer legt diese Angaben schriftlich vor.

(8) ¹For the calculation of the work shift, the employer shall call upon the employee in writing to present a list of work shifts he has performed with another employer. ²The employee shall present this information in writing.

Siebter Abschnitt
Straf- und Bußgeldvorschriften

Chapter 7
Penalties and Fines

§ 22
Bußgeldvorschriften

Section 22
Fines

(1) Ordnungswidrig handelt, wer als Arbeitgeber vorsätzlich oder fahrlässig

(1) An administrative offense shall be deemed to be committed by an employer who, intentionally or negligently,

1. entgegen §§ 3, 6 Abs. 2 oder § 21 a Abs. 4, jeweils auch in Verbindung mit § 11 Abs. 2, einen Arbeitnehmer über die Grenzen der Arbeitszeit hinaus beschäftigt,
2. entgegen § 4 Ruhepausen nicht, nicht mit der vorgeschriebenen Mindestdauer oder nicht rechtzeitig gewährt,
3. entgegen § 5 Abs. 1 die Mindestruhezeit nicht gewährt oder entgegen § 5 Abs. 2 die Verkürzung der Ruhezeit durch Verlängerung einer anderen Ruhezeit nicht oder nicht rechtzeitig ausgleicht,
4. einer Rechtsverordnung nach § 8 Satz 1, § 13 Abs. 1 oder 2 oder § 24 zuwiderhandelt, soweit sie für einen bestimmten Tatbestand auf diese Bußgeldvorschrift verweist,
5. entgegen § 9 Abs. 1 einen Arbeitnehmer an Sonn- oder Feiertagen beschäftigt,
6. entgegen § 11 Abs. 1 einen Arbeitnehmer an allen Sonntagen beschäftigt oder entgegen § 11 Abs. 3 einen

1. assigns an employee to work beyond the limits of permissible working time in contravention of section 3, 6 (2) or section 21 a (4), in connection with section 11 (2),
2. does not grant a rest break or grants one below the minimum duration or does not grant one at the proper time, in contravention of section 4,
3. does not grant the minimum rest time in contravention of section 5 (1), or does not in due time compensate for the reduction of the rest time by lengthening another rest time, in contravention of section 5 (2),
4. acts in breach of an ordinance pursuant to section 8 sentence 1, section 13 (1) or (2) or section 24, insofar as that ordinance stipulates a fine in punishment for a specific act,
5. schedules an employee to work on Sundays or holidays in contravention of section 9 (1),
6. schedules an employee to work on all Sundays in contravention of section 11 (1), or does not grant a sub-

Ersatzruhetag nicht oder nicht rechtzeitig gewährt,

7. einer vollziehbaren Anordnung nach § 13 Abs. 3 Nr. 2 zuwiderhandelt,
8. entgegen § 16 Abs. 1 die dort bezeichnete Auslage oder den dort bezeichneten Aushang nicht vornimmt,
9. entgegen § 16 Abs. 2 oder § 21a Abs. 7 Aufzeichnungen nicht oder nicht richtig erstellt oder nicht für die vorgeschriebene Dauer aufbewahrt oder
10. entgegen § 17 Abs. 4 eine Auskunft nicht, nicht richtig oder nicht vollständig erteilt, Unterlagen nicht oder nicht vollständig vorlegt oder nicht einsendet oder entgegen § 17 Abs. 5 Satz 2 eine Maßnahme nicht gestattet.

(2) Die Ordnungswidrigkeit kann in den Fällen des Absatzes 1 Nr. 1 bis 7, 9 und 10 mit einer Geldbuße bis zu fünfzehntausend Euro, in den Fällen des Absatzes 1 Nr. 8 mit einer Geldbuße bis zu zweitausendfünfhundert Euro geahndet werden.

§ 23
Strafvorschriften

(1) Wer eine der in § 22 Abs. 1 Nr. 1 bis 3, 5 bis 7 bezeichneten Handlungen

1. vorsätzlich begeht und dadurch Gesundheit oder Arbeitskraft eines Arbeitnehmers gefährdet oder
2. beharrlich wiederholt,

wird mit Freiheitsstrafe bis zu einem Jahr oder mit Geldstrafe bestraft.

(2) Wer in den Fällen des Absatzes 1 Nr. 1 die Gefahr fahrlässig verursacht, wird mit Freiheitsstrafe bis zu sechs Monaten oder mit Geldstrafe bis zu 180 Tagessätzen bestraft.

---

stitute day off or does not grant it within the deadline in contravention of section 11 (3),

7. acts in breach of an enforceable directive pursuant to section 13 (3) no. 2,
8. does not display or post the documents set forth in section 16 (1) in contravention of that provision,
9. does not make the record set forth in section 16 (2) or section 21a (7) in contravention of that provision, or does not make it correctly or does not keep it for the prescribed length of time,
10. in contravention of section 17 (4), does not provide information or gives incorrect or incomplete information, does not present documents or presents them incompletely or does not submit them, or, in contravention of section 17 (5) sentence 2, does not permit a measure set forth therein to be taken.

(2) An administrative offense in the cases of subsection (1) nos. 1 to 7, 9 and 10 shall be punished by a fine of up to 15,000 euro, in the cases of subsection (1) no. 8 by a fine of up to 2,500 euro.

Section 23
Criminal Law Provisions

(1) Whosoever, with regard to the actions set forth in section 22 (1) nos. 1 to 3, 5 to 7

1. intentionally commits such an act, thus endangering an employee's health or ability to work, or
2. persistently repeats such an act

shall be punished by imprisonment of up to one year or by a fine.

(2) Whosoever, in the case of subsection (1) no. 1, negligently endangers an employee, shall be punished by imprisonment of up to six months or with a fine of up to 180 days of per diem payments (*Tagessätze*).

Achter Abschnitt
Schlussvorschriften

§ 24
Umsetzung von zwischenstaatlichen Vereinbarungen und Rechtsakten der EG

Die Bundesregierung kann mit Zustimmung des Bundesrates zur Erfüllung von Verpflichtungen aus zwischenstaatlichen Vereinbarungen oder zur Umsetzung von Rechtsakten des Rates oder der Kommission der Europäischen Gemeinschaften, die Sachbereiche dieses Gesetzes betreffen, Rechtsverordnungen nach diesem Gesetz erlassen.

§ 25
Übergangsregelung für Tarifverträge

[1] Enthält ein am 1. Januar 2004 bestehender oder nachwirkender Tarifvertrag abweichende Regelungen nach § 7 Abs. 1 oder 2 oder § 12 Satz 1, die den in diesen Vorschriften festgelegten Höchstrahmen überschreiten, bleiben diese tarifvertraglichen Bestimmungen bis zum 31. Dezember 2006 unberührt. [2] Tarifverträgen nach Satz 1 stehen durch Tarifvertrag zugelassene Betriebsvereinbarungen sowie Regelungen nach § 7 Abs. 4 gleich.

Chapter 8
Concluding Provisions

Section 24
Application of International Agreements and Legal Instruments of the EG

The Federal Government may, with the consent of the Upper House of Parliament, enact ordinances for the purpose of fulfilling obligations arising from international agreements or the application of legal instruments of the Council or Commission of the European Community pertaining to the content of this Act.

Section 25
Interim Regulation for Collective Bargaining Agreements

[1] Should on 1 January 2004 an existing or retroactively applicable collective bargaining agreement contain provisions in deviation from section 7 (1) or (2) or section 12 sentence 1 which exceed the maximum limits set forth in these provisions, these contractual clauses shall not be affected until 31 December 2006. [2] Collective bargaining agreements pursuant to sentence 1 are equivalent to works agreements permitted by collective bargaining agreements as well as provisions pursuant to section 7 (4).

XV. Maternity Protection Act (Mutterschutzgesetz – MuSchG)

of 20 June 2000 (Federal Law Gazette I p. 2318)

in the amended version of 17 March 2009

Erster Abschnitt
Allgemeine Vorschriften

§ 1
Geltungsbereich

Dieses Gesetz gilt
1. für Frauen, die in einem Arbeitsverhältnis stehen,
2. für weibliche in Heimarbeit Beschäftigte und ihnen Gleichgestellte (§ 1 Abs. 1 und 2 des Heimarbeitsgesetzes vom 14. März 1951 BGBl. I S. 191), soweit sie am Stück mitarbeiten.

§ 2
Gestaltung des Arbeitsplatzes

(1) Wer eine werdende oder stillende Mutter beschäftigt, hat bei der Einrichtung und der Unterhaltung des Arbeitsplatzes einschließlich der Maschinen, Werkzeuge und Geräte und bei der Regelung der Beschäftigung die erforderlichen Vorkehrungen und Maßnahmen zum Schutze von Leben und Gesundheit der werdenden oder stillenden Mutter zu treffen.

(2) Wer eine werdende oder stillende Mutter mit Arbeiten beschäftigt, bei denen sie ständig stehen oder gehen muss, hat für sie eine Sitzgelegenheit zum kurzen Ausruhen bereitzustellen.

(3) Wer eine werdende oder stillende Mutter mit Arbeiten beschäftigt, bei denen sie ständig sitzen muss, hat ihr Gelegenheit zu kurzen Unterbrechungen ihrer Arbeit zu geben.

Chapter 1
General Provisions

Section 1
Scope of Application

This Act applies
1. to women who are in an employment relationship
2. female persons employed to work at home and comparable persons (section 1 (1) and (2) of the Home Work Act *(Heimarbeitsgesetz)* of 14 March 1951 – Federal Law Gazette I p. 191), insofar as they work together on a single project.

Section 2
Design of the Workplace

(1) Anyone employing an expectant or nursing mother shall take the necessary precautions and measures for the protection of expectant or nursing mother's life and health in setting up and maintaining the workplace, including the machines, tools, equipment, and in regulating her work activity.

(2) Anyone employing an expectant or nursing mother in work which requires continuous standing or walking shall provide her with an opportunity to sit and take a short rest.

(3) Anyone employing an expectant or nursing mother in work which requires continuous sitting shall give her the opportunity to take short breaks from her work.

(4) Die Bundesregierung wird ermächtigt, durch Rechtsverordnung mit Zustimmung des Bundesrates

1. den Arbeitgeber zu verpflichten, zur Vermeidung von Gesundheitsgefährdungen der werdenden oder stillenden Mütter oder ihrer Kinder Liegeräume für diese Frauen einzurichten und sonstige Maßnahmen zur Durchführung des in Absatz 1 enthaltenen Grundsatzes zu treffen,
2. nähere Einzelheiten zu regeln wegen der Verpflichtung des Arbeitgebers zur Beurteilung einer Gefährdung für die werdenden oder stillenden Mütter, zur Durchführung der notwendigen Schutzmaßnahmen und zur Unterrichtung der betroffenen Arbeitnehmerinnen nach Maßgabe der insoweit umzusetzenden Artikel 4 bis 6 der Richtlinie 92/85/EWG des Rates vom 19. Oktober 1992 über die Durchführung von Maßnahmen zur Verbesserung der Sicherheit und des Gesundheitsschutzes von schwangeren Arbeitnehmerinnen, Wöchnerinnen und stillenden Arbeitnehmerinnen am Arbeitsplatz (ABl. EG Nr. L 348 S. 1).

(5) Unabhängig von den auf Grund des Absatzes 4 erlassenen Vorschriften kann die Aufsichtsbehörde in Einzelfällen anordnen, welche Vorkehrungen und Maßnahmen zur Durchführung des Absatzes 1 zu treffen sind.

(4) The Federal Government shall be empowered to enact ordinances with the consent of the upper house of parliament *(Bundesrat)*

1. obligating the employer to set up rooms in which expectant or nursing mothers can lie down and to take further measures for the implementation of the principle embodied in subsection (1), so as to avoid dangers to the health of expectant or nursing mothers or their children.
2. regulating details concerning the employer's obligation to assess a danger to expectant or nursing mothers, to carry out the necessary protective measures and to inform the affected employees pursuant to Articles 4 to 6 of the as yet to be implemented [European] Council Directive 92/85/EEC of 19 October 1992 on the introduction of measures to encourage improvements in the safety and health at work of pregnant workers and workers who have recently given birth or are breastfeeding which shall be implemented in this Act.

(5) In addition to the regulations issued on the basis of subsection (4), the supervisory authority may, in individual cases, issue an order stipulating the precautions and measures to be taken in implementing subsection (1).

Zweiter Abschnitt
Beschäftigungsverbote

Chapter 2
Prohibitions of Employment

§ 3
Beschäftigungsverbote für werdende Mütter

Section 3
Prohibitions of Employment of Expectant Mothers

(1) Werdende Mütter dürfen nicht beschäftigt werden, soweit nach ärztlichem Zeugnis Leben oder Gesundheit von Mutter oder Kind bei Fortdauer der Beschäftigung gefährdet ist.

(1) Expectant mothers may not be employed if, according to a physician's certificate, the mother or child's life or health would be endangered by a continuance of her employment.

(2) Werdende Mütter dürfen in den letzten sechs Wochen vor der Entbindung nicht beschäftigt werden, es sei denn, dass sie sich zur Arbeitsleistung ausdrücklich bereit erklären; die Erklärung kann jederzeit widerrufen werden.

(2) Expectant mothers shall not be employed in the last six weeks prior to delivery, unless they explicitly declare their willingness to work, which declaration may be revoked at any time.

§ 4
Weitere Beschäftigungsverbote

Section 4
Additional Prohibitions of Employment

(1) Werdende Mütter dürfen nicht mit schweren körperlichen Arbeiten und nicht mit Arbeiten beschäftigt werden, bei denen sie schädlichen Einwirkungen von gesundheitsgefährdenden Stoffen oder Strahlen von Staub, Gasen oder Dämpfen, von Hitze, Kälte oder Nässe, von Erschütterungen oder Lärm ausgesetzt sind.

(1) Expectant mothers may not be assigned to heavy physical work or work in which they are exposed to harmful effects of hazardous substances or rays, of dust, gases or fumes, of heat, cold or dampness, of vibrations or noise.

(2) [1]Werdende Mütter dürfen insbesondere nicht beschäftigt werden

(2) Expectant mothers shall in particular not be employed

1. mit Arbeiten, bei denen regelmäßig Lasten von mehr als fünf kg Gewicht oder gelegentlich Lasten von mehr als zehn kg Gewicht ohne mechanische Hilfsmittel von Hand gehoben, bewegt oder befördert werden. [2]Sollen größere Lasten mit mechanischen Hilfsmitteln von Hand gehoben, bewegt oder befördert werden, so darf die körperliche Beanspruchung der werdenden Mutter nicht größer sein als bei Arbeiten nach Satz 1,
2. nach Ablauf des fünften Monats der Schwangerschaft mit Arbeiten, bei denen sie ständig stehen müssen, soweit diese Beschäftigung täglich vier Stunden überschreitet,
3. mit Arbeiten, bei denen sie sich häufig erheblich strecken oder beugen oder bei denen sie dauernd hocken oder sich gebückt halten müssen,
4. mit der Bedienung von Geräten und Maschinen aller Art mit hoher Fußbeanspruchung, insbesondere von solchen mit Fußantrieb,
5. mit dem Schälen von Holz,
6. mit Arbeiten, bei denen sie infolge ihrer Schwangerschaft in besonde-

1. in work in which loads exceeding five kilos are regularly, or loads exceeding ten kilos are occasionally lifted, moved or carried by hand without mechanical aids. Where heavier loads are to be lifted, moved or carried by hand with mechanical aids, the physical demands on the expectant mother shall not be greater than those for the work pursuant to sentence 1,
2. after the expiration of the fifth month of pregnancy, in work in which they must continually stand, insofar as such employment exceeds four hours daily,
3. in work in which they must frequently and considerably stretch or bend or in which she must continuously squat or stoop,
4. in the operation of equipment and machines of all kinds with extensive strain on the feet, especially those with foot drives,
5. to strip bark from logs,
6. in work in which, as a result of their pregnancy, expectant mothers are

rem Maße der Gefahr, an einer Berufskrankheit zu erkranken, ausgesetzt sind oder bei denen durch das Risiko der Entstehung einer Berufskrankheit eine erhöhte Gefährdung für die werdende Mutter oder eine Gefahr für die Leibesfrucht besteht,

7. nach Ablauf des dritten Monats der Schwangerschaft auf Beförderungsmitteln,

8. mit Arbeiten, bei denen sie erhöhten Unfallgefahren, insbesondere der Gefahr auszugleiten, zu fallen oder abzustürzen, ausgesetzt sind.

(3) [1] Die Beschäftigung von werdenden Müttern mit

1. Akkordarbeit und sonstigen Arbeiten, bei denen durch ein gesteigertes Arbeitstempo ein höheres Entgelt erzielt werden kann,

2. Fließarbeit mit vorgeschriebenem Arbeitstempo

ist verboten. [2] Die Aufsichtsbehörde kann Ausnahmen bewilligen, wenn die Art der Arbeit und das Arbeitstempo eine Beeinträchtigung der Gesundheit von Mutter oder Kind nicht befürchten lassen. [3] Die Aufsichtsbehörde kann die Beschäftigung für alle werdenden Mütter eines Betriebes oder einer Betriebsabteilung bewilligen, wenn die Voraussetzungen des Satzes 2 für alle im Betrieb oder in der Betriebsabteilung beschäftigten Frauen gegeben sind.

(4) Die Bundesregierung wird ermächtigt, zur Vermeidung von Gesundheitsgefährdungen der werdenden oder stillenden Mütter und ihrer Kinder durch Rechtsverordnung mit Zustimmung des Bundesrates

1. Arbeiten zu bestimmen, die unter die Beschäftigungsverbote der Absätze 1 und 2 fallen,

2. weitere Beschäftigungsverbote für werdende und stillende Mütter vor und nach der Entbindung zu erlassen.

(5) [1] Die Aufsichtsbehörde kann in Einzelfällen bestimmen, ob eine Arbeit

particularly exposed to the danger of contracting an occupational disease or the risk of contracting an occupational disease increases the danger to the expectant mother or the fetus,

7. after expiration of the third month of pregnancy, on transportation systems,

8. in work in which they are exposed to increased risk of accidents, particularly the risk of slipping, tripping or falling.

(3) [1] The assignment of expectant mothers to

1. piecework and other work in which a higher remuneration can be achieved through an accelerated working speed,

2. assembly-line work with a prescribed working speed

is prohibited. [2] The supervisory authority may approve exceptions if the kind of work and the working speed do not give reason to fear that the health of mother or child will be impaired. [3] The supervisory authority may approve the assignment of all expectant mothers to an establishment or department of an establishment if the condition set forth in sentence 2 is met for all women employed in that establishment or department.

(4) To avoid endangering the health of expectant or nursing mothers and their children, the Federal Government shall be empowered to enact ordinances with the consent of the Upper House of Parliament

1. to define which work assignments fall under the prohibition of employment set forth in subsections (1) and (2),

2. to issue additional prohibitions of employment for expectant and nursing mothers before and after delivery.

(5) [1] The supervisory authority may, in individual cases, determine whether a

unter die Beschäftigungsverbote der Absätze 1 bis 3 oder einer von der Bundesregierung gemäß Absatz 4 erlassenen Verordnung fällt. ²Sie kann in Einzelfällen die Beschäftigung mit bestimmten anderen Arbeiten verbieten.

work assignment falls under the prohibitions of employment set forth in subsections (1) to (3) or an ordinance issued by the Federal Government pursuant to subsection (4). ²It may, in individual cases, prohibit the certain other work assignments.

§ 5
Mitteilungspflicht, ärztliches Zeugnis

Section 5
Duty to Notify, Physician's Certificate

(1) ¹Werdende Mütter sollen dem Arbeitgeber ihre Schwangerschaft und den mutmaßlichen Tag der Entbindung mitteilen, sobald ihnen ihr Zustand bekannt ist. ²Auf Verlangen des Arbeitgebers sollen sie das Zeugnis eines Arztes oder einer Hebamme vorlegen. ³Der Arbeitgeber hat die Aufsichtsbehörde unverzüglich von der Mitteilung der werdenden Mutter zu benachrichtigen. ⁴Er darf die Mitteilung der werdenden Mutter Dritten nicht unbefugt bekannt geben.

(1) ¹Expectant mothers shall notify the employer of their pregnancy and the probable delivery date as soon as their condition is known to them. ²At the employer's request they shall present a certificate issued by a physician or a midwife. ³The employer shall inform the supervisory authority of the expectant mother's notification without delay. ⁴Unless authorized, he may not disclose the expectant mother's notification to a third party.

(2) ¹Für die Berechnung der in § 3 Abs. 2 bezeichneten Zeiträume vor der Entbindung ist das Zeugnis eines Arztes oder einer Hebamme maßgebend; das Zeugnis soll den mutmaßlichen Tag der Entbindung angeben. ²Irrt sich der Arzt oder die Hebamme über den Zeitpunkt der Entbindung, so verkürzt oder verlängert sich diese Frist entsprechend.

(2) ¹In computing the periods prior to delivery as set forth in section 3 (2), the certificate issued by a physician or a midwife shall be decisive; the certificate shall indicate the probable delivery date. ²If the physician or midwife is in error as to the delivery date, this period shall be shortened or extended accordingly.

(3) Die Kosten für die Zeugnisse nach den Absätzen 1 und 2 trägt der Arbeitgeber.

(3) The employer shall bear the cost of the certificates pursuant to subsections (1) and (2).

§ 6
Beschäftigungsverbote nach der Entbindung

Section 6
Prohibitions of Employment After Delivery

(1) ¹Mütter dürfen bis zum Ablauf von acht Wochen, bei Früh- und Mehrlingsgeburten bis zum Ablauf von zwölf Wochen nach der Entbindung nicht beschäftigt werden. ²Bei Frühgeburten und sonstigen vorzeitigen Entbindungen verlängern sich die Fristen nach Satz 1 zusätzlich um den Zeitraum der

(1) ¹Mothers shall not be employed until eight weeks, and in the case of premature or multiple births, twelve weeks, after delivery. ²In the case of premature births and other premature deliveries, the periods pursuant to sentence 1 shall additionally be extended by the duration of the protective period

Schutzfrist nach § 3 Abs. 2, der nicht in Anspruch genommen werden konnte. ³Beim Tod ihres Kindes kann die Mutter auf ihr ausdrückliches Verlangen ausnahmsweise schon vor Ablauf dieser Fristen, aber noch nicht in den ersten zwei Wochen nach der Entbindung, wieder beschäftigt werden, wenn nach ärztlichem Zeugnis nichts dagegen spricht. ⁴Sie kann ihre Erklärung jederzeit widerrufen.

(2) Frauen, die in den ersten Monaten nach der Entbindung nach ärztlichem Zeugnis nicht voll leistungsfähig sind, dürfen nicht zu einer ihre Leistungsfähigkeit übersteigenden Arbeit herangezogen werden.

(3) ¹Stillende Mütter dürfen mit den in § 4 Abs. 1, 2 Nr. 1, 3, 4, 5, 6 und 8 sowie Abs. 3 Satz 1 genannten Arbeiten nicht beschäftigt werden. ²Die Vorschriften des § 4 Abs. 3 Satz 2 und 3 sowie Abs. 5 gelten entsprechend.

pursuant to section 3 (2) which could not be utilized. ³If her child should die, the mother may, at her explicit request and as an exceptional case, resume her employment prior to their expiration, but not within the first two weeks after delivery, provided that a physician certifies that there is no objection to her doing so. ⁴She can revoke her declaration at any time.

(2) Women who, according to a physician's certificate, are not fully able to work in the first months after the delivery, shall not be required to work beyond their ability to perform.

(3) ¹Nursing mothers shall not be assigned to the work referred to in section 4 (1) and (2) nos. 1, 3, 4, 5, 6 and 8 as well as in subsection (3) sentence 1. ²The provisions of section 4 (3) sentences 2 and 3, as well as subsection (5) shall apply *mutatis mutandis*.

§ 7
Stillzeit

Section 7
Nursing Periods

(1) ¹Stillenden Müttern ist auf ihr Verlangen die zum Stillen erforderliche Zeit, mindestens aber zweimal täglich eine halbe Stunde oder einmal täglich eine Stunde freizugeben. ²Bei einer zusammenhängenden Arbeitszeit von mehr als acht Stunden soll auf Verlangen zweimal eine Stillzeit von mindestens 45 Minuten oder, wenn in der Nähe der Arbeitsstätte keine Stillgelegenheit vorhanden ist, einmal eine Stillzeit von mindestens 90 Minuten gewährt werden. ³Die Arbeitszeit gilt als zusammenhängend, soweit sie nicht durch eine Ruhepause von mindestens zwei Stunden unterbrochen wird.

(2) ¹Durch die Gewährung der Stillzeit darf ein Verdienstausfall nicht eintreten. ²Die Stillzeit darf von stillenden Müttern nicht vor- oder nachgearbeitet und nicht auf die in dem Arbeitszeitgesetz oder in anderen Vorschriften fest-

(1) ¹Nursing mothers are be given, at their request, the necessary free time for nursing, but at least half an hour twice daily or one hour once daily. ²For a continuous working time of more than eight hours, two nursing periods shall be granted upon request of at least 45 minutes each or, if there are no nursing facilities in the vicinity of the place of work, one nursing period of at least 90 minutes. ³Working time shall be deemed to be continuous unless it is interrupted by a rest period of at least two hours.

(2) ¹No loss from earnings shall result from the granting of the nursing period. ²Nursing time may not be made up by nursing mothers before or after work and or be deducted from the rest periods prescribed in the Hours of Em-

gesetzten Ruhepausen angerechnet werden.

(3) Die Aufsichtsbehörde kann in Einzelfällen nähere Bestimmungen über Zahl, Lage und Dauer der Stillzeiten treffen; sie kann die Einrichtung von Stillräumen vorschreiben.

(4) ¹Der Auftraggeber oder Zwischenmeister hat den in Heimarbeit Beschäftigten und den ihnen Gleichgestellten für die Stillzeit ein Entgelt von 75 vom Hundert eines durchschnittlichen Stundenverdienstes, mindestens aber 0,38 Euro für jeden Werktag zu zahlen. ²Ist die Frau für mehrere Auftraggeber oder Zwischenmeister tätig, so haben diese das Entgelt für die Stillzeit zu gleichen Teilen zu gewähren. ³Auf das Entgelt finden die Vorschriften der §§ 23 bis 25 des Heimarbeitsgesetzes vom 14. März 1951 (BGBl. I S. 191) über den Entgeltschutz Anwendung.

§ 8
Mehrarbeit, Nacht- und Sonntagsarbeit

(1) Werdende und stillende Mütter dürfen nicht mit Mehrarbeit, nicht in der Nacht zwischen 20 und 6 Uhr und nicht an Sonn- und Feiertagen beschäftigt werden.

(2) ¹Mehrarbeit im Sinne des Absatzes 1 ist jede Arbeit, die

1. von Frauen unter 18 Jahren über 8 Stunden täglich oder 80 Stunden in der Doppelwoche,
2. von sonstigen Frauen über 8¹/₂ Stunden täglich oder 90 Stunden in der Doppelwoche

hinaus geleistet wird. ²In die Doppelwoche werden die Sonntage eingerechnet.

(3) Abweichend vom Nachtarbeitsverbot des Absatzes 1 dürfen werdende Mütter in den ersten vier Monaten der

ployment Act *(Arbeitszeitgesetz)* or other regulations.

(3) The supervisory authority may, in individual cases, enact more detailed provisions as to the number, location and duration of nursing periods; it may require that nursing rooms be set up.

(4) ¹The principal or intermediary *(Zwischenmeister)* shall pay women working at home, and those in an equivalent position, remuneration equal 75 percent of their average hourly earning for nursing time, but at least 0.38 euro for every working day *(Werktag)*. ²If a woman works for two or more principals or intermediaries, they shall equally share payment of the remuneration for the nursing time. ³The provisions on protection of remuneration set forth in sections 23 to 25 of the Home Work Act *(Heimarbeitsgesetz)* of 14 March 1951 (Federal Law Gazette I p. 191) shall apply to the remuneration.

Section 8
Overtime, Night Work and Sunday Work

(1) Expectant or nursing mothers may not be assigned to work overtime, at night between 8:00 p.m. and 6:00 a.m. or on Sundays and public holidays.

(2) ¹Overtime within the meaning of subsection (1) shall be any work performed by

1. women under 18 years of age for more than 8 hours a day or 80 hours in a period of two weeks,
2. other women for more than 8¹/₂ hours a day or 90 hours in a period of two weeks.

²Such two week period also includes Sundays.

(3) Notwithstanding the prohibition of night work pursuant to subsection (1), expectant mothers in the first four

Schwangerschaft und stillende Mütter beschäftigt werden

1. in Gast- und Schankwirtschaften und im Übrigen Beherbergungswesen bis 22 Uhr,
2. in der Landwirtschaft mit dem Melken von Vieh ab 5 Uhr,
3. als Künstlerinnen bei Musikaufführungen, Theatervorstellungen und ähnlichen Aufführungen bis 23 Uhr.

(4) Im Verkehrswesen, in Gast- und Schankwirtschaften und im übrigen Beherbergungswesen, im Familienhaushalt, in Krankenpflege- und in Badeanstalten, bei Musikaufführungen, Theatervorstellungen, anderen Schaustellungen, Darbietungen oder Lustbarkeiten dürfen werdende oder stillende Mütter, abweichend von Absatz 1, an Sonn- und Feiertagen beschäftigt werden, wenn ihnen in jeder Woche einmal eine ununterbrochene Ruhezeit von mindestens 24 Stunden im Anschluss an eine Nachtruhe gewährt wird.

(5) ¹An in Heimarbeit Beschäftigte und ihnen Gleichgestellte, wie werdende oder stillende Mütter sind, darf Heimarbeit nur in solchem Umfang und mit solchen Fertigungsfristen ausgegeben werden, dass sie von der werdenden Mutter voraussichtlich während einer 8-stündigen Tagesarbeitszeit, von der stillenden Mutter voraussichtlich während einer $7^{1}/_{4}$-stündigen Tagesarbeitszeit an Werktagen ausgeführt werden kann. ²Die Aufsichtsbehörde kann in Einzelfällen nähere Bestimmungen über die Arbeitsmenge treffen; falls ein Heimarbeitsausschuss besteht, hat sie diesen vorher zu hören.

(6) Die Aufsichtsbehörde kann in begründeten Einzelfällen Ausnahmen von den vorstehenden Vorschriften zulassen.

months of pregnancy and nursing mothers may be employed

1. in restaurants and bars and otherwise in the hotel industry until 10:00 p.m.,
2. in agriculture in the milking of cattle from 5:00 a.m. on,
3. as artists in musical, theatrical or similar performances until 11:00 p.m.

(4) Notwithstanding the provisions in subsection (1), expectant or nursing mothers may be employed on Sundays and public holidays in the transportation business, as domestic workers in a family household, in restaurants, bars or otherwise in the hotel industry, in hospitals and swimming facilities, in musical and theatrical performances, other exhibitions, presentations or entertainment, if once each week they are granted an uninterrupted rest period of at least 24 hours following an overnight rest period.

(5) ¹Expectant or nursing mothers working at home, and those in an equivalent position, may only be assigned work at home to the extent that and with deadlines for completion such that they can probably be carried out by expectant mothers by working an eight-hour day and by nursing mothers working a $7^{1}/_{4}$-hour day on working days. ²The supervisory authority may enact more detailed provisions on the amount of work; if a home work committee exists, the supervisory authority shall consult with it first.

(6) The supervisory authority may in certain justified cases grant exceptions to the above provisions.

Abschnitt 2a
Mutterschaftsurlaub

§§ 8a bis 8d
(weggefallen)

Chapter 2a
Maternity Leave

Section 8a to Section 8d
(repealed)

Dritter Abschnitt **Kündigung**	**Chapter 3** **Termination**
§ 9 **Kündigungsverbot**	**Section 9** **Prohibition of Dismissal**

(1) ¹Die Kündigung gegenüber einer Frau während der Schwangerschaft und bis zum Ablauf von vier Monaten nach der Entbindung ist unzulässig, wenn dem Arbeitgeber zur Zeit der Kündigung die Schwangerschaft oder Entbindung bekannt war oder innerhalb zweier Wochen nach Zugang der Kündigung mitgeteilt wird; das Überschreiten dieser Frist ist unschädlich, wenn es auf einem von der Frau nicht zu vertretenden Grund beruht und die Mitteilung unverzüglich nachgeholt wird. ²Die Vorschrift des Satzes 1 gilt für Frauen, die den in Heimarbeit Beschäftigten gleichgestellt sind, nur, wenn sich die Gleichstellung auch auf den Neunten Abschnitt – Kündigung – des Heimarbeitsgesetzes vom 14. März 1951 (BGBl. I S. 191) erstreckt.

(1) ¹Dismissal of a woman during pregnancy and in the first four months following delivery shall be unlawful if the employer was aware of the pregnancy or delivery at the time it gave notice of dismissal or is informed of such within two weeks after the notice of dismissal was served; if this time period is exceeded, no repercussions shall ensue if the delay was due to reasons beyond the woman's control and the notification was then made without undue delay. ²The provision set forth in sentence 1 shall apply to women in an equivalent position to those working at home only if the equivalence also extends to the Ninth Chapter (dismissal) of the Home Work Act of 14 March 1951 (Federal Law Gazette I p. 191).

(2) Kündigt eine schwangere Frau, gilt § 5 Abs. 1 Satz 3 entsprechend.

(2) If a pregnant woman gives notice of dismissal, section 5 (1) sentence 3 shall apply *mutatis mutandis*.

(3) ¹Die für den Arbeitsschutz zuständige oberste Landesbehörde oder die von ihr bestimmte Stelle kann in besonderen Fällen, die nicht mit dem Zustand einer Frau während der Schwangerschaft oder ihrer Lage bis zum Ablauf von vier Monaten nach der Entbindung in Zusammenhang stehen, ausnahmsweise die Kündigung für zulässig erklären. ²Die Kündigung bedarf der schriftlichen Form und sie muss den zulässigen Kündigungsgrund angeben.

(3) ¹The highest State authority responsible for protection of employees or the office designated by it may, in special cases, which are not associated with a woman's condition during her pregnancy or her situation in the first four months after delivery, declare a dismissal to be permissible. ²The dismissal must be in written form and state the permissible grounds for dismissal.

(4) In Heimarbeit Beschäftigte und ihnen Gleichgestellte dürfen während der Schwangerschaft und bis zum Ablauf von vier Monaten nach der Entbindung nicht gegen ihren Willen bei der Ausgabe von Heimarbeit ausgeschlossen

(4) Women working at home and those in an equivalent position may not be excluded from receiving assignments to work at home against their will during the pregnancy and for the first four months after delivery; the provisions

werden; die Vorschriften der §§ 3, 4, 6 und 8 Abs. 5 bleiben unberührt.

set forth in sections 3, 4, 6 and 8 (5) remain unaffected.

§ 9 a
(weggefallen)

Section 9 a
(repealed)

§ 10
Erhaltung von Rechten

(1) Eine Frau kann während der Schwangerschaft und während der Schutzfrist nach der Entbindung (§ 6 Abs. 1) das Arbeitsverhältnis ohne Einhaltung einer Frist zum Ende der Schutzfrist nach der Entbindung kündigen.

(2) ¹Wird das Arbeitsverhältnis nach Absatz 1 aufgelöst und wird die Frau innerhalb eines Jahres nach der Entbindung in ihrem bisherigen Betrieb wieder eingestellt, so gilt, soweit Rechte aus dem Arbeitsverhältnis von der Dauer der Betriebs- oder Berufszugehörigkeit oder von der Dauer der Beschäftigungs- oder Dienstzeit abhängen, das Arbeitsverhältnis als nicht unterbrochen. ²Dies gilt nicht, wenn die Frau in der Zeit von der Auflösung des Arbeitsverhältnisses bis zur Wiedereinstellung bei einem anderen Arbeitgeber beschäftigt war.

Section 10
Retention of Rights

(1) A woman may terminate the employment relationship during her pregnancy and during the protection period following the delivery (section 6 (1)) as of the end of the protection period without needing to observe a notice period.

(2) ¹If the employment relationship is dissolved pursuant to subsection (1) and the woman's employment is reinstated in her former workplace within one year after delivery, the employment relationship shall be deemed to have not been interrupted to the extent that rights arising from the employment relationship are contingent upon the amount of time she has worked for an establishment or in a classification or the amount of time she has work in one occupation or upon the length of the term of employment or service. ²This shall not apply if the woman was employed by another employer during the period between the dissolution of the employment relationship and its reinstatement.

Vierter Abschnitt
Leistungen

Chapter 4
Benefits

§ 11
Arbeitsentgelt bei Beschäftigungsverboten

(1) ¹Den unter den Geltungsbereich des § 1 fallenden Frauen ist, soweit sie nicht Mutterschaftsgeld nach den Vorschriften der Reichsversicherungsordnung beziehen können, vom Arbeitgeber mindestens der Durchschnittsverdienst der letzten 13 Wochen oder der letzten

Section 11
Remuneration in Case of Prohibition of Employment

(1) ¹The employer shall continue to pay the women falling within the purview of section 1 at least their average earnings in the last thirteen weeks or the last three months prior to the commencement of the month in which pregnancy occurred, unless they can receive maternity bene-

drei Monate vor Beginn des Monats, in dem die Schwangerschaft eingetreten ist, weiter zu gewähren, wenn sie wegen eines Beschäftigungsverbots nach § 3 Abs. 1, §§ 4, 6 Abs. 2 oder 3 oder wegen des Mehr-, Nacht- oder Sonntagsarbeitsverbots nach § 8 Abs. 1, 3 oder 5 teilweise oder völlig mit der Arbeit aussetzen. ²Dies gilt auch, wenn wegen dieser Verbote die Beschäftigung oder die Entlohnungsart wechselt. ³Wird das Arbeitsverhältnis erst nach Eintritt der Schwangerschaft begonnen, so ist der Durchschnittsverdienst aus dem Arbeitsentgelt der ersten 13 Wochen oder drei Monate der Beschäftigung zu berechnen. ⁴Hat das Arbeitsverhältnis nach Satz 1 oder 3 kürzer gedauert, so ist der kürzere Zeitraum der Berechnung zugrunde zu legen. ⁵Zeiten, in denen kein Arbeitsentgelt erzielt wurde, bleiben außer Betracht.

(2) ¹Bei Verdiensterhöhungen nicht nur vorübergehender Natur, die während oder nach Ablauf des Berechnungszeitraums eintreten, ist von dem erhöhten Verdienst auszugehen. ²Verdienstkürzungen, die im Berechnungszeitraum infolge von Kurzarbeit, Arbeitsausfällen oder unverschuldeter Arbeitsversäumnis eintreten, bleiben für die Berechnung des Durchschnittsverdienstes außer Betracht. ³Zu berücksichtigen sind dauerhafte Verdienstkürzungen, die während oder nach Ablauf des Berechnungszeitraums eintreten und nicht auf einem mutterschutzrechtlichen Beschäftigungsverbot beruhen.

(3) Die Bundesregierung wird ermächtigt, durch Rechtsverordnung mit Zustimmung des Bundesrates Vorschriften über die Berechnung des Durchschnittsverdienstes im Sinne der Absätze 1 und 2 zu erlassen.

fits pursuant to the provisions of the Imperial Insurance Regulations (*Reichsversicherungsordnung*), if they suspend their work activities in whole or in part due to a prohibition of employment pursuant to section 3 (1), sections 4, 6 (2) or (3) or due to the prohibition of overtime, night work and Sunday work pursuant to section 8 (1), (3) or (5). ²This also applies if the employment or type of remuneration changes due to these prohibitions. ³If the employment relationship commences after the occurrence of pregnancy, then the average earnings shall be calculated from the remuneration of the first thirteen weeks or three months of the employment. ⁴Where the employment relationship pursuant to sentence 1 or 3 has lasted for a briefer time, then the shorter time period shall be the basis for the calculation. ⁵Periods in which no employment remuneration was achieved shall not be taken into account.

(2) ¹In case of a non-temporary increase in earnings during or after the end of the calculation period, the calculation shall be based on these increased earnings. ²Reductions in earnings which occur during the calculation period as a result of short time, loss of working time or an absence from work without fault, shall not be taken into account in calculating the average earnings. ³Permanent reductions in earnings which occur during or after the calculation period has expired and are not due to a prohibition of work under the maternity protection statutes shall be taken into account.

(3) The Federal Government shall be empowered to enact ordinances with the consent of the upper house of parliament on the calculation of average earnings within the meaning of subsections (1) and (2).

§ 12

(*weggefallen*)

Section 12

(*repealed*)

§ 13
Mutterschaftsgeld

(1) Frauen, die Mitglied einer gesetzlichen Krankenkasse sind, erhalten für die Zeit der Schutzfristen des § 3 Abs. 2 und des § 6 Abs. 1 sowie für den Entbindungstag Mutterschaftsgeld nach den Vorschriften der Reichsversicherungsordnung oder des Gesetzes über die Krankenversicherung der Landwirte über das Mutterschaftsgeld.

(2) [1]Frauen, die nicht Mitglied einer gesetzlichen Krankenkasse sind, erhalten, wenn sie bei Beginn der Schutzfrist nach § 3 Abs. 2 in einem Arbeitsverhältnis stehen oder in Heimarbeit beschäftigt sind, für die Zeit der Schutzfristen des § 3 Abs. 2 und des § 6 Abs. 1 sowie für den Entbindungstag Mutterschaftsgeld zu Lasten des Bundes in entsprechender Anwendung der Vorschriften der Reichsversicherungsordnung über das Mutterschaftsgeld, höchstens jedoch insgesamt 210 Euro. [2]Das Mutterschaftsgeld wird diesen Frauen auf Antrag vom Bundesversicherungsamt gezahlt. [3]Die Sätze 1 und 2 gelten für Frauen entsprechend, deren Arbeitsverhältnis während ihrer Schwangerschaft oder der Schutzfrist des § 6 Abs. 1 nach Maßgabe von § 9 Abs. 3 aufgelöst worden ist.

(3) Frauen, die während der Schutzfristen des § 3 Abs. 2 oder des § 6 Abs. 1 von einem Beamten- in ein Arbeitsverhältnis wechseln, erhalten von diesem Zeitpunkt an Mutterschaftsgeld entsprechend den Absätzen 1 und 2.

§ 14
Zuschuss zum Mutterschaftsgeld

(1) [1]Frauen, die Anspruch auf Mutterschaftsgeld nach § 200 Abs. 1, 2 Satz 1

Section 13
Maternity Benefits

(1) For the time of the protection periods set forth in section 3 (2) and section 6 (1) as well as for the day of giving birth, women belonging to statutory health insurance schemes shall receive maternity benefits pursuant to the provisions of the Imperial Insurance Regulations or the Act on Health Insurance for Farmers regarding maternity benefits.

(2) [1]Women not belonging to statutory health insurance schemes shall receive maternity payments during the protection periods set forth in section 3 (2) and section 6 (1), and maternity benefits for the day of delivery, at the expense of the Federal Government in corresponding application of the provisions of the Imperial Insurance Regulations regarding maternity benefits, but no more than a total of 210 euro, provided that, at the commencement of the protection period pursuant to section 3 (2), they were in an employment relationship or working at home or her employment relationship was permissibly dissolved by her employer during her pregnancy. [2]Maternity benefits shall be granted to those women upon application by the Federal Insurance Agency *(Bundesversicherungsamt)*. [3]Sentences 1 and 2 apply *mutatis mutandis* for women whose employment relationship was dissolved during their pregnancy or the protective period set forth in section 6 (1) on the basis of section 9 (3).

(3) Women whose status changes from a civil servant to an employee during the protective periods set forth in section 3 (2) or section 6 (1) shall from that point on receive maternity benefits in accordance with subsections (1) and (2).

Section 14
Contribution to Maternity Benefits

(1) [1]Women having a claim to maternity benefits pursuant to section 200 (1) and

bis 4 und Abs. 3 der Reichsversicherungsordnung, § 29 Abs. 1, 2 und 4 des Gesetzes über die Krankenversicherung der Landwirte oder § 13 Abs. 2, 3 haben, erhalten während ihres bestehenden Arbeitsverhältnisses für die Zeit der Schutzfristen des § 3 Abs. 2 und § 6 Abs. 1 sowie für den Entbindungstag von ihrem Arbeitgeber einen Zuschuss in Höhe des Unterschiedsbetrages zwischen 13 Euro und dem um die gesetzlichen Abzüge verminderten durchschnittlichen kalendertäglichen Arbeitsentgelt. ²Das durchschnittliche kalendertägliche Arbeitsentgelt ist aus den letzten drei abgerechneten Kalendermonaten, bei wöchentlicher Abrechnung aus den letzten 13 abgerechneten Wochen vor Beginn der Schutzfrist nach § 3 Abs. 2 zu berechnen. ³Nicht nur vorübergehende Erhöhungen des Arbeitsentgeltes, die während der Schutzfristen des § 3 Abs. 2 und § 6 Abs. 1 wirksam werden, sind ab diesem Zeitpunkt in die Berechnung einzubeziehen. ⁴Einmalig gezahltes Arbeitsentgelt (§ 23a des Vierten Buches Sozialgesetzbuch) sowie Tage, an denen infolge von Kurzarbeit, Arbeitsausfällen oder unverschuldeter Arbeitsversäumnis kein oder ein vermindertes Arbeitsentgelt erzielt wurde, bleiben außer Betracht. ⁵Zu berücksichtigen sind dauerhafte Verdienstkürzungen, die während oder nach Ablauf des Berechnungszeitraums eintreten und nicht auf einem mutterschutzrechtlichen Beschäftigungsverbot beruhen. ⁶Ist danach eine Berechnung nicht möglich, so ist das durchschnittliche kalendertägliche Arbeitsentgelt einer gleichartig Beschäftigten zugrunde zu legen.

(2) Frauen, deren Arbeitsverhältnis während ihrer Schwangerschaft oder

(2) sentences 2 to 4 and (3) of the Imperial Insurance Regulations (*Reichsversicherungsordnung*), section 29 (1), (2) and (4) of the Act on Health Insurance for Farmers (*Krankenversicherung der Landwirte*) or section 13 (2) and (3) of this Act shall receive, during their existing employment relationship, for the duration of the protection periods set forth in section 3 (2) and section 6 (1), as well as for the day of delivery, a contribution from their employer amounting to the difference between 13 euro and the average remuneration per calendar day minus the statutory deductions. ²The average remuneration per calendar day shall to be calculated from the last three calendar months accounted for or, in case of a weekly accounting, from the last thirteen weeks accounted for, prior to the commencement of the protection period pursuant to section 3 (2). ³Non-temporary increases in the average remuneration which go into effect during the protection periods set forth in section 3 (2) and section 6 (1) shall be incorporated into the calculation as of that point in time. ⁴ One-off remuneration payments (section 23a of the Fourth Book of the Social Code – (*Viertes Buch Sozialgesetzbuch*)) as well as days on which no remuneration or less remuneration was achieved due to short time, loss of working hours or an absence from work without fault, shall not be taken into account. ⁵Permanent reductions in earnings which occur during or after the calculation period has expired and are not due to a prohibition of work under the maternity protection statutes shall be taken into account. ⁶If a calculation on that basis is not possible, then it shall be based on the average remuneration for employment per day for a comparable employment. ⁷If such a calculation is not possible, then the average remuneration per calendar day of a person similarly employed shall be taken as the basis.

(2) Women whose employment relationship has been dissolved during

während der Schutzfrist des § 6 Abs. 1 nach Maßgabe von § 9 Abs. 3 aufgelöst worden ist, erhalten bis zum Ende dieser Schutzfrist den Zuschuss nach Absatz 1 von der für die Zahlung des Mutterschaftsgeldes zuständigen Stelle.

(3) Absatz 2 gilt entsprechend, wenn der Arbeitgeber wegen eines Insolvenzereignisses im Sinne des § 183 Abs. 1 Satz 1 des Dritten Buches Sozialgesetzbuch seinen Zuschuss nach Absatz 1 nicht zahlen kann.

(4) [1] Der Zuschuss nach den Absätzen 1 bis 3 entfällt für die Zeit, in der Frauen die Elternzeit nach dem Bundeselterngeld- und Elternzeitgesetz in Anspruch nehmen oder in Anspruch genommen hätten, wenn deren Arbeitsverhältnis nicht während ihrer Schwangerschaft oder während der Schutzfrist des § 6 Abs. 1 vom Arbeitgeber zulässig aufgelöst worden wäre. [2] Dies gilt nicht, soweit sie eine zulässige Teilzeitarbeit leisten.

their pregnancy or the protection period set forth in section 6 (1) on the basis of section 9 (3) shall receive up to the end of this protection period the employer's contribution pursuant to subsection (1) from the agency competent for paying the maternity benefits.

(3) Subsection (2) applies *mutatis mutandis* if the employer cannot pay its contribution pursuant to subsection (1) due to an insolvency proceeding within the meaning of section 183 (1) sentence 1 of the Third Book of the Social Security Code *(Drittes Buch Sozialgesetzbuch)*.

(4) [1] The contribution pursuant to subsections (1) to (3) shall not be granted during the period in which the women lay claim to parental leave pursuant to the Federal Parental Benefit and Parental Leave Act *(Bundeselterngeld- und Elternzeitgesetz)* or would have laid claim to it had their employment relationship not been permissibly dissolved by their employer during their pregnancy or during the protective period set forth in section 6 (1). [2] This shall not apply where they perform permissible part-time work.

§ 15
Sonstige Leistungen bei Schwangerschaft und Mutterschaft

Frauen, die in der gesetzlichen Krankenversicherung versichert sind, erhalten auch die folgenden Leistungen bei Schwangerschaft und Mutterschaft nach den Vorschriften der Reichsversicherungsordnung oder des Gesetzes über die Krankenversicherung der Landwirte:

1. ärztliche Betreuung und Hebammenhilfe,
2. Versorgung mit Arznei-, Verband- und Heilmitteln,
3. stationäre Entbindung,
4. häusliche Pflege,
5. Haushaltshilfe.

Section 15
Other Pregnancy and Maternity Benefits

Women belonging to statutory health insurance schemes shall also receive the following pregnancy and maternity benefits pursuant to the provisions of the Imperial Insurance Regulations or the Act on Health Insurance for Farmers:

1. medical care, as well as midwife assistance,
2. provision of medicines, dressings and therapeutic preparations,
3. inpatient delivery,
4. nursing care at home,
5. help in the household.

§ 16
Freistellung für Untersuchungen

¹Der Arbeitgeber hat die Frau für die Zeit freizustellen, die zur Durchführung der Untersuchungen im Rahmen der Leistungen der gesetzlichen Krankenversicherung bei Schwangerschaft und Mutterschaft erforderlich ist. ²Entsprechendes gilt zugunsten der Frau, die nicht in der gesetzlichen Krankenversicherung versichert ist. ³Ein Entgeltausfall darf hierdurch nicht eintreten.

§ 17
Erholungsurlaub

¹Für den Anspruch auf bezahlten Erholungsurlaub und dessen Dauer gelten die Ausfallzeiten wegen mutterschutzrechtlicher Beschäftigungsverbote als Beschäftigungszeiten. ²Hat die Frau ihren Urlaub vor Beginn der Beschäftigungsverbote nicht oder nicht vollständig erhalten, so kann sie nach Ablauf der Fristen den Resturlaub im laufenden oder im nächsten Urlaubsjahr beanspruchen.

Fünfter Abschnitt
Durchführung des Gesetzes

§ 18
Auslage des Gesetzes

(1) In Betrieben und Verwaltungen, in denen regelmäßig mehr als drei Frauen beschäftigt werden, ist ein Abdruck dieses Gesetzes an geeigneter Stelle zur Einsicht auszulegen oder auszuhängen.

(2) Wer Heimarbeit ausgibt oder abnimmt, hat in den Räumen der Ausgabe und Abnahme einen Abdruck dieses Gesetzes an geeigneter Stelle zur Einsicht auszulegen oder auszuhängen.

Section 16
Release from Work for Examinations

¹The employer shall release women from their work responsibilities for the time necessary for examinations within the scope of the services rendered to pregnant women and mothers by the statutory health insurance scheme. ²The same shall apply *mutatis mutandis* to the benefit of women who are not insured in the statutory health insurance scheme. ³A loss of remuneration shall not result therefrom.

Section 17
Vacation

¹With respect to the claim for vacation time and its duration, the time away from work due to the prohibition of employment under the maternity protection regulations shall be counted as work periods. ²If the woman did not receive her vacation time in full prior to the onset of the prohibition of employment, she may lay claim to the remaining vacation time after the periods have expired or during the next vacation year.

Chapter 5
Implementation of the Act

Section 18
Display of the Act

(1) In establishments and administrative offices in which more than three women are regularly employed, a copy of this Act shall be displayed or posted for inspection at a suitable location.

(2) Whoever assigns or accepts work done at home shall display or post a copy of this Act at a suitable location in the rooms in which the assignment and acceptance are performed.

§ 19
Auskunft

(1) Der Arbeitgeber ist verpflichtet, der Aufsichtsbehörde auf Verlangen

1. die zur Erfüllung der Aufgaben dieser Behörde erforderlichen Angaben wahrheitsgemäß und vollständig zu machen,
2. die Unterlagen, aus denen Namen, Beschäftigungsart und -zeiten der werdenden und stillenden Mütter sowie Lohn- und Gehaltszahlungen ersichtlich sind, und alle sonstigen Unterlagen, die sich auf die zu Nummer 1 zu machenden Angaben beziehen, zur Einsicht vorzulegen oder einzusenden.

(2) Die Unterlagen sind mindestens bis zum Ablauf von zwei Jahren nach der letzten Eintragung aufzubewahren.

§ 20
Aufsichtsbehörden

(1) Die Aufsicht über die Ausführung der Vorschriften dieses Gesetzes und der auf Grund dieses Gesetzes erlassenen Vorschriften obliegt den nach Landesrecht zuständigen Behörden (Aufsichtsbehörden).

(2) ¹Die Aufsichtsbehörden haben dieselben Befugnisse und Obliegenheiten wie nach § 139b der Gewerbeordnung die dort genannten besonderen Beamten. ²Das Grundrecht der Unverletzlichkeit der Wohnung (Artikel 13 des Grundgesetzes) wird insoweit eingeschränkt.

Sechster Abschnitt
Straftaten und Ordnungswidrigkeiten

§ 21
Straftaten und Ordnungswidrigkeiten

(1) Ordnungswidrig handelt der Arbeitgeber, der vorsätzlich oder fahrlässig

Section 19
Information

(1) When called upon to do so by the supervisory authority, the employer shall be obligated to

1. provide accurate and complete information necessary for the fulfilment of the authority's duties,
2. present for inspection or submit documents showing the name, type of employment and working hours of the expectant and nursing mothers, as well as wage and salary payments, and all other documents referring to the data to be provided pursuant to no. 1.

(2) The documents shall be retained for at least two years following the last entry.

Section 20
Supervisory Authorities

(1) Supervision of the implementation of the provisions of this Act and of the regulations enacted pursuant to this Act is the duty of the authorities (supervisory authorities) which competent under the state laws.

(2) ¹The supervisory authorities shall have the same rights and duties as the special officials designated in section 139b of the Trade Law (*Gewerbeordnung*). ²The constitutional right of the inviolability of the home (Article 13 of the Basic Law – *Grundgesetz*) is restricted to this extent.

Chapter 6
Criminal and Administrative Offenses

Section 21
Criminal and Administrative Offenses

(1) An employer is guilty of an administrative offense who intentionally or negligently violates

1. den Vorschriften der §§ 3, 4 Abs. 1 bis 3 Satz 1 oder § 6 Abs. 1 bis 3 Satz 1 über die Beschäftigungsverbote vor und nach der Entbindung,
2. den Vorschriften des § 7 Abs. 1 Satz 1 oder Abs. 2 Satz 2 über die Stillzeit,
3. den Vorschriften des § 8 Abs. 1 oder 3 bis 5 Satz 1 über Mehr-, Nacht- oder Sonntagsarbeit,
4. den auf Grund des § 4 Abs. 4 erlassenen Vorschriften, soweit sie für einen bestimmten Tatbestand auf diese Bußgeldvorschrift verweisen,
5. einer vollziehbaren Verfügung der Aufsichtsbehörde nach § 2 Abs. 5, § 4 Abs. 5, § 6 Abs. 3 Satz 2, § 7 Abs. 3 oder § 8 Abs. 5 Satz 2 Halbsatz 1,
6. den Vorschriften des § 5 Abs. 1 Satz 3 über die Benachrichtigung,
7. der Vorschrift des § 16 Satz 1, auch in Verbindung mit Satz 2, über die Freistellung für Untersuchungen oder
8. den Vorschriften des § 18 über die Auslage des Gesetzes oder des § 19 über die Einsicht, Aufbewahrung und Vorlage der Unterlagen und über die Auskunft

zuwiderhandelt.

(2) Die Ordnungswidrigkeit nach Absatz 1 Nr. 1 bis 5 kann mit einer Geldbuße bis zu fünfzehntausend Euro, die Ordnungswidrigkeit nach Absatz 1 Nr. 6 bis 8 mit einer Geldbuße bis zu zweitausendfünfhundert Euro geahndet werden.

(3) Wer vorsätzlich eine der in Absatz 1 Nr. 1 bis 5 bezeichneten Handlungen begeht und dadurch die Frau in ihrer Arbeitskraft oder Gesundheit gefährdet, wird mit Freiheitsstrafe bis zu einem Jahr oder mit Geldstrafe bestraft.

(4) Wer in den Fällen des Absatzes 3 die Gefahr fahrlässig verursacht, wird mit Freiheitsstrafe bis zu sechs Monaten oder mit Geldstrafe bis zu einhundertachtzig Tagessätzen bestraft.

1. the provisions of sections 3, 4 (1) to (3) sentence 1 or Section 6 (1) to (3) sentence 1 regarding prohibitions of employment before and after delivery,
2. the provisions of section 7 (1) sentence 1 or (2) sentence 2 regarding nursing time,
3. the provisions of section 8 (1) or (3) to (5) sentence 1 regarding overtime, night work and Sunday work,
4. the provisions enacted pursuant to section 4 (4) where they refer to these administrative fine provisions for a specific offence,
5. an enforceable administrative order of the supervisory authorities pursuant to section 2 (5), section 4 (5), section 6 (3) sentence 2, section 7 (3) or section 8 (5) first half of sentence 2,
6. the provisions of section 5 (1) sentence 3 regarding notification,
7. the provisions of section 16 sentence 1, also in connection with sentence 2, regarding release from work for examinations or,
8. the provisions of section 18 regarding the display of this Act or of section 19 regarding the inspection, preservation and presentation of documents and regarding information.

(2) An administrative offense pursuant to subsection (1) nos. 1 to 5 may be subject to a fine of up to 15,000 euro, administrative offenses pursuant to subsection (1) nos. 6 to 8 may be subject to a fine of up to 2,500 euro.

(3) Any person who intentionally commits one of the acts described in subsection (1) nos. 1 to 5, thereby endangering the woman's working capacity or health, shall be sentenced to imprisonment for up to one year or fined.

(4) Any person who negligently brings about the cases of endangerment set forth in subsection (3) shall be sentenced to imprisonment for up to six months or be fined up to 180 daily rates *(Tagessätze)*.

§§ 22, 23
(weggefallen)

Sections 22, 23
(repealed)

Siebter Abschnitt
Schlussvorschriften

Chapter 7
Final Provisions

§ 24
In Heimarbeit Beschäftigte

Section 24
(Women Working at Home)

Für die in Heimarbeit Beschäftigten und die ihnen Gleichgestellten gelten

The following provisions in this Act shall apply to women working at home and those in an equivalent position:

1. die §§ 3, 4 und 6 mit der Maßgabe, dass an die Stelle der Beschäftigungsverbote das Verbot der Ausgabe von Heimarbeit tritt,

2. § 2 Abs. 4, § 5 Abs. 1 und 3, § 9 Abs. 1, § 11 Abs. 1, § 13 Abs. 2, die §§ 14, 16, 19 Abs. 1 und § 21 Abs. 1 mit der Maßgabe, dass an die Stelle des Arbeitgebers der Auftraggeber oder Zwischenmeister tritt.

1. sections 3, 4 and 6, with the exception that the prohibitions of employment shall be replaced by a prohibition of assignment of work to be done at home,

2. section 2 (4), section 5 (1) and (3), section 9 (1), section 11 (1), section 13 (2), sections 14, 16, 19 (1) and section 21 (1), with the exception that the employer shall be replaced by the principal or intermediary.

§ 25
(weggefallen)

Section 25
(repealed)

XVI. Federal Parental Benefit and Parental Leave Act (Bundeselterngeld- und Elternzeitgesetz – BEEG)

of 5 December 2006 (Federal Law Gazette I p. 2748)

in the amended version of 28 March 2009

(excerpts)

Zweiter Abschnitt
Elternzeit für Arbeitnehmerinnen und Arbeitnehmer

Chapter 2
Parental Leave for Employees

§ 15
Anspruch auf Elternzeit

Section 15
Claim to Parental Leave

(1) ¹Arbeitnehmerinnen und Arbeitnehmer haben Anspruch auf Elternzeit, wenn sie

1. a) mit ihrem Kind,
   b) mit einem Kind, für das sie die Anspruchsvoraussetzungen nach § 1 Abs. 3 oder 4 erfüllen, oder
   c) mit einem Kind, das sie in Vollzeitpflege nach § 33 des Achten Buches Sozialgesetzbuch aufgenommen haben,

   in einem Haushalt leben und
2. dieses Kind selbst betreuen und erziehen.

²Nicht sorgeberechtigte Elternteile und Personen, die nach Satz 1 Nr. 1 Buchstabe b und c Elternzeit nehmen können, bedürfen der Zustimmung des sorgeberechtigten Elternteils.

(1 a) Anspruch auf Elternzeit haben Arbeitnehmer und Arbeitnehmerinnen auch, wenn sie mit ihrem Enkelkind in einem Haushalt leben und dieses Kind selbst betreuen und erziehen und

1. ein Elternteil des Kindes minderjährig ist oder
2. ein Elternteil des Kindes sich im letzten oder vorletzten Jahr einer Ausbildung befindet, die vor Vollendung

(1) ¹Employees shall have a claim to parental leave if they live together in a household

1. a) with their child,
   b) with a child for whom they meet the prerequisites for the claim as set forth in section 1 (3) or (4), or
   c) with a child whom they have taken into their care for the purpose of full-time fostering (section 33 of the Eighth Book of the Social Security Code *(Achtes Buch Sozialgesetzbuch)*)

   and
2. care for and raise this child themselves.

²Parents without custody and persons who are allowed to take parental leave pursuant to sentence 1 no. 1b and c shall require the consent of the parent with custody.

(1 a) Employees shall also have a claim to parental leave if they live with their grandchild in a household and care for and raise this child themselves and

1. one parent of the child is a minor or
2. one parent of the child is in the last or penultimate year of a vocational training that commenced before the

des 18. Lebensjahres begonnen wurde und die Arbeitskraft des Elternteils im Allgemeinen voll in Anspruch nimmt. Der Anspruch besteht nur für Zeiten, in denen keiner der Elternteile des Kindes selbst Elternzeit beansprucht.

(2) ¹Der Anspruch auf Elternzeit besteht bis zur Vollendung des dritten Lebensjahres eines Kindes. ²Die Zeit der Mutterschutzfrist nach § 6 Abs. 1 des Mutterschutzgesetzes wird auf die Begrenzung nach Satz 1 angerechnet. ³Bei mehreren Kindern besteht der Anspruch auf Elternzeit für jedes Kind, auch wenn sich die Zeiträume im Sinne von Satz 1 überschneiden. ⁴Ein Anteil der Elternzeit von bis zu zwölf Monaten ist mit Zustimmung des Arbeitgebers auf die Zeit bis zur Vollendung des achten Lebensjahres übertragbar; dies gilt auch, wenn sich die Zeiträume im Sinne von Satz 1 bei mehreren Kindern überschneiden. ⁵Bei einem angenommenen Kind und bei einem Kind in Vollzeit- oder Adoptionspflege kann Elternzeit von insgesamt bis zu drei Jahren ab der Aufnahme bei der berechtigten Person, längstens bis zur Vollendung des achten Lebensjahres des Kindes genommen werden; die Sätze 3 und 4 sind entsprechend anwendbar, soweit sie die zeitliche Aufteilung regeln. ⁶Der Anspruch kann nicht durch Vertrag ausgeschlossen oder beschränkt werden.

(3) ¹Die Elternzeit kann, auch anteilig, von jedem Elternteil allein oder von beiden Elternteilen gemeinsam genommen werden. ²Satz 1 gilt in den Fällen des Absatzes 1 Satz 1 Nr. 1 Buchstabe b und c entsprechend.

(4) ¹Der Arbeitnehmer oder die Arbeitnehmerin darf während der Elternzeit nicht mehr als 30 Wochenstunden erwerbstätig sein. ²Eine im Sinne des § 23 des Achten Buches Sozialgesetzbuch geeignete Tagespflegeperson kann bis zu fünf Kinder in Tagespflege betreuen, auch wenn die wöchentliche Betreu-

parent reached the age of 18 and generally takes up the parent's entire labor power.

This claim shall only exist for times in which neither of the parents of the child themselves lay claim to parental leave.

(2) ¹The claim to parental leave lasts until the child's third birthday. ²The duration of the maternity protection period pursuant to section 6 (1) of the Maternity Protection Act *(Mutterschutzgesetz)* shall be credited against the limitation pursuant to sentence 1. ³In the case of two or more children, the claim for paternal leave exists for each child, even if the time periods pursuant to sentence 1 should overlap. ⁴A portion of up to twelve months of the parental leave can be transferred with the employer's consent to the period up to the child's eighth birthday, even if in the case of two or more children the time periods pursuant to sentence 1 overlap. ⁵In the case of an adopted or fulltime foster child and a child living with the employee during the adoption process, parental leave can be taken for up to three years after the authorized person has taken the child into his or her care, but at most up to the child's eighth birthday; sentences 3 and 4 shall apply *mutatis mutandis* with respect to the apportionment of the time. ⁶This claim cannot be excluded or restricted by contract.

(3) ¹Parental leave may be taken by either parent alone, also pro rata, or by both parents together. ²Sentence 1 shall apply *mutatis mutandis* in the cases set forth in subsection (1) sentence 1 no. 1 b and c.

(4) ¹Employees may not work for more than 30 hours per week during the parental leave. ²A childcare worker who is suitable within the meaning of section 23 of the Eighth Book of the Social Security Code may care for up to five children, even if the childcare time per week exceeds 30 hours. ³Part-time work

ungszeit 30 Stunden übersteigt. ³Teilzeitarbeit bei einem anderen Arbeitgeber oder selbständige Tätigkeit nach Satz 1 bedürfen der Zustimmung des Arbeitgebers. ⁴Dieser kann sie nur innerhalb von vier Wochen aus dringenden betrieblichen Gründen schriftlich ablehnen.

(5) ¹Der Arbeitnehmer oder die Arbeitnehmerin kann eine Verringerung der Arbeitszeit und ihre Ausgestaltung beantragen. ²Über den Antrag sollen sich der Arbeitgeber und der Arbeitnehmer oder die Arbeitnehmerin innerhalb von vier Wochen einigen. ³Der Antrag kann mit der schriftlichen Mitteilung nach Absatz 7 Satz 1 Nr. 5 verbunden werden. ⁵Unberührt bleibt das Recht, sowohl die vor der Elternzeit bestehende Teilzeitarbeit unverändert während der Elternzeit fortzusetzen, soweit Absatz 4 beachtet ist, als auch nach der Elternzeit zu der Arbeitszeit zurückzukehren, die vor Beginn der Elternzeit vereinbart war.

(6) Der Arbeitnehmer oder die Arbeitnehmerin kann gegenüber dem Arbeitgeber, soweit eine Einigung nach Absatz 5 nicht möglich ist, unter den Voraussetzungen des Absatzes 7 während der Gesamtdauer der Elternzeit zweimal eine Verringerung seiner oder ihrer Arbeitszeit beanspruchen.

(7) ¹Für den Anspruch auf Verringerung der Arbeitszeit gelten folgende Voraussetzungen:
1. Der Arbeitgeber beschäftigt, unabhängig von der Anzahl der Personen in Berufsbildung, in der Regel mehr als 15 Arbeitnehmer und Arbeitnehmerinnen,
2. das Arbeitsverhältnis in demselben Betrieb oder Unternehmen besteht ohne Unterbrechung länger als sechs Monate,
3. die vertraglich vereinbarte regelmäßige Arbeitszeit soll für mindestens zwei Monate auf einen Umfang zwischen 15 und 30 Wochenstunden verringert werden,

with another employer or freelance work pursuant to sentence 1 shall require the consent of the employer, who may only withhold such consent within four weeks in writing and on urgent operational grounds.

(5) ¹The employee may apply for a reduction in the working time and its implementation. ²The employee and employer should agree within four weeks on this request. ³This request may be combined with the written notice pursuant to subsection (7) sentence 1 no. 5. ⁴This shall not affect the employee's right to maintain unchanged during the parental leave the part-time work he or she had prior to the parental leave, subject to compliance with subsection (4), or to resume after the parental leave the working time he or she had agreed upon prior to the parental leave.

(6) If no agreement can be reached pursuant to subsection (5), the employee may, subject to the prerequisites set forth in subsection (7), demand a reduction of the working time twice during the entire parental leave period.

(7) ¹A claim for reduction of working time is subject to the following prerequisites:
1. The employer regularly employs more than 15 employees, not counting trainees,
2. the employment relationship has existed for more than six consecutive months in the same establishment or company,
3. the contractual working time is to be reduced for at least two months to between 15 and 30 hours per week,

4. dem Anspruch stehen keine dringenden betrieblichen Gründe entgegen und
5. der Anspruch wurde dem Arbeitgeber sieben Wochen vor Beginn der Tätigkeit schriftlich mitgeteilt.

²Der Antrag muss den Beginn und den Umfang der verringerten Arbeitszeit enthalten. ³Die gewünschte Verteilung der verringerten Arbeitszeit soll im Antrag angegeben werden. ⁴Falls der Arbeitgeber die beanspruchte Verringerung der Arbeitszeit ablehnen will, muss er dies innerhalb von vier Wochen mit schriftlicher Begründung tun. ⁵Soweit der Arbeitgeber der Verringerung der Arbeitszeit nicht oder nicht rechtzeitig zustimmt, kann der Arbeitnehmer oder die Arbeitnehmerin Klage vor den Gerichten für Arbeitssachen erheben.

4. the claim is not opposed by any urgent operational grounds, and
5. the claim was communicated to the employer in writing seven weeks before the reduced working time begins.

²The request must state the beginning date and the scope of the reduced working hours. ³The desired distribution of the reduced working hours should be stated in the request. ⁴If the employer wishes to deny the claim for reduction of working time, it must do so within four weeks with a written substantiation. ⁵If the employer does not consent to the reduction in working time at all, or not in a timely manner, the employee may file charges before the courts for labor matters.

§ 16
Inanspruchnahme der Elternzeit

(1) ¹Wer Elternzeit beanspruchen will, muss sie spätestens sieben Wochen vor Beginn schriftlich vom Arbeitgeber verlangen und gleichzeitig erklären, für welche Zeiten innerhalb von zwei Jahren Elternzeit genommen werden soll. ²Bei dringenden Gründen ist ausnahmsweise eine angemessene kürzere Frist möglich. ³Nimmt die Mutter die Elternzeit im Anschluss an die Mutterschutzfrist, wird die Zeit der Mutterschutzfrist nach § 6 Abs. 1 des Mutterschutzgesetzes auf den Zeitraum nach Satz 1 angerechnet. ⁴Nimmt die Mutter die Elternzeit im Anschluss an einen auf die Mutterschutzfrist folgenden Erholungsurlaub, werden die Zeit der Mutterschutzfrist nach § 6 Abs. 1 des Mutterschutzgesetzes und die Zeit des Erholungsurlaubs auf den Zweijahreszeitraum nach Satz 1 angerechnet. ⁵Die Elternzeit kann auf zwei Zeitabschnitte verteilt werden; eine Verteilung auf weitere Zeitabschnitte ist nur mit der Zustimmung des Arbeitgebers möglich.

Section 16
Utilization of Parental Leave

(1) ¹If an employee wishes to claim parental leave, he or she must demand in writing that the employer grant parental leave at least seven weeks, in other cases at least eight weeks in advance of commencement, designating the period within two years in which parental leave is to be taken. ²Where urgent grounds exist, a reasonable shorter notice period shall also be possible in exceptional cases. ³If the mother takes the parental leave immediately following the maternity protection period, the duration of the maternity protection period pursuant to section 6 (1) of the Maternity Protection Act shall be set off against the period set forth in sentence 1. ⁴If the mother takes the parental leave immediately following vacation which is taken after the maternity protection period, the duration of the maternity protection period pursuant to section 6 (1) of the Maternity Protection Act and the vacation time shall be set off against the two-year period set forth

⁶Der Arbeitgeber hat dem Arbeitnehmer oder der Arbeitnehmerin die Elternzeit zu bescheinigen.

(2) Können Arbeitnehmerinnen und Arbeitnehmer aus einem von ihnen nicht zu vertretenden Grund eine sich unmittelbar an die Mutterschutzfrist des § 6 Abs. 1 des Mutterschutzgesetzes anschließende Elternzeit nicht rechtzeitig verlangen, können sie dies innerhalb einer Woche nach Wegfall des Grundes nachholen.

(3) ¹Die Elternzeit kann vorzeitig beendet oder im Rahmen des § 15 Abs. 2 verlängert werden, wenn der Arbeitgeber zustimmt. ²Die vorzeitige Beendigung wegen der Geburt eines weiteren Kindes oder wegen eines besonderen Härtefalls im Sinne des § 7 Abs. 2 Satz 3 kann der Arbeitgeber nur innerhalb von vier Wochen aus dringenden betrieblichen Gründen schriftlich ablehnen. ³Die Arbeitnehmerin kann ihre Elternzeit nicht wegen der Mutterschutzfristen des § 3 Abs. 2 und § 6 Abs. 1 des Mutterschutzgesetzes vorzeitig beenden; dies gilt nicht während ihrer zulässigen Teilzeitarbeit. ⁴Eine Verlängerung kann verlangt werden, wenn ein vorgesehener Wechsel in der Anspruchsberechtigung aus einem wichtigen Grund nicht erfolgen kann.

(4) Stirbt das Kind während der Elternzeit, endet diese spätestens drei Wochen nach dem Tod des Kindes.

(5) Eine Änderung in der Anspruchsberechtigung hat der Arbeitnehmer oder die Arbeitnehmerin dem Arbeitgeber unverzüglich mitzuteilen.

in sentence 1. ⁵The parental leave can be divided into two time intervals; a division into additional intervals shall only be possible with the employer's consent. ⁶The employer must certify the parental leave for the employee.

(2) Should the employees fail to apply for parental leave immediately following the maternal protection period pursuant to section 6 (1) of the Maternity Protection Act in a timely manner due to reasons beyond their control, they may submit such application within one week after such reasons no longer pertain.

(3) ¹The parental leave may be ended early or within the framework of section 15 (2) with the employer's consent. ²The employer may only deny early termination due to the birth of another child or a special hardship case within the meaning of section 7 (2) sentence 3 in writing within four weeks on urgent operational grounds. ³A female employee may not terminate her parental leave early due to the maternal protection periods set forth in section 3 (2) and section 6 (1) of the Maternity Protection Act; this shall not apply during her permissible part-time work. ⁴An extension may be requested if an anticipated change in the grounds for the claim cannot be effected for good cause.

(4) If the child should die during the parental leave, it shall end no later than three weeks after the death of the child.

(5) The employee shall notify the employer of any change in the grounds for the claim without undue delay.

§ 17
Urlaub

(1) ¹Der Arbeitgeber kann den Erholungsurlaub, der dem Arbeitnehmer oder der Arbeitnehmerin für das Ur-

Section 17
Vacation

(1) ¹The employer may reduce the vacation to which the employee is entitled for the vacation year by one twelfth for

laubsjahr zusteht, für jeden vollen Kalendermonat der Elternzeit um ein Zwölftel kürzen. ²Dies gilt nicht, wenn der Arbeitnehmer oder die Arbeitnehmerin während der Elternzeit bei seinem oder ihrem Arbeitgeber Teilzeitarbeit leistet.

(2) Hat der Arbeitnehmer oder die Arbeitnehmerin den ihm oder ihr zustehenden Urlaub vor dem Beginn der Elternzeit nicht oder nicht vollständig erhalten, hat der Arbeitgeber den Resturlaub nach der Elternzeit im laufenden oder im nächsten Urlaubsjahr zu gewähren.

(3) Endet das Arbeitsverhältnis während der Elternzeit oder wird es im Anschluss an die Elternzeit nicht fortgesetzt, so hat der Arbeitgeber den noch nicht gewährten Urlaub abzugelten.

(4) Hat der Arbeitnehmer oder die Arbeitnehmerin vor Beginn der Elternzeit mehr Urlaub erhalten, als ihm oder ihr nach Absatz 1 zusteht, kann der Arbeitgeber den Urlaub, der dem Arbeitnehmer oder der Arbeitnehmerin nach dem Ende der Elternzeit zusteht, um die zu viel gewährten Urlaubstage kürzen.

each full calendar month for which the employee takes parental leave. ²Sentence 1 shall not apply if the employee works part-time for the employer during the parental leave.

(2) If the employee has not taken all the vacation days to which he or she is entitled prior to the commencement of parental leave, the employer shall grant the remaining vacation days following the parental leave in the current or following vacation year.

(3) If the employment relationship ends during the parental leave or is not continued after the parental leave, the employer shall compensate the employee for vacation days not taken.

(4) If the employee has taken more vacation days prior to the parental leave than he or she is entitled to under subsection (1), the employer may reduce the vacation days to which the employee is entitled after the parental leave by the excess number of vacation days taken.

§ 18
Kündigungsschutz

(1) ¹Der Arbeitgeber darf das Arbeitsverhältnis ab dem Zeitpunkt, von dem an Elternzeit verlangt worden ist, höchstens jedoch acht Wochen vor Beginn der Elternzeit und während der Elternzeit nicht kündigen. ²In besonderen Fällen kann ausnahmsweise eine Kündigung für zulässig erklärt werden. ³Die Zulässigkeitserklärung erfolgt durch die für den Arbeitsschutz zuständige oberste Landesbehörde oder die von ihr bestimmte Stelle. ⁴Die Bundesregierung kann mit Zustimmung des Bundesrates allgemeine Verwaltungsvorschriften zur Durchführung des Satzes 2 erlassen.

Section 18
Protection Against Dismissal

(1) ¹The employer may not terminate the employment relationship as of the moment at which parental leave has been requested, but at most eight weeks prior to the commencement of the parental leave or during the parental leave. ²A dismissal may be declared permissible in special exceptional cases. ³The declaration of permissibility shall be issued by the highest state authority responsible for protection of workers or an authority designated by it. ⁴The Federal Government may, with the consent of the upper house of parliament, issue general administrative regulations to implement sentence 2.

(2) Absatz 1 gilt entsprechend, wenn Arbeitnehmer oder Arbeitnehmerinnen

1. während der Elternzeit bei demselben Arbeitgeber Teilzeitarbeit leisten oder
2. ohne Elternzeit in Anspruch zu nehmen, Teilzeitarbeit leisten und Anspruch auf Elterngeld nach § 1 während des Bezugszeitraums nach § 4 Abs. 1 haben.

§ 19
Kündigung zum Ende der Elternzeit

Der Arbeitnehmer oder die Arbeitnehmerin kann das Arbeitsverhältnis zum Ende der Elternzeit nur unter Einhaltung einer Kündigungsfrist von drei Monaten kündigen.

§ 20
Zur Berufsbildung Beschäftigte, in Heimarbeit Beschäftigte

(1) [1] Die zu ihrer Berufsbildung Beschäftigten gelten als Arbeitnehmer oder Arbeitnehmerinnen im Sinne dieses Gesetzes. [2] Die Elternzeit wird auf Berufsbildungszeiten nicht angerechnet.

(2) [1] Anspruch auf Elternzeit haben auch die in Heimarbeit Beschäftigten und die ihnen Gleichgestellten (§ 1 Abs. 1 und 2 des Heimarbeitsgesetzes), soweit sie am Stück mitarbeiten. [2] Für sie tritt an die Stelle des Arbeitgebers der Auftraggeber oder Zwischenmeister und an die Stelle des Arbeitsverhältnisses das Beschäftigungsverhältnis.

§ 21
Befristete Arbeitsverträge

(1) Ein sachlicher Grund, der die Befristung eines Arbeitsverhältnisses rechtfertigt, liegt vor, wenn ein Arbeitnehmer oder eine Arbeitnehmerin zur Vertretung eines anderen Arbeitneh-

(2) Subsection (1) shall apply *mutatis mutandis* if an employee

1. works part-time for the same employer during the parental leave or
2. works part-time without claiming parental leave and has a claim to parental allowances pursuant to section 1 during the reference period pursuant to section 4 (1).

Section 19
Termination at the End of Parental Leave

The employee may only terminate the employment relationship as of the end of the parental leave upon observance of a three-month termination notice period.

Section 20
Trainees, Home Workers

(1) [1] Trainees shall be deemed to be employees within the meaning of this Act. [2] The parental leave shall not be set off against the trainee period.

(2) [1] Persons working in the home and those in an equivalent position (section 1 (1) and (2) of the Home Work Act *(Heimarbeitgesetz)*) shall be entitled to parental leave if they work on a piecework basis. [2] In such cases, the commissioner of the work or the intermediate master craftsman *(Zwischenmeister)* shall take the place of the employer, and the work relationship shall take the place of the employment relationship.

Section 21
Limited Term Employment Agreements

(1) Material grounds justifying the limitation of the term of an employment relationship shall exist if an employee is hired to take the place of another employer for the duration of the period in

mers oder einer anderen Arbeitnehmerin für die Dauer eines Beschäftigungsverbotes nach dem Mutterschutzgesetz, einer Elternzeit, einer auf Tarifvertrag, Betriebsvereinbarung oder einzelvertraglicher Vereinbarung beruhenden Arbeitsfreistellung zur Betreuung eines Kindes oder für diese Zeiten zusammen oder für Teile davon eingestellt wird.

(2) Über die Dauer der Vertretung nach Absatz 1 hinaus ist die Befristung für notwendige Zeiten einer Einarbeitung zulässig.

(3) Die Dauer der Befristung des Arbeitsvertrags muss kalendermäßig bestimmt oder bestimmbar oder den in den Absätzen 1 und 2 genannten Zwecken zu entnehmen sein.

(4) [1] Der Arbeitgeber kann den befristeten Arbeitsvertrag unter Einhaltung einer Frist von mindestens drei Wochen, jedoch frühestens zum Ende der Elternzeit, kündigen, wenn die Elternzeit ohne Zustimmung des Arbeitgebers vorzeitig endet und der Arbeitnehmer oder die Arbeitnehmerin die vorzeitige Beendigung der Elternzeit mitgeteilt hat. [2] Satz 1 gilt entsprechend, wenn der Arbeitgeber die vorzeitige Beendigung der Elternzeit in den Fällen des § 16 Abs. 3 Satz 2 nicht ablehnen darf.

(5) Das Kündigungsschutzgesetz ist im Falle des Absatzes 4 nicht anzuwenden.

(6) Absatz 4 gilt nicht, soweit seine Anwendung vertraglich ausgeschlossen ist.

(7) [1] Wird im Rahmen arbeitsrechtlicher Gesetze oder Verordnungen auf die Zahl der beschäftigten Arbeitnehmer und Arbeitnehmerinnen abgestellt, so sind bei der Ermittlung dieser Zahl Arbeitnehmer und Arbeitnehmerinnen, die sich in der Elternzeit befinden oder zur Betreuung eines Kindes freigestellt sind, nicht mitzuzählen, solange für sie aufgrund von Absatz 1 ein Vertreter

which employment is prohibited pursuant to the Maternity Protection Act, of parental leave, of release from work responsibilities in order to care for a child under the provisions of a collective bargaining agreement, a works agreement or an individual agreement, or for these periods added together or for parts of such periods.

(2) The limited term may be extended beyond the period of replacement set forth in subsection (1), if necessary to work the replacement employee in.

(3) The limited term of the employment agreement must be determined or determinable on a calendar basis or discernable from the purposes set forth in subsections (1) and (2).

(4) [1] The employer may terminate the limited term employment agreement with a notice period of at least three weeks, but at the earliest as of the end of the parental leave if the parental leave is terminated early without the employer's consent and the employee has notified the employer such early termination. [2] Sentence 1 applies *mutatis mutandis* if the employer may not refuse the early termination of the parental leave in the cases set forth in section 16 (3) sentence 2.

(5) In the cases set forth in subsection (4) the Protection Against Unfair Dismissals Act *(Kündigungsschutzgesetz)* shall not apply.

(6) Subsection (4) shall not apply where its application is excluded by contract.

(7) [1] If, within the framework of employment law statutes or ordinances, the number of employees is taken as a basis for calculation, the employees on parental leave or released from their work responsibilities in order to care for a child shall not be included in this calculation as long as a replacement has been hired pursuant to subsection (1). [2] This shall not apply if the replacement

oder eine Vertreterin eingestellt ist. ²Dies gilt nicht, wenn der Vertreter oder die Vertreterin nicht mitzuzählen ist. ³Die Sätze 1 und 2 gelten entsprechend, wenn im Rahmen arbeitsrechtlicher Gesetze oder Verordnungen auf die Zahl der Arbeitsplätze abgestellt wird.

is not to be included in the count. ³Sentences 1 and 2 shall apply *mutatis mutandis* if the number of jobs is used as a basis for calculation in the framework of employment law statutes or ordinance.

XVII. Social Security Code III (3. Sozialgesetzbuch – SGB)

of 24 March 1997 (Federal Law Gazette I p. 594)

in the amended version of 3 August 2010

(excerpts)

§ 143
Ruhen des Anspruchs bei Arbeitsentgelt und Urlaubsabgeltung

(1) Der Anspruch auf Arbeitslosengeld ruht während der Zeit, für die der Arbeitslose Arbeitsentgelt erhält oder zu beanspruchen hat.

(2) ¹Hat der Arbeitslose wegen Beendigung des Arbeitsverhältnisses eine Urlaubsabgeltung erhalten oder zu beanspruchen, so ruht der Anspruch auf Arbeitslosengeld für die Zeit des abgegoltenen Urlaubs. ²Der Ruhenszeitraum beginnt mit dem Ende des die Urlaubsabgeltung begründenden Arbeitsverhältnisses.

(3) ¹Soweit der Arbeitslose die in den Absätzen 1 und 2 genannten Leistungen (Arbeitsentgelt im Sinne des § 115 des Zehnten Buches) tatsächlich nicht erhält, wird das Arbeitslosengeld auch für die Zeit geleistet, in der der Anspruch auf Arbeitslosengeld ruht. ²Hat der Arbeitgeber die in den Absätzen 1 und 2 genannten Leistungen trotz des Rechtsübergangs mit befreiender Wirkung an den Arbeitslosen oder an einen Dritten gezahlt, hat der Bezieher des Arbeitslosengeldes dieses insoweit zu erstatten.

Section 143
Suspension of the Claim in the Case of Remuneration for Work and Compensation for Vacation Not Taken

(1) The claim to unemployment benefits shall be suspended during the time in which the unemployed person receives or has a claim to remuneration for work.

(2) ¹If the unemployed person has received or has a claim for compensation for vacation not taken due to the termination of the employment relationship, the claim for unemployment benefits shall be suspended for the vacation time so compensated. ²The period of suspension shall commence with the end of the employment relationship underlying the compensation for vacation time.

(3) ¹Where the unemployed person does not actually receive the payments set forth in subsections (1) and (2) (remuneration for work within the meaning of section 115 of the Tenth Book), unemployment benefits shall also be granted for the period during which the claim for unemployment benefits is suspended. ²If the employer has made the payments set forth in subsections (1) and (2) to the unemployed person or a third party despite the transfer of rights with discharging effect, the recipient of the unemployment benefits shall reimburse these benefits in the amount of such payments.

§ 143a
Ruhen des Anspruchs bei Entlassungsentschädigung

(1) [1]Hat der Arbeitslose wegen der Beendigung des Arbeitsverhältnisses eine Abfindung, Entschädigung oder ähnliche Leistung (Entlassungsentschädigung) erhalten oder zu beanspruchen und ist das Arbeitsverhältnis ohne Einhaltung einer der ordentlichen Kündigungsfrist des Arbeitgebers entsprechenden Frist beendet worden, so ruht der Anspruch auf Arbeitslosengeld von dem Ende des Arbeitsverhältnisses an bis zu dem Tage, an dem das Arbeitsverhältnis bei Einhaltung dieser Frist geendet hätte. [2]Diese Frist beginnt mit der Kündigung, die der Beendigung des Arbeitsverhältnisses vorausgegangen ist, bei Fehlen einer solchen Kündigung mit dem Tage der Vereinbarung über die Beendigung des Arbeitsverhältnisses. [3]Ist die ordentliche Kündigung des Arbeitsverhältnisses durch den Arbeitgeber ausgeschlossen, so gilt bei

1. zeitlich unbegrenztem Ausschluss eine Kündigungsfrist von 18 Monaten,
2. Zeitlich begrenztem Ausschluss oder bei Vorliegen der Voraussetzungen für eine fristgebundene Kündigung aus wichtigem Grund die Kündigungsfrist, die ohne den Ausschluss der ordentlichen Kündigung maßgebend gewesen wäre.

[4]Kann dem Arbeitnehmer nur bei Zahlung einer Entlassungsentschädigung ordentlich gekündigt werden, so gilt eine Kündigungsfrist von einem Jahr. [5]Hat der Arbeitslose auch eine Urlaubsabgeltung (§ 143 Abs. 2) erhalten oder zu beanspruchen, verlängert sich der Ruhenszeitraum nach Satz 1 um die Zeit des abgegoltenen Urlaubs. [6]Leistungen, die der Arbeitgeber für den Arbeitslosen, dessen Arbeitsverhältnis frühestens mit Vollendung des 55. Lebensjahres beendet wird, unmittelbar für dessen Rentenversicherung nach

Section 143a
Suspension of the Claim in Case of Compensation for Dismissal

(1) [1]If the unemployed person has received or has a claim to severance pay, compensation or a similar payment due to the termination of the employment relationship (dismissal compensation) and if the employment relationship was terminated without observing one of the ordinary termination notice periods applicable for the employer, the claim for unemployment benefits shall be suspended as of the end of the employment relationship until the day on which the employment relationship would have ended if such a notice period had been observed. [2]This notice period shall commence with the dismissal notice preceding the termination of the employment relationship; if no such dismissal notice is rendered, then with the date of the agreement to end the employment relationship. [3]If an ordinary termination of the employment relationship by the employer is excluded, then

1. if such exclusion is for an unlimited period, the notice period shall be 18 months,
2. if such exclusion is for a limited period or if the prerequisites for a dismissal with notice for good cause exist, the notice period shall be that which would have applied if an ordinary termination had not been excluded.

[4]If the employee can only be ordinarily dismissed with payment of dismissal compensation, a one-year termination notice period shall apply. [5]If the unemployed person has also received or has a claim to compensation for vacation has not taken (section 143 (2)), the suspension period shall be extended pursuant to sentence 1 by the length of the vacation time for which compensation is paid. [6]Payments the employer makes for the unemployed person whose employment relationship was terminated before he reached the age of 55 that

§ 187 a Abs. 1 des Sechsten Buches aufwendet, bleiben unberücksichtigt. ⁷Satz 6 gilt entsprechend für Beiträge des Arbeitgebers zu einer berufsständischen Versorgungseinrichtung.

(2) ¹Der Anspruch auf Arbeitslosengeld ruht nach Absatz 1 längstens ein Jahr. ²Er ruht nicht über den Tag hinaus,

1. bis zu dem der Arbeitslose bei Weiterzahlung des während der letzten Beschäftigungszeit kalendertäglich verdienten Arbeitsentgelts einen Betrag in Höhe von sechzig Prozent der nach Absatz 1 zu berücksichtigenden Entlassungsentschädigung als Arbeitsentgelt verdient hätte,

2. an dem das Arbeitsverhältnis infolge einer Befristung, die unabhängig von der Vereinbarung über die Beendigung des Arbeitsverhältnisses bestanden hat, geendet hätte oder

3. an dem der Arbeitgeber das Arbeitsverhältnis aus wichtigem Grunde ohne Einhaltung einer Kündigungsfrist hätte kündigen können.

³Der nach Satz 2 Nr. 1 zu berücksichtigende Anteil der Entlassungsentschädigung vermindert sich sowohl für je fünf Jahre des Arbeitsverhältnisses in demselben Betrieb oder Unternehmen als auch für je fünf Lebensjahre nach Vollendung des fünfunddreißigsten Lebensjahres um je fünf Prozent; er beträgt nicht weniger als fünfundzwanzig Prozent der nach Absatz 1 zu berücksichtigenden Entlassungsentschädigung. ⁴Letzte Beschäftigungszeit sind die am Tag des Ausscheidens aus dem Beschäftigungsverhältnis abgerechneten Entgeltabrechnungszeiträume der letzten zwölf Monate; § 130 Abs. 2 Satz 1 Nr. 3 und Abs. 3 gilt entsprechend. ⁵Arbeitsentgeltkürzungen infolge von Krankheit, Kurzarbeit, Arbeitsausfall oder Arbeitsversäumnis bleiben außer Betracht.

went directly to his old-age pension insurance pursuant to section 187a (1) of the Sixth Book, shall not be taken into account. ⁷Sentence 6 applies *mutatis mutandis* for contributions the employer makes to a pension organization for particular professions.

(2) ¹The claim for unemployment benefits shall be suspended pursuant to subsection (1) for a maximum of one year. ²It shall not be suspended beyond the day

1. up to which, had payment of the remuneration earned per day in the most recent working period continued, the unemployed person would have earned as remuneration a sum in the amount of 60 percent of the dismissal compensation to be taken into account pursuant to subsection (1),

2. on which the employment relationship would have ended due to a limitation of the term of the employment, independent of the agreement terminating the employment relationship or

3. on which the employer would have been able to terminate the employment relationship for cause without observing a notice period.

³The dismissal compensation to be taken into account pursuant to sentence 2 no. 1 shall be reduced by five percent both for every five years of employment in the same establishment or company and for every five years of age after reaching the age of 35; it shall not amount to less than 25 percent of the dismissal compensation to be taken into account pursuant to subsection (1). ⁴The most recent working period is defined as the remuneration accounting periods accounted for the twelve months preceding the last day of employment; section 130 (2) sentence 1 no. 3 and subsection (3) applies *mutatis mutandis*. ⁵Reductions in remuneration due to sickness, short-time work, loss of working time or unexcused absence from work shall not be taken into account.

(3) Hat der Arbeitslose wegen Beendigung des Beschäftigungsverhältnisses unter Aufrechterhaltung des Arbeitsverhältnisses eine Entlassungsentschädigung erhalten oder zu beanspruchen, gelten die Absätze 1 und 2 entsprechend.

(4) ¹Soweit der Arbeitslose die Entlassungsentschädigung (Arbeitsentgelt im Sinne des § 115 des Zehnten Buches) tatsächlich nicht erhält, wird das Arbeitslosengeld auch für die Zeit geleistet, in der der Anspruch auf Arbeitslosengeld ruht. ²Hat der Verpflichtete die Entlassungsentschädigung trotz des Rechtsübergangs mit befreiender Wirkung an den Arbeitslosen oder an einen Dritten gezahlt, hat der Bezieher des Arbeitslosengeldes dieses insoweit zu erstatten.

(3) If the unemployed person has received or has a claim to dismissal compensation due to a termination of the employment relationship while the working relationship is maintained, subsections (1) and (2) apply *mutatis mutandis*.

(4) ¹If the unemployed person has not actually received the dismissal compensation (remuneration within the meaning of section 115 of the Tenth Book), unemployment benefits shall also be paid for the period in which the claim for such benefits is suspended. ²If the obligated party paid the dismissal compensation to the unemployed person or a third party despite the transfer of rights with discharging effect, the recipient of the unemployment benefits shall reimburse these benefits in the amount of such dismissal compensation.

§ 144
Ruhen bei Sperrzeit

(1) ¹Hat der Arbeitnehmer sich versicherungswidrig verhalten, ohne dafür einen wichtigen Grund zu haben, ruht der Anspruch für die Dauer einer Sperrzeit. ²Versicherungswidriges Verhalten liegt vor, wenn

1. der Arbeitslose das Beschäftigungsverhältnis gelöst oder durch ein arbeitsvertragswidriges Verhalten Anlass für die Lösung des Beschäftigungsverhältnisses gegeben und dadurch vorsätzlich oder grob fahrlässig die Arbeitslosigkeit herbeigeführt hat (Sperrzeit bei Arbeitsaufgabe),

2. der bei der Agentur für Arbeit als arbeitsuchend gemeldete Arbeitnehmer (§ 38 Abs. 1) oder der Arbeitslose trotz Belehrung über die Rechtsfolgen eine von der Agentur für Arbeit unter Benennung des Arbeitgebers und der Art der Tätigkeit

Section 144
Suspension of the Claim in Case of a Period of Disqualification

(1) ¹If the unemployed person has conducted himself in violation of the conditions for eligibility without providing good cause for doing so, his claim shall be suspended for a disqualification period. ²A violation of the conditions for eligibility occurs if

1. the unemployed person has dissolved the employment relationship or provided grounds for the dissolution of the employment relationship by his conduct in breach of his employment agreement, and if he has thereby brought about the unemployment intentionally or through gross negligence (disqualification period in the case of abandonment of job),

2. the employee who has been registered with the Employment Agency as looking for work (section 38 (1)) or the unemployed person does not accept or take up employment offered by the Employment Agency, naming the employer and the type of work in-

angebotene Beschäftigung nicht annimmt oder nicht antritt oder die Anbahnung eines solchen Beschäftigungsverhältnisses, insbesondere das Zustandekommen eines Vorstellungsgespräches, durch sein Verhalten verhindert (Sperrzeit bei Arbeitsablehnung),
3. der Arbeitslose trotz Belehrung über die Rechtsfolgen die von der Agentur für Arbeit geforderten Eigenbemühungen nicht nachweist (Sperrzeit bei unzureichenden Eigenbemühungen),
4. der Arbeitslose sich weigert, trotz Belehrung über die Rechtsfolgen an einer Maßnahme nach § 46 oder einer Maßnahme zur beruflichen Ausbildung oder Weiterbildung oder einer Maßnahme zur Teilhabe am Arbeitsleben teilzunehmen (Sperrzeit bei Ablehnung einer beruflichen Eingliederungsmaßnahme),
5. der Arbeitslose die Teilnahme an einer in Nummer 4 genannten Maßnahme abbricht oder durch maßnahmewidriges Verhalten Anlass für den Ausschluss aus einer dieser Maßnahmen gibt (Sperrzeit bei Abbruch einer beruflichen Eingliederungsmaßnahme),
6. der Arbeitslose einer Aufforderung der Agentur für Arbeit, sich zu melden oder zu einem ärztlichen oder psychologischen Untersuchungstermin zu erscheinen (§ 309), trotz Belehrung über die Rechtsfolgen nicht nachkommt oder nicht nachgekommen ist (Sperrzeit bei Meldeversäumnis),
7. der Arbeitslose seiner Meldepflicht nach § 38 Abs. 1 nicht nachgekommen ist (Sperrzeit bei verspäteter Arbeitsuchendmeldung).

³ Der Arbeitnehmer hat die für die Beurteilung eines wichtigen Grundes maßgebenden Tatsachen darzulegen und nachzuweisen, wenn diese in seiner

volved, despite being instructed of the legal consequences thereof or prevents the initiation of such an employment relationship, in particular the conducting of an employment interview by his behavior (disqualification period in the case of refusal to work),
3. the unemployed person does not provide proof of his own efforts as required by the Employment Agency despite being instructed of the legal consequences thereof, (disqualification period in the case of insufficient own efforts,
4. the unemployed person refuses to take part in a measure pursuant to section 46 or a professional training or further education program or a program for the professional integration of disabled persons, despite being instructed of the legal consequences thereof (disqualification period in the case of rejection of a professional integration measure),
5. the unemployed person discontinues his participation in one of the measures set forth in no. 4 or gives cause by conduct in violation of the measure for his exclusion from one of these measures (disqualification period in the case of discontinuation of a professional integration measure)
6. the unemployed person fails, or has failed, to comply with a demand by the Employment Agency that he registers with it or keeps an appointment for a medical or psychological examination (section 309), despite being instructed of the legal consequences thereof (disqualification period in the case of failure to register),
7. the unemployed person fails to comply with his duty to register pursuant to section 38 (1) (disqualification period in the case of delayed registration as looking for work).

³ The employee shall present and demonstrate the facts relevant for assessing good cause if they are within his sphere or his area of responsibility. ⁴ Employ-

Sphäre oder in seinem Verantwortungsbereich liegen. ⁴Beschäftigungen im Sinne des Satzes 2 Nr. 1 und 2 sind auch Arbeitsbeschaffungsmaßnahmen (§ 27 Abs. 3 Nr. 5).

(2) ¹Die Sperrzeit beginnt mit dem Tag nach dem Ereignis, das die Sperrzeit begründet, oder, wenn dieser Tag in eine Sperrzeit fällt, mit dem Ende dieser Sperrzeit. ²Werden mehrere Sperrzeiten durch dasselbe Ereignis begründet, folgen sie in der Reihenfolge des Absatzes 1 Satz 2 Nr. 1 bis 7 einander nach.

(3) ¹Die Dauer der Sperrzeit bei Arbeitsaufgabe beträgt zwölf Wochen. ²Sie verkürzt sich

1. auf drei Wochen, wenn das Arbeitsverhältnis innerhalb von sechs Wochen nach dem Ereignis, das die Sperrzeit begründet, ohne eine Sperrzeit geendet hätte,
2. auf sechs Wochen, wenn
    a) das Arbeitsverhältnis innerhalb von zwölf Wochen nach dem Ereignis, das die Sperrzeit begründet, ohne eine Sperrzeit geendet hätte oder
    b) eine Sperrzeit von zwölf Wochen für den Arbeitslosen nach den für den Eintritt der Sperrzeit maßgebenden Tatsachen eine besondere Härte bedeuten würde.

(4) Die Dauer der Sperrzeit bei Arbeitsablehnung, bei Ablehnung einer beruflichen Eingliederungsmaßnahme oder bei Abbruch einer beruflichen Eingliederungsmaßnahme beträgt

1. im Falle des erstmaligen versicherungswidrigen Verhaltens dieser Art drei Wochen,
2. im Falle des zweiten versicherungswidrigen Verhaltens dieser Art sechs Wochen,
3. in den übrigen Fällen zwölf Wochen.

ment within the meaning of sentence 2 nos. 1 and 2 shall also be job creation measures (section 27 (3) no. 5).

(2) ¹Such disqualification period shall commence on the day after the incident which causes the disqualification period or, if such day falls within a disqualification period, with the end of such disqualification period. ²If two or more disqualification periods are caused by the same event, they shall follow each other consecutively in the order set forth in subsection (1) sentence 2 nos. 1 to 7.

(3) ¹The duration of the disqualification period in the case of abandonment of job shall be twelve weeks. ²This period shall be reduced

1. to three weeks if the employment relationship would have ended within six weeks after the event causing the disqualification period without a disqualification period,
2. to six weeks if
    a) the employment relationship would have ended within twelve weeks after the event causing the disqualification period without a disqualification period or
    b) a disqualification period of twelve weeks would represent an unreasonable hardship for the unemployed person in light of the circumstances relevant to the imposition of the disqualification period.

(4) The duration of the disqualification period in the case of refusal to work, in the case of rejection of a professional integration measure or in the case of discontinuation of a professional integration measure shall be

1. three weeks, if such conduct in violation of the conditions for eligibility occurs for the first time,
2. six weeks, if such conduct in violation of the conditions for eligibility occurs for the second time,
3. twelve weeks in all other cases.

| Im Falle der Arbeitsablehnung oder der Ablehnung einer beruflichen Eingliederungsmaßnahme nach der Meldung zur frühzeitigen Arbeitsuche (§ 38 Abs. 1) im Zusammenhang mit der Entstehung des Anspruchs gilt Satz 1 entsprechend. | In the case of refusal to work or rejection of a professional integration measure after registering as looking for work early (section 38 (1)) in connection with the creation of a claim, sentence 1 applies *mutatis mutandis*. |

(5) Die Dauer einer Sperrzeit bei unzureichenden Eigenbemühungen beträgt zwei Wochen.

(5) The length of a disqualification period in the case of insufficient own efforts shall be two weeks.

(6) Die Dauer einer Sperrzeit bei Meldeversäumnis oder bei verspäteter Arbeitsuchendmeldung beträgt eine Woche.

(6) The length of a disqualification period in the case of a failure to register or delayed registration as looking for work shall be one week.

Siebter Titel
Erstattungspflichten für Arbeitgeber

Part 7
Employer's Duty to Reimburse

§ 147a
Erstattungspflicht des Arbeitgebers

Section 147a
Employer's Duty to Reimburse

(1) ¹Der Arbeitgeber, bei dem der Arbeitslose innerhalb der letzten vier Jahre vor dem Tag der Arbeitslosigkeit, durch den nach § 124 Abs. 1 die Rahmenfrist bestimmt wird, mindestens 24 Monate in einem Versicherungspflichtverhältnis gestanden hat, erstattet der Bundesagentur vierteljährlich das Arbeitslosengeld für die Zeit nach Vollendung des 57. Lebensjahres des Arbeitslosen, längstens für 32 Monate. ²Die Erstattungspflicht tritt nicht ein, wenn das Arbeitsverhältnis vor Vollendung des 55. Lebensjahres des Arbeitslosen beendet worden ist, der Arbeitslose auch die Voraussetzung für eine der in § 142 Abs. 1 Nr. 2 bis 4 genannten Leistungen oder für eine Rente wegen Berufsunfähigkeit erfüllt oder der Arbeitgeber darlegt und nachweist, dass

(1) ¹The employer with whom the unemployed person was in a compulsory insurance relationship for at least 24 months within the last four years up to the date of unemployment, through which the framework notice period pursuant to section 124 (1) is determined, shall reimburse quarterly the Federal Employment Agency for the unemployment benefits for the period after the unemployed person reaches the age of 57, for a maximum of 32 months. ²The duty to reimburse shall not apply if the employment relationship was terminated before the unemployed person reached the age of 55, the unemployed person also meets the prerequisite for benefits set forth in section 142 (1) nos. 2 to 4 or for a pension due to inability to work or the employer demonstrates and proves

1. der Arbeitslose innerhalb der letzten zwölf Jahre vor dem Tag der Arbeitslosigkeit, durch den nach § 124 Abs. 1 die Rahmenfrist bestimmt wird, weniger als zehn Jahre zu ihm in einem Arbeitsverhältnis gestanden hat,

1. that within the last 12 years before the first day of unemployment through which the framework notice period is determined pursuant to section 124 (1), the unemployed person had been in an employment relation-

2. er in der Regel nicht mehr als 20 Arbeitnehmer ausschließlich der zu ihrer Berufsausbildung Beschäftigten beschäftigt; § 3 Abs. 1 Satz 2 bis 6 des Aufwendungsausgleichsgesetzes gilt entsprechend mit der Maßgabe, daß das Kalenderjahr maßgebend ist, das dem Kalenderjahr vorausgeht, in dem die Voraussetzungen des Satzes 1 für die Erstattungspflicht erfüllt sind,
3. der Arbeitslose das Arbeitsverhältnis durch Kündigung beendet und weder eine Abfindung noch eine Entschädigung oder ähnliche Leistung wegen der Beendigung des Arbeitsverhältnisses erhalten oder zu beanspruchen hat,
4. er das Arbeitsverhältnis durch sozial gerechtfertigte Kündigung beendet hat; § 7 des Kündigungsschutzgesetzes findet keine Anwendung; die Agentur für Arbeit ist an eine rechtskräftige Entscheidung des Arbeitsgerichts über die soziale Rechtfertigung einer Kündigung gebunden,

5. er bei Beendigung des Arbeitsverhältnisses berechtigt war, das Arbeitsverhältnis aus wichtigem Grund ohne Einhaltung einer Kündigungsfrist oder mit sozialer Auslauffrist zu kündigen,
6. sich die Zahl der Arbeitnehmer in dem Betrieb, in dem der Arbeitslose zuletzt mindestens zwei Jahre beschäftigt war, um mehr als drei Prozent innerhalb eines Jahres vermindert und unter den in diesem Zeitraum ausscheidenden Arbeitnehmern der Anteil der Arbeitnehmer, die das 55. Lebensjahr vollendet haben, nicht höher ist als es ihrem Anteil an der Gesamtzahl der im Betrieb Beschäftigten zu Beginn des Jahreszeitraumes entspricht. Vermindert sich die Zahl der Beschäftigten im gleichen Zeitraum um mindestens zehn Prozent, verdoppelt sich

ship with it for a total of less than 10 years,
2. that as a rule it does not have more than 20 employees, excluding trainees; section 3 (1) sentences 2 to 6 of the Equalization of Expenditures Act (*Aufwendungsausgleichsgesetz*) applies *mutatis mutandis* provided that the relevant calendar year is that preceding the calendar year in which the prerequisites for the reimbursement duty set forth in sentence 1 have been met,
3. that the unemployed person resigned from the employment relationship and did not receive or have a claim to severance pay or compensation or similar payment due to the termination of the employment relationship,
4. that it terminated the employment relationship due to a socially justified dismissal; section 7 of the Protection Against Unfair Dismissal Act (*Kündigungsschutzgesetz – KSchG*) shall not apply; the Employment Agency is bound to a final and nonappealable decision by the labor court on the social justification of the dismissal,
5. that once the employment relationship came to an end it was entitled to terminate the employment relationship for cause without observing a dismissal notice period or with a social expiration period,
6. that the number of employees in the establishment in which the unemployed person last worked for at least two years has decreased by more than three percent within one year and that of the employees leaving the company during this period, the percentage who were 55 of age or older does not exceed the percentage such employees comprise of the total number of employees in the establishment at the beginning of the annual period. If the number of employees decreases by at least ten percent in the same period, the percentage of the older employees which

der Anteil der älteren Arbeitnehmer, der bei der Verminderung der Zahl der Arbeitnehmer nicht überschritten werden darf. Rechnerische Bruchteile werden aufgerundet. Wird der gerundete Anteil überschritten, ist in allen Fällen eine Einzelfallentscheidung erforderlich,

7. der Arbeitnehmer im Rahmen eines kurzfristigen drastischen Personalabbaus von mindestens 20 Prozent aus dem Betrieb, in dem er zuletzt mindestens zwei Jahre beschäftigt war, ausgeschieden ist und dieser Personalabbau für den örtlichen Arbeitsmarkt von erheblicher Bedeutung ist.

(2) Die Erstattungspflicht entfällt, wenn der Arbeitgeber

1. darlegt und nachweist, dass in dem Kalenderjahr, das dem Kalenderjahr vorausgeht, für das der Wegfall geltend gemacht wird, die Voraussetzungen für den Nichteintritt der Erstattungspflicht nach Absatz 1 Satz 2 Nr. 2 erfüllt sind, oder
2. insolvenzfähig ist und darlegt und nachweist, dass die Erstattung für ihn eine unzumutbare Belastung bedeuten würde, weil durch die Erstattung der Fortbestand des Unternehmens oder die nach Durchführung des Personalabbaus verbleibenden Arbeitsplätze gefährdet wären. Insoweit ist zum Nachweis die Vorlage einer Stellungnahme einer fachkundigen Stelle erforderlich.

(3) ¹Die Erstattungsforderung mindert sich, wenn der Arbeitgeber darlegt und nachweist, dass er

1. nicht mehr als 40 Arbeitnehmer oder
2. nicht mehr als 60 Arbeitnehmer

im Sinne des Absatzes 1 Satz 2 Nr. 2 beschäftigt, um zwei Drittel im Falle der Nummer 1 und um ein Drittel im Falle der Nummer 2. ²Für eine nachträgliche Minderung der Erstattungsforderung gilt Absatz 2 Nr. 1 entsprechend.

may not be exceeded in reducing the number of employees shall be doubled. Mathematical fractions shall be rounded off. If the rounded off percentage is exceeded, it will be necessary in every case to make a decision based on the individual case,

7. that the employee left the establishment in which he had most recently worked for at least two years within the framework of a drastic reduction in personnel on short notice of at least 20 percent and this reduction in personnel was of substantial significance for the local labor market.

(2) The duty to reimburse shall not apply if the employer

1. demonstrates and proves that in the calendar year preceding the calendar year for which the non-applicability of the duty is asserted, the prerequisites for such non-applicability pursuant to subsection (1) sentence 2 no. 2 have been met, or
2. is eligible for insolvency proceedings and demonstrates and proves that the reimbursement would create an unreasonable hardship for it because it would jeopardize the continued existence of the company or the jobs remaining after the reduction in personnel has been carried out. Proof in this case shall require an expert opinion.

(3) ¹If the employer demonstrates and proves that it has

1. no more than 40 employees or
2. no more than 60 employees

within the meaning of subsection (1) sentence 2 no. 2, the reimbursement claim shall be reduced by two thirds in the case of no. 1 and by one third in the case of no. 2. ²For a subsequent reduction of the reduction claim subsection (2) no. 1 applies *mutatis mutandis*.

(4) Die Verpflichtung zur Erstattung des Arbeitslosengeldes schließt die auf diese Leistung entfallenden Beiträge zur Kranken-, Pflege- und Rentenversicherung ein.

(5) ¹Konzernunternehmen im Sinne des § 18 des Aktiengesetzes gelten bei der Ermittlung der Beschäftigungszeiten als ein Arbeitgeber. ²Die Erstattungspflicht richtet sich gegen den Arbeitgeber, bei dem der Arbeitnehmer zuletzt in einem Arbeitsverhältnis gestanden hat.

(6) ¹Die Agentur für Arbeit berät den Arbeitgeber auf Verlangen über Voraussetzungen und Umfang der Erstattungsregelung. ²Auf Antrag des Arbeitgebers entscheidet die Agentur für Arbeit im voraus, ob die Voraussetzungen des Absatzes 1 Satz 2 Nr. 6 oder 7 erfüllt sind.

(7) ¹Der Arbeitslose ist auf Verlangen der Agentur für Arbeit verpflichtet, Auskünfte zu erteilen, sich bei der Agentur für Arbeit persönlich zu melden oder sich einer ärztlichen oder psychologischen Untersuchung zu unterziehen, soweit das Entstehen oder der Wegfall des Erstattungsanspruchs von dieser Mitwirkung abhängt. ²Voraussetzung für das Verlangen der Agentur für Arbeit ist, dass bei der Agentur für Arbeit Umstände in der Person des Arbeitslosen bekannt sind, die für das Entstehen oder den Wegfall der Erstattungspflicht von Bedeutung sind. ³Die §§ 65 und 65a des Ersten Buches gelten entsprechend.

(8) ¹Der Erstattungsanspruch verjährt in vier Jahren nach Ablauf des Kalenderjahres, für das das Arbeitslosengeld zu erstatten ist. ²§ 50 Abs. 4 Satz 2 und 3 des Zehnten Buches gilt entsprechend.

(4) The obligation to reimburse unemployment benefits includes the contributions to health, nursing care and old-age pension insurance accruing to such benefits.

(5) ¹In calculating the periods of employment, corporate groups within the meaning of section 18 of the Stock Corporation Act *(Aktiengesetz – AktG)* shall be deemed to constitute one employer. ²The reimbursement duty is directed against the employer with which the employee was most recently in an employment relationship.

(6) ¹The Employment Agency shall advise the employer upon request on the prerequisites for and scope of the reimbursement regulation. ²Upon the employer's application, the Employment Agency shall determine in advance whether the prerequisites set forth in subsection (1) sentence 2 nos. 6 or 7 are met.

(7) ¹At the request of the Employment Agency, the unemployed person shall be obligated to provide information, to report personally to the Employment Agency or submit to a medical or psychological examination where the onset or discontinuation of the reimbursement duty is dependent upon such co-operation. ²In order for the Employment Agency to be able to make such a request, it must be aware of personal circumstance affecting the unemployed person which are of significance for the onset or discontinuation of the reimbursement duty. ³Sections 65 and 65a of the First Book apply *mutatis mutandis.*

(8) ¹The claim for reimbursement shall become statute-barred four years after the expiration of the calendar year for which the unemployment benefits are to be reimbursed. ²Section 50 (4) sentences 2 and 3 of the Tenth Book applies *mutatis mutandis.*

XVIII. Social Security Code IV (4. Sozialgesetzbuch – SGB)

of 23 December 1976 (Federal Law Gazette I p. 3845)

in the amended version of 12 November 2009

(excerpts)

§ 7
Beschäftigung

(1) [1]Beschäftigung ist die nichtselbständige Arbeit, insbesondere in einem Arbeitsverhältnis. [2]Anhaltspunkte für eine Beschäftigung sind eine Tätigkeit nach Weisungen und eine Eingliederung in die Arbeitsorganisation des Weisungsgebers.

(1 a) [1]Eine Beschäftigung besteht auch in Zeiten der Freistellung von der Arbeitsleistung von mehr als einem Monat, wenn

1. während der Freistellung Arbeitsentgelt aus einem Wertguthaben nach § 7b fällig ist und
2. das monatlich fällige Arbeitsentgelt in der Zeit der Freistellung nicht unangemessen von dem für die vorausgegangenen zwölf Kalendermonate abweicht, in denen Arbeitsentgelt bezogen wurde.

[2]Beginnt ein Beschäftigungsverhältnis mit einer Zeit der Freistellung, gilt Satz 1 Nr. 2 mit der Maßgabe, dass das monatlich fällige Arbeitsentgelt in der Zeit der Freistellung nicht unangemessen von dem für die Zeit der Arbeitsleistung abweichen darf, mit der das Arbeitsentgelt später erzielt werden soll. [3]Eine Beschäftigung gegen Arbeitsentgelt besteht während der Zeit der Freistellung auch, wenn die Arbeitsleistung, mit der das Arbeitsentgelt später erzielt werden soll, wegen einer im Zeitpunkt der Vereinbarung nicht vorhersehbaren vorzeitigen Beendigung des Beschäftigungsverhältnisses

Section 7
Employment

(1) [1]Employment is non-independent work, in particular in an employment relationship. [2]The existence of employment is indicated by the presence of activities carried out by direction and an integration into the work organization of the issuer of the directions.

(1 a) [1]Even during a period of release from work duties for more than one month, employment shall exist if

1. remuneration is payable during the release period out of a valuation credit pursuant to section 7b and
2. the monthly remuneration payable during the release period does not disproportionately differ from that of the preceding twelve calendar months in which remuneration was received.

[2]If an employment relationship commences with a release period, sentence 1 no. 2 shall apply provided that monthly remuneration payable during the release period does not disproportionately differ from that for the period in which work which is to be remunerated is performed. [3]Employment for remuneration exists during the release period as well if the work which is to be remunerated can no longer be performed due to a premature termination of the employment relationship which could not have been foreseen at the time of the conclusion of the employment agreement. [4]On conclusion of the

nicht mehr erbracht werden kann. ⁴Die Vertragsparteien können beim Abschluss der Vereinbarung nur für den Fall, dass Wertguthaben wegen der Beendigung der Beschäftigung auf Grund verminderter Erwerbsfähigkeit, des Erreichens einer Altersgrenze, zu der eine Rente wegen Alters beansprucht werden kann, oder des Todes des Beschäftigten nicht mehr für Zeiten einer Freistellung von der Arbeitsleistung verwendet werden können, einen anderen Verwendungszweck vereinbaren. ⁵Die Sätze 1 bis 4 gelten nicht für Beschäftigte, auf die Wertguthaben übertragen werden. ⁶Bis zur Herstellung einheitlicher Einkommensverhältnisse im Inland werden Wertguthaben, die durch Arbeitsleistung im Beitrittsgebiet erzielt werden, getrennt erfasst; sind für die Beitrags- oder Leistungsberechnung im Beitrittsgebiet und im Übrigen Bundesgebiet unterschiedliche Werte vorgeschrieben, sind die Werte maßgebend, die für den Teil des Inlandes gelten, in dem das Wertguthaben erzielt worden ist.

(1b) Die Möglichkeit eines Arbeitnehmers zur Vereinbarung flexibler Arbeitszeiten gilt nicht als eine die Kündigung des Arbeitsverhältnisses durch den Arbeitgeber begründende Tatsache im Sinne des § 1 Abs. 2 Satz 1 des Kündigungsschutzgesetzes.

(2) Als Beschäftigung gilt auch der Erwerb beruflicher Kenntnisse, Fertigkeiten oder Erfahrungen im Rahmen betrieblicher Berufsbildung.

(3) ¹Eine Beschäftigung gegen Arbeitsentgelt gilt als fortbestehend, solange das Beschäftigungsverhältnis ohne Anspruch auf Arbeitsentgelt fortdauert, jedoch nicht länger als einen Monat. ²Eine Beschäftigung gilt auch als fortbestehend, wenn Arbeitsentgelt aus einem der Deutschen Rentenversicherung Bund übertragenen Wertguthaben

agreement the parties may agree to another purpose of use only for the case that valuation credits can no longer be used because the employment has been terminated either due to the diminished capacity to work, the achievement of pensionable age or the death of the employee. ⁵Sentences 1 to 4 shall not apply to employees to whom valuation credit is to be transferred. ⁶Until the creation of a uniform domestic earning capacity valuation credits which are to be attained through employment in an acceding territory will be separately recorded; if different values are prescribed for the calculation of contributions or benefits in the acceding territory and in other Federal territories, then the values which are applicable for the part of Germany in which the valuation credit has been attained are authoritative.

(1b) The ability of an employee to agree to flexible working hours shall not be deemed to constitute a circumstance justifying termination of the employment relationship by the employer within the meaning of section 1 (1) sentence 2 of the Protection Against Unfair Dismissal Act (*Kündigungsschutzgesetz – KSchG*).

(2) The acquisition of professional knowledge, skills or experience within the scope of a company's professional training program shall also be deemed to constitute employment.

(3) ¹Employment for remuneration shall be deemed to remain in existence as long as the employment relationship continues without a claim to remuneration, but no longer than one month. ²Employment shall also be deemed to remain in existence if remuneration out of a valuation credit transferred to the German Pension Insurance Federal In-

bezogen wird. ³Satz 1 gilt nicht, wenn Krankengeld, Krankentagegeld, Verletztengeld, Versorgungskrankengeld, Übergangsgeld oder Mutterschaftsgeld oder nach gesetzlichen Vorschriften Erziehungsgeld oder Elterngeld bezogen oder Elternzeit in Anspruch genommen oder Wehrdienst oder Zivildienst geleistet wird. ⁴Satz 1 gilt auch nicht für die Inanspruchnahme von Pflegezeit im Sinne des § 3 des Pflegezeitgesetzes.

stitution *(Deutsche Rentenversicherung Bund).* ³Sentence 1 shall not apply if sickness benefits, injury benefits, disabled persons entitlement to sick pay, bridge payments or maternity benefits or educational allowances or parental benefits pursuant to the statutory provisions are drawn or parental leave is claimed or military or alternative civil service is being performed. ⁴Sentence 1 shall also not apply to the utilization of nursing care leave within the meaning of section 3 of the Nursing Care Leave Act (Pflegezeitgesetz).

§ 7a
Anfrageverfahren

Section 7a
Inquiry Proceeding

(1) ¹Die Beteiligten können schriftlich eine Entscheidung beantragen, ob eine Beschäftigung vorliegt, es sei denn, die Einzugsstelle oder ein anderer Versicherungsträger hatte im Zeitpunkt der Antragstellung bereits ein Verfahren zur Feststellung einer Beschäftigung eingeleitet. ²Die Einzugsstelle hat einen Antrag nach Satz 1 zu stellen, wenn sich aus der Meldung des Arbeitgebers (§ 28a) ergibt, dass der Beschäftigte Ehegatte, Lebenspartner oder Abkömmling des Arbeitgebers oder geschäftsführender Gesellschafter einer Gesellschaft mit beschränkter Haftung ist. ³Über den Antrag entscheidet abweichend von § 28h Abs. 2 die Deutsche Rentenversicherung Bund.

(1) ¹The concerned parties may apply in writing for a decision as to whether an employment exists, unless the collecting agency or another insurance carrier had already initiated a proceeding to ascertain employment before such application was filed. ²The collecting agency shall file an application pursuant to sentence 1 if the employer's notification (section 28a) shows that the employed person is a spouse, life partner or descendent of the employer or managing shareholder of a limited liability company. ³Notwithstanding section 28h (2), the decision on the application shall be made by the German Pension Insurance Federal Institution *(Deutsche Rentenversicherung Bund).*

(2) Die Deutsche Rentenversicherung Bund entscheidet auf Grund einer Gesamtwürdigung aller Umstände des Einzelfalles, ob eine Beschäftigung vorliegt.

(2) The German Pension Insurance Federal Institution shall determine on the basis of an overall evaluation of all circumstances involved in the individual case whether or not a case of employment exists.

(3) ¹Die Deutsche Rentenversicherung Bund teilt den Beteiligten schriftlich mit, welche Angaben und Unterlagen sie für ihre Entscheidung benötigt. ²Sie setzt den Beteiligten eine angemessene Frist, innerhalb der diese die Angaben zu machen und die Unterlagen vorzulegen haben.

(3) ¹The German Pension Insurance Federal Institution shall inform the concerned parties in writing what information and documents it requires to make its decision. ²It shall set a reasonable time period within which the parties must provide such information and documents.

(4) Die Deutsche Rentenversicherung Bund teilt den Beteiligten mit, welche Entscheidung sie zu treffen beabsichtigt, bezeichnet die Tatsachen, auf die sie ihre Entscheidung stützen will, und gibt den Beteiligten Gelegenheit, sich zu der beabsichtigten Entscheidung zu äußern.

(5) Die Deutsche Rentenversicherung Bund fordert die Beteiligten auf, innerhalb einer angemessenen Frist die Tatsachen anzugeben, die eine Widerlegung begründen, wenn diese die Vermutung widerlegen wollen.

(6) [1] Wird der Antrag nach Absatz 1 innerhalb eines Monats nach Aufnahme der Tätigkeit gestellt und stellt die Deutsche Rentenversicherung Bund ein versicherungspflichtiges Beschäftigungsverhältnis fest, tritt die Versicherungspflicht mit der Bekanntgabe der Entscheidung ein, wenn der Beschäftigte

1. zustimmt und
2. er für den Zeitraum zwischen Aufnahme der Beschäftigung und der Entscheidung eine Absicherung gegen das finanzielle Risiko von Krankheit und zur Altersvorsorge vorgenommen hat, die der Art nach den Leistungen der gesetzlichen Krankenversicherung und der gesetzlichen Rentenversicherung entspricht.

[2] Der Gesamtsozialversicherungsbeitrag wird erst zu dem Zeitpunkt fällig, zu dem die Entscheidung, dass eine Beschäftigung vorliegt, unanfechtbar geworden ist.

(7) [1] Widerspruch und Klage gegen Entscheidungen, dass eine Beschäftigung vorliegt, haben aufschiebende Wirkung. [2] Eine Klage auf Erlass der Entscheidung ist abweichend von § 88 Abs. 1 des Sozialgerichtsgesetzes nach Ablauf von drei Monaten zulässig.

(4) The German Pension Insurance Federal Institution shall inform the concerned parties what decision it intends to make, describe the circumstances on which it wishes to base its decision and give the parties an opportunity to take a position on the intended decision.

(5) The German Pension Insurance Federal Institution shall call upon the concerned parties to state the circumstances justifying a refutation within a reasonable period of time if they wish to refute the presumption of employment.

(6) [1] If the application pursuant to subsection (1) is filed within one month of the commencement of the work activity and if the German Pension Insurance Federal Institution ascertains that an employment relationship subject to social insurance regulations exists, the duty to pay social insurance contributions shall ensue with the announcement of the decision, provided that the employed person

1. consents thereto and
2. had taken out insurance against the financial risk of illness and for old age benefits, of a type corresponding to statutory health insurance and old age insurance during the period between the commencement of the work and the decision.

[2] The joint social insurance contribution shall only become payable once the decision that employment exists is final and can no longer be contested.

(7) [1] Objections to and legal actions against a decision that employment exists shall have a suspensive effect. [2] Notwithstanding section 88 (1) of the Social Court Act *(Sozialgerichtsgesetz)*, an action for issuance of the decision shall be permitted after three months have elapsed.

§ 7 b
Wertguthabenvereinbarung

Eine Wertguthabenvereinbarung liegt vor, wenn
1. der Aufbau des Wertguthabens auf Grund einer schriftlichen Vereinbarung erfolgt,
2. diese Vereinbarung nicht das Ziel der flexiblen Gestaltung der werktäglichen oder wöchentlichen Arbeitszeit oder den Ausgleich betrieblicher Produktions- und Arbeitszeitzyklen verfolgt,
3. Arbeitsentgelt in das Wertguthaben eingebracht wird, um es für Zeiten der Freistellung von der Arbeitsleistung oder der Verringerung der vertraglich vereinbarten Arbeitszeit zu entnehmen,
4. das aus dem Wertguthaben fällige Arbeitsentgelt mit einer vor oder nach der Freistellung von der Arbeitsleistung oder der Verringerung der vertraglich vereinbarten Arbeitszeit erbrachten Arbeitsleistung erzielt wird und
5. das fällige Arbeitsentgelt insgesamt 400 Euro monatlich übersteigt, es sei denn, die Beschäftigung wurde vor der Freistellung als geringfügige Beschäftigung ausgeübt.

§ 7 c
Verwendung von Wertguthaben

(1) Das Wertguthaben auf Grund einer Vereinbarung nach § 7 b kann in Anspruch genommen werden
1. für gesetzlich geregelte vollständige oder teilweise Freistellungen von der Arbeitsleistung oder gesetzlich geregelte Verringerungen der Arbeitszeit, insbesondere für Zeiten,
   a) in denen der Beschäftigte nach § 3 des Pflegezeitgesetzes vom 28. Mai 2008 (BGBl. I S. 874, 896) in der jeweils geltenden Fassung einen pflegebedürftigen nahen Angehörigen in häuslicher Umgebung pflegt,

Section 7 b
Valuation Credit Agreement

A valuation credit agreement exists if
1. the valuation credit is built up on the basis of a written agreement,
2. this agreement does not pursue the goal of a flexible structuring of the working hours per working day or per week or an equalization of operational production and working time cycles,
3. remuneration is contributed to the valuation credit so that it can be withdrawn for periods of release from work duties or a reduction of the contractually agreed upon working time,
4. the remuneration payable out of the valuation credit is achieved with the performance of work before or after the release from work duties or the reduction of the contractually agreed upon working hours and
5. the total payable remuneration exceeds 400 euro per month, unless the employment was performed as insignificant employment prior to the release.

Section 7 c
Use of Valuation Credits

(1) The valuation credit can be utilized on the basis of an agreement pursuant to section 7 b
1. for complete or partial releases from work duties that are regulated by statute or reductions of working hours that are regulated by statute, in particular for periods of time,
   a) in which the employee is caring for a close relative requiring care in a home environment pursuant to section 3 of the Nursing Care Leave Act of 28 May 2008 (Federal Law Gazette I pp. 874, 896) as it may change from time to time,

b) in denen der Beschäftigte nach § 15 des Bundeselterngeld- und Elternzeitgesetzes ein Kind selbst betreut und erzieht,

c) für die der Beschäftigte eine Verringerung seiner vertraglich vereinbarten Arbeitszeit nach § 8 des Teilzeit- und Befristungsgesetzes verlangen kann; § 8 des Teilzeit- und Befristungsgesetzes gilt mit der Maßgabe, dass die Verringerung der Arbeitszeit auf die Dauer der Entnahme aus dem Wertguthaben befristet werden kann,

2. für vertraglich vereinbarte vollständige oder teilweise Freistellungen von der Arbeitsleistung oder vertraglich vereinbarte Verringerungen der Arbeitszeit, insbesondere für Zeiten,
   a) die unmittelbar vor dem Zeitpunkt liegen, zu dem der Beschäftigte eine Rente wegen Alters nach dem Sechsten Buch bezieht oder beziehen könnte oder
   b) in denen der Beschäftigte an beruflichen Qualifizierungsmaßnahmen teilnimmt.

(2) Die Vertragsparteien können die Zwecke, für die das Wertguthaben in Anspruch genommen werden kann, in der Vereinbarung nach § 7b abweichend von Absatz 1 auf bestimmte Zwecke beschränken.

§ 7d
Führung und Verwaltung von Wertguthaben

(1) Wertguthaben sind als Arbeitsentgeltguthaben einschließlich des darauf entfallenden Arbeitgeberanteils am Gesamtsozialversicherungsbeitrag zu führen. Die Arbeitszeitguthaben sind in Arbeitsentgelt umzurechnen.

(2) Arbeitgeber haben Beschäftigte mindestens einmal jährlich in Textform über die Höhe ihres im Wertguthaben

---

b) in which the employee is caring for and raising a child himself or herself pursuant to section 15 of the Federal Parental Benefit and Parental Leave Act,

c) for which the employee can demand a reduction of his or her contractually agreed upon working time pursuant to section 8 of the Part-Time and Limited Term Employment Act; section 8 of the Part-Time and Limited Term Employment Act applies with the proviso that the reduction of the working hours can be limited to the duration of the withdrawal from the valuation credit,

2. for contractually agreed upon whole or partial releases from work duties or contractually agreed upon reductions of working hours, in particular for times,
   a) immediately preceding the point in time at which, due to his or her age, the employee receives or could receive a pension pursuant to the Sixth Book or
   b) in which the employee participates in professional qualification measures.

(2) Notwithstanding subsection (1), in the agreement pursuant to section 7b, the parties can limit the purposes for which the valuation credit can be utilized to specific purposes.

Section 7d
Maintenance and Management of Valuation Credits

(1) Valuation credits shall be maintained as remuneration credits, including the employer's share of the joint social insurance contribution accruing to them. The working time credits shall be converted to remuneration.

(2) Employer shall inform employees at least once each year in text form of the amount of their remuneration

enthaltenen Arbeitsentgeltguthabens zu unterrichten.

(3) Für die Anlage von Wertguthaben gelten die Vorschriften über die Anlage der Mittel von Versicherungsträgern nach dem Vierten Titel des Vierten Abschnitts entsprechend, mit der Maßgabe, dass eine Anlage in Aktien oder Aktienfonds bis zu einer Höhe von 20 Prozent zulässig und ein Rückfluss zum Zeitpunkt der Inanspruchnahme des Wertguthabens mindestens in der Höhe des angelegten Betrages gewährleistet ist. Ein höherer Anlageanteil in Aktien oder Aktienfonds ist zulässig, wenn

1. dies in einem Tarifvertrag oder auf Grund eines Tarifvertrages in einer Betriebsvereinbarung vereinbart ist oder
2. das Wertguthaben nach der Wertguthabenvereinbarung ausschließlich für Freistellungen nach § 7c Absatz 1 Nummer 2 Buchstabe a in Anspruch genommen werden kann.

§ 7e
Insolvenzschutz

(1) Die Vertragsparteien treffen im Rahmen ihrer Vereinbarung nach § 7 Abs. 1b durch den Arbeitgeber zu erfüllende Vorkehrungen, um das Wertguthaben einschließlich des darin enthaltenen Gesamtsozialversicherungsbeitrages gegen das Risiko der Insolvenz des Arbeitgebers vollständig abzusichern, soweit

1. ein Anspruch auf Insolvenzgeld nicht besteht und wenn
2. das Wertguthaben des Beschäftigten einschließlich des darin enthaltenen Gesamtsozialversicherungsbeitrages einen Betrag in Höhe der monatlichen Bezugsgröße übersteigt.

In einem Tarifvertrag oder auf Grund eines Tarifvertrages in einer Betriebsvereinbarung kann ein von Satz 1 Nr. 2 abweichender Betrag vereinbart werden.

(2) Zur Erfüllung der Verpflichtung

credit contained in the valuation credit.

(3) Investments of valuation credits shall be governed by the provisions on investments of funds of insurers pursuant to the Fourth Title of the Fourth Chapter *mutatis mutandis*, subject to the proviso that an investment in shares or equity funds is permissible up to an amount of 20 percent and that a recoupment at the time of the utilization of the valuation credit is ensured, at least in the amount of the invested sum. A greater investment percentage in shares or equity funds is permissible if

1. this has been agreed upon in a collective bargaining agreement or on the basis of a collective bargaining agreement in a works agreement or
2. under the valuation credit agreement, the valuation credit can be utilized exclusively for releases pursuant to section 7c (1) no. 2 a.

Section 7e
Insolvency Protection

(1) The contractual parties shall take precautionary measures within the scope of their agreement pursuant to section 7 (1b) that are to be fulfilled by the employer in order to completely secure the valuation credits, including the joint social insurance contribution contained therein against the risk of the employer's insolvency, provided that

1. no claim to insolvency benefits exists and if
2. the employee's valuation credit, including the joint social insurance contribution contained therein, exceeds the amount of the monthly reference figure.

It is possible to agree to an amount that departs from sentence 1 no. 2 in a collective bargaining agreement or on the basis of a collective bargaining agreement in a works agreement.

(2) In order to fulfill the obligation set

nach Absatz 1 sind Wertguthaben unter Ausschluss der Rückführung durch einen Dritten zu führen, der im Fall der Insolvenz des Arbeitgebers für die Erfüllung der Ansprüche aus dem Wertguthaben für den Arbeitgeber einsteht, insbesondere in einem Treuhandverhältnis, das die unmittelbare Übertragung des Wertguthabens in das Vermögen des Dritten und die Anlage des Wertguthabens auf einem offenen Treuhandkonto oder in anderer geeigneter Weise sicherstellt. Die Vertragsparteien können in der Vereinbarung nach § 7b ein anderes, einem Treuhandverhältnis im Sinne des Satzes 1 gleichwertiges Sicherungsmittel vereinbaren, insbesondere ein Versicherungsmodell oder ein schuldrechtliches Verpfändungs- oder Bürgschaftsmodell mit ausreichender Sicherung gegen Kündigung.

(3) Keine geeigneten Vorkehrungen sind bilanzielle Rückstellungen sowie zwischen Konzernunternehmen (§ 18 des Aktiengesetzes) begründete Einstandspflichten, insbesondere Bürgschaften, Patronatserklärungen oder Schuldbeitritte.

(4) Der Arbeitgeber hat den Beschäftigten unverzüglich über die Vorkehrungen zum Insolvenzschutz in geeigneter Weise schriftlich zu unterrichten, wenn das Wertguthaben die in Absatz 1 Satz 1 Nummer 2 genannten Voraussetzungen erfüllt.

(5) Hat der Beschäftigte den Arbeitgeber schriftlich aufgefordert, seinen Verpflichtungen nach den Absätzen 1 bis 3 nachzukommen und weist der Arbeitgeber dem Beschäftigten nicht innerhalb von zwei Monaten nach der Aufforderung die Erfüllung seiner Verpflichtung zur Insolvenzsicherung des Wertguthabens nach, kann der Beschäftigte die Vereinbarung nach § 7b mit sofortiger Wirkung kündigen; das Wertguthaben ist nach Maßgabe des § 23b Absatz 2 aufzulösen.

forth in subsection (1), valuation credits must be maintained to the exclusion of a repayment by a third party, who in the event of the insolvency of the employer, is responsible for the fulfillment of the claims arising from the valuation credits for the employer, in particular in a trust relationship that ensures the direct transfer of the valuation credit to the assets of the third party and the deposit of the valuation credit into an open trust account or in some other suitable manner. The contractual parties can provide in the agreement pursuant to section 7b for a different form of security equivalent to a trust within the meaning of sentence 1, in particular an insurance model or a contractual pledge or suretyship model with adequate security against termination.

(3) Accruals in the balance sheets and obligations to assume liabilities that are entered into between group companies (section 18 of the Stock Corporation Act), in particular suretyships, letters of comfort or accessions to debt are not suitable precautionary measures.

(4) The employer shall inform the employees of the precautionary measures to protect against insolvency in an appropriate manner writing if the valuation credit meets the prerequisites set forth in subsection 1 sentence 1 no. 2.

(5) If the employee has called upon the employer in writing to meet its obligations pursuant to subsections (1) to (3) and if the employer does not provide proof to the employee that it has met its obligation to secure the valuation credit against insolvency within two months of being called upon to do so, the employee can terminate the agreement pursuant to section 7b with immediate effect; the valuation credit shall then be dissolved in accordance with section 23b (2).

(6) Stellt der Träger der Rentenversicherung bei der Prüfung des Arbeitgebers nach § 28p fest, dass

1. für ein Wertguthaben keine Insolvenzschutzregelung getroffen worden ist,
2. die gewählten Sicherungsmittel nicht geeignet sind im Sinne des Absatzes 3,
3. die Sicherungsmittel in ihrem Umfang das Wertguthaben um mehr als 30 Prozent unterschreiten oder
4. die Sicherungsmittel den im Wertguthaben enthaltenen Gesamtsozialversicherungsbeitrag nicht umfassen,

weist er in dem Verwaltungsakt nach § 28p Absatz 1 Satz 5 den in dem Wertguthaben enthaltenen und vom Arbeitgeber zu zahlenden Gesamtsozialversicherungsbeitrag aus. Weist der Arbeitgeber dem Träger der Rentenversicherung innerhalb von zwei Monaten nach der Feststellung nach Satz 1 nach, dass er seiner Verpflichtung nach Absatz 1 nachgekommen ist, entfällt die Verpflichtung zur sofortigen Zahlung des Gesamtsozialversicherungsbeitrages. Hat der Arbeitgeber den Nachweis nach Satz 2 nicht innerhalb der dort vorgesehenen Frist erbracht, ist die Vereinbarung nach § 7b als von Anfang an unwirksam anzusehen; das Wertguthaben ist aufzulösen.

(7) Kommt es wegen eines nicht geeigneten oder nicht ausreichenden Insolvenzschutzes zu einer Verringerung oder einem Verlust des Wertguthabens, haftet der Arbeitgeber für den entstandenen Schaden. Ist der Arbeitgeber eine juristische Person oder eine Gesellschaft ohne Rechtspersönlichkeit haften auch die organschaftlichen Vertreter gesamtschuldnerisch für den Schaden. Der Arbeitgeber oder ein organschaftlicher Vertreter haften nicht, wenn sie den Schaden nicht zu vertreten haben.

(8) Eine Beendigung, Auflösung oder Kündigung der Vorkehrungen zum Insolvenzschutz vor der bestimmungs-

(6) Should the social security carrier ascertain upon auditing the employer pursuant to section 28p that

1. no insolvency protection regulation has been adopted for a valuation credit,
2. the security measures are not suitable within the meaning of subsection (3),
3. the scope of the security measures falls more than 30 percent below the valuation credit or
4. the security measures do not cover the joint social insurance contribution contained in the valuation credit,

it shall report the joint social insurance contribution that is contained in the valuation credit and is to be paid by the employer in the administrative act pursuant to section 28p (1) sentence 5. Should the employer provide proof to the social security carrier within two months of the determination pursuant to sentence 1 that it has met its obligation pursuant to subsection (1), it will no longer be obligated to pay the joint social insurance contribution immediately. If the employer does not provide the proof pursuant to sentence 2 within the time period set forth therein, the agreement pursuant to section 7b shall be deemed to have been invalid from its outset; the valuation credit shall be dissolved.

(7) Should the valuation credit be reduced or lost due to an unsuitable or insufficient insolvency protection, the employer shall bear liability for the damage incurred. If the employer is a legal entity or a company without legal personality, its legal representatives will bear joint liability for the damage. The employer or a legal representative shall not bear liability if they are not responsible for the damage.

(8) The precautionary insolvency protection measures cannot be cancelled, dissolved or terminated prior to the

gemäßen Auflösung des Wertguthabens ist unzulässig, es sei denn, die Vorkehrungen werden mit Zustimmung des Beschäftigten durch einen mindestens gleichwertigen Insolvenzschutz abgelöst.

(9) Die Absätze 1 bis 8 finden keine Anwendung gegenüber dem Bund, den Ländern, Gemeinden, Körperschaften, Stiftungen und Anstalten des öffentlichen Rechts, über deren Vermögen die Eröffnung des Insolvenzverfahrens nicht zulässig ist, sowie solchen juristischen Personen des öffentlichen Rechts, bei denen der Bund, ein Land oder eine Gemeinde kraft Gesetzes die Zahlungsfähigkeit sichert.

§ 7 f
Übertragung von Wertguthaben

(1) Bei Beendigung der Beschäftigung kann der Beschäftigte durch schriftliche Erklärung gegenüber dem bisherigen Arbeitgeber verlangen, dass das Wertguthaben nach § 7 b

1. auf den neuen Arbeitgeber übertragen wird, wenn dieser mit dem Beschäftigten eine Wertguthabenvereinbarung nach § 7 b abgeschlossen und der Übertragung zugestimmt hat,
2. auf die Deutsche Rentenversicherung Bund übertragen wird, wenn das Wertguthaben einschließlich des Gesamtsozialversicherungsbeitrages einen Betrag in Höhe des Sechsfachen der monatlichen Bezugsgröße übersteigt; die Rückübertragung ist ausgeschlossen.

Nach der Übertragung sind die mit dem Wertguthaben verbundenen Arbeitgeberpflichten vom neuen Arbeitgeber oder von der Deutschen Rentenversicherung Bund zu erfüllen.

(2) Im Fall der Übertragung auf die Deutsche Rentenversicherung Bund kann der Beschäftigte das Wertguthaben für Zeiten der Freistellung von der Arbeitsleistung und Zeiten der Verrin-

contractual dissolution of the valuation credit unless the precautionary measures are replaced with the employee's consent by insolvency protection of at least equivalent value.

(9) Subsections (1) to (8) shall have no application vis-à-vis the Federal Government, the Federal States, municipalities, corporations, foundations and institutions under public law, against whose assets no insolvency proceedings can permissibly be opened, as well as those legal entities under public law whose solvency is ensured by the Federal Government, a Federal State, or a municipality by force of law.

Section 7 f
Transfer of valuation credits

(1) In the event of a termination of the employment relationship, the employee can demand by written declaration to the former employer that the valuation credit pursuant to section 7 b

1. be transferred to the new employer if it has concluded a valuation credit agreement pursuant to section 7 b with the employee and consented to the transfer,
2. be transferred to the German Pension Insurance Federal Institution (*Deutsche Rentenversicherung Bund*) if the valuation credit, including the joint social insurance contribution, exceeds a sum six times that of the monthly reference figure; a return transfer shall be excluded.

Following the transfer, the employer duties associated with the valuation credits shall be fulfilled by the new employer or the German Pension Insurance Federal Institution.

(2) In the event of a transfer to the German Pension Insurance Federal Institution, the employee may utilize the valuation credit for periods in which he is released from work duties and peri-

gerung der vertraglich vereinbarten Arbeitszeit nach § 7c Absatz 1 sowie auch außerhalb eines Arbeitsverhältnisses für die in § 7c Absatz 1 Nummer 2 Buchstabe a genannten Zeiten in Anspruch nehmen. Der Antrag ist spätestens einen Monat vor der begehrten Freistellung schriftlich bei der Deutschen Rentenversicherung Bund zu stellen; in dem Antrag ist auch anzugeben, in welcher Höhe Arbeitsentgelt aus dem Wertguthaben entnommen werden soll; dabei ist § 7 Absatz 1a Satz 1 Nummer 2 zu berücksichtigen.

(3) Die Deutsche Rentenversicherung Bund verwaltet die ihr übertragenen Wertguthaben einschließlich des darin enthaltenen Gesamtsozialversicherungsbeitrages als ihr übertragene Aufgabe bis zu deren endgültiger Auflösung getrennt von ihrem sonstigen Vermögen treuhänderisch. Die Wertguthaben sind nach den Vorschriften über die Anlage der Mittel von Versicherungsträgern nach dem Vierten Titel des Vierten Abschnitts anzulegen. Die der Deutschen Rentenversicherung Bund durch die Übertragung, Verwaltung und Verwendung von Wertguthaben entstehenden Kosten sind vollständig vom Wertguthaben in Abzug zu bringen und in der Mitteilung an den Beschäftigten nach § 7d Absatz 2 gesondert auszuweisen.

ods of a reduction of the contractually agreed upon working time pursuant to section 7c (1), as well as outside of an employment relationship for the time periods set forth in section 7c (1) no. 2 a. The application shall be filed in writing no later than one month prior to the desired release with the German Pension Insurance Federal Institution; the application shall also state the amount of remuneration that is to be withdrawn from the valuation credits, taking into account section 7 (1a) sentence 1 no. 2.

(3) The German Pension Insurance Federal Institution shall manage the valuation credits transferred to it, including the joint social insurance contribution contained therein, in trust as a task transferred to it up to its final dissolution, separate from its other assets. The valuation credits shall be invested in accordance with the provisions on the investment of funds of insurers set forth in the fourth Title of the Fourth Chapter. The costs incurred by German Pension Insurance Federal Institution due to the transfer, management and use of valuation credits shall be deducted in full from the valuation credit and reported separately in the communication to the employees pursuant to section 7d (2).

§ 7g
Bericht der Bundesregierung

Section 7g
Report of the Federal Government

Die Bundesregierung berichtet den gesetzgebenden Körperschaften bis zum 31. März 2012 über die Auswirkungen des Gesetzes zur Verbesserung der Rahmenbedingungen für die Absicherung flexibler Arbeitszeitregelungen und zur Änderung anderer Gesetze vom 21. Dezember 2008 (BGBl. I S. 2940), insbesondere über die Entwicklung der Inanspruchnahme und Nutzung der Wertguthaben, den Umfang und die Kosten der an die Deut-

The Federal Government shall report to the legislative corporations by 31 March 2012 on the impact of the Law for Improvement of Framework Conditions for Coverage of Flexible Working Arrangements and for Amendment of Other Laws (*Gesetz zur Verbesserung der Rahmenbedingungen für die Absicherung flexibler Arbeitszeitregelungen und zur Änderung anderer Gesetze*) of 21 December 2008 (Federal Law Gazette. I p. 2940), in particular on the develop-

sche Rentenversicherung Bund übertragenen Wertguthaben und der wegen Insolvenz des Arbeitgebers ersatzlos aufgelösten Wertguthaben und sonstigen Arbeitszeitguthaben, und macht gegebenenfalls Vorschläge für eine Weiterentwicklung des Insolvenzschutzes.

ment of the utilization and use of the valuation credits, the scope and the costs of the valuation credits transferred to the German Pension Insurance Federal Institution and of the valuation credits and other working time credits that were dissolved without replacement due to the employer's insolvency, and make proposals for a further development of the insolvency protection if appropriate.

§ 8
Geringfügige Beschäftigung und geringfügige selbständige Tätigkeit

(1) Eine geringfügige Beschäftigung liegt vor, wenn

1. das Arbeitsentgelt aus dieser Beschäftigung regelmäßig im Monat 400 Euro nicht übersteigt,
2. die Beschäftigung innerhalb eines Kalenderjahres auf längstens zwei Monate oder 50 Arbeitstage nach ihrer Eigenart begrenzt zu sein pflegt oder im Voraus vertraglich begrenzt ist, es sei denn, dass die Beschäftigung berufsmäßig ausgeübt wird und ihr Entgelt 400 Euro im Monat übersteigt.

(2) ¹Bei der Anwendung des Absatzes 1 sind mehrere geringfügige Beschäftigungen nach Nummer 1 oder Nummer 2 sowie geringfügige Beschäftigungen nach Nummer 1 mit Ausnahme einer geringfügigen Beschäftigung nach Nummer 1 und nicht geringfügige Beschäftigungen zusammenzurechnen. ²Eine geringfügige Beschäftigung liegt nicht mehr vor, sobald die Voraussetzungen des Absatzes 1 entfallen. ³Wird beim Zusammenrechnen nach Satz 1 festgestellt, dass die Voraussetzungen einer geringfügigen Beschäftigung nicht mehr vorliegen, tritt die Versicherungspflicht erst mit dem Tag ein, an dem die Entscheidung über die Versicherungspflicht nach § 37 des Zehnten Buches durch die Einzugsstelle nach § 28i Satz 5 oder einen anderen Träger der Rentenversicherung bekannt gege-

Section 8
Insignificant Employment and Insignificant Freelance Activity

(1) Insignificant employment (*geringfügige Beschäftigung*) exists if

1. the remuneration for this work does not regularly exceed 400 euro per month,
2. the employment, by its nature, tends to be or is contractually limited in advance to a maximum of two months or 50 working days within a calendar year, unless the employment is performed as a profession and the remuneration exceeds 400 euro per month.

(2) ¹In applying subsection (1), multiple insignificant employments pursuant to no. 1 or no. 2, as well as insignificant employments pursuant to no. 1, with the exception of one insignificant employment pursuant to no. 1 and non-insignificant employment shall be added together. ²An employment is no longer insignificant once the prerequisites set forth in subsection (1) cease to exist. ³If, in performing the calculation pursuant to sentence 1 it is established that the prerequisites set forth in sentence 1 no longer exist, the duty to make insurance contributions shall only commence on the day on which the decision on the insurance obligation pursuant to section 37 of the Tenth Book by the collecting agency pursuant to section 28i sentence 5 or another carrier of the old-age pension insurance is

ben wird. ⁴Dies gilt nicht, wenn der Arbeitgeber vorsätzlich oder grob fahrlässig versäumt hat, den Sachverhalt für die versicherungsrechtliche Beurteilung der Beschäftigung aufzuklären.

(3) ¹Die Absätze 1 und 2 gelten entsprechend, soweit an Stelle einer Beschäftigung eine selbständige Tätigkeit ausgeübt wird. ²Dies gilt nicht für das Recht der Arbeitsförderung.

announced. ⁴This shall not apply if the employer has, intentionally or due to gross negligence, failed to ascertain the facts of the matter for the assessment of the employment under insurance law.

(3) ¹Subsections (1) and (2) shall apply *mutatis mutandis* where freelance work is performed instead of an employment. ²This shall not apply to the regulations governing the right to promotion of employment *(Arbeitsförderung)*.

Zweiter Titel
Verfahren und Haftung bei der Beitragszahlung

Part 2
Procedure of and Liability for the Payment of Contributions

§ 28 d
Gesamtsozialversicherungsbeitrag

Section 28 d
Joint Social Insurance Contribution

¹Die Beiträge in der Kranken- oder Rentenversicherung für einen kraft Gesetzes versicherten Beschäftigten oder Hausgewerbetreibenden sowie der Beitrag aus Arbeitsentgelt aus einer versicherungspflichtigen Beschäftigung nach dem Recht der Arbeitsförderung werden als Gesamtsozialversicherungsbeitrag gezahlt. ²Satz 1 gilt auch für den Beitrag zur Pflegeversicherung für einen in der Krankenversicherung kraft Gesetzes versicherten Beschäftigten. ³Die nicht nach dem Arbeitsentgelt zu bemessenden Beiträge in der landwirtschaftlichen Krankenversicherung für einen kraft Gesetzes versicherten Beschäftigten gelten zusammen mit den Beiträgen zur Rentenversicherung und Arbeitsförderung im Sinne des Satzes 1 ebenfalls als Gesamtsozialversicherungsbeitrag.

¹The contributions to health or old age insurance for an employee ensured by force of law or a person engaged in work in the home, as well as the contribution from the remuneration paid in an employment subject to the social insurance regulations pursuant to the laws governing the promotion of employment shall be paid as a joint social insurance contribution. ²Sentence 1 shall also apply for the contribution to nursing care insurance for an employee covered by health insurance by force of law. ³The contributions to agricultural health insurance for an employee covered by force of law, which are not calculated according to the remuneration, shall also, together with the contributions to the old age pension insurance employment promotion within the meaning of sentence 1, be deemed to constitute joint social insurance contributions.

§ 28 e
Zahlungspflicht, Vorschuss

Section 28 e
Duty to Make Payments, Advance Payments

(1) ¹Den Gesamtsozialversicherungsbeitrag hat der Arbeitgeber und in den

(1) ¹The joint social insurance contribution must be paid by the employer and

Fällen der nach §7f Absatz 1 Satz 1 Nummer 2 auf die Deutsche Rentenversicherung Bund übertragenen Wertguthaben die Deutsche Rentenversicherung Bund zu zahlen. ²Die Zahlung des vom Beschäftigten zu tragenden Teils des Gesamtsozialversicherungsbeitrags gilt als aus dem Vermögen des Beschäftigten erbracht. ³Ist ein Träger der Kranken- oder Rentenversicherung oder die Bundesagentur für Arbeit der Arbeitgeber, gilt der jeweils für diesen Leistungsträger oder, wenn eine Krankenkasse der Arbeitgeber ist, auch der für die Pflegekasse bestimmte Anteil am Gesamtsozialversicherungsbeitrag als gezahlt; dies gilt für die Beiträge zur Rentenversicherung auch im Verhältnis der Träger der Rentenversicherung untereinander.

(2) ¹Für die Erfüllung der Zahlungspflicht des Arbeitgebers haftet bei einem wirksamen Vertrag der Entleiher wie ein selbstschuldnerischer Bürge, soweit ihm Arbeitnehmer gegen Vergütung zur Arbeitsleistung überlassen worden sind. ²Er kann die Zahlung verweigern, solange die Einzugsstelle den Arbeitgeber nicht gemahnt hat und die Mahnfrist nicht abgelaufen ist. ³Zahlt der Verleiher das vereinbarte Arbeitsentgelt oder Teile des Arbeitsentgelts an den Leiharbeitnehmer, obwohl der Vertrag nach § 9 Nr. 1 des Arbeitnehmerüberlassungsgesetzes unwirksam ist, so hat er auch den hierauf entfallenden Gesamtsozialversicherungsbeitrag an die Einzugsstelle zu zahlen. ⁴Hinsichtlich der Zahlungspflicht nach Satz 3 gilt der Verleiher neben dem Entleiher als Arbeitgeber; beide haften insoweit als Gesamtschuldner.

(2a) Für die Erfüllung der Zahlungspflicht, die sich für den Arbeitgeber knappschaftlicher Arbeiten im Sinne von § 134 Absatz 4 des Sechsten Buches

where valuation credits have been transferred to the German Pension Insurance Federal Institution in the cases pursuant to section 7f (1) sentence 1 no. 2, they must be paid by the German Pension Insurance Federal Institution. ²The payment of the portion of the joint social insurance contribution that is to be borne by the employee shall be deemed to be rendered from the assets of the employee. ³If a carrier of health or old-age pension insurance or the Federal Employment Agency is the employer, the share of their respective insurance carrier or, if a health insurance fund is the employer, also the share of the joint social insurance contribution earmarked for the nursing care insurance shall be deemed to be paid; this applies to the old-age pension insurance contributions also within the old-age pension insurance carriers' relationship to each other.

(2) ¹In the case of leased employees, where a valid contract exists, the lessee shall be liable for the fulfillment of the employer's duty to pay contributions as an absolute guarantor provided that employees are leased to it to work for pay. ²The lessee may refuse to pay as long as the collecting agency has not sent a reminder to the employer and the deadline for payment has not expired. ³If the lessor pays the agreed remuneration or part thereof to the leased employee, even though the contract pursuant to section 9 (1) of the Act Regulating the Commercial Leasing of Employees (*Arbeitnehmerüberlassungsgesetz – AÜG*) is invalid, then it must pay the joint social insurance contribution accruing to it to the collecting agency. ⁴With respect to the duty to pay pursuant to sentence 3, the lessor, along with the lessee, shall be deemed to be the employer; both are joint and severally liable to that extent.

(2a) In the case of mining work within the meaning of section 134 (4) of the Sixth Book, the employer of the mining operation with which the work is geo-

ergibt, haftet der Arbeitgeber des Bergwerkbetriebes, mit dem die Arbeiten räumlich und betrieblich zusammenhängen, wie ein selbstschuldnerischer Bürge. Der Arbeitgeber des Bergwerksbetriebes kann die Befriedigung verweigern, solange die Einzugsstelle den Arbeitgeber der knappschaftlichen Arbeiten nicht gemahnt hat und die Mahnfrist nicht abgelaufen ist.

(3) Für die Erfüllung der Zahlungspflicht des Arbeitgebers von Seeleuten nach § 13 Absatz 1 Satz 2 haften Arbeitgeber und Reeder als Gesamtschuldner.

(3a) [1] Ein Unternehmer des Baugewerbes, der einen anderen Unternehmer mit der Erbringung von Bauleistungen im Sinne des § 175 Abs. 2 des Dritten Buches beauftragt, haftet für die Erfüllung der Zahlungspflicht dieses Unternehmers oder eines von diesem Unternehmer beauftragten Verleihers wie ein selbstschuldnerischer Bürge. [2] Satz 1 gilt entsprechend für die vom Nachunternehmer gegenüber ausländischen Sozialversicherungsträgern abzuführenden Beiträge. [3] Absatz 2 Satz 2 gilt entsprechend.

(3b) [1] Die Haftung nach Absatz 3a entfällt, wenn der Unternehmer nachweist, dass er ohne eigenes Verschulden davon ausgehen konnte, dass der Nachunternehmer oder ein von ihm beauftragter Verleiher seine Zahlungspflicht erfüllt. [2] Ein Verschulden des Unternehmers ist ausgeschlossen, soweit und solange er Fachkunde, Zuverlässigkeit und Leistungsfähigkeit des Nachunternehmers oder des von diesem beauftragten Verleihers durch eine Präqualifikation nachweist, die die Eignungsvoraussetzungen nach § 8 der Vergabe- und Vertragsordnung für Bauleistungen Teil A in der Fassung der Bekanntmachung vom 20. März 2006 (BAnz. Nummer 94a vom 18. Mai 2006) erfüllt.

(3c) [1] Ein Unternehmer, der Bauleistungen im Auftrag eines anderen Unter-

graphically and operationally associated shall be liable for the fulfillment of the employer's duty to pay contributions as an absolute guarantor. The employer of the mining operation can refuse to fulfill this duty as long as the collecting agency has not sent a reminder to the employer of the miners and the deadline for payment has not expired.

(3) For the fulfillment of the payment duty of the employer of sailors pursuant to section 13 (1) sentence 2, the employer and the ship-owner shall be jointly and severally liable.

(3a) [1] A contractor in the construction industry who commissions another contractor to render construction work within the meaning of section 175 (2) of the Third Book, shall be liable for fulfillment of the payment duties of that contractor or a lessor commissioned by it as an absolute guarantor. [2] Sentence 1 applies *mutatis mutandis* for the contributions to be paid by the subcontractor to foreign social security carriers. [3] Subsection (2) sentence 2 applies *mutatis mutandis*.

(3b) [1] The liability pursuant to subsection (3a) shall not be imposed if the contractor can prove that, without being at fault, he was able to presume that the subcontractor or a lessor commissioned by him would meet his payment obligations. [2] Fault on the part of the contractor shall be excluded as long as and to the extent that it provides proof of the specialized knowledge, reliability and capability of the subcontractor or a commissioned lessor of leased employees by means of a pre-qualification that meets the suitability prerequisites set forth in section 8 of the Award Rules for Building Works Part A in the version of the promulgation of 20 March 2006 (Federal Gazette no. 94a of 18 May 2006).

(3c) [1] A contractor who performs construction work on behalf of another

nehmers erbringt, ist verpflichtet, auf Verlangen der Einzugstelle Firma und Anschrift dieses Unternehmers mitzuteilen. ²Kann der Auskunftsanspruch nach Satz 1 nicht durchgesetzt werden, hat ein Unternehmer, der einen Gesamtauftrag für die Erbringung von Bauleistungen für ein Bauwerk erhält, der Einzugsstelle auf Verlangen Firma und Anschrift aller Unternehmer, die von ihm mit der Erbringung von Bauleistungen beauftragt wurden, zu benennen.

(3 d) ¹Absatz 3a gilt ab einem geschätzten Gesamtwert aller für ein Bauwerk in Auftrag gegebenen Bauleistungen von 275 000 Euro. ²Für die Schätzung gilt § 3 der Vergabeverordnung vom 9. Januar 2001 (BGBl. I S. 110), die zuletzt durch Artikel 3 Abs. 1 des Gesetzes vom 16. Mai 2001 (BGBl. I S. 876) geändert worden ist.

(3 e) ¹Die Haftung des Unternehmers nach Absatz 3a erstreckt sich in Abweichung von der dort getroffenen Regelung auf das von dem Nachunternehmer beauftragte nächste Unternehmen, wenn die Beauftragung des unmittelbaren Nachunternehmers bei verständiger Würdigung der Gesamtumstände als ein Rechtsgeschäft anzusehen ist, dessen Ziel vor allem die Auflösung der Haftung nach Absatz 3a ist. ²Maßgeblich für die Würdigung ist die Verkehrsanschauung im Baubereich. ³Ein Rechtsgeschäft im Sinne dieser Vorschrift, das als Umgehungstatbestand anzusehen ist, ist in der Regel anzunehmen,

a) wenn der unmittelbare Nachunternehmer weder selbst eigene Bauleistungen noch planerische oder kaufmännische Leistungen erbringt oder
b) wenn der unmittelbare Nachunternehmer weder technisches noch planerisches oder kaufmännisches Fach-

contractor shall be obligated to provide the name and address of that contractor at the request of the collecting agency. ²If the right to receive information pursuant to sentence 1 cannot be enforced, a contractor who receives an overall commission to perform construction work for a construction project shall provide to the collecting agency upon request the name and address of all contractors it has contracted to perform construction work.

(3 d) ¹Subsection (3 a) shall apply where the estimated total value of all the construction work commissioned for a construction project comes to at least 275,000 euro. ²The estimate shall be subject to section 3 of the Ordinance on the Awarding of Contracts (*Vergabeverordnung*) of 9 January 2001 (Federal Law Gazette I p. 110), which was most recently amended by Article 3 (1) of the Act of 16 May 2001 (Federal Law Gazette I p. 876).

(3 e) ¹The contractor's liability pursuant to subsection (3 a) shall, notwithstanding the provision set forth therein, extend to the next contractor commissioned by the subcontractor if the commissioning of the direct subcontractor is to be deemed a legal transaction in light of a reasonable assessment of the overall circumstances, the primary goal of which is the dissolution of the liability pursuant to subsection (3 a). ²This assessment shall be decisively based on the prevailing opinion in the construction industry. ³A legal transaction within the meaning of this provision that is to be deemed to constitute an attempt to circumvent such liability shall be presumed as a rule,

a) if the direct subcontractor neither performs its own construction work nor renders planning or commercial services or
b) if the direct subcontractor does not employ trained staff in either the technical or the planning or the

personal in nennenswertem Umfang beschäftigt oder

c) wenn der unmittelbare Nachunternehmer in einem gesellschaftsrechtlichen Abhängigkeitsverhältnis zum Hauptunternehmer steht.

Besonderer Prüfung bedürfen die Umstände des Einzelfalles vor allem in den Fällen, in denen der unmittelbare Nachunternehmer seinen handelsrechtlichen Sitz außerhalb des Europäischen Wirtschaftsraums hat.

(3f) ¹Der Unternehmer kann den Nachweis nach Absatz 3b Satz 2 an Stelle der Präqualifikation auch durch Vorlage einer Unbedenklichkeitsbescheinigung der zuständigen Einzugsstelle für den Nachunternehmer oder den von diesem beauftragten Verleiher erbringen. ²Die Unbedenklichkeitsbescheinigung enthält Angaben über die ordnungsgemäße Zahlung der Sozialversicherungsbeiträge und die Zahl der gemeldeten Beschäftigten. ³Die Bundesregierung berichtet unter Beteiligung des Normenkontrollrates über die Wirksamkeit und Reichweite der Generalunternehmerhaftung für Sozialversicherungsbeiträge im Baugewerbe, insbesondere über die Haftungsfreistellung nach Satz 1 und nach Absatz 3b, den gesetzgebenden Körperschaften im Jahr 2012.

(4) Die Haftung umfasst die Beiträge und Säumniszuschläge, die infolge der Pflichtverletzung zu zahlen sind, sowie die Zinsen für gestundete Beiträge (Beitragsansprüche).

(5) Die Satzung der Einzugsstelle kann bestimmen, unter welchen Voraussetzungen vom Arbeitgeber Vorschüsse auf den Gesamtsozialversicherungsbeitrag verlangt werden können.

commercial area to an appreciable extent or

c) if the direct subcontractor is in a dependent relationship to the main contractor as defined by company law.

The circumstances of the individual case must be particularly examined in cases in which the direct subcontractor has its registered domicile outside of the European Economic Area.

(3f) ¹The contractor can also provide the proof pursuant to subsection (3b) sentence 2 in lieu of the pre-qualification by presenting a tax clearance issued by the collection agency competent for the subcontractor or the lessor of leased employees commissioned by it. ²This tax clearance contains information on the proper payment of social insurance contributions and the number of reported employees. ³The Federal Government shall, with the participation of the regulatory control council, report to the legislative corporations in the year 2012 on the validity and range of the contractor liability for social insurance contributions in the construction industry, in particular on the exemption from liability pursuant to sentence 1 and subsection (3b).

(4) The liability covers the contributions and default charges to be paid as a consequence of a breach of duty, as well as the interest for extended deadlines for contributions (contribution claims).

(5) The bylaws of the collecting agency may determine the conditions under which advances on the social insurance contribution payments may be demanded of an employer.

§ 28f
Aufzeichnungspflicht, Nachweise der Beitragsabrechnung und der Beitragszahlung

(1) ¹Der Arbeitgeber hat für jeden Beschäftigten, getrennt nach Kalenderjah-

Section 28f
Recording Duty, Proof of Accounting for and Payment of Contributions

(1) ¹The employer shall maintain wage records for each employee within the

ren, Lohnunterlagen im Geltungsbereich dieses Gesetzes in deutscher Sprache zu führen und bis zum Ablauf des auf die letzte Prüfung (§ 28p) folgenden Kalenderjahres geordnet aufzubewahren. ²Satz 1 gilt nicht hinsichtlich der Beschäftigten in privaten Haushalten. ³Die landwirtschaftlichen Krankenkassen können wegen der mitarbeitenden Familienangehörigen Ausnahmen zulassen. ⁴Für die Aufbewahrung der Beitragsabrechnungen und der Beitragsnachweise gilt Satz 1.

(1a) Bei der Ausführung eines Dienst- oder Werkvertrages im Baugewerbe hat der Unternehmer die Lohnunterlagen und die Beitragsabrechnung so zu gestalten, dass eine Zuordnung der Arbeitnehmer, des Arbeitsentgelts und des darauf entfallenden Gesamtsozialversicherungsbeitrags zu dem jeweiligen Dienst- oder Werkvertrag möglich ist.

(2) ¹Hat ein Arbeitgeber die Aufzeichnungspflicht nicht ordnungsgemäß erfüllt und können dadurch die Versicherungs- oder Beitragspflicht oder die Beitragshöhe nicht festgestellt werden, kann der prüfende Träger der Rentenversicherung den Beitrag in der Kranken-, Pflege- und Rentenversicherung und zur Arbeitsförderung von der Summe der vom Arbeitgeber gezahlten Arbeitsentgelte geltend machen. ²Satz 1 gilt nicht, soweit ohne unverhältnismäßig großen Verwaltungsaufwand festgestellt werden kann, dass Beiträge nicht zu zahlen waren oder Arbeitsentgelt einem bestimmten Beschäftigten zugeordnet werden kann. ³Soweit der prüfende Träger der Rentenversicherung die Höhe der Arbeitsentgelte nicht oder nicht ohne unverhältnismäßig großen Verwaltungsaufwand ermitteln kann, hat er diese zu schätzen. ⁴Dabei ist für das monatliche Arbeitsentgelt eines Beschäftigten das am Beschäftigungsort ortsübliche Arbeitsentgelt mit zu berücksichtigen. ⁵Der prüfende Träger der Rentenversicherung hat einen auf Grund der Sätze 1, 3 und 4 ergangenen Bescheid insoweit zu widerru-

scope of application of this Code in German, divided by calendar year, and preserve them in good order until the end of the calendar year following the most recent audit (section 28p). ²Sentence 1 shall not apply with respect to employees working in private households. ³The agricultural health insurance funds may permit exceptions for working family members. ⁴Sentence 1 shall also apply to the preservation of contribution accounts and proofs of payment.

(1a) In performing a service or work agreement in the construction industry, the contractor shall draw up the payroll documents and the contribution calculation in such a way that each employee, his remuneration and the overall social security contribution accrued can be attributed to the respective service or work agreement.

(2) ¹If an employer has not properly fulfilled its duty to keep records and if the duty to take out insurance or make contributions or the amount of such contributions therefore cannot be ascertained, the auditing carrier of the old-age pension insurance may assert a claim for the contribution to the health, nursing care and old-age pension insurance and for the promotion of employment from the sum of the remuneration payments made by the employer. ²Sentence 1 shall not apply if it is possible to ascertain without an unreasonable amount of administrative effort that no contributions need to be paid or remuneration can be attributed to a certain employee. ³Where the auditing carrier of the old-age pension insurance cannot conduct its investigation at all or not without an unreasonable amount of administrative effort, it shall make an estimation. ⁴In estimating the monthly remuneration of an employee it shall also take into account the customary remuneration in the location of the employment. ⁵The auditing carrier of the old-age pension insurance shall revoke a notice issued on the

fen, als nachträglich Versicherungs- oder Beitragspflicht oder Versicherungsfreiheit festgestellt und die Höhe des Arbeitsentgelts nachgewiesen werden. ⁶Die von dem Arbeitgeber auf Grund dieses Bescheides geleisteten Zahlungen sind insoweit mit der Beitragsforderung zu verrechnen.

(3) ¹Der Arbeitgeber hat der Einzugsstelle einen Beitragsnachweis zwei Arbeitstage vor Fälligkeit der Beiträge durch Datenübertragung zu übermitteln; dies gilt nicht hinsichtlich der Beschäftigten in privaten Haushalten bei Verwendung von Haushaltsschecks. ²Übermittelt der Arbeitgeber den Beitragsnachweis nicht zwei Arbeitstage vor Fälligkeit der Beträge, so kann die Einzugsstelle das für die Beitragsberechnung maßgebende Arbeitsentgelt schätzen, bis der Nachweis ordnungsgemäß übermittelt wird. ³Der Beitragsnachweis gilt für die Vollstreckung als Leistungsbescheid der Einzugsstelle und im Insolvenzverfahren als Dokument zur Glaubhaftmachung der Forderungen der Einzugsstelle. ⁴Im Beitragsnachweis ist auch die Steuernummer des Arbeitgebers anzugeben, wenn der Beitragsnachweis die Pauschsteuer für geringfügig Beschäftigte enthält.

(4) ¹Arbeitgeber, die den Gesamtsozialversicherungsbeitrag an mehrere Orts- oder Innungskrankenkassen zu zahlen haben, können bei

1. dem jeweils zuständigen Bundesverband oder
2. einer Orts- oder Innungskrankenkasse

(beauftragte Stelle) für die jeweilige Kassenart beantragen, dass der beauftragten Stelle der jeweilige Beitragsnachweis eingereicht wird. ²Dies gilt auch für Arbeitgeber, die den Gesamtsozialversicherungsbeitrag an mehrere Betriebskrankenkassen oder landwirt-

basis of sentences 1, 3 and 4 to the extent that the duty to take out insurance or pay contributions, or the freedom from such duty, can be subsequently ascertained and the amount of the remuneration can be proven. ⁶The payments made by the employer on the basis of this notice shall be set off against the claim for contributions.

(3) ¹The employer shall submit proof of payment of contributions to the collecting agency by data transmission two working days before the contributions fall due; this shall not apply with respect to employees working in private households where household checks are used. ²If the employer fails to transmit the proof of contributions two working days before the contributions fall due, the collecting agency may estimate the remuneration on which the calculation of the contributions is to be based until such proof has been properly transmitted. ³For enforcement purposes, the proof of contributions shall be deemed to constitute notice of performance by the collecting agency and in insolvency proceedings, the document providing prima facie evidence of the collecting agency's claims. ⁴The proof of contributions shall also give the employer's taxpayer's reference number if the proof of contributions contains the lump sum tax for insignificant employment.

(4) ¹Employers who need to pay the joint social insurance contribution to multiple local or guild health insurance funds may apply to

1. the respective competent federal association or
2. a local or guild health insurance fund

(authorized agency) for the respective type of fund to have the respective proof of contribution submitted to the authorized agency. ²This applies also to employers who need to pay the joint social insurance contribution to multiple works health insurance funds or agricul-

schaftliche Krankenkassen zu zahlen haben, gegenüber dem jeweiligen Bundesverband. ³Gibt die beauftragte Stelle dem Antrag statt, hat sie die zuständigen Einzugsstellen zu unterrichten. ⁴Im Falle des Satzes 1 erhält die beauftragte Stelle auch den Gesamtsozialversicherungsbeitrag, den sie arbeitstäglich durch Überweisung unmittelbar an folgende Stellen weiterzuleiten hat:
1. die Beiträge zur Kranken- und Pflegeversicherung an die zuständigen Einzugsstellen,
2. die Beiträge zur Rentenversicherung gemäß § 28k,
3. die Beiträge zur Arbeitsförderung an die Bundesagentur für Arbeit.

⁵Die beauftragte Stelle hat die für die zuständigen Einzugsstellen bestimmten Beitragsnachweise an diese weiterzuleiten. ⁶Die Träger der Pflegeversicherung, der Rentenversicherung und die Bundesagentur für Arbeit können den Beitragsnachweis sowie den Eingang, die Verwaltung und die Weiterleitung ihrer Beiträge bei der beauftragten Stelle prüfen. ⁷§ 28q Abs. 2 und 3 sowie § 28r Abs. 1 und 2 gelten entsprechend.

(5) ¹Abweichend von Absatz 1 Satz 1 sind die am 31. Dezember 1991 im Beitrittsgebiet vorhandenen Lohnunterlagen mindestens bis zum 31. Dezember 2011 vom Arbeitgeber aufzubewahren. ²Die Pflicht zur Aufbewahrung erlischt, wenn der Arbeitgeber die Lohnunterlagen dem Betroffenen aushändigt oder die für die Rentenversicherung erforderlichen Daten bescheinigt, frühestens jedoch mit Ablauf des auf die letzte Prüfung der Träger der Rentenversicherung bei dem Arbeitgeber folgenden Kalenderjahres, und wenn ein Unternehmen aufgelöst wird.

§ 28 g
Beitragsabzug

¹Der Arbeitgeber und in den Fällen der nach § 7f Absatz 1 Satz 1 Nummer 2

tural health insurance funds, who can apply to the respective Federal Association. ³If the authorized agency approves the application, it shall inform the competent collecting agency. ⁴In the case of sentence 1, the authorized agency shall also receive the joint social insurance contribution which it shall forward without delay to the following agencies by bank transfer on each working day:
1. the contributions for health and nursing care insurance to the competent collecting agencies,
2. the contributions for old-age pension insurance pursuant to section 28 k,
3. the contributions for employment promotion to the Federal Employment Agency.

⁵The authorized agency shall forward the proofs of contributions to the competent collecting agencies for which they are intended. ⁶The carrier of the nursing care insurance, the old-age pension insurance and the Federal Employment Agency may inspect the proof of contribution as well as the receipt, administration and forwarding of their contributions at the authorized agency. ⁷Section 28q (2) and (3) and section 28r (1) and (2) apply *mutatis mutandis*.

(5) Notwithstanding subsection (1) sentence 1, the wage records on hand in the former German Democratic Republic on 31 December 1991 shall be preserved by the employer at least until 31 December 2011. ¹The duty to preserve shall expire when the employer hands the wage records over to the affected person or certifies the data necessary for the old-age pension insurance, but at the earliest at the end of the calendar year following the last inspection by the carriers of the old-age pension insurance on the employer's premises and when a company is dissolved.

Section 28 g
Deduction for Contribution

¹The employer, and where the valuation credits are transferred to the Ger-

auf die Deutsche Rentenversicherung Bund übertragenen Wertguthaben die Deutsche Rentenversicherung Bund hat gegen den Beschäftigten einen Anspruch auf den vom Beschäftigten zu tragenden Teil des Gesamtsozialversicherungsbeitrags. ²Dieser Anspruch kann nur durch Abzug vom Arbeitsentgelt geltend gemacht werden. ³Ein unterbliebener Abzug darf nur bei den drei nächsten Lohn- oder Gehaltszahlungen nachgeholt werden, danach nur dann, wenn der Abzug ohne Verschulden des Arbeitgebers unterblieben ist. ⁴Die Sätze 2 und 3 gelten nicht, wenn der Beschäftigte seinen Pflichten nach § 28o Abs. 1 vorsätzlich oder grob fahrlässig nicht nachkommt oder er den Gesamtsozialversicherungsbeitrag allein trägt oder solange der Beschäftigte nur Sachbezüge erhält.

man Pension Insurance Federal Institution pursuant to section 7f (1) sentence 1 no. 2, the German Pension Insurance Federal Institution, shall have a claim against the employee for the portion of the joint social insurance contribution to be borne by the employee. ²This claim may only be asserted by deduction from the remuneration. ³A failure to perform a deduction may only be remedied in the next three wage or salary payments, and thereafter only if the failure to perform the deduction was not the fault of the employer. ⁴Sentences 2 and 3 shall not apply if the employee intentionally or with gross negligence failed to perform his duties pursuant to section 28o (1) or he bears the joint social insurance contribution alone or as long as the employee merely receives benefits in kind.

§ 28h
Einzugsstellen

(1) ¹Der Gesamtsozialversicherungsbeitrag ist an die Krankenkassen (Einzugsstellen) zu zahlen. ²Die Einzugsstelle überwacht die Einreichung des Beitragsnachweises und die Zahlung des Gesamtsozialversicherungsbeitrags. Beitragsansprüche, die nicht rechtzeitig erfüllt worden sind, hat die Einzugsstelle geltend zu machen.

(2) ¹Die Einzugsstelle entscheidet über die Versicherungspflicht und Beitragshöhe in der Kranken-, Pflege- und Rentenversicherung sowie nach dem Recht der Arbeitsförderung; sie erlässt auch den Widerspruchsbescheid. ²Soweit die Einzugsstelle die Höhe des Arbeitsentgelts nicht oder nicht ohne unverhältnismäßig großen Verwaltungsaufwand ermitteln kann, hat sie dieses zu schätzen. ³Dabei ist für das monatliche Arbeitsentgelt des Beschäftigten das am Beschäftigungsort ortsübliche Arbeitsentgelt mit zu berücksichtigen. ⁴Die nach § 28i Satz 5 zuständige Einzugsstelle prüft die Einhaltung der Arbeitsentgeltgrenze bei geringfügiger Be-

Section 28h
Collecting Agencies

(1) ¹The joint social insurance contribution shall be paid to the health insurance funds (collecting agencies). ²The collecting agency shall oversee the submission of the proof of contributions and the joint social insurance contribution. ³The collecting agency shall assert contribution claims that are not fulfilled in a timely manner.

(2) ¹The collecting agency decides on the duty to take out insurance and amount of contributions to the health, nursing care and old-age pension insurance, as well as pursuant to the employment promotion laws; it also issues the objection notice. ²If the collecting agency cannot ascertain the amount of the remuneration at all or not without an unreasonable amount of administrative effort, it shall make an estimation. ³In estimating the monthly remuneration of an employee it shall also take into account the customary remuneration in the location of the employment. ⁴The competent collection agency pursuant to section 28i sentence 5 shall

schäftigung nach den §§ 8 und 8a und entscheidet bei deren Überschreiten über die Versicherungspflicht in der Kranken-, Pflege- und Rentenversicherung sowie nach dem Recht der Arbeitsförderung; sie erlässt auch den Widerspruchsbescheid.

(3) [1]Bei Verwendung eines Haushaltsschecks vergibt die Einzugsstelle im Auftrag der Bundesagentur für Arbeit die Betriebsnummer des Arbeitgebers, berechnet den Gesamtsozialversicherungsbeitrag und die Umlagen nach dem Aufwendungsausgleichsgesetz und zieht diese vom Arbeitgeber im Wege des Lastschriftverfahrens ein. [2]Die Einzugsstelle meldet bei Beginn und Ende der Beschäftigung und zum Jahresende der Datenstelle der Träger der Rentenversicherung die für die Rentenversicherung und die Bundesagentur für Arbeit erforderlichen Daten eines jeden Beschäftigten. [3]Die Einzugsstelle teilt dem Beschäftigten den Inhalt der abgegebenen Meldung schriftlich mit.

(4) Bei Verwendung eines Haushaltsschecks bescheinigt die Einzugsstelle dem Arbeitgeber zum Jahresende

1. den Zeitraum, für den Beiträge zur Rentenversicherung gezahlt wurden, und
2. die Höhe des Arbeitsentgelts (§ 14 Abs. 3), des von ihm getragenen Gesamtsozialversicherungsbeitrags und der Umlagen.

verify compliance with remuneration limits for insignificant employment pursuant to sections 8 and 8a and if they have been exceeded, decide on the duty to take out health, nursing care and old-age pension insurance as well as according to the right of promotion of employment; it shall also issue the objection notice.

(3) [1]Where a household check is used, the collecting agency shall assign the employer's number on behalf of the Federal Employment Agency, calculate the amount of the joint social insurance contribution and the assessments pursuant to the Equalization of Expenditures Act (*Aufwendungsausgleichsgesetz*) and collect it from the employer by way of direct debiting. [2]The collecting agency shall announce at the beginning and end of the employment and at the end of the year of the old-age pension insurance carrier's data agency the data for each employee which is necessary for the old-age pension insurance and the Federal Employment Agency. [3]The collecting agency shall inform the employee in writing of the content of the announcement made.

(4) [1]Where a household check is used, the collecting agency shall certify to the employer at the end of the year

1. the period for which the mandatory old-age pension insurance contributions have been paid and
2. the amount of the remuneration (section 14 (3)) of the joint social insurance contribution and the assessments born by it.

§ 28i
Zuständige Einzugsstelle

[1]Zuständige Einzugsstelle für den Gesamtsozialversicherungsbeitrag ist die Krankenkasse, von der die Krankenversicherung durchgeführt wird. [2]Für Beschäftigte, die bei keiner Krankenkasse versichert sind, werden Beiträge zur Rentenversicherung und zur Arbeitsför-

Section 28i
Competent Collecting Agencies

[1]The collecting agency competent for the joint social insurance contribution is the health insurance fund which administers the health insurance. [2]For employees who are not insured with a health insurance fund, contributions to old-age pension insurance and promotion of em-

derung an die Einzugsstelle gezahlt, die der Arbeitgeber in entsprechender Anwendung des § 175 Abs. 3 Satz 2 des Fünften Buches gewählt hat. ³Zuständige Einzugsstelle ist in den Fällen des § 28 f Abs. 2 die nach § 175 Abs. 3 Satz 3 des Fünften Buches bestimmte Krankenkasse. ⁴Zuständige Einzugsstelle ist in den Fällen des § 2 Abs. 3 die Deutsche Rentenversicherung Knappschaft-Bahn-See. ⁵Bei geringfügigen Beschäftigungen ist zuständige Einzugsstelle die Deutsche Rentenversicherung Knappschaft-Bahn-See als Träger der Rentenversicherung.

ployment shall be paid to the collecting agency selected by the employer in analogous application of section 175 (3) sentence 2 of the Fifth Book. ³In the cases set forth in section 28 f (2), the competent collecting agency shall be the health insurance fund determined pursuant to section 175 (3) sentence 3 of the Fifth Book. ⁴The competent collecting agency in the cases set forth in section 2 (3) is the German Pension Fund Mining-Rail-Sea *(Deutsche Rentenversicherung Knappschaft-Bahn-See)*. ⁵In the case of insignificant employment, the competent collecting agency shall be the German Pension Fund Mining-Rail-Sea as the carrier of the old-age pension insurance.

§ 28 k
Weiterleitung von Beiträgen

Section 28 k
Forwarding of Contributions

(1) ¹Die Einzugsstelle leitet dem zuständigen Träger der Pflegeversicherung, der Rentenversicherung und der Bundesagentur für Arbeit die für diese gezahlten Beiträge einschließlich der Zinsen auf Beiträge und Säumniszuschläge arbeitstäglich weiter; dies gilt entsprechend für die Weiterleitung der Beiträge zur gesetzlichen Krankenversicherung an den Gesundheitsfonds. ²Die Deutsche Rentenversicherung Bund teilt den Einzugsstellen die zuständigen Träger der Rentenversicherung und deren Beitragsanteil spätestens bis zum 31. Oktober eines jeden Jahres für das folgende Kalenderjahr mit. ³Die Deutsche Rentenversicherung Bund legt den Verteilungsschlüssel für die Aufteilung der Beitragseinnahmen der allgemeinen Rentenversicherung auf die einzelnen Träger unter Berücksichtigung der folgenden Parameter fest:

(1) ¹The collecting agency shall forward to the competent carriers of the nursing care insurance, the old-age pension insurance and the Federal Employment Agency the contributions paid for them, including interest on contributions and default charges every working day; this applies mutatis mutandis for the forwarding of the contributions to the statutory health insurance to the health care fund. ²The German Pension Insurance Federal Institution *(Deutsche Rentenversicherung Bund)* shall inform the collecting agencies of the competent carriers of the old-age pension insurance and its share of the contributions by no later than 31 October of each year for the following calendar year. ³The German Pension Insurance Federal Institution shall determine the allocation formula for the division of the contribution revenues of the general old-age pension insurance between the individual carriers, taking into account the following parameters:

1. Für die Aufteilung zwischen Deutsche Rentenversicherung Bund und Regionalträgern:
    a) Für 2005 die prozentuale Aufteilung der gezahlten Pflichtbeiträge zur Rentenversicherung der Arbei-

1. For the division between the German Pension Insurance Federal Institution and regional carriers:
    a) For 2005 the percentage division of the mandatory contributions paid between the blue-collar workers'

ter und der Rentenversicherung der Angestellten im Jahr 2003,

b) Fortschreibung dieser Anteile in den folgenden Jahren unter Berücksichtigung der Veränderung des Anteils der bei den Regionalträgern Pflichtversicherten gegenüber dem jeweiligen vorvergangenen Kalenderjahr.

2. Für die Aufteilung der Beiträge unter den Regionalträgern:
Das Verhältnis der Pflichtversicherten dieser Träger untereinander.

3. Für die Aufteilung zwischen Deutsche Rentenversicherung Bund und Deutsche Rentenversicherung Knappschaft-Bahn-See:

Das Verhältnis der in der allgemeinen Rentenversicherung Pflichtversicherten dieser Träger untereinander.

(2) ¹Bei geringfügigen Beschäftigungen werden die Beiträge zur Krankenversicherung an den Gesundheitsfond, bei Versicherten in der landwirtschaftlichen Krankenversicherung an den Spitzenverband der landwirtschaftlichen Sozialversicherung weitergeleitet. ²Das Nähere zur Bestimmung des Anteils des Spitzenverbandes der landwirtschaftlichen Sozialversicherung, insbesondere über eine pauschale Berechnung und Aufteilung, vereinbaren die Spitzenverbände der beteiligten Träger der Sozialversicherung.

old-age pension insurance *(Rentenversicherung der Arbeiter)* and white-collar workers' old-age pension insurance *(Rentenversicherung der Angestellten)* in the year 2003,

b) continuation of these shares in the following years, taking into account the change in the share of the persons covered by mandatory insurance with the regional carriers in comparison to the previous calendar year.

2. For the division of the contributions between the regional carriers:
The proportional relationship of the persons covered by mandatory insurance with these carriers to each other.

3. For the division between the German Pension Insurance Federal Institution and the German pension insurance company Deutsche Rentenversicherung Knappschaft-Bahn-See:

The proportional relationship of the persons covered by mandatory general old-age insurance with these carriers to each other.

(2) ¹In the case of insignificant employment, the contributions to the health insurance shall be passed on to the Health Care Fund (Gesundheitsfond), in the case of persons incurred in the agricultural health insurance, the contributions shall be passed on to the Central Agricultural Social Insurance Fund *(Spitzenverband der landwirtschaftlichen Sozialversicherung)*. ²The central associations of the participating social insurance carriers shall agree in more detail on how to determine the share of the Federal Association of Agricultural Health Insurance Funds, in particular with regard to a lump sum calculation and division.

§ 281
Vergütung

(1) ¹Die Einzugsstellen, die Träger der Rentenversicherung und die Bundes-

Section 281
Fees

(1) ¹The collecting agencies, the carriers of the old-age pension insurance and the Federal Employment Agency shall

agentur für Arbeit erhalten für
1. die Geltendmachung der Beitragsansprüche,
2. den Einzug, die Verwaltung, die Weiterleitung, die Abrechnung und die Abstimmung der Beiträge,
3. die Prüfung bei den Arbeitgebern,
4. die Durchführung der Meldeverfahren,
5. die Ausstellung der Sozialversicherungsausweise und
6. die Durchführung des Haushaltsscheckverfahrens, soweit es über die Verfahren nach den Nummern 1 bis 5 hinausgeht und Aufgaben der Sozialversicherung betrifft,

eine pauschale Vergütung, mit der alle dadurch entstehenden Kosten abgegolten werden, dies gilt entsprechend für die Künstlersozialkasse. ²Die Höhe und die Verteilung der Vergütung werden durch Vereinbarung zwischen dem Spitzenverband Bund der Krankenkassen, der Deutschen Rentenversicherung Bund, der Bundesagentur für Arbeit und der Künstlersozialkasse geregelt; vor dem Abschluss und vor Änderungen der Vereinbarung ist der Spitzenverband der landwirtschaftlichen Sozialversicherung anzuhören. ³In der Vereinbarung ist auch für den Fall, dass eine Einzugsstelle ihre Pflichten nicht ordnungsgemäß erfüllt und dadurch erhebliche Beitragsrückstände entstehen, festzulegen, dass sich die Vergütung für diesen Zeitraum angemessen mindert.

Die Deutsche Rentenversicherung Knappschaft-Bahn-See wird ermächtigt, die ihr von den Krankenkassen nach Satz 1 zustehende Vergütung mit den nach § 28 k Absatz 2 Satz 1 an den Gesundheitsfonds weiterzuleitenden Beiträgen zur Krankenversicherung für geringfügige Beschäftigungen aufzurechnen.

(1 a) *(weggefallen)*

(2) Soweit die Einzugsstellen oder die beauftragten Stellen (§ 28 f Abs. 4) bei der Verwaltung von Fremdbeiträgen

receive a lump sum fee for
1. the assertion of contribution claims,
2. the collection, administration, forwarding, accounting and coordination of the contributions,
3. the auditing of the employers,
4. the execution of the registration procedures,
5. the issuing of the social insurance ID cards and
6. the execution of the household check procedures, where they go beyond nos. 1 to 5 and involve social security responsibilities,

with which all costs incurred shall be discharged, this applies analogously for the Artists' Social Welfare Fund *(Künstlersozialkasse)*. ²The amount and distribution of the remuneration shall be regulated by the Central Federal Association of the Health Insurance Funds (Spitzenverband Bund der Krankenkassen), the German Pension Insurance Federal Institution, the Federal Employment Agency and the Artists' Social Welfare Fund; the Central Agricultural Social Insurance Fund must be heard prior to the conclusion or amendment of the agreement. ³The agreement shall also stipulate that in the event that a collecting agency does not carry out its duties properly, resulting in substantial outstanding contributions, the remuneration for this period of time will be reduced appropriately.

The German Pension Fund Mining-Rail-Sea shall be empowered to set off the fees from the health insurance funds to which it is entitled pursuant to sentence 1 against the contributions to health insurance for insignificant employment that are to be forwarded to the health care fund pursuant to section 28 k (2) sentence 1.

(1 a) *(repealed)*

(2) Where the collecting agencies or the commissioned agencies (section 28 f (4)) draw a profit from the administration

Gewinne erzielen, wird deren Aufteilung durch Vereinbarungen zwischen den Krankenkassen oder ihren Verbänden und der Deutschen Rentenversicherung Bund sowie der Bundesagentur für Arbeit geregelt.

of outside contributions, their allocation shall be regulated by agreements between the health insurance funds or their associations and the German Pension Insurance Federal Institution *(Deutsche Rentenversicherung Bund)* as well as the Federal Employment Agency.

XIX. Social Security Code IX (9. Sozialgesetzbuch – SGB IX)

of 19 June 2001 (Federal Law Gazette I p. 1046)

in the amended version of 5 August 2010

(excerpts)

§ 2
Behinderung

(1) [1]Menschen sind behindert, wenn ihre körperliche Funktion, geistige Fähigkeit oder seelische Gesundheit mit hoher Wahrscheinlichkeit länger als sechs Monate von dem für das Lebensalter typischen Zustand abweichen und daher ihre Teilhabe am Leben in der Gesellschaft beeinträchtigt ist. [2]Sie sind von Behinderung bedroht, wenn die Beeinträchtigung zu erwarten ist.

(2) Menschen sind im Sinne des Teils 2 schwerbehindert, wenn bei ihnen ein Grad der Behinderung von wenigstens 50 vorliegt und sie ihren Wohnsitz, ihren gewöhnlichen Aufenthalt oder ihre Beschäftigung auf einem Arbeitsplatz im Sinne des § 73 rechtmäßig im Geltungsbereich dieses Gesetzbuches haben.

(3) Schwerbehinderten Menschen gleichgestellt werden sollen behinderte Menschen mit einem Grad der Behinderung von weniger als 50, aber wenigstens 30, bei denen die übrigen Voraussetzungen des Absatzes 2 vorliegen, wenn sie infolge ihrer Behinderung ohne die Gleichstellung einen geeigneten Arbeitsplatz im Sinne des § 73 nicht erlangen oder nicht behalten können (gleichgestellte behinderte Menschen).

Section 2
Disability

(1) [1]People are disabled if their bodily functions, mental abilities or psychological health will most probably deviate from the condition typical for their age for more than six months and thus their participation in society is impaired. [2]They face a threat of being disabled if the impairment is to be anticipated.

(2) People are severely disabled within the meaning of Part 2 if the degree of their disability is at least 50 and their registered domicile, their normal place of residence or their employment in a workplace within the meaning of section 73 is legally located within the scope of this Code.

(3) Disabled persons with a degree of disability of less than 50 but at least 30, shall be placed on an equal footing with severely disabled persons if they meet the other prerequisites set forth in subsection (2) and if, as a result of their disability, they cannot obtain or retain a suitable job within the meaning of section 73 without such equal treatment (disabled persons treated as severely disabled persons).

§ 68
Geltungsbereich

(1) Die Regelungen dieses Teils gelten für schwerbehinderte und diesen gleichgestellte behinderte Menschen.

Section 68
Scope of Application

(1) The provisions of this Part apply to severely disabled persons and disabled persons treated as severely disabled persons.

(2) ¹Die Gleichstellung behinderter Menschen mit schwerbehinderten Menschen (§ 2 Abs. 3) erfolgt auf Grund einer Feststellung nach § 69 auf Antrag des behinderten Menschen durch die Bundesagentur für Arbeit. ²Die Gleichstellung wird mit dem Tag des Eingangs des Antrags wirksam. ³Sie kann befristet werden.

(3) Auf gleichgestellte behinderte Menschen werden die besonderen Regelungen für schwerbehinderte Menschen mit Ausnahme des § 125 und des Kapitels 13 angewendet.

(4) ¹Schwerbehinderten Menschen gleichgestellt sind auch behinderte Jugendliche und junge Erwachsene (§ 2 Abs. 1) während der Zeit einer Berufsausbildung in Betrieben und Dienststellen, auch wenn der Grad der Behinderung weniger als 30 beträgt oder ein Grad der Behinderung nicht festgestellt ist. ²Der Nachweis der Behinderung wird durch eine Stellungnahme der Agentur für Arbeit oder durch einen Bescheid über Leistungen zur Teilhabe am Arbeitsleben erbracht. ³Die besonderen Regelungen für schwerbehinderte Menschen, mit Ausnahme des § 102 Abs. 3 Nr. 2 Buchstabe c, werden nicht angewendet.

(2) ¹The treatment of disabled persons as severely disabled persons (section 2 (3)) shall arise on the basis of a determination pursuant to section 69 by the Federal Employment Agency upon the application of the disabled person. ²Such equal treatment shall go into effect on the day the application is delivered. ³It may be subject to a limited term.

(3) Disabled persons treated as severely disabled persons shall be subject to the special regulations for severely disabled persons with the exception of section 125 and Chapter 13.

(4) ¹Disabled youths and young adults (section 2 (1)) shall be placed on an equal footing with severely disabled persons during their professional training in establishments and civil service workplaces, even if the degree of their disability is less than 30 or a degree of disability has not yet been determined. ²The proof of the disability shall be obtained through an expert opinion of the Employment Agency or an order regarding benefits to enable participation in the working life. ³The special provisions for severely disabled persons, with the exception of section 102 (3) no. 2 c, shall not be applied.

§ 81
Pflichten des Arbeitgebers und Rechte schwerbehinderter Menschen

(1) ¹Die Arbeitgeber sind verpflichtet zu prüfen, ob freie Arbeitsplätze mit schwerbehinderten Menschen, insbesondere mit bei der Agentur für Arbeit arbeitslos oder arbeitsuchend gemeldeten schwerbehinderten Menschen, besetzt werden können. ²Sie nehmen frühzeitig Verbindung mit der Agentur für Arbeit auf. ³Die Bundesagentur für Arbeit oder ein Integrationsfachdienst schlägt den Arbeitgebern geeignete schwerbehinderte Menschen vor. ⁴Über die Vermittlungsvorschläge und vorlie-

Section 81
Duties of the Employer and Rights of Severely Disabled Persons

(1) ¹The employers shall be obligated to ascertain whether job vacancies can be filled with severely disabled persons, in particular with those registered with the Employment Agency as unemployed or seeking employment. ²They shall contact the Employment Agency in good time. ³The Federal Employment Agency or a specialized integration service commissioned by it shall propose suitable severely disabled persons to the employers. ⁴The employers shall inform the severely disabled em-

gende Bewerbungen von schwerbehinderten Menschen haben die Arbeitgeber die Schwerbehindertenvertretung und die in § 93 genannten Vertretungen unmittelbar nach Eingang zu unterrichten. ⁵Bei Bewerbungen schwerbehinderter Richter und Richterinnen wird der Präsidialrat unterrichtet und gehört, soweit dieser an der Ernennung zu beteiligen ist. ⁶Bei der Prüfung nach Satz 1 beteiligen die Arbeitgeber die Schwerbehindertenvertretung nach § 95 Abs. 2 und hören die in § 93 genannten Vertretungen an. ⁷Erfüllt der Arbeitgeber seine Beschäftigungspflicht nicht und ist die Schwerbehindertenvertretung oder eine in § 93 genannte Vertretung mit der beabsichtigten Entscheidung des Arbeitgebers nicht einverstanden, ist diese unter Darlegung der Gründe mit ihnen zu erörtern. ⁸Dabei wird der betroffene schwerbehinderte Mensch angehört. ⁹Alle Beteiligten sind vom Arbeitgeber über die getroffene Entscheidung unter Darlegung der Gründe unverzüglich zu unterrichten. ¹⁰Bei Bewerbungen schwerbehinderter Menschen ist die Schwerbehindertenvertretung nicht zu beteiligen, wenn der schwerbehinderte Mensch die Beteiligung der Schwerbehindertenvertretung ausdrücklich ablehnt.

(2) ¹Arbeitgeber dürfen schwerbehinderte Beschäftigte nicht wegen ihrer Behinderung benachteiligen. ²Im Einzelnen gelten hierzu die Regelungen des Allgemeinen Gleichbehandlungsgesetzes.

(3) ¹Die Arbeitgeber stellen durch geeignete Maßnahmen sicher, dass in ihren Betrieben und Dienststellen wenigstens die vorgeschriebene Zahl schwerbehinderter Menschen eine möglichst dauerhafte behinderungsgerechte Beschäftigung finden kann. ²Absatz 4 Satz 2 und 3 gilt entsprechend.

ployees' representation and the representational bodies designated in section 93 of the proposals and applications from severely disabled persons immediately upon receiving them. ⁵In the case of applications of severely disabled judges, the presidential council of the judiciary (*Präsidialrat*) shall be informed and consulted if it is to participate in their appointment. ⁶In performing the ascertainment pursuant to sentence 1, the employers shall involve the severely disabled employees' representation pursuant to section 95 (2) and consult with the representational bodies designated in section 93. ⁷If the employer does not comply with its duty to employ severely disabled persons and if the severely disabled employees' representation or one of the representational bodies designated in section 93 is not in agreement with the employer's intended decision, the employer must explain and state the grounds for the decision. ⁸In this context, the affected severely disabled person will be heard. ⁹The employer shall inform all the parties concerned of the decision made and state the grounds for it without delay. ¹⁰In the case of applications of severely disabled persons the severely disabled employees' representation shall not be involved if the severely disabled person explicitly rejects its involvement.

(2) ¹Employers may not discriminate against severely disabled persons on the grounds of their disability. ²Specifically, the provisions of the General Equal Treatment Act (*Allgemeines Gleichbehandlungsgesetz*) shall apply.

(3) ¹The employer shall take suitable measures to ensure that in its establishments and civil service workplaces at least the prescribed number of severely disabled persons can find suitable and possibly permanent employment. ²Subsection (4) sentences 2 and 3 apply mutatis mutandis.

(4) ¹Die schwerbehinderten Menschen haben gegenüber ihren Arbeitgebern Anspruch auf

1. Beschäftigung, bei der sie ihre Fähigkeiten und Kenntnisse möglichst voll verwerten und weiterentwickeln können,
2. bevorzugte Berücksichtigung bei innerbetrieblichen Maßnahmen der beruflichen Bildung zur Förderung ihres beruflichen Fortkommens,
3. Erleichterungen im zumutbaren Umfang zur Teilnahme an außerbetrieblichen Maßnahmen der beruflichen Bildung,
4. behinderungsgerechte Einrichtung und Unterhaltung der Arbeitsstätten einschließlich der Betriebsanlagen, Maschinen und Geräte sowie der Gestaltung der Arbeitsplätze, des Arbeitsumfeldes, der Arbeitsorganisation und der Arbeitszeit, unter besonderer Berücksichtigung der Unfallgefahr,
5. Ausstattung ihres Arbeitsplatzes mit den erforderlichen technischen Arbeitshilfen

unter Berücksichtigung der Behinderung und ihrer Auswirkungen auf die Beschäftigung. ²Bei der Durchführung der Maßnahmen nach den Nummern 1, 4 und 5 unterstützt die Bundesagentur für Arbeit und die Integrationsämter die Arbeitgeber unter Berücksichtigung der für die Beschäftigung wesentlichen Eigenschaften der schwerbehinderten Menschen. ³Ein Anspruch nach Satz 1 besteht nicht, soweit seine Erfüllung für den Arbeitgeber nicht zumutbar oder mit unverhältnismäßigen Aufwendungen verbunden wäre oder soweit die staatlichen oder berufsgenossenschaftlichen Arbeitsschutzvorschriften oder beamtenrechtliche Vorschriften entgegenstehen.

(5) ¹Die Arbeitgeber fördern die Einrichtung von Teilzeitarbeitsplätzen. ²Sie werden dabei von den Integrationsämtern unterstützt. ³Schwerbehinderte Menschen haben einen Anspruch auf

(4) ¹ Severely disabled persons have a claim against their employers for

1. employment in which they can utilize and develop their skills and knowledge to the greatest possible extent,
2. preferential treatment in internal measures for professional training to further their professional advancement,
3. facilitation, to a reasonable extent, of their participation in external vocational training programs,
4. accommodations for the disabled with respect to installations and maintenance of the workplace, including the operational facilities, machines and equipment, as well as the structuring of the jobs, the work environment, the work organization and working time, taking the danger of accidents particularly into account,
5. equipment of the workplace with the requisite technical work aids

taking into account the handicap and its effects upon the employment. ²In carrying out the measures set forth in nos. 1, 4 and 5, the Federal Employment Agency and Integration Authorities (*Integrationsämter*) shall support the employers, taking into account the qualities of severely disabled persons which are essential for the employment. ³No claim pursuant to sentence 1 shall exist where its fulfilment would be unreasonable for the employer or entail unreasonable expense or it would be in contravention of the national or professional associations' regulations for the protection of employees or regulations applicable to civil servants.

(5) ¹The employers shall promote the establishment of part-time jobs. ²The Integration Authority shall support them in this endeavour. ³Severely disabled persons shall have a claim to

Teilzeitbeschäftigung, wenn die kürzere Arbeitszeit wegen Art oder Schwere der Behinderung notwendig ist; Absatz 4 Satz 3 gilt entsprechend.

part-time work if shorter working hours are necessary due to the type or severity of their disability; subsection (4) sentence 3 applies *mutatis mutandis*.

§ 85
Erfordernis der Zustimmung

Die Kündigung des Arbeitsverhältnisses eines schwerbehinderten Menschen durch den Arbeitgeber bedarf der vorherigen Zustimmung des Integrationsamtes.

Section 85
Consent Requirement

The termination of the employment relationship of a severely disabled person by the employer requires the prior consent of the Integration Authority.

§ 86
Kündigungsfrist

Die Kündigungsfrist beträgt mindestens vier Wochen.

Section 86
Dismissal Notice Period

The dismissal notice period shall be at least four weeks.

§ 87
Antragsverfahren

(1) ¹Die Zustimmung zur Kündigung beantragt der Arbeitgeber bei dem für den Sitz des Betriebes oder der Dienststelle zuständigen Integrationsamt schriftlich. ²Der Begriff des Betriebes und der Begriff der Dienststelle im Sinne des Teils 2 bestimmen sich nach dem Betriebsverfassungsgesetz und dem Personalvertretungsrecht.

(2) Das Integrationsamt holt eine Stellungnahme des Betriebsrates oder Personalrates und der Schwerbehindertenvertretung ein und hört den schwerbehinderten Menschen an.

(3) Das Integrationsamt wirkt in jeder Lage des Verfahrens auf eine gütliche Einigung hin.

Section 87
Application Procedure

(1) ¹The employer shall apply in writing to the Integration Authority competent for the seat of the establishment or the civil service workplace for its consent to a dismissal. ²The terms "establishment" and "civil service workplace" within the meaning of Part 2 are defined in the Works Constitution Act (*Betriebsverfassungsgesetz*) and the staff representation laws (*Personalvertretungsrecht*).

(2) The Integration Authority shall obtain an expert opinion from the works council or staff council and the severely disabled employees' representation and grant the severely disabled person a hearing.

(3) The Integration Authority shall work toward an amicable resolution at every stage of the proceeding.

§ 88
Entscheidung des Integrationsamtes

(1) Das Integrationsamt soll die Entscheidung, falls erforderlich auf Grund

Section 88
Decision by the Integration Authority

(1) The Integration Authority shall reach its decision, if necessary on the

mündlicher Verhandlung, innerhalb eines Monats vom Tage des Eingangs des Antrages an treffen.

(2) ¹Die Entscheidung wird dem Arbeitgeber und dem schwerbehinderten Menschen zugestellt. ²Der Bundesagentur für Arbeit wird eine Abschrift der Entscheidung übersandt.

(3) Erteilt das Integrationsamt die Zustimmung zur Kündigung, kann der Arbeitgeber die Kündigung nur innerhalb eines Monats nach Zustellung erklären.

(4) Widerspruch und Anfechtungsklage gegen die Zustimmung des Integrationsamtes zur Kündigung haben keine aufschiebende Wirkung.

(5) ¹In den Fällen des § 89 Abs. 1 Satz 1 und Abs. 3 gilt Absatz 1 mit der Maßgabe, dass die Entscheidung innerhalb eines Monats vom Tage des Eingangs des Antrages an zu treffen ist. ¹Wird innerhalb dieser Frist eine Entscheidung nicht getroffen, gilt die Zustimmung als erteilt. ³Die Absätze 3 und 4 gelten entsprechend.

§ 89
Einschränkungen der Ermessensentscheidung

(1) ¹Das Integrationsamt erteilt die Zustimmung bei Kündigungen in Betrieben und Dienststellen, die nicht nur vorübergehend eingestellt oder aufgelöst werden, wenn zwischen dem Tage der Kündigung und dem Tage, bis zu dem Gehalt oder Lohn gezahlt wird, mindestens drei Monate liegen. ²Unter der gleichen Voraussetzung soll es die Zustimmung auch bei Kündigungen in Betrieben und Dienststellen erteilen, die nicht nur vorübergehend wesentlich eingeschränkt werden, wenn die Gesamtzahl der weiterhin beschäftigten schwerbehinderten Menschen zur Erfüllung der Beschäftigungspflicht nach § 71 ausreicht. ³Die Sätze 1 und 2 gelten nicht, wenn eine Weiterbeschäftigung auf einem anderen Arbeitsplatz dessel-

basis of an oral hearing, within one month of the day of receipt of the application.

(2) ¹The decision shall be served to the employer and the severely disabled person. ²The Federal Employment Agency shall be sent a copy of the decision.

(3) If the Integration Authority consents to the dismissal, the employer may only declare the dismissal within one month after being served with the decision.

(4) Objections and actions to contest the Integration Authority's consent to the dismissal shall not have a suspensive effect.

(5) ¹In the cases of section 89 (1) sentence 1 and (3), subsection (1) shall apply subject to the proviso that the decision must be made within one month of the day of receipt of the application. ²If no decision is made within this period, consent shall be deemed to have been granted. ³Subsections (3) and (4) apply *mutatis mutandis*.

Section 89
Restrictions on Discretionary Decisions

(1) ¹The Integration Authority shall render its consent to dismissals in establishments and civil service workplaces which have been closed down or dissolved, not merely on a temporary basis, if the date of the dismissal and the date on which the salary or wage is paid are at least three months apart. ²Under the same condition, it shall also render its consent to dismissals in establishments and civil service workplaces which have been substantially cut back, not merely on a temporary basis, if the total number of severely disabled persons who continue to be employed there is sufficient to comply with the employment duty pursuant to section 71. ³Sentences 1 and 2 shall not apply if continued em-

ben Betriebes oder derselben Dienststelle oder auf einem freien Arbeitsplatz in einem anderen Betrieb oder einer anderen Dienststelle desselben Arbeitgebers mit Einverständnis des schwerbehinderten Menschen möglich und für den Arbeitgeber zumutbar ist.

(2) Das Integrationsamt soll die Zustimmung erteilen, wenn dem schwerbehinderten Menschen ein anderer angemessener und zumutbarer Arbeitsplatz gesichert ist.

(3) Ist das Insolvenzverfahren über das Vermögen des Arbeitgebers eröffnet, soll das Integrationsamt die Zustimmung erteilen, wenn

1. der schwerbehinderte Mensch in einem Interessenausgleich namentlich als einer der zu entlassenden Arbeitnehmer bezeichnet ist (§ 125 der Insolvenzordnung),
2. die Schwerbehindertenvertretung beim Zustandekommen des Interessenausgleichs gemäß § 95 Abs. 2 beteiligt worden ist,
3. der Anteil der nach dem Interessenausgleich zu entlassenden schwerbehinderten Menschen an der Zahl der beschäftigten schwerbehinderten Menschen nicht größer ist als der Anteil der zu entlassenden übrigen Arbeitnehmer an der Zahl der beschäftigten übrigen Arbeitnehmer und
4. die Gesamtzahl der schwerbehinderten Menschen, die nach dem Interessenausgleich bei dem Arbeitgeber verbleiben sollen, zur Erfüllung der Beschäftigungspflicht nach § 71 ausreicht.

§ 90
Ausnahmen

(1) Die Vorschriften dieses Kapitels gelten nicht für schwerbehinderte Menschen,

ployment in another workplace of the same establishment or civil service workplace or in a vacant position in another establishment or civil service workplace of the same employer is possible with the agreement of the severely disabled person and reasonable for the employer.

(2) The Integration Authority shall render its consent if another suitable and reasonable position has been secured for the severely disabled person.

(3) If insolvency proceedings have been opened against the employer's assets, the Integration Authority shall render its consent if

1. the severely disabled person is mentioned by name in a reconciliation of interests *(Interessenausgleich)* as one of the employees to be laid off (section 125 of the Insolvency Act – *Insolvenzordnung*),
2. the representation for severely disabled employees has participated in bringing about the reconciliation of interests pursuant to section 95 (2),
3. the proportion of the severely disabled persons to be laid off pursuant to the reconciliation of interests to the number of severely disabled employees does not exceed the proportion of the other employees to be laid off to the number of other employees and
4. the total number of severely disabled persons who are to remain with the employer pursuant to the reconciliation of interests is sufficient to comply with the employment duty pursuant to section 71.

Section 90
Exceptions

(1) The provisions of this Chapter shall not apply to severely disabled persons

1. deren Arbeitsverhältnis zum Zeitpunkt des Zugangs der Kündigungserklärung ohne Unterbrechung noch nicht länger als sechs Monate besteht oder
2. die auf Stellen im Sinne des § 73 Abs. 2 Nr. 2 bis 5 beschäftigt werden oder
3. deren Arbeitsverhältnis durch Kündigung beendet wird, sofern sie
   a) das 58. Lebensjahr vollendet haben und Anspruch auf eine Abfindung, Entschädigung oder ähnliche Leistung auf Grund eines Sozialplanes haben oder
   b) Anspruch auf Knappschaftsausgleichsleistung nach dem Sechsten Buch oder auf Anpassungsgeld für entlassene Arbeitnehmer des Bergbaus haben,

wenn der Arbeitgeber ihnen die Kündigungsabsicht rechtzeitig mitgeteilt hat und sie der beabsichtigten Kündigung bis zu deren Ausspruch nicht widersprechen.

(2) Die Vorschriften dieses Kapitels finden ferner bei Entlassungen, die aus Witterungsgründen vorgenommen werden, keine Anwendung, sofern die Wiedereinstellung der schwerbehinderten Menschen bei Wiederaufnahme der Arbeit gewährleistet ist.

(2a) Die Vorschriften dieses Kapitels finden ferner keine Anwendung, wenn zum Zeitpunkt der Kündigung die Eigenschaft als schwerbehinderter Mensch nicht nachgewiesen ist oder das Versorgungsamt nach Ablauf der Frist des § 69 Abs. 1 Satz 2 eine Feststellung wegen fehlender Mitwirkung nicht treffen konnte.

(3) Der Arbeitgeber zeigt Einstellungen auf Probe und die Beendigung von Arbeitsverhältnissen schwerbehinderter Menschen in den Fällen des Absatzes 1 Nr. 1 unabhängig von der Anzeigepflicht nach anderen Gesetzen dem Integrationsamt innerhalb von vier Tagen an.

1. whose employment relationship at the time of receipt of the declaration of dismissal has not lasted longer than six months without interruption or
2. who are employed in positions within the meaning of section 73 (2) nos. 2 to 5 or
3. whose employment relationship was terminated by dismissal, where they
   a) have reached the age of 58 and have a claim to severance payment, compensatory damages or similar payments on the basis of a social plan *(Sozialplan)* or
   b) have a claim to miners' equalization benefits pursuant to the Sixth Book or adaptation benefits for dismissed mine workers,

provided that the employer informed them of the intention to dismiss in a timely manner and they did not object to the intended dismissal before it was declared.

(2) The provisions of this Chapter shall further not apply with respect to dismissals performed due to bad weather, provided that it is ensured that the disabled persons will be reinstated once the work is resumed.

(2a) The provisions of this Chapter shall further not apply if at the time of the termination the severe disability of the person has not been proven or the Pension Office *(Versorgungsamt)* was unable to make a determination after the time period set forth in section 69 (1) sentence 2 expired for lack of cooperation.

(3) The employer shall notify the Integration Authority of hirings on a probationary basis and terminations of employment relationships of severely disabled persons in the cases set forth in subsection (1) no. 1 within four days, independent of the notification duty pursuant to other statutes.

§ 91
Außerordentliche Kündigung

(1) Die Vorschriften dieses Kapitels gelten mit Ausnahme von § 86 auch bei außerordentlicher Kündigung, soweit sich aus den folgenden Bestimmungen nichts Abweichendes ergibt.

(2) ¹Die Zustimmung zur Kündigung kann nur innerhalb von zwei Wochen beantragt werden; maßgebend ist der Eingang des Antrages bei dem Integrationsamt. ²Die Frist beginnt mit dem Zeitpunkt, in dem der Arbeitgeber von den für die Kündigung maßgebenden Tatsachen Kenntnis erlangt.

(3) ¹Das Integrationsamt trifft die Entscheidung innerhalb von zwei Wochen vom Tage des Eingangs des Antrages an. ²Wird innerhalb dieser Frist eine Entscheidung nicht getroffen, gilt die Zustimmung als erteilt.

(4) Das Integrationsamt soll die Zustimmung erteilen, wenn die Kündigung aus einem Grunde erfolgt, der nicht im Zusammenhang mit der Behinderung steht.

(5) Die Kündigung kann auch nach Ablauf der Frist des § 626 Abs. 2 Satz 1 des Bürgerlichen Gesetzbuchs erfolgen, wenn sie unverzüglich nach Erteilung der Zustimmung erklärt wird.

(6) Schwerbehinderte Menschen, denen lediglich aus Anlass eines Streiks oder einer Aussperrung fristlos gekündigt worden ist, werden nach Beendigung des Streiks oder der Aussperrung wieder eingestellt.

§ 92
Erweiterter Beendigungsschutz

¹Die Beendigung des Arbeitsverhältnisses eines schwerbehinderten Menschen bedarf auch dann der vorherigen Zustimmung des Integrationsamtes, wenn sie im Falle des Eintritts einer teilwei-

Section 91
Termination for Cause

(1) The provisions of this Chapter apply, with the exception of section 86, in the case of terminations for cause as well, unless the following provisions determine otherwise.

(2) ¹The consent to the termination may only be applied for within two weeks; the time of delivery of the application to the Integration Authority shall be decisive in determining observance of this time period. ²The time period shall commence once the employer obtains knowledge of the facts decisively relevant to the dismissal.

(3) ¹The Integration Authority shall reach a decision within two weeks of the date of delivery of the application. ²If no decision is made within this period, consent shall be deemed to have been rendered.

(4) The Integration Authority shall render its consent if the dismissal was performed for reasons unrelated to the disability.

(5) The dismissal may also be performed after expiration of the time period set forth in section 626 (2) sentence 1 of the German Civil Code if it is declared immediately following the rendering of the consent.

(6) Severely disabled persons who are dismissed without notice merely on the occasion of a strike or lockout shall be reinstated after the strike or lockout comes to an end.

Section 92
Extended Protection Against Termination

¹The termination of the employment relationship with a severely disabled person shall require the prior consent of the Integration Authority even if it is due to the emergence of a partial de-

sen Erwerbsminderung, der Erwerbsminderung auf Zeit, der Berufsunfähigkeit oder der Erwerbsunfähigkeit auf Zeit ohne Kündigung erfolgt. ²Die Vorschriften dieses Kapitels über die Zustimmung zur ordentlichen Kündigung gelten entsprechend.

crease in earning capacity, a temporary decrease in earning capacity, an occupational disability or a temporary total disability and no dismissal has been performed. ²The provisions of this Chapter on the consent to ordinary dismissals apply mutatis mutandis.

Kapitel 5
Betriebs-, Personal-, Richter-, Staatsanwalts- und Präsidialrat, Schwerbehindertenvertretung, Beauftragter des Arbeitgebers

Chapter 5
Works Council, Staff Council, Judiciary Council, Public Prosecutors' Council and Presidential Council of the Judiciary, Severely Disabled Employees' Representation, Employer's Representative

§ 93
Aufgaben des Betriebs-, Personal-, Richter-, Staatsanwalts- und Präsidialrates

Section 93
Tasks of the Works Council, Staff Council, Judiciary Council, Public Prosecutors' Council and Presidential Council of the Judiciary

¹Betriebs-, Personal-, Richter-, Staatsanwalts- und Präsidialrat fördern die Eingliederung schwerbehinderter Menschen. ²Sie achten insbesondere darauf, dass die dem Arbeitgeber nach den §§ 71, 72 und 81 bis 84 obliegenden Verpflichtungen erfüllt werden; sie wirken auf die Wahl der Schwerbehindertenvertretung hin.

¹The works council, staff council, judiciary council, public prosecutors' council and presidential council of the judiciary shall promote the integration of disabled persons. ²They shall particularly ensure that the employer's obligations pursuant to sections 71, 72 and 81 to 84 are fulfilled; they shall work toward the election of a representational body for disabled persons.

§ 94
Wahl und Amtszeit der Schwerbehindertenvertretung

Section 94
Election and Term of the Representation for Severely Disabled Persons

(1) ¹In Betrieben und Dienststellen, in denen wenigstens fünf schwerbehinderte Menschen nicht nur vorübergehend beschäftigt sind, werden eine Vertrauensperson und wenigstens ein stellvertretendes Mitglied gewählt, das die Vertrauensperson im Falle der Verhinderung durch Abwesenheit oder Wahrnehmung anderer Aufgaben vertritt. ²Ferner wählen bei Gerichten, de-

(1) ¹In establishments and civil service workplaces in which at least five severely disabled persons work, not just on a temporary basis, a representative and at least a deputy member shall be elected to stand in for the representative in his absence or if he is engaged in other tasks. ²Additionally, in courts to which at least five severely disabled judges belong, these judges shall elect a

nen mindestens fünf schwerbehinderte Richter oder Richterinnen angehören, diese einen Richter oder eine Richterin zu ihrer Schwerbehindertenvertretung. ³Satz 2 gilt entsprechend für Staatsanwälte oder Staatsanwältinnen, soweit für sie eine besondere Personalvertretung gebildet wird. ⁴Betriebe oder Dienststellen, die die Voraussetzungen des Satzes 1 nicht erfüllen, können für die Wahl mit räumlich nahe liegenden Betrieben des Arbeitgebers oder gleichstufigen Dienststellen derselben Verwaltung zusammengefasst werden; soweit erforderlich, können Gerichte unterschiedlicher Gerichtszweige und Stufen zusammengefasst werden. ⁵Über die Zusammenfassung entscheidet der Arbeitgeber im Benehmen mit dem für den Sitz der Betriebe oder Dienststellen einschließlich Gerichten zuständigen Integrationsamt.

(2) Wahlberechtigt sind alle in dem Betrieb oder der Dienststelle beschäftigten schwerbehinderten Menschen.

(3) ¹Wählbar sind alle in dem Betrieb oder der Dienststelle nicht nur vorübergehend Beschäftigten, die am Wahltage das 18. Lebensjahr vollendet haben und dem Betrieb oder der Dienststelle seit sechs Monaten angehören; besteht der Betrieb oder die Dienststelle weniger als ein Jahr, so bedarf es für die Wählbarkeit nicht der sechsmonatigen Zugehörigkeit. ²Nicht wählbar ist, wer kraft Gesetzes dem Betriebs-, Personal-, Richter-, Staatsanwalts- oder Präsidialrat nicht angehören kann.

(4) Bei Dienststellen der Bundeswehr, bei denen eine Vertretung der Soldaten nach dem Bundespersonalvertretungsgesetz zu wählen ist, sind auch schwerbehinderte Soldaten und Soldatinnen wahlberechtigt und auch Soldaten und Soldatinnen wählbar.

(5) ¹Die regelmäßigen Wahlen finden alle vier Jahre in der Zeit vom 1. Ok-

judge to their representation for severely disabled persons. ³Sentence 2 shall apply mutatis mutandis for public prosecutors where a special staff representational body is created for them. ⁴Establishments or civil service workplaces which do not fulfill the prerequisites of sentence 1 may be combined for the election with other establishments of the employer or civil service workplaces on the same level of the same administrative body which are located close by; where necessary, courts of different judicial branches and levels may be combined. ⁵The employer shall decide on the combination in consultation with the Integration Authority responsible for the seat of the establishment or civil service workplaces, including courts.

(2) All severely disabled employees in the establishment or civil service workplaces shall be eligible to vote.

(3) ¹Persons eligible for election are all employees in the establishment or civil service workplace who are not just employed on a temporary basis who have reached the age of 18 on the day of the election and have been employed in the establishment or civil service workplace for at least six months; if the establishment or civil service workplace has been in existence for less than one year, the six-month employment requirement shall not apply. ²Anyone who by law may not belong to a works council, staff council, judiciary council, public prosecutors' council or presidential council of the judiciary shall not be eligible for election.

(4) In the case of workplaces of the army, where a representation for the soldiers is to be elected pursuant to the Federal Staff Representation Act *(Bundespersonalvertretungsgesetz)*, severely disabled soldiers are also eligible to vote and be elected.

(5) ¹The regular elections shall be held every four years in the period from

tober bis 30. November statt. ²Außerhalb dieser Zeit finden Wahlen statt, wenn

1. das Amt der Schwerbehindertenvertretung vorzeitig erlischt und ein stellvertretendes Mitglied nicht nachrückt,
2. die Wahl mit Erfolg angefochten worden ist oder
3. eine Schwerbehindertenvertretung noch nicht gewählt ist.

³Hat außerhalb des für die regelmäßigen Wahlen festgelegten Zeitraumes eine Wahl der Schwerbehindertenvertretung stattgefunden, wird die Schwerbehindertenvertretung in dem auf die Wahl folgenden nächsten Zeitraum der regelmäßigen Wahlen neu gewählt. ⁴Hat die Amtszeit der Schwerbehindertenvertretung zum Beginn des für die regelmäßigen Wahlen festgelegten Zeitraums noch nicht ein Jahr betragen, wird die Schwerbehindertenvertretung im übernächsten Zeitraum für regelmäßige Wahlen neu gewählt.

(6) ¹Die Vertrauensperson und das stellvertretende Mitglied werden in geheimer und unmittelbarer Wahl nach den Grundsätzen der Mehrheitswahl gewählt. ²Im Übrigen sind die Vorschriften über die Wahlanfechtung, den Wahlschutz und die Wahlkosten bei der Wahl des Betriebs-, Personal-, Richter-, Staatsanwalts- oder Präsidialrates sinngemäß anzuwenden. ³In Betrieben und Dienststellen mit weniger als 50 wahlberechtigten schwerbehinderten Menschen wird die Vertrauensperson und das stellvertretende Mitglied im vereinfachten Wahlverfahren gewählt, sofern der Betrieb oder die Dienststelle nicht aus räumlich weit auseinander liegenden Teilen besteht. ⁴Ist in einem Betrieb oder einer Dienststelle eine Schwerbehindertenvertretung nicht gewählt, so kann das für den Betrieb oder die Dienststelle zuständige Integrationsamt zu einer Versammlung schwerbehinderter Menschen zum Zwecke der Wahl eines Wahlvorstandes einladen.

1 October to 30 November. ²Elections shall be held outside of this period if

1. the term of the representative for severely disabled employees' representation expires prematurely and no deputy member takes his place,
2. the election is successfully contested or
3. no severely disabled employees' representation has yet been elected.

³If an election for the severely disabled employees' representation has been held outside of the regular election period, the representation shall be newly elected in the next regular election period following the election. ⁴If the severely disabled employees' representation has not yet served for one year at the beginning of the regular election period, it shall be newly elected in the regular election period following the next election.

(6) ¹The representative and deputy shall be elected in secret and direct balloting according to the principles of majority voting. ²Otherwise, the provisions on contesting, protection and the costs of elections of the election of the works council, staff council, judiciary council, public prosecutors' council and presidential council of the judiciary shall be applied mutatis mutandis. ³In establishments and civil service workplace with fewer than 50 disabled persons eligible to vote, the representative and deputy shall be elected in a simplified election procedure, provided that the establishment or the civil service workplaces does not consist of portions geographically distant from each other. ⁴If no severely disabled employees' representation is elected in an establishment or civil service workplace, that Integration Authority responsible for the establishment or civil service workplace may send an invitation to a meeting of severely disabled persons for the purpose of electing an electoral board.

(7) ¹Die Amtszeit der Schwerbehindertenvertretung beträgt vier Jahre. ²Sie beginnt mit der Bekanntgabe des Wahlergebnisses oder, wenn die Amtszeit der bisherigen Schwerbehindertenvertretung noch nicht beendet ist, mit deren Ablauf. ³Das Amt erlischt vorzeitig, wenn die Vertrauensperson es niederlegt, aus dem Arbeits-, Dienst- oder Richterverhältnis ausscheidet oder die Wählbarkeit verliert. ⁴Scheidet die Vertrauensperson vorzeitig aus dem Amt aus, rückt das mit der höchsten Stimmenzahl gewählte stellvertretende Mitglied für den Rest der Amtszeit nach; dies gilt für das stellvertretende Mitglied entsprechend. ⁵Auf Antrag eines Viertels der wahlberechtigten schwerbehinderten Menschen kann der Widerspruchsausschuss bei dem Integrationsamt (§ 119) das Erlöschen des Amtes einer Vertrauensperson wegen grober Verletzung ihrer Pflichten beschließen.

(7) ¹The term of office of the severely disabled employees' representation shall be four years. ²It shall commence with the announcement of the election results or, if the term of the previous representation has not yet ended, once it comes to an end. ³The term shall expire prematurely if the representative resigns from office, resigns from the employment, service or judge relationship or loses his eligibility to hold office. ⁴If the representative prematurely steps down from his position, the deputy member with the highest number of votes shall replace him for the rest of the term; this applies for the deputy member mutatis mutandis. ⁵Upon a motion by one-fourth of the disabled persons eligible to vote, the objection committee of the Integration Authority (section 119) may resolve that a representative's term of office has expired due to gross breach of duty.

§ 95
Aufgaben der Schwerbehindertenvertretung

Section 95
Responsibilities of the Severely Disabled Employees' Representation

(1) ¹Die Schwerbehindertenvertretung fördert die Eingliederung schwerbehinderter Menschen in den Betrieb oder die Dienststelle, vertritt ihre Interessen in dem Betrieb oder der Dienststelle und steht ihnen beratend und helfend zur Seite. ²Sie erfüllt ihre Aufgaben insbesondere dadurch, dass sie

(1) ¹The severely disabled employees' representation shall promote the integration of severely disabled employees in the establishment or civil service workplace, represent their interests in the establishment or civil service workplace and provide them with advice and assistance. ²It shall fulfill its responsibilities in particular by

1. darüber wacht, dass die zugunsten schwerbehinderter Menschen geltenden Gesetze, Verordnungen, Tarifverträge, Betriebs- oder Dienstvereinbarungen und Verwaltungsanordnungen durchgeführt, insbesondere auch die dem Arbeitgeber nach den §§ 71, 72 und 81 bis 84 obliegenden Verpflichtungen erfüllt werden,

2. Maßnahmen, die den schwerbehinderten Menschen dienen, insbeson-

1. monitoring the compliance with the statutes, ordinances, collective bargaining agreements, works or civil service workplaces agreements and administrative ordinances benefiting severely disabled persons, in particular the obligations imposed upon the employer pursuant to sections 71, 72 and 81 to 84,

2. applying to the competent authorities for measures which serve se-

dere auch präventive Maßnahmen, bei den zuständigen Stellen beantragt, 3. Anregungen und Beschwerden von schwerbehinderten Menschen entgegennimmt und, falls sie berechtigt erscheinen, durch Verhandlung mit dem Arbeitgeber auf eine Erledigung hinwirkt; sie unterrichtet die schwerbehinderten Menschen über den Stand und das Ergebnis der Verhandlungen. ³Die Schwerbehindertenvertretung unterstützt Beschäftigte auch bei Anträgen an die nach § 69 Abs. 1 zuständigen Behörden auf Feststellung einer Behinderung, ihres Grades und einer Schwerbehinderung sowie bei Anträgen auf Gleichstellung an die Agentur für Arbeit. ⁴In Betrieben und Dienststellen mit in der Regel mehr als 100 schwerbehinderten Menschen kann sie nach Unterrichtung des Arbeitgebers das mit der höchsten Stimmenzahl gewählte stellvertretende Mitglied zu bestimmten Aufgaben heranziehen, in Betrieben und Dienststellen mit mehr als 200 schwerbehinderten Menschen, das mit der nächsthöchsten Stimmzahl gewählte weitere stellvertretende Mitglied. ⁵Die Heranziehung zu bestimmten Aufgaben schließt die Abstimmung untereinander ein. (2) ¹Der Arbeitgeber hat die Schwerbehindertenvertretung in allen Angelegenheiten, die einen einzelnen oder die schwerbehinderten Menschen als Gruppe berühren, unverzüglich und umfassend zu unterrichten und vor einer Entscheidung anzuhören; er hat ihr die getroffene Entscheidung unverzüglich mitzuteilen. ²Die Durchführung oder Vollziehung einer ohne Beteiligung nach Satz 1 getroffenen Entscheidung ist auszusetzen, die Beteiligung ist innerhalb von sieben Tagen nachzuholen; sodann ist endgültig zu entscheiden. ³Die Schwerbehindertenvertretung hat das Recht auf Beteiligung am Verfahren nach § 81 Abs. 1 und beim Vorliegen	verely disabled persons, including in particular preventative measures, 3. accepting suggestions and complaints from severely disabled persons and, if they appear justified, working toward negotiations with the employer to resolve the issue; it shall inform the severely disabled persons of the status and results of the negotiations. ³The severely disabled employees' representation shall also support employees in filing applications to the authorities competent for the implementation of the Federal Pension Act (*Bundesversorgungsgesetz*) for determination of a disability, its degree and a severe disability, as well as applications to the Employment Agency for equal treatment. ⁴In establishments and civil service workplaces employing regularly over 100 severely disabled persons, it may involve the deputy member receiving the greatest number of votes in specific tasks after informing the employer, in establishments and civil service workplaces with more than 200 severely disabled persons, the additional deputy member with the next greatest number of votes. ⁵The involvement in specific tasks includes the coordination among them. (2) ¹The employer shall inform the severely disabled employees' representation with respect to all matters affecting an individual severely disabled person or the severely disabled employees as a group completely and without undue delay and consult with it before making a decision; the employer shall inform the severely disabled employees' representation of the decision made without delay. ²The implementation or enforcement of a decision made without participation pursuant to sentence 1 shall be suspended and participation shall be effected within seven days; a final decision shall then be made. ³The severely disabled employees' represen-

von Vermittlungsvorschlägen der Bundesagentur für Arbeit nach § 81 Abs. 1 oder von Bewerbungen schwerbehinderter Menschen das Recht auf Einsicht in die entscheidungsrelevanten Teile der Bewerbungsunterlagen und Teilnahme an Vorstellungsgesprächen.

(3) ¹Der schwerbehinderte Mensch hat das Recht, bei Einsicht in die über ihn geführte Personalakte oder ihn betreffende Daten des Arbeitgebers die Schwerbehindertenvertretung hinzuzuziehen. ²Die Schwerbehindertenvertretung bewahrt über den Inhalt der Daten Stillschweigen, soweit sie der schwerbehinderte Mensch nicht von dieser Verpflichtung entbunden hat.

(4) ¹Die Schwerbehindertenvertretung hat das Recht, an allen Sitzungen des Betriebs-, Personal-, Richter-, Staatsanwalts- oder Präsidialrates und deren Ausschüssen sowie des Arbeitsschutzausschusses beratend teilzunehmen; sie kann beantragen, Angelegenheiten, die einzelne oder die schwerbehinderten Menschen als Gruppe besonders betreffen, auf die Tagesordnung der nächsten Sitzung zu setzen. ²Erachtet sie einen Beschluss des Betriebs-, Personal-, Richter-, Staatsanwalts- oder Präsidialrates als eine erhebliche Beeinträchtigung wichtiger Interessen schwerbehinderter Menschen oder ist sie entgegen Absatz 2 Satz 1 nicht beteiligt worden, wird auf ihren Antrag der Beschluss für die Dauer von einer Woche vom Zeitpunkt der Beschlussfassung an ausgesetzt; die Vorschriften des Betriebsverfassungsgesetzes und des Personalvertretungsrechtes über die Aussetzung von Beschlüssen gelten entsprechend. ³Durch die Aussetzung wird eine Frist nicht verlängert. ⁴In den Fällen des § 21e Abs. 1 und 3 des Gerichtsverfassungsgesetzes ist die Schwerbehindertenvertretung, außer in Eilfällen, auf Antrag eines betroffenen schwerbehin-

tation shall have the right to participate in proceedings pursuant to section 81 (1) and, where employment proposals have been made by the Federal Employment Agency, pursuant to section 81 (1) or where applications have been submitted by disabled persons, it shall have the right to inspect the application documents relevant for making a decision and participate in the job interviews.

(3) ¹A severely disabled person has the right to involve the severely disabled employees' representation in the inspection of the personnel file kept on him or the employer's data affecting him. ²The disabled employees' representation shall maintain secrecy regarding the content of the data unless the severely disabled person has released it from this obligation.

(4) ¹The severely disabled employees' representation shall have the right to attend all sessions of the works council, staff council, judiciary council, public prosecutors' council and presidential council of the judiciary and their committees as well as the industrial protection committee in an advisory capacity; it may move to have matters affecting individual severely disabled persons or severely disabled employees as a group put on the agenda for the next meeting. ²If it considers that a resolution by the works council, staff council, judiciary council, public prosecutors' council and presidential council of the judiciary represents a major impairment of important interests of severely disabled persons or if it has not been allowed to participate pursuant to subsection (2) sentence 1, upon its motion the resolution shall be suspended for a period of one week from the time of its adoption; the provisions of the Works Constitution Act and the staff representation laws on the suspension of resolutions shall apply mutatis mutandis. ³The suspension shall not cause a time period to be extended. ⁴In the cases set forth in section 21e subsections (1) and

derten Richters oder einer schwerbehinderten Richterin vor dem Präsidium des Gerichtes zu hören.

(5) Die Schwerbehindertenvertretung wird zu Besprechungen nach § 74 Abs. 1 des Betriebsverfassungsgesetzes, § 66 Abs. 1 des Bundespersonalvertretungsgesetzes sowie den entsprechenden Vorschriften des sonstigen Personalvertretungsrechtes zwischen dem Arbeitgeber und den in Absatz 4 genannten Vertretungen hinzugezogen.

(6) ¹Die Schwerbehindertenvertretung hat das Recht, mindestens einmal im Kalenderjahr eine Versammlung schwerbehinderter Menschen im Betrieb oder in der Dienststelle durchzuführen. ²Die für Betriebs- und Personalversammlungen geltenden Vorschriften finden entsprechende Anwendung.

(7) Sind in einer Angelegenheit sowohl die Schwerbehindertenvertretung der Richter und Richterinnen als auch die Schwerbehindertenvertretung der übrigen Bediensteten beteiligt, so handeln sie gemeinsam.

(8) Die Schwerbehindertenvertretung kann an Betriebs- und Personalversammlungen in Betrieben und Dienststellen teilnehmen, für die sie als Schwerbehindertenvertretung zuständig ist, und hat dort ein Rederecht, auch wenn die Mitglieder der Schwerbehindertenvertretung nicht Angehörige des Betriebes oder der Dienststelle sind.

(3) of the Judicature Act (*Gerichtsverfassungsgesetz*), the severely disabled employees' representation shall, except in urgent cases, be given a hearing before the presidium of the court at the request of an affected severely disabled person or a disabled judge.

(5) The severely disabled employees' representation shall be included in consultations pursuant to section 74 (1) of the Works Constitution Act, section 66 (1) of the Federal Staff Representation Act (*Bundespersonalvertretungsgesetz*), as well as the corresponding provisions of the other staff representation laws between the employer and the representational bodies mentioned in subsection (4).

(6) ¹The severely disabled employees' representation shall have the right to hold a meeting of severely disabled persons in the establishment or the civil service workplace at least once in each calendar year. ²The provisions for works council and staff meetings shall apply mutatis mutandis.

(7) If both the severely disabled employees' representation of the judges and that of the other civil service employees are affected by a matter, they shall act jointly.

(8) The severely disabled employees' representation may attend works council and staff meetings in establishments and civil service workplaces for which it is competent as the disabled employees' representation and shall have a right to speak in such meetings, even if the members of the disabled employees' representation are not employees at the establishment or civil service workplace.

§ 96
Persönliche Rechte und Pflichten der Vertrauenspersonen der schwerbehinderten Menschen

(1) Die Vertrauenspersonen führen ihr Amt unentgeltlich als Ehrenamt.

Section 96
Personal Rights and Duties of the Severely Disabled Employees' Representatives

(1) The representatives shall hold their office in an honorary capacity with no remuneration.

(2) Die Vertrauenspersonen dürfen in der Ausübung ihres Amtes nicht behindert oder wegen ihres Amtes nicht benachteiligt oder begünstigt werden; dies gilt auch für ihre berufliche Entwicklung.

(3) ¹Die Vertrauenspersonen besitzen gegenüber dem Arbeitgeber die gleiche persönliche Rechtsstellung, insbesondere den gleichen Kündigungs-, Versetzungs- und Abordnungsschutz wie ein Mitglied des Betriebs-, Personal-, Staatsanwalts- oder Richterrates. ²Das stellvertretende Mitglied besitzt während der Dauer der Vertretung und der Heranziehung nach § 95 Abs. 1 Satz 4 die gleiche persönliche Rechtsstellung wie die Vertrauensperson, im Übrigen die gleiche Rechtsstellung wie Ersatzmitglieder der in Satz 1 genannten Vertretungen.

(4) ¹Die Vertrauenspersonen werden von ihrer beruflichen Tätigkeit ohne Minderung des Arbeitsentgelts oder der Dienstbezüge befreit, wenn und soweit es zur Durchführung ihrer Aufgaben erforderlich ist. ²Sind in den Betrieben und Dienststellen in der Regel wenigstens 200 schwerbehinderte Menschen beschäftigt, wird die Vertrauensperson auf ihren Wunsch freigestellt; weiter gehende Vereinbarungen sind zulässig. ³Satz 1 gilt entsprechend für die Teilnahme an Schulungs- und Bildungsveranstaltungen, soweit diese Kenntnisse vermitteln, die für die Arbeit der Schwerbehindertenvertretung erforderlich sind. ⁴Satz 3 gilt auch für das mit der höchsten Stimmenzahl gewählte stellvertretende Mitglied, wenn wegen

1. ständiger Heranziehung nach § 95,
2. häufiger Vertretung der Vertrauensperson für längere Zeit,
3. absehbaren Nachrückens in das Amt der Schwerbehindertenvertretung in kurzer Frist

(2) The representatives may not be impaired in the exercise of their function or placed at a disadvantage or receive preferential treatment due to their office; this also applies to their professional advancement.

(3) ¹The representatives shall have the same legal position vis-à-vis the employer from a personal point of view, specifically the same protection against termination, transfer and delegation as a member of the works council, staff council, public prosecutors' council or judiciary council. ²The deputy representative shall have the same legal position from a personal point of view as the representative during the term of the representation and involvement in tasks pursuant to section 95 (1) sentence 4, and otherwise the same legal position as deputy members of the bodies mentioned in sentence 1.

(4) ¹The representatives shall be released from their work duties without a reduction in pay where and to the extent this is necessary for the performance of their duties. ²If at least 200 disabled persons are regularly employed in the establishments and civil service workplaces, the representatives shall be released at their request; agreements beyond that are permissible. ³Sentence 1 applies *mutatis mutandis* to participation in training and further education events provided that they impart knowledge necessary for the work of the severely disabled employees' representation. ⁴Sentence 3 shall also apply to the deputy elected with the most votes if his participation in such events is necessary because

1. he is consistently involved in tasks pursuant to section 95,
2. he frequently stands in for the representative for a lengthy period,
3. it is foreseeable that he will be replacing the representative shortly.

die Teilnahme an Bildungs- und Schulungsveranstaltungen erforderlich ist.

(5) ¹Freigestellte Vertrauenspersonen dürfen von inner- oder außerbetrieblichen Maßnahmen der Berufsförderung nicht ausgeschlossen werden. ²Innerhalb eines Jahres nach Beendigung ihrer Freistellung ist ihnen im Rahmen der Möglichkeiten des Betriebes oder der Dienststelle Gelegenheit zu geben, eine wegen der Freistellung unterbliebene berufliche Entwicklung in dem Betrieb oder der Dienststelle nachzuholen. Für Vertrauenspersonen, die drei volle aufeinander folgende Amtszeiten freigestellt waren, erhöht sich der genannte Zeitraum auf zwei Jahre.

(6) Zum Ausgleich für ihre Tätigkeit, die aus betriebsbedingten oder dienstlichen Gründen außerhalb der Arbeitszeit durchzuführen ist, haben die Vertrauenspersonen Anspruch auf entsprechende Arbeits- oder Dienstbefreiung unter Fortzahlung des Arbeitsentgelts oder der Dienstbezüge.

(7) ¹Die Vertrauenspersonen sind verpflichtet,
1. über ihnen wegen ihres Amtes bekannt gewordene persönliche Verhältnisse und Angelegenheiten von Beschäftigten im Sinne des § 73, die ihrer Bedeutung oder ihrem Inhalt nach einer vertraulichen Behandlung bedürfen, Stillschweigen zu bewahren und
2. ihnen wegen ihres Amtes bekannt gewordene und vom Arbeitgeber ausdrücklich als geheimhaltungsbedürftig bezeichnete Betriebs- oder Geschäftsgeheimnisse nicht zu offenbaren und nicht zu verwerten.

²Diese Pflichten gelten auch nach dem Ausscheiden aus dem Amt. ³Sie gelten nicht gegenüber der Bundesagentur für Arbeit, den Integrationsämtern und den Rehabilitationsträgern, soweit deren Aufgaben den schwerbehinderten Menschen gegenüber es erfordern, gegenüber den Vertrauenspersonen in den Stufenvertretungen (§ 97) sowie ge-

(5) ¹Representatives released from their work duties may not be excluded from internal or external professional advancement measures. ²Within one year after the release comes to an end, they shall be given an opportunity to the extent possible in the establishment or the civil service workplace to make up for a professional development in the establishment or civil service workplace that he had missed due to the release. ³For representatives that were released for three full consecutive terms, the above time period shall be increased to two years.

(6) As compensation for activities they must perform outside of working hours for operational or official reasons, the representatives shall have a claim to the corresponding amount of free time with continued payment of remuneration.

(7) ¹The representatives shall be obligated
1. to maintain silence with respect to the personal circumstances and matters of employees within the meaning of section 73 of which they learn due to their office, where the significance or the content of such information require confidential treatment and
2. to refrain from disclosing or utilizing trade or business secrets which they learn due to their office and which the employer has explicitly designated as confidential.

²These duties shall also apply after the representative leaves office. ³They shall not apply vis-à-vis the Federal Employment Agency, the Integration Authorities and the rehabilitation providers, where their responsibilities to disabled persons so require, vis-à-vis the representatives in the level representations (section 97) and vis-à-vis the

genüber den in § 79 Abs. 1 des Betriebsverfassungsgesetzes und den in den entsprechenden Vorschriften des Personalvertretungsrechtes genannten Vertretungen, Personen und Stellen.

(8) ¹Die durch die Tätigkeit der Schwerbehindertenvertretung entstehenden Kosten trägt der Arbeitgeber. ²Das Gleiche gilt für die durch die Teilnahme des mit der höchsten Stimmenzahl gewählten stellvertretenden Mitglieds an Schulungs- und Bildungsveranstaltungen nach Absatz 4 Satz 3 entstehenden Kosten.

(9) Die Räume und der Geschäftsbedarf, die der Arbeitgeber dem Betriebs-, Personal-, Richter-, Staatsanwalts- oder Präsidialrat für dessen Sitzungen, Sprechstunden und laufende Geschäftsführung zur Verfügung stellt, stehen für die gleichen Zwecke auch der Schwerbehindertenvertretung zur Verfügung, soweit ihr hierfür nicht eigene Räume und sächliche Mittel zur Verfügung gestellt werden.

§ 97
Konzern-, Gesamt-, Bezirks- und Hauptschwerbehindertenvertretung

(1) ¹Ist für mehrere Betriebe eines Arbeitgebers ein Gesamtbetriebsrat oder für den Geschäftsbereich mehrerer Dienststellen ein Gesamtpersonalrat errichtet, wählen die Schwerbehindertenvertretungen der einzelnen Betriebe oder Dienststellen eine Gesamtschwerbehindertenvertretung. ²Ist eine Schwerbehindertenvertretung nur in einem der Betriebe oder in einer der Dienststellen gewählt, nimmt sie die Rechte und Pflichten der Gesamtschwerbehindertenvertretung wahr.

(2) ¹Ist für mehrere Unternehmen ein Konzernbetriebsrat errichtet, wählen die Gesamtschwerbehinderten-

representative bodies, persons and agencies mentioned in section 79 (1) of the Works Constitution Act and the corresponding provisions of the staff representation laws.

(8) ¹The costs incurred by the activities of the severely disabled employees' representation shall be borne by the employer. ²The same shall hold for the cost of the participation of the deputy member receiving the most votes in training and further educational events pursuant to subsection (4) sentence 3.

(9) The office space and clerical requirements the employer makes available to the works council, staff council, judiciary council, public prosecutors' council and presidential council of the judiciary for their sessions, consulting hours and ongoing management shall be made available to the severely disabled employees' representative for the same purpose unless they are provided with their own rooms and equipment.

Section 97
Group, Joint, District and Primary Severely Disabled Employees' Representation

(1) ¹If a joint works council has been established for two or more establishments of an employer or a joint staff council for the area of operations of two or more civil service workplaces, the severely disabled employees' representations of the individual establishments or civil service workplaces shall elect a joint severely disabled employees' representation. ²If a severely disabled employees' representation has only been elected in one of the establishments or civil service workplaces, it shall take on the rights and duties of the joint severely disabled employees' representation.

(2) ¹If a group works council has been established for two or more companies, the joint severely disabled employees'

vertretungen eine Konzernschwerbehindertenvertretung. ²Besteht ein Konzernunternehmen nur aus einem Betrieb, für den eine Schwerbehindertenvertretung gewählt ist, hat sie das Wahlrecht wie eine Gesamtschwerbehindertenvertretung.

(3) ¹Für den Geschäftsbereich mehrstufiger Verwaltungen, bei denen ein Bezirks- oder Hauptpersonalrat gebildet ist, gilt Absatz 1 sinngemäß mit der Maßgabe, dass bei den Mittelbehörden von deren Schwerbehindertenvertretung und den Schwerbehindertenvertretungen der nachgeordneten Dienststellen eine Bezirksschwerbehindertenvertretung zu wählen ist. ²Bei den obersten Dienstbehörden ist von deren Schwerbehindertenvertretung und den Bezirksschwerbehindertenvertretungen des Geschäftsbereichs eine Hauptschwerbehindertenvertretung zu wählen; ist die Zahl der Bezirksschwerbehindertenvertretungen niedriger als zehn, sind auch die Schwerbehindertenvertretungen der nachgeordneten Dienststellen wahlberechtigt.

(4) ¹Für Gerichte eines Zweiges der Gerichtsbarkeit, für die ein Bezirks- oder Hauptrichterrat gebildet ist, gilt Absatz 3 entsprechend. ²Sind in einem Zweig der Gerichtsbarkeit bei den Gerichten der Länder mehrere Schwerbehindertenvertretungen nach § 94 zu wählen und ist in diesem Zweig kein Hauptrichterrat gebildet, ist in entsprechender Anwendung von Absatz 3 eine Hauptschwerbehindertenvertretung zu wählen. ³Die Hauptschwerbehindertenvertretung nimmt die Aufgabe der Schwerbehindertenvertretung gegenüber dem Präsidialrat wahr.

(5) Für jede Vertrauensperson, die nach den Absätzen 1 bis 4 neu zu wählen ist,

representations shall elect a group severely disabled employees' representation. ²If a group company consists of only one establishment for which a severely disabled employees' representation has been elected, it shall have the voting rights of a joint severely disabled employees' representation.

(3) ¹For the area of operations of multi-level administrative agencies in which a district or main staff council has been established, subsection (1) shall apply analogously with the proviso that for the mid-level authorities a district severely disabled persons' representation shall be created from their severely disabled persons' representation and that of the subordinate civil service workplaces. ²In the case of the highest administrative agencies, a main severely disabled persons' representation shall be created from their severely disabled employees' representation and the district severely disabled persons' representations; if the number of district severely disabled persons' representations is less than ten, the severely disabled persons' representations in the lower level civil service workplaces shall also be entitled to vote.

(4) ¹For courts in a branch of the judiciary for which a district or main judge's council has been formed, subsection (3) shall apply *mutatis mutandis*. ²If two or more severely disabled employees' representations are to be formed in a branch of the judiciary in the courts of the states pursuant to section 94 and if no main judge's council has been formed in this branch, a main severely disabled employees' representation shall be elected in analogous application of subsection (3). ³The main severely disabled employees' representation shall carry out the tasks of the severely disabled employees' representation vis-à-vis the presidential council of the judiciary.

(5) For each representative to be newly elected pursuant to subsections (1) to

wird wenigstens ein stellvertretendes Mitglied gewählt.

(6) ¹Die Gesamtschwerbehindertenvertretung vertritt die Interessen der schwerbehinderten Menschen in Angelegenheiten, die das Gesamtunternehmen oder mehrere Betriebe oder Dienststellen des Arbeitgebers betreffen und von den Schwerbehindertenvertretungen der einzelnen Betriebe oder Dienststellen nicht geregelt werden können, sowie die Interessen der schwerbehinderten Menschen, die in einem Betrieb oder einer Dienststelle tätig sind, für die eine Schwerbehindertenvertretung nicht gewählt ist; dies umfasst auch Verhandlungen und den Abschluss entsprechender Integrationsvereinbarungen. ²Satz 1 gilt entsprechend für die Konzern-, Bezirks- und Hauptschwerbehindertenvertretung sowie für die Schwerbehindertenvertretung der obersten Dienstbehörde, wenn bei einer mehrstufigen Verwaltung Stufenvertretungen nicht gewählt sind. ³Die nach Satz 2 zuständige Schwerbehindertenvertretung ist auch in persönlichen Angelegenheiten schwerbehinderter Menschen, über die eine übergeordnete Dienststelle entscheidet, zuständig; sie gibt der Schwerbehindertenvertretung der Dienststelle, die den schwerbehinderten Menschen beschäftigt, Gelegenheit zur Äußerung. ⁴Satz 3 gilt nicht in den Fällen, in denen der Personalrat der Beschäftigungsbehörde zu beteiligen ist.

(7) § 94 Abs. 3 bis 7, § 95 Abs. 1 Satz 4, Abs. 2, 4, 5 und 7 und § 96 gelten entsprechend, § 94 Abs. 5 mit der Maßgabe, dass die Wahl der Gesamt- und Bezirksschwerbehindertenvertretungen in der Zeit vom 1. Dezember bis 31. Januar, die der Konzern- und Hauptschwerbehindertenvertretungen in der Zeit vom 1. Februar bis 31. März stattfindet.

(4), at least one deputy member shall be elected.

(6) ¹The joint severely disabled employees' representation represents the interests of the severely disabled persons in matters concerning the entire company or two or more establishments or civil service workplaces of the employer and cannot be resolved by the severely disabled employees' representations of the individual establishments or civil service workplaces, as well as the interests of the severely disabled persons work in an establishment or a civil service workplace for which no severely disabled employees' representation has been elected; this also includes negotiations and the conclusion of the respective integration agreements. ²Sentence 1 applies *mutatis mutandis* for group, district and main severely disabled employees' representations as well as for the severely disabled employees' representations in the highest agency authority if representations for the various levels in a multilevel administrative agency are not elected. ³The competent severely disabled employees' representation pursuant to sentence 2 shall also be competent in personal matters concerning severely disabled persons over which a superior agency decides; such superior agency shall give the severely disabled employees' representation of the civil service workplace employing the severely disabled persons an opportunity to express itself. ⁴Sentence 4 shall not apply in the cases in which the staff council of the highest level of authority is to be involved.

(7) Section 94 subsections (3) to (7), Section 95 (1) sentence 4, (2), (4), (5) and (7) and section 96 apply *mutatis mutandis* and section 94 (5) subject to the proviso that the election of the joint and district severely disabled employees' representations shall be held in the period from 1 December to 31 January and that of the group and main severely disabled employees' representations shall be held from 1 February to 31 March.

(8) § 95 Abs. 6 gilt für die Durchführung von Versammlungen der Vertrauens- und der Bezirksvertrauenspersonen durch die Gesamt-, Bezirks- oder Hauptschwerbehindertenvertretung entsprechend.

(8) Section 95 (6) shall apply *mutatis mutandis* for the holding of meetings of the representatives and district representatives by the joint, district or main severely disabled employees' representations.

§ 98
Beauftragter des Arbeitgebers

[1] Der Arbeitgeber bestellt einen Beauftragten, der ihn in Angelegenheiten schwerbehinderter Menschen verantwortlich vertritt; falls erforderlich, können mehrere Beauftragte bestellt werden. [2] Der Beauftragte soll nach Möglichkeit selbst ein schwerbehinderter Mensch sein. [3] Der Beauftragte achtet vor allem darauf, dass dem Arbeitgeber obliegende Verpflichtungen erfüllt werden.

Section 98
Employer's Representative

[1] The employer shall appoint a representative to represent it with authority in matters concerning severely disabled persons; if necessary, two or more representatives may be appointed. [2] The representative shall, if possible, be a severely disabled person himself. [3] The representative shall primarily see to it that the employer's obligations are met.

§ 99
Zusammenarbeit

(1) Arbeitgeber, Beauftragter des Arbeitgebers, Schwerbehindertenvertretung und Betriebs-, Personal-, Richter-, Staatsanwalts- oder Präsidialrat arbeiten zur Teilhabe schwerbehinderter Menschen am Arbeitsleben in dem Betrieb oder der Dienststelle eng zusammen.

(2) [1] Die in Absatz 1 genannten Personen und Vertretungen, die mit der Durchführung des Teils 2 beauftragten Stellen und die Rehabilitationsträger unterstützen sich gegenseitig bei der Erfüllung ihrer Aufgaben. [2] Vertrauensperson und Beauftragter des Arbeitgebers sind Verbindungspersonen zur Bundesagentur für Arbeit und zu dem Integrationsamt.

Section 99
Cooperation

(1) The employer, employer's representative, severely disabled employees' representation and district, staff, judiciary, public prosecutors' council or the presidential council of the judiciary shall work closely together to ensure the participation of severely disabled persons in the working life in the establishment or civil service workplace.

(2) [1] The persons and representations mentioned in subsection (1), the authorities responsible for carrying out Part 2 and rehabilitation providers shall mutually support each other in the fulfillment of their tasks. [2] Severely disabled employees' representatives and employers' representatives shall be the liaison persons to the Federal Employment Agency and the Integration Authority.

§ 100
Verordnungsermächtigung

Die Bundesregierung wird ermächtigt, durch Rechtsverordnung mit Zustim-

Section 100
Empowerment to Issue Ordinances

The Federal Government shall be empowered to issue ordinances with the

mung des Bundesrates nähere Vorschriften über die Vorbereitung und Durchführung der Wahl der Schwerbehindertenvertretung und ihrer Stufenvertretungen zu erlassen.

consent of the upper house of parliament (*Bundesrat*) concerning the preparation for and conducting of the election of the severely disabled employees' representations and the representations on higher levels.

§ 125
Zusatzurlaub

Section 125
Additional Vacation

(1) [1] Schwerbehinderte Menschen haben Anspruch auf einen bezahlten zusätzlichen Urlaub von fünf Arbeitstagen im Urlaubsjahr; verteilt sich die regelmäßige Arbeitszeit des schwerbehinderten Menschen auf mehr oder weniger als fünf Arbeitstage in der Kalenderwoche, erhöht oder vermindert sich der Zusatzurlaub entsprechend. [2] Soweit tarifliche, betriebliche oder sonstige Urlaubsregelungen für schwerbehinderte Menschen einen längeren Zusatzurlaub vorsehen, bleiben sie unberührt.

(1) [1] Severely disabled employees shall have a claim to additional paid vacation days in the amount of five working days per vacation year; if the severely disabled person's regular working time is divided over more or less than five working days per calendar week, the number of additional vacation days shall be increased or decreased accordingly. [2] Where vacation provisions in collective bargaining agreements, on establishment level or other provisions call for a longer additional vacation period for severely disabled persons, such provisions shall remain unaffected.

(2) [1] Besteht die Schwerbehinderteneigenschaft nicht während des gesamten Kalenderjahres, so hat der schwerbehinderte Mensch für jeden vollen Monat der im Beschäftigungsverhältnis vorliegenden Schwerbehinderteneigenschaft einen Anspruch auf ein Zwölftel des Zusatzurlaubs nach Absatz 1 Satz 1. [2] Bruchteile von Urlaubstagen, die mindestens einen halben Tag ergeben, sind auf volle Urlaubstage aufzurunden. [3] Der so ermittelte Zusatzurlaub ist dem Erholungsurlaub hinzuzurechnen und kann bei einem nicht im ganzen Kalenderjahr bestehenden Beschäftigungsverhältnis nicht erneut gemindert werden.

(2) [1] If the person is not severely disabled during the entire calendar year, he shall have a claim to one-twelfth of the additional vacation days pursuant to subsection (1) sentence 1 for each month in which he was severely disabled during his employment. [2] Fractions of vacation days amounting to at least half of one day shall be rounded up to a full vacation day. [3] The additional vacation days calculated in this manner shall be added to the normal vacation days and may not be reduced again if the employment relationship does not exist in the entire calendar year.

(3) Wird die Eigenschaft als schwerbehinderter Mensch nach § 69 Abs. 1 und 2 rückwirkend festgestellt, finden auch für die Übertragbarkeit des Zusatzurlaubs in das nächste Kalenderjahr die dem Beschäftigungsverhältnis zugrunde liegenden urlaubsrechtlichen Regelungen Anwendung.

(3) If a person is retroactively classified as a severely disabled person pursuant to section 69 (1) and (2) the transferability of the additional vacation days to the next calendar year shall also be governed by the legal provisions on vacations which apply to the employment relationship.

XX. Law Pertaining to Companies with Limited Liability (GmbH-Gesetz)

of 20 April 1892

in the amended version of 31 July 2009

(excerpts)

Chapter 1
Formation of company

Section 6
Managing Director

(1) The company must have one or more managing directors.

(2) ¹Only a natural person with unlimited legal capacity can serve as managing director. A person cannot be a managing director who

1. as a ward is subject in whole or in part to a reservation of consent in the handling of his or her financial affairs, (section 1903 of the German Civil Code),
2. has been prohibited from engaging in an occupation, a line of work, a business or a line of business due to a court judgment or an enforceable decision by an administrative authority if and to the extent that such prohibition corresponds in full or in part to the company's object,
3. has been convicted of one or more intentional offenses involving
   a) a failure to file a petition for the opening of insolvency proceedings (delay in filing for insolvency),
   b) pursuant to sections 283 to 283 d of the German Criminal Code *(Strafgesetzbuch)* (insolvency offences),
   c) the making of false statements pursuant to section 82 of this Act or section 399 of the Stock Corporation Act *(Aktiengesetz),*

d) der unrichtigen Darstellung nach § 400 des Aktiengesetzes, § 331 des Handelsgesetzbuchs, § 313 des Umwandlungsgesetzes oder § 17 des Publizitätsgesetzes oder

e) nach den §§ 263 bis 264a oder den §§ 265b bis 266a des Strafgesetzbuchs zu einer Freiheitsstrafe von mindestens einem Jahr

verurteilt worden ist; dieser Ausschluss gilt für die Dauer von fünf Jahren seit der Rechtskraft des Urteils, wobei die Zeit nicht eingerechnet wird, in welcher der Täter auf behördliche Anordnung in einer Anstalt verwahrt worden ist.

Satz 2 Nr. 3 gilt entsprechend bei einer Verurteilung im Ausland wegen einer Tat, die mit den in Satz 2 Nr. 3 genannten Taten vergleichbar ist.

(3) ¹Zu Geschäftsführern können Gesellschafter oder andere Personen bestellt werden. ²Die Bestellung erfolgt entweder im Gesellschaftsvertrag oder nach Maßgabe der Bestimmungen des dritten Abschnitts.

(4) Ist im Gesellschaftsvertrag bestimmt, dass sämtliche Gesellschafter zur Geschäftsführung berechtigt sein sollen, so gelten nur die der Gesellschaft bei Festsetzung dieser Bestimmung angehörenden Personen als die bestellten Geschäftsführer.

(5) Gesellschafter, die vorsätzlich oder grob fahrlässig einer Person, die nicht Geschäftsführer sein kann, die Führung der Geschäfte überlassen, haften der Gesellschaft solidarisch für den Schaden, der dadurch entsteht, dass diese Person die ihr gegenüber der Gesellschaft bestehenden Obliegenheiten verletzt.

d) the making of misrepresentations pursuant to section 400 of the Stock Corporation Act, section 331 of the German Commercial Code (*Handelsgesetzbuch*), section 313 of the Transformations Act (*Umwandlungsgesetz*) or section 17 of the Disclosure Act (*Publizitätsgesetz*) or

e) pursuant to sections 263 to 264a or sections 265b to 266a of the German Criminal Code and sentenced to imprisonment for at least one year;

this exclusion shall apply for a period of five years from the date of the final conviction, not counting the duration of the perpetrator's confinement to an institution by order of the authorities.

Sentence 2 no. 3 applies *mutatis mutandis* to a conviction in a foreign jurisdiction of offences which are comparable to those offences designated in sentence 2 no 3.

(3) ¹Shareholders or other persons can be appointed managing directors. ²The appointment is effected either through the articles of association or according to the provisions of the Third Chapter.

(4) If the articles of association provide that all shareholders are entitled to manage the company, only such persons as are shareholders of the company when this provision is adopted shall be deemed to be the appointed managing directors.

(5) Shareholders who, intentionally or due to gross negligence, allow a person who cannot be a managing director to manage the business shall bear joint liability toward the company for the damage that is incurred because this person violates his or her obligations toward the company.

Abschnitt 3
Vertretung der Gesellschaft

§ 35
Vertretung durch Geschäftsführer

(1) Die Gesellschaft wird durch die Geschäftsführer gerichtlich und außergerichtlich vertreten. Hat eine Gesellschaft keinen Geschäftsführer (Führungslosigkeit), wird die Gesellschaft für den Fall, dass ihr gegenüber Willenserklärungen abgegeben oder Schriftstücke zugestellt werden, durch die Gesellschafter vertreten.

(2) [1] Sind mehrere Geschäftsführer bestellt, sind sie alle nur gemeinschaftlich zur Vertretung der Gesellschaft befugt, es sei denn, dass der Gesellschaftsvertrag etwas anderes bestimmt. [2] Ist der Gesellschaft gegenüber eine Willenserklärung abzugeben, genügt die Abgabe gegenüber einem Vertreter der Gesellschaft nach Absatz 1. [3] An die Vertreter der Gesellschaft nach Absatz 1 können unter der im Handelsregister eingetragenen Geschäftsanschrift Willenserklärungen abgegeben und Schriftstücke für die Gesellschaft zugestellt werden. [4] Unabhängig hiervon können die Abgabe und die Zustellung auch unter der eingetragenen Anschrift der empfangsberechtigten Person nach § 10 Abs. 2 Satz 2 erfolgen.

(3) [1] Befinden sich alle Geschäftsanteile der Gesellschaft in der Hand eines Gesellschafters oder daneben in der Hand der Gesellschaft und ist er zugleich deren alleiniger Geschäftsführer, so ist auf seine Rechtsgeschäfte mit der Gesellschaft § 181 des Bürgerlichen Gesetzbuchs anzuwenden. [2] Rechtsgeschäfte zwischen ihm und der von ihm vertretenen Gesellschaft sind, auch wenn er nicht alleiniger Geschäftsführer ist, unverzüglich nach ihrer Vornahme in eine Niederschrift aufzunehmen.

Chapter 3
Representation of the Company

Section 35
Representation by the Managing Directors

(1) The company is represented by the managing directors in and out of court. If a company does not have a managing director (leaderlessness), where declarations of intent are rendered to it or documents are served to it, the company shall be represented by the shareholders.

(2) [1] If two or more managing directors have been appointed, they shall all only be authorized to represent the company jointly, unless otherwise provided in the articles of association. [2] If a declaration of intent is to be submitted to the company, a submission to a representative of the company pursuant to subsection (1) shall suffice. [3] Declarations of intent and documents can be served to the representatives of the company pursuant to subsection (1) for the company at the business address recorded in the Commercial Register. [4] Independent of this, the submission and service can also be effected at the registered address of the persons authorized to take receipt pursuant to section 10 (2) sentence 2.

(3) [1] If all shares of the company are held by one shareholder or by one shareholder and the company and if the shareholder is also the sole managing director of the company, section 181 of the German Civil Code applies to his legal transactions with the company. [2] Legal transactions between him and the company represented by him shall, promptly upon their undertaking, be put in writing, even if he is not the sole managing director.

§ 35 a
Angaben auf Geschäftsbriefen

(1) ¹Auf allen Geschäftsbriefen gleichviel welcher Form, die an einen bestimmten Empfänger gerichtet werden, müssen die Rechtsform und der Sitz der Gesellschaft, das Registergericht des Sitzes der Gesellschaft und die Nummer, unter der die Gesellschaft in das Handelsregister eingetragen ist, sowie alle Geschäftsführer und, sofern die Gesellschaft einen Aufsichtsrat gebildet und dieser einen Vorsitzenden hat, der Vorsitzende des Aufsichtsrats mit dem Familiennamen und mindestens einem ausgeschriebenen Vornamen angegeben werden. ²Werden Angaben über das Kapital der Gesellschaft gemacht, so müssen in jedem Fall das Stammkapital sowie, wenn nicht alle in Geld zu leistenden Einlagen eingezahlt sind, der Gesamtbetrag der ausstehenden Einlagen angegeben werden.

(2) Der Angaben nach Absatz 1 Satz 1 bedarf es nicht bei Mitteilungen oder Berichten, die im Rahmen einer bestehenden Geschäftsverbindung ergehen und für die üblicherweise Vordrucke verwendet werden, in denen lediglich die im Einzelfall erforderlichen besonderen Angaben eingefügt zu werden brauchen.

(3) ¹Bestellscheine gelten als Geschäftsbriefe im Sinne des Absatzes 1. ²Absatz 2 ist auf sie nicht anzuwenden.

(4) ¹Auf allen Geschäftsbriefen und Bestellscheinen, die von einer Zweigniederlassung einer Gesellschaft mit beschränkter Haftung mit Sitz im Ausland verwendet werden, müssen das Register, bei dem die Zweigniederlassung geführt wird, und die Nummer des Registereintrags angegeben werden; im übrigen gelten die Vorschriften der Absätze 1 bis 3 für die Angaben bezüglich der Haupt- und der Zweigniederlassung, soweit nicht das ausländische Recht Abweichungen nötig macht. ²Befindet sich die ausländische

Section 35 a
Information on Business Letters

(1) ¹All business letters, regardless of their form directed to a specific addressee shall contain details of the legal form and domicile of the company, the registry court of the company's domicile and the company's number in the commercial register, as well as the surname and at least one first name written in full of all of the managing directors and, where the company has formed a supervisory board which has a chairman, the chairman of the supervisory board. ²Where details of the company's share capital are given, there shall be included the amount of the registered share capital and the total of contributions outstanding unless all contributions to be paid in cash have been paid in.

(2) The information listed in subsection (1) sentence 1 need not be included on notifications and reports issued in connection with an existing business relationship, and where it is customary to use pre-printed forms on which only the particular details necessary for each case have to be inserted.

(3) ¹Order forms are deemed to be business letters within the meaning of subsection (1). ²Subsection (2) does not apply to them.

(4) ¹All business letters and order forms used by a branch of a limited liability company with foreign domicile shall bear an indication of the commercial register with which the branch is registered and the number of its entry; in all other cases, the provisions of subsections (1) to (3) shall apply for the information regarding the principal place of business and the branch to the extent that foreign law does not require a deviation. ²If the foreign company is in liquidation, this fact, along with the names of all of the liquidators, shall be indicated.

Gesellschaft in Liquidation, so sind auch diese Tatsache sowie alle Liquidatoren anzugeben.

§ 36
(weggefallen)

Section 36
(repealed)

§ 37
Beschränkungen der Vertretungsbefugnis

(1) Die Geschäftsführer sind der Gesellschaft gegenüber verpflichtet, die Beschränkungen einzuhalten, welche für den Umfang ihrer Befugnis, die Gesellschaft zu vertreten, durch den Gesellschaftsvertrag oder, soweit dieser nicht ein anderes bestimmt, durch die Beschlüsse der Gesellschafter festgesetzt sind.

(2) ¹Gegen dritte Personen hat eine Beschränkung der Befugnis der Geschäftsführer, die Gesellschaft zu vertreten, keine rechtliche Wirkung. ²Dies gilt insbesondere für den Fall, dass die Vertretung sich nur auf gewisse Geschäfte oder Arten von Geschäften erstrecken oder nur unter gewissen Umständen oder für eine gewisse Zeit oder an einzelnen Orten stattfinden soll, oder dass die Zustimmung der Gesellschafter oder eines Organs der Gesellschaft für einzelne Geschäfte erforderlich ist.

Section 37
Limitations of the Power to Represent

(1) The managing directors are obligated vis-à-vis the company to observe restrictions on their power to represent the company imposed by the articles of association or, in the absence of other provisions, by shareholders' resolutions.

(2) ¹Restrictions on the right of the managing directors to represent the company have no legal effect vis-à-vis third parties. ²This relates especially to the case where representation extends only to certain transactions or types of transactions, or is only valid under certain circumstances or for a certain period of time or at certain locations, or where the approval by the shareholders or by a body of the company is required for individual transactions.

§ 38
Widerruf der Bestellung

(1) Die Bestellung der Geschäftsführer ist zu jeder Zeit widerruflich, unbeschadet der Entschädigungsansprüche aus bestehenden Verträgen.

(2) ¹Im Gesellschaftsvertrag kann die Zulässigkeit des Widerrufs auf den Fall beschränkt werden, dass wichtige Gründe denselben notwendig machen. ²Als solche Gründe sind insbesondere grobe Pflichtverletzung oder Unfähigkeit zur ordnungsmäßigen Geschäftsführung anzusehen.

Section 38
Revocation of appointment

(1) The appointment of the managing directors can be revoked at any time without prejudice to the indemnification claims resulting from existing contracts.

(2) ¹The articles of association can restrict the right of revocation to the case where important reasons make it necessary. ²Such reasons would be deemed to be especially gross breach of duty and inability to manage the company properly.

§ 39
Anmeldung der Geschäftsführer

(1) Jede Änderung in den Personen der Geschäftsführer sowie die Beendigung der Vertretungsbefugnis eines Geschäftsführers ist zur Eintragung in das Handelsregister anzumelden.

(2) Der Anmeldung sind die Urkunden über die Bestellung der Geschäftsführer oder über die Beendigung der Vertretungsbefugnis in Urschrift oder öffentlich beglaubigter Abschrift beizufügen.

(3) [1]Die neuen Geschäftsführer haben in der Anmeldung zu versichern, dass keine Umstände vorliegen, die ihrer Bestellung nach § 6 Abs. 2 Satz 2 Nr. 2 und 3 sowie Satz 3 entgegenstehen und dass sie über ihre unbeschränkte Auskunftspflicht gegenüber dem Gericht belehrt worden sind. [2]§ 8 Abs. 3 Satz 2 ist anzuwenden.

Section 39
Filing for Registration of the Managing Directors

(1) Every change in the managing directors as well as the termination of a managing director's power of representation must be filed for registration in the commercial register.

(2) There must be attached to the filing the documents recording the appointment of the managing director or the termination of the power of representation in original or as officially authenticated copies.

(3) [1]The new managing directors must confirm in the filing that no circumstances exist which would hinder their appointment pursuant to section 6 (2) sentence 2 nos. 2 and 3, as well as sentence 3. and that they have been duly advised of their unrestricted duty to provide information to the court. [2]Section 8 (3) sentence 2 applies.

§ 43
Haftung der Geschäftsführer

(1) Die Geschäftsführer haben in den Angelegenheiten der Gesellschaft die Sorgfalt eines ordentlichen Geschäftsmannes anzuwenden.

(2) Geschäftsführer, welche ihre Obliegenheiten verletzen, haften der Gesellschaft solidarisch für den entstandenen Schaden.

(3) [1]Insbesondere sind sie zum Ersatz verpflichtet, wenn den Bestimmungen des § 30 zuwider Zahlungen aus dem zur Erhaltung des Stammkapitals erforderlichen Vermögen der Gesellschaft gemacht oder den Bestimmungen des § 33 zuwider eigene Geschäftsanteile der Gesellschaft erworben worden sind. [2]Auf den Ersatzanspruch finden die Bestimmungen in § 9b Abs. 1 entsprechende Anwendung. [3]Soweit der Ersatz zur Befriedigung der Gläubiger der Gesellschaft erforderlich ist, wird die Verpflichtung der Geschäftsführer da-

Section 43
Liability of the Managing Directors

(1) The managing directors shall apply in the affairs of the company the care of a prudent businessman.

(2) Managing directors who are in breach of their duties are jointly and severally liable to the company for damages sustained.

(3) [1]They have especially an obligation to pay compensation if, in contravention of the provisions of section 30, payments have been made out of company assets required to preserve the registered share capital or if, in contravention of the provisions of section 33, the company has acquired its own shares. [2]The provisions of section 9b (1) apply *mutatis mutandis* to the claim for compensation. [3]To the extent that the compensation is required to satisfy the company's creditors, the managing directors' obligation is not cancelled by

durch nicht aufgehoben, dass dieselben in Befolgung eines Beschlusses der Gesellschafter gehandelt haben.

(4) Die Ansprüche auf Grund der vorstehenden Bestimmungen verjähren in fünf Jahren.

the fact that they acted in accordance with a shareholders' resolution.

(4) Claims based on the foregoing provisions are barred by statute after five years.

§ 43a
Kreditgewährung aus Gesellschaftsvermögen

¹Den Geschäftsführern, anderen gesetzlichen Vertretern, Prokuristen oder zum gesamten Geschäftsbetrieb ermächtigten Handlungsbevollmächtigten darf Kredit nicht aus dem zur Erhaltung des Stammkapitals erforderlichen Vermögen der Gesellschaft gewährt werden. ²Ein entgegen Satz 1 gewährter Kredit ist ohne Rücksicht auf entgegenstehende Vereinbarungen sofort zurückzugewähren.

Section 43a
Granting of Loans from Company Assets

¹Company assets required to preserve the share capital may not be used to grant loans to managing directors, other legal representatives, holders of general signing powers and authorized signatories with powers extending to the whole business. ²Loans extended in contravention of sentence 1 are repayable immediately regardless of any agreement to the contrary.

§ 44
Stellvertreter von Geschäftsführern

Die für die Geschäftsführer gegebenen Vorschriften gelten auch für Stellvertreter von Geschäftsführern.

Section 44
Deputy Managing Directors

The provisions relating to managing directors also apply to deputy managing directors.

§ 45
Rechte der Gesellschafter

(1) Die Rechte, welche den Gesellschaftern in den Angelegenheiten der Gesellschaft, insbesondere in Bezug auf die Führung der Geschäfte zustehen, sowie die Ausübung derselben bestimmen sich, soweit nicht gesetzliche Vorschriften entgegenstehen, nach dem Gesellschaftsvertrag.

(2) In Ermangelung besonderer Bestimmungen des Gesellschaftsvertrags finden die Vorschriften der §§ 46 bis 51 Anwendung

Section 45
Rights of the Shareholders

(1) The shareholders' rights in relation to the affairs of the company, especially as regards the management of the business, and how these rights are to be exercised, are governed by the articles of association, unless statutory provisions provide otherwise.

(2) In the absence of specific provisions in the articles of association, the regulations set out in sections 46 to 51 apply.

§ 46
Aufgabenkreis der Gesellschafter

Der Bestimmung der Gesellschafter unterliegen:

Section 46
Subject of Shareholders' Resolutions

Shareholders' resolutions are required for the following:

1. die Feststellung des Jahresabschlusses und die Verwendung des Ergebnisses;	1. approval of the annual financial statements and use of results;
1a. die Entscheidung über die Offenlegung eines Einzelabschlusses nach internationalen Rechnungslegungsstandards (§ 325 Abs. 2a des Handelsgesetzbuchs) und über die Billigung des von den Geschäftsführern aufgestellten Abschlusses;	1a. decision on the disclosure of an individual financial statement according to international accounting standards (section 325 (2a) of the German Commercial Code) and on the approval of the financial statement prepared by the managing directors;
1b. die Billigung eines von den Geschäftsführern aufgestellten Konzernabschlusses;	1b. approval of a group financial statement prepared by the managing directors;
2. die Einforderung der Einlagen;	2. calls for payment of the capital contributions;
3. die Rückzahlung von Nachschüssen;	3. repayment of additional contributions;
4. die Teilung, Zusammenlegung sowie die Einziehung von Geschäftsanteilen;	4. partition, consolidation and redemption of shares;
5. die Bestellung und die Abberufung von Geschäftsführern sowie die Entlastung derselben;	5. appointment and removal of managing directors as well as formal approval of their conduct of the business;
6. die Maßregeln zur Prüfung und Überwachung der Geschäftsführung;	6. measures to check and supervise management;
7. die Bestellung von Prokuristen und von Handlungsbevollmächtigten zum gesamten Geschäftsbetrieb;	7. appointment of holders of general signing powers and of authorized signatories with powers extending to the whole business;
8. die Geltendmachung von Ersatzansprüchen, welche der Gesellschaft aus der Gründung oder Geschäftsführung gegen Geschäftsführer oder Gesellschafter zustehen, sowie die Vertretung der Gesellschaft in Prozessen, welche sie gegen die Geschäftsführer zu führen hat.	8. lodging the company's claims for compensation vis-à-vis managing directors or shareholders connected with the formation or management, and representing the company in lawsuits against the managing directors.

§ 47
Abstimmung

Section 47
Voting

(1) Die von den Gesellschaftern in den Angelegenheiten der Gesellschaft zu treffenden Bestimmungen erfolgen durch Beschlussfassung nach der Mehrheit der abgegebenen Stimmen.

(1) The decisions to be made by the shareholders on company affairs shall be effected by resolutions passed by a majority of the votes cast.

(2) Jeder Euro eines Geschäftsanteils gewährt eine Stimme.

(2) Each euro of a share grants one vote.

(3) Vollmachten bedürfen zu ihrer Gültigkeit der Textform.

(3) Proxies must be in writing in order to be valid.

(4) ¹Ein Gesellschafter, welcher durch die Beschlussfassung entlastet oder von einer Verbindlichkeit befreit werden soll, hat hierbei kein Stimmrecht und darf ein solches auch nicht für andere ausüben. ²Dasselbe gilt von einer Beschlussfassung, welche die Vornahme eines Rechtsgeschäfts oder die Einleitung oder Erledigung eines Rechtsstreits gegenüber einem Gesellschafter betrifft.

(4) ¹A shareholder may not vote or exercise voting powers on behalf of others where a resolution is to be passed to formally approve his conduct of business or release him from a liability. ²The same applies for a resolution relating to the conclusion of a legal transaction or to the initiation or termination of a lawsuit against a shareholder.

§ 48
Gesellschafterversammlung

(1) Die Beschlüsse der Gesellschafter werden in Versammlungen gefasst.

(2) Der Abhaltung einer Versammlung bedarf es nicht, wenn sämtliche Gesellschafter in Textform mit der zu treffenden Bestimmung oder mit der schriftlichen Abgabe der Stimmen sich einverstanden erklären.

(3) Befinden sich alle Geschäftsanteile der Gesellschaft in der Hand eines Gesellschafters oder daneben in der Hand der Gesellschaft, so hat er unverzüglich nach der Beschlussfassung eine Niederschrift aufzunehmen und zu unterschreiben.

Section 48
Shareholders' Meetings

(1) Shareholders' resolutions are passed at meetings.

(2) A meeting need not be held if all of the shareholders declare in writing their agreement with the decision to be taken or with the casting of votes by written ballot.

(3) If all of the company's shares are held by one shareholder or by one shareholder and the company, he must prepare and sign minutes without undue delay after the resolution is passed.

§ 49
Einberufung der Versammlung

(1) Die Versammlung der Gesellschafter wird durch die Geschäftsführer berufen.

(2) Sie ist außer den ausdrücklich bestimmten Fällen zu berufen, wenn es im Interesse der Gesellschaft erforderlich erscheint.

(3) Insbesondere muss die Versammlung unverzüglich berufen werden, wenn aus der Jahresbilanz oder aus einer im Laufe des Geschäftsjahres aufgestellten Bilanz sich ergibt, dass die Hälfte des Stammkapitals verloren ist.

Section 49
Convening Shareholders' Meetings

(1) Shareholders' meetings are convened by the managing directors.

(2) In addition to the cases expressly provided for, they shall be convened where it appears necessary in the interest of the company.

(3) In particular, a shareholders' meeting shall be convened without delay if it is apparent from the annual financial statements or from a balance sheet prepared at an interim date that one-half of the registered share capital is lost.

XXI. Stock Corporation Act (Aktiengesetz – AktG)

of 6 September 1965 (Federal Law Gazette I p. 1089)

in the amended version of 31 July 2009

(excerpts)

Chapter 1
Management Board

Section 76
Management of the Stock Corporation

(1) The management board shall manage the company on its own responsibility.

(2) ¹The management board may comprise one or more persons. ²In the case of companies with a share capital of over three million euro, the management board shall comprise no less than two persons; unless the articles provide for it to consist of one person. ³The provisions governing the appointment of a labor relations director to the management board shall remain unaffected.

(3) ¹Only a natural person with full legal capacity may be a management board member. ²A person cannot be a management board member who

1. as a ward is subject in whole or in part to a reservation of consent in the handling of his or her financial affairs (section 1903 of the German Civil Code),

2. has been prohibited from engaging in an occupation, a line of work, a business or a line of business due to a court judgment or an enforceable decision by an administrative authority if and to the extent that such prohibition corresponds in full or in part to the company's object,

3. wegen einer oder mehrerer vorsätzlich begangener Straftaten
   a) des Unterlassens der Stellung des Antrags auf Eröffnung des Insolvenzverfahrens (Insolvenzverschleppung),
   b) nach den §§ 283 bis 283d des Strafgesetzbuchs (Insolvenzstraftaten),
   c) der falschen Angaben nach § 399 dieses Gesetzes oder § 82 des Gesetzes betreffend die Gesellschaften mit beschränkter Haftung,
   d) der unrichtigen Darstellung nach § 400 dieses Gesetzes, § 331 des Handelsgesetzbuchs, § 313 des Umwandlungsgesetzes oder § 17 des Publizitätsgesetzes,
   e) nach den §§ 263 bis 264a oder den §§ 265b bis 266a des Strafgesetzbuchs zu einer Freiheitsstrafe von mindestens einem Jahr

verurteilt worden ist; dieser Ausschluss gilt für die Dauer von fünf Jahren seit der Rechtskraft des Urteils, wobei die Zeit nicht eingerechnet wird, in welcher der Täter auf behördliche Anordnung in einer Anstalt verwahrt worden ist.

Satz 2 Nr. 3 gilt entsprechend bei einer Verurteilung im Ausland wegen einer Tat, die mit den in Satz 2 Nr. 3 genannten Taten vergleichbar ist.

3. has been convicted of one or more intentional offenses involving
   a) a failure to file a petition for the opening of insolvency proceedings (delay in filing for insolvency),
   b) pursuant to sections 283 to 283d of the German Criminal Code (Strafgesetzbuch) (insolvency offences),
   c) the making of false statements pursuant to section 399 of this Act or section 82 of the Limited Liability Companies Act,
   d) the making of misrepresentations pursuant to section 400 of this Act, section 331 of the German Commercial Code (Handelsgesetzbuch), section 313 of the Transformations Act (Umwandlungsgesetz) or section 17 of the Disclosure Act (Publizitätsgesetz),
   e) pursuant to sections 263 to 264a or sections 265b to 266a of the German Criminal Code and sentenced to imprisonment for at least one year;

this exclusion shall apply for a period of five years from the date of the final conviction, not counting the duration of the perpetrator's confinement to an institution by order of the authorities.

Sentence 2 no. 3 applies *mutatis mutandis* to a conviction in a foreign jurisdiction of offences which are comparable to those offences designated in sentence 2 no 3.

§ 77
Geschäftsführung

(1) ¹Besteht der Vorstand aus mehreren Personen, so sind sämtliche Vorstandsmitglieder nur gemeinschaftlich zur Geschäftsführung befugt. ²Die Satzung oder die Geschäftsordnung des Vorstands kann Abweichendes bestimmen; es kann jedoch nicht bestimmt werden, dass ein oder mehrere Vorstandsmitglieder Meinungsverschiedenheiten im

Section 77
Management

(1) ¹If the management board comprises more than one person, the management board members may only manage the company jointly. ²The articles of association or the rules of procedure for the management board may provide otherwise; however, they may not provide that one or more management board members can resolve differences of opi-

Vorstand gegen die Mehrheit seiner Mitglieder entscheiden.

(2) ¹Der Vorstand kann sich eine Geschäftsordnung geben, wenn nicht die Satzung den Erlass der Geschäftsordnung dem Aufsichtsrat übertragen hat oder der Aufsichtsrat eine Geschäftsordnung für den Vorstand erlässt. ²Die Satzung kann Einzelfragen der Geschäftsordnung bindend regeln. ³Beschlüsse des Vorstands über die Geschäftsordnung müssen einstimmig gefasst werden.

nion within the management board against the majority of its members.

(2) ¹The management board may issue rules of procedure for itself unless the articles of association confer the authority to issue such rules of procedure upon the supervisory board or the supervisory board issues rules of procedure for the management board. ²The articles of association may contain binding provisions regarding specific matters concerning the rules of procedure. ³Resolutions by the management board regarding the rules of procedure shall require a unanimous vote.

§ 78
Vertretung

Section 78
Representation

(1) Der Vorstand vertritt die Gesellschaft gerichtlich und außergerichtlich. Hat eine Gesellschaft keinen Vorstand (Führungslosigkeit), wird die Gesellschaft für den Fall, dass ihr gegenüber Willenserklärungen abgegeben oder Schriftstücke zugestellt werden, durch den Aufsichtsrat vertreten.

(1) The management board shall represent the company in and out of court. If a company does not have a management board (leaderlessness), where declarations of intent are rendered to it or documents are served to it, the company shall be represented by the supervisory board.

(2) ¹Besteht der Vorstand aus mehreren Personen, so sind, wenn die Satzung nichts anderes bestimmt, sämtliche Vorstandsmitglieder nur gemeinschaftlich zur Vertretung der Gesellschaft befugt. ²Ist eine Willenserklärung gegenüber der Gesellschaft abzugeben, so genügt die Abgabe gegenüber einem Vorstandsmitglied oder im Fall des Absatzes 1 Satz 2 gegenüber einem Aufsichtsratsmitglied. ³An die Vertreter der Gesellschaft nach Absatz 1 können unter der im Handelsregister eingetragenen Geschäftsanschrift Willenserklärungen gegenüber der Gesellschaft abgegeben und Schriftstücke für die Gesellschaft zugestellt werden. Unabhängig hiervon können die Abgabe und die Zustellung auch unter der eingetragenen Anschrift der empfangsberechtigten Person nach § 39 Abs. 1 Satz 2 erfolgen.

(2) ¹If the management board comprises more than one person, the management board members shall represent the company jointly, unless the articles of association provide otherwise. ²If a declaration of intent is to be rendered to the company, it shall suffice if it is rendered to a management board member or, in the case of subsection (1) sentence 2, a supervisory board member. ³Declarations of intent and documents can be served to the representatives of the company pursuant to subsection (1) for the company at the business address recorded in the Commercial Register. ⁴Independent of this, the submission and service can also be effected at the registered address of the persons authorized to take receipt pursuant to section 39 (1) sentence 2.

(3) ¹Die Satzung kann auch bestimmen, dass einzelne Vorstandsmitglieder allein oder in Gemeinschaft mit einem Prokuristen zur Vertretung der Gesellschaft befugt sind. ²Dasselbe kann der Aufsichtsrat bestimmen, wenn die Satzung ihn hierzu ermächtigt hat. Absatz 2 Satz 2 gilt in diesen Fällen sinngemäß.

(4) ¹Zur Gesamtvertretung befugte Vorstandsmitglieder können einzelne von ihnen zur Vornahme bestimmter Geschäfte oder bestimmter Arten von Geschäften ermächtigen. ²Dies gilt sinngemäß, wenn ein einzelnes Vorstandsmitglied in Gemeinschaft mit einem Prokuristen zur Vertretung der Gesellschaft befugt ist.

(3) ¹The articles of association may also provide that particular management board members can represent the company by acting either alone or jointly with a procuration officer *(Prokurist)*. ²The supervisory board may also provide this if authorized to do so by the articles of association. ³Subsection (2) sentence 2 shall apply analogously in such cases.

(4) ¹Management board members authorized to represent the company jointly may authorize individual members to engage in certain transactions or kinds of transactions. ²The same shall apply analogously if a management board member is authorized to represent the company by acting jointly with a procuration officer.

§ 79
Zeichnung durch Vorstandsmitglieder

(weggefallen)

Section 79
Signatures of Management Board Members

(repealed)

§ 80
Angaben auf Geschäftsbriefen

(1) ¹Auf allen Geschäftsbriefen gleichviel welcher Form, die an einen bestimmten Empfänger gerichtet werden, müssen die Rechtsform und der Sitz der Gesellschaft, das Registergericht des Sitzes der Gesellschaft und die Nummer, unter der die Gesellschaft in das Handelsregister eingetragen ist, sowie alle Vorstandsmitglieder und der Vorsitzende des Aufsichtsrats mit dem Familiennamen und mindestens einem ausgeschriebenen Vornamen angegeben werden. ²Der Vorsitzende des Vorstands ist als solcher zu bezeichnen. ³Werden Angaben über das Kapital der Gesellschaft gemacht, so müssen in jedem Fall das Grundkapital sowie, wenn auf die Aktien der Ausgabebetrag nicht vollständig eingezahlt ist, der Gesamtbetrag der ausstehenden Einlagen angegeben werden.

Section 80
Business Letters

(1) ¹All business letters, regardless of their form, directed to a specific recipient shall state the company's legal form and seat, the court of registration of the company's seat, the number under which the company has been registered in the Commercial Register, and the last name and at least one first name written in full of each management board member and the chairman of the supervisory board. ²The chairman of the management board shall be designated as such. ³If information is provided regarding the company's capital, the amount of the share capital shall in any event be stated and, if the issue price has not been fully paid in, the aggregate amount of the outstanding contributions.

(2) Der Angaben nach Absatz 1 Satz 1 und 2 bedarf es nicht bei Mitteilungen oder Berichten, die im Rahmen einer bestehenden Geschäftsverbindung ergehen und für die üblicherweise Vordrucke verwendet werden, in denen lediglich die im Einzelfall erforderlichen besonderen Angaben eingefügt zu werden brauchen.

(3) ¹Bestellscheine gelten als Geschäftsbriefe im Sinne des Absatzes 1. ²Absatz 2 ist auf sie nicht anzuwenden.

(4) ¹Auf allen Geschäftsbriefen und Bestellscheinen, die von einer Zweigniederlassung einer Aktiengesellschaft mit Sitz im Ausland verwendet werden, müssen das Register, bei dem die Zweigniederlassung geführt wird, und die Nummer des Registereintrags angegeben werden; im übrigen gelten die Vorschriften der Absätze 1 bis 3 für die Angaben bezüglich der Haupt- und der Zweigniederlassung, soweit nicht das ausländische Recht Abweichungen nötig macht. ²Befindet sich die ausländische Gesellschaft in Abwicklung, so sind auch diese Tatsache sowie alle Abwickler anzugeben.

(2) The information pursuant to subsection (1) sentences 1 and 2 need not be provided in communications or reports which are made in the course of an existing business relationship and for which printed forms are customarily used in which only the particulars of the specific transaction need be inserted.

(3) Order forms shall be deemed to be business letters within the meaning of subsection (1). Subsection (2) shall not apply to such order forms.

(4) ¹All business letters and order forms which are used by a branch of a stock corporation having its seat outside of Germany shall state the commercial register into which the branch has been entered and the registration number; in all other respects the provisions of subsections (1) to (3) for the information regarding the principal place of business and the branch shall apply except where otherwise required by the foreign law. ²If the foreign company is in the process of liquidation, this fact and the names all liquidators must also be stated.

§ 81
Änderung des Vorstands und der Vertretungsbefugnis seiner Mitglieder

(1) Jede Änderung des Vorstands oder der Vertretungsbefugnis eines Vorstandsmitglieds hat der Vorstand zur Eintragung in das Handelsregister anzumelden.

(2) Der Anmeldung sind die Urkunden über die Änderung in Urschrift oder öffentlich beglaubigter Abschrift beizufügen.

(3) ¹Die neuen Vorstandsmitglieder haben in der Anmeldung zu versichern, dass keine Umstände vorliegen, die ihre Bestellung nach § 76 Abs. 3 Satz 2 Nr. 2 und 3 sowie Satz 3 entgegenstehen, und dass sie über

Section 81
Change in the Management Board and in the Authority of its Members to Represent the Company

(1) The management board shall apply for entry into the commercial register of any change in the management board or in the authority of a management board member to represent the company.

(2) The originals or officially certified copies of the documents concerning such change shall be appended to the application.

(3) ¹New management board members shall certify in the application that no circumstances exist which preclude their appointment pursuant to section 76 (3) sentence 2 nos. 2 and 3, as well as sentence 3 and that they have been advised

ihre unbeschränkte Auskunftspflicht gegenüber dem Gericht belehrt worden sind. ²§ 37 Abs. 2 Satz 2 ist anzuwenden.

(4) *(weggefallen)*

of their obligation to make full disclosure to the court. ²Section 37 (2) sentence 2 shall apply.

(4) *(repealed)*

§ 82
Beschränkungen der Vertretungs- und Geschäftsführungsbefugnis

(1) Die Vertretungsbefugnis des Vorstands kann nicht beschränkt werden.

(2) Im Verhältnis der Vorstandsmitglieder zur Gesellschaft sind diese verpflichtet, die Beschränkungen einzuhalten, die im Rahmen der Vorschriften über die Aktiengesellschaft die Satzung, der Aufsichtsrat, die Hauptversammlung und die Geschäftsordnungen des Vorstands und des Aufsichtsrats für die Geschäftsführungsbefugnis getroffen haben.

Section 82
Restrictions on the Authority to Represent and Manage

(1) The management board's authority to represent the company may not be restricted.

(2) The management board members shall be obligated vis-à-vis the company to comply with the restrictions regarding their authority to manage the company which, in accordance with the provisions governing stock corporations, are imposed by the articles of association, the supervisory board, the shareholders' meeting and the rules of procedure for the management board and the supervisory board.

§ 83
Vorbereitung und Ausführung von Hauptversammlungsbeschlüssen

(1) ¹Der Vorstand ist auf Verlangen der Hauptversammlung verpflichtet, Maßnahmen, die in die Zuständigkeit der Hauptversammlung fallen, vorzubereiten. ²Das gleiche gilt für die Vorbereitung und den Abschluss von Verträgen, die nur mit Zustimmung der Hauptversammlung wirksam werden. ³Der Beschluss der Hauptversammlung bedarf der Mehrheiten, die für die Maßnahmen oder für die Zustimmung zu dem Vertrag erforderlich sind.

(2) Der Vorstand ist verpflichtet, die von der Hauptversammlung im Rahmen ihrer Zuständigkeit beschlossenen Maßnahmen auszuführen.

Section 83
Preparation and Execution of Resolutions of Shareholders' Meeting

(1) ¹The management board shall, at the request of the shareholders' meeting, prepare any matter falling within the competence of the shareholders' meeting. ²The same shall apply to the preparation and execution of agreements which will become effective only with the consent of the shareholders' meeting. ³The resolution of the shareholders' meeting shall require the same majority as is required for the resolution on the respective matter or, for the granting of consent to such agreements.

(2) The management board shall be obligated to execute any resolution adopted by the shareholders' meeting with respect to matters falling within the competence of the shareholders' meeting.

§ 84
Bestellung und Abberufung des Vorstands

(1) ¹Vorstandsmitglieder bestellt der Aufsichtsrat auf höchstens fünf Jahre. ²Eine wiederholte Bestellung oder Verlängerung der Amtszeit, jeweils für höchstens fünf Jahre, ist zulässig. ³Sie bedarf eines erneuten Aufsichtsratsbeschlusses, der frühestens ein Jahr vor Ablauf der bisherigen Amtszeit gefasst werden kann. ⁴Nur bei einer Bestellung auf weniger als fünf Jahre kann eine Verlängerung der Amtszeit ohne neuen Aufsichtsratsbeschluss vorgesehen werden, sofern dadurch die gesamte Amtszeit nicht mehr als fünf Jahre beträgt. ⁵Dies gilt sinngemäß für den Anstellungsvertrag; er kann jedoch vorsehen, dass er für den Fall einer Verlängerung der Amtszeit bis zu deren Ablauf weiter gilt.

(2) Werden mehrere Personen zu Vorstandsmitgliedern bestellt, so kann der Aufsichtsrat ein Mitglied zum Vorsitzenden des Vorstands ernennen.

(3) ¹Der Aufsichtsrat kann die Bestellung zum Vorstandsmitglied und die Ernennung zum Vorsitzenden des Vorstands widerrufen, wenn ein wichtiger Grund vorliegt. ²Ein solcher Grund ist namentlich grobe Pflichtverletzung, Unfähigkeit zur ordnungsmäßigen Geschäftsführung oder Vertrauensentzug durch die Hauptversammlung, es sei denn, dass das Vertrauen aus offenbar unsachlichen Gründen entzogen worden ist. ³Dies gilt auch für den vom ersten Aufsichtsrat bestellten Vorstand. ⁴Der Widerruf ist wirksam, bis seine Unwirksamkeit rechtskräftig festgestellt ist. ⁵Für die Ansprüche aus dem Anstellungsvertrag gelten die allgemeinen Vorschriften.

Section 84
Appointment and Removal of the Management Board

(1) ¹The supervisory board shall appoint the management board members for a term not exceeding five years. ²Such appointment may be renewed or the term of office may be extended, provided that the term of each such renewal or extension does not exceed five years. ³Such renewal or extension shall require a new supervisory board resolution which may be adopted no earlier than one year before the current term of office expires. ⁴The term of office may only be extended without a new supervisory board resolution if the appointment was for a term of less than five years, provided that the aggregate term of office will not, as a result of such extension, exceed five years. ⁵The same shall apply analogously to the service agreement; such agreement may, however, provide that in the event of an extension of the term of office, the agreement will continue in effect until the expiration of such term.

(2) If more than one person is appointed as management board member, the supervisory board may appoint one of the members as the chairman of the management board.

(3) ¹The supervisory board may revoke the appointment of a management board member or the appointment of a member as chairman of the management board for cause (*wichtiger Grund*). ²Such cause shall in particular include a gross breach of duty, inability to manage the company properly, or a vote of no-confidence by the shareholders' meeting, unless such vote of no-confidence was passed for manifestly arbitrary reasons. ³The same shall also apply to the management board appointed by the first supervisory board. ⁴Such revocation shall be valid until rendered invalid by a judicial decision which has become final and can no longer be appealed. ⁵Rights arising under the service agree-

(4) Die Vorschriften des Gesetzes über die Mitbestimmung der Arbeitnehmer in den Aufsichtsräten und Vorständen der Unternehmen des Bergbaus und der Eisen und Stahl erzeugenden Industrie vom 21. Mai 1951 (Bundesgesetzbl. I S. 347) – Montan-Mitbestimmungsgesetz – über die besonderen Mehrheitserfordernisse für einen Aufsichtsratsbeschluss über die Bestellung eines Arbeitsdirektors oder den Widerruf seiner Bestellung bleiben unberührt.

(4) [1] The provisions of the Act on the Codetermination of Employees in the Supervisory Board and Management Boards in the Mining and Iron and Steel Producing Industries of 21 May 1951 (Federal Law Gazette I p. 347) – the "Coal and Steel Codetermination Act" *(Montan-Mitbestimmungsgesetz)* – regarding the special majority requirements for resolutions of the supervisory board on the appointment of a labor relations director to the management board or the revocation of such appointment shall remain unaffected.

§ 85
Bestellung durch das Gericht

(1) [1] Fehlt ein erforderliches Vorstandsmitglied, so hat in dringenden Fällen das Gericht auf Antrag eines Beteiligten das Mitglied zu bestellen. [2] Gegen die Entscheidung ist die Beschwerde zulässig.

(2) Das Amt des gerichtlich bestellten Vorstandsmitglieds erlischt in jedem Fall, sobald der Mangel behoben ist.

(3) [1] Das gerichtlich bestellte Vorstandsmitglied hat Anspruch auf Ersatz angemessener barer Auslagen und auf Vergütung für seine Tätigkeit. [2] Einigen sich das gerichtlich bestellte Vorstandsmitglied und die Gesellschaft nicht, so setzt das Gericht die Auslagen und die Vergütung fest. [3] Gegen die Entscheidung ist die Beschwerde zulässig; die Rechtsbeschwerde ist ausgeschlossen. Aus der rechtskräftigen Entscheidung findet die Zwangsvollstreckung nach der Zivilprozessordnung statt.

Section 85
Appointment by the Court

(1) [1] If the management board does not have the requisite number of members, the court shall, in urgent cases, make the necessary appointments upon application by one of the parties concerned. [2] A complaint may be lodged against such decisions.

(2) The office of a court-appointed management board member shall in any case expire as soon as the vacancy has been filled.

(3) [1] The court-appointed management board member shall be entitled to reimbursement for reasonable cash expenses and remuneration for his services. [2] If the court-appointed management board member and the company do not reach agreement, the court shall fix the amount of the expenses and remuneration. [3] A complaint may be lodged against this decision; a complaint on points of law only is barred. [5] A final and non-appealable decision may be enforced in accordance with the provisions of the Code of Civil Procedure *(Zivilprozessordnung)*.

§ 86
Gewinnbeteiligung der Vorstandsmitglieder

(weggefallen)

Section 86
Participation in Profits by Management Board Members

(repealed)

§ 87
Grundsätze für die Bezüge der Vorstandsmitglieder

(1) ¹Der Aufsichtsrat hat bei der Festsetzung der Gesamtbezüge des einzelnen Vorstandsmitglieds (Gehalt, Gewinnbeteiligungen, Aufwandsentschädigungen, Versicherungsentgelte, Provisionen, anreizorientierte Vergütungszusagen wie zum Beispiel Aktienbezugsrechte und Nebenleistungen jeder Art) dafür zu sorgen, dass diese in einem angemessenen Verhältnis zu den Aufgaben und Leistungen des Vorstandsmitglieds sowie zur Lage der Gesellschaft stehen und die übliche Vergütung nicht ohne besondere Gründe übersteigen. Die Vergütungsstruktur ist bei börsennotierten Gesellschaften auf eine nachhaltige Unternehmensentwicklung auszurichten. Variable Vergütungsbestandteile sollen daher eine mehrjährige Bemessungsgrundlage haben; für außerordentliche Entwicklungen soll der Aufsichtsrat eine Begrenzungsmöglichkeit vereinbaren. ²Satz 1 gilt sinngemäß für Ruhegehalt, Hinterbliebenenbezüge und Leistungen verwandter Art.

(2) ¹Verschlechtert sich die Lage der Gesellschaft nach der Festsetzung so, dass die Weitergewährung der Bezüge nach Absatz 1 unbillig für die Gesellschaft wäre, so soll der Aufsichtsrat oder im Falle des § 85 Abs. 3 das Gericht auf Antrag des Aufsichtsrats die Bezüge auf die angemessene Höhe herabsetzen. ²Ruhegehalt, Hinterbliebenenbezüge und Leistungen verwandter Art können nur in den ersten drei Jahren nach Ausscheiden aus der Gesellschaft nach Satz 1 herabgesetzt werden.. ³Durch eine Herabsetzung wird der Anstellungsvertrag im übrigen nicht berührt. ⁴Das Vorstandsmitglied kann jedoch seinen Anstellungsvertrag für den Schluss des nächsten Kalendervierteljahrs mit einer Kündigungsfrist von sechs Wochen kündigen.

Section 87
Principles Governing Remuneration of Management Board Members

(1) ¹The supervisory board shall, in determining the aggregate remuneration of any management board member (salary, profit participation, reimbursement of expenses, insurance premiums, commissions, incentive-oriented remuneration commitments, such as stock options, for example, and additional benefits of any kind), ensure that it bears a reasonable relationship to such member's duties and performance, as well as the condition of the company and do not exceed the customary remuneration without special grounds for doing so. At listed companies, the remuneration structure must be geared towards sustainable company development. Variable remuneration components should therefore be based on a multi-year assessment; in the event of extraordinary developments, the supervisory board should agree on a compensation cap. ² Sentence 1 shall apply analogously to retirement pay, benefits to surviving dependents and similar payments.

(2) ¹Should the condition of the company deteriorate following this determination such that continuation of payment of the remuneration pursuant to in subsection (1) would be inequitable to the company, the supervisory board, or, in the case of section 85 (3), the court upon application by the supervisory board, should reduce the remuneration to an appropriate amount. ²Retirement pay, benefits to surviving dependents and similar payments can only be reduced pursuant to sentence 1 in the first three years after resignation from the company. Such reduction shall not affect the other terms of the service agreement. ³The management board member may, however, terminate his service agreement of the end of the next calendar quarter upon giving six weeks' notice.

(3) Wird über das Vermögen der Gesellschaft das Insolvenzverfahren eröffnet und kündigt der Insolvenzverwalter den Anstellungsvertrag eines Vorstandsmitglieds, so kann es Ersatz für den Schaden, der ihm durch die Aufhebung des Dienstverhältnisses entsteht, nur für zwei Jahre seit dem Ablauf des Dienstverhältnisses verlangen.

§ 88
Wettbewerbsverbot

(1) [1]Die Vorstandsmitglieder dürfen ohne Einwilligung des Aufsichtsrats weder ein Handelsgewerbe betreiben noch im Geschäftszweig der Gesellschaft für eigene oder fremde Rechnung Geschäfte machen. [2]Sie dürfen ohne Einwilligung auch nicht Mitglied des Vorstands oder Geschäftsführer oder persönlich haftender Gesellschafter einer anderen Handelsgesellschaft sein. [3]Die Einwilligung des Aufsichtsrats kann nur für bestimmte Handelsgewerbe oder Handelsgesellschaften oder für bestimmte Arten von Geschäften erteilt werden.

(2) [1]Verstößt ein Vorstandsmitglied gegen dieses Verbot, so kann die Gesellschaft Schadenersatz fordern. [2]Sie kann statt dessen von dem Mitglied verlangen, dass es die für eigene Rechnung gemachten Geschäfte als für Rechnung der Gesellschaft eingegangen gelten lässt und die aus Geschäften für fremde Rechnung bezogene Vergütung herausgibt oder seinen Anspruch auf die Vergütung abtritt.

(3) [1]Die Ansprüche der Gesellschaft verjähren in drei Monaten seit dem Zeitpunkt, in dem die übrigen Vorstandsmitglieder und die Aufsichtsratsmitglieder von der zum Schadensersatz verpflichtenden Handlung Kenntnis erlangen oder ohne grobe Fahrlässigkeit erlangen müssten. [2]Sie verjähren ohne Rücksicht auf diese Kenntnis oder grob fahrlässige Unkenntnis in fünf Jahren von ihrer Entstehung an.

(3) If insolvency proceedings have been instituted against the company's assets and the insolvency receiver has given notice of termination of a management board member's service agreement, such member may claim compensation for damage incurred as a result of such termination only for the two years following the termination.

Section 88
Prohibition of Competition

(1) [1]Management board members may not engage in any trade or enter into any transaction in the company's line of business on their own behalf or on behalf of others without the consent of the supervisory board. [2]Nor may they, without such consent, be a management board member, or a managing director or general partner of another commercial enterprise. [3]The supervisory board's consent may be granted only for a specific commercial enterprise, or for specific kinds of transactions.

(2) [1]If a management board member violates this prohibition, the company may claim damages. [2]Alternatively, the company may require that such member treat any transactions made on his own behalf as having been made on behalf of the company and surrender to the company any remuneration received for transactions made on behalf of another person or assign his rights to such remuneration.

(3) [1]The company's claims shall become statute barred three months after the date on which the other management board members and the supervisory board obtained knowledge of the act giving rise to the claim for damages or should have obtained such knowledge if they were not grossly negligent. [2]Irrespective of such knowledge or lack of knowledge due to gross negligence, such claims shall become statute barred five years after they have arisen.

§ 89
Kreditgewährung an Vorstandsmitglieder

(1) ¹Die Gesellschaft darf ihren Vorstandsmitgliedern Kredit nur auf Grund eines Beschlusses des Aufsichtsrats gewähren. ²Der Beschluss kann nur für bestimmte Kreditgeschäfte oder Arten von Kreditgeschäften und nicht für länger als drei Monate im voraus gefasst werden. ³Er hat die Verzinsung und Rückzahlung des Kredits zu regeln. ⁴Der Gewährung eines Kredits steht die Gestattung einer Entnahme gleich, die über die dem Vorstandsmitglied zustehenden Bezüge hinausgeht, namentlich auch die Gestattung der Entnahme von Vorschüssen auf Bezüge. ⁵Dies gilt nicht für Kredite, die ein Monatsgehalt nicht übersteigen.

(2) ¹Die Gesellschaft darf ihren Prokuristen und zum gesamten Geschäftsbetrieb ermächtigten Handlungsbevollmächtigten Kredit nur mit Einwilligung des Aufsichtsrats gewähren. ²Eine herrschende Gesellschaft darf Kredite an gesetzliche Vertreter, Prokuristen oder zum gesamten Geschäftsbetrieb ermächtigte Handlungsbevollmächtigte eines abhängigen Unternehmens nur mit Einwilligung ihres Aufsichtsrats, eine abhängige Gesellschaft darf Kredite an gesetzliche Vertreter, Prokuristen oder zum gesamten Geschäftsbetrieb ermächtigte Handlungsbevollmächtigte des herrschenden Unternehmens nur mit Einwilligung des Aufsichtsrats des herrschenden Unternehmens gewähren. ³Absatz 1 Satz 2 bis 5 gilt sinngemäß.

(3) ¹Absatz 2 gilt auch für Kredite an den Ehegatten, Lebenspartner oder an ein minderjähriges Kind eines Vorstandsmitglieds, eines anderen gesetzlichen Vertreters, eines Prokuristen oder eines zum gesamten Geschäftsbetrieb ermächtigten Handlungsbevollmächtigten. ²Er gilt ferner für Kredite

Section 89
Extension of Credit to Management Board Members

(1) ¹The company may only extend credit to management board members on the basis of a resolution adopted by the supervisory board. ²Such resolution may authorize only specific credit transactions or specific kinds of credit transactions, and not for more than three months in advance. ³Such resolution shall contain provisions regarding the payment of interest on, and repayment of, any loan. ⁴The granting of a loan shall be equivalent to the permission to make withdrawals in excess of the remuneration due to the management board member, including specifically permission to obtain advances on his remuneration. ⁵This shall not apply to loans, the amount of which does not exceed one month's salary.

(2) ¹The company may extend credit to its procuration officers and general managers (Handlungsbevollmächtigte) only with the consent of the supervisory board. ²A controlling company may extend credit to legal representatives, procuration officers or general managers of a controlled enterprise only with the consent of its supervisory board; a controlled company may extend credit to legal representatives, procuration officers or general managers of the controlling company only with the consent of the supervisory board of the controlling company. ³Subsection (1) sentences 2 to 5 shall apply analogously.

(3) ¹Para. (2) shall also apply with respect to credits to the spouse, life partner or a minor child of a management board member or other legal representatives, procuration officer or general manager. ²It shall also apply to credits granted to any third party acting on behalf of any such persons or on behalf of

an einen Dritten, der für Rechnung dieser Personen oder für Rechnung eines Vorstandsmitglieds, eines anderen gesetzlichen Vertreters, eines Prokuristen oder eines zum gesamten Geschäftsbetrieb ermächtigten Handlungsbevollmächtigten handelt.

(4) ¹Ist ein Vorstandsmitglied, ein Prokurist oder ein zum gesamten Geschäftsbetrieb ermächtigter Handlungsbevollmächtigter zugleich gesetzlicher Vertreter oder Mitglied des Aufsichtsrats einer anderen juristischen Person oder Gesellschafter einer Personenhandelsgesellschaft, so darf die Gesellschaft der juristischen Person oder der Personenhandelsgesellschaft Kredit nur mit Einwilligung des Aufsichtsrats gewähren; Absatz 1 Satz 2 und 3 gilt sinngemäß. ²Dies gilt nicht, wenn die juristische Person oder die Personenhandelsgesellschaft mit der Gesellschaft verbunden ist oder wenn der Kredit für die Bezahlung von Waren gewährt wird, welche die Gesellschaft der juristischen Person oder der Personenhandelsgesellschaft liefert.

(5) Wird entgegen den Absätzen 1 bis 4 Kredit gewährt, so ist der Kredit ohne Rücksicht auf entgegenstehende Vereinbarungen sofort zurückzugewähren, wenn nicht der Aufsichtsrat nachträglich zustimmt.

(6) Ist die Gesellschaft ein Kreditinstitut oder Finanzdienstleistungsinstitut, auf das § 15 des Gesetzes über das Kreditwesen anzuwenden ist, gelten anstelle der Absätze 1 bis 5 die Vorschriften des Gesetzes über das Kreditwesen.

a management board member, other legal representative, procuration officer or general manager.

(4) ¹If a management board member, procuration officer or general manager is also a legal representative or member of the supervisory board of another legal entity or member of a commercial partnership (*Personenhandelsgesellschaft*), the company may extend credit to such legal entity or commercial partnership only with the consent of the supervisory board; subsection (1) sentences 2 and 3 shall apply analogously. ²This shall not apply if such legal entity or commercial partnership is affiliated with the company or if the credit is extended to finance the payment of goods which the company supplies to such legal entity or commercial partnership.

(5) Any credit extended in violation of the provisions set forth in subsections (1) to (4) shall be repaid immediately, notwithstanding any agreement to the contrary, unless the supervisory board renders its subsequent consent.

(6) If the company is a bank or financial services institution to which section 15 of the Banking Act (*Gesetz über das Kreditwesen*) applies, the provisions of the Banking Act shall apply in lieu of subsections (1) to (5).

§ 90
Berichte an den Aufsichtsrat

(1) ¹Der Vorstand hat dem Aufsichtsrat zu berichten über

1. die beabsichtigte Geschäftspolitik und andere grundsätzliche Fragen der Unternehmensplanung (insbesondere die Finanz-, Investitions-

Section 90
Reports to the Supervisory Board

(1) ¹The management board shall report to the supervisory board on:

1. intended business policy and other essential matters regarding corporate planning (in particular the financial, investment and personnel planning),

und Personalplanung), wobei auf Abweichungen der tatsächlichen Entwicklung von früher berichteten Zielen unter Angabe von Gründen einzugehen ist;	whereby deviations of the actual development from the goals reported on earlier shall be discussed, stating the reasons for such deviation;
2. die Rentabilität der Gesellschaft, insbesondere die Rentabilität des Eigenkapitals;	2. the profitability of the company, in particular the return on equity;
3. den Gang der Geschäfte, insbesondere den Umsatz, und die Lage der Gesellschaft;	3. the progress of the business, in particular turnover, and the condition of the company;
4. Geschäfte, die für die Rentabilität oder Liquidität der Gesellschaft von erheblicher Bedeutung sein können.	4. transactions which may have a material impact upon the profitability or liquidity of the company.
Ist die Gesellschaft Mutterunternehmen (§ 290 Abs. 1, 2 des Handelsgesetzbuchs), so hat der Bericht auch auf Tochterunternehmen und auf Gemeinschaftsunternehmen (§ 310 Abs. 1 des Handelsgesetzbuchs) einzugehen. [2]Außerdem ist dem Vorsitzenden des Aufsichtsrats aus sonstigen wichtigen Anlässen zu berichten; als wichtiger Anlass ist auch ein dem Vorstand bekanntgewordener geschäftlicher Vorgang bei einem verbundenen Unternehmen anzusehen, der auf die Lage der Gesellschaft von erheblichem Einfluss sein kann.	[2]If the company is a parent company (section 290 (1) and (2) of the German Commercial Code), the report shall also discuss subsidiaries and joint ventures (section 310 (1) of the Commercial Code). [3]In addition, reports to the chairman of the supervisory board shall be made on the occasion of other significant events; a business transaction involving an affiliated enterprise which becomes known to the management board and which could have a material impact upon the condition of the company shall also be considered to be a significant event in this sense.
(2) Die Berichte nach Absatz 1 Satz 1 Nr. 1 bis 4 sind wie folgt zu erstatten:	(2) Reports pursuant to subsection (1) sentence 1 nos. 1 to 4 shall be made as follows:
1. die Berichte nach Nummer 1 mindestens einmal jährlich, wenn nicht Änderungen der Lage oder neue Fragen eine unverzügliche Berichterstattung gebieten;	1. reports pursuant to no. 1 not less than once a year, unless changes in circumstances or new issues necessitate an immediate report;
2. die Berichte nach Nummer 2 in der Sitzung des Aufsichtsrats, in der über den Jahresabschluss verhandelt wird;	2. reports pursuant to no. 2 at the supervisory board meeting to approve of the annual financial statements;
3. die Berichte nach Nummer 3 regelmäßig, mindestens vierteljährlich;	3. reports pursuant to no. 3 regularly, but not less than once per quarter;
4. die Berichte nach Nummer 4 möglichst so rechtzeitig, dass der Aufsichtsrat vor Vornahme der Geschäfte Gelegenheit hat, zu ihnen Stellung zu nehmen.	4. reports pursuant to no. 4 early enough, if possible, to enable the supervisory board to express its opinion before such transactions are entered into.
(3) [1]Der Aufsichtsrat kann vom Vorstand jederzeit einen Bericht verlangen	(3) [1]The supervisory board may at any time request a report from the manage-

über Angelegenheiten der Gesellschaft, über ihre rechtlichen und geschäftlichen Beziehungen zu verbundenen Unternehmen sowie über geschäftliche Vorgänge bei diesen Unternehmen, die auf die Lage der Gesellschaft von erheblichem Einfluss sein können. ²Auch ein einzelnes Mitglied kann einen Bericht, jedoch nur an den Aufsichtsrat, verlangen.

(4) ¹Die Berichte haben den Grundsätzen einer gewissenhaften und getreuen Rechenschaft zu entsprechen. ²Sie sind möglichst rechtzeitig und, mit Ausnahme des Berichts nach Absatz 1 Satz 3, in der Regel in Textform zu erstatten.

(5) ¹Jedes Aufsichtsratsmitglied hat das Recht, von den Berichten Kenntnis zu nehmen. ²Soweit die Berichte in Textform erstattet worden sind, sind sie auch jedem Aufsichtsratsmitglied auf Verlangen zu übermitteln, soweit der Aufsichtsrat nichts anderes beschlossen hat. ³Der Vorsitzende des Aufsichtsrats hat die Aufsichtsratsmitglieder über die Berichte nach Absatz 1 Satz 2 spätestens in der nächsten Aufsichtsratssitzung zu unterrichten.

ment board on the company's affairs, its legal and business relationships with affiliated companies and on the business transactions of such companies which may have a material impact upon the condition of the company. ²Individual members may also request such a report but only to the supervisory board.

(4) ¹The reports shall comply with the principles of conscientious and accurate reporting. ²They shall be prepared in a timely manner, if possible, and with the exception of the report pursuant to subsection (1) sentence 3, in text form as a rule.

(5) ¹Each supervisory board member shall have the right to take note of the reports. ²If the reports have been made in text form, they shall be conveyed to each supervisory board member upon demand, unless the supervisory board has resolved otherwise. ³The chairman of the supervisory board shall inform the supervisory board members of reports made pursuant to subsection (1) sentence 2 at the latest during the next supervisory board meeting.

§ 91
Organisation, Buchführung

(1) Der Vorstand hat dafür zu sorgen, dass die erforderlichen Handelsbücher geführt werden.

(2) Der Vorstand hat geeignete Maßnahmen zu treffen, insbesondere ein Überwachungssystem einzurichten, damit den Fortbestand der Gesellschaft gefährdende Entwicklungen früh erkannt werden.

Section 91
Organization, Accounting

(1) The management board shall ensure that the requisite commercial books of account are maintained.

(2) The management board shall take appropriate measures, in particular the installation of a monitoring system so that developments endangering the company's continued existence can be identified early.

§ 92
Vorstandspflichten bei Verlust, Überschuldung oder Zahlungsunfähigkeit

(1) Ergibt sich bei Aufstellung der Jahresbilanz oder einer Zwischenbilanz

Section 92
Duties of the Management Board in the Event of Losses, Overindebtedness or Insolvency

(1) ¹If upon preparation of the annual balance sheet or an interim balance

oder ist bei pflichtmäßigem Ermessen anzunehmen, dass ein Verlust in Höhe der Hälfte des Grundkapitals besteht, so hat der Vorstand unverzüglich die Hauptversammlung einzuberufen und ihr dies anzuzeigen.

(2) [1] Nachdem die Zahlungsunfähigkeit der Gesellschaft eingetreten ist oder sich ihre Überschuldung ergeben hat, darf der Vorstand keine Zahlungen leisten. [2] Dies gilt nicht von Zahlungen, die auch nach diesem Zeitpunkt mit der Sorgfalt eines ordentlichen und gewissenhaften Geschäftsleiters vereinbar sind. Die gleiche Verpflichtung trifft den Vorstand für Zahlungen an Aktionäre, soweit diese zur Zahlungsunfähigkeit der Gesellschaft führen mussten, es sei denn, dies war auch bei Beachtung der in § 93 Abs. 1 Satz 1 bezeichneten Sorgfalt nicht erkennbar.

§ 93
Sorgfaltspflicht und Verantwortlichkeit der Vorstandsmitglieder

(1) [1] Die Vorstandsmitglieder haben bei ihrer Geschäftsführung die Sorgfalt eines ordentlichen und gewissenhaften Geschäftsleiters anzuwenden. [2] Eine Pflichtverletzung liegt nicht vor, wenn das Vorstandsmitglied bei einer unternehmerischen Entscheidung vernünftigerweise annehmen durfte, auf der Grundlage angemessener Information zum Wohle der Gesellschaft zu handeln. [3] Über vertrauliche Angaben und Geheimnisse der Gesellschaft, namentlich Betriebs- oder Geschäftsgeheimnisse, die den Vorstandsmitgliedern durch ihre Tätigkeit im Vorstand bekanntgeworden sind, haben sie Stillschweigen zu bewahren. [4] Die Pflicht des Satzes 3 gilt nicht gegenüber einer nach § 342b des Handelsgesetzbuchs anerkannten Prüfstelle im Rahmen einer von dieser durchgeführten Prüfung.

sheet it becomes apparent, or if in the exercise of proper judgement it must be assumed, that the company has incurred a loss equal to one half of the share capital, the management board shall convene a shareholders' meeting without delay and inform the meeting thereof.

(2) [1] After the onset of the company's inability to pay or once it has become apparent that it is overindebted, the management board may not make any payments. [2] This shall not apply to payments which, even after this point, are consistent with the due care of a prudent and conscientious manager. The same obligation shall be incumbent on the management board with regard to payments to shareholders where they would necessarily lead to the company's inability to pay, unless this was not discernible even when exercising the due care designated in section 93 (1) sentence 1.

Section 93
Duty of Care and Responsibility of Management Board Members

(1) [1] In managing the company's business the management board members shall exercise the due care of a prudent and conscientious manager. [2] A breach of duty shall not exist if, in making an entrepreneurial decision, the management board member could reasonably assume that he is acting on the basis of adequate information for the benefit of the company. [3] They shall maintain confidentiality with respect to confidential information and company secrets, particularly trade or business secrets, which have become known to the management board members as a result of the service on the management board. [4] The duty set forth in sentence 3 shall not apply vis-à-vis an auditing firm which is recognized pursuant to section 342b of the Commercial Code in the course of an audit conducted by this firm.

(2) ¹Vorstandsmitglieder, die ihre Pflichten verletzen, sind der Gesellschaft zum Ersatz des daraus entstehenden Schadens als Gesamtschuldner verpflichtet. ²Ist streitig, ob sie die Sorgfalt eines ordentlichen und gewissenhaften Geschäftsleiters angewandt haben, so trifft sie die Beweislast. Schließt die Gesellschaft eine Versicherung zur Absicherung eines Vorstandsmitglieds gegen Risiken aus dessen beruflicher Tätigkeit für die Gesellschaft ab, ist ein Selbstbehalt von mindestens 10 Prozent des Schadens bis mindestens zur Höhe des Eineinhalbfachen der festen jährlichen Vergütung des Vorstandsmitglieds vorzusehen.

(3) Die Vorstandsmitglieder sind namentlich zum Ersatz verpflichtet, wenn entgegen diesem Gesetz

1. Einlagen an die Aktionäre zurückgewährt werden,
2. den Aktionären Zinsen oder Gewinnanteile gezahlt werden,
3. eigene Aktien der Gesellschaft oder einer anderen Gesellschaft gezeichnet, erworben, als Pfand genommen oder eingezogen werden,
4. Aktien vor der vollen Leistung des Ausgabebetrags ausgegeben werden,
5. Gesellschaftsvermögen verteilt wird,
6. Zahlungen entgegen § 92 Abs. 2 geleistet werden,
7. Vergütungen an Aufsichtsratsmitglieder gewährt werden,
8. Kredit gewährt wird,
9. bei der bedingten Kapitalerhöhung außerhalb des festgesetzten Zwecks oder vor der vollen Leistung des Gegenwerts Bezugsaktien ausgegeben werden.

(4) ¹Der Gesellschaft gegenüber tritt die Ersatzpflicht nicht ein, wenn die Handlung auf einem gesetzmäßigen Beschluss der Hauptversammlung beruht. ²Dadurch, dass der Aufsichtsrat die Handlung gebilligt hat, wird

(2) ¹Management board members who breach their duties shall be jointly and severally liable to the company for any resulting damage. ²If there is a dispute as to whether they exercised the due care of a prudent and conscientious manager, they shall bear the burden of proof. Should the company take out insurance to secure a management board member against risks arising from his or her professional activity for the company, it shall provide for a deductible of at least ten percent of the damage up to at least one and one-half times the amount of the fixed annual remuneration of the management board member.

(3) The management board members shall, in particular, be liable for damages if, contrary to this Act:

1. contributions are repaid to shareholders;
2. shareholders are paid interest or dividends;
3. company shares or shares of another company are subscribed, acquired, taken as a pledge or redeemed;
4. share certificates are issued before the issue price has been fully paid;
5. company assets are distributed;
6. payments are made in violation of section 92 (2);
7. remuneration is paid to members of the supervisory board;
8. credit is extended;
9. in connection with a conditional capital increase, pre-emptive shares are issued other than for the specified purpose or prior to full payment of the consideration.

(4) ¹Liability to the company for damages shall not be incurred if the action was in accordance with a lawful resolution of the shareholders' meeting. ²Liability for damages shall not be precluded by the fact that the supervisory

die Ersatzpflicht nicht ausgeschlossen. ³Die Gesellschaft kann erst drei Jahre nach der Entstehung des Anspruchs und nur dann auf Ersatzansprüche verzichten oder sich über sie vergleichen, wenn die Hauptversammlung zustimmt und nicht eine Minderheit, deren Anteile zusammen den zehnten Teil des Grundkapitals erreichen, zur Niederschrift Widerspruch erhebt. ⁴Die zeitliche Beschränkung gilt nicht, wenn der Ersatzpflichtige zahlungsunfähig ist und sich zur Abwendung des Insolvenzverfahrens mit seinen Gläubigern vergleicht oder wenn die Ersatzpflicht in einem Insolvenzplan geregelt wird.

(5) ¹Der Ersatzanspruch der Gesellschaft kann auch von den Gläubigern der Gesellschaft geltend gemacht werden, soweit sie von dieser keine Befriedigung erlangen können. ²Dies gilt jedoch in anderen Fällen als denen des Absatzes 3 nur dann, wenn die Vorstandsmitglieder die Sorgfalt eines ordentlichen und gewissenhaften Geschäftsleiters gröblich verletzt haben; Absatz 2 Satz 2 gilt sinngemäß. ³Den Gläubigern gegenüber wird die Ersatzpflicht weder durch einen Verzicht oder Vergleich der Gesellschaft noch dadurch aufgehoben, dass die Handlung auf einem Beschluss der Hauptversammlung beruht. ⁴Ist über das Vermögen der Gesellschaft das Insolvenzverfahren eröffnet, so übt während dessen Dauer der Insolvenzverwalter oder der Sachwalter das Recht der Gläubiger gegen die Vorstandsmitglieder aus.

(6) Die Ansprüche aus diesen Vorschriften verjähren in fünf Jahren.

board has consented to the act. ³The company may not waive or conclude a settlement on a damages claim until three years have passed after the claim has arisen, and then only with the consent of the shareholders' meeting and provided that no minority whose aggregate holding equals or exceeds one-tenth of the share capital records an objection in the minutes. ⁴This time limitation shall not apply if the person liable for damages is insolvent and enters into a composition with his creditors to avoid bankruptcy proceedings or if the liability to pay damages is included in an insolvency plan.

(5) ¹The company's claim for damages may also be asserted by the company's creditors to the extent that they are unable to obtain satisfaction from the company. ²However, this shall only apply in cases other than those set forth in subsection (3), where the management board members have grossly breached the duty of care of a prudent and conscientious manager; subsection (2) sentence 2 shall apply analogously. ³The duty to pay damages to the creditors shall not be extinguished by a waiver or compromise by the company or by the fact that the act that caused the damage was based on a resolution of the shareholders' meeting. ⁴If insolvency proceedings have been initiated against the company's assets, the insolvency receiver shall exercise the creditors' rights against the management board members for the duration of these proceedings.

(6) Claims under the above provisions shall become statute barred in five years.

§ 94
Stellvertreter von Vorstandsmitgliedern

Die Vorschriften für die Vorstandsmitglieder gelten auch für ihre Stellvertreter.

Section 94
Deputies of Management Board Members

The provisions relating to management board members shall also apply to their deputies.

Zweiter Abschnitt
Aufsichtsrat

§ 95
Zahl der Aufsichtsratsmitglieder

¹Der Aufsichtsrat besteht aus drei Mitgliedern. ²Die Satzung kann eine bestimmte höhere Zahl festsetzen. ³Die Zahl muss durch drei teilbar sein. ⁴Die Höchstzahl der Aufsichtsratsmitglieder beträgt bei Gesellschaften mit einem Grundkapital
bis zu 1.500.000 Euro neun,
von mehr als 1.500.000 Euro fünfzehn,
von mehr als 10.000.000 Euro einundzwanzig.
⁵Durch die vorstehenden Vorschriften werden hiervon abweichende Vorschriften des Gesetzes über die Mitbestimmung der Arbeitnehmer vom 4. Mai 1976 (Bundesgesetzbl. I S. 1153), des Montan-Mitbestimmungsgesetzes und des Gesetzes zur Ergänzung des Gesetzes über die Mitbestimmung der Arbeitnehmer in den Aufsichtsräten und Vorständen der Unternehmen des Bergbaus und der Eisen und Stahl erzeugenden Industrie vom 7. August 1956 (Bundesgesetzbl. I S. 707) – Mitbestimmungsergänzungsgesetz – nicht berührt.

§ 96
Zusammensetzung des Aufsichtsrats

(1) Der Aufsichtsrat setzt sich zusammen

bei Gesellschaften, für die das Mitbestimmungsgesetz gilt, aus Aufsichtsratsmitgliedern der Aktionäre und der Arbeitnehmer,

bei Gesellschaften, für die das Montan-Mitbestimmungsgesetz gilt, aus Aufsichtsratsmitgliedern der Aktionäre und der Arbeitnehmer und aus weiteren Mitgliedern,

Chapter 2
Supervisory Board

Section 95
Number of Members of the Supervisory Board

¹The supervisory board shall comprise three members. ²The articles of association may provide for a specific higher number. ³Such number must be divisible by three. ⁴The maximum number of members of the supervisory board for companies with a share capital of:
up to 1,500,000 euro shall be nine,
more than 1,500,000 euro shall be fifteen,
more than 10,000,000 euro shall be twenty-one.
⁵These provisions shall not affect any conflicting provisions set forth in the Employees Codetermination Act (*Mitbestimmungsgesetz*) of 4 May 1976 (Federal Law Gazette I p. 1153), the Coal and Steel Codetermination Act (*Montan-Mitbestimmungsgesetz*) and the Supplemental Act to the Act on the Codetermination of Employees in the Supervisory Boards and Management Boards in the Mining and the Iron and Steel Producing Industries of 7 August 1956 (Federal Law Gazette I p. 707) – ("the Supplemental Codetermination Act" – *Mitbestimmungsergänzungsgesetz*).

Section 96
Composition of the Supervisory Board

(1) The supervisory board shall:

in the case of companies to which the Codetermination Act applies, comprise representatives of the shareholders and the employees;

in the case of companies to which the Coal and Steel Codetermination Act applies, comprise representatives of the shareholders and the employees and additional members;

bei Gesellschaften, für die die §§ 5 bis 13 des Mitbestimmungsergänzungsgesetzes gelten, aus Aufsichtsratsmitgliedern der Aktionäre und der Arbeitnehmer und aus einem weiteren Mitglied,

bei Gesellschaften, für die das Drittelbeteiligungsgesetz gilt, aus Aufsichtsratsmitgliedern der Aktionäre und der Arbeitnehmer,

bei Gesellschaften, für die das Gesetz über die Mitbestimmung der Arbeitnehmer bei einer grenzüberschreitenden Verschmelzung gilt, aus Aufsichtsratsmitgliedern der Aktionäre und der Arbeitnehmer,

bei den übrigen Gesellschaften nur aus Aufsichtsratsmitgliedern der Aktionäre.

(2) Nach anderen als den zuletzt angewandten gesetzlichen Vorschriften kann der Aufsichtsrat nur zusammengesetzt werden, wenn nach § 97 oder nach § 98 die in der Bekanntmachung des Vorstands oder in der gerichtlichen Entscheidung angegebenen gesetzlichen Vorschriften anzuwenden sind.

in the case of companies to which sections 5 to 13 of the Supplemental Codetermination Act applies, comprise representatives of the shareholders and the employees and one additional member;

in the case of companies to which the One-Third Participation Act applies, comprise representatives of the shareholders and the employees;

in the case of companies to which the Act Governing the Codetermination of the Employees in the Event of a Cross-Border Merger applies, comprise representatives of the shareholders and the employees;

in the case of all other companies, comprise representatives of the shareholders only.

(2) The supervisory board may only be established otherwise than in accordance with the statutory provisions last applied if, pursuant to section 97 or section 98, other statutory provisions are to be applied that have been specified in an announcement by the management board or a judicial decision.

§ 97
Bekanntmachung über die Zusammensetzung des Aufsichtsrats

Section 97
Announcement Concerning Composition of the Supervisory Board

(1) [1]Ist der Vorstand der Ansicht, daß der Aufsichtsrat nicht nach den für ihn maßgebenden gesetzlichen Vorschriften zusammengesetzt ist, so hat er dies unverzüglich in den Gesellschaftsblättern und gleichzeitig durch Aushang in sämtlichen Betrieben der Gesellschaft und ihrer Konzernunternehmen bekanntzumachen. [2]In der Bekanntmachung sind die nach Ansicht des Vorstands maßgebenden gesetzlichen Vorschriften anzugeben. [3]Es ist darauf hinzuweisen, dass der Aufsichtsrat nach diesen Vorschriften zusammengesetzt wird, wenn nicht Antragsberechtigte nach § 98 Abs. 2 innerhalb eines Monats nach der Bekanntma-

(1) [1]If the management board is of the opinion that the composition of the supervisory board is not in compliance with the applicable statutory provisions, it shall promptly announce this in the company's designated journals, and simultaneously, in notices displayed in all establishments of the company and of the members of its group. [2]The announcement shall specify the statutory provisions which are relevant in the opinion of the management board. [3]The announcement shall state that the supervisory board will be composed in accordance with such provisions, unless parties authorized pursuant to section 98 (2) apply to the competent court

chung im elektronischen Bundesanzeiger das nach § 98 Abs. 1 zuständige Gericht anrufen.

(2) ¹Wird das nach § 98 Abs. 1 zuständige Gericht nicht innerhalb eines Monats nach der Bekanntmachung im elektronischen Bundesanzeiger angerufen, so ist der neue Aufsichtsrat nach den in der Bekanntmachung des Vorstands angegebenen gesetzlichen Vorschriften zusammenzusetzen. ²Die Bestimmungen der Satzung über die Zusammensetzung des Aufsichtsrats, über die Zahl der Aufsichtsratsmitglieder sowie über die Wahl, Abberufung und Entsendung von Aufsichtsratsmitgliedern treten mit der Beendigung der ersten Hauptversammlung, die nach Ablauf der Anrufungsfrist einberufen wird, spätestens sechs Monate nach Ablauf dieser Frist insoweit außer Kraft, als sie den nunmehr anzuwendenden gesetzlichen Vorschriften widersprechen. ³Mit demselben Zeitpunkt erlischt das Amt der bisherigen Aufsichtsratsmitglieder. ⁴Eine Hauptversammlung, die innerhalb der Frist von sechs Monaten stattfindet, kann an Stelle der außer Kraft tretenden Satzungsbestimmungen mit einfacher Stimmenmehrheit neue Satzungsbestimmungen beschließen.

(3) Solange ein gerichtliches Verfahren nach §§ 98, 99 anhängig ist, kann eine Bekanntmachung über die Zusammensetzung des Aufsichtsrats nicht erfolgen.

pursuant to section 98 (1) within one month from the date of the announcement in the electronic Federal Gazette *(Bundesanzeiger)*.

(2) ¹If no application is made to the competent court pursuant to section 98 (1) within one month from the date of the announcement in the electronic Federal Gazette, the new supervisory board shall be composed in accordance with the statutory provisions specified in the management board's announcement. ²To the extent that the provisions in the articles of association regarding the composition of the supervisory board, the number of members in the supervisory board and the election, removal and delegation of supervisory board members conflict with the statutory provisions now to be applied, they shall cease to be effective as of the adjournment of the first shareholders' meeting convened after the expiration of such one month period, but no later than six months after the expiration of such period. ³The term of office of the pervious members of the supervisory board shall also expire as of the same date. ⁴A shareholders' meeting held within such six month period may, by simple majority, adopt new provisions to replace those provisions in the articles of association which are to cease to be effective.

(3) No announcement concerning the composition of the supervisory board may be made while judicial proceedings pursuant to section 98 and section 99 are pending.

§ 98
Gerichtliche Entscheidung über die Zusammensetzung des Aufsichtsrats

(1) Ist streitig oder ungewiss, nach welchen gesetzlichen Vorschriften der Aufsichtsrat zusammenzusetzen ist, so entscheidet darüber auf Antrag ausschließlich das Landgericht, in dessen Bezirk die Gesellschaft ihren Sitz hat.

Section 98
Judicial Decision Concerning Composition of the Supervisory Board

(1) If it is disputed or uncertain which statutory provisions are to be applied to the composition of the supervisory board, the exclusive competency to rule on such an issue, upon application, shall lie with the Regional Court *(Landgericht)* of the district in which the company has its seat.

(2) ¹Antragsberechtigt sind

1. der Vorstand,
2. jedes Aufsichtsratsmitglied,
3. jeder Aktionär,
4. der Gesamtbetriebsrat der Gesellschaft oder, wenn in der Gesellschaft nur ein Betriebsrat besteht, der Betriebsrat,
5. der Gesamt- oder Unternehmenssprecherausschuss der Gesellschaft oder, wenn in der Gesellschaft nur ein Sprecherausschuss besteht, der Sprecherausschuss,
6. der Gesamtbetriebsrat eines anderen Unternehmens, dessen Arbeitnehmer nach den gesetzlichen Vorschriften, deren Anwendung streitig oder ungewiss ist, selbst oder durch Delegierte an der Wahl von Aufsichtsratsmitgliedern der Gesellschaft teilnehmen, oder, wenn in dem anderen Unternehmen nur ein Betriebsrat besteht, der Betriebsrat,
7. der Gesamt- oder Unternehmenssprecherausschuss eines anderen Unternehmens, dessen Arbeitnehmer nach den gesetzlichen Vorschriften, deren Anwendung streitig oder ungewiss ist, selbst oder durch Delegierte an der Wahl von Aufsichtsratsmitgliedern der Gesellschaft teilnehmen, oder, wenn in dem anderen Unternehmen nur ein Sprecherausschuss besteht, der Sprecherausschuss,
8. mindestens ein Zehntel oder einhundert der Arbeitnehmer, die nach den gesetzlichen Vorschriften, deren Anwendung streitig oder ungewiss ist, selbst oder durch Delegierte an der Wahl von Aufsichtsratsmitgliedern der Gesellschaft teilnehmen,
9. Spitzenorganisationen der Gewerkschaften, die nach den gesetzlichen Vorschriften, deren Anwendung streitig oder ungewiss ist, ein Vorschlagsrecht hätten,

(2) ¹The following shall be empowered to file an application with the court:

1. the management board;
2. each member of the supervisory board;
3. each shareholder;
4. the joint works council of the company or, if the company has only one works council, that works council;
5. the joint or enterprise spokesperson's committee of the company or, if the company has only one spokesperson's committee, that spokesperson's committee,
6. the joint works council of another enterprise whose employees participate directly or through delegates in the election of members of the supervisory board of the company pursuant to the statutory provisions whose application is disputed or uncertain, or, if the other enterprise has only one works council, that works council;
7. the joint or enterprise spokesperson's committee of another company whose employees participate directly or through delegates in the election of members of the supervisory board of the company pursuant to the statutory provisions whose application is disputed or uncertain, or, if the other enterprise has only one spokesperson's committee, that spokesperson's committee,
8. at least one-tenth or one hundred of the employees who participate directly or through delegates in the election of members of the supervisory board of the company pursuant to the statutory provisions whose application is disputed or uncertain;
9. the central organizations of the labor unions which would have a right to nominate members, pursuant to the statutory provisions whose application is disputed or uncertain;

10. Gewerkschaften, die nach den gesetzlichen Vorschriften, deren Anwendung streitig oder ungewiss ist, ein Vorschlagsrecht hätten.

²Ist die Anwendung des Mitbestimmungsgesetzes oder die Anwendung von Vorschriften des Mitbestimmungsgesetzes streitig oder ungewiss, so sind außer den nach Satz 1 Antragsberechtigten auch je ein Zehntel der wahlberechtigten in § 3 Abs. 1 Nr. 1 des Mitbestimmungsgesetzes bezeichneten Arbeitnehmer oder der wahlberechtigten leitenden Angestellten im Sinne des Mitbestimmungsgesetzes antragsberechtigt.

(3) Die Absätze 1 und 2 gelten sinngemäß, wenn streitig ist, ob der Abschlussprüfer das nach § 3 oder § 16 des Mitbestimmungsergänzungsgesetzes maßgebliche Umsatzverhältnis richtig ermittelt hat.

(4) ¹Entspricht die Zusammensetzung des Aufsichtsrats nicht der gerichtlichen Entscheidung, so ist der neue Aufsichtsrat nach den in der Entscheidung angegebenen gesetzlichen Vorschriften zusammenzusetzen. ²§ 97 Abs. 2 gilt sinngemäß mit der Maßgabe, daß die Frist von sechs Monaten mit dem Eintritt der Rechtskraft beginnt.

§ 99
Verfahren

(1) Auf das Verfahren ist das Gesetz über das Verfahren in Familiensachen und in den Angelegenheiten der freiwilligen Gerichtsbarkeit anzuwenden, soweit in den Absätzen 2 bis 5 nichts anderes bestimmt ist.

(2) ¹Das Landgericht hat den Antrag in den Gesellschaftsblättern bekanntzu-

10. labor unions which would have a right to nominate members, pursuant to the statutory provisions whose application is disputed or uncertain.

²If either the application of the Codetermination Act or the application of certain provisions of the Codetermination Act is disputed or uncertain, then in addition to those entitled to make an application pursuant to sentence 1, one-tenth of the employees designated in section 3 (1) no. 1 of the Codetermination Act who are eligible to vote, or one-tenth of the managerial employees within the meaning of the Codetermination Act who are eligible to vote, shall also be entitled to make an application to the court.

(3) Subsections (1) and (2) shall apply analogously in the event of a dispute as to whether the auditor has correctly determined the relevant turnover ratio pursuant to section 3 or section 16 of the Supplemental Codetermination Act.

(4) ¹If the composition of the supervisory board does not comply with the decision of the court, the new supervisory board shall be composed in accordance with the statutory provisions cited in the decision. ²Section 97 (2) shall apply analogously, with the exception that the six month period shall commence on the date on which such decision becomes final and can no longer be appealed.

Section 99
Procedure

(1) The procedure shall be governed by the provisions of the Act on Proceedings in Family Matters and Voluntary Jurisdiction *(Gesetz über das Verfahren in Familiensachen und in den Angelegenheiten der freiwilligen Gerichtsbarkeit – FamFG)*, unless otherwise set forth in subsections (2) to (5).

(2) ¹The Regional Court shall announce the application in the company's desig-

machen. ²Der Vorstand und jedes Aufsichtsratsmitglied sowie die nach § 98 Abs. 2 antragsberechtigten Betriebsräte, Sprecherausschüsse, Spitzenorganisationen und Gewerkschaften sind zu hören.

(3) ¹Das Landgericht entscheidet durch einen mit Gründen versehenen Beschluss. ²Gegen die Entscheidung des Landgerichts findet die Beschwerde statt. ³Sie kann nur auf eine Verletzung des Rechts gestützt werden; § 72 Abs. 1 Satz 2 und § 74 Abs. 2 und 3 des Gesetzes über das Verfahren in Familiensachen und in den Angelegenheiten der freiwilligen Gerichtsbarkeit sowie § 547 der Zivilprozessordnung gelten sinngemäß. ⁴Die Beschwerde kann nur durch die Einreichung einer von einem Rechtsanwalt unterzeichneten Beschwerdeschrift eingelegt werden. ⁵Die Landesregierung kann durch Rechtsverordnung die Entscheidung über die Beschwerde für die Bezirke mehrerer Oberlandesgerichte einem der Oberlandesgerichte oder dem Obersten Landesgericht übertragen, wenn dies der Sicherung einer einheitlichen Rechtsprechung dient. ⁶Die Landesregierung kann die Ermächtigung auf die Landesjustizverwaltung übertragen.

(4) ¹Das Gericht hat seine Entscheidung dem Antragsteller und der Gesellschaft zuzustellen. ²Es hat sie ferner ohne Gründe in den Gesellschaftsblättern bekanntzumachen. ³Die Beschwerde steht jedem nach § 98 Abs. 2 Antragsberechtigten zu. ⁴Die Beschwerdefrist beginnt mit der Bekanntmachung der Entscheidung im elektronischen Bundesanzeiger, für den Antragsteller und die Gesellschaft jedoch nicht vor der Zustellung der Entscheidung.

(5) ¹Die Entscheidung wird erst mit der Rechtskraft wirksam. ²Sie wirkt für und gegen alle. ³Der Vorstand hat

nated journals. ²The management board and each member of the supervisory board as well as the works councils, spokesperson's committees, central organizations and labor unions which are empowered pursuant to section 98 (2) shall be heard.

(3) ¹The Regional Court shall render a decision setting out the grounds on which it is based. ²A complaint may be filed against this Regional Court decision. ³ It may only be based on a violation of the law; section 72 (1) sentence 2 and section 74 (2) and (3) of the Act on Proceedings in Family Matters and Voluntary Jurisdiction as well as section 547 of the Code of Civil Procedure (*Zivilprozeßordnung*) shall apply analogously. ⁴Such complaint may only be made by filing a notice of complaint signed by an attorney. ⁵The state government may by ordinance transfer jurisdiction for several districts to one Higher Regional Court, or to the Highest Regional Court (*Oberstes Landesgericht*), so as to ensure uniformity of decisions. ⁶The state government may transfer such authority to the ministry of justice of that state.

(4) ¹The court shall serve its decision to the party that filed the application and to the company. ²Furthermore, the court shall announce its decision in the company's journals without setting out the grounds for the decision. ³A complaint may be lodged by any party empowered pursuant to section 98 (2). ⁴The time period in which the complaint must be lodged shall commence on the date on which the decision was announced in the electronic Federal Gazette but, in the case of the applicant party and the company, not before delivery of the decision.

(5) ¹The decision shall become effective only once it has become final and can no longer be appealed. ²Such decision shall

die rechtskräftige Entscheidung unverzüglich zum Handelsregister einzureichen.

(6) ¹Für die Kosten des Verfahrens gilt die Kostenordnung. ³Für das Verfahren des ersten Rechtszugs wird das Vierfache der vollen Gebühr erhoben. ³Für das Verfahren über ein Rechtsmittel wird die gleiche Gebühr erhoben; dies gilt auch dann, wenn das Rechtsmittel Erfolg hat. ⁴Wird der Antrag oder das Rechtsmittel zurückgenommen, bevor es zu einer Entscheidung kommt, so ermäßigt sich die Gebühr auf die Hälfte. ⁵Der Geschäftswert ist von Amts wegen festzusetzen. ⁶Er bestimmt sich nach § 30 Abs. 2 der Kostenordnung mit der Maßgabe, dass der Wert regelmäßig auf 50.000 Euro anzunehmen ist. ⁷Schuldner der Kosten ist die Gesellschaft. ⁸Die Kosten können jedoch ganz oder zum Teil dem Antragsteller auferlegt werden, wenn dies der Billigkeit entspricht. ⁹Kosten der Beteiligten werden nicht erstattet.

§ 100
Persönliche Voraussetzungen für Aufsichtsratsmitglieder

(1) ¹Mitglied des Aufsichtsrats kann nur eine natürliche, unbeschränkt geschäftsfähige Person sein. ²Ein Betreuer, der bei der Besorgung seiner Vermögensangelegenheiten ganz oder teilweise einem Einwilligungsvorbehalt (§ 1903 des Bürgerlichen Gesetzbuchs) unterliegt, kann nicht Mitglied des Aufsichtsrats sein.

(2) ¹Mitglied des Aufsichtsrats kann nicht sein, wer

1. bereits in zehn Handelsgesellschaften, die gesetzlich einen Aufsichtsrat zu bilden haben, Aufsichtsratsmitglied ist,
2. gesetzlicher Vertreter eines von der Gesellschaft abhängigen Unternehmens ist,

have effect for and against everyone. ³The management board shall promptly submit the final and binding decision to the Commercial Register.

(6) ¹The cost of the proceedings shall be determined pursuant to the Act on Court Costs *(Kostenordnung)*. ²For proceedings before the court of first instance, four times the full fee shall be assessed. ³For proceedings on a legal remedy, the same amount shall be assessed; this applies even if the legal remedy is successful. ⁴If the application or the legal remedy is withdrawn before a decision is rendered, the fees shall be reduced by one-half. ⁵The court shall, ex officio, determine the value of the subject matter of the proceedings. ⁶This value shall be determined in accordance with section 30 (2) of the Act on Court Costs, provided that as a rule, it is assumed to amount to fifty thousand euro. ⁷The company shall be liable for the costs. ⁸The applicant party shall, however, be liable for all or part of the costs if equity so requires. ⁹The parties' own costs shall not be reimbursed.

Section 100
Personal Qualifications of Members of the Supervisory Board

(1) ¹Only a natural person with full legal capacity may be a member of the supervisory board. ²A person under guardianship whose property affairs are subject, in whole or in part, to reservations of consent (section 1903 of the German Civil Code) may not be a member of the supervisory board.

(2) ¹A person may not be a member of the supervisory board who:

1. is already a member of the supervisory board of ten commercial companies which are required by law to form a supervisory board,
2. is the legal representative of a dependent enterprise controlled by the company,

3. gesetzlicher Vertreter einer anderen Kapitalgesellschaft ist, deren Aufsichtsrat ein Vorstandsmitglied der Gesellschaft angehört, oder
4. in den letzten zwei Jahren Vorstandsmitglied derselben börsennotierten Gesellschaft war, es sei denn, seine Wahl erfolgt auf Vorschlag von Aktionären, die mehr als 25 Prozent der Stimmrechte an der Gesellschaft halten.

[2] Auf die Höchstzahl nach Satz 1 Nr. 1 sind bis zu fünf Aufsichtsratssitze nicht anzurechnen, die ein gesetzlicher Vertreter (beim Einzelkaufmann der Inhaber) des herrschenden Unternehmens eines Konzerns in zum Konzern gehörenden Handelsgesellschaften, die gesetzlich einen Aufsichtsrat zu bilden haben, inne hat. [3] Auf die Höchstzahl nach Satz 1 Nr. 1 sind Aufsichtsratsämter im Sinne der Nummer 1 doppelt anzurechnen, für die das Mitglied zum Vorsitzenden gewählt worden ist.

(3) Die anderen persönlichen Voraussetzungen der Aufsichtsratsmitglieder der Arbeitnehmer sowie der weiteren Mitglieder bestimmen sich nach dem Mitbestimmungsgesetz, dem Montan-Mitbestimmungsgesetz, dem Mitbestimmungsergänzungsgesetz, dem Drittelbeteiligungsgesetz und dem Gesetz über die Mitbestimmung der Arbeitnehmer bei einer grenzüberschreitenden Verschmelzung.

(4) Die Satzung kann persönliche Voraussetzungen nur für Aufsichtsratsmitglieder fordern, die von der Hauptversammlung ohne Bindung an Wahlvorschläge gewählt oder auf Grund der Satzung in den Aufsichtsrat entsandt werden.

(5) Bei Gesellschaften im Sinn des § 264d des Handelsgesetzbuchs muss mindestens ein unabhängiges Mitglied des Aufsichtsrats über Sachverstand auf den Gebieten Rechnungslegung oder Abschlussprüfung verfügen.

3. is the legal representative of another corporation whose supervisory board includes a member of the company's management board, or
4. was a member of the management board of the same listed company in the past two years, unless his or her election resulted from a proposal by shareholders holding more than 25 percent of the voting rights in the company.

[2] In determining the maximum number pursuant to sentence 1 no. 1, no account shall be taken of up to five seats a legal representative (or, in the case of a sole proprietorship, the owner) of the controlling enterprise of a group has on supervisory boards of commercial enterprises belonging to such group which are required by law to form a supervisory board. [3] In computing the maximum number pursuant to sentence 1 no. 1, if the member has been elected chairman of a supervisory board, his seat within the meaning of no. 1 shall be counted twice.

(3) The further personal qualifications of the representatives of the employees and the additional members of the supervisory board shall be determined pursuant to the Codetermination Act, the Coal and Steel Codetermination Act, the Supplemental Codetermination Act, the One-Third Participation Act and the Act Governing the Codetermination of the Employees in the Event of a Cross-Boundary Merger.

(4) The articles of association may stipulate personal qualifications only for those supervisory board members who are elected by the shareholders' meeting without being bound by nominations or are appointed to the supervisory board pursuant to the articles of association.

(5) In the case of companies within the meaning of section 264d of the German Commercial Code, at least one independent member of the supervisory board must have expert knowledge in the areas of accounting or auditing.

§ 101
Bestellung der Aufsichtsratsmitglieder

(1) ¹Die Mitglieder des Aufsichtsrats werden von der Hauptversammlung gewählt, soweit sie nicht in den Aufsichtsrat zu entsenden oder als Aufsichtsratsmitglieder der Arbeitnehmer nach dem Mitbestimmungsgesetz, dem Mitbestimmungsergänzungsgesetz, dem Drittelbeteiligungsgesetz oder dem Gesetz über die Mitbestimmung der Arbeitnehmer bei einer grenzüberschreitenden Verschmelzung zu wählen sind. ²An Wahlvorschläge ist die Hauptversammlung nur gemäß §§ 6 und 8 des Montan-Mitbestimmungsgesetzes gebunden.

(2) ¹Ein Recht, Mitglieder in den Aufsichtsrat zu entsenden, kann nur durch die Satzung und nur für bestimmte Aktionäre oder für die jeweiligen Inhaber bestimmter Aktien begründet werden. ²Inhabern bestimmter Aktien kann das Entsendungsrecht nur eingeräumt werden, wenn die Aktien auf Namen lauten und ihre Übertragung an die Zustimmung der Gesellschaft gebunden ist. ³Die Aktien der Entsendungsberechtigten gelten nicht als eine besondere Gattung. ⁴Die Entsendungsrechte können insgesamt höchstens für ein Drittel der sich aus dem Gesetz oder der Satzung ergebenden Zahl der Aufsichtsratsmitglieder der Aktionäre eingeräumt werden.

(3) ¹Stellvertreter von Aufsichtsratsmitgliedern können nicht bestellt werden. ²Jedoch kann für jedes Aufsichtsratsmitglied mit Ausnahme des weiteren Mitglieds, das nach dem Montan-Mitbestimmungsgesetz oder dem Mitbestimmungsergänzungsgesetz auf Vorschlag der übrigen Aufsichtsratsmitglieder gewählt wird, ein Ersatzmitglied bestellt werden, das Mitglied des Aufsichtsrats wird, wenn das Aufsichtsratsmitglied vor Ablauf seiner Amtszeit wegfällt. ³Das Ersatzmitglied kann nur gleichzeitig mit dem

Section 101
Appointment of Supervisory Board Members

(1) ¹Supervisory board members shall be elected by the shareholders' meeting, unless they are to be delegated to the supervisory board or elected as employee representatives pursuant to the Codetermination Act, the Supplemental Codetermination Act, the One-Third Participation Act, or the Act Governing the Codetermination of the Employees in the Event of a Cross-Boundary Merger. ²The shareholders' meeting shall be bound by nominations only pursuant to sections 6 and 8 of the Coal and Steel Codetermination Act.

(2) ¹The right to delegate members to the supervisory board may only be granted by the articles of association and only to certain shareholders or the holders of certain shares. ²The right to delegate may be granted to holders of certain shares only if such shares are registered and their transfer requires the consent of the company. ³Shares held by persons with the right to delegate shall not be deemed to constitute a separate class. ⁴The delegation right may be granted to no more than one-third of the shareholder representatives in the supervisory board as determined by statute or the articles of association.

(3) ¹Deputies of supervisory board members may not be appointed. ²However, a substitute member may be appointed for each supervisory board member, with the exception of the additional member to be elected pursuant to the Coal and Steel Codetermination Act or the Supplemental Codetermination Act, upon nomination by the other supervisory board members, who shall become a supervisory board member if the regular member ceases to hold office prior to the expiration of his term of office. ³Such substitute member

Aufsichtsratmitglied bestellt werden. ⁴Auf seine Bestellung sowie die Nichtigkeit und Anfechtung seiner Bestellung sind die für das Aufsichtsratsmitglied geltenden Vorschriften anzuwenden.

may only be appointed simultaneously with the supervisory board member. ⁴The provisions governing supervisory board members shall govern the appointment and the nullity and contestation of the appointment of substitute members.

§ 102
Amtszeit der Aufsichtsratsmitglieder

(1) ¹Aufsichtsratsmitglieder können nicht für längere Zeit als bis zur Beendigung der Hauptversammlung bestellt werden, die über die Entlastung für das vierte Geschäftsjahr nach dem Beginn der Amtszeit beschließt. ²Das Geschäftsjahr, in dem die Amtszeit beginnt, wird nicht mitgerechnet.

(2) Das Amt des Ersatzmitglieds erlischt spätestens mit Ablauf der Amtszeit des weggefallenen Aufsichtsratsmitglieds.

Section 102
Term of Office of Supervisory Board Members

(1) ¹Supervisory board members may not be appointed for a period of time extending beyond the adjournment of the shareholders' meeting which resolves on the discharging of the management for the fourth business year following the commencement of their term of office. ²The business year in which their term of office commences shall not be taken into account.

(2) The term of office of a substitute member shall expire at the latest with the expiration of the term of office of the supervisory board member who no longer holds office.

§ 103
Abberufung der Aufsichtsratsmitglieder

(1) ¹Aufsichtsratsmitglieder, die von der Hauptversammlung ohne Bindung an einen Wahlvorschlag gewählt worden sind, können von ihr vor Ablauf der Amtszeit abberufen werden. ²Der Beschluss bedarf einer Mehrheit, die mindestens drei Viertel der abgegebenen Stimmen umfasst. ³Die Satzung kann eine andere Mehrheit und weitere Erfordernisse bestimmen.

(2) ¹Ein Aufsichtsratsmitglied, das auf Grund der Satzung in den Aufsichtsrat entsandt ist, kann von dem Entsendungsberechtigten jederzeit abberufen und durch ein anderes ersetzt werden. ²Sind die in der Satzung bestimmten Voraussetzungen des Entsendungsrechts weggefallen, so kann die Haupt-

Section 103
Removal of Supervisory Board Members

(1) ¹Supervisory board members who have been elected by the shareholders' meeting without being bound by nominations may be removed by virtue a shareholders' resolution before their term of office expires. ²Such resolution shall require a majority of at least three-fourths of the votes cast. ³The articles of association may provide for a different majority and additional requirements.

(2) ¹The person with the right to delegate may at any time remove a supervisory board member who has been delegated to the supervisory board pursuant to the articles of association and replace him with another person. ²If the conditions for his right of delegation as set forth in the articles of association no

versammlung das entsandte Mitglied mit einfacher Stimmenmehrheit abberufen.

(3) ¹Das Gericht hat auf Antrag des Aufsichtsrats ein Aufsichtsratsmitglied abzuberufen, wenn in dessen Person ein wichtiger Grund vorliegt. ²Der Aufsichtsrat beschließt über die Antragstellung mit einfacher Mehrheit. ³Ist das Aufsichtsratsmitglied auf Grund der Satzung in den Aufsichtsrat entsandt worden, so können auch Aktionäre, deren Anteile zusammen den zehnten Teil des Grundkapitals oder den anteiligen Betrag von einer Million Euro erreichen, den Antrag stellen. ⁴Gegen die Entscheidung ist die Beschwerde zulässig.

(4) Für die Abberufung der Aufsichtsratsmitglieder, die weder von der Hauptversammlung ohne Bindung an einen Wahlvorschlag gewählt worden sind noch auf Grund der Satzung in den Aufsichtsrat entsandt sind, gelten außer Absatz 3 das Mitbestimmungsgesetz, das Montan-Mitbestimmungsgesetz, das Mitbestimmungsergänzungsgesetz, das Drittelbeteiligungsgesetz, das SE-Beteiligungsgesetz und das Gesetz über die Mitbestimmung der Arbeitnehmer bei einer grenzüberschreitenden Verschmelzung.

(5) Für die Abberufung eines Ersatzmitglieds gelten die Vorschriften über die Abberufung des Aufsichtsratsmitglieds, für das es bestellt ist.

longer apply, the shareholders' meeting may remove the delegated member by a simple majority of votes.

(3) ¹Upon application by the supervisory board, the court shall remove a supervisory board member for cause relating to the person of that member. ²The supervisory board shall resolve to file such an application by simple majority. ³If the supervisory board member was delegated to the supervisory board pursuant to the articles of association, shareholders whose aggregate holding amounts to one-tenth of the share capital or a proportionate sum of one million euro may also file such an application. ⁴A complaint may be lodged against the court's decision.

(4) The Codetermination Act, the Coal and Steel Codetermination Act, the Supplemental Codetermination Act, the One-Third Participation Act, the Participation of Employees (European Companies) Act and the Act Governing the Codetermination of the Employees in the Event of a Cross-Boundary Merger shall apply, in addition to subsection (3), to the removal of supervisory board members who were neither elected by the shareholders' meeting without being bound by nominations nor delegated to the supervisory board pursuant to the articles of association.

(5) The provisions governing the removal of a substitute supervisory board member shall be the same as those applicable to the supervisory board member he replaced.

§ 104
Bestellung durch das Gericht

(1) ¹Gehört dem Aufsichtsrat die zur Beschlussfähigkeit nötige Zahl von Mitgliedern nicht an, so hat ihn das Gericht auf Antrag des Vorstands, eines Aufsichtsratsmitglieds oder eines Aktionärs auf diese Zahl zu ergänzen. ²Der Vorstand ist verpflichtet, den An-

Section 104
Appointment by the Court

(1) ¹If the supervisory board does not have enough members to constitute a quorum, the court shall, upon application by the management board, a supervisory board member or a shareholder, add the necessary number of members. ²The management board shall be obli-

trag unverzüglich zu stellen, es sei denn, dass die rechtzeitige Ergänzung vor der nächsten Aufsichtsratssitzung zu erwarten ist. ³Hat der Aufsichtsrat auch aus Aufsichtsratsmitgliedern der Arbeitnehmer zu bestehen, so können auch den Antrag stellen

1. der Gesamtbetriebsrat der Gesellschaft oder, wenn in der Gesellschaft nur ein Betriebsrat besteht, der Betriebsrat, sowie, wenn die Gesellschaft herrschendes Unternehmen eines Konzerns ist, der Konzernbetriebsrat,
2. der Gesamt- oder Unternehmenssprecherausschuss der Gesellschaft oder, wenn in der Gesellschaft nur ein Sprecherausschuss besteht, der Sprecherausschuss sowie, wenn die Gesellschaft herrschendes Unternehmen eines Konzerns ist, der Konzernsprecherausschuss,
3. der Gesamtbetriebsrat eines anderen Unternehmens, dessen Arbeitnehmer selbst oder durch Delegierte an der Wahl teilnehmen, oder, wenn in dem anderen Unternehmen nur ein Betriebsrat besteht, der Betriebsrat,
4. der Gesamt- oder Unternehmenssprecherausschuss eines anderen Unternehmens, dessen Arbeitnehmer selbst oder durch Delegierte an der Wahl teilnehmen, oder, wenn in dem anderen Unternehmen nur ein Sprecherausschuss besteht, der Sprecherausschuss,
5. mindestens ein Zehntel oder einhundert der Arbeitnehmer, die selbst oder durch Delegierte an der Wahl teilnehmen,
6. Spitzenorganisationen der Gewerkschaften, die das Recht haben, Aufsichtsratsmitglieder der Arbeitnehmer vorzuschlagen,
7. Gewerkschaften, die das Recht haben, Aufsichtsratsmitglieder der Arbeitnehmer vorzuschlagen.

⁴Hat der Aufsichtsrat nach dem Mitbestimmungsgesetz auch aus Aufsichtsratsmitgliedern der Arbeitnehmer zu

gated to file such an application without delay, unless it is expected that the necessary seats on the supervisory board will be filled prior to the next supervisory board meeting. ³If the supervisory board must also include representatives of the employees, such application may also be filed by:

1. the joint works council of the company or, if the company has only one works council, that works council and, if the company is the controlling enterprise of a group, the group works council,
2. the joint or enterprise spokesperson's committee of the company or, if the company has only one spokesperson's committee, the spokesperson's committee as well as, if the company in the controlling enterprise of a group, the group spokesperson's committee,
3. the joint works council of another company whose employees participate in the election directly or through delegates or, if such other company has only one works council, that works council,
4. the joint or enterprise spokesperson's committee of another company whose employees participate directly or through delegates in the election, or, if the other enterprise has only one spokesperson's committee, that spokesperson's committee,
5. at least one-tenth or one hundred of the employees who participate in the election directly or through delegates,
6. the central organizations of labor unions which have the right to nominate employee representatives to the supervisory board,
7. labor unions which have the right to nominate employee representatives to the supervisory board.

⁴If the supervisory board is required to include employee representatives pursuant to the Codetermination Act, then

bestehen, so sind außer den nach Satz 3 Antragsberechtigten auch je ein Zehntel der wahlberechtigten in § 3 Abs. 1 Nr. 1 des Mitbestimmungsgesetzes bezeichneten Arbeitnehmer oder der wahlberechtigten leitenden Angestellten im Sinne des Mitbestimmungsgesetzes antragsberechtigt. ⁵Gegen die Entscheidung ist die Beschwerde zulässig.

(2) ¹Gehören dem Aufsichtsrat länger als drei Monate weniger Mitglieder als die durch Gesetz oder Satzung festgesetzte Zahl an, so hat ihn das Gericht auf Antrag auf diese Zahl zu ergänzen. ²In dringenden Fällen hat das Gericht auf Antrag den Aufsichtsrat auch vor Ablauf der Frist zu ergänzen. ³Das Antragsrecht bestimmt sich nach Absatz 1. ⁴Gegen die Entscheidung ist die Beschwerde zulässig.

(3) Absatz 2 ist auf einen Aufsichtsrat, in dem die Arbeitnehmer ein Mitbestimmungsrecht nach dem Mitbestimmungsgesetz, dem Montan-Mitbestimmungsgesetz oder dem Mitbestimmungsergänzungsgesetz haben, mit der Maßgabe anzuwenden,

1. dass das Gericht den Aufsichtsrat hinsichtlich des weiteren Mitglieds, das nach dem Montan-Mitbestimmungsgesetz oder dem Mitbestimmungsergänzungsgesetz auf Vorschlag der übrigen Aufsichtsratsmitglieder gewählt wird, nicht ergänzen kann,

2. dass es stets ein dringender Fall ist, wenn dem Aufsichtsrat, abgesehen von dem in Nummer 1 genannten weiteren Mitglied, nicht alle Mitglieder angehören, aus denen er nach Gesetz oder Satzung zu bestehen hat.

(4) ¹Hat der Aufsichtsrat auch aus Aufsichtsratsmitgliedern der Arbeit-

in addition to those parties empowered to file an application pursuant to sentence 3, one-tenth of the employees designated in section 3 (1) no. 1 of the Co-determination Act who are eligible to vote or one-tenth of the managerial employees within the meaning of the Codetermination Act who are eligible to vote, shall also be empowered to file such an application. ⁵A complaint may be lodged against the court's decision.

(2) ¹If the supervisory board has had fewer members than required by statute or the articles of association for more than three months, the court shall, upon application, add the necessary number of members. ²In urgent cases the court shall, upon application, restore the supervisory board to the requisite number even before this period has expired. ³The right to file such an application shall be governed by subsection (1). ⁴A complaint may be lodged against the court's decision.

(3) Subsection (2) shall apply to a supervisory board in which the employees have a right to codetermination pursuant to the provisions of the Codetermination Act, the Coal and Steel Codetermination Act or the Supplemental Codetermination Act, provided, however, that:

1. the court may not restore the supervisory board to the requisite number by appointing the additional member who is to be elected upon nomination by the other supervisory board members pursuant to the Coal and Steel Codetermination Act or the Supplemental Codetermination Act.

2. an urgent case shall always be deemed to exist if the supervisory board does not have the full number of members required pursuant to the statutes or the articles of association, not including the additional member referred to in no. 1.

(4) ¹If the supervisory board is required to include employee representatives as

nehmer zu bestehen, so hat das Gericht ihn so zu ergänzen, dass das für seine Zusammensetzung maßgebende zahlenmäßige Verhältnis hergestellt wird. ²Wenn der Aufsichtsrat zur Herstellung seiner Beschlussfähigkeit ergänzt wird, gilt dies nur, soweit die zur Beschlussfähigkeit nötige Zahl der Aufsichtsratsmitglieder die Wahrung dieses Verhältnisses möglich macht. ³Ist ein Aufsichtsratsmitglied zu ersetzen, das nach Gesetz oder Satzung in persönlicher Hinsicht besonderen Voraussetzungen entsprechen muss, so muss auch das vom Gericht bestellte Aufsichtsratsmitglied diesen Voraussetzungen entsprechen. ⁴Ist ein Aufsichtsratsmitglied zu ersetzen, bei dessen Wahl eine Spitzenorganisation der Gewerkschaften, eine Gewerkschaft oder die Betriebsräte ein Vorschlagsrecht hätten, so soll das Gericht Vorschläge dieser Stellen berücksichtigen, soweit nicht überwiegende Belange der Gesellschaft oder der Allgemeinheit der Bestellung des Vorgeschlagenen entgegenstehen; das gleiche gilt, wenn das Aufsichtsratsmitglied durch Delegierte zu wählen wäre, für gemeinsame Vorschläge der Betriebsräte der Unternehmen, in denen Delegierte zu wählen sind.

(5) Das Amt des gerichtlich bestellten Aufsichtsratsmitglieds erlischt in jedem Fall, sobald der Mangel behoben ist.

(6) ¹Das gerichtlich bestellte Aufsichtsratsmitglied hat Anspruch auf Ersatz angemessener barer Auslagen und, wenn den Aufsichtsratsmitgliedern der Gesellschaft eine Vergütung gewährt wird, auf Vergütung für seine Tätigkeit. ²Auf Antrag des Aufsichtsratsmitglieds setzt das Gericht die Auslagen und die Vergütung fest. ³Gegen die Entscheidung ist die Beschwerde zulässig; die Rechtsbeschwerde ist ausgeschlossen. ⁴Aus der rechtskräftigen Entscheidung findet die Zwangsvollstreckung nach der Zivilprozessordnung statt.

well, the court shall appoint additional members in such a way as to establish the numerical ratio required for the composition of the supervisory board. ²If appointments are to be made to the supervisory board in order to establish a quorum, this shall apply only if the number of supervisory board members required for a quorum permits such a ratio to prevail. ³If a supervisory board member is to be replaced who must meet special personal criteria under the law or the articles of association, the supervisory board member appointed by the court must also meet such criteria. ⁴If a supervisory board member is to be replaced whom a central organization of labor unions, a labor union or the works councils would have the right to nominate, the court shall take into account the nominations of such parties, unless appointment of the nominated person would contravene overriding interests of the company or the general public; if the supervisory board member is to be elected by delegates, the same shall apply to joint nominations by the works councils of the companies in which delegates are to be elected.

(5) The term of office of the court-appointed supervisory board member shall in any event expire as soon as the deficiency has been remedied.

(6) ¹The supervisory board member shall be entitled to reimbursement of reasonable cash expenses and, if remuneration is granted to regular supervisory board members of the company, to remuneration for his services. ²Upon application by such supervisory board member, the court shall stipulate such expenses and remuneration. ³ A complaint may be lodged against its decision; complaint on points of law only shall be precluded. ⁴A decision which has become final and can no longer be appealed may be enforced pursuant to the Code of Civil Procedure.

§ 105
Unvereinbarkeit der Zugehörigkeit zum Vorstand und zum Aufsichtsrat

(1) Ein Aufsichtsratsmitglied kann nicht zugleich Vorstandsmitglied, dauernd Stellvertreter von Vorstandsmitgliedern, Prokurist oder zum gesamten Geschäftsbetrieb ermächtigter Handlungsbevollmächtigter der Gesellschaft sein.

(2) ¹Nur für einen im voraus begrenzten Zeitraum, höchstens für ein Jahr, kann der Aufsichtsrat einzelne seiner Mitglieder zu Stellvertretern von fehlenden oder verhinderten Vorstandsmitgliedern bestellen. ²Eine wiederholte Bestellung oder Verlängerung der Amtszeit ist zulässig, wenn dadurch die Amtszeit insgesamt ein Jahr nicht übersteigt. ³Während ihrer Amtszeit als Stellvertreter von Vorstandsmitgliedern können die Aufsichtsratsmitglieder keine Tätigkeit als Aufsichtsratsmitglied ausüben. ⁴Das Wettbewerbsverbot des § 88 gilt für sie nicht.

Section 105
Incompatibility of Membership on Both the Management Board and the Supervisory Board

(1) A supervisory board member may not at the same time be a management board member, a permanent deputy management board member, a procuration officer or general manager of the company.

(2) ¹The supervisory board may appoint individual members as deputies for absent or incapacitated management board members for a term to be fixed in advance, not to exceed one year. ²Such appointment may be renewed or the term of office extended, provided, however, that the aggregate term of office does not exceed one year. ³During their term of office as deputies of management board members, the supervisory board members may not exercise the functions of a supervisory board member. ⁴The prohibition of competition pursuant to section 88 shall not apply to them.

§ 106
Bekanntmachung der Änderungen im Aufsichtsrat

Der Vorstand hat bei jeder Änderung in den Personen der Aufsichtsratsmitglieder unverzüglich eine Liste der Mitglieder des Aufsichtsrats, aus welcher Name, Vorname, ausgeübter Beruf und Wohnort der Mitglieder ersichtlich ist, zum Handelsregister einzureichen; das Gericht hat nach § 10 des Handelsgesetzbuchs einen Hinweis darauf bekannt zu machen, dass die Liste zum Handelsregister eingereicht worden ist.

Section 106
Announcement of Changes in the Supervisory Board

With every change in the composition of the supervisory board, the management board shall submit to the Commercial Register without delay a list of the members of the supervisory board, stating their first and last names, professions and residential addresses; pursuant to section 10 of the Commercial Code, the Court must announce that the list has been submitted to the Commercial Register.

§ 107
Innere Ordnung des Aufsichtsrats

(1) ¹Der Aufsichtsrat hat nach näherer Bestimmung der Satzung aus seiner

Section 107
Internal Organization of the Supervisory Board

(1) ¹The supervisory board shall elect from its midst a chairman and at least

Mitte einen Vorsitzenden und mindestens einen Stellvertreter zu wählen. ²Der Vorstand hat zum Handelsregister anzumelden, wer gewählt ist. ³Der Stellvertreter hat nur dann die Rechte und Pflichten des Vorsitzenden, wenn dieser behindert ist.

(2) ¹Über die Sitzungen des Aufsichtsrats ist eine Niederschrift anzufertigen, die der Vorsitzende zu unterzeichnen hat. ²In der Niederschrift sind der Ort und der Tag der Sitzung, die Teilnehmer, die Gegenstände der Tagesordnung, der wesentliche Inhalt der Verhandlungen und die Beschlüsse des Aufsichtsrats anzugeben. ³Ein Verstoß gegen Satz 1 oder Satz 2 macht einen Beschluss nicht unwirksam. ⁴Jedem Mitglied des Aufsichtsrats ist auf Verlangen eine Abschrift der Sitzungsniederschrift auszuhändigen.

(3) ¹Der Aufsichtsrat kann aus seiner Mitte einen oder mehrere Ausschüsse bestellen, namentlich, um seine Verhandlungen und Beschlüsse vorzubereiten oder die Ausführung seiner Beschlüsse zu überwachen. ²Er kann insbesondere einen Prüfungsausschuss bestellen, der sich mit der Überwachung des Rechnungslegungsprozesses, der Wirksamkeit des internen Kontrollsystems, des Risikomanagementsystems und des internen Revisionssystems sowie der Abschlussprüfung, hier insbesondere der Unabhängigkeit des Abschlussprüfers und der vom Abschlussprüfer zusätzlich erbrachten Leistungen, befasst. ³Die Aufgaben nach Absatz 1 Satz 1, § 59 Abs. 3, § 77 Abs. 2 Satz 1, § 84 Abs. 1 Satz 1 und 3, Abs. 2 und Abs. 3 Satz 1, § 87 Abs. 1 und Abs. 2 Satz 1 und 2, § 111 Abs. 3, §§ 171, 314 Abs. 2 und 3 sowie Beschlüsse, dass bestimmte Arten von Geschäften nur mit Zustimmung des Aufsichtsrats vorgenommen werden dürfen, können einem Ausschuss nicht an Stelle des Aufsichtsrats zur Beschlussfassung überwiesen werden. ⁴Dem Aufsichtsrat ist regelmäßig

one deputy chairman in accordance with the applicable provisions of the articles of association. ²The management board shall report the persons elected to the Commercial Register. ³The deputy chairman shall have the rights and duties of the chairman only if the latter is incapacitated.

(2) ¹Minutes shall be kept of the supervisory board meetings and signed by the chairman. ²The minutes shall state the place and date of the meeting, the persons attending, the items on the agenda, the essential contents of the proceedings, and the resolutions adopted by the supervisory board. ³A violation of the provisions of sentence 1 or 2 shall not invalidate a resolution. ⁴A copy of the minutes of the meeting shall be provided upon request to each supervisory board member.

(3) ¹The supervisory board may appoint from its midst one or more committees, in particular to prepare its deliberations and resolutions or to supervise the implementation of its resolutions. ²In particular it may appoint an audit committee to monitor the accounting process, the effectiveness of the internal control system, the risk management system and the internal auditing system, as well as the audit of the financial statements, in particular the independence of the audit and the additional services rendered by the auditor. ³However, neither the duties pursuant to subsection (1) sentence 1, section 59 (3), section 77 (2) sentence 1, section 84 (1) sentences 1 and 3, (2) and (3) sentence 1, section 87 (1) and (2) sentences 1 and 2, section 111 (3), sections 171 and 314 (2) and (3) nor resolutions providing that specific types of transactions may be entered into only with the consent of the supervisory board, may be referred to a committee for resolution in lieu of the supervisory board. ⁴The supervisory board shall be informed of the work of the committees on a regular basis.

über die Arbeit der Ausschüsse zu berichten.

(4) Richtet der Aufsichtsrat einer Gesellschaft im Sinn des § 264 d des Handelsgesetzbuchs einen Prüfungsausschuss im Sinn des Absatzes 3 Satz 2 ein, so muss mindestens ein Mitglied die Voraussetzungen des § 100 Abs. 5 erfüllen.

(4) Should the supervisory board of a company within the meaning of section 264 d of the German Commercial Code establish an audit committee within the meaning of subsection (3) sentence 2, at least one of the members must meet the prerequisites set out in section 100 (5).

§ 108
Beschlussfassung des Aufsichtsrats

Section 108
Resolutions of the Supervisory Board

(1) Der Aufsichtsrat entscheidet durch Beschluss.

(1) The supervisory board shall decide by resolution.

(2) [1] Die Beschlussfähigkeit des Aufsichtsrats kann, soweit sie nicht gesetzlich geregelt ist, durch die Satzung bestimmt werden. [2] Ist sie weder gesetzlich noch durch die Satzung geregelt, so ist der Aufsichtsrat nur beschlussfähig, wenn mindestens die Hälfte der Mitglieder, aus denen er nach Gesetz oder Satzung insgesamt zu bestehen hat, an der Beschlussfassung teilnimmt. [3] In jedem Fall müssen mindestens drei Mitglieder an der Beschlussfassung teilnehmen. [4] Der Beschlussfähigkeit steht nicht entgegen, dass dem Aufsichtsrat weniger Mitglieder als die durch Gesetz oder Satzung festgesetzte Zahl angehören, auch wenn das für seine Zusammensetzung maßgebende zahlenmäßige Verhältnis nicht gewahrt ist.

(2) [1] Where the quorum required for the supervisory board is not determined by statute, it may be set by the articles of association. [2] If the quorum is not set by statute or the articles of association, the supervisory board shall only have a quorum if at least one-half of the number of members it is required to have pursuant to statute or the articles of association participate in the adoption of the resolution. [3] In any event at least three members shall be required to participate in the adoption of a resolution. [4] If the supervisory board has fewer members than the number required by statute or the articles of association this shall not prejudice the presence of a quorum, even if the numerical ratio required for its composition is not maintained.

(3) [1] Abwesende Aufsichtsratsmitglieder können dadurch an der Beschlussfassung des Aufsichtsrats und seiner Ausschüsse teilnehmen, dass sie schriftliche Stimmabgaben überreichen lassen. [2] Die schriftlichen Stimmabgaben können durch andere Aufsichtsratsmitglieder überreicht werden. [3] Sie können auch durch Personen, die nicht dem Aufsichtsrat angehören, übergeben werden, wenn diese nach § 109 Abs. 3 zur Teilnahme an der Sitzung berechtigt sind.

(3) [1] Supervisory board members who are not present may take part in the adoption of a resolution of the supervisory board or of any committee thereof by having written votes submitted. [2] The written votes may be submitted by other supervisory board members. [3] They may also be submitted by persons who are not supervisory board members, provided that such persons are entitled to attend the meeting pursuant to section 109 (3).

(4) Schriftliche, fernmündliche oder andere vergleichbare Formen der Beschlussfassung des Aufsichtsrats und seiner Ausschüsse sind vorbehaltlich einer näheren Regelung durch die Satzung oder eine Geschäftsordnung des Aufsichtsrats nur zulässig, wenn kein Mitglied diesem Verfahren widerspricht.

(4) Resolutions of the supervisory board and its committees may only be adopted in writing, telephone or other comparable forms, subject to a more detailed regulation by the articles of association or rules of procedure, if no member objects to such procedure.

§ 109
Teilnahme an Sitzungen des Aufsichtsrats und seiner Ausschüsse

Section 109
Attendance of Meetings of the Supervisory Board and its Committees

(1) ¹An den Sitzungen des Aufsichtsrats und seiner Ausschüsse sollen Personen, die weder dem Aufsichtsrat noch dem Vorstand angehören, nicht teilnehmen. ²Sachverständige und Auskunftspersonen können zur Beratung über einzelne Gegenstände zugezogen werden.

(1) ¹Persons who are not supervisory board or management board members may not attend meetings of the supervisory board and its committees. ²Experts and persons needed to provide information may be invited for consultation on individual matters.

(2) Aufsichtsratsmitglieder, die dem Ausschuss nicht angehören, können an den Ausschusssitzungen teilnehmen, wenn der Vorsitzende des Aufsichtsrats nichts anderes bestimmt.

(2) Supervisory board members who are not members of a committee may attend meetings of such committee, unless the chairman of the supervisory board determines otherwise.

(3) Die Satzung kann zulassen, dass an den Sitzungen des Aufsichtsrats und seiner Ausschüsse Personen, die dem Aufsichtsrat nicht angehören, an Stelle von verhinderten Aufsichtsratsmitgliedern teilnehmen können, wenn diese sie hierzu in Textform ermächtigt haben.

(3) The articles of association may permit persons who are not supervisory board members to attend meetings of the supervisory board and its committees in place of supervisory board members who are unable to attend, provided that such members have authorized such persons to attend in writing.

(4) Abweichende gesetzliche Vorschriften bleiben unberührt.

(4) Statutory provisions which depart from these provisions shall not be affected.

§ 110
Einberufung des Aufsichtsrats

Section 110
Convening of Supervisory Board Meetings

(1) ¹Jedes Aufsichtsratsmitglied oder der Vorstand kann unter Angabe des Zwecks und der Gründe verlangen, dass der Vorsitzende des Aufsichtsrats unverzüglich den Aufsichtsrat einberuft. ²Die Sitzung muss binnen zwei

(1) ¹Each supervisory board or the management board member may, upon stating the grounds therefore, request that the chairman of the supervisory board promptly convene a supervisory board meeting. ²The meeting shall be held

Wochen nach der Einberufung stattfinden.

(2) Wird dem Verlangen nicht entsprochen, so kann das Aufsichtsratsmitglied oder der Vorstand unter Mitteilung des Sachverhalts und der Angabe einer Tagesordnung selbst den Aufsichtsrat einberufen.

(3) Der Aufsichtsrat muss zwei Sitzungen im Kalenderhalbjahr abhalten. In nichtbörsennotierten Gesellschaften kann der Aufsichtsrat beschließen, dass eine Sitzung im Kalenderhalbjahr abzuhalten ist.

§ 111
Aufgaben und Rechte des Aufsichtsrats

(1) Der Aufsichtsrat hat die Geschäftsführung zu überwachen.

(2) [1] Der Aufsichtsrat kann die Bücher und Schriften der Gesellschaft sowie die Vermögensgegenstände, namentlich die Gesellschaftskasse und die Bestände an Wertpapieren und Waren, einsehen und prüfen. [2] Er kann damit auch einzelne Mitglieder oder für bestimmte Aufgaben besondere Sachverständige beauftragen. [3] Er erteilt dem Abschlussprüfer den Prüfungsauftrag für den Jahres- und den Konzernabschluss gemäß § 290 des Handelsgesetzbuchs.

(3) [1] Der Aufsichtsrat hat eine Hauptversammlung einzuberufen, wenn das Wohl der Gesellschaft es fordert. [2] Für den Beschluss genügt die einfache Mehrheit.

(4) [1] Maßnahmen der Geschäftsführung können dem Aufsichtsrat nicht übertragen werden. [2] Die Satzung oder der Aufsichtsrat hat jedoch zu bestimmen, dass bestimmte Arten von Geschäften nur mit seiner Zustimmung vorgenommen werden dürfen. [3] Verweigert der Aufsichtsrat seine Zustimmung, so kann der Vorstand verlangen, dass die Hauptversammlung

within two weeks from the date on which notice thereof has been given.

(2) If the request is not complied with, the supervisory board member or the management board may themselves call a meeting of the supervisory board upon stating the facts of the matter and the agenda.

(3) The supervisory board must hold two meetings each calendar half-year. In the case of companies which are not listed on the stock exchange, the supervisory board may resolve to meet once each calendar half-year.

Section 111
Duties and Rights of the Supervisory Board

(1) The supervisory board shall supervise the management of the company.

(2) [1] The supervisory board may inspect and examine the company's books and records, its assets, in particular cash, securities and merchandise. [2] The supervisory board may also commission individual members or, for specific assignments, special experts, to carry this out. [3] It shall mandate the auditor to audit the annual financial statements and the consolidated financial statements pursuant to section 290 of the Commercial Code.

(3) [1] The supervisory board shall call a shareholders' meeting whenever the interests of the company so require. [2] Any resolution to do so shall require a simple majority.

(4) [1] Management responsibilities may not be conferred on the supervisory board. [2] However, the articles of association or the supervisory board must stipulate that specific types of transactions may be entered into only with the consent of the supervisory board. [3] If the supervisory board refuses to grant its consent, the management board may request that a shareholders' meeting re-

über die Zustimmung beschließt. ⁴Der Beschluss, durch den die Hauptversammlung zustimmt, bedarf einer Mehrheit, die mindestens drei Viertel der abgegebenen Stimmen umfasst. ⁵Die Satzung kann weder eine andere Mehrheit noch weitere Erfordernisse bestimmen.

(5) Die Aufsichtsratsmitglieder können ihre Aufgaben nicht durch andere wahrnehmen lassen.

§ 112
Vertretung der Gesellschaft gegenüber Vorstandsmitgliedern

¹Vorstandsmitgliedern gegenüber vertritt der Aufsichtsrat die Gesellschaft gerichtlich und außergerichtlich. ²§ 78 Abs. 2 Satz 2 gilt entsprechend.

§ 113
Vergütung der Aufsichtsratsmitglieder

(1) ¹Den Aufsichtsratsmitgliedern kann für ihre Tätigkeit eine Vergütung gewährt werden. ²Sie kann in der Satzung festgesetzt oder von der Hauptversammlung bewilligt werden. ³Sie soll in einem angemessenen Verhältnis zu den Aufgaben der Aufsichtsratsmitglieder und zur Lage der Gesellschaft stehen. ³Ist die Vergütung in der Satzung festgesetzt, so kann die Hauptversammlung eine Satzungsänderung, durch welche die Vergütung herabgesetzt wird, mit einfacher Stimmenmehrheit beschließen.

(2) ¹Den Mitgliedern des ersten Aufsichtsrats kann nur die Hauptversammlung eine Vergütung für ihre Tätigkeit bewilligen. ²Der Beschluss kann erst in der Hauptversammlung gefasst werden, die über die Entlastung der Mitglieder des ersten Aufsichtsrats beschließt.

solve whether to grant such consent. ⁴The shareholders' resolution to grant such consent shall require a majority of at least three-fourths of the votes cast. ⁵The articles of association may neither require a different majority nor stipulate additional requirements.

(5) Supervisory board members may not confer their responsibilities on other persons.

Section 112
Representation of the Company as against Management Board Members

¹The supervisory board shall represent the company both in and out of court as against the management board members. ²Section 78 (2) sentence 2 applies *mutatis mutandis*.

Section 113
Remuneration of Supervisory Board Members

(1) ¹The supervisory board members may receive remuneration for their services. ²Such remuneration may be set in the articles of association or authorized by the shareholders' meeting. ³Such remuneration shall bear a reasonable relationship to the supervisory board members' duties and the condition of the company. ⁴If the remuneration is set in the articles, the shareholders' meeting may, by simple majority, resolve to amend the articles of association to reduce this remuneration.

(2) ¹Remuneration of the members of the first supervisory board for their services may only be authorized by shareholders' resolution. ²Such a resolution may be adopted only in the shareholders' meetings which decide on the discharge of the members of the first supervisory board.

(3) ¹Wird den Aufsichtsratsmitgliedern ein Anteil am Jahresgewinn der Gesellschaft gewährt, so berechnet sich der Anteil nach dem Bilanzgewinn, vermindert um einen Betrag von mindestens vier vom Hundert der auf den geringsten Ausgabebetrag der Aktien geleisteten Einlagen. ²Entgegenstehende Festsetzungen sind nichtig.

(3) ¹If supervisory board members are granted a share of the company's annual profit, such share shall be computed on the basis of the net retained profits, reduced by an amount of no less than four percent of the contributions made on the lowest issued price of the shares. ²Any provisions to the contrary shall be null and void.

§ 114
Verträge mit Aufsichtsratsmitgliedern

(1) Verpflichtet sich ein Aufsichtsratsmitglied außerhalb seiner Tätigkeit im Aufsichtsrat durch einen Dienstvertrag, durch den ein Arbeitsverhältnis nicht begründet wird, oder durch einen Werkvertrag gegenüber der Gesellschaft zu einer Tätigkeit höherer Art, so hängt die Wirksamkeit des Vertrags von der Zustimmung des Aufsichtsrats ab.

(2) ¹Gewährt die Gesellschaft auf Grund eines solchen Vertrags dem Aufsichtsratsmitglied eine Vergütung, ohne dass der Aufsichtsrat dem Vertrag zugestimmt hat, so hat das Aufsichtsratsmitglied die Vergütung zurückzugewähren, es sei denn, dass der Aufsichtsrat den Vertrag genehmigt. ²Ein Anspruch des Aufsichtsratsmitglieds gegen die Gesellschaft auf Herausgabe der durch die geleistete Tätigkeit erlangten Bereicherung bleibt unberührt; der Anspruch kann jedoch nicht gegen den Rückgewähranspruch aufgerechnet werden.

Section 114
Contracts with Supervisory Board Members

(1) If, in addition to his services on the supervisory board, a supervisory board member enters into a contract with the company for the provision of professional services which does not establish an employment relationship, or to undertake a special assignment, any such contract shall require the consent of the supervisory board in order to be valid.

(2) ¹If, pursuant to any such contract, the company grants remuneration to a supervisory board member without the supervisory board having consented to such contract, that supervisory board member shall repay this remuneration, unless the supervisory board subsequently approves the contract. ²Any claim of the supervisory board member against the company for restitution of the enrichment obtained by the services performed shall remain unaffected; however, such claim may not be set off against the company's claim for repayment of the remuneration.

§ 115
Kreditgewährung an Aufsichtsratsmitglieder

(1) ¹Die Gesellschaft darf ihren Aufsichtsratsmitgliedern Kredit nur mit Einwilligung des Aufsichtsrats gewähren. ²Eine herrschende Gesellschaft darf Kredite an Aufsichtsratsmitglieder eines abhängigen Unternehmens nur mit Einwilligung ihres Aufsichts-

Section 115
Extension of Credit to Supervisory Board Members

(1) ¹The company may extend credit to supervisory board members only with the consent of the supervisory board. ²A controlling company may extend credit to supervisory board members of a controlled enterprise only with the consent of its supervisory board; a controlled

rats, eine abhängige Gesellschaft darf Kredite an Aufsichtsratsmitglieder des herrschenden Unternehmens nur mit Einwilligung des Aufsichtsrats des herrschenden Unternehmens gewähren. ³Die Einwilligung kann nur für bestimmte Kreditgeschäfte oder Arten von Kreditgeschäften und nicht für länger als drei Monate im voraus erteilt werden. ⁴Der Beschluss über die Einwilligung hat die Verzinsung und Rückzahlung des Kredits zu regeln. ⁵Betreibt das Aufsichtsratsmitglied ein Handelsgewerbe als Einzelkaufmann, so ist die Einwilligung nicht erforderlich, wenn der Kredit für die Bezahlung von Waren gewährt wird, welche die Gesellschaft seinem Handelsgeschäft liefert.

(2) Absatz 1 gilt auch für Kredite an den Ehegatten, Lebenspartner oder an ein minderjähriges Kind eines Aufsichtsratsmitglieds und für Kredite an einen Dritten, der für Rechnung dieser Personen oder für Rechnung eines Aufsichtsratsmitglieds handelt.

(3) ¹Ist ein Aufsichtsratsmitglied zugleich gesetzlicher Vertreter einer anderen juristischen Person oder Gesellschafter einer Personenhandelsgesellschaft, so darf die Gesellschaft der juristischen Person oder der Personenhandelsgesellschaft Kredit nur mit Einwilligung des Aufsichtsrats gewähren; Absatz 1 Satz 3 und 4 gilt sinngemäß. ²Dies gilt nicht, wenn die juristische Person oder die Personenhandelsgesellschaft mit der Gesellschaft verbunden ist oder wenn der Kredit für die Bezahlung von Waren gewährt wird, welche die Gesellschaft der juristischen Person oder der Personenhandelsgesellschaft liefert.

(4) Wird entgegen den Absätzen 1 bis 3 Kredit gewährt, so ist der Kredit ohne Rücksicht auf entgegenstehende Vereinbarungen sofort zurückzugewähren, wenn nicht der Aufsichtsrat nachträglich zustimmt.

company may extend credit to supervisory board members of the controlling enterprise only with the consent of the supervisory board of the controlling enterprise. ³Such consent may be granted only for specific credit transactions or kinds of credit transactions, and not for more than three months in advance. ⁴The resolution on such consent shall stipulate the payment of interest on, and repayment of, any loan. ⁵If the supervisory board member operates a business as a sole proprietor, such consent shall not be required if the credit is extended to finance the payment of goods which the company supplies to his business.

(2) Para. (1) shall also apply to credits to the spouse, life partner or a minor child of a supervisory board member and to any third person acting on the account of any such person or of a supervisory board member.

(3) ¹If a supervisory board member is also a legal representative of another legal entity or a member of a commercial partnership, the company may extend credit to such legal entity or commercial partnership only with the consent of the supervisory board; subsection (1) sentences 3 and 4 shall apply analogously. ²This shall not apply if such legal entity or commercial partnership is affiliated with the company or if the credit is extended to finance the payment of goods which the company supplies to such legal entity or commercial partnership.

(4) Any credit extended in violation of the provisions of subsections (1) to (3) shall be repaid immediately, irrespective of any agreement to the contrary, unless the supervisory board subsequently consents.

(5) Ist die Gesellschaft ein Kreditinstitut oder Finanzdienstleistungsinstitut, auf das § 15 des Gesetzes über das Kreditwesen anzuwenden ist, gelten anstelle der Absätze 1 bis 4 die Vorschriften des Gesetzes über das Kreditwesen.

(5) If the company is a bank or a financial services institution to which section 15 of the Banking Act applies, the provisions of the Banking Act shall apply in lieu of subsections (1) to (4).

§ 116
Sorgfaltspflicht und Verantwortlichkeit der Aufsichtsratsmitglieder

Section 116
Duty of Care and Responsibility of Supervisory Board Members

[1] Für die Sorgfaltspflicht und Verantwortlichkeit der Aufsichtsratsmitglieder gilt § 93 mit Ausnahme des Absatzes 2 Satz 3 über die Sorgfaltspflicht und Verantwortlichkeit der Vorstandsmitglieder sinngemäß. [2] Die Aufsichtsratsmitglieder sind insbesondere zur Verschwiegenheit über erhaltene vertrauliche Berichte und vertrauliche Beratungen verpflichtet. [3] Sie sind namentlich zum Ersatz verpflichtet, wenn sie eine unangemessene Vergütung festsetzen (§ 87 Absatz 1).

[1] Section 93 regarding the duty of care and responsibility of the management board members shall, with the exception of subsection (2) sentence 3, apply analogously to the duty of care and responsibility of the supervisory board members. [2] The supervisory board members are in particular obligated to maintain confidentiality with regard to confidential reports and consultations. [3] They shall be personally liable for damages if they set an unreasonable remuneration (section 87 (1)).

Dritter Abschnitt
Benutzung des Einflusses auf die Gesellschaft

Chapter 3
Exertion of Influence on the Company

§ 117
Schadenersatzpflicht

Section 117
Liability for Damages

(1) [1] Wer vorsätzlich unter Benutzung seines Einflusses auf die Gesellschaft ein Mitglied des Vorstands oder des Aufsichtsrats, einen Prokuristen oder einen Handlungsbevollmächtigten dazu bestimmt, zum Schaden der Gesellschaft oder ihrer Aktionäre zu handeln, ist der Gesellschaft zum Ersatz des ihr daraus entstehenden Schadens verpflichtet. [2] Er ist auch den Aktionären zum Ersatz des ihnen daraus entstehenden Schadens verpflichtet, soweit sie, abgesehen von einem Schaden, der ihnen durch Schädigung der Gesellschaft zugefügt worden ist, geschädigt worden sind.

(1) [1] Any person who, by willfully exerting his influence on the company, induces a management board member or the supervisory board, a procuration officer or a general manager to act to the disadvantage of the company or its shareholders, shall be liable to the company for any resulting damage. [2] Such person shall also be liable to the shareholders for any resulting damage insofar as they have sustained a loss apart from the loss they sustained due to the damage incurred by the company.

(2) ¹Neben ihm haften als Gesamtschuldner die Mitglieder des Vorstands und des Aufsichtsrats, wenn sie unter Verletzung ihrer Pflichten gehandelt haben. ²Ist streitig, ob sie die Sorgfalt eines ordentlichen und gewissenhaften Geschäftsleiters angewandt haben, so trifft sie die Beweislast. ³Der Gesellschaft und auch den Aktionären gegenüber tritt die Ersatzpflicht der Mitglieder des Vorstands und des Aufsichtsrats nicht ein, wenn die Handlung auf einem gesetzmäßigen Beschluss der Hauptversammlung beruht. ⁴Dadurch, dass der Aufsichtsrat die Handlung gebilligt hat, wird die Ersatzpflicht nicht ausgeschlossen.

(3) Neben ihm haftet ferner als Gesamtschuldner, wer durch die schädigende Handlung einen Vorteil erlangt hat, sofern er die Beeinflussung vorsätzlich veranlasst hat.

(4) Für die Aufhebung der Ersatzpflicht gegenüber der Gesellschaft gilt sinngemäß § 93 Abs. 4 Satz 3 und 4.

(5) ¹Der Ersatzanspruch der Gesellschaft kann auch von den Gläubigern der Gesellschaft geltend gemacht werden, soweit sie von dieser keine Befriedigung erlangen können. ²Den Gläubigern gegenüber wird die Ersatzpflicht weder durch einen Verzicht oder Vergleich der Gesellschaft noch dadurch aufgehoben, dass die Handlung auf einem Beschluss der Hauptversammlung beruht. ³Ist über das Vermögen der Gesellschaft das Insolvenzverfahren eröffnet, so übt während dessen Dauer der Insolvenzverwalter oder der Sachwalter das Recht der Gläubiger aus.

(6) Die Ansprüche aus diesen Vorschriften verjähren in fünf Jahren.

(7) Diese Vorschriften gelten nicht, wenn das Mitglied des Vorstands oder des Aufsichtsrats, der Prokurist oder

(2) ¹In addition to such person, the management board members and the supervisory board shall be jointly and severally liable if they have acted in breach of their duties. ²They shall bear the burden of proof in the event of a dispute as to whether or not they employed the care of a diligent and conscientious manager. ³The management board members and the supervisory board shall not be liable to the company or the shareholders for damage if they acted pursuant to a lawful resolution of the shareholders' meeting. ⁴However, liability for damages shall not be precluded by the fact that the supervisory board had consented to the act.

(3) In addition to such person, any person who has willfully caused undue influence to be exerted and obtained an advantage from the act which caused the damage shall also be jointly and severally liable.

(4) Section 93 (4) sentences 3 and 4 shall apply analogously to the removal of liability for damages to the company.

(5) ¹The company's claim for damages may also be asserted by its creditors if they are unable to obtain satisfaction from the company. ²Liability for damages to the creditors shall not be extinguished by a waiver or the conclusion of a settlement by the company nor by the fact that the act which caused the damage was based on a resolution of the shareholders' meeting. ³If insolvency proceedings have been initiated against the company assets, the insolvency receiver or the trustee shall exercise the rights of the creditors in the course of such proceedings.

(6) Claims under the above provisions shall be statute barred after a period of five years.

(7) These provisions shall not apply if the management board member or the supervisory board member, the procura-

der Handlungsbevollmächtigte durch Ausübung

1. der Leitungsmacht auf Grund eines Beherrschungsvertrags oder
2. der Leitungsmacht einer Hauptgesellschaft (§ 319), in die die Gesellschaft eingegliedert ist,

zu der schädigenden Handlung bestimmt worden ist.

tion officer or the general manager was induced to engage in the act causing damage by the exercise of:

1. the power to issue directives under a control agreement; or
2. the power of a principal company (section 319) into which the company has been integrated to issue directives.

XXII. Labor Court Act (Arbeitsgerichtsgesetz – ArbGG)

of 2 July 1979 (Federal Law Gazette I p. 853)

in the amended version of 30 July 2009

(excerpts)

Erster Teil
Allgemeine Vorschriften

§ 1
Gerichte für Arbeitssachen

Die Gerichtsbarkeit in Arbeitssachen – §§ 2 bis 3 – wird ausgeübt durch die Arbeitsgerichte – §§ 14 bis 31 –, die Landesarbeitsgerichte – §§ 33 bis 39 – und das Bundesarbeitsgericht – §§ 40 bis 45 – (Gerichte für Arbeitssachen).

§ 2
Zuständigkeit im Urteilsverfahren

(1) Die Gerichte für Arbeitssachen sind ausschließlich zuständig für

1. bürgerliche Rechtsstreitigkeiten zwischen Tarifvertragsparteien oder zwischen diesen und Dritten aus Tarifverträgen oder über das Bestehen oder Nichtbestehen von Tarifverträgen;

2. bürgerliche Rechtsstreitigkeiten zwischen tariffähigen Parteien oder zwischen diesen und Dritten aus unerlaubten Handlungen, soweit es sich um Maßnahmen zum Zwecke des Arbeitskampfs oder um Fragen der Vereinigungsfreiheit einschließlich des hiermit im Zusammenhang stehenden Betätigungsrechts der Vereinigungen handelt;

3. bürgerliche Rechtsstreitigkeiten zwischen Arbeitnehmern und Arbeitgebern

    a) aus dem Arbeitsverhältnis;

Part 1
General Provisions

Section 1
Courts for Labor Matters

The jurisdiction in labor matters – sections 2 to 3 – is exercised by the labor courts – sections 14 to 31 –, the State labor courts – sections 33 to 39 – and the Federal Labor Court – sections 40 to 45 – (courts for labor matters).

Section 2
Subject Matter Jurisdiction in Judgment Procedures

(1) The courts for labor matters have exclusive jurisdiction in

1. civil litigation between parties to a collective bargaining agreement or between them and third parties relating to collective bargaining agreements or as to the existence or non-existence of collective bargaining agreements;

2. civil litigation between parties capable of collectively bargaining or between them and third parties relating to torts insofar as it relates to measures for the purpose of the labor disputes or to questions of freedom to associate including the related right of the associations to act;

3. civil litigation between employees and employers

    a) relating to the employment relationship;

b) über das Bestehen oder Nichtbestehen eines Arbeitsverhältnisses;

c) aus Verhandlungen über die Eingehung eines Arbeitsverhältnisses und aus dessen Nachwirkungen;

d) aus unerlaubten Handlungen, soweit diese mit dem Arbeitsverhältnis im Zusammenhang stehen;

e) über Arbeitspapiere;

4. bürgerliche Rechtsstreitigkeiten zwischen Arbeitnehmern oder ihren Hinterbliebenen und

a) Arbeitgebern über Ansprüche, die mit dem Arbeitsverhältnis in rechtlichem oder unmittelbar wirtschaftlichem Zusammenhang stehen;

b) gemeinsamen Einrichtungen der Tarifvertragsparteien oder Sozialeinrichtungen des privaten Rechts über Ansprüche aus dem Arbeitsverhältnis oder Ansprüche, die mit dem Arbeitsverhältnis in rechtlichem oder unmittelbar wirtschaftlichem Zusammenhang stehen,

soweit nicht die ausschließliche Zuständigkeit eines anderen Gerichts gegeben ist;

5. bürgerliche Rechtsstreitigkeiten zwischen Arbeitnehmern oder ihren Hinterbliebenen und dem Träger der Insolvenzsicherung über Ansprüche auf Leistungen der Insolvenzsicherung nach dem Vierten Abschnitt des Ersten Teils des Gesetzes zur Verbesserung der betrieblichen Altersversorgung;

6. bürgerliche Rechtsstreitigkeiten zwischen Arbeitgebern und Einrichtungen nach Nummer 4 Buchstabe b und Nummer 5 sowie zwischen diesen Einrichtungen, soweit nicht die ausschließliche Zuständig-keit eines anderen Gerichts gegeben ist;

7. bürgerliche Rechtsstreitigkeiten zwischen Entwicklungshelfern und Trägern des Entwicklungsdienstes nach dem Entwicklungshelfergesetz;

b) regarding the existence or non-existence of an employment relationship;

c) relating to negotiations as to the entering into an employment relationship and relating to its subsequent effects;

d) relating to torts insofar as they are related to the employment relationship;

e) regarding employment re-cords;

4. civil litigation between employees or their survivors and

a) employers regarding claims having a legal or direct commercial connection with the employment relationship;

b) joint institutions of the parties to a collective bargaining agreement or social institutions with private legal status regarding claims resulting from the employment relationship or claims having a legal or direct commercial connection with the employment relationship

unless another court has the exclusive jurisdiction;

5. civil litigation between employees or their survivors and the carriers of the insolvency insurance regarding claims for insolvency insurance benefits pursuant to the Fourth Chapter of the First Part of the Act for the Improvement of Company Pension Plans;

6. civil litigation between employers and institutions pursuant to no. 4b) and no. 5, as well as between these institutions unless another court has exclusive jurisdiction;

7. civil litigation between development aid workers and the institutions in charge of the development service, pursuant of the Act for Development Aid Workers;

8. bürgerliche Rechtsstreitigkeiten zwischen den Trägern des freiwilligen sozialen oder ökologischen Jahres oder den Einsatzstellen und Freiwilligen nach dem Jugendfreiwilligendienstegesetz;
9. bürgerliche Rechtsstreitigkeiten zwischen Arbeitnehmern aus gemeinsamer Arbeit und aus unerlaubten Handlungen, soweit diese mit dem Arbeitsverhältnis im Zusammenhang stehen;
10. bürgerliche Rechtsstreitigkeiten zwischen behinderten Menschen im Arbeitsbereich von Werkstätten für behinderte Menschen und den Trägern der Werkstätten aus den in § 138 des Neunten Buches Sozialgesetzbuch geregelten arbeitnehmerähnlichen Rechtsverhältnissen.

(2) Die Gerichte für Arbeitssachen sind auch zuständig für bürgerliche Rechtsstreitigkeiten zwischen Arbeitnehmern und Arbeitgebern,

a) die ausschließlich Ansprüche auf Leistung einer festgestellten oder festgesetzten Vergütung für eine Arbeitnehmererfindung oder für einen technischen Verbesserungsvorschlag nach § 20 Abs. 1 des Gesetzes über Arbeitnehmererfindungen zum Gegenstand haben;
b) die als Urheberrechtsstreitsachen aus Arbeitsverhältnissen ausschließlich Ansprüche auf Leistung einer vereinbarten Vergütung zum Gegenstand haben.

(3) Vor die Gerichte für Arbeitssachen können auch nicht unter die Absätze 1 und 2 fallende Rechtsstreitigkeiten gebracht werden, wenn der Anspruch mit einer bei einem Arbeitsgericht anhängigen oder gleichzeitig anhängig werdenden bürgerlichen Rechtsstreitigkeit der in den Absätzen 1 und 2 bezeichneten Art in rechtlichem oder unmittelbar wirtschaftlichem Zusammenhang steht und für seine Geltendmachung nicht die ausschließliche Zuständigkeit eines anderen Gerichts gegeben ist.

8. civil litigation between the institutions in charge of the voluntary social or ecological year or the assigning bodies and volunteers pursuant to the Youth Volunteer Service Act;
9. civil litigation between workers resulting from joint work and from torts insofar as these are related to the employment relationship.
10. civil litigation between disabled persons in the work area of workshops for disabled persons and the sponsors of workshops under the legal circumstances set forth in section 138 of the Ninth Book of the Social Security Code (*Sozialgesetzbuch IX – SGB IX*).

(2) The courts for labor matters shall also have jurisdiction in civil litigation between employees and employers

a) which relates exclusively to claims for the payment of an ascertained or fixed remuneration for an employee's invention or for a suggestion regarding technical improvements pursuant to section 20 (1) of the Employees' Inventions Act (*Gesetz über Arbeitnehmererfindungen*);
b) which, as a copyright litigation matter arising from an employment relationship, involves exclusively claims for the payment of an agreed remuneration.

(3) Litigation not falling under subsections (1) and (2) may also be brought before the courts for labor matters if the claim has a legal or direct economic connection with civil lawsuits as described in subsections (1) and (2) which are pending or will become pending at the same time and provided that no other court has exclusive jurisdiction over the assertion of such claims.

(4) Auf Grund einer Vereinbarung können auch bürgerliche Rechtsstreitigkeiten zwischen juristischen Personen des Privatrechts und Personen, die kraft Gesetzes allein oder als Mitglieder des Vertretungsorgans der juristischen Person zu deren Vertretung berufen sind, vor die Gerichte für Arbeitssachen gebracht werden.

(5) In Rechtsstreitigkeiten nach diesen Vorschriften findet das Urteilsverfahren statt.

(4) On the basis of an agreement, civil litigation between legal entities with private legal status and persons who have been appointed to represent them by force of law alone or as members of the representative body of a legal entity may also be brought before the courts for labor matters.

(5) In litigation pursuant to these provisions, the judgment procedure applies.

§ 2a
Zuständigkeit im Beschlussverfahren

(1) Die Gerichte für Arbeitssachen sind ferner ausschließlich zuständig für

1. Angelegenheiten aus dem Betriebsverfassungsgesetz, soweit nicht für Maßnahmen nach seinen §§ 119 bis 121 die Zuständigkeit eines anderen Gerichts gegeben ist;
2. Angelegenheiten aus dem Sprecherausschussgesetz, soweit nicht für Maßnahmen nach seinen §§ 34 bis 36 die Zuständigkeit eines anderen Gerichts gegeben ist;
3. Angelegenheiten aus dem Mitbestimmungsgesetz, dem Mitbestimmungsergänzungsgesetz und dem Drittelbeteiligungsgesetz, soweit über die Wahl von Vertretern der Arbeitnehmer in den Aufsichtsrat und über ihre Abberufung mit Ausnahme der Abberufung nach § 103 Abs. 3 des Aktiengesetzes zu entscheiden ist;
3a. Angelegenheiten aus den §§ 94, 95, 139 des Neunten Buches Sozialgesetzbuch
3b. Angelegenheiten aus dem Gesetz über Europäische Betriebsräte, soweit nicht für Maßnahmen nach seinen §§ 43 bis 45 die Zuständigkeit eines anderen Gerichts gegeben ist;
3c. Angelegenheiten aus § 51 des Berufsbildungsgesetzes;

Section 2a
Subject Matter Jurisdiction in Order Procedures

(1) Additionally the courts for labor matters have exclusive jurisdiction over

1. matters relating to the Works Constitution Act, unless the jurisdiction of another court exists for measures pursuant to sections 119 to 121 thereof;
2. matters relating to the Spokespersons' Committee Act *(Sprecherausschussgesetz)*, unless the jurisdiction of another court exists for measures pursuant to sections 34 to 36 thereof;
3. matters relating to the Codetermination Act, the Supplemental Codetermination Act and the One-Third Participation Act insofar as it is to be decided as to the election of employees', representatives to the supervisory board or as to their removal, except the removal pursuant to section 103 (3) of the Stock Corporation Act;
3a. matters relating to sections 94, 95, 139 of the Social Security Code IX
3b. matters relating to the Act on European Works Councils, unless the jurisdiction of another court exists for measures pursuant to sections 43 to 45 thereof
3c. matters relating to section 51 of the Vocational Training Act *(Berufsbildungsgesetz)*;

3d. Angelegenheiten aus dem SE-Beteiligungsgesetz vom 22. Dezember 2004 (BGBl. I S. 3675, 3686) mit Ausnahme der §§ 45 und 46 und nach den §§ 34 bis 39 nur insoweit, als über die Wahl von Vertretern der Arbeitnehmer in das Aufsichts- oder Verwaltungsorgan sowie deren Abberufung mit Ausnahme der Abberufung nach § 103 Abs. 3 des Aktiengesetzes zu entscheiden ist;

3e. Angelegenheiten aus dem SCE-Beteiligungsgesetz vom 14. August 2006 (BGBl. I S. 1911, 1917) mit Ausnahme der §§ 47 und 48 und nach den §§ 34 bis 39 nur insoweit, als über die Wahl von Vertretern der Arbeitnehmer in das Aufsichts- oder Verwaltungsorgan sowie deren Abberufung zu entscheiden ist;

3f. Angelegenheiten aus dem Gesetz über die Mitbestimmung der Arbeitnehmer bei einer grenzüberschreitenden Verschmelzung vom 21. Dezember 2006 (BGBl. I S. 3332) mit Ausnahme der §§ 34 und 35 und nach den §§ 23 bis 28 nur insoweit, als über die Wahl von Vertretern der Arbeitnehmer in das Aufsichts- oder Verwaltungsorgan sowie deren Abberufung mit Ausnahme der Abberufung nach § 103 Abs. 3 des Aktiengesetzes zu entscheiden ist;

4. die Entscheidung über die Tariffähigkeit und die Tarifzuständigkeit einer Vereinigung.

(2) In Streitigkeiten nach diesen Vorschriften findet das Beschlussverfahren statt.

3d. matters relating to the Participation of Employees (European Companies) Act *(SE-Beteiligungsgesetz)* of 22 December 2004 (Federal Law Gazette I pp 3675, 3686) with the exception of sections 45 and 46 and pursuant to sections 34 to 39 only to the extent that a decision must be made regarding the election of representatives of the employees to the supervisory board or administrative body, as well as their dismissal, with the exception of dismissals pursuant to section 103 (3) of the German Stock Corporation Act;

3e. matters relating to the Participation of Employees European Cooperative Societies Act *(SCE-Beteiligungsgesetz)* of 14 August 2006 (Federal Law Gazette I pp. 1911, 1917) with the exception of sections 47 and 48 and pursuant to sections 34 to 39 only to the extent that a decision must be made regarding the election of representatives of the employees to the supervisory board or administrative body, as well as their dismissal;

3f. matters relating to the Act of the Co-determination of Employees in the Event of a Cross-Boundary Merger of December 2006 (Federal Law Gazette I p. 3332), with the exception of sections 34 and 35, and pursuant to sections 23 through 28 only with the extent that a decision is to be made regarding the election of the employees' representatives to the supervisory board or administrative body, as well as their dismissal, with the exception of dismissals that are governed by section 103 para. (3) of the Stock Corporation Act *(Aktiengesetz – AktG)*;

4. decisions as to the capacity and competence of an association to bargain collectively.

(2) In the litigation pursuant to this provision, the order procedure applies.

§ 3
Zuständigkeit in sonstigen Fällen

Die in den §§ 2 und 2a begründete Zuständigkeit besteht auch in den Fällen, in denen der Rechtsstreit durch einen Rechtsnachfolger oder durch eine Person geführt wird, die kraft Gesetzes an Stelle des sachlich Berechtigten oder Verpflichteten hierzu befugt ist.

§ 4
Ausschluss der Arbeitsgerichtsbarkeit

In den Fällen des § 2 Abs. 1 und 2 kann die Arbeitsgerichtsbarkeit nach Maßgabe der §§ 101 bis 110 ausgeschlossen werden.

§ 5
Begriff des Arbeitnehmers

(1) [1] Arbeitnehmer im Sinne dieses Gesetzes sind Arbeiter und Angestellte sowie die zu ihrer Berufsausbildung Beschäftigten. [2] Als Arbeitnehmer gelten auch die in Heimarbeit Beschäftigten und die ihnen Gleichgestellten (§ 1 des Heimarbeitsgesetzes vom 14. März 1951 – Bundesgesetzbl. I S. 191 –) sowie sonstige Personen, die wegen ihrer wirtschaftlichen Unselbständigkeit als arbeitnehmerähnliche Personen anzusehen sind. [3] Als Arbeitnehmer gelten nicht in Betrieben einer juristischen Person oder einer Personengesamtheit Personen, die kraft Gesetzes, Satzung oder Gesellschaftsvertrags allein oder als Mitglieder des Vertretungsorgans zur Vertretung der juristischen Person oder der Personengesamtheit berufen sind.

(2) Beamte sind als solche keine Arbeitnehmer.

(3) [1] Handelsvertreter gelten nur dann als Arbeitnehmer im Sinne dieses Gesetzes, wenn sie zu dem Personenkreis gehören, für den nach § 92a des Handelsgesetzbuchs die untere Grenze der vertraglichen Leistungen des Unter-

Section 3
Jurisdiction in Other Cases

The jurisdiction established by sections 2 and 2a also exists in the cases in which the litigation is pursued by a legal successor or a person who is by law competent instead of the person entitled or obligated in rem.

Section 4
Exclusion of Jurisdiction of Labor Courts

In the cases set forth in section 2 subsections (1) and (2) the jurisdiction of the labor courts can be excluded subject to sections 101 to 110.

Section 5
Definition of the Employee

(1) [1] Employees within the meaning of this Act are workers or salaried employees as well as persons employed in occupational training. [2] Persons employed to work at home and those deemed equivalent to them (section 1 of the Act regarding Work to be Performed at Home *(Heimarbeitsgesetz)* of 14 March 1951 – Federal Law Gazette I p. 191 –) are deemed employees as well as other persons who are regarded similar to employees because of their economic dependence. [3] In establishments of a legal entity or of a partnership, persons who are appointed pursuant to statute, articles of association or partnership agreement to represent the legal entity or the partnership alone or as a member of the representative body are not deemed employees.

(2) Civil servants are as such not employees.

(3) [1] Commercial agents are only then deemed employees within the meaning of this Act if they belong to the category of persons for which the lower limit of the contractual benefits of the entrepreneur can be fixed pursuant to sec-

nehmers festgesetzt werden kann, und wenn sie während der letzten sechs Monate des Vertragsverhältnisses, bei kürzerer Vertragsdauer während dieser, im Durchschnitt monatlich nicht mehr als 1.000 Euro auf Grund des Vertragsverhältnisses an Vergütung einschließlich Provision und Ersatz für im regelmäßigen Geschäftsbetrieb entstandene Aufwendungen bezogen haben. ²Das Bundesministerium für Arbeit und Soziales und das Bundesministerium der Justiz können im Einvernehmen mit dem Bundesministerium für Wirtschaft und Technologie die in Satz 1 bestimmte Vergütungsgrenze durch Rechtsverordnung, die nicht der Zustimmung des Bundesrates bedarf, den jeweiligen Lohn- und Preisverhältnissen anpassen.

tion 92a of the Commercial Code and if during the last six months of the contractual relationship or, in case of a shorter period, during this, they have received, by reason of the contractual relationship, as remuneration including commission and reimbursement for expenses incurred in the ordinary course of the business, a monthly average not exceeding 1.000 euro. ²The Federal Ministry of Labor and Social Affairs and the Federal Ministry of Justice can, in agreement with the Federal Ministry of Economics and Technology, adjust by administrative regulations which do not require the consent of the Federal Council, the remuneration limit as designated in the first sentence to the current wage and price situation.

§ 6
Besetzung der Gerichte für Arbeitssachen

(1) Die Gerichte für Arbeitssachen sind mit Berufsrichtern und mit ehrenamtlichen Richtern aus den Kreisen der Arbeitnehmer und Arbeitgeber besetzt.

(2) *(weggefallen)*

Section 6
Composition of Courts for Labor Matters

(1) The courts for labor matters shall be composed of professional judges and lay judges from employee and employer groups.

(2) *(repealed)*

§ 6a
Allgemeine Vorschriften über das Präsidium und die Geschäftsverteilung

Für die Gerichte für Arbeitssachen gelten die Vorschriften des Zweiten Titels des Gerichtsverfassungsgesetzes nach Maßgabe der folgenden Vorschriften entsprechend:

1. Bei einem Arbeitsgericht mit weniger als drei Richterplanstellen werden die Aufgaben des Präsidiums durch den Vorsitzenden oder, wenn zwei Vorsitzende bestellt sind, im Einvernehmen der Vorsitzenden wahrgenommen. Einigen sich die Vorsitzenden nicht, so entscheidet das Präsidium des Landesarbeitsgerichts oder, soweit ein solches nicht besteht, der Präsident dieses Gerichts.

Section 6a
General Provisions on the Presidium and the Allocation of Responsibility

For the courts for labor matters, the provisions of the Second Title of the Judicature Act *(Gerichtsverfassungsgesetz)* shall apply subject to the following provisions:

1. For a labor court with less than three authorized judgeships, the responsibilities of the presidium shall be carried out by the presiding judge, or, if two presiding judges have been appointed, by their mutual agreement. If the presiding judges cannot agree, then the presidium of the regional labor court shall decide, or if no such court exists, the president of this court.

2. Bei einem Landesarbeitsgericht mit weniger als drei Richterplanstellen werden die Aufgaben des Präsidiums durch den Präsidenten, soweit ein zweiter Vorsitzender vorhanden ist, im Benehmen mit diesem wahrgenommen.
3. Der aufsichtführende Richter bestimmt, welche richterlichen Aufgaben er wahrnimmt.
4. Jeder ehrenamtliche Richter kann mehreren Spruchkörpern angehören.
5. Den Vorsitz in den Kammern der Arbeitsgerichte führen die Berufsrichter.

§ 7
Geschäftsstelle, Aufbringung der Mittel

(1) ¹Bei jedem Gericht für Arbeitssachen wird eine Geschäftsstelle eingerichtet, die mit der erforderlichen Zahl von Urkundsbeamten besetzt wird. ²Die Einrichtung der Geschäftsstelle bestimmt bei dem Bundesarbeitsgericht das Bundesministerium für Arbeit und Soziales im Benehmen mit dem Bundesministerium der Justiz. ³Die Einrichtung der Geschäftsstelle bestimmt bei den Arbeitsgerichten und Landesarbeitsgerichten die zuständige oberste Landesbehörde.

(2) ¹Die Kosten der Arbeitsgerichte und der Landesarbeitsgerichte trägt das Land, das sie errichtet. ²Die Kosten des Bundesarbeitsgerichts trägt der Bund.

§ 8
Gang des Verfahrens

(1) Im ersten Rechtszug sind die Arbeitsgerichte zuständig.

(2) Gegen die Urteile der Arbeitsgerichte findet die Berufung an die Landesarbeitsgerichte nach Maßgabe des § 64 Abs. 1 statt.

(3) Gegen die Urteile der Landesarbeitsgerichte findet die Revision an

2. For a regional labor court with less than three authorized judgeships, the responsibilities of the presidium shall be carried out by the president, or, if a second presiding judge has been appointed, in cooperation with him.
3. The supervising judge shall determine what judicial responsibilities he will carry out.
4. Each honorary judge may belong to two or more panels of judges.
5. The professional judges shall preside over the chambers of the labor courts.

Section 7
Court Registry, Provision of Funds

(1) ¹For each court handling labor and employment matters, a registry shall be established which shall be staffed with the necessary number of registrars. ²The establishment of the registry for the Federal Labor Court shall be directed by the Federal Ministry for Labor and Social Affairs in cooperation with the Federal Ministry of Justice. ³The establishment of the registry for the labor courts and regional labor courts shall be directed by the competent highest state authorities.

(2) ¹The costs of the labor courts and the regional labor courts shall be borne by the state that establishes it. ²The costs of the Federal Labor court shall be borne by the federal government.

Section 8
Course of proceedings

(1) In the first instance the labor courts are competent.

(2) Against the judgments of the labor courts, the appeal to the State labor courts exists pursuant to section 64 (1).

(3) Against the judgments of the State labor courts, the appeal on points of

das Bundesarbeitsgericht nach Maßgabe des § 72 Abs. 1 statt.	law to the Federal Labor Court exists pursuant to section 72 (1).
(4) Gegen die Beschlüsse der Arbeitsgerichte und ihrer Vorsitzenden im Beschlussverfahren findet die Beschwerde an das Landesarbeitsgericht nach Maßgabe des § 87 statt.	(4) Against the orders of the labor courts and their chairmen in order procedures, the appeal to the State labor courts exists pursuant to section 87.
(5) Gegen die Beschlüsse der Landesarbeitsgerichte im Beschlussverfahren findet die Rechtsbeschwerde an das Bundesarbeitsgericht nach Maßgabe des § 92 statt.	(5) Against the orders of the State labor courts in order procedures, the appeal on points of law to the Federal Labor Court exists pursuant to section 92.

§ 9
Allgemeine Verfahrensvorschriften

Section 9
Rules of Procedure for Court Proceedings

(1) Das Verfahren ist in allen Rechtszügen zu beschleunigen.

(1) The proceeding shall be expedited in all instances.

(2) Die Vorschriften des Gerichtsverfassungsgesetzes über Zustellungs- und Vollstreckungsbeamte, über die Aufrechterhaltung der Ordnung in der Sitzung, über die Gerichtssprache, über die Wahrnehmung richterlicher Geschäfte durch Referendare und über Beratung und Abstimmung gelten in allen Rechtszügen entsprechend.

(2) The provisions of the Judicature Act on court service and enforcement officials, the maintenance of order in the sessions, the language used in court, the assumption of judicial matters by clerks *(Referendare)* and regarding advice and consultation shall apply in all instances *mutatis mutandis*.

(3) [1] Die Vorschriften über die Wahrnehmung der Geschäfte bei den ordentlichen Gerichten durch Rechtspfleger gelten in allen Rechtszügen entsprechend. [2] Als Rechtspfleger können nur Beamte bestellt werden, die die Rechtspflegerprüfung oder die Prüfung für den gehobenen Dienst bei der Arbeitsgerichtsbarkeit bestanden haben.

(3) [1] The provisions on the assumption of matters before the ordinary courts by judicial officers *(Rechtspfleger)* shall apply in all instances *mutatis mutandis*. [2] Only permanent status civil servants *(Beamte)* may be appointed as judicial officers who have passed the judicial officer's test or higher-level civil service test.

(4) Zeugen und Sachverständige erhalten eine Entschädigung oder Vergütung nach dem Justizvergütungs- und -entschädigungsgesetz.

(4) Witnesses and experts shall be receive compensation or remuneration pursuant to the Court Remuneration and Compensation Act *(Justizvergütungs- und -entschädigungsgesetz)*.

(5) [1] Alle mit einem befristeten Rechtsmittel anfechtbaren Entscheidungen enthalten die Belehrung über das Rechtsmittel. [2] Soweit ein Rechtsmittel nicht gegeben ist, ist eine entsprechende Belehrung zu erteilen. [3] Die Frist für ein Rechtsmittel beginnt nur, wenn die

(5) [1] All decisions which can be contested with a remedy for a limited period of time shall contain instruction on such remedy. [2] Where no remedy exists, instruction to that effect shall be rendered. [3] The time period for a remedy commences only if the party or trial

Partei oder der Beteiligte über das Rechtsmittel und das Gericht, bei dem das Rechtsmittel einzulegen ist, die Anschrift des Gerichts und die einzuhaltende Frist und Form schriftlich belehrt worden ist. ⁴Ist die Belehrung unterblieben oder unrichtig erteilt, so ist die Einlegung des Rechtsmittels nur innerhalb eines Jahres seit Zustellung der Entscheidung zulässig, außer wenn die Einlegung vor Ablauf der Jahresfrist infolge höherer Gewalt unmöglich war oder eine Belehrung dahin erfolgt ist, dass ein Rechtsmittel nicht gegeben sei; § 234 Abs. 1, 2 und § 236 Abs. 2 der Zivilprozessordnung gelten für den Fall höherer Gewalt entsprechend.

participant has been instructed in writing about the legal remedy, court with which the remedy is to be filed, the official address of the court and the time and formal provisions to be observed. ⁴If no such instruction is given or it is given incorrectly, the filing of the remedy shall only be permitted within one year after the decision has been served, unless it was impossible to file the remedy within one year due to force majeure or the parties were instructed that no remedies exist; section 234 (1), (2) and section 236 (2) of the Code of Civil Procedure *(Zivilprozessordnung)* shall apply for cases of force majeure *mutatis mutandis*.

§ 10
Parteifähigkeit

Section 10
Party Capacity

Parteifähig im arbeitsgerichtlichen Verfahren sind auch Gewerkschaften und Vereinigungen von Arbeitgebern sowie Zusammenschlüsse solcher Verbände; in den Fällen des § 2a Abs. 1 Nr. 1 bis 3f sind auch die nach dem Betriebsverfassungsgesetz, dem Sprecherausschussgesetz, dem Mitbestimmungsgesetz, dem Mitbestimmungsergänzungsgesetz, dem Drittelbeteiligungsgesetz, dem § 139 des Neunten Buches Sozialgesetzbuch, dem § 51 des Berufsbildungsgesetzes und den zu diesen Gesetzen ergangenen Rechtsverordnungen sowie die nach dem Gesetz über Europäische Betriebsräte, dem SE-Beteiligungsgesetz, dem SCE-Beteiligungsgesetz und dem Gesetz über die Mitbestimmung der Arbeitnehmer bei einer grenzüberschreitenden Verschmelzung beteiligten Personen und Stellen Beteiligte. Parteifähig im arbeitsgerichtlichen Verfahren sind in den Fällen des § 2a Abs. 1 Nr. 4 auch die beteiligten Vereinigungen von Arbeitnehmern und Arbeitgebern sowie die oberste Arbeitsbehörde des Bundes oder derjenigen Länder, auf deren Bereich sich die Tätigkeit der Vereinigung erstreckt.

Trade unions and employers' associations, and combinations of such organizations, may also be parties to a labor court proceeding; parties are, in the cases set forth in section 2a (1) nos. 1 to 3f, the persons and institutions participating pursuant to the Works Constitution Act, the Spokespersons' Committee Act, the Codetermination Act, the Supplemental Codetermination Act, the One-Third Participation Act, section 139 of the Ninth Book of the Social Security Code , section 51 of the Vocational Training Act and the administrative regulations enacted with respect to such Acts, as well as the participating persons and agencies pursuant to the European Works Council Act *(Gesetz über Euroäische Betriebsräte)*, the Participation of Employees European Companies Act *(SE-Beteiligungsgesetz)*, the Participation of Employees European Cooperative Societies Act *(SCE-Beteiligungsgesetz)* and the Act Governing the Codetermination of the Employees in the Event of a Cross-Boundary Merger. In the cases of section 2a (1) no. 4 the participating employees' or employers' associations involved as well as the highest labor authority of the federal government or of those states in whose territory the

association operates may also be parties to a labor court proceeding.

§ 11
Prozessvertretung

Section 11
Legal Representation

(1) ¹Die Parteien können vor dem Arbeitsgericht den Rechtsstreit selbst führen. ²Parteien, die eine fremde oder ihnen zum Zweck der Einziehung auf fremde Rechnung abgetretene Geldforderung geltend machen, müssen sich durch einen Rechtsanwalt als Bevollmächtigten vertreten lassen, soweit sie nicht nach Maßgabe des Absatzes 2 zur Vertretung des Gläubigers befugt wären oder eine Forderung einziehen, deren ursprünglicher Gläubiger sie sind.

(1) ¹The parties may conduct legal dispute themselves before the labor court ²Parties that assert a monetary claim of another or one that has been assigned to them for the purpose of collection must be represented by an attorney as authorized representative where they would not be authorized to represent the creditor pursuant to subsection (2) or collect on a claim of which they are the original creditor.

(2) ¹Die Parteien können sich durch einen Rechtsanwalt als Bevollmächtigten vertreten lassen. ²Darüber hinaus sind als Bevollmächtigte vor dem Arbeitsgericht vertretungsbefugt nur

(2) ¹The parties can be represented by an attorney as authorized representative. ²Beyond that, persons are entitled to represent before the labor court as authorized representatives only if they are

1. Beschäftigte der Partei oder eines mit ihr verbundenen Unternehmens (§ 15 des Aktiengesetzes); Behörden und juristische Personen des öffentlichen Rechts einschließlich der von ihnen zur Erfüllung ihrer öffentlichen Aufgaben gebildeten Zusammenschlüsse können sich auch durch Beschäftigte anderer Behörden oder juristischer Personen des öffentlichen Rechts einschließlich der von ihnen zur Erfüllung ihrer öffentlichen Aufgaben gebildeten Zusammenschlüsse vertreten lassen,

1. employees of the party or an affiliated company (section 15 of the Stock Corporation Act); public authorities and legal public law entities, including associations formed by them to fulfill their public tasks can also be represented by employees of other public authorities and legal public law entities, including associations formed by them to fulfill their public tasks,

2. volljährige Familienangehörige (§ 15 der Abgabenordnung, § 11 des Lebenspartnerschaftsgesetzes), Personen mit Befähigung zum Richteramt und Streitgenossen, wenn die Vertretung nicht im Zusammenhang mit einer entgeltlichen Tätigkeit steht,

2. adult family members (section 15 of the Fiscal Code of Germany, section 11 of the Civil Partnership Act), persons qualified to serve as judges and act as litigant parties, if such representation is not in connection with a remunerative activity,

3. selbständige Vereinigungen von Arbeitnehmern mit sozial- oder berufspolitischer Zwecksetzung für ihre Mitglieder,

3. independent employees associations with objectives of social or professional policy for their members,

4. Gewerkschaften und Vereinigungen von Arbeitgebern sowie Zusammen-

4. trade unions and employer associations as well as groups of such asso-

schlüsse solcher Verbände für ihre Mitglieder oder für andere Verbände oder Zusammenschlüsse mit vergleichbarer Ausrichtung und deren Mitglieder,

5. juristische Personen, deren Anteile sämtlich im wirtschaftlichen Eigentum einer der in Nummer 4 bezeichneten Organisationen stehen, wenn die juristische Person ausschließlich die Rechtsberatung und Prozessvertretung dieser Organisation und ihrer Mitglieder oder anderer Verbände oder Zusammenschlüsse mit vergleichbarer Ausrichtung und deren Mitglieder entsprechend deren Satzung durchführt, und wenn die Organisation für die Tätigkeit der Bevollmächtigten haftet.

[3] Bevollmächtigte, die keine natürlichen Personen sind, handeln durch ihre Organe und mit der Prozessvertretung beauftragten Vertreter.

(3) [1] Das Gericht weist Bevollmächtigte, die nicht nach Maßgabe des Absatzes 2 vertretungsbefugt sind, durch unanfechtbaren Beschluss zurück. Prozesshandlungen eines nicht vertretungsbefugten Bevollmächtigten und Zustellungen oder Mitteilungen an diesen Bevollmächtigten sind bis zu seiner Zurückweisung wirksam. [2] Das Gericht kann den in Absatz 2 Satz 2 Nr. 1 bis 3 bezeichneten Bevollmächtigten durch unanfechtbaren Beschluss die weitere Vertretung untersagen, wenn sie nicht in der Lage sind, das Sach- und Streitverhältnis sachgerecht darzustellen.

(4) [1] Vor dem Bundesarbeitsgericht und dem Landesarbeitsgericht müssen sich die Parteien, außer im Verfahren vor einem beauftragten oder ersuchten Richter und bei Prozesshandlungen, die vor dem Urkundsbeamten der Geschäftsstelle vorgenommen werden können, durch Prozessbevollmächtigte vertreten lassen. [2] Als Bevollmächtigte sind außer Rechtsanwälten nur die in

ciations for their members or for other associations or groups of associations having a comparable orientation and their members,

5. legal entities whose shares are all in the economic ownership of one of the organizations designated in no. 4 if the legal entity carries out the legal advice and representation in court of such organization and its members or other associations or groups of associations having a comparable orientation and their members in accordance with their articles of association and if the organization bears liability for the activity of the authorized representative.

[3] Authorized representatives who are not natural persons act through their governing bodies and the representatives engaged as legal counsel in court.

(3) [1] The court shall reject authorized representatives who are not entitled to represent in accordance with subsection (2) by issuing an incontestable order. Any actions performed in court by an authorized representative who are not entitled to represent and papers served or messages conveyed to such authorized representative shall be valid up to his rejection. [2] The court can, by incontestable order, prohibit the authorized representatives designated in subsection (2) sentence 2 nos. 1 to 3 from performing any further representation if they are not in a position to present the facts of the matter and of the dispute in a proper manner.

(4) [1] In cases before the Federal Labor Court and the Regional Labor Court, exception in proceedings before a commissioned (beauftragter Richter) or requested judge (ersuchter Richter) and for court actions that can be carried out before the court registrars, the parties must be represented by a person authorized to represent them in court. [2] Apart from attorneys, only those

Absatz 2 Satz 2 Nr. 4 und 5 bezeichneten Organisationen zugelassen. ³Diese müssen in Verfahren vor dem Bundesarbeitsgericht durch Personen mit Befähigung zum Richteramt handeln. ⁴Eine Partei, die nach Maßgabe des Satzes 2 zur Vertretung berechtigt ist, kann sich selbst vertreten; Satz 3 bleibt unberührt.

(5) ¹Richter dürfen nicht als Bevollmächtigte vor dem Gericht auftreten, dem sie angehören. Ehrenamtliche Richter dürfen, außer in den Fällen des Absatzes 2 Satz 2 Nr. 1, nicht vor einem Spruchkörper auftreten, dem sie angehören. ²Absatz 3 Satz 1 und 2 gilt entsprechend.

(6) ¹In der Verhandlung können die Parteien mit Beiständen erscheinen. Beistand kann sein, wer in Verfahren, in denen die Parteien den Rechtsstreit selbst führen können, als Bevollmächtigter zur Vertretung in der Verhandlung befugt ist. ²Das Gericht kann andere Personen als Beistand zulassen, wenn dies sachdienlich ist und hierfür nach den Umständen des Einzelfalls ein Bedürfnis besteht. ³Absatz 3 Satz 1 und 3 und Absatz 5 gelten entsprechend. ⁴Das von dem Beistand Vorgetragene gilt als von der Partei vorgebracht, soweit es nicht von dieser sofort widerrufen oder berichtigt wird.

oreganizations designated in subsection (2) sentence 2 nos. 4 and 5 shall be admitted as authorized representatives. ³These organizations must act before the Federal Labor Court through persons qualified to serve as judges. ⁴A party who is entitled to represent according to sentence 2 can represent himself; sentence 3 remains unaffected.

(5) ¹Judges may not appear before the court they belong to as authorized representatives. Honorary judges may, except in the cases of subsection (2) sentence 2 no. 1, not appear before a panel of judges to which they belong. ²Subsection (3) sentences 1 and 2 applies mutatis mutandis.

(6) ¹The party may appear in the proceeding with legal advisers (Beistände). A person may act as an advisor who is entitled to represent as an authorized representative in proceedings in which the parties can conduct the legal dispute themselves. ²The court may admit other persons as advisers if this is pertinent and a need exists under the circumstances of the individual case. ³Subsection (3) sentences 1 and 3 and subsection (5) apply mutatis mutandis. ⁴Statements made to the court by the advisor shall be deemed to have been made by the party to the extent they are immediately revoked or corrected by the party.

§ 11 a
Beiordnung eines Rechtsanwalts, Prozesskostenhilfe

(1) ¹Einer Partei, die außerstande ist, ohne Beeinträchtigung des für sie und ihre Familie notwendigen Unterhalts die Kosten des Prozesses zu bestreiten, und die nicht durch ein Mitglied oder einen Angestellten einer Gewerkschaft oder einer Vereinigung von Arbeitgebern vertreten werden kann, hat der Vorsitzende des Arbeitsgerichts auf ihren Antrag einen Rechtsanwalt beizuordnen, wenn die Gegenpartei durch einen Rechtsanwalt vertreten ist. ²Die

Section 11 a
Assignment of an Attorney, Legal Aid

(1) ¹If party is not in a position to pay the costs of the legal proceeding without impairing the support necessary to maintain himself and his family and cannot be represented by a member or employee of a trade union or an employers' association, the presiding labor court judge may assign him a lawyer upon request if the other party is represented by a lawyer. ²The party shall be informed of the right to make such a request.

Partei ist auf ihr Antragsrecht hinzuweisen.

(2) Die Beiordnung kann unterbleiben, wenn sie aus besonderen Gründen nicht erforderlich ist, oder wenn die Rechtsverfolgung offensichtlich mutwillig ist.

(2a) Die Absätze 1 und 2 gelten auch für die grenzüberschreitende Prozesskostenhilfe innerhalb der Europäischen Union nach der Richtlinie 2003/8/EG des Rates vom 27. Januar 2003 zur Verbesserung des Zugangs zum Recht bei Streitsachen mit grenzüberschreitendem Bezug durch Festlegung gemeinsamer Mindestvorschriften für die Prozesskostenhilfe in derartigen Streitsachen (ABl. EG Nr. L 26 S. 41, ABl. EU Nr. L 32 S. 15).

(3) Die Vorschriften der Zivilprozessordnung über die Prozesskostenhilfe und über die grenzüberschreitende Prozesskostenhilfe innerhalb der Europäischen Union nach der Richtlinie 2003/8/EG gelten in Verfahren vor den Gerichten für Arbeitssachen entsprechend.

(4) Das Bundesministerium für Arbeit und Soziales wird ermächtigt, zur Vereinfachung und Vereinheitlichung des Verfahrens durch Rechtsverordnung mit Zustimmung des Bundesrates Formulare für die Erklärung der Partei über ihre persönlichen und wirtschaftlichen Verhältnisse (§ 117 Abs. 2 der Zivilprozessordnung) einzuführen.

§ 12
Kosten

¹Die Justizverwaltungskostenordnung und die Justizbeitreibungsordnung gelten entsprechend, soweit sie nicht unmittelbar Anwendung finden. ²Bei Einziehung der Gerichts- und Verwaltungskosten leisten die Vollstreckungsbehörden der Justizverwaltung oder die sonst nach Landesrecht zuständigen Stellen den Gerichten für Arbeitssachen

(2) The assignment need not be carried out if it is unnecessary for special reasons or the legal prosecution is obviously malicious.

(2a) Subsections (1) and (2) shall also apply to the cross-boarder legal aid within the European Union pursuant to the Council Directive 2003/8/EC of 27 January 2003 to improve access to justice in cross-boarder disputes by establishing minimum common rules relating to legal aid for such disputes (OJ L 26 p. 41).

(3) The provisions of the Code of Civil Procedure on legal aid and of cross-boarder legal aid within the European Union pursuant to the Council Directive 2003/8/EC shall apply *mutatis mutandis* to cases before the courts for labor matters.

(4) In order to simplify and unify the proceeding, the Federal Ministry for Labor and Social Affairs shall be empowered to issue an ordinance with the consent of the Upper House of Parliament *(Bundesrat)* introducing preprinted forms for the party's declaration on its personal and economic circumstances (section 117 (2) of the Code of Civil Procedure).

Section 12
Costs

¹The Ordinance on Costs in the Area of Administration of Justice *(Justizverwaltungskostenordnung)* and the Justice Recovery of Fees Ordinance *(Justizbeitreibungsordnung)* apply *mutatis mutandis* where they are not directly applicable. ²Where court and administrative costs are collected, the enforcement agencies of the administration of justice

Amtshilfe, soweit sie diese Aufgaben nicht als eigene wahrnehmen. ³Vollstreckungsbehörde ist für die Ansprüche, die beim Bundesarbeitsgericht entstehen, die Justizbeitreibungsstelle des Bundesarbeitsgerichts.

or the court bodies that otherwise have jurisdiction over labor matters pursuant to state law shall provide official support where they do not assume these tasks as their own. ³The enforcement agency for claims arising before the Federal Labor Court shall be the justice recovery agency of the Federal Labor Court.

§ 12a
Kostentragungspflicht

(1) ¹In Urteilsverfahren des ersten Rechtszugs besteht kein Anspruch der obsiegenden Partei auf Entschädigung wegen Zeitversäumnis und auf Erstattung der Kosten für die Zuziehung eines Prozessbevollmächtigten oder Beistands. ²Vor Abschluss der Vereinbarung über die Vertretung ist auf den Ausschluss der Kostenerstattung nach Satz 1 hinzuweisen. ³Satz 1 gilt nicht für Kosten, die dem Beklagten dadurch entstanden sind, dass der Kläger ein Gericht der ordentlichen Gerichtsbarkeit, der allgemeinen Verwaltungsgerichtsbarkeit, der Finanz- oder Sozialgerichtsbarkeit angerufen und dieses den Rechtsstreit an das Arbeitsgericht verwiesen hat.

(2) ¹Werden im Urteilsverfahren des zweiten Rechtszugs die Kosten nach § 92 Abs. 1 der Zivilprozessordnung verhältnismäßig geteilt und ist die eine Partei durch einen Rechtsanwalt, die andere Partei durch einen Verbandsvertreter nach § 11 Abs. 2 Satz 2 Nr. 4 und 5 vertreten, so ist diese Partei hinsichtlich der außergerichtlichen Kosten so zu stellen, als wenn sie durch einen Rechtsanwalt vertreten worden wäre. ²Ansprüche auf Erstattung stehen ihr jedoch nur insoweit zu, als ihr Kosten im Einzelfall tatsächlich erwachsen sind.

Section 12a
Duty to bear costs

(1) ¹In judgment proceedings in the first instance, no claim for compensation of the successful party exists because of the time spent or for reimbursement of the costs of engaging a litigation representative or a counsel. ²Prior to concluding an agreement regarding representation, the exclusion of cost reimbursements pursuant to sent. 1 must be pointed out. ³Sent. 1 shall not apply to costs incurred by the defendant because of the plaintiff's commencing proceedings before a court of ordinary jurisdiction, of general administrative jurisdiction, of finance or social jurisdiction and such court transferring the litigation to the labor court.

(2) ¹In a judgment procedure in the second instance, the costs are divided proportionally pursuant to section 92 (1) of the Code of Civil Procedure (Zivilprozessordnung) and, if the one party is representative by an attorney at law and the other party by an association representative pursuant to section 11 (2) sentence 2 nos. 4 and 5, then this party shall be treated with respect to noncourt costs as if it had been represented by an attorney at law. ²However, it has only claims to reimbursement to the extent costs have actually been incurred by it in the individual case.

XXIII. Act Regulating the Commercial Leasing of Employees (Arbeitnehmerüberlassungsgesetz – AÜG)

of 7 August 1972 (Federal Law Gazette I p. 1393)

in the amended version of 2 March 2009

(excerpts)

§ 1
Erlaubnispflicht

(1) ¹Arbeitgeber, die als Verleiher Dritten (Entleihern) Arbeitnehmer (Leiharbeitnehmer) gewerbsmäßig zur Arbeitsleistung überlassen wollen, bedürfen der Erlaubnis. ²Die Abordnung von Arbeitnehmern zu einer zur Herstellung eines Werkes gebildeten Arbeitsgemeinschaft ist keine Arbeitnehmerüberlassung, wenn der Arbeitgeber Mitglied der Arbeitsgemeinschaft ist, für alle Mitglieder der Arbeitsgemeinschaft Tarifverträge desselben Wirtschaftszweiges gelten und alle Mitglieder auf Grund des Arbeitsgemeinschaftsvertrages zur selbständigen Erbringung von Vertragsleistungen verpflichtet sind. ³Für einen Arbeitgeber mit Geschäftssitz in einem anderen Mitgliedstaat des Europäischen Wirtschaftsraumes ist die Abordnung von Arbeitnehmern zu einer zur Herstellung eines Werkes gebildeten Arbeitsgemeinschaft auch dann keine Arbeitnehmerüberlassung, wenn für ihn deutsche Tarifverträge desselben Wirtschaftszweiges wie für die anderen Mitglieder der Arbeitsgemeinschaft nicht gelten, er aber die übrigen Voraussetzungen des Satzes 2 erfüllt.

(2) Werden Arbeitnehmer Dritten zur Arbeitsleistung überlassen und übernimmt der Überlassende nicht die üblichen Arbeitgeberpflichten oder das Arbeitgeberrisiko (§ 3 Abs. 1 Nr. 1 bis 3), so wird vermutet, dass der Überlassende Arbeitsvermittlung betreibt.

Section 1
Duty to Obtain Permit

(1) ¹Employers who, as lessors wish to commercially lease out employees (leased employees) to third parties (clients) for work shall require a permit. ²The delegation of employees to a team formed in order to produce a work shall not constitute leasing of employees if the employer is a member of such team, collective bargaining agreements apply to all members of the team and all members are obligated to render contractual performance independently on the basis of the team contract. ³For an employer domiciled in another member state of the European Economic Area, the delegation of employees to a team formed in order to produce a work shall not constitute leasing of employees even if the employer is not subject to the German collective bargaining agreements for the same economic sector as the other members of the team, but it meets the other prerequisites set forth in sentence 2.

(2) If employees are leased to third parties to perform work and if the lessor does not assume the usual employer duties or the employer risk (section 3 (1) nos. 1 to 3), it shall be presumed that the lessor is operating an employment agency.

(3) Dieses Gesetz ist mit Ausnahme des § 1b Satz 1, des § 16 Abs. 1 Nr. 1b und Abs. 2 bis 5 sowie der §§ 17 und 18 nicht anzuwenden auf die Arbeitnehmerüberlassung

1. zwischen Arbeitgebern desselben Wirtschaftszweiges zur Vermeidung von Kurzarbeit oder Entlassungen, wenn ein für den Entleiher und Verleiher geltender Tarifvertrag dies vorsieht,
2. zwischen Konzernunternehmen im Sinne des § 18 des Aktiengesetzes, wenn der Arbeitnehmer seine Arbeit vorübergehend nicht bei seinem Arbeitgeber leistet, oder
3. in das Ausland, wenn der Leiharbeitnehmer in ein auf der Grundlage zwischenstaatlicher Vereinbarungen begründetes deutsch-ausländisches Gemeinschaftsunternehmen verliehen wird, an dem der Verleiher beteiligt ist.

(3) With the exception of section 1b sentence 1, section 16 (1) no. 1b and (2) to (5) as well as sections 17 and 18, this Act shall not be applicable to the leasing of employees

1. between employers in the same economic sector in order to avoid short-time work or dismissal, if so provided in a collective bargaining agreement applicable to the lessor and the client,
2. between companies in a single group within the meaning of section 18 of the Stock Corporation Act (Aktiengesetz), if the employee temporarily does not work for his/her employer or
3. in foreign countries, if the leased employee is leased to a joint venture between a German and a non-German company formed on the basis of bilateral agreements and the lessor participates in such joint venture.

§ 9
Unwirksamkeit

Section 9
Invalidity

Unwirksam sind:

1. Verträge zwischen Verleihern und Entleihern sowie zwischen Verleihern und Leiharbeitnehmern, wenn der Verleiher nicht die nach § 1 erforderliche Erlaubnis hat,
2. Vereinbarungen, die für den Leiharbeitnehmer für die Zeit der Überlassung an einen Entleiher schlechtere als die im Betrieb des Entleihers für einen vergleichbaren Arbeitnehmer des Entleihers geltenden wesentlichen Arbeitsbedingungen einschließlich des Arbeitsentgelts vorsehen, es sei denn, der Verleiher gewährt dem zuvor arbeitslosen Leiharbeitnehmer für die Überlassung an einen Entleiher für die Dauer von insgesamt höchstens sechs Wochen mindestens ein Nettoarbeitsentgelt in Höhe des Betrages, den der Leiharbeitnehmer zuletzt als Arbeitslosengeld erhalten hat; Letzteres gilt nicht, wenn mit demsel-

The following shall be invalid:

1. Contracts between lessors and clients as well as between lessors and leased employees if the lessor does not have the permit set forth in section 1,
2. agreements under which the essential working conditions for the leased employee during the period of the lease to a client are worse than those prevailing for a comparable employee in that client's operation, including with respect to remuneration, unless the lessor grants the previously unemployed leased employee at least a net remuneration in the amount of the payment he most recently received as unemployment benefits for a lease to a client lasting no more than six weeks in total; the latter shall not apply if a leased employment relationship had already existed with the same lessor; a collec-

ben Verleiher bereits ein Leiharbeitsverhältnis bestanden hat; ein Tarifvertrag kann abweichende Regelungen zulassen; im Geltungsbereich eines solchen Tarifvertrages können nicht tarifgebundene Arbeitgeber und Arbeitnehmer die Anwendung der tariflichen Regelungen vereinbaren,

3. Vereinbarungen, die dem Entleiher untersagen, den Leiharbeitnehmer zu einem Zeitpunkt einzustellen, in dem dessen Arbeitsverhältnis zum Verleiher nicht mehr besteht; dies schließt die Vereinbarung einer angemessenen Vergütung zwischen Verleiher und Entleiher für die nach vorangegangenem Verleih oder mittels vorangegangenem Verleih erfolgte Vermittlung nicht aus,

4. Vereinbarungen, die dem Leiharbeitnehmer untersagen, mit dem Entleiher zu einem Zeitpunkt, in dem das Arbeitsverhältnis zwischen Verleiher und Leiharbeitnehmer nicht mehr besteht, ein Arbeitsverhältnis einzugehen.

tive bargaining agreement may contain provisions departing from this regulation; within the scope of application of such a collective bargaining agreement, employers and employees not bound by this agreement may agree that the provision therein are to apply,

3. agreements prohibiting the client from hiring the leased employee at a time at which the employment relationship with the lessor no longer exists; this does not exclude agreements for an appropriate remuneration between the lessor and the client for brokering that was carried out after or by means of the previous lease,

4. agreements prohibiting the leased employee from entering into an employment relationship with the client at a time at which the employment relationship between the lessor and the leased employee no longer exists.

§ 10
Rechtsfolgen bei Unwirksamkeit

(1) [1] Ist der Vertrag zwischen einem Verleiher und einem Leiharbeitnehmer nach § 9 Nr. 1 unwirksam, so gilt ein Arbeitsverhältnis zwischen Entleiher und Leiharbeitnehmer zu dem zwischen dem Entleiher und dem Verleiher für den Beginn der Tätigkeit vorgesehenen Zeitpunkt als zustande gekommen; tritt die Unwirksamkeit erst nach Aufnahme der Tätigkeit beim Entleiher ein, so gilt das Arbeitsverhältnis zwischen Entleiher und Leiharbeitnehmer mit dem Eintritt der Unwirksamkeit als zustande gekommen. [2] Das Arbeitsverhältnis nach Satz 1 gilt als befristet, wenn die Tätigkeit des Leiharbeitnehmers bei dem Entleiher nur befristet vorgesehen war und ein die Befristung des Arbeitsverhältnisses sachlich rechtfertigender Grund vorliegt. [3] Für das Arbeitsverhältnis nach Satz 1 gilt die zwischen dem Verleiher und dem Ent-

Section 10
Legal Consequences of Invalidity

(1) [1] If the contract between a lessor and a leased employee is invalid pursuant to section 9 no. 1, an employment relationship between a client and a leased employee shall be deemed to have been concluded at the time at which the work is to commence as set forth in the contract between the client and the lessor; if the invalidity only occurs after the work with the client has commenced, the employment relationship between the client and the leased employee shall be deemed to have been concluded upon the onset of the invalidity. [2] The employment relationship pursuant to sentence 1 shall be deemed to run for an limited term if the leased employee's work for the client was only to run for a limited term and there are objective ground justifying restricting the employment relationship to a limited term. [3] For an employment relationship pursuant to

leiher vorgesehene Arbeitszeit als vereinbart. ⁴Im übrigen bestimmen sich Inhalt und Dauer dieses Arbeitsverhältnisses nach den für den Betrieb des Entleihers geltenden Vorschriften und sonstigen Regelungen; sind solche nicht vorhanden, gelten diejenigen vergleichbarer Betriebe. ⁵Der Leiharbeitnehmer hat gegen den Entleiher mindestens Anspruch auf das mit dem Verleiher vereinbarte Arbeitsentgelt.

(2) ¹Der Leiharbeitnehmer kann im Fall der Unwirksamkeit seines Vertrags mit dem Verleiher nach § 9 Nr. 1 von diesem Ersatz des Schadens verlangen, den er dadurch erleidet, dass er auf die Gültigkeit des Vertrags vertraut. ²Die Ersatzpflicht tritt nicht ein, wenn der Leiharbeitnehmer den Grund der Unwirksamkeit kannte.

(3) ¹Zahlt der Verleiher das vereinbarte Arbeitsentgelt oder Teile des Arbeitsentgelts an den Leiharbeitnehmer, obwohl der Vertrag nach § 9 Nr. 1 unwirksam ist, so hat er auch sonstige Teile des Arbeitsentgelts, die bei einem wirksamen Arbeitsvertrag für den Leiharbeitnehmer an einen anderen zu zahlen wären, an den anderen zu zahlen. ²Hinsichtlich dieser Zahlungspflicht gilt der Verleiher neben dem Entleiher als Arbeitgeber; beide haften insoweit als Gesamtschuldner.

(4) Der Leiharbeitnehmer kann im Falle der Unwirksamkeit der Vereinbarung mit dem Verleiher nach § 9 Nr. 2 von diesem die Gewährung der im Betrieb des Entleihers für einen vergleichbaren Arbeitnehmer des Entleihers geltenden wesentlichen Arbeitsbedingungen einschließlich des Arbeitsentgelts verlangen.

(5) *(weggefallen)*

§ 11
Sonstige Vorschriften über das Leiharbeitsverhältnis

(1) ¹Der Nachweis der wesentlichen Vertragsbedingungen des Leiharbeits-

sentence 1, the working time shall be that which was agreed to by the lessor and the client. ⁴In all other respects, the content and duration of this employment relationship shall be determined by the statutory and other provisions applicable to the client's operation; if none exist, then those of comparable operations shall apply. ⁵The leased employee shall have a claim against the client for at least the amount of remuneration agreed to with the lessor.

(2) ¹In the event of the invalidity of the leased employee's contract with the lessor pursuant to section 9 no. 1, the leased employee may demand compensation for the damage he/she suffered by relying on the validity of the contract. ²The duty to pay damages shall not apply if the leased employee was aware of the grounds for the invalidity.

(3) ¹If the lessor pays the agreed remuneration for work or part thereof to the leased employee even though the contract is invalid pursuant to section 9 no. 1, the lessor must also pay others the part of the remuneration he would have need to pay to others had the contract been valid. ²With respect to this duty to pay, both the lessor and the client are deemed to be employers; to that extent, both are jointly and severally liable.

(4) In the event that the agreement with the lessor is invalid pursuant to section 9 no. 2, the leased employee may demand that the lessor grant him/her the essential working conditions, including remuneration, prevailing in the client's operation for a comparable employee of the client.

(5) *(repealed)*

Section 11
Other Provisions on Leased Employment Relationships

(1) ¹The documentation of the essential contractual provisions of the leased

verhältnisses richtet sich nach den Bestimmungen des Nachweisgesetzes. ²Zusätzlich zu den in § 2 Abs. 1 des Nachweisgesetzes genannten Angaben sind in die Niederschrift aufzunehmen:

1. Firma und Anschrift des Verleihers, die Erlaubnisbehörde sowie Ort und Datum der Erteilung der Erlaubnis nach § 1,
2. Art und Höhe der Leistungen für Zeiten, in denen der Leiharbeitnehmer nicht verliehen ist.

(2) ¹Der Verleiher ist ferner verpflichtet, dem Leiharbeitnehmer bei Vertragsschluss ein Merkblatt der Erlaubnisbehörde über den wesentlichen Inhalt dieses Gesetzes auszuhändigen. ²Nichtdeutsche Leiharbeitnehmer erhalten das Merkblatt und den Nachweis nach Absatz 1 auf Verlangen in ihrer Muttersprache. ³Die Kosten des Merkblatts trägt der Verleiher.

(3) ¹Der Verleiher hat den Leiharbeitnehmer unverzüglich über den Zeitpunkt des Wegfalls der Erlaubnis zu unterrichten. ²In den Fällen der Nichtverlängerung (§ 2 Abs. 4 Satz 3), der Rücknahme (§ 4) oder des Widerrufs (§ 5) hat er ihn ferner auf das voraussichtliche Ende der Abwicklung (§ 2 Abs. 4 Satz 4) und die gesetzliche Abwicklungsfrist (§ 2 Abs. 4 Satz 4 letzter Halbsatz) hinzuweisen.

(4) ¹§ 622 Abs. 5 Nr. 1 des Bürgerlichen Gesetzbuchs ist nicht auf Arbeitsverhältnisse zwischen Verleihern und Leiharbeitnehmern anzuwenden. ²Das Recht des Leiharbeitnehmers auf Vergütung bei Annahmeverzug des Verleihers (§ 615 Satz 1 des Bürgerlichen Gesetzbuchs) kann nicht durch Vertrag aufgehoben oder beschränkt werden; § 615 Satz 2 des Bürgerlichen Gesetzbuchs bleibt unberührt. Das Recht des Leiharbeitnehmers auf Vergütung kann

employment relationship shall be based on the provisions of the Documentation Act *(Nachweisgesetz)*. ²In addition to the information set forth in section 2 (1) of the Documentation Act, the following information shall be included in the record:

1. Company name and address of the lessor, the permitting authority and city and date of the granting of the permit pursuant to section 1,
2. type and amount of the benefits for periods in which the employee is not leased out.

(2) ¹Upon conclusion of the contract, the lessor shall further be obligated to hand the leased employee an informational leaflet from the permitting authority on the essential content of this Act. ² Non-German leased employees shall receive the leaflet and the document pursuant to subsection (1) in their native language upon request. ³The costs of the informational leaflet shall be borne by the lessor.

(3) ¹The lessor shall inform the leased employee without delay of the date on which the permit ceases to apply. ²In the event of the non-extension (section 2 (4) sentence 3), withdrawal (section 4) or revocation (section 5) of the permit, the lessor shall further inform the leased employee of the anticipated end of the work assignment (section 2 (4) sentence 4) and the statutory limitation of the extension to complete a work assignment (section 2 (4) last half of sentence 4).

(4) ¹Section 622 (5) no. 1 of the German Civil Code *(Bürgerliches Gesetzbuch)* shall not be applicable to employment relationships between lessors and leased employees. ²The leased employee's right to remuneration in case of default of acceptance (section 615 sentence 1 of the German Civil Code) may not be nullified or restricted by contract; Section 615 sentence 2 of the German Civil Code remains unaffected. The leased employee's right to remuneration can

durch Vereinbarung von Kurzarbeit für die Zeit aufgehoben werden, für die dem Leiharbeitnehmer Kurzarbeitergeld nach dem Dritten Buch Sozialgesetzbuch gezahlt wird; eine solche Vereinbarung kann das Recht des Leiharbeitnehmers auf Vergütung bis längstens zum 31. Dezember 2010 ausschließen.	be nullified by an agreement to short-time work for the period in which the leased employee is paid in accordance with the Third Book of the Social Security Code; such an agreement can exclude the leased employee's right to remuneration until no later than 31 December 2010.
(5) [1] Der Leiharbeitnehmer ist nicht verpflichtet, bei einem Entleiher tätig zu sein, soweit dieser durch einen Arbeitskampf unmittelbar betroffen ist. [2] In den Fällen eines Arbeitskampfs nach Satz 1 hat der Verleiher den Leiharbeitnehmer auf das Recht, die Arbeitsleistung zu verweigern, hinzuweisen.	(5) [1] The leased employee shall not be obligated to work for a client that is directly affected by a labor dispute. [2] In the event of a labor dispute pursuant to sentence 1, the lessor shall inform the leased employee of his/her right to refuse to work.
(6) [1] Die Tätigkeit des Leiharbeitnehmers bei dem Entleiher unterliegt den für den Betrieb des Entleihers geltenden öffentlich-rechtlichen Vorschriften des Arbeitsschutzrechts; die hieraus sich ergebenden Pflichten für den Arbeitgeber obliegen dem Entleiher unbeschadet der Pflichten des Verleihers. [2] Insbesondere hat der Entleiher den Leiharbeitnehmer vor Beginn der Beschäftigung und bei Veränderungen in seinem Arbeitsbereich über Gefahren für Sicherheit und Gesundheit, denen er bei der Arbeit ausgesetzt sein kann, sowie über die Maßnahmen und Einrichtungen zur Abwendung dieser Gefahren zu unterrichten. [3] Der Entleiher hat den Leiharbeitnehmer zusätzlich über die Notwendigkeit besonderer Qualifikationen oder beruflicher Fähigkeiten oder einer besonderen ärztlichen Überwachung sowie über erhöhte besondere Gefahren des Arbeitsplatzes zu unterrichten.	(6) [1] The leased employee's work for the client is subject to the public law statutes governing industrial safety applicable to the client's operation; the resulting duties for the employer shall also be incumbent upon the client, irrespective of the duties of the lessor. [2] In particular, the client shall inform the leased employee before the work commences, and in the event of changes in his/her working area, of the health and safety dangers to which he/she can be exposed in the course of the work, as well as of measures and facilities for averting such dangers. [3] The client shall additionally inform the leased employee of the necessity of special qualifications or professional skills or special medical supervision, as well as of increased dangers at the workplace.
(7) Hat der Leiharbeitnehmer während der Dauer der Tätigkeit bei dem Entleiher eine Erfindung oder einen technischen Verbesserungsvorschlag gemacht, so gilt der Entleiher als Arbeitgeber im Sinne des Gesetzes über Arbeitnehmererfindungen.	(7) If the leased employee has made an invention or technical suggestion for improvement in the course of his/her work for the client, the client shall be deemed to be the employer within the meaning of the Act on Employee Inventions *(Gesetz über Arbeitnehmererfindungen)*.

§ 12
Rechtsbeziehungen zwischen Verleiher und Entleiher

(1) [1]Der Vertrag zwischen dem Verleiher und dem Entleiher bedarf der Schriftform. [2]In der Urkunde hat der Verleiher zu erklären, ob er die Erlaubnis nach § 1 besitzt. [3]Der Entleiher hat in der Urkunde anzugeben, welche besonderen Merkmale die für den Leiharbeitnehmer vorgesehene Tätigkeit hat und welche berufliche Qualifikation dafür erforderlich ist sowie welche im Betrieb des Entleihers für einen vergleichbaren Arbeitnehmer des Entleihers wesentlichen Arbeitsbedingungen einschließlich des Arbeitsentgelts gelten; Letzteres gilt nicht, soweit die Voraussetzungen einer der beiden in § 3 Abs. 1 Nr. 3 und § 9 Nr. 2 genannten Ausnahmen vorliegen.

(2) [1]Der Verleiher hat den Entleiher unverzüglich über den Zeitpunkt des Wegfalls der Erlaubnis zu unterrichten. [2]In den Fällen der Nichtverlängerung (§ 2 Abs. 4 Satz 3), der Rücknahme (§ 4) oder des Widerrufs (§ 5) hat er ihn ferner auf das voraussichtliche Ende der Abwicklung (§ 2 Abs. 4 Satz 4) und die gesetzliche Abwicklungsfrist (§ 2 Abs. 4 Satz 4 letzter Halbsatz) hinzuweisen.

(3) *(weggefallen)*

§ 13
Auskunftsanspruch des Leiharbeitnehmers

Der Leiharbeitnehmer kann im Falle der Überlassung von seinem Entleiher Auskunft über die im Betrieb des Entleihers für einen vergleichbaren Arbeitnehmer des Entleihers geltenden wesentlichen Arbeitsbedingungen einschließlich des Arbeitsentgelts verlangen; dies gilt nicht, soweit die Voraussetzungen einer der beiden in § 3 Abs. 1 Nr. 3 und § 9 Nr. 2 genannten Ausnahmen vorliegen.

Section 12
Legal Relationships Between the Lessor and the Client

(1) [1]The contract between the lessor and the client must be in written form. [2]The lessor shall declare in the document whether he has a permit pursuant to section 1. [3]The client shall describe in the document the special features of the work the leased employee is to do, the professional qualifications that are necessary and the essential working conditions prevailing in the client's operation for comparable employees of the client, including the remuneration; the latter shall not apply if the prerequisites for one of the two exceptions mentioned in section 3 (1) no. 3 und section 9 no. 2 have been met.

(2) [1]The lessor shall inform the client without delay of the date on which the permit ceases to apply. [2]In the event of the non-extension (section 2 (4) sentence 3), withdrawal (section 4) or revocation (section 5) of the permit, the lessor shall further inform the client of the anticipated end of the work assignment (section 2 (4) sentence 4) and the statutory limitation of the extension to complete a work assignment (section 2 (4) last half of sentence 4).

(3) *(repealed)*

Section 13
Leased Employee's Claim for Disclosure of Information

In the event that a leased employee is leased, he/she may demand that the client provide information on the prevailing working conditions in the client's operation for a comparable employee of the client, including remuneration; this shall not apply if the prerequisites for one of the two exceptions mentioned in section 3 (1) no. 3 und section 9 no. 2 have been met.

§ 14
Mitwirkungs- und Mitbestimmungsrechte

(1) Leiharbeitnehmer bleiben auch während der Zeit ihrer Arbeitsleistung bei einem Entleiher Angehörige des entsendenden Betriebs des Verleihers.

(2) ¹Leiharbeitnehmer sind bei der Wahl der Arbeitnehmervertreter in den Aufsichtsrat im Entleiherunternehmen und bei der Wahl der betriebsverfassungsrechtlichen Arbeitnehmervertretungen im Entleiherbetrieb nicht wählbar. ²Sie sind berechtigt, die Sprechstunden dieser Arbeitnehmervertretungen aufzusuchen und an den Betriebs- und Jugendversammlungen im Entleiherbetrieb teilzunehmen. ³Die §§ 81, 82 Abs. 1 und die §§ 84 bis 86 des Betriebsverfassungsgesetzes gelten im Entleiherbetrieb auch in Bezug auf die dort tätigen Leiharbeitnehmer.

(3) ¹Vor der Übernahme eines Leiharbeitnehmers zur Arbeitsleistung ist der Betriebsrat des Entleiherbetriebs nach § 99 des Betriebsverfassungsgesetzes zu beteiligen. ²Dabei hat der Entleiher dem Betriebsrat auch die schriftliche Erklärung des Verleihers nach § 12 Abs. 1 Satz 2 vorzulegen. ³Er ist ferner verpflichtet, Mitteilungen des Verleihers nach § 12 Abs. 2 unverzüglich dem Betriebsrat bekanntzugeben.

(4) Die Absätze 1 und 2 Satz 1 und 2 sowie Absatz 3 gelten für die Anwendung des Bundespersonalvertretungsgesetzes sinngemäß.

§ 15
Ausländische Leiharbeitnehmer ohne Genehmigung

(1) Wer als Verleiher einen Ausländer, der einen erforderlichen Aufenthaltstitel nach § 4 Abs. 3 des Aufenthaltsgesetzes, eine Aufenthaltsgestattung oder

Section 14
Participation and Codetermination Rights

(1) Even while working for a client, leased employees shall remain employees of the lessor's establishment.

(2) ¹Leased employees shall not be eligible for election to the post of employees' representative in the supervisory board or to the employees' representational bodies under the Works Constitution Act *(Betriebsverfassungsgesetz)* in the client's company. ²They shall be entitled to avail themselves of the employee representative bodies' consultation hours and participate in the works and youth assemblies at the client's establishment. ³Sections 81 and 82 (1) and sections 84 to 86 of the Works Constitution Act shall apply in the client's establishment also with respect to the leased employees working there.

(3) ¹Before a leased employee is leased to perform a job, the works council of the client's establishment shall be involved in the decision making process pursuant to section 99 of the Works Constitution Act, whereby the client shall also present the works council with the lessor's written declaration pursuant to section 12 (1) sentence 2. ²The client shall further inform the works council of communications from the lessor pursuant to section 12 (2) without delay.

(4) Subsections (1) and (2), sentences 1 and 2 and subsection (3) shall apply *mutatis mutandis* to the application of the Federal Personnel Representation Act *(Bundespersonalvertretungsgesetz)*.

Section 15
Foreign Leased Employees Without a Permit

(1) A lessor who leases a foreigner who does not have the requisite residence title *(Aufenthaltstitel)* pursuant to section 4 (3) of the Residence Act *(Aufent-*

eine Duldung, die zur Ausübung der Beschäftigung berechtigen, oder eine Genehmigung nach § 284 Abs. 1 des Dritten Buches Sozialgesetzbuch nicht besitzt, entgegen § 1 einem Dritten ohne Erlaubnis überlässt, wird mit Freiheitsstrafe bis zu drei Jahren oder mit Geldstrafe bestraft.

(2) ¹In besonders schweren Fällen ist die Strafe Freiheitsstrafe von sechs Monaten bis zu fünf Jahren. ²Ein besonders schwerer Fall liegt in der Regel vor, wenn der Täter gewerbsmäßig oder aus grobem Eigennutz handelt.

§ 15 a
Entleih von Ausländern ohne Genehmigung

(1) ¹Wer als Entleiher einen ihm überlassenen Ausländer, der einen erforderlichen Aufenthaltstitel nach § 4 Abs. 3 des Aufenthaltsgesetzes, eine Aufenthaltsgestattung oder eine Duldung, die zur Ausübung der Beschäftigung berechtigen, oder eine Genehmigung nach § 284 Abs. 1 des Dritten Buches Sozialgesetzbuch nicht besitzt, zu Arbeitsbedingungen des Leiharbeitsverhältnisses tätig werden lässt, die in einem auffälligen Missverhältnis zu den Arbeitsbedingungen deutscher Leiharbeitnehmer stehen, die die gleiche oder eine vergleichbare Tätigkeit ausüben, wird mit Freiheitsstrafe bis zu drei Jahren oder mit Geldstrafe bestraft. ²In besonders schweren Fällen ist die Strafe Freiheitsstrafe von sechs Monaten bis zu fünf Jahren; ein besonders schwerer Fall liegt in der Regel vor, wenn der Täter gewerbsmäßig oder aus grobem Eigennutz handelt.

(2) Wer als Entleiher
1. gleichzeitig mehr als fünf Ausländer, die einen erforderlichen Aufenthaltstitel nach § 4 Abs. 3 des Aufenthaltsgesetzes, eine Aufenthaltsgestattung oder eine Duldung, die zur Aus-

haltsgesetz), a residence permit or a temporary suspension of deportation (Duldung) entitling the holder to enter into employment, or a permit pursuant to section 284 (1) sentence 1 of the Third Book of the Social Security Code (Sozialgesetzbuch), to a third party without permission in violation of section 1 shall be subject to imprisonment for up to three years or a fine.

(2) ¹In particularly serious cases a lessor can be sentenced to imprisonment for between six months and five years. ²As a rule, a particularly serious case exists if the offender is acting commercially or out of gross self-interest.

Section 15 a
Leasing of Foreigners Without a Permit

(1) ¹A client who allows a foreign employee it has leased who does not have the requisite residence title pursuant to section 4 (3) of the Residence Act, a residence permit or a temporary suspension of deportation entitling the holder to enter into employment, or a permit pursuant to section 284 (1) sentence 1 of the Third Book of the Social Security Code to work under lease employment working conditions which are blatantly disproportionate to the working conditions of German leased employees carrying out the same or comparable activity shall be subject to imprisonment for up to three years or a fine. ²In particularly serious cases a client can be sentenced to imprisonment for between six months and five years. ³As a rule, a particularly serious case exists if the offender is acting commercially or out of gross self-interest.

(2) A client who
1. allows more than five foreigners who do not have the requisite residence title pursuant to section 4 (3) of the Residence Act, a residence permit or a temporary suspension of deporta-

übung der Beschäftigung berechtigen, oder eine Genehmigung nach § 284 Abs. 1 des Dritten Buches Sozialgesetzbuch nicht besitzen, tätig werden läßt oder	tion entitling the holder to enter into employment, or a permit pursuant to section 284 (1) sentence 1 of the Third Book of the Social Security Code to work at the same time or
2. eine in § 16 Abs. 1 Nr. 2 bezeichnete vorsätzliche Zuwiderhandlung beharrlich wiederholt,	2. repeatedly commits one of the intentional offenses set forth in section 16 (1) no. 2
wird mit Freiheitsstrafe bis zu einem Jahr oder mit Geldstrafe bestraft. Handelt der Täter aus grobem Eigennutz, ist die Strafe Freiheitsstrafe bis zu drei Jahren oder Geldstrafe.	shall be subject to imprisonment for up to one year or a fine. If the offender is acting out of blatant self-interest he can be sentenced to imprisonment for up to three years or a fine.

XXIV. Law on Documenting Essential Applicable Conditions for Employment Relationships (Nachweisgesetz – NachwG)

of 20 July 1995 (Federal Law Gazette I p. 946)

in the amended version of 13 July 2001

(excerpts)

§ 1 Anwendungsbereich	Section 1 Scope
Dieses Gesetz gilt für alle Arbeitnehmer, es sei denn, dass sie nur zur vorübergehenden Aushilfe von höchstens einem Monat eingestellt werden.	This Act is applicable for all employees unless they have been hired as temporary employees for no more than one month.

§ 2 Nachweispflicht
Section 2 Duty of Documentation

(1) ¹Der Arbeitgeber hat spätestens einen Monat nach dem vereinbarten Beginn des Arbeitsverhältnisses die wesentlichen Vertragsbedingungen schriftlich niederzulegen, die Niederschrift zu unterzeichnen und dem Arbeitnehmer auszuhändigen. ²In die Niederschrift sind mindestens aufzunehmen:

1. der Name und die Anschrift der Vertragsparteien,
2. der Zeitpunkt des Beginns des Arbeitsverhältnisses,
3. bei befristeten Arbeitsverhältnissen: die vorhersehbare Dauer des Arbeitsverhältnisses,
4. der Arbeitsort oder, falls der Arbeitnehmer nicht nur an einem bestimmten Arbeitsort tätig sein soll, ein Hinweis darauf, dass der Arbeitnehmer an verschiedenen Orten beschäftigt werden kann,
5. eine kurze Charakterisierung oder Beschreibung der vom Arbeitnehmer zu leistenden Tätigkeit,
6. die Zusammensetzung und die Höhe des Arbeitsentgelts einschließ-

(1) ¹No later than one month after the agreed upon commencement of the employment relationship the employer shall record the essential contractual terms in writing, sign the record and hand it over to the employee. ²This record shall contain at least the following information:

1. the name and address of the parties to the agreement,
2. the date of commencement of the employment relationship,
3. in the case of fixed term employment relationships: the anticipated duration of the employment relationship,
4. the location of the workplace or, if the employee will not only be working at one workplace, a reference to the fact that the employee can be assigned to work at various locations,
5. a brief characterization or description of the activity to be performed by the employee,
6. the composition and amount of the remuneration, including the extra

lich der Zuschläge, der Zulagen, Prämien und Sonderzahlungen sowie anderer Bestandteile des Arbeitsentgelts und deren Fälligkeit,	pay, incentive payments and special payments, as well as other components of the remuneration and their payability,
7. die vereinbarte Arbeitszeit,	7. the agreed upon working time,
8. die Dauer des jährlichen Erholungsurlaubs,	8. the length of the annual vacation,
9. die Fristen für die Kündigung des Arbeitsverhältnisses,	9. the notice periods for terminating the employment relationship,
10. ein in allgemeiner Form gehaltener Hinweis auf die Tarifverträge, Betriebs- oder Dienstvereinbarungen, die auf das Arbeitsverhältnis anzuwenden sind.	10. a general reference to the collective bargaining agreements, works or service agreements applicable to the employment relationship.
³Der Nachweis der wesentlichen Vertragsbedingungen in elektronischer Form ist ausgeschlossen. ⁴Bei Arbeitnehmern, die eine geringfügige Beschäftigung nach § 8 Abs. 1 Nr. 1 des Vierten Buches Sozialgesetzbuch ausüben, ist außerdem der Hinweis aufzunehmen, dass der Arbeitnehmer in der gesetzlichen Rentenversicherung die Stellung eines versicherungspflichtigen Arbeitnehmers erwerben kann, wenn er nach § 5 Abs. 2 Satz 2 des Sechsten Buches Sozialgesetzbuch auf die Versicherungsfreiheit durch Erklärung gegenüber dem Arbeitgeber verzichtet.	³The essential contractual terms cannot be documented in electronic form. ⁴In the case of employees engaged in insignificant employment (*geringfügige Beschäftigung*) pursuant to section 8 (1) no. 1 of the Fourth Book of the Social Security Code (*Sozialgesetzbuch*), the record shall further contain a reference to the fact that the employee can acquire the position of an employee subject to contributions to the statutory pension insurance fund if he/she waives the exemption from compulsory insurance pursuant to section 5 (2) sentence 2 of the Sixth Book of the Social Security Code by declaration to the employer.
(2) Hat der Arbeitnehmer seine Arbeitsleistung länger als einen Monat außerhalb der Bundesrepublik Deutschland zu erbringen, so muss die Niederschrift dem Arbeitnehmer vor seiner Abreise ausgehändigt werden und folgende zusätzliche Angaben enthalten:	(2) If the employee is to perform his/her activities outside of the Federal Republic of Germany for more than one month, the record must be handed over to the employee before his/her departure and contain the following additional information:
1. die Dauer der im Ausland auszuübenden Tätigkeit,	1. the duration of the activity to be carried out abroad,
2. die Währung, in der das Arbeitsentgelt ausgezahlt wird,	2. the currency in which the remuneration will be paid,
3. ein zusätzliches mit dem Auslandsaufenthalt verbundenes Arbeitsentgelt und damit verbundene zusätzliche Sachleistungen,	3. an additional remuneration in connection with the stay abroad and associated additional benefits,
4. die vereinbarten Bedingungen für die Rückkehr des Arbeitnehmers.	4. the agreed conditions for the employee's return.
(3) ¹Die Angaben nach Absatz 1 Satz 2 Nr. 6 bis 9 und Absatz 2 Nr. 2 und 3	(3) ¹The information to be provided pursuant to subsection (1) sentence 2

können ersetzt werden durch einen Hinweis auf die einschlägigen Tarifverträge, Betriebs- oder Dienstvereinbarungen und ähnlichen Regelungen, die für das Arbeitsverhältnis gelten. ²Ist in den Fällen des Absatzes 1 Satz 2 Nr. 8 und 9 die jeweilige gesetzliche Regelung maßgebend, so kann hierauf verwiesen werden.

(4) Wenn dem Arbeitnehmer ein schriftlicher Arbeitsvertrag ausgehändigt worden ist, entfällt die Verpflichtung nach den Absätzen 1 und 2, soweit der Vertrag die in den Absätzen 1 bis 3 geforderten Angaben enthält.

nos. 6 to 9 and subsection (2) nos. 2 and 3 may be replaced by a reference to the relevant collective bargaining agreements, works or service agreements and similar provisions applicable to the employment relationship. ²If in the cases of subsection (1) sentence 2 nos. 8 and 9 the respective statutory provision is decisive, reference may be made thereto.

(4) If the employee is given a written employment agreement, the obligations set forth in subsections (1) and (2) will not apply, provided that the agreement contains the information set forth in subsections (1) to (3).

§ 3
Änderung der Angaben

¹Eine Änderung der wesentlichen Vertragsbedingungen ist dem Arbeitnehmer spätestens einen Monat nach der Änderung schriftlich mitzuteilen. ²Satz 1 gilt nicht bei einer Änderung der gesetzlichen Vorschriften, Tarifverträge, Betriebs- oder Dienstvereinbarungen und ähnlichen Regelungen, die für das Arbeitsverhältnis gelten.

Section 3
Changing the Information

¹A change in the essential contractual conditions must be communicated to the employee no later than one month after the change has been effected. ²Sent. 1 shall not apply in the case of a change in the statutory provisions, collective bargaining agreements, works or service agreements or similar provisions applicable to the employment relationship.

§ 5
Unabdingbarkeit

Von den Vorschriften dieses Gesetzes kann nicht zuungunsten des Arbeitnehmers abgewichen werden.

Section 5
Mandatory Nature

No deviation from this statute may be made to the detriment of the employee.

Glossary of Key Words
(English/German)

A

Aftereffect Nachwirkung
Annual wage tax adjustment Lohnsteuerjahresausgleich
Asset deal Vermögenkauf
Attendance bonus Anwesenheitsprämie

B

Benevolent funds Unterstützungskasse
Blocking period Sperrzeit
Blue collar worker Arbeiter

C

Capital formation benefits vermögenswirksame Leistungen
Codetermination Act Mitbestimmungsgesetz
Codetermination right Mitbestimmungsrecht
Collective Bargaining Agreement Register Tarifregister
Collective bargaining agreement on pay Lohn-/Gehaltstarifvertrag
Collective bargaining agreement Tarifvertrag
Collective Bargaining Agreements Act Tarifvertragsgesetz
Commission Provision
Company car Dienstwagen
Company pension plan betriebliche Altersvorsorge
Company practice betriebliche Übung
Compelling operational reasons dringende betriebliche Gründe
Compelling operational requirements dringende betriebliche Erfordernisse
Conciliation board Einigungsstelle
Conciliation hearing Güteverhandlung
Conduct-related dismissals verhaltensbedingte Kündigung
Confidentiality clause Verschwiegenheitsklausel
Consultation with the works council Anhörung des Betriebsrats
Continuation of Remuneration Act – Entgeltfortzahlungsgesetz
Corporate codetermination Unternehmensmitbestimmung
Covenant of non-competition Wettbewerbsverbot

D

Data protection Datenschutz
Default in acceptance Annahmeverzug
Direct insurance Direktversicherung
Direct pension Direktzusage
Directives Weisungen
Dismissal for operational reasons betriebsbedingte Kündigung
Dismissal for variation of contract Änderungskündigung
Dismissal on suspicion Verdachtskündigung
Dismissal without notice fristlose Kündigung
Dismissial notice period Kündigungsfrist
Division Sparte

E

Economic committee Wirtschaftsausschuss
Employee Arbeitnehmer
Employee accident insurance Unfallversicherung
Employer Arbeitgeber
Employers' Association Arbeitgeberverband
Employment and labor law Arbeitsrecht
Employment agreement Arbeitsvertrag
Employment agreement with a fixed term befristeter Arbeitsvertrag
Employment law Individualarbeitsrecht

Enterprise Unternehmen
Entrepreneurial decision Unternehmerentscheidung
Establishment Betrieb
European Works Council Europäischer Betriebsrat
Executive employment agreement Dienstvertrag
Executive employee leitender Angestellter
Exercise price (stock options) Ausübungspreis (Aktienoptionen)

F

Favorability principle Günstigkeitsprinzip
Federal Educational Allowance Act – Bundeserziehungsgeldgesetz
Federal Labor Court Bundesarbeitsgericht
Federal Vacation Act – Bundesurlaubsgesetz
Forfeiture clause (stock options) Verfallsklausel (Aktienoptionen)
Framework collective bargaining agreement Manteltarifvertrag
Framework collective bargaining agreement on general working and employment conditions Manteltarifvertrag
Freelancer freier Mitarbeiter/Selbständiger

G

General protection against dismissal allgemeiner Kündigungsschutz
German Civil Code Bürgerliches Gesetzbuch
German Commercial Code Handelsgesetzbuch
German Federal Employment Agency Bundesagentur für Arbeit
Granting agreement (stock option) Gewährungsvertrag (Aktienoptionen)
Group Konzern
Group works council Konzernbetriebsrat

H

Health insurance Krankenversicherung
Home and institutional care insurance Pflegeversicherung
Hiring Einstellung
Hours of Employment Act – Arbeitszeitgesetz

I

Independent contractor freier Mitarbeiter/Selbständiger
Industrial Action Arbeitskampf
Insignificant employment geringfügige Beschäftigung

J

Joint works council Gesamtbetriebsrat

L

Labor Court Arbeitsgericht
Labor Court Act Arbeitsgerichtsgesetz
Labor law kollektives Arbeitsrecht
Labor Office Agentur für Arbeit
Labor Protection Law Arbeitsschutzrecht
Leasing of employees Arbeitnehmerüberlassung
Legal entity juristische Person
Letter of reference Zeugnis
Liability Verschulden/Haftung
Limited liability company Gesellschaft mit beschränkter Haftung (GmbH)
Limited Liability Companies Act GmbH-Gesetz

M

Managerial employee leitender Angestellter
Managing director Geschäftsführer
Mass dismissals Massenentlassung
Maternity protection Mutterschutz
Merger Verschmelzung/Zusammenlegung

N

Negative health prognosis negative Gesundheitsprognose

O

Operational changes Betriebsänderung
Ordinary termination with prior notice ordentliche Kündigung

P

Parental leave Elternzeit
Part-time work Teilzeitarbeit
Pension insurance Rentenversicherung
Pension funds Pensionsfonds
Pension guaranty fund Pensionssicherungsverein
Person-related dismissal personenbedingte Kündigung
Persons with disabilities Schwerbehinderte
Persons with Disabilities Act Schwerbehindertengesetz
Piecework rates Akkordarbeit
Power of attorney Vollmacht
Principle of equal treatment Gleichbehandlungsgrundsatz
Probationary period Probezeit
Procuration officer Prokurist
Professional associations Berufsgenossenschaften
Protection Against Unfair Dismissals Act Kündigungsschutzgesetz
Pseudo-independence Scheinselbständigkeit

R

Radiation Ausstrahlung
Reconciliation of interests Interessenausgleich
Regional Court Landgericht
Regulatory arrangement Regelungsabrede
Residence title Aufenthaltstitel
Retirement fund Pensionsfonds

S

Section of an establishment Betriebsteil
Self-assessment wage tax return Lohnsteueranmeldung
Seniority Betriebszugehörigkeit
Severance pay Abfindung
Share deal Anteilskauf
Shareholders' meeting Gesellschafterversammlung
Short-time work Kurzarbeit
Sickness allowance Krankengeld
Social plan Sozialplan
Social Security Code Sozialgesetzbuch
Social security law Sozialversicherungsrecht
Social selection Sozialauswahl
Split-up Spaltung
Spokesperson's committee Sprecherausschuss
Staff pension fund Pensionskasse
Regional Labor Court of Appeal Landesarbeitsgericht
State Agency for Employment Landesagentur für Arbeit
Statutory Pension Insurance Rentenversicherung
Statutory Social Insurance gesetzliche Sozialversicherung
Stock corporation Aktiengesellschaft
Stock corporation Act Aktiengesetz
Stock options Aktienoptionen
Stream of income principle Lohnzuflussprinzip
Strike Streik
Suspension periods Ruhezeiten

T

Tax law Steuerrecht
Termination Kündigung
Total social insurance contribution Gesamtsozialversicherungsbeitrag
Trade union Gewerkschaft
Trade union social plan tariflicher Sozialplan
Transfer Versendung
Transfer of business Betriebsübergang
Transformation Umwandlung
Transitional mandate Übergangsmandat

U

Undertaking Unternehmen
Unemployment insurance Arbeitslosenversicherung
Union Gewerkschaft

V

Vacation Urlaub
Voluntary staff bonus Gratifikation/ Sonderleistung
Voluntary works agreement freiwillige Betriebsvereinbarung

W

Waiting period Wartezeit
Warning Abmahnung
Weighing of interests Interessenabwägung
White-collar worker Angestellter
Withholding tax deduction procedure Lohnsteuerabzugsverfahren
Working days Arbeitstage
Works agreement Betriebsvereinbarung
Works council Betriebsrat
Works meeting Betriebsversammlung
Written form Schriftform

Y

Youth and Trainee Representative Body Jugend- und Auszubildendenvertretung

Glossar

A

Abgabenordnung Tax Code
Abfindung severance pay
Abmahnung warning
AGB-Kontrolle review of employment agreements for compliance with §§ 305–310 German Civil Code (BGB)
Agentur für Arbeit Employment Agency
Akkordarbeit piecework rates
Aktienoptionen stock options
Aktiengesellschaft stock corporation
Aktiengesetz Stock Corporation Act
Allgemeines Gleichbehandlungsgesetz General Equal Treatment Act
allgemeine Ortskrankenkassen local health care funds
allgemeiner Kündigungsschutz general protection against dismissal
Änderungskündigung dismissal for variation of contract
Angestellter white collar worker
Anhörung des Betriebsrats consultation with the works council
Annahmeverzug default in acceptance
Anteilskauf share deal
Anwesenheitsprämie attendance bonus
Arbeiter blue collar worker
Arbeitgeber employer
Arbeitgeberverband employers' association
Arbeitnehmer employee
arbeitnehmerähnliche Person persons similar to employees
Arbeitnehmer-Entsendegesetz Posted Workers Law
Arbeitnehmererfindungsgesetz Employee Inventions Act
Arbeitnehmerüberlassung leasing of employees
Arbeitnehmerüberlassungsgesetz Act Regulating the Commercial Leasing of Employees; Personnel Leasing Act
Arbeitsgericht labor court
Arbeitsgerichtsgesetz Labor Court Act
Arbeitskampf industrial action
Arbeitslosenversicherung unemployment insurance
Arbeitsplatzschutzgesetz Job Protection Act
Arbeitsrecht employment and labor law
Arbeitsschutzrecht employment health and safety laws
Arbeitsschutzgesetz Law on Safety and Health at Work
Arbeitstag working day
Arbeitsvertrag employment agreement
Arbeitszeitgesetz Hours of Employment Act
Aufenthaltserlaubnis residence permit
Aufenthaltsgesetz Residence Law for EEA Nationals
Aufenthaltstitel residence title
Ausländergesetz Alien Act
Auslandstätigkeitserlass Edict on Employment Abroad
Auslauffrist expiration period
Aufsichtsbehörde competent authority
Aufsichtsrat supervisory board
außerordentliche Kündigung dismissal for cause
Ausstrahlung radiation
Ausübungspreis (Aktienoptionen) exercise price (stock options)
Auszubildende(r) apprentice

B

befristeter Arbeitsvertrag employment agreement for a fixed term
berechtigtes Interesse legitimate interest
Berufsbildungsgesetz Vocational Training Act
Berufsgenossenschaften professional associations
Beschlußverfahren procedures for resolving disputes between the employer and works council
Besitzgesellschaft company holding the fixed assets

Betrieb establishment
betriebliche Altersvorsorge company pension plan
betriebliche Übung company practice
Betriebsänderung operational changes
betriebsbedingte Kündigung dismissal for operational reasons
Betriebsaufspaltung business unit division
Betriebsgesellschaft operating company
Betriebsrat works council
Betriebsratsanhörung hearing of the works council
Betriebsrätegesetz Works Council Act
Betriebsteil section of an establishment
Betriebsübergang transfer of business
Betriebsvereinbarung (written) works agreement
Betriebsversammlung works meeting
Betriebsverfassungsgesetz Works Constitution Act
Betriebszugehörigkeit seniority
Bundesagentur für Arbeit German Federal Employment Agency
Bundesarbeitsgericht Federal Labor Court
Bundesaufsichtsamt für das Versicherungswesen Federal Supervisory Office for Insurance Companies
Bundesdatenschutzgesetz Federal Data Protection Act
Bundeselterngeld- und Elternzeitgesetz Federal Parental Allowance and Parental Leave Act
Bundeserziehungsgeldgesetz Federal Educational Allowance Act
Bundesimmissionsschutzgesetz Federal Emissions Protection Act
Bundessozialhilfegesetz Federal Social Assistance Act
Bundesurlaubsgesetz Federal Vacation Act
Bundesversicherungsanstalt für Angestellte (BfA) Federal Social Insurance Office for Salaried Employees
Bürgerliches Gesetzbuch German Civil Code

D

Datenschutz data protection
Deutscher Gewerkschaftsbund German Trade Union Association
Dienststelle civil service office
Dienstvertrag executive employment agreement
Dienstwagen company car
Direktversicherung direct insurance policies
Direktzusage direct pension commitment
dringende betriebliche Erfordernisse compelling operational requirements
dringende betriebliche Gründe compelling operational reasons
Drittelbeteiligungsgesetz One-Third Participation Act

E

EG-Vertrag Treaty Establishing the European Community
Einigungsstelle conciliation board
Einigungsvertrag Unification Treaty
Einkommensteuergesetz Income Tax Act
Einstellung hiring
Elterngeld parental allowance
Elternzeit parental leave
entfristete Kündigung extraordinary dismissal with ordinary notice periods
Entgeltfortzahlungsgesetz Act on Payment of Wages and Salaries on Holidays and in Case of Illness (Continuation of Remuneration Act)
Entgeltumwandlung deferred compensation
Ersatzkassen substitute funds
Erstes Arbeitsrechtsbereinigungsgesetz First Labor Law Simplification Act
Europäischer Betriebsrat European works council

F

Feiertage statutory holidays
Finanzamt tax authority
Firmentarifvertrag company agreements

German/English

freier Mitarbeiter freelancer/independent contractor
Freistellung „garden-leave" (i.e. the employer releases the employee from his/her work responsibilities after giving notice)
freiwillige Betriebsvereinbarung voluntary works agreement
Fremdgeschäftsführer dependent managing director
fristlose Kündigung dismissal without notice

G

Gehaltstarifvertrag collective bargaining agreement on pay („pay agreement")
geringfügige Beschäftigung insignificant employment
Gesamtbetriebsrat joint works council
Gesamtsozialversicherungsbeitrag total social insurance contribution
Geschäftsführer managing director
Gesellschaft mit beschränkter Haftung limited liability company
Gesellschafterversammlung shareholders' meeting
Gesetz über Betriebsärzte, Sicherheitsingenieure und andere Fachkräfte für Arbeitssicherheit Act on Works Physicians, Safety Engineers and Other Specialists for Employee Safety
Gesetz über den Versicherungsvertrag Insurance Policies Act
Gesetz über die Beaufsichtigung der privaten Versicherungsunternehmungen Supervision of Private Insurance Companies Act
Gesetz über Teilzeitarbeit und befristete Arbeitsverträge (TzBfG) Part-Time and Limited Term Employment Act
Gesetz zum Schutz der Beschäftigten vor sexueller Belästigung am Arbeitsplatz Act to Protect Employees Against Sexual Harassment on the Job
Gesetz zur Verbesserung der betrieblichen Altersvorsorge Act for the Improvement of Company Pension Plans
gesetzliche Sozialversicherung statutory social insurance
Gewährungsvertrag (Aktienoptionen) Granting Agreement (Stock Options)
Gewerkschaft trade union
Gleichbehandlungsgrundsatz principle of equal treatment
Gratifikation voluntary staff bonus
Grundgesetz Basic Law
Günstigkeitsprinzip favorability principle or rule
Güteverhandlung conciliation hearing

H

Haftung liability
Handelsgesetzbuch German Commercial Code
Hauptfürsorgestelle competent authority for the protection of disabled persons
Heimarbeitsgesetz Home Work Act

I

Individualarbeitsrecht employment law
Integrationsamt integration authority
Interessenabwägung weighing of interests
Interessenausgleich reconciliation of interests

J

Jugend- und Auszubildendenvertretung youth and trainee representative body
Jugendarbeitsschutzgesetz a) Young Persons in Employment Protection Act b) Youth Labor Protection Act
juristische Person legal entity

K

Kaufmann businessman, merchant
kollektives Arbeitsrecht labor law
Kommanditgesellschaft auf Aktien partnership limited by shares
Konzern group
Konzernbetriebsrat group works council

Krankengeld sickness allowance
Krankenkasse statutory health insurance schemes
Krankenversicherung health insurance
Kündigung termination
Kündigungsfrist dismissal notice period
Kündigungsschutzgesetz (KSchG) – Protection Against (Unfair) Dismissials Act
Kurzarbeit Short-time work

L

Ladenschlussgesetz (LadenschlussG) Shop Closing Hours Act
Landesarbeitsamt State Employment Agency
Landesarbeitsgericht Regional Labor Court of Appeal
Landesversicherungsanstalt für Arbeiter State Insurance Institute for Wage Workers
Landgericht Regional Court
leitende(r) Angestellte(r) executive, managerial employee
Lohn-/Gehaltstarifvertrag collective bargaining agreement on pay
Lohnsteuerabzugsverfahren withholding tax deduction procedure
Lohnsteueranmeldung self-assessment wage tax return
Lohnsteuerjahresausgleich annual wage tax adjustment
Lohnzuflussprinzip „stream of income" principle

M

Manteltarifvertrag framework collective bargaining agreement on general working and employment conditions; „framework agreement"
Massenentlassung mass dismissals
Mitbestimmungsgesetz (MitbestG) Codetermination Act
Mitbestimmungsrecht codetermination right
Montan-Mitbestimmungsgesetz Act Concerning the Codetermination of Employees in the Supervisory Boards and Management Boards in the Mining and the Iron and Steel Manufacturing Industry

Mutterschutz maternity protection
Mutterschutzgesetz (MuSchG) Maternity Protection Act

N

Nachweisgesetz (NachWG) Documentation Act
Nachwirkung aftereffect
natürliche Person natural person
negative Gesundheitsprognose negative health prognosis
Niederlassungserlaubnis settlement permit

O

ordentliche Kündigung ordinary termination with prior notice

P

Pensionsfonds retirement fund
Pensionskasse staff pension fund
Pensions-Sicherungs-Verein Pension Guaranty Fund (i. e. carrier of the insolvency insurance)
personenbedingte Kündigung person-related dismissal
Pflegeversicherung home and institutional care insurance
Prämie incentive
Probezeit probationary period
Prokurist procuration officer, procurial officer (i. e. holder of full commercial powers of attorney)
Provision commission

R

Regelungsabrede regulatory arrangement
Rentenversicherung statutory pension insurance
Ruhegeldgesetz Pension Act
Ruhezeiten suspension periods

S

Scheinselbständigkeit pseudo-independence
Scheinselbständige(r) pseudo-independent employee
Schriftform written form

schwerbehinderte Menschen persons with disabilities
Schwerbehindertengesetz (SchwerbG) Persons with Disabilities Act
Selbständiger freelancer/independent contractor
Sitz (einer Gesellschaft) seat, domicile
Sonderleistung voluntary staff bonus
Sozialauswahl social selection
Sozialgesetzbuch Social Security Code
Sozialplan social plan
Sozialversicherungsrecht social security laws
Spaltung split-up
Sparte division
Sperrzeit blocking period
Sprecherausschuss spokespersons' committee
Sprecherausschussgesetz Spokespersons' Committee Act
Stammhausbindungsvertrag parent company binding agreement
Steuerrecht tax law
Streik strike

T

Tantieme profit sharing
tariflicher Sozialplan trade union social plan
Tarifregister Collective Bargaining Agreements Register
Tarifvertrag collective bargaining agreement
Tarifvertragsgesetz (TVG) – Collective Bargaining Agreements Act

U

Übergangsmandat transitional mandate
Umwandlung transformation
Umwandlungsgesetz (UmwG) Transformation Act
Unfallversicherung employee accident insurance
Unternehmen enterprise, undertaking
Unternehmensmitbestimmung corporate codetermination
Unternehmerentscheidung entrepreneurial decision
Unterstützungskasse benevolent funds
Urlaub vacation
Urlaubsentgelt vacation pay

V

Verbandstarifvertrag association agreements
Verdachtskündigung dismissal on suspicion of unlawful conduct
ver.di (Vereinte Dienstleistungsgewerkschaft) public service workers union
Verfallsklausel (Aktienoptionen) forfeiture clause (stock options)
verhaltensbedingte Kündigung termination due to conduct
Vermögenskauf asset deal
vermögenswirksame Leistungen capital formation benefits
Verordnung über den Kinderarbeitsschutz Ordinance Protecting Against the Employment of Children
Verschmelzung merger
Verschulden fault
Verschwiegenheitsklausel confidentiality clause
Versendung transfer
Versicherungsaufsichtsgesetz Insurance Supervisory Act
Versicherungsverein auf Gegenseitigkeit Federal Supervisory Office for Insurance Companies; carrier of the insolvency insurance
Versorgungsanstalt des Bundes und der Länder Federal and State Pension Office
Versorgungsbezüge pension benefits
vertrauensvolle Zusammenarbeit mutual trust and cooperation
Vollmacht power of attorney
Vorstand – management board
Vorstandsmitglied member of the management board

W

Wahlordnung election code
Wahlvorstand election committee
Wartezeit waiting period
Weisungen directives, instructions

Werktag working day
Wettbewerbsverbot covenant of non-competition
wichtiger Grund (aus wichtigem Grund) cause [for termination] (for cause)
Wirtschaftsausschuss economic committee/economic affairs committee
wohlwollend favorable to the employee (letter of reference)

Z

Zeugnis Letter of reference
Zivilprozessordnung Code of Civil Procedure
Zulage/Zuschlag supplemental pay
Zwischenzeugnis interim reference